THE
MILITARY
BALANCE
2019

published by

for

The International Institute for Strategic Studies
ARUNDEL HOUSE | 6 TEMPLE PLACE | LONDON | WC2R 2PG | UK

THE MILITARY BALANCE 2019

The International Institute for Strategic Studies
ARUNDEL HOUSE | 6 TEMPLE PLACE | LONDON | WC2R 2PG | UK

DIRECTOR-GENERAL AND CHIEF EXECUTIVE **Dr John Chipman**
DIRECTOR FOR DEFENCE AND MILITARY ANALYSIS **Dr Bastian Giegerich**
EDITOR **James Hackett**
ASSOCIATE EDITOR **Nicholas Payne**

MILITARY AEROSPACE **Douglas Barrie** MRAeS
LAND WARFARE **Brigadier (Retd) Benjamin Barry**
MILITARY FORCES AND EQUIPMENT **Henry Boyd**
NAVAL FORCES AND MARITIME SECURITY **Nick Childs**
DEFENCE ECONOMICS **Dr Lucie Béraud-Sudreau**
RESEARCH AND ANALYSIS **Joseph Dempsey, Yvonni-Stefania Efstathiou, Amanda Lapo, Yohann Michel, Robert Mitchell, Meia Nouwens, Michael Tong, Tom Waldwyn**

EDITORIAL **Clea Gibson, Alexander Goodwin, Sara Hussain, Jill Lally, Gaynor Roberts, Sam Stocker, Carolyn West**
DESIGN, PRODUCTION, INFORMATION GRAPHICS **John Buck, Kelly Verity**
CARTOGRAPHY **John Buck, Kelly Verity**
RESEARCH SUPPORT **Peter Bowman, Jennifer Chandler, Katrina Marina, Joel McGrath, Alina Ragge**

This publication has been prepared by the Director-General and Chief Executive of the Institute and his Staff, who accept full responsibility for its contents. The views expressed herein do not, and indeed cannot, represent a consensus of views among the worldwide membership of the Institute as a whole.

FIRST PUBLISHED February 2019

© The International Institute for Strategic Studies 2019
All rights reserved. No part of this publication may be reproduced, stored, transmitted, or disseminated, in any form, or by any means, without prior written permission from Taylor & Francis, to whom all requests to reproduce copyright material should be directed, in writing.

ISBN 978-1-85743-988-5
ISSN 0459-7222

Cover images: FRONT: An F-35B lands on HMS *Queen Elizabeth* (Kyle Heller/MoD via Getty); a Chinese J-20 at Airshow China 2018 (VCG via Getty); a US F-16 pilot readies for a sortie (USAF/Samuel King Jr.); the destroyer USS *Dewey* launches a *Tomahawk* cruise missile (US Navy/Devin M. Langer). BACK: A Boeing B-52 G *Stratofortress* armed with two AGM-28 air-to-surface-missiles (Ullstein Bild via Getty), c.1960; a Russian TEL and an inset image of an SSC-X-4 ground-launched cruise missile, c.1988 (US DoD); Israeli armed forces during the Yom Kippur War, October 1973 (Gabriel Duval/AFP/Getty).

The Military Balance (ISSN 0459-7222) is published annually by Routledge Journals, an imprint of Taylor & Francis, 4 Park Square, Milton Park, Abingdon, Oxfordshire OX14 4RN, UK.

A subscription to the institution print edition, ISSN 0459-7222, includes free access for any number of concurrent users across a local area network to the online edition, ISSN 1479-9022.

All subscriptions are payable in advance and all rates include postage. Journals are sent by air to the USA, Canada, Mexico, India, Japan and Australasia. Subscriptions are entered on an annual basis, i.e. January to December. Payment may be made by sterling cheque, dollar cheque, international money order, National Giro, or credit card (Amex, Visa, Mastercard).

Please send subscription orders to: USA/Canada: Taylor & Francis Inc., Journals Department, 530 Walnut Street, Suite 850, Philadelphia, PA 19106, USA. UK/Europe/Rest of World: Routledge Journals, T&F Customer Services, T&F Informa UK Ltd., Sheepen Place, Colchester, Essex, CO3 3LP, UK. Email: subscriptions@tandf.co.uk

Contents

Indexes of Tables, Figures and Maps 4
Editor's Introduction 5

Part One **Capabilities, Trends and Economics**

Domain trends 7

Chapter 1 **Defence and military analysis** 9
Sixty years of *The Military Balance* 9; Challenges in nuclear-arms control: past and present 13;
Quantum computing and defence 18

Chapter 2 **Comparative defence statistics** 21
Defence budgets and expenditure 21; Soviet (VVS and PVO) and Russian Aerospace Forces (VKS), 1989–2018 23;
Brigade structures: China, Russia and the United States 24; Principal advanced anti-air-warfare surface combatants and
operators, 1998–2018 25; Key defence statistics 26

Chapter 3 **North America** 28
Regional trends in 2018 28;   Armed forces data section 44;
United States: defence policy and economics 30;   Arms procurements and deliveries 63
Canada: defence policy 42;

Chapter 4 **Europe** 66
Regional trends in 2018 66;   UK: defence policy 82;
Regional defence policy and economics 68;   Armed forces data section 87;
North Atlantic and the High North 77;   Arms procurements and deliveries 163
Sweden: defence policy and economics 78;

Chapter 5 **Russia and Eurasia** 166
Regional trends in 2018 166;   Armed forces data section 184;
Russia: defence policy and economics 168;   Arms procurements and deliveries 219
Belarus: defence policy and economics 178;

Chapter 6 **Asia** 222
Regional trends in 2018 222;   Thailand: defence policy and economics 242;
Regional defence policy and economics 224;   Armed forces data section 247;
China: defence policy and economics 232;   Arms procurements and deliveries 317
Japan: defence policy 241;

Chapter 7 **Middle East and North Africa** 320
Regional trends in 2018 320;   Gulf region: training and sustainability 329;
Regional defence policy and economics 322;   Armed forces data section 332;
Iraq: rebuilding the armed forces 327;   Arms procurements and deliveries 377

Chapter 8 **Latin America and the Caribbean** 380
Regional trends in 2018 380;   Mexico: defence policy 391;
Regional defence policy and economics 382;   Armed forces data section 393;
Chile: defence policy and economics 387;   Arms procurements and deliveries 436

Chapter 9 **Sub-Saharan Africa** 438
Regional trends in 2018 438;   Armed forces data section 451;
Regional defence policy and economics 440;   Arms procurements and deliveries 501
South Africa: defence policy and economics 446;

Part Two **Reference**

Explanatory notes 503
Principal land definitions 507; Principal naval definitions 508; Principal aviation definitions 509

List of abbreviations for data sections 511

International comparisons of defence expenditure and military personnel 513

Index of country/territory abbreviations 519

Index of countries and territories 520

Index of **TABLES**

1. NDAA 2019 authorisation: equipment acquisitions and upgrades ... 32
2. US National Defense Budget Function and other selected budgets 1999, 2009–19 ... 37
3. US Navy build-up: shipbuilding proposals ... 39
4. US FY2018 defence-budget request: top 15 equipment programmes by value ... 63
5. US fixed-wing fighter-aircraft exports, 2010–Oct 2018 ... 64
6. Canada: maritime procurement programmes, by order date ... 64
7. NATO transformation, 2014–19 ... 70
8. Denmark: planned increases in defence spending, 2018–23 ... 75
9. EU PADR projects: companies involved per EU member ... 76
10. European frigate programmes and principal weapons systems ... 164
11. Russian defence expenditure as % of GDP ... 175
12. Australia: top five acquisition programmes in 2018, by approved expenditure ... 229
13. India: procurements from Russia and the United States, 2000–18 ... 231
14. Republic of Korea: naval platform procurement programmes, by contract date ... 318
15. Japan FY2019 defence-budget request: top ten new equipment acquisition programmes by value ... 318
16. Reported Russian defence exports to Algeria: recently completed and ongoing, by contract date ... 378
17. Saudi Arabia: top ten arms orders in 2017–18, by order date ... 379
18. Gulf Cooperation Council states: new fighter/ground-attack aircraft contracts, 2005–present ... 379
19. Iraq: selected procurement contracts, 2010–18 ... 379
20. SANDF budget by programme (in rand/US$ at yearly exchange rates) ... 449
21. South Africa: major equipment-procurement programmes ... 502
22. List of abbreviations for data sections ... 511
23. International comparisons of defence expenditure and military personnel ... 513
24. Index of country/territory abbreviations ... 519
25. Index of countries and territories ... 520

Index of **FIGURES**

1. Major landmarks in arms control, 1944–2017 ... 16

North America
2. Lockheed Martin F-35 *Lightning* II: sensor suite ... 35
3. US defence expenditure as % of GDP ... 37
4. Boeing: P-8A *Poseidon* Multi-Mission Maritime Aircraft (MMA) ... 65

Europe
5. Europe regional defence expenditure as % of GDP ... 74
6. Europe defence spending by country and sub-region, 2017 ... 74
7. UK: selected equipment reductions, 1989 and 2018 ... 83
8. *Queen Elizabeth*-class aircraft carriers ... 84
9. Europe: selected ongoing or completed procurement priorities in 2018 ... 163
10. Airbus Defence & Space: A400M heavy transport aircraft; A400M deliveries ... 165

Russia and Eurasia
11. Russia: *Kalibr* missile family ... 174
12. Russia: estimated total military expenditure as % of GDP ... 176
13. Russian Air Force: new tactical fighter deliveries, 2010–17 ... 219
14. Russian next-generation armoured-vehicle programmes: progress as of late 2018 ... 220
15. Admiralty Shipyards: Project 636 *Varshavyanka* (Improved *Kilo*) and Project 677 *Lada* (*St Petersburg*) attack submarines ... 221

Asia
16. Asia defence spending by country and sub-region, 2017 ... 226
17. Asia regional defence expenditure as % of GDP ... 228
18. Indo-Pacific defence spending, 2018 (US$bn, current) ... 228
19. Asia: selected ongoing or completed procurement priorities in 2018 ... 317
20. Rosoboronexport/Heavy Vehicles Factory: T-90S *Bhishma* Indian T-90S contracts, by date ... 319

Middle East and North Africa
21. North Africa defence expenditure 2017: sub-regional breakdown ... 324
22. Saudi Arabia defence expenditure as % of GDP ... 325
23. Middle East and North Africa: selected ongoing or completed procurement priorities in 2018 ... 377

Latin America and the Caribbean
24. Latin America and the Caribbean defence spending by country and sub-region ... 384
25. Latin America and the Caribbean regional defence expenditure as % of GDP ... 386
26. Latin America and the Caribbean: selected ongoing or completed procurement priorities in 2018 ... 436
27. Naval Group: Programa de Desenvolvimento de Submarinos (PROSUB) ... 437

Sub-Saharan Africa
28. China: military engagement in Africa ... 443
29. Sub-Saharan Africa regional defence expenditure as % of GDP ... 445
30. Sub-Saharan Africa: selected ongoing or completed procurement priorities in 2018 ... 501

Index of **MAPS**

1. Europe regional defence spending ... 73
2. Sweden military facilities ... 80
3. Russian forces in Crimea, 2018 ... 172
4. Russia and Eurasia regional defence spending ... 176
5. Belarus: principal military bases ... 181
6. Asia regional defence spending ... 227
7. Chinese military facilities in the South China Sea ... 234
8. Thailand: principal military bases ... 243
9. Middle East and North Africa regional defence spending ... 325
10. Latin America and the Caribbean regional defence spending ... 385
11. Chile: key military bases and defence-industrial facilities ... 388
12. Sub-Saharan Africa regional defence spending ... 444

Editor's Introduction

This 2019 edition of *The Military Balance* is published 60 years after it first appeared as an 11-page pamphlet in late 1959. The international security environment is again as uncertain today as it was then. Great-power competition still dominates contemporary Western policy discussions, but now it is not only Moscow's actions that generate attention. China perhaps represents even more of a challenge, as it introduces yet more advanced military systems and is engaged in a strategy to improve its forces' ability to operate at distance from the homeland. At the same time, while Western armed forces – particularly after Russia seized Crimea in 2014 – are refocusing on more traditional security challenges, though characterised by disruptive new elements, they are having to do this alongside, not instead of, the range of post-9/11 tasks.

The threat from terrorists persists, as does the impact of conflict and instability in Africa. And while the war in the Middle East against the Islamic State, also known as ISIS or ISIL, might have succeeded in eradicating its territorial base, ISIS could revert to insurgent tactics. Meanwhile, the civil war in Syria grinds on, with the regime in the ascendant. Tentative diplomatic progress at the end of 2018 raised hopes that the effects of the conflict in Yemen might be alleviated, if not an immediate end brought to the war. In Asia, the unexpected North Korean moratorium on missile testing led to renewed diplomatic contact on the peninsula, and between Pyongyang and Washington. However, although summits continued, there remained no progress on the issue of North Korea's denuclearisation. In Europe, NATO's eastern members worry about Russia, while simmering conflict continues in eastern Ukraine. In late 2018, Russia began flexing its muscles once more, this time in the Sea of Azov.

Defence spending

In early April 2019, NATO foreign ministers are due to convene to mark the Alliance's 70th anniversary, just days after the United Kingdom's scheduled departure from the European Union. They will celebrate the Alliance's accomplishments, though likely be aware that while external actors may be bent on undermining Euro-Atlantic cohesion, uncertainty also comes from within.

US President Donald Trump returned to a familiar theme at the July 2018 NATO summit. The US, he said, 'might do its own thing' unless European allies started spending more on defence. Although defence spending in NATO's European members grew by 4.2% in 2018, it is likely that Trump will, at the Alliance's anniversary gathering, again press Europe to spend more. In mid-2018 he said that European states should increase defence spending to 2% of GDP 'immediately'. As of late 2018, doing this would mean that NATO European states would have to find an extra US$102 billion, on top of the amount they currently spend.

Global defence spending in 2018 amounted to over US$1.67 trillion. This was an increase of more than US$80bn over the previous year and reflected higher spending in Western states, notably the United States. Indeed, the US has driven the global rise in spending, with a 5% real-terms budget increase between 2017 and 2018; in 2018, the US accounted for 45% of the global increase in defence spending, in constant 2010 dollars.

China sets the pace

China's military modernisation has been striking for the speed of development and breadth of its ambition to modernise the People's Liberation Army by 2035 and create 'world-class forces' by 2049. This ambition is supported by defence spending that has been on a relentlessly upward trajectory. Between 1998 and 2018, China's official defence budget grew, on average, annually by 10% in real terms. Between 2017 and 2018, there was a slight deceleration caused by slower economic growth, but the defence budget still grew year-on-year by nearly 6%.

Naval shipbuilding is focusing more than before on large, high-capability surface combatants. Indeed, Chinese naval capability is entering a new phase, designed to facilitate long-distance operations and heighten operational tempo. The simultaneous launch of two Type-055 cruisers in June 2018 meant that four had been launched in just over a year, and at least four more are under construction. China's first indigenous aircraft carrier began sea trials in 2018, as did the first Type-055. The carrier is based on the *Liaoning*, formerly a Soviet vessel: China's next carrier looks set to be its first truly domestic design, with improved capability to undertake more conventional carrier operations.

China's air force, meanwhile, continues to improve its capacity for tactical air combat. Testing of the Chengdu J-20 heavy fighter continued in 2018 and entry into front-line service seems closer. It appears that the PL-15 extended range active-radar-guided air-to-air missile (AAM) has started entering service. Likely fitted with an active electronically scanned array seeker, it marks a considerable improvement in the air force's AAM inventory. Furthermore, China's long-rumoured next-generation bomber moved closer to public recognition, when the H-20 designation was mentioned in state-controlled media in 2018.

China is making these moves during a time Beijing terms a 'strategic opportunity'. It has decided that any risk involved in implementing these changes is worth bearing now, because the danger of major conflict with a large power is relatively low. As a result, Beijing hopes that when this period of strategic opportunity ends, its armed forces will be able to match or even outmatch those of peer competitors. For the moment, though, China's military power remains latent and there are still areas of weakness, such as in anti-submarine warfare and amphibious operations. However, China continues to take strides towards addressing these deficiencies and is engaged on an improved training and exercise regime enabling it to test operational capability, as well as assess progress towards its modernisation goals.

Russia matters

Russia too remains a focus of Western security concern, not only because of its own military-modernisation programme but also because of its use of military power in seizing Crimea; its continued and sometimes provocative military behaviour in the Euro-Atlantic area; and continuing support for the Syrian regime of President Bashar al-Assad. New airborne-forces formations were activated in Crimea, a key air base was modernised and S-400 (SA-21 *Growler*) air-defence system replaced the previous S-300 (SA-10 *Grumble*/SA-20 *Gargoyle*) on the peninsula. The S-400 system has increased Moscow's potential reach in the Black Sea region.

There has been renewed interest from Moscow in nuclear- and dual-capable weapons systems. The *Avangard* hypersonic glide vehicle reportedly entered series production in 2018, while Russia also revealed the *Burevestnik* (SSC-X-9 *Skyfall*) nuclear-powered cruise missile. So far, two batches of the SSC-X-9 have been manufactured and tested, with only limited results. More successfully, and less publicly, Moscow is assessed to have continued to deploy the 9M729 (SSC-8 *Screwdriver*) ground-launched cruise missile. The SSC-8 is the cruise missile that, Washington said, led it at the end of 2018 to initiate the 60-day formal withdrawal process from the 1987 Intermediate-Range Nuclear Forces Treaty. But economic challenges mean that Russia's defence acquisitions have slowed in recent years. In contrast, because of more consistent increases in its defence spending, China does not face the same restrictions.

Ways of war

Advanced military systems and technical knowledge continue to spread. Some of these systems, such as hypersonic weapons, might hold at risk distant targets previously deemed safe; they might also compress the decision space for the defending force. Armed forces are looking to develop capabilities in other areas like cyber, space, robotics, directed energy and quantum technologies. China, for instance, has a national plan to develop artificial intelligence technology and is accelerating moves to improve civil–military integration.

Western states are reassessing previously held assumptions of advantage; for instance, that access to the global commons and freedom to operate in the electromagnetic spectrum are uncontested. They still retain an edge over adversaries, but the gap is narrowing. The pace of change may mean that in future, advantages – if they exist at all – may be held only fleetingly, before the other side catches up.

Western states can try to stay ahead by investing significantly in research and development and by boosting ties with the commercial high-technology sector. But in the West this is not always a smooth process. Faster acquisitions processes and improved coordination between armed services over military procurements might improve the speed with which systems are fielded. Innovation could be improved so that the urgency of operational innovation is maintained in peacetime, and that risk-taking in innovation is encouraged. In addition, more highly qualified people need to be recruited and retained by armed forces, which also need more flexible career structures.

Another approach is to accept this situation: not just that contestation is normal but that there is an increasingly level playing field. Western states could look to adapt plans and capabilities to this reality. One way would be to create 'moments of advantage', where rapidly focused military power across all domains could create operational overmatch even in an environment that is routinely contested. This idea is associated in the US with the multi-domain-battle concept.

Whatever strategies may be pursued, armed forces need also to plan on the assumption that their networks will be targeted by adversaries and that jamming and, more insidiously, spoofing, may become routine. They also need to become used to operating in a consistently contested information environment. Indeed, this may be more apparent as innovative adversaries seek to achieve strategic effect by operating below the threshold of war; attacks may happen as much in peacetime as in war. More resilient weapons and networks may help, enabling troops to fight in a degraded electromagnetic environment, but so too will better training and ensuring that the lessons of recent wars are not lost: the next fight might be at range and over the horizon, but it might also be urban.

Russia is a worry for Washington, but perhaps not so much in the long term. For the US, the 'pacing threat' in the 2025–30 time frame remains China. Signs of Washington's concern were again evident in 2018. US Air Force chiefs began publicly advocating that squadron numbers increase to 386 by 2025–30; this came just a couple of years after US Navy leaders advocated that the fleet increase to 355 ships. One reason for this is that, in the Asia-Pacific, the US is aware it faces the 'tyranny of distance'.

It is clear that China's military modernisation is leading others to reassess their own plans. Some states in the Asia-Pacific, such as Australia and Japan, are reshaping their procurements to include more advanced weapons systems, including next-generation combat aircraft, advanced air-defence weapons and better submarines. China fields – and is developing – a range of weapons that would complicate the planning of armed forces trying to enter the South China Sea, particularly under combat conditions. While China may have halted its land-reclamation and island-building programme in the South China Sea, it has instead concentrated on building up facilities and weapons on features there, implicitly exerting pressure on both its near neighbours and other regional states looking to exercise freedom of navigation.

China's modernising armed forces are being seen more often in more places. But while they may be engaged on a wider range of missions, they are still developing and remain operationally untested. China may have arrived strategically, but it has yet to arrive militarily. However, the progress it is making towards fielding better-equipped and -trained armed forces means that day continues to grow closer.

Domain trends

Defence economics

- Global defence spending picked up by 1.8% in real terms between 2017 and 2018. The rise in 2018 was driven by the United States, which increased its defence budget by 5% in real terms between 2017 and 2018. The US thereby accounted for 45% of global defence-spending increases in 2018.

- As a result of this increase, global military expenditure has bounced back from its low point in 2014, when lower energy prices led oil and gas exporters in particular to curb their defence outlays.

- There is still a serious lack of transparency over military expenditures in the Middle East and North Africa. There is no assessment available for conflict-afflicted countries (Libya, Syria, Yemen) or particularly opaque states (Qatar, UAE), while data is unreliable for other countries in the region (Bahrain, Oman, Saudi Arabia) because of lack of detailed publicly released information and likely off-budget funding.

- According to available data, Middle Eastern states continued to dedicate the largest share of GDP to defence and security by a wide margin. Among the world's top ten defence spenders by share of GDP, eight were from the Middle East (Algeria, Iran, Iraq, Israel, Jordan, Kuwait, Oman and Saudi Arabia), ranging from more than 4% to 11% of GDP. This reflects security concerns in a conflict-torn region but also over-prioritisation of defence compared to other policy sectors. The rest of the top-ten list comprises other states facing security challenges – Afghanistan and Mali.

- Defence-related revenue for eight out of the ten defence-focused Chinese state-owned enterprises indicates that, in 2016, seven of these were in the top 20 of the world's largest defence firms. Three of these – China South Industries Group Corporation (CSGC), Aviation Industry Corporation of China (AVIC) and China North Industries Group Corporation (NORINCO) – appeared in the top ten.

Land

- Armoured fighting vehicle inventories are being modernised rather than simply replaced. The high cost of producing new designs, in light of the quantities required, has resulted in many new vehicle programmes being delayed or cancelled. This has led many countries to instead upgrade and extend the life of existing platforms rather than replacing them.

- Armoured utility vehicles, cheaper and less complex than traditional land platforms, are continuing to prove popular with armies engaged in operations against asymmetric adversaries and with nascent armoured-vehicle manufacturers, as they offer a cheaper entry point into the market.

- The proliferation of surface-to-surface conventional ballistic- and cruise-missile capabilities continues, albeit slowly, as states see them as usefully cost-effective ways to hold at risk the military and civilian targets of stronger potential adversaries. In turn, this trend is helping to drive rising interest in missile-defence systems.

- Development work continues on advanced unmanned ground vehicles. However, initial military interest seems more directed towards unmanned or optionally manned logistics and support vehicles, rather than in the development of combat platforms.

- The renewed possibility of high-intensity conflict with peer competitors continues to preoccupy Western armies, though the operations on which they are currently engaged largely consist of training, logistics and fires support to local actors. At the same time, they are increasingly aware that the growing trend of urbanisation may make future combat increasingly challenging. Adequately addressing this will require more investment in bespoke, including urban, training facilities.

Maritime

- There is an increasing emphasis on blue-water capabilities. Power-projection capabilities, such as amphibious and land-attack capabilities, remain in demand and will continue to spread, but there is a renewed focus on the ability to engage at sea as well as from the sea. In turn, the growing complexity of the maritime domain is leading to a general rise in capability requirements for naval vessels, particularly for principal surface combatants like frigates, but also for smaller surface combatants and patrol vessels.

- Navies, particularly long-established forces, are emphasising the need to boost ship numbers, following years of fleet reductions. This is driven by a more complex and competitive maritime domain and is leading states to examine ways not just of increasing new procurements but also sustaining existing capabilities in service for longer.

- The proliferation of submarine capabilities is driving a new or renewed focus on anti-submarine capabilities. This is shifting the emphasis not only of procurements but also of training and deployments compared to recent experience.

- The proliferation and renewal of conventional offensive capabilities continues, particularly of anti-ship missiles. This will drive requirements for new means of distributing offensive capabilities ever more widely among fleets. At the same time, the increased missile threat is driving greater interest in maritime missile defences, and investment in this area will likely increase.

- There is increased interest in introducing innovative capabilities in the maritime domain, such as uninhabited and directed-energy systems; a number of these systems have started to be fielded and this will likely increase in pace. This will inevitably influence judgements over fleet composition and employment.

Aerospace

- Very high-speed glide vehicles and cruise missiles are being pursued by China, Russia and the United States as a means of countering missile defences. Russia could field a hypersonic glide vehicle, the *Avangard*, as early as 2019. Several other countries, including France, India and Japan, are also exploring the possible development of weapons capable of hypersonic (Mach 5+) speed.
- Russia and the US are looking to break a speed barrier that has limited the maximum speed of helicopters for almost 50 years. Both countries have high-speed designs in flight-test, both exploring different means of raising significantly the top speed of new designs.
- Although the US and partner nations are introducing into their inventories the F-35 fighter/ground-attack aircraft, several are also extending the lives of the previous aircraft 'generation'. This is in part due to F-35 programme delays and, in the US in particular, the annual rate of acquisition. Lower funding for this than originally planned has led the air force to extend the life of some of its fighter fleet, including the F-16C/D.
- Several air forces are in the process of revamping their air-to-air missile (AAM) inventories. The United Kingdom is introducing the *Meteor* rocket-ramjet-powered beyond-visual-range radar-guided AAM; the US is exploring what might follow the AIM-120 AMRAAM; and China now looks to be introducing into service the PL-15 radar-guided AAM. Meanwhile, Russia has introduced into service the R-77-1 (AA-12B *Adder*) and continues upgrade work, while testing of the Indian *Astra* radar-guided AAM is nearing completion.
- China, Russia and the US all now have next-generation bombers in various stages of design and development. The US B-21 *Raider* will enter service during the second half of the 2020s and could be joined by a Chinese design before the end of that decade. Russia, while working on a low-observable design to meet its PAK-DA future-bomber requirement, also plans to put an upgraded Tu-160 *Blackjack* into production.

Cyber

- The past year witnessed significant changes in national policies and military doctrines regarding cyberspace. EU and NATO states have taken a firmer stance in publicly attributing cyber attacks, and they have also declared their intentions to engage adversaries in cyberspace and through concerted diplomatic and economic sanctions.
- Multinational companies are improving their own cyber defences, as well as influencing internet-governance policy and adapting to regulatory measures at the global level.
- Governments and regional blocs are beginning to impose incentives and disincentives at the level of individual persons or companies – perhaps because extraterritorial pressures have so far proven largely ineffective vis-à-vis other sovereign states. There were four major examples in 2018 of the public attribution of cyber operations: the attribution by seven nations of the NotPetya malware attack to the Russian armed forces; US indictments of Russian military-intelligence organisations for interference in the 2016 US presidential election; German, UK and US alerts that Russia was targeting their critical-infrastructure networks; and the Dutch-led response to an attempted Russian cyber operation against the Organisation for the Prohibition of Chemical Weapons. These indicate collective Western resolve to publicly confront perceived Russian cyber activities.
- In order to improve deterrence, moves are under way to change the perceived utility of cyber operations for foreign actors. To this end, the US is increasingly producing criminal indictments, identifying individuals from China, Iran, North Korea and Russia. They may never face extradition and prosecution, but the professional disadvantages associated with being publicly revealed in such a way may in the future alter the personal decision calculus of foreign hackers. The EU and the US are seeking to use economic sanctions against individual hackers and corporate entities in a similar way.
- Several nations, including Australia, France, Germany, the UK and the US, have all publicised both their offensive cyber capabilities and their willingness to use them for national defence. US military doctrine, in particular, has adopted a more confrontational tone, asserting in the Department of Defense 2018 Cyber Strategy that the US will 'defend forward to disrupt or halt malicious cyber activity at its source, including activity that falls below the level of armed conflict'. Coupled with commitments from Denmark, Estonia, the Netherlands, the UK and US to use their cyber capabilities for NATO's collective defence, such doctrines may presage a more conflictual online environment. While nation-states are drawing lines in the sand regarding foreign cyber operations, they are breaking down the silos among their own military units to capitalise on, and boost, functional cooperation.

Chapter One
Sixty years of *The Military Balance*

This 2019 edition of *The Military Balance* marks 60 years since the publication first appeared, in late 1959, as a slim pamphlet of just 11 pages. The latest edition has been compiled by the IISS's Defence and Military Analysis Programme, the Institute's largest research team with 14 permanent staff. That first volume was produced single-handedly by Alastair Buchan, the first Director of what was then called The Institute for Strategic Studies. The Foreword stated that it was published 'as a contribution to the growing concern that is developing throughout the world about the arms race'. It is apparent, from these early editions, that the focus was very much on nuclear capabilities and missile systems. The rationale behind the first pamphlet was that there would be considerable value in collating published information 'into one simple comparative analysis […] in order to provide a firmer basis, not only of the discussion of "the balance of terror", but of the problems of disarmament'.

It is also true that the appearance of that first volume stemmed in part from concerns expressed to the Director by senior Western defence officials about a lack of public understanding over the size and nature of the Soviet military challenge to Europe. Indeed, the short paper *Making Headway, The First Five Years of the ISS* said that 'the responsible private citizen ... had little but occasional official statements and the sensational reports of newspapers to judge whether, for instance, there was a "missile gap", how strong the Russian army was, or what was the state of India's defences'.

Today, the problem is of a different character. There is a torrent of accessible information from a profusion of sources. But making sense of it all is another matter. Indeed, for an audience that is reacquainting itself with the degree to which information can be manipulated, there is still a place for sober, evidence-based and independent sources of information and analysis, like *The Military Balance*.

The book evolves

The amount of data in the book has significantly increased over the years. The first volume – called *The Soviet Union and The NATO Powers, The Military Balance* – contained information on just 15 states. The tenth edition in 1968–69, now solely titled *The Military Balance* (as it had been since the 1963–64 edition), contained information on 59 states; in the 2019 book, the tally is at 171. As Sir Michael Howard has pointed out, Alastair Buchan and his successors were 'later to lament that they had got themselves stuck with the title *The Military Balance*, providing as it does so stark and conceptually misleading an idea of the complex nature of military power'. But, he continued, 'stuck they are, and "MilBal" has become the Institute's flagship'.

In some respects the increase in the number of countries assessed in the book has reflected the internationalisation of the Institute, from the early 1960s onwards, in terms of the composition of its Council, the scope of its research activity as well as its staffing. The word 'International' was adopted as a prefix by the organisation in the early 1970s. Not 20 years ago, the editorial team for *The Military Balance* was mainly composed of former commissioned officers from the UK armed forces. Today we are an overwhelmingly civilian and increasingly international team. The way in which we display our data has also changed significantly over the years. Today, the book contains detailed lists of military organisations subdivided according to role, while military equipment is broken down according to its type. In doing this, we are mindful of the need to maintain categories that can be compared between states, as well as the wish of the Institute's Council in 1964 that *The Military Balance* retain the compression of the original edition, so making it easier to find information. This also helps ensure that the book remains portable. The 2019 edition may be heavier than the first, but it remains a one-volume publication that can easily be carried in an attaché case.

This is one of the features that continues to distinguish *The Military Balance* from other publications in the field. In deciding which information to prioritise in the book, we are mindful that we cannot accommodate the complete range of military systems operated by states. We display data that we think is essential to national military power. Naturally, this starts with strategic systems, and then progresses through combat weapons systems and combat support equipment. We are more selective on the latter and particularly so when it comes to combat service support (such as logistics and transport) although, of course, we realise that these capacities are vital to armed forces. And it means that some readers may disagree with us on our choices.

A comparable dataset

Another distinguishing feature, enabled by the book's concision, is the capacity it provides to compare data categories between country entries. Indeed, this quickly became one of its principal features, exemplified early on by its comparative tables of strategic nuclear systems. The ability to compare, over time, the same categories of organisation and equipment (as well as defence economics) data was helped by the introduction of formal data categorisation. This function developed incrementally, though for equipment it was greatly helped by the public emergence of equipment definitions as part of the discussions over conventional arms control in Europe. Importantly, these were then used by the states that were party to these agreements. The same could be said for the emergence of counting rules associated with strategic-arms-limitation agreements.

Of course, because of the breadth of our data, even developments like this did not meet all our needs. For instance, the equipment lists for arms-control agreements might only contain definitions for the equipment within the scope of these agreements – so excluding a range of national military equipment. The Institute therefore has its own ways of more formally categorising military equipment, again to assist in the process of comparing across countries. We publish information on these judgements in our 'Explanatory Notes'. Sometimes, countries disagree with them and tell us so. But we have to adopt a system that enables the comparison of equipment and forces between states. These comparative approaches remain valuable. *The Military Balance* still publishes its table of 'international comparisons of defence expenditure and military personnel' as well as a range of other comparative tables and charts. These days, governments use our data in public forums for reasons including its reliability and its accessibility; indeed, because it is unclassified, governments may feel more comfortable publishing *Military Balance* data than releasing their own.

The Military Balance+

The launch, in early 2017, of the Military Balance+ interactive digital database started a new era not just in the way we present our defence information, but also in the way that it can be used. We created a searchable system that allows users to query the data for themselves and provides the option to download our defence data in spreadsheet form. This is a significant change for our customers, who now no longer have to laboriously type our information into their own database; now they can download our information and integrate it in a fraction of the time taken previously. The database also allows us to diverge from the focus on concision. We do not have to employ so many abbreviations online and have the ability to include more data categories without the restrictions imposed by a bound book. It also allows us to move away from an annual publication cycle. We will retain the printed book, but this will in time provide us with a platform to present perhaps more discrete datasets, as well as conduct more analysis of our information.

Assessing military power

In its early years, senior Institute staff were concerned not just that *The Military Balance* remain concise, but that it remain a primarily quantitative publication. Indeed, one of the reasons for the establishment of the complementary *Strategic Survey* in 1967 was that the Institute needed a publication where matters of defence policy could be analysed, allowing *The Military Balance* to focus on quantitative assessments. But over recent decades, we have again introduced into the book analysis of defence plans, and the regional security environments within which nations frame their defence policies. This reflects the view that solely examining equipment, and examining military capabilities quantitatively, tells only part of the story of national military power. Understanding more about national defence policy is important too, as it gives the analyst information about what a nation might envisage as tasks for its armed forces. Policies can be used as guides against which to measure inventories and procurement plans: are these, for instance, well matched against the roles intended for armed forces? A range of other factors are also important in these more qualitative assessments. Operational experience is one, as is robust military training, and we track in our database information on key military exercises undertaken by states as well as their deployments. Also noteworthy is an understanding of the legislative steps that countries need to take before they can actually deploy their armed forces; it is easier for some than others. We cover additional areas in our 'capability summaries', such as a country's alliance relations and its defence-industrial base. But these are only indicators. Indeed, if *The Military Balance* was to engage in more thoroughgoing qualitative studies, it might have to also compare between states factors including doctrine, organisation, training, materiel, leadership and education, personnel, facilities and interoperability (collectively termed DOTMLPFI by NATO), with the trade-offs between thoroughness and concision that this would entail.

Focusing on the future

That said, there are questions now over what areas of military power we may look to assess, and to quantify, so as to still generate useful comparative assessments in future. Should we sharpen our focus on aspects of 'traditional' post-Second World War military power that are once more absorbing the attention of governments, such as strategic nuclear forces and manoeuvre warfare capabilities, at the expense of, say, systems useful in constabulary roles? Of course, an answer to the question 'how important are these weapons' may depend in large part on the location in which you happen to be sitting when the question is posed. And the Institute is mindful of the interests of its global membership and worldwide readership, as well as the reality that 'non-traditional' security challenges can fairly rapidly become more traditional.

Whether to include some new weapons systems may be seen as relatively clear-cut decisions – in time we can perhaps expect hypersonic systems to begin featuring in aerospace inventories – though these would still require clear methodological guidelines. But these decisions are harder to make for dual-use systems. For instance, in the 1980s there were suggestions that we should include more on space-based capabilities – the US Strategic Defense Initiative was noted in mid-decade by an external analyst as a possible area of focus. For space, which has relatively recently emerged as a conflict domain, it is difficult to determine how relevant some civilian satellites may be to military power. For example, armed forces may have access to bandwidth on civilian communications satellites, but determining which satellites are subject to these agreements may be problematic. They may also have access to remote-sensing satellites. However, these judgements are more straightforward when it comes to early-warning satellites.

New capabilities are emerging, like cyber power, autonomous systems, robotics and more technologically enabled systems, such as command-and-control networks improved with artificial intelligence and machine learning. A key challenge for analysts, and certainly for us working with comparative data, is first to begin understanding how to assess these. In recent years we have begun to look at proxies for making judgements about military cyber power; for instance, does a country have a military cyber organisation, or has it declared an offensive cyber capability? We are now engaged on a more thoroughgoing project to define metrics to measure cyber power. Of course, a key problem we will face is that cyber power is not solely a military phenomenon. It is critical to military systems, but also vital to economic and energy security, and much of the expertise may lie in the private sector. Nonetheless, our task is to identify categories that the Institute can begin to assess, and a methodology that it can apply in doing so.

As we gather our data, now and in the future, we adhere to an established formula. The Institute is independent and owes no allegiance to any government. We still, each year, solicit comments from countries on the data we publish, and to this end we maintain lines of communication with ministries of defence and armed forces. These contacts allow us not just to solicit information, but also to engage in a dialogue about data points through the year. We also regularly contact specialists outside government and we conduct continual open-source information gathering. With the volume of information in the public domain growing near-exponentially, this cuts two ways. For instance, increasing print and online imagery is a valuable aid to the analyst, but its practical utility depends on judgements we make, including over veracity. However, the judgements we make are ours alone.

From its inception, *The Military Balance* proved its value. Its data was used as a key source by the media from the first editions, and over the years it has also been used by governments and officials compiling their own defence publications. Examples include Marshal Vasily Sokolovsky's 1962 book *Military Strategy*, documents, speeches and publications by ministries of defence including the UK Ministry of Defence and the US Department of Defense, testimony to the US Congress, reports by other think tanks and even the 1980s Soviet propaganda pamphlets entitled *Whence the Threat to Peace*, issued as a riposte to the Pentagon's *Soviet Military Power*. In some cases, of course, organisations will use our information selectively. Selecting and collating the information is not straightforward. In 1964, it was said that four months of intensive work went into the production of the book. By 1968, this had grown to six to nine months. Now, production of the book and database is a year-round activity.

For many of those who work on and use our data, the book is a mine of information. Equipment has come and gone during these 60 years, such as the F-111 and the SR-71, but careful examination of the information indicates that there are also significant elements of continuity. For instance, some defence equipment has been in service throughout the 60 years. This includes the *Centurion*, T-34, T-54 and T-55 tanks and the MiG-21, Tu-95 and Tu-16 aircraft (variants of the latter serving as China's H-6 bomber) and the U-2 and B-52. The current plan is for the B-52 to still be in service in 2050 (it first flew in 1952, six years before the ISS was founded). *Sherman* main battle tanks only disappeared from our data in the last year, when we assessed that they were no longer in active Paraguayan service (three remain as recovery vehicles in Mexico). At the same time, for the defence specialist the books offer a window on plans that failed to carry through – the first edition notes that 'the supersonic TSR-2 will replace the *Canberra* for tactical purposes'. Those who began producing the book intended it to provide an authoritative basis of accessible information on which debates around military affairs could be centred. We still retain that ambition.

Challenges in nuclear-arms control: past and present

Nuclear-arms control is back at the centre of international-security debates. Although agreements related to the control of arms and the conduct of warfare have existed for centuries, the modern concept of arms control emerged as a result of the scholarly debate at the dawn of the Cold War about how to avoid a future conflict, particularly one involving nuclear weapons. The current group of treaties that define arms control – conventional, nuclear and other 'weapons of mass destruction' (WMD) – served the world well in managing the Cold War and the period of relative peace that followed.

However, arms-control regimes have come under increasing pressure since the late 1990s and are now in a period of unprecedented crisis. Should the Intermediate-Range Nuclear Forces (INF) Treaty and New START collapse, the world may be without any bilateral nuclear-arms-control agreements between the two states with the largest nuclear arsenals – Russia and the United States – for the first time since the 1960s. The risk is that the absence of arms control between these two powers may lead to an arms race with unpredictable consequences and instability that could lead to a new Cold War or potentially even to conflict.

Defining terms

The US launched the first nuclear-arms-control effort, the Baruch Plan, in 1946, under which the US would transfer control of its arsenal to the United Nations in exchange for a verifiable ban on nuclear weapons, to be followed by the elimination of the US nuclear inventory. This proposal failed, not least because the Soviet Union was quickly developing its own nuclear arsenal. Early efforts towards disarmament (including competing proposals throughout the 1950s and 1960s in the Committee on Disarmament) failed largely because they focused on eliminating the weapons, as though they were the cause of international conflicts, rather than a symptom of them. Scholars therefore sought a better approach.

The best definition of arms control to emerge from the early thinking of Cold War theorists is by Thomas C. Schelling and Morton H. Halperin in their seminal 1961 book, *Strategy and Arms Control*. This book defined the term to include 'all the forms of military cooperation between potential enemies in the interest of reducing the likelihood of war, its scope and violence if it occurs, and the political and economic costs of being prepared for it'. They also highlighted how 'common interest' between adversaries could lead to cooperation to avoid conflict, as well as asserting that arms control could include reductions or increases in weapons – as long as it focused on establishing stability and reducing the incentive for either side to initiate conflict.

Arms control was seen as a way not just to prevent nuclear war, but also to manage the arms race and competition for new weapons systems, as well as a means to buy time in order to solve underlying political conflicts. Setting a clearer context and meaning for arms control and its adoption within national strategies helped policymakers and publics alike not only to embrace arms control but also begin to find ways of implementing it.

The Cuban Missile Crisis focuses minds

The US, USSR and UK had been discussing a ban on testing since the late 1950s, but it was the Cuban Missile Crisis in 1962 that gave the US and Soviet political and military leadership the political will to embrace arms control, and particularly nuclear-arms control, as a way to manage tensions and risks during the Cold War.

The first tentative steps towards limiting the nuclear-arms race came days after the end of the Cuban Missile Crisis, with then Soviet premier Nikita Khrushchev's proposals to limit nuclear risks. This led to an agreement that established a direct communications link between Moscow and Washington in June 1963 (the 'hotline' agreement) and the Partial Nuclear Test Ban Treaty in August 1963, which limited tests by the Soviet Union, the United Kingdom and the US (but not China or France). The goodwill achieved led to the start of US–USSR talks on stopping the spread of nuclear weapons, first in space, resulting in the Outer Space Treaty of January 1967, and then globally, resulting in a joint draft treaty by the US and USSR on the Non-Proliferation of Nuclear Weapons (NPT) in August 1967. The NPT entered into force in 1970, legally limiting the number of countries that could possess nuclear weapons.

The golden age of Cold War arms control

Early successes in US–USSR talks helped build support among NATO members for arms control, as expressed in the December 1967 Report of the Council on the Future Tasks of the Alliance (known as the Harmel Report). The Harmel Report defined the original dual-track approach of deterrence and dialogue, which led directly to NATO's so-called 'Reykjavik signal' of 1968, which called for multilateral nuclear- and conventional-arms-control talks with the Warsaw Pact, known as the Mutual and Balanced Force Reductions (MBFR). The Harmel Report also led NATO to support the launch of the Conference on Security and Co-operation in Europe (CSCE), which led to the Helsinki process, resulting in the Helsinki Final Act of 1975 (which included transparency over large-scale military exercises). In parallel, bilateral US–USSR negotiations resulted in three key agreements in May 1972: the Agreement on the Prevention of Incidents On and Over the High Seas (INCSEA); the Strategic Arms Limitation Talks (SALT); and the Anti-Ballistic Missile (ABM) Treaty. This momentum also led to the negotiation and signature (but not ratification) of SALT II (1979). Global efforts to address other WMD resulted in the Biological and Toxin Weapons Convention (BTWC) of 1972, which entered into force in 1975.

The SS-20 crisis and the INF Treaty

Despite the progress on arms control, tensions between the US and USSR increased through the 1970s. A notable escalation occurred with the Soviet introduction of a new, destabilising nuclear missile in Europe, the 15Zh45 (SS-20 *Saber*) in 1977. The SS-20 was a direct threat to stability because of its effectiveness as a first-strike weapon. Critically, it was road-mobile and harder to strike than a fixed launcher. It was also solid-fuelled, and therefore ready to launch in minutes rather than the hours it took to prepare a liquid-fuelled rocket. The SS-20 also was highly accurate, with multiple warheads, unlike the 8K63 (SS-4 *Sandal*) and 8K65 (SS-5 *Skean*) missiles it replaced, which required far higher-yield nuclear warheads to damage their targets reliably. Because of this, the SS-4 and SS-5 missiles were seen as retaliatory rather than first-strike weapons. However, the introduction of the SS-20 led NATO allies to worry that the Soviet Union intended to launch a first strike (including SS-20s and shorter-range nuclear systems) to knock out NATO command-and-control systems and key airfields and seaports in Europe and prevent the US and Canada from bringing reinforcements from North America. This scenario would give Washington a stark choice after a first strike: to retaliate against Soviet targets and risk strikes on the continental US, or to 'de-couple' from Europe and allow the battlefield to be contained only on the territory of European NATO and Warsaw Pact states.

NATO reacted to the introduction of the SS-20 by reaching a second 'dual-track' decision in December 1979, declaring that, on the one hand, NATO would restore deterrence through basing a similar nuclear-weapon system in Europe – the *Pershing* II ground-launched ballistic missile (GLBM) and BGM-109G *Gryphon* ground-launched cruise missile (GLCM) – thus eliminating any perceived Soviet first-strike advantage. On the other hand, NATO would offer a route to reduce now-mutual risks through nuclear-arms control: specifically, a ban on ground-launched missiles with a range between 1,000 kilometres and 5,500 km in the European theatre. NATO member states met intensively from 1979 onwards to design and agree to the parameters of a treaty, which continued through the negotiations. Bilateral US–USSR talks, augmented by consultation among NATO member states before and after each round of talks, began in 1981 but collapsed in 1983 with the deployment of the *Pershing* II ballistic-missile and *Gryphon* cruise-missile systems in Europe. Like the SS-20, both of these systems were road-mobile and solid-fuelled. However, following a pivotal summit between then US president Ronald Reagan and then Soviet premier Mikhail Gorbachev in Reykjavik in 1986, both sides agreed to a global ban on Soviet and US intermediate-range ground-launched missiles and shorter-range systems. The INF Treaty, signed in 1987, banned GLBMs and GLCMs with ranges between 1,000 km and 5,500 km ('intermediate-range missiles', according to the treaty text) and 'shorter-range' GLBMs and GLCMs with ranges between 500 km and 1,000 km.

Helsinki and the end of the Cold War

Meanwhile, through the CSCE process, the Helsinki Final Act chapter on military transparency became the Stockholm Document of 1986, which contained more extensive and mandatory military-transparency rules, especially over military exercises, known as Confidence- and Security-Building Measures. The

Stockholm Document was expanded and updated in 1990, renamed the Vienna Document, further updated in 1992, 1994 and 1999, and is now known as the Vienna Document 2011. The MBFR talks ended in 1989 without producing a treaty, but the wide-ranging talks, which included discussion of nuclear weapons and aerial verification, resulted in the Conventional Armed Forces in Europe (CFE) Treaty in 1990. The aerial-verification regime was turned into its own treaty, the Open Skies Treaty, which provides the right to overfly all territory of each party (signed in 1992, but did not enter into force until 2002). On the bilateral track, success on the INF Treaty led to agreement on START in 1991, which, along with the CFE Treaty, provided verifiable, transparent reductions in the Cold War conventional and nuclear arsenals.

Enthusiasm for arms control and disarmament continued after the end of the Cold War, with the US and USSR (later Russia) announcing unilateral limits on short-range nuclear forces, known as the Presidential Nuclear Initiatives (PNI) of 1991 and 1992. A year later, Russia and the US subsequently agreed to ban multiple independently targetable re-entry vehicles (MIRVs) in START II (which did not enter into force). Other successful arms-control efforts included the ban on chemical weapons, known as the Chemical Weapons Convention (CWC), which was signed in 1993 and entered into force in 1997. Less successful was the call for a ban on the production of fissile material, the proposed Fissile Material Cut-Off Treaty, which has been on the agenda of the UN Conference on Disarmament since 1995 without leading to a treaty, and the Comprehensive Nuclear-Test-Ban Treaty (CTBT), which was signed in 1996, but is still not in force. The Agreement on the Adaptation of the CFE Treaty suffered a similar fate in 1999, with the treaty signed but still not in force. Critics of arms control began to push back on the underlying concept and framework (especially regarding the reliance on bilateral US–Russia treaties), while concerns over unaddressed non-compliance with existing agreements emerged in the context of a range of agreements, including the BTWC, CFE, CWC, INF, NPT and PNI.

A new form of arms control

Discussion over the utility of arms control came to the forefront of security debates with the US decision to withdraw from the ABM Treaty in 2002. Russia retaliated by withdrawing its ratification of the START II Treaty and pursuing MIRV-capable strategic missile systems. Then US president George W. Bush sought to introduce a new paradigm for bilateral nuclear-arms control with Russia, submitting a short and simple draft of a politically binding agreement to limit deployed systems. However, Russia insisted the treaty be legally binding, and the result was the Strategic Offensive Reductions Treaty (SORT). SORT lacked verification, instead requiring each side to declare that it had reduced the total number of its operationally deployed strategic nuclear warheads. SORT was superseded by the 2010 Treaty on Measures for the Further Reduction and Limitation of Strategic Offensive Arms, known as New START. Russia and the US returned to a pattern of more complex agreements that included verifiable elimination of nuclear delivery systems and limits on strategic delivery systems and deployed weapons that would reduce numbers down to levels not seen since the late 1950s. In February 2018, both parties announced they had reached the central limits of New START. However, the treaty did not limit MIRV-capable systems and, with the new administration of President Donald Trump, the US may be returning to the SORT approach of simple but non-verifiable agreements, instead of verifiable arms control. (For instance, John Bolton – now national security advisor to President Trump – as long ago as 2010 wrote critically of New START's 'myopic focus on Russian arms levels' and advocated greater flexibility over launchers.) Russia, in the meantime, rejected then US president Barack Obama's offer of further reductions in strategic nuclear weapons as proposed in his Berlin speech of June 2013.

SS-20 crisis redux

Since then, the crisis of arms-control compliance has worsened. Russia's willingness to violate the INF Treaty in pursuit of dual-capable, precision ground-launched cruise missiles of short and intermediate range, in the context of its pursuit of a broader set of strike capabilities, is of particular concern for stability. Its introduction of the 9M729 (SSC-8 *Screwdriver*), a road-mobile, dual-capable GLCM with a range likely greater than 2,000 km, has reintroduced the spectre of credible nuclear first strike to Europe for the first time in a generation. At the very least, Russia's unwillingness to take decisive and transparent steps to allay any concerns about the system or, more specifically, to destroy it in a verifiable way, has unsettled European states.

Figure 1 Major landmarks in arms control, 1944–2017

1940s
- 1944 US first atomic test
- 1945 US first atomic use
- 1946 Baruch Plan
- 1949 NATO formed
- 1949 Russia first atomic test

1950s
- 1954 US nuclear weapons deployed in Europe
- 1955 Warsaw Pact formed

1960s
- 1960 France first atomic test
- 1962 Cuban Missile Crisis
- 1963 Partial Nuclear Test Ban Treaty; Hotline Agreement
- 1964 China first atomic test
- 1966 US nuclear weapons in Europe peak (7,000)
- 1967 Harmel Report; Outer Space Treaty
- 1968 Treaty on the Non-Proliferation of Nuclear Weapons (NPT) signed; Mutual and Balanced Force Reduction (MBFR) talks launched

1970s
- 1970 NPT entry into force
- 1972 Strategic Arms Limitation Talks (SALT), Anti-Ballistic Missile Treaty; Agreement on the Prevention of Incidents on and over the High Seas, Biological and Toxin Weapons Convention signed
- 1974 Threshold Test Ban Treaty
- 1975 Helsinki Final Act
- 1977 Russia deploys SS-20 missiles
- 1979 NATO dual-track decision; SALT II

1980s
- 1981 Intermediate-range Nuclear Forces (INF) Treaty negotiations begin
- 1983 US *Pershing* II missiles deployed; INF negotiations halt
- 1986 US–Soviet Reykjavik Summit; Stockholm Document
- 1987 INF Treaty signed; global nuclear stockpiles peak at 64,000
- 1989 MBFR talks replaced by Conventional Armed Forces in Europe (CFE) talks

1990s
- 1990 CFE Treaty; Vienna Document
- 1991 Strategic Arms Reduction Treaty (START) I signed
- 1992 Open Skies Treaty signed
- 1993 START II signed; Chemical Weapons Convention signed (1997 entry into force)
- 1995 NPT indefinite extension
- 1999 Adapted CFE Treaty signed; Comprehensive Nuclear Test Ban Treaty signed

2000s
- 2002 Strategic Offensive Reductions Treaty (SORT) signed
- 2002 Open Skies entry into force

2010s
- 2010 New START Treaty
- 2017 Nuclear Weapon Ban Treaty signed

Instead, Russia has pursued counter-charges that the US had considered settled in the 1990s, while denying the existence of the system in bilateral talks from 2013 to 2017. In response, first the Obama administration and then the Trump administration sought to increase political, military and economic pressure on Russia to return to compliance and maintain allied support (including NATO and Asian allies). In December 2017, Russia admitted the existence of the system, but denied it was a treaty violation, though it gave no further explanation and made no effort to resolve US concerns during 2018. As a result of Russia's action, the US declared Russia in violation of the INF Treaty in July 2014 and has been seeking support from allies for additional steps, while Russia continues to deny it is in violation. On 4 December, the US said it had found Russia in 'material breach' of the treaty and that it would suspend its obligations 'as a remedy effective in 60 days unless Russia returns to full and verifiable compliance'.

What's next?

With little prospect of a positive resolution of the challenges facing the INF Treaty, nuclear-arms control is at a critical stage. If Russia continues to violate the INF Treaty, the extension of New START, which expires in 2021, is hard to envision. Some in the Trump administration suggest that they could pursue another SORT-type agreement, but while that likely is not Russia's preference – Moscow arguably would prefer verification, plus legal limitations – both sides may find that they currently have neither the funds nor the inclination to engage in a strategic nuclear-arms race. Both Moscow and Washington are already investing significant sums in nuclear-force modernisation, as they strive to reach their modernisation targets within New START limits. However, both countries have been developing air- and sea-launched intermediate-range missile systems for some time, and ground-launched systems are more likely to join the mix should the INF Treaty collapse. In addition, other states are developing and deploying such missile systems, in particular China, with the majority of its nuclear weapons delivered by intermediate-range ground-launched systems. Indeed, it has been argued that technology and the proliferation of related know-how are passing the INF Treaty by. More countries are seeking precision-guided, dual-capable cruise-missile technology, as other advanced systems suited to first-strike capabilities pass from drawing board to deployment, including long-range cruise missiles, hypersonic missiles and boost-glide systems.

One possible way forward was proposed by the US and Russia in October 2007 in a joint statement at the 62nd session of the UN General Assembly. In the face of the proliferation of intermediate- and shorter-range missiles, both sides proposed that additional countries (especially China) could join a call to renounce 'ground-launched ballistic and cruise missiles with ranges between 500 and 5,500 kilometers, leading to the destruction of any such missiles, and the cessation of associated programs'. While this proposal did not gain traction at the time, the spread of such systems – both nuclear-capable and conventional – has grown and the potential threat they pose has become clearer. (In addition, the current impasse over membership in the Missile Technology Control Regime (MTCR), with Russia blocking applications for new membership and China not yet permitted to join due to concerns over its export-control regime, has prevented the MTCR from fully achieving its aims.) The joint 2007 proposal could even be expanded to include a ban on the development, production and deployment of such systems, along with verifiable destruction provisions. It is likely that, to succeed today, such an agreement would also have to involve air- and sea-launched systems. It could mean revisiting the idea – discussed as part of the original INF Treaty proposals – of introducing regional limits on intermediate-range missile systems, rather than an outright ban.

Other issues will need to be addressed too, including shorter-range nuclear weapons and new technical problems. The latter includes long-distance hypersonic weapons and the challenge they pose in compressing a defender's decision space; the related role of artificial intelligence in military decision-making loops; lethal autonomous weapons; and how to (and whether it is possible to) deter cyber attacks (which could potentially target early-warning or nuclear-command-and-control facilities). While arriving at the frameworks capable of managing even one of these challenges could be problematic, surviving a new, more complex, less predictable and more multipolar equivalent of the Cold War could be even more difficult.

Quantum computing and defence

The integration of quantum technologies currently represents one of the most anticipated advances for armed forces, yet their precise impact remains difficult to predict. Although economical applications and widespread use are still years away, there is little doubt that they will have disruptive effect when they are employed at scale. In May 2018, the head of quantum computing at technology firm Intel suggested that 'if 10 years from now we have a quantum computer with a few thousand qubits, that would certainly change the world in the same way the first microprocessor did'. (A qubit, or quantum bit, is the basic unit of information in a quantum computer, analogous to a bit in a standard computer.) But while quantum technology is expected to eventually have far-reaching effects for military forces, intelligence services and law-enforcement agencies, it is unclear how far it will alter the traditional balance of power among states, or between states and non-state actors.

Potential military applications

The field of quantum information science is giving rise to multiple new defence-related applications that are often grouped together under the single moniker 'quantum', but which merit independent consideration. Quantum key distribution (QKD), quantum cryptanalysis and quantum sensing all promise to significantly affect strategic security in differing ways. For example, QKD provides a near-term advantage for defenders to secure their communications, while quantum cryptanalysis is an inherently offensive capability, though one that is maturing at a slower pace. Generalised quantum computing will offer many other possibilities, but they are too uncertain at this stage to permit concerted analysis of their second-order effects.

The most common form of quantum encryption is the transmission of cryptographic keys (i.e., QKD) using quantum 'superpositions' of photons during the initiation of secure communications sessions. In keeping with Heisenberg's uncertainty principle, the exact states of the photons are indeterminate until they are isolated and measured – only then do they exhibit a specific state of polarisation. As the very process of intercepting (or 'eavesdropping' on) a qubit irreversibly changes it, QKD offers a valuable means of knowing if communications have been intercepted and examined (e.g., through a 'man-in-the-middle' attack). This is analogous to using tamper-resistant envelopes for sending letters via the standard postal network. QKD technology is applicable to existing systems for encrypted communications, but until the last few years it had faced implementation challenges over long distances, thereby rendering it impractical outside limited environments.

Quantum cryptanalysis refers to the specific application of quantum computing for decrypting encoded messages. Current encryption standards primarily rely upon mathematical algorithms for encoding data, which are effectively unbreakable in any reasonable period of time. For example, US military-grade, Advanced Encryption Standard 256-bit encryption would theoretically require billions of years for modern computers to crack the code through brute-force methods (i.e., 'trial-and-error' of all possible solutions). Quantum computers, however, will eventually be able to replace sequential trial-and-error methods for processing such complex mathematical problems with alternate means to consider many possibilities simultaneously. The promise of quantum cryptanalysis is so alluring that some countries are already beginning to collect encrypted foreign communications with the expectation that they will be able to extract valuable secrets from that data in the future. When quantum cryptanalysis does become available, it will significantly affect international relations by making broadcast (or intercepted) communications open to decryption. For countries that extensively rely on encryption to secure military operations, diplomatic correspondence or other sensitive data, this could be a watershed event.

In September 2018, the United States published its National Strategic Overview for Quantum Information Science, which defined quantum sensing as 'leveraging quantum mechanics to enhance the fundamental accuracy of measurements and/or enabling new regimes or modalities for sensors and measurement'. Such new capabilities would afford clear military advantages. The United Kingdom's Defence Science Expert Committee has highlighted the potential importance of improved gravity sensors (quantum gravimeters), which could detect moving masses under water, such as submarines. Superconducting magnetometers that use quantum technology to measure miniscule changes in magnetic fields could also be used to locate enemy submarines, while quantum radar could be used to detect even low-observable aircraft. As the UK Defence Science and Technology Laboratory has said, 'it is anticipated that new militarily disruptive technologies (e.g., novel communications or radar modalities) will be enabled'. Quantum technologies already form part of developments related to the miniaturisation of atomic clocks, which are useful for position, navigation and timing purposes.

Quantum computing will likely provide other disruptive applications, although it is too early in the research-and-development phase to foresee what inventions lie ahead or how friendly forces or adversaries may leverage them. Quantum computing will not entirely supplant classical computing methods based on transistors and silicon microchips. Instead, quantum computing should best be conceived of as an alternative, complementary and even synergistic technology that will be able to solve some problems that current computers cannot, but which will most likely also be comparatively ineffective, or only marginally better, for solving other problems at which current computers excel.

National programmes

Several nations are heavily investing in quantum research to gain economic and military advantage. The dual-use nature of quantum computing means that private companies and universities will also play key roles in inventing and adapting these new technologies. In its March 2018 submission to the UK House of Commons Science and Technology Committee, the Institute of Physics asserted that 'the UK needs to convert its strong research base into commercial products, by deepening connections between academia and industry, and capitalising on relevant industrial strengths'. The extent to which a nation-state can marshal resources to prioritise the development of military applications may prove a decisive edge in this new technological race.

China was an early leader in quantum research and development. In 2016, Beijing initiated an effort to achieve major breakthroughs in quantum technologies by 2030, and that same year it launched the world's first quantum satellite, which teleported a photon to Earth in 2017. The *Micius* satellite has now successfully completed QKD from orbit to ground stations in Xinglong, China, and Graz, Austria. In 2017, China also established the first long-distance, terrestrial quantum-communication link between Beijing and Shanghai. These scientific achievements represent landmark initiatives that could secure China's government communications against foreign observation – at least until post-quantum cryptanalysis becomes a functional reality. The planned US$10-billion National Laboratory for Quantum Information Sciences in Hefei, Anhui province, will lead the nation's drive for quantum computing and sensing.

The US is another possible leader in the race to realise quantum applications for defence. Since 2016, the government has sponsored over US$200 million in quantum research, and in 2018 the Department of Energy and the National Science Foundation committed another US$250m to support quantum sensing, computing and communications through two- to five-year grant awards. Among the armed forces, the US Army Research Office funds extensive research in quantum computing, while the US Air Force sees it as transformative technology for information and space warfare. But even more relevant may be private-sector companies such as Google, IBM, Intel and Microsoft, which have been conducting quantum research for almost a decade. In the West, they – along with the Canadian company D-Wave Systems – are leading the development of quantum computers that may run the quantum-enabled military platforms of the future.

Collectively, European nations are also investing substantially and making significant advances. The European Commission's quantum-technologies flagship programme will be a large-scale research initiative in the order of €1bn (US$1.1bn) over a ten-year period. It is intended to focus on four main areas of quantum technology: communication, computation, simulation and sensing. In 2013, the UK government announced a five-year investment of £270m (US$422m) for its own National Quantum Technologies Programme, which is intended to 'create a coherent government, industry and academic quantum technology community', and quantum technologies were in late 2018 the subject of a UK Parliamentary inquiry. French President Emmanuel Macron signed a memorandum of understanding with Australia's then-prime minister Malcolm Turnbull in May 2018 on a joint venture between the two countries to develop and commercialise a quantum silicon integrated circuit. This joint venture will combine the efforts of the Australian company Silicon Quantum Computing and the French research institute Commissariat à l'énergie atomique et aux énergies alternatives. Finally, in September 2018, Germany announced new funding for quantum-technologies research worth €650m (US$771m) for the period 2018–22.

Russia is also investing in quantum computing, at the Russian Quantum Center, but it has not committed the same level of resources as other nations and remains behind China and the US. That may partially correlate with the overall decline in Russian scientific-research capacity since the 1990s. President Vladimir Putin has, however, reportedly raised national spending on research and development (R&D) to 1% of Russia's gross domestic product, with R187bn (US$3bn) earmarked for fundamental scientific R&D in 2018. Nonetheless, the recent breakthroughs in quantum information science have not been driven by Russian researchers, as is evident from vocal US concerns about a growing 'quantum gap' with China, without similar attention to threats from Russia in this field.

Quantum supremacy

The term 'quantum supremacy' refers to the ability of a quantum computer to perform tasks beyond the capability of today's most powerful conventional supercomputers. Google announced a 72-qubit processor in 2018 – surpassing IBM's record the previous year of 50 qubits – and said that its new chip might achieve quantum supremacy within a year. But it is not just the number of qubits that matters; rather, a combination of factors – including the 'depth' of a quantum circuit, or how many logical operations it can perform before errors proliferate – affect the true computational power that IBM researchers have termed 'quantum volume'. Intel shares the view that quantum technologies are incredibly complex and will require significant time to perfect commercial applications.

It is also worth considering what quantum technologies might mean for geopolitics. There are grounds for concern that the advent of quantum technologies will only exacerbate the digital divide among nations and increase security disparities. For example, quantum cryptanalysis could theoretically be a great equaliser, but in reality it may only become available to wealthy, advanced countries who can afford to operate the required assets. If a select handful of countries can both force transparency on their adversaries' communications and safeguard their own through QKD or post-quantum-encryption algorithms, then hegemonic relationships might persist. The same could hold true for massive data processing to deliver real-time intelligence and operational advantages to technically advanced states. This potential new security dilemma was raised during the 4th European Cybersecurity Forum in Krakow, Poland, in October 2018.

Conversely, the development and widespread diffusion of quantum technologies might over time reduce the comparative advantage of some powers. If every government can secure its communications, process intelligence data with heretofore-unprecedented scale and speed, and detect foreign military assets in the air or under the sea, then a levelling effect might be observed. All that can be certain at this stage is that technical quantum supremacy is both inevitable and close to hand, and that the disruptive effects of quantum technologies will likely lead countries to change their defence postures.

Chapter Two
Comparative defence statistics

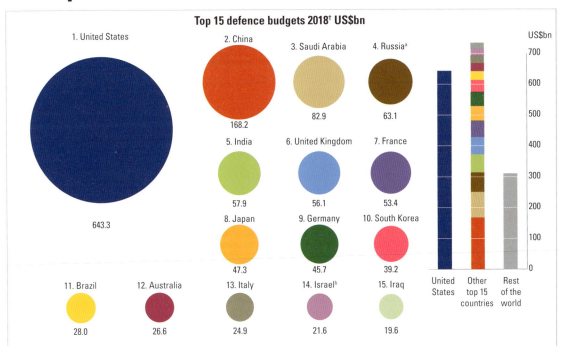

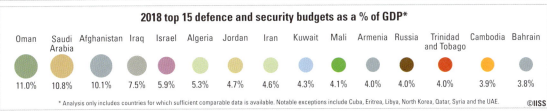

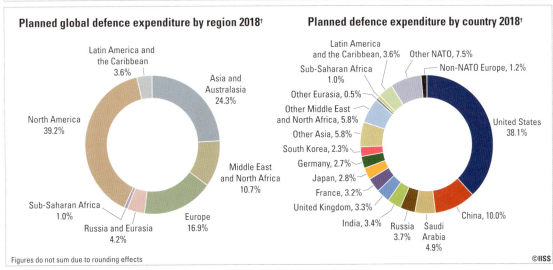

22 THE MILITARY BALANCE 2019

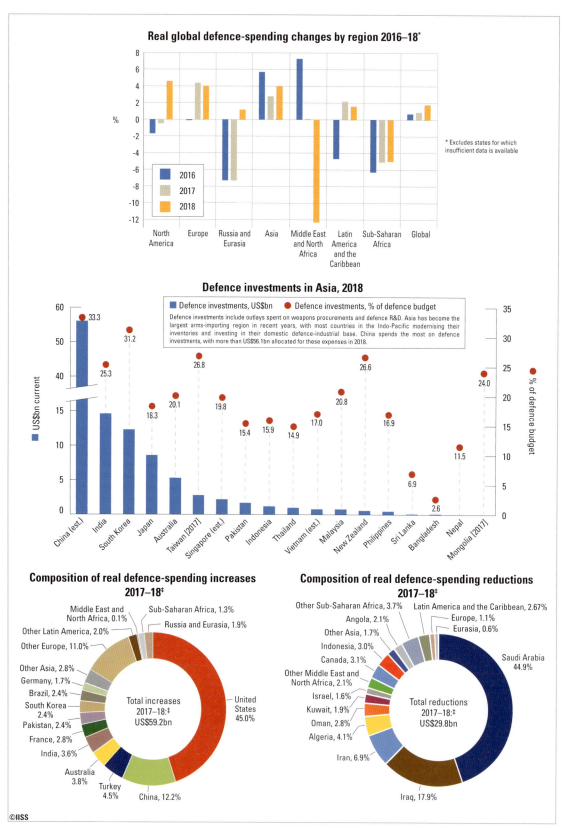

Comparative defence statistics

Soviet (VVS and PVO) and Russian Aerospace Forces (VKS), 1989–2018

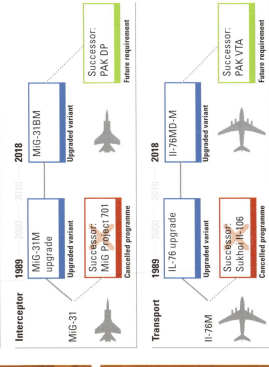

Russia's Aerospace Forces (VKS) have benefited from a decade of sustained investment allowing the delivery of new and upgraded combat aircraft and air-launched weapons. This, however, has relied on designs already in development or service when the Soviet Union collapsed; plans then for successor types of combat aircraft were abandoned in the early 1990s.

While upgrades of types already in service – such as the Su-27 *Flanker* – have belatedly entered the inventory, all new designs were shelved. As of late 2018, the VKS is once again attempting to address those same requirements. Ambitions to introduce the Sukhoi Su-57 heavy fighter into service are yet to be realised, while other military-aircraft plans are being revised. A mix of budgetary constraints combined with overly optimistic development schedules have combined to slow the introduction of the Su-57.

Ambitions to acquire a new bomber to meet the PAK DA requirement also appear to have been revised, with the project delayed and the aircraft re-cast as a complement to the new Tu-160M2 variant of the Soviet-era Tu-160 *Blackjack*.

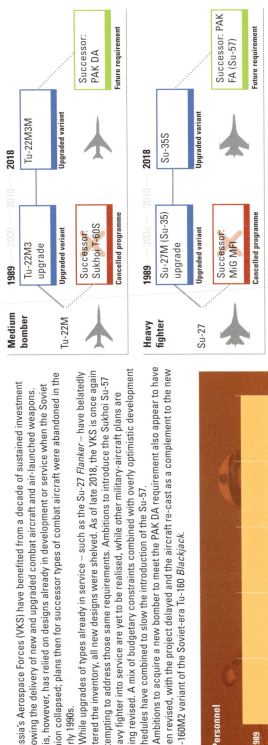

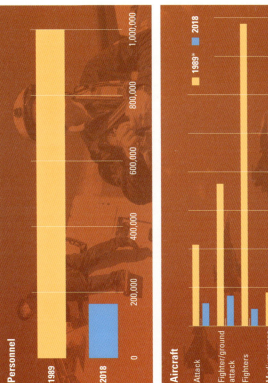

*1989 figure combines air-force and air-defence-force aircraft

Brigade structures: China, Russia and the United States

The armies of the United States (from 2003), Russia (from 2008) and China (from 2017) have shifted from division-based structures to new brigade-centric organisations for their manoeuvre forces. Combat support and combat service-support units, previously held separately at divisional level, have been moved into combat brigades. For Russia and the US, these changes were originally based on a judgement that there was a reduced prospect of high-intensity operations and, in the US case, on the ability to achieve air dominance. As a result, the US brigade combat team (BCT) designs are relatively light on fires and combat support. While subsequent revisions have added a third manoeuvre battalion and another combat-engineer company, the latest iteration of the US armored BCT still has only one battalion allocated to fire support, combat support and combat service support, and no organic air defence. The equivalent Russian motor-rifle brigade, by contrast, allocates more battalions to these roles, reflecting the importance of ground-based fire support in Russian doctrine and, perhaps, concerns over the relative weakness of Russian air capabilities. The new Chinese design appears to be a compromise between the two, with more support units than the US approach, but not as many as the Russian version, though there is possibly a higher headcount than either. In recent years there has been renewed attention in Russia and the West on potential high-intensity operations and both Russia and the US have begun re-emphasising division-level operations, Moscow going so far as to re-establish some previously downsized divisions. Whether the Chinese will eventually follow suit remains to be seen.

US: Armored Brigade Combat Team

China: Combined Arms Brigade (Heavy)

Russia: Motor-Rifle Brigade (with BMP infantry fighting vehicle)
In addition to the battalions shown, a motor-rifle brigade includes company-level electronic-warfare; chemical, biological, radiological and nuclear; and medical units.

© IISS

Comparative defence statistics

Principal advanced anti-air-warfare surface combatants and operators, 1998–2018

The US Navy brought into service the *Aegis* combat management system in the 1980s. Introduced after lengthy research and development, this was a step change in surface-ship anti-air-warfare (AAW) capabilities. *Aegis* was developed in response to a significant increase in the aircraft and anti-ship-missile threat, particularly that of saturation attack. Compared to existing systems, it comprised fixed phased-array radar and an integrated combat system, as well as better surface-to-air missiles. This improved processing, reaction time and channels of fire, and provided an extended engagement envelope. The first *Aegis*-equipped warship, the cruiser USS *Ticonderoga*, was commissioned in 1983. A further significant development took place in 1986 with the introduction of the multiple-cell vertical launch system (VLS) in place of trainable twin-arm missile launchers. Other navies followed suit, either by adopting *Aegis* or developing phased-array/active electronically scanned radar systems and VLS. Japan was an early adopter of *Aegis*. A number of medium-sized European navies rapidly made the step up in capability, either adopting *Aegis* or parts of it, whereas France, Italy and the United Kingdom developed their own systems. From 2005, China joined the club, and now has Type-052C and Type-052D destroyers, and will have Type-055 cruisers, though there may be question marks over the capabilities of some of the combat systems involved. But while Asia has nearly caught up with Europe in terms of numbers of these platforms, and looks set to forge ahead, the United States still fields more surface combatants with these capabilities than all other operators combined. US and Japanese *Aegis* ships also have a ballistic-missile-defence capability.

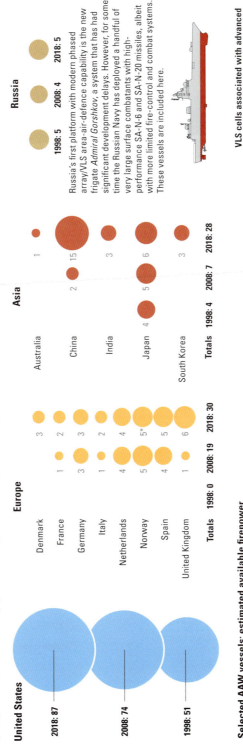

Selected AAW vessels: estimated available firepower

The US Navy's *Ticonderoga*-class cruisers are the oldest *Aegis*-equipped platforms, though they have been significantly updated. Their replacement will be critical for the US Navy. South Korea's KDD III *Sejong* class is the largest *Aegis* platform so far. China's Type-052D destroyers are about to be joined by the Type-055 cruisers, at an estimated 10,000–13,000 tonnes with 112 cells. US and Asian combatants in this class tend to have larger VLS magazines than their European counterparts (including Australia's Spanish-designed *Hobart* class). However, the cells cannot be reloaded at sea, although the US Navy is looking into this.

US: *Ticonderoga* class
10,000 tonnes FLD
122 VLS cells

South Korea: KDD III
11,000 tonnes FLD
80 (+48 ASW/LACM) VLS cells

China: Type-052D
7,500 tonnes FLD
64 VLS cells

Australia: *Hobart* class
6,300 tonnes FLD
48 VLS cells

France: *Forbin* class
7,050 tonnes FLD
48 VLS cells

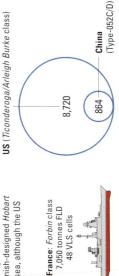

Russia's first platform with modern phased array/VLS area-air-defence capability is the new frigate *Admiral Gorshkov*, a system that has had significant development delays. However, for some time the Russian Navy has deployed a handful of very large surface combatants with high-performance SA-N-6 and SA-N-20 missiles, albeit with more limited fire-control and combat systems. These vessels are included here.

Helge Ingstad, foundered 8 Nov 2018. Salvage doubtful. FLD: full-load displacement. AAW: the capability to engage airborne threats, including aircraft and missiles

Key defence statistics

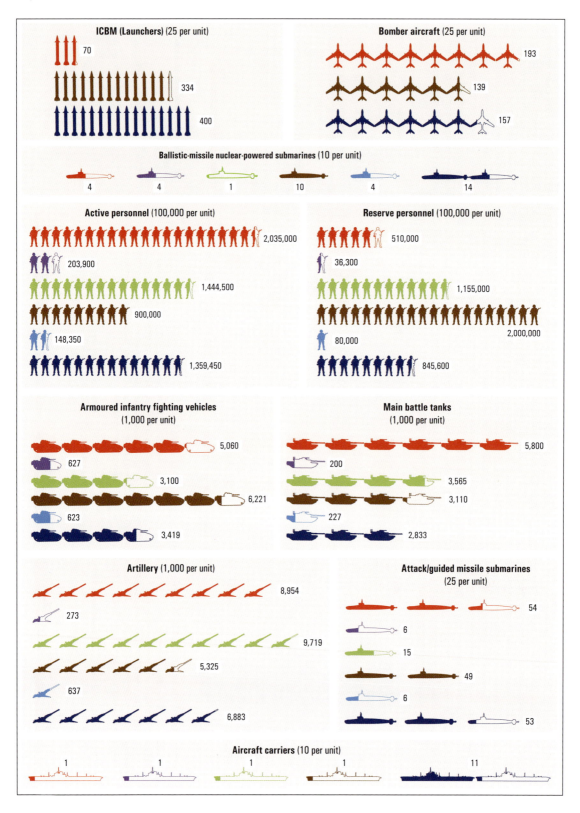

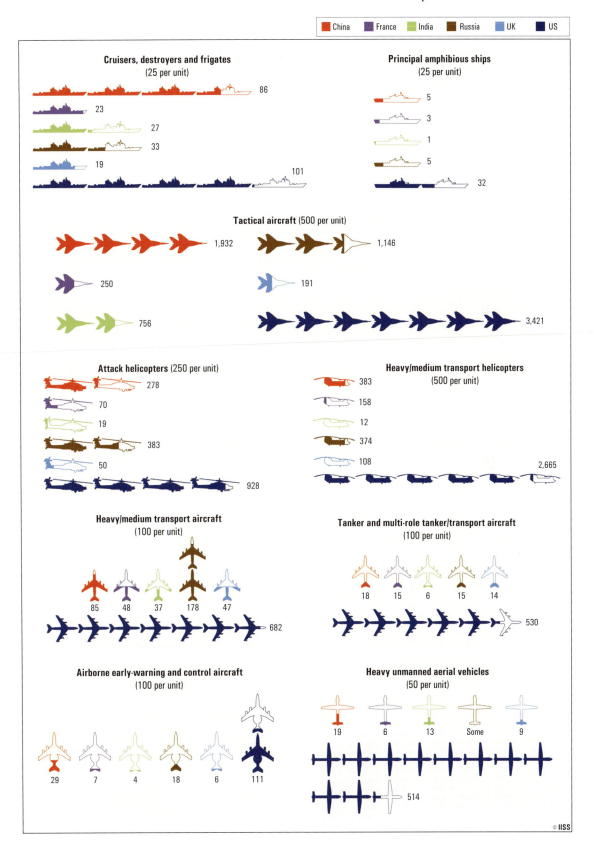

Chapter Three
North America

- The 2018 Nuclear Posture Review committed to nuclear modernisation, including development of low-yield warheads for SLBMs and, in the longer term, a modern nuclear-armed sea-launched cruise missile.
- Pentagon efforts to partner with Silicon Valley and technology firms to accelerate innovation have met some opposition from the sector, including refusal by Google staff to participate in the *Project Maven* AI initiative.
- The US army is fielding specially trained Security Force Assistance Brigades to provide trainers, advisors and mentors to partner other nations' forces. It continues to balance the requirements of ongoing missions with the reorientation to traditional tasks, also improving its combat-training centres and hastening their reorientation to high-end combat.
- The US Air Force continues to face the challenge of an ageing inventory combined with the lower pace of delivery of replacement types. USAF chiefs are advocating an expanded number of operational squadrons: the target mentioned is 386 by 2030.
- Any question of whether the Pentagon wanted to sustain two combat aircraft manufacturers (Lockheed Martin plus one other) appears to have been resolved with Boeing picking trainer, tanker UAV, and helicopter orders that will help sustain its military business.
- The US Navy continues to try to balance rebuilding readiness with achieving early progress towards increasing platform numbers to achieve a 355-ship battle force target.
- After delays, Canada announced that a consortium led by Lockheed Martin (with the UK Type-26 design) was the preferred bidder for its Canadian Surface Combatant programme.

Lockheed Martin F-35 fleet numbers

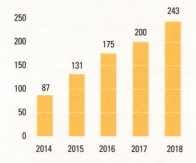

Boeing P-8A *Poseidon* fleet numbers

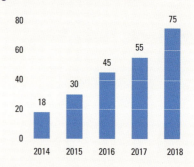

US expeditionary support and transport / logistics and supply vessels, 2014–18

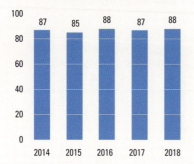

US principal surface combatants, 2014–18

(aircraft carriers, cruisers, destroyers, frigates)

Regional defence policy and economics   30 ▶

Armed forces data section   44 ▶

Arms procurements and deliveries   63 ▶

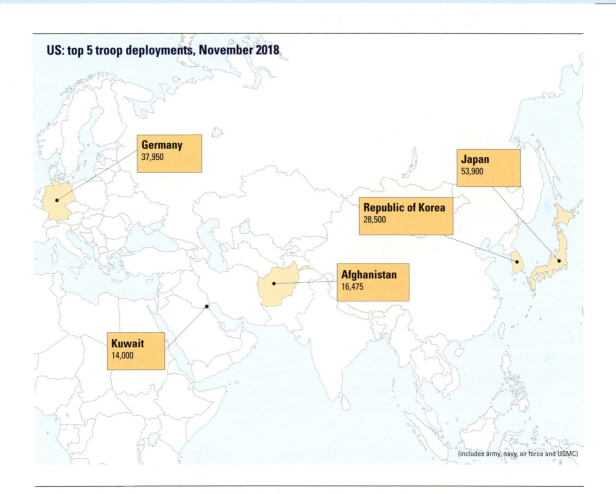

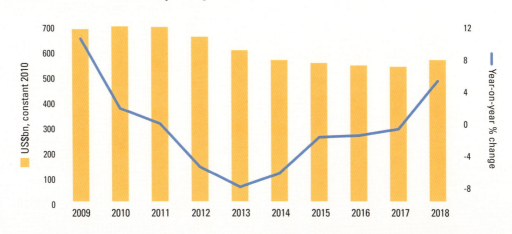

North America

UNITED STATES

Towards the end of its first year in power, the administration of US President Donald Trump began to release national-security documents that elaborated its political priorities. Trump wrote of his 2017 National Security Strategy (NSS) that 'we are charting a new and very different course'. His administration has done so in two important ways: by prioritising the return of great-power competition; and by unsettling Washington's closest allies.

Strategy documents

The strategy of 'principled realism' described by the December 2017 NSS is a narrative arc of military strength and generous institution building by the United States that surrendered American advantages and empowered and emboldened potential rivals. The contrast with the 2015 NSS is clear. That document, released by the Obama administration, affirmed 'America's leadership role within a rules-based international order that works best through empowered citizens, responsible states, and effective regional and international organizations'. The 2017 version flips the perspective from an international order of increasing cooperation to one of increased competition and of 'intertwined, long-term challenges that demand our sustained national attention and commitment'. It acknowledges that US advantages long taken for granted are shrinking relative to challengers and commits to prioritise US efforts to manage great-power competition from China and Russia.

Priorities from the NSS carried through into the 2018 National Defense Strategy (NDS), and into the Department of Defense's (DoD's) budget requests. The NDS states that 'inter-state strategic competition, not terrorism, is now the primary concern in U.S. national security'. Great-power challengers, rogue states (Iran and North Korea) and transnational threats shape the NDS and reprioritise spending in the defence budget. The language is stark. The United States' 'competitive military advantage has been eroding'. The US armed forces have 'no preordained right to victory on the battlefield', and tough choices need to be made in order 'to field a lethal, resilient, and rapidly adapting Joint Force'. It departs from the NSS in stressing the primacy of diplomacy in Washington's international engagement and emphasising the essential contributions of allies – the document contains multiple references to their importance.

In its February 2018 Nuclear Posture Review, the DoD provided more detail on its long-stated assertion that Russia was in violation of the 1987 Intermediate-Range Nuclear Forces (INF) Treaty, and committed the US to nuclear modernisation, including the development of low-yield warheads for submarine-launched ballistic missiles and, in the longer term, a modern nuclear-armed sea-launched cruise missile. The DoD also committed to robust missile defences. However, as of November it had yet to release its Missile Defense Review. Formerly the Ballistic Missile Defense Review, this new version is expected to focus also on hypersonic threats and advocate an enhanced detection and tracking architecture, including in space.

Congress largely complied with the administration's defence strategy and spending priorities, agreeing the US$716-billion top line during budget negotiations in March and passing the 2018 National Defense Authorization Act (NDAA) on schedule for the first time in a decade and with wide bipartisan support (the vote was 85–10 in the Senate, 351–66 in the House of Representatives). The budget deal extends only until 2020, however, making sustained support questionable.

The DoD's force-sizing construct has likewise been brought into alignment with the focus on great-power competition; but it also emphasises that the ability to defeat aggression by a major power, while deterring opportunistic aggression and disrupting imminent threats from terrorism and 'weapons of mass destruction', will require the fully mobilised joint force in wartime. While that appears to be an expanded construct, the previous force-sizing construct had focused on steady-state (rather than full wartime mobilisation) capacity.

While Congress authorised an increase in end-strength for the force, the DoD is programming money first to restore readiness that had eroded under Budget Control Act (BCA) 2011 spending caps. The US$33bn shortfall identified in 2017 by Secretary of Defense James Mattis has been filled, mostly by Congress ignoring the administration's reduction of Overseas Contingency Operations (OCO) funding. A Congress led by the president's own party has been activist in foreign and defence policy to stay the president's hand. Examples include continuing State Department funding despite administration efforts to reduce it by nearly 30%; supporting NATO in advance of the Brussels Summit; rejecting Russia's request to question US diplomats (which Trump had agreed with President Vladimir Putin to allow); and legislating against the withdrawal of US troops from South Korea or Europe without the secretary of defense's approval.

Alliance relations

The authors of the NSS have been commended for blunting the tone of President Trump's 'America First' campaign speeches and producing a strategy document more amenable to sustaining existing rules, alliances and institutions. However, the president's own views were unchanged, as the gap between his speech presenting the document and the NSS illustrated: 'We have made clear that countries that are immensely wealthy should reimburse the United States for the cost of defending them. This is a major departure from the past, but a fair and necessary one.'

While President Trump considers that he is 'strengthening even our strongest alliances', other members of these alliances do not agree. NATO allies have been left reeling from their interactions with the president, who refers to their own defence spending as money owed to the US and seems not to consider as relevant the legacy of shared sacrifice in war. Trump derailed the G7 meeting in June 2018, refusing to sign the communiqué and publicly denigrating Canada's Prime Minister Justin Trudeau. Trump also seems to consider the European Union as much of a foe as China, at least in trade terms. Unilateral US withdrawal from the Iranian nuclear deal – even after acknowledgement by the director of national intelligence and the secretaries of state and defense that Iran was in compliance with the agreement – and the subsequent imposition of secondary sanctions on European firms, led Heiko Maas, the German foreign minister, to suggest an international payments system independent of US influence. Trump's announcement that the US would withdraw from the INF Treaty also unsettled Washington's European allies. And talk of a 'bloody nose' attack under consideration by the US on North Korea alarmed both South Korea and Japan. Meanwhile, personal diplomacy by the president with North Korea and Russia left a trail of confusion about what he had agreed – North Korea maintains the US agreed to sign a peace treaty as a precursor to denuclearisation, while the White House maintains the opposite.

Those insults and alarms have come despite strenuous efforts by the departments of state and defense to sustain policy cooperation, and similarly strenuous restraint by allies in consenting to give President Trump the policy successes he claims. The 2018 NATO summit produced policy outcomes that could have been a significant success for the administration: renewed commitment by all allies to increased defence spending; a new Atlantic Command, headquartered in Norfolk, Virginia, to protect reinforcement routes and data cables in the Atlantic; and formal agreement on a force of 30 battalions, 30 air squadrons and 30 ships to be deployable within 30 days. (The US had, earlier in May, announced it would reinstate its 2nd Fleet, focused on the Atlantic; the fleet had been disestablished in 2011.) President Trump, however, preferred friction with allies before his Helsinki summit with President Putin. Indeed, where the administration has made advances, this has arguably been down to the work of government departments. Examples include the DoD's trilateral cooperation with Finland and Sweden, intelligence-sharing arrangements with India and further rotational deployments of US troops to Poland and the Baltic states.

Secretary of Defense Mattis, meanwhile, adroitly worked with both parties in Congress and closely with allies. That task became more difficult with the firing of Secretary of State Rex Tillerson and National Security Advisor H.R. McMaster. Their replacements, Mike Pompeo and John Bolton, are more closely aligned with the president's views than their predecessors and are reshaping their staffs in similar directions, leaving the DoD less latitude for independent policies. At the same time, President Trump appears to be growing in confidence about his own judgement on national-security issues and, analysts understand, impatient at the legal, legislative and bureaucratic processes that make the DoD less responsive than he expects it to be. Examples include the Space Force, proposed as the sixth US military service, and Trump's desire for a large military parade.

The incoherent policy atmosphere of the Trump administration always held the prospect for significant DoD changes, such as ending military exercises on the Korean Peninsula or banning military service by transgender or non-US citizens, and corroding civil–military norms by giving political speeches to military audiences or associating the DoD with immigration policies. But administration-personnel appointments in 2018 increase the likelihood of White House activism and effectiveness in imposing the president's political agenda on the Pentagon.

US Army

The 2018 US NDS's emphasis on inter-state strategic competition has led the US Army to continue its refocus from counter-insurgency towards also preparing for high-intensity combat against peer competitors. The Fiscal Year (FY) 2017 NDAA allocated resources for this task, and the 2019 NDAA accelerates this trend.

Readiness gains have been significant. Army Chief of Staff General Mark Milley testified before the Senate Armed Services Committee on 12 April 2018 that the readiness of active army brigade combat teams (BCTs) had increased from 30% a year before to 50% in May 2018. The army's goal is to achieve 66% for the regular army and 33% for the reserve component by 2022. Readiness, in this context, means that the units are fully staffed and equipped and immediately able to conduct decisive operations if ordered. This status is validated by a rotation though one of the Combat Training Centers (CTCs).

The army continues to improve the CTCs and hasten their reorientation to high-end combat. In 2018, there were 20 rotations to these centres, including four for reserve components. According to General Milley's testimony, these rotations are 'focused on the high-end fight, replicating near-peer competitor capabilities, including increased enemy lethality, degraded communications, persistent observation, and a contested environment'.

The army is also balancing the demand to produce ready units with high-end combat skills with the enduring missions in Afghanistan and elsewhere to counter irregular adversaries. In February 2018, the army established and deployed its first Security Force Assistance Brigade (SFAB) to Afghanistan. SFABs are designed to provide focused attention and expertise to the advisory mission. General Milley said that the SFAB comprises 'the chain of command of an infantry brigade combat team from staff sergeant on up'. This approach means conventional BCTs will no longer need to be repurposed from their conventional-warfare focus. SFABs also serve as a hedge for high-end missions, as they can be rapidly filled with junior officers and soldiers to become a full infantry BCT. The army plans to field a total of six SFABs, including one in the National Guard.

Some 150,000 soldiers remain deployed in support of US combatant commands. For the European Deterrence Initiative (EDI), 1,500 additional soldiers are planned join the 33,000 already in Europe by 2020. This increase includes a field-artillery brigade headquarters, two multiple-rocket-launcher battalions and a short-range air-defence battalion. The 2019 NDAA continues to increase authorised army-personnel levels to support improved readiness and meet new missions. Active-duty end-strength is expected to rise by 4,000 in FY2019 to 487,500 (the army's goal is

Table 1 **NDAA 2019 authorisation: equipment acquisitions and upgrades**

Equipment	Type	Source	Base	OCO	RDT&E	Sum
66 AH-64E *Apache*	Atk Hel	New build and upgrade	US$1.2bn	-	-	US$1.2bn
55 UH-60M/HH-60M *Black Hawk*	Med Tpt Hel/CSAR Hel	New build	US$1.1bn	US$21m	-	US$1.1bn
8 MH-47G *Chinook*	Hvy Tpt Hel (Spec Ops)	Upgrade	US$99m	US$25m	-	US$124m
135 M1A2C *Abrams*	MBT	Upgrade	US$1.1bn	US$455m	-	US$1.5bn
Mobile Protected Firepower programme	Tank	Development	-	-	US$319m	US$319m
61 M2A4/M7A4 *Bradley*	IFV	Upgrade	-	US$205m	-	US$205m
45 M109A7 *Paladin*	155 mm SP Arty	Upgrade	US$462m	US$67m	-	US$569m
197 Armoured Multi-purpose Vehicles (AMPV)	APC(T)	New build	US$449m	US$231m	-	US$679m
3,390 Joint Light Tactical Vehicles (JLTV)	AUV	New build	US$1.3bn	-	-	US$1.3bn

500,000), while the National Guard and army reserve will remain at 343,500 and 199,500 respectively.

Army equipment programmes are also accelerating, particularly plans to modernise Armored BCTs. The 2019 NDAA authorises a range of equipment for this purpose (see Table 1).

The army is also upgrading two BCT sets of *Stryker* vehicles to the latest version and *Abrams* tanks with the *Trophy* active-protection system, a battle-tested Israeli design. Nevertheless, these modernisation efforts are, as Milley told the Senate Armed Services Committee, upgrading 'technologies and ideas that come out of the '60s and '70s'. Congress allocated additional funds for modernisation programmes during the committee stages of the NDAA, particularly for research, development, test and evaluation.

Addressing peer competitors

The army took several important decisions in 2017–18 in a bid to close capability gaps with peer competitors. In December 2017, it published 'Multi-Domain Battle: Evolution of Combined Arms for the 21st Century: 2025–2040', since renamed 'Multi-Domain Operations'. This is the service's evolving concept for how it intends to seize the advantage from potential adversaries and restore a credible conventional deterrent and war-fighting capability against peer competitors.

Addressing peer-competitor challenges has spurred the army to prioritise modernisation efforts. In October 2017, it created eight cross-functional teams to address its most important capability challenges: long-range precision fires; next-generation combat vehicles; future vertical lift; network command, control, communication and intelligence; assured positioning, navigation and timing; air and missile defence; soldier lethality; and the synthetic training environment.

In November 2017, the army created an Army Modernization Task Force, which culminated in June 2018 with the establishment of US Army Futures Command (AFC), the most significant reorganisation of the service since the creation of the Training and Doctrine Command (TRADOC) in the 1970s. AFC began operations on 1 July.

Army Futures Command

AFC is the army's fourth four-star command, joining TRADOC, US Army Forces Command and US Army Materiel Command (AMC). Based in Austin, Texas, AFC has three subordinate organisations: Futures and Concepts; Combat Development; and Combat Systems. These are drawn principally from the AMC and TRADOC and include the Army Capabilities Integration Center; the Capability Development and Integration Centers and their battle labs, currently part of the TRADOC Centers of Excellence (such as manoeuvre and fires); the TRADOC Analysis Center; the Research, Development and Engineering Command; and the Army Materiel Systems Analysis Activity.

As a result, TRADOC is no longer responsible for building the future army. Instead, as the order announcing the creation of the AFC noted, 'TRADOC recruits, trains, and educates the Army's Soldiers; develops leaders; supports training in units; develops doctrine; establishes standards; and builds the Army by developing and integrating operational and functional concepts and organizational designs for the fielded force'.

US Navy and US Coast Guard

The US Navy (USN) spent 2018 dealing with issues including the continuing fallout from the ship collisions in the western Pacific in 2017; the debate over how – and how quickly – to achieve the target of a 355-ship fleet; and the beginnings of a change in posture arising from the NDS's reference to the return of great-power competition.

Multiple senior officers, chiefly based in the western Pacific, left their posts in the wake of the collisions. Investigations identified some specific and systemic failures. A particular problem among forward-deployed surface forces in the western Pacific was that training and readiness standards were affected by the demands of a growing operational tempo. While the lessons identified have focused particularly on surface naval forces in the Pacific, many are seen to apply to other parts of the surface navy.

Some recommendations have proved contentious – such as consolidating force-generation responsibilities, including for the Pacific, under Fleet Forces Command in Norfolk, Virginia. The challenge is that operational demands are, if anything, increasing, and thereby sharpening the dilemma over how to restore readiness levels while also seeking to grow the fleet.

As if to underline the operational tempo, in May 2018 the USN carried out its first two-ship freedom-of-navigation operation in its recent series of such missions in the South China Sea, and a two-destroyer transit of the Taiwan Strait in July. At the same time, mechanical problems sidelined two major amphibious ships that were due to participate in the 2018 *Rim of the Pacific* (RIMPAC) exercise, an indicator of readiness challenges in the amphibious force.

Meanwhile, the discussion continues over the target for a 355-ship fleet, including over whether it is even an appropriate goal. There is also pressure from the navy, Congress and defence companies over how best to achieve early results in terms of growing numbers and capability. Some estimates have suggested that reaching the 355-ship goal could take until 2050, unless more urgent approaches are found. Strategies proposed have included modernising and extending the lives of current platforms – for example, keeping *Arleigh Burke*-class destroyers in service for at least 45 years – and accelerating aircraft-carrier and submarine procurement schedules. At the same time, the navy has been preparing a new force-structure assessment that could modify the target fleet size, though this depends on new estimates of the likely requirement for key platforms, such as submarines; the likely impact on the capabilities of new programmes like the FFG(X) next-generation frigate; as well as, possibly, a new squeeze on funding in the coming years.

The USN has looked to fill capability gaps in response to an increasingly contested maritime space. It chose the Norwegian-designed Naval Strike Missile to fulfil its requirement for an over-the-horizon anti-ship weapon for the Littoral Combat Ship, while the firing of a submarine-launched *Harpoon* anti-ship missile by the USS *Olympia* during RIMPAC – the first such launch from a US submarine in more than two decades – signalled the likely return of the weapon and capability to the US inventory.

In April, there was no fleet carrier in the Middle East region when USN forces launched *Tomahawk* cruise-missile strikes on Syrian targets following an alleged chemical-weapons attack by the Assad regime. This highlights a situation that seems set to become increasingly regular as the navy adopts a more dynamic deployment model, in part to increase tactical unpredictability. Indeed, the navy is likely to rely increasingly on allies and the use of big-deck amphibious ships to provide limited fixed-wing naval-aviation capabilities to supplement its carriers.

The carrier USS *Harry S. Truman*, which might normally have been expected to deploy to the Middle East, remained instead in the Mediterranean and North Atlantic for a shortened period of three months at sea. This was one of the clearest examples of how the navy is looking to reshape its posture to move away from inflexible standing commitments in order to prepare for more high-end operations. Another was the re-establishment of the 2nd Fleet to refocus on delivering naval capability across the North Atlantic.

The 2nd Fleet's area of operations will extend into the Arctic, an area of increased significance also for the US Coast Guard. In March 2016, the navy and coastguard issued a request for proposals for the design and construction of up to three new heavy icebreakers. The coastguard was also due to commission a seventh new *Legend*-class national-security cutter as Congress continued to debate adding numbers to the inventory. Originally intended to be a class of eight ships, Congress has approved funding for 11, and has been considering adding a twelfth. The coastguard is also trying to balance requirements for smaller offshore-patrol cutters and fast-response cutters as it seeks to recapitalise its fleet.

US Air Force

The US Air Force (USAF) has for the better part of this decade been focused on the challenge from current and emerging competitors, while at the same time maintaining a commitment to counter-insurgency and counter-terrorism operations. Its problem is not that China is now emerging as a major aerospace power, which it had anticipated, but that Russia is attempting to reclaim its great-power status. The USAF again has to plan for European contingencies in parallel to the Indo-Pacific. Air Force Secretary Heather Wilson has said that 'the Air Force is too small for what the nation is asking us to do'.

Moreover, the air force does not have time to draw breath as it moves to address the deteriorating security environment, nor can it rely solely on over-matching the technology of a potential peer or near-peer adversary. The absolute gap between the US and China and Russia continues to close. Both are close to introducing fifth-generation combat aircraft, while China might begin to field a bomber aircraft with a reduced radar signature in the second half of the next decade. Beijing and Moscow are also pursuing advanced guided weapons.

Sustained combat operations are placing stress on the air force. William Roper, then air-force assistant secretary, said in March 2018 that 'cost-effective modernization is a top Air Force priority, and the need for it has never been more pressing. Twenty-six years of continuous combat operations has done more than just take a toll on Airmen and equipment; it has

Figure 2 **Lockheed Martin F-35** *Lightning* II: sensor suite

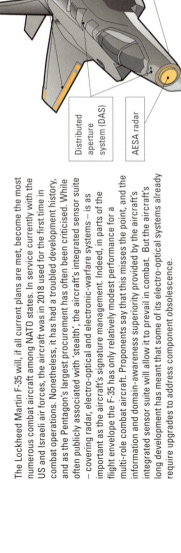
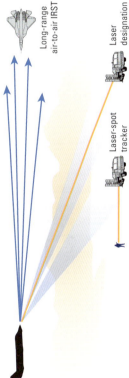
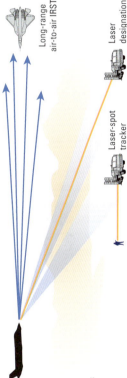

The Lockheed Martin F-35 will, if all current plans are met, become the most numerous combat aircraft among NATO states. In service currently with the US and Israeli air forces, the aircraft was in 2018 used for the first time in combat operations. Nonetheless, it has had a troubled development history, and as the Pentagon's largest procurement has often been criticised. While often publicly associated with 'stealth', the aircraft's integrated sensor suite – covering radar, electro-optical and electronic-warfare systems – is as important as the aircraft's signature management. Indeed, in parts of the flight envelope the F-35 has only relatively modest performance for a multi-role combat aircraft. Proponents say that this misses the point, and the information and domain-awareness superiority provided by the aircraft's integrated sensor suite will allow it to prevail in combat. But the aircraft's long development has meant that some of its electro-optical systems already require upgrades to address component obsolescence.

AESA radar

The Northrop Grumman APG-81 active electronically scanned array (AESA) multi-mode radar is the primary sensor used to detect surface and air targets beyond visual range. Detailed performance figures are classified. The radar, operating at the X-band, uses a slightly upward canted array to reduce radar reflectivity. The AESA is fixed, which limits its scan to plus or minus 60 degrees off bore-sight, but obviates the need for a mechanical re-positioner. As well as providing air- and surface-target detection and identification, the radar can be used for electronic attack and ground moving-target indicator and synthetic aperture radar modes.

Electro-optical targeting system

The Lockheed Martin electro-optical targeting system (EOTS) is a chin-mounted infrared search-and-track and laser designator. It provides passive detection of air and surface targets. The system housing is intended to maintain a low radar cross section: a pylon-mounted pod would increase the aircraft's radar signature. The EOTS is now being upgraded. Known as Advanced EOTS, this project is intended to improve performance, address component obsolescence and give better imagery and longer-range detection.

AAS-37 distributed aperture system

The Northrop Grumman AAS-37 distributed aperture system provides the pilot with imagery from six electro-optical sensors around the aircraft. The AAS-37 is used for day and night navigation, negating the need for night-vision goggles in the case of the latter. It can also provide warning of missile launches.

Features:

- Internally mounted
- Long-range, high-resolution
- Navigation forward-looking infrared (NAVFLIR), targeting forward-looking infrared (FLIR), infrared search and track (IRST) functions
- Air-to-surface targeting FLIR
- Air-to-air imaging
- Digital continuous zoom

allowed the national security environment to change while our time, talent, and treasure were otherwise engaged.' That said, it also provided the USAF with greater operational experience than China or Russia.

The USAF is operating combat-aircraft types for longer, and at a higher rate of use, than expected. This is the cumulative result of funding constraints, development delays, shifting priorities, and a more demanding and unpredictable security environment. Legacy tactical fleets are being retained for longer than previously planned. The F-15E *Strike Eagle* is now expected to remain in the inventory until 2040, while the last F-16C/D *Fighting Falcon*s might not be withdrawn until almost 2050. The average age of an aircraft in the air force's tactical combat fleet is 25 years. Stresses on people and aircraft, and changing security challenges, have led the air-force hierarchy to advocate an expanded number of operational squadrons. The 'air force we need', said Wilson in September, 'has 386 operational squadrons by 2030'.

Modernisation priorities

The workhorse of the future fighter fleet, the F-35A *Lightning* II, entered operational squadron service in 2017, and the air force plans to buy 258 aircraft between 2019 and 2024. Development concerns appear to have been for the most part overcome, while the aircraft's unit cost is also reducing. The cost for the low-rate initial production (LRIP) 10 batch was US$94.3 million, and this is expected to be cut further in LRIP 11. That said, the USAF and other F-35 customers were during the course of 2018 increasingly worried by support costs. USAF Chief of Staff General David Goldfein said he was 'concerned' about the issue. The risk is that greater-than-anticipated sustainment costs over the life of the programme would affect the planned procurement budget.

As of September 2018, the air force planned to receive its first 18 Boeing KC-46A *Pegasus* tanker aircraft by the end of April 2019, 20 months later than originally planned. Development problems with some of the aircraft's systems continued to be an issue during 2018. The air force intends to buy 179 KC-46As, with the type being used to first replace the McDonnell Douglas KC-10A *Extender*, 59 of which remain in service.

The air force's third procurement priority is the Northrop Grumman B-21 *Raider* low-observable bomber. This will replace the B-2 *Spirit* and the B-1B *Lancer* in the nuclear and conventional roles respectively. A critical design review was due for the programme at the end of 2018, and the first aircraft are meant to begin entering the inventory in the second half of the 2020s. This aggressive schedule continues to suggest that the still-classified detailed design may be well progressed. The air force's bomber road map sees the B-2 leave the inventory by 2032, with the B-1B following by 2036. The B-52H *Stratofortress* will remain in service until the 2050s, supplementing the planned 100-plus B-21s.

Critical to the B-52H in the nuclear-deterrent role is the Long-range Stand-off (LRSO) cruise missile, which will replace the AGM-86 nuclear-armed cruise missile. Lockheed Martin and Raytheon are developing designs for the LRSO – which is associated with the AGM-180/181 designation – under technology-maturation and risk-reduction contracts.

Performance characteristics of the LRSO requirement have not been made public, though the air force has been more forthcoming about two high-speed-weapons projects, both being developed by Lockheed Martin – the AGM-183A Air-launched Rapid Response Weapon (ARRW) and the Hypersonic Conventional Strike Weapon (HCSW). The USAF's renewed and public activity in the hypersonic domain is in part a response to Chinese and Russian pursuit of such technology. Meanwhile, the air-launched Hypersonic Air-breathing Weapon Concept (HAWC) is also being pursued by the air force. Other notable announcements in the year included the selection of a Boeing–SAAB team as the preferred bidder for the T-X trainer contract – giving Boeing a continuing stake in the design and manufacture of combat-capable fixed-wing aircraft – and the firm's contract-win, alongside Leonardo, in the programme to replace the UH-1N with the MH-139 in the liaison role for intercontinental-ballistic-missile personnel.

The USAF is also having to navigate President Trump's demand that an independent Space Force be set up, and the implications of this for the air force's Space Command. The president's idea to create a space service has not met with universal approval, with some opponents arguing it is a distraction.

DEFENCE ECONOMICS

The FY2019 budget for national-defence (discretionary 050 budget authority) spending totalled US$716 billion. This funding breaks down into US$617.1bn in base spending for the DoD, augmented by US$69bn in OCO funding. Of the remainder, US$21.9bn is requested for atomic-energy defence activities, chiefly managed by the Department of Energy, with the last US$8bn allotted to other defence activities, principally counter-terrorism operations conducted by the Federal Bureau of Investigation.

Discretionary 050 budget authority is the most commonly cited measure of US defence spending. It is the value classified as 'national defense' for the purposes of the spending caps instituted by the BCA of 2011, though the OCO account is exempt from these caps. The discretionary 050 budget authority request excludes US$10.8bn in mandatory defence spending, such as concurrent-receipt military retirement benefits; US$5.3bn in discretionary Foreign Military Financing (FMF) programmes managed by the State Department; US$11.7bn of discretionary and mandatory spending for the US Coast Guard (which operates under the Department of Homeland Security); and US$193bn for discretionary and mandatory veterans' benefits and services.

Budget authority is distinct from annual federal outlays in that it authorises some spending for later years. The 050 discretionary and mandatory budget requests for FY2019 would result in US$688.9bn in outlays between 1 October 2018 and 30 September 2019, if spent according to plan. The IISS uses annual outlays for its defence-budget figures.

The DoD component of the 050 spending request breaks down as follows: US$182bn for the US Army, US$194.1bn for the US Navy and US Marine Corps,

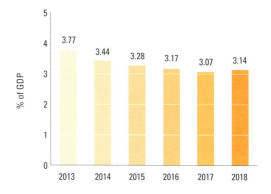

[1] Figures refer to the National Defense (050) Budget Function (Outlays) as a % of GDP

▲ Figure 3 **US defence expenditure** as % of GDP[1]

Table 2 **US National Defense Budget Function**[1] **and other selected budgets**[2] **1999, 2009–19**

US$ in billions, current year dollars	National Defense Budget Function		Atomic Energy Defense Activities	Other Defense Activities	Total National Defense			Department of Homeland Security	Department of Veterans Affairs	Total Federal Government Outlays	Total Federal Budget Surplus/ Deficit
					Discretionary						
FY	BA	Outlay	BA	BA	BA	BA	Outlay	BA	BA		
1999	278.4	261.2	12.4	1.4	292.2	288.3	274.8	N/A	44.1	1,701.8	125.6
2009	667.5	636.7	23.0	7.1	697.6	694.8	661.0	46.0	96.9	3,517.7	-1,412.7
2010	695.6	666.7	18.2	7.3	721.2	714.1	693.5	45.4	124.3	3,457.1	-1,294.4
2011	691.5	678.1	18.5	7.0	717.0	710.1	705.6	41.6	122.8	3,603.1	-1,299.6
2012	655.4	650.9	18.3	7.7	681.4	669.6	677.9	45.9	124.0	3,536.9	-1,087.0
2013	585.2	607.8	17.5	7.4	610.2	600.4	633.4	61.9	136.0	3,454.6	-679.5
2014	595.7	577.9	18.4	8.2	622.3	606.2	603.5	44.1	165.7	3,506.1	-484.6
2015	570.9	562.5	19.0	8.5	598.4	585.9	589.7	45.3	160.5	3,688.4	-438.5
2016	595.7	565.4	20.1	8.3	624.1	606.9	593.4	46.0	163.3	3,852.6	-584.7
2017	626.2	568.9	21.4	8.7	656.3	634.1	598.7	62.3	178.8	3,981.6	-665.4
2018*	652.9	612.5	21.9	8.4	683.2	674.6	643.3	73.8	184.2	4,173.0	-832.6
2019*	696.1	656.9	23.1	8.6	726.8	716.0	688.6	51.0	192.7	4,406.7	-984.4

Notes
FY = Fiscal Year (1 October–30 September)
* (request)

[1] The National Defense Budget Function subsumes funding for the DoD, the Department of Energy Atomic Energy Defense Activities and some smaller support agencies (including Federal Emergency Management and Selective Service System). It does not include funding for International Security Assistance (under International Affairs), the Veterans Administration, the US Coast Guard (Department of Homeland Security), nor for the National Aeronautics and Space Administration (NASA). Funding for civil projects administered by the DoD is excluded from the figures cited here.

[2] Early in each calendar year, the US government presents its defence budget to Congress for the next fiscal year, which begins on 1 October. The government also presents its Future Years Defense Program (FYDP), which covers the next fiscal year plus the following five. Until approved by Congress, the budget is called the Budget Request; after approval, it becomes the Budget Authority (BA).

US$194.2bn for the air force and US$115.8bn for defence-wide activities. The army receives nearly half of all OCO, while the air force is allocated one-quarter, and the remainder is more or less evenly divided between the navy and defence-wide activities. The distributions of both base and OCO spending by department are typical of recent years.

By functional category, the DoD funding request for 2019 equates to US$283.5bn for operations and maintenance, US$152.9bn for military personnel, US$144.3bn for procurement, US$92.4bn for research, development, test and evaluation (RDT&E), US$9.8bn for military construction, US$1.6bn for family housing, and US$1.6bn for revolving and management funds. Relative to FY2018-enacted appropriations, this represents a 2.3% decline in nominal procurement spending and a 4.8% increase to military personnel. There are nominal increases to both the operations and maintenance and RDT&E accounts. Each is less than a percentage point above inflation, which is estimated by the Congressional Budget Office at 2.2% in FY2018 and 2.0% in FY2019. Using enacted appropriations as a baseline better reflects congressional involvement in the budget process.

Two-year budget deal to amend the BCA

Annual 050 defence-budget growth from 2018 to 2019 was 2.1% in nominal terms, or roughly pacing inflation, which means that there has been no real increase in buying power. The 2018 Bipartisan Budget Act (BBA18) essentially reset the floor of base defence spending in 2018. This led to 10.6% growth in enacted appropriations from 2017 to 2018 before allowing the 2019 budget to grow with inflation from that new spending floor. Taken together, the 2018 and 2019 budgets represent a US$165bn increase above BCA spending caps for 050 discretionary budget authority in those two years. In FY2019, combined base and OCO discretionary 050 budget authority will be the highest since 2011, when adjusted for inflation.

How did these higher budgets transpire? President Donald Trump and the DoD leadership requested US$603bn in base discretionary national-defence spending in FY2018, far in excess of the US$549bn spending cap for that year. However, this is typical of budget requests after passage of the BCA: the Obama administration similarly submitted requests in excess of the spending caps for discretionary spending each year. On 9 February 2018, Congress passed the BBA18, which raised the base defence-spending caps to US$629bn and US$647bn in 2018 and 2019, respectively – an increase of US$165bn. Along with OCO spending and a series of additional smaller emergency-spending requests owing to North Korean provocations and hurricane relief, Congress appropriated a total of US$700.9bn in discretionary 050 budget authority for 2018. This figure was above the 2018 budget request, but in line with unofficial top-line figures advanced by the House and Senate Armed Services committees in late 2016 and early 2017. As such, Congress was the primary driving force behind the defence-budget increases.

Unusually, the president's 2019 defence-budget request was released before appropriations for FY2018 were fully known. The final appropriation for FY2018 did not occur until 23 March 2018, about a month after the release of the FY2019 request and 175 days into FY2018. White House and Pentagon officials based their 2019 request on the two-year BBA18 deal reached earlier in the year by Congress. BBA18 raised spending caps on defence and non-defence spending to pave the way for 2018 appropriations and the 2019 request.

Force structure

The final 2018 defence appropriations added 8,500 active-duty military personnel above the FY2018 request: 7,500 for the army and 1,000 for the marine corps. The 2019 budget requests a further 15,600 active-duty personnel from 2018 levels: 4,000 soldiers, 7,500 sailors, 4,000 airmen and 100 marines. The pay raise for 2018 was 2.4%, and the requested pay raise for 2019 is 2.6%, the largest in nine fiscal years.

While the 2019 NDAA resources the 2019 military-personnel request completely, congressional appropriators, who actually allocate the spending, only funded about 7,000 of the 15,600 personnel requested to instead fund modernisation priorities. A similar approach was adopted by the Senate in their draft NDAA, but abandoned in the final law (P.L. 115-232, signed by the president on 13 August 2018).

Most of this bolstered end-strength will address combat-readiness shortfalls by restoring ground units and naval-vessel crews to optimal strengths, and by addressing the air force's shortages in pilots and maintenance personnel. In FY2019, the army will continue to stand up its Security Force Assistance Brigades. The air force is adding a net of one active fighter squadron to its total force. The Department of the Navy projects no changes to marine-corps force structure and the addition of seven new active warships.

The 2019 defence-budget request also includes end-strength projections out to 2023. The navy and army would like to grow by 9,500 personnel each (active and reserve) above the FY2019 request, while the air force would like to add 11,400 and the marines just 300. These levels suggest few major force-structure changes in the near future. To use the army as an example, the projected active force of 495,500 in FY2023 would be just over the troop levels in the last full year of the Obama presidency, but far below President Trump's campaign promise of a 540,000-person active army.

Modernisation and the National Defense Strategy

The 2019 defence budget is the first to implement the precepts of the new NDS, released in January 2018. Pursuant to the strategy's reorientation of threats, the character of the budget suggests the DoD is pursuing a capability-based build-up rather than a capacity-driven one. Force structure will remain more or less steady, and modernisation will concentrate on developing next-generation systems.

Navy shipbuilding is a prime example. Congress appropriated 14 ships in 2018 and the White House requested ten more in FY2019 (see Table 3). Congress ended up adding two Littoral Combat Ships, an Expeditionary Fast Transport Vessel and a cable ship, as well as funds for the future procurement of another destroyer and two amphibious ships. But despite plans to sustain similar production rates for the next few years, the overall fleet is projected to peak at 326 vessels in 2023. It will not attain this size again until 2036, as the retirement rate of hulls outpaces production.

Naval-aviation procurement is down relative to 2018 appropriations, but tracks closely to the planning for 2019 that was included in last year's budget request. Programmes with notable decreases include the request for nine F-35C Joint Strike Fighters (down from ten in FY2018), 20 F-35Bs (down from 24), four KC-130J tanker/transport aircraft (down from six) and seven V-22 *Osprey* tilt-rotor aircraft (down from 14).

Conversely, the procurement picture for the marines is relatively positive, with notable additions including US$191m for communications equipment and an extra US$94m to procure new HIMARS rocket artillery systems.

The army in late 2017 unveiled its 'big six' modernisation priorities: long-range precision fires; next-generation combat vehicles; future vertical lift; networks and communications/intelligence, surveillance and reconnaissance; air and missile defence; and soldier lethality. The service has reallocated over 80% of its science and technology funding to support these, although this encompasses just 22% of army RDT&E, or US$2.4bn dollars.

While the army pursues new equipment, it is slowing procurement of legacy systems. After expanded helicopter purchases in 2018, aviation-procurement funding is down by more than 30% in the 2019 request. Nonetheless, upgrades continue unabated. More *Abrams* tanks have been slated for the *Abrams* improvement programme, and the 2019 request funds enough commercial off-the-shelf active protection systems to outfit 261 tanks (enough for three brigades). And procurement of the new armoured personnel carrier (AMPV) to replace the M113 is up by 90 units compared to 2018 appropriations (for a total request of 197).

In 2019, the air force is due to receive 87% of all new research and development dollars relative to 2018 appropriations. Importantly, this increase is to

Table 3 **US Navy build-up: shipbuilding proposals**

Congress ship appropriation, 2018	White House FY2019 request
1 Nuclear-powered aircraft carrier	
2 Destroyers with AShMs	3 Destroyers with AShMs
2 Nuclear-powered attack submarines	2 Nuclear-powered attack submarines
3 Littoral Combat Ships	1 Littoral Combat Ship
1 LX(R) landing platform dock	
1 Expeditionary Sea Base	1 Expeditionary Sea Base
1 Expeditionary Fast Transport Vessel	
1 Fleet-replenishment oiler	2 Fleet-replenishment oilers
1 Towing, salvage and rescue ship	1 Towing, salvage and rescue ship
1 Oceanographic survey ship	

unclassified air-force accounts: there is no nominal increase to classified RDT&E. The majority of new funding is directed into four space programmes: Evolved Expendable Launch Vehicles, Evolved Space-based Infrared Radar System, Navstar GPS and research into 'operationally responsive space'.

While space programmes benefited from increased RDT&E, the procurement picture is less bright, falling by US$1.2bn relative to 2018 appropriations. This decline is exaggerated by Congress's contentious decision to add two Wideband Global SATCOM satellites, which the air force did not request, into 2018 appropriations at a cost of US$595m.

Aircraft procurement is also lagging for three main reasons. The first relates to the cancelled plan to recapitalise the JSTARS surveillance aircraft, possibly with a new aircraft, in favour of alternatives still in development. Secondly, delays in KC-46 tanker production have resulted in US$151m in further losses to the procurement programme. Finally, the 2019 budget requests only 48 F-35As, compared to 56 included in 2018 appropriations.

OCO and emergency spending

The 2019 request for OCO totals US$69bn, a slight increase from 2018's appropriated US$65.9bn. However, the 2018 OCO appropriation was bolstered by a further US$5.8bn in emergency funding passed separately in December 2017 and February 2018. US$1.2bn of that amount was for hurricane relief, with the rest intended to repair the USS *Fitzgerald* and USS *John S. McCain*, augment ballistic-missile-defence capabilities and increase troop levels in Afghanistan. There is no equivalent supplemental budget request for any type of emergency spending in 2019.

The significant change to OCO is the US$6.5bn request for the EDI, significantly more than that requested in 2018 or enacted in 2017 (US$4.8bn and US$3.4bn, respectively).

NORAD: watching Northern America's skies and seas

The deteriorating security environment and likely impact of climate change have reinvigorated interest in replacing the North Warning System (NWS). Part of the sensor suite for the US–Canada North American Aerospace Defense Command (NORAD), this had until recently appeared to be a Cold War-era relic. At the same time, a sign both of Canada's interest in the Arctic and its growing capabilities there can be seen in the country's May 2018 decision to extend its air-defence identification zone to cover the country's entire Arctic archipelago.

Following the 9/11 attacks, the NWS became part of the defence against any further aerial threat from terrorists. At the same time, its traditional role of providing early warning of state-orchestrated air attack diminished. An increase in Russian long-range bomber flights skirting Canada's air-defence identification zone has – when combined with increased accessibility to the Arctic – not only refocused attention on potential threats from the north, but also resulted in steps to upgrade early-warning capabilities. Canada and the United States are engaged in studies examining options to replace the NWS, and an analysis will notionally be completed by 2020. Initial deliveries of a replacement capability might begin in 2026.

Radar coverage

The original US–Canada joint North American Air Defense Command was established in 1957, with responsibility for the Distant Early Warning radar network of FPS-19 long-range and FPS-23 low-level radars, commonly known as the DEW Line. The former radar could detect a bomber-size target flying at medium altitude at a range of 160 nautical miles. In the 1980s, the DEW Line was supplanted by the NWS.

The NWS consists of a chain of medium- and long-range radars providing air surveillance and early warning. In Canada, eleven AN/FPS-117 long-range radars are supported by 36 AN/FPS-124 short-range systems. The FPS-117 entered service in 1988 and the FPS-124 in 1990. Radar data is collated at the Royal Canadian Air Force's 22 Wing, also known as the Canadian Air Defence Sector. There are also three NWS sites in Alaska. Following assessment, and if required, radar information is then forwarded to NORAD at Peterson Air Force Base in Colorado. The NWS improved the capacity to detect Soviet-era cruise missiles, though capability in this area remained only partial. Developments in combat-aircraft and cruise-missile technology are now driving requirements for the technologies that will succeed the present radar system.

For example, Russia has already introduced into service an air-launched cruise missile with a reduced radar signature, the Kh-101/102 (AS-23A/B *Kodiak*). Depending on the version, this missile has an estimated maximum range of either 4,000 kilometres or 5,000 km, and a cruise altitude of around 50 metres. The Russian

More than US$3.2bn of the EDI increase is allocated to prepositioning equipment, which represents half of the total EDI request. Of that US$3.2bn, 77% goes toward the army's goal of establishing equipment sets to support a division-sized force based around two Armored Brigade Combat Teams (one upgraded with active protection systems), two fires brigades, supporting air defence and ancillary units. Ten percent of the total is for additional *Patriot* PAC-3 MSE air-defence systems and long-range air-launched cruise missiles (JASSM-ER), with most of the remainder allocated to Air Force Deployable Airbase Systems.

Total spending for Central Command train-and-equip operations remains steady, though with a shift away from Iraq and Syria toward Afghanistan. The Afghan Security Forces Fund request is for US$5.2bn, up from the 2018 appropriation of US$4.7bn. Conversely, the 2018 appropriation for train-and-equip activities to counter the Islamic State, also known as ISIS or ISIL, was US$1.8bn; the 2019 request totals US$1.4bn. Like FY2018, the 2019 request supports an end-strength of 11,958 in Afghanistan and 5,765 in counter-ISIS operations in Iraq and Syria, but increases personnel assigned to in-theatre support of both operations from 56,310 to 59,463.

Future Years Defense Program

The 2019 defence-budget request was the first completed by the Trump administration to include a Future Years Defense Program (FYDP), which projects spending from FY2019 through FY2023.

In general, trends in future years are consistent with the approach of the 2019 budget request. Annualised growth in discretionary national-defence spending between FY2018 and FY2023 is 2.1%, nearly identical with projected annual inflation in the US. The result is flat or declining defence spending when measured in constant dollars. Projected expenditures closely track the spending levels advanced by the last

Navy, meanwhile, is fielding the 3M14 (SS-N-30A *Kalibr*) cruise missile on both ships and submarines, which has an engagement range in excess of 2,000 km. While these missiles are subsonic, Russia is also developing hypersonic cruise missiles for its aerospace and naval forces.

These, however, are far from the only demands that will be placed upon the NWS replacement architecture. Low-observable combat-aircraft technology is no longer limited to the US and a handful of its allies. Russia continues to develop a design to meet its PAK DA bomber requirement that is widely held to have signature management at the heart of its design, though progress on this design is likely to depend on the trajectory of the Russian defence budget. NORAD's new surveillance network, however, is planned to be in operation well beyond 2050.

Surveillance requirements

Canada's All Domain Situational Awareness programme is attempting to identify the relevant technologies and approaches for future surveillance needs. As well as aerospace, maritime surface and sub-surface surveillance are part of the requirement. The notional timescale is to identify an approach by 2021, select the contractor(s) by 2023 and award a contract in 2024. The overall upgrade programme will likely take at least a decade to implement. Canada already uses its RADARSAT constellation for maritime surveillance, and this is likely to feature further in the architecture of a replacement NWS. The extent to which satellites will provide elements of the required aerospace surveillance has yet to become clear.

Maritime surveillance will also be supported by the acquisition of a long-range uninhabited aerial vehicle. Delivery of the yet-to-be-selected system is due in the mid-2020s. Maritime surveillance is increasing in prominence with the impact of climate change on the Northwest Passage, and the waterways across Canada's north linking the Pacific and Atlantic oceans on average becoming navigable for longer periods each year.

Other considerations include the extent to which resilience is required. During the Cold War, the DEW and NWS were tripwire systems. Their static radars were vulnerable to attack but were unlikely to be particularly high-value targets. It is likely that resilience considerations will form part of the planning process for the replacement architecture.

While the exact suite of sensors remains to be determined, as does the degree to which these are ground- or space-based, the requirement for them is enduring. Economic, ecological and security interests in the Arctic region will only grow, and because of these factors, the recapitalisation of Canada's and the United States' northern air-, and now maritime-, surveillance capacity will almost certainly remain a priority for Ottawa and Washington.

DoD plans completed before the enactment of the BCA 2011. In other words, the Pentagon is planning to restore funding to pre-sequestration levels without factoring in real growth to undo shortfalls brought about by the spending caps.

Projections of spending by public law title are available only for base accounts. They show that spending on base RDT&E is projected to decline by 6% in nominal terms by 2023. Spending on military personnel and procurement both outpace inflation and average overall budget growth. Because these accounts often have significant OCO components, it is not possible to project their exact values.

While Pentagon and White House leaders seem intent on quickly folding OCO back into the base budget, owing to both real and imagined criticisms of OCO, they are likely to have as little success as recent administrations – mostly due to the continuation of the BCA into 2020 and 2021. Yet FYDP plans beyond 2019 may not come to fruition. The BCA remains in effect for FY2020 and FY2021, meaning a further two-year budget agreement is necessary to secure the requested administration budgets. Without such a deal, base national-defence spending in FY2020 and FY2021 would fall by US$171bn, or about 13% of the total request.

Resourcing the FYDP would require a budget deal even larger than BBA18, which was over twice as large as the 2013 and 2015 budget deals combined, making it unlikely. The decline of OCO spending (which is exempt from budgets caps), compounding national debt and potential legislative changes stemming from the 2018 midterm elections could all prevent such a large deal from materialising.

Foreign Military Financing programmes

Outside the national-defence account, the State Department requested US$5.3bn in discretionary spending for FMF. This amount is in line with last year's request for US$5.1bn. Both of these figures reflect the Trump administration's objective of reducing State Department spending. Given congressional pushback to such proposals, the request should be viewed as a poor predictor of actual expenditures. Last year, for example, Congress appropriated US$6.1bn for FMF – close to the 2017 request (US$6.3bn).

Comparing the 2018 and 2019 requests still reveals useful information about relative changes in priorities. Funding for Israel increased from US$3.1bn to US$3.3bn, reflecting a new bilateral ten-year agreement for US$34bn in FMF contributions between 2019 and 2028. One condition of that deal is a gradual elimination of Israel's ability to convert one-quarter of received FMF funds into local currency to purchase Israeli products. Elsewhere, requested FMF spending on Pakistan reduced from US$100m to US$80m. Meanwhile, the 2018 request for a single 'Global' account worth US$201m was reduced to US$75m to improve budgetary oversight. This was augmented by a series of new, separate requests for individual countries (Colombia, Lebanon, the Philippines, Tunisia, Ukraine and Vietnam) totalling US$172m. However, requests for Egypt (US$1.3bn), Jordan (US$350m) and general administration remain unchanged.

CANADA

Delivering on the pledges of the Liberal government's 2017 defence-policy review remains the focus of Canadian defence. This report promised adaptation to a new and more challenging security environment, with a subtext that Canada would aim to maintain and strengthen international commitments and engagement.

Deployments

Canada has been deploying small but significant capability packages. In some areas, these commitments have been modestly boosted. At the July NATO summit in Brussels, Prime Minister Justin Trudeau announced a four-year extension – to March 2023 – of Canada's contribution to the Alliance's Enhanced Forward Presence in Europe. Canada leads the multinational battlegroup in Latvia. The announcement also indicated that the mission would grow from 455 to 540 personnel.

Canada's maritime commitment to NATO – a frigate deployed to the European theatre – was bolstered from February 2018 by the extended deployment to European waters of the submarine HMCS *Windsor*. While these *Victoria*-class vessels have operated before in the North Atlantic, this was the first-ever deployment of one by Canada to the Mediterranean. Trudeau also announced in July that Canada would take command of a new NATO training and capacity-building mission in Iraq. Up to 250 Canadian personnel will deploy up to late 2019.

A submarine also featured in Canada's broader efforts to project power, particularly in the Asia-Pacific. From September 2017, the Vancouver Island-homeported HMCS *Chicoutimi* began a seven-month deployment to the region, the first by a Royal Canadian Navy (RCN) submarine since the 1960s. At the end of July, the frigate HMCS *Calgary* also deployed to the region for five months, while Canada deployed 1,000 personnel to the US-led *Rim of the Pacific* (RIMPAC) exercise, including two frigates, two coastal-defence vessels and the new interim auxiliary oiler MV *Asterix*, which joined the fleet in January, thereby filling a major capability gap. The Asia-Pacific saw other capabilities deployed, including to help monitor compliance with UN sanctions against North Korea. And, after some delay, in July 2018 Canada began deploying the first of eight helicopters, plus some 250 personnel, to support the UN stabilisation mission in Mali. Amid these activities, questions continued about the Canadian forces' capabilities, their ability to sustain operational tempo and the future defence programme.

Procurement

Canada's long-running plans to recapitalise its combat-aircraft fleet, currently based on ageing CF-18 *Hornet*s, have been further complicated by a trade dispute between Ottawa and Boeing over a complaint by the latter against the Canadian firm Bombardier. Canada abandoned an expected interim purchase of 18 F/A-18E/F *Super Hornet*s. Instead, it is purchasing a similar number of second-hand F/A-18s from Australia.

Also, in December 2017, Canada formally launched a new competition to find a long-term successor aircraft to replace the previous administration's contentious plan to purchase 65 F-35A *Lightning* IIs (although Canada remains an industrial partner in the programme). The aim of the new plan is to select a design by early 2022, with the first of 88 new aircraft to be delivered in 2025. The list of 'eligible suppliers' for the procurement comprises Airbus Defence and Space (with Eurofighter *Typhoon*), Boeing Defense (*Super Hornet*), Dassault Aviation (*Rafale*), Lockheed Martin (F-35 *Lightning*) and Saab (*Gripen*).

The arrival of the converted merchant ship *Asterix* heralded a welcome revival of Canada's own afloat-support capacity. Until then, since the retirement of the *Protecteur* and *Preserver*, the RCN had been relying on help from the Chilean and Spanish navies. Canada's Joint Support Ship programme is intended to provide a new long-term afloat-support capability based on the German Navy's *Berlin* class. However, by 2018 the estimated cost of the project had increased by more than 40%. Initial construction began in June 2018, although detailed design of the two planned vessels had yet to be finalised, raising fears about potential additional cost increases and further delays. The RCN had been targeting delivery dates of 2022 and 2023 for the two ships, already somewhat later than originally planned, but these may now stretch by a further year or two.

In October 2018, after a series of delays, the Canadian government announced that it had selected the consortium led by Lockheed Martin, offering the BAE Systems Type-26 design, as the preferred bidder for its future Canadian Surface Combatant (CSC) programme. The other contending consortiums were offering versions of the Dutch *De Zeven Provinciën* and the Spanish F-105 frigate designs. A fixed-price bid from Italy's Fincantieri in November 2017, based on the FREMM design, was rejected by Canada as being outside the prescribed procurement process.

Canada still intends for construction of the CSC to begin in the early 2020s, and that a 'full complement' of 15 vessels will be procured to replace the current frigates and recently retired destroyers on a one-for-one basis. This remains an ambitious target. Meanwhile, the navy aims to modernise the current *Victoria*-class submarines in order to keep them effective until the mid-2030s. By then, however, their age will make this a challenge (the boats were launched in the UK between 1986 and 1993), as will any ambition to replace them.

The first *Harry DeWolf*-class Arctic offshore-patrol ship was launched in September 2018, and the government later said it will buy a sixth. There has been criticism that these vessels are under-equipped for their roles in what could become an increasingly challenging theatre of operations. The Canadian government has also been negotiating for the conversion of three modern commercial icebreakers to Canadian Coast Guard service on the model of the urgent requirement that led to the conversion of the MV *Asterix*.

Canada CAN

Canadian Dollar $		2017	2018	2019
GDP	C$	2.15tr	2.24tr	
	US$	1.65tr	17.3tr	
per capita	US$	45,095	46,733	
Growth	%	3.0	2.1	
Inflation	%	1.6	2.6	
Def exp [a]	C$	29.2bn	27.6bn	
	US$	22.5bn	21.4bn	
Def bdgt [b]	C$	24.1bn	23.5bn	
	US$	18.6bn	18.9bn	
US$1= C$		1.298	1.291	

[a] NATO definition
[b] Department of National Defence and Veterans Affairs

Population 35,881,659

Age	0–14	15–19	20–24	25–29	30–64	65 plus
Male	7.9%	2.8%	3.2%	3.5%	23.7%	8.5%
Female	7.5%	2.7%	3.0%	3.3%	23.4%	10.6%

Capabilities

Canada's armed forces are focused principally on territorial defence, as well as contributing important capabilities to international missions, principally through NATO. The 2017 defence review reaffirmed commitments to NATO, but also to modernising capabilities, including cyber power. Canada operates a volunteer force with high standards of training. The review promised to increase regular and reserve forces, with particular enhancements in the areas of cyber and intelligence. Deployments, although relatively small scale, underscore a determination to maintain a power-projection capability and international engagement. Canada's leadership of a NATO battlegroup in Latvia highlights a continuing capability to deploy medium-sized land formations. It has also contributed to NATO's air-policing mission. Meanwhile, the deployments of frigates and submarines to the NATO theatre and the Pacific demonstrate continuing blue-water naval capabilities. The 2017 review pledged to finally deliver on a range of delayed procurements aimed at making the services more suitable to future operations. It raised the target for a new-generation fighter to 88 aircraft, but a trade dispute with Boeing saw Canada turn to Australia to purchase second-hand F/A-18s to supplement its current fleet. In October 2018, the government selected the Lockheed Martin-led consortium and its BAE Systems Type-26 frigate design as the preferred bidder for Canada's future surface combatant. Canada maintains a well-developed range of mainly small and medium-sized defence firms. The strongest sector is in combat vehicles and components, though the naval sector has recently developed.

ACTIVE 66,600 (Army 23,000 Navy 8,300 Air Force 12,000 Other 23,300) Paramilitary 4,500

RESERVE 27,000 (Army 17,000 Navy 4,600 Air 2,100 Other 3,300)

ORGANISATIONS BY SERVICE

Space
EQUIPMENT BY TYPE
SATELLITES • SPACE SURVEILLANCE 1 *Sapphire*

Army 23,000
FORCES BY ROLE
MANOEUVRE
  Mechanised
    1 (1st) mech bde gp (1 armd regt, 2 mech inf bn, 1 lt inf bn, 1 arty regt, 1 cbt engr regt, 1 log bn)
    2 (2nd & 5th) mech bde gp (1 armd recce regt, 2 mech inf bn, 1 lt inf bn, 1 arty regt, 1 cbt engr regt, 1 log bn)
COMBAT SUPPORT
  1 engr regt
  3 MP pl
AIR DEFENCE
  1 SAM regt
EQUIPMENT BY TYPE
ARMOURED FIGHTING VEHICLES
  MBT 82: 42 *Leopard* 2A4 (trg role); 20 *Leopard* 2A4M (upgraded); 20 *Leopard* 2A6M (52 *Leopard* 1C2 in store)
  RECCE ε120 LAV-25 *Coyote*
  IFV 550: 141 LAV-III *Kodiak*; 409 LAV 6.0
  APC 443
    APC (T) 268: 235 M113; 33 M577 (CP)
    APC (W) 175 LAV *Bison* (incl 10 EW, 32 amb, 32 repair, 64 recovery)
  AUV 455: 7 *Cougar*; 448 TAPV
ENGINEERING & MAINTENANCE VEHICLES
  AEV 23: 5 *Buffalo*; 18 *Wisent* 2
  ARV 12 BPz-3 *Büffel*
ANTI-TANK/ANTI-INFRASTRUCTURE
  MSL • MANPATS TOW-2
  RCL 84mm *Carl Gustav*
ARTILLERY 287
  TOWED 163 **105mm** 126: 98 C3 (M101); 28 LG1 MkII; **155mm** 37 M777
  MOR 124: **81mm** 100; **SP 81mm** 24 LAV *Bison*
UNMANNED AERIAL VEHICLES • ISR • Light *Skylark*
AIR DEFENCE • SAM • Point-defence *Starburst*

Reserve Organisations 17,000

Canadian Rangers 5,000 Reservists
Provide a limited military presence in Canada's northern, coastal and isolated areas. Sovereignty, public-safety and surveillance roles
FORCES BY ROLE
MANOEUVRE
  Other
    5 (patrol) ranger gp (187 patrols)

Army Reserves 12,000 Reservists
Most units have only coy-sized establishments
FORCES BY ROLE
COMMAND
  10 bde gp HQ

MANOEUVRE
  Reconnaissance
    18 recce regt (sqn)
  Light
    51 inf regt (coy)
COMBAT SUPPORT
  16 fd arty regt (bty)
  3 indep fd arty bty
  10 cbt engr regt (coy)
  1 EW regt (sqn)
  4 int coy
  10 sigs regt (coy)
COMBAT SERVICE SUPPORT
  10 log bn (coy)
  3 MP coy

Royal Canadian Navy 8,300
EQUIPMENT BY TYPE
SUBMARINES • SSK 4:
  4 *Victoria* (ex-UK *Upholder*) with 6 single 533mm TT with Mk48 *Sea Arrow* HWT (2 currently non-operational)
PRINCIPAL SURFACE COMBATANTS • FRIGATES • FFGHM 12:
  12 *Halifax* with 2 quad lnchr with RGM-84 Block II *Harpoon* AShM, 2 octuple Mk48 VLS with RIM-7P *Sea Sparrow* SAM/RIM-162C ESSM SAM, 2 twin 324mm ASTT with Mk46 LWT, 1 *Phalanx* CIWS, 1 57mm gun (capacity 1 SH-3 (CH-124) *Sea King* ASW hel)
MINE WARFARE
  MINE COUNTERMEASURES • MCO 12 *Kingston* (also used in patrol role)
LOGISTICS AND SUPPORT 10
  AORH 1 *Asterix* (*Resolve*) (capacity 2 CH-148 *Cyclone* ASW hel)
  AX 9: AXL 8 *Orca*; AXS 1 *Oriole*

Reserves 4,600 reservists
24 units tasked with crewing 10 of the 12 MCOs, harbour defence & naval control of shipping

Royal Canadian Air Force (RCAF) 12,000
FORCES BY ROLE
FIGHTER/GROUND ATTACK
  4 sqn with F/A-18A/B *Hornet* (CF-18AM/BM)
ANTI-SUBMARINE WARFARE
  1 sqn with SH-3 *Sea King* (CH-124)
  1 sqn with CH-148 *Cyclone*
MARITIME PATROL
  2 sqn with P-3 *Orion* (CP-140 *Aurora*)
SEARCH & RESCUE/TRANSPORT
  3 sqn with AW101 *Merlin* (CH-149 *Cormorant*); C-130H/H-30 (CC-130) *Hercules*
  1 sqn with DHC-5 (CC-115) *Buffalo*
TANKER/TRANSPORT
  1 sqn with A310/A310 MRTT (CC-150/CC-150T)
  1 sqn with KC-130H
TRANSPORT
  1 sqn with C-17A (CC-177) *Globemaster*
  1 sqn with CL-600 (CC-144B)
  1 sqn with C-130J-30 (CC-130) *Hercules*
  1 (utl) sqn with DHC-6 (CC-138) *Twin Otter*
TRAINING
  1 OCU sqn with F/A-18A/B *Hornet* (CF-18AM/BM)
  1 OCU sqn with C-130H/H-30/J (CC-130) *Hercules*
  1 OCU sqn with CH-148 *Cyclone*
  1 OCU sqn with Bell 412 (CH-146 *Griffon*)
  1 sqn with P-3 *Orion* (CP-140 *Aurora*)
TRANSPORT HELICOPTER
  5 sqn with Bell 412 (CH-146 *Griffon*)
  3 (cbt spt) sqn with Bell 412 (CH-146 *Griffon*)
  1 (Spec Ops) sqn with Bell 412 (CH-146 *Griffon* – OPCON Canadian Special Operations Command)
  1 sqn with CH-47F (CH-147F) *Chinook*
EQUIPMENT BY TYPE
AIRCRAFT 95 combat capable
  FGA 77: 59 F/A-18A (CF-18AM) *Hornet*; 18 F/A-18B (CF-18BM) *Hornet*
  ASW 18 P-3 *Orion* (CP-140M *Aurora*)
  TKR/TPT 7: 2 A310 MRTT (CC-150T); 5 KC-130H
  TPT 47: **Heavy** 5 C-17A (CC-177) *Globemaster* III; **Medium** 25: 6 C-130H (CC-130) *Hercules*; 2 C-130H-30 (CC-130) *Hercules*; 17 C-130J-30 (CC-130) *Hercules*; **Light** 10: 6 DHC-5 (CC-115) *Buffalo*; 4 DHC-6 (CC-138) *Twin Otter*; **PAX** 7: 3 A310 (CC-150 *Polaris*); 4 CL-600 (CC-144B/C)
  TRG 4 DHC-8 (CT-142)
HELICOPTERS
  ASW 26: 11 SH-3 (CH-124) *Sea King* (to be withdrawn end 2018); 15 CH-148 *Cyclone* (6 more Block 2 hels delivered but not yet accepted)
  MRH 68 Bell 412 (CH-146 *Griffon*)
  TPT 29: **Heavy** 15 CH-47F (CH-147F) *Chinook*; **Medium** 14 AW101 *Merlin* (CH-149 *Cormorant*)
RADARS 53
  AD RADAR • NORTH WARNING SYSTEM 47: 11 AN/FPS-117 (range 200nm); 36 AN/FPS-124 (range 80nm)
  STRATEGIC 6: 4 Coastal; 2 Transportable
AIR-LAUNCHED MISSILES
  ASM AGM-65 *Maverick*
  AAM • IR AIM-9L *Sidewinder*; SARH AIM-7M *Sparrow*
  ARH AIM-120C AMRAAM
BOMBS
  Laser-guided: GBU-10/GBU-12/GBU-16 *Paveway* II; GBU-24 *Paveway* III
  INS/GPS-guided: GBU-31 JDAM; GBU-38 JDAM; GBU-49 *Enhanced Paveway* II

NATO Flight Training Canada
EQUIPMENT BY TYPE
AIRCRAFT
  TRG 45: 26 T-6A *Texan* II (CT-156 *Harvard* II); 19 *Hawk* 115 (CT-155) (advanced wpns/tactics trg)

Contracted Flying Services – Southport
EQUIPMENT BY TYPE
AIRCRAFT
  TPT • **Light** 7 Beech C90B *King Air*
  TRG 11 G-120A
HELICOPTERS
  MRH 9 Bell 412 (CH-146)
  TPT • **Light** 7 Bell 206 *Jet Ranger* (CH-139)

Canadian Special Operations Forces Command 1,500

FORCES BY ROLE
SPECIAL FORCES
   1 SF regt (Canadian Special Operations Regiment)
   1 SF unit (JTF 2)
COMBAT SERVICE SUPPORT
   1 CBRN unit (Canadian Joint Incident Response Unit – CJIRU)
TRANSPORT HELICOPTER
   1 (spec ops) sqn, with Bell 412 (CH-146 *Griffon* – from the RCAF)
EQUIPMENT BY TYPE
NBC VEHICLES 4 LAV *Bison* NBC
HELICOPTERS • MRH 10 Bell 412 (CH-146 *Griffon*)

Canadian Forces Joint Operational Support Group

FORCES BY ROLE
COMBAT SUPPORT
   1 engr spt coy
   1 (close protection) MP coy
   1 (joint) sigs regt
COMBAT SERVICE SUPPORT
   1 (spt) log unit
   1 (movement) log unit

Paramilitary 4,500

Canadian Coast Guard 4,500

Incl Department of Fisheries and Oceans; all platforms are designated as non-combatant

EQUIPMENT BY TYPE
PATROL AND COASTAL COMBATANTS 69
   PSOH 1 *Leonard J Cowley*
   PSO 1 *Sir Wilfred Grenfell* (with hel landing platform)
   PCO 13: 2 *Cape Roger*; 1 *Gordon Reid*; 9 *Hero*; 1 *Tanu*
   PCC 1 *Harp*
   PB 53: 1 *Post*; 1 *Quebecois*; 1 *Vakta*; 10 Type-300A; 36 Type-300B; 1 *S. Dudka*; 1 *Simmonds* (on loan from RCMP); 2 *Baie de Plaisance*
AMPHIBIOUS • LANDING CRAFT • UCAC 4 Type-400
LOGISTICS AND SUPPORT 42
   ABU 7
   AG 4
   AGB 15
   AGOR 8 (coastal and offshore fishery vessels)
   AGOS 8
HELICOPTERS • MRH 7 Bell 412EP • **TPT** 19: **Medium** 1 S-61; **Light** 18: 3 Bell 206L *Long Ranger*; 15 Bell 429

Cyber

In June 2017, Canada's defence-policy review said that Canada 'will develop the capability to conduct active cyber operations focused on external threats to Canada in the context of government-authorized military missions'. This was because a 'purely defensive' cyber posture was 'no longer sufficient'. In November 2017, the first transferees were stood up in the new 'cyber operator' role; civilian recruitment was due to start in 2018 and reservist recruitment in 2019. Canada published a cyber-security strategy in October 2010 and an action plan on implementation in 2013. The armed forces' Information Management Group (IMG) is responsible for electronic warfare and network defence. The Canadian Force Information Operations Group, under the IMG, commands the Canadian Forces Information Operations Group Headquarters; the Canadian Forces Electronic Warfare Centre; the Canadian Forces Network Operation Centre, which is the national operational cyber-defence unit permanently assigned to support Canadian Forces operations; and other units.

DEPLOYMENT

ALBANIA: OSCE • Albania 1
BOSNIA-HERZEGOVINA: OSCE • Bosnia and Herzegovina 2
CARIBBEAN: *Operation Caribbe* 1 MCO
CYPRUS: UN • UNFICYP (*Operation Snowgoose*) 1
DEMOCRATIC REPUBLIC OF THE CONGO: UN • MONUSCO (*Operation Crocodile*) 8
EGYPT: MFO (*Operation Calumet*) 68; 1 MP team
IRAQ: *Operation Inherent Resolve* (*Impact*) 370; 1 SF trg gp; 1 med unit; 1 hel flt with 4 Bell 412 (CH-146 *Griffon*) hel
KUWAIT: *Operation Inherent Resolve* (*Impact*) 1 A310 MRTT (C-150T); 2 C-130J-30 *Hercules* (CC-130J)
LATVIA: NATO • Enhanced Forward Presence (*Operation Reassurance*) 350; 1 mech inf bn HQ; 1 mech inf coy(+); LAV 6.0; M777
MALI: UN • MINUSMA (*Operation Presence*) 138: 1 hel sqn with 3 CH-47F (CH-147F) *Chinook*; 5 Bell 412 (CH-145 *Griffon*)
MEDITERRANEAN SEA: NATO • SNMG 2: 1 FFGHM
MIDDLE EAST: UN • UNTSO (*Operation Jade*) 4 obs
PACIFIC OCEAN: *Operation Caribbe* 2 MCO
ROMANIA: NATO • Air Policing 135; 5 F/A-18A *Hornet* (CF-18)
SERBIA: NATO • KFOR • *Joint Enterprise* (*Operation Kobold*) 5; OSCE • Kosovo 2
SOUTH SUDAN: UN • UNMISS (*Operation Soprano*) 5; 5 obs
UKRAINE: *Operation Unifier* 200; OSCE • Ukraine 35

FOREIGN FORCES

United Kingdom BATUS 400; 1 trg unit; 1 hel flt with SA341 *Gazelle* AH1
United States 150

United States US

United States Dollar $		2017	2018	2019
GDP	US$	19.5tr	20.5tr	
per capita	US$	59,792	62,518	
Growth	%	2.2	2.9	
Inflation	%	2.1	2.4	
Def exp [a]	US$	686bn	706bn	
Def bdgt [b]	US$	599bn	643bn	689bn

[a] NATO definition
[b] National Defense Budget Function (50) outlays. Includes DoD funding, as well as funds for nuclear-weapons-related activities undertaken by the Department of Energy. Excludes some military retirement and healthcare costs.

Population   329,256,465

Age	0–14	15–19	20–24	25–29	30–64	65 plus
Male	9.5%	3.3%	3.4%	3.7%	22.3%	7.1%
Female	9.1%	3.1%	3.3%	3.5%	22.8%	8.9%

Capabilities

The United States remains the world's most capable military power, with a unique ability to project power on a global basis. The Pentagon's 2018 National Defense Strategy refocused priorities on the return of renewed 'great-power competition' and called for a reversal in reductions in the size of the joint force. A new Nuclear Posture Review backed the development of low-yield warheads and a nuclear-capable sea-launched cruise missile. A missile-defence review is pending, and the direction to create a space force has fuelled debate over the best way to integrate space into national-security policy. The US is NATO's most capable member, and has defence-treaty obligations to, among others, Australia, the Philippines, Japan, South Korea and Thailand. The US maintains an all-volunteer force, including significant reserves, with high levels of training throughout all command and service levels. However, readiness remains a major concern. Modernisation priorities include a renewal of strategic nuclear capabilities, including a new class of ballistic-missile submarine and a new long-range bomber, and a major recapitalisation of air assets across the services. A major declared priority for the current administration is a long-term naval build-up to a 355-ship combat fleet. The US also continues to actively develop its defensive and offensive cyber capabilities. The country has the strongest defence industry globally, with a dominant position in the international defence market, although a report initiated by President Trump warned that key areas of the defence-industrial base were eroding, which could have consequences for the defence supply chain.

ACTIVE 1,359,450 (Army 476,200 Navy 329,850 Air Force 325,900 US Marine Corps 185,400 US Coast Guard 42,100)

RESERVE 845,600 (Army 524,000 Navy 100,950 Air Force 176,150 Marine Corps Reserve 38,350 US Coast Guard 6,150)

ORGANISATIONS BY SERVICE

US Strategic Command
HQ at Offutt AFB (NE). Five missions: US nuclear deterrent; missile defence; global strike; info ops; ISR

US Navy
EQUIPMENT BY TYPE
SUBMARINES • STRATEGIC • SSBN 14 *Ohio* with up to 24 UGM-133A *Trident* D-5/D-5LE nuclear SLBM, 4 single 533mm TT with Mk48 *Sea Arrow* HWT

US Air Force • Global Strike Command
FORCES BY ROLE
MISSILE
  9 sqn with LGM-30G *Minuteman* III
BOMBER
  5 sqn with B-52H *Stratofortress*
  2 sqn with B-2A *Spirit* (+1 ANG sqn personnel only)
EQUIPMENT BY TYPE
SURFACE-TO-SURFACE MISSILE LAUNCHERS
  ICBM • **Nuclear** 400 LGM-30G *Minuteman* III (1 Mk12A or Mk21 re-entry veh per missile)
AIRCRAFT
  BBR 66: 20 B-2A *Spirit*; 46 B-52H *Stratofortress*
AIR-LAUNCHED MISSILES
  ALCM • **Nuclear** AGM-86B

Strategic Defenses – Early Warning
North American Aerospace Defense Command (NORAD) – a combined US–CAN org
EQUIPMENT BY TYPE
RADAR
  NORTH WARNING SYSTEM 50: 14 AN/FPS-117 (range 200nm); 36 AN/FPS-124 (range 80nm)
  SOLID STATE PHASED ARRAY RADAR SYSTEM (SSPARS) 5: 2 AN/FPS-123 Early Warning Radar located at Cape Cod AFS (MA) and Clear AFS (AK); 3 AN/FPS-132 Upgraded Early Warning Radar located at Beale AFB (CA), Thule (GL) and Fylingdales Moor (UK)
  SPACETRACK SYSTEM 10: 1 AN/FPS-85 Spacetrack Radar at Eglin AFB (FL); 6 contributing radars at Cavalier AFS (ND), Clear (AK), Thule (GL), Fylingdales Moor (UK), Beale AFB (CA) and Cape Cod (MA); 3 Spacetrack Optical Trackers located at Socorro (NM), Maui (HI), Diego Garcia (BIOT)
  PERIMETER ACQUISITION RADAR ATTACK CHARACTERISATION SYSTEM (PARCS) 1 AN/FPQ-16 at Cavalier AFS (ND)
  DETECTION AND TRACKING RADARS 5 located at Kwajalein Atoll, Ascension Island, Australia, Kaena Point (HI), MIT Lincoln Laboratory (MA)
  GROUND BASED ELECTRO OPTICAL DEEP SPACE SURVEILLANCE SYSTEM (GEODSS) Socorro (NM), Maui (HI), Diego Garcia (BIOT)
  STRATEGIC DEFENCES – MISSILE DEFENCES
  SEA-BASED: *Aegis* engagement cruisers and destroyers

LAND-BASED: 40 ground-based interceptors at Fort Greely (AK); 4 ground-based interceptors at Vandenburg AFB (CA)

Space

EQUIPMENT BY TYPE
SATELLITES 137
  COMMUNICATIONS 43: 4 AEHF; 6 DSCS-III; 2 *Milstar*-I; 3 *Milstar*-II; 5 MUOS; 1 PAN-1 (P360); 5 SDS-III; 2 SDS-IV; 6 UFO; 9 WGS SV2
  NAVIGATION/POSITIONING/TIMING 31: 12 NAVSTAR Block IIF; 19 NAVSTAR Block IIR/IIRM
  METEOROLOGY/OCEANOGRAPHY 6 DMSP-5
  ISR 16: 5 FIA *Radar*; 5 *Evolved Enhanced/Improved Crystal* (visible and infrared imagery); 2 *Lacrosse* (*Onyx* radar imaging satellite); 1 NRO L-76; 1 ORS-1; 1 *TacSat*-4; 1 *TacSat*-6
  ELINT/SIGINT 27: 2 *Mentor* (advanced *Orion*); 3 Advanced *Mentor*; 4 *Mercury*; 1 NRO L-67; 1 *Trumpet*; 4 Improved *Trumpet*; 12 SBWASS (Space Based Wide Area Surveillance System; Naval Ocean Surveillance System)
  SPACE SURVEILLANCE 6: 4 GSSAP; 1 SBSS (Space Based Surveillance System); 1 ORS-5
  EARLY WARNING 8: 4 DSP; 4 SBIRS *Geo*-1

US Army 476,200

FORCES BY ROLE
Sqn are generally bn sized and tp are generally coy sized
COMMAND
  3 (I, III & XVIII AB) corps HQ
  1 (2nd) inf div HQ
SPECIAL FORCES
  (see USSOCOM)
MANOEUVRE
  Armoured
  1 (1st) armd div (2 (2nd & 3rd ABCT) armd bde (1 armd recce sqn, 2 armd bn, 1 armd inf bn, 1 SP arty bn, 1 cbt engr bn, 1 CSS bn); 1 (1st SBCT) mech bde (1 armd recce sqn, 3 mech inf bn, 1 arty bn, 1 cbt engr bn, 1 CSS bn); 1 MRL bde HQ; 1 log bde; 1 (hy cbt avn) hel bde)
  1 (1st) cav div (3 (1st–3rd ABCT) armd bde (1 armd recce sqn, 2 armd bn, 1 armd inf bn, 1 SP arty bn, 1 cbt engr bn, 1 CSS bn); 1 MRL bde (1 MRL bn); 1 log bde; 1 (hy cbt avn) hel bde)
  1 (1st) inf div (2 (1st & 2nd ABCT) armd bde (1 armd recce sqn, 2 armd bn, 1 armd inf bn, 1 SP arty bn, 1 cbt engr bn, 1 CSS bn); 1 log bde; 1 (cbt avn) hel bde)
  1 (3rd) inf div (2 (1st & 2nd ABCT) armd bde (1 armd recce sqn, 2 armd bn, 1 armd inf bn, 1 SP arty bn, 1 cbt engr bn, 1 CSS bn); 1 lt inf bn; 1 MRL bde HQ; 1 log bde; 1 (cbt avn) hel bde)
  Mechanised
  1 (4th) inf div (1 (3rd ABCT) armd bde (1 armd recce sqn, 2 armd bn, 1 armd inf bn, 1 SP arty bn, 1 cbt engr bn, 1 CSS bn); 1 (1st SBCT) mech bde (1 armd recce sqn, 3 mech inf bn, 1 arty bn, 1 cbt engr bn, 1 CSS bn); 1 (2nd IBCT) lt inf bde (1 recce sqn, 3 inf bn, 1 arty bn, 1 cbt engr bn, 1 CSS bn); 1 MRL bde HQ; 1 log bde; 1 (hy cbt avn) hel bde)
  1 (7th) inf div (2 (1st & 2nd SBCT, 2nd ID) mech bde (1 armd recce sqn, 3 mech inf bn, 1 arty bn, 1 cbt engr bn, 1 CSS bn))
  1 (1st SBCT, 25th ID) mech bde (1 armd recce sqn, 3 mech inf bn, 1 arty bn, 1 cbt engr bn, 1 CSS bn)
  2 (2nd & 3rd CR) mech bde (1 armd recce sqn, 3 mech sqn, 1 arty sqn, 1 cbt engr sqn, 1 CSS sqn)
  Light
  1 (10th Mtn) inf div (3 (1st–3rd IBCT) lt inf bde (1 recce sqn, 3 inf bn, 1 arty bn, 1 cbt engr bn, 1 CSS bn); 1 log bde; 1 (cbt avn) hel bde)
  1 (25th) inf div (2 (2 & 3rd IBCT) inf bde (1 recce sqn, 2 inf bn, 1 arty bn, 1 cbt engr bn, 1 CSS bn); 1 log bde; 1 (cbt avn) hel bde)
  2 (Sy Force Assist) inf bde(-)
  Air Manoeuvre
  1 (82nd) AB div (1 (1st AB BCT) AB bde (1 recce bn, 1 mech coy; 3 para bn, 1 arty bn, 1 cbt engr bn, 1 CSS bn); 2 (2nd & 3rd AB BCT) AB bde (1 recce bn, 3 para bn, 1 arty bn, 1 cbt engr bn, 1 CSS bn); 1 (cbt avn) hel bde; 1 log bde)
  1 (101st) air aslt div (3 (1st–3rd AB BCT) AB bde (1 recce bn, 3 para bn, 1 arty bn, 1 cbt engr bn, 1 CSS bn); 1 (cbt avn) hel bde; 1 log bde)
  1 (173rd AB BCT) AB bde (1 recce bn, 2 para bn, 1 arty bn, 1 cbt engr bn, 1 CSS bn)
  1 (4th AB BCT, 25th ID) AB bde (1 recce bn, 2 para bn, 1 arty bn, 1 cbt engr bn, 1 CSS bn)
  Other
  1 (11th ACR) trg armd cav regt (OPFOR) (2 armd cav sqn, 1 CSS bn)
COMBAT SUPPORT
  3 MRL bde (2 MRL bn)
  1 MRL bde (4 MRL bn)
  4 engr bde
  2 EOD gp (2 EOD bn)
  10 int bde
  2 int gp
  4 MP bde
  1 NBC bde
  3 (strat) sigs bde
  4 (tac) sigs bde
COMBAT SERVICE SUPPORT
  2 log bde
  3 med bde
  1 tpt bde
HELICOPTER
  2 (cbt avn) hel bde
  1 (cbt avn) hel bde HQ
AIR DEFENCE
  5 SAM bde

Reserve Organisations

Army National Guard 335,200 reservists
Normally dual-funded by DoD and states. Civil-emergency responses can be mobilised by state governors. Federal government can mobilise ARNG for major domestic emergencies and for overseas operations

FORCES BY ROLE
COMMAND
  8 div HQ
SPECIAL FORCES
  (see USSOCOM)
MANOEUVRE
  Reconnaissance
  1 armd recce sqn
  Armoured
  5 (ABCT) armd bde (1 armd recce sqn, 2 armd bn, 1 armd inf bn, 1 SP arty bn, 1 cbt engr bn, 1 CSS bn)
  Mechanised
  2 (SBCT) mech bde (1 armd recce sqn, 3 mech inf bn, 1 arty bn, 1 cbt engr bn, 1 CSS bn)
  Light
  14 (IBCT) lt inf bde (1 recce sqn, 3 inf bn, 1 arty bn, 1 cbt engr bn, 1 CSS bn)
  6 (IBCT) lt inf bde (1 recce sqn, 2 inf bn, 1 arty bn, 1 cbt engr bn, 1 CSS bn)
  4 lt inf bn
  Air Manoeuvre
  1 AB bn
COMBAT SUPPORT
  8 arty bde
  1 SP arty bn
  8 engr bde
  1 EOD regt
  3 int bde
  3 MP bde
  1 NBC bde
  2 (tac) sigs bde
  18 (Mnv Enh) cbt spt bde
COMBAT SERVICE SUPPORT
  9 log bde
  17 (regional) log spt gp
HELICOPTER
  8 (cbt avn) hel bde
  5 (theatre avn) hel bde
AIR DEFENCE
  3 SAM bde

Army Reserve 188,800 reservists
Reserve under full command of US Army. Does not have state-emergency liability of Army National Guard
FORCES BY ROLE
SPECIAL FORCES
  (see USSOCOM)
COMBAT SUPPORT
  4 engr bde
  4 MP bde
  2 NBC bde
  2 sigs bde
  3 (Mnv Enh) cbt spt bde
COMBAT SERVICE SUPPORT
  9 log bde
  11 med bde
HELICOPTER
  1 (theatre avn) hel bde

Army Stand-by Reserve 700 reservists
Trained individuals for mobilisation

EQUIPMENT BY TYPE
ARMOURED FIGHTING VEHICLES
  MBT 2,386: 775 M1A1 SA *Abrams*; 1,611 M1A2 SEPv2 *Abrams* (ε3,500 more M1A1/A2 *Abrams* in store)
  ASLT 134 M1128 *Stryker* MGS
  RECCE 1,745: ε1,200 M3A2/A3 *Bradley*; 545 M1127 *Stryker* RV (ε800 more M3 *Bradley* in store)
  IFV 2,931: ε14 LAV-25; ε2,500 M2A2/A3 *Bradley*; 334 M7A3/SA BFIST (OP); 83 M1296 *Styker Dragoon*; (ε2,000 more M2 *Bradley* in store)
  APC 10,547
    APC (T) ε5,000 M113A2/A3 (ε8,000 more in store)
    APC (W) 2,613: 1,773 M1126 *Stryker* ICV; 348 M1130 *Stryker* CV (CP); 188 M1131 *Stryker* FSV (OP); 304 M1133 *Stryker* MEV (Amb)
  PPV 2,934: 2,633 *MaxxPro Dash*; 301 *MaxxPro* LWB (Amb)
  AUV 9,016: 2,900 M1117 ASV; 465 M1200 *Armored Knight* (OP); 5,651 M-ATV
ENGINEERING & MAINTENANCE VEHICLES
  AEV 531: 113 M1 ABV; 250 M9 ACE; 168 M1132 *Stryker* ESV
  ARV 1,177+: 360 M88A1; 817 M88A2 (ε1,000 more M88A1 in store); some M578
  VLB 60: 20 REBS; 40 *Wolverine* HAB
  MW 3+: *Aardvark* JSFU Mk4; some *Husky* 2G; 3+ *Hydrema* 910 MCV-2; M58/M59 MICLIC; M139; *Rhino*
NBC VEHICLES 234 M1135 *Stryker* NBCRV
ANTI-TANK/ANTI-INFRASTRUCTURE
  MSL
    SP 1,133: 133 M1134 *Stryker* ATGM; ε1,000 M1167 HMMWV TOW
    MANPATS FGM-148 *Javelin*
  RCL 84mm *Carl Gustav*
ARTILLERY 5,411
  SP 155mm 965: 900 M109A6; 65 M109A7 (ε500 more M109A6 in store)
  TOWED 1,339: **105mm** 821 M119A2/3; **155mm** 518 M777A2
  MRL 227mm 600: 375 M142 HIMARS; 225 M270A1 MLRS
  MOR 2,507: **81mm** 990 M252; **120mm** 1,076 M120/M1064A3; **SP 120mm** 441 M1129 *Stryker* MC
SURFACE-TO-SURFACE MISSILE LAUNCHERS
  SRBM • Conventional MGM-140A/B ATACMS; MGM-168 ATACMS (All launched from M270A1 MLRS or M142 HIMARS MRLs)
AMPHIBIOUS 116
  PRINCIPAL AMPHIBIOUS SHIPS 8
    LSL 8 *Frank Besson* (capacity 24 *Abrams* MBT)
  LANDING CRAFT 70
    LCU 34 LCU-2000
    LCM 36 LCM 8 (capacity either 1 MBT or 200 troops)
AIRCRAFT
  ISR 19: 14 RC-12X *Guardrail*; 5 RC-12 *Guardrail* (trg)
  ELINT 8: 5 EO-5C ARL-M (COMINT/ELINT); 2 EO-5B ARL-C (COMINT); 1 TO-5C (trg)
  TPT 156: **Light** 152: 113 Beech A200 *King Air* (C-12 *Huron*); 28 Cessna 560 *Citation* (UC-35A/B); 11 SA-227 *Metro* (C-26B/E); **PAX** 4: 1 Gulfstream IV (C-20F); 2 Gulfstream V (C-37A); 1 Gulfstream G550 (C-37B)
  TRG 4 T-6D *Texan* II

HELICOPTERS
ATK 714: 464 AH-64D *Apache*; 250 AH-64E *Apache*
SAR 249: 19 HH-60L *Black Hawk*; 230 HH-60M *Black Hawk* (medevac)
TPT 2,822: **Heavy** 450 CH-47F *Chinook*; **Medium** 1,884: 250 UH-60A *Black Hawk*; 914 UH-60L *Black Hawk*; 720 UH-60M *Black Hawk*; **Light** 488: 423 UH-72A *Lakota*; 65 UH-1H/V *Iroquois*
TRG ε50 TH-67 *Creek*

UNMANNED AERIAL VEHICLES 388
CISR • Heavy 152 MQ-1C *Gray Eagle*
ISR • Medium 236 RQ-7B *Shadow*

AIR DEFENCE • SAM 1,183+
Long-range 480 MIM-104D/E/F *Patriot* PAC-2 GEM/PAC-2 GEM-T/PAC-3/PAC-3 MSE
Short-range NASAMS
Point-defence 703+: FIM-92 *Stinger*; 703 M1097 *Avenger*

MISSILE DEFENCE • Long-range 42 THAAD

AIR-LAUNCHED MISSILES
ASM AGM-114 *Hellfire*

US Navy 329,850

Comprises 2 Fleet Areas, Atlantic and Pacific. 6 Fleets: 2nd – Atlantic; 3rd – Pacific; 4th – Caribbean, Central and South America; 5th – Indian Ocean, Persian Gulf, Red Sea; 6th – Mediterranean; 7th – W. Pacific; plus Military Sealift Command (MSC); Naval Reserve Force (NRF). For Naval Special Warfare Command, see US Special Operations Command

EQUIPMENT BY TYPE
SUBMARINES 67
STRATEGIC • SSBN 14 *Ohio* opcon US STRATCOM with up to 24 UGM-133A *Trident* D-5/D-5LE nuclear SLBM, 4 single 533mm TT with Mk48 *Sea Arrow* HWT
TACTICAL 53
SSGN 49:
4 *Ohio* (mod) with total of 154 *Tomahawk* LACM, 4 single 533mm TT with Mk48 *Sea Arrow* HWT
7 *Los Angeles* with 1 12-cell VLS with *Tomahawk* LACM, 4 single 533mm TT with Mk48 *Sea Arrow* HWT
22 *Los Angeles* (Imp) with 1 12-cell VLS with *Tomahawk* LACM, 4 single 533mm TT with Mk48 *Sea Arrow* HWT
10 *Virginia* Flight I/II with 1 12-cell VLS with *Tomahawk* LACM, 4 single 533mm TT with Mk48 ADCAP mod 6 HWT
6 *Virginia* Flight III with 2 6-cell VLS with *Tomahawk* LACM, 4 single 533mm TT with Mk48 ADCAP mod 6 HWT
SSN 4:
1 *Los Angeles* with 4 single 533mm TT with Mk48 *Sea Arrow* HWT
3 *Seawolf* with 8 single 660mm TT with up to 45 *Tomahawk* LACM/Mk48 *Sea Arrow* HWT

PRINCIPAL SURFACE COMBATANTS 112
AIRCRAFT CARRIERS • CVN 11
1 *Gerald R. Ford* with 2 octuple Mk29 mod 5 GMLS with RIM-162D ESSM SAM, 2 Mk49 mod 3 GMLS with RIM-116 RAM SAM, 2 Mk 15 *Phalanx* CIWS (typical capacity 75+ F/A-18E/F *Super Hornet* FGA ac; F-35C *Lightning* II FGA ac (IOC planned 02/2019); E-2D *Hawkeye* AEW&C ac; EA-18G *Growler* EW ac; MH-60R *Seahawk* ASW hel; MH-60S *Knighthawk* MRH hel)
10 *Nimitz* with 2 8-cell Mk29 GMLS with RIM-162 ESSM SAM, 2 Mk49 GMLS with RIM-116 SAM, 2 Mk 15 *Phalanx* CIWS (typical capacity 55 F/A-18 *Hornet* FGA ac; F-35C *Lightning* II FGA ac (IOC planned 02/2019); 4 EA-18G *Growler* EW ac; 4 E-2C/D *Hawkeye* AEW ac; 6 H-60 *Seahawk* hel)

CRUISERS • CGHM 23:
22 *Ticonderoga* with *Aegis* Baseline 5/6/8/9 C2, 2 quad lnchr with RGM-84 *Harpoon* AShM, 2 61-cell Mk41 VLS with SM-2ER SAM/SM-3 SAM/SM-6 SAM/*Tomahawk* LACM, 2 triple 324mm ASTT with Mk54 LWT, 2 Mk 15 *Phalanx* Block 1B CIWS, 2 127mm guns (capacity 2 MH-60R *Seahawk*/MH-60S *Knight Hawk* hels)
1 *Zumwalt* with 20 4-cell Mk57 VLS with RIM-162 ESSM SAM/SM-2ER SAM/ASROC ASW/*Tomahawk* LACM, 2 155mm guns (capacity 2 MH-60R *Seahawk* ASW hel or 1 MH-60R *Seahawk* ASW hel and 3 *Fire Scout* UAV)

DESTROYERS 65
DDGHM 37 *Arleigh Burke* Flight IIA with *Aegis* Baseline 5/6/7/9 C2, 1 29-cell Mk41 VLS with ASROC ASW/SM-2ER SAM/SM-3 SAM/SM-6 SAM/*Tomahawk* LACM, 1 61-cell Mk41 VLS with ASROC ASW/SM-2ER SAM/SM-3 SAM/SM-6 SAM/*Tomahawk* LACM, 2 triple 324mm ASTT with Mk54 LWT, 2 Mk 15 *Phalanx* Block 1B CIWS, 1 127mm gun (capacity 2 MH-60R *Seahawk*/MH-60S *Knight Hawk* hels)
DDGM 28 *Arleigh Burke* Flight I/II with *Aegis* Baseline 5/9 C2, 2 quad lnchr with RGM-84 *Harpoon* AShM, 1 32-cell Mk41 VLS with ASROC ASW/SM-2ER SAM/SM-3 SAM/SM-6 SAM/*Tomahawk* LACM, 1 64-cell Mk41 VLS with ASROC ASW/SM-2 ER SAM/*Tomahawk* LACM, 2 Mk49 GMLS with RIM-116 RAM SAM, 2 triple 324mm ASTT with Mk54 LWT, 2 Mk 15 *Phalanx* Block 1B CIWS (4 with 2 SeaRAM instead of *Phalanx*), 1 127mm gun, 1 hel landing platform (of which two suffered major damage in collisions)

FRIGATES • FFHM 13:
6 *Freedom* with 1 21-cell Mk49 lnchr with RIM-116 RAM Block 2 SAM, 1 57mm gun (capacity 2 MH-60R/S *Seahawk* hel or 1 MH-60 with 3 MQ-8 *Fire Scout* UAV)
7 *Independence* with 1 11-cell SeaRAM lnchr with RIM-116 SAM, 1 57mm gun (capacity 2 MH-60R/S *Seahawk* hel and 3 MQ-8 *Fire Scout* UAV)

PATROL AND COASTAL COMBATANTS 61
PCFG 10 *Cyclone* with 1 quad Mk 208 lnchr with BGM-176B *Griffin* B SSM
PCF 3 *Cyclone*
PBF 6 Mk VI
PBR 42

MINE WARFARE • MINE COUNTERMEASURES 11
MCO 11 *Avenger* with 1 SLQ-48 MCM system, 1 SQQ-32(V)3 Sonar (mine hunting)

COMMAND SHIPS • LCC 2 *Blue Ridge* with 2 Mk 15 *Phalanx* Block 1B CIWS (capacity 3 LCPL; 2 LCVP; 700

troops; 1 med hel) (of which 1 vessel partially crewed by Military Sealift Command personnel)

AMPHIBIOUS
  PRINCIPAL AMPHIBIOUS SHIPS 32
    LHA 1 *America* with 2 octuple Mk29 GMLS with RIM-162D ESSM SAM; 2 Mk49 GMLS with RIM-116 RAM SAM, 2 Mk 15 *Phalanx* CIWS (capacity 6 F-35B *Lightning* II FGA ac; 12 MV-22B *Osprey* tpt ac; 4 CH-53E *Sea Stallion* hel; 7 AH-1Z *Viper*/UH-1Y *Iroquois* hel; 2 MH-60 hel)
    LHD 8 *Wasp* with 2 octuple Mk29 GMLS with RIM-7M/RIM-7P *Sea Sparrow* SAM, 2 Mk49 GMLS with RIM-116 RAM SAM, 2 Mk 15 *Phalanx* Block 1B CIWS (capacity: 6 AV-8B *Harrier* II FGA or F-35B *Lightning* II FGA ac; 4 CH-53E *Sea Stallion* hel; 6 MV-22B *Osprey* tpt ac; 4 AH-1W/Z hel; 3 UH-1Y hel; 3 LCAC(L); 60 tanks; 1,687 troops)
    LPD 11 *San Antonio* with 2 21-cell Mk49 GMLS with RIM-116 SAM (capacity 2 CH-53E *Sea Stallion* hel or 2 MV-22 *Osprey*; 2 LCAC(L); 14 AAAV; 720 troops)
    LSD 12:
      4 *Harpers Ferry* with 2 Mk 49 GMLS with RIM-116 SAM, 2 *Phalanx* Mk15 CIWS, 1 hel landing platform (capacity 2 LCAC(L); 40 tanks; 500 troops)
      8 *Whidbey Island* with 2 Mk49 GMLS with RIM-116 SAM, 2 *Phalanx* Mk15 CIWS, 1 hel landing platform (capacity 4 LCAC(L); 40 tanks; 500 troops)
  LANDING CRAFT 245
    LCU 32 LCU-1600 (capacity either 2 M1 *Abrams* MBT or 350 troops)
    LCP 108: 75 LCPL; 33 Utility Boat
    LCM 25: 10 LCM-6; 15 LCM-8
    LCAC 80 LCAC(L) (capacity either 1 MBT or 60 troops (undergoing upgrade programme))
  LOGISTICS AND SUPPORT 14
    AFDL 1 *Dynamic*
    AGOR 5 (all leased out): 1 *Ocean*; 3 *Thomas G. Thompson*; 1 *Kilo Moana*
    ARD 2
    AX 1 *Prevail*
    ESB 1 *Lewis B. Puller* (capacity 4 MH-53/MH-60 hel)
    SSA 2 (for testing)
    SSAN 1 (for propulsion plant training)
    UUV 1 *Cutthroat* (for testing)

Naval Reserve Forces 100,950

Selected Reserve 58,200

Individual Ready Reserve 42,750

Naval Inactive Fleet

Notice for reactivation:
60–90 days minimum (still on naval vessel register)

EQUIPMENT BY TYPE
AMPHIBIOUS 7
  LHA 3 *Tarawa* • **LPD** 4 *Austin*
LOGISTICS AND SUPPORT 4
  AOE 2 *Supply*
  ARS 2 *Safeguard*

Military Sealift Command (MSC)

Fleet Oiler (PM1)
EQUIPMENT BY TYPE
LOGISTICS AND SUPPORT 15
  AOR 15 *Henry J. Kaiser* with 1 hel landing platform

Special Mission (PM2)
EQUIPMENT BY TYPE
LOGISTICS AND SUPPORT 22
  AGM 3: 1 *Howard O. Lorenzen*; 1 *Invincible* (commercial operator); 1 Sea-based X-band Radar
  AGOR 6 *Pathfinder*
  AGOS 5: 1 *Impeccable* (commercial operator); 4 *Victorious*
  AGS 1 *Waters*
  AS 7 (long-term chartered, of which 1 *C-Champion*, 1 *Malama*, 1 *Dominator*, 4 *Arrowhead*)

Prepositioning (PM3)
EQUIPMENT BY TYPE
LOGISTICS AND SUPPORT 27
  AG 2: 1 *V Adm K.R. Wheeler*; 1 *Fast Tempo*
  AK 4: 2 *LTC John U.D. Page*; 1 *Maj. Bernard F. Fisher*; 1 *CPT David I. Lyon*
  AKEH 2 *Lewis and Clark*
  AKR 10: 2 *Bob Hope*; 1 *Stockham*; 7 *Watson*
  AKRH 5 *2nd Lt John P. Bobo*
  AP 2: 1 *Guam*; 1 *Westpac Express*
  ESD 2 *Montford Point*

Service Support (PM4)
EQUIPMENT BY TYPE
LOGISTICS AND SUPPORT 9
  AH 2 *Mercy* with 1 hel landing platform
  ARS 2 *Safeguard*
  AS 2 *Emory S Land*
  ATF 3 *Powhatan*

Sealift (PM5)
(At a minimum of 4 days' readiness)
EQUIPMENT BY TYPE
LOGISTICS AND SUPPORT 23
  AOT 6 (long-term chartered, of which 1 *Empire State*; 1 *Galveston*; 1 *Lawrence H. Gianella*; 1 *Maersk Peary*; 1 SLNC *Pax*; 1 SLNC *Goodwill*)
  AK 7: 1 *Ocean Crescent*; 3 *Sgt Matej Kocak*; 1 *1st Lt Harry L. Martin*; 1 *LCpl Roy M. Wheat*; 1 *Sea Eagle* (long-term chartered)
  AKR 10: 5 *Bob Hope*; 2 *Gordon*; 2 *Shughart*; 1 *Watson*

Fleet Ordnance and Dry Cargo (PM6)
EQUIPMENT BY TYPE
LOGISTICS AND SUPPORT 14
  AOE 2 *Supply*
  AKEH 12 *Lewis and Clark*

Afloat Staging Command Support (PM7)
EQUIPMENT BY TYPE
LOGISTICS AND SUPPORT 2
  ARC 1 *Zeus*

ESB 1 *Lewis B. Puller* (capacity 4 MH-53 hel/4 MV-22 tiltrotor; 250 troops)

Expeditionary Fast Transport (PM8)
EQUIPMENT BY TYPE
LOGISTICS AND SUPPORT 9
    EPF 9 *Spearhead*

US Maritime Administration (MARAD)

National Defense Reserve Fleet
EQUIPMENT BY TYPE
LOGISTICS AND SUPPORT 19
    AGOS 2 *General Rudder*
    AGM 2: 1 *Pacific Collector*; 1 *Pacific Tracker*
    AK 6: 1 *Cape Ann* (breakbulk); 1 *Cape Chalmers* (breakbulk); 2 *Cape Farewell*; 1 *Cape Nome* (breakbulk); 1 *Del Monte* (breakbulk)
    AOT 3 *Paul Buck*
    AP 4: 1 *Empire State* VI; 1 *Golden Bear*; 1 *Kennedy*; 1 *State of Maine*
    AX 2: 1 *Freedom Star*; 1 *Kings Pointer*

Ready Reserve Force
Ships at readiness up to a maximum of 30 days
EQUIPMENT BY TYPE
LOGISTICS AND SUPPORT 43
    ACS 6: 2 *Flickertail State*; 1 *Gopher State*; 3 *Keystone State*
    AK 4: 2 *Wright* (breakbulk); 2 *Cape May* (heavy lift)
    AKR 33: 1 *Adm W.M. Callaghan*; 4 *Algol*; 4 *Cape Capella*; 1 *Cape Decision*; 4 *Cape Ducato*; 1 *Cape Edmont*; 1 *Cape Henry*; 2 *Cape Hudson*; 2 *Cape Knox*; 4 *Cape Island*; 1 *Cape Orlando*; 1 *Cape Race*; 1 *Cape Trinity*; 2 *Cape Trinity*; 2 *Cape Victory*; 2 *Cape Washington*

Naval Aviation 98,600

10 air wg. Average air wing comprises 8 sqns: 4 with F/A-18; 1 with MH-60R; 1 with EA-18G; 1 with E-2C/D; 1 with MH-60S

FORCES BY ROLE
FIGHTER/GROUND ATTACK
    2 sqn with F/A-18C *Hornet*
    19 sqn with F/A-18E *Super Hornet*
    11 sqn with F/A-18F *Super Hornet*
    2 sqn with F-35C *Lightning* II
ANTI-SUBMARINE WARFARE
    11 sqn with MH-60R *Seahawk*
    1 ASW/CSAR sqn with HH-60H *Seahawk*
    3 ASW/ISR sqn with MH-60R *Seahawk*; MQ-8B *Fire Scout*
ELINT
    1 sqn with EP-3E *Aries* II
ELINT/ELECTRONIC WARFARE
    13 sqn with EA-18G *Growler*
MARITIME PATROL
    3 sqn with P-3C *Orion*
    8 sqn with P-8A *Poseidon*
    1 sqn (forming) with P-8A *Poseidon*
AIRBORNE EARLY WARNING & CONTROL
    6 sqn with E-2C *Hawkeye*
    3 sqn with E-2D *Hawkeye*

COMMAND & CONTROL
    2 sqn with E-6B *Mercury*
MINE COUNTERMEASURES
    2 sqn with MH-53E *Sea Dragon*
TRANSPORT
    2 sqn with C-2A *Greyhound*
TRAINING
    1 (FRS) sqn with EA-18G *Growler*
    1 (FRS) sqn with C-2A *Greyhound*; E-2C/D *Hawkeye*; TE-2C *Hawkeye*
    1 sqn with E-6B *Mercury*
    2 (FRS) sqn with F/A-18A/A+/B/C/D *Hornet*; F/A-18E/F *Super Hornet*
    2 (FRS) sqn with F-35C *Lightning* II
    1 (FRS) sqn with MH-53 *Sea Dragon*
    2 (FRS) sqn with MH-60S *Knight Hawk*; HH-60H *Seahawk*
    2 (FRS) sqn with MH-60R *Seahawk*
    1 sqn with P-3C *Orion*
    1 (FRS) sqn with P-3C *Orion*; P-8A *Poseidon*
    6 sqn with T-6A/B *Texan* II
    2 sqn with T-44C *Pegasus*
    5 sqn with T-45C *Goshawk*
    3 hel sqn with TH-57B/C *Sea Ranger*
    1 (FRS) UAV sqn with MQ-8B *Fire Scout*; MQ-8C *Fire Scout*
TRANSPORT HELICOPTER
    14 sqn with MH-60S *Knight Hawk*
    1 tpt hel/ISR sqn with MH-60S *Knight Hawk*; MQ-8B *Fire Scout*
ISR UAV
    1 sqn with MQ-4C *Triton*

EQUIPMENT BY TYPE
AIRCRAFT 1,007 combat capable
    FGA 736: 23 F-35C *Lightning* II; 10 F-16A *Fighting Falcon*; 4 F-16B *Fighting Falcon*; 10 F/A-18A/A+ *Hornet*; 9 F/A-18B *Hornet*; 90 F/A-18C *Hornet*; 30 F/A-18D *Hornet*; 290 F/A-18E *Super Hornet*; 270 F/A-18F *Super Hornet*
    ASW 140: 65 P-3C *Orion*; 75 P-8A *Poseidon*
    EW 131 EA-18G *Growler**
    ELINT 9 EP-3E *Aries* II
    AEW&C 80: 50 E-2C *Hawkeye*; 30 E-2D *Hawkeye*
    C2 16 E-6B *Mercury*
    TKR 3: 1 KC-130R *Hercules*; 1 KC-130T *Hercules*; 1 KC-130J *Hercules*
    TPT • Light 60: 4 Beech A200 *King Air* (C-12C *Huron*); 6 Beech A200 *King Air* (UC-12F *Huron*); 8 Beech A200 *King Air* (UC-12M *Huron*); 33 C-2A *Greyhound*; 2 DHC-2 *Beaver* (U-6A); 7 SA-227-BC *Metro* III (C-26D)
    TRG 582: 44 T-6A *Texan* II; 232 T-6B *Texan* II; 7 T-38C *Talon*; 55 T-44C *Pegasus*; 242 T-45C *Goshawk*; 2 TE-2C *Hawkeye*
HELICOPTERS
    ASW 225 MH-60R *Seahawk*
    MRH 271 MH-60S *Knight Hawk* (Multi Mission Support)
    MCM 28 MH-53E *Sea Dragon*
    ISR 3 OH-58C *Kiowa*
    CSAR 11 HH-60H *Seahawk*

TPT 13: **Heavy** 2 CH-53E *Sea Stallion*; **Medium** 3 UH-60L *Black Hawk*; **Light** 8: 5 UH-72A *Lakota*; 2 UH-1N *Iroquois*; 1 UH-1Y *Venom*
TRG 119: 43 TH-57B *Sea Ranger*; 76 TH-57C *Sea Ranger*
UNMANNED AERIAL VEHICLES • ISR 91
Heavy 41: 1 MQ-4C *Triton*; 20 MQ-8B *Fire Scout*; 16 MQ-8C *Fire Scout*; 4 RQ-4A *Global Hawk* (under evaluation and trials); **Medium** 35 RQ-2B *Pioneer*; **Light** 15 RQ-21A *Blackjack*
AIR-LAUNCHED MISSILES
AAM • **IR** AIM-9M *Sidewinder*; **IIR** AIM-9X *Sidewinder* II; **SARH** AIM-7 *Sparrow*; **ARH** AIM-120C-5/C-7/D AMRAAM
ASM AGM-65F *Maverick*; AGM-114B/K/M *Hellfire*; APKWS
AShM AGM-84D *Harpoon*; AGM-119A *Penguin* 3
ARM AGM-88B/C/E HARM/AARGM
ALCM • **Conventional** AGM-84E/H/K SLAM/SLAM-ER
BOMBS
Laser-guided: GBU-10/12/16 *Paveway* II; GBU-24 *Paveway* III
INS/GPS guided: GBU-31/32/38 JDAM; Enhanced *Paveway* II; GBU-54 Laser JDAM; AGM-154A/C/C-1 JSOW

Naval Aviation Reserve
FORCES BY ROLE
FIGHTER/GROUND ATTACK
 1 sqn with F/A-18A+ *Hornet*
ANTI-SUBMARINE WARFARE
 1 sqn with MH-60R *Seahawk*
ELECTRONIC WARFARE
 1 sqn with EA-18G *Growler*
MARITIME PATROL
 2 sqn with P-3C *Orion*
TRANSPORT
 5 log spt sqn with B-737-700 (C-40A *Clipper*)
 2 log spt sqn with Gulfstream III/IV (C-20D/G); Gulfstream V/G550 (C-37A/B)
 4 sqn with C-130T *Hercules*
 1 sqn with KC-130T *Hercules*
TRAINING
 2 (aggressor) sqn with F-5F/N *Tiger* II
 1 (aggressor) sqn with F/A-18A+ *Hornet*
TRANSPORT HELICOPTER
 2 sqn with HH-60H *Seahawk*
EQUIPMENT BY TYPE
 AIRCRAFT 77 combat capable
 FTR 31: 2 F-5F *Tiger* II; 29 F-5N *Tiger* II
 FGA 29 F/A-18A+ *Hornet*
 ASW 12 P-3C *Orion*
 EW 5 EA-18G *Growler**
 TKR 5 KC-130T *Hercules*
 TPT 41: **Medium** 18 C-130T *Hercules*; **PAX** 23: 15 B-737-700 (C-40A *Clipper*); 1 Gulfstream III (C-20D); 3 Gulfstream IV (C-20G); 1 Gulfstream V (C-37A); 3 Gulfstream G550 (C-37B)
HELICOPTERS
 ASW 7 MH-60R *Seahawk*
 MCM 7 MH-53E *Sea Dragon*
 CSAR 16 HH-60H *Seahawk*

US Marine Corps 185,400
3 Marine Expeditionary Forces (MEF), 3 Marine Expeditionary Brigades (MEB), 7 Marine Expeditionary Units (MEU) drawn from 3 div. An MEU usually consists of a battalion landing team (1 SF coy, 1 lt armd recce coy, 1 recce pl, 1 armd pl, 1 amph aslt pl, 1 inf bn, 1 arty bty, 1 cbt engr pl), an aviation combat element (1 medium-lift sqn with attached atk hel, FGA ac and AD assets) and a composite log bn, with a combined total of about 2,200 personnel. Composition varies with mission requirements
FORCES BY ROLE
SPECIAL FORCES
 (see USSOCOM)
MANOEUVRE
 Reconnaissance
 3 (MEF) recce coy
 Amphibious
 1 (1st) mne div (2 armd recce bn, 1 recce bn, 1 tk bn, 2 mne regt (4 mne bn), 1 mne regt (3 mne bn), 1 amph aslt bn, 1 arty regt (3 arty bn, 1 MRL bn), 1 cbt engr bn, 1 EW bn, 1 int bn, 1 sigs bn)
 1 (2nd) mne div (1 armd recce bn, 1 recce bn, 1 tk bn, 3 mne regt (3 mne bn), 1 amph aslt bn, 1 arty regt (2 arty bn), 1 cbt engr bn, 1 EW bn, 1 int bn, 1 sigs bn)
 1 (3rd) mne div (1 recce bn, 1 inf regt (3 inf bn), 1 arty regt (2 arty bn), 1 cbt spt bn (1 armd recce coy, 1 amph aslt coy, 1 cbt engr coy), 1 EW bn, 1 int bn, 1 sigs bn)
COMBAT SERVICE SUPPORT
 3 log gp
EQUIPMENT BY TYPE
ARMOURED FIGHTING VEHICLES
 MBT 447 M1A1 *Abrams*
 IFV 488 LAV-25
 APC • **APC (W)** 207 LAV variants (66 CP; 127 log; 14 EW)
 AAV 1,200 AAV-7A1 (all roles)
 AUV 2,429: 1,725 *Cougar*; 704 M-ATV
ENGINEERING & MAINTENANCE VEHICLES
 AEV 42 M1 ABV
 ARV 185: 60 AAVRA1; 45 LAV-R; 80 M88A1/2
 MW 38 *Buffalo*; some *Husky* 2G
 VLB 6 Joint Aslt Bridge
ANTI-TANK/ANTI-INFRASTRUCTURE •
 MSL
 SP 106 LAV-AT
 MANPATS FGM-148 *Javelin*; FGM-172B SRAW-MPV; TOW
ARTILLERY 1,452
 TOWED 812: **105mm**: 331 M101A1; **155mm** 481 M777A2
 MRL **227mm** 40 M142 HIMARS
 MOR 600: **81mm** 535 M252; **SP 81mm** 65 LAV-M; **120mm** (49 EFSS in store for trg)
UNMANNED AERIAL VEHCILES
 ISR • **Light** 100 BQM-147 *Exdrone*
AIR DEFENCE • SAM • **Point-defence** FIM-92 *Stinger*

Marine Corps Aviation 34,700

3 active Marine Aircraft Wings (MAW) and 1 MCR MAW

FORCES BY ROLE

FIGHTER
  1 sqn with F/A-18A++ *Hornet*
  5 sqn with F/A-18C *Hornet*
  4 sqn with F/A-18D *Hornet*

FIGHTER/GROUND ATTACK
  5 sqn with AV-8B *Harrier* II
  3 sqn with F-35B *Lightning* II

ELECTRONIC WARFARE
  1 sqn with EA-6B *Prowler*

COMBAT SEARCH & RESCUE/TRANSPORT
  1 sqn with Beech A200/B200 *King Air* (UC-12F/M *Huron*); Beech 350 *King Air* (UC-12W *Huron*); Cessna 560 *Citation Ultra/Encore* (UC-35C/D); DC-9 *Skytrain* (C-9B *Nightingale*); Gulfstream IV (C-20G); HH-1N *Iroquois*

TANKER
  3 sqn with KC-130J *Hercules*

TRANSPORT
  14 sqn with MV-22B *Osprey*
  2 sqn (forming) with MV-22B *Osprey*

TRAINING
  1 sqn with AV-8B *Harrier* II; TAV-8B *Harrier*
  1 sqn with F/A-18B/C/D *Hornet*
  1 sqn with F-35B *Lightning* II
  1 sqn with MV-22B *Osprey*
  1 hel sqn with AH-1W *Cobra*; AH-1Z *Viper*; HH-1N *Iroquois*; UH-1Y *Venom*
  1 hel sqn with CH-53E *Sea Stallion*

ATTACK HELICOPTER
  2 sqn with AH-1W *Cobra*; UH-1Y *Venom*
  5 sqn with AH-1Z *Viper*; UH-1Y *Venom*

TRANSPORT HELICOPTER
  8 sqn with CH-53E *Sea Stallion*
  1 (VIP) sqn with MV-22B *Osprey*; VH-3D *Sea King*; VH-60N *Presidential Hawk*

ISR UAV
  3 sqn with RQ-21A *Blackjack*

AIR DEFENCE
  2 bn with M1097 *Avenger*; FIM-92 *Stinger* (can provide additional heavy-calibre support weapons)

EQUIPMENT BY TYPE

AIRCRAFT 452 combat capable
  FGA 443: 61 F-35B *Lightning* II; 5 F-35C *Lightning* II; 45 F/A-18A++ *Hornet*; 7 F/A-18B *Hornet*; 107 F/A-18C *Hornet*; 92 F/A-18D *Hornet*; 110 AV-8B *Harrier* II; 16 TAV-8B *Harrier*
  EW 9 EA-6B *Prowler**
  TKR 45 KC-130J *Hercules*
  TPT 20: **Light** 17: 5 Beech A200/B200 *King Air* (UC-12F/M *Huron*); 5 Beech 350 *King Air* (C-12W *Huron*); 7 Cessna 560 *Citation Ultra/Encore* (UC-35C/D); **PAX** 3: 2 DC-9 *Skytrain* (C-9B *Nightingale*); 1 Gulfstream IV (C-20G)
  TRG 3 T-34C *Turbo Mentor*
TILTROTOR • **TPT** 306 MV-22B *Osprey*
HELICOPTERS
  ATK 177: 77 AH-1W *Cobra*; 100 AH-1Z *Viper*
  SAR 4 HH-1N *Iroquois*
  TPT 286: **Heavy** 139: 138 CH-53E *Sea Stallion*; 1 CH-53K *King Stallion*; **Medium** 19: 8 VH-60N *Presidential Hawk* (VIP tpt); 11 VH-3D *Sea King* (VIP tpt); **Light** 128 UH-1Y *Venom*

UNMANNED AERIAL VEHICLES
  ISR • **Light** 80 RQ-21A *Blackjack*

AIR DEFENCE
  SAM • **Point-defence** FIM-92 *Stinger*; M1097 *Avenger*

AIR-LAUNCHED MISSILES
  AAM • **IR** AIM-9M *Sidewinder*; **IIR** AIM-9X *Sidewinder* II; **SARH** AIM-7P *Sparrow*; **ARH** AIM-120C AMRAAM
  ASM AGM-65E/F IR *Maverick*; AGM-114 *Hellfire*; AGM-176 *Griffin*; APKWS
  AShM AGM-84D *Harpoon*
  ARM AGM-88 HARM
  LACM AGM-84E/H/K SLAM/SLAM-ER

BOMBS
  Laser-guided GBU-10/12/16 *Paveway* II
  INS/GPS guided GBU-31 JDAM; AGM-154A/C/C-1 JSOW

Reserve Organisations

Marine Corps Reserve 38,350

FORCES BY ROLE

MANOEUVRE
  Reconnaissance
  2 MEF recce coy
  Amphibious
  1 (4th) mne div (1 armd recce bn, 1 recce bn, 2 mne regt (3 mne bn), 1 amph aslt bn, 1 arty regt (2 arty bn, 1 MRL bn), 1 cbt engr bn, 1 int bn, 1 sigs bn)

COMBAT SERVICE SUPPORT
  1 log gp

Marine Corps Aviation Reserve 12,000 reservists

FORCES BY ROLE

FIGHTER
  1 sqn with F/A-18A++ *Hornet*

TANKER
  2 sqn with KC-130J/T *Hercules*

TRANSPORT
  2 sqn with MV-22B *Osprey*

TRAINING
  1 sqn with F-5F/N *Tiger* II

ATTACK HELICOPTER
  2 sqn with AH-1W *Cobra*; UH-1Y *Venom*

TRANSPORT HELICOPTER
  1 sqn with CH-53E *Sea Stallion*

ISR UAV
  1 sqn with RQ-21A *Blackjack*

EQUIPMENT BY TYPE

AIRCRAFT 23 combat capable
  FTR 12: 1 F-5F *Tiger* II; 11 F-5N *Tiger* II
  FGA 11 F/A-18A++ *Hornet*
  TKR 20: 7 KC-130J *Hercules*; 13 KC-130T *Hercules*
  TPT • **Light** 7: 2 Beech 350 *King Air* (UC-12W *Huron*); 5 Cessna 560 *Citation Ultra/Encore* (UC-35C/D)

TILTROTOR • TPT 12 MV-22B *Osprey*
HELICOPTERS
ATK 37 AH-1W *Cobra*
TPT 32: **Heavy** 6 CH-53E *Sea Stallion*; **Light** 26 UH-1Y *Venom*
UNMANNED AERIAL VEHICLES
ISR • **Light** 20 RQ-21A *Blackjack*

Marine Stand-by Reserve 700 reservists
Trained individuals available for mobilisation

US Coast Guard 42,100 (military); 8,500 (civilian)

9 districts (4 Pacific, 5 Atlantic)
EQUIPMENT BY TYPE
PATROL AND COASTAL COMBATANTS 160
PSOH 23: 1 *Alex Haley*; 13 *Famous*; 3 *Hamilton*; 6 *Legend*
PCO 42: 14 *Reliance* (with 1 hel landing platform); 28 *Sentinel* (Damen 4708)
PCC 22 *Island*
PBI 73 *Marine Protector*
LOGISTICS AND SUPPORT 78
ABU 52: 16 *Juniper*; 4 WLI; 14 *Keeper*; 18 WLR
AG 13: 1 *Cosmos*; 4 *Pamlico*; 8 *Anvil*
AGB 12: 9 *Bay*; 1 *Mackinaw*; 1 *Healy*; 1 *Polar* (1 *Polar* in reserve)
AXS 1 *Eagle*

US Coast Guard Aviation
EQUIPMENT BY TYPE
AIRCRAFT
SAR 20: 11 HC-130H *Hercules*; 9 HC-130J *Hercules*
TPT 34: **Medium** 14 C-27J *Spartan*; **Light** 18 CN235-200 (HC-144A – MP role); PAX 2 Gulfstream V (C-37A)
HELICOPTERS
SAR 146: 44 MH-60T *Jayhawk*; 102 AS366G1 (MH-65C/D) *Dauphin* II

US Air Force (USAF) 325,900

Almost the entire USAF (plus active force ANG and AFR) is divided into 10 Aerospace Expeditionary Forces (AEF), each on call for 120 days every 20 months. At least 2 of the 10 AEFs are on call at any one time, each with 10,000–15,000 personnel, 90 multi-role ftr and bbr ac, 31 intra-theatre refuelling aircraft and 13 aircraft for ISR and EW missions

Global Strike Command (GSC)
2 active air forces (8th & 20th); 8 wg
FORCES BY ROLE
SURFACE-TO-SURFACE MISSILE
9 ICBM sqn with LGM-30G *Minuteman* III
BOMBER
4 sqn with B-1B *Lancer*
2 sqn with B-2A *Spirit*
5 sqn (incl 1 trg) with B-52H *Stratofortress*
COMMAND & CONTROL
1 sqn with E-4B
TRANSPORT HELICOPTER
3 sqn with UH-1N *Iroquois*

Air Combat Command (ACC)
2 active air forces (9th & 12th); 12 wg. ACC numbered air forces provide the air component to CENTCOM, SOUTHCOM and NORTHCOM
FORCES BY ROLE
FIGHTER
3 sqn with F-22A *Raptor*
FIGHTER/GROUND ATTACK
4 sqn with F-15E *Strike Eagle*
4 sqn with F-16C/D *Fighting Falcon* (+6 sqn personnel only)
1 sqn with F-35A *Lightning* II
1 sqn with F-35A *Lightning* II (forming)
GROUND ATTACK
3 sqn with A-10C *Thunderbolt* II (+1 sqn personnel only)
ELECTRONIC WARFARE
1 sqn with EA-18G *Growler* (personnel only – USN aircraft)
2 sqn with EC-130H *Compass Call*
ISR
2 sqn with E-8C J-STARS (personnel only)
5 sqn with OC-135/RC-135/WC-135
2 sqn with U-2S
AIRBORNE EARLY WARNING & CONTROL
5 sqn with E-3B/C/G *Sentry*
COMBAT SEARCH & RESCUE
2 sqn with HC-130J *Combat King* II
2 sqn with HH-60G *Pave Hawk*
TRAINING
1 sqn with A-10C *Thunderbolt* II
1 sqn with E-3B/C *Sentry*
2 sqn with F-15E *Strike Eagle*
1 sqn with F-22A *Raptor*
1 sqn with RQ-4A *Global Hawk*; TU-2S
5 UAV sqn with MQ-9A *Reaper*
COMBAT/ISR UAV
7 sqn with MQ-9A *Reaper*
2 sqn with RQ-170 *Sentinel*
ISR UAV
2 sqn with EQ-4B/RQ-4B *Global Hawk*

Pacific Air Forces (PACAF)
Provides the air component of PACOM, and commands air units based in Alaska, Hawaii, Japan and South Korea. 3 active air forces (5th, 7th, & 11th); 8 wg
FORCES BY ROLE
FIGHTER
2 sqn with F-15C/D *Eagle*
2 sqn with F-22A *Raptor* (+1 sqn personnel only)
FIGHTER/GROUND ATTACK
5 sqn with F-16C/D *Fighting Falcon*
GROUND ATTACK
1 sqn with A-10C *Thunderbolt* II
AIRBORNE EARLY WARNING & CONTROL
2 sqn with E-3B/C *Sentry*
COMBAT SEARCH & RESCUE
1 sqn with HH-60G *Pave Hawk*
TANKER
1 sqn with KC-135R (+1 sqn personnel only)

TRANSPORT
1 sqn with B-737-200 (C-40B); Gulfstream V (C-37A)
2 sqn with C-17A *Globemaster*
1 sqn with C-130J-30 *Hercules*
1 sqn with Beech 1900C (C-12J); UH-1N *Huey*
TRAINING
1 (aggressor) sqn with F-16C/D *Fighting Falcon*

United States Air Forces Europe (USAFE)

Provides the air component to both EUCOM and AFRICOM. 1 active air force (3rd); 5 wg

FORCES BY ROLE
FIGHTER
1 sqn with F-15C/D *Eagle*
FIGHTER/GROUND ATTACK
2 sqn with F-15E *Strike Eagle*
3 sqn with F-16C/D *Fighting Falcon*
COMBAT SEARCH & RESCUE
1 sqn with HH-60G *Pave Hawk*
TANKER
1 sqn with KC-135R *Stratotanker*
TRANSPORT
1 sqn with C-130J-30 *Hercules*
2 sqn with Gulfstream V (C-37A); Learjet 35A (C-21A); B-737-700 (C-40B)

Air Mobility Command (AMC)

Provides strategic and tactical airlift, air-to-air refuelling and aeromedical evacuation. 1 active air force (18th); 12 wg and 1 gp

FORCES BY ROLE
TANKER
4 sqn with KC-10A *Extender*
9 sqn with KC-135R/T *Stratotanker* (+2 sqn with personnel only)
TRANSPORT
1 VIP sqn with B-737-200 (C-40B); B-757-200 (C-32A)
1 VIP sqn with Gulfstream V (C-37A)
1 VIP sqn with VC-25 *Air Force One*
2 sqn with C-5M *Super Galaxy*
8 sqn with C-17A *Globemaster* III (+1 sqn personnel only)
1 sqn with C-130H *Hercules* (+1 sqn personnel only)
5 sqn with C-130J-30 *Hercules* (+1 sqn personnel only)
1 sqn with Gulfstream V (C-37A)
2 sqn with Learjet 35A (C-21A)

Air Education and Training Command

1 active air force (2nd), 10 active air wg and 1 gp

FORCES BY ROLE
TRAINING
1 sqn with C-17A *Globemaster* III
1 sqn with C-130J-30 *Hercules*
4 sqn with F-16C/D *Fighting Falcon*
4 sqn with F-35A *Lightning* II
1 sqn with KC-46A *Pegasus* (forming)
1 sqn with KC-135R *Stratotanker*
5 (flying trg) sqn with T-1A *Jayhawk*
10 (flying trg) sqn with T-6A *Texan* II
10 (flying trg) sqn with T-38C *Talon*
1 UAV sqn with MQ-9A *Reaper*

EQUIPMENT BY TYPE
SURFACE-TO-SURFACE MISSILE LAUNCHERS
ICBM • **Nuclear** 400 LGM-30G *Minuteman* III (1 Mk12A or Mk21 re-entry veh per missile)
AIRCRAFT 1,466 combat capable
BBR 139: 61 B-1B *Lancer*; 20 B-2A *Spirit*; 58 B-52H *Stratofortress* (46 nuclear capable)
FTR 264: 95 F-15C *Eagle*; 10 F-15D *Eagle*; 159 F-22A *Raptor*
FGA 922: 211 F-15E *Strike Eagle*; 443 F-16C *Fighting Falcon*; 114 F-16D *Fighting Falcon*; 154 F-35A *Lightning* II
ATK 141 A-10C *Thunderbolt* II
EW 14 EC-130H *Compass Call*
ISR 41: 2 E-9A; 4 E-11A; 2 OC-135B *Open Skies*; 27 U-2S; 4 TU-2S; 2 WC-135 *Constant Phoenix*
ELINT 22: 8 RC-135V *Rivet Joint*; 9 RC-135W *Rivet Joint*; 3 RC-135S *Cobra Ball*; 2 RC-135U *Combat Sent*
AEW&C 31: 11 E-3B *Sentry*; 3 E-3C *Sentry*; 17 E-3G *Sentry*
C2 4 E-4B
TKR 156: 126 KC-135R *Stratotanker*; 30 KC-135T *Stratotanker*
TKR/TPT 59 KC-10A *Extender*
CSAR 15 HC-130J *Combat King* II
TPT 331: **Heavy** 182: 36 C-5M *Super Galaxy*; 146 C-17A *Globemaster* III; **Medium** 104 C-130J/J-30 *Hercules*; **Light** 23: 4 Beech 1900C (C-12J); 19 Learjet 35A (C-21A); **PAX** 22: 4 B-737-700 (C-40B); 4 B-757-200 (C-32A); 12 Gulfstream V (C-37A); 2 VC-25A *Air Force One*
TRG 1,127: 178 T-1A *Jayhawk*; 444 T-6A *Texan* II; 505 T-38A/C *Talon*
HELICOPTERS
CSAR 74 HH-60G *Pave Hawk*
TPT • **Light** 62 UH-1N *Huey*
UNMANNED AERIAL VEHICLES 244
CISR • **Heavy** 200 MQ-9A *Reaper*
ISR • **Heavy** 44: 3 EQ-4B; 31 RQ-4B *Global Hawk*; ε10 RQ-170 *Sentinel*
AIR DEFENCE • **SAM** • **Point-defence** FIM-92 *Stinger*
AIR-LAUNCHED MISSILES
AAM • **IR** AIM-9 *Sidewinder*; **IIR** AIM-9X *Sidewinder* II; **SARH** AIM-7M *Sparrow*; **ARH** AIM-120C/D AMRAAM
ASM AGM-65D/G *Maverick*; AGM-130A; AGM-176 *Griffin*; APKWS
ALCM • **Nuclear** AGM-86B (ALCM); **Conventional** AGM-86C (CALCM); AGM-86D (penetrator); AGM-158 JASSM; AGM-158B JASSM-ER
ARM AGM-88A/B HARM
EW MALD/MALD-J
BOMBS
Laser-guided GBU 10/12/16 *Paveway* II, GBU-24 *Paveway* III; GBU-28
INS/GPS guided GBU 31/32/38 JDAM; GBU-54 Laser JDAM; GBU-15 (with BLU-109 penetrating warhead or Mk84); GBU-39B Small Diameter Bomb (250lb); GBU-43B MOAB; GBU-57A/B MOP; Enhanced *Paveway* III

Reserve Organisations

Air National Guard 107,450 reservists
FORCES BY ROLE
BOMBER
1 sqn with B-2A *Spirit* (personnel only)

FIGHTER
  5 sqn with F-15C/D *Eagle*
  1 sqn with F-22A *Raptor* (+1 sqn personnel only)
FIGHTER/GROUND ATTACK
  11 sqn with F-16C/D *Fighting Falcon*
GROUND ATTACK
  4 sqn with A-10C *Thunderbolt* II
ISR
  1 sqn with E-8C J-STARS
COMBAT SEARCH & RESCUE
  1 sqn with HC-130P/N *Combat King*
  1 sqn with HC-130J *Combat King* II (forming)
  1 sqn with MC-130P *Combat Shadow*
  3 sqn with HH-60G *Pave Hawk*
TANKER
  17 sqn with KC-135R *Stratotanker* (+1 sqn personnel only)
  3 sqn with KC-135T *Stratotanker*
TRANSPORT
  1 sqn with B-737-700 (C-40C)
  6 sqn with C-17A *Globemaster* (+2 sqn personnel only)
  12 sqn with C-130H *Hercules*
  1 sqn with C-130H/LC-130H *Hercules*
  2 sqn with C-130J-30 *Hercules*
  1 sqn with WC-130H *Hercules*
TRAINING
  1 sqn with C-130H *Hercules*
  1 sqn with F-15C/D *Eagle*
  4 sqn with F-16C/D *Fighting Falcon*
  1 sqn with MQ-9A *Reaper*
COMBAT/ISR UAV
  11 sqn with MQ-9A *Reaper*
EQUIPMENT BY TYPE
AIRCRAFT 579 combat capable
  FTR 157: 127 F-15C *Eagle*; 10 F-15D *Eagle*; 20 F-22A *Raptor*
  FGA 336: 291 F-16C *Fighting Falcon*; 45 F-16D *Fighting Falcon*
  ATK 86 A-10C *Thunderbolt* II
  ISR 16 E-8C J-STARS
  ELINT 11 RC-26B *Metroliner*
  CSAR 10: 2 HC-130N *Combat King*; 3 HC-130P *Combat King*; 5 HC-130J *Combat King* II
  TKR 172: 148 KC-135R *Stratotanker*; 24 KC-135T *Stratotanker*
  TPT 218: **Heavy** 50 C-17A *Globemaster* III; **Medium** 165: 123 C-130H *Hercules*; 20 C-130J/J-30 *Hercules*; 10 LC-130H *Hercules*; 4 MC-130P *Combat Shadow*; 8 WC-130H *Hercules*; **PAX** 3 B-737-700 (C-40C)
  HELICOPTERS • **CSAR** 18 HH-60G *Pave Hawk*
  UNMANNED AERIAL VEHICLES • **CISR** • **Heavy** 35 MQ-9A *Reaper*

Air Force Reserve Command 68,700 reservists
FORCES BY ROLE
BOMBER
  1 sqn with B-52H *Stratofortress* (personnel only)
FIGHTER
  2 sqn with F-22A *Raptor* (personnel only)
FIGHTER/GROUND ATTACK
  2 sqn with F-16C/D *Fighting Falcon* (+1 sqn personnel only)
  1 sqn with F-35A *Lightning* II (personnel only)
GROUND ATTACK
  1 sqn with A-10C *Thunderbolt* II (+2 sqn personnel only)
ISR
  1 (Weather Recce) sqn with WC-130J *Hercules*
AIRBORNE EARLY WARNING & CONTROL
  1 sqn with E-3B/C *Sentry* (personnel only)
COMBAT SEARCH & RESCUE
  1 sqn with HC-130N *Combat King*
  2 sqn with HH-60G *Pave Hawk*
TANKER
  4 sqn with KC-10A *Extender* (personnel only)
  7 sqn with KC-135R *Stratotanker* (+2 sqn personnel only)
TRANSPORT
  1 (VIP) sqn with B-737-700 (C-40C)
  2 sqn with C-5M *Super Galaxy* (+1 sqn personnel only)
  3 sqn with C-17A *Globemaster* (+9 sqn personnel only)
  6 sqn with C-130H *Hercules*
  1 sqn with C-130J-30 *Hercules*
  1 (Aerial Spray) sqn with C-130H *Hercules*
TRAINING
  1 (aggressor) sqn with A-10C *Thunderbolt* II; F-15C/E *Eagle*; F-16 *Fighting Falcon*; F-22A *Raptor* (personnel only)
  1 sqn with A-10C *Thunderbolt* II
  1 sqn with B-52H *Stratofortress*
  1 sqn with C-5M *Super Galaxy*
  1 sqn with F-16C/D *Fighting Falcon*
  5 (flying training) sqn with T-1A *Jayhawk*; T-6A *Texan* II; T-38C *Talon* (personnel only)
COMBAT/ISR UAV
  2 sqn with MQ-9A *Reaper* (personnel only)
ISR UAV
  1 sqn with RQ-4B *Global Hawk* (personnel only)
EQUIPMENT BY TYPE
AIRCRAFT 126 combat capable
  BBR 18 B-52H *Stratofortress*
  FGA 53: 49 F-16C *Fighting Falcon*; 4 F-16D *Fighting Falcon*
  ATK 55 A-10C *Thunderbolt* II
  ISR 10 WC-130J *Hercules* (Weather Recce)
  CSAR 6 HC-130N *Combat King*
  TKR 70 KC-135R *Stratotanker*
  TPT 104: **Heavy** 42: 16 C-5M *Super Galaxy*; 26 C-17A *Globemaster* III; **Medium** 58: 48 C-130H *Hercules*; 10 C-130J-30 *Hercules*; **PAX** 4 B-737-700 (C-40C)
  HELICOPTERS • **CSAR** 16 HH-60G *Pave Hawk*

Civil Reserve Air Fleet
Commercial ac numbers fluctuate
AIRCRAFT • **TPT** 517 international (391 long-range and 126 short-range); 36 national

Air Force Stand-by Reserve 16,858 reservists
Trained individuals for mobilisation

US Special Operations Command
(USSOCOM) 63,150; 6,550 (civilian)

Commands all active, reserve and National Guard Special Operations Forces (SOF) of all services based in CONUS

Joint Special Operations Command
Reported to comprise elite US SOF, including Special Forces Operations Detachment Delta ('Delta Force'), SEAL Team 6 and integral USAF support

US Army Special Operations Command
34,100

FORCES BY ROLE
SPECIAL FORCES
  5 SF gp (4 SF bn, 1 spt bn)
  1 ranger regt (3 ranger bn; 1 cbt spt bn)
COMBAT SUPPORT
  1 civil affairs bde (5 civil affairs bn)
  1 psyops gp (3 psyops bn)
  1 psyops gp (4 psyops bn)
COMBAT SERVICE SUPPORT
  1 (sustainment) log bde (1 sigs bn)
HELICOPTER
  1 (160th SOAR) hel regt (4 hel bn)
EQUIPMENT BY TYPE
ARMOURED FIGHTING VEHICLES
  APC • **APC (W)** 28: 16 M1126 *Stryker* ICV; 12 *Pandur*
  AUV 640 M-ATV
ARTILLERY 20
  MOR • **120mm** 20 XM905 EMTAS
HELICOPTERS
  MRH 51 AH-6M/MH-6M *Little Bird*
  TPT 141: **Heavy** 69 MH-47G *Chinook*; **Medium** 72 MH-60M *Black Hawk*
UAV
  CISR • **Heavy** 12 MQ-1C *Gray Eagle*
  ISR • **Light** 29: 15 XPV-1 *Tern*; 14 XPV-2 *Mako*
  TPT • **Heavy** 28 CQ-10 *Snowgoose*

Reserve Organisations

Army National Guard
FORCES BY ROLE
SPECIAL FORCES
  2 SF gp (3 SF bn)

Army Reserve
FORCES BY ROLE
COMBAT SUPPORT
  2 psyops gp
  4 civil affairs comd HQ
  8 civil affairs bde HQ
  32 civil affairs bn (coy)

US Navy Special Warfare Command 9,850
FORCES BY ROLE
SPECIAL FORCES
  8 SEAL team (total: 48 SF pl)
  2 SEAL Delivery Vehicle team

Reserve Organisations

Naval Reserve Force
FORCES BY ROLE
SPECIAL FORCES
  8 SEAL det
  10 Naval Special Warfare det
  2 Special Boat sqn
  2 Special Boat unit
  1 SEAL Delivery Vehicle det

US Marine Special Operations Command
(MARSOC) 3,000

FORCES BY ROLE
SPECIAL FORCES
  1 SF regt (3 SF bn)
COMBAT SUPPORT
  1 int bn
COMBAT SERVICE SUPPORT
  1 spt gp

Air Force Special Operations Command
(AFSOC) 16,200

FORCES BY ROLE
GROUND ATTACK
  1 sqn with AC-130J *Ghostrider*
  1 sqn with AC-130U *Spectre*
  1 sqn with AC-130W *Stinger* II
TRANSPORT
  3 sqn with CV-22B *Osprey*
  1 sqn with DHC-8; Do-328 (C-146A)
  2 sqn with MC-130H *Combat Talon*
  3 sqn with MC-130J *Commando* II
  3 sqn with PC-12 (U-28A)
TRAINING
  1 sqn with M-28 *Skytruck* (C-145A)
  1 sqn with CV-22A/B *Osprey*
  1 sqn with HC-130J *Combat King* II; MC-130J *Commando* II
  1 sqn with Bell 205 (TH-1H *Iroquois*)
  1 sqn with HH-60G *Pave Hawk*; UH-1N *Huey*
COMBAT/ISR UAV
  2 sqn with MQ-9 *Reaper*
EQUIPMENT BY TYPE
AIRCRAFT 37 combat capable
  ATK 37: 12 AC-130J *Ghostrider*; 13 AC-130U *Spectre*; 12 AC-130W *Stinger* II
  CSAR 3 HC-130J *Combat King* II
  TPT 97: **Medium** 49: 14 MC-130H *Combat Talon* II; 35 MC-130J *Commando* II; **Light** 48: 9 Do-328 (C-146A); 4 M-28 *Skytruck* (C-145A); 35 PC-12 (U-28A)
TILT-ROTOR 49 CV-22A/B *Osprey*
HELICOPTERS
  CSAR 3 HH-60G *Pave Hawk*
  TPT • **Light** 34: 28 Bell 205 (TH-1H *Iroquois*); 6 UH-1N *Huey*
UNMANNED AERIAL VEHICLES • **CISR** • **Heavy** 30 MQ-9 *Reaper*

Reserve Organisations

Air National Guard
FORCES BY ROLE
ELECTRONIC WARFARE
   1 sqn with C-130J *Hercules*/EC-130J *Commando Solo*
ISR
   1 sqn with Beech 350ER *King Air* (MC-12W *Liberty*)
TRANSPORT
   1 flt with B-737-200 (C-32B)
EQUIPMENT BY TYPE
AIRCRAFT
   EW 3 EC-130J *Commando Solo*
   ISR 13 Beech 350ER *King Air* (MC-12W *Liberty*)
   TPT 5: **Medium** 3 C-130J *Hercules*; **PAX** 2 B-757-200 (C-32B)

Air Force Reserve
FORCES BY ROLE
TRAINING
   1 sqn with AC-130U *Spectre* (personnel only)
   1 sqn with M-28 *Skytruck* (C-145A) (personnel only)
COMBAT/ISR UAV
   1 sqn with MQ-9 *Reaper* (personnel only)

Cyber

The Department of Defense (DoD) released a new Cyber Strategy in September 2018. It said that China and Russia were conducting persistent campaigns in and through cyberspace that posed a long-term strategic risk to the US and its allies. The US, the document continued, 'will defend forward to disrupt or halt malicious cyber activity at its source, including activity that falls below the level of armed conflict'. The same month, the US released a National Cyber Strategy that said as well as US vulnerability to peacetime cyber attacks, the 'risk is growing' that adversaries 'will conduct cyber attacks against the United States during a crisis short of war'.

Cyber Command was elevated to the level of a unified combatant command in May 2018 (it was previously a sub-unified command under US Strategic Command), and the DoD is continuing to examine the possibility of separating Cyber Command from the National Security Agency.

Cyber Command requested a budget of US$647m for FY2018, representing a 16% increase on the previous year. Its Cyber Mission Force (CMF) of 133 teams reached IOC in October 2016 and the DoD said in May 2018 that it had reached FOC in May 2018. The air force plans to merge offensive and defensive cyber operations into a full-spectrum cyber capability called the Cyber Operations Squadron by 2026. In June, the DoD published a new edition of the joint doctrinal paper that defines the roles and responsibilities for cyberspace operations conducted by the US armed forces. A month later, the air force formally initiated the request-for-proposal process to develop a cyber-weapons system for US Cyber Command, known as the 'Unified Platform'. High-level DoD cyber exercises include the defence-focused Cyber Flag and Cyber Guard series, which involve broader actors from across government and includes critical-national-infrastructure scenarios.

DARPA's Plan X programme has been funding research on cyber warfare since 2013. According to the army, this 'gives commanders a way to see and respond to key cyber terrain in the same way they react to actions on the physical battlefield, and enables synchronizing cyber effects with key related war-fighting functions such as intelligence, signal, information operations and electronic warfare'.

In October 2012, then-president Barack Obama signed Presidential Policy Directive 20 (PPD-20), the purpose of which was to establish clear standards for US federal agencies in confronting threats in cyberspace. Among other provisions, PPD-20 stated that presidential approval is required for any cyber operations with 'significant consequences', although it was reported in August 2018 that President Trump had rescinded the directive.

DEPLOYMENT

AFGHANISTAN: NATO • *Operations Resolute Support* 8,475; 1 div HQ; 1 ARNG div HQ (fwd); 1 spec ops bn; 3 inf bde(-); 1 inf bn; 1 ARNG inf bn; 1 mne regt(-); 1 arty bty with M777A2; 1 ARNG MRL bty with M142 HIMARS; 1 EOD bn; 1 (cbt avn) hel bde with AH-64E *Apache*; CH-47F *Chinook*; UH-60 *Black Hawk*; 1 FGA sqn with F-16C *Fighting Falcon*; 1 atk sqn with A-10C *Thunderbolt* II; 1 EW sqn with EC-130H *Compass Call*; 1 ISR gp with MC-12W *Liberty*; 1 ISR unit with RC-12X *Guardrail*; 1 tpt sqn with C-130J-30 *Hercules*; 1 CSAR sqn with HH-60G *Pave Hawk*; 1 CISR UAV sqn with MQ-9A *Reaper*; 1 ISR UAV unit with RQ-21A *Blackjack*
US Central Command • *Operation Freedom's Sentinel* 8,000

ARABIAN SEA: US Central Command • US Navy • 5th Fleet: 1 SSGN; 1 DDGHM; 1 LSD; **Combined Maritime Forces** • TF 53: 1 AE; 2 AKE; 1 AOH; 3 AO

ARUBA: US Southern Command • 1 Forward Operating Location

ASCENSION ISLAND: US Strategic Command • 1 detection and tracking radar at Ascension Auxiliary Air Field

ATLANTIC OCEAN: US Northern Command • US Navy • 2nd Fleet: 6 SSBN; 20 SSGN; 4 CVN; 10 CGHM; 11 DDGHM; 7 DDGM; 3 FFHM; 3 PCF; 2 LHD; 3 LPD; 5 LSD

AUSTRALIA: US Pacific Command • 1,500; 1 SEWS at Pine Gap; 1 comms facility at Pine Gap; 1 SIGINT stn at Pine Gap; **US Strategic Command** • 1 detection and tracking radar at Naval Communication Station Harold E Holt

BAHRAIN: US Central Command • 5,000; 1 HQ (5th Fleet); 2 AD bty with MIM-104E/F *Patriot* PAC-2/3

BELGIUM: US European Command • 900

BOSNIA-HERZEGOVINA: OSCE • Bosnia and Herzegovina 6

BRITISH INDIAN OCEAN TERRITORY: US Strategic Command • 300; 1 Spacetrack Optical Tracker at Diego Garcia; 1 ground-based electro-optical deep space surveillance system (*GEODSS*) at Diego Garcia

US Pacific Command • 1 MPS sqn (MPS-2 with equipment for one MEB) at Diego Garcia with 2 AKRH; 3 AKR; 1 AKEH; 1 ESD; 1 naval air base at Diego Garcia, 1 support facility at Diego Garcia

BULGARIA: US European Command • 150; 1 armd inf coy with M1A2 SEPv2 *Abrams*; M2A3 *Bradley*

CAMEROON: US Africa Command • 300; MQ-1C *Gray Eagle*

CANADA: US Northern Command • 150

CENTRAL AFRICAN REPUBLIC: UN • MINUSCA 8

COLOMBIA: US Southern Command • 50

CUBA: US Southern Command • 1,000 (JTF-GTMO) at Guantánamo Bay

CURACAO: US Southern Command • 1 Forward Operating Location

DEMOCRATIC REPUBLIC OF THE CONGO: UN • MONUSCO 3

DJIBOUTI: US Africa Command • 4,700; 1 tpt sqn with C-130H/J-30 *Hercules*; 1 spec ops sqn with MC-130H/J; PC-12 (U-28A); 1 CSAR sqn with HH-60G *Pave Hawk*; 1 CISR UAV sqn with MQ-9A *Reaper*; 1 naval air base

EGYPT: MFO 454; elm 1 ARNG recce bn; 1 ARNG spt bn

EL SALVADOR: US Southern Command • 1 Forward Operating Location (Military, DEA, USCG and Customs personnel)

GERMANY: US Africa Command • 1 HQ at Stuttgart
US European Command • 37,950; 1 Combined Service HQ (EUCOM) at Stuttgart–Vaihingen
  US Army 23,000
  FORCES BY ROLE
  1 HQ (US Army Europe (USAREUR)) at Heidelberg; 1 div HQ (fwd); 1 SF gp; 1 recce bn; 2 armd bn; 1 mech bde(-); 1 fd arty bn; 1 (cbt avn) hel bde(-); 1 (cbt avn) hel bde HQ; 1 int bde; 1 MP bde; 1 sigs bde; 1 spt bde; 1 (APS) armd bde eqpt set
  EQUIPMENT BY TYPE
  M1A2 SEPv2 *Abrams*; M2A3/M3A3 *Bradley*; M1296 *Stryker Dragoon*, M109A6; M777A2; AH-64D *Apache*; CH-47F *Chinook*; UH-60M *Black Hawk*; HH-60M *Black Hawk*
  US Navy 500
  USAF 13,100
  FORCES BY ROLE
  1 HQ (US Air Force Europe (USAFE)) at Ramstein AB; 1 HQ (3rd Air Force) at Ramstein AB; 1 ftr wg at Spangdahlem AB with 1 ftr sqn with 24 F-16C/D *Fighting Falcon*; 1 tpt wg at Ramstein AB with 14 C-130J-30 *Hercules*; 2 Gulfstream V (C-37A); 5 Learjet 35A (C-21A); 1 B-737-700 (C-40B)
  USMC 1,350

GREECE: US European Command • 400; 1 naval base at Makri; 1 naval base at Souda Bay; 1 air base at Iraklion

GREENLAND (DNK): US Strategic Command • 160; 1 AN/FPS-132 Upgraded Early Warning Radar and 1 Spacetrack Radar at Thule

GUAM: US Pacific Command • 6,000; 4 SSGN; 1 MPS sqn (MPS-3 with equipment for one MEB) with 2 AKRH; 4 AKR; 1 ESD; 1 AKEH; 1 bbr sqn with 6 B-52H *Stratofortress*; 1 tkr sqn with 12 KC-135R *Stratotanker*; 1 tpt hel sqn with MH-60S; 1 SAM bty with THAAD; 1 air base; 1 naval base

HONDURAS: US Southern Command • 380; 1 avn bn with CH-47F *Chinook*; UH-60 *Black Hawk*

HUNGARY: US European Command • 100; 1 armd recce tp; M3 *Bradley*

IRAQ: US Central Command • *Operation Inherent Resolve* 5,000; 1 div HQ; 1 cav bde(-); 1 EOD pl; 1 atk hel sqn with AH-64D *Apache*

ISRAEL: US Strategic Command • 1 AN/TPY-2 X-band radar at Mount Keren

ITALY: US European Command • 12,750
  US Army 4,200; 1 AB bde(-)
  US Navy 4,000; 1 HQ (US Navy Europe (USNAVEUR)) at Naples; 1 HQ (6th Fleet) at Gaeta; 1 MP sqn with 4 P-8A *Poseidon* at Sigonella
  USAF 4,350; 1 ftr wg with 2 ftr sqn with 21 F-16C/D *Fighting Falcon* at Aviano; 1 CSAR sqn with 8 HH-60G *Pave Hawk* at Aviano
  USMC 200

JAPAN: US Pacific Command • 53,900
  US Army 2,700; 1 corps HQ (fwd); 1 SF gp; 1 avn bn; 1 SAM bn
  US Navy 20,250; 1 HQ (7th Fleet) at Yokosuka; 1 base at Sasebo; 1 base at Yokosuka
  FORCES BY ROLE
  3 FGA sqn at Iwakuni with 10 F/A-18E *Super Hornet*; 1 FGA sqn at Iwakuni with 10 F/A-18F *Super Hornet*; 2 EW sqn at Iwakuni/Misawa with 5 EA-18G *Growler*; 1 AEW&C sqn at Iwakuni with 5 E-2D *Hawkeye*; 2 ASW hel sqn at Atsugi with 12 MH-60R; 1 tpt hel sqn at Atsugi with 12 MH-60S
  EQUIPMENT BY TYPE
  1 CVN; 3 CGHM; 2 DDGHM; 8 DDGM (2 non-op); 1 LCC; 4 MCO; 1 LHD; 1 LPD; 2 LSD
  USAF 12,150
  FORCES BY ROLE
  1 HQ (5th Air Force) at Okinawa – Kadena AB; 1 ftr wg at Misawa AB with (2 ftr sqn with 22 F-16C/D *Fighting Falcon*); 1 wg at Okinawa – Kadena AB with (2 ftr sqn with 27 F-15C/D *Eagle*; 1 ftr sqn with 14 F-22A *Raptor*; 1 tkr sqn with 15 KC-135R *Stratotanker*; 1 AEW&C sqn with 2 E-3B/C *Sentry*; 1 CSAR sqn with 10 HH-60G *Pave Hawk*); 1 tpt wg at Yokota AB with 10 C-130J-30 *Hercules*; 3 Beech 1900C (C-12J); 1 Spec Ops gp at Okinawa – Kadena AB with (1 sqn with 5 MC-130H *Combat Talon*; 1 sqn with 5 MC-130J *Commando II*; 1 unit with 5 CV-22 *Osprey*); 1 ISR sqn with RC-135 *Rivet Joint*; 1 ISR UAV flt with 5 RQ-4A *Global Hawk*
  USMC 18,800
  FORCES BY ROLE
  1 mne div; 1 mne regt HQ; 1 arty regt HQ; 1 recce bn; 1 mne bn; 1 amph aslt bn; 1 arty bn; 1 FGA sqn

with 12 F/A-18C *Hornet*; 1 FGA sqn with 12 F/A-18D *Hornet*; 1 FGA sqn with 12 F-35B *Lightning* II; 1 tkr sqn with 15 KC-130J *Hercules*; 2 tpt sqn with 12 MV-22B *Osprey*

US Strategic Command • 1 AN/TPY-2 X-band radar at Shariki; 1 AN/TPY-2 X-Band radar at Kyogamisaki

JORDAN: US Central Command • *Operation Inherent Resolve* 2,300: 1 FGA sqn with 12 F-15E *Strike Eagle*; 1 CISR UAV sqn with 12 MQ-9A *Reaper*

KOREA, REPUBLIC OF: US Pacific Command • 28,500
US Army 19,200

FORCES BY ROLE

1 HQ (8th Army) at Seoul; 1 div HQ (2nd Inf) located at Tongduchon; 1 armd bde; 1 (cbt avn) hel bde; 1 MRL bde; 1 AD bde; 1 SAM bty with THAAD

EQUIPMENT BY TYPE

M1A2 SEPv2 *Abrams*; M2A2/M3A3 *Bradley*; M109A6; M270A1 MLRS; AH-64D *Apache*; CH-47F *Chinook*; UH-60L/M *Black Hawk*; MIM-104 *Patriot*; FIM-92A *Avenger*; 1 (APS) armd bde eqpt set
US Navy 250
USAF 8,800

FORCES BY ROLE

1 (AF) HQ (7th Air Force) at Osan AB; 1 ftr wg at Osan AB with (1 ftr sqn with 20 F-16C/D *Fighting Falcon*; 1 atk sqn with 24 A-10C *Thunderbolt* II); 1 ftr wg at Kunsan AB with (2 ftr sqn with 20 F-16C/D *Fighting Falcon*); 1 ISR sqn at Osan AB with U-2S
USMC 250

KUWAIT: US Central Command • 14,000; 1 ARNG armd bde; 1 ARNG (cbt avn) hel bde; 1 spt bde; 1 FGA sqn with 12 F-16C *Fighting Falcon*; 1 tpt sqn with 12 MV-22B *Osprey*; 1 CISR UAV sqn with MQ-9A *Reaper*; 2 AD bty with MIM-104E/F *Patriot* PAC-2/3; 1 (APS) armd bde set; 1 (APS) inf bde set

LATVIA: US European Command • 60; 1 tpt hel flt; 5 UH-60M *Black Hawk*

LIBYA: UN • UNSMIL 1 obs

MALI: UN • MINUSMA 24

MARSHALL ISLANDS: US Strategic Command • 1 detection and tracking radar at Kwajalein Atoll

MEDITERRANEAN SEA: US European Command • US Navy • 6th Fleet: 2 DDGHM; 6 DDGM; 1 LPD; 1 LCC

MIDDLE EAST: UN • UNTSO 2 obs

MOLDOVA: OSCE • Moldova 1

NETHERLANDS: US European Command • 400

NIGER: US Africa Command • 800

NORWAY: US European Command • 1,000; 1 mne bn; 1 (USMC) MEU eqpt set; 1 (APS) SP 155mm arty bn set

PACIFIC OCEAN: US Pacific Command • US Navy • 3rd Fleet: 8 SSBN; 21 SSGN; 4 SSN; 4 CVN; 10 CGHM; 21 DDGHM; 6 DDGM; 9 FFHM; 3 MCO; 1 LHA; 3 LHD; 5 LPD; 3 LSD

PERSIAN GULF: US Central Command • US Navy • 5th Fleet: 1 CGHM; 1 LHA; 1 LPD; 1 LSD; 10 PCFG; 6 (Coast Guard) PCC
Combined Maritime Forces • CTF-152: 4 MCO; 1 ESB

PHILIPPINES: US Pacific Command • *Operation Pacific Eagle - Philippines* 250

POLAND: NATO • Enhanced Forward Presence 774; 1 ARNG armd bn with M1A1 AIM *Abrams*; M2A2 ODS *Bradley*; M109A6
US European Command • 2,100; 1 armd bde HQ; 1 armd cav sqn(-) with M1A2 SEPv2 *Abrams*; M3A3 *Bradley*; 1 SP arty bn with M109A6; 1 atk hel flt with 4 AH-64D *Apache*; 1 tpt hel flt with 8 UH-60 *Black Hawk*

PORTUGAL: US European Command • 250; 1 spt facility at Lajes

QATAR: US Central Command • 10,000: 1 bbr sqn with 6 B-1B *Lancer*; 1 ISR sqn with 4 RC-135 *Rivet Joint*; 1 ISR sqn with 4 E-8C JSTARS; 1 tkr sqn with 24 KC-135R/T *Straotanker*; 1 tpt sqn with 4 C-17A *Globemaster*; 4 C-130H/J-30 *Hercules*; 2 AD bty with MIM-104E/F *Patriot* PAC-2/3
US Strategic Command • 1 AN/TPY-2 X-band radar

ROMANIA: US European Command • 1,150; 1 armd inf bn HQ; 2 armd/armd inf coy with M1A2 SEPv2 *Abrams*; M2A3 *Bradley*; 1 tpt hel flt with UH-60L *Black Hawk*

SAUDI ARABIA: US Central Command • 500

SERBIA : NATO • KFOR • *Joint Enterprise* 685; elm 1 ARNG inf bde HQ; 1 recce bn; 1 hel flt with UH-60; **OSCE** • Kosovo 5

SINGAPORE: US Pacific Command • 200; 1 log spt sqn; 1 spt facility

SOMALIA: US Africa Command • 500

SOUTH SUDAN: UN • UNMISS 7

SPAIN: US European Command • 3,200; 1 air base at Morón; 1 naval base at Rota

SYRIA: US Central Command • *Operation Inherent Resolve* 2,000+; 1 ranger unit; 1 mne bn; 1 arty bty with M777A2; 1 MRL bty with M142 HIMARS

THAILAND: US Pacific Command • 300

TURKEY: US European Command • 1,700; 1 tkr sqn with 14 KC-135; 1 ELINT flt with EP-3E *Aries* II; 1 air base at Incirlik; 1 support facility at Ankara; 1 support facility at Izmir
US Strategic Command • 1 AN/TPY-2 X-band radar at Kürecik

UKRAINE: JMTG-U 220 (trg mission); **OSCE** • Ukraine 70

UNITED ARAB EMIRATES: US Central Command • 5,000: 1 ftr sqn with 6 F-22A *Raptor*; 1 ISR sqn with 4 U-2; 1 AEW&C sqn with 4 E-3 *Sentry*; 1 tkr sqn with 12 KC-10A; 1 ISR UAV sqn with RQ-4 *Global Hawk*; 2 AD bty with MIM-104E/F *Patriot* PAC-2/3

UNITED KINGDOM: US European Command • 9,250

FORCES BY ROLE

1 ftr wg at RAF Lakenheath with 1 ftr sqn with 24 F-15C/D *Eagle*, 2 ftr sqn with 23 F-15E *Strike Eagle*; 1 ISR

sqn at RAF Mildenhall with OC-135/RC-135; 1 tkr wg at RAF Mildenhall with 15 KC-135R/T *Stratotanker*; 1 spec ops gp at RAF Mildenhall with (1 sqn with 8 CV-22B *Osprey*; 1 sqn with 8 MC-130J *Commando* II)

US Strategic Command • 1 AN/FPS-132 Upgraded Early Warning Radar and 1 Spacetrack Radar at Fylingdales Moor

FOREIGN FORCES

Germany Air Force: trg units with 40 T-38 *Talon*; 69 T-6A *Texan* II; 24 *Tornado* IDS; • Missile trg at Fort Bliss (TX)

Netherlands 1 hel trg sqn with AH-64D *Apache*; CH-47D *Chinook*

Singapore Air Force: trg units with F-16C/D; 12 F-15SG; AH-64D *Apache*; 6+ CH-47D *Chinook* hel

Arms procurements and deliveries – North America

Selected events in 2018

- In June, Northrop Grumman acquired Orbital ATK for US$7.8bn and assumed US$1.4bn of debt. Orbital ATK is the main supplier of solid rocket motors for US military missile systems and Northrop Grumman is one of four US companies capable of supplying missile systems. The US Federal Trade Commission approved the acquisition, provided that Northrop Grumman sell solid rocket motors to other missile manufacturers on a non-discriminatory basis. Orbital will become a division of Northrop Grumman and be renamed Northrop Grumman Innovation Systems.

- In September, the US Air Force selected the MH-139 helicopter offered by Boeing and Leonardo to replace its fleet of UH-1N *Hueys* used by forces guarding intercontinental-ballistic-missile sites and performing VIP and search-and-rescue duties. The other two contenders were based on the omnipresent UH-60 *Black Hawk*. Boeing was awarded a US$2.4bn contract in September to supply up to 84 MH-139s.

- The Department of Defense published a report in September on the US defence-industrial base, concluding that it faced significant challenges, including uncertain US government spending, a decline in domestic manufacturing capability and capacity, and a less skilled workforce. The health of the country's 'lower tier' manufacturers and the United States' dependence on foreign sole-source suppliers of key materials, such as rare earth elements, were highlighted as risks for the future. The report made a number of recommendations, including strengthening oversight of foreign investments, expanding direct investment in lower-tier manufacturing, diversifying sources of supply and efforts to promote STEM.

- In October, Canada selected the vessel for its Canadian Surface Combatant programme. The Lockheed Martin Canada and BAE Systems Global Combat Ship design is based on the United Kingdom's Type-26 frigate. Canada plans to build 15 vessels at an estimated cost of C$56–60bn (US$43.4–46.5bn). Halifax-based Irving Shipbuilding is the prime contractor, and deliveries are expected to begin in the mid-2020s.

- L-3 Technologies and Harris Corporation announced in October that they were to merge and form L-3 Harris Technologies. The companies state that this will create the sixth-largest defence company in the US. The merger has to be approved by various government offices but could be completed by mid-2019.

Table 4 **US FY2018 defence-budget request: top 15 equipment programmes by value**

Equipment	Type	Quantity	Value (US$)	Service	Prime contractor
Virginia class	SSGN	2	7.29bn	US Navy	General Dynamics Electric Boat
F-35A *Lightning* II	FGA ac	48	4.67bn	US Air Force	Lockheed Martin
Columbia class	SSBN	-	3.00bn	US Navy	General Dynamics Electric Boat
KC-46A *Pegasus*	Tkr ac	15	2.56bn	US Air Force	Boeing
F-35B *Lightning* II	FGA ac	20	2.54bn	US Marine Corps	Lockheed Martin
B-21 *Raider*	Bbr ac	R&D	2.31bn	US Air Force	Northrop Grumman
F/A-18E/F *Super Hornet*	FGA ac	24	1.99bn	US Navy	Boeing
P-8A *Poseidon*	ASW ac	10	1.98bn	US Navy	Boeing
Gerald R. Ford	CVN	-	1.65bn	US Navy	Newport News Shipbuilding
JLTV	AUV	3,390	1.32bn	US Army	Oshkosh Defense
F-35C *Lightning* II	FGA ac	9	1.28bn	US Navy	Lockheed Martin
CH-53K	Hvy tpt hel	8	1.27bn	US Marine Corps	Boeing
PAC-3MSE	SAM	240	1.13bn	US Army	Lockheed Martin
UH-60M *Black Hawk*	Med tpt hel	50	1.12bn	US Army	Sikorsky
John Lewis class	AOR	2	1.09bn	US Navy	General Dynamics NASSCO

Table 5 US fixed-wing fighter-aircraft exports, 2010–Oct 2018

Country	Equipment	2010	2011	2012	2013	2014	2015	2016	2017	Oct 2018
Australia	F-35A					2				8
Egypt	F-16C/D			7	20					
Indonesia	F-16C/D					5	4	5	4	2
Iraq	F-16C/D						4	10	7	
Israel	F-35I							2	7	3
Italy	F-16A/B			3						
Italy	F-35A							6*	2*	2*
Italy	F-35B									1*
Japan	F-35A							1	1*	4*
Morocco	F-16C/D	3	13	6						
Netherlands	F-35A			1	1					
Norway	F-35A							2	6	6
Pakistan	F-16C/D	14	14	1						
Saudi Arabia	F-15SA							4	26	17
Singapore	F-15	4		2				8		
South Korea	F-15K	2	2	3						
South Korea	F-35A									3
Turkey	F-16C/D		3	11						
Turkey	F-35A									2
United Arab Emirates	F-16	3	3	1						
United Kingdom	F-35B			2	1			5	6	2
	Total = 276	26	35	37	22	7	10	37	59	43

*final assembly outside US

Table 6 Canada: maritime procurement programmes, by order date

Programme	Equipment	Type	Quantity	Value (C$)	Value (US$)	Prime contractors	Order date
Maritime Helicopter Project	CH-148 *Cyclone*	ASW hel	28	3.2bn	2.46bn	Sikorsky	Nov 2004
Victoria In-Service Support Contract (VISSC)	*Victoria* class	SSK	4	2.6bn	2.44bn	Babcock Canada	Jun 2008
Halifax-class modernisation and frigate life-extension	*Halifax* class	FFGHM	12	4.3bn	3.10bn	Lockheed Martin Canada	Nov 2008
Arctic and Offshore Patrol Ships	*Harry DeWolf* class	PSOH	5	3.6bn	2.81bn	Irving Shipbuilding	Mar 2015
Joint Support Ship	*Protecteur* class	AORH	2	3.4bn	2.63bn	Vancouver Shipyards	Jun 2018
Canadian Surface Combatant	Global Combat Ship (UK Type-26 mod)	FFGHM	15	56–60bn	43.4–46.5bn	Irving Shipbuilding	-

Figure 4 Boeing: P-8A *Poseidon* Multi-Mission Maritime Aircraft (MMA)

The US Navy (USN) had taken delivery of over 70 P-8A aircraft by mid-2018. Although there have been some delays (it took 18 months for full-rate production to begin), production was by mid-2018 months ahead of schedule. The P-8A is derived from a pre-existing and tested design – Boeing's 737-800 commercial airliner. Military specifications are incorporated during the normal build process instead of being retrofitted. This process, called 'in-line production' by Boeing, is, in combination with additional pre-delivery flights, reported to have saved several millions of dollars from unit costs. Also, the USN has for the P-8A adopted a 'Spiral Development' acquisition process, where capability elements are defined early and are then bought, tested and added incrementally. This allows the aircraft to more rapidly reach initial operating capability as well as generating savings from a more predictable build schedule. Foreign sales have also helped, with four confirmed customers (Australia, India, Norway and the United Kingdom) and three more sales pending

(New Zealand, Saudi Arabia and South Korea). The FY2011 US Defense Budget Request noted 117 P-8As with an average unit cost estimated at US$229.45 million. This had decreased to US$206.23m in the FY2019 request.

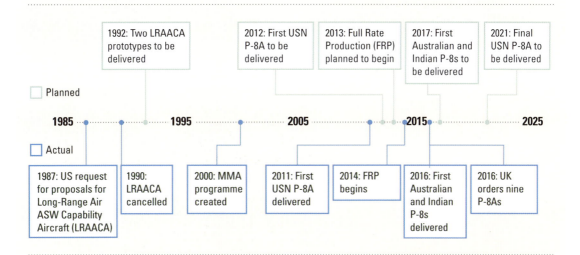

Prime contractor
Boeing (US)

Selected subcontractors
BAE Systems, Inc. (US)
Bharat Electronics Ltd (IND)*
CFM International (FRA and US)
GE Aviation (US)
HAL (IND)*
Northrop Grumman (US)
Raytheon (US)
Spirit Aerosystems (US)
Telephonics (US)*

*Indian P-8I *Neptune* variant

*Planned delivery schedule at time of Lot order

© IISS

Chapter Four
Europe

- While NATO continued to implement a demanding transformation agenda but struggled to shake off the discomfort of internal divisions, the EU progressed a large number of defence-cooperation initiatives. This demonstrated political convergence on the issue, but these had yet to yield any significant improvement to military capability.
- At its Brussels Summit, NATO said it would create a Cyber Operations Centre and two new commands: a Joint Force Command dealing with transatlantic lines of communication, and a Joint Support and Enabling Command to strengthen logistics capacity and military mobility.
- Exercise *Trident Juncture*, which took place in and offshore Norway in October, was NATO's largest exercise in decades. It saw the deployment of the VJTF, and some 50,000 troops in total, plus partner countries Finland and Sweden.
- The EU's PESCO initiative released two batches of projects, and while the second list (released in November) contains more projects related to specific military requirements, it still does not fully address strategic-capability gaps, including in strategic airlift, that were identified in the EU's June 2018 Capability Development Plan.
- Industrial and military logic supports a single European combat-aircraft development, but politics has seen two rival projects emerge, one from France and Germany and another from the UK.
- There is renewed emphasis in NATO on the maritime domain, intended to add credibility to the Enhanced Forward Presence and particularly NATO's ability to sustain this through transatlantic reinforcement.
- NATO European member states increased their total defence spending by 4.2% between 2017 and 2018.

Active military personnel – top 10
(15,000 per unit)

Turkey	355,200
France	203,900
Germany	179,400
Italy	171,050
United Kingdom	148,350
Greece	142,350
Spain	120,350
Poland	117,800
Romania	69,300
Netherlands	35,400

Europe defence spending, 2018 – top 5

United States US$643.3bn

Total European spending US$284.6bn

United Kingdom	France	Germany	Italy	Spain
56.1	53.4	45.7	24.9	15.1

Regional defence policy and economics 68 ▶
Armed forces data section 87 ▶
Arms procurements and deliveries 163 ▶

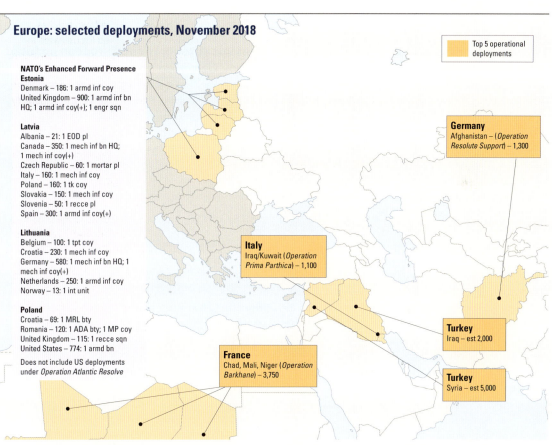

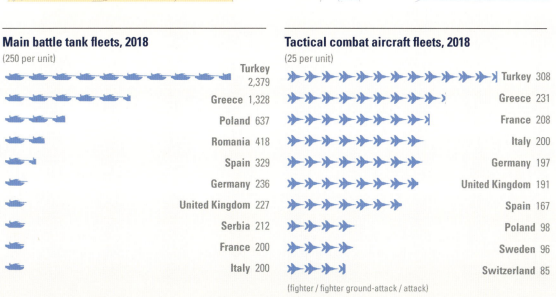

Europe

Defence establishments in Europe have continued to adapt in the face of a complex threat environment. There are sustained efforts to increase defence spending, adjust military forces and equipment capabilities, and introduce additional multinational defence initiatives. Concern about Russia's military modernisation and its application of force in Syria and Ukraine was matched in 2018 by a growing sense among policymakers that Moscow was acting within European societies, seeking to undermine societal coherence and exert political coercion. For example, in March 2018, former Russian military-intelligence officer Sergei Skripal was poisoned by a weapons-grade nerve agent, believed to be of Russian origin. Skripal had been convicted in Russia of spying for the United Kingdom, and after his release in a spy swap had been living in the UK. In April, Russian military-intelligence officers were caught by the Dutch security services as they attempted to mount a surveillance and cyber operation against the Organisation for the Prohibition of Chemical Weapons (OPCW), based in The Hague. The OPCW had earlier identified the agent used against Skripal. These events added to a growing list of Russian meddling conducted on European soil.

Meanwhile, amid fears that external actors were bent on undermining cohesion in Europe, uncertainty also came from within. During the July 2018 NATO summit in Brussels, US President Donald Trump, ignoring recent and planned future increases in defence spending among European NATO allies, suggested that the US 'might do its own thing' unless European allies started to spend more on defence. While several European governments found reassurance in the commitment to NATO expressed by Secretary of Defense James Mattis, others argued that it was not sustainable to expect US policy to proceed against the expressed position of the US president. Mattis, visiting Paris in October 2018, had urged European observers to ignore some of the divisive headlines, suggesting that 'actions speak loudest'. Indeed, the US government had reinforced its military presence in Europe and, notwithstanding Trump's rhetoric, funds for the Pentagon's European Deterrence Initiative continued to grow. Nonetheless, recurring rumours that Mattis might either resign or be fired added to the unease in European capitals.

Strategic autonomy and European ambition

German Chancellor Angela Merkel concluded in 2017 that the US was no longer necessarily a reliable partner. In a series of speeches and opinion-editorial pieces in July and August 2018, Heiko Maas, foreign minister in the Merkel cabinet, began 'making plans for a new world order' in which Europe would form a counterweight for situations in which the US 'crosses the line'. Maas suggested that an alliance of multilateralists, including Canada, Japan and South Korea, as well as like-minded Europeans, was needed to protect the international order, based on multilateralism, cooperation and the rule of law.

In contrast, the UK took a more measured approach. Still consumed by domestic political divisions over its exit from the European Union (Brexit) and negotiations over the terms of withdrawal, on 16 July Prime Minister Theresa May referred to the crisis created by Trump's suggestion merely as an 'additional session' of the NATO summit. Indeed, May suggested that Trump 'has made a difference' primarily by focusing 'the eyes of those around the table on the question of the 2% commitment'. Earlier, May explained at February's Munich Security Conference that the UK was 'unconditionally committed' to European security and that a new security partnership should govern this policy area between the EU and the UK after Brexit. While many of her counterparts across the continent welcomed the sentiment, a final agreement on Brexit – at least one that was agreed in the UK – proved elusive well into the autumn. The possibility that an acrimonious withdrawal from the EU would make security and defence cooperation more difficult was as real as it was unintended.

In contrast, France was pursuing ideas for a more autonomous posture, first outlined in September 2017 in a speech by President Emmanuel Macron. This is perhaps unsurprising given the long-standing desire in Paris for a significant degree of European independence in security and defence matters. Macron's major idea was for a European Intervention

Initiative. Though details remained sketchy, this would see a group of European nations use existing military assets and units to provide rapid-response capabilities for crisis management. In June 2018, nine countries (Belgium, Denmark, Estonia, France, Germany, the Netherlands, Portugal, Spain and the UK) signed a letter of intent (LOI) to pursue this initiative. The LOI makes clear that the initiative is not about creating formations for operations, but rather is meant to establish a 'non-binding forum of European participating states' with the 'ultimate objective ... to develop a shared strategic culture'. Participating governments have discussed some associated measures, including enhanced cooperation on strategic foresight and intelligence sharing; scenario development and planning; support to operations; and an exchange on lessons learned and doctrine. Paris was keen to maintain some distance between its initiative and formal EU security and defence structures but some partners, including Berlin, wanted a closer link, and the LOI suggests that the European Intervention Initiative should contribute to ongoing defence-collaboration efforts within the EU. Nonetheless, the fact that Denmark, which has an opt-out from EU military cooperation, and Brexit-focused Britain joined France's initiative showed the benefits of not directly associating it with Brussels.

Among European governments, there seem to be at least three different schools of thought over what European strategic autonomy might ultimately mean. For the UK, strategic autonomy – to the extent that it was seen as desirable at all – seems to mean the ability to provide a stronger European contribution to transatlantic burden sharing. For Germany, strategic autonomy referred to the ability to provide a counterweight to the US in face of existing policy differences, while for France it implied the ability to take military action independent of the US. On the multinational level, an interesting paradox emerged in 2018. Whereas NATO continued to implement a demanding transformation agenda started at its Wales Summit in 2014, but struggled to shake off

NATO summit propels transformation

At its 11–12 July 2018 summit in Brussels, NATO added yet more layers to its post-2014 adaptation process. Based on US suggestions, and according to US diplomats closely associated with Secretary of Defense James Mattis, a new readiness initiative was agreed committing NATO member states collectively to have 30 battalions, 30 air squadrons and 30 naval combat vessels ready to use in 30 days. In the run-up to the summit, several European NATO members expressed concern about the lack of detail related to the readiness initiative and what precisely was expected of them. Known as the 'four thirties', this goal is meant to be achieved by 2020. In October 2018, General Curtis Scaparrotti, NATO Supreme Allied Commander Europe (SACEUR), was reported as saying that 'perhaps the most important thing that has changed [in NATO] is the mindset that we have to get up every day now and be ready to deal with a real threat. That is a fundamental change.' Although progress on delivering the readiness initiative will be closely watched in Washington, NATO commanders point to the underlying shift in approach indicated by the initiative. Collective defence and hard-security concerns are once again at the heart of Alliance thinking, and the organisation is focused on recovering high-readiness capability, as well as the capacity to move and deploy large formations.

At the Brussels Summit, NATO also agreed measures to improve military mobility and defined a new plan for SACEUR to examine the administrative challenges of moving military personnel and assets across countries. The NATO Command Structure (NCS) was adjusted following an internal review, which had revealed shortcomings when measured against the declared political–military level of ambition. NATO will create a Cyber Operations Centre as well as two new commands: a Joint Force Command dealing with transatlantic lines of communication to be based in Norfolk, Virginia, and a Joint Support and Enabling Command to be based in Germany. Both commands should strengthen logistics capacity and support military mobility, and mean that the NCS will grow again in terms of personnel (by about 1,200) after severe post-Cold War cuts that saw staff levels reduced from about 22,000 posts at the end of the Cold War to some 6,800 at the start of 2018.

On 25 October, NATO launched its biggest exercise in decades, with the two-week-long *Trident Juncture 2018* bringing together some 50,000 troops from NATO member states, plus partner countries Finland and Sweden, to exercise in Norway, the Baltic Sea and the North Atlantic. In early October, it was announced that the US aircraft carrier USS *Harry S. Truman* and its strike group would join the exercise.

NATO also launched a training and capacity-building mission in Iraq, to be led by Canada and set to begin before the end of 2018, and agreed to conduct more exercises focused on southern-flank scenarios and contingencies.

Table 7 NATO transformation, 2014–19

Faced with multiple external security challenges on its eastern and southern flanks and internal challenges to Alliance coherence, NATO in 2014 embarked on a significant transformation process, seeking to strengthen its ability to conduct its core tasks of collective defence, crisis management and cooperative security. In its public pronouncements, NATO stresses that it has adopted a 360-degree approach to threats, but the initiatives launched in successive meetings of NATO heads of state and government demonstrate a clear focus on modernising NATO's approach to and capabilities for collective defence, which is mostly seen as being under threat on its eastern flank.

Policy initiative	Content	Intended effect	Assessment and status
Wales Summit (2014)			
Readiness Action Plan	■ Rotational continuous presence of land, sea and air forces and military activity in the eastern part of the Alliance ■ Enlarge the NATO Response Force (NRF) ■ Establish Very High Readiness Joint Task Force (VJTF) ■ Establish permanent command-and-control presence and force enablers on the territories of eastern allies ■ Increase readiness and capabilities of Headquarters Multinational Corps Northeast ■ An enhanced exercise programme	■ Strengthen collective-defence and crisis-management capability through improved readiness ■ Reassure eastern allies through on-the-ground presence and military activity	■ Intensified air policing, AWACS flights and maritime-patrol activities ■ NRF expansion from 13,000 to 40,000 troops ■ VJTF established as multinational brigade with up to five manoeuvre battalions; most ready to deploy in 2–7 days ■ NATO Force Integration Units established in BLG, EST, HUN, LVA, LTU, POL, ROM and SVK ■ Expanded frequency, size and scope of NATO exercises
Addressing hybrid-warfare threats	■ Enhance strategic communications ■ Develop hybrid exercise scenarios ■ Strengthen coordination with other organisations	■ Improve ability to deter and respond to hybrid attacks	■ NATO Strategic Communications Centre of Excellence established ■ Hybrid scenarios included in exercise programme ■ Higher degree of coordination with EU on hybrid threats
Defence Investment Pledge	■ Maintain 2% of GDP defence-spending levels or aim to reach this level by 2024 ■ Maintain 20% of defence-spending share on major equipment and R&D or aim to reach this level by 2024	■ Close capability gaps through higher spending and focus on defence investment ■ Achieve more balanced burden-sharing among allies	■ 13% real-terms increase in NATO–European defence spending between 2014 and 2018, but still below 2008 levels ■ Number of NATO member states meeting the 2% and/or the 20% target is growing
Framework Nations Concept (FNC)	■ Create groupings of allies, each led by one framework nation, to develop and deploy capabilities	■ Encourage multinational pursuit of agreed NATO defence-planning goals and provide formed units for operations	■ GER, ITA and UK set up FNC groupings ■ GER focus is on capability development and provision of formed units; ITA focus on capability development; and UK focus on operations
Enhanced Cyber Defence Policy	■ Establish cyber defence as a part of collective defence	■ Strengthen deterrence in cyberspace	■ Clarification that a cyber attack could lead to an Article 5 response ■ Increased cooperation with the private sector
Defence and Related Security Capacity Building Initiative (DCB)	■ Support, advise and assist third countries with DCB ■ Complementary approach to EU, OSCE and United Nations	■ Strengthen links to partner nations ■ Enable NATO's ability to project stability without deploying large combat forces	■ DCB activities launched, including in GEO, IRQ, JOR, MDA and TUN ■ Attempt to build on NATO experience with advise and assist, training and mentoring activities
Warsaw Summit (2016)			
Enhanced Forward Presence (EFP)	■ Deploy one multinational battalion-sized battlegroup each to EST, LVA, LTU and POL ■ Tailored forward presence for the Southeast/Black Sea region	■ Boost deterrence by establishing a multinational tripwire force, triggering an allied response in the case of aggression	■ Fully deployed as of June 2017, with CAN, GER, the UK and the US serving as framework EFP nations ■ Strength as of August 2018 was 4,743 troops

Table 7 NATO transformation, 2014–19

Reinforcement strategy	■ Call on member states to deliver heavy and high-end forces in line with NATO defence-planning priorities	■ Provide a credible solution to address 'anti-access/area-denial' threats from Russia	■ Some evidence that European NATO members are adjusting procurement activity and force structures to focus on collective-defence tasks ■ Implementation likely to stretch through the 2020s
Cyber Defence Pledge	■ Cyberspace recognised as an operational domain in its own right ■ Prioritise enhanced cyber defences for national networks and infrastructure	■ Improved ability to respond to cyber attacks ■ Improved national resilience in the face of cyber attacks	■ Does not alter NATO's defensive approach to cyber, but recognition of cyber as an operational domain is likely to drive policies, plans and information exchange in this area
NATO Baseline Requirements for National Resilience	■ NATO support to civil preparedness in areas such as continuity of government and essential services or the security of critical national infrastructure	■ Strengthened capacity to deal with hybrid threats ■ Agreed resilience guidelines	■ Reminder that NATO allies, according to Article 3 of the North Atlantic Treaty, need to contribute to collective defence by being able to resist attack
Intelligence and Security Division	■ Establish Joint Intelligence and Security Division (JISD) ■ Appoint assistant secretary-general (ASG) for Intelligence and Security	■ Improve NATO's ability to draw on a wide range of intelligence resources ■ Make efficient use of intelligence provided by allies	■ ASG appointed in December 2016 and JISD stood up in 2017 ■ Increased production of joint intelligence, but beyond the JISD intelligence work in NATO remains fragmented
Joint Declaration EU–NATO	■ Define priority areas for substantial cooperation: countering hybrid threats, operational cooperation, cyber security and defence; capability development; defence industrial and R&D cooperation, increased coordination of exercises; defence and security capacity building	■ Revive EU–NATO strategic partnership ■ Strengthen the case for complementary capabilities ■ Task staffs with implementation	■ List of 74 specific actions agreed, across the identified priority areas ■ Regular progress reports presented to EU and NATO; some evidence of increased exercise coordination ■ Joint declaration in July 2018 focused on military mobility, CBRN, and the women, peace and security agenda
Brussels Meeting of Heads of State and Government (2017)			
Action Plan for the Fight Against Terrorism	■ NATO membership in the Global Coalition to Defeat ISIS ■ Establish a terrorism intelligence cell and appoint a coordinator to oversee NATO's efforts in the fight against terrorism	■ Demonstrate NATO contributions to the international fight against terrorism ■ Increase activity on NATO's southern flank	■ NATO AWACS flights now conduct air-surveillance and airspace-management tasks for the coalition; NATO nations to provide air-to-air refuelling capability ■ Training mission in Iraq launched by NATO in 2018 to strengthen the capacity of Iraqi forces
Brussels Summit (2018)			
NATO Readiness Initiative	■ Allies will offer an additional 30 major naval combatants, 30 heavy or medium manoeuvre battalions, 30 combat air squadrons and enabling forces at 30 days readiness or less (the 'four 30s' concept)	■ Ensure NATO has access to combat-ready forces at high readiness ■ Strengthen NATO's capacity for rapid response and reinforcement of forward-deployed forces	■ Readiness initiative to be implemented by 2020 ■ Initiative will not lead to new forces being stood up, but focus on the readiness of existing forces ■ Driven by the US; European buy-in unclear at end of 2018
Military Mobility	■ Improve military mobility by: shortening border-crossing times; diplomatic clearance for military movements; identifying main and alternative supply routes; and exercising military-mobility tasks	■ Strengthen NATO capacity to rapidly deploy and sustain forces ■ Achieve better coordination in peacetime, crisis and conflict	■ NATO aims to cooperate with the EU, which has regulatory responsibility in key areas. The EU also can make money available to support the development of mobility-relevant defence infrastructure
NATO Command Structure (NCS)	■ Create a Cyberspace Operations Centre ■ Establish a Joint Force Command and a Joint Support and Enabling Command	■ Enhance situational awareness of operational activity in cyberspace ■ Rebuild NATO capacity to conduct large-scale collective-defence operations	■ A review of NATO's command structure said the NCS was not fit for purpose after significant post-Cold War cuts ■ New elements in the NCS reflect new threats, as well as a return to supporting large troop movements and complex logistics for collective defence

the discomfort created by internal divisions, the EU progressed a large number of defence-cooperation initiatives, demonstrating political convergence on the issue, but these had yet to yield any significant improvement to military capability.

EU defence cooperation takes shape

The EU focused on implementing plans drawn up in 2017 to strengthen defence cooperation. In December 2017, member states formally launched Permanent Structured Cooperation (PESCO), a concept that foresees far-reaching defence collaboration among EU member states to develop their military capability. When originally conceived, access to PESCO was supposed to be governed by demanding criteria regarding military capability and political will. In contrast, PESCO as adopted in 2017 is a much more inclusive undertaking, with softer criteria for those wishing to join. As a result, all EU member states except for Denmark, Malta and the UK are taking part. A first batch of 17 projects was launched in March 2018. European governments, perhaps surprised themselves by the rapid progress during 2017 towards agreement on PESCO, largely committed to projects that were already under way. It was hardly a surprise, therefore, when initial statements from participating governments suggested that more ambitious ventures would be put forward for the second batch of PESCO projects. This second list, released in November, contains more projects directly focused on specific military requirements, but still does not address strategic capability gaps including in the areas of heavy transport and strategic airlift.

During summer 2018, it became apparent that the EU felt it had succeeded, for the first time, in putting in place all elements necessary to generate military capabilities to support EU security and defence aspirations. The Capability Development Plan (CDP) sets common capability-development priorities for EU members. The CDP was revised in 2018 to take account of the suggestion, in the 2016 EU Global Strategy, that the Union should be able to protect its citizens. It singled out as priority items ground-combat capabilities, enhanced logistics and medical capabilities, air mobility, air superiority, the integration of military air capabilities, naval manoeuvrability, underwater control, space-based information and communications services, information superiority and cyber operations. This revised set of priorities points to more high-end military capabilities than the EU's recent operational activity would imply. Coordination with the NATO Defence Planning Process is also foreseen.

The priorities set in the CDP would feed into the Coordinated Annual Review on Defence (CARD), which would see member states report on their capability plans, with EU institutions monitoring alignment with CDP priorities and identifying opportunities for cooperation among member states. A CARD pilot phase was under way in 2018. Then, PESCO would draw on CARD results to plan and implement projects in support of the CDP. PESCO projects in turn would at least partially draw on the European Defence Fund (EDF) that would make EU funds available to support defence research and development, and ultimately capability development. PESCO projects would be eligible for a higher rate of EDF funding than other projects (30% instead of 20%), and some governments have already indicated their preference to restrict EDF funding to PESCO projects altogether. The plan is that enhanced European military capabilities result from this process of priority setting, de facto harmonisation of capability-development processes and planning of projects co-financed with EU funding. These capabilities would be directly related to the EU's level of ambition and compatible with NATO. At the end of 2018, this theory of EU capability development had crystallised into the EU's main defence effort, though it remained essentially untested.

DEFENCE ECONOMICS

Ten years after the financial crash, European economies have broadly recovered. In 2017, the euro area boasted its fastest growth rate in the past decade, at 2.4%, but the rate of economic output slowed down in 2018 to 2.0%. Central and Eastern European states, such as Slovakia (3.9% GDP growth in 2018), Latvia (3.7%) and Slovenia (4.5%), were particularly dynamic. Outside the eurozone, Romania and Poland also achieved strong economic output in 2018, at 4.0% and 4.4% respectively.

European Union Structural and Investment Funds contributed to the recovery in Central and Eastern Europe. For example, in 2017, the IMF calculated that EU funds made up half of the public investment in Romania and Hungary. According to the World Bank, EU funding was equivalent to more than 4% of GDP for some Central European countries, often in the form of Cohesion Funds for infrastructure projects.

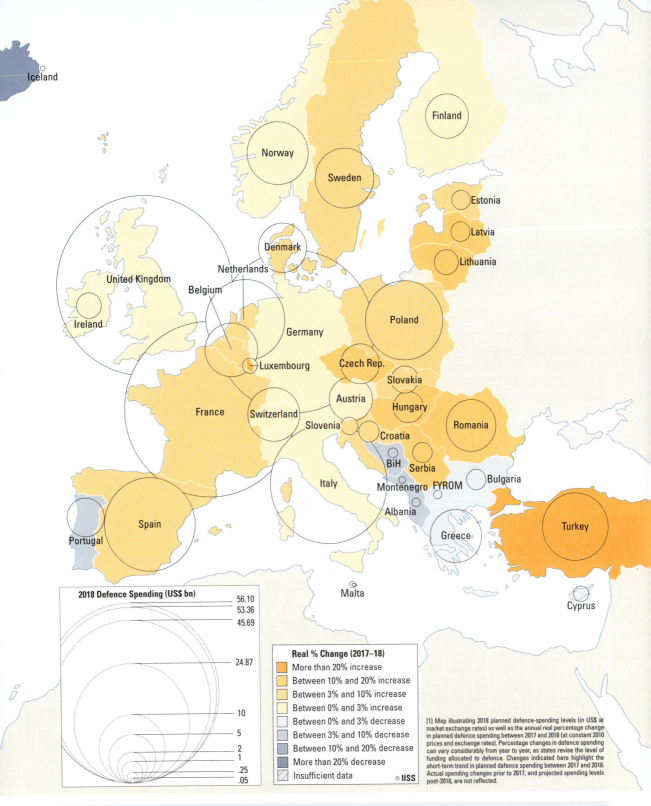

▲ Map 1 **Europe regional defence spending**[1]

Sub-regional groupings referred to in defence economics text: Central Europe (Austria, Czech Republic, Germany, Hungary, Poland, Slovakia and Switzerland), Northern Europe (Denmark, Estonia, Finland, Latvia, Lithuania, Norway and Sweden), Southern Europe (Cyprus, Greece, Italy, Malta, Portugal and Spain), Southeastern Europe (Bulgaria, Romania and Turkey), the Balkans (Albania, Bosnia-Herzegovina, Croatia, FYROM, Montenegro, Serbia and Slovenia) and Western Europe (Belgium, France, Iceland, Ireland, Luxembourg, the Netherlands and the United Kingdom).

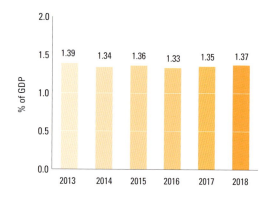

Figure 5 **Europe regional defence expenditure** as % of GDP

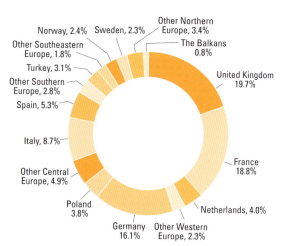

Other Western Europe – Belgium, Iceland, Ireland, Luxembourg
Other Central Europe – Austria, Czech Republic, Hungary, Slovakia, Switzerland
Other Northern Europe – Denmark, Estonia, Finland, Latvia, Lithuania
Other Southern Europe – Cyprus, Malta, Portugal
The Balkans – Albania, Bosnia-Herzegovina, Croatia, FYROM, Montenegro, Serbia, Slovenia
Other Southeastern Europe – Bulgaria, Romania

© IISS

Figure 6 **Europe defence spending by country and sub-region, 2017**

Low interest rates since the 2008 crisis also contributed to Europe's economic growth, by stimulating credit and investment. Governments' expenditure on interest payments fell, in turn reducing debt-to-GDP ratios in 2018. There are, however, some early signs of tightening monetary policy, which will raise the costs of debt servicing. In August 2018, the Bank of England increased its interest rate by a quarter of a percentage point to 0.75% – the highest level since 2009. By August 2018, the Czech National Bank had raised its interest rate five times in the year. Although the European Central Bank will keep its interest rate at its present level until mid-2019, by the end of 2018 it is set to normalise its monetary policy by looking to end quantitative easing.

This overall positive picture does not mask the difficulties experienced in some countries. Italy's right–left coalition proposed a public-spending increase in its first budget, combining tax cuts with the introduction of a minimum basic income. The budget plan proved unpopular with Europe's financial authorities and risks aggravating Italy's debt, which already stands at 130% of GDP. In the United Kingdom, although unemployment continues to fall, down to 4.1% in 2018, growth has slowed in comparison to its continental neighbours. The UK's GDP grew by 2.3% in 2015, but then slowed to 1.7% in 2017 and 1.4% in 2018. The IMF explained this deceleration by pointing to the effect of the fall in the pound in slowing real-term income growth, as well as reduced investment in the country because of uncertainty surrounding the UK's decision to withdraw from the EU. Further south, while Turkey experienced a growth rate of 3.5% in 2018, its currency weakened considerably in the summer due to tariffs imposed by the United States over a detained US citizen. This in turn helped propel inflation in Turkey to an estimated annual 15% in 2018.

Defence spending and procurement

Within this context, Europe's military spending continued to grow at a steady pace, rising by 4.0% in real terms in 2018, slightly down from 4.4% in 2017. Nominal increases between 2017 and 2018 for the region's biggest spenders were 4.3% in France, 4.1% in Germany and 3.2% in the UK.

This overall trend of rising defence spending is set to continue. The French parliament voted in 2018 for a seven-year forward plan for defence spending. The *Loi de Programmation Militaire* forecasts that the budget will rise to €44.0 billion (US$53.2bn) by 2023, excluding pensions, from a figure of €34.2bn (US$40.6bn) in 2018. The increase will fund a recruitment drive for 6,000 civilian and military staff, the bulk of which will bolster the cyber-defence and intelligence services. The extra funding will also enable new equipment purchases, including the modernisation of France's nuclear deterrent. (This is expected to cost €25.0bn (US$29.3bn) between 2019 and 2023.) In 2019, the priority focus is on expeditionary capabilities and sustainability, with the expected delivery of six *Reaper* uninhabited aerial vehicles (UAVs), one more A400M transport aircraft, two KC-130J tankers, the modernisation of one KC-130H tanker/transport, and one A330 MRTT for resupply and strategic airlift. Unsurprisingly, these reflect the requirements and lessons from France's continuing overseas military operations.

While the increase in defence spending in France benefits from a political consensus, there was less unanimity in Germany after the new coalition government was formed in March 2018. However, the budget for 2019 was eventually settled at €42.9bn (US$50.2bn), including pensions, which at 11.4% is a significant increase in nominal terms compared to 2018 (€38.5bn, or US$45.7bn).

In the UK, the National Audit Office reported potential shortfalls in the Ministry of Defence's (MoD's) 2018-28 Equipment Plan, at a minimum of £7.0bn (US$9.4bn), including £5.9bn (US$7.9bn) in the next four years. Despite these, treasury documents indicate a continued increase in the core defence budget (excluding pensions and other non-MoD funding sources) from £37.0bn (US$49.5bn) in 2018 to £37.9bn (US$49.2bn) in 2019. The MoD also benefited from £800 million in extra funding in the course of the year, including £600m (US$803m) for the *Dreadnought* programme. There is greater political consensus in Baltic and Nordic countries, where governments have announced spending increases. In Denmark, for instance, government and opposition parties agreed to increase defence spending, with significant annual steps taking the Danish defence budget over DKK38.7bn (US$6.3bn) by 2023.

In Sweden, a report initiated by the previous government and published in early 2018 called for spending increases totalling SEK168bn (US$19bn) between 2021 and 2030. The increase was justified, according to the report's authors, by the rising costs of replacing and maintaining military equipment. In Finland, the defence budget increased to €3.1bn (US$3.7bn) in 2019, up from €2.9bn (US$3.4bn) in 2018, largely due to the Squadron 2020 naval recapitalisation programme. Budgets are also rising in Estonia, to more than €600m (US$770m) by 2022, and Latvia, where the government expected to spend €182m (US$216m) in defence investments in 2018.

Defence-spending increases in European Union member states will, in a few years, be supplemented by money spent by the EU on defence objectives.

Table 8 **Denmark: planned increases in defence spending, 2018–23**

Currency	2018	2019	2020	2021	2022	2023
Yearly increases (DKKbn)	0.8	0.8	1.7	1.9	2.8	4.8
Yearly increases (US$bn)	0.127	0.125	0.268	0.302	0.450	0.779
Defence budget (DKKbn)	26.7	27.5	29.2	31.1	33.9	38.7
Defence budget (US$bn)	4.2	4.3	4.6	4.9	5.5	6.3

Source: Danish Defence Agreement 2018–2023

The European Commission's proposals for the multi-annual financial framework 2021–27 include €13bn (US$15bn) over the course of the seven-year period dedicated to defence research and capability development. Another €6.5bn (US$7.7bn) will be dedicated to military mobility. Nonetheless, and despite the increase in member states' defence budgets, cooperation in defence programmes is still seen as the best way to rationalise spending and generate economies of scale. That said, joint projects have in the past not always proven to be cheaper than domestic ones. In 2018, France and Germany committed to work jointly on a future tank programme (the Main Ground Combat System) and combat aircraft (the Future Combat Air Systems). Other areas of potential cooperation include cruise missiles, swarming UAVs, satellites and maritime-patrol aircraft. EU-level initiatives such as the Permanent Structured Cooperation (PESCO) framework may also in future make a difference. PESCO is specifically designed to foster defence cooperation among member states, including on arms procurement.

Defence industry

As well as PESCO, the European Defence Fund (EDF) allocates EU funding to support cooperative defence research and capability-development projects. Paving the way for the full introduction of the EDF, the EU has introduced two mechanisms. The Preparatory Action for Defence Research (PADR) will disburse €90m (US$107m) and the European Defence Industrial Development Programme (EDIDP) €500m (US$593m) until 2020. Then, between 2021 and 2027, these mechanisms will be taken over by the EDF. The EU proposes to support all or part of the research and capability-development projects, with the key pre-condition that they are undertaken by three companies from three countries.

Table 9 EU PADR projects: companies involved per EU member

	Pythia	Ocean 2020	GOSSRA	Vestlife	AcamsII	Total per country
Austria						0
Belgium		●				1
Bulgaria	●					1
Croatia						0
Cyprus						0
Czech Republic						0
Denmark		●				1
Estonia		●				1
Finland		●		●		2
France	●	●●●●			●	6
Germany		●●●●●	●		●	7
Greece		●●●●				4
Hungary						0
Ireland						0
Italy	●●●	●●●●● ●●●●	●●	●		15
Latvia						0
Lithuania		●●			●	3
Luxembourg						0
Malta						0
Netherlands		●	●	●	●	4
Poland	●	●●	●			4
Portugal		●	●	●	●●	5
Romania	●					1
Slovakia						0
Slovenia						0
Spain		●●●●	●●	●●		8
Sweden		●●	●		●	4
United Kingdom	●	●●●				4
Total per project	**8**	**41***	**9**	**6**	**7**	

*Total excludes NATO participation. Source: EDA
Pythia: strategic technology foresight; **Ocean 2020:** demonstrator for uninhabited systems to support maritime-security missions; **GOSSRA:** Generic Open Soldier System Reference Architecture; **Vestlife:** ballistic and CBRN protection of military personnel; **AcamsII:** adaptive camouflage system

involved respectively across three project areas.

With the EDF, the EU is introducing a mechanism to support innovation in defence research: 5% of the fund will be dedicated to disruptive technology and innovative equipment. This comes in the wake of a broader push across large European arms-producing states to foster innovation in light of defence-technology advances elsewhere, particularly those led by China and the US.

This motivation could also be seen in France, where the 2018 budget allocated €4.7bn (US$5.6bn) for defence research and development (R&D). There have also been a range of new institutional frameworks in recent years. To rationalise these various mechanisms, in early 2018 the French defence ministry created an agency dedicated to defence innovation, linked to the DGA, the defence-procurement and technology agency, with a €1bn (US$1.2bn) budget. Within this, an Innovation Defence Lab will be tasked to identify civilian innovations that can be used for military purposes.

The UK has also set up new mechanisms to facilitate defence innovation. The 2017 Defence R&D budget came to £3.1bn (US$4.0bn). A UK Defence Solutions Centre (UKDSC), established in 2017, runs an innovation competition to generate new technologies relevant for defence. The UKDSC also hosts an Innovation and Collaborative Engagement Lab that brings together experts from innovative technology sectors. In 2016, the UK launched the Defence Innovation Initiative, which includes a Defence and Security Accelerator and a Defence Innovation Fund, which was allocated £800m (US$1.1bn) over ten years.

The PADR currently supports five projects, which reveal interesting patterns (see Table 9). Italy is the most involved state, with 15 firms and research organisations committed to four out of the five projects. Leonardo leads the most significant, Ocean 2020, which received a €35m grant (US$41.5m) and aims to integrate uninhabited platforms for naval surveillance. Spain and Germany come behind Italy, with eight and seven bodies

Germany is looking to establish similar institutional frameworks. Berlin allocated €1.1bn

(US$1.3bn) for defence R&D in 2018. The Bundeswehr created a Cyber Innovation Hub in 2017, funded with €15m (US$17m) over three years. Germany's new defence-innovation agency, the Agentur für Disruptive Innovationen in der Cybersicherheit und Schlüsseltechnologien, was due to be established before the end of 2018.

Turkey's defence-industrial base is also strongly backed by the government. The lira's fall in mid-2018 could complicate Turkish procurement of foreign platforms, in particular F-35 combat aircraft, but also foreign-supplied parts for Turkish programmes, such as the indigenous combat aircraft (the TF-X) and the *Altay* main battle tank. However, indigenous procurements are relatively sheltered from the currency crisis.

Turkey has an ambitious goal to become self-sufficient in defence procurement by 2023. According to NATO, Turkey allocates more than 30% of its defence expenditure to weapons procurement and defence R&D. In 2018, 28.5% of all the country's R&D spending was dedicated to defence, amounting to TL3.26bn (US$636m). This has allowed Turkey to develop its defence industry and become a significant exporter. In 2017, according to the Defence and Aerospace Industry Manufacturers Association, aerospace and other defence exports reached US$1.8bn. Turkey's total aerospace (including civil aviation) and defence-industry revenue grew by 7.2% between 2013 (US$5.1bn) and 2018 (US$6.7bn).

NORTH ATLANTIC AND THE HIGH NORTH

There is now renewed emphasis in NATO on the maritime domain, centred on the North Atlantic and the 'High North'. This is intended to add credibility to the Alliance's Enhanced Forward Presence (EFP) strategy, and particularly NATO's ability to sustain this through transatlantic reinforcement, within the context of a perceived growth in the potential Russian threat in this arena, notably in submarine activity.

NATO's response has included the agreement to create a new joint-force command based in Norfolk, Virginia. This command will be focused on maritime security and sustaining transatlantic reinforcement. Meanwhile, in July 2018, the US Navy re-established its 2nd Fleet in order to refocus its activities in the North Atlantic area. In addition, 2018 saw an extended US Navy aircraft-carrier deployment in European waters, including a first foray by a US Navy carrier into the Arctic Circle in more than two decades.

Nonetheless, Russian force levels – including submarines – remain substantially lower than those of Soviet forces at the end of the Cold War. It is also difficult to assess the numbers of submarine sorties. These may remain relatively low by historical standards, but the potency of individual Russian platforms, together with the reduction in NATO anti-submarine-warfare (ASW) and blue-water naval capabilities since the end of the Cold War, suggest that Russian capabilities would pose a significant challenge to Alliance forces.

NATO navies have been interested in the arrival of the *Yasen* (*Severodvinsk*)-class cruise-missile submarine (SSGN) *Severodvinsk*. Although the design has its origins in the Cold War, it only became operational in 2016, is notably quiet, and carries a significant inventory of both land-attack and anti-ship missiles. A number of improved versions of this submarine are under construction or planned. Modernisation of Russia's *Antey* (*Oscar*-II)-class SSGNs is also under way.

There is also a renewed emphasis on traditional maritime strategic focal points, such as the transit routes of the Greenland–Iceland–United Kingdom (GIUK) Gap, but the character of the potential threat to these is less certain. It may be less a general threat to sea lines of communication and more one of individual platforms putting specific high-level NATO assets at risk. The UK, for example, has highlighted increased Russian activity associated with the Royal Navy's ballistic-missile-submarine base at Faslane, in Scotland. However, there might also be a threat to specific high-value naval formations: for example, targeting just one vessel carrying transatlantic reinforcements could have significant strategic effect.

Among other responses, the US has been refurbishing its base facilities in Keflavik, Iceland, in order to station P-8A *Poseidon* maritime-patrol aircraft there, in part to cover the GIUK Gap. Norway and the UK are also buying P-8s, and cooperation between all three is planned. A critical US capability in the Cold War was its underwater sound-surveillance system (SOSUS), placed in the vicinity of the GIUK Gap to track submarines. There have been reports of recent upgrade work, and further development of NATO and US acoustic-surveillance capabilities may be under consideration.

Meanwhile, Russia has continued to invest in precision long-range weapons, ranging from air-defence to land-attack cruise missiles. All of these pose a potential challenge to NATO's ability to manoeuvre and add to Russia's ability to defend in depth – including protecting Russia's ballistic-missile-submarine force through a revived 'bastion' concept in the Arctic Circle.

In late 2017, the then-chief of the UK Defence Staff highlighted concerns about the potential Russian threat to the undersea-cable infrastructure. Threats to such infrastructure are not new, but modern societies are more reliant on these cables than previously. There are particular concerns about Russia's development of surface 'mother ships' and submarines that can host a variety of deep-ocean mini-submarines.

There is also concern that the 'High North' could become an arena of strategic competition. Reducing sea ice will potentially increase significantly the utility of polar shipping routes, particularly the Northern Sea Route, and increase access to and the value of energy and other natural resources. Russia has a direct stake in this and has been taking steps to strengthen its capabilities in the High North. However, other states are also being prompted to refocus on and revive their ability to operate in this region (hence the return in 2018, after more than a decade, of a Royal Navy submarine to an under-ice exercise) and also drawing in other major actors, notably China.

SWEDEN

Russia's annexation of Crimea in 2014 and its support of separatists in eastern Ukraine were a clear indication to the Swedish security and defence community that Russia's increased involvement in the affairs of neighbouring states now posed a challenge to the hitherto-benign security environment in the Baltic. This situation was reflected in a May 2014 report by the Swedish Defence Commission. This document, which set out objectives for security policy and defence developments over the next five years, noted that the territorial defence of Sweden was once again the primary task for the Swedish Armed Forces (SAF). At the same time, having been subject to repeated reductions in the 1990s and early 2000s, no further cuts were announced in defence spending or organisation.

The subsequent defence bill, agreed by parliament in 2015, said that the war-fighting capability of the SAF needed to be strengthened along with defence cooperation with other countries and organisations, within the restrictions of a non-aligned policy. In addition, initial steps were taken to reactivate the Cold War-era 'total defence' concept, in terms of planning and preparatory actions involving national and local government agencies, as well as private enterprises and civil society. Another outcome was that the trend of falling defence expenditure levelled out and started to rise in absolute terms, although not as a percentage of GDP.

Defence priorities

These new priorities are notable in part because of the limited interest that hitherto had been paid to defence-related issues across the political spectrum. During the Cold War, defence issues were prominent in Swedish society and in government policy. Sweden's priorities changed during the 1980s, and particularly after the collapse of the Soviet Union in 1991, in light of the development of a more favourable security situation in the Baltic region and the desire by politicians to release defence funds for other areas of government spending. Swedish defence policy in the 1990s and early 2000s was largely focused on peace-support operations, first in the western Balkans and later in Afghanistan. Other areas of importance were procurement and defence-industry issues, such as the recurrent upgrades to the JAS-39C/D *Gripen* combat aircraft and related export drives.

In the wake of the deep force reductions that took place between 1990 and 2005 and the suspension of peacetime conscription in 2010, the armed forces and security issues had become less 'visible' to the population. About two-thirds of defence-related infrastructure was closed in the years after the Cold War, with this process accelerating in the late 1990s and early 2000s. Before 1990, almost every county in Sweden hosted either an army garrison, an air-force wing or a naval base, and the vast majority of men had military experience from their time as conscripts. (Until it was suspended in 2010, only Swedish men were conscripted.) In recent years, administrations have therefore tried to revive awareness of defence issues among the population. An example of this was the distribution in June 2018 of a civil-defence brochure called 'If crisis or war comes'. Sent to all Swedish households, this pamphlet contained information on emergency preparedness, total defence and the warning systems used to alert citizens in various contingencies.

The renewed interest in security and defence has spurred debate on the merits of Swedish military non-alignment versus NATO membership. Sweden's political parties are divided on this issue. The Social Democrats, the Green Party, the Left Party and the Swedish Democrats are in favour of continued non-alignment. The Social Democrats say that a shift in Swedish policy would be destabilising for the Baltic Sea region. Others say that NATO membership would force Sweden to raise its defence spending, and this money would be better spent on areas including foreign aid and domestic welfare. Concerns about Alliance membership also include the politics of some members, and the possession of nuclear weapons by three allies.

At the other end of the spectrum are parties that formed the government between 2006 and 2014. The Moderate Party, the Liberal Party, the Center Party and the Christian Democratic Party are all publicly in favour of Swedish NATO membership, though it is not high on their agenda. Proponents of membership say that this should have the support of a majority of the population and that any application should be made in tandem with Finland. However, opinion polls show that Swedish opinion is divided. A poll in Sweden's biggest daily newspaper in January 2018 showed that the public was 43% in favour of NATO membership, 37% against and 25% undecided. A previous poll from July 2017 published by the public television company showed 32% in favour, 43% against and 25% undecided. Historically, the percentage of the Swedish population against NATO membership has been higher than that in favour.

Defence cooperation

Despite its non-aligned status, Sweden has continued a policy of close cooperation with NATO in several areas, in addition to long-standing membership of the Partnership for Peace programme and contributions to Alliance-led operations. Cooperation has been deepened by membership of the enhanced-opportunities programme for partner countries, along with Finland, and implementation of the 2014 host-nation support agreement with NATO. Sweden has also taken part, as a partner country, in several NATO exercises, such as CMX 2016 and *Trident Juncture* 2018. Aside from cooperation with NATO, as a member of the European Union Sweden has supported the development of the Permanent Structured Cooperation (PESCO), launched in late 2017. In terms of peace-support operations, Sweden's major troop contribution has since 2015 been an intelligence, surveillance and reconnaissance unit deployed to the UN-led operation in Mali, MINUSMA.

Sweden is a firm supporter of Nordic Defence Cooperation (NORDEFCO), and is due to chair the mechanism in 2019. However, the most significant recent developments in defence cooperation are several agreements on peacetime cooperation with countries such as the United Kingdom and the United States in order to, among other things, boost interoperability. Bilateral cooperation with Finland is particularly important and includes operational planning for joint action in various contingencies including war, if activated by the political authorities in the two countries.

The armed forces

The present-day Swedish Armed Forces is largely a product of the 2004 defence bill. This was the third in a succession of defence decisions (1995/1996, 1999/2001 and 2004) that reduced the size of the armed forces and defence funding. Parliament stated in 2004 that the basis for the SAF's posture should be that there were no military threats of any significance and that this would be the case for the foreseeable future. An additional assumption was that any changes would come with at least ten years' notice (the ten-year rule was dropped in 2010, two years after the war in Georgia). This move meant that operational planning for territorial defence was discontinued; consequently, there was no need for wartime organisation or a mobilisation system. The armed forces were mainly tasked with taking part in international operations and maintaining existing military skills. Readiness requirements differed between units, ranging from days to years, in order to economise because of scarce resources. With the exception of coastal artillery, most military units were maintained to some degree, although numbers were in many cases small, with correspondingly limited operational capability. In 2010, the government suspended conscription, as part of a move towards an all-volunteer force. However, the end of conscription was not matched by the number of volunteers needed to fill posts. According to the ministry, 'all-volunteer recruitment hasn't provided the Armed Forces with enough trained personnel' and readiness was suffering. The armed forces were short of '1,000 active squad leaders, soldiers and sailors as well as 7,000 reservists' in 2016. Announcing the return of conscript service from the beginning of 2018, defence authorities said that recruitment would be both voluntary and conscript-based and would be gender-neutral, with both men and women now subject to the draft.

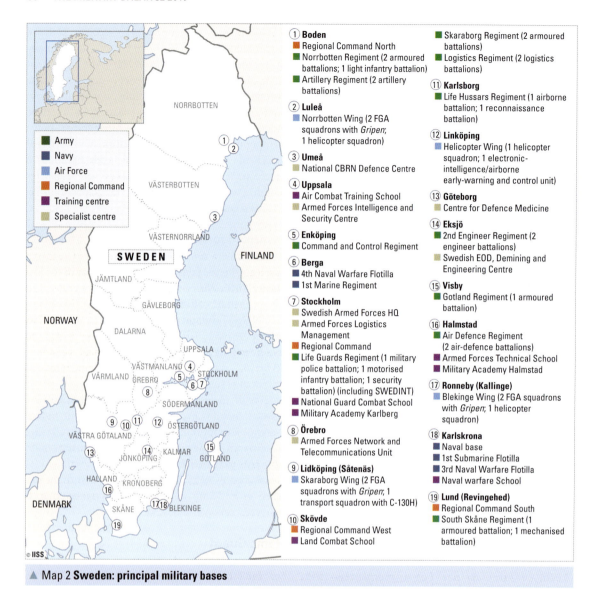

▲ Map 2 **Sweden: principal military bases**

Army

The Swedish Army comprises two mechanised brigades with units including armour (with *Leopard* 2 main battle tanks), mechanised infantry (with CV9040 infantry fighting vehicles), artillery, engineering, air-defence and auxiliary units. The southern brigade is headquartered in Skövde, while the northern brigade is headquartered in Boden. As well as these two brigades, there are more specialised units, such as ranger and intelligence battalions, and a chemical, biological, radiological and nuclear company. The army has experienced difficulty in filling personnel-intensive units with volunteers and will benefit from the decision to reintroduce conscription.

An important outcome of the 2015 defence bill was to once again garrison the island of Gotland. As a result, a mechanised battlegroup has been permanently based there since 2017. New barracks and maintenance facilities have been built outside Visby, near training facilities that were not dismantled when the armoured regiment stationed there was disbanded in 2005. Indeed this unit, the Gotland Regiment, was itself revived in 2018, at least in name. Gotland was also central to Sweden's large *Aurora* military exercise in 2017.

Ongoing army procurements include self-propelled mortars, *Archer* self-propelled artillery pieces, and short-range anti-aircraft missiles. Elements of the CV90 and *Leopard* 2 MBT fleets, delivered in the 1990s, are being refurbished and upgraded. In August 2018, in order to boost the capability of its air-defence network, the government decided to acquire the US-made *Patriot* surface-to-air missile system. This will replace the 1960s-vintage *Hawk* and is one of Sweden's major defence procurements in the near term.

Navy

Sweden's main naval base is at Karlskrona, with a supplementary base located outside Stockholm. There is also a harbour and replenishment facilities in Gothenburg on the west coast. The main operational components of the navy are two naval-warfare flotillas, a submarine flotilla and an amphibious battalion equipped with fast assault craft. The navy was the principal beneficiary of the change to voluntary recruitment in 2010, as it was able to recruit specialists more directly, and its units operate modern vessels such as the *Visby*-class corvettes and the *Gotland*-class submarines. The level of interoperability with other countries is high, especially so in the case of Finland; the navy plays an important role in bilateral operational defence cooperation.

The navy frequently takes part in multilateral exercises, such as BALTOPS. Like the army, its main limitation is its small size (five corvettes, five submarines, four missile boats, as well as smaller vessels for counter-mine operations, logistics support and surveillance), though it has responsibility for one of the longest coastlines in Europe.

Current naval procurements include a new signals-intelligence ship, the new A26 submarine class (with two on order) and new anti-ship missiles (RBS-15 Mk4) for the *Visby* corvettes. In addition, two *Gotland*-class submarines, two *Göteborg*-class corvettes and the amphibious battalion's fleet of fast assault craft are being refurbished and upgraded.

Air force

The air force's main task of monitoring Swedish airspace and securing the territorial integrity has proven more demanding over the last few years due to the assertive behaviour of Russian forces in the Baltic Sea area. Its inventory includes Saab JAS-39 C/D *Gripen* multi-role fighters organised into six squadrons based at Luleå, Ronneby and Såtenäs. The last C/D version was delivered to the Swedish Air Force in 2015. The *Gripen*'s operational capability was significantly boosted by the integration in 2016 of the *Meteor* long-range air-to-air missile; its armament till then included AIM-120 AMRAAM and IRIS-T air-to-air missiles, RBS-15 air-to-surface missiles and GBU-49 laser-guided bombs. Alternative bases for fighter wings exist at Uppsala and at Gotland. However, the deteriorating security environment has highlighted the need to disperse the fighter squadrons to wartime locations during periods of heightened readiness. This concept was developed by the air force during the Cold War but only limited infrastructure, materiel and dedicated personnel remain after the reductions of the 1990s and early 2000s.

For airlift, a transport squadron of six C-130Hs is based at Såtenäs. Sweden is also a member of the SAC Heavy Airlift Wing in Hungary, which operates three C-17s. The SAF's fleet of AW 109, UH-60M *Black Hawk* and NH90 helicopters is organised in a combined helicopter wing, with three squadrons for ground-based and naval operations. The naval version of NH90 is capable of conducting anti-submarine operations.

The air force is the dominant service in terms of research and development and procurement. Indeed, the largest proportion of the defence-materiel budget is taken up by development and production of the new JAS-39 *Gripen* E. The Swedish government has ordered 60 in total. The 'E' variant's first flight took place in mid-2017. The aircraft are expected to be delivered between 2020 and 2026.

Home Guard

The volunteer-based Home Guard serves as Sweden's territorial force. It includes nearly 22,000 troops in 40 battalions and can be mobilised in hours, according to the armed forces. This was tested in a large mobilisation exercise in mid-2018. Its main tasks include the protection of military installations and navy and air-force bases, as well as surveillance and intelligence gathering. The Home Guard also supports the emergency services in disasters, such as the forest fires in summer 2018.

Some elements of the Home Guard are tactically mobile and the coastal units are equipped with fast boats. Mortars, radio equipment and transport vehicles have recently been either procured or transferred from the army. The Home Guard's personnel establishment has in recent years been stable. However, the reintroduction of conscription and basic military training will also be important for future recruitment to the Home Guard. In many parts of Sweden, it represents the sole military presence, which makes the Home Guard an important link between the public and the armed forces.

Defence economics

The Swedish economy is growing and is expected to continue to do so in the near future. According to the IMF, GDP growth for 2018 will be 2.4%, which is above the forecast for the euro area (2.0%). The labour market is strong but unemployment is not expected to fall much further from the current level of 6.3%, due to a slowdown in job creation and the labour force growing as a result of immigration.

The Swedish defence budget has risen from US$5.99 billion in 2013 to US$6.54bn in 2018, when measured in constant (2010) US dollars. Defence spending in Sweden in 2018 amounts to 1.12% of GDP compared to 1.54% in Norway, 1.23% in Finland and 1.20% in Denmark. According to an agreement reached in 2017 between the Social Democrats, the Green Party, the Moderate Party and the Center Party, the defence budget should rise by US$300 million each year from 2018–20. In spite of this, the SAF reported in spring 2018 that it needs even more funding in order to fulfil the aims of the 2015 defence bill. This was supported by a government-appointed public inquiry, which in February 2018 said that the acquisition of new equipment, in-service support and equipment maintenance for the SAF were underfunded by at least US$700m between 2018 to 2025.

The next long-term defence bill is planned for 2020. The Swedish Defence Commission (with representatives from all parties in parliament) is expected to report back to government in May 2019 their recommendations for defence policy for the years 2021–25. One of the major issues for political negotiations will be generating a sustainable level of defence spending beyond 2020. Several parties in parliament have argued in favour of a substantial increase during the 2020s, aimed at reaching 2% of GDP in the latter half of the decade.

As late as 2000 Sweden spent 2% of GDP on defence, according to *Military Balance* figures. Any government would need significant political will to today pursue similar funding aspirations. And were such a funding boost to transpire, the challenge for the Swedish Armed Forces would then be to absorb the effective doubling of its budget at the same time as transforming its defence posture.

UNITED KINGDOM

The United Kingdom's armed forces retain significant deployable combat power, but under-staffing and a forward equipment programme that has been labelled 'unaffordable' limit their current and future military capabilities. While UK Defence Secretary Gavin Williamson has announced a 'Modernising Defence Programme', the likelihood of acquiring the funds necessary to deliver this appears low, raising the possibility of further reductions.

The 2010 UK Strategic Defence and Security Review (SDSR) reduced the UK armed forces' conventional military capability by about one-third, and the judgement that the country's defence-policy goals and equipment programmes were unaffordable led to a reduction in military ambition. However, the 2015 SDSR resulted in the decision to invest in equipment modernisation in order to deliver the more capable 'Joint Force 2025'. Orders were placed for F-35B *Lightning* II Joint Strike Fighters, AH-64E *Apache* helicopters, MQ-9B *Sky Guardian* (dubbed *Protector* in UK service) uninhabited aerial vehicles (UAVs) and P-8A *Poseidon* maritime-patrol aircraft. The financial strategy to achieve this was based on 0.5% real-terms growth to the defence budget each year, more effective control of equipment-programme-cost growth and ambitious targets for internal efficiency savings.

Modernising defence

By late 2017, a year after the UK National Security Council concluded that threats from domestic terrorism, cyberspace, and Russia's military and 'hybrid' challenges were materialising more rapidly than envisaged, it was clear that the defence programme was again running into financial trouble. One reason was that the 2016 referendum vote to leave the European Union devalued the pound and increased the cost of buying foreign equipment. Another was that the costs of some future equipment programmes, particularly submarine and nuclear capabilities, were growing faster than anticipated, while many of the Ministry of Defence's (MoD's) efficiency savings had not materialised.

In January 2018, Williamson announced that he would lead a 'Modernising Defence Programme' scrutinising the MoD and its business and equipment-procurement processes, in order to identify savings and ways to increase efficiency. Another strand of this review is to decide on the UK's current and future capabilities. Williamson has said he would press for more funds, while he and the service chiefs have made explicit statements about the increasing Russian threat to the UK and its forces. At the time of writing, it was unclear when this plan would be published.

However, in November 2018 the UK's National Audit Office assessed the equipment plan as 'unaffordable', pointing towards a major shortfall in the forward equipment programme's funding. The £186.4-billion (US$249bn) plan had an affordability gap of at least £7.0bn (US$9.4bn), of which £5.9bn (US$7.9bn) will occur in the next four years. The MoD is looking for efficiency and costs-saving measures as a result of these funding challenges. During 2018, leaks indicated three operational-capability-reduction packages under consideration. The combination of an unaffordable equipment plan, a high proportion of new equipment projects being at risk and increasing levels of under-staffing raise difficult choices for the MoD, with a high probability of further cuts to the armed forces' conventional capability. These circumstances also increase the considerable challenge of funding any capability enhancements that might be proposed by the Modernising Defence Programme.

Equipment and operations

Amid this challenging financial environment, the UK nonetheless continued to order and introduce new equipment into service. In 2018, fixed-wing trials began for HMS *Queen Elizabeth*. The carrier transited to the US east coast where the UK's newly acquired F-35B aircraft landed on the vessel for the first time. The MoD also announced it would procure the E-7 airborne early-warning aircraft and rejoin the *Boxer* armoured-vehicle programme for its Mechanised Infantry Vehicle requirement. Together with *Ajax* tracked vehicles, the wheeled *Boxer* is envisaged as being a key component of the army's future Strike

▼ Figure 7 **UK: selected equipment reductions, 1989 and 2018**

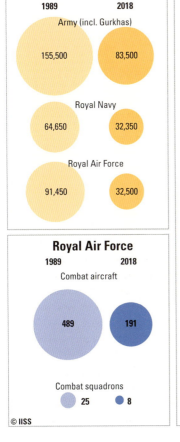

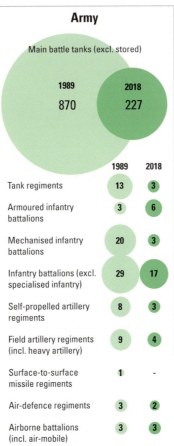

Figure 8 *Queen Elizabeth*-class aircraft carriers

HMS *Queen Elizabeth* and its sister ship *Prince of Wales* will, in full carrier-strike configuration, offer a power-projection capability far greater than that of their immediate predecessors, and probably second only to US Navy strike carriers. Studies to replace the *Invincible*-class light aircraft carriers began in the mid-1990s. The 1998 Strategic Defence Review announced plans for two new larger vessels, able to carry up to 50 aircraft. The project was controversial from the start and suffered multiple delays and cost increases. The two ships themselves are unique for their size (of 65,000 tonnes) in being configured for short take-off and vertical landing (STOVL) without catapults or arrestor gear. Some critics regard this as sub-optimal, because of the relatively short range and payload limitations of the F-35B STOVL variant of the Joint Strike Fighter, as well as the ships' inability to accommodate conventional fixed-wing airborne early-warning aircraft. Furthermore, there are doubts as to whether they will regularly deploy their full complement (at least 36) of F-35s. The 2015 Strategic Defence and Security Review announced that the ships would be given enhanced amphibious assault carrier (LPH) features likely to include improved accommodation and equipment facilities for an embarked force. There is some concern over using such high-value platforms in the LPH role, and that adding such a requirement could have a detrimental effect on the development of a full carrier-strike capability. Nevertheless, it seems likely that they will be employed as more flexible platforms for joint operations than traditional carriers. Notwithstanding an abortive plan in 2010 to fit them with catapults and arrestor gear, this remains an option during their expected 50-year service lives – not least to accommodate new uninhabited air systems – and they possess features to enable such adaption.

Briefing rooms
- Integrated and comprehensive complex
- Optimised aviation-mission planning

Integrated electric propulsion
- Two gas turbines
- Four diesel generators
- 112MW power
- Maximum speed of 27+ knots
- Capacity for future systems, including electromagnetic catapult and directed-energy weapons

Weapons
- Magazines
- Highly automated weapons-handling system
- Significant reduction in crew requirement

Crewing
- Lean crewing with extensive use of remote systems to reduce full-life costs
- Original complement of 679 likely to rise to nearer 900, with an air group of 900
- Reduced crewing an area of innovation and potential operational risk
- New USS *Gerald R. Ford* (at 100,000 tonnes) will likely have a crew of about 2,600 and an air group of 2,400

Twin-island design
- Allows separation of main propulsion units for increased survivability
- Enables better location of flying control in aft island for improved flight-deck operations

Ski-jump
- Built at 12.5 degrees
- Improves F-35B short-take-off performance

© IISS

Europe 85

▼ Figure 8 *Queen Elizabeth*-class aircraft carriers

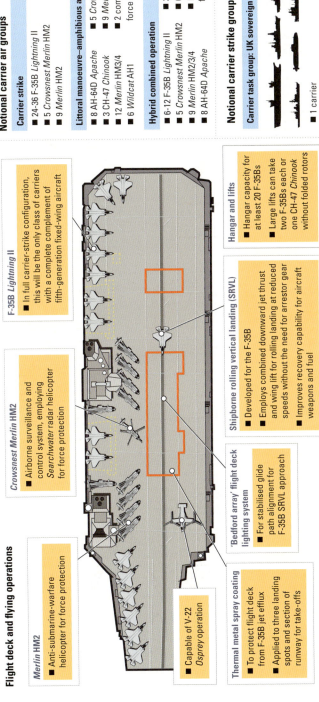

Notional carrier air groups

Carrier strike
- 24–36 F-35B *Lightning* II
- 5 *Crowsnest* Merlin HM2
- 9 Merlin HM2

Littoral manoeuvre–amphibious assault carrier (LPH)
- 8 AH-64D *Apache*
- 3 CH-47 *Chinook*
- 12 Merlin HM3/4
- 6 Wildcat AH1
- 5 *Crowsnest* Merlin HM2
- 9 Merlin HM2
- 2 company embarked force (250 personnel)

Hybrid combined operation
- 6–12 F-35B *Lightning* II
- 5 *Crowsnest* Merlin HM2
- 9 Merlin HM2/3/4
- 8 AH-64D *Apache*
- 3 CH-47 *Chinook*
- 6 Wildcat AH1
- Embarked special forces

Notional carrier strike groups

Carrier task group: UK sovereign
- 1 carrier
- 2 Type-45 destroyers
- 2 Type-23/-26 frigates
- 1 *Astute*-class submarine
- 2 auxiliaries

Coalition task group: possible additional units
- 2 US *Arleigh Burke*-class destroyers
- 2 European frigates

The Royal Navy has postulated a sovereign carrier group as above for a high-threat environment. The more contested the environment, the more support, including from allies, that would be required. Two carriers will allow a continuous availability of one ship, but operating both together would likely overstretch RN resources for the foreseeable future, except in an extreme emergency.

Flight deck and flying operations

Merlin HM2
- Anti-submarine-warfare helicopter for force protection

Thermal metal spray coating
- To protect flight deck from F-35B jet efflux
- Applied to three landing spots and section of runway for take-offs

- Capable of V-22 *Osprey* operation

'Bedford array' flight deck lighting system
- For stabilised glide path alignment for F-35B SRVL approach

Crowsnest Merlin HM2
- Airborne surveillance and control system, employing *Searchwater* radar helicopter for force protection

F-35B *Lightning* II
- In full carrier-strike configuration, this will be the only class of carriers with a complete complement of fifth-generation fixed-wing aircraft

Hangar and lifts
- Hangar capacity for at least 20 F-35Bs
- Large lifts can take two F-35Bs each or one CH-47 *Chinook* without folded rotors

Shipborne rolling vertical landing (SRVL)
- Developed for the F-35B
- Employs combined downward jet thrust and wing lift for rolling landing at reduced speeds without the need for arrestor gear
- Improves recovery capability for aircraft weapons and fuel

UK aircraft-carrier capability-regeneration timeline, 2016–26

2016	*Crowsnest* Airborne Surveillance and Control contract signed
2017	*Queen Elizabeth* commissioned; *Prince of Wales* officially named; *Queen Elizabeth* begins sea trials
2018	*Queen Elizabeth* F-35B flying trials begin
2019	Royal Navy accepts *Prince of Wales* from builders
2020	*Crowsnest* initial operating capability; Carrier strike initial operating capability
2021	*Queen Elizabeth* first operational deployment with UK and possibly US Marine Corps F-35Bs embarked
2022	*Crowsnest* full operating capability
2023	*Prince of Wales* full operating capability in LPH role; Carrier strike full operating capability (24 F-35Bs available for carrier operations)
2026	Carrier-Enabled Power Projection full operating capability (full range of capabilities and full task group with new support shipping)

Brigades. Although the defence secretary said that there were no plans to decommission the two landing-platform-dock (LPD) amphibious ships, the landing-platform-helicopter (LPH) HMS *Ocean* was decommissioned and sold to Brazil.

While the UK's global deployments persist, personnel strength has continued to fall across the services. Under-staffing increased by 1.3% in 2018, an overall deficit of 6.2%, compared with 3.3% in 2016. There are particular deficiencies in numbers of pilots, intelligence specialists and engineers, especially nuclear engineers. These shortages result, in part, from pay being below comparable civilian levels. The MoD claims it has sufficient personnel to meet its operational requirements, and while the army could probably draw on its reserve, the navy and air force reserves are smaller and lack many key capabilities.

Uncertain prospects

It is unlikely that efficiency savings alone will release funds of the order required to tackle the current financial difficulties. The July 2018 Major Projects Review said that there is considerable risk in many future equipment projects, with almost half being graded amber ('successful delivery is in doubt') or red ('successful delivery appears to be unachievable'), the latter including future nuclear reactors, *Astute* submarines, *Protector* UAVs and the upgraded *Warrior* infantry fighting vehicle. Many of the programmes at risk are crucial to delivering the capabilities required by Joint Force 2025. Furthermore, without significant improvements in pay, allowances, accommodation and training, the chances of the services approaching full strength are likely to be remote.

Financial commitments to other areas by the government, and uncertainty over the near-term trajectory of the economy after the UK withdraws from the EU, make it unlikely that there will be a significant increase in the defence budget. This reduces the MoD's room for manoeuvre in balancing existing and future capability requirements, and means that further reductions to the conventional capabilities of the UK's armed forces may be likely.

Albania ALB

Albanian Lek		2017	2018	2019
GDP	lek	1.55tr	1.65tr	
	US$	13.1bn	15.1bn	
per capita	US$	4,545	5,261	
Growth	%	3.8	4.0	
Inflation	%	2.0	2.3	
Def exp [a]	lek	17.2bn	19.5bn	
	US$	145m	178m	
Def bdgt [b]	lek	13.0bn	14.3bn	15.7bn
	US$	110m	131m	
FMA (US)	US$	2.4m	0m	
US$1=lek		118.80	109.35	

[a] NATO definition

[b] Excludes military pensions

Population 3,057,220

Ethnic groups: Albanian 82.6%; Greek 0.9%; Romani 0.3%; Macedonian 0.2%; other or unspecified 15.7%

Age	0–14	15–19	20–24	25–29	30–64	65 plus
Male	9.5%	4.2%	4.9%	4.8%	20.5%	5.6%
Female	8.5%	3.8%	4.6%	4.6%	22.5%	6.3%

Capabilities

Principal missions for Albania's armed forces include territorial defence, internal security, disaster-relief tasks, and small-scale peacekeeping or training deployments. Tirana is looking to improve the operational readiness of its mechanised infantry battalion in order to fulfil obligations to NATO, which it joined in 2009. Other priorities include improving border management and information sharing to prevent transnational crime and terrorism. Greece and Italy police Albania's airspace. Albania contributes to EU missions but does not possess an independent expeditionary capability. Most Soviet-era equipment has been sold. Limited defence modernisation under the Long-term Development Plan 2016–25 is proceeding, but progress has so far been restricted to small numbers of helicopters. However, the contract for the purchase of the Integrated Surveillance System for Albanian Airspace was approved in November 2017. The navy is expected to receive upgrades to vessels that have been or still are deployed in the Aegean Sea. In late 2018, the prime minister announced that NATO will invest in modernising the Kucove air base. Albania has little in the way of domestic defence industry, with no ability to design and manufacture modern military platforms. Nevertheless, the country has some publicly owned defence companies that are capable of producing small arms, explosives and ammunition.

ACTIVE 8,000 (Land Force 3,000 Naval Force 650 Air Force 550 Other 3,800) **Paramilitary 500**

ORGANISATIONS BY SERVICE

Land Force 3,000
FORCES BY ROLE
SPECIAL FORCES
  1 SF bn
  1 cdo bn
MANOEUVRE
Light
  3 lt inf bn
COMBAT SUPPORT
  1 mor bty
  1 NBC coy
EQUIPMENT BY TYPE
ARMOURED FIGHTING VEHICLES
  APC • **PPV** 3 *Maxxpro Plus*
ARTILLERY • **MOR** 93: **82mm** 81; **120mm** 12

Naval Force 650
EQUIPMENT BY TYPE
PATROL AND COASTAL COMBATANTS • **PBF** 5
  Archangel

Coast Guard
EQUIPMENT BY TYPE
PATROL AND COASTAL COMBATANTS 22
  PB 9: 4 *Iluria* (Damen Stan Patrol 4207); 3 Mk3 *Sea Spectre*; 2 (other)
  PBR 13: 4 Type-227; 1 Type-246; 1 Type-303; 7 Type-2010

Air Force 550
EQUIPMENT BY TYPE
HELICOPTERS
  TPT 27: **Medium** 4 AS532AL *Cougar*; **Light** 22: 1 AW109; 5 Bell 205 (AB-205); 7 Bell 206C (AB-206C); 8 Bo-105; 2 H145

Regional Support Brigade 700
FORCES BY ROLE
COMBAT SUPPORT
  1 cbt spt bde (1 engr bn, 1 (rescue) engr bn, 1 CIMIC det)

Military Police
FORCES BY ROLE
COMBAT SUPPORT
  1 MP bn
EQUIPMENT BY TYPE
ARMOURED FIGHTING VEHICLES
  AUV IVECO LMV

Logistics Brigade 1,200
FORCES BY ROLE
COMBAT SERVICE SUPPORT
  1 log bde (1 tpt bn, 2 log bn)

DEPLOYMENT

AFGHANISTAN: NATO • *Operation Resolute Support* 136
BOSNIA-HERZEGOVINA: EU • EUFOR • *Operation Althea* 1
LATVIA: NATO • Enhanced Forward Presence 21; 1 EOD pl
MALI: EU • EUTM Mali 4
MEDITERRANEAN SEA: NATO • SNMG 2: 1 PB
SERBIA: NATO • KFOR 28; **OSCE** • Kosovo 3
UKRAINE: OSCE • Ukraine 9

FOREIGN FORCES

Armenia OSCE 1
Austria OSCE 1
Bosnia-Herzegovina OSCE 1
Bulgaria OSCE 1
Canada OSCE 1
Georgia OSCE 1
Germany OSCE 3
Italy OSCE 1
Macedonia (FYROM) OSCE 2
Moldova OSCE 1
Serbia OSCE 1
United Kingdom OSCE 2

Austria AUT

Euro €		2017	2018	2019
GDP	€	370bn	387bn	
	US$	417bn	459bn	
per capita	US$	47,347	51,708	
Growth	%	3.0	2.8	
Inflation	%	2.2	2.0	
Def bdgt [a]	€	2.80bn	2.85bn	2.89bn
	US$	3.16bn	3.38bn	
US$1=€		0.89	0.84	

[a] Includes military pensions

Population	8,793,370				
Age	0–14	15–19	20–24	25–29	30–64	65 plus
Male	7.2%	2.6%	3.1%	3.3%	24.4%	8.4%
Female	6.8%	2.5%	3.0%	3.3%	24.6%	10.9%

Capabilities

Austria remains constitutionally non-aligned, but is an EU member and actively engaged in the Common Security and Defence Policy. Defence-policy objectives are based on the 2013 National Security Strategy, the 2014 Defence Strategy and the 2015 Military Strategy, including providing military capabilities to maintain sovereignty and territorial integrity, to enable military assistance to the civil authorities and to participate in crisis-management missions abroad. A 2017 defence plan included structural changes at the operational and tactical command-and-control level; Vienna is also planning to boost its rapid-response capability and to stand up new Jäger battalions. In addition, army brigades will specialise according to roles, such as rapid response, mechanised (heavy), air-mobile (light) and mountain warfare. Initial steps were taken in 2017 but implementation appears incomplete. While not a NATO member, Austria joined NATO's Partnership for Peace framework in 1995 and has since participated in NATO-led crisis-management operations. In April 2018, the government announced modest budget increases to support training and exercises. The level of ambition for crisis response is to be able to deploy and sustain a minimum (on average) of 1,100 troops. In August 2018, several options were discussed to replace Austria's *Typhoon* aircraft, including upgrades to the existing fleet as well as replacement of the existing airframes. Protected mobility is a modernisation priority for 2018 and 2019, and a range of armoured vehicles are due to enter service. Austria's defence-industrial base is comprised of some 100 companies with significant niche capabilities and international ties in the areas of weapons and ammunitions, communications equipment and vehicles.

ACTIVE 21,200 (Land Forces 11,550 Air 2,700 Support 6,950)

Conscript liability 6 months recruit trg, 30 days reservist refresher trg for volunteers; 120–150 days additional for officers, NCOs and specialists. Authorised maximum wartime strength of 55,000

RESERVE 157,900 (Joint structured 27,700; Joint unstructured 130,200)

Some 12,000 reservists a year undergo refresher trg in tranches

ORGANISATIONS BY SERVICE

Land Forces 11,550
FORCES BY ROLE
MANOEUVRE
  Armoured
  1 (4th) armd inf bde (1 recce/SP arty bn, 1 tk bn, 2 armd inf bn, 1 spt bn)
  Mechanised
  1 (3rd) mech inf bde (1 recce/SP arty bn, 2 mech inf bn, 1 mot inf bn; 1 cbt engr bn, 1 spt bn)
  Light
  1 (7th) lt inf bde (1 recce bn, 3 inf bn, 1 cbt engr bn, 1 spt bn)
  1 (6th) mtn inf bde (3 mtn inf bn, 1 cbt engr bn, 1 spt bn)
EQUIPMENT BY TYPE
ARMOURED FIGHTING VEHICLES
  MBT 56 *Leopard* 2A4
  AIFV 112 *Ulan*
  APC • APC (W) 78 *Pandur*
  AUV 157: 29 *Dingo* 2; 128 IVECO LMV
ENGINEERING & MAINTENANCE VEHICLES
  ARV 30: 20 4KH7FA-SB; 10 M88A1
NBC VEHICLES 12 *Dingo* 2 AC NBC
ANTI-TANK/ANTI-INFRASTRUCTURE
  MSL • MANPATS *Bill* 2 (PAL 2000)
ARTILLERY 114
  SP 155mm 24 M109A5ÖE
  MOR 120mm 90 sGrW 86 (10 more in store)

Air Force 2,700

The Air Force is part of Joint Forces Comd and consists of 2 bde; Air Support Comd and Airspace Surveillance Comd
FORCES BY ROLE
FIGHTER
  2 sqn with *Typhoon*
ISR
  1 sqn with PC-6B *Turbo Porter*
TRANSPORT
  1 sqn with C-130K *Hercules*
TRAINING
  1 trg sqn with Saab 105Oe*
  1 trg sqn with PC-7 *Turbo Trainer*
TRANSPORT HELICOPTER
  2 sqn with Bell 212 (AB-212)
  1 sqn with OH-58B *Kiowa*

1 sqn with S-70A *Black Hawk*
2 sqn with SA316/SA319 *Alouette* III
AIR DEFENCE
2 bn
1 radar bn
EQUIPMENT BY TYPE
AIRCRAFT 33 combat capable
FTR 15 Eurofighter *Typhoon* Tranche 1
TPT 11: **Medium** 3 C-130K *Hercules*; **Light** 8 PC-6B *Turbo Porter*
TRG 32: 12 PC-7 *Turbo Trainer*; 18 Saab 105Oe*; 2 DA40NG
HELICOPTERS
MRH 24 SA316/SA319 *Alouette* III
ISR 10 OH-58B *Kiowa*
TPT 32: **Medium** 9 S-70A-42 *Black Hawk*; **Light** 23 Bell 212 (AB-212)
AIR DEFENCE
SAM • Point-defence *Mistral*
GUNS 35mm 24 Z-FIAK system (6 more in store)
AIR-LAUNCHED MISSILES • AAM • IIR IRIS-T

Special Operations Forces

FORCES BY ROLE
SPECIAL FORCES
2 SF gp
1 SF gp (reserve)

Support 6,950

Support forces comprise Joint Services Support Command and several agencies, academies and schools

Cyber

The implementation plan for the 2013 National Cyber Security Strategy is nearly complete; the strategy will be reviewed in the near term. An Austrian cyber-security law, based on the EU Network and Information Systems (NIS) Directive, took effect in late 2018, and a national NIS authority is to be created. A national Cyber Security Steering Group coordinates cyber-security-related matters on the strategic-operational level on a whole-of-government approach. The defence ministry is responsible for strategic planning and direction. The ministry's Cyber Defence Board (led by the cyber coordinator) provides strategic planning and direction. The defence structures/organisation within the Cyber Defence Centre reached full operating capability at the end of 2017. A CIS and Cyber Security Centre will be subordinated to the Joint Support and Enabling Command and will assume overall responsibility for cyber defence at the operational level. There is an operational centralised Computer Security Incident Response Capability, based on the armed forces' milCERT.

DEPLOYMENT

AFGHANISTAN: NATO • *Operation Resolute Support* 17
ALBANIA: OSCE • Albania 1
BOSNIA-HERZEGOVINA: EU • EUFOR • *Operation Althea* 344; 1 inf bn HQ; 2 inf coy; 1 hel unit
CYPRUS: UN • UNFICYP 5
LEBANON: UN • UNIFIL 182; 1 log coy
MALI: EU • EUTM Mali 12; UN • MINUSMA 3
MIDDLE EAST: UN • UNTSO 4 obs
MOLDOVA: OSCE • Moldova 1
SERBIA: NATO • KFOR 508; 1 recce coy; 2 mech inf coy; 1 log coy; OSCE • Kosovo 1
UKRAINE: OSCE • Ukraine 14
WESTERN SAHARA: UN • MINURSO 7 obs

Belgium BEL

Euro €		2017	2018	2019
GDP	€	437bn	452bn	
	US$	494bn	536bn	
per capita	US$	43,488	46,979	
Growth	%	1.7	1.5	
Inflation	%	2.2	2.2	
Def exp [a]	€	4.00bn	4.20bn	
	US$	4.51bn	4.98bn	
Def bdgt [b]	€	4.00bn	4.20bn	4.19bn
	US$	4.51bn	4.98bn	
US$1=€		0.89	0.84	

[a] NATO definition
[b] Includes military pensions

Population 11,570,762

Age	0–14	15–19	20–24	25–29	30–64	65 plus
Male	8.8%	2.8%	3.0%	3.3%	23.3%	8.1%
Female	8.4%	2.7%	2.9%	3.2%	23.1%	10.5%

Capabilities

In July 2016, the government published its strategic vision for defence up to 2030. Brussels intends to stabilise Belgium's defence effort and then provide for growth after 2020. It also envisages a reduced personnel component of around 25,000. However, a large number of impending service retirements means that a gradual increase in recruitment is planned. Belgium also continues to pursue high readiness levels and deployable niche capabilities. NATO membership is central to defence policy, as are the EU and the UN. Due to its limited force size, Belgium often collaborates with neighbours and has committed with Denmark and the Netherlands to form a composite combined special-operations command. Belgium can deploy forces for a small-scale overseas operation and maintains overseas deployments on EU and UN missions. The government is investing in short-term requirements related to aircraft readiness, personal equipment and land-forces vehicles. As part of the defence plan, the government envisages launching five investment projects for fighter aircraft, frigates, mine-countermeasures vessels, UAVs and land-combat vehicles. The air force has selected the F-35 *Lightning* II to replace its F-16s. Belgium has an advanced, export-focused defence industry, focusing on components and subcontracting, though in FN Herstal it has one of the world's largest manufacturers of small arms.

ACTIVE 26,550 (Army 9,750 Navy 1,450 Air 5,700 Medical Service 1,250 Joint Service 8,400)

RESERVE 5,100

ORGANISATIONS BY SERVICE

Land Component 9,750
FORCES BY ROLE
SPECIAL FORCES
  1 spec ops regt (1 SF gp, 1 cdo bn, 1 para bn)
MANOEUVRE
  Mechanised
  1 mech bde (1 ISR bn; 3 mech bn; 2 lt inf bn; 1 arty bn; 2 engr bn; 2 sigs gp; 2 log bn)
COMBAT SUPPORT
  1 EOD unit
  1 MP coy
COMBAT SERVICE SUPPORT
  1 log bn
EQUIPMENT BY TYPE
ARMOURED FIGHTING VEHICLES
  ASLT 18 *Piranha* III-C DF90
  RECCE 36 *Pandur Recce*
  IFV 19 *Piranha* III-C DF30
  APC • APC (W) 78: 64 *Piranha* III-C; 14 *Piranha* III-PC (CP)
  AUV 656: 220 *Dingo* 2 (inc 52 CP); 436 IVECO LMV
ENGINEERING & MAINTENANCE VEHICLES
  AEV 8 *Piranha* III-C
  ARV 13: 4 *Pandur*; 9 *Piranha* III-C
  VLB 4 *Leguan*
ANTI-TANK/ANTI-INFRASTRUCTURE
  MSL • MANPATS *Spike*-MR
ARTILLERY 60
  TOWED 105mm 14 LG1 MkII
  MOR 46: **81mm** 14; **120mm** 32

Naval Component 1,450
EQUIPMENT BY TYPE
PRINCIPAL SURFACE COMBATANTS 2
  FRIGATES • FFGHM 2 *Leopold* I (ex-NLD *Karel Doorman*) with 2 quad lnchr with *Harpoon* AShM, 1 16-cell Mk48 VLS with RIM-7P *Sea Sparrow* SAM, 4 single Mk32 324mm ASTT with Mk46 LWT, 1 *Goalkeeper* CIWS, 1 76mm gun (capacity 1 med hel)
PATROL AND COASTAL COMBATANTS
  PCC 2 *Castor*
MINE WARFARE • MINE COUNTERMEASURES
  MHC 5 *Flower* (*Tripartite*)
LOGISTICS AND SUPPORT 3
  AGFH 1 *Godetia* (log spt/comd) (capacity 1 *Alouette* III)
  AGOR 1 *Belgica*
  AXS 1 *Zenobe Gramme*

Naval Aviation
(part of the Air Component)
EQUIPMENT BY TYPE
HELICOPTERS
  ASW 4 NH90 NFH
  MRH 3 SA316B *Alouette* III

Air Component 5,700
FORCES BY ROLE
FIGHTER/GROUND ATTACK/ISR
  4 sqn with F-16AM/BM *Fighting Falcon*
SEARCH & RESCUE
  1 sqn with *Sea King* Mk48
TRANSPORT
  1 sqn with A321; ERJ-135 LR; ERJ-145 LR; *Falcon* 900B
  1 sqn with C-130H *Hercules*
TRAINING
  1 OCU sqn with F-16AM/BM *Fighting Falcon*
  1 sqn with SF-260D/M
  1 BEL/FRA unit with *Alpha Jet**
  1 OCU unit with AW109
TRANSPORT HELICOPTER
  2 sqn with AW109 (ISR)
ISR UAV
  1 sqn with RQ-5A *Hunter* (B-*Hunter*)
EQUIPMENT BY TYPE
AIRCRAFT 76 combat capable
  FTR 58: 48 F-16AM *Fighting Falcon*; 10 F-16BM *Fighting Falcon*
  TPT 16: **Medium** 10 C-130H *Hercules*; **Light** 4: 2 ERJ-135 LR; 2 ERJ-145 LR; **PAX** 2: 1 A321; 1 *Falcon* 900B
  TRG 50: 18 *Alpha Jet**; 9 SF-260D; 23 SF-260M
HELICOPTERS
  ASW 4 NH90 NFH opcon Navy
  MRH 3 SA316B *Alouette* III opcon Navy
  SAR 3 *Sea King* Mk48 (to be replaced by NH90 NFH)
  TPT 17: **Medium** 4 NH90 TTH; **Light** 13 AW109 (ISR) (7 more in store)
UNMANNED AERIAL VEHICLES
  ISR • Heavy 12 RQ-5A *Hunter* (B-*Hunter*) (1 more in store)
AIR-LAUNCHED MISSILES
  AAM • IR AIM-9M *Sidewinder*; **IRR** AIM-9X *Sidewinder* II; **ARH** AIM-120B AMRAAM
BOMBS
  Laser-guided: GBU-10/GBU-12 *Paveway* II; GBU-24 *Paveway* III
  INS/GPS guided: GBU-31 JDAM; GBU-38 JDAM; GBU-54 Laser JDAM (dual-mode)

Medical Service 1,250
FORCES BY ROLE
COMBAT SERVICE SUPPORT
  4 med unit
  1 fd hospital
EQUIPMENT BY TYPE
ARMOURED FIGHTING VEHICLES
  APC • APC (W) 10: 4 *Pandur* (amb); 6 *Piranha* III-C (amb)
  AUV 10 *Dingo* 2 (amb)

Cyber
The defence ministry released the Belgian Defence Cyber Security Strategy in 2014, outlining three pillars of its cyber-security capability: Cyber Defence, Cyber Intelligence and Cyber Counter-Offensive, with 'full operational capacity' by 2020. A 'Strategic Vision for Defence' covering the period 2016–30 was published in June 2016. In this, the cyber mandate was updated, including not only cyber

defence and intelligence but also offensive capabilities. According to the defence ministry, this capability must, on the one hand, ensure an appropriate level of cyber security for Belgian weapons and communication systems, while on the other it must also be able to identify, manipulate or distort an opponent's networks and systems. A cyber-intelligence pillar guarantees the necessary situational understanding to guarantee freedom of action. The defence ministry is developing its Cyber Security Operations Centre, which provides a second layer of cyber defence. All other types of cyber operations (response, exploitation, influence, offensive) are the responsibility of the centralised cyber capability.

DEPLOYMENT

AFGHANISTAN: NATO • *Operation Resolute Support* 78

DEMOCRATIC REPUBLIC OF THE CONGO: UN • MONUSCO 1; 1 obs

FRANCE: NATO • Air Component 28 *Alpha Jet* located at Cazaux/Tours

IRAQ: *Operation Inherent Resolve* 30

JORDAN: *Operation Inherent Resolve (Desert Falcon)* 30

LITHUANIA: NATO • Enhanced Forward Presence 100; 1 tpt coy; **NATO** • Baltic Air Policing 4 F-16AM *Fighting Falcon*

MALI: EU • EUTM Mali 20; **UN** • MINUSMA 130; 1 recce unit; 1 tpt flt with 1 C-130H *Hercules*

MIDDLE EAST: UN • UNTSO 1 obs

NORTH SEA: NATO • SNMCMG 1: 1 MHC

UKRAINE: OSCE • Ukraine 1

FOREIGN FORCES

United States US European Command: 900

Bosnia-Herzegovina BIH

Convertible Mark			2017	2018	2019
GDP		mark	31.5bn	33.0bn	
		US$	18.2bn	20.0bn	
per capita		US$	5,181	5,704	
Growth		%	3.0	3.2	
Inflation		%	1.2	1.4	
Def bdgt		mark	286m	284m	
		US$	165m	172m	
FMA (US)		US$	4m	0m	
US$1=mark			1.74	1.65	

Population   3,849,891

Ethnic groups: Bosniac 50.1% Serb 30.7% Croat 15.4% Other or unspecified 3.7%

Age	0–14	15–19	20–24	25–29	30–64	65 plus
Male	6.9%	2.8%	3.1%	3.7%	26.5%	5.7%
Female	6.4%	2.7%	2.9%	3.5%	27.0%	8.8%

Capabilities

The armed forces' primary goals are to defend territorial integrity and contribute to peacekeeping missions and civilian-support operations. Bosnia-Herzegovina joined NATO's Partnership for Peace in 2006 and a Membership Action Plan was presented in 2010. Its aspiration to join NATO has been delayed due to unresolved defence-property issues. The country is reforming its armed forces and modernising its equipment in accordance with its Defence Review, Development and Modernisation Plan for 2017–27 and its NATO aspirations. The armed forces are professional and represent all three ethnic groups. However, low salaries likely negatively affect recruitment and retention. Bosnia-Herzegovina contributes to NATO missions and has deployed personnel to *Operation Resolute Support* in Afghanistan, but the armed forces have no capacity to independently deploy and self-sustain beyond national borders. The inventory comprises mainly ageing Soviet-era equipment. There is an aspiration to procure new Western armoured vehicles and helicopters, but financial constraints have limited progress. Bosnia-Herzegovina has little in the way of a domestic defence industry, with only the capability to produce small arms, ammunition and explosives.

ACTIVE 10,500 (Armed Forces 10,500)

ORGANISATIONS BY SERVICE

Armed Forces 10,500

1 ops comd; 1 spt comd

FORCES BY ROLE
MANOEUVRE
  Light
  3 inf bde (1 recce coy, 3 inf bn, 1 arty bn)
COMBAT SUPPORT
  1 cbt spt bde (1 tk bn, 1 engr bn, 1 EOD bn, 1 int bn, 1 MP bn, 1 CBRN coy, 1 sigs bn)
COMBAT SERVICE SUPPORT
  1 log comd (5 log bn)
EQUIPMENT BY TYPE
ARMOURED FIGHTING VEHICLES
  MBT 45 M60A3
  APC • **APC (T)** 20 M113A2
ENGINEERING & MAINTENANCE VEHICLES
  VLB MTU
  MW *Bozena*
ANTI-TANK/ANTI-INFRASTRUCTURE • **MSL**
   SP 60: 8 9P122 *Malyutka*; 9 9P133 *Malyutka*; 32 BOV-1; 11 M-92
   MANPATS 9K11 *Malyutka* (AT-3 *Sagger*); 9K111 *Fagot* (AT-4 *Spigot*); 9K115 *Metis* (AT-7 *Saxhorn*); HJ-8; *Milan*
ARTILLERY 224
  TOWED 122mm 100 D-30
  MRL 122mm 24 APRA-40
  MOR 120mm 100 M-75

Air Force and Air Defence Brigade 800

FORCES BY ROLE
HELICOPTER
  1 sqn with Bell 205; Mi-8MTV *Hip*; Mi-17 *Hip* H
  1 sqn with Mi-8 *Hip*; SA-342H/L *Gazelle* (HN-42/45M)
AIR DEFENCE
  1 AD bn

EQUIPMENT BY TYPE
AIRCRAFT
FGA (7 J-22 *Orao* in store)
ATK (6 J-1 (J-21) *Jastreb*; 3 TJ-1(NJ-21) *Jastreb* all in store)
ISR (2 RJ-1 (IJ-21) *Jastreb** in store)
TRG (1 G-4 *Super Galeb* (N-62)* in store)
HELICOPTERS
MRH 13: 4 Mi-8MTV *Hip*; 1 Mi-17 *Hip* H; 1 SA-341H *Gazelle* (HN-42); 7 SA-342L *Gazelle* (HN-45M)
TPT 21: **Medium** 8 Mi-8 *Hip* **Light** 13 Bell 205 (UH-1H *Iroquois*)
TRG 1 Mi-34 *Hermit*
AIR DEFENCE
SAM
Short-range 20 2K12 *Kub* (SA-6 *Gainful*)
Point-defence 7+: 6 9K31 *Strela*-1 (SA-9 *Gaskin*); 9K34 *Strela*-3 (SA-14 *Gremlin*); 1 9K35M3 *Strela*-10M3 (SA-13 *Gopher*); 9K310 (SA-16 *Gimlet*)
GUNS 764
SP 169: **20mm** 9 BOV-3 SPAAG; **30mm** 154: 38 M53; 116 M-53/59; **57mm** 6 ZSU-57-2
TOWED 586: **20mm** 468: 32 M55A2, 4 M38, 1 M55 A2B1, 293 M55A3/A4, 138 M75; **23mm** 29 ZU-23,**30mm** 33 M-53; **37mm** 7 Type-55; **40mm** 49: 31 L60, 16 L70, 2 M-12

DEPLOYMENT
AFGHANISTAN: NATO • *Operation Resolute Support* 63
ALBANIA: OSCE • Albania 1
ARMENIA/AZERBAIJAN: OSCE • Minsk Conference 1
CENTRAL AFRICAN REPUBLIC: EU • EUTM RCA 2
DEMOCRATIC REPUBLIC OF THE CONGO: UN • MONUSCO 3 obs
MALI: UN • MINUSMA 2
SERBIA: OSCE • Kosovo 10
UKRAINE: OSCE • Ukraine 50

FOREIGN FORCES
Part of EUFOR – *Operation Althea* unless otherwise stated
Albania 1
Austria 344; 1 inf bn HQ; 2 inf coy
Azerbaijan OSCE 1
Bulgaria 11
Canada OSCE 2
Chile 15
Czech Republic 2 • OSCE 1
Germany OSCE 1
Greece 2
Hungary 164; 1 inf coy • OSCE 1
Ireland 5 • OSCE 1
Italy 5 • OSCE 6
Macedonia (FYORM) 3
Moldova OSCE 1
Netherlands OSCE 1
Poland 39
Romania 48
Russia OSCE 2
Serbia OSCE 1
Slovakia 41
Slovenia 14
Spain 2 • OSCE 3
Switzerland 21
Turkey 249; 1 inf coy
United Kingdom 2; • OSCE 3
United States OSCE 6

Bulgaria BLG

Bulgarian Lev L		2017	2018	2019
GDP	L	98.6bn	105bn	
	US$	56.9bn	63.7bn	
per capita	US$	8,077	9,080	
Growth	%	3.6	3.6	
Inflation	%	1.2	2.6	
Def exp [a]	L	1.26bn	1.64bn	
	US$	724m	991m	
Def bdgt [b]	L	1.17bn	1.19bn	
	US$	677m	724m	
FMA (US)	US$	5m	0m	
US$1=L		1.73	1.65	

[a] NATO definition
[b] Excludes military pensions

Population	7,057,504					
Age	0–14	15–19	20–24	25–29	30–64	65 plus
Male	7.5%	2.6%	2.6%	3.3%	25.2%	7.8%
Female	7.1%	2.2%	2.4%	3.1%	25.0%	11.5%

Capabilities

The armed forces' main priority is defending state sovereignty and territorial integrity. Bulgaria is in the process of implementing the Programme for the Development of the Defence Capabilities of the Bulgarian Armed Forces 2020. In March 2018, the National Assembly adopted a new National Security Strategy that includes cyber and transportation security for the first time, while attention was also paid to hybrid threats. A NATO member, Bulgaria enjoys close ties with the US. With only limited numbers of combat aircraft itself, Bulgaria's airspace is protected by NATO's Air Policing Mission. It has reached several bilateral defence-cooperation agreements with regional states. Sofia has increased the military retirement age and reduced the maximum age for recruitment in an attempt to cope with personnel shortages. Training is prioritised for those units intended for international operations and those with certain readiness levels declared to NATO and the EU. Bulgaria regularly trains and exercises with NATO partners and regional allies. The country contributes to NATO and EU missions but has little logistics-support capability. Despite long-term plans for reform, the armed forces still rely heavily on ageing Soviet-era equipment. In May 2018, Bulgaria approved the purchase of new or used fighter aircraft to replace its MiG-29s, as well as the acquisition of core combat capabilities to enable the formation of battalion battlegroups within the mechanised brigades. The navy is prioritising the procurement of a multi-purpose patrol vessel and the modernisation of its frigates to boost its presence in the Black Sea. Bulgaria's defence industry exports small arms but has limited capacity to design and manufacture platforms.

ACTIVE 31,300 (Army 15,300 Navy 3,450 Air 6,700 Central Staff 5,850)

RESERVE 3,000 (Joint 3,000)

ORGANISATIONS BY SERVICE

Army 16,300
FORCES BY ROLE
MANOEUVRE
Reconnaissance
  1 recce bn
Mechanised
  2 mech bde (4 mech inf bn, 1 SP arty bn, 1 cbt engr bn, 1 log bn, 1 SAM bn)
Light
  1 mtn inf regt
COMBAT SUPPORT
1 arty regt (1 fd arty bn, 1 MRL bn)
1 engr regt (1 cbt engr bn, 1 ptn br bn, 1 engr spt bn)
1 NBC bn
COMBAT SERVICE SUPPORT
1 log regt
EQUIPMENT BY TYPE
ARMOURED FIGHTING VEHICLES
  MBT 90 T-72M1/M2
  IFV 160: 90 BMP-1; 70 BMP-23
  APC 120
    APC (T) 100 MT-LB
    APC (W) 20 BTR-60
  AUV 17 M1117 ASV
ENGINEERING & MAINTENANCE VEHICLES
  AEV MT-LB
  ARV T-54/T-55; MTP-1; MT-LB
  VLB BLG67; TMM
ANTI-TANK/ANTI-INFRASTRUCTURE
  MSL
    SP 24 9P148 *Konkurs* (AT-5 *Spandrel*)
    MANPATS 9K111 *Fagot* (AT-4 *Spigot*); 9K111-1 *Konkurs* (AT-5 *Spandrel*); (9K11 *Malyutka* (AT-3 *Sagger*) in store)
  GUNS 126: **85mm** (150 D-44 in store); **100mm** 126 MT-12
ARTILLERY 311
  SP 122mm 48 2S1
  TOWED 152mm 24 D-20
  MRL 122mm 24 BM-21
  MOR 120mm 215 2S11 SP *Tundzha*
SURFACE-TO-SURFACE MISSILE LAUNCHERS
  SRBM • Conventional 9K79 *Tochka* (SS-21 *Scarab*)
AIR DEFENCE
  SAM • Point-defence 9K32 *Strela* (SA-7 *Grail*)‡; 24 9K33 *Osa* (SA-8 *Gecko*)
  GUNS 400
    SP 23mm ZSU-23-4
    TOWED 23mm ZU-23; **57mm** S-60; **100mm** KS-19

Navy 3,450
EQUIPMENT BY TYPE
PRINCIPAL SURFACE COMBATANTS • FRIGATES • 4
  FFM 3 *Drazki* (ex-BEL *Wielingen*) with 1 octuple Mk29 GMLS with RIM-7P *Sea Sparrow* SAM, 2 single 533mm ASTT with L5 HWT, 1 sextuple 375mm MLE 54 Creusot-Loire A/S mor, 1 100mm gun (Fitted for but not with 2 twin lnchr with MM38 *Exocet* AShM)
  FF 1 *Smeli* (ex-FSU *Koni*) with 2 RBU 6000 *Smerch* 2 A/S mor, 2 twin 76mm guns
PATROL AND COASTAL COMBATANTS 3
  PCFG 1 *Mulnaya*† (ex-FSU *Tarantul* II) with 2 twin lnchr with P-15M *Termit*-M (SS-N-2C *Styx*) AShM, 2 AK630M CIWS, 1 76mm gun
  PCT 2 *Reshitelni* (ex-FSU *Pauk* I) with 4 single 406mm TT, 2 RBU 1200 A/S mor, 1 76mm gun
MINE COUNTERMEASURES 6
  MHC 1 *Tsibar* (Tripartite – ex-BEL *Flower*)
  MSC 3 *Briz* (ex-FSU *Sonya*)
  MSI 2 *Olya* (ex-FSU)
AMPHIBIOUS 1
  LCM 1 *Vydra* (capacity either 3 MBT or 200 troops)
LOGISTICS AND SUPPORT 8: 2 **AGS**; 2 **AOL**; 1 **ARS**; 2 **ATF**; 1 **AX**

Naval Aviation
EQUIPMENT BY TYPE
HELICOPTERS • ASW 2 AS565MB *Panther*

Air Force 6,700
FORCES BY ROLE
FIGHTER/ISR
  1 sqn with MiG-29A/UB *Fulcrum*
TRANSPORT
  1 sqn with An-30 *Clank*; C-27J *Spartan*; L-410UVP-E; PC-12M
TRAINING
  1 sqn with L-39ZA *Albatros**
  1 sqn with PC-9M
ATTACK HELICOPTER
  1 sqn with Mi-24D/V *Hind* D/E
TRANSPORT HELICOPTER
  1 sqn with AS532AL *Cougar*; Bell 206 *Jet Ranger*; Mi-17 *Hip* H
EQUIPMENT BY TYPE
AIRCRAFT 21 combat capable
  FTR 15: 12 MiG-29A *Fulcrum*†; 3 MiG-29UB *Fulcrum*†
  FGA (Some MiG-21bis *Fishbed*/MiG-21UM *Mongol* B in store)
  ISR 1 An-30 *Clank*
  TPT 7: **Medium** 3 C-27J *Spartan*; **Light** 4: 1 An-2T *Colt*; 2 L-410UVP-E; 1 PC-12M
  TRG 12: 6 L-39ZA *Albatros**; 6 PC-9M (basic)
HELICOPTERS
  ATK 6 Mi-24D/V *Hind* D/E
  MRH 5 Mi-17 *Hip* H
  TPT 18: **Medium** 12 AS532AL *Cougar*; **Light** 6 Bell 206 *Jet Ranger*
UNMANNED AERIAL VEHICLES • EW *Yastreb*-2S

AIR DEFENCE
SAM
Long-range S-200 (SA-5 *Gammon*); S-300 (SA-10 *Grumble*)
Medium-range S-75 *Dvina* (SA-2 *Guideline*)
Short-range S-125 *Pechora* (SA-3 *Goa*); 2K12 *Kub* (SA-6 *Gainful*)
AIR-LAUNCHED MISSILES
AAM • IR R-3 (AA-2 *Atoll*)‡ R-73 (AA-11 *Archer*) **SARH** R-27R (AA-10 *Alamo* A)
ASM Kh-29 (AS-14 *Kedge*); Kh-25 (AS-10 *Karen*)

Special Forces
FORCES BY ROLE
SPECIAL FORCES
1 spec ops bde (1 SF bn, 1 para bn)

DEPLOYMENT
AFGHANISTAN: NATO • *Operation Resolute Support* 158
ALBANIA: OSCE • Albania 1
BLACK SEA: NATO • SNMCMG 2: 1 MHC
BOSNIA-HERZEGOVINA: EU • EUFOR • *Operation Althea* 11
MALI: EU • EUTM Mali 5
SERBIA: NATO • KFOR 23; **OSCE •** Kosovo 2
UKRAINE: OSCE • Ukraine 43

FOREIGN FORCES
United States US European Command: 150; 1 armd inf coy; M1A2 SEPv2 *Abrams*; M2A3 *Bradley*

Croatia CRO

Croatian Kuna k		2017	2018	2019
GDP	k	365bn	381bn	
	US$	54.8bn	60.0bn	
per capita	US$	13,271	14,637	
Growth	%	2.8	2.8	
Inflation	%	1.1	1.6	
Def exp [a]	k	4.55bn	4.96bn	
	US$	694m	781m	
Def bdgt	k	4.39bn	4.82bn	5.08bn
	US$	658m	758m	
FMA (US)	US$	1m	0m	
US$1=k		6.67	6.35	

[a] NATO definition

Population 4,270,480

Ethnic groups: Croatian 90.4% Serbian 4.3% Bosniac 0.7% Italian 0.4% Hungarian 0.3% Other or unspecified 3.9 %

Age	0–14	15–19	20–24	25–29	30–64	65 plus
Male	7.3%	2.7%	3.0%	3.1%	24.3%	7.7%
Female	6.9%	2.6%	2.9%	3.0%	24.8%	11.6%

Capabilities
Principal tasks for the armed forces include defending national sovereignty and territorial integrity as well as tackling terrorism and contributing to international missions. Croatia joined NATO in 2009, having reformed its armed forces to create a small professional force, with a focus on international peacekeeping duties. Economic challenges have delayed further defence modernisation. The Act on Service in the Croatian Armed Forces was amended in 2018, aiming to improve conditions of service. Zagreb has defence-cooperation agreements with Bosnia-Herzegovina, Hungary and Romania, and personnel frequently train with regional and international allies. Croatia participates in NATO and EU missions, including in Afghanistan. The inventory is almost entirely composed of ageing Soviet-era equipment. Modernisation objectives include the acquisition of helicopters, while Zagreb has selected second-hand Israeli F-16Ds to replace its MiG-21 aircraft fleet. Croatia has a small defence industry, focused on small arms, ammunition, explosives and naval systems.

ACTIVE 15,200 (Army 10,750 Navy 1,300 Air 1,300 Joint 1,850) **Paramilitary 3,000**
Conscript liability Voluntary conscription, 8 weeks

RESERVE 18,350 (Army 18,350)

ORGANISATIONS BY SERVICE

Joint 1,850 (General Staff)
FORCES BY ROLE
SPECIAL FORCES
1 SF bn

Army 10,750
FORCES BY ROLE
MANOEUVRE
Armoured
1 armd bde (1 tk bn, 1 armd bn, 2 armd inf bn, 1 SP arty bn, 1 ADA bn, 1 cbt engr bn)
Light
1 mot inf bde (2 mech inf bn, 2 mot inf bn, 1 fd arty bn, 1 ADA bn, 1 cbt engr bn)
Other
1 inf trg regt
COMBAT SUPPORT
1 arty/MRL regt
1 AT regt
1 engr regt
1 int bn
1 MP regt
1 NBC bn
1 sigs regt
COMBAT SERVICE SUPPORT
1 log regt
AIR DEFENCE
1 ADA regt
EQUIPMENT BY TYPE
ARMOURED FIGHTING VEHICLES
MBT 75 M-84
IFV 101 M-80
APC 198
APC (T) 14 BTR-50

APC (W) 132: 6 BOV-VP; 126 Patria AMV (incl variants)
PPV 52: 32 *Maxxpro Plus*; 20 RG-33 HAGA (amb)
AUV 172: 10 IVECO LMV; 162 M-ATV
ENGINEERING & MAINTENANCE VEHICLES
ARV M84AI; WZT-3; 6 *Maxxpro Recovery*
VLB 5 MT-55A
MW 2: 1 *Bozena*; 1 *Rhino*
ANTI-TANK/ANTI-INFRASTRUCTURE • MSL
SP 41 POLO BOV 83
MANPATS 9K11 *Malyutka* (AT-3 *Sagger*); 9K111 *Fagot* (AT-4 *Spigot*); 9K111-1 *Konkurs* (AT-5 *Spandrel*); 9K115 *Metis* (AT-7 *Saxhorn*)
ARTILLERY 259
SP 20: **122mm** 8 2S1; **155mm** 12 PzH 2000
TOWED 107: **122mm** 53 D-30; **130mm** 36 M-46H1; **155mm** 18 M1H1
MRL 28: **122mm** 27: 6 M91 *Vulkan*; 21 BM-21 *Grad*; **128mm** 1 LOV RAK M91 R24
MOR 104: **82mm** 29 LMB M96; **120mm** 75: 70 M-75; 5 UBM 52
AIR DEFENCE
SAM • Point-defence 8 *Strela*-10; 9K310 *Igla*-1 (SA-16 *Gimlet*)
GUNS 96
SP 20mm 39 BOV-3 SP
TOWED 20mm 65 M55A4

Navy 1,300

Navy HQ at Split
EQUIPMENT BY TYPE
PATROL AND COASTAL COMBATANTS 5
PCFG 1 *Končar* with 2 twin lnchr with RBS15B Mk I AShM, 1 AK630 CIWS, 1 57mm gun
PCG 4:
2 *Kralj* with 4 single lnchr with RBS15B Mk I AShM, 1 AK630 CIWS, 1 57mm gun (with minelaying capability)
2 *Vukovar* (ex-FIN *Helsinki*) with 4 single lnchr with RBS15B Mk I AShM, 1 57mm gun
MINE WARFARE • MINE COUNTERMEASURES •
MHI 1 *Korcula*
AMPHIBIOUS • LANDING CRAFT 5:
LCT 2 *Cetina* (with minelaying capability)
LCVP 3: 2 Type-21; 1 Type-22
LOGISTICS AND SUPPORT • AKL 1
COASTAL DEFENCE • AShM 3 RBS15K

Marines

FORCES BY ROLE
MANOEUVRE
Amphibious
1 indep mne coy

Coast Guard

FORCES BY ROLE
Two divisions, headquartered in Split (1st div) and Pula (2nd div)
EQUIPMENT BY TYPE
PATROL AND COASTAL COMBATANTS • PB 4 *Mirna*

LOGISTICS AND SUPPORT
AKL 1 PT-71
AX 2

Air Force and Air Defence 1,300

FORCES BY ROLE
FIGHTER/GROUND ATTACK
1 (mixed) sqn with MiG-21bis/UMD *Fishbed*
TRANSPORT
1 sqn with An-32 *Cline*
TRAINING
1 sqn with PC-9M; Z-242L
1 hel sqn with Bell 206B *Jet Ranger* II
TRANSPORT HELICOPTER
2 sqn with Mi-8MTV *Hip* H; Mi-8T *Hip* C; Mi-171Sh
EQUIPMENT BY TYPE
AIRCRAFT 11 combat capable
FGA 11: 8 MiG-21bis *Fishbed*; 3 MiG-21UMD *Fishbed*
TPT • Light 2 An-32 *Cline*
TRG 22: 17 PC-9M; 5 Z-242L
HELICOPTERS
MRH 27: 11 Mi-8MTV *Hip* H; 16 OH-58D *Kiowa Warrior*
TPT 21: **Medium** 13: 3 Mi-8T *Hip* C; 10 Mi-171Sh; **Light** 8 Bell 206B *Jet Ranger* II
UNMANNED AERIAL VEHICLES
ISR • Medium *Hermes* 450
AIR DEFENCE • SAM
Point-defence 9K31 *Strela*-1 (SA-9 *Gaskin*); 9K34 *Strela*-3 (SA-14 *Gremlin*); 9K310 *Igla*-1 (SA-16 *Gimlet*)
AIR-LAUNCHED MISSILES
AAM • IR R-3S (AA-2 *Atoll*)‡; R-60; R-60MK (AA-8 *Aphid*)
ASM AGM-114 *Hellfire*

Special Forces Command

FORCES BY ROLE
SPECIAL FORCES
2 SF gp

Paramilitary 3,000

Police 3,000 armed

DEPLOYMENT

AFGHANISTAN: NATO • *Operation Resolute Support* 123
INDIA/PAKISTAN: UN • UNMOGIP 9 obs
LEBANON: UN • UNIFIL 1
LITHUANIA: NATO • Enhanced Forward Presence 230; 1 mech inf coy with Patria AMV; M-ATV
POLAND: NATO • Enhanced Forward Presence 69; 1 MRL bty with M91 *Vulkan*
SERBIA: NATO • KFOR 35; 1 hel unit with Mi-8 *Hip* OSCE • Kosovo 1
UKRAINE: OSCE • Ukraine 11
WESTERN SAHARA: UN • MINURSO 6 obs

Cyprus CYP

Euro €		2017	2018	2019
GDP	€	19.2bn	20.2bn	
	US$	21.7bn	24.0bn	
per capita	US$	25,380	27,865	
Growth	%	3.9	4.0	
Inflation	%	0.7	0.8	
Def bdgt	€	352m	352m	357m
	US$	397m	417m	
US$1=€		0.89	0.84	

Population   1,237,088

Age	0–14	15–19	20–24	25–29	30–64	65 plus
Male	8.0%	3.1%	4.4%	4.8%	25.5%	5.2%
Female	7.6%	2.7%	3.6%	4.0%	24.2%	6.9%

Capabilities

The National Guard is focused on protecting the island's territorial integrity and sovereignty, and safeguarding Cyprus's EEZ. Its main objective is to deter any Turkish incursion, and to provide enough opposition until military support can be provided by Greece, its primary ally. Cyprus has been enhancing its defence cooperation with Greece, including on cyber defence. Nicosia has also pledged deeper military ties with Israel, while France has renewed and enhanced its defence-cooperation agreement with Cyprus, with plans to develop facilities for French vessels on the island. Having reduced conscript liability in 2016, Nicosia began recruiting additional contract-service personnel, as part of the effort to modernise and professionalise its forces. Cyprus exercises with several international partners, most notably France, Greece and Israel. External deployments have been limited to some officers joining EU and UN missions. Cyprus has little logistics capability to support operations abroad. Equipment comprises a mix of Soviet-era and modern European systems. Cyprus has little in the way of a domestic defence industry, with no ability to design and manufacture modern equipment. The government is looking for opportunities to cooperate with the Greek defence industry.

ACTIVE 15,000 (National Guard 15,000)
Paramilitary 750
Conscript liability 14 months

RESERVE 50,000 (National Guard 50,000)
Reserve service to age 50 (officers dependent on rank; military doctors to age 60)

ORGANISATIONS BY SERVICE

National Guard 15,000 (incl conscripts)
FORCES BY ROLE
SPECIAL FORCES
  1 comd (regt) (1 SF bn)
MANOEUVRE
  Armoured
  1 lt armd bde (2 armd bn, 1 armd inf bn)
  Mechanised
  4 (1st, 2nd, 6th & 7th) lt mech bde
  Light
  1 (4th) lt inf bde
  2 (2nd & 8th) lt inf regt
COMBAT SUPPORT
  1 arty comd (8 arty bn)
COMBAT SERVICE SUPPORT
  1 (3rd) spt bde
EQUIPMENT BY TYPE
ARMOURED FIGHTING VEHICLES
  MBT 134: 82 T-80U; 52 AMX-30B2
  RECCE 69 EE-9 *Cascavel*
  IFV 43 BMP-3
  APC 294
    APC (T) 168 *Leonidas*
    APC (W) 126 VAB (incl variants)
ENGINEERING & MAINTENANCE VEHICLES
  ARV 3: 2 AMX-30D; 1 BREM-1
ANTI-TANK/ANTI-INFRASTRUCTURE
  MSL
    SP 33: 15 EE-3 *Jararaca* with *Milan*; 18 VAB with HOT
    MANPATS *Milan*
  RCL 106mm 144 M40A1
  GUNS • TOWED 100mm 20 M-1944
ARTILLERY 432
  SP 155mm 24: 12 Mk F3; 12 *Zuzana*
  TOWED 84: **105mm** 72 M-56; **155mm** 12 TR-F-1
  MRL 22: **122mm** 4 BM-21; **128mm** 18 M-63 *Plamen*
  MOR 302: **81mm** 170 E-44 (70+ M1/M9 in store); **107mm** 20 M2/M30; **120mm** 112 RT61
AIR DEFENCE
  SAM
    Medium-range 4 9K37M1 *Buk* M1-2 (SA-11 *Gadfly*)
    Short-range 18: 12 *Aspide*; 6 9K331 *Tor*-M1 (SA-15 *Gauntlet*)
    Point-defence *Mistral*
  GUNS • TOWED 60: **20mm** 36 M-55; **35mm** 24 GDF-003 (with *Skyguard*)

Maritime Wing
FORCES BY ROLE
COMBAT SUPPORT
  1 (coastal defence) AShM bty with MM40 *Exocet* AShM
EQUIPMENT BY TYPE
PATROL AND COASTAL COMBATANTS 6
  PCC 2: 1 *Alasia* (ex-OMN *Al Mabrukha*) with 1 hel landing platform; 1 OPV 62 (ISR *Sa'ar* 4.5 derivative)
  PBF 4: 2 Rodman 55; 2 *Vittoria*
COASTAL DEFENCE • AShM 3 MM40 *Exocet*

Air Wing
EQUIPMENT BY TYPE
AIRCRAFT
  TPT • Light 1 BN-2B *Islander* **TRG** 1 PC-9
HELICOPTERS
  ATK 11 Mi-35P *Hind* E
  MRH 7: 3 AW139 (SAR); 4 SA342L1 *Gazelle* (with HOT for anti-armour role)
  TPT • Light 2 Bell 206L3 *Long Ranger*

Paramilitary 750+

Armed Police 500+

FORCES BY ROLE
MANOEUVRE
  Other
    1 (rapid-reaction) paramilitary unit
EQUIPMENT BY TYPE
ARMOURED FIGHTING VEHICLES
  APC • APC (W) 2 VAB VTT
HELICOPTERS • MRH 4: 2 AW139; 2 Bell 412SP

Maritime Police 250

EQUIPMENT BY TYPE
PATROL AND COASTAL COMBATANTS 10
  PBF 5: 2 *Poseidon*; 1 *Shaldag*; 2 *Vittoria*
  PB 5 SAB-12

DEPLOYMENT

LEBANON: UN • UNIFIL 2

FOREIGN FORCES

Argentina UNFICYP 244; 2 inf coy; 1 hel flt
Austria UNFICYP 5
Bangladesh UNFICYP 2
Brazil UNFICYP 2
Canada UNFICYP 1
Chile UNFICYP 12
Greece Army: 950; ε200 (officers/NCO seconded to Greek-Cypriot National Guard)
Hungary UNFICYP 11
Pakistan UNFICYP 1
Paraguay UNFICYP 12
Serbia UNFICYP 2
Slovakia UNFICYP 242; 1 inf coy; 1 engr pl
United Kingdom 2,260; 2 inf bn; 1 hel sqn with 4 Bell 412 *Twin Huey* • Operation Inherent Resolve (*Shader*) 500: 1 FGA sqn with 8 *Tornado* GR4; 6 *Typhoon* FGR4; 2 *Sentinel* R1; 1 A330 MRTT *Voyager* KC3; 2 C-130J *Hercules* • UNFICYP (*Operation Tosca*) 278: 1 recce coy

TERRITORY WHERE THE GOVERNMENT DOES NOT EXERCISE EFFECTIVE CONTROL

Data here represents the de facto situation on the northern section of the island. This does not imply international recognition as a sovereign state.

Capabilities

ACTIVE 3,000 (Army 3,000) **Paramilitary** 150
Conscript liability 15 months

RESERVE 15,000
Reserve liability to age 50

ORGANISATIONS BY SERVICE

Army ε3,000

FORCES BY ROLE
MANOEUVRE
  Light
    5 inf bn
    7 inf bn (reserve)
EQUIPMENT BY TYPE
ANTI-TANK/ANTI-INFRASTRUCTURE
  MSL • MANPATS *Milan*
  RCL • 106mm 36
ARTILLERY • MOR • 120mm 73

Paramilitary

Armed Police ε150

FORCES BY ROLE
SPECIAL FORCES
  1 (police) SF unit

Coast Guard

PATROL AND COASTAL COMBATANTS 6
  PCC 5: 2 SG45/SG46; 1 *Rauf Denktash*; 2 US Mk 5
  PB 1

FOREIGN FORCES

TURKEY
Army ε33,800

FORCES BY ROLE
1 corps HQ; 1 SF regt; 1 armd bde; 2 mech inf div; 1 mech inf regt; 1 arty regt; 1 avn comd
EQUIPMENT BY TYPE
ARMOURED FIGHTING VEHICLES
  MBT 287 M48A5T2
  IFV 147 ACV AIFV
  APC • APC (T) 492: 106 ACV AAPC (incl variants); 386 M113 (incl variants)
ANTI-TANK/ANTI-INFRASTRUCTURE
  MSL
    SP 60 ACV TOW
    MANPATS *Milan*
  RCL 106mm 219 M40A1
ARTILLERY 643
  SP 155mm 174: 30 M44T; 144 M52T1
  TOWED 84: 105mm 36 M101A1; 155mm 36 M114A2; 203mm 12 M115
  MRL 122mm 9 T-122
  MOR 376: 81mm 171; 107mm 70 M30; 120mm 135 HY-12
PATROL AND COASTAL COMBATANTS 1 PB
AIRCRAFT • TPT • Light 3 Cessna 185 (U-17)
HELICOPTERS • TPT 3 Medium 2 AS532UL *Cougar*
Light 1 Bell 205 (UH-1H *Iroquois*)
AIR DEFENCE
  SAM Point-defence FIM-92 *Stinger*
  GUNS • TOWED 150: 20mm 122: 44 Rh 202; 78 GAI-D01; 35mm 28 GDF-003

Czech Republic CZE

Czech Koruna Kc		2017	2018	2019
GDP	Kc	5.05tr	5.24tr	
	US$	216bn	245bn	
per capita	US$	20,402	23,085	
Growth	%	4.3	3.1	
Inflation	%	2.4	2.3	
Def exp [a]	Kc	52.7bn	58.8bn	
	US$	2.26bn	2.74bn	
Def bdgt [b]	Kc	52.5bn	58.9bn	66.7bn
	US$	2.25bn	2.75bn	
US$1=Kc		23.38	21.43	

[a] NATO definition
[b] Includes military pensions

Population	10,686,269					
Age	0–14	15–19	20–24	25–29	30–64	65 plus
Male	7.8%	2.3%	2.7%	3.4%	25.2%	7.9%
Female	7.4%	2.1%	2.5%	3.2%	24.5%	11.1%

Capabilities

The 2015 national-security strategy states that NATO is central to Czech security, while the 2017 defence strategy points to Russian assertiveness, an arc of instability to the south and southeast of Europe and information warfare, including cyber attacks, as core security challenges. In February 2017, the Czech Republic signed a letter of intent with Germany to affiliate the 4th Czech Rapid Deployment Brigade with the 10th German Armoured Division under NATO's Framework Nations Concept. In the same year, a bilateral agreement with Slovakia addressed mutual air-defence issues. It was announced in 2018 that the two countries will cooperate on procurement tenders. The government plans to increase personnel numbers and adopted an Active Reserve Law in 2016, which aims to incentivise engagement in the reserves. However, recruitment and retention remains a challenge. The armed forces are able to deploy on a variety of international crisis-management operations, including NATO's Enhanced Forward Presence in the Baltic states. The defence ministry announced plans at the end of 2017 to upgrade existing military training and simulation facilities by 2025. The government is trying to replace legacy equipment in order to both modernise the armed forces and reduce dependence on Russia for spare parts and services. Modernisation priorities include infantry fighting vehicles, self-propelled howitzers, multi-role helicopters, transport aircraft, short-range air-defence systems and UAVs. The defence-industrial base includes development and manufacturing capability, in particular relating to small arms, vehicles, and training and light attack aircraft. The holding company Czechoslovak Group brings together several companies across the munitions, vehicles and aerospace sectors.

ACTIVE 23,200 (Army 12,250 Air 5,850 Other 3,650)

ORGANISATIONS BY SERVICE

Army 12,250
FORCES BY ROLE
MANOEUVRE
  Reconnaissance
    1 ISR/EW regt (1 recce bn, 1 EW bn)
  Armoured
    1 (7th) mech bde (1 tk bn, 2 armd inf bn, 1 mot inf bn)
  Mechanised
    1 (4th) rapid reaction bde (2 mech inf bn, 1 mot inf bn, 1 AB bn)
COMBAT SUPPORT
  1 (13th) arty regt (2 arty bn)
  1 engr regt (3 engr bn, 1 EOD bn)
  1 CBRN regt (2 CBRN bn)
COMBAT SERVICE SUPPORT
  1 log regt (2 log bn, 1 maint bn)

Active Reserve
FORCES BY ROLE
COMMAND
  14 (territorial defence) comd
MANOEUVRE
  Armoured
    1 armd coy
  Light
    14 inf coy (1 per territorial comd) (3 inf pl, 1 cbt spt pl, 1 log pl)

EQUIPMENT BY TYPE
ARMOURED FIGHTING VEHICLES
  MBT 30 T-72M4CZ (89 T-72 in store)
  RECCE (34 BPzV *Svatava* in store)
  IFV 227: 120 BMP-2; 107 *Pandur* II (incl variants); (98 BMP-1; 65 BMP-2 all in store)
  APC
    APC (T) (17 OT-90 in store)
  AUV 21 *Dingo* 2; IVECO LMV
ENGINEERING & MAINTENANCE VEHICLES
  ARV 10 VPV-ARV (12 more in store); VT-55A; VT-72M4
  VLB 6 MT-55A (3 more in store)
  MW Bozena 5; UOS-155 *Belarty*
ANTI-TANK/ANTI-INFRASTRUCTURE
  MSL • MANPATS 9K111-1 *Konkurs* (AT-5 *Spandrel*); FGM-148 *Javelin*; Spike-LR
  RCL 84mm *Carl Gustaf*
ARTILLERY 96
  SP 152mm 48 M-77 *Dana* (38 more in store)
  MOR 48: 120mm 40 M-1982; (45 more in store); SP 120mm 8 SPM-85

Air Force 5,850
Principal task is to secure Czech airspace. This mission is fulfilled within NATO Integrated Extended Air Defence System (NATINADS) and, if necessary, by means of the Czech national reinforced air-defence system. The air force also provides CAS for army SAR, and performs a tpt role

FORCES BY ROLE
FIGHTER/GROUND ATTACK
  1 sqn with *Gripen* C/D
  1 sqn with L-159 ALCA; L-159T
TRANSPORT
  2 sqn with A319CJ; C295M; CL-601 *Challenger*; L-410 *Turbolet*; Yak-40 *Codling*
TRAINING
  1 sqn with L-39ZA *Albatros**; L-159 ALCA; L-159T

ATTACK HELICOPTER
 1 sqn with Mi-24/Mi-35 *Hind*
TRANSPORT HELICOPTER
 1 sqn with Mi-17 *Hip* H; Mi-171Sh
 1 sqn with Mi-8 *Hip*; Mi-17 *Hip* H; PZL W-3A *Sokol*
AIR DEFENCE
 1 (25th) SAM regt (2 AD gp)
EQUIPMENT BY TYPE
AIRCRAFT 44 combat capable
 FGA 14: 12 *Gripen* C; 2 *Gripen* D
 ATK 21: 16 L-159 ALCA; 5 L-159T
 TPT 15: **Light** 12: 4 C295M; 6 L-410 *Turbolet*; 2 Yak-40 *Codling*; **PAX** 3: 2 A319CJ; 1 CL-601 *Challenger*
 TRG 9 L-39ZA *Albatros**
HELICOPTERS
 ATK 17: 7 Mi-24 *Hind* D; 10 Mi-35 *Hind* E
 MRH 5 Mi-17 *Hip* H
 TPT • **Medium** 30: 4 Mi-8 *Hip*; 16 Mi-171Sh; 10 PZL W3A *Sokol*
AIR DEFENCE • SAM
 Point-defence 9K35 *Strela*-10 (SA-13 *Gopher*); 9K32 *Strela*-2‡ (SA-7 *Grail*) (available for trg RBS-70 gunners); RBS-70
AIR-LAUNCHED MISSILES
 AAM • IR AIM-9M *Sidewinder*; ARH AIM-120C-5 AMRAAM
BOMBS
 Laser-guided: GBU *Paveway*

Other Forces

FORCES BY ROLE
SPECIAL FORCES
 1 SF gp
MANOEUVRE
 Other
  1 (presidential) gd bde (2 bn)
  1 (honour guard) gd bn (2 coy)
COMBAT SUPPORT
 1 int gp
 1 (central) MP comd
 3 (regional) MP comd
 1 (protection service) MP comd

Cyber

A Cyber Security Act entered into force in January 2015 and a new National Cyber Security Strategy and an Action Plan for 2015–20 were published. The former states that the country will look 'to increase national capacities for active cyber defence and cyber attack countermeasures'. The National Cyber and Information Security Agency was established on 1 August 2017 as the central body of state administration for cyber security, including the protection of classified information in the area of information and communications systems and cryptographic protection, which was previously the responsibility of the National Security Agency. The defence ministry is developing its own cyber-defence capabilities according to specific tasks based on EU or NATO documents and the requirements of the National Action Plan. The defence ministry security director also leads on cyber security.

DEPLOYMENT

AFGHANISTAN: NATO • *Operation Resolute Support* 281
BOSNIA-HERZEGOVINA: EU • EUFOR • *Operation Althea* 2; OSCE • Bosnia and Herzegovina 1
CENTRAL AFRICAN REPUBLIC: UN • MINUSCA 3 obs
DEMOCRATIC REPUBLIC OF THE CONGO: UN • MONUSCO 1; 1 obs
EGYPT: MFO 18; 1 C295M
IRAQ: *Operation Inherent Resolve* 30
LATVIA: NATO • Enhanced Forward Presence 60; 1 mor pl
MALI: EU • EUTM Mali 41; UN • MINUSMA 3; 2 obs
SERBIA: NATO • KFOR 10; OSCE • Kosovo 1; UN • UNMIK 2 obs
SYRIA/ISRAEL: UN • UNDOF 3
UKRAINE: OSCE • Ukraine 14

Denmark DNK

Danish Krone kr		2017	2018	2019
GDP	kr	2.15tr	2.23tr	
	US$	326bn	355bn	
per capita	US$	56,631	61,227	
Growth	%	2.3	2.0	
Inflation	%	1.1	1.4	
Def exp [a]	kr	25.0bn	26.7bn	
	US$	3.78bn	4.25bn	
Def bdgt [b]	kr	25.0bn	26.7bn	27.5bn
	US$	3.78bn	4.25bn	
US$1=kr		6.60	6.29	

[a] NATO definition
[b] Includes military pensions

Population	5,809,502					
Age	0–14	15–19	20–24	25–29	30–64	65 plus
Male	8.4%	3.3%	3.4%	3.2%	22.3%	8.6%
Female	8.0%	3.1%	3.3%	3.1%	22.6%	10.6%

Capabilities

Danish military capabilities remain compact but effective despite pressures on spending and deployments. In January 2018, the government issued a new defence agreement for 2018–23, envisaging increased defence spending to deal with a deteriorating security environment. In particular, it is intended to strengthen deterrence, cyber defence and Denmark's role in international operations, as well as the armed forces' ability to support civilian authorities in national-security tasks. Denmark plans to set up a heavy brigade with ground-based air-defence capabilities and a light infantry battalion to take on patrol and guard missions in support of the police. Denmark also intends to strengthen naval air defence, as well as anti-submarine-warfare capabilities. Ties to NATO, NOR-DEFCO and other regional neighbours have increased. A defence agreement, aimed at deterring Russia, was signed in April 2015 with other Nordic states. Denmark is an EU member but has opted out of military cooperation under the Common Security and Defence Policy. The new defence agreement foresees that national service is retained and that the annual conscript intake should rise. Procurement of the F-35A to replace the country's ageing F-16AM/BM fleet was confirmed in June 2016. However, the strain of transitioning to the new platform could temporarily reduce Denmark's ability to contribute to NATO air-policing tasks. Industrial support from Terma, Denmark's largest defence company, may have been important to the F-35 procurement decision, as some key sub-components and composites are produced by the firm. The defence-industrial base is focused on exports to Europe and North America and is mainly active in defence electronics and the design and manufacture of components and subsystems.

ACTIVE 14,500 (Army 6,900 Navy 2,200 Air 2,900 Joint 2,500)

Conscript liability 4–12 months, most voluntary

RESERVES 45,700 (Army 34,300 Navy 5,300 Air Force 4,750 Service Corps 1,350)

ORGANISATIONS BY SERVICE

Army 6,900

Div and bde HQ are responsible for trg only; if necessary, can be transformed into operational formations

FORCES BY ROLE
COMMAND
  1 div HQ
  2 bde HQ
MANOEUVRE
  Reconnaissance
  1 recce bn
  1 ISR bn
  Armoured
  1 tk bn
  Mechanised
  3 mech inf bn
  2 mech inf bn(-)
COMBAT SUPPORT
  1 SP arty bn
  1 cbt engr bn
  1 CBRN/construction bn
  1 EOD coy
  1 int bn
  1 MP bn
  3 sigs bn
COMBAT SERVICE SUPPORT
  2 log bn
  1 maint bn
  1 spt bn
EQUIPMENT BY TYPE
ARMOURED FIGHTING VEHICLES
  MBT 38 *Leopard* 2A5 (12 more in store)
  IFV 44 CV9035 MkIII
  APC 226
    APC (T) 125 M113 (incl variants); (306 more in store awaiting disposal)
    APC (W) 101: 79 *Piranha* III (incl variants); 22 *Piranha* V
  AUV 120: 84 *Eagle* IV; 36 *Eagle* V
ENGINEERING & MAINTENANCE VEHICLES
  ARV 10 *Bergepanzer* 2
  VLB 6 *Biber*
  MW 14 910-MCV-2

ANTI-TANK/ANTI-INFRASTRUCTURE
  RCL 84mm 186 *Carl Gustav*
ARTILLERY 24
  SP 155mm 12 M109A3 (being replaced by CAESAR)
  MOR • TOWED 120mm 12 Soltam K6B1
AIR DEFENCE • SAM • Point-defence FIM-92 *Stinger*

Navy 2,200

EQUIPMENT BY TYPE
PRINCIPAL SURFACE COMBATANTS 3
  DESTROYERS • DDGHM 3 *Iver Huitfeldt* with 4 quad lnchr with RGM-84L *Harpoon* Block II AShM, 1 32-cell Mk41 VLS (to be fitted with SAM), 2 12-cell Mk56 VLS with RIM-162 SAM, 2 twin 324mm TT with MU90 LWT, 1 *Millennium* CIWS, 2 76mm guns (capacity 1 med hel)
PATROL AND COASTAL COMBATANTS 13
  PSOH 4 *Thetis* 1 76mm gun (capacity 1 MH-60R *Seahawk*)
  PSO 3 *Knud Rasmussen* with 1 76mm gun, 1 hel landing platform
  PCC 6 *Diana*
MINE WARFARE • MINE COUNTERMEASURES 6
  MCI 4 MSF MK-I
  MSD 2 *Holm*
LOGISTICS AND SUPPORT 11
  ABU 2 (primarily used for MARPOL duties)
  AE 1 *Sleipner*
  AG 2 *Absalon* (flexible support ships) with 4 quad lnchr with RGM-84L *Harpoon* Block II AShM, 3 12-cell Mk 56 VLS with RIM-162 ESSM SAM, 2 twin 324mm TT with MU90 LWT, 2 *Millennium* CIWS, 1 127mm gun (capacity 2 AW101 *Merlin*; 2 LCP, 7 MBT or 40 vehicles; 130 troops)
  AGS 2 *Holm*
  AKL 2 *Seatruck*
  AXS 2 *Svanen*

Air Force 2,900

Tactical Air Command
FORCES BY ROLE
FIGHTER/GROUND ATTACK
  2 sqn with F-16AM/BM *Fighting Falcon*
ANTI-SUBMARINE WARFARE
  1 sqn with *Super Lynx* Mk90B
SEARCH & RESCUE/TRANSPORT HELICOPTER
  1 sqn with AW101 *Merlin*
  1 sqn with AS550 *Fennec* (ISR)
TRANSPORT
  1 sqn with C-130J-30 *Hercules*; CL-604 *Challenger* (MP/VIP)
TRAINING
  1 unit with MFI-17 *Supporter* (T-17)
EQUIPMENT BY TYPE
AIRCRAFT 44 combat capable
  FTR 44: 34 F-16AM *Fighting Falcon*; 10 F-16BM *Fighting Falcon* (30 operational)
  TPT 8: **Medium** 4 C-130J-30 *Hercules*; **PAX** 4 CL-604 *Challenger* (MP/VIP)
  TRG 27 MFI-17 *Supporter* (T-17)

HELICOPTERS
 ASW 9: 6 *Super Lynx* Mk90B; 3 MH-60R *Seahawk*
 MRH 8 AS550 *Fennec* (ISR) (4 more non-operational)
 TPT • Medium 13 AW101 *Merlin* (8 SAR; 5 Tpt)
AIR-LAUNCHED MISSILES
 AAM • IR AIM-9L *Sidewinder*; IIR AIM-9X *Sidewinder* II; ARH AIM-120B AMRAAM
 ASM AGM-65 *Maverick*
BOMBS
 Laser-guided EGBU-12/GBU-24 *Paveway* II/III
 INS/GPS guided GBU-31 JDAM

Control and Air Defence Group
1 Control and Reporting Centre, 1 Mobile Control and Reporting Centre. 4 Radar sites

Special Operations Command
FORCES BY ROLE
SPECIAL FORCES
 1 SF unit
 1 diving unit

Reserves

Home Guard (Army) 34,300 reservists (to age 50)
FORCES BY ROLE
MANOEUVRE
 Light
 2 regt cbt gp (3 mot inf bn, 1 arty bn)
 5 (local) def region (up to 2 mot inf bn)

Home Guard (Navy) 4,500 reservists (to age 50)
EQUIPMENT BY TYPE
PATROL AND COASTAL COMBATANTS 30
 PB 30: 17 MHV800; 1 MHV850; 12 MHV900

Home Guard (Air Force) 4,750 reservists (to age 50)

Home Guard (Service Corps) 1,350 reservists

Cyber
A National Strategy for Cyber and Information Security was released in December 2014. The Centre for Cyber Security (CFCS) is situated within the Danish Defence Intelligence Service. The CFCS is Denmark's national information and communications technology (ICT) security authority with three primary responsibilities: contribute to protecting Denmark against cyber threats; assist in securing a solid and robust ICT critical infrastructure; and warn of, protect against and counter cyber attacks. The 2018–23 Defence Agreement will lead to a significant increase in the CFCS's resources. In addition to existing cyber-defence capabilities, Denmark has developed a capacity to conduct defensive and offensive military operations in cyberspace that will become fully operational in 2019.

DEPLOYMENT

AFGHANISTAN: NATO • *Operation Resolute Support* 160
ESTONIA: NATO • Enhanced Forward Presence 186; 1 armd inf coy with CV9035
IRAQ: *Operation Inherent Resolve* 190; 1 SF gp; 1 trg team
KUWAIT: *Operation Inherent Resolve* 20
MALI: UN • MINUSMA 1
MEDITERRANEAN SEA: NATO • SNMG 1: 1 AG
MIDDLE EAST: UN • UNTSO 11 obs
SERBIA: NATO • KFOR 35
SOUTH SUDAN: UN • UNMISS 11
UKRAINE: OSCE • Ukraine 8
UNITED ARAB EMIRATES: *Operation Inherent Resolve* 20

Estonia EST

Euro €		2017	2018	2019
GDP	€	23.0bn	24.8bn	
	US$	26.0bn	29.5bn	
per capita	US$	19,735	22,417	
Growth	%	4.9	3.7	
Inflation	%	3.7	3.0	
Def Exp [a]	€	479m	524m	
	US$	541m	624m	
Def bdgt [b]	€	481m	538m	614m
	US$	544m	641m	
FMA (US)	US$	10m	0m	
US$1=€		0.89	0.84	

[a] NATO definition
[b] Includes military pensions

Population 1,244,288

Ethnic groups: Estonian 70%; Russian 25%; Ukranian 1.7%; Belarusian 1%; other or unspecified 2.3%

Age	0–14	15–19	20–24	25–29	30–64	65 plus
Male	8.3%	2.2%	2.4%	3.6%	23.4%	6.7%
Female	7.9%	2.1%	2.2%	3.3%	24.6%	13.1%

Capabilities
Estonia has small active armed forces and is reliant on NATO membership as a security guarantor. Security policy is predicated on the goals of ensuring sovereignty and territorial integrity, and there is concern over Russian security policy and military activity. The government's 2017–26 National Defence Development Plan (NDDP) reflects the worsening security environment in the Baltic region. The active armed forces are supplemented by a reserve component. In June 2018 Estonia joined the French-inspired European Intervention Force. A NATO battlegroup based in Estonia became operational in mid-2017 as part of the Alliance's Enhanced Forward Presence. The country's Amari air base hosts a NATO Baltic Air Policing detachment. Estonia is also a member of the UK-led multinational Joint Expeditionary Force. Cyber security is a strength, and Tallinn hosts NATO's Cybersecurity Centre of Excellence. The NDDP notes a desire to increase the annual conscript intake and the total number of active personnel. There is very limited organic capability to deploy beyond borders, though Estonian forces take part in EU, NATO and UN missions abroad on a small scale. The NDDP identifies the need for additional armoured mobility and armoured firepower, anti-armour weapons and increased munitions stocks. The country has a niche defence-industrial capability, including ship repair and digital systems.

ACTIVE 6,600 (Army 5,700 Navy 400 Air 500)
Defence League 15,800
Conscript liability 8 or 11 months (depending on specialisation; conscripts cannot be deployed)

RESERVE 12,000 (Joint 12,000)

ORGANISATIONS BY SERVICE

Army 2,500; 3,200 conscript (total 5,700)
4 def region. All units except one inf bn are reserve based
FORCES BY ROLE
MANOEUVRE
  Light
  1 (1st) bde (1 recce coy, 3 inf bn, 1 arty bn, 1 AD bn, 1 cbt engr bn, 1 spt bn)
  1 (2nd) inf bde (1 inf bn, 1 spt bn)
COMBAT SUPPORT
  1 sigs bn
COMBAT SERVICE SUPPORT
  1 log bn

Defence League 15,800
15 Districts
EQUIPMENT BY TYPE
ARMOURED FIGHTING VEHICLES
  IFV 28 CV9035EE (incl 2 CP)
  APC 158
    APC (W) 151: 56 XA-180 *Sisu*; 80 XA-188 *Sisu*; 15 BTR-80
    PPV 7 *Mamba*
ENGINEERING & MAINTENANCE VEHICLES
  AEV 2 Pioneerpanzer 2 *Dachs*
  ARV 2 BPz-2
  VLB 2 *Biber*
ANTI-TANK/ANTI-INFRASTRUCTURE
  MSL • MANPATS FGM-148 *Javelin*; Milan
  RCL 160+; **106mm**: 30 M40A1; **84mm** *Carl Gustav*; **90mm** 130 PV-1110
ARTILLERY 376
  TOWED 66: **122mm** 42 D-30 (H 63); **155mm** 24 FH-70
  MOR 310: **81mm** 131: 41 B455; 10 NM 95; 80 M252; **120mm** 179: 14 2B11; 165 M/41D
AIR DEFENCE
  SAM • Point-defence *Mistral*
  GUNS • TOWED 23mm ZU-23-2

Navy 300; 100 conscript (total 400)
EQUIPMENT BY TYPE
MINE WARFARE • MINE COUNTERMEASURES 4
  MCCS 1 *Tasuja* (ex-DNK *Lindormen*)
  MHC 3 *Admiral Cowan* (ex-UK *Sandown*) (1 in refit)

Air Force 500
FORCES BY ROLE
TRANSPORT
  1 sqn with An-2 *Colt*
TRANSPORT HELICOPTER
  1 sqn with R-44 *Raven* II

EQUIPMENT BY TYPE
AIRCRAFT • TPT • Light 2 An-2 *Colt*
HELICOPTERS • TPT • Light 4 R-44 *Raven* II

Special Operations Forces
FORCES BY ROLE
SPECIAL FORCES
  1 spec ops bn

Paramilitary

Border Guard
The Estonian Border Guard is subordinate to the Ministry of the Interior. Air support is provided by the Estonian Border Guard Aviation Corps
EQUIPMENT BY TYPE
PATROL AND COASTAL COMBATANTS 13
  PCO 2: 1 *Kati*; 1 *Kindral Kurvits*
  PCC 1 *Kou* (FIN *Silma*)
  PB 10: 1 *Pikker*; 1 *Raju* (Baltic 4500WP); 1 *Valve*; 8 (other)
AMPHIBIOUS • LANDING CRAFT • LCU 3
LOGISTICS & SUPPORT • AGF 1 *Balsam*
AIRCRAFT • TPT • Light 2 L-410
HELICOPTERS • MRH 3 AW139

Cyber
Estonia adopted a national Cyber Security Strategy in 2008 and in 2009 added a Cyber Security Council to the government's Security Committee, which supports strategic-level, inter-agency cooperation. Tallinn hosts the NATO Cooperative Cyber Security Centre of Excellence and the NATO *Locked Shields* cyber exercise takes place annually in Estonia, as has the Cyber Coalition exercise since 2013. A Cyber Security Strategy for 2014–17 advocated greater integration of capability. A Defence Cyber Command became operational in August 2018, with full operating capability reportedly expected by 2023.

DEPLOYMENT

AFGHANISTAN: NATO • *Operation Resolute Support* 40
IRAQ: *Operation Inherent Resolve* 7
LEBANON: UN • UNIFIL 38
MALI: *Operation Barkhane* 50; **EU •** EUTM Mali 4; **UN •** MINUSMA 3
MIDDLE EAST: UN • UNTSO 3 obs
MOLDOVA: OSCE • Moldova 1
SERBIA: NATO • KFOR 2
UKRAINE: OSCE • Ukraine 3

FOREIGN FORCES
All **NATO** Enhanced Forward Presence unless stated
Denmark 186; 1 armd inf coy
Germany NATO Baltic Air Policing 6 Eurofighter *Typhoon*
United Kingdom 900; 1 armd inf bn HQ; 1 armd inf coy (+); 1 engr sqn

Finland FIN

Euro €		2017	2018	2019
GDP	€	224bn	233bn	
	US$	253bn	277bn	
per capita	US$	45,927	50,068	
Growth	%	2.8	2.6	
Inflation	%	0.8	1.2	
Def bdgt [a]	€	2.83bn	2.87bn	3.14bn
	US$	3.20bn	3.41bn	
US$1=€		0.89	0.84	

[a] Excludes military pensions

Population   5,537,364

Age	0–14	15–19	20–24	25–29	30–64	65 plus
Male	8.4%	2.8%	3.1%	3.2%	22.6%	9.2%
Female	8.0%	2.6%	2.9%	3.1%	22.2%	11.9%

Capabilities

Finland's armed forces are primarily focused on territorial defence. The country's long border with Russia has focused attention on Russia's military capabilities and plans. The 2017 Defence Report argues that changes in the security environment have increased the demands on the armed forces and stresses that financial constraints are forcing trade-offs between long-term procurement plans and operational readiness. An EU member state, Finland's principal multilateral defence relationships include NORDEFCO and the Northern Group, as well as strong bilateral cooperation with Sweden and the US; it is building close ties with NATO short of membership. In 2017, Finland joined a multinational cooperation programme for air-to-ground precision-guided munitions set up by a group of NATO member states. The country's largest deployment is to the UNIFIL mission but it also contributes to NATO operations and the international counter-ISIS coalition. In 2015, the air force launched the HX Fighter Programme to replace its F/A-18s. A request for quotations was issued in April 2018 and the replacement aircraft is expected to be selected in 2021. Under Finland's Squadron 2020 programme, the navy will replace patrol boats and minelayers with corvette-sized vessels capable of operating in shallow water and cold weather. Finland's defence industry consists largely of privately owned SMEs, concentrating on niche products for international markets, but it also features some internationally competitive larger companies producing wheeled armoured vehicles and turreted mortar systems.

ACTIVE 21,500 (Army 15,300 Navy 3,500 Air 2,700)
Paramilitary 2,700
Conscript liability 165, 255 or 347 days (latter for NCOs, officers or those on 'especially demanding' duties)

RESERVE 216,000 (Army 170,000 Navy 20,000 Air 26,000) **Paramilitary 11,500**
18,000 reservists a year do refresher training: total obligation 80 days (150 for NCOs, 200 for officers) between conscript service and age 50 (NCOs and officers to age 60)

ORGANISATIONS BY SERVICE

Army 5,000; 10,300 conscript (total 15,300)
FORCES BY ROLE
Finland's army maintains a mobilisation strength of about 285,000. In support of this requirement, two conscription cycles, each for about 13,500 conscripts, take place each year. After conscript training, reservist commitment is to the age of 60. Reservists are usually assigned to units within their local geographical area. All service appointments or deployments outside Finnish borders are voluntary for all members of the armed services. All brigades are reserve based

Reserve Organisations 170,000
FORCES BY ROLE
SPECIAL FORCES
  1 SF bn
MANOEUVRE
  Armoured
    2 armd BG (regt)
  Mechanised
    2 (Karelia & Pori Jaeger) mech bde
  Light
    3 (Jaeger) bde
    6 lt inf bde
COMBAT SUPPORT
  1 arty bde
  1 AD regt
  7 engr regt
  3 sigs bn
COMBAT SERVICE SUPPORT
  Some log unit
HELICOPTER
  1 hel bn

EQUIPMENT BY TYPE
ARMOURED FIGHTING VEHICLES
  MBT 80 *Leopard* 2A6 (100 *Leopard* 2A4 in store)
  IFV 212: 110 BMP-2/-2MD; 102 CV9030FIN
  APC 613
    APC (T) 142: 40 MT-LBu; 102 MT-LBV
    APC (W) 471: 260 XA-180/185 *Sisu*; 101 XA-202 *Sisu* (CP); 48 XA-203 *Sisu*; 62 AMV (XA-360)
ENGINEERING & MAINTENANCE VEHICLES
  ARV 27: 15 MTP-LB; 12 VT-55A
  VLB 27: 12 BLG-60M2; 6 *Leopard* 2S; 9 SISU *Leguan*
  MW *Aardvark* Mk 2; KMT T-55; 6 *Leopard* 2R CEV; RA-140 DS
ANTI-TANK/ANTI-INFRASTRUCTURE
  MSL • MANPATS NLAW; *Spike*-MR; *Spike*-LR
ARTILLERY 681
  SP 122mm 40: 4 K9 *Thunder*; 36 2S1 *Gvozdika* (PsH 74)
  TOWED 324: **122mm** 234 D-30 (H 63); **130mm** 36 M-46 (K 54); **155mm** 54 K 83/GH-52 (K 98)
  MRL 56: **122mm** 34 RM-70; **227mm** 22 M270 MLRS
  MOR 279+: **81mm** Krh/71; **120mm** 261 Krh/92; **SP 120mm** 18 XA-361 AMOS
HELICOPTERS
  MRH 7: 5 Hughes 500D; 2 Hughes 500E
  TPT • Medium 20 NH90 TTH
UNMANNED AERIAL VEHICLES
  ISR • Medium 11 ADS-95 *Ranger*
AIR DEFENCE
  SAM
    Short-range 44: 20 *Crotale* NG (ITO 90); 24 NASAMS II FIN (ITO 12)
    Point-defence 16+: 16 ASRAD (ITO 05); FIM-92 *Stinger* (ITO 15); RBS 70 (ITO 05/05M)

GUNS 400+: **23mm** ItK 95/ZU-23-2 (ItK 61); **35mm** ItK 88;
SP 35mm *Leopard* 2 ITK *Marksman*

Navy 1,600; 1,900 conscript (total 3,500)
FORCES BY ROLE
Naval Command HQ located at Turku; with two subordinate Naval Commands (Gulf of Finland and Archipelago Sea); 1 Naval bde; 3 spt elm (Naval Materiel Cmd, Naval Academy, Naval Research Institute)
EQUIPMENT BY TYPE
PATROL AND COASTAL COMBATANTS 20
  PCGM 4 *Hamina* with 4 RBS15SF3 (MTO-85M) AShM, 1 octuple VLS with *Umkhonto*-IR (ITO2004) SAM, 1 57mm gun
  PBF 12 *Jehu* (U-700) (capacity 24 troops)
  PBG 4 *Rauma* with 6 RBS15SF3 (MTO-85M) AShM
MINE WARFARE 15
  MINE COUNTERMEASURES 10
    MCC 3 *Katanpää*
    MSI 7: 4 *Kiiski*; 3 *Kuha*
  MINELAYERS • ML 5:
    2 *Hameenmaa* with 1 octuple VLS with *Umkhonto*-IR (ITO2004) SAM, 2 RBU 1200 A/S mor, up to 100–120 mines, 1 57mm gun
    3 *Pansio* with 50 mines
AMPHIBIOUS • LANDING CRAFT 51
  LCM 1 *Kampela*
  LCP 50
LOGISTICS AND SUPPORT 7
  AG 3: 1 *Louhi*; 2 *Hylje*
  AX 4: 3 *Fabian Wrede*; 1 *Lokki*

Coastal Defence
FORCES BY ROLE
MANOEUVRE
  Amphibious
  1 mne bde
COMBAT SUPPORT
  1 cbt spt bde (1 AShM bty)
EQUIPMENT BY TYPE
COASTAL DEFENCE
  AShM 4 RBS15K
  ARTY • 130mm 30 K-53tk (static)
ANTI-TANK/ANTI-INFRASTRUCTURE
  MSL • MANPATS *Spike* (used in AShM role)

Air Force 1,950; 750 conscript (total 2,700)
3 Air Comds: Satakunta (West), Karelia (East), Lapland (North)
FORCES BY ROLE
FIGHTER/GROUND ATTACK
  3 sqn with F/A-18C/D *Hornet*
ISR
  1 (survey) sqn with Learjet 35A
TRANSPORT
  1 flt with C295M
  4 (liaison) flt with PC-12NG
TRAINING
  1 sqn with *Hawk* Mk50/51A/66* (air-defence and ground-attack trg)
  1 unit with L-70 *Vinka*

EQUIPMENT BY TYPE
AIRCRAFT 107 combat capable
  FGA 62: 55 F/A-18C *Hornet*; 7 F/A-18D *Hornet*
  MP 1 F-27-400M
  ELINT 1 C295M
  TPT • Light 10: 2 C295M; 3 Learjet 35A (survey; ECM trg; tgt-tow); 5 PC-12NG
  TRG 74: 1 G-115EA; 29 *Hawk* Mk50/51A*; 16 *Hawk* Mk66*; 28 L-70 *Vinka*
AIR-LAUNCHED MISSILES
  AAM • IR AIM-9 *Sidewinder*; **IIR** AIM-9X *Sidewinder*;
  ARH AIM-120C AMRAAM
  LACM Conventional AGM-158 JASSM
BOMBS
  INS/GPS-guided GBU-31 JDAM; AGM-154C JSOW

Paramilitary
Border Guard 2,700
Ministry of Interior. 4 Border Guard Districts and 2 Coast Guard Districts
FORCES BY ROLE
MARITIME PATROL
  1 sqn with Do-228 (maritime surv); AS332 *Super Puma*; Bell 412 (AB-412) *Twin Huey*; Bell 412EP (AB-412EP) *Twin Huey*; AW119KE *Koala*
EQUIPMENT BY TYPE
PATROL AND COASTAL COMBATANTS 45
  PSO 1 *Turva* with 1 hel landing platform
  PCC 3: 2 *Tursas*; 1 *Merikarhu*
  PB 41
AMPHIBIOUS • LANDING CRAFT • UCAC 6
AIRCRAFT • TPT • Light 2 Do-228
HELICOPTERS
  MRH 5: 3 Bell 412 (AB-412) *Twin Huey*; 2 Bell 412EP (AB-412EP) *Twin Huey*
  TPT 9: **Medium** 5 AS332 *Super Puma*; **Light** 4 AW119KE *Koala*

Reserve 11,500 reservists on mobilisation

Cyber
The 2017–20 Implementation Plan for Finland's Cyber Security said that the defence ministry would develop and maintain a comprehensive cyber-defence capability for their statutory tasks, including a cyber-attack capability. The 2013 national cyber strategy and the defence forces internal concept encompass intelligence as well as offensive and defensive cyber capabilities. Full operating capability is planned by 2020. The defence forces published a Cyber Defence Concept in 2016 and created an internal implementation plan to generate the required capabilities. The cyber division is organised under the defence forces' C5 Agency. The European Centre of Excellence for Countering Hybrid Threats was established in Helsinki in April 2017.

DEPLOYMENT

AFGHANISTAN: NATO • *Operation Resolute Support* 29

IRAQ: *Operation Inherent Resolve* 100; 1 trg team

LEBANON: UN • UNIFIL 300; elm 1 mech inf bn; 1 maint coy
MALI: EU • EUTM Mali 1; UN • MINUSMA 4
MIDDLE EAST: UN • UNTSO 18 obs
SERBIA: NATO • KFOR 20
SOMALIA: EU • EUTM Somalia 7
UKRAINE: OSCE • Ukraine 23

France FRA

Euro €		2017	2018	2019
GDP	€	2.29tr	2.36tr	
	US$	2.59tr	2.79tr	
per capita	US$	39,933	42,931	
Growth	%	2.3	1.6	
Inflation	%	1.2	1.9	
Def exp [a]	€	40.9bn	42.7bn	
	US$	46.1bn	50.7bn	
Def bdgt [b]	€	43.1bn	45.0bn	46.5bn
	US$	48.7bn	53.4bn	
US$1=€		0.89	0.84	

[a] NATO definition
[b] Includes pensions

Population	67,364,357					
Age	0–14	15–19	20–24	25–29	30–64	65 plus
Male	9.5%	3.1%	2.9%	3.0%	22.0%	8.4%
Female	9.1%	2.9%	2.8%	2.9%	22.2%	11.1%

Capabilities

France maintains globally deployed forces that are also engaged on enduring operations in Africa. The 2017 Strategic Review reiterated operational commitments in sub-Saharan Africa and the Middle East, as well as a continued presence in the Asia-Pacific. The Programme Budget Law for 2019–25 set out defence-budget increases to support these goals. France plays a leading military role in the EU, NATO and the UN. In 2018, Paris launched the European Intervention Initiative, joined by nine other European countries, intended to foster a common strategic culture and develop the ability to jointly deploy quickly in case of crises. French forces are experienced and well trained, taking part in a range of NATO and other multinational exercises. Deployments abroad have demonstrated the ability to support expeditionary forces independently; however, the more recent focus on domestic security has reduced training levels and limited the ability to deploy more troops overseas. Some strategic military air-transport requirements are dependent on allies and external contractors. The high operational tempo has increased the stress on equipment. The Programme Budget Law seeks to remedy this with a budget increase for maintenance, reform of aerospace maintenance, and accelerated modernisation of multi-role tanker transport and refuelling aircraft. France has a sophisticated defence industry, exemplified by companies such as Dassault, MBDA and Nexter, with most procurements undertaken domestically and strong exports. However, President Macron has called for increased European defence-industrial cooperation. France is also seeking to invest in future technologies and supports start-ups and innovation in the defence domain.

ACTIVE 203,900 (Army 114,450 Navy 35,300 Air 40,800, Other Staffs 13,350) **Paramilitary 103,400**

RESERVE 36,300 (Army 21,650 Navy 5,400 Air 5,550 Other Staffs 3,700) **Paramilitary 40,000**

ORGANISATIONS BY SERVICE

Strategic Nuclear Forces

Navy 2,200
EQUIPMENT BY TYPE
SUBMARINES • STRATEGIC • SSBN 4
 1 *Le Triomphant* with 16 M45 SLBM with 6 TN-75 nuclear warheads, 4 single 533mm TT with F17 Mod 2 HWT/SM39 *Exocet* AShM (in refit until 2018/19)
 3 *Le Triomphant* with 16 M51 SLBM with 6 TN-75 nuclear warheads, 4 single 533mm TT with F17 Mod 2 HWT/SM39 *Exocet* AShM
AIRCRAFT • FGA 20 *Rafale* M F3 with ASMPA msl

Air Force 1,800

Air Strategic Forces Command
FORCES BY ROLE
STRIKE
 1 sqn with *Rafale* B with ASMPA msl
 1 sqn with *Rafale* B with ASMPA msl (forming)
TANKER
 1 sqn with C-135FR; KC-135 *Stratotanker*
EQUIPMENT BY TYPE
AIRCRAFT 20 combat capable
 FGA 20 *Rafale* B
 TKR/TPT 11 C-135FR
 TKR 3 KC-135 *Stratotanker*

Paramilitary

Gendarmerie 40

Space
EQUIPMENT BY TYPE
SATELLITES 7
 COMMUNICATIONS 3: 2 *Syracuse*-3 (designed to integrate with UK *Skynet* & ITA *Sicral*); 1 *Athena-Fidus* (also used by ITA)
 ISR 4: 2 *Helios* (2A/2B); 2 *Pleiades*

Army 114,450
Regt and BG normally bn size
FORCES BY ROLE
COMMAND
 1 corps HQ (CRR-FR)
 2 div HQ
MANOEUVRE
 Reconnaissance
 1 recce regt
 Armoured
 1 (2nd) armd bde (2 tk regt, 3 armd inf regt, 1 SP arty regt, 1 engr regt)

1 (7th) armd bde (1 tk regt, 1 armd BG, 3 armd inf regt, 1 SP arty regt, 1 engr regt)
1 armd BG (UAE)
Mechanised
1 (6th) lt armd bde (2 armd cav regt, 1 armd inf regt, 1 mech inf regt, 1 mech inf regt(-), 1 SP arty regt, 1 engr regt)
1 (FRA/GER) mech bde (1 armd cav regt, 1 mech inf regt)
1 mech regt (Djibouti)
Light
1 (27th) mtn bde (1 armd cav regt, 3 mtn inf regt, 1 arty regt, 1 engr regt)
3 inf regt (French Guiana & French West Indies)
1 inf regt (New Caledonia)
1 inf bn (Côte d'Ivoire)
1 inf coy (Mayotte)
Air Manoeuvre
1 (11th) AB bde (1 armd cav regt, 4 para regt, 1 arty regt, 1 engr regt, 1 spt regt)
1 AB regt (La Réunion)
1 AB bn (Gabon)
Amphibious
1 (9th) amph bde (2 armd cav regt, 1 armd inf regt, 2 mech inf regt, 1 SP arty regt, 1 engr regt)
Other
4 SMA regt (French Guiana, French West Indies & Indian Ocean)
3 SMA coy (French Polynesia, Indian Ocean & New Caledonia)
COMBAT SUPPORT
1 MRL regt
2 engr regt
2 EW regt
1 int bn
1 CBRN regt
5 sigs regt
COMBAT SERVICE SUPPORT
5 tpt regt
1 log regt
1 med regt
3 trg regt
HELICOPTER
1 (4th) hel bde (3 hel regt)
ISR UAV
1 UAV regt
AIR DEFENCE
1 SAM regt

Special Operation Forces 2,200
FORCES BY ROLE
SPECIAL FORCES
2 SF regt
HELICOPTER
1 hel regt

Reserves 21,650 reservists
Reservists form 79 UIR (Reserve Intervention Units) of about 75 to 152 troops, for 'Proterre' – combined land projection forces bn, and 23 USR (Reserve Specialised Units) of about 160 troops, in specialised regt

EQUIPMENT BY TYPE
ARMOURED FIGHTING VEHICLES
MBT 200 *Leclerc*
ASLT 248 AMX-10RC
RECCE 1,516: 70 ERC-90F4 *Sagaie*; 1,446 VBL/VB2L
IFV 627: 517 VBCI VCI; 110 VBCI VPC (CP)
APC 2,338
  APC (T) 53 BvS-10
  APC (W) 2,285: 2,200 VAB; 85 VAB VOA (OP)
AUV 16 *Aravis*
ENGINEERING & MAINTENANCE VEHICLES
AEV 54 AMX-30EBG
ARV 48+: 30 AMX-30D; 18 *Leclerc* DNG; VAB-EHC
VLB 67: 39 EFA; 18 PTA; 10 SPRAT
MW 24+: AMX-30B/B2; 4 *Buffalo*; 20 *Minotaur*
NBC VEHICLES 40 VAB NRBC
ANTI-TANK/ANTI-INFRASTRUCTURE • MSL
SP 110 VAB *Milan*
MANPATS *Eryx*; FGM-148 *Javelin*; *Milan*; MMP
ARTILLERY 273+
SP 155mm 109: 32 AU-F-1; 77 CAESAR
TOWED 155mm 12 TR-F-1
MRL 227mm 12 M270 MLRS
MOR 140+: **81mm** LLR 81mm; **120mm** 140 RT-F-1
AIRCRAFT • TPT • Light 13: 5 PC-6B *Turbo Porter*; 5 TBM-700; 3 TBM-700B
HELICOPTERS
ATK 70: 38 *Tiger* HAP; 32 *Tiger* HAD
MRH 110: 18 AS555UN *Fennec*; 92 SA341F/342M *Gazelle* (all variants)
TPT 157: **Heavy** 8 H225M *Caracal* (CSAR); **Medium** 114: 26 AS532UL *Cougar*; 36 NH90 TTH; 52 SA330 *Puma*; **Light** 35 H120 *Colibri* (leased)
UNMANNED AERIAL VEHICLES
ISR • Medium 23 SDTI (*Sperwer*)
AIR DEFENCE • SAM • Point-defence *Mistral*

Navy 35,300
EQUIPMENT BY TYPE
SUBMARINES 10
  STRATEGIC • SSBN 4:
    1 *Le Triomphant* opcon Strategic Nuclear Forces with 16 M45 SLBM with 6 TN-75 nuclear warheads, 4 single 533mm TT with F17 Mod 2 HWT/SM39 *Exocet* AShM (currently undergoing modernisation programme to install M51 SLBM; expected completion 2018/19)
    3 *Le Triomphant* opcon Strategic Nuclear Forces with 16 M51 SLBM with 6 TN-75 nuclear warheads, 4 single 533mm TT with F17 Mod 2 HWT/SM39 *Exocet* AShM
  TACTICAL • SSN 6:
    6 *Rubis* with 4 single 533mm TT with F17 Mod 2 HWT/SM39 *Exocet* AShM
PRINCIPAL SURFACE COMBATANTS 24
  AIRCRAFT CARRIERS 1
    CVN 1 *Charles de Gaulle* with 4 Sylver A43 octuple VLS with *Aster* 15 SAM, 2 sextuple *Sadral* lnchr with *Mistral* SAM (capacity 35–40 *Rafale* M/E-2C *Hawkeye*/AS365 *Dauphin*)
  DESTROYERS • DDGHM 12:
    2 *Cassard* with 2 quad lnchr with MM40 *Exocet* Block 2 AShM, 1 Mk13 GMLS with SM-1MR SAM, 2

sextuple *Sadral* lnchr with *Mistral* SAM, 2 single 533mm ASTT with L5 Mod 4 HWT, 1 100mm gun (capacity 1 AS565SA *Panther* ASW hel)

2 *Forbin* with 2 quad lnchr with MM40 *Exocet* Block 3 AShM, 4 8-cell *Sylver* A50 VLS with *Aster* 30 SAM, 2 8-cell *Sylver* A50 VLS with *Aster* 15 SAM, 2 twin 324mm ASTT with MU90, 2 76mm gun (capacity 1 NH90 TTH hel)

1 *Georges Leygues* with 2 quad lnchr with MM40 *Exocet* AShM, 1 octuple lnchr with *Crotale* SAM, 2 sextuple *Sadral* lnchr with *Mistral* SAM, 2 single 533mm ASTT with L5 HWT, 1 100mm gun (capacity 2 *Lynx* hel)

3 *Georges Leygues* (mod) with 2 quad lnchr with MM40 *Exocet* AShM, 1 octuple lnchr with *Crotale* SAM, 2 twin *Simbad* lnchr with *Mistral* SAM, 2 single 324mm ASTT with MU90 LWT, 1 100mm gun (capacity 2 *Lynx* hel)

4 *Aquitaine* with 2 8-cell *Sylver* A70 VLS with MdCN (SCALP Naval) LACM, 2 quad lnchr with MM40 *Exocet* Block 3 AShM, 2 8-cell *Sylver* A43 VLS with *Aster* 15 SAM, 2 twin B515 324mm ASTT with MU90 LWT, 1 76mm gun (capacity 1 NH90 NFH hel)

FRIGATES • FFGHM 11:

6 *Floreal* with 2 single lnchr with MM38 *Exocet* AShM, 1 twin *Simbad* lnchr with *Mistral* SAM, 1 100mm gun (capacity 1 AS565SA *Panther* hel)

5 *La Fayette* with 2 quad lnchr with MM40 *Exocet* Block 3 AShM, 1 octuple lnchr with *Crotale* SAM (space for fitting 2 octuple VLS lnchr for *Aster* 15/30), 1 100mm gun (capacity 1 AS565SA *Panther*/SA321 *Super Frelon* hel)

PATROL AND COASTAL COMBATANTS 20

FSM 7 *D'Estienne d'Orves* with 1 twin *Simbad* lnchr with *Mistral* SAM, 4 single ASTT, 1 100mm gun

PSO 3 *d'Entrecasteaux* with 1 hel landing platform

PCC 5: 2 *L'Audacieuse*; 3 *Flamant*

PCO 5: 2 *La Confiance*, 1 *Lapérouse*; 1 *Le Malin*; 1 *Fulmar*

MINE WARFARE • MINE COUNTERMEASURES 17

MCD 4 *Vulcain*

MHC 3 *Antarès*

MHO 10 *Éridan*

AMPHIBIOUS

PRINCIPAL AMPHIBIOUS SHIPS 3

LHD 3 *Mistral* with 2 twin *Simbad* lnchr with *Mistral* SAM (capacity up to 16 NH90/SA330 *Puma*/AS532 *Cougar*/*Tiger* hel; 2 LCAC or 4 LCM; 13 MBTs; 50 AFVs; 450 troops)

LANDING CRAFT 38

LCT 4 EDA-R

LCM 9 CTM

LCVP 25

LOGISTICS AND SUPPORT 34

ABU 1 *Telenn Mor*

AG 3 *Chamois*

AGE 2: 1 *Corraline*; 1 *Lapérouse* (used as trials ships for mines and divers)

AGI 1 *Dupuy de Lome*

AGM 1 *Monge*

AGOR 2: 1 *Pourquoi pas?* (used 150 days per year by Ministry of Defence; operated by Ministry of Research and Education otherwise); 1 *Beautemps-beaupré*

AGS 3 *Lapérouse*

AORH 3 *Durance* with 1-3 twin *Simbad* lnchr with *Mistral* SAM (capacity 1 SA319 *Alouette* III/AS365 *Dauphin*/*Lynx*)

ATF 2 *Malabar*

ATS 2 *Loire* (BSAH)

AXL 10: 8 *Léopard*; 2 *Glycine*

AXS 4: 2 *La Belle Poule*; 2 other

Naval Aviation 6,500

FORCES BY ROLE

STRIKE/FIGHTER/GROUND ATTACK

2 sqn with *Rafale* M F3

1 sqn (forming) with *Rafale* M F3

ANTI-SURFACE WARFARE

1 sqn with AS565SA *Panther*

ANTI-SUBMARINE WARFARE

2 sqn (forming) with NH90 NFH

1 sqn with *Lynx* Mk4

MARITIME PATROL

2 sqn with *Atlantique* 2

1 sqn with *Falcon* 20H *Gardian*

1 sqn with *Falcon* 50MI

AIRBORNE EARLY WARNING & CONTROL

1 sqn with E-2C *Hawkeye*

SEARCH & RESCUE

1 sqn with AS365N/F *Dauphin* 2

TRAINING

1 sqn with EMB 121 *Xingu*

1 unit with SA319B *Alouette* III

1 unit with *Falcon* 10MER

1 unit with CAP 10M

EQUIPMENT BY TYPE

AIRCRAFT 54 combat capable

FGA 42 *Rafale* M F3

ASW 12 *Atlantique* 2 (10 more in store)

AEW&C 3 E-2C *Hawkeye*

SAR 4 *Falcon* 50MS

TPT 26: **Light** 11 EMB-121 *Xingu*; **PAX** 15: 6 *Falcon* 10MER; 5 *Falcon* 20H *Gardian*; 4 *Falcon* 50MI

TRG 7 CAP 10M

HELICOPTERS

ASW 38: 16 *Lynx* Mk4; 22 NH90 NFH

MRH 45: 9 AS365N/F/SP *Dauphin* 2; 2 AS365N3; 16 AS565SA *Panther*; 18 SA319B *Alouette* III

AIR-LAUNCHED MISSILES

AAM • IR R-550 *Magic* 2; **IIR** *Mica* IR; **ARH** *Mica* RF

ASM AASM; AS-30L

AShM AM39 *Exocet*

LACM Nuclear ASMPA

BOMBS

Laser-guided: GBU-12 *Paveway* II

Marines 2,000

Commando Units 550

FORCES BY ROLE

MANOEUVRE

Reconnaissance

1 recce gp

Amphibious
2 aslt gp
1 atk swimmer gp
1 raiding gp
COMBAT SUPPORT
1 cbt spt gp
COMBAT SERVICE SUPPORT
1 spt gp

Fusiliers-Marin 1,450
FORCES BY ROLE
MANOEUVRE
Other
2 sy gp
7 sy coy

Reserves 5,400 reservists

Air Force 40,800
FORCES BY ROLE
STRIKE
1 sqn with *Rafale* B with ASMPA msl
1 sqn with *Rafale* B with ASMPA msl (forming)
SPACE
1 (satellite obs) sqn
FIGHTER
1 sqn with *Mirage* 2000-5
1 sqn with *Mirage* 2000B/C
FIGHTER/GROUND ATTACK
3 sqn with *Mirage* 2000D
1 (composite) sqn with *Mirage* 2000-5/D (Djibouti)
2 sqn with *Rafale* B/C
1 sqn with *Rafale* B/C (UAE)
ELECTRONIC WARFARE
1 flt with C-160G *Gabriel* (ESM)
AIRBORNE EARLY WARNING & CONTROL
1 (Surveillance & Control) sqn with E-3F *Sentry*
SEARCH & RESCUE/TRANSPORT
4 sqn with C-160R *Transall*; CN235M; SA330 *Puma*; AS555 *Fennec* (Djibouti, French Guiana, Gabon, Indian Ocean & New Caledonia)
TANKER
1 sqn with C-135FR; KC-135 *Stratotanker*
TANKER/TRANSPORT
2 sqn with C-160R *Transall*
TRANSPORT
1 sqn with A310-300; A330; A340-200 (on lease)
1 sqn with A400M
1 sqn with C-130H/H-30 *Hercules*; C-160R *Transall*
1 sqn with C-130H/H-30/J-30 *Hercules*
2 sqn with CN235M
1 sqn with *Falcon* 7X (VIP); *Falcon* 900 (VIP); *Falcon* 2000
3 flt with TBM-700A
1 (mixed) gp with C-160 *Transall*; DHC-6-300 *Twin Otter*
TRAINING
1 OCU sqn with *Mirage* 2000D
1 OCU sqn with *Rafale* B/C
1 OCU sqn with SA330 *Puma*; AS555 *Fennec*
1 OCU unit with C-160 *Transall*
1 (aggressor) sqn with *Alpha Jet**

4 sqn with *Alpha Jet**
3 sqn with Grob G120A-F; TB-30 *Epsilon*
1 sqn with EMB-121
TRANSPORT HELICOPTER
2 sqn with AS555 *Fennec*
2 sqn with AS332C/L *Super Puma*; SA330 *Puma*; H225M
ISR UAV
1 sqn with MQ-9A *Reaper*
AIR DEFENCE
3 sqn with *Crotale* NG; SAMP/T
1 sqn with SAMP/T
EQUIPMENT BY TYPE
SATELLITES see Space
AIRCRAFT 292 combat capable
FTR 41: 35 *Mirage* 2000-5/2000C; 6 *Mirage* 2000B
FGA 167: 67 *Mirage* 2000D; 52 *Rafale* B; 48 *Rafale* C
ELINT 2 C-160G *Gabriel* (ESM)
AEW&C 4 E-3F *Sentry*
TKR 3 KC-135 *Stratotanker*
TKR/TPT 12: 1 A330 MRTT; 11 C-135FR
TPT 130: **Heavy** 14 A400M; **Medium** 34: 5 C-130H *Hercules*; 9 C-130H-30 *Hercules*; 2 C-130J-30 *Hercules*; 18 C-160R *Transall*; **Light** 70: 19 CN235M-100; 8 CN235M-300; 5 DHC-6-300 *Twin Otter*; 23 EMB-121 *Xingu*; 15 TBM-700; **PAX** 12: 3 A310-300; 1 A330; 2 A340-200 (on lease); 2 *Falcon* 7X; 2 *Falcon* 900 (VIP); 2 *Falcon* 2000
TRG 153: 84 *Alpha Jet**; 18 Grob G120A-F (leased); 25 TB-30 *Epsilon* (incl many in storage); 6 PC-21; 13 SR20 (leased); 7 SR22 (leased)
HELICOPTERS
MRH 37 AS555 *Fennec*
TPT 36: **Heavy** 11 H225M *Caracal*; **Medium** 25: 1 AS332C *Super Puma*; 4 AS332L *Super Puma*; 20 SA330B *Puma*
UNMANNED AERIAL VEHICLES
CISR • **Heavy** 6 MQ-9A *Reaper* (unarmed)
AIR DEFENCE • **SAM Long-range** 8 SAMP/T; **Short-range** 12 *Crotale* NG
AIR-LAUNCHED MISSILES
AAM • **IR** R-550 *Magic* 2; **IIR** *Mica* IR; **ARH** *Mica* RF
ASM AASM; AS-30L; *Apache*
LACM
Nuclear ASMPA
Conventional SCALP EG
BOMBS
Laser-guided: GBU-12 *Paveway* II

Security and Intervention Brigade
FORCES BY ROLE
SPECIAL FORCES
3 SF gp
MANOEUVRE
Other
24 protection units
30 (fire fighting and rescue) unit

Reserves 5,550 reservists

Paramilitary 103,400

Gendarmerie 103,400; 40,000 reservists
EQUIPMENT BY TYPE
ARMOURED FIGHTING VEHICLES
  ASLT 28 VBC-90
  APC • APC (W) 153 VXB-170 (VBRG-170)
ARTILLERY • MOR 81mm some
PATROL AND COASTAL COMBATANTS 38
  PB 38: 2 *Athos*; 4 *Géranium*; 24 VCSM; 8 VSMP
HELICOPTERS • TPT • Light 60: 25 AS350BA *Ecureuil*; 20 H135; 15 H145

Cyber

In mid-December 2016, the French defence ministry published a new cyber-security doctrine based on a concept of active defence, whereby a newly formed military-cyber corps is authorised to pre-emptively identify, trace and track potential attackers, neutralise such attacks on a pre-emptive basis and retaliate against attacks on the basis of an escalation model that also allows for kinetic responses. Cyber defence is formally designated an art of war and is to be taught to France's entire officer corps. The military-cyber corps, staffed largely by the foreign-intelligence service, will report directly to the chief of the general staff. The new doctrine acknowledges the presence of a Tailored Access Unit, which has been in existence for over 30 years and is deployed overseas to provide covert coverage of specific targets. The military-cyber corps personnel level is scheduled to rise to 2,600, supplemented by a reserve force, which itself is scheduled to rise to 4,400. The February 2018 strategic review of cyber defence noted four operational areas for cyber: protection, intelligence, judicial investigation and 'military action', which can use 'active cyber warfare' and allow 'national defence operations'.

DEPLOYMENT

ARABIAN SEA: Combined Maritime Forces • CTF-150: 2 FFGHM

BURKINA FASO: *Operation Barkhane* 250; 1 SF gp; 1 H225M; 1 SA342 *Gazelle*

CENTRAL AFRICAN REPUBLIC: EU • EUTM RCA 40 **UN** • MINUSCA 10; 1 UAV unit

CHAD: *Operation Barkhane* 1,500; 1 mech inf BG; 1 FGA det with 4 *Mirage* 2000C/D; 1 tpt det with 1 C-130H; 4 CN235M

CÔTE D'IVOIRE: 950; 1 (Marine) inf bn

DEMOCRATIC REPUBLIC OF THE CONGO: UN • MONUSCO 2

DJIBOUTI: 1,450; 1 (Marine) combined arms regt with (2 recce sqn, 2 inf coy, 1 arty bty, 1 engr coy); 1 hel det with 2 SA330 *Puma*; 1 SA342 *Gazelle*; 1 LCM; 1 FGA sqn with 4 *Mirage* 2000-5; 1 SAR/tpt sqn with 1 C-160 *Transall*; 2 SA330 *Puma*

EGYPT: MFO 1

FRENCH GUIANA: 2,100: 1 (Foreign Legion) inf regt; 1 (Marine) inf regt; 1 SMA regt; 2 PCO; 1 tpt sqn with 3 CN235M; 5 SA330 *Puma*; 4 AS555 *Fennec*; 3 gendarmerie coy; 1 AS350BA *Ecureuil*; 1 H145

FRENCH POLYNESIA: 1,180: 1 SMA coy; 1 naval HQ at Papeete; 1 FFGHM; 1 PSO; 1 PCO; 1 AFS; 3 *Falcon* 200 *Gardian*; 1 SAR/tpt sqn with 2 CN235M

FRENCH WEST INDIES: 1,000; 1 (Marine) inf regt; 2 SMA regt; 2 FFGHM; 1 AS565SA *Panther*; 1 SA319 *Alouette* III; 1 naval base at Fort de France (Martinique); 4 gendarmerie coy; 1 PB; 2 AS350BA *Ecureuil*

GABON: 350; 1 AB bn

GERMANY: 2,000 (incl elm Eurocorps and FRA/GER bde); 1 (FRA/GER) mech bde (1 armd cav regt, 1 mech inf regt)

GULF OF GUINEA: *Operation Corymbe* 1 LHD; 1 FSM

INDIAN OCEAN: 2,000 (incl La Réunion and TAAF); 1 (Marine) para regt; 1 (Foreign Legion) inf coy; 1 SMA regt; 1 SMA coy; 2 FFGHM; 1 PCO; 1 LCM; 1 naval HQ at Port-des-Galets (La Réunion); 1 naval base at Dzaoudzi (Mayotte); 1 Falcon 50M; 1 SAR/tpt sqn with 2 CN235M; 5 gendarmerie coy; 1 SA319 *Alouette* III

IRAQ: *Operation Inherent Resolve* (*Chammal*) 500; 1 SF gp; 1 trg unit; 1 SP arty bty with 4 CAESAR

JORDAN: *Operation Inherent Resolve* (*Chammal*) 8 *Rafale* F3; 1 *Atlantique* 2

LEBANON: UN • UNIFIL 669; 1 mech inf bn(-); 1 maint coy; VBL; VBCI; VAB; *Mistral*

MALI: *Operation Barkhane* 1,750; 1 mech inf BG; 1 log bn; 1 hel unit with 4 *Tiger*; 3 NH90 TTH; 6 SA330 *Puma*; 4 SA342 *Gazelle*; **EU** • EUTM Mali 13; **UN** • MINUSMA 24

NEW CALEDONIA: 1,660; 1 (Marine) mech inf regt; 1 SMA coy; 6 ERC-90F1 *Lynx*; 1 FFGHM; 1 PSO; 2 PCC; 1 base with 2 *Falcon* 200 *Gardian* at Nouméa; 1 tpt unit with 2 CN235 MPA; 3 SA330 *Puma*; 4 gendarmerie coy; 2 AS350BA *Ecureuil*

NIGER: *Operation Barkhane* 500; 1 FGA det with 2 *Mirage* 2000C; 2 *Mirage* 2000D; 1 tkr/tpt det with 1 C-135FR; 1 C-160 *Transall*; 1 UAV det with 4 MQ-9A *Reaper*

QATAR: *Operation Inherent Resolve* (*Chammal*) 1 E-3F *Sentry*

SENEGAL: 350; 1 *Falcon* 50MI

SYRIA: *Operation Inherent Resolve* (*Chammal*) 1 SF unit

UKRAINE: OSCE • Ukraine 18

UNITED ARAB EMIRATES: 650: 1 armd BG (1 tk coy, 1 arty bty); *Leclerc*; CAESAR; •: *Operation Inherent Resolve* (*Chammal*); 1 FGA sqn with 6 *Rafale* F3

WESTERN SAHARA: UN • MINURSO 2 obs

FOREIGN FORCES

Belgium 28 *Alpha Jet* trg ac located at Cazaux/Tours
Germany 400 (GER elm Eurocorps)
Singapore 200; 1 trg sqn with 12 M-346 *Master*

Germany GER

Euro €		2017	2018	2019
GDP	€	3.28tr	3.40tr	
	US$	3.70tr	4.03tr	
per capita	US$	44,769	48,670	
Growth	%	2.5	1.9	
Inflation	%	1.7	1.8	
Def exp [a]	€	40.4bn	41.9bn	
	US$	45.7bn	49.7bn	
Def bdgt [b]	€	37.0bn	38.5bn	42.9bn
	US$	41.8bn	45.7bn	
US$1=€		0.89	0.84	

[a] NATO definition
[b] Includes military pensions

Population 80,457,737

Age	0–14	15–19	20–24	25–29	30–64	65 plus
Male	6.6%	2.5%	2.7%	3.1%	24.5%	9.7%
Female	6.2%	2.4%	2.6%	3.0%	24.3%	12.4%

Capabilities

The 2016 defence white paper committed Germany to a leadership role in European defence. It also emphasised the importance of NATO and the need for the armed forces to contribute to collective-defence tasks. The 2018 Konzeption der Bundeswehr underlines that collective- and territorial-defence tasks will drive current military-modernisation efforts and are of equal standing with international crisis-management operations. The key implication for defence modernisation is that Germany will need to invest in readiness and return to fully equipping operational units, after having experimented in recent years with rotating equipment among units depending on their deployment or training demands. Germany is aligning its defence-planning process with capability goals derived from multinational guidance. Berlin has been a key sponsor of the Framework Nations Concept and in the EU led the drive to implement Permanent Structured Cooperation on defence. Close military cooperation has been established, including the affiliation of units, with the Czech Republic, France, the Netherlands and Romania. The defence ministry has announced the objective of increasing authorised active force numbers but this will be challenging, given recruitment and retention problems after conscription was suspended in 2011. The armed forces are also struggling to improve their readiness levels in light of increasing demands on NATO's eastern flank. In 2019, Germany will be the framework nation for NATO's Very High Readiness Joint Task Force land component. Shortages of spare parts and maintenance problems are reported in all three services. Germany's defence-industrial base is able to design and manufacture equipment to meet requirements across all military domains, with strengths in land and naval systems. The government is pursuing a policy of closer defence-industrial cooperation in Europe.

ACTIVE 179,400 (Army 61,700 Navy 15,900 Air 27,600 Joint Support Service 27,400 Joint Medical Service 19,950 Cyber 12,700; Other 14,150)
Conscript liability Voluntary conscription only. Voluntary conscripts can serve up to 23 months

RESERVE 28,250 (Army 6,500 Navy 1,200 Air 3,300 Joint Support Service 11,500 Joint Medical Service 3,300 Other 2,450)

ORGANISATIONS BY SERVICE

Space
EQUIPMENT BY TYPE
SATELLITES 7
  COMMUNICATIONS 2 COMSATBw (1 & 2)
  ISR 5 SAR-*Lupe*

Army 61,700
FORCES BY ROLE
COMMAND
  elm 2 (1 GNC & MNC NE) corps HQ
MANOEUVRE
  Armoured
  1 (1st) armd div (1 (9th) armd bde (1 armd recce bn, 1 tk bn, 2 armd inf bn, 1 lt inf bn, 1 cbt engr bn, 1 spt bn); 1 (21st) armd bde (1 armd recce bn, 1 tk bn, 1 armd inf bn, 1 lt inf bn, 1 cbt engr bn, 1 spt bn); 1 (41st) mech inf bde (1 armd recce bn, 2 armd inf bn, 1 lt inf bn, 1 cbt engr bn, 1 sigs coy, 1 spt bn); 1 tk bn (for NLD 43rd Bde); 1 SP arty bn; 1 sigs coy)
  1 (10th) armd div (1 (12th) armd bde (1 armd recce bn, 1 tk bn, 2 armd inf bn, 1 cbt engr bn, 1 sigs coy, 1 spt bn); 1 (37th) mech inf bde (1 armd recce bn, 1 tk bn, 2 armd inf bn, 1 engr bn, 1 sigs coy, 1 spt bn); 1 (23rd) mtn inf bde (1 recce bn, 3 mtn inf bn, 1 cbt engr bn, 1 spt bn); 1 SP arty bn; 1 SP arty trg bn; 2 mech inf bn (GER/FRA bde); 1 arty bn (GER/FRA bde); 1 cbt engr coy (GER/FRA bde); 1 spt bn (GER/FRA bde))
  Air Manoeuvre
  1 (rapid reaction) AB div (1 SOF bde (2 SOF bn); 1 AB bde (2 recce coy, 2 para regt, 2 cbt engr coy); 1 atk hel regt; 2 tpt hel regt; 1 sigs coy)

EQUIPMENT BY TYPE
ARMOURED FIGHTING VEHICLES
  MBT 236: 217 *Leopard* 2A5/A6; 19 *Leopard* 2A7
  RECCE 185: 169 *Fennek* (incl 14 engr recce, 14 fires spt); 16 *Wiesel*
  IFV 578: 357 *Marder* 1A3/A4/A5; 221 *Puma*
  APC 1,246
    APC (T) 507: 345 Bv-206D/S; 162 M113 (inc variants)
    APC (W) 739: 208 *Boxer* (inc CP and trg variants); 531 TPz-1 *Fuchs* (inc variants)
  AUV 683: 247 *Dingo* 2; 363 *Eagle* IV/V; 73 *Wiesel* 1 Mk20 (with 20mm gun)
ENGINEERING & MAINTENANCE VEHICLES
  AEV 42 *Dachs*
  ARV 134: 89 BPz-2 1; 45 BPz-3 *Büffel*
  VLB 53: 22 *Biber*; 1 *Leopard* 2 with *Leguan*; 30 M3
  MW 24 *Keiler*
NBC VEHICLES 8 TPz-1 *Fuchs* NBC
ANTI-TANK/ANTI-INFRASTRUCTURE • MSL
  SP 102 *Wiesel* with TOW
  MANPATS *Milan*; *Spike-LR* (MELLS)
ARTILLERY 223
  SP 155mm 113 PzH 2000
  MRL 227mm 20 M270 MLRS
  MOR 90: **120mm** 60 *Tampella*; **SP 120mm** 30 M113 with *Tampella*

HELICOPTERS
ATK 67 *Tiger*
TPT 118: **Medium** 63 NH90; **Light** 55: 41 Bell 205 (UH-1D *Iroquois*); 14 H135
UNMANNED AERIAL VEHICLES
ISR 128: **Medium** 44 KZO; **Light** 84 LUNA

Navy 15,900
EQUIPMENT BY TYPE
SUBMARINES • TACTICAL • SSK 6:
6 Type-212A with 6 single 533mm TT with DM2A4 *Seehecht* HWT
PRINCIPAL SURFACE COMBATANTS 14
DESTROYERS • DDGHM 7:
4 *Brandenburg* with 2 twin lnchr with MM38 *Exocet* AShM, 1 16-cell Mk41 VLS with RIM-7M/P, 2 Mk49 GMLS with RIM-116 RAM SAM, 2 twin 324mm ASTT with MU90 LWT, 1 76mm gun (capacity 2 *Sea Lynx* Mk88A hel)
3 *Sachsen* with 2 quad Mk141 lnchr with RGM-84F *Harpoon* AShM, 1 32-cell Mk41 VLS with SM-2MR/RIM-162B ESSM SAM, 2 21-cell Mk49 GMLS with RIM-116 RAM SAM, 2 triple Mk32 324mm ASTT with MU90 LWT, 1 76mm gun (capacity; 2 *Sea Lynx* Mk88A hel)
FRIGATES 7
FFGHM 2 *Bremen* with 2 quad Mk141 lnchr with RGM-84A/C *Harpoon* AShM, 1 octuple Mk29 GMLS with RIM-7M/P *Sea Sparrow* SAM, 2 Mk49 GMLS with RIM-116 RAM SAM, 2 twin 324mm ASTT with Mk46 LWT, 1 76mm gun (capacity 2 *Sea Lynx* Mk88A hel)
FFGM 5 *Braunschweig* (K130) with 2 twin lnchr with RBS15 AShM, 2 Mk49 GMLS each with RIM-116 RAM SAM, 1 76mm gun, 1 hel landing platform
MINE WARFARE • MINE COUNTERMEASURES 24
MHO 10 *Frankenthal* (2 used as diving support)
MSO 2 *Ensdorf*
MSD 12 *Seehund*
AMPHIBIOUS • LCU 1 Type-520
LOGISTICS AND SUPPORT 22
AFSH 3 *Berlin* (Type-702) (capacity 2 *Sea King* Mk41 hel; 2 RAMs)
AG 4: 2 *Schwedeneck* (Type-748); 2 *Stollergrund* (Type-745)
AGI 3 *Oste* (Type-423)
AGOR 1 *Planet* (Type-751)
AOR 6 *Elbe* (Type-404) with 1 hel landing platform (2 specified for PFM support; 1 specified for SSK support; 3 specified for MHC/MSC support)
AOT 2 *Rhön* (Type-704)
APB 2: 1 *Knurrhahn*; 1 *Ohre*
AXS 1 *Gorch Fock*

Naval Aviation 2,000
EQUIPMENT BY TYPE
AIRCRAFT 8 combat capable
ASW 8 AP-3C *Orion*
TPT • **Light** 2 Do-228 (pollution control)
HELICOPTERS
ASW 22 *Lynx* Mk88A
SAR 21 *Sea King* Mk41

Naval Special Forces Command
FORCES BY ROLE
SPECIAL FORCES
1 SF coy

Sea Battalion
FORCES BY ROLE
MANOEUVRE
Amphibious
1 mne bn

Air Force 27,600
FORCES BY ROLE
FIGHTER
3 wg (2 sqn with Eurofighter *Typhoon*)
FIGHTER/GROUND ATTACK
1 wg (2 sqn with *Tornado* IDS)
1 wg (2 sqn with Eurofighter *Typhoon* (multi-role))
ISR
1 wg (1 ISR sqn with *Tornado* ECR/IDS; 2 UAV sqn with *Heron*)
TANKER/TRANSPORT
1 (special air mission) wg (3 sqn with A310 MRTT; A319; A340; AS532U2 *Cougar* II; *Global* 5000)
TRANSPORT
1 wg (total: 1 sqn with C-160D *Transall*)
1 wg (3 sqn (forming) with A400M *Atlas*)
TRAINING
1 sqn located at Holloman AFB (US) with *Tornado* IDS
1 unit (ENJJPT) located at Sheppard AFB (US) with T-6 *Texan* II; T-38A
1 hel unit located at Fassberg
TRANSPORT HELICOPTER
1 tpt hel wg (3 sqn with CH-53G/GA/GE/GS *Stallion*; 1 sqn with H145M)
AIR DEFENCE
1 wg (3 SAM gp) with MIM-104C/F *Patriot* PAC-2/3
1 AD gp with ASRAD *Ozelot*; C-RAM *Mantis* and trg unit
1 AD trg unit located at Fort Bliss (US) with MIM-104C/F *Patriot* PAC-2/3
3 (tac air ctrl) radar gp

Air Force Regiment
FORCES BY ROLE
MANOEUVRE
Other
1 sy regt
EQUIPMENT BY TYPE
AIRCRAFT 217 combat capable
FTR 129 Eurofighter *Typhoon*
ATK 68 *Tornado* IDS
ATK/EW 20 *Tornado* ECR*
TKR/TPT 4 A310 MRTT
TPT 53: **Heavy** 21 A400M; **Medium** 23 C-160D *Transall*;
PAX 9: 1 A310; 2 A340 (VIP); 2 A319; 4 *Global* 5000
TRG 109: 69 T-6A *Texan* II, 40 T-38A
HELICOPTERS
MRH 15 H145M
TPT 73: **Heavy** 70 CH-53G/GA/GS/GE *Stallion*; **Medium** 3 AS532U2 *Cougar* II (VIP)

UNMANNED AERIAL VEHICLES • ISR • Heavy 8
Heron 1
AIR DEFENCE
  SAM
    Long-range 30 MIM-104C/F Patriot PAC-2/PAC-3
    Point-defence 10 ASRAD Ozelot (with FIM-92 Stinger)
  GUNS 35mm 12 C-RAM Mantis
AIR-LAUNCHED MISSILES
  AAM • IR AIM-9L/Li Sidewinder; **IIR** IRIS-T; **ARH** AIM-120B AMRAAM
  LACM Taurus KEPD 350
  ARM AGM-88B HARM
BOMBS
  Laser-guided GBU-24 Paveway III, GBU-54 JDAM

Joint Support Service 27,400

FORCES BY ROLE
COMBAT SUPPORT
  3 MP regt
  2 NBC bn
COMBAT SERVICE SUPPORT
  6 log bn
  1 spt regt
EQUIPMENT BY TYPE
ARMOURED FIGHTING VEHICLES
  APC • APC (W) 74 TPz-1 Fuchs (inc variants)
  AUV 451: 206 Dingo 2; 245 Eagle IV/V
ENGINEERING & MAINTENANCE VEHICLES
  ARV 59: 29 BPz-2; 30 BPz-3 Büffel
NBC VEHICLES 35 TPz-1 Fuchs A6/A7/A8 NBC

Joint Medical Services 19,900

FORCES BY ROLE
COMBAT SERVICE SUPPORT
  4 med regt
EQUIPMENT BY TYPE
ARMOURED FIGHTING VEHICLES
  APC • APC (W) 109: 72 Boxer (amb); 37 TPz-1 Fuchs (amb)
  AUV 42 Eagle IV/V (amb)

Cyber & Information Command 12,700

FORCES BY ROLE
COMBAT SUPPORT
  4 EW bn
  6 sigs bn

Cyber

Germany issued a Cyber Security Strategy in February 2011. The National Cyber Security Council, an inter-ministerial body at state-secretary level, analyses cyber-related issues. A National Cyber Response Centre was set up at the Federal Office for Information Security in April 2011. In 2016, Germany boosted its cyber capabilities by implementing far-reaching reforms. A new Directorate-General Cyber/IT (CIT) was created within the Federal Ministry of Defence, with two divisions for Cyber/IT Governance and IT Services/Information Security. The director-general serves as chief information officer and point of contact for other federal ministries and agencies. The director-general's tasks include advancing technical cyber/IT capabilities and guiding cyber policies. A Cyber and Information Space Command (KdoCIR) led by a chief of staff for Cyber and Information Space (InspCIR) was launched in April 2017. The overall aim of these reforms is to assign current capabilities to areas of responsibility, protect Bundeswehr and national cyber and IT infrastructure, and improve capabilities in order to better respond to cyber attacks. Germany's defence minister stated in April 2017 that the armed forces could respond with offensive cyber operations if networks are attacked.

DEPLOYMENT

AFGHANISTAN: NATO • Operation Resolute Support 1,300; 1 bde HQ; 1 recce bn; 1 hel flt with CH-53; 1 UAV flt with 3 Heron 1 UAV

ALBANIA: OSCE • Albania 3

ARMENIA/AZERBAIJAN: OSCE • Minsk Conference 1

BLACK SEA: NATO • SNMCMG 2: 1 AOR

BOSNIA-HERZEGOVINA: OSCE • Bosnia & Herzegovina 1

DJIBOUTI: EU • Operation Atalanta 1 AP-3C Orion

ESTONIA: NATO • Baltic Air Policing 6 Eurofighter Typhoon

FRANCE: 400 (incl GER elm Eurocorps)

IRAQ: 110 (trg spt)

JORDAN: Operation Inherent Resolve 300; 4 Tornado ECR; 1 A310 MRTT

LEBANON: UN • UNIFIL 112; 1 FFGM

LIBYA: UN • UNISMIL 2 obs

LITHUANIA: NATO • Enhanced Forward Presence 580; 1 mech inf bn HQ; 1 mech inf coy(+) with Leopard 2A6; Boxer

MALI: EU • EUTM Mali 147; **UN •** MINUSMA 430; 1 sy coy; 1 int coy; 1 UAV sqn

MEDITERRANEAN SEA: EU • EU NAVFOR MED: 1 FFGHM; **NATO •** SNMG 2: 1 FFGHM

MOLDOVA: OSCE • Moldova 1

NIGER: Operation Barkhane 2 C-160 Transall

NORTH SEA: NATO • SNMCMG 1: 1 MHO

POLAND: 100 (GER elm MNC-NE)

SERBIA: NATO • KFOR 440; **OSCE •** Kosovo 7

SOUTH SUDAN: UN • UNMISS 3; 11 obs

SUDAN: UN • UNAMID 7

UKRAINE: OSCE • Ukraine 28

UNITED STATES: Trg units with 40 T-38 Talon; 69 T-6A Texan II at Goodyear AFB (AZ)/Sheppard AFB (TX); 1 trg sqn with 14 Tornado IDS at Holloman AFB (NM); NAS Pensacola (FL); Fort Rucker (AL); Missile trg at Fort Bliss (TX)

WESTERN SAHARA: UN • MINURSO 3 obs

FOREIGN FORCES

France 2,000; 1 (FRA/GER) mech bde (1 armd cav regt, 1 mech inf regt)

United Kingdom 3,750; 1 armd bde(-) (1 tk regt, 1 armd inf bn); 1 SP arty regt; 1 maint regt; 1 med regt
United States
US Africa Command: **Army**; 1 HQ at Stuttgart
US European Command: 37,950; 1 combined service HQ (EUCOM) at Stuttgart-Vaihingen

Army 23,000; 1 HQ (US Army Europe (USAREUR) at Heidelberg; 1 div HQ (fwd); 1 SF gp; 1 recce bn; 2 armd bn; 1 mech bde(-); 1 arty bn; 1 (cbt avn) hel bde(-); 1 (cbt avn) hel bde HQ; 1 int bde; 1 MP bde; 1 sigs bde; 1 spt bde; 1 ARNG SAM bde(-); 1 (APS) armd bde eqpt set; M1A2 SEPv2 *Abrams*; M2A2 *Bradley*; *Stryker Dragoon*; M109A6; M119A3; M777A2; AH-64D *Apache*; CH-47F *Chinook*; UH-60L/M *Black Hawk*; HH-60M *Black Hawk*; M1097 Avenger
Navy 500
USAF 13,100; 1 HQ (US Airforce Europe (USAFE)) at Ramstein AB; 1 HQ (3rd Air Force) at Ramstein AB; 1 ftr wg at Spangdahlem AB with 1 ftr sqn with 24 F-16CJ *Fighting Falcon*; 1 airlift wg at Ramstein AB with 14 C-130J-30 *Hercules*; 2 Gulfstream V (C-37A); 5 Learjet 35A (C-21A); 1 B-737-700 (C-40B)
USMC 1,350

Greece GRC

Euro €		2017	2018	2019
GDP	€	178bn	183bn	
	US$	201bn	218bn	
per capita	US$	18,637	20,311	
Growth	%	1.4	2.0	
Inflation	%	1.1	0.7	
Def exp [a]	€	4.21bn	4.11bn	
	US$	4.76bn	4.90bn	
Def bdgt [b]	€	4.19bn	4.11bn	4.23bn
	US$	4.73bn	4.90bn	
US$1=€		0.89	0.84	

[a] NATO definition
[b] Includes military pensions

Population 10,761,523

Age	0–14	15–19	20–24	25–29	30–64	65 plus
Male	7.1%	2.4%	2.5%	2.7%	24.9%	9.2%
Female	6.7%	2.3%	2.4%	2.7%	25.3%	11.8%

Capabilities

Greece's 2014 National Military Strategy identifies the country's principal defence objectives as safeguarding sovereignty and territorial integrity. The armed forces would also be expected to support Cyprus in the event of a conflict. The Force Structure 2013–27 document set out plans to make the armed forces more flexible, rapidly deployable and cost-effective. Greece is a NATO member and leads an EU battlegroup. In recent years, defence-cooperation agreements have been signed with Cyprus, Egypt and Israel. In 2018, talks began on an enhanced US presence in the country. The Mutual Defense Cooperation Agreement is the cornerstone of US–Greece defence cooperation and provides for a naval-support facility and an airfield at Souda Bay in Crete. The armed forces are conscript based, although Athens is looking to become fully professional. However, financial difficulties and widespread abuse of the deferment process have slowed plans. Training levels are reportedly good, with a focus by the armed forces on joint operational training. Greece's deployments involve limited numbers of personnel and focus on the near abroad, although the country contributes to EU, NATO and UN missions. Greece is modernising and upgrading its stored P-3B *Orion* aircraft to strengthen its maritime-patrol and anti-submarine-warfare capability. Rotary-wing transport capability is being boosted and most of the F-16 fleet is being upgraded. Procurement priorities include the procurement of multi-purpose frigates and a new combat aircraft. Greece has an extensive defence industry focused on the domestic market, capable of manufacturing and developing naval vessels, subsystems, ammunition and small arms.

ACTIVE 142,350 (Army 93,500 Navy 16,250 Air 21,000 Joint 11,600) **Paramilitary 4,000**
Conscript liability 9 months army; 12 months navy and air force

RESERVE 220,500 (Army 181,500 Navy 5,000 Air 34,000)

ORGANISATIONS BY SERVICE

Army 48,500; 45,000 conscripts (total 93,500)

Units are manned at 3 different levels – Cat A 85% fully ready, Cat B 60% ready in 24 hours, Cat C 20% ready in 48 hours (requiring reserve mobilisation). 3 military regions

FORCES BY ROLE
COMMAND
    2 corps HQ (incl NRDC-GR)
    1 armd div HQ
    3 mech inf div HQ
    1 inf div HQ
SPECIAL FORCES
    1 SF comd
    1 cdo/para bde
MANOEUVRE
  Reconnaissance
    4 recce bn
  Armoured
    4 armd bde (2 armd bn, 1 mech inf bn, 1 SP arty bn)
  Mechanised
    10 mech inf bde (1 armd bn, 2 mech bn, 1 SP arty bn)
  Light
    2 inf regt
  Air Manoeuvre
    1 air mob bde
    1 air aslt bde
  Amphibious
    1 mne bde
COMBAT SUPPORT
    2 MRL bn
    3 AD bn (2 with I-*Hawk*, 1 with *Tor* M1)
    3 engr regt
    2 engr bn
    1 EW regt
    10 sigs bn
COMBAT SERVICE SUPPORT
    1 log corps HQ
    1 log div (3 log bde)

HELICOPTER
1 hel bde (1 hel regt with (2 atk hel bn), 2 tpt hel bn, 4 hel bn)

EQUIPMENT BY TYPE
ARMOURED FIGHTING VEHICLES
  MBT 1,328: 170 *Leopard* 2A6HEL; 183 *Leopard* 2A4; 500 *Leopard* 1A4/5; 100 M60A1/A3; 375 M48A5
  RECCE 242 VBL
  IFV 398 BMP-1
  APC • APC (T) 2,407: 86 *Leonidas* Mk1/2; 2,108 M113A1/A2; 213 M577 (CP)
ENGINEERING & MAINTENANCE VEHICLES
  ARV 261: 12 *Büffel*; 43 BPz-2; 94 M88A1; 112 M578
  VLB 12+: 12 *Biber*; *Leguan*
  MW *Giant Viper*
ANTI-TANK/ANTI-INFRASTRUCTURE
  MSL
    SP 557: 195 HMMWV with 9K135 *Kornet*-E (AT-14 *Spriggan*); 362 M901
    MANPATS 9K111 *Fagot* (AT-4 *Spigot*); *Milan*; TOW
  RCL 84mm *Carl Gustav*; **90mm** EM-67; **SP 106mm** 581 M40A1
ARTILLERY 3,609
  SP 587: **155mm** 442: 418 M109A1B/A2/A3GEA1/A5; 24 PzH 2000; **203mm** 145 M110A2
  TOWED 557: **105mm** 351: 333 M101; 18 M-56; **155mm** 206 M114
  MRL 145: **122mm** 109 RM-70; **227mm** 36 M270 MLRS
  MOR 2,320: **81mm** 1,700; **107mm** 620 M30 (incl 231 SP)
SURFACE-TO-SURFACE MISSILE LAUNCHERS
  SRBM • Conventional MGM-140A ATACMS (launched from M270 MLRS)
AIRCRAFT • TPT • Light 18: 1 Beech 200 *King Air* (C-12C) 2 Beech 200 *King Air* (C-12R/AP *Huron*); 15 Cessna 185 (U-17A/B)
HELICOPTERS
  ATK 28: 19 AH-64A *Apache*; 9 AH-64D *Apache*
  TPT 140: **Heavy** 24: 18 CH-47D *Chinook*; 6 CH-47SD *Chinook*; **Medium** 14 NH90 TTH; **Light** 102: 88 Bell 205 (UH-1H *Iroquois*); 14 Bell 206 (AB-206) *Jet Ranger*
UNMANNED AERIAL VEHICLES
  ISR • Medium 4 *Sperwer*
AIR DEFENCE
  SAM 155
    Medium-range 42 MIM-23B I-*Hawk*
    Short-range 21 9K331 *Tor*-M1 (SA-15 *Gauntlet*)
    Point-range 92+: 38 9K33 *Osa*-M (SA-8B *Gecko*); 54 ASRAD HMMWV; FIM-92 *Stinger*
  GUNS • TOWED 727: **20mm** 204 Rh 202; **23mm** 523 ZU-23-2

National Guard 33,000 reservists
Internal security role
FORCES BY ROLE
MANOEUVRE
  Light
    1 inf div
  Air Manoeuvre
    1 para regt

COMBAT SUPPORT
  8 arty bn
  4 AD bn
COMBAT SUPPORT
  1 hel bn

Navy 14,200; 2,050 conscript (total 16,250)
EQUIPMENT BY TYPE
SUBMARINES • TACTICAL • SSK 11:
  3 *Poseidon* (GER Type-209/1200) with 8 single 533mm TT with SUT HWT
  1 *Poseidon* (GER Type-209/1200) (modernised with AIP technology) with 8 single 533mm TT with SUT HWT
  3 *Glavkos* (GER Type-209/1100) with 8 single 533mm TT with UGM-84C *Harpoon* AShM/SUT HWT
  4 *Papanikolis* (GER Type-214) with 8 single 533mm TT with UGM-84C *Harpoon* AShM/SUT HWT
PRINCIPAL SURFACE COMBATANTS 13
  FRIGATES • FFGHM 13:
    4 *Elli* Batch I (ex-NLD *Kortenaer* Batch 2) with 2 quad Mk141 lnchr with RGM-84A/C *Harpoon* AShM, 1 octuple Mk29 GMLS with RIM-7M/P *Sea Sparrow* SAM, 2 twin 324mm ASTT with Mk46 LWT, 1 *Phalanx* CIWS, 1 76mm gun (capacity 2 Bell 212 (AB-212) hel or 1 S-70B *Seahawk* hel)
    2 *Elli* Batch II (ex-NLD *Kortenaer* Batch 2) with 2 quad Mk141 lnchr with RGM-84A/C *Harpoon* AShM, 1 octuple Mk29 GMLS with RIM-7M/P *Sea Sparrow* SAM, 2 twin 324mm ASTT with Mk46 LWT, 2 *Phalanx* CIWS, 2 76mm gun (capacity 2 Bell 212 (AB-212) hel or 1 S-70B *Seahawk* hel)
    3 *Elli* Batch III (ex-NLD *Kortenaer* Batch 2) with 2 quad Mk141 lnchr with RGM-84A/C *Harpoon* AShM, 1 octuple Mk29 lnchr with RIM-7M/P *Sea Sparrow* SAM, 2 twin 324mm ASTT with Mk46 LWT, 1 *Phalanx* CIWS, 1 76mm gun (capacity 2 Bell 212 (AB-212) hel)
    4 *Hydra* (GER MEKO 200) with 2 quad lnchr with RGM-84G *Harpoon* AShM, 1 16-cell Mk48 Mod 5 VLS with RIM-162 ESSM SAM, 2 triple 324mm ASTT each with Mk46 LWT, 2 *Phalanx* CIWS, 1 127mm gun (capacity 1 S-70B *Seahawk* ASW hel)
PATROL AND COASTAL COMBATANTS 33
  CORVETTES • FSGM 5 *Roussen* (*Super Vita*) with 2 quad lnchr with MM40 *Exocet* Block 2 AShM, 1 21-cell Mk49 GMLS with RIM-116 RAM SAM, 1 76mm gun
  PCFG 12:
    2 *Kavaloudis* (FRA *La Combattante* IIIB) with 6 single lnchr with RB 12 *Penguin* AShM, 2 single 533mm TT with SST-4 HWT, 2 76mm gun
    3 *Kavaloudis* (FRA *La Combattante* IIIB) with 2 twin lnchr with RGM-84C *Harpoon* AShM, 2 single 533mm TT with SST-4 HWT, 2 76mm gun
    2 *Laskos* (FRA *La Combattante* III) with 4 MM38 *Exocet* AShM, 2 single 533mm TT with SST-4 HWT, 2 76mm gun
    2 *Laskos* (FRA *La Combattante* III) with 2 twin lnchr with RGM-84C *Harpoon* AShM, 2 single 533mm TT with SST-4 HWT, 2 76mm gun
    1 *Votsis* (ex-GER *Tiger*) with 2 twin Mk-141 lnchr with RGM-84C *Harpoon* AShM, 1 76mm gun

2 *Votsis* (ex-GER *Tiger*) with 2 twin MM38 *Exocet* AShM, 1 76mm gun
PCO 8:
2 *Armatolos* (DNK *Osprey*) with 1 76mm gun
2 *Pirpolitis* with 1 76mm gun
4 *Machitis* with 1 76mm gun
PB 8: 4 *Andromeda* (NOR *Nasty*); 2 *Stamou*; 2 *Tolmi*
MINE COUNTERMEASURES 4
MHO 4: 2 *Evropi* (ex-UK *Hunt*); 2 *Evniki* (ex-US *Osprey*)
AMPHIBIOUS
LANDING SHIPS • LST 5:
5 *Chios* (capacity 4 LCVP; 300 troops) with 1 76mm gun, 1 hel landing platform
LANDING CRAFT 15
LCU 5
LCA 7
LCAC 3 *Kefallinia* (*Zubr*) with 2 AK630 CIWS (capacity either 3 MBT or 10 APC (T); 230 troops)
LOGISTICS AND SUPPORT 25
ABU 2
AG 2 *Pandora*
AGOR 1 *Naftilos*
AGS 2: 1 *Stravon*; 1 *Pytheas*
AOR 2 *Axios* (ex-GER *Luneburg*)
AORH 1 *Prometheus* (ITA *Etna*) with 1 Phalanx CIWS
AOT 4 *Ouranos*
AWT 6 *Kerkini*
AXS 5

Coastal Defence
EQUIPMENT BY TYPE
COASTAL DEFENCE • AShM 2 MM40 *Exocet*

Naval Aviation
FORCES BY ROLE
ANTI-SUBMARINE WARFARE
1 div with S-70B *Seahawk*; Bell 212 (AB-212) ASW
EQUIPMENT BY TYPE
AIRCRAFT • ASW (5 P-3B *Orion* in store undergoing modernisation)
HELICOPTERS
ASW 18: 7 Bell 212 (AB-212) ASW; 11 S-70B *Seahawk*
AIR-LAUNCHED MISSILES
ASM AGM-114 *Hellfire*
AShM AGM-119 *Penguin*

Air Force 18,800; 2,200 conscripts (total 21,000)

Tactical Air Force
FORCES BY ROLE
FIGHTER/GROUND ATTACK
1 sqn with F-4E *Phantom* II
3 sqn with F-16CG/DG Block 30/50 *Fighting Falcon*
3 sqn with F-16CG/DG Block 52+ *Fighting Falcon*
2 sqn with F-16C/D Block 52+ ADV *Fighting Falcon*
1 sqn with *Mirage* 2000-5EG/BG Mk2
1 sqn with *Mirage* 2000EG/BG
AIRBORNE EARLY WARNING
1 sqn with EMB-145H *Erieye*

EQUIPMENT BY TYPE
AIRCRAFT 231 combat capable
FGA 231: 34 F-4E *Phantom* II; 70 F-16CG/DG Block 30/50 *Fighting Falcon*; 55 F-16CG/DG Block 52+; 30 F-16 C/D Block 52+ ADV *Fighting Falcon;* 19 *Mirage* 2000-5EG Mk2; 5 *Mirage* 2000-5BG Mk2; 16 *Mirage* 2000EG; 2 *Mirage* 2000BG
AEW 4 EMB-145AEW (EMB-145H) *Erieye*
AIR-LAUNCHED MISSILES
AAM • IR AIM-9L/P *Sidewinder*; R-550 *Magic* 2;
IIR IRIS-T; *Mica* IR; **ARH** AIM-120B/C AMRAAM; *Mica* RF
ASM AGM-65A/B/G *Maverick*
LACM SCALP EG
AShM AM39 *Exocet*
ARM AGM-88 HARM
BOMBS
Electro-optical guided: GBU-8B HOBOS
Laser-guided: GBU-10/12/16 *Paveway* II; GBU-24 *Paveway* III; GBU-50 *Enhanced Paveway* II
INS/GPS-guided GBU-31 JDAM; AGM-154C JSOW

Air Defence
FORCES BY ROLE
AIR DEFENCE
6 sqn/bty with MIM-104A/B/D *Patriot/Patriot* PAC-1 SOJC/*Patriot* PAC-2 GEM
2 sqn/bty with S-300PMU-1 (SA-10C *Grumble*)
12 bty with *Skyguard*/RIM-7 *Sparrow*/guns; *Crotale* NG/GR; *Tor*-M1 (SA-15 *Gauntlet*)
EQUIPMENT BY TYPE
AIR DEFENCE
SAM
Long-range 48: 36 MIM-104A/B/D *Patriot/Patriot* PAC-1 SOJC/PAC-2 GEM; 12 S-300PMU-1 (SA-10C *Grumble*)
Short-range 13+: 9 *Crotale* NG/GR; 4 9K331 *Tor*-M1 (SA-15 *Gauntlet*); some *Skyguard/Sparrow*
GUNS • 30mm 35+ *Artemis*-30

Air Support Command
FORCES BY ROLE
SEARCH & RESCUE/TRANSPORT HELICOPTER
1 sqn with AS332C *Super Puma* (SAR/CSAR)
1 sqn with AW109; Bell 205A (AB-205A) (SAR); Bell 212 (AB-212 - VIP, tpt)
TRANSPORT
1 sqn with C-27J *Spartan*
1 sqn with C-130B/H *Hercules*
1 sqn with EMB-135BJ *Legacy*; ERJ-135LR; Gulfstream V
EQUIPMENT BY TYPE
AIRCRAFT
TPT 26: **Medium** 23: 8 C-27J *Spartan*; 5 C-130B *Hercules*; 10 C-130H *Hercules*; **Light** 2: 1 EMB-135BJ *Legacy*; 1 ERJ-135LR; **PAX** 1 Gulfstream V
HELICOPTERS
TPT 31: **Medium** 12 AS332C *Super Puma*; **Light** 19: 12 Bell 205A (AB-205A) (SAR); 4 Bell 212 (AB-212) (VIP, Tpt); 3 AW109

Air Training Command

FORCES BY ROLE

TRAINING
2 sqn with T-2C/E *Buckeye*
2 sqn with T-6A/B *Texan* II
1 sqn with T-41D

EQUIPMENT BY TYPE
AIRCRAFT • TRG 91: 28 T-2C/E *Buckeye*; 20 T-6A *Texan* II; 25 T-6B *Texan* II; 18 T-41D

Paramilitary

Coast Guard and Customs 4,000

EQUIPMENT BY TYPE
PATROL AND COASTAL COMBATANTS 124:
  PCC 3
  PCO 1 *Gavdos* (Damen 5009)
  PBF 54
  PB 66
AIRCRAFT • TPT • Light 4: 2 Cessna 172RG *Cutlass*; 2 TB-20 *Trinidad*
HELICOPTERS
SAR: 3 AS365N3

Cyber

A new Joint Cyber Command in the Hellenic National Defence General Staff was established in 2014, replacing the existing Cyber Defence Directorate. The National Policy on Cyber Defence was published in March 2018.

DEPLOYMENT

AFGHANISTAN: NATO • *Operation Resolute Support* 5

BOSNIA-HERZEGOVINA: EU • EUFOR • *Operation Althea* 1

CYPRUS: Army 950 (ELDYK army); ε200 (officers/NCOs seconded to Greek-Cypriot National Guard) (total 1,150); 1 mech bde (1 armd bn, 2 mech inf bn, 1 arty bn); 61 M48A5 MOLF MBT; 80 *Leonidas* APC; 12 M114 arty; 6 M110A2 arty

LEBANON: UN • UNIFIL 148; 1 FFGHM

MALI: EU • EUTM Mali 2

MEDITERRANEAN SEA: NATO • SNMG 2: 1 FFGHM; 1 PCO; 1 MHO

SERBIA: NATO • KFOR 116; 1 inf coy
OSCE • Kosovo 1

UKRAINE: OSCE • Ukraine 23

FOREIGN FORCES

United States US European Command: 400; 1 naval base at Makri; 1 naval base at Soudha Bay; 1 air base at Iraklion

Hungary HUN

Hungarian Forint f		2017	2018	2019
GDP	f	38.2tr	40.8tr	
	US$	139bn	156bn	
per capita	US$	14,209	16,016	
Growth	%	4.0	4.0	
Inflation	%	2.4	2.8	
Def exp [a]	f	403bn	444bn	
	US$	1.47bn	1.70bn	
Def bdgt [b]	f	354bn	427bn	513bn
	US$	1.29bn	1.64bn	
US$1=f		274.27	261.03	

[a] NATO definition
[b] Excludes military pensions

Population 9,825,704

Age	0–14	15–19	20–24	25–29	30–64	65 plus
Male	7.6%	2.7%	3.0%	3.2%	24.0%	7.2%
Female	7.1%	2.5%	2.8%	3.1%	24.9%	11.9%

Capabilities

Hungary published a National Security Strategy and National Military Strategy in 2012. Territorial defence and the ability to participate in NATO and other international operations are central tenets of the military strategy, including the medium-term aim of having forces capable of taking part in high-intensity operations. Hungary is also implementing the Zrínyi 2026 national defence and armed-forces modernisation plan, announced in December 2016. Hungary coordinates policy with the other member states of the Visegrád Group, including on defence, and hosts the NATO Centre of Excellence for Military Medicine. At the end of 2017, the ministry of defence announced that Hungary would resume pilot training in 2018. In 2017, the defence ministry established the Military Augmentation Preparation and Training Command to improve recruitment, training and military education. The armed forces participate in international crisis-management missions, notably in the Balkans, Afghanistan and Iraq, but have very limited organic capacity to deploy forces beyond national borders. Increasing migration pressure has involved the armed forces in internal border-control operations, assisting national police forces. Announced equipment-modernisation priorities focus on individual soldier equipment and fixed- and rotary-wing aircraft. The defence ministry focused on the air-force-related elements of Zrínyi 2026 in 2018, in part to assist with the transport of troops to international missions. Hungary's defence-industrial base is limited, though the defence ministry set up an inter-ministerial working group to boost domestic capacity in the small-arms sector.

ACTIVE 27,800 (Army 10,450 Air 5,750 Joint 11,600)
Paramilitary 12,000

RESERVE 20,000

ORGANISATIONS BY SERVICE

Hungary's armed forces have reorganised into a joint force

Land Component 10,450 (incl riverine element)

FORCES BY ROLE
SPECIAL FORCES
  1 SF regt

MANOEUVRE
Reconnaissance
1 ISR regt
Mechanised
1 (5th) mech inf bde (3 mech inf bn, 1 cbt engr coy, 1 sigs coy, 1 log bn)
1 (25th) mech inf bde (1 tk bn; 2 mech inf bn, 1 arty bn, 1 AT bn, 1 log bn)
COMBAT SUPPORT
1 engr regt
1 EOD/rvn regt
1 CBRN bn
1 sigs regt
COMBAT SERVICE SUPPORT
1 log regt
EQUIPMENT BY TYPE
ARMOURED FIGHTING VEHICLES
MBT 44 T-72M1
IFV 120 BTR-80A
APC 272
APC (W) 260 BTR-80
PPV 12 Maxxpro Plus
ENGINEERING & MAINTENANCE VEHICLES
AEV BAT-2
ARV VT-55A
VLB BLG-60; MTU; TMM
NBC VEHICLES 24+: 24 K90 CBRN Recce; PSZH-IV CBRN Recce
ANTI-TANK/ANTI-INFRASTRUCTURE
MSL • MANPATS 9K111 *Fagot* (AT-4 *Spigot*); 9K111-1 *Konkurs* (AT-5 *Spandrel*)
ARTILLERY 31
TOWED 152mm 31 D-20
MOR 82mm
PATROL AND COASTAL COMBATANTS • PBR 2
MINE COUNTERMEASURES • MSR 4 *Nestin*

Air Component 5,750

FORCES BY ROLE
FIGHTER/GROUND ATTACK
1 sqn with *Gripen* C/D
TRANSPORT
1 sqn with An-26 *Curl*
TRAINING
1 sqn with Z-143LSi; Z-242L
ATTACK HELICOPTER
1 sqn with Mi-24 *Hind*
TRANSPORT HELICOPTER
1 sqn with Mi-8 *Hip*; Mi-17 *Hip* H
AIR DEFENCE
1 SAM regt (9 bty with *Mistral*; 3 bty with 2K12 *Kub* (SA-6 *Gainful*))
1 radar regt
EQUIPMENT BY TYPE
AIRCRAFT 14 combat capable
FGA 14: 12 *Gripen* C; 2 *Gripen* D
TPT 6: Light 4 An-26 *Curl*; PAX 2 A319
TRG 4: 2 Z-143LSi; 2 Z-242L
HELICOPTERS
ATK 11: 3 Mi-24D *Hind* D; 6 Mi-24V *Hind* E; 2 Mi-24P *Hind* F
MRH 7 Mi-17 *Hip* H
TPT • Medium 3 Mi-8 *Hip* (10 in store)
AIR DEFENCE
SAM • Point-defence 16 2K12 *Kub* (SA-6 *Gainful*); *Mistral*
AIR-LAUNCHED MISSILES
AAM • IR AIM-9 *Sidewinder*; SARH R-27 (AA-10 *Alamo* A); ARH AIM-120C AMRAAM
ASM AGM-65 *Maverick*; 3M11 *Falanga* (AT-2 *Swatter*); 9K114 *Shturm*-V (AT-6 *Spiral*)
BOMBS • Laser-guided *Paveway* II

Paramilitary 12,000

Border Guards 12,000 (to reduce)

Ministry of Interior
FORCES BY ROLE
MANOEUVRE
Other
1 (Budapest) paramilitary district (7 rapid reaction coy)
11 (regt/district) paramilitary regt
EQUIPMENT BY TYPE
ARMOURED FIGHTING VEHICLES
APC • APC (W) 68 BTR-80

Cyber

A National Cyber Security Centre was established in 2015 by uniting the GovCERT-Hungary and the National Electronic Information Security Authority. The centre is supervised by the interior ministry (MoI). There is also a National Cybersecurity Coordination Council, a National Cybersecurity Forum and a cyber coordinator for cyber security at the governmental level. The Information Security Centre for Critical Systems and Facilities operated by the MoI's National Disaster Management Directorate has responsibility for critical-infrastructure protection, including of information. The Cyber Defence Centre (CDC) was established in 2016 within the Military National Security Service for security management, vulnerability assessment and for incident handling in the defence sector. Since the end of 2017, the CDC has operated a 24/7 computer-incident response capability.

DEPLOYMENT

AFGHANISTAN: NATO • *Operation Resolute Support* 111
BOSNIA-HERZEGOVINA: EU • *Operation Althea* 164; 1 inf coy; **OSCE** • Bosnia & Herzegovina 1
CENTRAL AFRICAN REPUBLIC: UN • MINUSCA 2; 2 obs
CYPRUS: UN • UNFICYP 11
IRAQ: *Operation Inherent Resolve* 164
LEBANON: UN • UNIFIL 10
MALI: EU • EUTM Mali 7
MOLDOVA: OSCE • Moldova 1
SERBIA: NATO • KFOR 388; 1 inf coy (KTM)
SOMALIA: EU • EUTM Somalia 4
UKRAINE: OSCE • Ukraine 28
WESTERN SAHARA: UN • MINURSO 2 obs

FOREIGN FORCES

United States US European Command: 100; 1 armd recce tp; M3A3 *Bradley*

Iceland ISL

Icelandic Krona Kr		2017	2018	2019
GDP	Kr	2.62tr	2.80tr	
	US$	24.5bn	26.7bn	
per capita	US$	70,248	75,700	
Growth	%	4.0	3.7	
Inflation	%	1.8	2.5	
Sy Bdgt [a]	Kr	5.87bn	4.28bn	6.75bn
	US$	54.9m	40.8m	
US$1=Kr		106.84	104.84	

[a] Coast Guard budget

Population	343,518					
Age	0–14	15–19	20–24	25–29	30–64	65 plus
Male	10.4%	3.3%	3.6%	3.7%	22.4%	6.8%
Female	10.0%	3.2%	3.4%	3.5%	22.1%	7.7%

Capabilities

Iceland is a NATO member but maintains only a coastguard service. In 2016, the country established a National Security Council to implement and monitor security policy. The coastguard controls the NATO Iceland Air Defence System, as well as a NATO Control and Reporting Centre that feeds into NATO air- and missile-defence and air-operations centres. Increased Russian air and naval activities in the Atlantic and close to NATO airspace have led to complaints from Iceland. Iceland considers its bilateral defence agreement with the US as an important pillar of its security policy and participates in the security-policy dialogue of NORDEFCO. Iceland hosts NATO and regional partners for exercises, transits and naval task groups, as well as the Icelandic Air Policing mission. Despite there being no standing armed forces, Iceland makes financial contributions and on occasion deploys civilian personnel to NATO missions. In late 2016, following a June joint declaration between the two countries, the US Navy began operating P-8 *Poseidon* maritime-patrol aircraft from Keflavik air base, and was reportedly upgrading hangars and other infrastructure at the site to enable regular, rotational patrols.

ACTIVE NIL Paramilitary 250

ORGANISATIONS BY SERVICE

Paramilitary

Iceland Coast Guard 250
EQUIPMENT BY TYPE
PATROL AND COASTAL COMBATANTS 3
    PSOH: 2 *Aegir*
    PSO 1 *Thor*
LOGISTICS AND SUPPORT • AGS 1 *Baldur*
AIRCRAFT • TPT • Light 1 DHC-8-300 (MP)
HELICOPTERS
    TPT • Medium 2 AS332L1 *Super Puma*

FOREIGN FORCES

Iceland Air Policing: Aircraft and personnel from various NATO members on a rotating basis

Ireland IRL

Euro €		2017	2018	2019
GDP	€	294bn	309bn	
	US$	332bn	366bn	
per capita	US$	68,711	75,192	
Growth	%	7.2	4.7	
Inflation	%	0.3	0.7	
Def bdgt [a]	€	921m	946m	994m
	US$	1.04bn	1.12bn	
US$1=€		0.89	0.84	

[a] Includes military pensions and capital expenditure

Population	5,068,050					
Age	0–14	15–19	20–24	25–29	30–64	65 plus
Male	11.0%	3.1%	2.9%	3.1%	23.8%	6.0%
Female	10.5%	3.0%	2.8%	3.1%	23.6%	7.0%

Capabilities

The armed forces' core mission is defending the state against armed aggression, although a 2015 white paper broadened the scope of the national-security risk assessment beyond traditional military and paramilitary threats. It listed inter- and intra-state conflict, cyber attacks, terrorism, emergencies and natural disasters, among others. The army maintains substantial EOD capabilities. Ireland is active in EU defence cooperation and continues to contribute to multinational operations. Its forces are well trained for their roles. Ireland is also working to establish a specialist reserve with relevant professional qualifications. It has sufficient logistic capability to sustain its UN deployments but has no strategic-airlift capacity. After the white paper, Dublin identified a large number of defence projects to be completed over a ten-year period. Key priorities include a mid-life upgrade for the army's *Piranha* armoured personnel carriers, EOD robots and UAVs. Ireland has a small defence industry. Specialist firms export drive-train technologies for land systems while aviation maintenance, repair and overhaul is principally focused on the civil sector.

ACTIVE 9,500 (Army 7,500 Navy 1,100 Air 900)

RESERVE 4,050 (Army 3,850 Navy 200)

ORGANISATIONS BY SERVICE

Army 7,500
FORCES BY ROLE
SPECIAL FORCES
  1 ranger coy
MANOEUVRE
  Reconnaissance
  1 armd recce sqn
  Mechanised
  1 mech inf coy
  Light
  1 inf bde (1 cav recce sqn, 4 inf bn, 1 arty regt (3 fd arty

bty, 1 AD bty), 1 fd engr coy, 1 sigs coy, 1 MP coy, 1 tpt coy)

1 inf bde (1 cav recce sqn, 3 inf bn, 1 arty regt (3 fd arty bty, 1 AD bty), 1 fd engr coy, 1 sigs coy, 1 MP coy, 1 tpt coy)

EQUIPMENT BY TYPE
ARMOURED FIGHTING VEHICLES
  RECCE 6 *Piranha* IIIH 30mm
  APC 101
    APC (W) 74: 56 *Piranha* III; 18 *Piranha* IIIH
    PPV 27 RG-32M
ANTI-TANK/ANTI-INFRASTURCTURE
  MSL • MANPATS FGM-148 *Javelin*
  RCL 84mm *Carl Gustav*
ARTILLERY 299
  TOWED • **105mm** 23: 17 L118 Light Gun; 6 L119 Light Gun
  MOR 275: **81mm** 180; **120mm** 95
AIR DEFENCE
  SAM • **Point-defence** RBS-70
  GUNS • **TOWED 40mm** 32 L/70 each with 8 *Flycatcher*

Reserves 3,850 reservists
FORCES BY ROLE
MANOEUVRE
  Reconnaissance
    1 (integrated) armd recce sqn
    2 (integrated) cav sqn
  Mechanised
    1 (integrated) mech inf coy
  Light
    14 (integrated) inf coy
COMBAT SUPPORT
  4 (integrated) arty bty
  2 engr gp
  2 MP coy
  3 sigs coy
COMBAT SERVICE SUPPORT
  2 med det
  2 tpt coy

Naval Service 1,100
EQUIPMENT BY TYPE
PATROL AND COASTAL COMBATANTS 8
  PSOH 1 *Eithne* with 1 57mm gun
  PSO 5: 2 *Roisin* with 1 76mm gun; 3 *Samuel Beckett* with 1 76mm gun
  PCO 2 *Orla* (ex-UK *Peacock*) with 1 76mm gun
  LOGISTICS AND SUPPORT • AXS 2

Air Corps 880
2 ops wg; 2 spt wg; 1 trg wg; 1 comms and info sqn
EQUIPMENT BY TYPE
AIRCRAFT
  MP 2 CN235 MPA
  TPT • **Light** 5: 4 Cessna FR-172H; 1 Learjet 45 (VIP)
  TRG 8 PC-9M
HELICOPTERS:
  MRH 6 AW139
  TPT • **Light** 2 H135 (incl trg/medevac)

DEPLOYMENT
BOSNIA-HERZEGOVINA: EU • EUFOR • *Operation Althea* 5; OSCE • Bosnia and Herzegovina 1
DEMOCRATIC REPUBLIC OF THE CONGO: UN • MONUSCO 4
LEBANON: UN • UNIFIL 353; elm 1 mech inf bn
MALI: EU • EUTM Mali 20
MEDITERRANEAN SEA: EU • EUNAVFOR MED 1 PSO
MIDDLE EAST: UN • UNTSO 13 obs
MOLDOVA: OSCE • Moldova 1
SERBIA: NATO • KFOR 12; OSCE • Kosovo 3
SYRIA/ISRAEL: UN • UNDOF 126; 1 inf coy
UKRAINE: OSCE • Ukraine 11
WESTERN SAHARA: UN • MINURSO 3 obs

Italy ITA

Euro €		2017	2018	2019
GDP	€	1.72tr	1.76tr	
	US$	1.94tr	2.09tr	
per capita	US$	31,997	34,349	
Growth	%	1.5	1.2	
Inflation	%	1.3	1.3	
Def exp [a]	€	21.2bn	21.2bn	
	US$	23.9bn	25.1bn	
Def bdgt [b]	€	20.3bn	21.0bn	21.0bn
	US$	22.9bn	24.9bn	
US$1=€		0.89	0.84	

[a] NATO definition
[b] Includes military pensions

Population   62,246,674

Age	0–14	15–19	20–24	25–29	30–64	65 plus
Male	7.0%	2.4%	2.5%	2.7%	24.4%	9.3%
Female	6.7%	2.3%	2.5%	2.8%	25.3%	12.3%

Capabilities

Italy is concerned by security challenges in the Euro-Atlantic environment, as well as from Europe's southern flank. The 2017–19 defence plan, building on the 2015 defence white paper, outlined a goal to reduce personnel numbers and improve joint activity between the services. NATO member Italy takes part in the Alliance's air-policing mission and since early 2017 has deployed to Latvia as part of the Enhanced Forward Presence. The EUNAVFOR-MED force is headquartered in Rome, while the US Navy 6th Fleet is based in Naples. Italian forces are well equipped and trained, though the white paper indicated a desire to improve joint training. The country takes part in and hosts NATO and other multinational exercises and continues to support NATO, EU and UN operations abroad. However, Italy is planning to gradually reduce its presence overseas to focus on Europe's southern flank. Italy's logistics capability is enabled by a fleet of medium transport aircraft and tankers. The white paper detailed capability-enhancement programmes including upgrades to main battle tanks and procurement of armoured fighting vehicles, counter-UAV systems and electronic-warfare capabilities. The expected retirement of much of the naval fleet has triggered a long-term replacement plan; funds are still being allocated for the FREMM frigate programme. F-35As have been ordered for the air force (and F-35Bs for naval aviation). Italy has an advanced defence industry, producing equipment across all the domains, with particular strengths in shipbuilding and aircraft and helicopter manufacturing. The country hosts Europe's F-35 final assembly and check-out facility at Cameri. Italy takes part in European defence-industrial cooperation projects, including PESCO projects.

ACTIVE 171,050 (Army 99,950 Navy 30,000 Air 41,100) Paramilitary 175,750

RESERVES 18,300 (Army 13,400 Navy 4,900)

ORGANISATIONS BY SERVICE

Space
EQUIPMENT BY TYPE
SATELLITES 9
  COMMUNICATIONS 4: 1 *Athena-Fidus* (also used by FRA); 3 *Sicral*
  ISR 5: 4 *Cosmo* (*Skymed*); 1 OPSAT-3000

Army 99,950
Regt are bn sized
FORCES BY ROLE
COMMAND
  1 (NRDC-ITA) corps HQ (1 spt bde, 1 sigs regt, 1 spt regt)
MANOEUVRE
  Mechanised
  1 (*Friuli*) div (1 (*Ariete*) armd bde (1 cav regt, 2 tk regt, 1 mech inf regt, 1 SP arty regt, 1 cbt engr regt, 1 log regt); 1 (*Pozzuolo del Friuli*) cav bde (1 cav regt, 1 amph regt, 1 arty regt, 1 cbt engr regt, 1 log regt); 1 (*Folgore*) AB bde (1 cav regt, 3 para regt, 1 arty regt, 1 cbt engr regt, 1 log regt); 1 (*Friuli*) air mob bde (1 air mob regt, 2 avn regt))
  1 (*Acqui*) div (1 (*Pinerolo*) mech bde (1 tk regt, 3 mech inf regt, 1 SP arty regt, 1 cbt engr regt, 1 log regt); 1 (*Granatieri*) mech bde (1 cav regt, 1 mech inf regt); 1 (*Garibaldi Bersaglieri*) mech bde (1 cav regt, 1 tk regt, 2 mech inf regt, 1 SP arty regt, 1 cbt engr regt, 1 log regt); 1 (*Aosta*) mech bde (1 cav regt, 3 mech inf regt, 1 SP arty regt, 1 cbt engr regt, 1 log regt); 1 (*Sassari*) lt mech bde (3 mech inf regt, 1 cbt engr regt, 1 log regt))
  Mountain
  1 (*Tridentina*) mtn div (2 mtn bde (1 cav regt, 3 mtn inf regt, 1 arty regt, 1 mtn cbt engr regt, 1 spt bn, 1 log regt))
COMBAT SUPPORT
  1 arty comd (1 arty regt, 1 MRL regt, 1 NBC regt)
  1 AD comd (2 SAM regt, 1 ADA regt)
  1 engr comd (2 engr regt, 1 CIMIC regt)
  1 EW/sigs comd (1 EW/ISR bde (1 EW regt, 1 int regt, 1 STA regt); 1 sigs bde with (7 sigs regt))
COMBAT SERVICE SUPPORT
  1 log comd (2 log regt, 4 med unit)
HELICOPTER
  1 hel bde (3 hel regt)

EQUIPMENT BY TYPE
ARMOURED FIGHTING VEHICLES
  MBT 200 C1 *Ariete*
  ASLT 259 B1 *Centauro*
  IFV 428: 200 VCC-80 *Dardo;* 208 VBM 8×8 *Freccia* (incl 36 with *Spike*-LR); 20 VBM 8×8 *Freccia* (CP)
  APC 828
    APC (T) 361: 245 Bv-206; 116 M113 (incl variants)
    APC (W) 428: 151 *Puma* 4×4; 277 *Puma* 6×6
  PPV 39 VTMM
  AUV 10 *Cougar*; IVECO LMV
  AAV 15: 14 AAVP-7; 1 AAVC-7
ENGINEERING & MAINTENANCE VEHICLES
  AEV 40 *Dachs*; M113
  ARV 138: 137 BPz-2; 1 AAVR-7
  VLB 64 *Biber*
  MW 9: 6 *Buffalo*; 3 *Miniflail*
NBC VEHICLES 14: 5 VBR NBC; 9 VBR NBC Plus
ANTI-TANK/ANTI-INFRASTRUCTURE
  MSL • MANPATS *Spike*; *Milan*
  RCL 80mm *Folgore*
ARTILLERY 1,018
  SP 155mm 193: 124 M109L; 69 PzH 2000
  TOWED 188: **105mm** 25 Oto Melara Mod 56; **155mm** 163 FH-70
  MRL 227mm 21 MLRS
  MOR 616: **81mm** 283 Expal; **120mm** 325: 183 Brandt; 142 RT-61 (RT-F1) **SP 120mm** 21 VBM 8×8 *Freccia*
AIRCRAFT • TPT • Light 6: 3 Do-228 (ACTL-1); 3 P-180 *Avanti*
HELICOPTERS
  ATK 36 AW129CBT *Mangusta*
  MRH 14 Bell 412 (AB-412) *Twin Huey*
  TPT 143: **Heavy** 27: 12 CH-47C *Chinook*; 15 CH-47F *Chinook*; **Medium** 39 NH90 TTH; **Light** 77: 6 AW109; 32 Bell 205 (AB-205); 26 Bell 206 *Jet Ranger* (AB-206); 13 Bell 212 (AB-212)
AIR DEFENCE
  SAM
    Long-range 16 SAMP/T
    Short-range 32 *Skyguard/Aspide*
    Point-defence FIM-92 *Stinger*
  GUNS • SP 25mm 64 SIDAM
AIR-LAUNCHED MISSILES
  ASM *Spike*-ER

Navy 30,000
EQUIPMENT BY TYPE
SUBMARINES • TACTICAL • SSK 8:
  4 *Pelosi* (imp *Sauro*, 3rd and 4th series) with 6 single 533mm TT with Type-A-184 HWT
  4 *Salvatore Todaro* (Type-212A) with 6 single 533mm TT with Type-A-184 Mod 3 HWT/DM2A4 HWT
PRINCIPAL SURFACE COMBATANTS 18
  AIRCRAFT CARRIERS • CVS 2:
    1 *Cavour* with 4 octuple VLS with *Aster* 15 SAM, 2 76mm guns (capacity mixed air group of 20 AV-8B *Harrier* II; AW101 *Merlin*; NH90; Bell 212)
    1 *G. Garibaldi* with 2 octuple *Albatros* lnchr with *Aspide* SAM, 2 triple 324mm ASTT with Mk46 LWT

(capacity mixed air group of 18 AV-8B *Harrier* II; AW101 *Merlin*; NH90; Bell 212)

DESTROYERS • DDGHM 11:

2 *Andrea Doria* with 2 quad lnchr with *Otomat* Mk2A AShM, 1 48-cell VLS with *Aster* 15/*Aster* 30 SAM, 2 single 324mm ASTT with MU90 LWT, 3 76mm guns (capacity 1 AW101 *Merlin*/NH90 hel)

2 *Luigi Durand de la Penne* (ex-*Animoso*) with 2 quad lnchr with *Otomat* Mk 2A AShM/*Milas* A/S, 1 Mk13 GMLS with SM-1MR SAM, 1 octuple *Albatros* lnchr with *Aspide* SAM, 2 triple 324mm ASTT with Mk46 LWT, 1 127mm gun, 3 76mm guns (capacity 1 NH90 or 2 Bell 212 (AB-212) hel)

3 *Bergamini* (GP) with 2 quad lnchr with *Otomat* Mk2A AShM, 1 16-cell VLS with *Aster* 15/*Aster* 30 SAM, 2 triple 324mm ASTT with MU90 LWT, 1 127mm gun, 1 76mm gun (capacity 2 AW101/NH90 hel)

4 *Bergamini* (ASW) with 2 quad lnchr with *Otomat* Mk2A AShM, 1 16-cell VLS with *Aster* 15/*Aster* 30 SAM, 2 triple 324mm ASTT with MU90 LWT, 2 76mm gun (capacity 2 AW101/NH90 hel)

FRIGATES • FFGHM 5 *Maestrale* with 4 single lnchr with *Otomat* Mk2 AShM, 1 octuple *Albatros* lnchr with *Aspide* SAM, 2 triple 324mm ASTT with Mk46 LWT, 1 127mm gun (capacity 1 NH90 or 2 Bell 212 (AB-212) hel)

PATROL AND COASTAL COMBATANTS 15

CORVETTES • FSM 1 *Minerva* 1 8-cell *Albatros* lnchr with *Aspide* SAM, 1 76mm gun

PSOH 10:

4 *Cassiopea* with 1 76mm gun (capacity 1 Bell 212 (AB-212) hel)

4 *Comandante Cigala Fuligosi* with 1 76mm gun (capacity 1 Bell 212 (AB-212)/NH90 hel)

2 *Sirio* (capacity 1 Bell 212 (AB-212) or NH90 hel)

PB 4 *Esploratore*

MINE WARFARE • MINE COUNTERMEASURES 10

MHO 10: 8 *Gaeta*; 2 *Lerici*

AMPHIBIOUS

PRINCIPAL AMPHIBIOUS SHIPS 3

LHD 3:

2 *San Giorgio* with 1 76mm gun (capacity 3-4 AW101/NH90/Bell 212; 3 LCM 2 LCVP; 30 trucks; 36 APC (T); 350 troops)

1 *San Giusto* with 1 76mm gun (capacity 2 AW101 *Merlin*/ NH90/Bell 212; 3 LCM 2 LCVP; 30 trucks; 36 APC (T); 350 troops)

LANDING CRAFT 24: 15 **LCVP**; 9 **LCM**

LOGISTICS AND SUPPORT 63

ABU 5 *Ponza*

AFD 9

AGE 3: 1 *Leonardo* (coastal); 1 *Raffaele Rosseti*; 1 *Vincenzo Martellota*

AGI 1 *Elettra*

AGOR 1 *Alliance*

AGS 3: 1 *Ammiraglio Magnaghi* with 1 hel landing platform; 2 *Aretusa* (coastal)

AKSL 6 *Gorgona*

AORH 3: 1 *Etna* with 1 76mm gun (capacity 1 AW101/NH90/Bell 212 hel); 2 *Stromboli* with 1 76mm gun (capacity 1 AW101/NH90 hel)

AOT 7 *Depoli*

ARSH 1 *Anteo* (capacity 1 Bell 212 (AB-212) hel)

ATS 6 *Ciclope*

AWT 7: 1 *Bormida*; 2 *Simeto*; 4 *Panarea*

AXL 3 *Aragosta*

AXS 8: 1 *Amerigo Vespucci*; 1 *Palinuro*; 1 *Italia*; 5 *Caroly*

Naval Aviation 2,200

FORCES BY ROLE

FIGHTER/GROUND ATTACK

1 sqn with AV-8B *Harrier* II; TAV-8B *Harrier* II

ANTI-SUBMARINE WARFARE/TRANSPORT

5 sqn with AW101 ASW *Merlin*; Bell 212 ASW (AB-212AS); Bell 212 (AB-212); NH90 NFH

MARITIME PATROL

1 flt with P-180

AIRBORNE EARLY WANRING & CONTROL

1 flt with AW101 AEW *Merlin*

EQUIPMENT BY TYPE

AIRCRAFT 17 combat capable

FGA 17: 14 AV-8B *Harrier* II; 2 TAV-8B *Harrier* II; 1 F-35B *Lightning* II

MP 3 P-180

HELICOPTERS

ASW 47: 10 AW101 ASW *Merlin*; 9 Bell 212 ASW; 28 NH90 NFH

AEW 4 AW101 AEW *Merlin*

TPT 15: **Medium** 11: 8 AW101 *Merlin*; 3 NH-90 MITT; **Light** 4 Bell 212 (AB-212)

AIR-LAUNCHED MISSILES

AAM • IR AIM-9L *Sidewinder*; **ARH** AIM-120 AMRAAM

ASM AGM-65 *Maverick*

AShM Marte Mk 2/S

Marines 3,000

FORCES BY ROLE

MANOEUVRE

Amphibious

1 mne regt (1 recce coy, 2 mne bn, 1 log bn)

1 (boarding) mne regt (2 mne bn)

1 landing craft gp

Other

1 sy regt (3 sy bn)

EQUIPMENT BY TYPE

ARMOURED FIGHTING VEHICLES

APC (T) 27: 24 VCC-1; 3 VCC-2

AAV 18: 15 AAVP-7; 2 AAVC-7

ENGINEERING & MAINTENANCE VEHICLES

ARV 1 AAVR-7

ANTI-TANK/ANTI-INFRASTRUCTURE

MSL• MANPATS *Milan*; *Spike*

ARTILLERY

MOR 32: **81mm** 18 Brandt; **120mm** 10 Brandt; **SP 120mm** 4 M106

AIR DEFENCE • SAM • Point-defence FIM-92 *Stinger*

Air Force 41,100

FORCES BY ROLE

FIGHTER

4 sqn with Eurofighter *Typhoon*

FIGHTER/GROUND ATTACK
1 sqn with AMX *Ghibli*
1 (SEAD/EW) sqn with *Tornado* ECR
2 sqn with *Tornado* IDS
1 sqn with F-35A *Lightning* II
FIGHTER/GROUND ATTACK/ISR
1 sqn with AMX *Ghibli*
MARITIME PATROL
1 sqn (opcon Navy) with ATR-72MP (P-72A)
TANKER/TRANSPORT
1 sqn with KC-767A
COMBAT SEARCH & RESCUE
1 sqn with AB-212 ICO
SEARCH & RESCUE
1 wg with AW139 (HH-139A); Bell 212 (HH-212); HH-3F *Pelican*
TRANSPORT
2 (VIP) sqn with A319CJ; AW139 (VH-139A); *Falcon* 50; *Falcon* 900 *Easy*; *Falcon* 900EX; SH-3D *Sea King*
2 sqn with C-130J/C-130J-30/KC-130J *Hercules*
1 sqn with C-27J *Spartan*
1 (calibration) sqn with P-180 *Avanti*
TRAINING
1 OCU sqn with Eurofighter *Typhoon*
1 sqn with MB-339PAN (aerobatic team)
1 sqn with MD-500D/E (NH-500D/E)
1 OCU sqn with *Tornado*
1 OCU sqn with AMX-T *Ghibli*
1 sqn with MB-339A
1 sqn with MB-339CD*
1 sqn with SF-260EA, 3 P2006T (T-2006A)
ISR UAV
1 sqn with MQ-9A *Reaper*; RQ-1B *Predator*
AIR DEFENCE
2 bty with *Spada*
EQUIPMENT BY TYPE
AIRCRAFT 211 combat capable
  FTR 86 Eurofighter *Typhoon*
  FGA 48: 31 AMX *Ghibli*; 8 AMX-T *Ghibli*; 9 F-35A *Lightning* II
  ATK 34 *Tornado* IDS
  ATK/EW 15 *Tornado* ECR*
  MP 2 ATR-72MP (P-72A)
  SIGINT 1 Beech 350 *King Air*
  AEW&C 2 Gulfstream G550 CAEW
  TKR/TPT 6: 4 KC-767A; 2 KC-130J *Hercules*
  TPT 74: **Medium** 31: 9 C-130J *Hercules*; 10 C-130J-30 *Hercules*; 12 C-27J *Spartan*; **Light** 35: 15 P-180 *Avanti*; 20 S-208 (liaison); **PAX** 8: 3 A319CJ; 2 *Falcon* 50 (VIP); 2 *Falcon* 900 *Easy*; 1 *Falcon* 900EX (VIP)
  TRG 109: 18 M-346; 21 MB-339A; 28 MB-339CD*; 16 MB-339PAN (aerobatics); 26 SF-260EA
HELICOPTERS
  MRH 54: 13 AW139 (HH-139A/VH-139A); 2 MD-500D (NH-500D); 39 MD-500E (NH-500E)
  CSAR 7 AW101 (HH-101A)
  SAR 12 HH-3F *Pelican*
  TPT 31: **Medium** 2 SH-3D *Sea King* (liaison/VIP); **Light** 29 Bell 212 (HH-212)/AB-212 ICO
UNMANNED AERIAL VEHICLES • ISR • Heavy 14: 9 MQ-9A *Reaper*; 5 RQ-1B *Predator*

AIR DEFENCE • SAM • Short SPADA
AIR-LAUNCHED MISSILES
  AAM • IR AIM-9L *Sidewinder*; **IIR** IRIS-T; **ARH** AIM-120B AMRAAM
  ARM AGM-88 HARM
  LACM SCALP EG/*Storm Shadow*
BOMBS
  Laser-guided/GPS: Enhanced *Paveway* II; Enhanced *Paveway* III

Joint Special Forces Command (COFS)

Army
FORCES BY ROLE
SPECIAL FORCES
  1 SF regt (9th *Assalto paracadutisti*)
  1 STA regt
  1 ranger regt (4th *Alpini paracadutisti*)
COMBAT SUPPORT
  1 psyops regt
TRANSPORT HELICOPTER
  1 spec ops hel regt

Navy (COMSUBIN)
FORCES BY ROLE
SPECIAL FORCES
  1 SF gp (GOI)
  1 diving gp (GOS)

Air Force
FORCES BY ROLE
SPECIAL FORCES
  1 wg (sqn) (17th *Stormo Incursori*)

Paramilitary

Carabinieri
FORCES BY ROLE
SPECIAL FORCES
  1 spec ops gp (GIS)

Paramilitary 175,750

Carabinieri 107,650
The Carabinieri are organisationally under the MoD. They are a separate service in the Italian Armed Forces as well as a police force with judicial competence

Mobile and Specialised Branch
FORCES BY ROLE
MANOEUVRE
  Other
  1 (mobile) paramilitary div (1 bde (1st) with (1 horsed cav regt, 11 mobile bn); 1 bde (2nd) with (1 (1st) AB regt, 2 (7th & 13th) mobile regt))
HELICOPTER
  1 hel gp
EQUIPMENT BY TYPE
ARMOURED FIGHTING VEHICLES
  APC • APC (T) 3 VCC-2
PATROL AND COASTAL COMBATANTS • PB 69

AIRCRAFT • TPT • **Light:** 1 P-180 *Avanti*
HELICOPTERS
  MRH 24 Bell 412 (AB-412)
  TPT • **Light** 19 AW109

Customs 68,100

(Servizio Navale Guardia Di Finanza)

EQUIPMENT BY TYPE
PATROL AND COASTAL COMBATANTS 179
  PCF 1 *Antonio Zara*
  PBF 146: 19 *Bigliani*; 24 *Corrubia*; 9 *Mazzei*; 62 V-2000; 32 V-5000/V-6000
  PB 32: 24 *Buratti*; 8 *Meatini*
LOGISTICS AND SUPPORT • AX 1 *Giorgio Cini*

Cyber

A Joint Integrated Concept on Computer Network Operations was approved in 2009, as was a Joint Interagency Concept on Cyberwarfare in 2014. The National Strategic Framework for Cyberspace Security, released in 2013, says that the defence ministry 'plans, executes and sustains Computer Network Operations in the cyber domain in order to prevent, localize and defend (actively and in-depth), oppose and neutralise all threats and/or hostile actions in the cyber domain'. Following the 2015 defence white paper, Italy created a Joint Cyber Command. This will achieve full operational capability in 2019. Initial focus is on network protection, including of deployed forces.

DEPLOYMENT

AFGHANISTAN: NATO • *Operation Resolute Support* 800; 1 mech inf bde HQ; 1 mech inf regt(-); 1 hel regt(-); AW129 *Mangusta*; NH90; RQ-7

ALBANIA: **OSCE** • Albania 1

BLACK SEA: **NATO** • SNMCMG 2: 1 MHO

BOSNIA-HERZEGOVINA: **EU** • EUFOR • *Operation Althea* 5; **OSCE** • Bosnia and Herzegovina 6

DJIBOUTI: 90

EGYPT: MFO 78; 3 PB

GULF OF ADEN & INDIAN OCEAN: EU • *Operation Atalanta* 1 DDGHM

INDIA/PAKISTAN: UN • UNMOGIP 2 obs

IRAQ: *Operation Inherent Resolve* (*Prima Parthica*) 845; 1 inf regt; 1 trg unit; 1 hel sqn with 4 NH90

KUWAIT: *Operation Inherent Resolve* (*Prima Parthica*) 255; 4 AMX; 2 MQ-9A *Reaper*; 1 KC-767A

LATVIA: NATO • Enhanced Forward Presence 160; 1 mech inf coy

LEBANON: UN • UNIFIL 1,043; 1 mech bde HQ; 1 mech inf bn; 1 MP coy; 1 hel bn

LIBYA: MIASIT 375; **UN** • UNSMIL 2 obs

MALI: EU • EUTM Mali 12; **UN** • MINUSMA 2

MEDITERRANEAN SEA: EU • EU NAVFOR MED: 1 LHD

NIGER: MISIN 70

SERBIA: NATO • KFOR 538; 1 mtn inf BG HQ; 1 Carabinieri unit; **OSCE** • Kosovo 10

SOMALIA: EU • EUTM Somalia 123

TURKEY: NATO • *Operation Active Fence* 130; 1 SAM bty with SAMP/T

UKRAINE: **OSCE** • Ukraine 26

UNITED ARAB EMIRATES: 120; 1 tpt flt with 2 C-130J *Hercules*

WESTERN SAHARA: UN • MINURSO 2 obs

FOREIGN FORCES

United States US European Command: 12,750
  Army 4,200; 1 AB IBCT(-)
  Navy 4,000; 1 HQ (US Navy Europe (USNAVEUR)) at Naples; 1 HQ (6th Fleet) at Gaeta; 1 ASW Sqn with 4 P-8A *Poseidon* at Sigonella
  USAF 4,350; 1 ftr wg with 2 ftr sqn with 21 F-16C/D *Fighting Falcon* at Aviano; 1 CSAR sqn with 8 HH-60G *Pave Hawk*
  USMC 200

Latvia LVA

Euro €		2017	2018	2019
GDP	€	26.9bn	28.9bn	
	US$	30.3bn	34.3bn	
per capita	US$	15,550	17,634	
Growth	%	4.5	3.7	
Inflation	%	2.9	2.7	
Def exp [a]	€	454m	576m	
	US$	513m	684m	
Def bdgt [b]	€	470m	576m	601m
	US$	531m	684m	
FMA (US)	US$	10m	0m	
US$1= €		0.89	0.84	

[a] NATO definition
[b] Includes military pensions

Population   1,923,559

Ethnic groups: Latvian 62%; Russian 27%; Belarusian 3%; Polish 2.2%

Age	0–14	15–19	20–24	25–29	30–64	65 plus
Male	7.8%	2.2%	2.6%	3.7%	23.3%	6.4%
Female	7.4%	2.1%	2.4%	3.5%	25.3%	13.1%

Capabilities

Latvia has small armed forces focused on maintaining national sovereignty and territorial integrity but the country depends on NATO membership as a security guarantor. Russia is Latvia's over-riding security concern, which in general drives security policy. The 2016 State Defence Concept set defence-strategic principles, priorities and activities. That same year, a National Armed Forces Development plan 2016–28 illustrated a capabilities-based planning process. Principal tasks are to develop and increase capabilities that would ensure early warning, detection and situational awareness, to increase combat readiness and to enhance the ability to counter hybrid threats. The armed forces are volunteer-based, although the option of moving to conscription was discussed, and rejected, in 2017. Latvia has no requirement and therefore no capacity to independently deploy and sustain forces beyond its national boundaries, although the armed forces have taken part in a range of NATO operations, and EU civilian and military missions. Land capabilities are part of the focus of the armed forces development plan – particularly for the mechanised land-force brigade and National Guard. Acquisition requirements include self-propelled howitzers, CVR(T), MANPADS and ATGW systems. The defence ministry also plans to improve combat readiness. Latvia has only niche defence-industrial capability, with cyber security a focus.

ACTIVE 6,210 (Army 1,400 Navy 480 Air 430 Joint Staff 3,300 National Guard 600)

RESERVE 15,900 (National Guard 7,750; Joint 8,150)

ORGANISATIONS BY SERVICE

Joint 3,300
FORCES BY ROLE
SPECIAL FORCES
  1 SF unit
COMBAT SUPPORT
  1 MP bn

Army 1,400
FORCES BY ROLE
MANOEUVRE
  Mechanised
  1 mech inf bde (2 mech inf bn, 1 cbt spt bn HQ, 1 CSS bn HQ)

National Guard 600; 7,750 part-time (8,350 total)
FORCES BY ROLE
MANOEUVRE
  Light
  1 (2nd) inf bde (4 inf bn; 1 engr bn)
  3 (1st, 3rd & 4th) inf bde (3 inf bn; 1 sy bn; 1 spt bn)
COMBAT SUPPORT
  1 cyber unit
  1 NBC coy
  1 psyops pl
EQUIPMENT BY TYPE
ARMOURED FIGHTING VEHICLES
  MBT 3 T-55 (trg)
  RECCE 81 FV107 *Scimitar* (incl variants)
ANTI-TANK/ANTI-INFRASTRUCTURE
  MANPATS *Spike*-LR
  RCL 84mm *Carl Gustav*; **90mm** 130 Pvpj 1110
ARTILLERY 123
  SP 155mm 47 M109A5ÖE
  TOWED 100mm 23 K-53
  MOR 53: **81mm** 28 L16; **120mm** 25 M120

Navy 480 (incl Coast Guard)
Naval Forces Flotilla separated into an MCM squadron and a patrol-boat squadron. LVA, EST and LTU have set up a joint naval unit, BALTRON, with bases at Liepaja, Riga, Ventspils (LVA), Tallinn (EST), Klaipeda (LTU). Each nation contributes 1–2 MCMVs
EQUIPMENT BY TYPE
PATROL AND COASTAL COMBATANTS 5
  PB 5 *Skrunda* (GER *Swath*)
MINE WARFARE • MINE COUNTERMEASURES 6
  MHO 5 *Imanta* (ex-NLD *Alkmaar/Tripartite*)
  MCCS 1 *Vidar* (ex-NOR)
LOGISTICS AND SUPPORT 1
  AXL 1 *Varonis* (comd and spt ship, ex-NLD)

Coast Guard
Under command of the Latvian Naval Forces
EQUIPMENT BY TYPE
PATROL AND COASTAL COMBATANTS
  PB 6: 1 *Astra*; 5 KBV 236 (ex-SWE)

Air Force 430
Main tasks are airspace control and defence, maritime and land SAR and air transportation
FORCES BY ROLE
TRANSPORT
  1 (mixed) tpt sqn with An-2 *Colt*; Mi-17 *Hip* H; PZL Mi-2 *Hoplite*
AIR DEFENCE
  1 AD bn
  1 radar sqn (radar/air ctrl)
AIRCRAFT • TPT • Light 4 An-2 *Colt*
HELICOPTERS
  MRH 4 Mi-17 *Hip* H
  TPT • Light 2 PZL Mi-2 *Hoplite*
AIR DEFENCE
  SAM • Point-defence RBS-70
  GUNS • TOWED 40mm 24 L/70

Paramilitary

State Border Guard
EQUIPMENT BY TYPE
PATROL AND COASTAL COMBATANTS
  PB 3: 1 *Valpas* (ex-FIN); 1 *Lokki* (ex-FIN); 1 *Randa*
HELICOPTERS
  TPT • Light 4: 2 Bell 206B (AB-206B) *Jet Ranger* II; 2 AW109E *Power*

Cyber
The Cyber Security Strategy of Latvia was published in 2014. Latvia established a military computer emergency-response team (MilCERT) unit in early 2016. The MilCERT monitors information and communication technologies of the defence ministry and institutions, including the armed forces. It cooperates closely with the national CERT, participates in international exercises and increases cyber-defence capabilities. A Cyber Defence Unit has been operational in the National Guard since 2014. Its goal is to ensure the formation of reserve cyber-defence capabilities and its main role is to support the MilCERT and the national CERT.

DEPLOYMENT

AFGHANISTAN: NATO • *Operation Resolute Support* 36

IRAQ: *Operation Inherent Resolve* 6

MALI: EU • EUTM Mali 3; **UN** • MINUSMA 17

NORTH SEA: NATO • SNMCMG 1: 1 MHO

UKRAINE: OSCE • Ukraine 7

FOREIGN FORCES

All **NATO** Enhanced Forward Presence unless stated
Albania 21; 1 EOD pl
Canada 350; 1 mech inf bn HQ; 1 mech inf coy(+)
Czech Republic 60; 1 mor pl
Italy 160; 1 mech inf coy
Poland 169; 1 tk coy
Slovakia 150; 1 mech inf coy
Slovenia 50; 1 CBRN pl(+)
Spain 300; 1 armd inf coy(+)
United States *Operation Atlantic Resolve*: 1 tpt hel flt; 5 UH-60M *Black Hawk*

Lithuania LTU

Euro €		2017	2018	2019
GDP	€	41.9bn	44.2bn	
	US$	47.3bn	52.5bn	
per capita	US$	16,731	18,857	
Growth	%	3.9	3.5	
Inflation	%	3.7	2.5	
Def exp [a]	€	724m	873m	
	US$	817m	1.04bn	
Def bdgt [b]	€	724m	891m	952m
	US$	817m	1.06bn	
FMA (US)	US$	10m	0m	
US$1=€		0.89	0.84	

[a] NATO definition
[b] Includes military pensions

Population 2,793,284

Ethnic groups: Lithuanian 84.2%; Polish 6.6%; Russians 5.8%; Belarusian 1.2%

Age	0–14	15–19	20–24	25–29	30–64	65 plus
Male	7.7%	2.7%	3.0%	3.4%	22.6%	6.7%
Female	7.3%	2.6%	2.8%	3.2%	25.0%	13.0%

Capabilities

Lithuania's small armed forces focus on maintaining territorial integrity and national sovereignty but the country relies on NATO membership for its security. Like the other Baltic states, it is reliant on NATO's air-policing deployment for a combat-aircraft capacity. Russia is the country's predominant security concern, and this shapes Lithuanian defence policy. In January 2017, Lithuania adopted a new National Security Strategy, reflecting the worsening regional security environment. Better combat readiness is an objective. Compulsory military service was reintroduced in 2015.

Lithuania has a limited medium-airlift capability, for use in supporting its forces on multinational deployed operations, and has no requirement for solely sovereign missions. It takes an active part in NATO and EU operations. The country is purchasing the NASAMS SAM system to improve its ground-based air defences. Lithuania has a small defence-industrial base, with niche capabilities, for instance in helicopter support and maintenance.

ACTIVE 19,850 (Army 12,400 Navy 750 Air 1,200 Other 5,500) **Paramilitary 14,400**

Conscript liability 9 months

RESERVE 6,700 (Army 6,700)

ORGANISATIONS BY SERVICE

Army 7,350; 5,050 active reserves (total 12,400)

FORCES BY ROLE
MANOEUVRE
  Mechanised
  1 (1st) mech bde (1 recce coy, 4 mech inf bn, 1 arty bn)
  Light
  1 (2nd) mot inf bde (2 mot inf bn, 1 arty bn)
COMBAT SUPPORT
  1 engr bn
COMBAT SERVICE SUPPORT
  1 trg regt

EQUIPMENT BY TYPE
ARMOURED FIGHTING VEHICLES
  IFV 4 *Boxer* (*Vilkas*) (in test)
  APC • APC (T) 238: 234 M113A1; 4 M577 (CP)
ENGINEERING & MAINTENANCE VEHICLES
  AEV 8 MT-LB
  ARV 6: 2 BPz-2; 4 M113
ANTI-TANK/ANTI-INFRASTRUCTURE
  MSL
    SP 10 M1025A2 HMMWV with FGM-148 *Javelin*
    MANPATS FGM-148 *Javelin*
  RCL 84mm *Carl Gustav*
ARTILLERY 64
  SP 16 PzH 2000
  TOWED 105mm 18 M101
  MOR 120mm 30: 5 2B11; 10 M/41D; 15 M113 with Tampella
AIR DEFENCE • SAM • Point-defence GROM

Reserves

National Defence Voluntary Forces 5,050 active reservists
FORCES BY ROLE
MANOEUVRE
  Other
  6 (territorial) def unit

Navy 760

LVA, EST and LTU established a joint naval unit, BALTRON, with bases at Liepaja, Riga, Ventpils (LVA), Tallinn (EST), Klaipeda (LTU)

EQUIPMENT BY TYPE
PATROL AND COASTAL COMBATANTS 4

PCC 4 *Zemaitis* (ex-DNK *Flyvefisken*) with 1 76mm gun
MINE WARFARE • MINE COUNTERMEASURES 4
MHC 3: 1 *Sūduvis* (ex-GER *Lindau*); 2 *Skulvis* (ex-UK *Hunt*)
MCCS 1 *Jotvingis* (ex-NOR *Vidar*)
LOGISTICS AND SUPPORT • AAR 1 *Šakiai*

Air Force 1,200

FORCES BY ROLE
AIR DEFENCE
  1 AD bn
EQUIPMENT BY TYPE
AIRCRAFT
  TPT 5: **Medium** 3 C-27J *Spartan*; **Light** 2 L-410 *Turbolet*
  TRG 1 L-39ZA *Albatros*
HELICOPTERS
  MRH 3 AS365M3 *Dauphin* (SAR)
  TPT • **Medium** 3 Mi-8 *Hip* (tpt/SAR)
AIR DEFENCE • SAM • Point-defence FIM-92 *Stinger*; RBS-70

Special Operation Force

FORCES BY ROLE
SPECIAL FORCES
  1 SF gp (1 CT unit; 1 Jaeger bn, 1 cbt diver unit)

Logistics Support Command 1,350

FORCES BY ROLE
COMBAT SERVICE SUPPORT
  1 log bn

Training and Doctrine Command 1,550

FORCES BY ROLE
COMBAT SERVICE SUPPORT
  1 trg regt

Other Units 2,600

FORCES BY ROLE
COMBAT SUPPORT
  1 MP bn

Paramilitary 14,400

Riflemen Union 11,000

State Border Guard Service 3,400

Ministry of Interior
EQUIPMENT BY TYPE
PATROL AND COASTAL COMBATANTS • PB 3: 1 *Lokki* (ex-FIN); 1 KBV 041 (ex-SWE); 1 KBV 101 (ex-SWE)
AMPHIBIOUS • LANDING CRAFT • UCAC 2 *Christina* (*Griffon* 2000)
AIRCRAFT • TPT • Light 1 Cessna 172RG
HELICOPTERS • TPT • Light 5: 1 BK-117 (SAR); 2 H120 *Colibri*; 2 H135

Cyber

In mid-2017, all cyber responsibilities were consolidated under the defence ministry. From the beginning of 2018, the ministry took on the role of leadership for Lithuania's overall cyber and state information resources (SIR) security and is now responsible for shaping national cyber-security policy. A unified National Cyber Security Centre under the defence ministry operates as the main national computer emergency-response unit for management of cyber incidents related to critical information infrastructure and SIR, public services, ISPs and digital-services providers. The law on cyber security was amended in mid-2018. The defence ministry prepared a National Cyber Security Strategy in cooperation with other state institutions and the private sector; this was adopted in August 2018. Lithuania is establishing a Regional Cyber Security Defense Center that will concentrate on practical aspects of cyber defence, including for NATO and its partners. Lithuania also in 2018 started a Cyber Rapid Response Teams and Mutual Assistance in Cybersecurity project within the PESCO framework.

DEPLOYMENT

AFGHANISTAN: NATO • *Operation Resolute Support* 50
CENTRAL AFRICAN REPUBLIC: EU • EUTM RCA 1
MALI: EU • EUTM Mali 2; **UN •** MINUSMA 38; 1 obs
NORTH SEA: NATO • SNMCMG 1: 1 MHC
SERBIA: NATO • KFOR 1
UKRAINE: JMTG-U 40; **OSCE •** Ukraine 2

FOREIGN FORCES

All **NATO** Enhanced Forward Presence unless stated
Belgium 250; 1 mech inf coy • **NATO** Baltic Air Policing 4 F-16AM *Fighting Falcon*
Croatia 230; 1 mech inf coy
Germany 580; 1 armd inf bn HQ; 1 mech inf coy(+)
Netherlands 250; 1 armd inf coy
Norway 13; 1 int unit

Luxembourg LUX

Euro €		2017	2018	2019
GDP	€	55.4bn	58.2bn	
	US$	62.5bn	69.0bn	
per capita	US$	105,863	113,954	
Growth	%	2.3	4.0	
Inflation	%	2.1	1.5	
Def exp [a]	€	288m	321m	
	US$	326m	381m	
Def bdgt	€	248m	341m	
	US$	280m	404m	
US$1=€		0.89	0.84	

[a] NATO definition

Population	605,764					
Age	0–14	15–19	20–24	25–29	30–64	65 plus
Male	8.6%	3.0%	3.3%	3.6%	25.1%	6.7%
Female	8.1%	2.9%	3.1%	3.5%	23.9%	8.3%

Capabilities

Luxembourg maintains a limited military capability to participate in European collective security and crisis management. Defence Guidelines for 2025 and Beyond were published at the end of 2017. They contain strong statements of support for NATO and EU security policy and contributions to international missions. They also outline ambitious modernisation plans, including a reorganisation of the army, which will take on joint responsibilities, including for ISR, a new air component and a military-cyber cell. Luxembourg has contributed troops to the multinational battlegroup in Lithuania as part of NATO's Enhanced Forward Presence. It is part of the European Multi-Role Tanker Transport Fleet programme, partially funding one A330 MRTT, but the Belgian and Dutch air forces are responsible for policing Luxembourg's airspace. Sustaining the army's personnel strength depends on better recruiting and retention and being able to recruit from other EU states. A review is under way, examining a specialised reserve of civilian experts. The defence guidelines envisage considerable equipment improvements and cooperative development of UAV capabilities with Belgium and the Netherlands. Ambitions for the new air component include tactical-airlift and medical-evacuation capabilities. There is a small but advanced space industry and some foreign defence firms have a presence, but the country is otherwise reliant on imports. A strategy for defence industry, innovation and research is to be developed as part of the new defence guidelines.

ACTIVE 900 (Army 900) Paramilitary 600

ORGANISATIONS BY SERVICE

Army 900
FORCES BY ROLE
MANOEUVRE
  Reconnaissance
  2 recce coy (1 to Eurocorps/BEL div, 1 to NATO pool of deployable forces)
EQUIPMENT BY TYPE
ARMOURED FIGHTING VEHICLES
  AUV 48 *Dingo 2*
ANTI-TANK/ANTI-INFRASTRUCTURE
  MSL • **MANPATS** NLAW; TOW
ARTILLERY • **MOR** 81mm 6

Paramilitary 600
  Gendarmerie 600

DEPLOYMENT

AFGHANISTAN: NATO • *Operation Resolute Support* 2
MALI: EU • *EUTM Mali* 2
MEDITERRANEAN SEA: EU • *EUNAVFOR MED* 2 *Merlin* IIIC (leased)

Macedonia, Former Yugoslav Republic FYROM

Macedonian Denar d		2017	2018	2019
GDP	d	620bn	642bn	
	US$	11.4bn	12.4bn	
per capita	US$	5,474	5,953	
Growth	%	0.0	1.6	
Inflation	%	1.4	1.8	
Def bdgt	d	6.24bn	6.50bn	
	US$	114m	125m	
FMA (US)	US$	3.6m	0m	
US$1=d		54.53	51.92	

Population 2,118,945

Ethnic groups: Macedonian 64.2%; Albanian 25.2%; Turkish 3.9%; Romani 2.7%; Serbian 1.8%; Bosniac 0.9%

Age	0–14	15–19	20–24	25–29	30–64	65 plus
Male	8.9%	3.3%	3.6%	3.8%	24.5%	5.8%
Female	8.3%	3.1%	3.4%	3.6%	24.2%	7.7%

Capabilities

The armed forces' primary goals are safeguarding the state's territorial integrity and sovereignty, as well as contributing to operations under the EU, NATO and UN umbrellas. A strategic defence review was released in 2018, which set out aims to optimise, reorganise and modernise the armed forces into a small, modern and flexible force. The review's 'Future armed forces 2028' concept calls for changes in the armed forces' structure, the consolidation of commands and headquarters, and a reorganised defence ministry. Skopje joined NATO's Membership Action Plan in 1999. NATO accession is subject to the resolution of the dispute with Greece over the country's name. The armed forces are fully professional and the country aims to train all units, particularly those with deployable capability, to NATO standards. A number of units are earmarked for participation in NATO-led operations. Skopje contributes to EU and NATO missions, with personnel deployed to *Operation Resolute Support* in Afghanistan. Participation in international peacekeeping missions has increased logistics capability. The country has modest maritime and air wings and relies on Soviet-era equipment. A 2014–23 modernisation plan is intended to update equipment to NATO standards, but progress has been limited. Among the priorities identified are the procurement of air-defence missile batteries and medium- and long-range anti-armour systems. There is little in the way of a domestic defence industry, with no ability to design and manufacture modern equipment.

ACTIVE 8,000 (Army 8,000) Paramilitary 7,600
RESERVE 4,850

ORGANISATIONS BY SERVICE

Army 8,000
FORCES BY ROLE
SPECIAL FORCES
  1 SF regt (1 SF bn, 1 Ranger bn)
MANOEUVRE
  Mechanised
  1 mech inf bde (1 tk bn, 4 mech inf bn, 1 arty bn, 1 engr bn, 1 NBC coy)

COMBAT SUPPORT
1 MP bn
1 sigs bn
COMBAT SERVICE SUPPORT
1 log bde (3 log bn)

Reserves
FORCES BY ROLE
MANOEUVRE Light
1 inf bde
EQUIPMENT BY TYPE
ARMOURED FIGHTING VEHICLES
MBT 31 T-72A
RECCE 10 BRDM-2
IFV 11: 10 BMP-2; 1 BMP-2K (CP)
APC 202
APC (T) 47: 9 *Leonidas*; 28 M113; 10 MT-LB
APC (W) 155: 57 BTR-70; 12 BTR-80; 2 *Cobra*; 84 TM-170 *Hermelin*
ANTI-TANK/ANTI-INFRASTRUCTURE
MSL • MANPATS *Milan*
RCL **57mm**; **82mm** M60A
ARTILLERY 126
TOWED 70: **105mm** 14 M-56; **122mm** 56 M-30 M-1938
MRL 17: **122mm** 6 BM-21; **128mm** 11
MOR 39: **120mm** 39

Marine Wing
EQUIPMENT BY TYPE
PATROL AND COASTAL COMBATANTS • PB 2 *Botica*

Aviation Brigade
FORCES BY ROLE
TRAINING
1 flt with Z-242; Bell 205 (UH-1H *Iroquois*)
ATTACK HELICOPTER
1 sqn with Mi-24K *Hind* G2; Mi-24V *Hind* E
TRANSPORT HELICOPTER
1 sqn with Mi-8MTV *Hip*; Mi-17 *Hip* H
AIR DEFENCE
1 AD bn
EQUIPMENT BY TYPE
AIRCRAFT
TPT • Light 1 An-2 *Colt*
TRG 5 Z-242
HELICOPTERS
ATK 4 Mi-24V *Hind* E (10: 2 Mi-24K *Hind* G2; 8 Mi-24V *Hind* E in store)
MRH 6: 4 Mi-8MTV *Hip*; 2 Mi-17 *Hip* H
TPT • Light 2 Bell 205 (UH-1H *Iroquois*)
AIR DEFENCE
SAM • Point-defence 8 9K35 *Strela*-10 (SA-13 *Gopher*); 9K310 *Igla*-1 (SA-16 *Gimlet*)
GUNS **40mm** 36 L20

Paramilitary
Police 7,600 (some 5,000 armed)
incl 2 SF units

EQUIPMENT BY TYPE
ARMOURED FIGHTING VEHICLES
APC • APC (T) M113; APC (W) BTR-80; TM-170 *Heimlin*
AUV *Ze'ev*
HELICOPTERS
MRH 1 Bell 412EP *Twin Huey*
TPT • Light 2: 1 Bell 206B (AB-206B) *Jet Ranger* II; 1 Bell 212 (AB-212)

DEPLOYMENT
AFGHANISTAN: NATO • Operation Resolute Support 44
ALBANIA: OSCE • Albania 2
BOSNIA-HERZEGOVINA: EU • EUFOR • Operation Althea 3; OSCE • Bosnia and Herzegovina 1
LEBANON: UN • UNIFIL 2
SERBIA: OSCE • Kosovo 14
UKRAINE: OSCE • Ukraine 31

Malta MLT

Euro €		2017	2018	2019
GDP	€	11.1bn	12.0bn	
	US$	12.6bn	14.3bn	
per capita	US$	27,327	30,555	
Growth	%	6.7	5.7	
Inflation	%	1.3	1.8	
Def bdgt [a]	€	57m	59m	
	US$	64m	70m	
US$1= €		0.89	0.84	

[a] Excludes military pensions

Population 449,043

Age	0–14	15–19	20–24	25–29	30–64	65 plus
Male	7.7%	2.7%	3.2%	3.5%	23.9%	8.8%
Female	7.3%	2.6%	3.0%	3.3%	23.2%	10.7%

Capabilities

The principal roles for the armed forces are maintaining external security and support for civil emergencies and to the police. There is also focus on maritime security in the Mediterranean. Malta is neutral but is a member of NATO's Partnership for Peace programme. The country also participates in bilateral and multilateral exercises. Although deployment capacity is limited, Malta has contributed to European missions. Italy has assisted Malta in meeting some security requirements, including air surveillance, while the European Internal Security Fund is funding some modernisation. Although there is some shipbuilding and ship-repair activity and a small aviation maintenance industry, none are defence-specific and Malta relies on imports to equip its armed forces.

ACTIVE 1,950 (Armed Forces 1,950)

RESERVE 180 (Emergency Volunteer Reserve Force 120 Individual Reserve 60)

ORGANISATIONS BY SERVICE

Armed Forces of Malta 1,950

FORCES BY ROLE
SPECIAL FORCES
  1 SF unit
MANOEUVRE
  Light
  1 (1st) inf regt (3 inf coy, 1 cbt spt coy)
COMBAT SUPPORT
  1 (3rd) cbt spt regt (1 cbt engr sqn, 1 EOD sqn, 1 maint sqn)
COMBAT SERVICE SUPPORT
  1 (4th) CSS regt (1 CIS coy, 1 sy coy)
EQUIPMENT BY TYPE
ARTILLERY • MOR 81mm L16
AIR DEFENCE • GUNS 14.5mm 1 ZPU-4

Maritime Squadron
Organised into 5 divisions: offshore patrol; inshore patrol; rapid deployment and training; marine engineering; and logistics
EQUIPMENT BY TYPE
PATROL AND COASTAL COMBATANTS 8
  PCO 1 *Emer*
  PCC 1 *Diciotti*
  PB 6: 4 Austal 21m; 2 *Marine Protector*
LOGISTICS AND SUPPORT 2
  AAR 2 *Cantieri Vittoria*

Air Wing
1 base party. 1 flt ops div; 1 maint div; 1 integrated log div; 1 rescue section
EQUIPMENT BY TYPE
AIRCRAFT
  TPT • Light 5: 3 Beech 200 *King Air* (maritime patrol); 2 BN-2B *Islander*
  TRG 3 *Bulldog* T MK1
HELICOPTERS
  MRH 6: 3 AW139 (SAR); 3 SA316B *Alouette* III

Montenegro MNE

Euro €		2017	2018	2019
GDP	€	4.24bn	4.53bn	
	US$	4.78bn	5.39bn	
per capita	US$	7,678	8,644	
Growth	%	4.3	3.7	
Inflation	%	2.4	2.8	
Def exp [a]	€	59m	71m	
	US$	66m	85m	
Def bdgt [b]	€	66m	67m	
	US$	75.0m	79.2m	
FMA (US)	US$	1m	0m	
US$1=€		0.89	0.84	

[a] NATO definition
[b] Includes military pensions

Population 614,249

Ethnic groups: Montenegrin 45% Serbian 28.7% Bosniac 8.6% Albanian 4.9% Croatian 1%

Age	0–14	15–19	20–24	25–29	30–64	65 plus
Male	7.5%	2.0%	2.3%	3.5%	28.4%	6.1%
Female	7.6%	2.6%	2.7%	3.3%	24.9%	9.0%

Capabilities
According to its defence strategy, Montenegro intends to develop an integrated defence system, capable of defending and preserving independence, sovereignty and national territory. However, the principal concern of the authorities is integrating Montenegro into the collective security system of NATO as well as the EU. Montenegro joined NATO in 2017. Montenegro that year accepted NATO's capability targets and has also been aligning its defence planning process with NATO standards. The country has signed defence agreements with Croatia, Slovenia and Poland in recent years. Reform and professionalism of the armed forces has been slow, and developments have been focused on structural issues around improving recruitment, outflow and professional development. The armed forces are not designed to have an expeditionary capability, and as such have little logistics capability to support deployments beyond national borders. Nevertheless, personnel have deployed to Afghanistan with NATO, affording them valuable experience. Podgorica intends to replace ageing Soviet-era equipment. Procurement priorities include light and medium helicopters and light armoured vehicles as well as improved communications capacities according to NATO standards. Future plans include the formation of a SOF unit and intelligence unit in the land forces. The country's defence industry is capable of producing small arms and ammunition.

ACTIVE 1,950 (Army 875 Navy 350 Air Force 225 Other 500) **Paramilitary 10,100**

ORGANISATIONS BY SERVICE

Army 875
FORCES BY ROLE
MANOEUVRE
  Reconnaissance
  1 recce coy
  Light
  1 mot inf bn
COMBAT SUPPORT
  1 MP coy
  1 sigs coy
COMBAT SERVICE SUPPORT
  1 log bn
EQUIPMENT BY TYPE
ARMOURED FIGHTING VEHICLES
  APC • APC (W) 8 BOV-VP M-86
ANTI-TANK/ANTI-INFRASTRUCTURE
  SP 9 BOV-1
  MSL • MANPATS 9K111 *Fagot* (AT-4 *Spigot*); 9K111-1 *Konkurs* (AT-5 *Spandrel*)
ARTILLERY 135
  TOWED 122mm 12 D-30
  MRL 128mm 18 M-63/M-94 *Plamen*
  MOR 105: 82mm 73; 120mm 32

Navy 350
1 Naval Cmd HQ with 4 operational naval units (patrol boat; coastal surveillance; maritime detachment; and SAR) with additional sigs, log and trg units with a separate coastguard element. Some listed units are in the process of decommissioning

EQUIPMENT BY TYPE
PATROL AND COASTAL COMBATANTS 5
  PSO 1 *Kotor* with 1 twin 76mm gun (1 further vessel in reserve)
  PCFG 2 *Rade Končar*† (of which 1 in refit) with 2 single lnchr with P-15 *Termit* (SS-N-2B *Styx*) AShM (missiles disarmed)
  PB 2 *Mirna* (Type-140) (Police units)
LOGISTICS AND SUPPORT 1
  AXS 1 *Jadran*†

Air Force 225
Golubovci (Podgorica) air base under army command
FORCES BY ROLE
TRAINING
  1 (mixed) sqn with G-4 *Super Galeb*; Utva-75 (none operational)
TRANSPORT HELICOPTER
  1 sqn with SA341/SA342L *Gazelle*
EQUIPMENT BY TYPE
AIRCRAFT • **TRG** (4 G-4 *Super Galeb* non-operational; 4 Utva-75 non-operational)
HELICOPTERS
  MRH 13 SA341/SA342L (HN-45M) *Gazelle*
  TPT • **Medium** 1 Bell 412EP *Twin Huey*

Paramilitary ε10,100

Montenegrin Ministry of Interior Personnel ε6,000

Special Police Units ε4,100

DEPLOYMENT
AFGHANISTAN: NATO • *Operation Resolute Support* 20
MALI: EU • EUTM Mali 1
UKRAINE: OSCE • Ukraine 3
WESTERN SAHARA: UN • MINURSO 2 obs

Multinational Organisations

Capabilities
The following represent shared capabilities held by contributors collectively rather than as part of national inventories.

ORGANISATIONS BY SERVICE

NATO AEW&C Force
Based at Geilenkirchen (GER). Original participating countries (BEL, CAN, DNK, GER, GRC, ITA, NLD, NOR, PRT, TUR, US) have been subsequently joined by 5 more (CZE, ESP, HUN, POL, ROM).
FORCES BY ROLE
AIRBORNE EARLY WARNING & CONTROL
  1 sqn with B-757 (trg); E-3A *Sentry* (NATO standard)

EQUIPMENT BY TYPE
AIRCRAFT
  AEW&C 16 E-3A *Sentry* (NATO standard)
  TPT • **PAX** 1 B-757 (trg)

Strategic Airlift Capability
Heavy Airlift Wing based at Papa air base (HUN). 12 participating countries (BLG, EST, FIN, HUN, LTU, NLD, NOR, POL, ROM, SVN, SWE, USA)
EQUIPMENT BY TYPE
AIRCRAFT • **TPT** • **Heavy** 3 C-17A *Globemaster* III

Strategic Airlift Interim Solution
Intended to provide strategic-airlift capacity pending the delivery of A400M aircraft by leasing An-124s. 14 participating countries (BEL, CZE, FIN, FRA, GER, GRC, HUN, LUX, NOR, POL, SVK, SVN, SWE, UK)
EQUIPMENT BY TYPE
AIRCRAFT • **TPT** • **Heavy** 2 An-124-100 (4 more available on 6–9 days' notice)

Netherlands NLD

Euro €		2017	2018	2019
GDP	€	737bn	767bn	
	US$	832bn	910bn	
per capita	US$	48,555	52,931	
Growth	%	2.9	2.8	
Inflation	%	1.3	1.4	
Def exp [a]	€	8.69bn	10.7bn	
	US$	9.81bn	12.7bn	
Def bdgt [b]	€	8.96bn	9.53bn	10.5bn
	US$	10.1bn	11.3bn	
US$1=€		0.89	0.84	

[a] NATO definition
[b] Includes military pensions

Population 17,151,228

Age	0–14	15–19	20–24	25–29	30–64	65 plus
Male	8.4%	3.1%	3.1%	3.2%	23.2%	8.5%
Female	8.0%	2.9%	3.0%	3.2%	23.2%	10.2%

Capabilities
The 2018 defence review tasks the armed forces with territorial defence and supporting national civil authorities with law-enforcement, disaster relief and humanitarian assistance. Dutch forces have integrated increasingly with NATO allies, particularly Germany. The army contains a Dutch–German tank battalion; there is also cooperation and integration with the German armed forces in the air and naval domains. The Netherlands has air-policing agreements with France, Belgium and Luxembourg and is a member of the UK-led Joint Expeditionary Force. The Netherlands, Belgium and Denmark have committed to forming a composite special-operations command. Dutch forces are fully professional and well trained and the Netherlands can deploy and sustain a medium-scale force for a single operation, or a small-scale joint force for an extended period. The Netherlands makes significant contributions to NATO and EU military operations globally. The

country has a modern European- and US-sourced equipment inventory. An agreement is in place with Belgium on the joint acquisition of new frigates and minehunters, while the air force is to acquire F-35 *Lightning* II combat aircraft. The Netherlands is part of the programme for a multinational NATO unit of A330 transport/tanker aircraft. The country has an advanced domestic defence industry focusing on armoured vehicles, naval ships and air-defence systems, but also hosts a range of international aerospace-company subsidiaries. Damen Schelde Naval Shipbuilding exports frigates, corvettes and fast-attack craft, while DutchAero manufactures engine components for the F-35. The country also collaborates with Germany on the *Boxer* and *Fennek* armoured vehicles.

ACTIVE 35,400 (Army 18,850 Navy 8,500 Air 8,050)
Military Constabulary 5,900
RESERVE 4,500 (Army 4,000 Navy 80 Air 420) Military Constabulary 160 Reserve liability to age 35 for soldiers/sailors, 40 for NCOs, 45 for officers

ORGANISATIONS BY SERVICE

Army 18,850
FORCES BY ROLE
COMMAND
  elm 1 (1 GNC) corps HQ
SPECIAL FORCES
  4 SF coy
MANOEUVRE Reconnaissance
  1 ISR bn (2 armd recce sqn, 1 EW coy, 2 int sqn, 1 UAV bty)
Mechanised
  1 (43rd) mech bde (1 armd recce sqn, 2 armd inf bn, 1 engr bn, 1 maint coy, 1 med coy)
  1 (13th) mech bde (1 recce sqn, 2 mech inf bn, 1 engr bn, 1 maint coy, 1 med coy)
Air Manoeuvre
  1 (11th) air mob bde (3 air mob inf bn, 1 engr coy, 1 med coy, 1 supply coy, 1 maint coy)
COMBAT SUPPORT
  1 SP arty bn (3 SP arty bty)
  1 AD comd (1 AD sqn; 1 AD bty)
  1 CIMIC bn
  1 engr bn
  2 EOD coy 1 (CIS) sigs bn 1 CBRN coy
COMBAT SERVICE SUPPORT
  1 med bn
  5 fd hospital
  3 maint coy
  2 tpt bn

Reserves 2,700 reservists
National Command
Cadre bde and corps tps completed by call-up of reservists (incl Territorial Comd)
FORCES BY ROLE
MANOEUVRE
  Light
    3 inf bn (could be mobilised for territorial def)

EQUIPMENT BY TYPE
ARMOURED FIGHTING VEHICLES
  RECCE 196 *Fennek*
  IFV 170 CV9035NL
  APC • APC (W) 200 *Boxer* (8 driver trg; 52 amb; 60 CP; 23 log)
  AUV 60 *Bushmaster* IMV
ENGINEERING & MAINTENANCE VEHICLES
  AEV 10: *Dachs*; 10 *Kodiak*
  ARV 25+: BPz-2; 25 BPz-3 *Büffel*
  VLB 13 *Legaun*
  MW *Bozena*
NBC VEHICLES 6 TPz-1 *Fuchs* NBC
ANTI-TANK/ANTI-INFRASTRUCTURE • MSL
  SP 40 *Fennek* MRAT
  MANPATS *Spike*-MR (*Gil*)
ARTILLERY 119:
  SP 155mm 18 PzH 2000
  MOR 101: **81mm** 83 L16/M1; **120mm** 18 Brandt
AIR DEFENCE • SAM
  Long-range 20 MIM-104D/F *Patriot* PAC-2 GEM/PAC-3 (TMD capable)
  Short-range 6 NASAMS II
  Point-defence 18+: FIM-92 *Stinger*; 18 *Fennek* with FIM-92 *Stinger*

Navy 8,500 (incl Marines)
EQUIPMENT BY TYPE
SUBMARINES • TACTICAL • SSK 4 *Walrus* with 4 single 533mm TT with Mk48 *Sea Arrow* HWT
PRINCIPAL SURFACE COMBATANTS 6
  DESTROYERS • DDGHM 4:
    3 *De Zeven Provinciën* with 2 quad Mk141 lnchr with RGM-84F *Harpoon* AShM, 1 40-cell Mk41 VLS with SM-2MR/ESSM SAM, 2 twin 324mm ASTT with Mk46 LWT, 1 *Goalkeeper* CIWS, 1 127mm gun (capacity 1 NH90 hel)
    1 *Zeven Provinciën* with 2 quad Mk141 lnchr with RGM-84F *Harpoon* AShM, 1 40-cell Mk41 VLS with SM-2MR/ESSM SAM, 2 twin 324mm ASTT with Mk46 LWT, 2 *Goalkeeper* CIWS, 1 127mm gun (capacity 1 NH90 hel)
  FRIGATES • FFGHM
    2 *Karel Doorman* with 2 quad Mk141 lnchr with RGM-84A/C *Harpoon* AShM, 1 16-cell Mk48 VLS with RIM-7P *Sea Sparrow* SAM, 2 twin 324mm ASTT with Mk46 LWT, 1 *Goalkeeper* CIWS, 1 76mm gun (capacity 1 NH90 hel)
PATROL AND COASTAL COMBATANTS
  PSOH 4 *Holland* with 1 76mm gun (capacity 1 NH90 hel)
MINE WARFARE • MINE COUNTERMEASURES
  MHO 6 *Alkmaar* (*Tripartite*)
AMPHIBIOUS
  PRINCIPAL AMPHIBIOUS SHIPS • LPD 2:
    1 *Rotterdam* with 2 *Goalkeeper* CIWS (capacity 6 NH90/AS532 *Cougar* hel; either 6 LCVP or 2 LCM and 3 LCVP; either 170 APC or 33 MBT; 538 troops)
    1 *Johan de Witt* with 2 *Goalkeeper* CIWS (capacity 6 NH90 hel or 4 AS532 *Cougar* hel; either 6 LCVP or 2 LCM and 3 LCVP; either 170 APC or 33 MBT; 700 troops)

LANDING CRAFT 17
   LCM 5 Mk9
   LCVP 12 Mk5

LOGISTICS AND SUPPORT 8
   AFSH 1 *Karel Doorman* with 2 *Goalkeeper* CIWS (capacity 6 NH90/AS532 *Cougar* or 2 CH-47F *Chinook* hel; 2 LCVP)
   AGS 2 *Snellius*
   AK 1 *Pelikaan*
   AOT 1 *Patria*
   AS 1 *Mercuur*
   AXL 1 *Van Kingsbergen*
   AXS 1 *Urania*

Marines 2,650

FORCES BY ROLE
SPECIAL FORCES
   1 SF gp (1 SF sqn, 1 CT sqn)
MANOEUVRE
   Amphibious
   2 mne bn
   1 amph aslt gp
COMBAT SERVICE SUPPORT
   1 spt gp (coy)

EQUIPMENT BY TYPE
ARMOURED FIGHTING VEHICLES
   APC • **APC (T)** 160: 87 Bv-206D; 73 BvS-10 *Viking*
ENGINEERING & MAINTENANCE VEHICLES
   ARV 4 BvS-10; 4 BPz-2
   MED 4 BvS-10
ANTI-TANK/ANTI-INFRASTRUCTURE
   MSL • **MANPATS** Spike-MR (*Gil*)
ARTILLERY • **MOR 81mm** 12 L16/M1
AIR DEFENCE • **SAM** • **Point-defence** FIM-92 *Stinger*

Air Force 8,050

FORCES BY ROLE
FIGHTER/GROUND ATTACK
   3 sqn with F-16AM/BM *Fighting Falcon*
ANTI-SUBMARINE WARFARE/SEARCH & RESCUE
   1 sqn with NH90 NFH
TANKER/TRANSPORT
   1 sqn with C-130H/H-30 *Hercules*
   1 sqn with KDC-10; Gulfstream IV
TRAINING
   1 OEU sqn with F-35A *Lightning* II
   1 sqn with PC-7 *Turbo Trainer*
   1 hel sqn with AH-64D *Apache*; CH-47D *Chinook* (based at Fort Hood, TX)
ATTACK HELICOPTER
   1 sqn with AH-64D *Apache*
TRANSPORT HELICOPTER
   1 sqn with AS532U2 *Cougar* II
   1 sqn with CH-47D/F *Chinook*

EQUIPMENT BY TYPE
AIRCRAFT 63 combat capable
   FTR 61 F-16AM/BM *Fighting Falcon*
   FGA 2 F-35A *Lightning* II (in test)
   TKR 2 KDC-10
   TPT 5: **Medium** 4: 2 C-130H *Hercules*; 2 C-130H-30 *Hercules*; **PAX** 1 Gulfstream IV
   TRG 13 PC-7 *Turbo Trainer*
HELICOPTERS
   ATK 28 AH-64D *Apache*
   ASW 12 NH90 NFH
   TPT 33: **Heavy** 17: 11 CH-47D *Chinook*; 6 CH-47F *Chinook*; **Medium** 16: 8 AS532U2 *Cougar* II; 8 NH90 TTH
AIR-LAUNCHED MISSILES
   AAM • **IR** AIM-9L/M *Sidewinder*; **IIR** AIM-9X *Sidewinder* II; **ARH** AIM-120B AMRAAM
   ASM AGM-114K *Hellfire*; AGM-65D/G *Maverick*
BOMBS
   Laser-guided GBU-10/GBU-12 *Paveway* II; GBU-24 *Paveway* III (all supported by LANTIRN)
   INS/GPS guided GBU-39 Small Diameter Bomb

Paramilitary

Royal Military Constabulary 5,900

Subordinate to the Ministry of Defence, but performs most of its work under the authority of other ministries

FORCES BY ROLE
MANOEUVRE
   Other
   5 paramilitary district (total: 28 paramilitary unit)

EQUIPMENT BY TYPE
ARMOURED FIGHTING VEHICLES
   APC • **APC (W)** 24 YPR-KMar

Cyber

A Defence Cyber Command (DCC) was launched in September 2014 and became operational in early 2017. It provides 'integrated military operational and offensive cyber capacity'. The DCC is situated in the army but comprises personnel from all the armed services. In late July 2018, the DCC came under the direct command of the commander of the armed forces in order to help the deployability of this capability. According to the defence ministry, 'the armed forces can attack, manipulate and disable the digital systems of opponents. Potential opponents might be other states, terrorist or other organisations, or hackers.' A Joint SIGINT Cyber Unit was stood up in 2014 under the General Intelligence and Security Service and the Dutch Military Intelligence and Security Service. An updated defence cyber strategy was published in November 2018.

DEPLOYMENT

AFGHANISTAN: NATO • *Operation Resolute Support* 160
BOSNIA-HERZEGOVINA: OSCE • Bosnia and Herzegovina 1
CARIBBEAN: 1 AFSH
IRAQ: *Operation Inherent Resolve* 150; 3 trg unit
JORDAN: *Operation Inherent Resolve* 150; 6 F-16AM *Fighting Falcon*
LEBANON: UN • UNIFIL 1

LITHUANIA: NATO • Enhanced Forward Presence 250; 1 armd inf coy

MALI: UN • MINUSMA 241; 1 recce coy

MEDITERRANEAN SEA: NATO • SNMG 1: 1 DDGHM

MIDDLE EAST: UN • UNTSO 13 obs

NORTH SEA: NATO • SNMCMG 1: 1 MHO

SERBIA: OSCE • Kosovo 1

SOUTH SUDAN: UN • UNMISS 6

SYRIA/ISRAEL: UN • UNDOF 2

UKRAINE: OSCE • Ukraine 6

UNITED STATES: 1 hel trg sqn with AH-64D *Apache*; CH-47D *Chinook* based at Fort Hood (TX)

FOREIGN FORCES

United States US European Command: 400

Norway NOR

Norwegian Kroner kr		2017	2018	2019
GDP	kr	3.30tr	3.57tr	
	US$	399bn	441bn	
per capita	US$	75,389	82,372	
Growth	%	1.9	2.1	
Inflation	%	1.9	1.9	
Def exp [a]	kr	53.5bn	57.5bn	
	US$	6.46bn	7.11bn	
Def bdgt [b]	kr	51.2bn	54.9bn	59.0
	US$	6.20bn	6.80bn	
US$1=kr		8.27	8.08	

[a] NATO definition
[b] Includes military pensions

Population	5,372,191					
Age	0–14	15–19	20–24	25–29	30–64	65 plus
Male	9.2%	3.1%	3.4%	3.6%	23.4%	7.7%
Female	8.8%	2.9%	3.2%	3.5%	22.2%	9.0%

Capabilities

Norway sustains small but well-equipped and highly trained armed forces. Territorial defence is at the heart of security policy. The Long Term Defence Plan, published in 2016, said that the armed forces needed further adjustments to address evolving security challenges at home and abroad. In October 2017, the defence ministry announced measures to strengthen capability in the High North. A USMC contingent has deployed to Vaernes, on a rotational basis, since January 2017. In August 2018, this was extended for up to five years and a second location at Setermonden added. The US will invest, through its European Deterrence Initiative, in infrastructure upgrades at Rygge Air Station to enable reinforcements in case of conflict. Norway is not an EU member, but it signed a cooperation agreement with the European Defence Agency in 2006. At any one time, around one-third of troops are conscripts. Norway maintains a small presence in a range of international crisis-management missions, including in Afghanistan, Iraq and in Jordan. Equipment recapitalisation is ongoing. Norway's first F-35A arrived in late 2017 and the government announced that it would procure four submarines as part of a strategic partnership with Germany. Large procurements will stretch budgets, with the F-35 alone reportedly taking up 32% of all procurement spending between 2018 and 2025. In June 2018, it was announced that a planned upgrade to Norway's main battle tank fleet would be abandoned until the mid-2020s. Norway has an advanced and diverse defence-industrial base with a high percentage of SMEs and a mix of private and state-owned companies.

ACTIVE 23,250 (Army 8,100 Navy 3,900 Air 3,600 Central Support 7,000 Home Guard 650)

Conscript liability 19 months maximum. Conscripts first serve 12 months from 19–28, and then up to 4–5 refresher training periods until age 35, 44, 55 or 60 depending on rank and function. Conscription was extended to women in 2015

RESERVE 40,000 (Home Guard 40,000)

Readiness varies from a few hours to several days

ORGANISATIONS BY SERVICE

Army 3,700; 4,400 conscript (total 8,100)

The armoured infantry brigade – Brigade North – trains new personnel of all categories and provides units for international operations. At any time around one-third of the brigade will be trained and ready to conduct operations. The brigade includes one high-readiness armoured battalion (Telemark Battalion) with combat support and combat service support units on high readiness

FORCES BY ROLE
MANOEUVRE
  Reconnaissance
    1 (GSV) bn (1 (border) recce coy, 1 ranger coy, 1 spt coy, 1 trg coy)
  Armoured
    1 armd inf bde (1 ISR bn, 2 armd bn, 1 lt inf bn, 1 arty bn, 1 engr bn, 1 MP coy, 1 CIS bn, 1 spt bn, 1 med bn)
  Light
    1 lt inf bn (His Majesty The King's Guards)

EQUIPMENT BY TYPE
ARMOURED FIGHTING VEHICLES
  MBT 36 *Leopard* 2A4
  RECCE 21 CV9030
  IFV 91: 76 CV9030N; 15 CV9030N (CP)
  APC 390
    APC (T) 315 M113 (incl variants)
    APC (W) 75 XA-186 *Sisu*/XA-200 *Sisu*
  AUV 190: 20 *Dingo* 2; 170 IVECO LMV
ENGINEERING & MAINTENANCE VEHICLES
  AEV 25: 16 CV90 STING; 8 M113 AEV; 1 *Wisent*-2
  ARV 6 BPz-2
  VLB 35: 26 *Leguan*; 9 *Leopard* 1
  MW 9 910 MCV-2
NBC VEHICLES 6 TPz-1 *Fuchs* NBC
ANTI-TANK/ANTI-INFRASTRUCTURE
  MANPATS FGM-148 *Javelin*
  RCL **84mm** *Carl Gustav*
ARTILLERY 202
  SP **155mm** 24 M109A3GN
  MOR 202: **81mm** 150 L16; SP **81mm** 28: 16 CV9030; 12 M125A2

Navy 2,100; 1,800 conscripts (total 3,900)

Joint Command – Norwegian National Joint Headquarters. The Royal Norwegian Navy is organised into four elements under the command of the chief of staff of the Navy: the naval units (*Kysteskadren*), the schools (*Sjoforsvarets Skoler*), the naval bases and the coastguard (*Kystvakten*)

FORCES BY ROLE
MANOEUVRE
Reconnaissance
1 ISR coy (Coastal Rangers)
COMBAT SUPPORT
1 EOD pl

EQUIPMENT BY TYPE
SUBMARINES • TACTICAL • SSK 6 *Ula* with 8 single 533mm TT with A3 *Seal* DM2 HWT
PRINCIPAL SURFACE COMBATANTS 4
DESTROYERS • DDGHM 4 *Fridtjof Nansen* with *Aegis* C2 (mod), 2 quad lnchr with NSM AShM, 1 8-cell Mk41 VLS with ESSM SAM, 2 twin 324mm ASTT with *Sting Ray* LWT, 1 76mm gun (capacity 1 NH90 hel) (1 other sank 11/2018; may be salvaged and returned to service)
PATROL AND COASTAL COMBATANTS 12:
  PCFG 6 *Skjold* with 8 single lnchr with NSM AShM, 1 76mm gun
  PBF 6 CB90N (capacity 20 troops)
MINE WARFARE • MINE COUNTERMEASURES 4:
  MSC 2 *Alta* with 1 twin *Simbad* lnchr with *Mistral* SAM
  MHC 2 *Oksoy* with 1 twin *Simbad* lnchr with *Mistral* SAM
LOGISTICS AND SUPPORT 5
  AGI 1 *Marjata* IV
  AGS 2: 1 *HU Sverdrup* II; 1 *Eger* (*Marjata* III) with 1 hel landing platform
  AXL 2 *Reine*

Coast Guard

EQUIPMENT BY TYPE
PATROL AND COASTAL COMBATANTS 13
  PSOH 3 *Nordkapp* with 1 57mm gun (capacity 1 med tpt hel)
  PSO 5: 3 *Barentshav*; 1 *Harstad*; 1 *Svalbard* with 1 57mm gun, 1 hel landing platform
  PCC 5 *Nornen*

Air Force 2,600 ; 1,000 conscript (total 3,600)

Joint Command – Norwegian National HQ

FORCES BY ROLE
FIGHTER/GROUND ATTACK
  2 sqn with F-16AM/BM *Fighting Falcon*
MARITIME PATROL
  1 sqn with P-3C *Orion*; P-3N *Orion* (pilot trg)
ELECTRONIC WARFARE
  1 sqn with *Falcon* 20C (EW, Flight Inspection Service)
SEARCH & RESCUE
  1 sqn with *Sea King* Mk43B; AW101
TRANSPORT
  1 sqn with C-130J-30 *Hercules*
TRAINING
  1 sqn with MFI-15 *Safari*
TRANSPORT HELICOPTER
  2 sqn with Bell 412SP *Twin Huey*
  1 sqn with NH90 (forming)
AIR DEFENCE
  1 bn with NASAMS II

EQUIPMENT BY TYPE
AIRCRAFT 79 combat capable
  FTR 57: 47 F-16AM *Fighting Falcon*; 10 F-16BM
  FGA 16 F-35A *Lightning* II
  ASW 6: 4 P-3C *Orion*; 2 P-3N *Orion* (pilot trg)
  EW 2 *Falcon* 20C
  TPT • Medium 4 C-130J-30 *Hercules*
  TRG 16 MFI-15 *Safari*
HELICOPTERS
  ASW 8 NH90 NFH
  SAR 17: 5 AW101; 12 *Sea King* Mk43B
  MRH 18: 6 Bell 412HP; 12 Bell 412SP
AIR DEFENCE
  SAM • Short-range NASAMS II
AIR-LAUNCHED MISSILES
  AAM • IR AIM-9L *Sidewinder*; **IIR** AIM-9X *Sidewinder* II; IRIS-T; **ARH** AIM-120B AMRAAM; AIM-120C AMRAAM
BOMBS
  Laser-guided EGBU-12 *Paveway* II
  INS/GPS guided JDAM

Special Operations Command (NORSOCOM)

FORCES BY ROLE
SPECIAL FORCES
  1 (armed forces) SF comd (2 SF gp)
  1 (navy) SF comd (1 SF gp)

Central Support, Administration and Command 6,150; 850 conscripts (total 7,000)

Central Support, Administration and Command includes military personnel in all joint elements and they are responsible for logistics and CIS in support of all forces in Norway and abroad

Home Guard 650 (40,000 reserves)

The Home Guard is a separate organisation, but closely cooperates with all services. The Home Guard is organised in 11 Districts with mobile Rapid Reaction Forces (3,000 troops in total) as well as reinforcements and follow-on forces (37,000 troops in total)

EQUIPMENT BY TYPE
PATROL AND COASTAL COMBATANTS • PB 11: 4 *Harek*; 2 *Gyda*; 5 *Alusafe* 1290

Cyber

The defence ministry is responsible for defending military networks and national coordination in armed conflict. The 2012 Cyber Security Strategy for Norway contained cross-governmental guidelines for cyber defence. Norwegian Armed Forces Cyber Defence supports the armed forces by establishing, operating and protecting networks. It is responsible for defending military networks against cyber attack. It also supports the armed forces at home and abroad with the establishment, operation, development and protection of communications systems, and is responsible for defending military networks against cyber attacks, as well as developing network defence.

DEPLOYMENT

AFGHANISTAN: NATO • *Operation Resolute Support* 70
EGYPT: MFO 3
IRAQ: *Operation Inherent Resolve* 60; 1 trg unit
JORDAN: *Operation Inherent Resolve* 60
LITHUANIA: NATO • Enhanced Forward Presence 13; 1 int unit
MALI: UN • MINUSMA 15
MIDDLE EAST: UN • UNTSO 14 obs
NORTH SEA: NATO • SNMG 1: 1 DDGHM; NATO • SNMCMG 1: 1 MHC
SERBIA: NATO • KFOR 2; OSCE • Kosovo 1
SOUTH SUDAN: UN • UNMISS 14
UKRAINE: OSCE • Ukraine 12

FOREIGN FORCES

United States US European Command: 1,000; 1 mne bn; 1 (USMC) MEU eqpt set; 1 (APS) 155mm SP Arty bn eqpt set

Poland POL

Polish Zloty z		2017	2018	2019
GDP	z	1.98tr	2.11tr	
	US$	525bn	549bn	
per capita	US$	13,821	14,469	
Growth	%	4.7	4.4	
Inflation	%	2.0	2.0	
Def exp [a]	z	37.5bn	41.8bn	
	US$	9.94bn	10.9bn	
Def bdgt [b]	z	37.7bn	41.5bn	44.7bn
	US$	9.98bn	10.8bn	
FMA (US)	US$	6.3m	0m	
US$1=z		3.78	3.84	

[a] NATO definition
[b] Includes military pensions

Population	38,420,687					
Age	0–14	15–19	20–24	25–29	30–64	65 plus
Male	7.6%	2.5%	3.0%	3.5%	25.2%	6.7%
Female	7.2%	2.4%	2.8%	3.4%	25.7%	10.2%

Capabilities

Territorial defence and NATO membership are central pillars of Poland's defence policy. The primary focus of the 2017–32 defence concept is to prepare the armed forces to provide a deterrent against Russian aggression. Russia is characterised as a direct threat to Poland and to a stable international order. The government continues to pursue a goal of permanently stationing US troops in the country. Security and defence cooperation also takes place through the Visegrád Group. There are also defence ties through the Bucharest Nine, which brings together NATO's eastern-flank countries. Warsaw has also established a fund to bolster its neighbours' defence-modernisation ambitions. The 2017–32 defence concept defines an ambition to restore divisions as tactical combat units, rather than administrative units. Recruitment is under way for the Territorial Defence Force, launched in 2017. Poland has some capacity to independently deploy forces beyond national borders. Defence-acquisition reform is planned but a national armaments strategy has yet to be released. A new armaments agency is due to be launched to consolidate responsibilities and establish stronger control over programmes. Poland intends to build up its own anti-access/area-denial capacity and in the 2017 Defence Concept expressed an interest in research into emerging technologies. Warsaw continues plans to strengthen its domestic defence-industrial base, much of which is now consolidated in the state-owned holding company PGZ, using technology transfers and international partnering. Beyond PGZ, several international defence primes have subsidiaries in Poland.

ACTIVE 117,800 (Army 61,200 Navy 7,000 Air Force 18,700 Special Forces 3,400 Territorial 14,000 Joint 13,500) Paramilitary 73,400

ORGANISATIONS BY SERVICE

Army 61,200

FORCES BY ROLE
COMMAND
  elm 1 (MNC NE) corps HQ
MANOEUVRE
  Reconnaissance
  3 recce regt
  Armoured
  1 (11th) armd cav div (2 armd bde, 1 mech bde, 1 arty regt)
  Mechanised
  1 (12th) div (2 mech bde, 1 (coastal) mech bde, 1 arty regt)
  1 (16th) div (1 armd bde, 2 mech bde, 1 arty regt)
  1 (18th) div (1 armd bde, 1 mech bde)
  Air Manoeuvre
  1 (6th) air aslt bde (3 air aslt bn)
  1 (25th) air cav bde (3 air cav bn, 2 tpt hel bn, 1 (casevac) med unit)
COMBAT SUPPORT
  2 engr regt
  1 ptn br regt
  2 chem def regt
COMBAT SUPPORT
  2 log bde
HELICOPTER
  1 (1st) hel bde (2 atk hel sqn with Mi-24D/V *Hind* D/E, 1 CSAR sqn with Mi-24V *Hind* E; PZL W-3PL *Gluszec*; 2 ISR hel sqn with Mi-2URP; 2 hel sqn with Mi-2)
AIR DEFENCE
  3 AD regt

EQUIPMENT BY TYPE
ARMOURED FIGHTING VEHICLES
  MBT 637: 142 *Leopard* 2A4; 105 *Leopard* 2A5; 232 PT-91 *Twardy*; 158 T-72A/T-72M1 (221 more in store)
  RECCE 407: 282 BRDM-2; 38 BWR; 87 BRDM-2 R5
  IFV 1,636: 1,277 BMP-1; 359 *Rosomak* IFV
  APC 257
    APC (T) WDSz (OP)

APC (W) 227: 211 *Rosomak* APC; 16 AWD RAK (CP)
PPV 30 *Maxxpro*
AUV 85: 40 *Cougar* (on loan from US); 45 M-ATV
ENGINEERING & MAINTENANCE VEHICLES
AEV 25+: IWT; MT-LB; 17 *Rosomak* WRT; 8 MID *Bizon*
ARV 69: 28 BPz-2; 15 MT-LB; 26 WZT-3M
VLB 62: 4 *Biber*; 48 BLG67M2; 10 MS-20 *Daglezja*
MW 18: 14 Bozena 4; ISM *Kroton*; 4 *Kalina* SUM
ANTI-TANK/ANTI-INFRASTRUCTURE
MSL • MANPATS 9K11 *Malyutka* (AT-3 *Sagger*); 9K111 *Fagot* (AT-4 *Spigot*); *Spike*-LR
ARTILLERY 815
SP 427: **122mm** 292 2S1 *Gvozdika*; **152mm** 111 M-77 *Dana*; **155mm** 24 *Krab*
MRL 122mm 180: 75 BM-21; 30 RM-70; 75 WR-40 *Langusta*
MOR 216: **98mm** 89 M-98; **120mm** 95 M120; **SP 120mm** 32 SMK120 RAK
HELICOPTERS
ATK 28 Mi-24D/V *Hind* D/E
MRH 64: 7 Mi-8MT *Hip*; 3 Mi-17 *Hip* H; 1 Mi-17AE *Hip* (aeromedical); 5 Mi-17-1V *Hip*; 16 PZL Mi-2URP *Hoplite*; 24 PZL W-3W/WA *Sokol*; 8 PZL W-3PL *Gluszec* (CSAR)
TPT 34: **Medium** 9: 7 Mi-8T *Hip*; 2 PZL W-3AE *Sokol* (aeromedical); **Light** 25 PZL Mi-2 *Hoplite*
AIR DEFENCE
SAM
Short-range 20 2K12 *Kub* (SA-6 *Gainful*)
Point-defence 84+: 9K32 *Strela*-2‡ (SA-7 *Grail*); 64 9K33 *Osa*-AK (SA-8 *Gecko*); 20 ZSU-23-4MP *Biala*; GROM; *Poprad*
GUNS 332
SP 23mm 8 ZSU-23-4
TOWED 23mm 324; 252 ZU-23-2; 72 ZUR-23-2KG/PG

Navy 7,000
EQUIPMENT BY TYPE
SUBMARINES • TACTICAL 3
SSK 3:
 2 *Sokol* (ex-NOR Type-207) with 8 single 533mm TT
 1 *Orzel* (ex-FSU *Kilo*) with 6 single 533mm TT each with 53-65 HWT (currently non-operational; has been in refit since 2014; damaged by fire in 2017)
PRINCIPAL SURFACE COMBATANTS 2
FRIGATES • FFGHM 2 *Pulaski* (ex-US *Oliver Hazard Perry*) with 1 Mk13 GMLS with RGM-84D/F *Harpoon* AShM/SM-1MR SAM, 2 triple 324mm ASTT with MU90 LWT, 1 *Phalanx* Block 1B CIWS, 1 76mm gun (capacity 2 SH-2G *Super Seasprite* ASW hel) (1 vessel used as training ship)
PATROL AND COASTAL COMBATANTS 4
CORVETTES • FSM 1 *Kaszub* with 2 quad lnchr with 9K32 *Strela*-2 (SA-N-5 *Grail*) SAM, 2 twin 533mm ASTT with SET-53 HWT, 2 RBU 6000 *Smerch* 2 A/S mor, 1 76mm gun
PCFGM 3:
 3 *Orkan* (ex-GDR *Sassnitz*) with 1 quad lnchr with RBS15 Mk3 AShM, 1 quad lnchr (manual aiming) with *Strela*-2 (SA-N-5 *Grail*) SAM, 1 AK630 CIWS, 1 76mm gun

MINE WARFARE • MINE COUNTERMEASURES 21
MCCS 1 *Kontradmirał Xawery Czernicki*
MHO 3 *Krogulec*
MSI 17: 1 *Gopło*; 12 *Gardno*; 4 *Mamry*
AMPHIBIOUS 8
LANDING SHIPS • LSM 5 *Lublin* (capacity 9 tanks; 135 troops)
LANDING CRAFT • LCU 3 *Deba* (capacity 50 troops)
LOGISTICS AND SUPPORT 20
AGI 2 *Moma*
AGS 8: 2 *Heweliusz*; 4 *Wildcat* 40; 2 (coastal)
AORL 1 *Baltyk*
AOL 1 *Moskit*
ARS 4: 2 *Piast*; 2 *Zbyszko*
ATF 2
AX 1 *Wodnik* with 1 twin AK230 CIWS
AXS 1 *Iskra*
COASTAL DEFENCE • AShM 12+: 12 NSM; MM40 *Exocet*
AIR DEFENCE • SAM
Short-range *Crotale* NG/GR

Naval Aviation 1,300
FORCES BY ROLE
ANTI SUBMARINE WARFARE/SEARCH & RESCUE
 1 sqn with Mi-14PL *Haze* A; Mi-14PL/R *Haze* C
 1 sqn with PZL W-3RM *Anakonda*; SH-2G *Super Seasprite*
MARITIME PATROL
 1 sqn with An-28RM; An-28E
TRANSPORT
 1 sqn with An-28TD; M-28B TD *Bryza*
 1 sqn with An-28TD; M-28B; Mi-17 *Hip* H; PZL Mi-2 *Hoplite*; PZL W-3T; 1 PZL W-3A
EQUIPMENT BY TYPE
AIRCRAFT
MP 10: 8 An-28RM *Bryza*; 2 An-28E *Bryza*
TPT • Light 4: 2 An-28TD *Bryza*; 2 M-28B TD *Bryza*
HELICOPTERS ASW 11: 7 Mi-14PL *Haze*; 4 SH-2G *Super Seasprite*
MRH 1 Mi-17 *Hip* H
SAR 8: 2 Mi-14PL/R *Haze* C; 4 PZL W-3RM *Anakonda*; 2 PZL W-3WA RM *Anakonda*
TPT • Light 7: 4 PZL Mi-2 *Hoplite*; 1 PZL W-3A; 2 PZL-W-3T

Air Force 18,700
FORCES BY ROLE
FIGHTER
 2 sqn with MiG-29A/UB *Fulcrum*
FIGHTER/GROUND ATTACK
 3 sqn with F-16C/D Block 52+ *Fighting Falcon*
FIGHTER/GROUND ATTACK/ISR
 2 sqn with Su-22M-4 *Fitter*
SEARCH AND RESCUE
 1 sqn with Mi-2; PZL W-3 *Sokol*
TRANSPORT
 1 sqn with C-130E; PZL M-28 *Bryza*
 1 sqn with C295M; PZL M-28 *Bryza*
TRAINING
 1 sqn with PZL-130 *Orlik*

1 sqn with TS-11 *Iskra*
1 hel sqn with SW-4 *Puszczyk*
TRANSPORT HELICOPTER
1 (Spec Ops) sqn with Mi-17 *Hip* H
1 (VIP) sqn with Mi-8; W-3WA *Sokol*
AIR DEFENCE
1 bde with S-125 *Neva* SC (SA-3 *Goa*); S-200C *Vega* (SA-5 *Gammon*)
EQUIPMENT BY TYPE
AIRCRAFT 98 combat capable
FTR 32: 25 MiG-29A *Fulcrum*; 7 MiG-29UB *Fulcrum*
FGA 66: 36 F-16C Block 52+ *Fighting Falcon*; 12 F-16D Block 52+ *Fighting Falcon*; 12 Su-22M4 *Fitter*; 6 Su-22UM3K *Fitter*
TPT 46: **Medium** 5 C-130E *Hercules*; **Light** 39: 16 C295M; 23 M-28 *Bryza* TD; **PAX** 2: 1 Gulfstream G550; 1 737-800
TRG 68: 8 M-346; 28 PZL-130 *Orlik*; 32 TS-11 *Iskra*
HELICOPTERS
MRH 8 Mi-17 *Hip* H
TPT 69: **Medium** 29: 9 Mi-8 *Hip*; 10 PZL W-3 *Sokol*; 10 PZL W-3WA *Sokol* (VIP); **Light** 40: 16 PZL Mi-2 *Hoplite*; 24 SW-4 *Puszczyk* (trg)
AIR DEFENCE • SAM
Long-range 1 S-200C *Vega* (SA-5 *Gammon*)
Short-range 17 S-125 *Neva* SC (SA-3 *Goa*)
AIR-LAUNCHED MISSILES
AAM • IR R-60 (AA-8 *Aphid*); R-73 (AA-11 *Archer*); AIM-9 *Sidewinder*; R-27T (AA-10B *Alamo*); **IIR** AIM-9X *Sidwinder* II; **ARH** AIM-120C AMRAAM
ASM AGM-65J/G *Maverick*; Kh-25 (AS-10 *Karen*); Kh-29 (AS-14 *Kedge*)
LACM Conventional AGM-158 JASSM

Special Forces 3,400
FORCES BY ROLE
SPECIAL FORCES
3 SF units (GROM, FORMOZA & cdo)
COMBAT SUPPORT/
1 cbt spt unit (AGAT)
COMBAT SERVICE SUPPORT
1 spt unit (NIL)

Territorial Defence Forces 14,000
FORCES BY ROLE
MANOEUVRE
Other
3 sy bde
10 sy bde (forming)

Paramilitary 73,400

Border Guards 14,300
Ministry of Interior

Maritime Border Guard 3,700
EQUIPMENT BY TYPE
PATROL AND COASTAL COMBATANTS 18
PCC 2 *Kaper*
PBF 6: 2 *Straznik*; 4 IC16M
PB 10: 2 *Wisloka*; 2 *Baltic* 24; 1 Project MI-6

AMPHIBIOUS • LANDING CRAFT • UCAC 2 *Griffon* 2000TDX

Prevention Units (Police) 59,100
Anti-terrorist Operations Bureau n.k.
Ministry of Interior

Cyber
The National Security Bureau issued a cyber-security doctrine in January 2015. The doctrine specifies significant tasks needed in order to build a national cyber-security capability. It was reported that the document noted the need to pursue 'active cyber defence, including offensive actions in cyberspace' and maintain 'readiness for cyberwar'. In November 2018, the defence ministry announced that the classified 2017–26 armed forces development plan had been agreed, noting references to the creation of cyber-defence forces.

DEPLOYMENT
AFGHANISTAN: NATO • Operation Resolute Support 315; **UN •** UNAMA 1 obs
ARMENIA/AZERBAIJAN: OSCE • Minsk Conference 1
BOSNIA-HERZEGOVINA: EU • EUFOR • Operation Althea 39
CENTRAL AFRICAN REPUBLIC: EU • EUTM RCA 1
DEMOCRATIC REPUBLIC OF THE CONGO: UN • MONUSCO 1 obs
IRAQ: Operation Inherent Resolve 130
LATVIA: NATO • Enhanced Forward Presence 160; 1 tk coy
ROMANIA: NATO • MNB-SE 225; 1 mech inf coy; *Rosomak*
SERBIA: NATO • KFOR 252; 1 inf coy; **OSCE •** Kosovo 1; **UN •** UNMIK 1 obs
SOUTH SUDAN: UN • UNMISS 1 obs
UKRAINE: OSCE • Ukraine 41
WESTERN SAHARA: UN • MINURSO 2 obs

FOREIGN FORCES
All NATO Enhanced Forward Presence unless stated
Croatia 69; 1 MRL bty with M91 *Vulkan*
Germany MNC-NE corps HQ: 100
Romania 120; 1 ADA bty; 1 MP coy
United Kingdom 115; 1 recce sqn
United States: 774; 1 ARNG armd bn with M1A1 AIM *Abrams*; M2A2 ODS *Bradley*; M109A6 • Operation Atlantic Resolve 2,100; 1 armd bde HQ; 1 armd cav sqn(-); 1 SP arty bn; M1A2 SEPv2 *Abrams*; M3A3 *Bradley*; M109A6; 1 atk hel flt with AH-64D *Apache*; 1 tpt hel flt with 8 UH-60 *Black Hawk*

Portugal PRT

Euro €		2017	2018	2019
GDP	€	193bn	201bn	
	US$	218bn	238bn	
per capita	US$	21,159	23,176	
Growth	%	2.7	2.3	
Inflation	%	1.6	1.7	
Def exp [a]	€	2.40bn	2.73bn	
	US$	2.71bn	3.24bn	
Def bdgt	€	2.24bn	2.18bn	
	US$	2.53bn	2.58bn	
US$1=€		0.89	0.84	

[a] NATO definition

Population	10,355,493					
Age	0–14	15–19	20–24	25–29	30–64	65 plus
Male	8.0%	3.0%	3.0%	3.2%	23.8%	7.9%
Female	7.4%	2.7%	2.6%	2.8%	24.2%	11.5%

Capabilities

Principal tasks for Portugal's all-volunteer armed forces are homeland defence, maritime security, multinational operations and responding to humanitarian disasters. The 2013 strategic review set out key defence tasks and envisaged a reduction in army strength and organisational change dividing the services into immediate reaction forces, permanent defence forces and modular forces. Investment plans support Portugal's ambition to field rapid-reaction and maritime-surveillance capabilities for territorial defence and multinational operations. The government in December 2018 approved a new military programme law for 2019–30; this has to be approved by parliament. The proposal is expected to boost local defence industry, leading to the acquisition of up to six KC-390 aircraft; six offshore patrol vessels; a replenishment tanker; and a multi-purpose logistics ship. There will be new investments in cyber security and in dual-use technologies. Portugal is an active member of NATO, and NATO's new cyber-security academy is being built there. It also contributes to EU military structures. There is a close relationship with former dependencies and with the US, which operates out of Lajes air base. The army plans to enhance electronic-warfare capacity, light armour and upgrade its *Leopard* 2A6s. The navy intends to upgrade its frigates and submarines and acquire patrol vessels and a logistic-support ship, while the air force plans to modernise its remaining F-16s and its P-3C *Orion* maritime-patrol aircraft. There is an active defence industry, though principally in relation to shipbuilding, broader maintenance tasks and the manufacture of components and small arms and light weapons.

ACTIVE 27,200 (Army 13,700 Navy 7,600 Air 5,900)
Paramilitary 24,700

RESERVE 211,950 (Army 210,000 Navy 1,250, Air Force 700)
Reserve obligation to age 35

ORGANISATIONS BY SERVICE

Army 13,700

5 territorial comd (2 mil region, 1 mil district, 2 mil zone)

FORCES BY ROLE
SPECIAL FORCES
1 SF bn
MANOEUVRE
Reconnaissance
1 ISR bn
Mechanised
1 mech bde (1 cav tp, 1 tk regt, 1 mech inf bn, 1 arty bn, 1 AD bty, 1 engr coy, 1 sigs coy, 1 spt bn)
1 (intervention) bde (1 cav tp, 1 recce regt, 2 mech inf bn, 1 arty bn, 1 AD bty, 1 engr coy, 1 sigs coy, 1 spt bn)
Air Manoeuvre
1 (rapid reaction) bde (1 cav tp, 1 cdo bn, 2 para bn, 1 arty bn, 1 AD bty, 1 engr coy, 1 sigs coy, 1 spt bn)
Other
1 (Azores) inf gp (2 inf bn, 1 AD bty)
1 (Madeira) inf gp (1 inf bn, 1 AD bty)
COMBAT SUPPORT
1 STA bty
1 engr bn (1 construction coy; 1 EOD unit; 1 ptn br coy; 1 CBRN coy)
1 EW coy
1 MP bn
1 psyops unit
1 CIMIC coy (joint)
1 sigs bn
COMBAT SERVICE SUPPORT
1 maint coy
1 log coy
1 tpt coy
1 med unit
AIR DEFENCE
1 AD bn

Reserves 210,000
FORCES BY ROLE
MANOEUVRE
Light
3 (territorial) def bde (on mobilisation)

EQUIPMENT BY TYPE
ARMOURED FIGHTING VEHICLES
MBT 37 *Leopard* 2A6
RECCE 30: 14 V-150 *Chaimite*; 16 VBL
IFV 30 *Pandur* II MK 30mm
APC 397
  APC (T) 239: 176 M113A1; 14 M113A2; 49 M577A2 (CP)
  APC (W) 158: 12 V-200 *Chaimite*; 146 *Pandur* II (incl variants)
ENGINEERING & MAINTENANCE VEHICLES
AEV M728
ARV 13: 6 M88A1, 7 *Pandur* II ARV
VLB M48
ANTI-TANK/ANTI-INFRASTRUCTURE
MSL
  SP 26: 17 M113 with TOW; 4 M901 with TOW; 5 *Pandur* II with TOW
  MANPATS *Milan*; TOW
RCL • **84mm** *Carl Gustav*; **90mm** M67; **106mm** 45 M40A1
ARTILLERY 321
  SP **155mm** 24: 6 M109A2; 18 M109A5

TOWED 63: **105mm** 39: 17 L119 Light Gun; 21 M101A1; 1 Model 56 pack howitzer; **155mm** 24 M114A1
MOR 234: **81mm** 143; **SP 81mm** 12: 2 M125A1; 10 M125A2; **107mm** 11 M30; **SP 107mm** 18: 3 M106A1; 15 M106A2; **120mm** 50 Tampella
AIR DEFENCE
SAM • **Point-defence** 20+: 1 M48A2 *Chaparral*; 19 M48A3 *Chaparral*; FIM-92 *Stinger*
GUNS • **TOWED 20mm** 20 Rh 202

Navy 7,600 (incl 1,250 Marines)
EQUIPMENT BY TYPE
SUBMARINES • **TACTICAL** • **SSK** 2 *Tridente* (GER Type-214) with 8 533mm TT with UGM-84L *Harpoon* Block II AShM/*Black Shark* HWT
PRINCIPAL SURFACE COMBATANTS 5
FRIGATES • **FFGHM** 5:
2 *Bartolomeu Dias* (ex-NLD *Karel Doorman*) with 2 quad Mk141 lnchr with RGM-84C *Harpoon* AShM, 1 16-cell Mk48 VLS with RIM-7M *Sea Sparrow* SAM, 2 Mk32 twin 324mm ASTT with Mk46 LWT, 1 *Goalkeeper* CIWS, 1 76mm gun (capacity: 1 *Lynx* Mk95 (*Super Lynx*) hel)
3 *Vasco Da Gama* with 2 quad Mk141 lnchr with RGM-84C *Harpoon* AShM, 1 octuple Mk 29 GMLS with RIM-7M *Sea Sparrow* SAM, 2 Mk32 triple 324mm ASTT with Mk46 LWT, 1 *Phalanx* Block 1B CIWS, 1 100mm gun (capacity 2 *Lynx* Mk95 (*Super Lynx*) hel)
PATROL AND COASTAL COMBATANTS 20
CORVETTES • **FS** 2:
1 *Baptista de Andrade* with 1 100mm gun, 1 hel landing platform
1 *Joao Coutinho* with 1 twin 76mm gun, 1 hel landing platform
PSO 3 *Viana do Castelo* with 1 hel landing platform
PCC 4: 2 *Cacine*; 2 *Tejo* (ex-DNK *Flyvisken*)
PBR 11: 1 *Albatroz*; 5 *Argos*; 4 *Centauro*; 1 *Rio Minho*
LOGISTICS AND SUPPORT 11
AGS 4: 2 *D Carlos* I (ex-US *Stalwart*); 2 *Andromeda*
AORL 1 *Bérrio* (ex-UK *Rover*) with 1 hel landing platform (for medium hel)
AXS 6: 1 *Sagres*; 1 *Creoula*; 1 *Polar*; 2 *Belatrix*; 1 *Zarco*

Marines 1,250
FORCES BY ROLE
SPECIAL FORCES
1 SF det
MANOEUVRE
Light
2 lt inf bn
COMBAT SUPPORT
1 mor coy
1 MP det
EQUIPMENT BY TYPE
ARTILLERY • **MOR 120mm** 30

Naval Aviation
EQUIPMENT BY TYPE
HELICOPTERS • **ASW** 5 *Lynx* Mk95 (*Super Lynx*)

Air Force 5,900
FORCES BY ROLE
FIGHTER/GROUND ATTACK
2 sqn with F-16AM/BM *Fighting Falcon*
MARITIME PATROL
1 sqn with P-3C *Orion*
ISR/TRANSPORT
1 sqn with C295M
COMBAT SEARCH & RESCUE
1 sqn with with AW101 *Merlin*
TRANSPORT
1 sqn with C-130H/C-130H-30 *Hercules*
1 sqn with *Falcon* 50
TRAINING
1 sqn with SA316 *Alouette* III
1 sqn with TB-30 *Epsilon*
EQUIPMENT BY TYPE
AIRCRAFT 35 combat capable
FTR 30: 26 F-16AM *Fighting Falcon*; 4 F-16BM *Fighting Falcon*
ASW 5 P-3C *Orion*
ISR: 7: 5 C295M (maritime surveillance), 2 C295M (photo recce)
TPT 13: **Medium** 5: 2 C-130H *Hercules*; 3 C-130H-30 *Hercules* (tpt/SAR); **Light** 5 C295M; **PAX** 3 *Falcon* 50 (tpt/VIP)
TRG 16 TB-30 *Epsilon*
HELICOPTERS
MRH 6 SA316 *Alouette* III (trg, utl)
TPT • **Medium** 12 AW101 *Merlin* (6 SAR, 4 CSAR, 2 fishery protection)
AIR-LAUNCHED MISSILES
AAM • **IR** AIM-9L/I *Sidewinder*; **ARH** AIM-120C AMRAAM
ASM AGM-65A *Maverick*
AShM AGM-84A *Harpoon*
BOMBS
Laser-guided/GPS GBU-49 *Enhanced Paveway* II
INS/GPS guided GBU-31 JDAM

Paramilitary 24,700

National Republican Guard 24,700
EQUIPMENT BY TYPE
PATROL AND COASTAL COMBATANTS 32
PBF 12
PB 20
HELICOPTERS • **MRH** 7 SA315 *Lama*

Cyber
The 2013 Cyber Defence Policy Guidance established a national cyber-defence structure. Portugal released a National Cyberspace Security Strategy in 2015. The strategic-military aspects of cyber defence are the responsibility of the Council of the Chiefs of Staff. A Cyber Defence Centre, under the chief of defence, reached full operating capability in 2017. Cyber-defence units within the three branches of the armed forces are responsible for responding to cyber attacks.

DEPLOYMENT

AFGHANISTAN: NATO • *Operation Resolute Support* 195

CENTRAL AFRICAN REPUBLIC: EU • EUTM RCA 45; **UN** • MINUSCA 165; 1 AB coy

IRAQ: *Operation Inherent Resolve* 34

MALI: EU • EUTM Mali 12; **UN** • MINUSMA 2

NORTH SEA: NATO • SNMG 1: 1 FFGHM

SERBIA: NATO • KFOR 3; **OSCE** • Kosovo 1

SOMALIA: EU • EUTM Somalia 4

UKRAINE: OSCE • Ukraine 2

WESTERN SAHARA: UN • MINURSO 1 obs

FOREIGN FORCES

United States US European Command: 250; 1 spt facility at Lajes

Romania ROM

New Lei		2017	2018	2019
GDP	lei	859bn	939bn	
	US$	212bn	239bn	
per capita	US$	10,786	12,189	
Growth	%	6.9	4.0	
Inflation	%	1.3	4.7	
Def exp [a]	lei	14.8bn	18.2bn	
	US$	3.64bn	4.63bn	
Def bdgt [b]	lei	14.8bn	18.2bn	19.5bn
	US$	3.64bn	4.63bn	
FMA (US)	US$	4.4m	0m	
US$1=lei		4.05	3.92	

[a] NATO definition
[b] Includes military pensions

Population		21,457,116				
Age	0–14	15–19	20–24	25–29	30–64	65 plus
Male	7.4%	2.7%	2.8%	3.6%	25.6%	6.6%
Female	7.0%	2.5%	2.6%	3.5%	26.0%	9.8%

Capabilities

Romania's armed forces are structured around territorial defence, support to NATO and EU missions and contributing to regional and global stability and security. Principal security threats include, according to the National Defence Strategy 2015–19 and the 2016 Military Strategy, Russia's increased presence in the Black Sea, hybrid warfare, cyber attacks and terrorism. The government has stated the intention to strengthen operational capabilities and develop its partnerships and cooperation with other NATO and EU members, and there is an ongoing programme to modernise and upgrade the armed forces to meet NATO standards. Bucharest has signed defence-cooperation agreements with regional allies. Nevertheless, it places a great value on its strategic partnership with the US. Romania hosts the *Aegis* Ashore ballistic-missile-defence system at Deveselu. Romania trains widely with its NATO and regional allies and contributes to EU and NATO missions. The inventory is mainly composed of ageing Soviet-era equipment, which is seen as a factor limiting capability. Acquisition plans include armoured vehicles, air-defence radars, surface-to-air missiles and corvettes. Acquisition of second-hand F-16s has enhanced Romania's air capabilities. Romania was once a significant weapons exporter, yet since 1989 the country's defence industry has struggled. Current production focuses on small arms and ammunition. However, Bucharest is looking to boost the industry through offset agreements and technology transfers.

ACTIVE 69,300 (Army 36,000 Navy 6,500 Air 10,300 Joint 16,500) **Paramilitary 57,000**

RESERVE 50,000 (Joint 50,000)

ORGANISATIONS BY SERVICE

Army 36,000

Readiness is reported as 70–90% for NATO-designated forces (1 div HQ, 1 mech bde, 1 inf bde & 1 mtn inf bde) and 40–70% for other forces

FORCES BY ROLE
COMMAND
  2 div HQ (2nd & 4th)
  elm 1 div HQ (MND-SE)
SPECIAL FORCES
  1 SF bde (2 SF bn, 1 para bn, 1 log bn)
MANOEUVRE
  Reconnaissance
  1 recce bde
  2 recce regt
  Mechanised
  5 mech bde (1 tk bn, 2 mech inf bn, 1 arty bn, 1 AD bn, 1 log bn)
  Light
  1 (MNB-SE) inf bde (3 inf bn, 1 arty bn, 1 AD bn, 1 log bn)
  2 mtn inf bde (3 mtn inf bn, 1 arty bn, 1 AD bn, 1 log bn)
COMBAT SUPPORT
  1 MRL bde (3 MRL bn, 1 STA bn, 1 log bn)
  2 arty regt
  1 engr bde (4 engr bn, 1 ptn br bn, 1 log bn)
  2 engr bn
  3 sigs bn
  1 CIMIC bn
  1 MP bn
  3 CBRN bn
COMBAT SERVICE SUPPORT
  3 spt bn
AIR DEFENCE
  3 AD regt

EQUIPMENT BY TYPE
ARMOURED FIGHTING VEHICLES
  MBT 418: 260 T-55AM; 104 TR-85; 54 TR-85 M1
  IFV 139: 38 MLI-84 (incl CP); 101 MLI-84M *Jderul*
  APC 851
    APC (T) 76 MLVM
    APC (W) 715: 69 B33 TAB *Zimbru*; 31 *Piranha* III; 2 *Piranha* V; 410 TAB-71 (incl variants); 203 TAB-77 (incl variants)
    PPV 60 *Maxxpro*
  AUV 427 TABC-79 (incl variants)
ENGINEERING & MAINTENANCE VEHICLES
  ARV 51: 3 BPz-2; 3 MLI-84M TEHEVAC; 5 TERA-71L; 40 TERA-77L

VLB 40 BLG-67
NBC VEHICLES 80 RCH-84
ANTI-TANK/ANTI-INFRASTRUCTURE
  MSL • SP 134: 12 9P122 *Malyutka* (AT-3 *Sagger*); 74 9P133 *Malyutka* (AT-3 *Sagger*); 48 9P148 *Konkurs* (AT-5 *Spandrel*)
  GUNS
    SP 100mm (23 SU-100 in store)
    TOWED 100mm 222 M-1977
ARTILLERY 1,087
  SP 122mm 24: 6 2S1; 18 Model 89
  TOWED 449: 122mm 98 (M-30) M-1938 (A-19); 152mm 351: 247 M-1981; 104 M-1985
  MRL 122mm 188: 134 APR-40; 54 LAROM
  MOR 426: SP 82mm 160: 80 TAB-71AR; 80 TABC-79AR; 120mm 266 M-1982
AIR DEFENCE
  SAM • Short-range 32 2K12 *Kub* (SA-6 *Gainful*)
  GUNS 60
    SP 35mm 36 *Gepard*
    TOWED 35mm 24 GDF-003

Navy 6,500

EQUIPMENT BY TYPE
PRINCIPAL SURFACE COMBATANTS 3
  DESTROYERS 3
    DDGH 1 *Marasesti* with 4 twin lnchr with P-15M *Termit*-M (SS-N-2C *Styx*) AShM, 2 triple 533mm ASTT with 53–65 HWT, 2 RBU 6000 *Smerch* 2 A/S mor, 2 twin 76mm guns (capacity 2 SA-316 (IAR-316) *Alouette* III hel)
    DDH 2 *Regele Ferdinand* (ex-UK Type-22), with 2 triple 324mm TT, 1 76mm gun (capacity 1 SA330 (IAR-330) *Puma*)
PATROL AND COASTAL COMBATANTS 24
  CORVETTES 4
    FSH 2 *Tetal* II with 2 twin 533mm ASTT, 2 RBU 6000 *Smerch* 2 A/S mor, 2 AK630 CIWS, 1 76mm gun (capacity 1 SA316 (IAR-316) *Alouette* III hel)
    FS 2 *Tetal* I with 2 twin 533mm ASTT with 53-65E HWT, 2 RBU 2500 *Smerch* 1 A/S mor, 2 twin 76mm guns
  PCFG 3 *Zborul* with 2 twin lnchr with P-15M *Termit*-M (SS-N-2C *Styx*) AShM, 2 AK630 CIWS, 1 76mm gun
  PCFT 3 *Naluca* with 4 single 533mm ASTT
  PCR 8:
    5 *Brutar* II with 2 BM-21 MRL, 1 100mm gun
    3 *Kogalniceanu* with 2 BM-21 MRL, 2 100mm guns
  PBR 6 VD141 (ex-MSR now used for river patrol)
MINE WARFARE 11
  MINE COUNTERMEASURES 10
    MSO 4 *Musca* with 2 RBU 1200 A/S mor, 2 AK230 CIWS
    MSR 6 VD141
  MINELAYERS • ML 1 *Corsar* with up to 120 mines, 2 RBU 1200 A/S mor, 1 57mm gun
LOGISTICS AND SUPPORT 8
  AE 2 *Constanta* with 2 RBU 1200 A/S mor, 2 twin 57mm guns
  AGOR 1 *Corsar*
  AGS 2: 1 *Emil Racovita*;1 *Catuneanu*

AOL 1 *Tulcea*
ATF 1 *Grozavu*
AXS 1 *Mircea*

Naval Infantry
FORCES BY ROLE
MANOEUVRE
  Light
    1 naval inf regt
EQUIPMENT BY TYPE
ARMOURED FIGHTING VEHICLES
  AUV 14: 11 ABC-79M; 3 TABC-79M

Air Force 10,300

FORCES BY ROLE
FIGHTER
  2 sqn with MiG-21 *Lancer* C
FIGHTER GROUND ATTACK
  1 sqn (forming) with with F-16AM/BM *Fighting Falcon*
GROUND ATTACK
  1 sqn with IAR-99 *Soim*
TRANSPORT
  1 sqn with An-30 *Clank*; C-27J *Spartan*
  1 sqn with C-130B/H *Hercules*
TRAINING
  1 sqn with IAR-99 *Soim*
  1 sqn with SA316B *Alouette* III (IAR-316B); Yak-52 (Iak-52)
TRANSPORT HELICOPTER
  2 (multi-role) sqn with IAR-330 SOCAT *Puma*
  3 sqn with SA330 *Puma* (IAR-330)
AIR DEFENCE
  1 AD bde
COMBAT SERVICE SUPPORT
  1 engr spt regt
EQUIPMENT BY TYPE
AIRCRAFT 56 combat capable
  FTR 12: 8 F-16AM *Fighting Falcon*; 4 F-16BM *Fighting Falcon*
  FGA 24: 6 MiG-21 *Lancer* B; 18 MiG-21 *Lancer* C
  ISR 2 An-30 *Clank*
  TPT • Medium 12: 7 C-27J *Spartan*; 4 C-130B *Hercules*; 1 C-130H *Hercules*
  TRG 32: 10 IAR-99*; 10 IAR-99C *Soim**; 12 Yak-52 (Iak-52)
HELICOPTERS
  MRH 30: 22 IAR-330 SOCAT *Puma*; 8 SA316B *Alouette* III (IAR-316B)
  TPT • Medium 36: 21 SA330L *Puma* (IAR-330L); 15 SA330M *Puma* (IAR-330M)
AIR DEFENCE • SAM • Medium-range 14: 6 S-75M3 *Volkhov* (SA-2 *Guideline*); 8 MIM-23 *Hawk* PIP III
AIR-LAUNCHED MISSILES
  AAM • IR AIM-9M *Sidewinder*; R-73 (AA-11 *Archer*); R-550 *Magic* 2; *Python* 3 ARH AIM-120C AMRAAM
  ASM *Spike*-ER
BOMBS
  Laser-guided GBU-12 *Paveway*
  INS/GPS guided GBU-38 JDAM

Paramilitary ε57,000

Gendarmerie ε57,000
Ministry of Interior

Cyber

Romania's 2013 and 2015 cyber-security strategies define the conceptual framework, aim, objectives, priorities and courses of action for providing cyber security at the national level. Romania's 2016 Military Strategy said the country needed to develop the legal framework to conduct operations in cyberspace. The defence ministry contains a military CERT. Romania is in 2019 due to join the NATO Cooperative Cyber Defence Centre of Excellence.

DEPLOYMENT

AFGHANISTAN: NATO • *Operation Resolute Support* 742; 1 inf bn

BOSNIA-HERZEGOVINA: EU • EUFOR • *Operation Althea* 48

CENTRAL AFRICAN REPUBLIC: EU • EUTM RCA 14

DEMOCRATIC REPUBLIC OF THE CONGO: UN • MONUSCO 4; 7 obs

INDIA/PAKISTAN: UN • UNMOGIP 2 obs

IRAQ: *Operation Inherent Resolve* 50

MALI: EU • EUTM Mali 3; **UN** • MINUSMA 3

POLAND: NATO • Enhanced Forward Presence 120; 1 ADA bty; 1 MP coy

SERBIA: NATO • KFOR 71; **UN** • UNMIK 1 obs

SOMALIA: EU • EUTM Somalia 3

SOUTH SUDAN: UN • UNMISS 2; 5 obs

UKRAINE: OSCE • Ukraine 36

FOREIGN FORCES

Canada NATO Air Policing: 135; 4 F/A-18A *Hornet* (CF-18)
Poland NATO MNB-SE 225; 1 mech inf coy; *Rosomak*
United States US European Command: 1,150; 1 armd inf bn HQ; 2 armd/armd inf coy; M1A2 SEPv2 *Abrams*; M2A3 *Bradley*; 1 tpt hel flt with 5 UH-60L *Black Hawk*

Serbia SER

Serbian Dinar d		2017	2018	2019
GDP	d	4.46tr	4.75tr	
	US$	41.4bn	47.7bn	
per capita	US$	5,901	6,815	
Growth	%	1.9	4.0	
Inflation	%	3.1	2.1	
Def bdgt	d	58.9bn	70.5bn	
	US$	546m	707m	
FMA (US)	US$	1.8m	0m	
US$1=d		107.76	99.74	

Population 7,078,110

Ethnic groups: Serbian 83.3%; Hungarian 3.35%; Romani 2.05%; Bosniac 2.02%; Croatian 0.8%

Age	0–14	15–19	20–24	25–29	30–64	65 plus
Male	7.5%	2.7%	3.1%	3.3%	24.6%	7.6%
Female	7.0%	2.6%	2.9%	3.1%	24.9%	10.8%

Capabilities

Serbia's armed forces focus on territorial defence, internal security and limited support to peacekeeping missions. According to the 2018 draft security strategy, key threats include separatism, religious and political extremism, and further international recognition of Kosovo. The armed forces are modernising to address long-term capability shortfalls and personnel shortages. Priorities include procurements; improving availability, maintenance and readiness levels; and bolstering air-defence systems. Serbia has agreed to deepen cooperation with NATO through an Individual Partnership Action Plan, though Belgrade does not aspire to join the Alliance. Serbia also maintains a close relationship with Russia, which in recent years has transferred military equipment to Serbia. The armed forces have reduced in size over the last decade, though annual recruitment goals are not being met. The armed forces also lack skilled technicians to operate and maintain advanced systems and suffer from a shortage of pilots. Serbia mostly trains with its Balkan neighbours, as well as Belarus, Russia and NATO countries. Serbia contributes to EU, OSCE and UN peacekeeping missions. Serbia's defence industry focuses on missile and artillery systems, and small arms and ammunition, but the country is reliant on external suppliers for major platforms. Serbia continues to develop its defence industry with a focus on the aerospace industry.

ACTIVE 28,150 (Army 13,250 Air Force and Air Defence 5,100 Training Command 3,000 Guards 1,600 Other MoD 5,200) **Paramilitary 3,700**
Conscript liability 6 months (voluntary)

RESERVE 50,150

ORGANISATIONS BY SERVICE

Army 13,250
FORCES BY ROLE
SPECIAL FORCES
1 SF bde (1 CT bn, 1 cdo bn, 1 para bn)
MANOEUVRE
  Mechanised
  1 (1st) bde (1 tk bn, 2 mech inf bn, 1 inf bn, 1 SP arty bn, 1 MRL bn, 1 AD bn, 1 engr bn, 1 log bn)
  3 (2nd, 3rd & 4th) bde (1 tk bn, 2 mech inf bn, 2 inf bn, 1 SP arty bn, 1 MRL bn, 1 AD bn, 1 engr bn, 1 log bn)
COMBAT SUPPORT
1 (mixed) arty bde (4 arty bn, 1 MRL bn, 1 spt bn)
2 ptn bridging bn
1 NBC bn
1 sigs bn
2 MP bn

Reserve Organisations
FORCES BY ROLE
MANOEUVRE
  Light
  8 (territorial) inf bde

EQUIPMENT BY TYPE
ARMOURED FIGHTING VEHICLES
  MBT 212: 199 M-84; 13 T-72
  RECCE 46 BRDM-2
  IFV 335: 323 M-80; 12 *Lazar-3*
  APC 83 • **APC(T)** 44: 12 BTR-50 (CP); 32 MT-LB (CP)
    APC (W) 39 BOV-VP M-86; some *Lazar-3*

AUV BOV M-16
ENGINEERING & MAINTENANCE VEHICLES
AEV IWT
ARV M84A1; T-54/T-55
VLB MT-55; TMM
ANTI-TANK/ANTI-INFRASTRUCTURE
MSL
SP 48 BOV-1 (M-83) with 9K11 *Malyutka* (AT-3 *Sagger*)
MANPATS 9K11 *Malyutka* (AT-3 *Sagger*); 9K111 *Fagot* (AT-4 *Spigot*)
RCL 90mm 6 M-79
ARTILLERY 443
SP 67+: 122mm 67 2S1 *Gvozdika*; 155mm B-52 NORA
TOWED 132: 122mm 78 D-30; 130mm 18 M-46; 152mm 36 M-84 NORA-A
MRL 81: 128mm 78: 18 M-63 *Plamen*; 60 M-77 *Organj*; 262mm 3 M-87 *Orkan*
MOR 163: 82mm 106 M-69; 120mm 57 M-74/M-75
AIR DEFENCE
SAM
Short-range 77 2K12 *Kub* (SA-6 *Gainful*);
Point-defence 17+: 12 9K31M *Strela*-1M (SA-9 *Gaskin*); 5 9K35M *Strela*-10M; 9K32M *Strela*-2M (SA-7 *Grail*)‡; *Šilo* (SA-16 *Gimlet*)
GUNS • TOWED 40mm 36 Bofors L/70

River Flotilla

The Serbian–Montenegrin navy was transferred to Montenegro upon independence in 2006, but the Danube flotilla remained in Serbian control. The flotilla is subordinate to the Land Forces

EQUIPMENT BY TYPE
PATROL AND COASTAL COMBATANTS 5
PBR 5: 3 Type-20; 2 others
MINE WARFARE • MINE COUNTERMEASURES 4
MSI 4 *Nestin* with 1 quad lnchr with *Strela* 2M (SA-N-5 *Grail*) SAM
AMPHIBOUS • LANDING CRAFT • LCVP 5 Type-22
LOGISTICS AND SUPPORT 2
AGF 1 *Kozara*
AOL 1

Air Force and Air Defence 5,100

FORCES BY ROLE
FIGHTER
1 sqn with MiG-21bis *Fishbed*; MiG-29 *Fulcrum*
FIGHTER/GROUND ATTACK
1 sqn with G-4 *Super Galeb**; J-22 *Orao*
ISR
2 flt with IJ-22 *Orao* 1*; MiG-21R *Fishbed* H*
TRANSPORT
1 sqn with An-2; An-26; Do-28; Yak-40 (Jak-40); 1 PA-34 *Seneca* V
TRAINING
1 sqn with G-4 *Super Galeb** (adv trg/light atk); SA341/342 *Gazelle*; Utva-75 (basic trg)
ATTACK HELICOPTER
1 sqn with SA341H/342L *Gazelle*; (HN-42/45); Mi-24 *Hind*
TRANSPORT HELICOPTER
2 sqn with Mi-8 *Hip*; Mi-17 *Hip* H; Mi-17V-5 *Hip*

AIR DEFENCE
1 bde (5 bn (2 msl, 3 SP msl) with S-125 *Neva* (SA-3 *Goa*); 2K12 *Kub* (SA-6 *Gainful*); 9K32 *Strela*-2 (SA-7 *Grail*); 9K310 *Igla*-1 (SA-16 *Gimlet*))
2 radar bn (for early warning and reporting)
COMBAT SUPPORT
1 sigs bn
COMBAT SERVICE SUPPORT
1 maint bn
EQUIPMENT BY TYPE
AIRCRAFT 63 combat capable
FTR 13+ : 2+ MiG-21bis *Fishbed*; 2+ MiG-21UM *Mongol* B; 5 MiG-29 *Fulcrum*; 4 MiG-29UB *Fulcrum*
FGA 17 J-22 *Orao* 1
ISR 12: 10 IJ-22R *Orao* 1*; 2 MiG-21R *Fishbed* H*
TPT • Light 10: 1 An-2 *Colt*; 4 An-26 *Curl*; 2 Do-28 *Skyservant*; 2 Yak-40 (Jak-40); 1 PA-34 *Seneca* V
TRG 42: 21 G-4 *Super Galeb**; 11 Utva-75; 10 *Lasta* 95
HELICOPTERS
ATK 2 Mi-24 *Hind*
MRH 52: 1 Mi-17 *Hip* H; 2 Mi-17V-5 *Hip*; 2 SA341H *Gazelle* (HI-42); 34 SA341H *Gazelle* (HN-42)/SA342L *Gazelle* (HN-45); 13 SA341H *Gazelle* (HO-42)/SA342L1 *Gazelle* (HO-45)
TPT • Medium 8 Mi-8T *Hip* (HT-40)
AIR DEFENCE
SAM
Short-range 15: 6 S-125 *Pechora* (SA-3 *Goa*); 9 2K12 *Kub* (SA-6 *Gainful*)
Point-defence 9K32 *Strela*-2 (SA-7 *Grail*)‡; 9K310 *Igla*-1 (SA-16 *Gimlet*)
GUNS • TOWED 40mm 24 Bofors L/70
AIR-LAUNCHED MISSILES
AAM • IR R-60 (AA-8 *Aphid*)
ASM AGM-65 *Maverick*; A-77 *Thunder*

Guards 1,600

FORCES BY ROLE
MANOEUVRE
Other
1 (ceremonial) gd bde (1 gd bn, 1 MP bn, 1 spt bn)

Paramilitary 3,700

Gendarmerie 3,700

EQUIPMENT BY TYPE
ARMOURED FIGHTING VEHICLES
APC • APC (W) 12+: some *Lazar-3*; 12 BOV-VP M-86
AUV BOV M-16 *Milos*

DEPLOYMENT

ALBANIA: OSCE • Albania 1

BOSNIA-HERZEGOVINA: OSCE • Bosnia and Herzegovina 1

CENTRAL AFRICAN REPUBLIC: EU • EUTM RCA 7; UN • MINUSCA 73; 2 obs; 1 med coy

CYPRUS: UN • UNFICYP 2

DEMOCRATIC REPUBLIC OF THE CONGO: UN • MONUSCO 1

LEBANON: UN • UNIFIL 177; 1 mech inf coy
MALI: EU • EUTM Mali 3
MIDDLE EAST: UN • UNTSO 1 obs
SOMALIA: EU • EUTM Somalia 6
UKRAINE: OSCE • Ukraine 16

TERRITORY WHERE THE GOVERNMENT DOES NOT EXERCISE EFFECTIVE CONTROL

Data here represents the de facto situation in Kosovo. This does not imply international recognition as a sovereign state. In February 2008, Kosovo declared itself independent. Serbia remains opposed to this, and while Kosovo has not been admitted to the United Nations, a number of states have recognised Kosovo's self-declared status.

Kosovo Security Force 2,500; reserves 800

The Kosovo Security Force (KSF) was formed in January 2009 as a non-military organisation with responsibility for crisis response, civil protection and EOD. In 2017, a proposal by Pristina to establish an army was opposed by Russia, Serbia, the US and NATO. Legislation to this effect was passed by Pristina in October 2018. In December, NATO said that should the KSF's mandate evolve, it would have to examine its level of engagement with the force. The KSF is armed with small arms and light vehicles only.

FOREIGN FORCES

All under Kosovo Force (KFOR) command unless otherwise specified
Albania 28 • OSCE 3
Armenia 40
Austria 508; 1 recce coy; 2 mech inf coy; 1 log coy • OSCE 1
Bosnia-Herzegovina OSCE 10
Bulgaria 23 • OSCE 2
Canada 5 • OSCE 2
Croatia 35; 1 hel flt with Mi-8 • OSCE 1
Czech Republic 10 • OSCE 1 • UNMIK 2 obs
Denmark 35
Estonia 2
Finland 20
Georgia OSCE 1
Germany 198 • OSCE 4
Greece 116; 1 inf coy • OSCE 1
Hungary 388; 1 inf coy (KTM)
Ireland 12 • OSCE 3
Italy 538; 1 mtn inf BG HQ; 1 Carabinieri unit • OSCE 11
Kyrgyzstan OSCE 2
Lithuania 1
Macedonia (FYROM) OSCE 14
Moldova 41 • OSCE 2 • UNMIK 1 obs
Netherlands OSCE 1
Norway 2 • OSCE 1
Poland 260; 1 inf coy • OSCE 1 • UNMIK 1 obs
Portugal 3 • OSCE 1
Romania 71 • UNMIK 1 obs
Russia OSCE 1
Slovenia 241; 1 mot inf coy; 1 MP unit; 1 hel unit
Spain OSCE 1
Sweden 2 • OSCE 3
Switzerland 190; 1 inf coy; 1 engr pl; 1 hel flt with AS332
Tajikistan OSCE 1
Turkey 299; 1 inf coy • UNMIK 1 obs
Ukraine 40 • OSCE 1 • UNMIK 3 obs
United Kingdom 24 • OSCE 5
United States 655; elm 1 ARNG inf bde HQ; 1 recce bn; 1 hel flt with UH-60 • OSCE 8

Slovakia SVK

Euro €		2017	2018	2019
GDP	€	85.0bn	90.2bn	
	US$	96.0bn	107bn	
per capita	US$	17,655	19,642	
Growth	%	3.4	3.9	
Inflation	%	1.3	2.6	
Def exp [a]	€	935m	1.09bn	
	US$	1.06bn	1.29bn	
Def bdgt	€	990m	1.08bn	1.15bn
	US$	1.12bn	1.28bn	
US$1=€		0.89	0.84	

[a] NATO definition

Population 5,445,040

Age	0–14	15–19	20–24	25–29	30–64	65 plus
Male	7.8%	2.6%	3.0%	3.6%	25.5%	6.0%
Female	7.4%	2.5%	2.8%	3.5%	25.8%	9.4%

Capabilities

Slovakia is trying to modernise its armed forces and replace obsolete equipment while contributing to international crisis-management missions. A defence white paper in September 2016 set out security priorities and a plan to increase defence capabilities. In 2017, the government approved a new defence strategy, a new military strategy and a Long-Term Defence Development Plan. A NATO and EU member state, Slovakia cooperates closely with the Visegrád Group framework. Bratislava has signed an agreement to enable air policing and closer integration of air-defence capabilities. After amending the law on conscription in 2017, Slovakia began to implement its Active Reserves pilot project in order to help address shortfalls in specialist capacities, including in engineering. Results of the pilot project fell short of expectations, and Slovakia passed legislation in early 2018 to improve the training conditions for active reservists from mid-2018 onwards. Slovakia has committed to deploying a company-sized unit to NATO's Enhanced Forward Presence and has also contributed to EU operations and UN peacekeeping missions. Bratislava is planning to replace its small fighter and rotary-wing-transport fleets. Coinciding with the July 2018 NATO summit, the government announced it had selected the F-16. There are also ambitions to replace land equipment and improve the level of technology in the armed forces. Part of Slovakia's defence-industrial base is organised within the state-controlled holding company DMD Group, including KONSTRUKTA Defence, which produces land systems. Other companies focus on maintenance, repair and overhaul services.

ACTIVE 15,850 (Army 6,250 Air 3,950 Central Staff 2,550 Support and Training 3,100)
Conscript liability 6 months

ORGANISATIONS BY SERVICE

Central Staff 2,550
FORCES BY ROLE
SPECIAL FORCES
1 (5th) spec ops bn

Army 6,250
FORCES BY ROLE
MANOEUVRE
  Armoured
    1 (2nd) armd bde (1 recce bn, 1 tk bn, 1 armd inf bn, 1 mot inf bn, 1 mixed SP arty bn)
  Mechanised
    1 (1st) mech bde (3 armd inf bn, 1 MRL bn, 1 engr bn, 1 NBC bn)
COMBAT SUPPORT
  1 MP bn
COMBAT SERVICE SUPPORT
  1 spt bde (2 log bn, 1 maint bn, 1 spt bn)
EQUIPMENT BY TYPE
ARMOURED FIGHTING VEHICLES
  MBT 30 T-72M
  RECCE 18 BPsVI
  IFV 249: 148 BMP-1; 91 BMP-2; 10 BVP-M
  APC 101+ APC (T) 72 OT-90
    APC (W) 22: 7 OT-64; 15 Tatrapan (6×6)
  PPV 7+ RG-32M
  AUV IVECO LMV
ENGINEERING & MAINTENANCE VEHICLES
  ARV MT-55; VT-55A; VT-72B; WPT-TOPAS
  VLB AM-50; MT-55A
  MW Bozena; UOS-155 Belarty
ANTI-TANK/ANTI-INFRASTRUCTURE
  SP 9S428 with *Malyutka* (AT-3 *Sagger*) on BMP-1; 9P135 *Fagot* (AT-4 *Spigot*) on BMP-2; 9P148 *Konkurs* (AT-5 *Spandrel*) on BRDM-2
  MANPATS 9K11 *Malyutka* (AT-3 *Sagger*); 9K111-1 *Konkurs* (AT-5 *Spandrel*)
  RCL 84mm Carl Gustav
ARTILLERY 68
  SP 19: 152mm 3 M-77 *Dana*; 155mm 16 M-2000 *Zuzana*
  TOWED 122mm 19 D-30
  MRL 30: 122mm 4 RM-70; 122/227mm 26 RM-70/85 MODULAR
AIR DEFENCE • SAM
  Point-defence 48+: 48 9K35 *Strela*-10 (SA-13 *Gopher*); 9K32 *Strela*-2 (SA-7 *Grail*); 9K310 *Igla*-1 (SA-16 *Gimlet*)

Air Force 3,950
FORCES BY ROLE
FIGHTER
  1 sqn with MiG-29AS/UBS *Fulcrum*
TRANSPORT
  1 flt with C-27J *Spartan*
  1 flt with L-410FG/T/UVP *Turbolet*
TRANSPORT HELICOPTER
  1 sqn with Mi-8 *Hip*; Mi-17 *Hip* H
  1 sqn with PZL MI-2 *Hoplite*
TRAINING
  1 sqn with L-39CM/ZA/ZAM *Albatros*

AIR DEFENCE
  1 bde with 2K12 *Kub* (SA-6 *Gainful*); 9K32 *Strela*-2 (SA-7 *Grail*); S-300 (SA-10 *Grumble*)
EQUIPMENT BY TYPE
AIRCRAFT 24 combat capable
  FTR 12: 10 MiG-29AS *Fulcrum*; 2 MiG-29UBS *Fulcrum*;
  TPT 10: Medium 2 C-27J *Spartan*; Light 8: 2 L-410FG *Turbolet*; 2 L-410T *Turbolet*; 4 L-410UVP *Turbolet*
  TRG 12: 6 L-39CM *Albatros**; 5 L-39ZA *Albatros**; 1 L-39ZAM *Albatros**
HELICOPTERS
  ATK (15: 5 Mi-24D *Hind* D; 10 Mi-24V *Hind* E all in store)
  MRH 13 Mi-17 *Hip* H
  TPT 9: Medium 3: 1 Mi-8 *Hip*; 2 UH-60M *Black Hawk* Light 6 PZL MI-2 *Hoplite*
AIR DEFENCE • SAM
  Long-range S-300PS (SA-10 *Grumble*)
  Short-range 2K12 *Kub* (SA-6 *Gainful*)
  Point-defence 9K32 *Strela*-2 (SA-7 *Grail*)‡
AIR-LAUNCHED MISSILES
  AAM • IR R-60 (AA-8 *Aphid*); R-73 (AA-11 *Archer*)
  SARH R-27R (AA-10A *Alamo*)
  ASM S5K/S5KO (57mm rockets); S8KP/S8KOM (80mm rockets)

DEPLOYMENT

AFGHANISTAN: NATO • *Operation Resolute Support* 36
BOSNIA-HERZEGOVINA: EU • EUFOR • *Operation Althea* 41
CYPRUS: UN • UNFICYP 242; 1 inf coy; 1 engr pl
LATVIA: NATO • Enhanced Forward Presence 150; 1 mech inf coy
MIDDLE EAST: UN • UNTSO 2 obs
UKRAINE: OSCE • Ukraine 12

Slovenia SVN

Euro €		2017	2018	2019
GDP	€	43.3bn	46.3bn	
	US$	48.9bn	55.0bn	
per capita	US$	23,654	26,586	
Growth	%	5.0	4.5	
Inflation	%	1.4	2.1	
Def exp [a]	€	422m	466m	
	US$	477m	553m	
Def bdgt [b]	€	420m	449m	
	US$	474m	532m	
US$1=€		0.89	0.84	

[a] NATO definition
[b] Includes military pensions

Population 2,102,126

Ethnic groups: Slovenian 83%; Serbian 2%; Croatian 1.8%; Bosniac 1%; other or unspecified 12.2%

Age	0–14	15–19	20–24	25–29	30–64	65 plus
Male	6.9%	2.3%	2.5%	3.0%	26.0%	8.0%
Female	6.5%	2.2%	2.4%	2.9%	25.9%	11.5%

Capabilities

Since joining NATO and the EU in 2004, territorial defence and the ability to take part in peace-support operations have been central to Slovenia's defence strategy. The defence ministry completed a Strategic Defence Review in December 2016. Its core conclusion was that the goals of the previous 2009 review had been missed and that capability development had stalled at a time when Europe's security environment had deteriorated. Underfunding and bureaucratic failure to implement the policy guidelines were singled out as key reasons. The main development goal to 2023 has been defined as the formation and equipping of two battalion-sized battlegroups. Doctrine will also be reviewed. Slovenia acts as the framework nation for the NATO Mountain Warfare Centre of Excellence. Because its small air wing is not equipped to provide air policing, Italy and Hungary currently provide this capability under NATO arrangements. The country contributes to EU, NATO and UN operations and exercises with other member states. Recruitment and retention continues to be a challenge. Slovenia started its third rotation to NATO's Enhanced Forward Presence in July 2018 where it contributes to the Canadian-led battlegroup. Continuing resource challenges mean that significant modernisation steps seem unlikely during the current Medium-Term Defence Programme to 2020. Slovenia's defence industry relies heavily on exports for its revenue and focuses on individual solider equipment, small arms and ammunition, and CBRN protection and detection.

ACTIVE 7,250 (Army 7,250)

RESERVE 1,500 (Army 1,500)

ORGANISATIONS BY SERVICE

Army 7,250
FORCES BY ROLE
Regt are bn sized
SPECIAL FORCES
 1 SF unit (1 spec ops coy, 1 CSS coy)
MANOEUVRE
 Mechanised
 1 (1st) mech inf bde (1 mech inf regt, 1 mtn inf regt, 1 cbt spt bn (1 ISR coy, 1 arty bty, 1 engr coy, 1 MP coy, 1 CBRN coy, 1 sigs coy, 1 SAM bty))
 1 (72nd) mech inf bde (2 mech inf regt, 1 cbt spt bn (1 ISR coy, 1 arty bty, 1 engr coy, 1 MP coy, 1 CBRN coy, 1 sigs coy, 1 SAM bty))
COMBAT SUPPORT
 1 EW coy
COMBAT SERVICE SUPPORT
 1 log bde (1 log regt, 1 maint regt (1 tk coy), 1 med regt)

Reserves
FORCES BY ROLE
MANOEUVRE
 Mountain
 2 inf regt (territorial – 1 allocated to each inf bde)
EQUIPMENT BY TYPE
ARMOURED FIGHTING VEHICLES
 MBT 14 M-84 (trg role) (32 more in store)
 APC 115+:
  APC (W) 115: 85 *Pandur* 6×6 (*Valuk*); 30 Patria 8×8 (*Svarun*)
  PPV *Cougar* 6×6 JERRV

ENGINEERING & MAINTENANCE VEHICLES
 ARV VT-55A
 VLB MT-55A
NBC VEHICLES 10 *Cobra* CBRN
ANTI-TANK/ANTI-INFRASTRUCTURE
 MSL • MANPATS *Spike* MR/LR
ARTILLERY 68
 TOWED • 155mm 18 TN-90
 MOR 50+: 82mm M-69; 120mm 50 MN-9/M-74
AIR DEFENCE • SAM • Point-defence 9K338 *Igla*-S (SA-24 *Grinch*)

Army Maritime Element 130
FORCES BY ROLE
SPECIAL FORCES
 1 SF unit
EQUIPMENT BY TYPE
PATROL AND COASTAL COMBATANTS 2
 PCC 1 *Triglav* III (RUS *Svetlyak*)
 PBF 1 *Super Dvora* MkII

Air Element 610
FORCES BY ROLE
TRANSPORT
 1 sqn with *Falcon* 2000EX; L-410 *Turbolet*; PC-6B *Turbo Porter*;
TRAINING
 1 unit with Bell 206 *Jet Ranger* (AB-206); PC-9M*; Z-143L; Z-242L
TRANSPORT HELICOPTER
 1 sqn with AS532AL *Cougar*; Bell 412 *Twin Huey*
COMBAT SERVICE SUPPORT
 1 maint sqn
EQUIPMENT BY TYPE
AIRCRAFT 9 combat capable
 TPT 4: Light 3: 1 L-410 *Turbolet*; 2 PC-6B *Turbo Porter*
 PAX 1 *Falcon* 2000EX
 TRG 19: 9 PC-9M*; 2 Z-143L; 8 Z-242L
HELICOPTERS
 MRH 8: 5 Bell 412EP *Twin Huey*; 2 Bell 412HP *Twin Huey*; 1 Bell 412SP *Twin Huey* (some armed)
 TPT 8: Medium 4 AS532AL *Cougar*; Light 4 Bell 206 *Jet Ranger* (AB-206)

DEPLOYMENT

AFGHANISTAN: NATO • *Operation Resolute Support* 8
BOSNIA-HERZEGOVINA: EU • EUFOR • *Operation Althea* 14
IRAQ: *Operation Inherent Resolve* 6
LATVIA: NATO • Enhanced Forward Presence 50; 1 recce pl
LEBANON: UN • UNIFIL 18
MALI: EU • EUTM Mali 4
MIDDLE EAST: UN • UNTSO 3 obs
SERBIA: NATO • KFOR 241; 1 mot inf coy; 1 MP unit; 1 hel unit
UKRAINE: OSCE • Ukraine 1

Spain ESP

Euro €		2017	2018	2019
GDP	€	1.16tr	1.21tr	
	US$	1.31tr	1.44tr	
per capita	US$	28,359	31,060	
Growth	%	3.0	2.7	
Inflation	%	2.0	1.8	
Def exp [a]	€	10.5bn	11.4bn	
	US$	11.9bn	13.5bn	
Def bdgt [b]	€	11.8bn	12.7bn	
	US$	13.4bn	15.1bn	
US$1=€		0.89	0.84	

[a] NATO definition
[b] Includes military pensions

Population	49,331,076					
Age	0–14	15–19	20–24	25–29	30–64	65 plus
Male	7.9%	2.5%	2.5%	2.9%	26.0%	7.7%
Female	7.5%	2.3%	2.3%	2.6%	25.6%	10.3%

Capabilities

The 2017 National Security Strategy indicated that Spain's defence policy was global in scope, though concerned by threats emanating from the Middle East and sub-Saharan Africa. The army began a force-structure review in 2015, which resulted in a reorganisation into multipurpose brigades with heavy, medium and light capabilities, optimised for deployable operations and with a greater emphasis on mechanised formations and special-operations forces. Spain is a member of NATO and continues to support NATO, EU and UN operations abroad. The country hosts one of NATO's two Combined Air Operations Centres, and the country's Joint Special Operations Command will provide the Special Operations Component Command for the NATO Response Force in 2018. The armed forces are well trained and there is a routine exercise programme for both domestic and multinational exercises. The country's equipment and logistic-support capability appears to be sufficient to meet its national commitments and contribution to NATO operations and exercises. In early 2018, Spain launched an equipment-modernisation plan, with funding for the modernisation of army *Chinook* helicopters, for the S-80 submarine programme and for military-communications satellites. Spain has reportedly expressed interest in acquiring the F-35 to replace its AV-8Bs. Madrid has also expressed willingness to join European combat aircraft replacement projects such as the Franco-German FCAS and announced that it will participate in funding the European MALE UAV project. Spain's defence industry manufactures across all domains and exports globally. Navantia is the principal, state-owned, shipbuilding firm. The industry is largely integrated within the European defence-industrial manufacturing base.

ACTIVE 120,350 (Army 69,250 Navy 20,100 Air 19,350 Joint 11,650) **Paramilitary 75,800**

RESERVE 15,150 (Army 9,200 Navy 2,900 Air 2,350 Other 700)

ORGANISATIONS BY SERVICE

Space
EQUIPMENT BY TYPE
SATELLITES • COMMUNICATIONS 2: 1 *Spainsat*; 1 *Xtar-Eur*

Army 69,250

The Land Forces High Readiness HQ Spain provides one NATO Rapid Deployment Corps HQ (NRDC-ESP)

FORCES BY ROLE
COMMAND
  1 corps HQ (CGTAD/NRDC-ESP) (1 int regt, 1 MP bn)
  2 div HQ
SPECIAL FORCES
  1 comd (4 spec ops bn, 1 int coy, 1 sigs coy, 1 log bn)
MANOEUVRE
  Reconnaissance
  1 armd cav regt (2 armd recce bn)
  Mechanised
  3 (10th, 11th & 12th) mech bde (1 armd regt (1 armd recce bn, 1 tk bn), 1 mech inf regt (1 armd inf bn, 1 mech inf bn), 1 lt inf bn, 1 SP arty bn, 1 AT coy, 1 AD coy, 1 engr bn, 1 int coy, 1 NBC coy, 1 sigs coy, 1 log bn)
  1 (1st) mech bde (1 armd regt (1 armd recce bn, 1 tk bn), 1 mech inf regt (1 armd inf bn, 1 mtn inf bn), 1 mtn inf bn, 1 SP arty bn, 1 AT coy, 1 AD coy, 1 engr coy, 1 NBC coy, 1 sigs coy, 1 log bn)
  2 (2nd/La Legion & 7th) lt mech bde (1 armd recce bn, 1 mech inf regt (2 mech inf bn), 1 lt inf bn, 1 fd arty bn, 1 AT coy, 1 AD coy, 1 engr bn, 1 int coy, 1 NBC coy, 1 sigs coy, 1 log bn)
  Air Manoeuvre
  1 (6th) bde (1 recce bn, 2 para bn, 1 lt inf bn, 1 fd arty bn, 1 AT coy, 1 AD coy, 1 engr bn, 1 int coy, 1 NBC coy, 1 sigs coy, 1 log bn)
  Other
  1 (Canary Islands) comd (1 lt inf bde (2 mech inf regt (1 mech inf bn), 1 lt inf regt (1 lt inf bn), 1 fd arty regt, 1 AT coy, 1 engr bn, 1 int coy, 1 NBC coy, 1 sigs coy, 1 log bn); 1 spt hel bn; 1 AD regt)
  1 (Balearic Islands) comd (1 inf regt)
  2 (Ceuta and Melilla) comd (1 recce regt, 1 mech inf bn, 1 inf bn, 1 arty regt, 1 engr bn, 1 sigs coy, 1 log bn)
COMBAT SUPPORT
  1 arty comd (1 arty regt; 1 MRL regt; 1 coastal arty regt)
  1 engr comd (2 engr regt, 1 bridging regt)
  1 EW/sigs bde (2 EW regt, 3 sigs regt)
  1 NBC regt
  1 CIMIC bn
COMBAT SERVICE SUPPORT
  1 log bde (5 log regt; 1 tpt regt)
  1 med bde (1 log unit, 2 med regt, 1 fd hospital unit)
HELICOPTER
  1 hel comd (1 atk hel bn, 2 spt hel bn, 1 tpt hel bn, 1 sigs bn, 1 log unit (1 spt coy, 1 supply coy))
AIR DEFENCE
  1 AD comd (3 SAM regt, 1 sigs unit)

EQUIPMENT BY TYPE
ARMOURED FIGHTING VEHICLES
 MBT 327: 108 *Leopard* 2A4; 219 *Leopard* 2E
 RECCE 271: 84 B1 *Centauro*; 187 VEC-M1
 IFV 227: 206 *Pizarro*; 21 *Pizarro* (CP)
 APC 895
  APC (T) 473: 20 Bv-206S; 453 M113 (incl variants)
  APC (W) 312 BMR-600/BMR-600M1
  PPV 110 RG-31
 AUV 260 IVECO LMV
ENGINEERING & MAINTENANCE VEHICLES
 AEV 34 CZ-10/25E
 ARV 72: 16 *Leopard* REC; 1 AMX-30; 3 BMR REC; 4 *Centauro* REC; 14 *Maxxpro* MRV; 12 M113; 22 M47
 VLB 16: 1 M47; 15 M60
 MW 6 *Husky* 2G
ANTI-TANK/ANTI-INFRASTRUCTURE
 MSL • MANPATS *Spike*-LR; TOW
ARTILLERY 1,560
 SP 155mm 96 M109A5
 TOWED 281: 105mm 217: 56 L118 Light Gun; 161 Model 56 pack howitzer; 155mm 64 SBT 155/52 SIAC
 MOR 1,183: 81mm 777; SP 81mm 4 VAMTAC with Cardom 81mm; 120mm 402
COASTAL DEFENCE • ARTY 155mm 19 SBT 155/52 APU SBT V07
HELICOPTERS
 ATK 21: 6 *Tiger* HAP-E; 15 *Tiger* HAD-E
 TPT 84: Heavy 17 CH-47D *Chinook* (HT-17D); Medium 40: 16 AS332B *Super Puma* (HU-21); 12 AS532UL *Cougar*; 6 AS532AL *Cougar*; 6 NH90 TTH; Light 27: 6 Bell 205 (HU-10B *Iroquois*); 5 Bell 212 (HU.18); 16 H135 (HE.26/HU.26)
UAV • ISR • Medium 6: 2 *Searcher* MkII-J (PASI); 4 *Searcher* MkIII (PASI)
AIR DEFENCE
 SAM
  Long-range 18 MIM-104C *Patriot* PAC-2
  Medium-range 38 MIM-23B I-*Hawk* Phase III
  Short-range 21: 8 NASAMS; 13 *Skyguard/Aspide*
  Point-defence *Mistral*
 GUNS • TOWED 35mm 67: 19 GDF-005; 48 GDF-007

Navy 20,100 (incl Naval Aviation and Marines)

EQUIPMENT BY TYPE
SUBMARINES • TACTICAL • SSK 3:
 3 *Galerna* with 4 single 533mm TT with F17 Mod 2/L5 HWT
PRINCIPAL SURFACE COMBATANTS 11
 DESTROYERS • DDGHM 5:
  5 *Alvaro de Bazan* with *Aegis* Baseline 5 C2, 2 quad Mk141 lnchr with RGM-84F *Harpoon* AShM, 1 48-cell Mk41 VLS with SM-2MR/RIM-162B *Sea Sparrow* SAM, 2 Mk32 Mod 9 SVTT twin 324mm ASTT with Mk46 LWT, 1 127mm gun (capacity 1 SH-60B *Seahawk* ASW hel)
 FRIGATES • FFGHM 6:
  6 *Santa Maria* with 1 Mk13 GMLS with RGM-84C *Harpoon* AShM/SM-1MR SAM, 2 Mk32 triple 324mm ASTT with Mk46 LWT, 1 *Meroka* mod 2 CIWS, 1 76mm gun (capacity 2 SH-60B *Seahawk* ASW hel)

AMPHIBIOUS
 PRINCIPAL AMPHIBIOUS SHIPS 3:
  LHD 1 *Juan Carlos* I (capacity 18 hel or 10 AV-8B FGA ac; 4 LCM-1E; 42 APC; 46 MBT; 900 troops)
  LPD 2 *Galicia* (capacity 6 Bell 212 or 4 SH-3D *Sea King* hel; 4 LCM or 2 LCM & 8 AAV; 130 APC or 33 MBT; 540 troops)
 LANDING CRAFT 12
  LCM 12 LCM 1E
LOGISTICS AND SUPPORT 2
 AORH 2: 1 *Patino* (capacity 3 Bell 212 or 2 SH-3D *Sea King* hel); 1 *Cantabria* (capacity 3 Bell 212 or 2 SH-3D *Sea King* hel)

Maritime Action Force

EQUIPMENT BY TYPE
PATROL AND COASTAL COMBATANTS 22
 PSOH 5 *Meteoro* (*Buques de Accion Maritima*) with 1 76mm gun
 PSO 5:
  3 *Alboran* each with 1 hel landing platform
  2 *Descubierta* with 1 76mm gun
 PCO 4 *Serviola* with 1 76mm gun
 PCC 3 *Anaga* with 1 76mm gun
 PB 4: 2 P-101; 2 *Toralla*
 PBR 1 *Cabo Fradera*
MINE WARFARE • MINE COUNTERMEASURES 6
 MHO 6 *Segura*
LOGISTICS AND SUPPORT 29
 AGI 1 *Alerta*
 AGOR 2 (with ice-strengthened hull, for polar research duties in Antarctica)
 AGS 3: 2 *Malaspina*; 1 *Castor*
 AK 2: 1 *Martin Posadillo* with 1 hel landing platform; 1 *El Camino Español*
 AP 1 *Contramaestre Casado* with 1 hel landing platform
 ASR 1 *Neptuno*
 ATF 3: 1 *Mar Caribe*; 1 *Mahon*; 1 *La Grana*
 AXL 8: 4 *Contramaestre*; 4 *Guardiamarina*
 AXS 8

Naval Aviation 850

FORCES BY ROLE
FIGHTER/GROUND ATTACK
 1 sqn with AV-8B *Harrier* II Plus
ANTI-SUBMARINE WARFARE
 1 sqn with SH-60B/F *Seahawk*
TRANSPORT
 1 (liaison) sqn with Cessna 550 *Citation* II; Cessna 650 *Citation* VII
TRAINING
 1 sqn with Hughes 500MD8
 1 flt with TAV-8B *Harrier*
TRANSPORT HELICOPTER
 1 sqn with Bell 212 (HU-18)
 1 sqn with SH-3D *Sea King*
EQUIPMENT BY TYPE
AIRCRAFT 13 combat capable
 FGA 13: 8 AV-8B *Harrier* II Plus; 4 AV-8B *Harrier* II (upgraded to II Plus standard); 1 TAV-8B *Harrier* (on lease from USMC)
 TPT • Light 4: 3 Cessna 550 *Citation* II; 1 Cessna 650 *Citation* VII

HELICOPTERS
ASW 21: 7 SH-3D *Sea King* (tpt); 12 SH-60B *Seahawk*; 2 SH-60F *Seahawk*
MRH 9 Hughes 500MD
TPT • Light 7 Bell 212 (HA-18)
AIR-LAUNCHED MISSILES
AAM • IR AIM-9L *Sidewinder*; **ARH** AIM-120 AMRAAM
ASM AGM-65G *Maverick*
AShM AGM-119 *Penguin*

Marines 5,350
FORCES BY ROLE
SPECIAL FORCES
1 spec ops bn
MANOEUVRE
Amphibious
1 mne bde (1 recce unit, 1 mech inf bn, 2 inf bn, 1 arty bn, 1 log bn)
Other
1 sy bde (5 mne garrison gp)
EQUIPMENT BY TYPE
ARMOURED FIGHTING VEHICLES
MBT 2 M60A3TTS
APC • APC (W) 34: 32 *Piranha* IIIC; 1 *Piranha* IIIC (amb); 1 *Piranha* IIIC EW (EW)
AAV 18: 16 AAV-7A1/AAVP-7A1; 2 AAVC-7A1 (CP)
ENGINEERING & MAINTENANCE VEHICLES
AEV 4 *Piranha* IIIC
ARV 2: 1 AAVR-7A1; 1 M88; 1 *Piranha* IIIC
ARTILLERY 30
SP 155mm 6 M109A2
TOWED 105mm 24 Model 56 pack howitzer
ANTI-TANK/ANTI-INFRASTRUCTURE
MSL • MANPATS *Spike*-LR; TOW-2
AIR DEFENCE • SAM • Point-defence *Mistral*

Air Force 19,350
The Spanish Air Force is organised in 3 commands – General Air Command, Combat Air Command and Canary Islands Air Command
FORCES BY ROLE
FIGHTER
2 sqn with Eurofighter *Typhoon*
FIGHTER/GROUND ATTACK
5 sqn with F/A-18A/B MLU *Hornet* (EF-18A/B MLU)
MARITIME PATROL
1 sqn with P-3A/M *Orion*
ISR
1 sqn with Beech C90 *King Air*
1 sqn with Cessna 550 *Citation* V; CN235 (TR-19A)
ELECTRONIC WARFARE
1 sqn with C-212 *Aviocar*; *Falcon* 20D
SEARCH & RESCUE
1 sqn with AS332B/B1 *Super Puma*; CN235 VIGMA
1 sqn with AS332B *Super Puma*; CN235 VIGMA
1 sqn with C-212 *Aviocar*; CN235 VIGMA
TANKER/TRANSPORT
1 sqn with KC-130H *Hercules*
TRANSPORT
1 VIP sqn with A310; *Falcon* 900

1 sqn with C-130H/H-30 *Hercules*; A400M
1 sqn with C-212 *Aviocar*
2 sqn with C295
1 sqn with CN235
TRAINING
1 OCU sqn with Eurofighter *Typhoon*
1 OCU sqn with F/A-18A/B (EF-18A/B MLU) *Hornet*
1 sqn with Beech F33C *Bonanza*
2 sqn with C-101 *Aviojet*
1 sqn with C-212 *Aviocar*
1 sqn with T-35 *Pillan* (E-26)
2 (LIFT) sqn with F-5B *Freedom Fighter*
1 hel sqn with H120 *Colibri*
1 hel sqn with S-76C
TRANSPORT HELICOPTER
1 sqn with AS332M1 *Super Puma*; AS532UL *Cougar* (VIP)
EQUIPMENT BY TYPE
AIRCRAFT 170 combat capable
FTR 83: 64 Eurofighter *Typhoon*; 19 F-5B *Freedom Fighter*
FGA 84: 20 F/A-18A *Hornet* (EF-18A); 52 EF-18A MLU; 12 EF-18B MLU
ASW 3 P-3M *Orion*
MP 8 CN235 VIGMA
ISR 2 CN235 (TR-19A)
EW 3: 1 C-212 *Aviocar* (TM.12D); 2 *Falcon* 20D
TKR 5 KC-130H *Hercules*
TPT 77: **Heavy** 3 A400M; **Medium** 7: 6 C-130H *Hercules*; 1 C-130H-30 *Hercules*; **Light** 59: 3 Beech C90 *King Air*; 22 Beech F33C *Bonanza*; 10 C-212 *Aviocar* (incl 9 trg); 13 C295; 8 CN235; 3 Cessna 550 *Citation* V (ISR); **PAX** 8: 2 A310; 1 B-707; 5 *Falcon* 900 (VIP)
TRG 98: 61 C-101 *Aviojet*; 37 T-35 *Pillan* (E-26)
HELICOPTERS
TPT 40: **Medium** 18: 9 AS332B/B1 *Super Puma*; 4 AS332M1 *Super Puma*; 3 AS332C1 *Super Puma*; 2 AS532UL *Cougar* (VIP); **Light** 22: 14 H120 *Colibri*; 8 S-76C
AIR DEFENCE • SAM
Short-range *Skyguard/Aspide*
Point-defence *Mistral*
AIR-LAUNCHED MISSILES
AAM • IR AIM-9L/JULI *Sidewinder*; **IIR** IRIS-T; **SARH** AIM-7P *Sparrow*; **ARH** AIM-120B/C AMRAAM
ARM AGM-88B HARM
ASM AGM-65G *Maverick*
AShM AGM-84D *Harpoon*
LACM Taurus KEPD 350
BOMBS
Laser-guided: GBU-10/12/16 *Paveway* II; GBU-24 *Paveway* III; EGBU-16 *Paveway* II; BPG-2000
INS/GPS guided: GBU-38 JDAM

Emergencies Military Unit (UME) 3,500
FORCES BY ROLE
COMMAND
1 div HQ
MANOEUVRE
Other
5 Emergency Intervention bn
1 Emergency Support and Intervention regt

COMBAT SUPPORT
1 sigs bn
HELICOPTER
1 hel bn opcon Army

Paramilitary 75,800

Guardia Civil 75,800
17 regions, 54 Rural Comds
FORCES BY ROLE
SPECIAL FORCES
8 (rural) gp
MANOEUVRE
Other
15 (traffic) sy gp
1 (Special) sy bn
EQUIPMENT BY TYPE
PATROL AND COASTAL COMBATANTS 64
PSO 1 with 1 hel landing platform
PCC 2
PBF 34
PB 27
AIRCRAFT • TPT • Light 2 CN235-300
HELICOPTERS
MRH 20: 2 AS653N3 *Dauphin*; 18 Bo-105ATH
TPT • Light 21: 8 BK-117; 13 H135

Cyber
A Joint Cyber Defense Command was set up in 2013, subordinate to Spain's chief of defence. In 2014, short-/medium-term goals included achieving full operating capability on 'CNDefense, CNExploitation, and CNAttack'. Spain's intelligence CERT coordinates CERT activities.

DEPLOYMENT
AFGHANISTAN: NATO • *Operation Resolute Support* 40
BLACK SEA: NATO • SNMCMG 2: 1 MHO
BOSNIA-HERZEGOVINA: EU • EUFOR • *Operation Althea* 2; OSCE • Bosnia and Herzegovina 3
CENTRAL AFRICAN REPUBLIC: EU • EUTM RCA 8
DJIBOUTI: EU • *Operation Atalanta* 1 P-3M *Orion*
GABON: *Operation Barkhane* 45; 1 C295M
GULF OF ADEN & INDIAN OCEAN: EU • *Operation Atalanta* 1 LPD
IRAQ: *Operation Inherent Resolve* 350; 2 trg unit
LATVIA: NATO • Enhanced Forward Presence 300; 1 armd inf coy(+)
LEBANON: UN • UNIFIL 630; 1 mech bde HQ; 1 mech inf bn(-); 1 engr coy; 1 sigs coy
MALI: EU • EUTM Mali 292; UN • MINUSMA 1
MEDITERRANEAN SEA: NATO • SNMG 2: 1 DDGHM;1 AORH; EU • EU NAVFOR MED: 1 FFGHM; 1 CN235
SENEGAL: *Operation Barkhane* 57; 1 C-130H *Hercules*
SERBIA: OSCE • Kosovo 1
SOMALIA: EU • EUTM Somalia 13

TURKEY: NATO • *Operation Active Fence* 149; 1 SAM bty with MIM-104C *Patriot* PAC-2
UKRAINE: OSCE • Ukraine 16

FOREIGN FORCES
United States US European Command: 3,200; 1 air base at Morón; 1 naval base at Rota

Sweden SWE

Swedish Krona Skr		2017	2018	2019
GDP	Skr	4.58tr	4.80tr	
	US$	536bn	555bn	
per capita	US$	52,925	53,867	
Growth	%	2.1	2.4	
Inflation	%	1.9	1.9	
Def bdgt	Skr	50.7bn	53.8bn	
	US$	5.94bn	6.22bn	
US$1=Skr		8.55	8.65	

Population	10,040,995					
Age	0–14	15–19	20–24	25–29	30–64	65 plus
Male	9.0%	2.7%	3.2%	3.6%	22.2%	9.4%
Female	8.5%	2.5%	3.0%	3.5%	21.7%	10.9%

Capabilities
Sweden's armed forces remain configured for territorial defence and there has been growing concern at Russian military activity in the Baltic area. There has also been a focus on increasing cooperation with neighbours and NATO in recent years. The 2016–20 defence bill set out the aims of strengthening operational capabilities and deepening multilateral and bilateral defence relationships. Sweden decided to relocate its service staffs from Stockholm to other locations in 2019 in order to provide better protection. There are plans to increase defence ties with the UK and the US. Concerns over readiness levels have led to greater cooperation with NATO and NORDEFCO. In May 2018, Sweden, Finland and the US signed a statement of intent to develop closer cooperation on exercises and interoperability. Readiness, exercises and training, as well as cyber defence, are spending priorities. Amid recruitment challenges, Sweden announced in March 2017 that it would reinstate conscription from January 2018. Sweden has started to re-garrison the island of Gotland. Readiness challenges in the air force triggered a discussion about extending the service life of the JAS-39C *Gripen* Cs beyond their intended 2026 retirement date, not least since the air force was slated to receive a lower number of JAS-39Es than requested. In August 2018, Sweden proceeded with the acquisition of the *Patriot* medium-range air-defence system. The country's export-oriented defence industry is privately owned and capable of meeting most of the armed forces' equipment needs, including for advanced combat aircraft and conventional submarines.

ACTIVE 29,750 (Army 6,850 Navy 2,100 Air 2,700 Other 18,100) **Voluntary Auxiliary Organisations 21,200**

Conscript liability 4–11 months, depending on branch (selective conscription; 4,000 in total, gender neutral)

ORGANISATIONS BY SERVICE

Army 6,850
The army has been transformed to provide brigade-sized task forces depending on the operational requirement

FORCES BY ROLE
COMMAND
  2 bde HQ
MANOEUVRE
  Reconnaissance
    1 recce bn
  Armoured
    5 armd bn
    1 armd BG
  Mechanised
    1 mech bn
  Light
    1 mot inf bn
    1 lt inf bn
  Air Manoeuvre
    1 AB bn
  Other
    1 sy bn
COMBAT SUPPORT
  2 arty bn
  2 engr bn
  2 MP coy
  1 CBRN coy
COMBAT SERVICE SUPPORT
  1 tpt coy
AIR DEFENCE
  2 AD bn

Reserves
FORCES BY ROLE
MANOEUVRE
  Other
    40 Home Guard bn

EQUIPMENT BY TYPE
ARMOURED FIGHTING VEHICLES
  MBT 120 Leopard 2A5 (Strv 122)
  IFV 396: 354 CV9040 (Strf 9040; incl CP); 42 Epbv 90 (OP)
  APC 1,083
    APC (T) 408: 258 Pbv 302; 150 BvS10 MkII
    APC (W) 315: 34 XA-180 Sisu (Patgb 180); 20 XA-202 Sisu (Patgb 202); 148 XA-203 Sisu (Patgb 203); 113 Patria AMV (XA-360/Patgb 360)
  PPV 360 RG-32M
ENGINEERING & MAINTENANCE VEHICLES
  AEV 6 Kodiak
  ARV 40: 14 Bgbv 120; 26 Bgbv 90
  VLB 3 Brobv 120
  MW 33+: Aardvark Mk2; 33 Area Clearing System
ANTI-TANK/ANTI-INFRASTRUCTURE
  MSL • MANPATS NLAW; RBS-55
  RCL 84mm Carl Gustav
ARTILLERY 305
  SP 155mm 23 Archer
  MOR 282; **81mm** 201 M/86; **120mm** 81 M/41D
AIR DEFENCE
  SAM
    Medium-range MIM-23B Hawk (RBS-97)
    Point-defence RBS-70
  GUNS • SP 40mm 30 Strv 90LV

Navy 1,250; 850 Amphibious (total 2,100)
EQUIPMENT BY TYPE
SUBMARINE • TACTICAL • SSK 5:
  3 Gotland (AIP fitted) with 2 single 400mm TT with Typ 431 LWT/Typ 451 LWT, 4 single 533mm TT with Typ 613 HWT/Typ 62 HWT
  2 Sodermanland (AIP fitted) with 3 single 400mm TT with Typ 431 LWT/Typ 451LWT, 6 single 533mm TT with Typ 613 HWT/Typ 62 HWT
PATROL AND COASTAL COMBATANTS 143
  CORVETTES • FSG 5 Visby with 8 RBS15 AShM, 4 single 400mm ASTT with Tp45 LWT, 1 57mm gun, 1 hel landing platform
  PCGT 4:
    2 Gälve with 4 twin lnchr with RBS15 Mk2 AShM, 4 single 400mm ASTT with Tp431 LWT, 4 Saab 601 A/S mor, 1 57mm gun
    2 Stockholm with 4 twin lnchr with RBS15 Mk2 AShM, 4 Saab 601 mortars, 4 single 400mm ASTT with Tp431 LWT, 1 57mm gun
  PBF 129 Combat Boat 90E/H/HS (capacity 18 troops)
  PB 5 Tapper (Type 80)
MINE WARFARE • MINE COUNTERMEASURES 7
  MCC 5 Koster
  MCD 2 Spårö (Styrsö mod)
AMPHIBIOUS • LANDING CRAFT 11
  LCVP 8 Trossbat
  LCAC 3 Griffon 8100TD
LOGISTICS AND SUPPORT 15
  AG 2: 1 Carlskrona with 2 57mm gun, 1 hel landing platform (former ML); 1 Trosso (spt ship for corvettes and patrol vessels but can also be used as HQ ship)
  AGF 2 Ledningsbåt 2000
  AGI 1 Orion
  AKL 1 Loke
  ARS 2: 1 Belos III; 1 Furusund (former ML)
  AX 5 Altair
  AXS 2: 1 Falken; 1 Gladan

Amphibious 850
FORCES BY ROLE
MANOEUVRE
  Amphibious
    1 amph bn
EQUIPMENT BY TYPE
ARTILLERY • MOR 81mm 12 M/86
COASTAL DEFENCE • AShM 8 RBS-17 Hellfire

Air Force 2,700
FORCES BY ROLE
FIGHTER/GROUND ATTACK/ISR
  6 sqn with JAS 39C/D Gripen

TRANSPORT/ISR/AEW&C
1 sqn with C-130H *Hercules* (Tp-84); KC-130H *Hercules* (Tp-84); Gulfstream IV SRA-4 (S-102B); S-100B/D *Argus*

TRAINING
1 unit with Sk-60

AIR DEFENCE
1 (fighter control and air surv) bn

EQUIPMENT BY TYPE
AIRCRAFT 96 combat capable
  FGA 96 JAS 39C/D *Gripen*
  ELINT 2 Gulfstream IV SRA-4 (S-102B)
  AEW&C 3: 1 S-100B *Argus*; 2 S-100D *Argus*
  TKR 1 KC-130H *Hercules* (Tp-84)
  TPT 8: **Medium** 5 C-130H *Hercules* (Tp-84); **Light** 2 Saab 340 (OS-100A/Tp-100C); **PAX** 1 Gulfstream 550 (Tp-102D)
  TRG 67 Sk-60W
UNMANNED AERIAL VEHICLES
  ISR • Medium 8 RQ-7 *Shadow* (AUV 3 *Örnen*)
AIR-LAUNCHED MISSILES
  ASM AGM-65 *Maverick* (RB-75)
  AShM RB-15F
  AAM • IR AIM-9L *Sidewinder* (RB-74); **IIR** IRIS-T (RB-98); **ARH** AIM-120B AMRAAM (RB-99); *Meteor*
BOMBS
  Laser-Guided GBU-12 *Paveway* II
  INS/GPS guided GBU-39 Small Diameter Bomb

Armed Forces Hel Wing
FORCES BY ROLE
TRANSPORT HELICOPTER
  3 sqn with AW109 (Hkp 15A); AW109M (Hkp-15B); NH90 (Hkp-14) (SAR/ASW); UH-60M *Black Hawk* (Hkp-16)

EQUIPMENT BY TYPE
HELICOPTERS
  ASW 5 NH90 ASW
  TPT 48: **Medium** 28: 15 UH-60M *Black Hawk* (Hkp-16); 13 NH90 TTH (Hkp-14); **Light** 20: 12 AW109 (Hkp-15A); 8 AW109M (Hkp-15B)

Special Forces
FORCES BY ROLE
SPECIAL FORCES
  1 spec ops gp
COMBAT SUPPORT
  1 cbt spt gp

Other 18,100
Includes staff, logistics and intelligence personnel
FORCES BY ROLE
COMBAT SUPPORT
  1 EW bn
  1 psyops unit
COMBAT SERVICE SUPPORT
  2 log bn
  1 maint bn
  4 med coy
  1 tpt coy

Cyber
Sweden has a national CERT, is involved in informal CERT communities and is a member of the European Government CERTs group. A national cyber-security strategy has also been adopted. Four ministries have a cyber remit: defence, foreign affairs, justice, and enterprise and industry. The Swedish Civil Contingencies Agency, which reports to the defence ministry, is in charge of supporting and coordinating security nationwide. According to the 2015 defence bill, 'cyber defence capabilities are an important part of the Swedish Defence. Vital systems must be protected from attack. This also requires the ability to carry out active operations in the cyber domain.' As well as strengthening capacity as part of the total-defence concept, Sweden sees international cooperation in cyber as vital.

DEPLOYMENT
AFGHANISTAN: NATO • *Operation Resolute Support* 29
CENTRAL AFRICAN REPUBLIC: EU • EUTM RCA 9
DEMOCRATIC REPUBLIC OF THE CONGO: UN • MONUSCO 1; 1 obs
INDIA/PAKISTAN: UN • UNMOGIP 5 obs
IRAQ: *Operation Inherent Resolve* 66
KOREA, REPUBLIC OF: NNSC • 5 obs
MALI: EU • EUTM Mali 6; **UN •** MINUSMA 241; 1 int coy
MIDDLE EAST: UN • UNTSO 6 obs
SERBIA: NATO • KFOR 2; **OSCE •** Kosovo 3
SOMALIA: EU • EUTM Somalia 4
SOUTH SUDAN: UN • UNMISS 2 obs
UKRAINE: OSCE • Ukraine 11
WESTERN SAHARA: UN • MINURSO 2 obs

Switzerland CHE

Swiss Franc fr		2017	2018	2019
GDP	fr	669bn	694bn	
	US$	679bn	709bn	
per capita	US$	80,637	83,583	
Growth	%	1.7	3.0	
Inflation	%	0.5	1.1	
Def bdgt [a]	fr	4.71bn	4.87bn	5.32bn
	US$	4.79bn	4.97bn	
US$1=fr		0.98	0.98	

[a] Includes military pensions

Population 8,292,809

Age	0–14	15–19	20–24	25–29	30–64	65 plus
Male	7.8%	2.7%	2.9%	3.2%	24.7%	8.0%
Female	7.4%	2.5%	2.8%	3.2%	24.6%	10.2%

Capabilities

The conscript-based armed forces are postured for territorial defence and limited participation in international peace-support operations. The government has begun to reduce its armed forces, reflecting an assessment that in the militia-based system not all personnel would realistically be available for active service. With permanent neutrality a core feature of foreign and security policy, Switzerland is not a member of any alliances, although it joined NATO's Partnership for Peace Programme in 1996 and on occasion contributes to NATO- and EU-led operations alongside its engagement in UN or OSCE missions. Switzerland does not participate in combat operations for peace-enforcement purposes and its deployments are limited in size. The 2016 armed-forces development plan emphasises improvements in readiness, training and equipment. The approach to readiness is changing to a flexible model in which different units are called up for active service gradually and on different timelines. Plans to replace F-5 *Tiger* II combat aircraft with the *Gripen* were scrapped after a national referendum rejected the proposal in May 2014. With Switzerland's air-policing capabilities diminished, in July 2018 the government relaunched its attempt to procure a new combat aircraft. The multi-stage selection process is expected to be completed by the end of 2020 and now includes replacement of the F/A18 *Hornet*, which will be life-extended through to 2030. Other priorities include upgrades to Switzerland's air-surveillance systems and transport helicopters. Switzerland's defence industry has limited design and manufacturing capabilities, with recognised capacity in the land-vehicles sector, which has links to North American companies.

ACTIVE 21,450 (Armed Forces 21,450)

Conscript liability 260-600 compulsory service days depending on rank. 18 or 23 weeks' training (depending on branch) generally at age 20, followed by 6 refresher trg courses (3 weeks each). Alternative service available.

RESERVE 134,800

Civil Defence 73,000 (51,000 Reserve)

ORGANISATIONS BY SERVICE

Armed Forces 2,950 active; 18,500 conscript (21,450 total)

Operations Command 72,600 on mobilisation

4 Territorial Regions. With the exception of military police all units are non-active

FORCES BY ROLE
COMMAND
  4 regional comd
SPECIAL FORCES
  2 SF bn
MANOEUVRE
  Armoured
  2 (1st & 11th) bde (1 recce bn, 1 tk bn, 2 armd inf bn, 1 SP arty bn, 1 engr bn, 1 sigs bn)
  Mechanised
  1 (4th) bde (2 recce bn, 2 SP arty bn, 1 ptn br bn)
  Light
  10 inf bn
  7 mtn inf bn
  1 mtn inf unit

COMBAT SUPPORT
  4 engr bn
  4 MP bn
  1 NBC bn
  1 int unit
COMBAT SUPPORT
  4 engr rescue bn
EQUIPMENT BY TYPE
ARMOURED FIGHTING VEHICLES
  MBT 134 *Leopard* 2 (Pz-87 *Leo*)
  IFV 186: 154 CV9030CH; 32 CV9030 (CP)
  APC 914
    APC (T) 238 M113A2 (incl variants)
    APC (W) 676: 346 *Piranha* II; 330 *Piranha* I/II/IIIC (CP)
  AUV 441 *Eagle* II
ENGINEERING & MAINTENANCE VEHICLES
  AEV 12 *Kodiak*
  ARV 25 *Büffel*
  MW 46: 26 Area Clearing System; 20 M113A2
NBC VEHICLES 12 *Piranha* IIIC CBRN
ANTI-TANK/ANTI-INFRASTRUCTURE
  MSL • SP 106 *Piranha* I TOW-2
ARTILLERY 433
  SP 155mm 133 M109 KAWEST
  MOR • 81mm 300 Mw-72
PATROL AND COASTAL COMBATANTS • PBR 11 *Aquarius*
AIR DEFENCE • SAM • Point-defence FIM-92 *Stinger*

Air Force 17,200 on mobilisation

FORCES BY ROLE
FIGHTER
  3 sqn with F-5E/F *Tiger* II
  3 sqn with F/A-18C/D *Hornet*
TRANSPORT
  1 sqn with Beech 350 *King Air*; DHC-6 *Twin Otter*; PC-6 *Turbo Porter*; PC-12
  1 VIP Flt with Beech 1900D; Cessna 560XL *Citation*; *Falcon* 900EX
TRAINING
  1 sqn with PC-7CH *Turbo Trainer*; PC-21
  1 sqn with PC-9 (tgt towing)
  1 OCU Sqn with F-5E/F *Tiger* II
TRANSPORT HELICOPTER
  6 sqn with AS332M *Super Puma*; AS532UL *Cougar*; H135M
ISR UAV
  1 sqn with ADS 95 *Ranger*
EQUIPMENT BY TYPE
AIRCRAFT 85 combat capable
  FTR 54: 42 F-5E *Tiger* II; 12 F-5F *Tiger* II
  FGA 31: 25 F/A-18C *Hornet*; 6 F/A-18D *Hornet*
  TPT 22: Light 21: 1 Beech 350 *King Air*; 1 Beech 1900D; 1 Cessna 560XL *Citation*; 1 DHC-6 *Twin Otter*; 15 PC-6 *Turbo Porter*; 1 PC-6 (owned by armasuisse, civil registration); 1 PC-12 (owned by armasuisse, civil registration); PAX 1 *Falcon* 900EX
  TRG 44: 28 PC-7CH *Turbo Trainer*; 8 PC-9; 8 PC-21
HELICOPTERS
  MRH 20 H135M

TPT • **Medium** 25: 15 AS332M *Super Puma*; 10 AS532UL *Cougar*
UNMANNED AERIAL VEHICLES
ISR • Medium 16 ADS 95 *Ranger* (4 systems)
AIR-LAUNCHED MISSILES • AAM • IR AIM-9P *Sidewinder*; **IIR** AIM-9X *Sidewinder* II; **ARH** AIM-120B/C-7 AMRAAM

Ground Based Air Defence (GBAD)

GBAD assets can be used to form AD clusters to be deployed independently as task forces within Swiss territory

EQUIPMENT BY TYPE
AIR DEFENCE
    SAM • Point *Rapier*; FIM-92 *Stinger*
    GUNS 35mm Some GDF with *Skyguard*

Armed Forces Logistic Organisation 9,650 on mobilisation

FORCES BY ROLE
COMBAT SERVICE SUPPORT
    1 log bde (6 log bn; 1 tpt bn; 6 med bn)

Command Support Organisation 11,150 on mobilisation

FORCES BY ROLE
COMBAT SERVICE SUPPORT
    1 spt bde

Training Command 37,350 on mobilisation
COMBAT SERVICE SUPPORT
    5 trg unit

Civil Defence 73,000 (51,000 Reserve)
(not part of armed forces)

Cyber

Five Swiss government organisations have responsibilities for cyber threats and responses: the Federal Intelligence Service; the Military Intelligence Service; the Command Support Organisation; Information Security and Facility Protection; and the Federal Office for Civil Protection. A National Cyber Defence Strategy was published in 2012. A national strategy for protection against cyber risks was adopted by the Federal Council in April 2018.

DEPLOYMENT

BOSNIA-HERZEGOVINA: EU • EUFOR • *Operation Althea* 21
DEMOCRATIC REPUBLIC OF THE CONGO: UN • MONUSCO 3
INDIA/PAKISTAN: UN • UNMOGIP 3 obs
KOREA, REPUBLIC OF: NNSC • 5 officers
MALI: UN • MINUSMA 6
MIDDLE EAST: UN • UNTSO 12 obs
SERBIA: NATO • KFOR 235 (military volunteers); 1 inf coy; 1 engr pl; 1 hel flt with AS332M *Super Puma*
UKRAINE: OSCE • Ukraine 8
WESTERN SAHARA: UN • MINURSO 2 obs

Turkey TUR

New Turkish Lira L		2017	2018	2019
GDP	L	3.11tr	3.66tr	
	US$	852bn	714bn	
per capita	US$	10,537	8,716	
Growth	%	7.4	3.5	
Inflation	%	11.1	15.0	
Def exp [a]	L	47.3bn	60.9bn	
	US$	13.0bn	11.9bn	
Def bdgt [b]	L	28.8bn	40.5bn	
	US$	7.89bn	7.90bn	
US$1=L		3.65	5.12	

[a] NATO definition
[b] Includes funding for Undersecretariat of Defence Industries

Population   81,257,239

Age	0–14	15–19	20–24	25–29	30–64	65 plus
Male	12.6%	4.2%	4.0%	4.0%	22.2%	3.4%
Female	12.1%	4.0%	3.8%	3.9%	21.8%	4.2%

Capabilities

Turkey has large, well-equipped armed forces that are primarily structured for national defence. Much recent activity has focused on internal security and cross-border operations in response to the continuing war in Syria. The Turkish Armed Forces 2033 Strategic Plan aims to modernise military equipment and the force structure. According to government officials, terrorism is the main security threat. Turkey is a NATO member and has provided access to its airspace and facilities for operations in Iraq and Syria. Following the attempted coup in July 2016, Ankara dismissed large numbers of officers from its armed forces, with the loss of experienced personnel affecting both operational effectiveness and training levels, especially in the air force. The armed forces train regularly, including with NATO allies. Turkish statements have indicated an intention to enhance its presence in Cyprus, possibly including a naval base in the northern part of the island. Equipment is mostly sourced from national firms. Ankara selected BMC to start series production for its first national main battle tank, a project that has been delayed for over two decades. Turkey is also developing a domestic fighter aircraft, with the delivery of F-35As in question as a result of US restrictions. To bolster air defence, Ankara signed a contract with Russia for S-400 missile systems. Under new laws, the president has authority over defence procurement and control over Turkey's top defence companies. Turkey has signed defence-cooperation agreements with a focus on exports and technology transfer, in an effort to boost its national defence industry and achieve defence-industrial autonomy. The defence industry is developing more sophisticated weapons platforms across all domains.

ACTIVE 355,200 (Army 260,200 Navy 45,000 Air 50,000) Paramilitary 156,800

Conscript liability 12 months (5.5 months for university graduates; 21 days for graduates with exemption)

RESERVE 378,700 (Army 258,700 Navy 55,000 Air 65,000)
Reserve service to age 41 for all services

ORGANISATIONS BY SERVICE

Space
EQUIPMENT BY TYPE
SATELLITES • ISR 2 *Gokturk*-1/2

Army ε260,200 (including conscripts)
FORCES BY ROLE
COMMAND
   4 army HQ
   9 corps HQ
SPECIAL FORCES
   8 cdo bde
   1 mtn cdo bde
   1 cdo regt
MANOEUVRE
   Armoured
   1 (52nd) armd div (2 armd bde, 1 mech bde)
   7 armd bde
   Mechanised
   2 (28th & 29th) mech div
   14 mech inf bde
   Light
   1 (23rd) mot inf div (3 mot inf regt)
   7 mot inf bde
COMBAT SUPPORT
   2 arty bde
   1 trg arty bde
   6 arty regt
   2 engr regt
AVIATION
   4 avn regt
   4 avn bn
EQUIPMENT BY TYPE
ARMOURED FIGHTING VEHICLES
   MBT 2,379: 316 *Leopard* 2A4; 170 *Leopard* 1A4; 227 *Leopard* 1A3; 100 M60A1; 650 M60A3; 166 M60T; 750 M48A5 T2 (2,000 M48A5 T1 in store)
   RECCE ε250 *Akrep*
   IFV 645 ACV AIFV
   APC 4,336
      APC (T) 3,636: 823 ACV AAPC; 2,813 M113/M113A1/M113A2
      PPV 700+: 50+ *Edjer Yaclin* 4×4; ε650 *Kirpi*
   AUV 882: 800+ *Cobra*; 82 *Cobra* II
ENGINEERING & MAINTENANCE VEHICLES
   AEV 12+: AZMIM; 12 M48; M113A2T2
   ARV 150: 12 *Leopard* 1; 105 M48T5; 33 M88A1
   VLB 88: 36 *Leguan*; 52 Mobile Floating Assault Bridge
   MW *Husky* 2G; *Tamkar*
ANTI-TANK/ANTI-INFRASTRUCTURE
   MSL
      SP 365 ACV TOW
      MANPATS 9K135 *Kornet*-E (AT-14 *Spriggan*); *Cobra*; *Eryx*; *Milan*
   RCL 3,869: **57mm** 923 M18; **75mm** 617; **106mm** 2,329 M40A1
ARTILLERY 7,799+
   SP 1,080: **155mm** 825: ε150 M44T1; 365 M52T (mod); ε310 T-155 *Firtina*; **175mm** 36 M107; **203mm** 219 M110A2
   TOWED 760+: **105mm** 75+ M101A1; **155mm** 523: 517 M114A1/M114A2; 6 *Panter*; **203mm** 162 M115
   MRL 146+: **107mm** 48; **122mm** ε36 T-122; **227mm** 12 M270 MLRS; **302mm** 50+ TR-300 *Kasirga* (WS-1)
   MOR 5,813+
      SP 1,443+: **81mm**; **107mm** 1,264 M106; **120mm** 179
      TOWED 4,370: **81mm** 3,792; **120mm** 578
SURFACE-TO-SURFACE MISSILE LAUNCHERS
   SRBM • Conventional MGM-140A ATACMS (launched from M270 MLRS); J-600T *Yildirim* (B-611/CH-SS-9 mod 1)
AIRCRAFT
   ISR 5 Beech 350 *King Air*
   TPT • Light 8: 5 Beech 200 *King Air*; 3 Cessna 421
   TRG 49: 45 Cessna T182; 4 T-42A *Cochise*
HELICOPTERS
   ATK 77: 18 AH-1P *Cobra*; 12 AH-1S *Cobra*; 5 AH-1W *Cobra*; 4 TAH-1P *Cobra*; 9 T129A; 29 T129B
   MRH 28 Hughes 300C
   TPT 225+: **Heavy** 7 CH-47F *Chinook*; **Medium** 77+: 29 AS532UL *Cougar*; 48+ S-70A *Black Hawk*; **Light** 141: 12 Bell 204B (AB-204B); ε45 Bell 205 (UH-1H *Iroquois*); 64 Bell 205A (AB-205A); 20 Bell 206 *Jet Ranger*
UNMANNED AERIAL VEHICLES
   CISR • Medium 33 *Bayraktar* TB2
   ISR • Heavy *Falcon* 600/*Firebee*; **Medium** CL-89; *Gnat*; **Light** *Harpy*
AIR DEFENCE
   SAM • Point-defence 148+: 70 *Altigan* PMADS octuple *Stinger* lnchr, 78 *Zipkin* PMADS quad *Stinger* lnchr; FIM-92 *Stinger*
   GUNS 1,664
      SP 35mm *Korkut*; **40mm** 262 M42A1
      TOWED 1,402: **20mm** 439 GAI-D01/Rh-202; **35mm** 120 GDF-001/GDF-003; **40mm** 843: 803 L/60/L/70; 40 T-1
AIR-LAUNCHED MISSILES
   ASM *Mizrak*-U (UMTAS)
BOMBS
   Laser-guided MAM-L; MAM-C

Navy ε45,000 (including conscripts)
EQUIPMENT BY TYPE
SUBMARINES • TACTICAL • SSK 12:
   4 *Atilay* (GER Type-209/1200) with 8 single 533mm ASTT with SST-4 HWT
   8 *Preveze*/*Gür* (GER Type-209/1400) with 8 single 533mm ASTT with UGM-84 *Harpoon* AShM/*Tigerfish* Mk2 HWT/DM2A4 HWT
PRINCIPAL SURFACE COMBATANTS 19
   FRIGATES • FFGHM 19:
      4 *Barbaros* (mod GER MEKO 200 F246 & F247) with 2 quad Mk141 lnchr with RGM-84C *Harpoon* AShM, 2 8-cell Mk41 VLS with RIM-162B ESSM SAM, 2 Mk32 triple 324mm ASTT with Mk46 LWT, 3 *Sea Zenith* CIWS, 1 127mm gun (capacity 1 Bell 212 (AB-212) hel)
      4 *Gabya* (ex-US *Oliver Hazard Perry* class) with 1 Mk13 GMLS with RGM-84C *Harpoon* AShM/SM-1MR SAM, 1 8-cell Mk41 VLS with RIM-162B ESSM SAM, 2 Mk32 triple 324mm ASTT with Mk46 LWT, 1 *Phalanx* Block 1B CIWS, 1 76mm gun (capacity 1 S-70B *Seahawk*/AB-212 ASW hel)

4 *Gabya* (ex-US *Oliver Hazard Perry* class) with 1 Mk13 GMLS with RGM-84C *Harpoon* AShM/SM-1MR SAM, 2 Mk32 triple 324mm ASTT with Mk46 LWT, 1 *Phalanx* Block 1B CIWS, 1 76mm gun (capacity 1 S-70B *Seahawk*/AB-212 ASW hel)

4 *Yavuz* (GER MEKO 200TN) with 2 quad Mk141 lnchr with RGM-84C *Harpoon* AShM, 1 octuple Mk29 GMLS with *Sea Sparrow* SAM, 2 Mk32 triple 324mm ASTT with Mk46 LWT, 3 *Sea Zenith* CIWS, 1 127mm gun (capacity 1 Bell 212 (AB-212) hel)

3 *Ada* with 2 quad lnchr with RCM-84C *Harpoon* AShM, 1 Mk49 21-cell lnchr with RIM-116 SAM, 2 Mk32 twin 324mm ASTT with Mk46 LWT, 1 76mm gun (capacity 1 S-70B *Seahawk* hel)

PATROL AND COASTAL COMBATANTS 52:
  CORVETTES • FSGM 6:
    6 *Burak* (ex-FRA *d'Estienne d'Orves*) with 2 single lnchr with MM38 *Exocet* AShM, 4 single 324mm ASTT with Mk46 LWT, 1 Mk54 A/S mor, 1 100mm gun
  PCFG 19:
    4 *Dogan* (GER Lurssen-57) with 2 quad lnchr with RGM-84A/C *Harpoon* AShM, 1 76mm gun
    9 *Kilic* with 2 quad Mk 141 lnchr with RGM-84C *Harpoon* AShM, 1 76mm gun
    4 *Rüzgar* (GER Lurssen-57) with 2 quad lnchr with RGM-84A/C *Harpoon* AShM, 1 76mm gun
    2 *Yildiz* with 2 quad lnchr with RGM-84A/C *Harpoon* AShM, 1 76mm gun
  PCC 16 *Tuzla*

MINE WARFARE • MINE COUNTERMEASURES 15:
  MHO 11: 5 *Engin* (FRA *Circe*); 6 *Aydin*
  MSC 4 *Seydi* (US *Adjutant*)

AMPHIBIOUS
  LANDING SHIPS • LST 5:
    2 *Bayraktar* with 1 hel landing platform (capacity 20 MBT; 250 troops)
    1 *Osman Gazi* with 1 *Phalanx* CIWS (capacity 4 LCVP; 17 tanks; 980 troops) (with 1 hel landing platform)
    2 *Sarucabey* with 1 *Phalanx* CIWS (capacity 11 tanks; 600 troops) (with 1 hel landing platform)
  LANDING CRAFT 30
    LCT 21: 2 C-120/130; 11 C-140; 8 C-151
    LCM 9: 1 C-310; 8 LCM 8

LOGISTICS AND SUPPORT 35
  ABU 2: 1 AG5; 1 AG6 with 1 76mm gun
  AGS 2: 1 *Cesme* (ex-US *Silas Bent*); 1 *Cubuklu*
  AOR 2 *Akar* with 1 twin 76mm gun, 1 *Phalanx* CIWS, 1 hel landing platform
  AOT 2 *Burak*
  AOL 1 *Gurcan*
  AP 1 *Iskenderun*
  ASR 3: 1 *Alemdar* with 1 hel landing platform; 2 *Isin* II
  ATF 9: 1 *Akbas*; 1 *Degirmendere*; 1 *Gazal*; 1 *Inebolu*; 5 *Onder*
  AWT 3 *Sogut*
  AXL 8
  AX 2 *Pasa* (ex-GER *Rhein*)

Marines 3,000
FORCES BY ROLE
MANOEUVRE
  Amphibious
    1 mne bde (3 mne bn; 1 arty bn)

Naval Aviation
FORCES BY ROLE
ANTI-SUBMARINE WARFARE
  2 sqn with Bell 212 ASW (AB-212 ASW); S-70B *Seahawk*
  1 sqn with ATR-72-600; CN235M-100; TB-20 *Trinidad*
EQUIPMENT BY TYPE
AIRCRAFT
  MP 6 CN235M-100
  TPT • Light 7: 2 ATR-72-600; 5 TB-20 *Trinidad*
HELICOPTERS
  ASW 29: 11 Bell 212 ASW (AB-212 ASW); 18 S-70B *Seahawk*

Air Force ε50,000
2 tac air forces (divided between east and west)
FORCES BY ROLE
FIGHTER/GROUND ATTACK
  1 sqn with F-4E *Phantom* 2020
  8 sqn with F-16C/D *Fighting Falcon*
ISR
  1 sqn with F-16C/D *Fighting Falcon*
  1 unit with *King Air* 350
AIRBORNE EARLY WARNING & CONTROL
  1 sqn (forming) with B-737 AEW&C
EW
  1 unit with CN235M EW
SEARCH & RESCUE
  1 sqn with AS532AL/UL *Cougar*
TANKER
  1 sqn with KC-135R *Stratotanker*
TRANSPORT
  1 sqn with A400M; C-160D *Transall*
  1 sqn with C-130B/E/H *Hercules*
  1 (VIP) sqn with Cessna 550 *Citation* II (UC-35); Cessna 650 *Citation* VII; CN235M; Gulfstream 550
  3 sqn with CN235M
  10 (liaison) flt with Bell 205 (UH-1H *Iroquois*); CN235M
TRAINING
  1 sqn with F-16C/D *Fighting Falcon*
  1 sqn with F-5A/B *Freedom Fighter*; NF-5A/B *Freedom Fighter*
  1 sqn with SF-260D
  1 sqn with KT-1T
  1 sqn with T-38A/M *Talon*
  1 sqn with T-41D *Mescalero*
AIR DEFENCE
  4 sqn with MIM-14 *Nike Hercules*
  2 sqn with *Rapier*
  8 (firing) unit with MIM-23 *Hawk*
MANOEUVRE
  Air Manoeuvre
    1 AB bde

EQUIPMENT BY TYPE
AIRCRAFT 308 combat capable
  FTR 27: 17 NF-5A *Freedom Fighter*; 10 NF-5B *Freedom Fighter* (48 F-5s being upgraded as LIFT)
  FGA 281: 20 F-4E *Phantom* 2020; 27 F-16C *Fighting Falcon* Block 30; 162 F-16C *Fighting Falcon* Block 50; 14 F-16C *Fighting Falcon* Block 50+; 8 F-16D Block 30 *Fighting Falcon*; 33 F-16D *Fighting Falcon* Block 50; 16 F-16D *Fighting Falcon* Block 50+; 1 F-35A *Lightning* II

ISR 5 Beech 350 *King Air*
EW 2+ CN235M EW
AEW&C 4 B-737 AEW&C
TKR 7 KC-135R *Stratotanker*
TPT 88: **Heavy** 7 A400M; **Medium** 31: 6 C-130B *Hercules*; 12 C-130E *Hercules*; 1 C-130H *Hercules*; 12 C-160D *Transall*; **Light** 49: 2 Cessna 550 *Citation* II (UC-35 - VIP); 2 Cessna 650 *Citation* VII; 45 CN235M; **PAX** 1 Gulfstream 550
TRG 168: 33 SF-260D; 70 T-38A/M *Talon*; 25 T-41D *Mescalero*; 40 KT-IT
HELICOPTERS
TPT 35: **Medium** 20: 6 AS532AL *Cougar* (CSAR); 14 AS532UL *Cougar* (SAR); **Light** 15 Bell 205 (UH-1H *Iroquois*)
UNMANNED AERIAL VEHICLES 29+
CISR • **Heavy** 8 ANKA-S
ISR 27+: **Heavy** 9+: some ANKA; 9 *Heron*; **Medium** 18 *Gnat* 750
AIR DEFENCE
SAM
Long-range MIM-14 *Nike Hercules*
Medium-range MIM-23 *Hawk*
Point-defence *Rapier*
AIR-LAUNCHED MISSILES
AAM • **IR** AIM-9S *Sidewinder*; *Shafrir* 2(‡); **IIR** AIM-9X *Sidewinder* II; **SARH** AIM-7E *Sparrow*; **ARH** AIM-120A/B AMRAAM
ARM AGM-88A HARM
ASM AGM-65A/G *Maverick*; *Popeye* I
LACM Coventional AGM-84K SLAM-ER
BOMBS
Electro-optical guided GBU-8B HOBOS (GBU-15)
INS/GPS guided AGM-154A JSOW; AGM-154C JSOW
Laser-guided MAM-C; MAM-L; *Paveway* I; *Paveway* II

Paramilitary 156,800

Gendarmerie 152,100

Ministry of Interior; Ministry of Defence in war
FORCES BY ROLE
SPECIAL FORCES
1 cdo bde
MANOEUVRE
Other
1 (border) paramilitary div
2 paramilitary bde
EQUIPMENT BY TYPE
ARMOURED FIGHTING VEHICLES
RECCE *Akrep*
APC 560+
APC (W) 560: 535 BTR-60/BTR-80; 25 *Condor*
PPV *Kirpi*
AUV *Cobra*; *Cobra* II
AIRCRAFT
ISR Some O-1E *Bird Dog*
TPT • **Light** 2 Do-28D
HELICOPTERS
ATK 4 T129B
MRH 19 Mi-17 *Hip* H

TPT 35: **Medium** 12 S-70A *Black Hawk*; **Light** 23: 8 Bell 204B (AB-204B); 6 Bell 205A (AB-205A); 8 Bell 206A (AB-206A) *Jet Ranger*; 1 Bell 212 (AB-212)
UNMANNED AERIAL VEHICLES
CISR • **Medium** 12 *Bayraktar* TB2
BOMBS
Laser-guided MAM-L; MAM-C

Coast Guard 4,700

EQUIPMENT BY TYPE
PATROL AND COASTAL COMBATANTS 104
PSOH 4 *Dost* with 1 76mm gun
PBF 60
PB 40
AIRCRAFT • **MP** 3 CN235 MPA
HELICOPTERS • **MRH** 8 Bell 412EP (AB-412EP – SAR)

DEPLOYMENT

AFGHANISTAN: NATO • *Operation Resolute Support* 506; 1 mot inf bn(-)

ARABIAN SEA & GULF OF ADEN: Combined Maritime Forces • CTF-151: 1 FFGHM

BLACK SEA: NATO • SNMCMG 2: 1 MHO

BOSNIA-HERZEGOVINA: EU • EUFOR • *Operation Althea* 249; 1 inf coy

CYPRUS (NORTHERN): ε33,800; 1 army corps HQ; 1 SF regt; 1 armd bde; 2 mech inf div; 1 mech inf regt; 1 arty regt; 1 avn comd; 287 M48A5T2; 147 ACV AIFV; 106 ACV AAPC (incl variants); 386 M113 (incl variants); 36 M101A1; 36 M114A2; 12 M115; 30 M44T; 144 M52T1; 9 T-122; 171 81mm mor; 70 M30; 135 HY-12; *Milan*; 60 ACV TOW; 219 M40A1; FIM-92 *Stinger*; 44 Rh 202; 78 GAI-D01; 16 GDF-003; 3 Cessna 185 (U-17); 2 AS532UL *Cougar*; 1 Bell 205 (UH-1H *Iroquois*); 1 PB

IRAQ: Army: 2,000; 1 armd BG

LEBANON: UN • UNIFIL 86; 1 PCFG

MEDITERRANEAN SEA: NATO • SNMG 2: 1 FFGHM; 1 PCC

QATAR: Army: 200 (trg team); 1 mech inf coy; 1 arty unit; 12+ ACV AIFV/AAPC; 2 T-155 *Firtina*

SERBIA: NATO • KFOR 291; 1 inf coy
UN • UNMIK 1 obs

SOMALIA: 200 (trg team); UN • UNSOM 1 obs

SYRIA: ε5,000; 1 cdo unit; 2 armd BG; 1 SAM unit; 1 gendarmerie unit

UKRAINE: OSCE • Ukraine 10

FOREIGN FORCES

Italy *Active Fence*: 130; 1 SAM bty with SAMP/T
Saudi Arabia *Inherent Resolve*: 6 F-15S *Eagle*
Spain *Active Fence*: 149; 1 SAM bty with MIM-104C *Patriot* PAC-2
United States US European Command: 1,700; 1 tkr sqn with 14 KC-135; 1 ELINT flt with EP-3E *Aries* II; 1 spt facility at Izmir; 1 spt facility at Ankara; 1 air base at Incirlik • US Strategic Command: 1 AN/TPY-2 X-band radar at Kürecik

United Kingdom UK

British Pound £		2017	2018	2019
GDP	£	2.04tr	2.10tr	
	US$	2.63tr	2.81tr	
per capita	US$	39,800	42,261	
Growth	%	1.7	1.4	
Inflation	%	2.7	2.5	
Def exp [a]	£	43.0bn	44.1bn	
	US$	55.4bn	59.0bn	
Def bdgt [b]	£	40.6bn	ε41.9bn	
	US$	52.4bn	ε56.1bn	
US$1=£		0.78	0.75	

[a] NATO definition

[b] Includes total departmental expenditure limits; costs of military operations; and external income earned by the MoD

Population	65,105,246					
Age	0–14	15–19	20–24	25–29	30–64	65 plus
Male	9.0%	2.8%	3.2%	3.5%	23.1%	8.1%
Female	8.5%	2.7%	3.1%	3.4%	22.5%	9.9%

Capabilities

The 2018 National Security Capability Review highlighted a range of security challenges, including from state-based threats and from terrorists. UK defence policy is based on using the armed forces to reduce direct threats by projecting stability abroad. Principal defence priorities are contributing to the counter-ISIS coalition and NATO tasks, including in Afghanistan and in Eastern Europe. The ministry of defence oversees all-volunteer armed forces. Joint Forces Command comprises key joint force elements, such as special-forces and military-cyber capabilities. The armed forces are relatively well balanced between combat, combat support and logistics, but many key capabilities are close to critical mass and all three services are short of personnel. A Modernising Defence Programme has been ongoing for most of 2018, but without additional funding further capability reductions are likely. This puts at risk the delivery of the 'Future Force 2025' intended to conduct combat against peer opponents. The US is the country's closest military ally. There is also a close intelligence relationship with the 'Five Eyes' nations and a growing military partnership with France. The UK has decided to retain military forces in Germany and leads the Combined Joint Expeditionary Force. A naval base has recently opened in Bahrain and the UK continues to support the FPDA in Southeast Asia. Force modernisation continues, but the defence budget is under pressure because of the fall in the value of the pound, the cost growth of major equipment programmes and the difficulty of achieving savings targets. Expeditionary logistic capability meets policy requirements, but peacetime logistic support within the UK is dependent on contractors. The country's sophisticated defence industry is a world leader in defence exports but cannot meet all of the UK's requirements.

ACTIVE 148,350 (Army 83,500 Navy 32,350 Air 32,500)

RESERVE 80,000 (Regular Reserve 43,600 (Army 29,450, Navy 6,550, Air 7,600); Volunteer Reserve 34,350 (Army 27,450, Navy 3,650, Air 3,250); Sponsored Reserve 2,050)

Includes both trained and those currently under training within the Regular Forces, excluding university cadet units

ORGANISATIONS BY SERVICE

Strategic Forces 1,000

Royal Navy
EQUIPMENT BY TYPE
SUBMARINES • STRATEGIC • SSBN 4:
  4 *Vanguard* with 1 16-cell VLS with UGM-133A *Trident* II D-5/D-5LE nuclear SLBM, 4 533mm TT with *Spearfish* HWT (each boat will not deploy with more than 40 warheads, but each missile could carry up to 12 MIRV; some *Trident* D-5 capable of being configured for sub-strategic role)
MSL • SLBM • Nuclear 48 UGM-133A *Trident* II D-5 (fewer than 160 declared operational warheads)

Royal Air Force
EQUIPMENT BY TYPE
RADAR • STRATEGIC 1 Ballistic Missile Early Warning System (BMEWS) at Fylingdales Moor

Space
EQUIPMENT BY TYPE
SATELLITES • COMMUNICATIONS 8: 1 NATO-4B; 3 *Skynet*-4; 4 *Skynet*-5

Army 80,400; 3,100 Gurkhas (total 83,500)

Regt normally bn size. Many cbt spt and CSS regt and bn have reservist sub-units

FORCES BY ROLE
COMMAND
1 (ARRC) corps HQ
MANOEUVRE
Armoured
1 (3rd) armd div (3 armd inf bde (1 armd recce regt, 1 tk regt, 2 armd inf bn, 1 mech inf bn); 1 log bde (5 log regt; 3 maint regt; 3 med regt))
Light
1 (1st) lt inf div (1 (4th) inf bde (1 recce regt, 1 lt mech inf bn; 2 lt inf bn); 1 (7th) inf bde (1 recce regt, 3 lt inf bn); 2 (11th & 160th) inf bde (2 lt inf bn); 1 (51st) inf bde (1 recce regt; 1 lt mech inf bn; 1 lt inf bn); 1 (38th) inf bde (1 lt inf bn); 1 (Spec Inf Gp) inf bde(-) (3 inf bn(-)); 1 log bde (2 log regt; 2 maint bn; 2 med regt))
2 lt inf bn (London)
1 (Gurkha) lt inf bn (Brunei)
Air Manoeuvre
1 (16th) air aslt bde (1 recce pl, 2 para bn, 1 (Gurkha) air mob bn, 1 fd arty regt, 1 cbt engr regt, 1 log regt, 1 med regt)
COMBAT SUPPORT
1 arty bde (3 SP arty regt, 2 fd arty regt)
1 engr bde (5 cbt engr regt, 2 EOD regt, 1 (MWD) EOD search regt, 1 engr regt, 1 (air spt) engr regt, 1 log regt)
1 (geographic) engr regt
1 ISR bde (1 STA regt, 1 EW regt, 3 int bn, 1 ISR UAV regt)
1 MP bde (3 MP regt)
1 sigs bde (7 sigs regt)
1 sigs bde (2 sigs regt; 1 (ARRC) sigs bn)
1 (77th) info ops bde (3 info ops gp, 1 spt gp, 1 engr spt/log gp)

COMBAT SERVICE SUPPORT
1 engr spt gp
1 log bde (3 log regt; 1 maint regt)
1 med bde (3 fd hospital)
AIR DEFENCE
2 AD regt

Reserves

Army Reserve 27,450 reservists

The Army Reserve (AR) generates individuals, sub-units and some full units. The majority of units are subordinate to regular formation headquarters and paired with one or more regular units

FORCES BY ROLE
MANOEUVRE
  Reconnaissance
  3 recce regt
  Armoured
  1 armd regt
  Light
  15 lt inf bn
  Air Manoeuvre
  1 para bn
COMBAT SUPPORT
  3 arty regt
  1 STA regt
  1 MRL regt
  3 engr regt
  4 int bn
  4 sigs regt
COMBAT SERVICE SUPPORT
  11 log regt
  6 maint regt
  4 med regt
  10 fd hospital
AIR DEFENCE
  1 AD regt
EQUIPMENT BY TYPE
ARMOURED FIGHTING VEHICLES
  MBT 227 *Challenger* 2
  RECCE 613: 197 *Jackal*; 110 *Jackal* 2; 130 *Jackal* 2A; 145 FV107 *Scimitar*; 31 *Scimitar* Mk2
  IFV 623: 466 FV510 *Warrior*; 88 FV511 *Warrior* (CP); 51 FV514 *Warrior* (OP); 18 FV515 *Warrior* (CP)
  APC 1,291
    APC (T) 895 *Bulldog* Mk3
    PPV 396 *Mastiff* (6×6)
  AUV 1,238: 399 *Foxhound*; 252 FV103 *Spartan* (incl variants); 23 *Spartan* Mk2 (incl variants); 396 *Panther* CLV; 168 *Ridgback*
ENGINEERING & MAINTENANCE VEHICLES
  AEV 92: 60 *Terrier*; 32 *Trojan*
  ARV 259: 80 *Challenger* ARRV; 28 FV106 *Samson*; 5 *Samson* Mk2; 105 FV512 *Warrior*; 41 FV513 *Warrior*
  MW 64 *Aardvark*
  VLB 70: 37 M3; 33 *Titan*
NBC VEHICLES 8 TPz-1 *Fuchs* NBC
ANTI-TANK/ANTI-INFRASTRUCTURE • MSL
  SP *Exactor* (*Spike* NLOS)
  MANPATS FGM-148 *Javelin*; NLAW

ARTILLERY 598
  SP 155mm 89 AS90
  TOWED 105mm 114 L118 Light Gun
  MRL 227mm 35 M270B1 MLRS
  MOR 81mm 360 L16A1
AMPHIBIOUS • LCM 3 Ramped Craft Logistic
AIR DEFENCE • SAM
  Point-defence 74: 60 FV4333 *Stormer* with *Starstreak*; 14 *Rapier* FSC; *Starstreak* (LML)

Joint Helicopter Command

Tri-service joint organisation including Royal Navy, Army and RAF units

Army

FORCES BY ROLE
ISR
  1 regt (1 sqn with BN-2 *Defender/Islander*; 1 sqn with SA341B *Gazelle* AH1)
ATTACK HELICOPTER
  1 regt (2 sqn with AH-64D *Apache*; 1 trg sqn with AH-64D *Apache*)
  1 regt (2 sqn with AH-64D *Apache*)
HELICOPTER
  1 regt (2 sqn with AW159 *Wildcat* AH1)
  1 (spec ops) sqn with AS365N3; SA341B *Gazelle* AH1
  1 flt with Bell 212 (Brunei)
  1 flt with SA341B *Gazelle* AH1 (Canada)
TRAINING
  1 hel regt (1 sqn with AH-64D *Apache*; 1 sqn with AS350B *Ecureuil*; 1 sqn with Bell 212; *Lynx* AH9A; SA341B *Gazelle* AH1)
ISR UAV
  1 ISR UAV regt
COMBAT SERVICE SUPPORT
  1 maint regt

Army Reserve

FORCES BY ROLE
HELICOPTER
  1 hel regt (4 sqn personnel only)

Royal Navy

FORCES BY ROLE
ATTACK HELICOPTER
  1 lt sqn with AW159 *Wildcat* AH1
TRANSPORT HELICOPTER
  2 sqn with AW101 *Merlin* HC3/3A/3i

Royal Air Force

FORCES BY ROLE
TRANSPORT HELICOPTER
  3 sqn with CH-47D/SD/F *Chinook* HC3/4/4A/6
  2 sqn with SA330 *Puma* HC2
TRAINING
  1 OCU sqn with CH-47D/SD/F *Chinook* HC3/4/4A/6; SA330 *Puma* HC2
EQUIPMENT BY TYPE
AIRCRAFT • TPT • Light 12: 9 BN-2T-4S *Defender*; 3 BN-2 *Islander* AL1

HELICOPTERS
ATK 50 AH-64D *Apache*
MRH 66: 5 AS365N3; 34 AW159 *Wildcat* AH1; 27 SA341B *Gazelle* AH1
TPT 122: **Heavy** 60: 38 CH-47D *Chinook* HC4/4A; 7 CH-47SD *Chinook* HC3; 1 CH-47SD *Chinook* HC5; 14 CH-47F *Chinook* HC6; **Medium** 48: 25 AW101 *Merlin* HC3/3A/3i; 23 SA330 *Puma* HC2; **Light** 14: 9 AS350B *Ecureuil*; 5 Bell 212
UNMANNED AERIAL VEHICLES • ISR • Medium 7 *Watchkeeper* (37+ more in store)

Royal Navy 32,350
EQUIPMENT BY TYPE
SUBMARINES 10
  STRATEGIC • SSBN 4:
    4 *Vanguard*, opcon Strategic Forces with 1 16-cell VLS with UGM-133A *Trident* II D-5/D-5LE nuclear SLBM, 4 single 533mm TT with *Spearfish* HWT (each boat will not deploy with more than 40 warheads, but each missile could carry up to 12 MIRV; some *Trident* D-5 capable of being configured for sub-strategic role)
  TACTICAL • SSN 6:
    3 *Trafalgar* with 5 single 533mm TT with UGM-109E *Tactical Tomahawk* Block IV (TACTOM) LACM/*Spearfish* HWT
    3 *Astute* with 6 single 533mm TT with UGM-109E *Tactical Tomahawk* Block IV (TACTOM) LACM/*Spearfish* HWT
PRINCIPAL SURFACE COMBATANTS 20
  AIRCRAFT CARRIERS • CV 1
    1 *Queen Elizabeth* (to be fitted with 3 Mk 15 *Phalanx* Block 1B CIWS) (future capacity 24 F-35B *Lightning* II, 14 *Merlin* HM2/*Wildcat* HMA2/CH-47 *Chinook* hel) (in trials)
  DESTROYERS 6
    DDGHM 3 *Daring* (Type-45) with 2 quad lnchr with RGM-84C *Harpoon*, 6 8-cell *Sylver* A50 VLS with *Sea Viper* (*Aster* 15 and *Aster* 30) SAM, 2 Mk 15 *Phalanx* Block 1B CIWS, 1 114mm gun (capacity 1 AW159 *Wildcat*/AW101 *Merlin* hel)
    DDHM 3 *Daring* (Type-45) with 6 8-cell *Sylver* A50 VLS with *Sea Viper* (*Aster* 15 and *Aster* 30) SAM, 2 Mk 15 *Phalanx* Block 1B CIWS, 1 114mm gun (capacity 1 AW159 *Wildcat*/AW101 *Merlin* hel)
  FRIGATES • FFGHM 13:
    8 *Duke* (Type-23) with 2 quad Mk141 lnchr with RGM-84C *Harpoon* AShM, 1 32-cell VLS with *Sea Wolf* SAM, 2 twin 324mm ASTT with *Sting Ray* LWT, 1 114mm gun (capacity either 2 AW159 *Wildcat* or 1 AW101 *Merlin* hel)
    5 *Duke* (Type-23) with 2 quad Mk141 lnchr with RGM-84C *Harpoon* AShM, 1 32-cell VLS with *Sea Ceptor* SAM, 2 twin 324mm ASTT with *Sting Ray* LWT, 1 114mm gun (capacity either 2 AW159 *Wildcat* or 1 AW101 *Merlin* hel)
PATROL AND COASTAL COMBATANTS 22
  PSO 4: 2 *River* Batch 1; 1 *River* Batch 1 (mod) with 1 hel landing platform; 1 *River* Batch 2 with 1 hel landing platform
  PBI 18: 16 *Archer* (trg); 2 *Scimitar*

MINE WARFARE • MINE COUNTERMEASURES 13
  MCO 6 *Hunt* (incl 4 mod *Hunt*)
  MHC 7 *Sandown* (1 additional decommissioned and used in trg role)
AMPHIBIOUS
  PRINCIPAL AMPHIBIOUS SHIPS 2
    LPD 2 *Albion* with 2 Mk 15 *Phalanx* Block 1B CIWS (capacity 2 med hel; 4 LCU or 2 LCAC; 4 LCVP; 6 MBT; 300 troops) (of which 1 at extended readiness)
LOGISTICS AND SUPPORT 4
  AGB 1 *Protector* with 1 hel landing platform
  AGS 3: 1 *Scott*; 2 *Echo* (all with 1 hel landing platform)

Royal Fleet Auxiliary
Support and miscellaneous vessels are mostly manned and maintained by the Royal Fleet Auxiliary (RFA), a civilian fleet owned by the UK MoD, which has approximately 1,950 personnel with type comd under Fleet Commander
AMPHIBIOUS • PRINCIPAL AMPHIBIOUS SHIPS 3
  LSD 3 *Bay* (capacity 4 LCU; 2 LCVP; 24 CR2 *Challenger* 2 MBT; 350 troops)
LOGISTICS AND SUPPORT 12
  AORH 5: 2 *Wave*; 1 *Fort Victoria* with 2 Mk 15 *Phalanx* CIWS; 2 *Tide* (capacity 1 AW159 *Wildcat*/AW101 *Merlin* hel)
  AFSH 2 *Fort Rosalie*
  AG 1 *Argus* (aviation trg ship with secondary role as primarily casualty-receiving ship)
  AKR 4 *Point* (not RFA manned)

Naval Aviation (Fleet Air Arm) 4,650
FORCES BY ROLE
ANTI-SUBMARINE WARFARE
  3 sqn with AW101 ASW *Merlin* HM2
  2 sqn with AW159 *Wildcat* HMA2
AIRBORNE EARLY WARNING
  1 sqn with *Merlin* Mk 2 *Crowsnest* (forming)
TRAINING
  1 sqn with Beech 350ER *King Air*
  1 sqn with G-115
  1 sqn with *Hawk* T1
EQUIPMENT BY TYPE
AIRCRAFT 12 combat capable
  TPT • Light 4 Beech 350ER *King Air* (*Avenger*)
  TRG 17: 5 G-115; 12 *Hawk* T1*
HELICOPTERS
  ASW 58: 28 AW159 *Wildcat* HMA2; 30 AW101 ASW *Merlin* HM2

Royal Marines 6,600
FORCES BY ROLE
MANOEUVRE
  Amphibious
    1 (3rd Cdo) mne bde (2 mne bn; 2 sy bn; 1 amph aslt sqn; 1 (army) arty regt; 1 (army) engr regt; 1 ISR gp (1 EW sqn; 1 cbt spt sqn; 1 sigs sqn; 1 log sqn), 1 log regt)
    1 landing craft sqn opcon Royal Navy
EQUIPMENT BY TYPE
ARMOURED FIGHTING VEHICLES
  APC (T) 99 BvS-10 Mk2 *Viking*

ANTI-TANK/ANTI-INFRASTUCTURE
  MSL • MANPATS FGM-148 *Javelin*
ARTILLERY 39
  TOWED 105mm 12 L118 Light Gun
  MOR 81mm 27 L16A1
PATROL AND COASTAL COMBATANTS • PB 2 *Island*
AMPHIBIOUS • LANDING CRAFT 30
  LCU 10 LCU Mk10 (capacity 4 *Viking* APC or 120 troops) LCVP 16 LCVP Mk5B (capacity 35 troops)
  UCAC 4 *Griffon* 2400TD
AIR DEFENCE • SAM • Point-defence *Starstreak*

Royal Air Force 32,500

FORCES BY ROLE
FIGHTER
  2 sqn with *Typhoon* FGR4/T3
FIGHTER/GROUND ATTACK
  3 sqn with *Typhoon* FGR4/T3
  1 sqn with F-35B *Lightning* II (forming)
GROUND ATTACK
  2 sqn with *Tornado* GR4/4A
ISR
  1 sqn with *Sentinel* R1
  1 sqn with *Shadow* R1
ELINT
  1 sqn with RC-135W *Rivet Joint*
AIRBORNE EARLY WARNING & CONTROL
  1 sqn with E-3D *Sentry*
SEARCH & RESCUE
  1 sqn with Bell 412EP *Griffin* HAR-2
TANKER/TRANSPORT
  2 sqn with A330 MRTT *Voyager* KC2/3
TRANSPORT
  1 (comms) sqn with AW109E/SP; BAe-146; BN-2A *Islander* CC2
  1 sqn with A400M *Atlas*
  1 sqn with C-17A *Globemaster*
  3 sqn with C-130J/J-30 *Hercules*
TRAINING
  1 OCU sqn with *Typhoon*
  1 OCU sqn with E-3D *Sentry*; *Sentinel* R1
  1 sqn with Beech 200 *King Air*
  1 sqn with EMB-312 *Tucano* T1
  2 sqn with *Hawk* T1/1A/1W
  1 sqn with *Hawk* T2
  3 sqn with *Tutor*
COMBAT/ISR UAV
  2 sqn with MQ-9A *Reaper*
EQUIPMENT BY TYPE
AIRCRAFT 250 combat capable
  FGA 154: 17 F-35B *Lightning* II (in test); 137 *Typhoon* FGR4/T3
  ATK 37 *Tornado* GR4/GR4A
  ISR 9: 4 *Sentinel* R1; 5 *Shadow* R1
  ELINT 3 RC-135W *Rivet Joint*
  AEW&C 6 E-3D *Sentry*
  TKR/TPT 14 A330 MRTT *Voyager* KC2/3
  TPT 61: Heavy 28: 20 A400M *Atlas*; 8 C-17A *Globemaster*; Medium 19: 6 C-130J *Hercules*; 13 C-130J-30 *Hercules*; Light 10: 5 Beech 200 *King Air* (on lease); 2 Beech 200GT *King Air* (on lease); 3 BN-2A *Islander* CC2; PAX 4 BAe-146 CC2/C3
  TRG 208: 5 EMB-500 *Phenom* 100; 39 EMB-312 *Tucano* T1 (39 more in store); 101 G-115E *Tutor*; 28 *Hawk* T2*; 31 *Hawk* T1/1A/1W* (ε46 more in store); 4 T-6C *Texan* II
HELICOPTERS
  MRH 5: 1 AW139; 4 Bell 412EP *Griffin* HAR-2
  TPT • Light 3: 2 AW109E; 1 AW109SP
UNMANNED AERIAL VEHICLES
  CISR • Heavy 9 MQ-9A *Reaper*
AIR-LAUNCHED MISSILES
  AAM • IR AIM-9L/L(I) *Sidewinder*; IIR ASRAAM; ARH AIM-120C-5 AMRAAM; *Meteor*
  ASM AGM-114 *Hellfire*; *Brimstone*; *Dual-Mode Brimstone*; *Brimstone* II
  ALCM *Storm Shadow*
BOMBS
  Laser/GPS-guided GBU-10 *Paveway* II; GBU-24 *Paveway* III; Enhanced *Paveway* II/III; *Paveway* IV

Royal Air Force Regiment

FORCES BY ROLE
MANOEUVRE
  Other
  6 sy sqn
COMBAT SUPPORT
  1 CBRN sqn

Tri-Service Defence Helicopter School

FORCES BY ROLE
TRAINING
  1 hel sqn with Bell 412EP *Griffin* HT1
  2 hel sqn with AS350B *Ecureuil*
EQUIPMENT BY TYPE
HELICOPTERS
  MRH 11 Bell 412EP *Griffin* HT1
  TPT • Light 27: 25 AS350B *Ecureuil*; 2 AW109E

Volunteer Reserve Air Forces

(Royal Auxiliary Air Force/RAF Reserve)
MANOEUVRE
  Other
  5 sy sqn
COMBAT SUPPORT
  2 int sqn
COMBAT SERVICE SUPPORT
  1 med sqn
  1 (air movements) sqn
  1 (HQ augmentation) sqn
  1 (C-130 Reserve Aircrew) flt

UK Special Forces

Includes Royal Navy, Army and RAF units
FORCES BY ROLE
SPECIAL FORCES
  1 (SAS) SF regt
  1 (SBS) SF regt
  1 (Special Reconnaissance) SF regt
  1 SF BG (based on 1 para bn)
AVIATION
  1 wg (includes assets drawn from 3 Army hel sqn, 1 RAF tpt sqn and 1 RAF hel sqn)

COMBAT SUPPORT
1 sigs regt

Reserve
FORCES BY ROLE
SPECIAL FORCES
2 (SAS) SF regt

Cyber

The National Cyber Security Centre plays a central role in coordinating the UK's cyber policy, and works with ministries and agencies to implement cyber-security programmes. A Joint Forces Cyber Group was set up in 2013, including a Joint Cyber Reserve, providing support to two Joint Cyber Units and other information-assurance units across the defence establishment. Increased concern about the potential of information operations in and through the cyber domain was central to the 2015 creation of 77 Brigade. The 2015 Strategic Defence and Security Review designated cyber a tier-one risk and stated that the UK would respond to a cyber attack in the same way as it would an equivalent conventional attack. In October 2016, the UK acknowledged publicly the use of offensive cyber capabilities against ISIS. In April 2016, it was announced that a Cyber Security Operations Centre would be established under the Ministry of Defence (MoD) and tasked with protecting the ministry's cyberspace. The Defence Cyber School was opened in March 2018. The UK is developing specialist rapid-response teams, trained to isolate, defend and respond to cyber threats and prepared to deploy around the UK and to operational theatres overseas. Through the National Offensive Cyber Programme – a partnership between the MoD and Government Communications Headquarters (GCHQ) since 2015 – the UK says it has strengthened its cyber capabilities and has continued to employ offensive cyber alongside the conventional capabilities of the armed forces.

DEPLOYMENT

AFGHANISTAN: NATO • *Operation Resolute Support* 1,100; 1 inf bn(+); 1 hel flt with 3 *Puma* HC2

ALBANIA: OSCE • Albania 2

ARABIAN SEA: *Operation Kipion* 1 DDHM; 1 LPD; 1 LSD

ARMENIA/AZERBAIJAN: OSCE • Minsk Conference 1

ASCENSION ISLAND: 20

ATLANTIC (NORTH)/CARIBBEAN: 1 LSD

ATLANTIC (SOUTH): 1 PSO

BAHRAIN: 160; 1 naval base

BELIZE: BATSUB 12

BOSNIA-HERZEGOVINA: EU • EUFOR • *Operation Althea* 2; **OSCE** • Bosnia and Herzegovina 3

BRITISH INDIAN OCEAN TERRITORY: 40; 1 navy/marine det

BRUNEI: 1,000; 1 (Gurkha) lt inf bn; 1 jungle trg centre; 1 hel flt with 3 Bell 212

CANADA: BATUS 370; 1 trg unit; 1 hel flt with SA341 *Gazelle* AH1

CYPRUS: 2,260; 2 inf bn; 1 SAR sqn with 4 Bell 412 *Griffin* HAR-2; 1 radar (on det); *Operation Shader* 500: 1 FGA sqn with 6 *Tornado* GR4; 6 *Typhoon* FGR4; 2 *Sentinel* R1; 1 E-3D *Sentry*; 1 A330 MRTT *Voyager* KC3; 2 C-130J *Hercules*; **UN** • UNFICYP (*Operation Tosca*) 278; 1 recce coy

DEMOCRATIC REPUBLIC OF THE CONGO: UN • MONUSCO (*Operation Percival*) 2

EGYPT: MFO 2

ESTONIA: NATO • Enhanced Forward Presence (*Operation Cabrit*) 900; 1 armd inf bn HQ; 1 armd inf coy(+); 1 engr sqn

FALKLAND ISLANDS: 1,200: 1 inf coy(+); 1 sigs unit; 1 AD det with *Rapier*; 1 PSO; 1 ftr flt with 4 *Typhoon* FGR4; 1 tkr/tpt flt with 1 A330 MRTT *Voyager*; 1 A400M; 1 hel flt with 2 *Chinook*

GERMANY: 3,750; 1 armd inf bde(-) (1 tk regt, 1 armd inf bn); 1 SP arty regt; 1 maint regt; 1 med regt

GIBRALTAR: 570 (incl Royal Gibraltar regt); 2 PB

IRAQ: *Operation Shader* 400; 2 inf bn(-); 1 engr sqn(-)

KENYA: BATUK 350; 1 trg unit

KUWAIT: *Operation Shader* 50; 1 CISR UAV sqn with 8 MQ-9A *Reaper*

LIBYA: UN • UNSMIL (*Operation Tramal*) 1 obs

MALI: *Operation Barkhane* 90; 1 hel flt with 3 *Chinook* HC3; **EU** • EUTM Mali 8; **UN** • MINUSMA (*Operation Newcombe*) 2

NEPAL: 60 (Gurkha trg org)

NIGERIA: 50 (trg team)

OMAN: 90

PERSIAN GULF: *Operation Kipion* 2 MCO; 2 MHC; 1 LSD

POLAND: NATO • Enhanced Forward Presence 115; 1 recce sqn

SERBIA: NATO • KFOR 24; **OSCE** • Kosovo 5

SOMALIA: EU • EUTM Somalia 4; **UN** • UNSOM (*Operation Praiser*) 43; 3 obs; **UN** • UNSOS (*Operation Catan*) 40; 2 obs

SOUTH SUDAN: UN • UNMISS (*Operations Trenton & Vogul*) 333; 1 engr coy

UKRAINE: *Operation Orbital* 53 (trg team); **OSCE** • Ukraine 65

UNITED ARAB EMIRATES: 200; 1 tpt/tkr flt with C-17A *Globemaster*; C-130J *Hercules*; A330 MRTT *Voyager*

FOREIGN FORCES

United States
US European Command: 9,250; 1 ftr wg at RAF Lakenheath (1 ftr sqn with 24 F-15C/D *Eagle*, 2 ftr sqn with 23 F-15E *Strike Eagle*); 1 ISR sqn at RAF Mildenhall with OC-135/RC-135; 1 tkr wg at RAF Mildenhall with 15 KC-135R/T *Stratotanker*; 1 spec ops gp at RAF Mildenhall (1 sqn with 8 CV-22B *Osprey*; 1 sqn with 8 MC-130J *Commando* II) • US Strategic Command: 1 AN/FPS-132 Upgraded Early Warning Radar and 1 *Spacetrack* radar at Fylingdales Moor

Arms procurements and deliveries – Europe

Selected events in 2018

- In April, France and Germany signed an agreement to collaborate on a Future Combat Air System (FCAS) that aims to replace the Dassault *Rafale* and the Eurofighter *Typhoon*. Dassault will lead on the project with the aim of producing prototypes for testing in the mid-2020s. A concept design issued by Airbus showed a low-observable, twin-engine fighter aircraft acting as part of a command-and-control network with other aircraft and unmanned systems. A model displayed by Dassault in late 2018 was broadly similar but was tailless, unlike the Airbus design which showed twin outwardly canted vertical stabilisers.

- The United Kingdom launched a Combat Air Strategy in July and displayed a concept model of a fighter aircraft that it hopes will begin replacing the *Typhoon* in the mid-2030s. The *Tempest* project is a collaboration between BAE Systems, Leonardo, MBDA and Rolls-Royce, although the UK is open to foreign partners to help share costs. The *Tempest* is a large, low-observable, twin-engined design with a flexible payload configuration. The UK plans to invest £2bn (US$2.7bn) over ten years in the project.

- The French defence ministry created a defence-innovation agency in September. The agency will focus on the research and development of key technologies, as well as the integration of civilian technologies into military equipment. This is simultaneous to a larger reform of the French procurement agency (DGA) that began in 2017 that seeks to speed up the procurement process and improve cooperation between the armed forces and industry.

- At the EURONAVAL trade show in Paris in October, French defence minister Florence Parly announced the start of an 18-month study phase to determine France's future aircraft-carrier requirements. The options include operating more than one carrier. Although only in the early stages of what will be a decades-long programme, the minister stated that a new French carrier must be capable of operating the Franco-German FCAS and that France was in discussions with the US over the acquisition of the General Atomics electromagnetic aircraft-launching system (EMALS) used on the USS *Gerald R. Ford* carrier.

- In October, Fincantieri and Naval Group announced a 50/50 joint venture (JV) to build ships for Italy and France, as well as export customers. Although the JV did not have any contracts at the time of writing, it is working towards offering a logistic-ship design to the French Navy based on a vessel being built for the Italian Navy. The JV will also bid for the mid-life upgrade of the French and Italian *Horizon*-class destroyers.

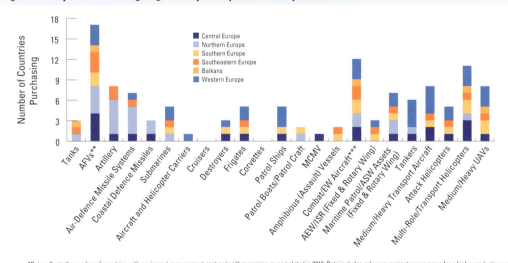

▼ Figure 9 **Europe: selected ongoing or completed procurement priorities in 2018**

*Data reflects the number of countries with equipment-procurement contracts either ongoing or completed in 2018. Data includes only procurement programmes for which a production contract has been signed. The data does not include upgrade programmes.
**Armoured fighting vehicles not including main battle tanks   ***Includes combat-capable training aircraft

© IISS

Table 10 European frigate programmes and principal weapons systems

Country	Class	Prime contractor	Contract date	Value (US$)	Quantity	Anti-ship missile	Surface-to-air missile	Torpedo	Naval gun
FRA	FREMM	(FRA) Naval Group	2005	8.3bn	6 (anti-submarine warfare)	MM40 *Exocet* (EUR) MBDA	*Aster* 15 (EUR) MBDA	MU90 (FRA/ITA) EuroTorp	Oto Melara 76/62 *Super Rapid* (ITA) Leonardo
					2 (air defence)		*Aster* 15/30 (EUR) MBDA		
	Frégates de Taille Intermédiaire		2017	4.28bn	5		*Aster* 30 (EUR) MBDA		
GER	Baden-Württemberg (F125)	(GER) TKMS	2007	3.69bn	4	RGM-84 *Harpoon* (US) Boeing (will be replaced by NSM (NOR) Kongsberg)	RIM-116 RAM (US) Raytheon/(GER) Diehl BGT	–	Oto Melara 127/64mm LW (ITA) Leonardo
	Köln (K130 Batch II)	(GER) Lürssen Werft	2017	2.25bn	5	RBS15 (SWE) Saab			Oto Melara 76/62 *Super Rapid* (ITA) Leonardo
ITA	FREMM	(ITA) Orizzonte Sistemi Navali	2006	6.76bn	4 (anti-submarine warfare) 6 (multi-role)	*Otomat/Teseo* (EUR) MBDA	*Aster* 15/30 (EUR) MBDA	MU90 (FRA/ITA) EuroTorp	Oto Melara 76/62 *Super Rapid* (ITA) Leonardo and Oto Melara 127/64mm LW (ITA) Leonardo
	Pattugliatori Polivalenti d'Altura	(ITA) Fincantieri, (ITA) Leonardo	2015	5.99bn*	2 (full)		*Aster* 15, 30 & 30 Block 1NT (EUR) MBDA	*Black Shark* (ITA) Leonardo	
					3 (light+)	–	*Aster* 30 (EUR) MBDA	*Black Shark* (ITA) Leonardo and *Black Arrow* (ITA) Leonardo	
					2 (light)	–	–	*Black Arrow* (ITA) Leonardo	
TUR	Ada (MILGEM)	(TUR) Istanbul Naval Shipyard	2004	n.k.	4	RGM-84 *Harpoon* (US) Boeing and/or ATMACA (TUR) Roketsan	RIM-116 RAM (US) Raytheon/(GER) Diehl BGT	Mk 46 (US) Raytheon	Oto Melara 76/62 *Super Rapid* (ITA) Leonardo
	Istanbul (G-MILGEM)		2005	n.k.	4		RIM-116 RAM (US) Raytheon/(GER) Diehl BGT and RIM-162 ESSM (US) Raytheon	Mk 46 (US) Raytheon	
UK	City (Type-26)	(UK) BAE Systems	2017	4.83bn	3 (8 planned)	T.B.D.	*Sea Ceptor* (CAMM) (EUR) MBDA	*Sting Ray* (UK) BAE Systems	BAE 5 inch 62-calibre Mk 45 (US) BAE Land Systems & Armaments

*Contract includes construction of a support vessel

▼ Figure 10 **Airbus Defence & Space: A400M heavy transport aircraft**

The A400M can trace its origins back to the early 1980s when Aérospatiale, British Aerospace, Lockheed and MBB proposed cooperating on a replacement for the C-130 *Hercules* and C-160 *Transall*.

A decade later, an eight-nation team (Belgium, France, Germany, Italy, Portugal, Spain, Turkey and the United Kingdom) under the European Future Large Aircraft Group (EUROFLAG) project, together with Airbus, submitted its proposal for a four-engine turboprop that would lie between the Lockheed Martin C-130J and the Boeing C-17A *Globemaster* in both size and cost.

Engine selection caused some controversy when, in May 2003, European consortium EUROPROP International's TP400-D6 was selected over Pratt & Whitney Canada's PW180. A €19.7 billion (US$22.3bn) fixed-price production contract was signed that month, with deliveries of 180 aircraft to the (by then) seven-nation group planned to take place between 2009 and 2021.

The programme has suffered delays and cost overruns. Issues with the Full Automatic Digital Engine Control (FADEC) and the gearbox meant that the prototype's maiden flight did not take place until late 2009, a year behind schedule. Airbus agreed to fund most development, and to a fixed-price contract, in part because it anticipated export sales of up to 200 aircraft. However, the cancellation of South Africa's order, and a 2010 contract renegotiation after Airbus reported cost overruns of €11.2bn (US$15.6bn), have proven challenging.

The overall order was cut from 180 to 170 and the seven nations agreed to pay an additional €3.5bn (US$4.7bn). The first series-production aircraft was not delivered until 2013. Despite this, the aircraft has been used on operations – including in Mali – where its ability to land on soft and short runways was demonstrated with some success.

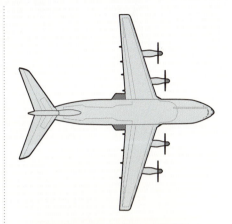

Prime contractor
Airbus Defence & Space (INTL)

Selected subcontractors
Denel Aerostructures (RSA)
Diehl Aerosystems (GER)
EUROPROP International (INTL)
GKN Aerospace (UK)
Indra (ESP)
Safran (FRA)
Thales (FRA)
Turkish Aerospace Industries (TUR)

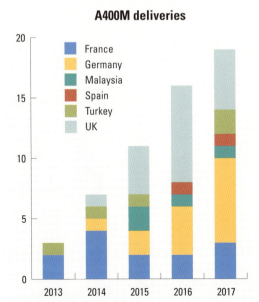

A400M deliveries

	2003 contract		2010 renegotiation	
Country	Quantity	Approx. share of cost*	Quantity	Approx. share of cost*
Belgium	7	€766.11m	7	€967.65m
France	50	€5.47bn	50	€6.91bn
Germany	60	€6.57bn	53	€7.33bn
Luxembourg	1	€109.44m	1	€138.34m
Spain	27	€2.96bn	27	€3.73bn
Turkey	10	€1.09bn	10	€1.38bn
UK	25	€2.74bn	22	€3.04bn
Total	180	€19.7bn (US$22.3bn)	170	€23.5bn (US$31.2bn)
Unit cost	1	€109.44m (US$123.7m)	1	€138.24m (US$183.4m)

*Based on division of total cost by quantity ordered

© IISS

Chapter Five
Russia and Eurasia

- Improving air-ground cooperation is a focus for the armed forces, exemplified by the appointment of a career ground-forces officer as C-in-C of the Russian Aerospace Forces. Russia is also working to refine its reconnaissance-strike complex.
- This is another lesson from Russia's operation in Syria, which remains a springboard for senior commanders; deployment there is important for promotion.
- Russia's Su-57 development is progressing at a modest pace. Meanwhile, improved versions of a previous generation, including the Su-35, are improving air force capabilities.
- Russia's Navy commissioned its first new truly blue-water principal surface combatant in some two decades, including with a new, potentially more capable air-defence system.
- The creation of information troops and reinstatement of the Main Directorate for Political-Military Affairs showed that Russia's command has sharpened its attention on confrontation in the information domain.
- Russia's surge of naval capabilities into the Eastern Mediterranean in late 2018 demonstrated its ability to potentially pose challenges to NATO and other navies in the region.

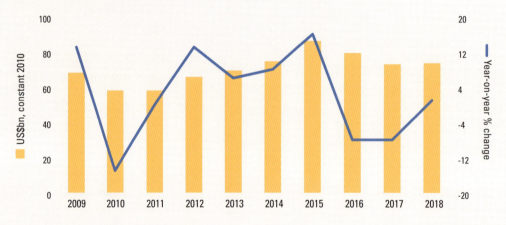

Russia real-terms total military expenditure, 2009–18 (US$bn, constant 2010)

Active military personnel – top 10
(25,000 per unit)

Russia 900,000
Ukraine 209,000
Azerbaijan 66,950
Uzbekistan 48,000
Belarus 45,350
Armenia 44,800
Kazakhstan 39,000
Turkmenistan 36,500
Georgia 20,650
Kyrgyzstan 10,900

Regional defence policy and economics	168 ▶
Armed forces data section	184 ▶
Arms procurements and deliveries	219 ▶

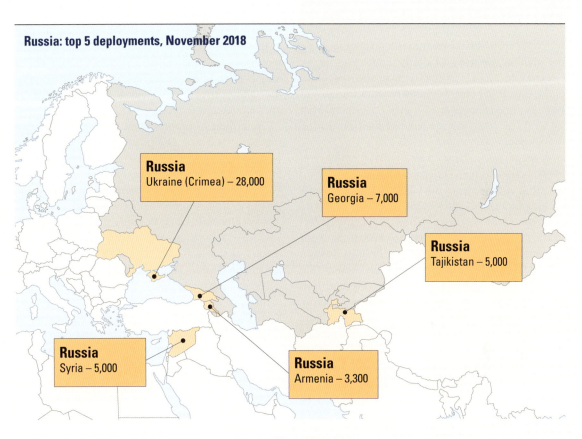

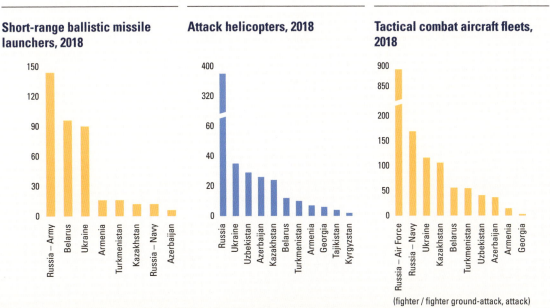

(fighter / fighter ground-attack, attack)

Russia and Eurasia

RUSSIA

In March 2018, Russia went to the polls in its latest presidential election. Vladimir Putin was again returned to office. Continuity was also the order of the day at the defence ministry: both Minister of Defence Sergei Shoigu and Chief of the General Staff General Valery Gerasimov retained their posts after the election.

Nonetheless, there were some personnel movements of note. Perhaps the most interesting reshuffle in the defence ministry in some years was the appointment of Colonel-General Sergei Surovikin, a career Ground Forces officer, as commander-in-chief of the Russian Aerospace Forces. Such an appointment is unprecedented not only in Russian but also Soviet history and perhaps reflects the officially stated rationale behind the selection – to improve cooperation between the Aerospace Forces and the Ground Forces. However, air-force officer Lieutenant-General Andrei Yudin kept his post as deputy to the commander-in-chief. Before taking on his new role, Surovikin had commanded Russia's armed forces in Syria for nine months and gained significant experience during 2017's major offensive against the Islamic State, also known as ISIS or ISIL.

Syria: battle laboratory

Russia's operation in Syria remains a springboard for senior commanders; deployment there is important for promotion. Since the mission began in late 2015, more than 500 Russian generals have rotated through the country on deployment. Indeed, the newly appointed commanders-in-chief of the Eastern and Central military districts have commanded Russian troops in Syria.

Moscow's mission in Syria has two principal priorities: firstly, to bolster the regime of its ally, Bashar al-Assad, and secondly, to use the deployment as a test bed for the development of joint operations and new weapons and tactics. For example, Russia has put its concept of a joint information battlespace into practice there, by providing troops with real-time information on friendly and adversary forces. The defence ministry has invested considerable effort in improving cooperation between units and refining the reconnaissance-strike complex. As part of this, Russia continues to work on modernising its reconnaissance capabilities, to detect and monitor targets in real time, and to reduce the time between the detection of a target and its engagement by artillery, aircraft or precision weapons.

According to reports from the Russian defence ministry, between the start of the mission in September 2015 and August 2018, the Aerospace Forces carried out 39,000 combat flights in Syria. A little over half of these were completed at night. These figures indicate improvements to both air capability and aircrew proficiency. But activity fell in 2018: from January to September, only 5,000 combat flights were carried out, which was reportedly a reduction on the previous year. This decline is largely due to the balance of power in the conflict changing in favour of the pro-government forces, which has allowed Russia to reduce its military presence in Syria. In summer 2018, a number of aircraft and helicopters returned to Russia, including, it was reported, all the new Mi-28 and Ka-52 attack helicopters. At the beginning of autumn, about 30 aircraft remained in Syria – the lowest number since the beginning of Russia's intervention.

The information dimension

The Syria campaign continues to be studied in Russian military academies, leading to a range of lessons for tactics and procurement. As well as lessons on the efficacy of weaponry, one of the most important relates to active information and psychological operations, which are used to suppress an opponent's will to resist. Alongside traditional methods, such as spreading leaflets, missions of this type have reportedly also been conducted in cyberspace.

Russia announced in 2017 that it had formed the Information Operations Troops. There is little information available in public on this group's activities, although it is understood that its covert activity is conducted mainly in cyberspace. In 2018, the defence ministry reinstated the Main Directorate for Military–Political Affairs, which has among its key responsibilities the management of propaganda and counter-propaganda, patriotic education and psychological support for the armed forces. The creation of these new organisations shows that the Russian command has sharpened its attention on confrontation in the information domain.

Personnel

As a result of Russia's demographic crisis of the 1990s, the number of young men each year reaching draft age remains low. Nonetheless, according to official statements, in 2017 the armed forces reached 95% of target strength. This is the result of the high number of contract personnel being recruited, which reached over 380,000 in early 2018. Consequently, the draft continues to be reduced. In spring 2018, 128,000 men were conscripted, less than in spring 2017. Around 260,000 recruits in total were expected to be conscripted over the course of 2018. The reduction in the draft will continue and the current plan is to have 499,200 contract personnel with only 150,000 conscripts in the armed forces by 2020.

Support units contain fewer contract personnel, freeing contractors to instead be employed in front-line combat units, including the Airborne Forces and marines, which are recruiting two battalion tactical groups of contract troops for each regiment or brigade. These units are intended to solve the problem of uneven training levels caused by the draft and demobilisation cycle for conscripts serving only one year. Overall, 126 battalion tactical groups wholly comprising contract troops have been formed in the Ground Forces and Airborne Forces. These are reported to be at constant combat readiness, which, for Russian analysts, is understood to mean around 24-hours readiness to move. Meanwhile, special forces, combined-arms units in Russia's peacekeeping forces (such as the 15th Separate Motor-rifle Brigade) and submarine crews are entirely staffed by contract personnel.

However, the contract-personnel level falls short of the goal set at the beginning of the reform effort, where the armed forces would be composed entirely of fully combat-ready units. Conscripts still represent a third of the armed forces and remain only marginally fit for real combat operations; it is understood that they have not been sent to Syria, even in support roles.

New weapons

On 1 March 2018, in his annual address to the Federal Assembly, Putin referred to the ongoing development of innovative strategic-weapons systems. Some of these were hitherto publicly unknown. *Burevestnik*, a nuclear-powered ultra-long-range cruise missile, is currently in test. According to Russian reports, *Peresvet* mobile lasers have been observed at Strategic Rocket Forces bases. A squadron of modernised MiG-31 fighters equipped with the *Kinzhal* hypersonic air-to-surface missile (modelled on the 9M723 (SS-26 *Stone*) ballistic missile from the *Iskander*-M system) is undergoing operational testing in the Southern Military District, in the Caspian Sea area. Less still is known about *Poseidon*, a nuclear-powered uninhabited underwater vehicle.

Specialists understand that these weapons are currently prototypes. It is unclear whether they will complete the test-and-development process. The first tests of the *Burevestnik* cruise missile were unsuccessful, and efforts are currently being directed towards developing an improved model.

However, there are fewer doubts about the RS-28 *Sarmat* (SS-X-29), the new liquid-fuelled, multiple independently targetable re-entry vehicle-equipped heavy intercontinental ballistic missile (ICBM), to be fitted out with the already-tested *Avangard* hypersonic glide vehicle. *Sarmat* is intended to replace the RS-20 (SS-18 *Satan*) ICBM.

Despite Putin's bold statements, these weapons are not 'game-changers'. They could be useful in terms of securing a second-strike capability, but they do not provide Russia with the capacity to mount successfully an immediate counterforce nuclear strike. It is possible that they are considered by Moscow only as a reliable guarantee of preserving Russia's second-strike retaliatory capability, or perhaps also a useful bargaining chip in any future arms-control negotiations.

Infrastructure

The construction of military bases along the border with Ukraine continues. The 152nd Logistics Brigade was reported as formed at Liski in Voronezh in February 2018. The 20th Combined Arms Army (CAA), based close to the border, is still forming. In addition to two motor-rifle divisions, the 20th CAA includes an anti-aircraft brigade, an artillery brigade, a missile brigade and a command-and-control brigade, the 9th Signal Brigade at Voronezh.

There have been no significant changes in the group of ground forces deployed to Crimea. However, the Airborne Forces activated the 171st Airborne Battalion in Feodosia in December 2017 and the Aerospace Forces replaced the 12th Regiment's

S-300PM1 (SA-20 *Gargoyle*) surface-to-air missile (SAM) systems with S-400s. The modernisation of Belbek airfield is the largest infrastructure project on the Crimean Peninsula. Once the second runway is complete, the airfield will be able to receive all types of strategic-aviation assets. In addition, a squadron of Tu-22M3 *Backfire* bombers equipped with anti-ship missiles (possibly Kh-32s) may be permanently stationed there, making the peninsula even more important to Moscow in asserting its control over the Black Sea.

Another significant development is the return of Russian carrier aviation to the NITKA land-based carrier simulator in Crimea. Before the peninsula was annexed, a new training centre was being built by Russia in Yeysk, on the shores of the Sea of Azov, though this was not completed. During summer 2018, both regiments of the navy's carrier-based fighters were training in Crimea.

Meanwhile, plans to boost Russia's military presence in the Arctic have slowed and a new Arctic motor-rifle brigade intended for the Yamal Peninsula in northwest Siberia has been put on hold. However, there are plans to build, before the end of 2019, a small air-defence base near Tiksi on Russia's northeast coast; there was a base near Tiksi during the Cold War.

At the same time, recent investments in Arctic airfields have proved their worth. After modernisation, in 2018 a Tu-160 *Blackjack* strategic bomber was for the first time able to land at Anadyr airfield in Chukotka. In the same year, a group of Tu-142 anti-submarine aircraft flew over the North Pole to the shores of Alaska for the first time in some years. The provision

Command and control

Russia's leadership often states that international affairs are entering a period of rapid change and sustained instability. President Vladimir Putin, for instance, has pointed to the simultaneous growth of international competition and the degradation of global governance mechanisms. Chief of the General Staff General Valery Gerasimov has discussed the evolution of the character of war, noting increasing international competition over energy, transit routes and access to markets. He emphasises that the reasons for the use of military force are broadening, and how quickly thriving states can now be reduced to violent chaos.

Moscow categorises threats into two groups. The first is the development of long-range, high-precision weapons and mobile forces. These capabilities increase the tempo of military activity, reducing operational pauses in action. The second is based on the broad use of political, economic, humanitarian, information and other non-military measures, applied in coordination with the protest potential of a population and supplemented by military measures. As a result, according to Gerasimov, it is increasingly important in contemporary conflicts to be able to defend the population and strategic sites and communications from the activity of special forces and saboteurs and manage the system of territorial defence.

Taken together, these have led to the view in Moscow that the (armed) protection of a state is not simply a military matter, but one that requires the consolidation of all agencies of state power. Indeed, Gerasimov has said that territorial defence can only be organised with the involvement of law-enforcement and security agencies.

Furthermore, a priority for Moscow is to improve the correlation between information management, decision-making and executive actors across the state, in order to improve responsiveness in times of crises. According to Gerasimov, such views are now expressed in the Defence Plan, a new form of strategic planning that emerged in early 2013 and was subsequently updated for the period 2016–20.

Despite the widespread view in the Euro-Atlantic community that Russian decision-making, apparently unhindered by democratic processes, is a simpler and faster process than in Western capitals, a number of issues complicate the picture for the Russian leadership.

Firstly, the chain of command has in the past often proved unreliable. For example, information – even on strategic questions, such as during the early days of the Ukraine crisis – is often inefficiently passed up the chain, hindering timely decision-making. In addition, instructions passed down the chain have sometimes been fulfilled only tardily or incompletely, even in implementing the strategic agenda set out in Putin's 2012 May decrees. The leadership is making considerable efforts to address such problems, but even if decision-making in Moscow becomes faster, the quality of the information on which decisions are based and the effectiveness of action once decisions have been taken are open to question.

Secondly, though organisations such as the Security Council and the Main Directorate for Special Projects (GUSP) exist to oversee such processes, it is often difficult to coordinate the activities of different ministries,

Ground forces

New units have formed incrementally in 2018, including a new (127th) motor-rifle division, formed out of some of the existing brigades of the 5th Army around Vladivostok, the upgrade of three of six Airborne Forces tank companies to battalions and the formation of a new tank battalion in Kaliningrad. The established tank and motor-rifle divisions appear to be moving towards achieving their full complement, although most still lack at least one of their planned regiments.

The planned gradual reduction in expenditure on equipment purchases was confirmed at the 'Armiya 2018' military exhibition, where contract agreements were down on 2017. In addition, a significant proportion of the equipment mock-ups seen in previous years are still not yet ready for serial production. At the show, it was announced that a total of 132 T-14 tanks and T-15 heavy infantry fighting vehicles would be delivered between 2018 and 2022. However, it was striking that there were no contracts to buy in quantity new light armoured vehicles. The *Kurganets*-25 tracked platform and the wheeled *Bumerang* will be produced only in small batches for testing in 2019–21.

Indeed, there has been continued emphasis on recapitalising existing vehicle fleets. The 2016 T-72B3 upgrade (with a more powerful engine and improved reactive armour) is currently being issued to tank regiments in the new motor-rifle divisions and all B3 models are expected to be retrofitted to this standard at some point. Deliveries of the BMP-2 infantry fighting vehicle upgraded with the *Berezhok* combat module (BMP-2M) began in the Central Military

agencies and departments – as well as actors at federal, regional and local levels – and between civilian and military authorities. The armed forces have criticised the civilian authorities for their lack of readiness, for example, and their slow implementation of military orders, as well as noting more practical problems in terms of logistics, transport, reconnaissance and communications. Indeed, in many ways, this is a reminder that Russia is not monolithic, and that numerous vested interests throughout the chain of command and across the various parts of the state mean that the orchestration of Russian state power is not always harmonious.

Recognising such problems, the authorities have looked to improve information management and synchronisation. Measures have included major exercises that not only rehearse rapid deployments over long distances, but also bring together actors from across the state, such as the central bank and various ministries, including transport, communications, health and agriculture.

Similarly, there have been strategic policing exercises, such as *Zaslon* 2015, while the armed forces have exercised with the National Guard – a force established in 2016 to combine the interior troops, special-forces and rapid-response troops, and other non-military armed forces in Russia – to rehearse the protection of strategically important locations (such as energy, industry and transport centres) against saboteurs and terrorists. Territorial-defence staffs are also being established to improve coordination between regional and military authorities.

Perhaps the most important development, however, has been the establishment of the National Defence Management Centre (NDMC), sometimes also known as the National Defence Control Centre. Mikhail Mizintsev, commander of the NDMC, has stated that the armed forces must be ready to react quickly to crises without having to endure a prolonged transition to a war footing – in other words, the goal is to minimise the mobilisation gap. The NDMC, which opened in 2014, facilitates this and has an extensive remit. It has three levels of command: a supreme command centre, which controls the strategic nuclear forces; a combat command centre, which monitors the global political–military situation and provides forecasting and analysis; and a centre that oversees everyday activities, coordinating the work of security ministries and departments in peacetime, including the Interior Ministry, foreign- and military-intelligence organisations, the Ministry of Emergencies and the Federal Security Service's Border Guards. Indeed, all defence-related information flows are narrowed into this single channel, to enable all military movement in Russia and international defence and security developments to be tracked in real time.

As the hub of a nationwide network of such centres, the NDMC is intended to unify all existing command and monitoring systems across Russia and act as a single point of coordination for information and control over all agencies. It also oversees information and cyber security, and monitors social networks, unrest and protests. Since being commissioned, the NDMC has also supervised equipment modernisation, strategic exercises and combat operations in Syria. It represents a new stage in the attempt to enhance and improve Russian command and control.

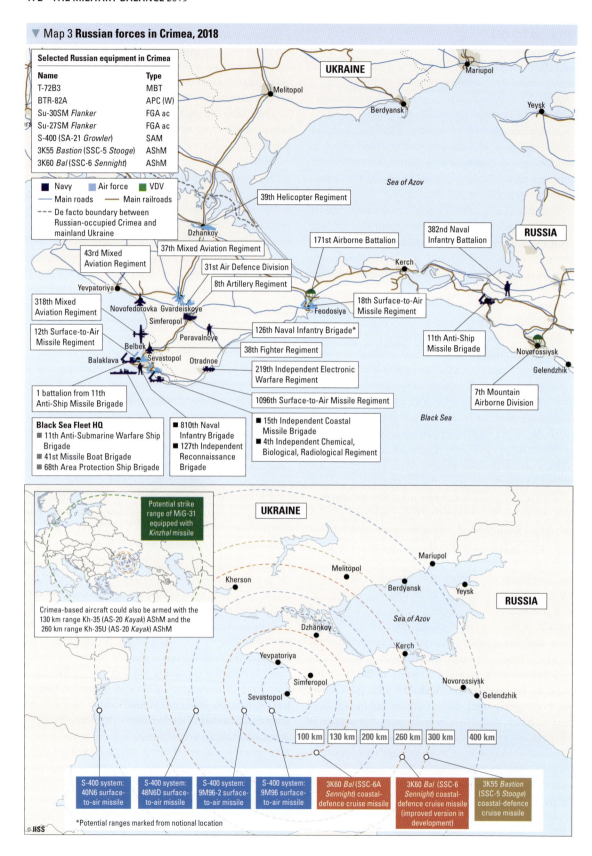

District in 2018. Further production of the *Tornado*-S 300 mm multiple-rocket launcher appears to have been complicated by a legal case brought against the manufacturer in July by the defence ministry.

Aerospace forces

The Russian Aerospace Forces (VKS) continued during 2018 to absorb the lessons from their ongoing involvement in Syria and to come to terms with the more modest ambitions of Russia's latest State Armament Programme (SAP 2018–27).

Besides allowing new and upgraded aircraft and weapons to be tested operationally, the Syria mission has provided valuable experience for air and ground crews. Workers from the defence-aerospace industry have also supported the deployment from the air base at Hmeimim in Syria.

The performance of Russian aircraft in Syria may have allowed the VKS to take a more sanguine view of the slow progress of the Su-57 being developed to meet its future multi-role fighter (PAK-FA) requirement. The Su-35S *Flanker* E made its operational debut in Syria, as did one of its primary air-to-air missiles, the R-77-1 (AA-12B *Adder*) active radar-guided medium-range weapon. This Su-35 iteration of the *Flanker* was originally conceived as an export-only product, but as the PAK-FA was delayed it was adopted by the air force as a gap-filler. Indications so far are that the SAP to 2027 only supports the acquisition of a small number of Su-57s (at least until 2023). Pre-production versions of the Su-57 are being flown with an interim engine, as the intended engine may not be ready for series production before 2023.

Further indications of more modest near- to medium-term acquisition aims for the VKS include the emphasis on upgrades to existing bomber types, and the intention to begin to build an upgraded variant of the Tu-160 *Blackjack*, the Tu-160M2. The latter features updated NK-32 engines (production of which has been restarted), increased range and updated avionics, which will serve as the basis for those to be used in the PAK-DA next-generation bomber requirement. Development continues of a new bomber design, Tupolev's Item 80, which is meant to meet the PAK-DA requirement, but the pace appears to have slowed. It is possible that PAK-DA may be viewed increasingly as a complement to, rather than a replacement for, the *Blackjack*. As Tu-160M2 and PAK-DA enter production, the Tu-95MS *Bear* strategic bomber may be gradually withdrawn.

However, the emphasis for the VKS remains the development and acquisition of a variety of stand-off air-to-surface weapons for the bomber fleet. As well as continuing to buy the Kh-101/Kh-102 (AS-23A/B *Kodiak*) long-range cruise missile, the development of both shorter- and apparently longer-range land-attack weapons is under way. The Kh-50 designation has been associated with a smaller cruise missile likely intended for internal carriage on aircraft whose weapons bay will not accommodate the larger Kh-101. Boosting the inventory of short-range air-launched precision-guided weapons is also a priority. The air force has relied on unguided free-fall bombs in Syria, in part reflecting the need to complete the development of or increase production rates on armaments projects now reaching fruition, such as the Kh-30 family of air-to-surface missiles.

Naval forces

At the end of July 2018, *Admiral Gorshkov* – the first Project 22350 frigate – was finally commissioned some 12 years after the ship was first laid down. This marked the introduction into service of the first new truly blue-water surface combatant in nearly two decades. At the same time, a second *Gorshkov*-class frigate was nearing completion, with four more in the pipeline, possibly to be followed by an improved and slightly enlarged version, the Project 22350M.

A factor in the effectiveness of these ships will be whether issues have been resolved with the development of their 3K96-2 (SA-NX-28) *Poliment-Redut* air-defence missile system. If so, this would mark a significant improvement in the Russian Navy's area air-defence capability.

In terms of legacy blue-water capabilities, the much-needed refit of Russia's sole aircraft carrier, *Admiral Kuznetsov*, got under way in 2018. Indications are that the work will focus on the refurbishment of propulsion and electronic systems, rather than any more substantial capability enhancements. Even so, the vessel is unlikely to be back in operation before the early 2020s; that could move further to the right after the damage in October 2018 to the large floating dry dock that carried the vessel.

It remains the case that the most significant recent trend in Russian naval capabilities has been the focus on the construction of relatively small surface platforms and submarines armed with long-range cruise and anti-ship missiles from the *Kalibr* family of weapons. Even here, new deliveries in 2018 were

Figure 11 Russia: *Kalibr* missile family

Russia's *Kalibr* family of anti-ship, land-attack and anti-submarine weapons includes subsonic and supersonic terminal-phase cruise missiles, the 3M54 (SS-N-27 *Sizzler*) anti-ship missile and the 3M14 (SS-N-30) land-attack cruise missile, as well as two rocket-boosted anti-submarine torpedoes, respectively 91R1 and 91RT2. Export versions are marketed under the *Club* banner, though some are range-limited to adhere to the Missile Technology Control Regime (MTCR). A subsonic anti-ship version of the 3M54 is also offered for export, but this does not appear to be part of the Russian Navy's system.

The 3M14 (SS-N-30) long-range cruise missile has design heritage from the Novator 3M10 *Granat* (SS-N-21 *Sampson*) subsonic cruise missile, first deployed in 1986. The 3M14 has a range in the order of 2,000 km, but the export derivative is restricted to just below the MTCR limit of 300 km. The 3M14 provides a conventional land-attack capability, particularly for smaller classes of Russian naval vessels. Strikes on Syria using 3M14 have been launched from conventional submarines (*Kalibr-PL*) and surface combatants (*Kalibr-NK*) in the Caspian Sea, up to 1,500 km away.

Club-S is in service with the navies of Algeria, China, India and Vietnam, aboard their *Kilo*-class submarines. Whilst only the sea-launched versions of *Club* are known to have been exported, other launch options are marketed. This includes the *Club-K* complex, which is designed to fit within a standard shipping container. An air-launched derivative has also been advertised as a possible development.

Russian Navy launch platforms

In addition to vessels built to launch *Kalibr* variants, Russia has announced plans to modify a number of existing vessels to enable the same capability. This includes eight *Antey* (*Oscar II*) guided-missile submarines (with up to 72 missiles per vessel), and the *Orlan* (*Kirov*) nuclear-powered cruisers.

● In service ● Planned

Submarines	*Yasen*
	Varshavyanka
Destroyers	*Admiral Gorshkov*
Frigates	*Admiral Grigorovich*
	Gepard
	Gremyashchiy
	Vasily Bykov
Corvettes	*Buyan-M*
	Karakurt

Ground-launched *Kalibr* derivatives

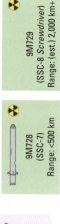

9M728 (SSC-7) Range: <500 km

9M729 (SSC-8 *Screwdriver*) Range: (est.) 2,000 km+

Russia has developed new ground-launched LACMs: the 9M728 (SSC-7) and the 9M729 (SSC-8 *Screwdriver*). Though their lineage has not been officially stated, the missiles are assessed as derived from the 3M14 *Kalibr* and they are able to carry both conventional and nuclear warheads. The shorter-range 9M728 can be launched from a variant of the 9K720 *Iskander-M* missile system. The launch vehicle can carry either or both 9M728 cruise and 9M723 ballistic missiles internally.

The longer-range SSC-8 is believed to be a version of the Russian Navy 3M14T, with an assessed range in excess of 2,000 km. The United States has formally protested against the apparent deployment of this system; the US–Russia Intermediate-Range Nuclear Forces Treaty prohibits ground-launched ballistic- and cruise-missile systems with ranges between 500 km and 5,500 km. (The treaty does not cover sea-launched missiles.)

Kalibr (domestic variants)

Kalibr-NK	*Kalibr-PL*
3M14T (SS-N-30) Range: 2,000 km+	3M14K (SS-N-30) Range: 2,000 km+

Land-attack cruise missiles (LACMs)

Club-N	*Club-S*	*Club-M/Club-K* *	*Club-A*
3M14TE (SS-N-30) Range: 275 km	3M14E (SS-N-30) Range: 275 km	3M14KE Range: 275 km	3M14AE

Anti-ship missiles (AShMs)

3M54T (SS-N-27A *Sizzler*)	3M54K (SS-N-27 *Sizzler*)		
3M54TE (SS-N-27 *Sizzler*) Range: 220 km	3M54E (SS-N-27 *Sizzler*) Range: 220 km	3M54KE Range: 220 km	3M54AE
3M54TE1 (SS-N-27B *Sizzler*) Range: 275 km	3M54E1 (SS-N-27 *Sizzler*) Range: 275 km	3M54KE1 Range: 275 km	3M54AE1

Anti-submarine missiles

91RT2 Range: 40 km Status unconfirmed	91R1 Range: 50 km Status unconfirmed	91RTE2 Range: 40 km	91RE1 Range: 50 km

▓	Ground-launched
▓	Surface-vessel-launched
▓	Submarine-launched
▓	Air-launched
☢	Assessed dual-capable

Club-K is a containerised system (using commercial ISO 20/40) and may also be mounted on ship decks

proceeding slowly. Nonetheless, the first of the improved Project 08851 *Yasen*-M-class submarines began sea trials in September 2018. Programmes to modernise the capabilities of a range of legacy large surface platforms also continue, at a relatively slow pace.

Also after a considerable delay, in June the navy commissioned the amphibious landing ship *Ivan Gren*, some 14 years after construction of the vessel began. A relatively modest 120 metres in length and displacing just 6,600 tonnes, the ship nevertheless represents a considerable improvement over the elderly inventory of amphibious shipping. A key question remains over the extent to which Moscow plans to invest in further improvements in this area; only two of these ships have been ordered so far.

The navy has additionally sought to achieve strategic effect by moving platforms between key theatres and undertaking some significant showcase deployments and concentrations of force. For example, in August 2018, the navy deployed a group of more than a dozen ships, including at least six *Kalibr*-equipped vessels, in the eastern Mediterranean. Although dubbed an exercise, they appeared ready to support Russian operations in Syria and to act as a deterrent to Western and other naval forces operating in the area. In June, the Northern Fleet carried out its largest Arctic exercise in a decade. Then, in September, the Pacific Fleet mounted an exercise involving more than 20 vessels, said to have been the largest since the end of the Cold War, followed quickly by a three-ship regional deployment. These developments appeared to mark a further increase in the level of Russian naval activity, demonstrating at least an ability to deploy in key regions, if not necessarily on a global scale.

Strategic Rocket Forces

Compared to other service arms, Russia's strategic nuclear forces remain relatively immune to budget cuts. Nevertheless, they too have lost one of their major projects. In December 2017, it was announced that development of the *Barguzin* mobile railway complex would be discontinued due to financial constraints, with the funds redirected to new strategic weapons.

The most important of these is the new RS-28 *Sarmat* (SS-X-29) heavy liquid-fuelled ICBM. Launch tests were carried out in December 2017 and twice more over the next six months, including a limited firing of the first-stage engines.

In 2018, the Strategic Rocket Forces completed the rearmament of three missile divisions with the RS-24 *Yars* (SS-27 mod 2) ICBM. The plan remains to replace all RS-12M *Topol* (SS-25 *Sickle*) and RS-12M2 *Topol*-M (SS-27 mod 1) ICBMs with *Yars* by 2021, though achieving this looks unlikely, given the production rates that would be required. Nonetheless, thanks to the rapid acquisition of new missiles, the Strategic Rocket Forces stand out as the most advanced branch of the Russian armed forces: as of 2018, some 79% of its weapons were classed as 'new'.

DEFENCE ECONOMICS

Defence spending

Russia's economy has exhibited only modest growth, or decline, since 2013. The economy grew by 1.5% in 2017 and 1.7% in 2018. Russia's Ministry of Economic Development is forecasting 2.0% growth in 2020, increasing to 3.3% by 2024, but new economic-policy initiatives will be needed if such a revival is to be achieved. By contrast, the IMF forecasts only 1.2% growth in 2023.

Under the State Armament Programme (SAP) 2011–20, Russian defence spending grew rapidly in real terms and as a share of GDP, peaking in 2015. Since then, the rate of growth has moderated and the GDP share is now declining (see Table 11). The SAP to 2020 was always regarded as a one-off process of quickly tackling years of meagre funding, permitting the transition to a more normal annual rate of arms procurement after a few years. This time has arrived and, according to the Ministry of Finance's plans,

Table 11 **Russian defence expenditure** as % of GDP

Year	'National defence' Trillion roubles	as % GDP	Total military expenditure[1] Trillion roubles	as % GDP
2018	2.830	2.88	3.935	4.00
2017	2.666[2]	2.90	3.712	4.03[2]
2016	2.982[2]	3.46	3.831	4.45[2]
2015	3.181	3.81	4.026	4.83
2014	2.479	3.13	3.224	4.07
2013	2.106	2.88	2.787	3.81
2012	1.812	2.66	2.505	3.67
2011	1.516	2.51	2.029	3.37

[1] According to NATO definition
[2] Excluding a one-off payment to reduce accumulated debts of defence-industry enterprises under the scheme of state-guaranteed credits.
2011–2017: actual spending; 2018: amended federal budget for 2018

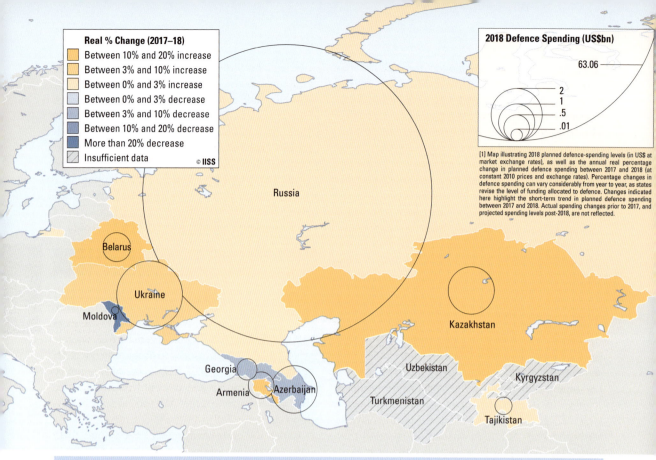

▲ Map 4 **Russia and Eurasia regional defence spending**[1]

revealed in July 2018, spending on 'national defence' (the budget chapter covering the defence ministry's military outlays) will increase to a modest extent in nominal terms in 2019–21. However, it is due to fall as a share of GDP from almost 2.9% in 2018 to 2.6% in 2021, resulting in a share of total military spending of approximately 3.6%. This corresponds to its level before the start of the SAP to 2020.

Understanding the trend of Russian military spending has been complicated by technical factors that have affected the reported defence budget. In 2016 and 2017, the 'national defence' chapter included substantial sums to cover past debts to the defence industry under the system of state-guaranteed credits. This was used to boost spending in the early years of the SAP. The debt settlement amounted to 792 billion roubles (US$11.8bn) in 2016 and 187bn roubles (US$3.2bn) in 2017. But these payments did not contribute to Russia's defence capability and should be excluded from any analysis of the trend of actual military expenditure. Excluding debt settlements, defence spending in nominal terms fell by 6% in 2016 and 11% in 2017, compared with the 28% growth in spending seen in 2015.

In 2017, an additional factor led to a reduction in the reported level of spending. As part of its campaign to tighten contract discipline and effective use of budget funding, the defence ministry decided late in the year to withhold payments to defence companies until contracts for the delivery of new weapons had been completed. The outcome was that more than 200bn roubles (US$3.4bn) was withheld,

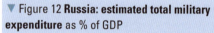
▼ Figure 12 **Russia: estimated total military expenditure** as % of GDP

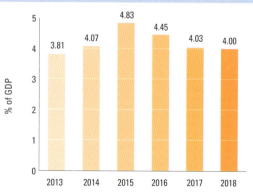

leading to a 6% underspend compared with the total federal budget allocation to 'national defence' in 2017. The withheld payments were disbursed in the early months of 2018, leading to an overspend that was not foreseen when the year's budget was adopted. An amended version of the budget law for 2018 was adopted in early July and this increased the allocation to 'national defence' by about 245bn roubles (US$3.9bn), covering additional outlays relating to the 2017 state defence order. The budget was amended again in November but with only a modest increase in defence spending. It remains to be seen whether the withholding of payments late in the year will become a regular practice.

A new State Armament Programme to 2027

With the formation of a new government following the start of Vladimir Putin's fourth term as president in May 2018, Yury Borisov, formerly deputy defence minister for procurement, replaced Dmitriy Rogozin as deputy prime minister responsible for oversight of the defence industry and first deputy chair of the Military-Industrial Commission (chaired by Putin). Borisov has a background in the electronics industry. His successor as deputy defence minister for procurement was Aleksey Krivoruchko, who was from 2014 to June 2018 general director of Kalashnikov, part of the Rostec state corporation.

Before his departure, Borisov had overseen the preparation of Russia's new SAP, replacing the one to 2020. Originally, this was to have been for the years 2016–25, but at the beginning of 2015 it was postponed until economic prospects were more certain. At first, it was expected to run from 2018 to 2025 but in 2017 it was decided that it should be a ten-year programme to 2027. President Vladimir Putin finally approved the new SAP in December 2017.

The state programme is classified. It is valued in current prices and only the first five years are operational; the second five are presented only in general terms. Total funding of the defence ministry's forces under the SAP to 2027 will be 19 trillion roubles (US$304bn); for the forces of other agencies, such as the Federal Security Service, the Russian National Guard and the Ministry of Emergencies, more than 3trn roubles (US$48.1bn) has been allocated. In nominal terms, the defence ministry will receive the same sum as under the previous programme, but in real terms probably only 50–60% of the sum allocated in the SAP to 2020. In addition, the defence ministry will receive 1trn roubles (US$16bn) for infrastructure investment directly related to the deployment of new weapons. It is not known what share of the ministry's allocation relates to the first five years of the SAP, but it is probably much more than the 31% allocated under the previous SAP to 2020. However, this time, probably because of the tense international situation, there has been no indication of the number of new systems to be delivered under the programme.

As before, strategic missiles have first priority. Acquisition of the RS-24 *Yars* (SS-27 mod 2) intercontinental ballistic missile (ICBM) will continue, and from around 2020 the new RS-28 *Sarmat* (SS-X-29) heavy ICBM should enter service. A number of old RS-18 (SS-19 *Stiletto*) ICBMs will be equipped with the new *Avangard* hypersonic boost-glide vehicle. The priority for the space forces will be to restore Russia's missile early-warning satellite network, with the re-equipping of the ground-based warning system with *Voronezh* radars nearing completion. The air-defence forces will receive more S-400 surface-to-air missile (SAM) systems, but from around 2020 they should begin to receive its successor, the delayed S-500 endo-atmospheric missile-defence system. The new medium-range S-350 *Vityaz* SAM should also enter service.

The air force will probably acquire a smaller number of new aircraft than under the previous SAP. A high priority will be the renewal of the transport-aircraft fleet, including introducing into service the Il-76MD-90A, starting production of the light Il-112 military transport and completing the development of the medium Il-276. However, the number of transports in service is unlikely to increase much before 2025. Rotary-wing development may be limited to upgraded versions of the Ka-52 and Mi-28N helicopters. Russia has made rapid progress in developing and deploying reconnaissance uninhabited aerial vehicles (UAVs) but still lacks a strike system, which is set to be a high priority under the new SAP. The heavy *Okhotnik*, being developed by the Sukhoi design bureau, may be the first real strike UAV to enter Russian service.

The *Armata* main battle tank will likely enter service with the ground forces but not in large numbers. As acknowledged by Borisov, *Armata* is too expensive for mass acquisition. Instead, procurement in quantity will focus on modernised T-72, T-80 and T-90 tanks. More *Terminator* combat vehicles and *Koalitsiya*-SV self-propelled howitzers will be acquired. Work on new robotic systems will likely be a priority under the new programme.

It is clear that the navy will receive very few, if any, heavy surface ships before 2027. More Project 22350 frigates and Project 20380 corvettes will be built, plus some new Project 20386 corvettes and a larger number of small missile ships armed with *Kalibr* and *Oniks* cruise missiles. Submarine building will focus on completing the series of Project 995A *Borey*-A ballistic-missile boats armed with *Bulava* missiles and Project 08851 *Yasen*-M multi-role submarines, though from the early 2020s construction is expected to begin on the first *Khaski*-class successor. The building of new non-nuclear submarines depends, to a large extent, on whether Russia is finally able to produce a viable air-independent propulsion unit.

Defence industry

Rogozin now heads the state corporation for the space-missile industry, Roscosmos, which was established in August 2015. This is now undergoing a major reorganisation, with the aim of improving efficiency after a series of costly launch failures.

The vast state corporation Rostec, headed by Sergey Chemezov, uniting 700 enterprises grouped into 15 holding companies, looks set to absorb the United Aircraft Corporation as an additional holding company, achieving full control of the entire aviation industry – fixed wing, helicopters, engines and avionics. Reorganisation of the United Shipbuilding Corporation now also seems likely, as it is one of the least effective corporate structures of the defence sector. The building of many new naval ships has been subject to long delays.

A significant development for the defence industry was the adoption in late 2017 of a government decree establishing new pricing principles for military products developed and produced under the state defence order. It is designed as a cost-saving measure and should increase profits for defence contractors, making possible the financing of more investment and re-equipping from company earnings rather than budget sources. It should also promote the development of more extensive subcontracting. This was discouraged by the old system of pricing, which left subcontractors with meagre profits. The new approach is now being introduced, but it will take some time before it is operational.

Meanwhile, the elaborate system to closely monitor the use of budget funding under the state defence order continues to function. While the defence industry still complains of excessive bureaucracy and intrusive monitoring, the procurement process should lead to fewer diversions of funding to other purposes and corruption associated with arms procurement. In response to sanctions, a specialised lead bank, Promsvyazbank – organised so as to minimise its vulnerability to sanction pressures – has been designated the principal bank for servicing the state defence order.

Arms exports

In 2017, for the third year running, Russian arms-manufacturing firms signed contracts totalling approximately US$15bn. Once again, sales of aircraft and air-defence systems accounted for a large proportion of total exports. By July 2018, China had received a regimental set of S-400s, while a deal for the system worth a reported US$2.5bn was concluded with Turkey, notwithstanding NATO opposition, with deliveries to begin in late 2019 or early 2020. India has signed a contract for the S-400, while several other countries, including Iraq, Saudi Arabia and Qatar, have expressed interest in buying it. Most of the 24 Su-35 fighters sold to China in November 2015 have been delivered, while in February 2018 a deal worth US$1.14bn was concluded with Indonesia for 11 Su-35s. India and Malaysia have also expressed interest in buying the aircraft. There is an expectation that Russia's use of a wide range of weaponry in Syria will boost export sales.

BELARUS

Belarus's armed forces are slowly completing their long transformation from the force that separated from the Soviet military into those of a middle-sized European country. While official documents underline the still-close military alliance with Russia, Minsk's position is more nuanced. In general, this stems from ad hoc decisions rather than deliberate policies by either Minsk or Moscow. Belarus lacks the funds for significant military investments and has its own distinct priorities, while Moscow is unwilling to invest much in its ally without gaining more control over Belarusian armed forces and facilities.

Security and defence policy

The Belarusian government rarely discusses its security policy in public. However, while Minsk has limited military goals, it is tailoring its armed forces to tackle contemporary security challenges. Indeed, Defence Minister Andrei Ravkov describes the armed forces' ongoing rearmament programme as 'selective'. In February 2018, the defence ministry revealed plans to reduce the army's stored weapons and materiel by a quarter in order to save costs, although the age of some of this equipment makes the prospect of selling it on unlikely. There are two principal drivers for security policy: political stability and relations with Russia.

Internal security

In numerous official statements and semi-official pronouncements, the government has demonstrated concern over the potential for civil unrest to turn into violent clashes and armed conflict, and perhaps prompt foreign intervention. In recent years, Belarusian defence officials have emphasised the need to be ready to cope with multiple security issues without external assistance. While leaders frequently say little on Russia's role in defending Belarus, President Alexander Lukashenko said in October 2018 that in case of a security crisis, there could not be 100% reliance 'even on Russia'. Earlier, in February Lukashenko suggested that Russia's leadership does not see the need to supply the armies of its allies. He also said that Minsk looks to 'arm and modernise' together with fellow Collective Security Treaty Organisation (CSTO) member states, although there is only public information on cooperation with Kazakhstan. Belarusian officials also highlight defence cooperation with China.

Ravkov described new challenges and threats facing the country late in the decade as including 'terrorist and extremist organisations actively [using] new concepts and mechanisms of regime change in other countries', advancing constitutional change and violating these states' 'territorial integrity by provoking internal armed conflicts'. Analysts assess that he also included powerful foreign states in this group of challenges. Minsk had observed events in eastern Ukraine and was keen to prevent the same happening in Belarus. In January 2016, Belarus adopted a new military doctrine, revising the previous version from 2001. Among potential military threats, the document emphasised 'hybrid warfare' and 'colour revolutions'. The former term implied Russian intervention of the kind Moscow undertook in eastern Ukraine, although Belarusian officials did not say so directly. The latter term refers to purported Western attempts at regime change of the sort alleged by Moscow to have occurred since the mid-2000s in Georgia and Ukraine, although Belarusian officials did not cite these as examples. Belarus's military exercises and rearmament programme reflect Minsk's preparation for these scenarios. However, there is little evidence that Minsk is preparing for any direct confrontation with Western states or NATO, even as an ally of Russia. According to the official military daily newspaper *Belorusskaya voennaya gazeta*, 'the preparation of Belarusian armed forces is aimed mostly at fighting terrorist groups and not engaging in any large-scale hostilities'.

Relations with Russia

For Minsk, cooperation with Russia does not mean that both countries should adhere to identical defence policies or views on security. Belarus elaborates a more nuanced opinion on NATO activities in the region and is more muted in public pronouncements than Moscow. In a 2015 television interview, Ravkov called the increasing NATO presence in the region 'a danger', but stressed that 'there is no military threat'. Unlike Moscow, Minsk remains committed to transparency by remaining in the Treaty on Conventional Armed Forces in Europe and opening up *Zapad* 2017 exercises that included Belarusian units to NATO and OSCE observers, as well as observers from neighbouring countries, including Ukraine.

That said, Minsk recognises Russia's security concerns and to an extent provides support for Russia's defence efforts. Belarus, which has limited economic potential and resources, leverages Moscow's use of Belarusian defence capacities and territory. Indeed, some elements of its armed forces may be more important to Russia than to Belarus, most notably air and missile defence. Analysts consider that Minsk maintains these capabilities mostly to play a role in the defence of Russia. It also enables Minsk to avoid the permanent basing of Russian forces in Belarusian territory, except for two highly specialised technical facilities – the Russian Navy's long-range low-frequency communications centre in Vileyka and the Hantsavichy early-warning radar, both of which were established in Soviet or early post-Soviet times. It is believed that Russia does not pay directly for either facility; in return the Belarusian military has free access to Russian military facilities such as the Ashuluk military training area. Analysts also understand that Belarus has access to economic and other benefits from the Kremlin, with these perhaps including subsidised oil and gas or access to markets.

Belarus's geography dictates much of its security policy. By the mid-2000s, it had NATO neighbours to the north and the west, and since 2014, Ukraine, to the south, has developed closer ties to the West. These developments left Minsk with the choice of either risking tension with the West or adjusting its policies. Minsk chose the latter by renouncing most of its earlier anti-Western rhetoric, increasing divergence with Russia on foreign policy and defence matters (higher transparency in exercises, maintaining its obligations under the Treaty on Conventional Armed Forces in Europe, increasing self-reliance in military policy), and increasing contacts with NATO and its member states. The geopolitical situation with regard to Russia, however, remained static. Belarus will always be important to Russia, as it is situated next to Russia's core regions around Moscow. Because of this, Moscow considers it necessary to have at least minimal air- and missile-defence capacities in Belarus, either under allied Belarusian command or Russian units in-country. While Moscow would like to increase its military capabilities in Belarus, with a view to NATO states' capacities to the west, in 2016 Minsk reportedly displayed reluctance to station Russian 9K720 *Iskander*-M (SS-26 *Stone*) short-range ballistic-missile systems under Russian command in Belarus as Moscow refused to supply the systems to Minsk. Prior to this, analysts had understood that Russia was interested in obtaining for its forces an air base in Belarus.

In 2016, Minsk and Moscow also completed the formalities around the adoption of the 2009 agreement on establishing a single air-defence system for Belarus and Russia. The agreement essentially formalised or confirmed already existing air-defence cooperation mechanisms. The main joint standby-alert duty arrangements (*sovmestnoe boevoe dezhurstvo*) began in 1996, in addition to information exchanges, joint training sessions and equipment supplies. The joint operation of Belarusian and Russian military units attached to this single air-defence system will be coordinated from the Russian air force's central command centre. For all other purposes, these units remain under national command, but this would change in the case of armed conflict, when a joint Belarus–Russia air-defence command would be established. In 2017, Minsk and Moscow amended the 2009 agreement by specifying and limiting its scope: in the original text, the joint command could be established in a 'period of a threat'; the amendments stipulated the establishment of such a command only in a 'period of immediate threat of aggression'.

In November 2017, the Belarus–Russia agreement on supplying a joint regional group of Belarusian and Russian troops entered force. Both parties agreed that each had to supply their own national army units, which shall become part of this group in case of an imminent conflict – there is no permanently staffed formation. Moscow has committed to supplying Minsk with equipment and arms only during an 'increasing military threat to the Union state [of Belarus and Russia] and in times of war'.

The armed forces

When the independent Belarusian armed forces formed in the 1990s, it was similar to its Russian counterpart in terms of doctrine, training, equipment and organisation, and officers moved between the two forces. Now the two armed forces have different missions, identities, structures, equipment and training. Belarus switched to a brigade-based organisational structure before Russia and kept that structure after Russia started re-establishing larger units. Belarus also maintains and modernises many of the platforms that Russia is phasing out and increasingly develops its own, sometimes in cooperation with other countries, such as China.

However, the Belarusian armed forces are deployed largely as they were in Soviet times. The existing Western and Northwestern operational commands, formed in 2001, reflect the tendency to not make changes to military deployments unless absolutely necessary. There have been some recent changes, such as a new air-defence regiment armed with *Tor*-M2E (SA-15 *Gauntlet*) surface-to-air missile (SAM) systems and a battalion of internal troops stationed near the Lithuanian border to guard the nuclear power plant under construction there.

Minsk has said it will retain obligatory military service for all men. Most of those drafted who have secondary education serve for 18 months, while those with a university degree serve for 12 months. Conscripts can be assigned to serve in the army, special forces, air defence and air force, internal troops or border troops. However, the army is looking to introduce a more flexible military-service system and unlike in Soviet times does not call up all conscripts. Conscripts with different educational backgrounds and qualifications serve different types of military service. According to official statements, in 2018, about 80% of conscripts were not immediately

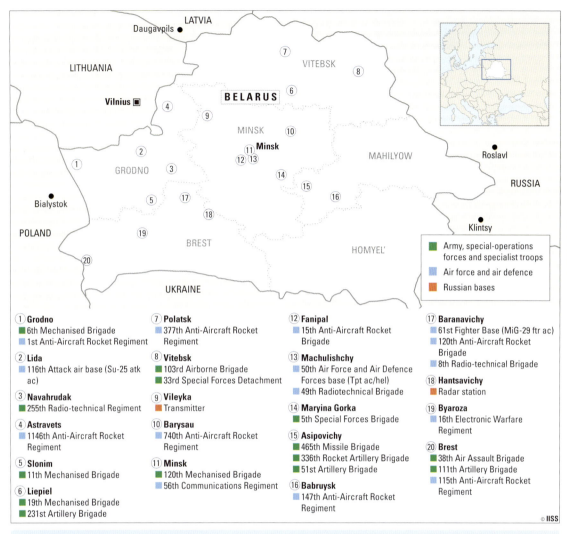

▲ Map 5 **Belarus: principal military bases**

drafted for full-time military service. The armed forces are increasing reserve service, which includes usually university-educated recruits serving for shorter periods over the course of two years. Later, these reserves attend refresher courses and take part in military exercises. Conscripts do not have the freedom to choose whether to do full conscription service or reserve service. Minsk is also looking to increase the professional component, and the share of professional servicemen and women in the army rose from 16% in 2014 to 20% at the beginning of 2018.

Army

While the army still contains remnants of the Soviet era, there are lines of modernisation. The government pays particular attention to special-operations forces and rocket and missile forces. No spending figures are published, but the intensive involvement of special-operations forces in exercises and the development of new weapons for the rocket and missile units provides evidence for this.

Minsk's reliance on Russia for air-defence equipment has led to lower levels of investment in that domain. In recent years, however, Belarus has only obtained from Russia some *Tor*-M2E SAM systems, second-hand S-300PS (SA-10 *Grumble*) SAM systems (for the air force), Yak-130 aircraft and Mi-8MTV-5 helicopters.

Minsk plans to modernise its T-72 tanks, in both Belarusian and Russian plants, and to purchase more Belarusian-manufactured armoured vehicles, namely the *Volat* V1 armoured utility vehicle and the *Kaiman* armoured reconnaissance vehicle, and the Belarusian-modernised BTR-70MB1 armoured personnel carrier. Planned acquisitions for 2018 included *Tor*-M2E air-defence systems and radars from Russia, and a number of uninhabited aerial vehicles (UAVs), including types designed for artillery targeting and reconnaissance.

Air force

The air force has been incrementally retiring sophisticated platforms, such as Su-24 and Su-27 combat aircraft and Mi-24 attack helicopters, without identified replacements. Officials insist that the Yak-130 training/light-attack aircraft can take on the roles of most of these systems. The delivery of 12 Su-30SM aircraft from Russia was due to start in 2018 but has been postponed.

Annual flying hours for pilots have increased but remain at a relatively low level. In the Soviet era, flying hours amounted to around 120 each year per fighter pilot; by the late 2010s, this had fallen to just 70–75 hours. Minsk considers the reduced capabilities of the Belarusian Air Force to be as much a problem for Russia as for Belarus. For many years, it seemed that Minsk expected Moscow to deliver newer aircraft, either for a symbolic fee or as payment in goods. Conversely, Moscow has unsuccessfully tried – since at least the beginning of 2013 – to have Minsk accept the deployment of a Russian Air Force regiment in Belarus.

Training and cooperation

Belarus has established military training departments offering various programmes in major civilian universities. After establishing an aviation-training capability in the 2000s, pilots can now train at the Military Academy and civilian Minsk State Higher Aviation College.

The armed forces train on a bilateral and multilateral basis with Russia but also with CSTO forces – the Belarusian 103rd Airborne Brigade is part of the CSTO Collective Rapid Reaction Force (KSOR) – as well as China. Belarusian special-operations troops trained with their Chinese counterparts most recently in 2018 in China, while People's Liberation Army troops last exercised in Belarus in 2017. In May 2018, Minsk also held its first joint drills with Kazakhstan. Belarus also takes part in NATO's Partnership for Peace programme and, according to the foreign ministry, there have been about 125 joint Belarus–NATO activities since 1997. In 2015–16, Belarus signed bilateral military-cooperation agreements with its three neighbouring NATO member countries, Latvia, Lithuania and Poland.

Army exercises mostly focus on counter-insurgency and urban warfare. Minsk has retired numerous types of equipment that would be required for offensive operations, especially armour and artillery, bombers and attack helicopters, and has abandoned some military facilities; for example, its only military-helicopter base is in Kobryn, on the border with Ukraine. Belarus has not purchased modern mechanised armoured vehicles in significant numbers, except for light-armoured platforms.

Defence economics and industry

Unlike its neighbours, Belarus has not responded to growing regional tensions with more than a modest defence-budget increase. From a low point of US$506 million in 2016, the 2018 budget reached US$629m. Indeed, not only does Minsk see no pressing need for larger investments in national security, it has little money for these. In 2012, Minsk urged Moscow to contribute to the financing of the Belarusian armed forces, stressing their importance to Russia. In February 2018, Lukashenko once again criticised Russia for failing to build up the armies of the CSTO members.

Little is spent on military equipment and Minsk looks to avoid imports, preferring to produce it domestically, even if this results in weaponry of only limited capability. That is particularly true of mechanised armoured vehicles. Indeed, Belarus's defence industry is one of the few sectors of national industry that is significantly developing. The armed forces' inventory is increasingly supplied by Belarusian firms, which is in itself an achievement. For a long time after independence, Belarusian industry only produced limited defence products, such as electronic and optical equipment and various components. Now, government officials openly articulate the aspiration to develop more defence products, particularly artillery and small arms. However, with the national budget constrained, defence firms are currently focused on improving their exports. According to the State Military Industrial Committee (SMIC) of Belarus, arms exports in 2017 were 15% up on the previous year, exceeding US$1 billion, though these figures are at variance with other public estimates, which place overall exports at around half that. Some Belarusian defence firms are in private hands, although they operate under the control of the SMIC.

According to an official SMIC statement, 54% of the 'international interaction' of the Belarusian defence industry involves Russian partners, which, if anything, indicates some success in internationalising Belarus's defence industries. Belarusian firms supply many of the components for Russian arms, such as electronics, tank sights and chassis for Russian missiles, including for Moscow's strategic nuclear systems. However, as early as 2010, Russia began to replace foreign components and Belarus has been no exception. However, it is understood that Moscow has so far failed to replace the Belarusian chassis in Russian missile systems or to buy the Minsk-based MZKT factory that produces them. Nonetheless, in the long term, Belarus's defence industry and the national defence-industrial base will be undermined by such efforts.

While most Belarusian defence products are modernised Soviet designs, there are some new products, including rockets and missiles. Belarus designed, with Chinese support, the *Polonez* multiple-launch rocket system, then developed and manufactured a missile for it. Together with China, Belarus has also for some time worked on designing a SAM system. In addition, Minsk is developing UAVs for the Belarusian armed forces. In 2016, it demonstrated a first-strike system, the *Burevestnik*-MB, which is armed with eight unguided 57 mm rockets, and two so-called 'kamikaze' mini-UAVs. Efforts to manufacture indigenous armoured vehicles started relatively recently. Two models of light armoured vehicle – the *Caiman* and the *Volat* V1 – and the BTR-70MB1 variant have been designed for the Belarusian armed forces.

Armenia ARM

Armenian Dram d		2017	2018	2019
GDP	d	5.57tr	6.14tr	
	US$	11.5bn	12.5bn	
per capita	US$	3,857	4,190	
Growth	%	7.5	6.0	
Inflation	%	0.9	3.0	
Def bdgt [a]	d	210bn	248bn	
	US$	435m	506m	
FMA (US)	US$	1m	0m	
US$1=d		482.70	490.17	

[a] Includes imported military equipment, excludes military pensions

Population	3,038,217					
Age	0–14	15–19	20–24	25–29	30–64	65 plus
Male	10.0%	3.0%	3.4%	4.3%	23.1%	4.7%
Female	8.7%	2.7%	3.3%	4.4%	25.3%	7.0%

Capabilities

The armed forces' main focus is territorial defence, given continuing tensions with neighbouring Azerbaijan over Nagorno-Karabakh. In early 2018, a Modernisation Programme was released for the period 2018–24. Despite economic constraints, the document outlined the ambitious goal of reorganising the command structure and modernising the equipment inventory. The programme includes sections on cyber- and information-domain capabilities. Armenia is a member of the CSTO and maintains strong defence ties with Russia, centred on equipment-procurement, technical-advice and personnel-training programmes. Military doctrine remains influenced by Russian thinking. Armenia is also engaged in a NATO Individual Partnership Action Plan. Conscription continues, but there is a growing cohort of professional officers. The armed forces have deployed on NATO and UN missions in Afghanistan, Kosovo and Lebanon, providing learning opportunities. Personnel train regularly and take part in annual CSTO exercises and with Russia in bilateral drills. Equipment is mainly of Russian origin. Agreements have been reached in recent years to purchase modern Russian systems. Serviceability and maintenance of mainly ageing aircraft have been a problem for the air force. There is some capacity to manufacture defence equipment for the domestic market, including electro-optics, light weapons and UAVs, but Armenia is reliant on Russia for other equipment platforms and systems.

ACTIVE 44,800 (Army 41,850 Air/AD Aviation Forces (Joint) 1,100 other Air Defence Forces 1,850)
Paramilitary 4,300
Conscript liability 24 months

RESERVE
Some mobilisation reported, possibly 210,000 with military service within 15 years

ORGANISATIONS BY SERVICE

Army 22,900; 18,950 conscripts (total 41,850)
FORCES BY ROLE
SPECIAL FORCES
  1 SF bde
MANOEUVRE
  Mechanised
  1 (1st) corps (1 recce bn, 1 tk bn, 2 MR regt, 1 maint bn)
  1 (2nd) corps (1 recce bn, 1 tk bn, 2 MR regt, 1 lt inf regt, 1 arty bn)
  1 (3rd) corps (1 recce bn, 1 tk bn, 4 MR regt, 1 lt inf regt, 1 arty bn, 1 MRL bn, 1 sigs bn, 1 maint bn)
  1 (4th) corps (4 MR regt; 1 SP arty bn; 1 sigs bn)
  1 (5th) corps (with 2 fortified areas) (1 MR regt)
  Other
  1 indep MR trg bde
COMBAT SUPPORT
  1 arty bde
  1 MRL bde
  1 AT regt
  1 AD bde
  2 AD regt
  2 (radiotech) AD regt
  1 engr regt

EQUIPMENT BY TYPE
ARMOURED FIGHTING VEHICLES
  MBT 109: 3 T-54; 5 T-55; 101 T-72A/B
  RECCE 12 BRM-1K (CP)
  IFV 231: 75 BMP-1; 6 BMP-1K (CP); 150 BMP-2
  APC • APC (W) 130: 8 BTR-60; 100 BTR-60 look-a-like; 18 BTR-70; 4 BTR-80
ENGINEERING & MAINTENANCE VEHICLES
  AEV MT-LB
  ARV BREhM-D; BREM-1
ANTI-TANK/ANTI-INFRASTRUCTURE
  MSL • SP 22+: 9 9P148 *Konkurs* (AT-5 *Spandrel*); 13 9P149 *Shturm* (AT-6 *Spiral*); 9K129 *Kornet*-E (AT-14 *Spriggan*)
ARTILLERY 232
  SP 38: **122mm** 10 2S1 *Gvozdika*; **152mm** 28 2S3 *Akatsiya*
  TOWED 131: **122mm** 69 D-30; **152mm** 62: 26 2A36 *Giatsint*-B; 2 D-1; 34 D-20
  MRL 57: **122mm** 47 BM-21 *Grad*; **273mm** 4 WM-80; **300mm** 6 9A52 *Smerch*
  MOR 120mm 12 M120
SURFACE-TO-SURFACE MISSILE LAUNCHERS
  SRBM • Conventional 16: 8 9K72 *Elbrus* (SS-1C *Scud* B); 4 9K79 *Tochka* (SS-21 *Scarab*); 4 9K720 *Iskander*-E
UNMANNED AERIAL VEHICLES
  ISR • Light 15 *Krunk*
AIR DEFENCE
  SAM
    Medium-range 2K11 *Krug* (SA-4 *Ganef*); S-75 *Dvina* (SA-2 *Guideline*); 9K37M *Buk*-M1 (SA-11 *Gadfly*)
    Short-range 2K12 *Kub* (SA-6 *Gainful*); S-125 *Pechora* (SA-3 *Goa*)
    Point-defence 9K33 *Osa* (SA-8 *Gecko*); 9K310 *Igla*-1 (SA-16 *Gimlet*); 9K38 *Igla* (SA-18 *Grouse*); 9K333 *Verba*; 9K338 *Igla*-S (SA-24 *Grinch*)
  GUNS
    SP 23mm ZSU-23-4
    TOWED 23mm ZU-23-2

Air and Air Defence Aviation Forces 1,100
1 Air & AD Joint Command

FORCES BY ROLE
GROUND ATTACK
1 sqn with Su-25/Su-25UBK *Frogfoot*
EQUIPMENT BY TYPE
AIRCRAFT 15 combat capable
ATK 15: 13 Su-25 *Frogfoot*; 2 Su-25UBK *Frogfoot*
TPT 4: **Heavy** 3 Il-76 *Candid;* **PAX** 1 A319CJ
TRG 14: 4 L-39 *Albatros*; 10 Yak-52
HELICOPTERS
ATK 7 Mi-24P *Hind*
ISR 4: 2 Mi-24K *Hind*; 2 Mi-24R *Hind* (cbt spt)
MRH 10 Mi-8MT (cbt spt)
C2 2 Mi-9 *Hip* G (cbt spt)
TPT • **Light** 7 PZL Mi-2 *Hoplite*
AIR DEFENCE • SAM • **Long-range** S-300PT (SA-10 *Grumble*); S-300PS (SA-10 *Grumble*)

Paramilitary 4,300

Police
FORCES BY ROLE
MANOEUVRE
Other
4 paramilitary bn
EQUIPMENT BY TYPE
ARMOURED FIGHTING VEHICLES
RECCE 5 BRM-1K (CP)
IFV 45: 44 BMP-1; 1 BMP-1K (CP)
APC • **APC (W)** 24 BTR-60/BTR-70/BTR-152
ABCV 5 BMD-1

Border Troops
Ministry of National Security
EQUIPMENT BY TYPE
ARMOURED FIGHTING VEHICLES
RECCE 3 BRM-1K (CP)
IFV 35 BMP-1
APC • **APC (W)** 23: 5 BTR-60; 18 BTR-70
ABCV 5 BMD-1

DEPLOYMENT

AFGHANISTAN: NATO • *Operation Resolute Support* 121
ALBANIA: OSCE • Albania 1
LEBANON: UN • UNIFIL 33
MALI: UN • MINUSMA 1
MOLDOVA: OSCE • Moldova 1
SERBIA: NATO • KFOR 40
UKRAINE: OSCE • Ukraine 2

FOREIGN FORCES
OSCE figures represent total Minsk Conference mission personnel in both Armenia and Azerbaijan
Bosnia-Herzegovina OSCE 1
Germany OSCE 1
Moldova OSCE 2
Poland OSCE 1

Russia 3,300: 1 mil base with (1 MR bde; 74 T-72; 80 BMP-1; 80 BMP-2; 12 2S1; 12 BM-21); 1 ftr sqn with 18 MiG-29 *Fulcrum*; 1 hel sqn with 8 Mi-24P *Hind*; 4 Mi-8MT *Hip*; 2 SAM bty with S-300V (SA-12 *Gladiator/Giant*); 1 SAM bty with 2K12 *Kub* (SA-6 *Gainful*)
United Kingdom OSCE 1

Azerbaijan AZE

Azerbaijani New Manat m		2017	2018	2019
GDP	m	69.1bn	77.5bn	
	US$	40.7bn	45.6bn	
per capita	US$	4,141	4,587	
Growth	%	0.1	1.3	
Inflation	%	13.0	3.5	
Def bdgt [a]	m	2.64bn	2.74bn	
	US$	1.55bn	1.61bn	
FMA (US)	US$	1m	0m	
US$1=m		1.70	1.70	

[a] Official defence budget. Excludes a significant proportion of procurement outlays

Population	10,046,516					
Age	0–14	15–19	20–24	25–29	30–64	65 plus
Male	12.3%	3.4%	4.0%	4.9%	22.3%	2.6%
Female	10.8%	2.9%	3.7%	4.7%	24.1%	4.2%

Capabilities

The armed forces' principal focus is territorial defence, in light of continuing tensions with neighbouring Armenia over Nagorno-Karabakh. A defence doctrine was adopted in 2010. Azerbaijan maintains a defence relationship with NATO and is in the fifth cycle (2017–19) of its NATO Individual Partnership Action Plan. Azerbaijan is looking to deepen ties with Belarus, Serbia, the UK and the US through military-cooperation agreements. Defence cooperation with Moscow is focused on equipment procurement and technical advice. Readiness within Azerbaijan's conscript-based armed services varies between units. Azerbaijan has taken part in multilateral exercises and its forces have trained with Turkish troops in bilateral drills. The armed forces have little expeditionary capability though they contribute to NATO's *Operation Resolute Support* in Afghanistan. Defence modernisation and procurement has been a focus in the past decade, to replace the ageing inventory of mainly Soviet-era equipment. The air force in particular suffers from maintenance problems. Recent orders include for air-defence and artillery systems and wheeled and tracked armoured vehicles, predominantly of Russian origin. Azerbaijan's limited but growing defence-industrial capabilities are centred on the Ministry of Defence Industry, which manages and oversees the production of small arms and light weapons. While the country is reliant on external suppliers for major defence-equipment platforms and systems, some defence companies have started to export to foreign markets.

ACTIVE 66,950 (Army 56,850 Navy 2,200 Air 7,900)
Paramilitary 15,000
Conscript liability 18 months (12 for graduates)

RESERVE 300,000
Some mobilisation reported; 300,000 with military service within 15 years

ORGANISATIONS BY SERVICE

Army 56,850
FORCES BY ROLE
COMMAND
  5 corps HQ
MANOEUVRE
  Mechanised
  4 MR bde
  Light
  19 MR bde
  Other
  1 sy bde
COMBAT SUPPORT
  1 arty bde
  1 arty trg bde
  1 MRL bde
  1 AT bde
  1 engr bde
  1 sigs bde
COMBAT SERVICE SUPPORT
  1 log bde
EQUIPMENT BY TYPE
ARMOURED FIGHTING VEHICLES
  MBT 439: 95 T-55; 244 T-72A/AV/B; 100 T-90S
  RECCE 15 BRM-1
  IFV 216: 43 BMP-1; 33 BMP-2; 88 BMP-3; 7 BTR-80A; 45+ BTR-82A
  APC 568
    APC (T) 336 MT-LB
    APC (W) 142: 10 BTR-60; 132 BTR-70
    PPV 90: 45 *Marauder*; 45 *Matador*
  AUV 65+: 35 *Cobra*; 30+ *Sand Cat*
  ABCV 20 BMD-1
ENGINEERING & MAINTENANCE VEHICLES
  AEV IMR-2; MT-LB
  ARV BREM-L *Brelianka*
  MW *Bozena*; GW-3 (minelayer)
ANTI-TANK/ANTI-INFRASTRUCTURE
  SP 10 9P157-2 *Khrizantema*-S (AT-15 *Springer*)
  MSL • MANPATS 9K11 *Malyutka* (AT-3 *Sagger*); 9K111 *Fagot* (AT-4 *Spigot*); 9K111-1 *Konkurs* (AT-5 *Spandrel*); 9K115 *Metis* (AT-7 *Saxhorn*); *Spike*-LR
ARTILLERY 598
  SP 96: **122mm** 46 2S1 *Gvozdika*; **152mm** 33: 6 2S3 *Akatsiya*; 18 2S19 *Msta*-S; 9 M-77 *Dana*; **155mm** 5 ATMOS 2000; **203mm** 12 2S7 *Pion*
  TOWED 207: **122mm** 129 D-30; **130mm** 36 M-46; **152mm** 42: 18 2A36 *Giatsint*-B; 24 D-20
  GUN/MOR 120mm 36: 18 2S9 NONA-S; 18 2S31 *Vena*
  MRL 147: **122mm** 60+: 43 BM-21 *Grad*; 9+ IMI *Lynx*; 8 RM-70 *Vampir*; **128mm** 12 RAK-12; **220mm** 18 TOS-1A; **300mm** 36: 30 9A52 *Smerch*; 6+ *Polonez*; **302mm** 21 T-300 *Kasirga*
  MOR 120mm 112: 5 *Cardom*; 107 M-1938 (PM-38)
SURFACE-TO-SURFACE MISSILE LAUNCHERS
  SRBM • Conventional 6: 2 IAI LORA; ε4 9M79 *Tochka* (SS-21 *Scarab*)

UNMANNED AERIAL VEHICLES
  ISR • Medium 3 *Aerostar*
AIR DEFENCE
  SAM
    Medium-range 2K11 *Krug* (SA-4 *Ganef*)
    Point-defence 9K33 *Osa* (SA-8 *Gecko*); 9K35 *Strela*-10 (SA-13 *Gopher*); 9K32 *Strela* (SA-7 *Grail*)‡; 9K34 *Strela*-3 (SA-14 *Gremlin*); 9K310 *Igla*-1 (SA-16 *Gimlet*); 9K338 *Igla*-S (SA-24 *Grinch*)
  GUNS
    SP 23mm ZSU-23-4
    TOWED 23mm ZU-23-2

Navy 2,200
EQUIPMENT BY TYPE
PATROL AND COASTAL COMBATANTS 11
  CORVETTES • FS 1 *Kusar* (ex-FSU *Petya II*) with 2 RBU 6000 *Smerch* 2 A/S mor, 2 twin 76mm gun
  PSO 2: 1 *Luga* (*Wodnik* 2) (FSU Project 888; additional trg role); 1 *Neftegaz* (Project B-92) (ex-Coast Guard)
  PCC 3: 2 *Petrushka* (FSU UK-3; additional trg role); 1 *Shelon* (ex-FSU Project 1388M)
  PB 3: 1 *Araz* (ex-TUR AB 25); 1 *Bryza* (ex-FSU Project 722); 1 *Poluchat* (ex-FSU Project 368)
  PBF 3 *Stenka*
MINE WARFARE • MINE COUNTERMEASURES 4
  MHC 4: 2 *Korund* (*Yevgenya*) (Project 1258); 2 *Yakhont* (FSU *Sonya*)
AMPHIBIOUS 6
  LSM 3: 1 *Polnochny A* (FSU Project 770) (capacity 6 MBT; 180 troops); 2 *Polnochny B* (FSU Project 771) (capacity 6 MBT; 180 troops)
  LCM 3: 2 T-4 (FSU); 1 *Vydra*† (FSU) (capacity either 3 MBT or 200 troops)
LOGISTICS AND SUPPORT • AGS 1 (FSU Project 10470)

Air Force and Air Defence 7,900
FORCES BY ROLE
FIGHTER
  1 sqn with MiG-29 *Fulcrum*; MiG-29UB *Fulcrum*
FIGHTER/GROUND ATTACK
  1 regt with Su-24 *Fencer*; Su-25 *Frogfoot*; Su-25UB *Frogfoot* B
TRANSPORT
  1 sqn with An-12 *Cub*; Yak-40 *Codling*
TRAINING
  1 sqn with L-39 *Albatros*
ATTACK/TRANSPORT HELICOPTER
  1 regt with Ka-32 *Helix C*; Mi-8 *Hip*; Mi-24 *Hind*; PZL Mi-2 *Hoplite*
EQUIPMENT BY TYPE
AIRCRAFT 37 combat capable
  FTR 16: 14 MiG-29 *Fulcrum*; 2 MiG-29UB *Fulcrum*
  ATK 21: 2 Su-24 *Fencer*†; 16 Su-25 *Frogfoot*; 3 Su-25UB *Frogfoot* B
  TPT 4: **Medium** 1 An-12 *Cub*; **Light** 3 Yak-40 *Codling*
  TRG 12 L-39 *Albatros*
HELICOPTERS
  ATK 26 Mi-24 *Hind*
  MRH: 20+ Mi-17-IV *Hip*

TPT 24: **Medium** 17: 1 Bell 412; 3 Ka-32 *Helix* C; 13 Mi-8 *Hip* **Light** 7 PZL Mi-2 *Hoplite*
UAV • ISR 16: **Heavy** 1 *Heron*; **Medium** 15: 4 *Aerostar*; 10+ *Hermes* 450; 1 *Hermes* 900
AIR DEFENCE • SAM
  Long-range S-200 *Vega* (SA-5 *Gammon*); S-300PM/PMU2
  Medium-range S-75 *Dvina* (SA-2 *Guideline*); 9K37M *Buk*-M1 (SA-11 *Gadfly*); *Buk*-MB; S-125-2TM *Pechora*-2TM (SA-26)
  Short-range *Abisr*
AIR-LAUNCHED MISSILES
  AAM • IR R-60 (AA-8 *Aphid*); R-73 (AA-11 *Archer*) **IR/SARH** R-27 (AA-10 *Alamo*)
  ASM *Barrier*-V

Paramilitary ε15,000

State Border Service ε5,000
Ministry of Internal Affairs
EQUIPMENT BY TYPE
ARMOURED FIGHTING VEHICLES
  IFV 168 BMP-1/BMP-2
  APC • **APC (W)** 19 BTR-60/70/80
ARTILLERY • MRL 122mm 3 T-122
HELICOPTERS • ATK 24 Mi-35M *Hind*
UNMANNED AERIAL VEHICLES
  ISR • **Medium** *Hermes* 900

Coast Guard
The Coast Guard was established in 2005 as part of the State Border Service
EQUIPMENT BY TYPE
PATROL AND COASTAL COMBATANTS 16
  PCG 3 *Sa'ar* 62 with 1 8-cell lnchr with *Spike* NLOS SSM, 1 hel landing platform
  PBF 9: 1 *Osa* II (FSU Project 205); 6 *Shaldag* V; 2 Silver Ships 48ft
  PB 4: 2 Baltic 150; 1 *Point* (US); 1 *Grif* (FSU *Zhuk*)
LOGISTICS AND SUPPORT 5
  ARS 1 *Iva* (FSU *Vikhr*)
  ATF 4 *Neftegaz* (Project B-92) (also used for patrol duties)

Internal Troops 10,000+
Ministry of Internal Affairs
EQUIPMENT BY TYPE
ARMOURED FIGHTING VEHICLES
  APC • **APC (W)** 7 BTR-60/BTR-70/BTR-80

DEPLOYMENT

AFGHANISTAN: NATO • *Operation Resolute Support* 120
BOSNIA-HERZEGOVINA: OSCE • Bosnia and Herzegovina 1
UKRAINE: OSCE • Ukraine 1

FOREIGN FORCES
OSCE figures represent total Minsk Conference mission personnel in both Armenia and Azerbaijan

Bosnia-Herzegovina OSCE 1
Germany OSCE 1
Moldova OSCE 2
Poland OSCE 1
United Kingdom OSCE 1

TERRITORY WHERE THE GOVERNMENT DOES NOT EXERCISE EFFECTIVE CONTROL

Nagorno-Karabakh was part of Azerbaijan, but mostly populated by ethnic Armenians. In 1988, when inter-ethnic clashes between Armenians and Azeris erupted in Azerbaijan, the local authorities declared their intention to secede and join Armenia. Baku rejected this and armed conflict erupted. A ceasefire was brokered in 1994; since then, Armenia has controlled most of Nagorno-Karabakh. While Armenia provides political, economic and military support to Nagorno-Karabakh, the region has declared itself independent – although this has not been recognised by any other state, including Armenia. Baku claims Nagorno-Karabakh and the occupied territories as part of Azerbaijan. Data presented here represents an assessment of the de facto situation.

Nagorno-Karabakh
Available estimates vary with reference to military holdings in Nagorno-Karabakh. Main battle tanks are usually placed at around 200–300 in number, with similar numbers for other armoured combat vehicles and artillery pieces, and small numbers of helicopters. Overall personnel-strength estimates are between 18,000 and 20,000. Some of the equipment listed may belong to Armenian forces.
EQUIPMENT BY TYPE
ARMOURED FIGHTING VEHICLES
  MBT T-72
  RECCE BRDM-2
  IFV BMP-1; BMP-2
ANTI-TANK/ANTI-INFRASTRUCTURE
  MSL
    SP 9P148 *Konkurs* (AT-5 *Spandrel*); 9P149 *Shturm* (AT-6 *Spiral*)
    MANPATS 9K111-1 *Konkurs* (AT-5 *Spandrel*)
  RCL 73mm SPG-9
ARTILLERY 232
  SP 122mm 2S1 *Gvozdika*; **152mm** 2S3 *Akatsiya*
  TOWED 122mm D-30; **152mm** 2A36 *Giatsint*-B; D-20
  MRL 122mm BM-21 *Grad*; **273mm** WM-80
  MOR 120mm M-74/M-75
SURFACE-TO-SURFACE MISSILE LAUNCHERS
  SRBM • **Conventional** 9K72 *Elbrus* (SS-1C *Scud* B)
HELICOPTERS
  ATK 5 Mi-24 *Hind*
  MRH 5 Mi-8MT *Hip*
AIR DEFENCE
  SAM
    Medium-range 2K11 *Krug* (SA-4 *Ganef*); S-75 *Dvina* (SA-2 *Guideline*)
    Short-range 2K12 *Kub* (SA-6 *Gainful*); S-125 *Pechora* (SA-3 *Goa*)

Point-defence 9K33 *Osa* (SA-8 *Gecko*); 9K310 *Igla*-1 (SA-16 *Gimlet*); 9K38 *Igla* (SA-18 *Grouse*)
GUNS
  SP 23mm ZSU-23-4
  TOWED 23mm ZU-23-2

Belarus BLR

Belarusian Ruble r		2017	2018	2019
GDP	r	105bn	115bn	
	US$	54.4bn	56.9bn	
per capita	US$	5,727.00	6,020.00	
Growth	%	2.4	4.0	
Inflation	%	6.0	5.5	
Def bdgt	r	1.03bn	1.22bn	
	US$	531m	604m	
US$1=r		1.93	2.02	
Population	9,527,543			

Age	0–14	15–19	20–24	25–29	30–64	65 plus
Male	8.1%	2.4%	2.8%	3.8%	24.4%	4.8%
Female	7.6%	2.3%	2.7%	3.7%	26.9%	10.2%

Capabilities

Located between Russia and NATO European members, the main task of Belarus's armed forces is maintaining territorial integrity. The country's latest military doctrine was approved in July 2016, and identified as security challenges 'hybrid methods' and 'colour revolutions'. It also called for smaller, more mobile forces with improved counter-terrorism capabilities. Belarus is a member of the CSTO. Russia remains the country's principal defence partner, though Minsk has also looked to improve defence cooperation with China and Turkey. The forces remain conscript-based and train regularly with other CSTO partners. There has been increased emphasis on the training of territorial-defence troops to allow them to better operate with the regular forces. There is a small heavy-airlift fleet that could be supplemented by civil transport aircraft, and Minsk has a special-forces brigade trained for the air-assault role. There is no requirement to independently deploy and sustain the armed forces, but they could do so as a part of the CSTO. Russia continues to be Minsk's main defence-equipment supplier. In recent years, Belarus has received air-defence systems and advanced combat-trainer/light-attack aircraft from Moscow. A small number of Su-30SM multi-role fighters is on order. The local defence industry manufactures vehicles, guided weapons and electronic-warfare systems, among other equipment. However, there is no capacity to design or manufacture modern combat aircraft. The sector also undertakes upgrade work for foreign customers.

ACTIVE 45,350 (Army 10,700 Air 11,750 Special Operations Forces 5,900 Joint 17,000) **Paramilitary 110,000**

Conscript liability 18 months (alternative service option)

RESERVE 289,500 (Joint 289,500 with mil service within last 5 years)

ORGANISATIONS BY SERVICE

Army 10,700
FORCES BY ROLE
COMMAND
  2 comd HQ (West & North West)
MANOEUVRE
  Mechanised
  2 mech bde
  2 mech bde(-)
COMBAT SUPPORT
  2 arty bde
  1 engr bde
  1 engr regt
EQUIPMENT BY TYPE
ARMOURED FIGHTING VEHICLES
  MBT 542: 527 T-72B; 15 T-72B3 mod
  RECCE 132 BRM-1; *Cayman* BRDM
  IFV 932 BMP-2
  APC • APC (T) 58 MT-LB
  AUV 8 CS/VN3B mod; GAZ *Tigr*
ENGINEERING & MAINTENANCE VEHICLES
  AEV BAT-2; IMR-2; MT-LB
  VLB 24: 20 MTU-20; 4 MT-55A
  MW UR-77
NBC VEHICLES BRDM-2RKhB; RKhM-4; RKhm-K
ANTI-TANK/ANTI-INFRASTRUCTURE • MSL
  SP 160: 75 9P148 *Konkurs*; 85 9P149 *Shturm*
  MANPATS 9K111 *Fagot* (AT-4 *Spigot*); 9K111-1 *Konkurs* (AT-5 *Spandrel*); 9K115 *Metis* (AT-7 *Saxhorn*)
ARTILLERY 583
  SP 333: **122mm** 125 2S1 *Gvozdika*; **152mm** 208: 125 2S3 *Akatsiya*; 71 2S5; 12 2S19 *Msta-S*
  TOWED **152mm** 72 2A65 *Msta-B*
  MRL 164: **122mm** 128 BM-21 *Grad*; **220mm** 36 9P140 *Uragan*
  MOR **120mm** 14 2S12
AIR DEFENCE
  SAM Point-defence 2K22 *Tunguska* (SA-19 *Grison*)
  GUNS • SP 23mm ZU-23-2 (tch)

Air Force and Air Defence Forces 11,750
FORCES BY ROLE
FIGHTER
  2 sqn with MiG-29/S/UB *Fulcrum*
GROUND ATTACK
  2 sqn with Su-25K/UBK *Frogfoot* A/B
TRANSPORT
  1 base with An-12 *Cub*; An-24 *Coke*; An-26 *Curl*; Il-76 *Candid*; Tu-134 *Crusty*
TRAINING
  Some sqn with L-39 *Albatros*
ATTACK HELICOPTER
  Some sqn with Mi-24 *Hind*
TRANSPORT HELICOPTER
  Some (cbt spt) sqn with Mi-8 *Hip*; Mi-8MTV-5 *Hip*; Mi-26 *Halo*
EQUIPMENT BY TYPE
AIRCRAFT 64 combat capable

FTR 34: 28 MiG-29 *Fulcrum*/MiG-29S *Fulcrum* C; 6 MiG-29UB *Fulcrum* B
FGA (21 Su-27/UB *Flanker* B/C non-operational/stored)
ATK 22 Su-25K/UBK *Frogfoot* A/B
TPT 8: **Heavy** 2 Il-76 *Candid* (+9 civ Il-76 available for mil use); **Light** 6: 1 An-24 *Coke*; 4 An-26 *Curl*; 1 Tu-134 *Crusty*
TRG 8+: Some L-39 *Albatros*; 8 Yak-130 *Mitten**
HELICOPTERS
ATK 12 Mi-24 *Hind*
TPT 26: **Heavy** 6 Mi-26 *Halo*; **Medium** 20: 8 Mi-8 *Hip*; 12 Mi-8MTV-5 *Hip*
AIR-LAUNCHED MISSILES
AAM • IR R-60 (AA-8 *Aphid*); R-73 (AA-11 *Archer*)
SARH R-27R (AA-10 *Alamo* A)
ASM Kh-25 (AS-10 *Karen*); Kh-29 (AS-14 *Kedge*)
ARM Kh-58 (AS-11 *Kilter*) (likely WFU)

Air Defence

AD data from Uzal Baranovichi EW radar

FORCES BY ROLE
AIR DEFENCE
 1 bde S-300PS (SA-10B *Grumble*)
 3 regt with S-300PS (SA-10 *Grumble*)
 1 bde with 9K37 *Buk* (SA-11 *Gadfly*); 9K332 *Tor*-M2E (SA-15 *Gauntlet*)
 1 regt with 9K322 *Tor*-M2E
 2 regt with 9K33 *Osa* (SA-8 *Gecko*)
EQUIPMENT BY TYPE
AIR DEFENCE • SAM
 Long-range S-300PS (SA-10 *Grumble*)
 Medium-range 9K37 *Buk* (SA-11 *Gadfly*)
 Short-range 17 9K332 *Tor*-M2E (SA-15 *Gauntlet*)
 Point-defence 9K33 *Osa* (SA-8 *Gecko*); 9K35 *Strela*-10 (SA-13 *Gopher*)

Special Operations Command 5,900

FORCES BY ROLE
SPECIAL FORCES
 1 SF bde
MANOEUVRE
 Mechanised
 2 mech bde
EQUIPMENT BY TYPE
ARMOURED FIGHTING VEHICLES
 APC • APC (W) 185: 32 BTR-70M1; 153 BTR-80
ARTILLERY 42
 TOWED 122mm 24 D-30
 GUN/MOR • TOWED 120mm 18 2B23 NONA-M1
ANTI-TANK/ANTI-INFRASTRUCTURE • MSL
 MANPATS 9K111 *Fagot* (AT-4 *Spigot*); 9K111-1 *Konkurs* (AT-5 *Spandrel*); 9K115 *Metis* (AT-7 *Saxhorn*)

Joint 17,000 (Centrally controlled units and MoD staff)

FORCES BY ROLE
SURFACE-TO-SURFACE MISSILE
 1 SRBM bde
COMBAT SUPPORT
 1 arty bde
 1 MRL bde
 2 engr bde
 1 EW unit
 1 NBC regt
 1 ptn bridging regt
 2 sigs bde
EQUIPMENT BY TYPE
ARMOURED FIGHTING VEHICLES
 APC • APC (T) 20 MT-LB
NBC VEHICLES BRDM-2RKhB; RKhM-4; RKhM-K
ARTILLERY 112
 SP 152mm 36 2S5 *Giatsint*-S
 TOWED 152mm 36 2A65 *Msta*-B
 MRL 300mm 40: 36 9A52 *Smerch*; 4 *Polonez*
SURFACE-TO-SURFACE MISSILE LAUNCHERS
 SRBM • **Conventional** 96: 36 9K79 *Tochka* (SS-21 *Scarab*); 60 9K72 *Elbrus* (SS-1C *Scud* B)

Paramilitary 110,000

State Border Troops 12,000
Ministry of Interior

Militia 87,000
Ministry of Interior

Internal Troops 11,000

DEPLOYMENT

LEBANON: UN • UNIFIL 5
UKRAINE: OSCE • Ukraine 7

Georgia GEO

Georgian Lari		2017	2018	2019
GDP	lari	38.0bn	41.6bn	
	US$	15.2bn	16.7bn	
per capita	US$	4,086.00	4,506.00	
Growth	%	5.0	5.5	
Inflation	%	6.0	2.8	
Def bdgt	lari	770m	802m	790m
	US$	307m	322m	
FMA (US)	US$	37m	0m	
US$1=lari		2.51	2.49	

Population	4,926,087					
Age	0–14	15–19	20–24	25–29	30–64	65 plus
Male	9.5%	2.8%	3.2%	4.1%	21.8%	6.4%
Female	8.7%	2.4%	3.0%	4.0%	24.2%	9.9%

Capabilities

Georgia's main security preoccupations concern Russian military deployments and the breakaway regions of Abkhazia and South Ossetia. A Strategic Defence Review 2017–20 was published in April 2017. This aimed at improving personnel structures, training facilities and equipment and stressed a 'total defence' approach involving the armed forces and civil society. The document noted the importance of Georgia's reserve component for this framework. A new defence white paper was published in 2017. Long-standing security cooperation with the US includes the Georgia Defence Readiness Program, designed to boost military capabilities. The armed forces are professional and are working to develop NATO compatibility, although conscription is still active. Despite participation in several NATO multinational exercises, readiness varies greatly between units and training levels tend to be variable. Georgia's armed forces have little expeditionary logistic capabilities, contributing only to NATO's *Resolute Support* mission in Afghanistan. The backbone of the armed forces' military equipment is legacy Soviet-era systems with varying degrees of obsolescence. The Major Systems Acquisitions Strategy 2019–25 outlines efforts to procure new equipment in several areas, including air defence, anti-tank systems, artillery, intelligence and aviation. The country has only recently begun to develop a defence-industrial base, and this is intended mainly to support the armed forces. The State Military Scientific-Technical Center has demonstrated some maintenance, repair, overhaul and design capabilities for the production of light armoured vehicles.

ACTIVE 20,650 (Army 19,050 National Guard 1,600)
Paramilitary 5,400
Conscript liability 12 months

ORGANISATIONS BY SERVICE

Army 15,000; 4,050 conscript (total 19,050)
FORCES BY ROLE
SPECIAL FORCES
 1 SF bde
MANOEUVRE
 Light
 5 inf bde
 Amphibious
 2 mne bn (1 cadre)
COMBAT SUPPORT
 2 arty bde
 1 engr bde
 1 sigs bn
 1 SIGINT bn
 1 MP bn
COMBAT SERVICE SUPPORT
 1 med bn
EQUIPMENT BY TYPE
ARMOURED FIGHTING VEHICLES
 MBT 123: 23 T-55AM2; 100 T-72B/SIM1
 RECCE 5: 1 BRM-1K; 4+ *Didgori*-2
 IFV 71: 25 BMP-1; 46 BMP-2
 APC 189+
  APC (T) 69+: 3+ *Lazika*; 66 MT-LB
  APC (W) 120+: 25 BTR-70; 19 BTR-80; *Cobra*; 8+ *Didgori*-1; 3+ *Didgori*-3; 65 *Ejder*
 AUV 10+: ATF *Dingo*; 10 *Cougar*
ENGINEERING & MAINTENANCE VEHICLES
 ARV IMR-2
ANTI-TANK/ANTI-INFRASTRUCTURE
 MSL • MANPATS 9K111 *Fagot* (AT-4 *Spigot*); 9K113 *Konkurs* (AT-5 *Spandrel*); FGM-148 *Javelin*
 GUNS • TOWED ε40: **85mm** D-44; **100mm** T-12
ARTILLERY 240
 SP 67: **122mm** 20 2S1 *Gvozdika*; **152mm** 46: 32 M-77 *Dana*; 13 2S3 *Akatsiya*; 1 2S19 *Msta-S*; **203mm** 1 2S7 *Pion*

 TOWED 71: **122mm** 58 D-30; **152mm** 13: 3 2A36 *Giatsint-B*; 10 2A65 *Msta-B*
 MRL 122mm 37: 13 BM-21 *Grad*; 6 GradLAR; 18 RM-70
 MOR 120mm 65: 14 2S12 *Sani*; 33 M-75; 18 M120
AIR DEFENCE • SAM
 Short-range *Spyder*-SR
 Point-defence *Grom*; *Mistral*-2; 9K32 *Strela*-2 (SA-7 *Grail*)‡; 9K35 *Strela*-10 (SA-13 *Gopher*); 9K36 *Strela*-3 (SA-14 *Gremlin*); 9K310 *Igla*-1 (SA-16 *Gimlet*)

Aviation and Air Defence Command 1,300 (incl 300 conscript)
1 avn base, 1 hel air base
EQUIPMENT BY TYPE
AIRCRAFT 3 combat capable
 ATK 3 Su-25KM *Frogfoot* (6 Su-25 *Frogfoot* in store)
 TPT • Light 9: 6 An-2 *Colt*; 1 Tu-134A *Crusty* (VIP); 2 Yak-40 *Codling*
 TRG 9 L-29 *Delfin*
HELICOPTERS
 ATK 6 Mi-24 *Hind*
 TPT 29: **Medium** 17 Mi-8T *Hip*; **Light** 12 Bell 205 (UH-1H *Iroquois*)
UNMANNED AERIAL VEHICLES
 ISR • Medium 1+ *Hermes* 450
AIR DEFENCE • SAM
 Medium-range 9K37 *Buk*-M1 (SA-11 *Gadfly*) (1-2 bn)
 Point-defence 8 9K33 *Osa* AK (SA-8B *Gecko*) (two bty); 9K33 *Osa* AKM (6-10 updated SAM systems)

National Guard 1,600 active reservists opcon Army
FORCES BY ROLE
MANOEUVRE
 Light
 1 inf bde

Paramilitary 5,400

Border Police 5,400

Coast Guard
HQ at Poti. The Navy was merged with the Coast Guard in 2009 under the auspices of the Georgian Border Police, within the Ministry of the Interior
EQUIPMENT BY TYPE
PATROL AND COASTAL COMBATANTS 21
 PBF 6: 4 Ares 43m; 1 *Kaan* 33; 1 *Kaan* 20
 PB 15: 1 *Akhmeta*; 2 *Dauntless*; 2 *Dilos* (ex-GRC); 1 *Kutaisi* (ex-TUR AB 25); 2 *Point*; 7 *Zhuk* (3 ex-UKR)
AMPHIBIOUS • LANDING CRAFT • LCM 1 *Vydra* (ex-BLG) (capacity either 3 MBT or 200 troops)

DEPLOYMENT

AFGHANISTAN: NATO • *Operation Resolute Support* 870; 1 lt inf bn: **UN •** UNAMA 2 obs

ALBANIA: OSCE • Albania 1

CENTRAL AFRICAN REPUBLIC: EU • EUTM RCA 35

MALI: EU • EUTM Mali 1
SERBIA: OSCE • Kosovo 1
UKRAINE: OSCE • Ukraine 22

TERRITORY WHERE THE GOVERNMENT DOES NOT EXERCISE EFFECTIVE CONTROL

Following the August 2008 war between Russia and Georgia, the areas of Abkhazia and South Ossetia declared themselves independent. Data presented here represents the de facto situation and does not imply international recognition as sovereign states.

FOREIGN FORCES

Russia 7,000; 1 mil base at Gudauta (Abkhazia) with (1 MR bde; 40 T-90A; 120 BTR-82A; 18 2S3; 12 2S12; 18 BM-21; some S-300 SAM; some atk hel); 1 mil base at Djava/Tskhinvali (S. Ossetia) with (1 MR bde; 40 T-72; 120 BMP-2; 36 2S3; 12 2S12)

Kazakhstan KAZ

Kazakhstani Tenge t		2017	2018	2019
GDP	t	52.0tr	59.9tr	
	US$	159bn	184bn	
per capita	US$	8,762	9,977	
Growth	%	4.0	3.7	
Inflation	%	7.4	6.4	
Def bdgt	t	412bn	517bn	610bn
	US$	1.27bn	1.59bn	
US$1=t		326.00	325.17	

Population 18,744,548

Ethnic groups: Kazakh 63.3%; Russian 23.7%; Uzbek 2.8%; Ukraninan 2.1%; Tatar 1.3%; German 1.1%; other or unspecified 5.7%

Age	0–14	15–19	20–24	25–29	30–64	65 plus
Male	12.8%	3.2%	3.7%	4.4%	20.8%	2.8%
Female	13.2%	3.1%	3.6%	4.3%	23.0%	5.1%

Capabilities

Kazakhstan's new military doctrine, adopted in October 2017, indicates a change in focus from countering violent extremism towards a wider concern for border security and hybrid threats to national security. In May 2018, a new military branch was created to protect against cyber threats. In the army, air-mobile units are held at the highest level of readiness. Kazakhstan entered a bilateral military agreement with Uzbekistan in September 2017 to cooperate on training and education, countering violent extremism and reducing militant movements in their region. Kazakhstan has a close defence relationship with Russia, reinforced by CSTO and SCO membership, and Moscow operates a radar station at Balkhash. In 2016, in an effort to improve training, Kazakhstan broadened the curriculum taught in military academies. Kazakhstan takes part in regional and CSTO exercises, including anti-terror drills. By regional standards, the armed forces are both relatively sizeable and well equipped, following the acquisition of significant amounts of new and upgraded materiel in recent years, primarily from Russia. Fighter/ground-attack aircraft seem to be a particular priority, with new orders placed in 2018. However, airworthiness across the air inventory remains problematic. Russia has also supplied Kazakhstan with S-300PS self-propelled surface-to-air missile systems as part of a Joint Air-Defence Agreement, boosting its long-range air-defence capability. Kazakhstan is growing its indigenous defence industry, and exports increased in 2017–18. A joint venture with South African firm Paramount Engineering will deliver *Arlan* 4x4 vehicles. Further joint ventures and production of rotary-wing and medium-lift fixed-wing aircraft are envisaged in cooperation with European companies.

ACTIVE 39,000 (Army 20,000 Navy 3,000 Air 12,000 MoD 4,000) **Paramilitary 31,500**
Conscript liability 12 months (due to be abolished)

ORGANISATIONS BY SERVICE

Army 20,000

4 regional comd: Astana, East, West and Southern
FORCES BY ROLE
MANOEUVRE
 Armoured
  1 tk bde
 Mechanised
  3 mech bde
 Air Manoeuvre
  4 air aslt bde
COMBAT SUPPORT
 3 arty bde
 1 SSM unit
 3 cbt engr bde
EQUIPMENT BY TYPE
ARMOURED FIGHTING VEHICLES
 MBT 300 T-72BA
 RECCE 100: 40 BRDM-2; 60 BRM-1
 IFV 607: 500 BMP-2; 107 BTR-80A
 APC 369+
  APC (T) 150 MT-LB
  APC (W) 209: 2 BTR-3E; 190 BTR-80; 17 *Cobra*
  PPV 10+ *Arlan*
ENGINEERING & MAINTENANCE VEHICLES
 AEV MT-LB
ANTI-TANK/ANTI-INFRASTRUCTURE
 MSL
  SP 3+: 3 BMP-T; HMMWV with 9K111-1 *Konkurs* (AT-5 *Spandrel*); 9P149 *Shturm* (MT-LB with AT-6 *Spiral*)
  MANPATS 9K111 *Fagot* (AT-4 *Spigot*); 9K111-1 *Konkurs* (AT-5 *Spandrel*); 9K115 *Metis* (AT-7 *Saxhorn*)
 GUNS 100mm 68 MT-12/T-12
ARTILLERY 611
 SP 246: **122mm** 126: 120 2S1 *Gvozdika*; 6 *Semser*; **152mm** 120 2S3 *Akatsiya*
 TOWED 150: **122mm** 100 D-30; **152mm** 50 2A65 *Msta*-B (**122mm** up to 300 D-30 in store)
 GUN/MOR 120mm 25 2S9 NONA-S
 MRL 127: **122mm** 100 BM-21 *Grad*; **220mm** 3 TOS-1A; **300mm** 24: 6 BM-30 *Smerch*; 18 IMI *Lynx* (with 50 msl) (**122mm** 100 BM-21 *Grad*; **220mm** 180 9P140 *Uragan* all in store)
 MOR 63 **SP 120mm** 18 *Cardom*; **120mm** 45 2B11 *Sani/* M120

SURFACE-TO-SURFACE MISSILE LAUNCHERS
SRBM • Conventional 12 9K79 *Tochka* (SS-21 *Scarab*)

Navy 3,000
EQUIPMENT BY TYPE
PATROL AND COASTAL COMBATANTS 12
  PCGM 2 *Kazakhstan* with 1 *Barrier*-BK lnchr with 4 RK-2B SSM, 1 *Arbalet*-K lnchr with 4 9K38 *Igla* (SA-18 *Grouse*), 1 AK306 CIWS
  PCC 1 *Kazakhstan* with 1 122mm MRL
  PBF 3 *Sea Dolphin*
  PB 6: 3 *Archangel*; 1 *Dauntless*; 1 *Turk* (AB 25); 1 Other
MINE WARFARE • MINE COUNTERMEASURES 1
  MCC 1 *Alatau* (Project 10750E) with 1 AK306 CIWS
LOGISTICS AND SUPPORT • AGS 1 *Zhaik*

Coastal Defence
FORCES BY ROLE
MANOEUVRE
  Mechanised
  1 naval inf bde
EQUIPMENT BY TYPE
ARMOURED FIGHTING VEHICLES
  IFV 70 BTR-82A

Air Force 12,000 (incl Air Defence)
FORCES BY ROLE
FIGHTER
  1 sqn with MiG-29/MiG-29UB *Fulcrum*
  2 sqn with MiG-31B/MiG-31BM *Foxhound*
FIGHTER/GROUND ATTACK
  1 sqn with MiG-27 *Flogger* D; MiG-23UB *Flogger* C
  1 sqn with Su-27/Su-27UB *Flanker*
  1 sqn with Su-27/Su-30SM *Flanker*
GROUND ATTACK
  1 sqn with Su-25 *Frogfoot*
TRANSPORT
  1 unit with Tu-134 *Crusty*; Tu-154 *Careless*
  1 sqn with An-12 *Cub*, An-26 *Curl*, An-30 *Clank*, An-72 *Coaler*, C295M
TRAINING
  1 sqn with L-39 *Albatros*
ATTACK HELICOPTER
  5 sqn with Mi-24V *Hind*
TRANSPORT HELICOPTER
  Some sqn with Bell 205 (UH-1H *Iroquois*); H145; Mi-8 *Hip*; Mi-17V-5 *Hip*; Mi-171Sh *Hip*; Mi-26 *Halo*
AIR DEFENCE
  Some regt with S-75M *Volkhov* (SA-2 *Guideline*); S-125 *Neva* (SA-3 *Goa*); S-300/S-300PS (SA-10/10B *Grumble*); 2K11 *Krug* (SA-4 *Ganef*); S-200 *Angara* (SA-5 *Gammon*); 2K12 *Kub* (SA-6 *Gainful*)
EQUIPMENT BY TYPE
AIRCRAFT 106 combat capable
  FTR 46: 12 MiG-29 *Fulcrum*; 2 MiG-29UB *Fulcrum*; 32 MiG-31/MiG-31BM *Foxhound*
  FGA 46: 12 MiG-27 *Flogger* D; 2 MiG-23UB *Flogger* C; 20 Su-27 *Flanker*; 4 Su-27UB *Flanker*; 8 Su-30SM
  ATK 14: 12 Su-25 *Frogfoot*; 2 Su-25UB *Frogfoot*
  ISR 1 An-30 *Clank*
  TPT 19: **Medium** 2 An-12 *Cub*; **Light** 16: 6 An-26 *Curl*, 2 An-72 *Coaler*; 6 C295; 2 Tu-134 *Crusty*; **PAX** 1 Tu-154 *Careless*
  TRG 18: 17 L-39 *Albatros*; 1 Z-242L
HELICOPTERS
  ATK 24: 20 Mi-24V *Hind* (some upgraded); 4 Mi-35M *Hind*
  MRH 26: 20 Mi-17V-5 *Hip*; 6 Mi-171Sh *Hip*
  TPT 14: **Heavy** 4 Mi-26 *Halo*; **Light** 10: 4 Bell 205 (UH-1H *Iroquois*); 6 H145
UNMANNED AERIAL VEHICLES
  CISR • **Heavy** 2 *Wing Loong* (GJ-1)
AIR DEFENCE • SAM
  Long-range S-200 *Angara* (SA-5 *Gammon*); S-300 (SA-10 *Grumble*); 40+ S-300PS (SA-10B *Grumble*)
  Medium-range 2K11 *Krug* (SA-4 *Ganef*); S-75M *Volkhov* (SA-2 *Guideline*)
  Short-range 2K12 *Kub* (SA-6 *Gainful*); S-125 *Neva* (SA-3 *Goa*)
  Point-defence 9K35 *Strela*-10 (SA-13 *Gopher*)
AIR-LAUNCHED MISSILES
  AAM • **IR** R-60 (AA-8 *Aphid*); R-73 (AA-11 *Archer*); **IR/SARH** R-27 (AA-10 *Alamo*); **SARH** R-33 (AA-9 *Amos*); **ARH** R-77 (AA-12A *Adder* – on MiG-31BM)
  ASM Kh-23 (AS-7 *Kerry*)‡; Kh-25 (AS-10 *Karen*); Kh-29 (AS-14 *Kedge*)
  ARM Kh-27 (AS-12 *Kegler*); Kh-58 (AS-11 *Kilter*)

Paramilitary 31,500

National Guard ε20,000
Ministry of Interior
AIRCRAFT
  TPT • **Medium** 1 Y-8F-200WA

State Security Service 2,500

Border Service ε9,000
Ministry of Interior
EQUIPMENT BY TYPE
AIRCRAFT 7: **Light** 6: 4 An-26 *Curl*; 1 An-74T; 1 An-74TK **PAX** 1 SSJ-100
HELICOPTERS • TPT • Medium 15: 1 Mi-171; 14 Mi-171Sh

Coast Guard
EQUIPMENT BY TYPE
PATROL AND COASTAL COMBATANTS 22
  PBF 11: 1 *Aibar* (Project 0210); 8 FC-19; 2 *Saygak*
  PB 11: 4 *Almaty*; 5 *Sardar*; 2 *Zhuk* (of which 1 may be operational)

DEPLOYMENT

MOLDOVA: OSCE • Moldova 2
UKRAINE: OSCE • Ukraine 5
WESTERN SAHARA: UN • MINURSO 5 obs

Kyrgyzstan KGZ

Kazakhstani Tenge t		2017	2018	2019
GDP	t	521bn	551bn	
	US$	7.57bn	8.01bn	
per capita	US$	1,208	1,254	
Growth	%	4.6	2.8	
Inflation	%	3.2	2.9	
Def bdgt	t	n.k	n.k	
	US$	n.k	n.k	
US$1=t		68.86	68.79	

Population 5,849,296

Ethnic groups: Kyrgyz 71.7%; Uzbek 14.3%; Russian 7.2%; Dungan 1.1%; Uyguy 0.9%; other or unspecified 4.8%

Age	0–14	15–19	20–24	25–29	30–64	65 plus
Male	15.6%	4.0%	4.3%	4.7%	18.4%	2.1%
Female	14.8%	3.9%	4.1%	4.6%	20.2%	3.4%

Capabilities

Although Kyrgyzstan is generally dependent on Russian assistance for its defence requirements, it has started to expand its ties with regional countries on issues such as defence-industrial cooperation. A July 2013 military doctrine detailed reforms including plans for enhanced command and control, more effective military logistics and a modern air-defence system. As part of Kyrgyzstan's effort to counter terrorism, the government ordered the creation of an inter-agency working group to devise an anti-extremism and anti-terrorism programme. There is a close strategic relationship with Russia and Kyrgyzstan is a member of both the CSTO and the SCO. Moscow maintains a military presence, including a squadron of Su-25SM ground-attack aircraft at Kant air base, which it has leased since 2003. Talk are ongoing over a possible second Russian base. In 2018, bilateral cooperation agreements were signed with Kazakhstan and Uzbekistan. Joint training is held with regional countries, including on anti-terror drills, but combat readiness remains an issue. Kyrgyzstan has a limited capability to deploy externally, and personnel are deployed to OSCE and UN missions in Ukraine, Serbia and South Sudan. The armed forces possess ageing land equipment and limited air capabilities, relying instead on Russian support, training and deployments. There is little local defence industry, although in 2018 Kazakhstan and Kyrgyzstan discussed defence-industrial cooperation and prospects for mutual supplies of military products.

ACTIVE 10,900 (Army 8,500 Air 2,400) Paramilitary 9,500

Conscript liability 18 months

ORGANISATIONS BY SERVICE

Army 8,500
FORCES BY ROLE
SPECIAL FORCES
  1 SF bde
MANOEUVRE
  Mechanised
  2 MR bde
  1 (mtn) MR bde

COMBAT SUPPORT
  1 arty bde
  1 AD bde
EQUIPMENT BY TYPE
ARMOURED FIGHTING VEHICLES
  MBT 150 T-72
  RECCE 30 BRDM-2
  IFV 320: 230 BMP-1; 90 BMP-2
  APC • APC (W) 55: 25 BTR-70; 20 BTR-70M; 10 BTR-80
ANTI-TANK/ANTI-INFRASTRUCTURE
  MSL • MANPATS 9K11 *Malyutka* (AT-3 *Sagger*); 9K111 *Fagot* (AT-4 *Spigot*); 9K111-1 *Konkurs* (AT-5 *Spandrel*)
  RCL 73mm SPG-9
  GUNS 100mm 36: 18 MT-12/T-12; 18 M-1944
ARTILLERY 228
  SP 122mm 18 2S1 *Gvozdika*
  TOWED 123: **122mm** 107: 72 D-30; 35 M-30 (M-1938); **152mm** 16 D-1
  GUN/MOR 120mm 12 2S9 NONA-S
  MRL 21: **122mm** 15 BM-21; **220mm** 6 9P140 *Uragan*
  MOR 120mm 54: 6 2S12; 48 M-120
AIR DEFENCE
  SAM • Point-defence 9K32 *Strela*-2 (SA-7 *Grail*)‡
  GUNS 48
    SP 23mm 24 ZSU-23-4
    TOWED 57mm 24 S-60

Air Force 2,400
FORCES BY ROLE
FIGHTER
  1 regt with L-39 *Albatros**
TRANSPORT
  1 regt with An-2 *Colt*; An-26 *Curl*
ATTACK/TRANSPORT HELICOPTER
  1 regt with Mi-24 *Hind*; Mi-8 *Hip*
AIR DEFENCE
  Some regt with S-125 *Pechora* (SA-3 *Goa*); S-75 *Dvina* (SA-2 *Guideline*); 2K11 *Krug* (SA-4 *Ganef*)
EQUIPMENT BY TYPE
AIRCRAFT 4 combat capable
  TPT • Light 6: 4 An-2 *Colt*; 2 An-26 *Curl*
  TRG 4 L-39 *Albatros**
HELICOPTERS
  ATK 2 Mi-24 *Hind*
  TPT • Medium 8 Mi-8 *Hip*
AIR DEFENCE • SAM
  Medium-range 2K11 *Krug* (SA-4 *Ganef*); S-75 *Dvina* (SA-2 *Guideline*)
  Short-range S-125 *Pechora* (SA-3 *Goa*)

Paramilitary 9,500

Border Guards 5,000 (KGZ conscript, RUS officers)

Internal Troops 3,500

National Guard 1,000

DEPLOYMENT

MOLDVOA: OSCE • Moldova 2
SERBIA: OSCE • Kosovo 2
SOUTH SUDAN: UN • UNMISS 1 obs
SUDAN: UN • UNAMID 1 obs
UKRAINE: OSCE • Ukraine 26

FOREIGN FORCES

Russia ε500 Military Air Forces: 13 Su-25SM *Frogfoot*; 2 Mi-8 *Hip*

Moldova MDA

Moldovan Leu L		2017	2018	2019
GDP	L	177bn	192bn	
	US$	9.56bn	11.4bn	
per capita	US$	2,694	3,227	
Growth	%	4.5	3.8	
Inflation	%	6.6	3.6	
Def bdgt	L	566m	616m	
	US$	30.6m	36.8m	
FMA (US)	US$	12.8m	0m	
US$1=L		18.50	16.76	
Population	3,437,720			

Age	0–14	15–19	20–24	25–29	30–64	65 plus
Male	9.4%	2.8%	3.3%	4.0%	24.1%	5.1%
Female	8.9%	2.6%	3.1%	3.8%	24.9%	7.9%

Capabilities

The primary role of Moldova's armed forces is to maintain territorial integrity, though their size means they would be unable to offer more than token resistance to a determined adversary. The forces are constitutionally neutral. In early 2017, a National Defence Strategy for 2017–21 was approved, including border defence, airspace control and protection, and improvements to the military-training system, as well as equipment-modernisation imperatives. Moldova continues to build relations with both European states and NATO. The country signed up to the NATO Defence Capacity Building Initiative in September 2014. Moldova is aiming to end mandatory conscription and develop professional armed forces. The Professional Army 2018–2021 programme was approved in June 2018. The services exercise regularly with NATO states. Moldova has no requirement or capability to independently deploy and support its forces overseas. However, service members have deployed as part of KFOR. The country has no defence-industrial capabilities beyond the basic maintenance of front-line equipment.

ACTIVE 5,150 (Army 3,250 Air 600 Logistic Support 1,300) **Paramilitary 900**

Conscript liability 12 months (3 months for university graduates)

RESERVE 58,000 (Joint 58,000)

ORGANISATIONS BY SERVICE

Army 1,300; 1,950 conscript (total 3,250)
FORCES BY ROLE
SPECIAL FORCES
 1 SF bn
MANOEUVRE
 Light
 3 mot inf bde
 1 lt inf bn
 Other
 1 gd bn
COMBAT SUPPORT
 1 arty bn
 1 engr bn
 1 NBC coy
 1 sigs bn
EQUIPMENT BY TYPE
ARMOURED FIGHTING VEHICLES
 APC 163
  APC (T) 69: 9 BTR-D; 60 MT-LB (variants)
  APC (W) 94: 13 BTR-80; 81 TAB-71
 ABCV 44 BMD-1
ANTI-TANK/ANTI-INFRASTRUCTURE
 MSL • MANPATS 9K111 *Fagot* (AT-4 *Spigot*); 9K111-1 *Konkurs* (AT-5 *Spandrel*)
 RCL 73mm SPG-9
 GUNS 100mm 37 MT-12
ARTILLERY 221
 TOWED 69: 122mm 17 (M-30) M-1938; 152mm 52: 21 2A36 *Giatsint*-B; 31 D-20
 GUN/MOR • SP 120mm 9 2S9 NONA-S
 MRL 220mm 11 9P140 *Uragan*
 MOR 132: 82mm 75 BM-37; 120mm 57: 50 M-1989; 7 PM-38
AIR DEFENCE • GUNS • TOWED 39: 23mm 28 ZU-23; 57mm 11 S-60

Air Force 600 (incl 250 conscripts)
FORCES BY ROLE
TRANSPORT
 1 sqn with An-2 *Colt*; Mi-8MTV-1/PS *Hip*; Yak-18
AIR DEFENCE
 1 regt with S-125 *Neva* (SA-3 *Goa*)
EQUIPMENT BY TYPE
AIRCRAFT
 TPT • Light 3: 2 An-2 *Colt*; 1 Yak-18
HELICOPTERS
 TPT • Medium 6: 2 Mi-8PS *Hip*; 4 Mi-8MTV-1 *Hip*
AIR DEFENCE • SAM • Short-range 3 S-125 *Neva* (SA-3 *Goa*)

Paramilitary 900

OPON 900 (riot police)
Ministry of Interior

DEPLOYMENT

ALBANIA: OSCE • Albania 1
ARMENIA/AZERBAIJAN: OSCE • Minsk Conference 2
BOSNIA-HERZEGOVINA: OSCE • Bosnia and Herzegovina 1
CENTRAL AFRICAN REPUBLIC: UN • MINUSCA 2; 3 obs
SERBIA: NATO • KFOR 41; OSCE • Kosovo 2; UN • UNMIK 1 obs
SOUTH SUDAN: UN • UNMISS 1; 2 obs
UKRAINE: OSCE • Ukraine 45

FOREIGN FORCES

Armenia OSCE 1
Austria OSCE 1
Estonia OSCE 1
Germany OSCE 1
Hungary OSCE 1
Ireland OSCE 1
Kazakhstan OSCE 2
Kyrgyzstan OSCE 2
Russia ε1,500 (including 400 peacekeepers) 7 Mi-24 *Hind*/Mi-8 *Hip*
Ukraine 10 mil obs (Joint Peacekeeping Force)
United States OSCE 1

Russia RUS

Russian Rouble r		2017	2018	2019
GDP	r	92.0tr	98.4tr	
	US$	1.58tr	1.58tr	
per capita	US$	10,956	10,950	
Growth	%	1.5	1.7	
Inflation	%	3.7	2.8	
Def exp [a]	r	3.71tr	3.93tr	
	US$	63.6bn	63.1bn	
Def bdgt	r	2.67tr	2.83tr	2.91tr
	US$	45.7bn	45.3bn	
US$1=r		58.34	62.40	

[a] Calculated to be comparable with the NATO definition of defence expenditure

Population 142,122,776

Ethnic groups: Tatar 3.71%; Armenian 0.8%; Bashkir 1.1%; Chechen 1%; Chuvash 1%

Age	0–14	15–19	20–24	25–29	30–64	65 plus
Male	8.8%	2.4%	2.4%	3.5%	24.5%	4.6%
Female	8.4%	2.3%	2.3%	3.4%	27.3%	10.0%

Capabilities

Russia supports capable conventional military forces and retains the second-largest nuclear arsenal in the world. The armed forces underpin an assertive foreign policy. Military aims are guaranteeing sovereignty and territorial integrity and maintaining and increasing Russia's influence in the near abroad and further afield. Russia is a leading member of both the CSTO and the SCO. The armed forces comprise a mix of volunteers and conscripts. Defence reforms launched in 2008 emphasised the shift from a conscript-based mass-mobilisation army to smaller, more professional ground forces. Morale has improved because of better pay, terms and conditions, and greater prestige associated with military service. The armed forces can independently deploy and sustain forces on a global scale, although at extended distances force size would be modest. Its air-led intervention in Syria shows Russia can deploy, sustain and maintain a high operational tempo for a fixed- and rotary-wing air force, along with the required force-protection package for the main operating base. Russia continues to modernise its nuclear and conventional weapons. The 2020 State Armament Programme (SAP) has been broadly successful, although several of the more ambitious procurement goals were not met. The follow-on programme, SAP 2027, continues the emphasis on modernisation, though some aims are more modest. Russia can design, develop and manufacture advanced nuclear and conventional weaponry. Its defence-industrial base, however, suffered from the lack of investment in the 1990s, and more recently from the loss of access to Ukrainian components. The defence-aerospace sector has been particularly successful in terms of exports, with the sale of combat aircraft and surface-to-air missile systems.

ACTIVE 900,000 (Army 280,000 Navy 150,000 Air 165,000 Strategic Rocket Force 50,000 Airborne 45,000 Special Operations Forces 1,000 Railway Troops 29,000 Command and Support 180,000) **Paramilitary 554,000**

Conscript liability 12 months (conscripts now can opt for contract service immediately, which entails a 24-month contract)

RESERVE 2,000,000 (all arms)
Some 2,000,000 with service within last 5 years; reserve obligation to age 50

ORGANISATIONS BY SERVICE

Strategic Deterrent Forces ε80,000 (incl personnel assigned from the Navy and Aerospace Forces)

Navy
EQUIPMENT BY TYPE
SUBMARINES • STRATEGIC • SSBN 10:
  1 *Kalmar* (*Delta* III) with 16 R-29RKU-02 *Statsiya*-02 (SS-N-18 *Stingray*) nuclear SLBM, 2 single 400mm TT with SET-72 LWT, 4 single 533mm TT with 53-65K HWT/SET-65K HWT/USET-80K *Keramika* HWT
  6 *Delfin* (*Delta* IV) with 16 R-29RMU2 *Sineva*/R-29RMU2.1 *Layner* (SS-N-23 *Skiff*) nuclear SLBM, 4 single 533mm TT with 53-65K HWT/SET-65K HWT/USET-80K *Keramika* HWT
  3 *Borey* (*Dolgorukiy*) with 16 *Bulava* (SS-N-32) nuclear SLBM, 6 single 533mm TT with USET-80K *Keramika* HWT/UGST *Fizikov* HWT
  (1 *Akula* (*Typhoon*)† in reserve for training with capacity for 20 *Bulava* (SS-N-32) nuclear SLBM, 6 single 533mm TT with 53-65K HWT/SET-65K HWT/USET-80K *Keramika* HWT)

Strategic Rocket Force Troops 50,000

3 Rocket Armies operating silo and mobile launchers organised in 12 divs. Regt normally with 10 silos (6 for RS-20/SS-18), or 9 mobile lnchr, and one control centre

FORCES BY ROLE
SURFACE-TO-SURFACE MISSILE
 9 ICBM regt with RS-12M *Topol* (SS-25 *Sickle*)
 8 ICBM regt with RS-12M2 *Topol*-M (SS-27 mod 1)
 3 ICBM regt with RS-18 (SS-19 *Stiletto*)
 9 ICBM regt with RS-20 (SS-18 *Satan*)
 10 ICBM regt with RS-24 *Yars* (SS-27 mod 2)
 4 ICBM regt (forming) with RS-24 *Yars* (SS-27 mod 2)

EQUIPMENT BY TYPE
SURFACE-TO-SURFACE MISSILE LAUNCHERS
 ICBM • **Nuclear** 334: ε63 RS-12M *Topol* (SS-25 *Sickle*) (mobile single warhead); 60 RS-12M2 *Topol*-M (SS-27 mod 1) silo-based (single warhead); 18 RS-12M2 *Topol*-M (SS-27 mod 1) road mobile (single warhead); 30 RS-18 (SS-19 *Stiletto*) (mostly mod 3, 6 MIRV per msl) (being withdrawn); 46 RS-20 (SS-18 *Satan*) (mostly mod 5, 10 MIRV per msl); 103 RS-24 *Yars* (SS-27 mod 2; ε3 MIRV per msl) road mobile; 14 RS-24 *Yars* (SS-27 mod 2; ε3 MIRV per msl) silo-based

Long-Range Aviation Command

FORCES BY ROLE
BOMBER
 1 sqn with Tu-160/Tu-160M1 *Blackjack*
 3 sqn with Tu-95MS/MS mod *Bear*

EQUIPMENT BY TYPE
AIRCRAFT
 BBR 76: 10 Tu-160 *Blackjack* with Kh-55SM (AS-15B *Kent*) nuclear LACM; 6 Tu-160M1 *Blackjack* with Kh-55SM (AS-15B *Kent*)/Kh-102 (AS-23 *Kodiak*) nuclear LACM; 46 Tu-95MS *Bear* H with Kh-55SM (AS-15B *Kent*) nuclear LACM; 14 Tu-95MS mod *Bear* H with Kh-55SM (AS-15B *Kent*)/Kh-102 (AS-23 *Kodiak*) nuclear LACM

Space Command

EQUIPMENT BY TYPE
SATELLITES 101
 COMMUNICATIONS 59: 2 *Blagovest*; 2 *Garpun*; 13 *Gonets*-D/M (dual-use); 3 Mod *Globus* (*Raduga*-1M); 4 *Meridian*; 3 *Parus*; 3 *Raduga*; 21 *Rodnik* (*Strela*-3M); 8 *Strela*-3
 EARLY WARNING 2 *Tundra*
 NAVIGATION/POSITIONING/TIMING 25 GLONASS
 ISR 10: 2 *Bars*-M; 1 GEO-IK 2; 1 *Kondor*; 1 *Kosmos*-2519; 2 *Persona*; 3 *Resurs*-P
 ELINT/SIGINT 5: 4 *Liana* (*Lotos*-S); 1 *Tselina*-2
RADAR 12; Russia leases ground-based radar stations in Baranovichi (Belarus) and Balkhash (Kazakhstan). It also has radars on its own territory at Lekhtusi (St Petersburg); Armavir (Krasnodar); Olenegorsk (Murmansk); Mishelevka (Irkuts); Kaliningrad; Pechora (Komi); Yeniseysk (Krasnoyarsk); Baranul (Altayskiy); Orsk (Orenburg) and Gorodets/Kovylkino (OTH)

Aerospace Defence Command

FORCES BY ROLE
AIR DEFENCE
 2 AD div HQ
 4 SAM regt with S-300PM1/PM2 (SA-20 *Gargoyle*)
 5 SAM regt with S-400 (SA-21 *Growler*); 96K6 *Pantsir*-S1 (SA-22 *Greyhound*)

EQUIPMENT BY TYPE
AIR DEFENCE • SAM 222
 Long-range 186: 90 S-300PM1/PM2 (SA-20 *Gargoyle*); 96 S-400 (SA-21 *Growler*)
 Short-range 36 96K6 *Pantsir*-S1 (SA-22 *Greyhound*)
MISSILE DEFENCE 68 53T6 (ABM-3 *Gazelle*)
RADAR 1 ABM engagement system located at Sofrino (Moscow)

Army ε280,000 (incl conscripts)

4 military districts (West (HQ St Petersburg), Centre (HQ Yekaterinburg), South (HQ Rostov-on-Don) & East (HQ Khabarovsk), each with a unified Joint Strategic Command

FORCES BY ROLE
COMMAND
 12 army HQ
 1 corps HQ
SPECIAL FORCES
 8 (Spetsnaz) SF bde
 1 (Spetsnaz) SF regt
MANOEUVRE
 Reconnaissance
 2 recce bde
 Armoured
 1 (4th) tk div (1 armd recce bn, 2 tk regt, 1 MR regt, 1 arty regt, 1 AD regt)
 1 (90th) tk div (1 armd recce bn, 2 tk regt, 1 MR regt, 1 arty regt)
 2 tk bde (1 armd recce bn, 3 tk bn, 1 MR bn, 1 arty bn, 1 MRL bn, 2 AD bn, 1 engr bn, 1 EW coy, 1 NBC coy)
 1 (3rd) MR div (1 armd recce bn, 1 tk regt, 2 MR regt, 1 arty regt)
 1 (144th) MR div (1 armd recce bn, 1 tk regt, 1 MR regt, 1 arty regt)
 1 (150th) MR div (1 armd recce bn, 2 tk regt, 1 MR regt; 1 arty regt, 1 AD regt)
 14 (BMP) MR bde (1 armd recce bn, 1 tk bn, 3 armd inf bn, 2 arty bn, 1 MRL bn, 1 AT bn, 2 AD bn, 1 engr bn, 1 EW coy, 1 NBC coy)
 Mechanised
 1 (2nd) MR div (1 armd recce bn, 1 tk regt, 2 MR regt, 1 arty regt, 1 AD regt)
 1 (42nd) MR div (1 armd recce bn, 3 MR regt, 1 arty regt)
 9 (BTR/MT-LB) MR bde (1 recce bn; 1 tk bn; 3 mech inf bn; 2 arty bn; 1 MRL bn; 1 AT bn; 2 AD bn; 1 engr bn; 1 EW coy; 1 NBC coy)
 2 MR bde (4–5 mech inf bn; 1 arty bn; 1 AD bn; 1 engr bn)
 3 (lt/mtn) MR bde (1 recce bn; 2 mech inf bn; 1 arty bn)
 1 (18th) MGA div (2 MGA regt; 1 arty regt; 1 tk bn; 2 AD bn)
SURFACE-TO-SURFACE MISSILE
 10 SRBM/GLCM bde with 9K720 *Iskander*-M (SS-26 *Stone*/SSC-7) (multiple brigades also with 9M729 (SSC-8 *Screwdriver*))
 1 SRBM bde with 9K79-1 *Tochka*-U (SS-21B *Scarab*)

COMBAT SUPPORT
9 arty bde
1 hy arty bde
4 MRL bde
4 engr bde
1 MP bde
5 NBC bde
10 NBC regt
COMBAT SERVICE SUPPORT
10 log bde
AIR DEFENCE
14 AD bde
EQUIPMENT BY TYPE
ARMOURED FIGHTING VEHICLES
MBT 2,750: 750 T-72B/BA; 800 T-72B3; 400 T-73B3 mod; 450 T-80BV/U; 350 T-90/T-90A (10,200 in store: 7,000 T-72/T-72A/B; 3,000 T-80B/BV/U; 200 T-90)
RECCE 1,700: 1,000 BRDM-2/2A (1,000+ BRDM-2 in store); 700 BRM-1K (CP)
IFV 5,140: 500 BMP-1; 3,000 BMP-2; 540 BMP-3; 100 BTR-80A; 1,000 BTR-82A/AM (8,500 in store: 7,000 BMP-1; 1,500 BMP-2)
APC 6,100+
  APC (T) 3,500+: some BMO-T; 3,500 MT-LB (2,000 MT-LB in store)
  APC (W) 2,600: 800 BTR-60 (all variants); 200 BTR-70 (all variants); 1,500 BTR-80; 100+ BPM-97 *Dozor* (4,000 BTR-60/70 in store)
  PPV *Typhoon*-K
AUV 100+: 100+ GAZ *Tigr*; some IVECO LMV
ENGINEERING & MAINTENANCE VEHICLES
AEV BAT-2; IMR; IMR-2; IMR-3; IRM; MT-LB
ARV BMP-1; BREM-1/64/K/L; BTR-50PK(B); M1977; MTP-LB; RM-G; T-54/55; VT-72A
VLB KMM; MT-55A; MTU; MTU-20; MTU-72; PMM-2
MW BMR-3M; GMX-3; MCV-2 (reported); MTK; MTK-2; UR-77
ANTI-TANK/ANTI-INFRASTRUCTURE
MSL
  SP BMP-T with 9K120 *Ataka* (AT-9 *Spiral* 2); 9P149 with 9K114 *Shturm* (AT-6 *Spiral*); 9P149M with 9K132 *Shturm*-SM (AT-9 *Spiral*-2); 9P157-2 with 9K123 *Khrizantema* (AT-15 *Springer*); 9P163-3 with 9M133 *Kornet* (AT-14 *Spriggan*); 9K128-1 *Kornet*-T (AT-14 *Spriggan*)
  MANPATS 9K111M *Fagot* (AT-4 *Spigot*); 9K111-1 *Konkurs* (AT-5 *Spandrel*); 9K115 *Metis* (AT-7 *Saxhorn*); 9K115-1 *Metis*-M (AT-13 *Saxhorn* 2); 9K115-2 *Metis*-M1 (AT-13 *Saxhorn* 2); 9K135 *Kornet* (AT-14 *Spriggan*)
RCL 73mm SPG-9
GUNS • TOWED 100mm 526 MT-12 (**100mm** 2,000 T-12/MT-12 in store)
ARTILLERY 4,342+
  SP 1,610: **122mm** 150 2S1 *Gvozdika*; **152mm** 1,400: 800 2S3 *Akatsiya*; 100 2S5 *Giatsint*-S; 500 2S19/2S19M1/2S19M2 *Msta*-S/SM; **203mm** 60 2S7M *Malka* (4,260 in store: **122mm** 2,000 2S1 *Gvozdika*; **152mm** 2,000: 1,000 2S3 *Akatsiya*; 850 2S5 *Giatsint*-S; 150 2S19 *Msta*-S; **203mm** 260 2S7 *Pion*)
  TOWED 150: **152mm** 150 2A65 *Msta*-B (12,415 in store: **122mm** 8,150: 4,400 D-30; 3,750 M-30 (M-1938); **130mm** 650 M-46; **152mm** 3,575: 1,100 2A36 *Giatsint*-B; 600 2A65 *Msta*-B; 1,075 D-20; 700 D-1 (M-1943); 100 M-1937 (ML-20); **203mm** 40 B-4M)
GUN/MOR 180+
  SP 120mm 80+: 30 2S23 NONA-SVK; 50+ 2S34
  TOWED 120mm 100 2B16 NONA-K
MRL 862+ **122mm** 550 BM-21 *Grad*/*Tornado*-G; **220mm** 200 9P140 *Uragan*; some 9K512 *Uragan*-1M; some TOS-1A; **300mm** 112: 100 9A52 *Smerch*; 12 9A54 *Tornado*-S (3,220 in store: **122mm** 2,420: 2,000 BM-21 *Grad*; 420 9P138; **132mm** 100 BM-13; **220mm** 700 9P140 *Uragan*)
MOR 1,540+: **82mm** 800+ 2B14; **120mm** 700 2S12 *Sani*; **240mm** 40 2S4 *Tulpan* (2,590 in store: **120mm** 1,900: 1,000 2S12 *Sani*; 900 M-1938 (PM-38); **160mm** 300 M-160; **SP 240mm** 390 2S4 *Tulpan*)
SURFACE-TO-SURFACE MISSILE LAUNCHERS
SRBM 144:
  Dual-capable 120 9K720 *Iskander*-M (SS-26 *Stone*)
  Conventional 24 9K79-1 *Tochka*-U (SS-21B *Scarab*) (some *Scud* in store)
GLCM • Dual-capable Some 9M728 (SSC-7); some 9M729 (SSC-8 *Screwdriver*)
UNMANNED AERIAL VEHICLES
ISR • Heavy Tu-243 *Reys*/Tu-243 *Reys* D (service status unclear); **Light** BLA-07; *Pchela*-1; *Pchela*-2
AIR DEFENCE
SAM 1,520+
  Long-range S-300V (SA-12 *Gladiator/Giant*); S-300V4 (SA-23)
  Medium-range 350: ε200 9K37M *Buk*-M1-2 (SA-11 *Gadfly*); ε90 9K317 *Buk*-M2 (SA-17 *Grizzly*); ε60 9K317M *Buk*-M3 (SA-17 *Grizzly*)
  Short-range 120+ 9K331/9K332 *Tor*-M/M1/M2/M2U (SA-15 *Gauntlet*) (9M338 msl entering service)
  Point-defence 1,050+: 250+ 2K22M *Tunguska* (SA-19 *Grison*); 400 9K33M3 *Osa*-AKM (SA-8B *Gecko*); 400 9K35M3 *Strela*-10 (SA-13 *Gopher*); 9K310 *Igla*-1 (SA-16 *Gimlet*); 9K34 *Strela*-3 (SA-14 *Gremlin*); 9K38 *Igla* (SA-18 *Grouse*); 9K333 *Verba*; 9K338 *Igla*-S (SA-24 *Grinch*)
GUNS
  SP 23mm ZSU-23-4
  TOWED 23mm ZU-23-2; **57mm** S-60

Reserves

Cadre formations
FORCES BY ROLE
MANOEUVRE
  Mechanised
  13 MR bde

Navy ε150,000 (incl conscripts)

4 major fleet organisations (Northern Fleet, Pacific Fleet, Baltic Fleet, Black Sea Fleet) and Caspian Sea Flotilla
EQUIPMENT BY TYPE
SUBMARINES 58
  STRATEGIC • SSBN 10:
    1 *Kalmar* (*Delta* III) with 16 R-29RKU-02 *Statsiya*-02 (SS-N-18 *Stingray*) nuclear SLBM, 2 single 400mm TT with SET-72 LWT, 4 single 533mm TT with 53-65K HWT/SET-65K HWT/USET-80K *Keramika* HWT

6 *Delfin* (*Delta* IV) with 16 R-29RMU2 *Sineva*/R-29RMU2.1 *Layner* (SS-N-23 *Skiff*) nuclear SLBM, 4 single 533mm TT with 53-65K HWT/SET-65K HWT/USET-80K *Keramika* HWT

3 *Borey* (*Dolgorukiy*) with 16 *Bulava* (SS-N-32) nuclear SLBM, 6 single 533mm TT with USET-80K *Keramika* HWT/UGST *Fizikov* HWT

(1 *Akula* (*Typhoon*)† in reserve for training with capacity for 20 *Bulava* (SS-N-32) nuclear SLBM, 6 single 533mm TT with 53-65K HWT/SET-65K HWT/USET-80K *Keramika* HWT)

TACTICAL 48

SSGN 9:

8 *Antey* (*Oscar* II) with 2 12-cell lnchr with 3M45 *Granit* (SS-N-19 *Shipwreck*) AShM, 2 single 650mm TT each with T-65 HWT/RPK-7 (SS-N-16 *Stallion*) ASW msl, 4 single 553mm TT with 53-65K HWT/SET-65K HWT/USET-80K *Keramika* HWT (of which 2 in refit)

1 *Yasen* (*Severodvinsk*) with 1 octuple VLS with 3M54K (SS-N-27 *Sizzler*) AShM/3M55 *Onyx* (SS-N-26 *Strobile*) AShM/3M14K (SS-N-30) dual-capable LACM; 10 single 533mm TT with USET-80K *Keramika* HWT/UGST *Fizikov* HWT

SSN 16:

9 *Schuka*-B (*Akula* I) with 4 single 533mm TT with 53-65K HWT/TEST-71M HWT/USET-80K *Keramika* HWT/3M10 *Granat* (SS-N-21 *Sampson*) nuclear LACM (weapons in store), 4 single 650mm TT with T-65 HWT/RPK-7 (SS-N-16 *Stallion*) ASW msl (of which 6 in refit)

2 *Schuka*-B (*Akula* II) with 4 single 533mm TT with 53-65K HWT/TEST-71M HWT/USET-80K *Keramika* HWT/3M10 *Granat* (SS-N-21 *Sampson*) nuclear LACM (weapons in store), 4 single 650mm TT with T-65 HWT/RPK-7 (SS-N-16 *Stallion*) ASW msl (of which 1 in refit)

2 *Kondor* (*Sierra* II) with 4 single 533mm TT with TEST-71M HWT/USET-80K *Keramika* HWT/3M10 *Granat* (SS-N-21 *Sampson*) nuclear LACM (weapons in store), 4 single 650mm TT with T-65 HWT

3 *Schuka* (*Victor* III) with 4 single 533mm TT with 53-65K HWT/SET-65K HWT/USET-80K *Keramika* HWT/3M10 *Granat* (SS-N-21 *Sampson*) nuclear LACM (weapons in store), 2 single 650mm TT with T-65 HWT

(1 *Barracuda* (*Sierra* I) (in reserve) with 6 single 533mm TT with TEST-71M HWT/USET-80K *Keramika* HWT/3M10 *Granat* (SS-N-21 *Sampson*) nuclear LACM (weapons in store))

SSK 23:

16 *Paltus* (*Kilo*) (of which 2 in refit) with 6 single 533mm TT with 53-65K HWT/TEST-71M HWT/USET-80K *Keramika* HWT

6 *Varshavyanka* (*Kilo*) with 6 single 533mm TT with 53-65K HWT/TEST-71M HWT/USET-80K *Keramika* HWT/3M54K (SS-N-27 *Sizzler*) AShM/3M14K (SS-N-30) dual-capable LACM

1 *Lada* (*Petersburg*) (in test) with 6 single 533mm TT with USET-80K *Keramika* HWT/3M54K (SS-N-27 *Sizzler*) AShM/3M14K (SS-N-30) dual-capable LACM

PRINCIPAL SURFACE COMBATANTS 35

AIRCRAFT CARRIERS • CV 1 *Admiral Kuznetsov* with 12 lnchr with 3M45 *Granit* (SS-N-19 *Shipwreck*) AShM, 24 8-cell 3S95 VLS with 3K95 *Kindzhal* (SA-N-9 *Gauntlet*) SAM, 2 RBU 12000 *Udav* 1 A/S mor, 8 *Kortik* CIWS with 3M11 (SA-N-11 *Grison*) SAM, 6 AK630M CIWS (capacity 18–24 Su-33 *Flanker* D Ftr ac; MiG-29KR FGA ac; 15 Ka-27 *Helix* ASW hel, 2 Ka-31R *Helix* AEW hel) (in refit since 2018)

CRUISERS 4

CGHMN 1:

1 *Orlan* (*Kirov*) with 20 lnchr with 3M45 *Granit* (SS-N-19 *Shipwreck*) AShM, 6 6-cell B-203A VLS with S-300F *Fort* (SA-N-6 *Grumble*) SAM, 6 6-cell B-203A VLS with S-300FM *Fort*-M (SA-N-20 *Gargoyle*) SAM, 16 octuple 3S95 VLS with 3K95 *Kindzhal* (SA-N-9 *Gauntlet*) SAM, 2 quintuple 533mm TT with RPK-6M *Vodopad*-NK (SS-N-16 *Stallion*) A/S msl, 1 RBU 6000 *Smerch* 2 A/S mor, 2 RBU 1000 *Smerch* 3 A/S mor, 6 *Kortik* CIWS with 9M311 (SA-N-11 *Grison*) SAM, 1 twin 130mm gun (capacity 3 Ka-27 *Helix* ASW hel) (1 other non-operational; undergoing extensive refit and planned to return to service in 2021)

CGHM 3:

3 *Atlant* (*Slava*) with 8 twin lnchr with 3M70 *Vulkan* (SS-N-12 mod 2 *Sandbox*) AShM, 8 octuple VLS with S-300F *Fort* (SA-N-6 *Grumble*) SAM/S-300FM *Fort* M (SA-N-20 *Gargoyle*) SAM, 2 twin lnchr with *Osa*-M (SA-N-4 *Gecko*) SAM, 2 quintuple 533mm ASTT with SET-65K HWT, 2 RBU 6000 *Smerch* 2 A/S mor, 6 AK630 CIWS, 1 twin 130mm gun (capacity 1 Ka-27 *Helix* ASW hel)

DESTROYERS 16

DDGHM 15:

5 *Sarych* (*Sovremenny*) with 2 quad lnchr with 3M80 *Moskit* (SS-N-22 *Sunburn*) AShM, 2 twin 3S90 lnchr with 9K30 *Uragan* (SA-N-7 *Gadfly*) SAM, 2 twin 533mm TT with 53-65K HWT/SET-65K HWT, 2 RBU 1000 *Smerch* 3 A/S mor, 4 AK630M CIWS, 2 twin 130mm guns (capacity 1 Ka-27 *Helix* ASW hel) (of which 1 in refit)

8 *Fregat* (*Udaloy* I) with 2 quad lnchr with URK-5 *Rastrub*-B (SS-N-14 *Silex*) AShM/ASW, 8 octuple 3S95 VLS with 3K95 *Kindzhal* (SA-N-9 *Gauntlet*) SAM, 2 quad 533mm ASTT with 53-65K HWT/SET-65K HWT, 2 RBU 6000 *Smerch* 2 A/S mor, 4 AK630M CIWS, 2 100mm guns (capacity 2 Ka-27 *Helix* ASW hel)

1 *Fregat* (*Udaloy* II) with 2 quad lnchr with 3M80 *Moskit* (SS-N-22 *Sunburn*) AShM, 8 octuple 3S95 VLS with 3K95 *Kindzhal* (SA-N-9 *Gauntlet*) SAM, 2 *Kortik* CIWS with 3M11 (SA-N-11 *Grison*) SAM, 2 quintuple 533mm ASTT with 53-65K HWT/SET-65K HWT, 2 RBU 6000 *Smerch* 2 A/S mor, 1 twin 130mm gun (capacity 2 Ka-27 *Helix* ASW hel)

1 *Admiral Gorshkov* (Project 22350) with 2 8-cell UKSK VLS with 3M14T (SS-N-30) dual-capable LACM/3M54T (SS-N-27 *Sizzler*) AShM/3M55

Oniks (SS-N-26 *Strobile*) AShM/91RT2 A/S msl, 4 8-cell VLS with 3K96-2 *Poliment-Redut* (SA-N-28) SAM, 2 quad 324mm TT with *Paket*-NK LWT, 2 *Palash* CIWS, 1 130mm gun (capacity 1 Ka-27 *Helix* ASW hel)

DDGM 1:

1 *Komsomolets Ukrainy* (*Kashin* mod) with 2 quad lnchr with 3M24 *Uran* (SS-N-25 *Switchblade*) AShM, 2 twin lnchr with *Volnya* (SA-N-1 *Goa*) SAM, 5 single 533mm ASTT with 53-65K HWT/SET-65K HWT, 2 RBU 6000 *Smerch* 2 A/S mor, 1 twin 76mm gun

FRIGATES 14

FFGHM 10:

3 *Admiral Grigorovich* (*Krivak* V) with 1 8-cell VLS with 3M54 (SS-N-27 *Sizzler*) AShM/3M55 *Oniks* (SS-N-26 *Strobile*) AShM/3M14 (SS-N-30) dual-capable LACM, 2 12-cell VLS with 9M317E *Shtil*-1 SAM, 2 twin 533mm TT with 53-65K HWT/SET-65K HWT, 1 RBU 6000 A/S mor, 2 AK630 CIWS, 1 100mm gun (capacity 1 Ka-27 *Helix* ASW hel)

2 *Jastreb* (*Neustrashimy*) with 2 quad lnchr with 3M24 *Uran* (SS-N-25 *Switchblade*) AShM, 4 octuple 3S95 VLS with 3K95 *Kindzhal* (SA-N-9 *Gauntlet*), 6 single 533mm ASTT with RPK-6M *Vodopad*-NK (SS-N-16 *Stallion*) A/S msl, 1 RBU 6000 *Smerch* 2 A/S mor, 2 *Kortik* CIWS with 3M11 (SA-N-11 *Grison*), 1 100mm gun (capacity 1 Ka-27 *Helix* ASW hel) (of which 1 in refit)

1 *Steregushchiy* (Project 20380) with 2 quad lnchr with 3M24 *Uran* (SS-N-25 *Switchblade*) AShM, 2 quad 324mm ASTT with *Paket*-NK LWT, 1 *Kortik*-M CIWS with 3M311 (SA-N-11 *Grison*) SAM, 2 AK630 CIWS, 1 100mm gun (capacity 1 Ka-27 *Helix* ASW hel)

4 *Steregushchiy* (Project 20380) with 2 quad lnchr with 3M24 *Uran* (SS-N-25 *Switchblade*) AShM, 3 4-cell 3S97 VLS with 3K96-3 *Redut* (SA-N-28) SAM (in test), 2 quad 324mm ASTT with *Paket*-NK LWT, 2 AK630 CIWS, 1 100mm gun (capacity 1 Ka-27 *Helix* ASW hel)

FFGM 4:

1 *Gepard* with 2 quad lnchr with 3M24 *Uran* (SS-N-25 *Switchblade*) AShM, 1 twin lnchr with *Osa*-M (SA-N-4 *Gecko*) SAM, 2 AK630 CIWS, 1 76mm gun

1 *Gepard* with 1 8-cell VLS with 3M14T *Kalibr*-NK (SS-N-30) dual-capable LACM/3M54T (SS-N-27 *Sizzler*) AShM/3M5S *Oniks* (SS-N-26 *Strobile*) AShM, 1 3K89 *Palma* CIWS with 9M337 *Sasna*-R SAM, 1 76mm gun

1 *Burevestnik* (*Krivak* I mod)† with 1 quad lnchr with URK-5 *Rastrub*-B (SS-N-14 *Silex*) AShM/ASW, 1 twin lnchr with *Osa*-M (SA-N-4 *Gecko*) SAM, 2 quad 533mm ASTT with 53-65K HWT/SET-65K HWT, 2 RBU 6000 *Smerch* 2 A/S mor, 2 twin 76mm guns

1 *Burevestnik* M (*Krivak* II) with 1 quad lnchr with URK-5 *Rastrub*-B (SS-N-14 *Silex*) AShM/ASW, 2 twin lnchr with *Osa*-M (SA-N-4 *Gecko* SAM), 2 quad 533mm ASTT with 53-65K HWT/SET-65K HWT, 2 RBU 6000 *Smerch* 2 A/S mor, 2 100mm guns

PATROL AND COASTAL COMBATANTS 105

CORVETTES 49

FSGM 20

6 *Buyan*-M (*Sviyazhsk*) with 1 octuple VLS with 3M54 (SS-N-27 *Sizzler*) AShM/3M14 (SS-N-30) dual-capable LACM, 2 sextuple lnchr with 3M47 *Gibka* (SA-N-10 *Grouse*) SAM, 1 AK630-M2 CIWS, 1 100mm gun

2 *Sivuch* (*Dergach*) with 2 quad lnchr with 3M80 *Moskit* (SS-N-22 *Sunburn*) AShM, 1 twin lnchr with 4K33AM *Osa*-M (SA-N-4 *Gecko*) SAM, 2 AK630M CIWS, 1 76mm gun

12 *Ovod* (*Nanuchka* III) with 2 triple lnchr with P-120 *Malakhit* (SS-N-9 *Siren*) AShM, 1 twin lnchr with *Osa*-MA2 (SA-N-4 *Gecko*) SAM, 1 AK630 CIWS, 1 76mm gun

FSM 29:

2 *Albatros* (*Grisha* III) with 1 twin lnchr with *Osa*-M (SA-N-4 *Gecko*) SAM, 2 twin 533mm ASTT, 2 RBU 6000 *Smerch* 2 A/S mor, 1 twin 57mm gun

18 *Albatros* (*Grisha* V) with 1 twin lnchr with *Osa*-M (SA-N-4 *Gecko*) SAM, 2 twin 533mm ASTT, 1 RBU 6000 *Smerch* 2 A/S mor, 1 76mm gun

3 *Buyan* (*Astrakhan*) with 1 sextuple lnchr with 3M47 *Gibka* (SA-N-10 *Grouse*) SAM, 1 A-215 *Grad*-M 122mm MRL, 2 AK306 CIWS, 1 100mm gun

6 *Parchim* II with 2 quad lnchr with *Strela*-2 (SA-N-5 *Grail*) SAM, 2 twin 533mm ASTT, 2 RBU 6000 *Smerch* 2 A/S mor, 1 AK630 CIWS, 1 76mm gun

PCFG 23:

5 *Molnya* (*Tarantul* II) with 2 twin lnchr with P-22 *Termit*-R (SS-N-2D Improved *Styx*) AShM, 2 AK630 MCIWS, 1 76mm gun

17 *Molnya* (*Tarantul* III) with 2 twin lnchr with 3M80 *Moskit* (SS-N-22 *Sunburn*) AShM, 2 AK630M CIWS, 1 76mm gun

1 *Molnya* (*Tarantul* III) with 2 twin lnchr with 3M80 *Moskit* (SS-N-22 *Sunburn*) AShM, 1 *Palma* CIWS, 1 76mm gun

PCF 1 *Molnya* (*Tarantul* III) with 2 AK630M CIWS, 1 76mm gun

PBF 13: 11 *Raptor* (capacity 20 troops); 2 *Mangust*

PBR 4 *Shmel* with 1 76mm gun

PB 15 *Grachonok*

MINE WARFARE • MINE COUNTERMEASURES 43

MCC 1 *Alexandrit* (Project 12700) with 1 AK306 CIWS

MHI 8: 7 *Sapfir* (*Lida*) with 1 AK306 CIWS; 1 *Malakhit* (*Olya*)

MHO 2 *Rubin* (*Gorya*) with 2 quad lnchr with *Strela*-2 (SA-N-5 *Grail*) SAM, 1 AK630 CIWS, 1 76mm gun

MSC 22: 20 *Yakhont* (*Sonya*) with 4 AK630 CIWS (some with 2 quad lnchr with *Strela*-2 (SA-N-5 *Grail*) SAM); 2 *Korund*-E (*Yevgenya*) (Project 1258E)

MSO 10: 9 *Akvamaren* (*Natya*); 1 *Agat* (*Natya* II) (all with 2 quad lnchr (manual aiming) with *Strela*-2 (SA-N-5 *Grail*) SAM, 2 RBU 1200 *Uragan* A/S mor, 2 twin AK230 CIWS

AMPHIBIOUS

LANDING SHIPS • LST 20:

12 Project 775 (*Ropucha* I/II) with 2 twin 57mm guns (capacity either 10 MBT and 190 troops or 24 APC (T) and 170 troops)

3 Project 775M (*Ropucha* III) with 2 AK630 CIWS, 1 76mm gun (capacity either 10 MBT and 190 troops or 24 APC (T) and 170 troops)

4 *Tapir* (*Alligator*) with 2-3 twin lnchr with *Strela-2* (SA-N-5 *Grail*) SAM, 2 twin 57mm guns (capacity 20 tanks; 300 troops)

1 *Ivan Gren* (Project 11711) with 1 AK630M-2 CIWS, 2 AK630M CIWS (capacity 1 Ka-29 *Helix* B hel; 13 MBT/36 AFV; 300 troops)

LANDING CRAFT 28

LCM 26: 9 *Akula* (*Ondatra*) (capacity 1 MBT); 5 *Dyugon* (capacity 5 APC or 100 troops); 12 *Serna* (Project 11770 (capacity 2 APC or 100 troops)

LCAC 2 *Pomornik* (*Zubr*) with 2 22-cell 140mm MS-227 *Ogon'* MRL, 2 AK630 CIWS (capacity 230 troops; either 3 MBT or 10 APC(T))

LOGISTICS AND SUPPORT 267

SSAN 9: 1 *Orenburg* (*Delta* III Stretch); 1 *Losharik*; 1 *Nelma* (X-Ray) (Project 1851); 2 *Halibut* (*Paltus*) (Project 18511); 3 *Kashalot* (*Uniform*); 1 *Podmoskovye* (Project 09787)

SSA 1 *Sarov* (Project 20120)

ABU 12: 8 *Kashtan*; 4 Project 419 (*Sura*)

AE 9: 7 *Muna*; 1 *Dubnyak*; *Akademik Kovalev* (Project 20181) with 1 hel landing platform

AEM 2: 1 *Kalma-3* (Project 1791R); 1 *Lama*

AFS 1 *Longvinik* (Project 23120)

AG 1 *Potok*

AGB 5: 1 *Dobrynya Mikitich*; 1 *Ilya Muromets*; 2 *Ivan Susanin*; 1 *Vladimir Kavraisky*

AGE 1 *Tchusovoy*

AGI 14: 2 *Alpinist*; 2 *Dubridium* (Project 1826); 1 *Moma*; 7 *Vishnya*; 2 *Yuri Ivanov*

AGM 1 *Marshal Nedelin*

AGOR 8: 1 *Akademik Krylov*; 1 *Igor Belousov*; 1 *Seliger*; 2 *Sibiriyakov*; 2 *Vinograd*; 1 *Yantar*

AGS 69: 8 *Biya*; 19 *Finik*; 7 *Kamenka*; 5 *Moma*; 9 *Onega*; 5 *Baklan* (Project 19920); 4 *Baklan* (Project 19920B); 2 *Vaygach*; 10 *Yug*

AGSH 1 *Samara*

AH 3 *Ob†*

AK 3: 2 *Irgiz*; 1 *Pevek* with 1 AK306 CIWS

AOL 9: 2 *Dubna*; 3 *Uda*; 4 *Altay* (mod)

AOR 3 *Boris Chilikin*

AORL 2: 1 *Kaliningradneft*; 1 *Olekma*

AOS 2 *Luza*

AR ε7 *Amur*

ARC 4: 3 *Emba*; 1 Improved *Klasma*

ARS 30: 1 *Kommuna*; 6 *Goryn*; 4 *Mikhail Rudnitsky*; 18 Project 23040; 1 *Zvezdochka* (Project 20180)

AS 3 Project 2020 (*Malina*)

ASR 1 *Elbrus*

ATF 55: 1 *Okhotsk*; 1 *Baklan*; ε3 *Katun*; 4 *Ingul*; 2 *Neftegaz*; 12 *Okhtensky*; 13 *Prometey*; 1 *Prut*; 4 *Sliva*; 14 *Sorum*

AWT 1 *Manych*

AXL 10: 8 *Petrushka*; 2 *Smolny* with 2 RBU 2500 A/S mor, 2 twin 76mm guns

Naval Aviation ε31,000

FORCES BY ROLE

FIGHTER

1 sqn with MiG-31B/BS *Foxhound*

1 sqn with Su-27/Su-27UB *Flanker*

1 regt with Su-33 *Flanker* D; Su-25UTG *Frogfoot*

FIGHTER/GROUND ATTACK

1 regt with MiG-29KR/KUBR *Fulcrum*

1 regt with MiG-31BM *Foxhound*; Su-24M/M2/MR *Fencer*

ANTI-SURFACE WARFARE/ISR

1 regt with Su-24M/MR *Fencer*; Su-30SM

1 sqn with Su-24M/MR *Fencer*

ANTI-SUBMARINE WARFARE

3 sqn with Il-38/Il-38N *May**; Il-18D; Il-20RT *Coot* A; Il-22 *Coot* B

8 sqn with Ka-27/Ka-29 *Helix*

1 sqn with Mi-14 *Haze* A

2 sqn with Tu-142MK/MZ/MR *Bear* F/J*

1 unit with Ka-31R *Helix*

MARITIME PATROL/TRANSPORT

1 sqn with An-26 *Curl*; Be-12 *Mail**; Mi-8 *Hip*

SEARCH & RESCUE/TRANSPORT

1 sqn with An-12PS *Cub*; An-26 *Curl*; Tu-134

TRANSPORT

1 sqn with An-12BK *Cub*; An-24RV *Coke*; An-26 *Curl*; An-72 *Coaler*; An-140

2 sqn with An-26 *Curl*; Tu-134

TRAINING

1 sqn with L-39 *Albatros*; Su-25UTG *Frogfoot*

1 sqn with An-140; Tu-134; Tu-154, Il-38 *May*

ATTACK/TRANSPORT HELICOPTER

1 sqn with Mi-24P *Hind*; Mi-8 *Hip*

TRANSPORT HELICOPTER

1 sqn with Mi-8 *Hip*

AIR DEFENCE

1 SAM regt with S-300PM1 (SA-20 *Gargoyle*)

1 SAM regt with S-300PM1 (SA-20 *Gargoyle*); S-300PS (SA-10B *Grumble*)

1 SAM regt with S-300PM1 (SA-20 *Gargoyle*); S-400 (SA-21 *Growler*); 96K6 Pantsir-S1 (SA-22 *Greyhound*)

1 SAM regt with S-300PS (SA-10B *Grumble*); S-400 (SA-21 *Growler*); 96K6 Pantsir-S1 (SA-22 *Greyhound*)

EQUIPMENT BY TYPE

AIRCRAFT 217 combat capable

FTR 67: 12 MiG-31B/BS *Foxhound*; 20 MiG-31BM *Foxhound*; 17 Su-33 *Flanker* D; 18 Su-27/Su-27UB *Flanker*

FGA 44: 19 MiG-29KR *Fulcrum*; 3 MiG-29KUBR *Fulcrum*; 22 Su-30SM

ATK 46: 41 Su-24M *Fencer*; 5 Su-25UTG *Frogfoot* (trg role)

ASW 44: 12 Tu-142MK/MZ *Bear* F; 10 Tu-142MR *Bear* J (comms); 15 Il-38 *May*; 7 Il-38N *May*

MP 5: 4 Be-12PS *Mail**; 1 Il-18D

ISR 12 Su-24MR *Fencer* E*

SAR 3 An-12PS *Cub*

ELINT 4: 2 Il-20RT *Coot* A; 2 Il-22 *Coot* B

TPT 49: **Medium** 2 An-12BK *Cub*; **Light** 45: 1 An-24RV *Coke*; 24 An-26 *Curl*; 6 An-72 *Coaler*; 4 An-140; 9 Tu-134; 1 Tu-134UBL; **PAX** 2 Tu-154M *Careless*

TRG 4 L-39 *Albatros*

HELICOPTERS

ATK 8 Mi-24P *Hind*

ASW 83: 41 Ka-27PL *Helix*; 22 Ka-27M *Helix*; 20 Mi-14 *Haze* A

EW 8 Mi-8 *Hip* J
AFW 2 Ka-31R *Helix*
SAR 56: 16 Ka-27PS *Helix* D; 40 Mi-14PS *Haze* C
TPT 41: **Medium** 35: 27 Ka-29 *Helix*; 4 Mi-8T *Hip*; 4 Mi-8MT *Hip*; **Light** 6 Ka-226T
AIR DEFENCE • SAM
Long-range 120: 56 S-300PM1 (SA-20 *Gargoyle*); 40 S-300PS (SA-10 *Grumble*); 24 S-400 (SA-21 *Growler*)
Short-range 12 96K6 *Pantsir*-S1 (SA-22 *Greyhound*)
AIR-LAUNCHED MISSILES
AAM • IR R-27T/ET (AA-10B/D *Alamo*); R-60 (AA-8 *Aphid*); R-73 (AA-11A *Archer*); ARH R-77-1 (AA-12B *Adder*); SARH R-27R/ER (AA-10A/C *Alamo*); R-33 (AA-9A *Amos*)
ARM Kh-25MP (AS-12 *Kegler*); Kh-31P (AS-17A *Krypton*); Kh-58 (AS-11 *Kilter*)
ASM Kh-59 (AS-13 *Kingbolt*); Kh-29T
AShM Kh-31A (AS-17B *Krypton*)

Naval Infantry (Marines) ε35,000

FORCES BY ROLE
COMMAND
3 corps HQ
SPECIAL FORCES
4 (OMRP) SF unit
11 (PDSS) cbt diver unit
MANOEUVRE
Reconnaissance
1 recce bde
Mechanised
3 MR bde
1 MR regt
6 naval inf bde
1 naval inf regt
SURFACE-TO-SURFACE MISSILE
1 SRBM/GLCM bde with 9K720 *Iskander*-M (SS-26 *Stone*/SSC-7)
COMBAT SUPPORT
2 arty bde
AIR DEFENCE
2 SAM regt with 9K33 *Osa* (SA-8 *Gecko*); *Strela*-1/*Strela*-10 (SA-9 *Gaskin*/SA-13 *Gopher*)
2 SAM regt with S-400 (SA-21 *Growler*); 96K6 *Pantsir*-S1 (SA-22 *Greyhound*)
1 SAM regt with S-300V4 (SA-23)
EQUIPMENT BY TYPE
ARMOURED FIGHTING VEHICLES
MBT 300: 50 T-72B; 200 T-72B3; 50 T-80BV
IFV 1,061: 400 BMP-2; 661 BTR-82A
APC 400
APC (T) 300 MT-LB
APC (W) 100 BTR-80
ANTI-TANK/ANTI-INFRASTRUCTURE
MSL
SP 60 9P148 with 9K111-1 *Konkurs* (AT-5 *Spandrel*); 9P149 with 9K114 *Shturm* (AT-6 *Spiral*); 9P157-2 with 9K123 *Khrisantema* (AT-15 *Springer*)
MANPATS 9K111-1 *Konkurs* (AT-5 *Spandrel*); 9K135 *Kornet* (AT-14 *Spriggan*)
GUNS 100mm T-12

ARTILLERY 383
SP 163: **122mm** 95 2S1 *Gvozdika*; **152mm** 68: 50 2S3 *Akatsiya*; 18 2S19 *Msta*-S
TOWED **152mm** 100: 50 2A36 *Giatsint*-B; 50 2A65 *Msta*-B
GUN/MOR 66
SP **120mm** 42: 12 2S23 NONA-SVK; 30 2S9 NONA-S
TOWED **120mm** 24 2B16 NONA-K
MRL 54: **122mm** 36 BM-21 *Grad*/*Tornado*-G; **220mm** 18 9P140 *Uragan*
SURFACE-TO-SURFACE MISSILE LAUNCHER
SRBM • Dual-capable 12 9K720 *Iskander*-M (SS-26 *Stone*)
GLCM • Dual-capable Some 9M728 (SSC-7)
AIR DEFENCE
SAM
Long-range 48+: 48 S-400 (SA-21 *Growler*); S-300V4 (SA-23)
Short-range 12 96K6 *Pantsir*-S1 (SA-22 *Greyhound*)
Point-defence 70+: 20 9K33 *Osa* (SA-8 *Gecko*); 50 9K31 *Strela*-1/9K35 *Strela*-10 (SA-9 *Gaskin*/SA-13 *Gopher*); 9K338 *Igla*-S (SA-24 *Grinch*)
GUNS **23mm** 60 ZSU-23-4

Coastal Missile and Artillery Troops 2,000

FORCES BY ROLE
COASTAL DEFENCE
5 AShM bde
1 AShM regt

EQUIPMENT BY TYPE
COASTAL DEFENCE
ARTY • SP **130mm** ε36 A-222 *Bereg*
AShM 76+: 36 3K60 *Bal* (SSC-6 *Sennight*); 40 3K55 *Bastion* (SSC-5 *Stooge*); some 4K44 *Redut* (SSC-1 *Sepal*); some 4K51 *Rubezh* (SSC-3 *Styx*)

Aerospace Forces ε165,000 (incl conscripts)

A joint CIS Unified Air Defence System covers RUS, ARM, BLR, KAZ, KGZ, TJK, TKM and UZB

FORCES BY ROLE
BOMBER
3 regt with Tu-22M3 *Backfire* C
3 sqn with Tu-95MS/MS mod *Bear*
1 sqn with Tu-160/Tu-160M1 *Blackjack*
FIGHTER
1 sqn with MiG-29/MiG-29UB *Fulcrum* (Armenia)
1 regt with MiG-31BM *Foxhound*
1 regt with MiG-31B/BS/BM *Foxhound*
1 regt with MiG-31B/BS/BM *Foxhound*; Su-27/Su-27UB *Flanker*
1 regt with Su-27/Su-27SM/Su-27UB *Flanker*; Su-30M2
2 regt with Su-30SM
FIGHTER/GROUND ATTACK
1 regt with MiG-31BM *Foxhound*; Su-27SM *Flanker*; Su-30M2; Su-30SM; Su-35S *Flanker*
1 regt with Su-27SM *Flanker*; Su-35S *Flanker*
1 regt with Su-35S *Flanker*; Su-30SM
1 regt with Su-27 *Flanker*; Su-27SM3 *Flanker*; Su-30M2
1 regt with Su-25 *Frogfoot*; Su-30SM

GROUND ATTACK
  1 regt with Su-24M/M2 *Fencer*; Su-34 *Fullback*
  1 regt with Su-24M *Fencer*; Su-25SM *Frogfoot*
  3 regt with Su-25SM/SM3 *Frogfoot*
  1 sqn with Su-25SM *Frogfoot* (Kyrgyzstan)
  3 regt with Su-34 *Fullback*
ISR
  2 regt with Su-24MR *Fencer**
  2 sqn with Su-24MR *Fencer**
  1 flt with An-30 *Clank*
AIRBORNE EARLY WARNING & CONTROL
  1 sqn with A-50/A-50U *Mainstay*
TANKER
  1 sqn with Il-78/Il-78M *Midas*
TRANSPORT
  6 regt/sqn with An-12BK *Cub*; An-26 *Curl*; Tu-134 *Crusty*; Tu-154 *Careless*; Mi-8 *Hip*
  1 regt with An-124 *Condor*; Il-76MD *Candid*
  1 regt with An-12BK *Cub*; Il-76MD *Candid*
  1 sqn with An-22 *Cock*
  3 regt with Il-76MD *Candid*
ATTACK/TRANSPORT HELICOPTER
  1 bde with Ka-52A *Hokum B*; Mi-28N *Havoc B*; Mi-35 *Hind*; Mi-26 *Halo*; Mi-8MTV-5 *Hip*
  1 bde with Ka-52A *Hokum B*; Mi-26 *Halo*; Mi-8 *Hip*
  1 bde with Mi-28N *Havoc B*; Mi-35 *Hind*; Mi-26 *Halo*; Mi-8 *Hip*
  2 regt with Ka-52A *Hokum B*; Mi-28N *Havoc B*; Mi-35 *Hind*; Mi-8 *Hip*
  1 regt with Ka-52A *Hokum B*; Mi-24P *Hind*; Mi-8PPA *Hip*; Mi-8 *Hip*
  1 regt with Ka-52A *Hokum B*; Mi-8 *Hip*
  1 regt with Mi-28N *Havoc B*; Mi-35 *Hind*; Mi-8 *Hip*
  1 regt with Mi-28N *Havoc B*; Mi-24P *Hind*; Mi-35 *Hind*; Mi-8 *Hip*
  2 regt with Mi-24P *Hind*; Mi-8 *Hip*
  2 sqn with Mi-24P *Hind*; Mi-8 *Hip*
AIR DEFENCE
  9 AD div HQ
  4 regt with 9K37M *Buk-M1-2*/9K317 *Buk-M2* (SA-11 *Gadfly*/SA-17 *Grizzly*); S-300V (SA-12 *Gladiator/Giant*)
  1 bde with S-300PS (SA-10 *Grumble*)
  4 regt with S-300PS (SA-10 *Grumble*)
  7 regt with S-300PM1/PM2 (SA-20 *Gargoyle*)
  9 regt with S-400 (SA-21 *Growler*); 96K6 *Pantsir*-S1 (SA-22 *Greyhound*)
EQUIPMENT BY TYPE
AIRCRAFT 1,223 combat capable
  BBR 139: 61 Tu-22M3 *Backfire C*; 1 Tu-22M3M *Backfire*; 1 Tu-22MR *Backfire* (1 in overhaul); 46 Tu-95MS *Bear*; 14 Tu-95MS mod *Bear*; 10 Tu-160 *Blackjack*; 6 Tu-160M1 *Blackjack*
  FTR 222: 70 MiG-29/MiG-29UB *Fulcrum*; 12 MiG-31B/31BS *Foxhound*; 80 MiG-31BM *Foxhound*; 50 Su-27 *Flanker*; 10 Su-27UB *Flanker*
  FGA 412: 44 MiG-29SMT *Fulcrum*; 6 MiG-29UBT *Fulcrum*; 47 Su-27SM *Flanker*; 19 Su-27SM3 *Flanker*; 20 Su-30M2; 91 Su-30SM; 112 Su-34 *Fullback*; 73 Su-35S *Flanker*
  ATK 264: 70 Su-24M/M2 *Fencer*; 40 Su-25 *Frogfoot*; 139 Su-25SM/SM3 *Frogfoot*; 15 Su-25UB *Frogfoot*
  ISR 87: 4 An-30 *Clank*; 79 Su-24MR *Fencer**; 2 Tu-214ON; 2 Tu-214R

EW 3 Il-22PP
ELINT 31: 14 Il-20M *Coot A*; 5 Il-22 *Coot B*; 12 Il-22M *Coot B*
AEW&C 18: 14 A-50 *Mainstay*; 4 A-50U *Mainstay*
C2 11: 4 Il-80 *Maxdome*; 2 Il-82; 4 Tu-214SR; 1 Tu-214PU-SBUS
TKR 15: 5 Il-78 *Midas*; 10 Il-78M *Midas*
TPT 427: **Heavy** 111: 9 An-124 *Condor*; 2 An-22 *Cock*; 99 Il-76MD *Candid*; 1 Il-76MD-M *Candid*; **Medium** 65 An-12BK *Cub*; **Light** 234: 114 An-26 *Curl*; 25 An-72 *Coaler*; 5 An-140; 9 An-148-100E; 27 L-410; 54 Tu-134 *Crusty*; **PAX** 17 Tu-154 *Careless*
TRG 227: 120 L-39 *Albatros*; 107 Yak-130 *Mitten**
HELICOPTERS
  ATK 375+: 117 Ka-52A *Hokum B*; 100 Mi-24D/V/P *Hind*; 90+ Mi-28N *Havoc B*; 8 Mi-28UB *Havoc*; 60+ Mi-35 *Hind*
  EW 27: 20 Mi-8PPA *Hip*; 7 Mi-8MTRP-1 *Hip*
  TPT 339: **Heavy** 33 Mi-26/Mi-26T *Halo*; **Medium** 306 Mi-8/Mi-8MT/Mi-8AMTSh/Mi-8AMTSh-VA/Mi-8MTV-5 *Hip*
  TRG 69: 19 Ka-226U; 50 Ansat-U
UNMANNED AERIAL VEHICLES
  ISR • **Medium** *Forpost* (*Searcher* II)
AIR DEFENCE • SAM 620:
  Long-range 490: 160 S-300PS (SA-10 *Grumble*); 150 S-300PM1/PM2 (SA-20 *Gargoyle*); 20 S-300V (SA-12 *Gladiator/Giant*); 160 S-400 (SA-21 *Growler*)
  Medium-range 80 9K37M *Buk*-M1-2/9K317 *Buk*-M2 (SA-11 *Gadfly*/SA-17 *Grizzly*)
  Short-range 50 96K6 *Pantsir*-S1/S2 (SA-22 *Greyhound*)
AIR-LAUNCHED MISSILES
  AAM • **IR** R-27T/ET (AA-10B/D *Alamo*); R-73 (AA-11 *Archer*); R-60T (AA-8 *Aphid*); **SARH** R-27R/ER (AA-10A/C *Alamo*); R-33/33S (AA-9 *Amos* A/B); **ARH** R-77-1 (AA-12B *Adder*); R-37M (AA-13A *Axehead*); **PRH** R-27P/EP (AA-10E/F *Alamo*)
  ARM Kh-25MP (AS-12A *Kegler*); Kh-25M (AS-12B *Kegler*); Kh-31P/PM (AS-17A/C *Krypton*); Kh-58 (AS-11 *Kilter*)
  ASM Kh-29 (AS-14 *Kedge*); Kh-38; Kh-59/Kh-59M (AS-13 *Kingbolt*/AS-18 *Kazoo*); *Kinzhal*; 9M114 *Kokon* (AT-6 *Spiral*); 9M120 *Ataka* (AT-9 *Spiral* 2); 9M120-1 *Vikhr* (AT-16 *Scallion*)
  AShM Kh-22 (AS-4 *Kitchen*); Kh-31A/AM (AS-17B/D *Krypton*); Kh-32 (entering service); Kh-35U (AS-20 *Kayak*)
  LACM
    Nuclear Kh-55SM (AS-15B *Kent*); Kh-102 (AS-23 *Kodiak*); **Conventional** Kh-101 (AS-23 *Kodiak*); Kh-555 (AS-22)
BOMBS
  Laser-guided KAB-500; KAB-1500L
  TV-guided KAB-500KR; KAB-1500KR; KAB-500OD; UPAB 1500
  INS/GLONASS-guided KAB-500S

Airborne Troops ε45,000
FORCES BY ROLE
SPECIAL FORCES
  1 (AB Recce) SF bde

MANOEUVRE
 Air Manoeuvre
 2 AB div (1 tk coy; 2 para/air aslt regt; 1 arty regt; 1 AD regt)
 2 AB div (2 para/air aslt regt; 1 arty regt; 1 AD regt)
 1 indep AB bde
 3 air aslt bde

EQUIPMENT BY TYPE
ARMOURED FIGHTING VEHICLES
 MBT 60 T-72B3
 IFV 20 BTR-82AM
 APC • APC (T) 776: 700 BTR-D; 76 BTR-MDM
 AUV GAZ *Tigr*; UAMZ *Toros*
 ABCV 1,291: 100 BMD-1; 1,000 BMD-2; 10 BMD-3; 30 BMD-4; 151 BMD-4M
ENGINEERING & MAINTENANCE VEHICLES
 ARV BREM-D; BREhM-D
ANTI-TANK/ANTI-INFRASTRUCTURE
 MSL
  SP 100 BTR-RD
  MANPATS 9K111 *Fagot* (AT-4 *Spigot*); 9K113 *Konkurs* (AT-5 *Spandrel*); 9K115 *Metis* (AT-7 *Saxhorn*); 9K115-1 *Metis*-M (AT-13 *Saxhorn* 2); 9K135 *Kornet* (AT-14 *Spriggan*)
 RCL 73mm SPG-9
 GUNS • SP 125mm 36+ 2S25 *Sprut*-SD
ARTILLERY 600+
 TOWED 122mm 150 D-30
 GUN/MOR • SP 120mm 250: 220 2S9 NONA-S; 30 2S9 NONA-SM; (500 2S9 NONA-S in store)
 MOR • TOWED 200+ **82mm** 150 2B14; **120mm** 50+ 2B23 NONA-M1
AIR DEFENCE
 SAM • Point-defence 30+: 30 *Strela*-10MN; 9K310 *Igla*-1 (SA-16 *Gimlet*); 9K38 *Igla* (SA-18 *Grouse*); 9K333 *Verba*; 9K338 *Igla*-S (SA-24 *Grinch*); 9K34 *Strela*-3 (SA-14 *Gremlin*)
 GUNS • SP 23mm 150 BTR-ZD

Special Operations Forces ε1,000
FORCES BY ROLE
SPECIAL FORCES
 2 SF unit

Railway Troops ε29,000
4 regional commands
FORCES BY ROLE
COMBAT SERVICE SUPPORT
 10 (railway) tpt bde

Russian Military Districts

Western Military District
HQ at St Petersburg

Army
FORCES BY ROLE
COMMAND
 3 army HQ
SPECIAL FORCES
 2 (Spetsnaz) SF bde

MANOEUVRE
 Reconnaissance
 1 recce bde
 Armoured
 1 tk div
 1 tk bde
 2 MR div
 Mechanised
 1 MR div
 3 MR bde
SURFACE-TO-SURFACE MISSILE
 2 SRBM/GLCM bde with *Iskander*-M
 1 SRBM bde with *Tochka*-U
COMBAT SUPPORT
 2 arty bde
 1 (hy) arty bde
 1 MRL bde
 1 engr bde
 1 MP bde
 1 NBC bde
 2 NBC regt
COMBAT SERVICE SUPPORT
 2 log bde
AIR DEFENCE
 3 AD bde

Reserves
FORCES BY ROLE
 MANOEUVRE
 Mechanised
 2 MR bde

Northern Fleet
EQUIPMENT BY TYPE
SUBMARINES 29
 STRATEGIC 8 **SSBN** (of which 1 in refit and 1 in reserve)
 TACTICAL 21: 4 **SSGN**; 11 **SSN** (of which 3 in refit and 1 in reserve); 6 **SSK** (of which 1 in refit)
PRINCIPAL SURFACE COMBATANTS 10: 1 **CV** (in refit); 1 **CGHMN** (1 other in refit); 1 **CGHM**; 7 **DDGHM**
PATROL AND COASTAL COMBATANTS 10: 2 **FSGM**; 6 **FSM**; 4 **PB**
MINE WARFARE • MINE COUNTERMEASURES 10: 1 **MHO**; 2 **MSO**; 7 **MSC**
AMPHIBIOUS 6: 4 **LST**; 2 **LCM**

Naval Aviation
FORCES BY ROLE
FIGHTER
 1 regt with Su-33 *Flanker* D; Su-25UTG *Frogfoot*
FIGHTER/GROUND ATTACK
 1 regt with MiG-29KR/KUBR *Fulcrum*
FIGHTER/GROUND ATTACK/ISR
 1 regt with MiG-31BM *Foxhound*; Su-24M/M2/MR *Fencer*
ANTI-SUBMARINE WARFARE
 1 sqn with Il-38 *May*; Il-20RT *Coot* A; Tu-134
 3 sqn with Ka-27/Ka-29 *Helix*
 1 sqn with Tu-142MK/MZ/MR *Bear* F/J

AIR DEFENCE
3 SAM regt with S-300PS (SA-10 *Grumble*); S-300PM1 (SA-20 *Gargoyle*); S-400 (SA-21 *Growler*); 96K6 Pantsir-S1 (SA-22 *Greyhound*)

EQUIPMENT BY TYPE
AIRCRAFT
FTR 38: 20 MiG-31BM *Foxhound*; 18 Su-33 *Flanker* D
FGA 25: 19 MiG-29KR *Fulcrum*; 4 MiG-29KUBR *Fulcrum*; 2 Su-30SM
ATK 18: 13 Su-24M *Fencer*; 5 Su-25UTG *Frogfoot* (trg role)
ASW 21: 10 Il-38 *May*; 11 Tu-142MK/MZ/MR *Bear F/J*
ISR 4 Su-24MR *Fencer**
ELINT 3: 2 Il-20RT *Coot A*; 1 Il-22 *Coot B*
TPT 9: 8 An-26 *Curl*; 1 Tu-134
HELICOPTERS
ASW Ka-27 *Helix A*
TPT • Medium Ka-29 *Helix B*; Mi-8 *Hip*
AIR DEFENCE • SAM
Long-range S-300PS (SA-10 *Grumble*); S-300PM1 (SA-20 *Gargoyle*); S-400 (SA-21 *Growler*)
Short-range 96K6 Pantsir-S1 (SA-22 *Greyhound*)

Naval Infantry
FORCES BY ROLE
COMMAND
1 corps HQ
MANOEUVRE
Mechanised
2 MR bde
1 naval inf bde

Coastal Artillery and Missile Troops
FORCES BY ROLE
COASTAL DEFENCE
1 AShM bde

Baltic Fleet
EQUIPMENT BY TYPE
SUBMARINES • TACTICAL • SSK 2
PRINCIPAL SURFACE COMBATANTS 8: 2 DDGHM; 6 FFGHM (of which 1 in refit)
PATROL AND COASTAL COMBATANTS 25: 6 FSGM; 6 FSM; 7 PCFG; 5 PBF; 1 PB
MINE WARFARE • MINE COUNTERMEASURES 12: 1 MCC; 5 MSC; 6 MHI
AMPHIBIOUS 13: 4 LST; 7 LCM; 2 LCAC

Naval Aviation
FORCES BY ROLE
FIGHTER
1 sqn with Su-27 *Flanker*
ANTI-SURFACE WARFARE/ISR
1 sqn with Su-24M/MR *Fencer*; Su-30SM
ANTI-SUBMARINE WARFARE
1 sqn with Ka-27/Ka-29 *Helix*
TRANSPORT
1 sqn with An-26 *Curl*; Tu-134 *Crusty*

ATTACK/TRANSPORT HELICOPTER
1 sqn with Mi-24P *Hind*; Mi-8 *Hip*
TRANSPORT HELICOPTER
1 sqn with Mi-8 *Hip*
EQUIPMENT BY TYPE
AIRCRAFT
FTR 18 Su-27/Su-27UB *Flanker*
FGA 8 Su-30SM
ATK 10 Su-24M *Fencer*
ISR 4 Su-24MR *Fencer**
TPT 8: 6 An-26 *Curl*; 2 Tu-134 *Crusty*
HELICOPTERS
ATK Mi-24P *Hind*
ASW Ka-27 *Helix*
TPT • Medium Ka-29 *Helix*; Mi-8 *Hip*

Naval Infantry
FORCES BY ROLE
COMMAND
1 corps HQ
MANOEUVRE
Mechanised
1 MR bde
1 MR regt
1 naval inf bde
SURFACE-TO-SURFACE MISSILE
1 SRBM/GLCM bde with *Iskander*-M
COMBAT SUPPORT
1 arty bde
AIR DEFENCE
3 SAM regt

Coastal Artillery and Missile Troops
FORCES BY ROLE
COASTAL DEFENCE
1 AShM regt

Military Air Force

6th Air Force & Air Defence Army
FORCES BY ROLE
FIGHTER
1 regt with Su-30SM
1 regt with MiG-31B/BS/BM *Foxhound*; Su-27 *Flanker*
1 regt with Su-27SM *Flanker*; Su-35S *Flanker*
GROUND ATTACK
1 regt with Su-34 *Fullback*
ISR
1 sqn with Su-24MR *Fencer*
1 flt with A-30 *Clank*
TRANSPORT
1 regt with An-12 *Cub*; An-26 *Curl*; Tu-134 *Crusty*
ATTACK HELICOPTER
1 bde with Ka-52A *Hokum B*; Mi-28N *Havoc B*; Mi-35 *Hind*; Mi-26 *Halo*; Mi-8MTV-5 *Hip*
1 regt with with Mi-24P/Mi-35 *Hind*; Mi-28N *Havoc B*; Mi-8 *Hip*
1 regt with Mi-24P *Hind*; Ka-52A *Hokum B*; Mi-8 *Hip*; Mi-8PPA *Hip*

AIR DEFENCE
1 SAM regt with 9K37M *Buk*-M1-2 (SA-11 *Gadfly*); S-300V (SA-12 *Gladiator/Giant*)
5 SAM regt with S-300PM1 (SA-20 *Gargoyle*)
1 SAM regt with S-400 (SA-21 *Growler*); 96K6 *Pantsir*-S1 (SA-22 *Greyhound*)

EQUIPMENT BY TYPE
AIRCRAFT
FTR 61: 31 MiG-31B/BS/BM *Foxhound*; 30 Su-27/Su-27UB *Flanker*
FGA 85: 12 Su-27SM *Flanker*; 24 Su-30SM; 24 Su-34 *Fullback*; 25 Su-35S *Flanker*
ISR 19: 4 An-30 *Clank*; 15 Su-24MR *Fencer**
TPT 12 An-12/An-26/Tu-134
HELICOPTERS
ATK 64+: 24 Ka-52A *Hokum* B; 16 Mi-24P *Hind*; 24 Mi-28N *Havoc* B; 12+ Mi-35 *Hind*
EW 10 Mi-8PPA *Hip*
TPT • Medium 50 Mi-8 *Hip*
AIR DEFENCE • SAM
Long-range S-300PM1 (SA-20 *Gargoyle*); S-300V (SA-12 *Gladiator/Giant*); S-400 (SA-21 *Growler*)
Medium-range 9K37M *Buk*-M1-2 (SA-11 *Gadfly*)
Short-range 96K6 *Pantsir*-S1 (SA-22 *Greyhound*)

Airborne Troops
FORCES BY ROLE
SPECIAL FORCES
1 (AB Recce) SF bde
MANOEUVRE
Air Manoeuvre
3 AB div

Central Military District
HQ at Yekaterinburg

Army
FORCES BY ROLE
COMMAND
2 army HQ
SPECIAL FORCES
2 (Spetsnaz) SF bde
MANOEUVRE
Armoured
1 tk div
3 MR bde
Mechanised
2 MR bde
2 (lt/mtn) MR bde
SURFACE-TO-SURFACE MISSILE
2 SRBM/GLCM bde with *Iskander*-M
COMBAT SUPPORT
2 arty bde
1 MRL bde
1 engr bde
2 NBC bde
2 NBC regt
COMBAT SERVICE SUPPORT
2 log bde
AIR DEFENCE
3 AD bde

Reserves
FORCES BY ROLE
MANOEUVRE
Mechanised
3 MR bde

Military Air Force
14th Air Force & Air Defence Army
FORCES BY ROLE
FIGHTER
1 regt with MiG-31BM *Foxhound*
1 regt with MiG-31B/BS/BM *Foxhound*
GROUND ATTACK
1 regt with Su-34 *Fullback*
1 sqn with Su-25SM *Frogfoot* (Kyrgyzstan)
ISR
1 sqn with Su-24MR *Fencer* E
TRANSPORT
1 regt with An-12 *Cub*; An-26 *Curl*; Tu-134 *Crusty*; Tu-154; Mi-8 *Hip*
ATTACK/TRANSPORT HELICOPTER
1 regt with Mi-24P *Hind*; Mi-8 *Hip*
1 sqn with Mi-24P *Hind*; Mi-8 *Hip* (Tajikistan)
AIR DEFENCE
3 regt with S-300PS (SA-10 *Grumble*)
1 bde with S-300PS (SA-10 *Grumble*)
1 regt with S-300PM1 (SA-20 *Gargoyle*)
2 regt with S-400 (SA-21 *Growler*); 96K6 *Pantsir*-S1 (SA-22 *Greyhound*)

EQUIPMENT BY TYPE
AIRCRAFT
FTR 40 MiG-31B/BS/BM *Foxhound*
FGA 12 Su-34 *Fullback*
ATK 25: 12 Su-24M *Fencer*; 13 Su-25SM *Frogfoot*
ISR 9 Su-24MR *Fencer* E
TPT 36 An-12 *Cub*/An-26 *Curl*/Tu-134 *Crusty*/Tu-154 *Careless*
HELICOPTERS
ATK 24 Mi-24 *Hind*
TPT 46: 6 Mi-26 *Halo*; 40 Mi-8 *Hip*
AIR DEFENCE • SAM
Long-range S-300PS (SA-10 *Grumble*); S-300PM1 (SA-20 *Gargoyle*); S-400 (SA-21 *Growler*)
Short-range 96K6 *Pantsir*-S1 (SA-22 *Greyhound*)

Airborne Troops
FORCES BY ROLE
MANOEUVRE
Air Manoeuvre
1 AB bde

Southern Military District
HQ located at Rostov-on-Don

Army
FORCES BY ROLE
COMMAND
3 army HQ
SPECIAL FORCES
3 (Spetsnaz) SF bde
1 (Spetsnaz) SF regt

MANOEUVRE
  Reconnaissance
    1 recce bde
  Armoured
    1 MR div
    3 MR bde
    1 MR bde (Armenia)
    1 MR bde (South Ossetia)
  Mechanised
    1 MR div
    1 MR bde
    1 MR bde (Abkhazia)
    1 (lt/mtn) MR bde
SURFACE-TO-SURFACE MISSILE
  2 SRBM/GLCM bde with *Iskander*-M
COMBAT SUPPORT
  2 arty bde
  1 MRL bde
  1 engr bde
  1 NBC bde
  2 NBC regt
COMBAT SERVICE SUPPORT
  2 log bde
AIR DEFENCE
  4 AD bde

Black Sea Fleet

The Black Sea Fleet is primarily based in Crimea, at Sevastopol, Karantinnaya Bay and Streletskaya Bay

EQUIPMENT BY TYPE
SUBMARINES • TACTICAL 7 **SSK** (of which 1 in refit)
PRINCIPAL SURFACE COMBATANTS 7: 1 **CGHM**; 1 **DDGM**; 3 **FFGHM**; 2 **FFGM**
PATROL AND COASTAL COMBATANTS 35: 4 **FSGM**; 6 **FSM**; 5 **PCFG**; 6 **PB**; 9 **PBF**; 2 **PBR**
MINE WARFARE • MINE COUNTERMEASURES 10: 1 **MHO**; 6 **MSO**; 2 **MSC**; 1 **MHI**
AMPHIBIOUS 10: 7 **LST**; 3 **LCM**

Naval Aviation
FORCES BY ROLE
FIGHTER
ANTI-SURFACE WARFARE/ISR
  1 regt with Su-24M/MR *Fencer*; Su-30SM
ANTI-SUBMARINE WARFARE
  1 sqn with Ka-27 *Helix*
  1 sqn with Mi-14 *Haze*
MARITIME PATROL/TRANSPORT
  1 sqn with An-26 *Curl*; Be-12PS *Mail**; Mi-8
EQUIPMENT BY TYPE
AIRCRAFT
  FGA 12 Su-30SM
  ATK 13 Su-24M *Fencer*
  ISR 4 Su-24MR *Fencer* E
  MP 3 Be-12PS *Mail**
  TPT 6 An-26
HELICOPTERS
  ASW Ka-27 *Helix*
  TPT • Medium Mi-8 *Hip* (MP/EW/Tpt)

Naval Infantry
FORCES BY ROLE
COMMAND
  1 corps HQ
MANOEUVRE
  Mechanised
    2 naval inf bde
COMBAT SUPPORT
  1 arty bde
AIR DEFENCE
  1 SAM regt

Coastal Artillery and Missile Troops
FORCES BY ROLE
COASTAL DEFENCE
  2 AShM bde

Caspian Sea Flotilla

EQUIPMENT BY TYPE
PRINCIPAL SURFACE COMBATANTS 2 **FFGM**
PATROL AND COASTAL COMBATANTS 8: 1 **FSGM**; 3 **FSM**; 1 **PCFG**; 1 **PB**; 2 **PBR**
MINE WARFARE • MINE COUNTERMEASURES 3: 2 **MSC**; 1 **MHI**
AMPHIBIOUS 9 **LCM**

Naval Infantry
FORCES BY ROLE
MANOEUVRE
  Mechanised
    1 naval inf regt

Military Air Force

4th Air Force & Air Defence Army
FORCES BY ROLE
FIGHTER
  1 regt with Su-30SM
  1 sqn with MiG-29 *Fulcrum* (Armenia)
FIGHTER/GROUND ATTACK
  1 regt with Su-27/Su-27SM *Flanker*; Su-30M2
  1 regt with Su-27/Su-27SM3 *Flanker*; Su-30M2
GROUND ATTACK
  1 regt with Su-24M *Fencer*; Su-25SM *Frogfoot*
  2 regt with Su-25SM/SM3 *Frogfoot*
  1 regt with Su-34 *Fullback*
ISR
  1 regt with Su-24MR *Fencer* E
TRANSPORT
  1 regt with An-12 *Cub*/Mi-8 *Hip*
ATTACK/TRANSPORT HELICOPTER
  1 bde with Mi-28N *Havoc* B; Mi-35 *Hind*; Mi-8 *Hip*; Mi-26 *Halo*
  1 regt with Mi-28N *Havoc* B; Mi-35 *Hind*; Mi-8 *Hip*
  2 regt with Ka-52A *Hokum* B; Mi-28N *Havoc* B; Mi-35 *Hind*; Mi-8AMTSh *Hip*
  1 sqn with Mi-24P *Hind*; Mi-8 *Hip* (Armenia)
AIR DEFENCE
  1 regt with 9K317 *Buk*-M2 (SA-17 *Grizzly*)
  1 regt with S-300PM1 (SA-20 *Gargoyle*)

3 regt with S-400 (SA-21 *Growler*); 96K6 *Pantsir*-S1 (SA-22 *Greyhound*)

EQUIPMENT BY TYPE
AIRCRAFT
  FTR 46: 12 MiG-29 *Fulcrum*; 34 Su-27 *Flanker*
  FGA 95: 12 Su-27SM *Flanker*; 12 Su-27SM3 *Flanker*; 14 Su-30M2; 21 Su-30SM; 36 Su-34 *Fullback*
  ATK 97: 12 Su-24M *Fencer*; 85 Su-25SM/SM3 *Frogfoot*
  ISR 24 Su-24MR *Fencer**
  TPT 12 An-12 *Cub*
HELICOPTERS
  ATK 117: 25 Ka-52A *Hokum B*; 44 Mi-28N *Havoc B*; 8 Mi-24P *Hind*; 40 Mi-35 *Hind*
  TPT 72: **Heavy** 10 Mi-26 *Halo*; **Medium** 62 Mi-8 *Hip*
AIR DEFENCE • SAM
  Long-range S-300PM1 (SA-20 *Gargoyle*); S-400 (SA-21 *Growler*)
  Medium-range 9K317 *Buk*-M2 (SA-17 *Grizzly*)
  Short-range 96K6 *Pantsir*-S1 (SA-22 *Greyhound*)

Airborne Troops
FORCES BY ROLE
MANOEUVRE
  Air Manoeuvre
  1 AB div
  1 air aslt bde

Eastern Military District
HQ located at Khabarovsk

Army
FORCES BY ROLE
COMMAND
  4 army HQ
SPECIAL FORCES
  1 (Spetsnaz) SF bde
MANOEUVRE
  Armoured
  1 tk bde
  6 MR bde
  Mechanised
  4 MR bde
  1 MGA div
SURFACE-TO-SURFACE MISSILE
  4 SRBM/GLCM bde with *Iskander*-M/K
COMBAT SUPPORT
  3 arty bde
  1 MRL bde
  1 engr bde
  1 NBC bde
  4 NBC regt
COMBAT SERVICE SUPPORT
  4 log bde
AIR DEFENCE
  4 AD bde

Reserves
FORCES BY ROLE
MANOEUVRE
  Mechanised
  8 MR bde

Pacific Fleet
EQUIPMENT BY TYPE
SUBMARINES 22
  STRATEGIC 4 **SSBN**
  TACTICAL 18: 5 **SSGN** (of which 3 in refit); 5 **SSN** (of which 4 in refit); 8 **SSK**
PRINCIPAL SURFACE COMBATANTS 8: 1 **CGHM**; 6 **DDGHM** (of which 2 in refit); 1 **FFGHM**
PATROL AND COASTAL COMBATANTS 25: 4 **FSGM**; 8 **FSM**; 10 **PCFG**; 3 **PB**
MINE WARFARE 8: 2 **MSO**; 6 **MSC**
AMPHIBIOUS 9: 4 **LST**; 5 **LCM**

Naval Aviation
FORCES BY ROLE
FIGHTER
  1 sqn with MiG-31B/BS *Foxhound*
ANTI-SUBMARINE WARFARE
  3 sqn with Ka-27/Ka-29 *Helix*
  2 sqn with Il-38 *May**; Il-18D; Il-22 *Coot B*
  1 sqn with Tu-142MK/MZ/MR *Bear F/J**
TRANSPORT
  2 sqn with An-12BK *Cub*; An-26 *Curl*; Tu-134
EQUIPMENT BY TYPE
AIRCRAFT
  FTR 12 MiG-31B/BS *Foxhound*
  ASW 23: 11 Tu-142MK/MZ/MR *Bear F/J*; 12 Il-38 *May*
  EW • ELINT 1 Il-22 *Coot B*
  TPT 6: 2 An-12BK *Cub*; 3 An-26 *Curl*; 1 Tu-134
HELICOPTERS
  ASW Ka-27 *Helix*
  TPT • **Medium** Ka-29 *Helix*; Mi-8 *Hip*

Naval Infantry
FORCES BY ROLE
MANOEUVRE
  Mechanised
  2 naval inf bde
AIR DEFENCE
  1 SAM regt

Coastal Artillery and Missile Troops
FORCES BY ROLE
COASTAL DEFENCE
  2 AShM bde

Military Air Force

11th Air Force & Air Defence Army
FORCES BY ROLE
FIGHTER/GROUND ATTACK
  1 regt with MiG-31BM *Foxhound*; Su-27SM *Flanker*; Su-30M2; Su-30SM; Su-35S *Flanker*
  1 regt with Su-35S *Flanker*; Su-30SM
  1 regt with Su-25 *Frogfoot*; Su-30SM
GROUND ATTACK
  1 regt with Su-24M/M2 *Fencer*; Su-34 *Fullback*
  1 regt with Su-25SM *Frogfoot*

ISR
1 regt with Su-24MR *Fencer E*
TRANSPORT
2 sqn with An-12 *Cub*/An-26 *Curl*/Tu-134 *Crusty*/Tu-154 *Careless*
ATTACK/TRANSPORT HELICOPTER
1 bde with Ka-52A *Hokum B*; Mi-8 *Hip*; Mi-26 *Halo*
1 regt with Ka-52A *Hokum B*; Mi-8 *Hip*; Mi-26 *Halo*
1 regt with Mi-24P *Hind*; Mi-8 *Hip*
AIR DEFENCE
2 regt with 9K37M *Buk*-M1-2 (SA-11 *Gadfly*); 9K317 Buk-M2 (SA-17 *Grizzly*); S-300V (SA-12 *Gladiator/Giant*)
1 regt with S-300PS (SA-10 *Grumble*)
3 regt with S-400 (SA-21 *Growler*); 96K6 *Pantsir*-S1 (SA-22 *Greyhound*)
EQUIPMENT BY TYPE
AIRCRAFT
FTR 20 MiG-31B/BS/BM *Foxhound*
FGA 120: 23 Su-27SM *Flanker*; 6 Su-30M2; 31 Su-30SM; 26 Su-34 *Fullback*; 34 Su-35S *Flanker*
ATK 102: 20 Su-24M *Fencer*; 10 Su-24M2 *Fencer*; 72 Su-25/Su-25SM *Frogfoot*
ISR 28 Su-24MR *Fencer E*
TPT 24: 22 An-12 *Cub*/An-26 *Curl*; 1 Tu-134 *Crusty*; 1 Tu-154 *Careless*
HELICOPTERS
ATK 36: 24 Ka-52A *Hokum B*; 12 Mi-24P *Hind*
TPT 60: **Heavy** 4 Mi-26 *Halo*; **Medium** 56 Mi-8 *Hip*
AIR DEFENCE • SAM
Long-range S-300PS (SA-10 *Grumble*); S-300V (SA-12 *Gladiator/Giant*); S-400 (SA-21 *Growler*)
Medium-range 9K317 *Buk*-M1-2 (SA-11 *Gadfly*); 9K317 *Buk*-M2 (SA-17 *Grizzly*)
Short-range 96K6 *Pantsir*-S1 (SA-22 *Greyhound*)

Airborne Troops
FORCES BY ROLE
MANOEUVRE
Air Manoeuvre
2 air aslt bde

Paramilitary 554,000

Border Guard Service ε160,000
Subordinate to Federal Security Service
FORCES BY ROLE
10 regional directorates
MANOEUVRE
Other
7 frontier gp
EQUIPMENT BY TYPE
ARMOURED FIGHTING VEHICLES
IFV/APC (W) 1,000 BMP/BTR
ARTILLERY 90:
SP 122mm 2S1 *Gvozdika*
GUN/MOR • SP 120mm 2S9 NONA-S
MOR 120mm 2S12 *Sani*

PRINCIPAL SURFACE COMBATANTS
FRIGATES • FFHM 3 *Nerey* (*Krivak* III) with 1 twin lnchr with *Osa-M* (SA-N-4 *Gecko*) SAM, 2 quad 533mm TT lnchr, 2 RBU 6000 *Smerch* 2 A/S mor, 1 100mm gun (capacity 1 Ka-27 *Helix A* ASW hel)
PATROL AND COASTAL COMBATANTS 191
PSO 5: 4 *Komandor*; 1 *Okean* (Project 22100) with 1 76mm gun, 1 hel landing platform
PCO 23: 8 *Alpinist* (Project 503); 1 *Sprut*; 12 *Okhotnik* (Project 22460) with 1 AK630M CIWS, 1 hel landing platform; 2 *Purga* with 1 hel landing platform
PCC 35: 5 *Molnya* II (*Pauk* II); 3 *Svetlyak* (Project 10410) with 2 AK306 CIWS; 18 *Svetlyak* (Project 10410) with 1 AK630M CIWS, 1 76mm gun; 8 *Svetlyak* (Project 10410) with 2 AK630M CIWS; 1 *Yakhont* with 2 AK306 CIWS
PCR 1 *Slepen* (*Yaz*) with 1 AK630 CIWS, 2 100mm guns
PBF 85: 55 *Mangust*; 3 *Mirazh* (Project 14310); 4 *Mustang*-2 (Project 18623); 21 *Sobol*; 2 *Sokzhoi* with 1 AK306 CIWS
PBR 30: 2 *Ogonek* with 1 AK306 CIWS; 2 *Ogonek* with 2 AK306 CIWS; 8 *Piyavka* with 1 AK630 CIWS; 18 *Moskit* (*Vosh*) with 1 AK630 CIWS, 1 100mm gun
PB 12: 2 *Morzh* (Project 1496M); 10 *Lamantin* (Project 1496M1)
LOGISTICS AND SUPPORT 37
AE 1 *Muna*
AGB 3 *Ivan Susanin* (primarily used as patrol ships) with 2AK630 CIWS, 1 76mm gun, 1 hel landing platform
AK 8 *Pevek* with 1 AK306 CIWS
AKSL 5 *Kanin*
AO 3: 1 *Ishim* (Project 15010); 2 *Envoron*
ATF 17: 16 *Sorum* (primarily used as patrol ships) with 2 AK230M CIWS; 1 *Sorum* (primarily used as patrol ship) with 2 AK306 CIWS
AIRCRAFT • TPT ε86: 70 An-24 *Coke*/An-26 *Curl*/An-72 *Coaler*/Il-76 *Candid*/Tu-134 *Crusty*/Yak-40 *Codling*; 16 SM-92
HELICOPTERS: ε200 Ka-28 (Ka-27) *Helix* ASW/Mi-24 *Hind* Atk/Mi-26 *Halo* Spt/Mi-8 *Hip* Spt

Federal Guard Service ε40,000–50,000
Org include elm of ground forces (mech inf bde and AB regt)
FORCES BY ROLE
MANOEUVRE
Mechanised
1 mech inf regt
Air Manoeuvre
1 AB regt
Other
1 (Presidential) gd regt

Federal Security Service Special Purpose Centre ε4,000
FORCES BY ROLE
SPECIAL FORCES
2 SF unit (Alfa and Vympel units)

National Guard ε340,000

FORCES BY ROLE
MANOEUVRE
  Other
    10 paramilitary div (2–5 paramilitary regt)
    17 paramilitary bde (3 mech bn, 1 mor bn)
    36 indep paramilitary rgt
    90 paramilitary bn (incl special motorised units)
  Aviation
    8 sqn
COMBAT SUPPORT
    1 arty regt
EQUIPMENT BY TYPE
ARMOURED FIGHTING VEHICLES
  RECCE some BRDM-2A
  IFV/APC (W) 1,650 BMP-2/BTR-70M/BTR-80/BTR-82A/BTR-82AM
ARTILLERY 35
  TOWED 122mm 20 D-30
  MOR 120mm 15 M-1938 (PM-38)
AIRCRAFT
  TPT 29: **Heavy** 9 Il-76 *Candid*; **Medium** 2 An-12 *Cub*; **Light** 18: 12 An-26 *Curl*; 6 An-72 *Coaler*
HELICOPTERS
  TPT 71: **Heavy** 10 Mi-26 *Halo*; **Medium** 60+: 60 Mi-8 *Hip*; some Mi-8AMTSh *Hip*; **Light** 1 Ka-226T

Cyber

The first official doctrinal statement on the role of the Russian military in cyberspace, the 'Conceptual Views on the Activity of the Russian Federation Armed Forces in Information Space', was released at the end of 2011, and described cyber-force tasks with little correlation to those of equivalent commands in the West. In particular, the document contains no mention of the possibility of offensive cyber activity. It is also entirely defensive in tone and focuses on force protection and the prevention of information warfare, including allowing for a military role in negotiating international treaties governing information security. In January 2012, then chief of the general staff Makarov gave a different picture of the three main tasks in this area: 'disrupting adversary information systems, including by introducing harmful software; defending our own communications and command systems'; and 'working on domestic and foreign public opinion using the media, Internet and more'. The third task is a reminder that, unlike some other nations with advanced cyber capabilities, Russia considers cyber warfare as an integral component of information warfare. Operations in Crimea from early 2014, in the wider information space concerning the conflict in Ukraine and allegations of influence activity in Western countries' elections demonstrate that Russian thinking and capacity has matured in these areas. In February 2017, Defence Minister Shoigu provided the first official acknowledgement that Russia had formed a new information-warfare branch of the armed forces.

DEPLOYMENT

ARMENIA: 3,300: 1 mil base with (1 MR bde; 74 T-72; 80 BMP-1; 80 BMP-2; 12 2S1; 12 BM-21); 1 sqn with 18 MiG-29 *Fulcrum*; 1 sqn with 8 Mi-24P *Hind*; 4 Mi-8MT *Hip*; 2 AD bty with S-300V (SA-12 *Gladiator/Giant*); 1 AD bty with 2K12 *Kub* (SA-6 *Gainful*)

BELARUS: 1 radar station at Baranovichi (*Volga* system; leased); 1 naval comms site

BOSNIA-HERZEGOVINA: OSCE • Bosnia and Herzegovina 2

DEMOCRATIC REPUBLIC OF THE CONGO: UN • MONUSCO 2; 14 obs

GEORGIA: 7,000; Abkhazia 1 mil base with (1 MR bde; 40 T-90A; 120 BTR-82A; 18 2S3; 12 2S12; 18 BM-21; some S-300 SAM; some atk hel); South Ossetia 1 mil base with (1 MR bde; 40 T-72; 120 BMP-2; 36 2S3; 12 2S12)

KAZAKHSTAN: 1 radar station at Balkash (*Dnepr* system; leased)

KYRGYZSTAN: ε500; 13 Su-25SM *Frogfoot*; 2 Mi-8 *Hip* spt hel

MEDITERRANEAN SEA: 2 SSK; 1 FFGHM; 1 FFGM; 1 AGI

MIDDLE EAST: UN • UNTSO 5 obs

MOLDOVA/TRANSDNIESTR: ε1,500 (including 441 peacekeepers); 2 MR bn; 100 MBT/AIFV/APC; 7 Mi-24 *Hind*; some Mi-8 *Hip*

SERBIA: OSCE • Kosovo 1

SOUTH SUDAN: UN • UNMISS 3; 2 obs

SUDAN: UN • UNISFA 1 obs

SYRIA: 5,000: 1 inf BG; 3 MP bn; 1 engr unit; ε10 T-72B3/T-90; ε20 BTR-82A; *Typhoon*-K; *Tigr*; 12 2A65; 4 9A52 *Smerch*; TOS-1A; 9K720 *Iskander*-M; 10 Su-24M *Fencer*; 6 Su-34; 4 Su-35S; 1 A-50 *Mainstay*; 1 Il-20M; 12 Mi-24P/Mi-35M *Hind*; 4 Mi-8AMTSh *Hip*; 1 AShM bty with 3K55 *Bastion*; 1 SAM bty with S-400; 1 SAM bty with S-300V4; 1 SAM bty with *Pantsir*-S1/S2; air base at Latakia; naval facility at Tartus

TAJIKISTAN: 5,000; 1 (201st) mil base with (40 T-72B1; 60 BMP-2; 80 BTR-82A; 40 MT-LB; 18 2S1; 36 2S3; 6 2S12; 12 9P140 *Uragan*); 4 Mi-24P *Hind*; 4 Mi-8MTV *Hip*

UKRAINE: Crimea: 28,000; 1 recce bde, 2 naval inf bde; 1 arty bde; 1 NBC regt; 40 T-72B3 MBT; 80 BMP-2 AIFV; 200 BTR-82A; 20 BTR-80 APC; 150 MT-LB; 18 2S1 arty; 18 2S19 arty; 12 BM-21 MRL; 1 AShM bde with 3K60 *Bal*; 3K55 *Bastion*; 1 FGA regt with Su-24M/MR; Su-30SM; 1 FGA regt with Su-27SM/SM3; Su-30M2; 1 FGA regt with Su-24M/Su-25SM; 1 atk/tpt hel regt; 1 ASW hel regt; 2 AD regt with S-400; *Pantsir*-S1; 1 Fleet HQ located at Sevastopol; 2 radar stations located at Sevastopol (*Dnepr* system) and Mukachevo (*Dnepr* system); Donetsk/Luhansk: 3,000 (reported); OSCE • Ukraine 39

WESTERN SAHARA: UN • MINURSO 16 obs

Tajikistan TJK

Tajikistani Somoni Tr		2017	2018	2019
GDP	Tr	61.1bn	67.4bn	
	US$	7.14bn	7.35bn	
per capita	US$	801	807	
Growth	%	7.1	5.0	
Inflation	%	7.3	5.8	
Def bdgt	Tr	1.66bn	1.99bn	
	US$	194m	217m	
US$1=Tr		8.55	9.16	

Population 8,604,882

Ethnic groups: Tajik 84.2%; Uzbek 12.2%; Kyrgyz 0.8%; Russian 0.5%; other or unspecified 2.3%

Age	0–14	15–19	20–24	25–29	30–64	65 plus
Male	16.3%	4.8%	4.5%	4.9%	17.9%	1.4%
Female	15.7%	4.6%	4.4%	4.7%	18.8%	2.0%

Capabilities

The Tajik armed forces have little capacity to deploy other than token forces and almost all equipment is of Soviet-era origin. Regional security and terrorism are concerns, due to the possibility that violence could spill over from Afghanistan. Tajikistan has been building its capability in this area by hosting a CSTO counter-terrorism exercise, and by taking part in stability and counter-terror exercises organised by US CENTCOM, hosting the 2017 iteration. Tajikistan is a member of the CSTO and there is a large Russian military presence at the 201st military base. In 2018, India and Tajikistan agreed to strengthen defence cooperation, in particular on counter-terrorism. Tajikistan has little capacity to deploy other than token forces but border deployments have been stepped up recently in response to regional security and terrorism concerns. In late 2016, a Military Cooperation Plan was signed with Russia. Moscow has indicated that Tajikistan is to receive military equipment, including aircraft. Some donations of personal equipment have been received from the US. Barring maintenance facilities, Tajikistan only has minimal defence-industrial capacity.

ACTIVE 8,800 (Army 7,300 Air Force/Air Defence 1,500) **Paramilitary 7,500**

Conscript liability 24 months

ORGANISATIONS BY SERVICE

Army 7,300
FORCES BY ROLE
MANOEUVRE
  Mechanised
  3 MR bde
  Air Manoeuvre
  1 air aslt bde
COMBAT SUPPORT
  1 arty bde
AIR DEFENCE
  1 SAM regt

EQUIPMENT BY TYPE
ARMOURED FIGHTING VEHICLES
  MBT 37: 30 T-72; 7 T-62
  IFV 23: 8 BMP-1; 15 BMP-2
  APC • APC (W) 23 BTR-60/BTR-70/BTR-80
ARTILLERY 23
  TOWED 122mm 10 D-30
  MRL 122mm 3 BM-21 Grad
  MOR 120mm 10
AIR DEFENCE • SAM
  Medium-range S-75 Dvina (SA-2 Guideline); S-125 Pechora-2M (SA-26)
  Point-defence 9K32 Strela-2 (SA-7 Grail)‡

Air Force/Air Defence 1,500
FORCES BY ROLE
TRANSPORT
  1 sqn with Tu-134A Crusty
ATTACK/TRANSPORT HELICOPTER
  1 sqn with Mi-24 Hind; Mi-8 Hip; Mi-17TM Hip H
EQUIPMENT BY TYPE
AIRCRAFT
  TPT • Light 1 Tu-134A Crusty
  TRG 4+: 4 L-39 Albatros; some Yak-52
HELICOPTERS
  ATK 4 Mi-24 Hind
  TPT • Medium 11 Mi-8 Hip/Mi-17TM Hip H

Paramilitary 7,500

Internal Troops 3,800

National Guard 1,200

Emergencies Ministry 2,500

Border Guards

DEPLOYMENT
SERBIA: OSCE • Kosovo 1
UKRAINE: OSCE • Ukraine 17

FOREIGN FORCES
Russia 5,000; 1 (201st) mil base with (40 T-72B1; 60 BMP-2; 80 BTR-82A; 40 MT-LB; 18 2S1; 36 2S3; 6 2S12; 12 9P140 Uragan); 4 Mi-24P Hind; 4 Mi-8MTV Hip

Turkmenistan TKM

Turkmen New Manat TMM		2017	2018	2019
GDP	TMM	133bn	150bn	
	US$	37.9bn	42.8bn	
per capita	US$	6,643	7,412	
Growth	%	6.5	6.2	
Inflation	%	8.0	9.4	
Def exp	TMM	n.k	n.k	
	US$	n.k	n.k	
USD1=TMM			3.50	3.50

Population 5,411,012

Ethnic groups: Turkmen 77%; Uzbek 9%; Russian 7%; Kazak 2%

Age	0–14	15–19	20–24	25–29	30–64	65 plus
Male	13.0%	4.2%	4.7%	4.9%	20.5%	2.1%
Female	12.7%	4.1%	4.7%	4.9%	21.3%	2.8%

Capabilities

Turkmenistan has concerns over potential regional spillover from the security situation in Afghanistan, but its armed forces lack significant capabilities and equipment. Turkmenistan has maintained a policy of neutrality since 1995 and confirmed this commitment in its 2016 military doctrine. This aimed to increase the armed forces' defensive capability in order to safeguard national interests and territorial integrity. Turkmenistan is not a member of the CSTO. While the ground forces are shifting from a Soviet-era divisional structure to a brigade system, progress is slow. The armed forces are largely conscript-based and reliant on Soviet-era equipment and doctrine, and the government has stated a requirement to improve conditions of service. Turkmenistan has participated in multinational exercises but has limited capacity to deploy externally and maintains no international deployments. The air force has a modest capability; however, most of the aircraft are of Soviet-era origin and have been stored or scrapped, and no significant new procurement has occurred. The 2016 military doctrine was intended to partly redress these issues. There are plans to strengthen the border guard with new equipment and facilities. Plans to bolster the naval forces have resulted in some procurements, leading to a modest improvement in the naval presence in the Caspian Sea. Barring maintenance facilities, Turkmenistan has little domestic defence industry, but is building a number of patrol vessels of Turkish design under licence.

ACTIVE 36,500 (Army 33,000 Navy 500 Air 3,000)
Paramilitary 5,000
Conscript liability 24 months

ORGANISATIONS BY SERVICE

Army 33,000
5 Mil Districts
FORCES BY ROLE
SPECIAL FORCES
  1 spec ops regt
MANOEUVRE
  Armoured
  1 tk bde
  Mechanised
  1 (3rd) MR div (1 tk regt; 3 MR regt, 1 arty regt)
  1 (22nd) MR div (1 tk regt; 1 MR regt, 1 arty regt)
  4 MR bde
  1 naval inf bde
  Other
  1 MR trg div
SURFACE-TO-SURFACE MISSILE
  1 SRBM bde with SS-1 *Scud*
COMBAT SUPPORT
  1 arty bde
  1 (mixed) arty/AT regt
  1 MRL bde
  1 AT regt
  1 engr regt
AIR DEFENCE
  2 SAM bde

EQUIPMENT BY TYPE†
ARMOURED FIGHTING VEHICLES
  MBT 654: 4 T-90S; 650 T-72/T-72UMG
  RECCE 260+: 200 BRDM-2; 60 BRM-1; Nimr *Ajban*
  IFV 1,038: 600 BMP-1/BMP-1M; 430 BMP-2; 4 BMP-3; 4 BTR-80A
  APC 902+
    APC (W) 874+: 120 BTR-60 (all variants); 300 BTR-70; 450 BTR-80; 4+ *Cobra*
    PPV 28+ *Kirpi*
  AUV 8 Nimr *Ajban* 440A
  ABCV 8 BMD-1
ANTI-TANK/ANTI-INFRASTRUCTURE
  MSL
    SP 58+: 8 9P122 *Malyutka*-M (AT-3 *Sagger* on BRDM-2); 8 9P133 *Malyutka*-P (AT-3 *Sagger* on BRDM-2); 2 9P148 *Konkurs* (AT-5 *Spandrel* on BRDM-2); 36 9P149 *Shturm* (AT-6 *Spiral* on MT-LB); 4+ *Baryer* (on *Karakal*)
    MANPATS 9K11 *Malyutka* (AT-3 *Sagger*); 9K111 *Fagot* (AT-4 *Spigot*); 9K111-1 *Konkurs* (AT-5 *Spandrel*); 9K115 *Metis* (AT-7 *Saxhorn*)
  GUNS 100mm 60 MT-12/T-12
ARTILLERY 765
  SP 122mm 40 2S1
  TOWED 457: **122mm** 350 D-30; **130mm** 6 M-46; **152mm** 101: 17 D-1; 72 D-20; 6 2A36 *Giatsint*-B; 6 2A65 *Msta*-B
  GUN/MOR 120mm 17 2S9 NONA-S
  MRL 154+: **122mm** 88: 18 9P138; 70 BM-21 *Grad*; RM-70; **220mm** 60 9P140 *Uragan*; **300mm** 6 9A52 *Smerch*
  MOR 97: **82mm** 31; **120mm** 66 M-1938 (PM-38)
SURFACE-TO-SURFACE MISSILE LAUNCHERS
  SRBM • Conventional 16 SS-1 *Scud*
UNMANNED AERIAL VEHICLES
  CISR • Heavy CH-3A; WJ-600
  ISR • Medium *Falco*
AIR DEFENCE
  SAM
    Short-range: FM-90; 2K12 *Kub* (SA-6 *Gainful*)
    Point-defence 53+: 40 9K33 *Osa* (SA-8 *Gecko*); 13 9K35 *Strela*-10 mod (SA-13 *Gopher*); 9K38 *Igla* (SA-18 *Grouse*);

9K32M *Strela*-2M (SA-7 *Grail*)‡; 9K34 *Strela*-3 (SA-14 *Gremlin*); *Mistral* (reported); QW-2
GUNS 70
  SP 23mm 48 ZSU-23-4
  TOWED 22+: **23mm** ZU-23-2; **57mm** 22 S-60
AIR-LAUNCHED MISSILES
  ASM CM-502KG; AR-1

Navy 500
EQUIPMENT BY TYPE
PATROL AND COASTAL COMBATANTS 4
  PCFG 2 *Edermen* (RUS *Molnya*) with 4 quad lnchr with 3M24E *Uran*-E (SS-N-25 *Switchblade*) AShM, 2 AK630 CIWS, 1 76mm gun
  PCGM 2 *Arkadag* (TUR *Tuzla*) with 2 twin lnchr with *Otomat* AShM, 2 twin *Simbad*-RC lnchr with *Mistral* SAM, 1 Roketsan A/S mor
LOGISTICS AND SUPPORT • AGHS 1 (Dearsan 41m)

Air Force 3,000
FORCES BY ROLE
FIGHTER
  2 sqn with MiG-29 *Fulcrum*; MiG-29UB *Fulcrum*;
GROUND ATTACK
  1 sqn with Su-25 *Frogfoot*
  1 sqn with Su-25MK *Frogfoot*
TRANSPORT
  1 sqn with An-26 *Curl*; Mi-8 *Hip*; Mi-24 *Hind*
TRAINING
  1 unit with L-39 *Albatros*
AIR DEFENCE
  Some sqn with S-75 *Dvina* (SA-2 *Guideline*); S-125 *Pechora* (SA-3 *Goa*); S-125 *Pechora*-2M (SA-26); S-200 *Angara* (SA-5 *Gammon*); FD-2000 (HQ-9); KS-1A (HQ-12)
EQUIPMENT BY TYPE
AIRCRAFT 55 combat capable
  FTR 24: 22 MiG-29A/S *Fulcrum*; 2 MiG-29UB *Fulcrum*
  ATK 31: 19 Su-25 *Frogfoot*; 12 Su-25MK *Frogfoot*
  TPT • Light 3: 1 An-26 *Curl*; 2 An-74TK *Coaler*
  TRG 2 L-39 *Albatros*
HELICOPTERS
  ATK 10 Mi-24P *Hind* F
  MRH 2+ AW139
  TPT 11: **Medium** 8: 6 Mi-8 *Hip*; 2 Mi-17V-V *Hip*; **Light** 3+ AW109
AIR-LAUNCHED MISSILES
  AAM • IR R-60 (AA-8 *Aphid*); R-73 (AA-11 *Archer*)
AIR DEFENCE • SAM
  Long-range S-200 *Angara* (SA-5 *Gammon*); FD-2000 (HQ-9)
  Medium-range S-75 *Dvina* (SA-2 *Guideline*); S-125 *Pechora*-2M (SA-26); KS-1A (HQ-12)
  Short-range S-125 *Pechora* (SA-3 *Goa*); S-125-2BM *Pechora*

Paramilitary 5,000

Federal Border Guard Service ε5,000
EQUIPMENT BY TYPE
PATROL AND COASTAL COMBATANTS 33
  PCGM 8 *Arkadag* (TUR *Tuzla*) with 2 twin lnchr with *Otomat* AShM, 2 twin *Simbad*-RC lnchr with *Mistral* SAM, 1 Roketsan A/S mor
  PBF 24: 10 *Bars*-12; 6 *Nazya* (Dearsan 33); 5 *Grif*-T; 3 *Sobol*
  PB 1 *Point*
AMPHIBIOUS • LCM 1 Dearsan LCM-1
HELICOPTERS
  MRH 2 AW139
  TPT 3+: **Medium** some Mi-8 *Hip*; **Light** 3 AW109

Ukraine UKR

Ukrainian Hryvnia h		2017	2018	2019
GDP	h	2.98tr	3.42tr	
	US$	112bn	126bn	
per capita	US$	2,656	2,964	
Growth	%	2.5	3.5	
Inflation	%	14.4	10.9	
Def bdgt [a]	h	74.4bn	88.6bn	
	US$	2.80bn	3.27bn	
FMA (US)	US$	99m	0m	
USD1=h		26.60	27.07	

[a] Including military pensions

Population	43,952,299					
Age	0–14	15–19	20–24	25–29	30–64	65 plus
Male	8.2%	2.2%	2.7%	3.6%	24.1%	5.5%
Female	7.7%	2.1%	2.6%	3.4%	26.9%	10.9%

Capabilities

Ukraine's overriding security concern is Russia's support for separatists in the east of the country. The armed forces were unable to offer any credible resistance to the Russian annexation of Crimea and struggled to combat the Russian-backed separatist forces. Defence policy is centred on maintaining sovereignty and territorial integrity. Ukraine adopted a revised doctrine in 2015 that identified Moscow as a 'military adversary', called for 'comprehensive reform' of the security sector and revoked the country's 'non-block status'. Military reforms since 2015 have addressed the weaknesses exposed in 2014. Ukraine joined the NATO Partnership for Peace programme in 1994, followed in 1997 by the creation of the NATO–Ukraine commission. In 2017, parliament identified NATO membership as a strategic goal. There are two conscript intakes per year, but the longer-term ambition is to professionalise the armed forces. The defence ministry's development programme aims to improve training, eventually aligning to NATO standards. The armed forces participate in bilateral and multinational exercises. Ukraine retains the notional capacity at least to deploy and sustain a modest force by air. Poor logistics capacity was exposed after 2014 and addressing this is a priority. The equipment inventory still consists predominantly of Soviet-era weaponry. Sustaining and in some cases upgrading these systems is a near-term concern, although much will need to be replaced over the coming decade. If not, the armed forces will face increasing problems with obsolescence. The country has a broad defence industry, though its capabilities remain shaped, and limited, by its Soviet heritage. Ukraine was a key provider of guided-weapons technologies in the Soviet Union. It retains the capability to build Soviet-era land systems and can maintain and modestly upgrade Soviet-era tactical combat aircraft.

ACTIVE 209,000 (Army 145,000 Navy 11,000 Air Force 45,000 Airborne 8,000 Special Operations Forces n.k.) **Paramilitary 88,000**

Conscript liability Army, Air Force 18 months, Navy 2 years. Minimum age for conscription raised from 18 to 20 in 2015

RESERVE 900,000 (Joint 900,000)

Military service within 5 years

ORGANISATIONS BY SERVICE

Army 145,000

4 regional HQ

FORCES BY ROLE
MANOEUVRE
  Reconnaissance
    5 recce bn
  Armoured
    3 tk bde
  Mechanised
    9 mech bde
    2 mtn bde
  Light
    4 mot inf bde
SURFACE-TO-SURFACE MISSILES
  1 SSM bde
COMBAT SUPPORT
  5 arty bde
  3 MRL regt
  1 engr regt
  1 EW regt
  1 EW bn
  2 EW coy
  1 CBRN regt
  4 sigs regt
COMBAT SERVICE SUPPORT
  3 maint regt
  1 maint coy
HELICOPTERS
  4 avn bde
AIR DEFENCE
  4 AD regt

Reserves

FORCES BY ROLE
MANOEUVRE
  Armoured
    3 tk bde
  Mechanised
    3 mech bde
  COMBAT SUPPORT
    1 arty bde

EQUIPMENT BY TYPE
ARMOURED FIGHTING VEHICLES
  MBT 854: 720 T-64/T-64BV/BM; 100 T-72AV/B1; 28 T-80BV; 6 T-84 *Oplot*; (94 T-80; 530 T-72; 578 T-64; 20 T-55 all in store)
  RECCE 548: 433 BRDM-2; 115 BRM-1K (CP)
  IFV 1,137: 193 BMP-1/BMP-1AK; 890 BMP-2; 4 BMP-3; 50+ BTR-3DA; some BTR-3E1; some BTR-4E *Bucephalus*
  APC 338
    APC (T) 15+: 15 BTR-D; some MT-LB
    APC (W) 313: 5 BTR-60; 215 BTR-70; 93 BTR-80
    PPV 10 *Kozak*-2
  ABCV 30: 15 BMD-1, 15 BMD-2
ENGINEERING & MAINTENANCE VEHICLES
  AEV 53 BAT-2; MT-LB
  ARV BREM-1; BREM-2; BREM-64; T-54/T-55
  VLB MTU-20
ANTI-TANK/ANTI-INFRASTRUCTURE
  MSL
    SP 9P149 with 9K114 *Shturm* (AT-6 *Spiral*)
    MANPATS 9K111 *Fagot* (AT-4 *Spigot*); 9K113 *Konkurs* (AT-5 *Spandrel*); FGM-148 *Javelin*; Stugna-P; *Corsar*
  GUNS 100mm ε500 MT-12/T-12
ARTILLERY 1,770
  SP 565+: **122mm** 271 2S1 *Gvozdika*; **152mm** 288: 235 2S3 *Akatsiya*; 18 2S5 *Giatsint*-S; 35 2S19 *Msta*-S; **203mm** 6+ 2S7 *Pion* (up to 90 2S7 *Pion* in store)
  TOWED 515+: **122mm** 75 D-30; **152mm** 440: 180 2A36 *Giatsint*-B; 130 2A65 *Msta*-B; 130+ D-20
  GUN/MOR • 120mm • TOWED 2 2B16 NONA-K
  MRL 348: **122mm** 203: 18 9P138; 185 BM-21 *Grad*; **220mm** 70 9P140 *Uragan*; **300mm** 75 9A52 *Smerch*
  MOR 120mm 340: 190 2S12 *Sani*; 30 M-1938 (PM-38); 120 M120-15
SURFACE-TO-SURFACE MISSILE LAUNCHERS
  SRBM • Conventional 90 9K79 *Tochka* (SS-21 *Scarab*)
HELICOPTERS
  ATK ε35 Mi-24 *Hind*
  MRH 1 *Lev*-1
  TPT • Medium ε24 Mi-8 *Hip*
AIR DEFENCE
  SAM
    Long-range Some S-300V (SA-12 *Gladiator*)
    Short-range 6 9K330 *Tor*-M
    Point-defence 9K35 *Strela*-10 (SA-13 *Gopher*); 9K33 *Osa*-AKM (SA-8 *Gecko*)
  GUNS
    SP 30mm 70 2S6
    TOWED 23mm ZU-23-2; **57mm** S-60
AIR-LAUNCHED MISSILES • ASM *Barrier*-V

Navy 11,000 (incl Naval Aviation and Naval Infantry)

After Russia's annexation of Crimea, HQ shifted to Odessa. Several additional vessels remain in Russian possession in Crimea

2 Regional HQ

EQUIPMENT BY TYPE
PRINCIPAL SURFACE COMBATANTS 1
  FRIGATES • FFHM 1 *Hetman Sagaidachny* (RUS *Krivak* III) with 1 twin lnchr with *Osa*-M (SA-N-4 *Gecko*) SAM, 2 quad 533mm ASTT with SET-65 HWT/53-65K HWT, 2 RBU 6000 *Smerch* 2 A/S mor, 2 AK630M CIWS, 1 100mm gun (capacity 1 Ka-27 *Helix* ASW hel)

PATROL AND COASTAL COMBATANTS 7
  CORVETTES • FS 1 *Grisha* (II) with 2 twin 533mm ASTT with SAET-60 HWT, 2 RBU 6000 *Smerch* 2 A/S mor, 2 57mm guns
  PHG 1 *Matka* (FSU *Vekhr*) with 2 single lnchr with P-15 *Termit*-M/R (SS-N-2C/D *Styx*) AShM, 1 AK630M CIWS, 1 76mm gun
  PBG 4 *Gyurza*-M (Project 51855) with 2 *Katran*-M IFV turret with 1 twin lnchr with *Baryer* ATGM
  PB 1 *Zhuk* (FSU *Grif*)
MINE WARFARE • MINE COUNTERMEASURES 1
  MHI 1 *Korund* (*Yevgenya*) (Project 1258)
AMPHIBIOUS
  LANDING SHIPS • LSM 1 *Polnochny* C (capacity 6 MBT; 180 troops)
  LANDING CRAFT • LCM 1 *Akula* (*Ondatra*)
LOGISTICS AND SUPPORT 10
  ABU 1 Project 419 (*Sura*)
  AG 1 *Bereza*
  AGI 1 *Muna*
  AKL 1
  AO 2 *Toplivo*
  AWT 1 *Sudak*
  AXL 3 *Petrushka*

Naval Aviation ε1,000
EQUIPMENT BY TYPE
FIXED-WING AIRCRAFT
  ASW (2 Be-12 *Mail* non-operational)
  TPT • Light (2 An-26 *Curl* in store)
HELICOPTERS
  ASW 7+: 4+ Ka-27 *Helix* A; 3 Mi-14PS/PL *Haze* A/C
  TPT • Medium 1 Ka-29 *Helix*-B

Naval Infantry ε2,000
FORCES BY ROLE
MANOEUVRE
  Light
  1 nav inf bde
  1 nav inf bn
EQUIPMENT BY TYPE
ARMOURED FIGHTING VEHICLES
  MBT 31 T-80BV
  IFV some BMP-1
  APC • APC (W) some BTR-60; some BTR-80
ARTILLERY
  SP 122mm 2S1 *Gvozdika*
  TOWED 152mm some 2A36 *Giatsint*-B

Air Forces 45,000
3 Regional HQ
FORCES BY ROLE
FIGHTER
  4 bde with MiG-29 *Fulcrum*; Su-27 *Flanker*; L-39 *Albatros*
FIGHTER/GROUND ATTACK
  2 bde with Su-24M *Fencer*; Su-25 *Frogfoot*
ISR
  2 sqn with Su-24MR *Fencer* E*
TRANSPORT
  3 bde with An-24; An-26; An-30; Il-76 *Candid*; Tu-134 *Crusty*
TRAINING
  Some sqn with L-39 *Albatros*
TRANSPORT HELICOPTER
  Some sqn with Mi-8; Mi-9; PZL Mi-2 *Hoplite*
AIR DEFENCE
  6 bde with 9K37M *Buk*-M1 (SA-11 *Gadfly*); S-300P/PS/PT (SA-10 *Grumble*)
  4 regt with 9K37M *Buk*-M1 (SA-11); S-300P/PS/PT (SA-10)
EQUIPMENT BY TYPE
AIRCRAFT ε125 combat capable
  FTR 71: ε37 MiG-29 *Fulcrum*; ε34 Su-27 *Flanker*
  FGA ε14 Su-24M *Fencer*
  ATK ε31 Su-25 *Frogfoot*
  ISR 12: 3 An-30 *Clank*; ε9 Su-24MR *Fencer* E*
  TPT 30: **Heavy** 5 Il-76 *Candid*; **Medium** 1 An-70; **Light** ε24: 3 An-24 *Coke*; ε20 An-26 *Curl*; 1 Tu-134 *Crusty*
  TRG ε32 L-39 *Albatros*
HELICOPTERS
  C2 ε14 Mi-9
  TPT 32: **Medium** ε30 Mi-8 *Hip*; **Light** 2 PZL Mi-2 *Hoplite*
AIR DEFENCE • SAM 322:
  Long-range 250 S-300P/PS/PT (SA-10 *Grumble*)
  Medium-range 72 9K37M *Buk*-M1 (SA-11 *Gadfly*)
AIR-LAUNCHED MISSILES
  AAM • IR R-60 (AA-8 *Aphid*); R-73 (AA-11 *Archer*)
  SARH R-27 (AA-10A *Alamo*)
  ASM Kh-25 (AS-10 *Karen*); Kh-29 (AS-14 *Kedge*)
  ARM Kh-25MP (AS-12 *Kegler*); Kh-58 (AS-11 *Kilter*); Kh-28 (AS-9 *Kyle*) (likely WFU)

High-Mobility Airborne Troops ε8,000
FORCES BY ROLE
MANOEUVRE
  Air Manoeuvre
  1 AB bde
  4 air mob bde
EQUIPMENT BY TYPE
ARMOURED FIGHTING VEHICLES
  IFV 75+: 30 BMD-1; 45 BMD-2; some BTR-3E1; some BTR-4 *Bucephalus*
  APC 180+
    APC (T) 25 BTR-D
    APC (W) 155+: 1 BTR-60; 2 BTR-70; 122 BTR-80; 30+ *Dozor*-B
ANTI-TANK/ANTI-INFRASTRUCTURE
  MSL • MANPATS 9K111 *Fagot* (AT-4 *Spigot*); 9K111-1 *Konkurs* (AT-5 *Spandrel*)
ARTILLERY 118
  TOWED • 122mm 54 D-30
  GUN/MOR • SP • 120mm 40 2S9 NONA-S
  MOR 120mm 24 2S12 *Sani*
AIR DEFENCE • GUNS • SP 23mm some ZU-23-2 (truck mounted)

Special Operations Forces n.k.
SPECIAL FORCES
  2 SF regt

Paramilitary 88,000

National Guard ε46,000
Ministry of Internal Affairs; 5 territorial comd
FORCES BY ROLE
MANOEUVRE
  Armoured
    Some tk bn
  Mechanised
    Some mech bn
  Light
    Some lt inf bn
EQUIPMENT BY TYPE
ARMOURED FIGHTING VEHICLES
  MBT T-64; T-64BV; T-64BM; T-72
  IFV 83: BTR-3; 32+ BTR-3E1; ε50 BTR-4 *Bucephalus*; 1 BMP-2
  APC 22+
    APC (W) BTR-70; BTR-80
    PPV 22+: Streit *Cougar*; Streit *Spartan*; 22 *Kozak*-2
ANTI-TANK/ANTI-INFRASTRUCTURE
  RCL 73mm some SPG-9
ARTILLERY
  TOWED 122mm some D-30
  MOR 120mm some
AIRCRAFT
  TPT • Light 24: 20 An-26 *Curl*; 2 An-72 *Coaler*; 2 Tu-134 *Crusty*
HELICOPTERS • TPT 8: Medium 7 Mi-8 *Hip*; Light 1 Mi-2MSB
AIR DEFENCE
  SAM • Point-defence 9K38 *Igla* (SA-18 *Grouse*)
  GUNS • SP 23mm some ZU-23-2 (truck mounted)

Border Guard ε42,000
FORCES BY ROLE
MANOEUVRE
  Light
    some mot inf gp
EQUIPMENT BY TYPE
ARMOURED FIGHTING VEHICLES
  APC • PPV 17 *Kozak*-2

Maritime Border Guard
The Maritime Border Guard is an independent subdivision of the State Commission for Border Guards and is not part of the navy
EQUIPMENT BY TYPE
PATROL AND COASTAL COMBATANTS 21
  PCT 1 *Pauk* I with 4 single 406mm TT, 2 RBU-1200 A/S mor, 1 76mm gun
  PCC 4 *Stenka*
  PB 12: 11 *Zhuk*; 1 *Orlan*
  PBR 4 *Shmel* with 1 76mm gun
LOGISTICS AND SUPPORT • AGF 1
  AIRCRAFT • TPT Medium An-8 *Camp*; Light An-24 *Coke*; An-26 *Curl*; An-72 *Coaler*
  HELICOPTERS • ASW: Ka-27 *Helix* A

Cyber

Ukraine remains the target of persistent and damaging cyber attacks, which have prompted greater state attention and international support. In June 2016, a National Cyber Security Coordination Centre was established, a year after the publication of the National Cyber Security Strategy. This centre is an agency of the National Security and Defence Council and consists of representatives from the defence ministry, the armed forces and the SBU (security service), among others. In early 2018, a Cyberthreats Response Center was opened, providing inter-agency coordination between the State Service of Special Communications and Information Protection of Ukraine, the state-security service and the national police. Through a Cyber Defence Trust Fund, NATO states are extending help to Ukraine in developing its technical capability to counter cyber attacks. According to NATO, this help will include establishing two Incident Management Centres. NATO members visited the Serhiy Korolylov Zhytomyr Military Institute in 2018, with a view to establishing a course on cyber security. Laboratory exercises as part of this visit included defensive and offensive cyber operations in support of a military scenario. Ukraine has also received bilateral assistance from a number of NATO member states in addressing cyber threats.

DEPLOYMENT

AFGHANISTAN: NATO • *Operation Resolute Support* 11
DEMOCRATIC REPUBLIC OF THE CONGO: UN • MONUSCO 255; 8 obs; 2 atk hel sqn
MOLDOVA: 10 obs
SERBIA: NATO • KFOR 40; OSCE • Kosovo 1; UN • UNMIK 3 obs
SOUTH SUDAN: UN • UNMISS 1; 3 obs
SUDAN: UN • UNISFA 2; 3 obs

FOREIGN FORCES

Albania OSCE 9
Armenia OSCE 2
Austria OSCE 14
Azerbaijan OSCE 1
Belarus OSCE 7
Belgium OSCE 1
Bosnia-Herzegovina OSCE 50
Bulgaria OSCE 43
Canada OSCE 35 • *Operation Unifier* 200
Croatia OSCE 11
Czech Republic OSCE 14
Denmark OSCE 8
Estonia OSCE 3
Finland OSCE 23
France OSCE 18
Georgia OSCE 22
Germany OSCE 28
Greece OSCE 23

Hungary OSCE 28
Ireland OSCE 11
Italy OSCE 26
Kazakhstan OSCE 5
Kyrgyzstan OSCE 26
Latvia OSCE 7
Lithuania OSCE 2 • JMTG-U 40
Macedonia (FYROM) OSCE 31
Moldova OSCE 45
Montenegro OSCE 3
Netherlands OSCE 6
Norway OSCE 12
Poland OSCE 41
Portugal OSCE 2
Romania OSCE 36
Russia OSCE 39
Serbia OSCE 16
Slovakia OSCE 12
Slovenia OSCE 1
Spain OSCE 16
Sweden OSCE 11
Switzerland OSCE 8
Tajikistan OSCE 17
Turkey OSCE 10
United Kingdom OSCE 65 • *Operation Orbital* 53
United States OSCE 70 • JMTG-U 220

TERRITORY WHERE THE GOVERNMENT DOES NOT EXERCISE EFFECTIVE CONTROL

In late February 2014, Russian forces occupied Crimea. The region then requested to join the Russian Federation after a referendum, in March, regarded as unconstitutional by the government in Kiev. Months after Russia's annexation of Crimea, fighting began in Ukraine's Donetsk and Luhansk oblasts, with separatist forces there allegedly operating with Russian support. Conflict in the east has persisted since that date. The information displayed for these forces reflects equipment that has been observed as employed in support of the separatist cause in eastern Ukraine. Data presented here represents the de facto situation and does not imply international recognition.

EASTERN UKRAINE SEPARATIST FORCES

ORGANISATIONS BY SERVICE

Donetsk People's Republic ε20,000
FORCES BY ROLE
SPECIAL FORCES
  2 (Spetsnaz) SF bn
MANOEUVRE
  Reconnaissance
  1 recce bn
  Armoured
  1 tk bn
  Light
  6 mot inf bde

COMBAT SUPPORT
  1 arty bde
  1 engr coy
  1 EW coy
COMBAT SERVICE SUPPORT
  1 log bn
AIR DEFENCE
  1 AD bn

Luhansk People's Republic ε14,000
FORCES BY ROLE
MANOEUVRE
  Reconnaissance
  1 recce bn
  Armoured
  1 tk bn
  Light
  4 mot inf bde
COMBAT SUPPORT
  1 arty bde
  1 engr coy
  1 EW coy
COMBAT SERVICE SUPPORT
  1 log bn
AIR DEFENCE
  1 AD bn
EQUIPMENT BY TYPE
ARMOURED FIGHTING VEHICLES
  MBT T-64BV; T-64B; T-64BM†; T-72B1; T-72BA
  RECCE BDRM-2
  IFV BMP-1; BMP-2; BTR-4
  APC
    APC (T) BTR-D; MT-LB; GT-MU
    APC (W) BTR-60; BTR-70; BTR-80
  ABCV BMD-1, BMD-2
ANTI-TANK/ANTI-INFRASTRUCTURE
  MSL 9K115 *Metis* (AT-7 *Saxhorn*); 9K135 *Kornet* (AT-14 *Spriggan*)
  RCL 73mm SPG-9
  GUNS 100mm MT-12
ARTILLERY
  SP 122mm 2S1 *Gvozdika*; **152mm** 2S3 *Akatsiya*; 2S19 *Msta-S*†; **203mm** 2S7 *Pion*
  TOWED 122mm D-30; **152mm** 2A65 *Msta-B*
  GUN/MOR
    SP 120mm 2S9 NONA-S
    TOWED 120mm 2B16 NONA-K
  MRL 122mm BM-21 *Grad*
  MOR 82mm 2B14; **120mm** 2B11 *Sani*
AIR DEFENCE
  SAM
    Short-range 9K332 *Tor*-M2 (SA-15 *Gauntlet*)
    Point-defence 2K22 *Tunguska* (SA-19 *Grison*); 9K32M *Strela*-2M (SA-7B *Grail*); 9K33 *Osa* (SA-8 *Gecko*); 9K35 *Strela*-10 (SA-13 *Gopher*); 9K38 *Igla* (SA-18 *Grouse*); GROM
  GUNS
    SP 23mm ZU-23-2 (tch/on MT-LB)
    TOWED 14.5mm ZPU-2; **57mm** S-60

FOREIGN FORCES

Russia Crimea: 28,000; 1 recce bde, 2 naval inf bde; 1 arty bde; 1 NBC bde; 40 T-72B3 MBT; 80 BMP-2 AIFV; 200 BTR-82A; 20 BTR-80 APC; 150 MT-LB; 18 2S1 arty; 18 2S19 arty; 12 BM-21 MRL; 1 AShM bde with 3K60 Bal; 3K55 *Bastion*; 1 FGA regt with Su-24M/MR; Su-30SM; 1 FGA regt with Su-27SM/SM3; Su-30M2; 1 FGA regt with Su-24M/Su-25SM; 1 atk/tpt hel regt; 1 ASW hel regt; 1 AD regt with S-300PM; 1 AD regt with S-400; 1 Fleet HQ located at Sevastopol; 2 radar stations located at Sevastopol (*Dnepr* system) and Mukachevo (*Dnepr* system) • Donetsk/Luhansk: 3,000 (reported)

Uzbekistan UZB

Uzbekistani Som s		2017	2018	2019
GDP	s	254tr	338tr	
	US$	48.8bn	43.3bn	
per capita	US$	1,520	1,326	
Growth	%	5.3	5.0	
Inflation	%	12.5	19.2	
Def exp	s	n.k	n.k	
	US$	n.k	n.k	
US$1=s		5203.03	7815.54	

Population 30,023,709

Ethnic groups: Uzbek 73%; Russian 6%; Tajik 5%; Kazakh 4%; Karakalpak 2%; Tatar 2%; Korean <1%; Ukrainian <1%

Age	0–14	15–19	20–24	25–29	30–64	65 plus
Male	12.1	4.2%	4.9%	5.2%	21.0%	2.3%
Female	11.5%	4.0%	4.7%	5.2%	21.7%	3.1%

Capabilities

Uzbekistan enacted a new military doctrine in early 2018, stressing heightened security concerns over terrorism and the potential spillover of instability from regional conflicts, particularly from Afghanistan. It also noted a requirement for military modernisation. The new doctrine also focuses on border security and hybrid-warfare concerns. Uzbekistan is a member of the SCO, but suspended its CSTO membership in 2012. It maintains bilateral defence ties with Moscow and in late 2018 a defence cooperation agreement was reported with India. The armed forces are army dominated and conscript-based. Uzbekistan has a limited capacity to deploy its forces externally and does not have any international deployments. The armed forces use mainly Soviet-era equipment. A sizeable air capability was inherited from the Soviet Union, but minimal recapitalisation in the intervening period has substantially reduced the active inventory. Logistical and maintenance shortcomings hinder aircraft availability. In recent years, there has been some procurement of rotary- and fixed-wing transport assets. Uzbekistan is reliant on foreign suppliers for advanced military equipment. A State Committee for the Defence Industry was established in late 2017 to organise domestic industry and defence orders. The 2018 defence doctrine calls for improvements to the domestic defence industry.

ACTIVE 48,000 (Army 24,500 Air 7,500 Joint 16,000)
Paramilitary 20,000
Conscript liability 12 months

ORGANISATIONS BY SERVICE

Army 24,500

4 Mil Districts; 2 op comd; 1 Tashkent Comd
FORCES BY ROLE
SPECIAL FORCES
  1 SF bde
MANOEUVRE
  Armoured
  1 tk bde
  Mechanised
  11 MR bde
  Air Manoeuvre
  1 air aslt bde
  1 AB bde
  Mountain
  1 lt mtn inf bde
COMBAT SUPPORT
  3 arty bde
  1 MRL bde
EQUIPMENT BY TYPE
ARMOURED FIGHTING VEHICLES
  MBT 340: 70 T-72; 100 T-64; 170 T-62
  RECCE 19: 13 BRDM-2; 6 BRM-1
  IFV 270 BMP-2
  APC 359
    APC (T) 50 BTR-D
    APC (W) 259: 24 BTR-60; 25 BTR-70; 210 BTR-80
    PPV 50 *Maxxpro+*
  ABCV 129: 120 BMD-1; 9 BMD-2
  AUV 11+: 7 *Cougar*; 4+ M-ATV
ENGINEERING & MAINTENANCE VEHICLES
  ARV 20 *Maxxpro* ARV
ANTI-TANK/ANTI-INFRASTRUCTURE
  MSL • MANPATS 9K11 *Malyutka* (AT-3 *Sagger*); 9K111 *Fagot* (AT-4 *Spigot*)
  GUNS 100mm 36 MT-12/T-12
ARTILLERY 487+
  SP 83+: **122mm** 18 2S1 *Gvozdika*; **152mm** 17+: 17 2S3 *Akatsiya*; 2S5 *Giatsint*-S (reported); **203mm** 48 2S7 *Pion*
  TOWED 200: **122mm** 60 D-30; **152mm** 140 2A36 *Giatsint*-B
  GUN/MOR 120mm 54 2S9 NONA-S
  MRL 108: **122mm** 60: 36 BM-21 *Grad*; 24 9P138; **220mm** 48 9P140 *Uragan*
  MOR 120mm 42: 5 2B11 *Sani*; 19 2S12 *Sani*; 18 M-120

Air Force 7,500

FORCES BY ROLE
FIGHTER
  1 sqn with MiG-29/MiG-29UB *Fulcrum*;
  1 sqn with Su-27/Su-27UB *Flanker*
GROUND ATTACK
  1 sqn with Su-24 *Fencer*
  1 sqn with Su-25/Su-25BM *Frogfoot*
ELINT/TRANSPORT
  1 regt with An-12/An-12PP *Cub*; An-26/An-26RKR *Curl*
TRANSPORT
  Some sqn with An-24 *Coke*; C295W; Tu-134 *Crusty*

TRAINING
1 sqn with L-39 *Albatros*

ATTACK/TRANSPORT HELICOPTER
1 regt with Mi-24 *Hind*; Mi-26 *Halo*; Mi-8 *Hip*;
1 regt with Mi-6 *Hook*; Mi-6AYa *Hook* C

EQUIPMENT BY TYPE
AIRCRAFT 41 combat capable
  FTR 12 MiG-29/MiG-29UB *Fulcrum* (18 more in store)
  FGA 13 Su-27/Su-27UB *Flanker* (11 more in store) (26 Su-17M (Su-17MZ)/Su-17UM-3 (Su-17UMZ) *Fitter* C/G non-operational)
  ATK 16: 12 Su-25/Su-25BM *Frogfoot*; 4 Su-24 *Fencer*
  EW/Tpt 26 An-12 *Cub* (med tpt)/An-12PP *Cub* (EW) **ELINT/Tpt** 13 An-26 *Curl* (lt tpt)/An-26RKR *Curl* (ELINT)
  TPT 7: **Heavy** 1 Il-76 *Candid*; **Light** 6: 1 An-24 *Coke*; 4 C295W; 1 Tu-134 *Crusty*
  TRG 14 L-39 *Albatros*
HELICOPTERS
  ATK 29 Mi-24 *Hind*
  TPT 69: **Heavy** 9: 8 H225M *Caracal*; 1 Mi-26 *Halo*; **Medium** 52 Mi-8 *Hip*; **Light** 8 AS350 *Ecureuil*
AIR DEFENCE • SAM 45
  Long-range S-200 *Angara* (SA-5 *Gammon*); FD-2000 (HQ-9)
  Medium-range S-75 *Dvina* (SA-2 *Guideline*)
  Short-range S-125 *Pechora* (SA-3 *Goa*)
AIR-LAUNCHED MISSILES
  AAM • IR R-60 (AA-8 *Aphid*); R-73 (AA-11 *Archer*); **IR/SARH** R-27 (AA-10 *Alamo*)
  ASM Kh-23 (AS-7 *Kerry*); Kh-25 (AS-10 *Karen*)
  ARM Kh-25P (AS-12 *Kegler*); Kh-28 (AS-9 *Kyle*); Kh-58 (AS-11 *Kilter*)

Paramilitary up to 20,000

Internal Security Troops up to 19,000
Ministry of Interior

National Guard 1,000
Ministry of Defence

Arms procurements and deliveries – Russia and Eurasia

Significant events in 2018

- Production of the S-500 *Prometey* ballistic-missile-defence and air-defence system began in March at the Nizhny Novgorod Machine-Building Plant (NMZ) and the Kirov Machine-Building Enterprise (KMP). US media reported in May that the S-500 managed to intercept a target at a range of 480 kilometres (a new record). Russia wants to begin S-500 deliveries to front-line units in 2020.

- Ukrainian aerospace firm Antonov signed an agreement with Boeing in July that will see the latter supply parts enabling Antonov to resume aircraft production. Prior to Russia's annexation of Crimea in 2014, Antonov sourced the majority of parts from Russia.

- In August, Russia contracted Sukhoi for the first two series-production Su-57 combat aircraft, which are planned to be delivered by the end of 2020. They will be fitted with the AL-41F-1 engine (*Izdeliye* 117) used by the Su-35S while development of the Su-57's new engine (*Izdeliye* 30) continues. Su-57s with the new engine are planned to be delivered from 2023.

- In September, Russia's Rostec sold 60% of NPO *Molniya* to Kalashnikov (51% of which is owned by Rostec). NPO Molniya is an aerospace design firm that supplies target drones to the Russian defence ministry and led the *Buran* space-shuttle programme, which was cancelled in 1993. In 2014, NPO Molniya was facing bankruptcy and unable to meet delivery deadlines but has since been revived. Kalashnikov hopes to expand into the space sector through the acquisition.

- President Vladimir Putin authorised the takeover of United Aircraft Corporation (UAC) by Rostec in October. This will consolidate all of Russia's military-aerospace industry into one entity and should make easier the funding of large aerospace projects. However, unlike UAC, Rostec is currently under sanctions by the US and the takeover could negatively affect Russian aerospace exports.

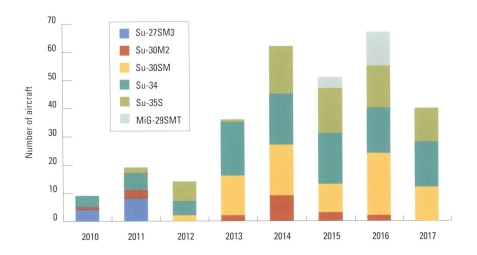

▼ Figure 13 **Russian Air Force: new tactical fighter deliveries, 2010–17**

Figure 14 Russian next-generation armoured-vehicle programmes: progress as of late 2018

Armata

T-14 MBT

T-15 IFV

T-16 ARV

Prime contractor
UralVagonZavod (UVZ)

Selected subcontractor/s
- Chelyabinsk Tractor Plant (2B-12-3A 1,500 hp engine)
- Factory No. 9 (2A82-1M 125 mm cannon)
- KBP Instrument Design Bureau (*Epokha* turret with 2A42 30 mm gun)
- KB Mashinostroyeniya (*Afganit* active-protection system)
- NII Stali (*Malakhit* passive armour complex)
- JSC Concern Sozvezdie (integrated tactical command-and-control system)

Planned in-service dates
(2015)	(late 2018)
2018	2020

Stage:
Low-rate initial production and state tests

Notes:
Deliveries of low-rate initial production batch ordered in 2015 (82 T-14, 41 T-15, 9 T-16) expected to complete in 2022

High costs may result in limited production run

Kurganets

B-10 APC

B-11 IFV

Prime contractor
KuganMashZavod (KMZ)

Selected subcontractor/s
- Yaroslavl Motor Plant (YaMZ-7801 700 hp engine)
- KBP Instrument Design Bureau (*Epokha* turret with 2A42 30 mm gun)
- JSC Concern Sozvezdie (integrated tactical command-and-control system)
- NII Stali (passive armour complex)

Planned in-service dates
(2015)	(late 2018)
2018	2021

Stage:
Low-rate initial production and factory tests

Notes:
Delays caused by technical issues and KMZ's financial difficulties

Bumerang

K-16 APC

K-17 IFV

Prime contractor
Military Industrial Group (VPK)

Selected subcontractor/s
- Arzamas Machine-Building Plant (AMZ) (vehicle manufacturer)
- Yaroslavl Motor Plant (YaMZ-780 700 hp engine)
- KBP Instrument Design Bureau (*Epokha* turret with 2A42 30 mm gun)
- NII Stali (passive armour complex)

Planned in-service dates
(2015)	(late 2018)
2019	2020

Stage:
Factory tests

Notes:
Factory tests planned to be completed in 2019

▼ Figure 15 **Admiralty Shipyards: Project 636 *Varshavyanka* (Improved *Kilo*) and Project 677 *Lada* (*St Petersburg*) attack submarines**

In 1975 the Rubin Design Bureau began work on a replacement for the Project 641/B (*Foxtrot* and *Tango*) submarines. The hull shape of the 641/B displayed a lineage from wartime-era submarines, but with the *Paltus* Project 877 (*Kilo*), Soviet designers opted for the more hydrodynamically efficient 'teardrop' shape that was becoming prevalent.

Between 1980 and 1997, over 40 *Kilo* submarines were built for the Soviet Union (and Russia) and other customers. The 877 design continued the Soviet preference for double-hulled submarines. Subsequently, 18 export variants (877EKM) optimised for warmer waters were sold. The incorporation of design refinements led to the production of a further model, the *Varshavyanka* Project 636 (Improved *Kilo*), intended for export, primarily to Warsaw Pact nations. Of these, two were sold to China, though a follow-on batch of ten improved Project 636Ms were delivered to Algeria and China. A subsequent variant, the Project 06361, was designed for Vietnam.

Both 636M and 06361 can operate the *Klub* family of cruise missiles. Work began in the late 1980s on a replacement for *Paltus*, although construction of the resulting Project 677 *Lada* boat did not begin until 1996. *Lada* is the first Russian conventionally powered submarine to have hydroplanes on the fin and, unlike *Kilo*, has a single hull. *Lada* has a smaller displacement than *Kilo*, with improved manoeuvrability.

However, the project has suffered from problems relating to the power plant and the air-independent propulsion (AIP) system. AIP will not be fitted onto those *Lada* boats that remain to be built under the contract. Likely because of the challenges with *Lada* builds, the Russian Navy ordered six domestic standard Project 06363 *Kilo* submarines in 2010 and 2011, which were delivered on schedule in 2014–16. The Russian Navy's decision to order a second batch may indicate confidence in the type, as well as a lack of available alternatives.

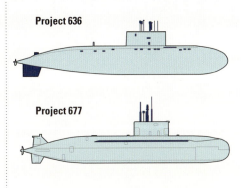

Project 636

Project 677

Prime contractor
Admiralty Shipyards (RUS)

Selected subcontractors
Gidropribor** (RUS)
Granit-Elektron (RUS)
Kolomensky Zavod (RUS)
NPO Avrora (RUS)
NPO Novator* (RUS)
Okeanpribor (RUS)
Rubin Design Bureau (RUS)

**Klub/Kalibr* cruise missiles ** Torpedoes*

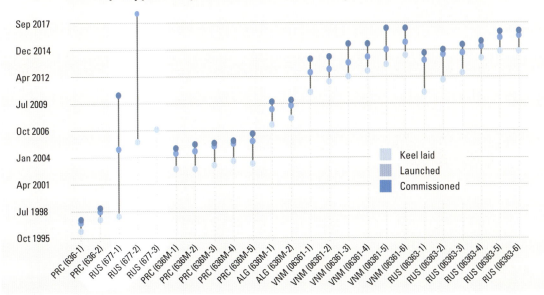

Chapter Six
Asia

- There is continuing concern in the West and regional countries over China's military modernisation.
- The PLAAF is moving ahead with the recapitalisation of its combat aircraft fleets, with obsolescent aircraft replaced with modern combat types. A successor to the H-6K medium-bomber is also in development. China also continues to expand its military presence in the South China Sea.
- Regional navies (Japan, South Korea, Australia) continue to develop or renew their ability to generate task-group-centred capabilities for enhanced blue-water operations. Japan's new defence programme guidelines were expected to reinforce 'cross-domain' capabilities. Japan is buying *Aegis* Ashore and looking into converting its *Izumo*-class vessels to carry the F-35B. Vietnam, meanwhile, continues to modernise its air and naval capabilities to complicate the deployment options of potential adversaries in the country's maritime littoral.
- Some of Asia's top defence spenders drove the regional increase in military expenditure. However, the detailed picture showed some contrasts as defence spending stagnated in Southeast Asia.
- Defence-industry modernisation continues across the region, albeit with varying degrees of success. In particular, India's progress remains hampered by slow and cumbersome bureaucratic processes.
- The unexpected North Korean moratorium on missile testing led to renewed diplomatic contact on the peninsula, and between Pyongyang and Washington. However, while summits continued, there remained no progress on the issue of North Korea's denuclearisation.
- India reported that its *Arihant* nuclear-powered ballistic missile submarine completed its first operational patrol.

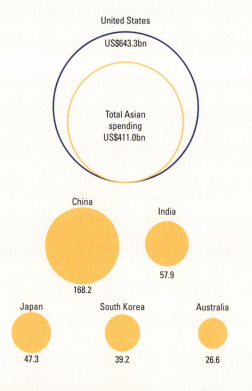

Asia defence spending, 2018 – top 5

United States US$643.3bn
Total Asian spending US$411.0bn
China 168.2
India 57.9
Japan 47.3
South Korea 39.2
Australia 26.6

Active military personnel – top 10
(25,000 per unit)

China 2,035,000
India 1,444,500
North Korea 1,280,000
Pakistan 654,000
South Korea 625,000
Vietnam 482,000
Myanmar 406,000
Indonesia 395,500
Thailand 360,850
Sri Lanka 255,000

Regional defence policy and economics	224 ▶
Armed forces data section	247 ▶
Arms procurements and deliveries	317 ▶

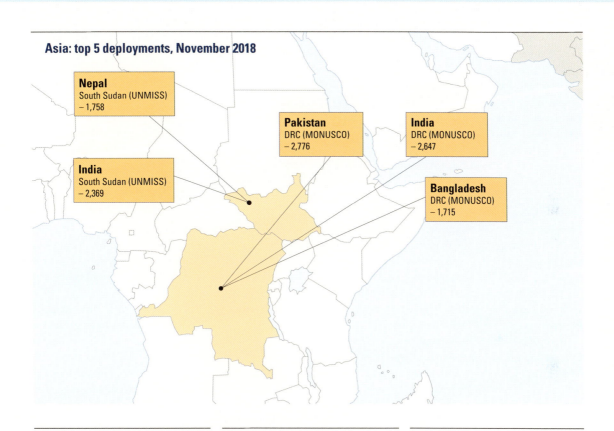

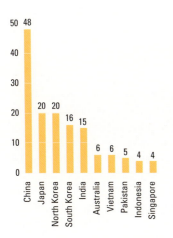

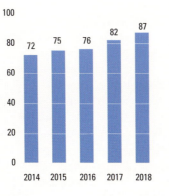

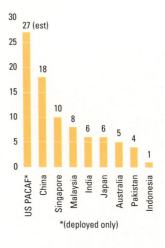

Asia

In late 2017 and early 2018, the crisis provoked by North Korea's nuclear-weapons and ballistic-missile programmes became the primary focus of attention in the region and beyond. The Trump administration increasingly viewed Pyongyang's capabilities as posing a direct threat to the United States. Of particular concern were North Korea's sixth nuclear test in September 2017 (which Pyongyang claimed involved a missile-ready, two-stage thermonuclear device) and the testing two months later of a *Hwasong*-15 intercontinental ballistic missile (ICBM), thought to be capable of reaching the continental US. For several months, there seemed a credible prospect that the US would feel compelled to attack North Korea with the aim of curtailing or eliminating the perceived threat. It was widely thought that this risked the possibility of escalation, to involve not just the US and the two Koreas, but also China and Japan, with unpredictable strategic and economic effects on the wider Asia-Pacific region and globally.

A diplomatic rapprochement between Seoul and Pyongyang in 2018 led the two countries' leaders to meet in April, May and September. As well as this surprising thaw in inter-Korean relations, the Singapore Summit in June 2018 between US President Donald Trump and North Korean leader Kim Jong-un, and bilateral negotiations over the following months, removed the immediate prospect of war. However, these developments by no means resolved the protracted and acutely dangerous dispute. In exchange for unspecified 'security guarantees' from the US, in Singapore Kim promised 'unwavering commitment to complete denuclearisation of the Korean Peninsula'. This phrase reflected North Korea's position that it would only agree to its own denuclearisation if the supposed threat posed by the United States' extended nuclear guarantee to South Korea was withdrawn.

Three weeks before the Singapore Summit, North Korea demolished tunnels at the Punggye-ri nuclear-test facility, and in July reportedly began dismantling facilities used to develop ballistic-missile engines at the Sohae satellite-launching station. However, these were apparently confidence-building measures rather than substantive steps towards disarmament. Furthermore, analysts questioned the level of destruction at Punggye-ri, and satellite imagery showed extensive continuing activity at the Yongbyon nuclear-research facility. Furthermore, US Secretary of State Mike Pompeo in late July told a Senate committee hearing that North Korea was continuing to produce enriched uranium for use in nuclear weapons. That same month, it was reported that Pyongyang appeared to be building new liquid-fuelled ICBMs at its Sanum-dong facility. Nevertheless, both South Korea and the US continued their intensive diplomacy with North Korea. In late September, Pompeo said that a second Trump–Kim summit was likely, and there was speculation that the US would reciprocate a commitment by Pyongyang on specific steps towards denuclearisation with a formal agreement – to which China would be a party – to end the Korean War.

Concerns over North Korea and the potential for conflict on the Korean Peninsula have exerted a significant influence on military developments in Northeast Asia. In late 2017, the US had deployed forces to the region on a scale that suggested to analysts either that it was planning for a preventive war against North Korea, or at the very least that the Pentagon was keen to deliver a message that Pyongyang should take its concerns seriously. B-52 and B-1 bombers and F-22 and F-35 combat aircraft all flew close to the peninsula in 2016 and 2017. Displaying as well as deploying its advanced military capabilities seemed to be a key element of US strategy. For the first time in more than a decade, by late October there were three US Navy carrier strike groups in the 7th Fleet area of operations in the western Pacific. In mid-November and early December, these forces engaged in major exercises with the Japanese and South Korean armed forces. While the South Korean administration led by Moon Jae-in, who became president in May 2017, has played a key role in facilitating the incipient peace process between the US and North Korea, it has continued South Korea's military-modernisation initiatives. Seoul is developing a conventional military deterrent based on the pre-emptive 'Kill Chain' capability (aimed at North Korea's missile and nuclear infrastructure, mobile launchers, and command, control and communications system); the Korean Air and Missile Defence system; and the Korean Massive Punishment and Retaliation (KMPR) strike capability targeting North Korea's political and military leadership.

Some analysts, however, consider that the KMPR strategy, at least, may have been somewhat downgraded by Seoul following the diplomatic activity in 2018. Although the Moon administration in September 2017 allowed the 'temporary' deployment to South Korea of four additional US Army Terminal High-Altitude Area Defense (THAAD) missile launchers, and in early 2018 reportedly ordered more *Taurus* KEPD-350 cruise missiles, an inter-Korean military agreement in September saw the two countries agree measures intended to lower tensions around the demilitarised zone, including setting up buffer zones, dismantling border posts and clearing landmines. And in October another South Korea–US military exercise (*Vigilant Ace*) was suspended, on top of the suspension of exercises including *Ulchi Freedom Guardian* announced shortly after the Singapore Summit. Nonetheless, South Korea's defence minister reportedly said in November that there 'shouldn't be any wavering' in South Korea's military-readiness posture. Japan has also made efforts to strengthen its defences against the security challenge from North Korea, notably through the Cabinet decision in December 2017 to purchase the *Aegis* Ashore missile-defence system.

The North Korea crisis unfolded alongside continuing concern in the West and regional countries – notably Japan – over China's growing defence spending, its efforts to enhance the capabilities of the People's Liberation Army (PLA), and evidence of its further militarisation of the features that it had occupied and had physically expanded since 2012 in the South China Sea. While the US still outspends China, Beijing's defence budget has continued to increase and the PLA has directed much of its growing budget towards efforts to improve its capabilities. The most obvious evidence of this has been the new equipment that is being brought into service, including a second aircraft carrier, more-capable ballistic missiles, improved submarines and new combat aircraft. At the same time, the PLA has been attempting to strengthen its capacity for warfare in the cyber, space and electronic-warfare arenas, while boosting the potential of China's national defence science, research and development, and industrial base through closer cooperation with the civilian high-technology sector. In combination, these efforts are yielding new capabilities that, alongside other improvements, will significantly strengthen China's maritime power-projection capabilities as well as the credibility of its nuclear deterrent.

Military capability is a complex phenomenon, however, and the PLA still suffers from important deficiencies, not least in vital areas such as anti-submarine warfare; intelligence, surveillance and reconnaissance; air-to-air refuelling; and joint-service operations. Even more significantly, it lacks recent direct experience of high-intensity operations, and the scale of the continuing purge of corrupt PLA officers may indicate problems with discipline and morale. The Chinese Communist Party's expressed goal of developing the PLA's capability so that it will be capable of 'winning wars' in three decades' time inadvertently highlights its present shortcomings and may be an ambitious target. The PLA's growing military capabilities increasingly complicate the United States' operational planning assumptions and could almost certainly inflict serious costs on the US armed forces if they were to have to force operational access to China's maritime littoral in the event of conflict. Nonetheless, the US remains the most important military power in the region, despite its need to project that power over considerable distances.

Some US allies and security partners worried about China have been unnerved by the Trump administration's unpredictability. However, substantial overall increases in US defence spending as well as the Department of Defense's continuing focus on strengthening US military capability – including the capacity to operate more closely with the armed forces of allies and partners in what it now calls the 'Indo-Pacific' region – are both in large part intended to mitigate China's military challenge. While the Trump administration nominally abandoned its predecessor's 'rebalance' to the Asia-Pacific, the US National Defense Strategy published in January 2018 gave pre-eminent attention to the Indo-Pacific and explicitly identified China and Russia as the primary 'strategic competitors'.

The US has not been alone in strengthening its military posture in the region in response to China's growing power. In Japan, Prime Minister Shinzo Abe's government has continued gradually to increase defence spending, which has allowed the Japan Self-Defense Forces to begin developing significant additional capabilities. While the immediate motivation for some capability-related developments, such as the acquisition of *Aegis* Ashore, has been the security challenge from North Korea, others – such as the incipient strike capability from Japan's growing force of F-35A combat aircraft – could potentially be used to project military power for wider purposes, against China as well as North Korea.

Under increasing political pressure from Beijing, and acutely aware that the cross-strait military balance has been shifting increasingly in China's favour, Taiwan's government has continued its efforts to strengthen the island's defence posture. It has been led since January 2016 by President Tsai Ing-wen of the Democratic Progressive Party, which favours a more distinct political identity for Taiwan. The Trump administration has supported Taipei's defence efforts, and in September 2018 announced the sale of spare parts and logistic support for Taiwanese military aircraft; this followed the agreement in June 2017 of a major arms package for Taiwan, including AGM-88 HARM air-to-surface anti-radiation missiles, torpedoes and technical support for early-warning radars.

In Southeast Asia, Vietnam has displayed the greatest resolution of any Association of Southeast Asian Nations (ASEAN) member in terms of attempting to deter Chinese interference with its interests in the South China Sea. To this end, Hanoi continues to modernise its naval and air arms as part of an effort to establish capabilities to complicate the deployment options of potential adversaries in the country's maritime littoral. Vietnam's state-controlled media reported during 2017 that India had not only agreed to supply, but had started delivering, *BrahMos* anti-ship cruise missiles to Vietnam, though this was denied by New Delhi in 2017 and 2018.

Elsewhere in Southeast Asia, more varied influences shape national-defence policies, strategies and military procurement. Singapore's defence spending has remained the largest of any Southeast Asian country, and the city-state has continued to invest heavily in major acquisition programmes. New equipment entering service in 2017–18 included A330 MRTT in-flight refuelling aircraft, *Aster* 30 SAMP/T medium-range ground-based air-defence systems and locally built *Independence*-class Littoral Mission Vessels, of which five of eight ships on order are now in service. A serious challenge for the country's armed forces is the impact of a declining national birth rate on the size of the conscript cohort, which is projected to decline by a third by 2030. In response, the acquisition of platforms requiring fewer personnel to operate is planned, including a new, locally developed armoured fighting vehicle and a next-generation howitzer.

DEFENCE ECONOMICS

In 2018, Asia was the main engine of global growth, according to the IMF, with GDP growth reaching 5.6%, thereby accounting for 60% of the global total. Within Asia, however, advanced economies slowed down between 2017 (2.4% GDP growth) and 2018 (2.1%), with the notable exception of Australia, where growth accelerated from 2.2% to 3.2%. The economies of Japan, Singapore, South Korea and Taiwan all decelerated. In contrast, the region's emerging markets and developing economies grew by 6.5%. The fastest-growing countries in 2018 were Bangladesh and India at 7.3%, followed by Cambodia (6.9%) and Laos (6.8%), then China and Vietnam both at 6.6%. India's economy in particular rebounded after important currency and tax reforms introduced since 2016, and after the implementation of policies regarding access to bank accounts, identity numbers and mobile phones.

As it is an export-oriented region, Asia largely benefited from improved global trade. Regional growth was also helped by infrastructure projects. Besides the investments linked to China's Belt and Road Initiative projects, there are important developments in India and Indonesia, among others.

▼ Figure 16 **Asia defence spending by country and sub-region, 2017**

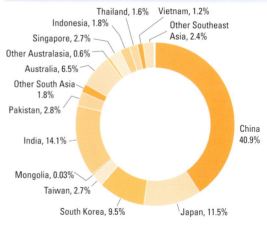

Note: analysis excludes North Korea and Laos due to insufficient data.

© IISS

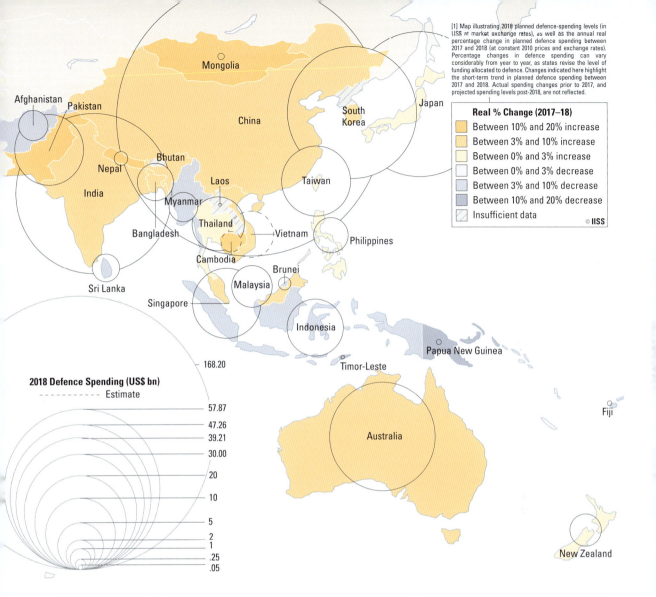

▲ Map 6 **Asia regional defence spending**[1]

However, countries with growing debt will likely face future challenges. In 2018, East Asian countries with high debt levels included China, Laos, Malaysia, Mongolia and Thailand, while Cambodia, Laos, Mongolia and Vietnam all had large fiscal deficits. This has led countries including China, Laos, Malaysia and Vietnam to renew fiscal-consolidation efforts, which might limit public spending and investments in the near term.

The trade showdown between the US and China will have a wider effect. Simulations run by international financial institutions show that the hikes in trade tariffs could influence regional growth. At the time of writing, it was too early to fully assess the impact of these measures, but there are potential economic consequences for Asia. For instance, if the full range of measures so far mooted are implemented, according to the IMF the effect would be to lower Chinese GDP by 1.6% over two years. The IMF also assessed that GDP growth could fall by 0.9% in South Korea, by 0.7% in India, Indonesia and Japan, and by 0.6% in Australia, Malaysia, the Philippines and Thailand.

Running counter to protectionist trends, some regional states are instead looking to new multilateral trade agreements. The Comprehensive and Progressive Agreement for Trans-Pacific Partnership, or the TPP-11, replaces the Trans-Pacific Partnership; the US pulled out of the negotiations for this following Donald Trump's election as US president. Ratification by at least six signatories is pending. In Southeast

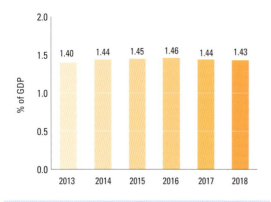

▲ Figure 17 **Asia regional defence expenditure** as % of GDP

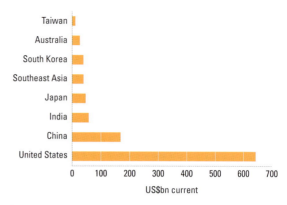

Southeast Asia includes Brunei, Cambodia, Indonesia, Malaysia, Myanmar, Philippines, Singapore, Thailand, Timor-Leste and Vietnam. No data available for Laos

▲ Figure 18 **Indo-Pacific defence spending, 2018** (US$bn, current)

Asia, the ASEAN Trade in Goods Agreement (ATIGA) will reduce tariffs among its member states, with full implementation expected in 2018.

Defence spending and procurement

Asian defence spending continues to increase. It grew by 4.0% in real terms between 2017 and 2018, picking up speed after a year of slower growth; the rate had been 2.8% between 2016 and 2017. Some of the region's top spenders drove the increase. In real terms, Australia's defence budget grew by 8.4%, China's by 5.7% and South Korea's by 4.5%.

In contrast, defence spending stagnated in Southeast Asia, with a regional decline of 0.6% between 2017 and 2018, though there was a more pronounced drop in some states, notably Indonesia where real-terms spending fell by 9.7%. This complex picture is a reminder that strong economic growth does not necessarily translate into strong defence-budget growth or high levels of defence expenditure. Governments in this sub-region are managing competing policy priorities; in Malaysia, for instance, there is a focus by the new government on healthcare. Overall, Southeast Asian states' defence budgets remain modest when compared to the rest of Asia; combined, they reach only the level of South Korea's defence budget (see Figure 18).

Consequently, procurement and defence research and development (R&D) spending for these countries remains constrained, compared to larger spenders in East Asia. For instance, Indonesia in 2018 dedicated 15.9% of its budget to these defence investments, which amounted to some US$1.16 billion, while in Malaysia and Vietnam these expenditures totalled US$804 million and US$821m respectively.

Among Southeast Asian countries, Singapore spends the most on procurement and defence R&D, with the estimated US$2.18bn spent on these in 2018 comprising just below 20% of its total defence budget. The city-state is making significant investments in its sophisticated air force. It is set to enhance its rotary-wing fleet with additional H225M *Caracal* and CH-47F *Chinook* helicopters, while the first of six A330 MRTT tankers was delivered in August 2018. The Singaporean government is also expected to decide, by the end of 2018, on whether to buy F-35 combat aircraft as the replacement for its F-16s.

Australia's increased defence budget is also dedicated largely to improving aerospace capacities. Indeed, air platforms comprise four of the top five acquisition projects for the Australian armed forces in the coming year (see Table 12). The first is the acquisition of F-35 combat aircraft; 72 will be bought in total and the first two were due to arrive in Australia in December 2018.

These procurement choices reflect Australia's concerns over regional security developments, including China's military progress, and a desire to acquire capabilities allowing it to act on its own as well as with like-minded states. For instance, Australia's procurement of P-8 maritime-patrol aircraft mirrors that in India. South Korea, meanwhile, has selected the P-8 for its future maritime-patrol-aircraft requirement.

Expenditures for naval programmes, such as the future submarines and frigates, will soon rise, with total programme costs projected at over A$50bn (US$37bn) and A$30bn (US$22bn) respectively. So

Table 12 **Australia: top five acquisition programmes in 2018, by approved expenditure**

Equipment ordered/procured	Project number/phase	Approved project expenditure, A$bn	Approved project expenditure, US$bn
F-35 combat aircraft	AIR6000 Phase 2A/B	15.51	11.51
Hobart-class air-warfare destroyer	SEA 4000 Phase 3	9.09	6.74
P-8A *Poseidon* maritime-patrol aircraft	AIR 7000 Phase 2	5.21	3.87
E-7A *Wedgetail* airborne early-warning aircraft	AIR 5077 Phase 3	3.87	2.87
MRH90 multi-role helicopter	AIR 9000 Phase 2	3.77	2.80

Source: Australian Government, Portfolio Budget Statements 2018–19, Defence Portfolio, Table 64: Top 30 Projects by 2018–19 Forecast Expenditure, p 120

far, total approved expenditure for Australia's future submarine design and construction is A$2.24bn (US$1.66bn) under phase 1B of the Sea 1000 project and A$395m (US$293m) for the future frigates under phase 1 of the Sea 5000 project.

Defence industry and markets

Contract negotiations were ongoing in late 2018 between Canberra and Naval Group regarding Australia's submarine programme. The French company was selected in 2016 to design and build 12 submarines based on the *Shortfin Barracuda* Block 1A design. A series of contracts has been signed since this announcement, but this situation illustrates the lengthy processes and challenges associated with implementing large equipment deals.

Even when it comes to long-established partnerships, arms transfers can be affected by disputes. In 2018, Japan and the US discussed Tokyo's concerns regarding the costs and processes of US Foreign Military Sales (FMS). Japan relies heavily on FMS, and the value of FMS deliveries increased from US$779m in 2010 to US$1.01bn in 2017. Japan's Audit Board has expressed concerns in recent years regarding the management of FMS, particularly over the F-35 programme. Japanese authorities, the watchdog said, had no knowledge on why prices had risen, that there were delays in the deliveries of parts and that there was a lack of coordination with Japanese firms involved in the manufacturing process. In 2018, defence ministers from both countries discussed 'improvements' to the FMS process, relating to delays in implementing procurement programmes, as well as reimbursements of Japanese overpayments on FMS transactions.

Meanwhile, South Korea was reclaiming outlays from Indonesia, concerning the KF-X joint combat-aircraft programme. According to press reports, Indonesia failed to pay approximately US$200m to South Korea for its share of the expenses, which amounted to 20% of the development costs. Seoul maintained that this did not delay the project, and that it was in discussions with Jakarta to reduce the latter's share in the programme. Indonesia was looking to the KF-X project to boost technology transfer to its own defence sector.

Developing a domestic defence-industrial base would, in theory, avoid such complications. Many states in the region are looking to do so. Possessing a defence-industrial sector would help with sovereign defence policymaking and would also – if they were to develop an export model – allow states to recoup through foreign earnings some of the investments made in the sector.

Vietnam is looking to rationalise its state-owned defence enterprises, notably through mergers. In mid-2018, a new regulation was intended to reduce the number of military-operated businesses from 88 to 17, to focus military-owned enterprises on defence tasks and to support economic development. However, this process of rationalisation began a decade ago, with little visible effect so far, though Vietnam's Military Telecommunications General Corporation changed its name to Viettel Military Industry and Telecom Group in early 2018.

In 2018, Australia took measures to support its defence-industrial base. The government launched a defence-export strategy in 2018, with the aim of Australia becoming one of the world's top-ten defence suppliers by 2028. The strategy created a new Australian Defence Export Office. The government also released A$20m (US$15m) of annual funding to support arms exports and opened an export credit line of A$3.8bn (US$2.9bn) for customers of Australian weapons systems. In April 2018, Canberra also released its Defence Industrial Capability Plan, following a 2016 Defence Industry Policy Statement. It identified priority areas for support to the defence industry, including on submarine capability, as well as land-combat vehicles and related technology upgrades, and included A$17m (US$13m) per year for grants to support small and medium-sized enterprises (SMEs) working in these areas. These new policies are intended to develop and support local manufacturers. Currently local companies are only dominant in shipbuilding, such as ASC and Austal. Other areas of Australia's defence-industrial base are dominated by foreign-owned prime contractors such as Raytheon Australia, BAE Systems Australia and Thales Australia.

Reform initiatives were also announced in South Korea in 2018, with a particular focus on developing SMEs. The Defense Acquisition Program Administration (DAPA) aims to diversify local defence suppliers, and boosting the role of SMEs is a key plank of DAPA's import-substitution policy. By raising the profile of SMEs and better integrating them into international defence supply chains, DAPA also hopes to enhance export results. In 2017, South Korea exported weapons worth US$3.19bn but intends to raise that figure to US$5bn by 2022. New offset guidelines are expected in early 2019 and may include requirements for foreign arms manufacturers to integrate locally made components into their weapons systems for South Korea's armed forces. The 'Defense Business Innovation Plan' launched in August 2018 focused on reforming procurement processes, but also contained initiatives to promote the domestic industrial base and

India: air- and naval-procurement update

Much of India's tactical combat-aircraft fleet is ageing and needs replacement, although urgency on this matter is not always apparent in New Delhi's procurement strategies. India first began to identify a multi-role fighter to fulfil its medium-combat-aircraft requirement some two decades ago, but it is only now near the beginning of a combat-aircraft procurement project to meet the bulk of this need. During the course of 2018, a limited interim acquisition of the French Dassault *Rafale* became mired in political allegations and counter-claims of corruption. Meanwhile, at least publicly, Indian enthusiasm to acquire a next-generation fighter from Russia was also on the wane.

A problem for the air force is that the strength of its tactical combat-aircraft squadrons remains well below target, at a time when both external acquisition projects and notional national development programmes are faltering. Furthermore, the rivals against which it baselines its needs – and in a worst-case scenario would face in a war on two fronts – are re-equipping their fleets. China and Pakistan are in the throes of recapitalising their combat-aircraft fleets and associated weapons inventories. Of the two, China constitutes by far the more significant challenge, and remains the main source of Islamabad's combat inventory. With the imminent service-entry of China's Chengdu J-20 fighter, India risks a situation where China has been able to develop and introduce into service its first low-observable combat aircraft in roughly the same time frame as that absorbed by Delhi in its failed attempts to buy an 'off-the-shelf' aircraft for its medium-fighter requirement.

That said, things seem to move faster in air defence. By the end of 2020 the air force will begin to receive the first of what is reported as a five-regiment order for the Russian S-400 (SA-21 *Growler*) long-range surface-to-air missile system, a deal for which was struck by New Delhi and Moscow in October 2018.

The Indian Navy has relied in the past on significant deliveries of platforms and weapons systems from Russia. However, the shortcomings of Russia's naval defence-industrial base are in part responsible for New Delhi's problems or delays in achieving its ambitious naval-expansion plans. Increasing focus on indigenous warship construction has produced its own problems, with Indian shipyards having a poor record of delivery. Meanwhile, government auditing reports have cited problems with Russian equipment supplies as being a factor in delayed naval programmes.

As a result, the Indian Navy has diversified its sources of supply; for example, it turned to Israel for the supply of its *Barak* 1 and *Barak* 8 air-defence systems. This has led to Indian warships being equipped with a complex mix of Israeli, Russian and Western systems. A growing strategic relationship with the United States is being driven by, and expressed in increasing discussions on, the naval-procurement front. An example is possible collaboration with the US on the design and equipping of India's planned second indigenous aircraft carrier. The US has filled a key maritime requirement with the supply of P-8 maritime-patrol aircraft (the P-8I *Neptune*), and looks like a strong contender to fill a navy requirement for new shipborne multi-role helicopters.

India still needs to overcome a slow and cumbersome bureaucratic process and a lack of adequate resources to deliver on its naval-programme ambitions; as in the air domain, New Delhi is increasingly conscious that it is being outpaced in this regard by Beijing.

Table 13 India: procurements from Russia and the United States, 2000–18

■ Russian systems   ■ US systems

2000 Su-30MKI *Flanker* H – FGA ac
Quantity: 140   **Value:** US$6.48bn
(IND) Hindustan Aeronautics (RUS licensed production)

2001 T-90S – MBT
Quantity: 124   **Value:** US$371.94m
(RUS) UralVagonZavod

2001 T-90S – MBT kits
Quantity: 186   **Value:** US$484.74m
(RUS) UralVagonZavod

2001 Il-38SD – ASW ac
Quantity: 5   **Value:** US$150m
(RUS) United Aircraft Corporation

2004 *Akula* II – SSN
Quantity: 1   **Value:** US$900m
(RUS) Government surplus lease

2004 *Kiev* class – CV
Quantity: 1   **Value:** US$2.35bn
(RUS) Government surplus

2004 MiG-29K/KUB *Fulcrum* – FGA ac
Quantity: 16   **Value:** US$794.21m
(RUS) United Aircraft Corporation

2004 T-90S – MBT
Quantity: 300   **Value:** n.k.
(IND) Ordnance Factory Board (RUS licensed production)

2005 9A52 *Smerch* – MRL
Quantity: 28   **Value:** εUS$396.48m
(RUS) NPO Splav

2006 *Talwar* II class (Pr. 11356) – FFGHM
Quantity: 3   **Value:** US$1.13bn
(RUS) Yantar Shipyard

2006 BMP-2K – IFV
Quantity: 123   **Value:** n.k.
(RUS) Kurganmashzavod

2007 9A52 *Smerch* – MRL
Quantity: 14   **Value:** εUS$217.75m
(RUS) NPO Splav

2007 Su-30MKI *Flanker* H – FGA ac
Quantity: 40 (of which 25 kits/semi-assembled)   **Value:** US$1.55bn
(RUS) United Aircraft Corporation

2007 T-90S – MBT
Quantity: 347 (of which 223 semi-assembled)
Value: US$1.22bn
(RUS) UralVagonZavod

2008 C-130J-30 *Hercules* – Med tpt ac
Quantity: 6   **Value:** US$962.45m
(US) Lockheed Martin

2008 Mi-17V-5 *Hip* H – MRH
Quantity: 80   **Value:** US$1.35bn
(RUS) Russian Helicopters

2009 P-8I *Neptune* – ASW ac
Quantity: 8   **Value:** US$2.1bn
(US) Boeing

2009 BMP-2 – IFV
Quantity: 236   **Value:** US$172.42m
(IND) Ordnance Factory Board (RUS licensed production)

2010 MiG-29K/KUB *Fulcrum* – FGA ac
Quantity: 29   **Value:** US$1.47bn
(RUS) United Aircraft Corporation

2011 BMP-2 – IFV
Quantity: 153   **Value:** US$117.19m
(IND) Ordnance Factory Board (RUS licensed production)

2011 C-17A *Globemaster* III – Hvy tpt hel
Quantity: 11   **Value:** US$4.7bn
(US) Boeing

2012 Su-30MKI *Flanker* H – FGA ac
Quantity: 42   **Value:** US$2.97bn
(RUS) United Aircraft Corporation

2012 Mi-17V-5 *Hip* H – MRH
Quantity: 71   **Value:** n.k.
(RUS) Russian Helicopters

2013 T-90S – MBT
Quantity: 236   **Value:** US$991.7m
(IND) Ordnance Factory Board (RUS licensed production)

2013 C-130J-30 *Hercules* – Med tpt ac
Quantity: 6   **Value:** US$1.01bn
(US) Lockheed Martin

2015 AH-64E *Apache* – Atk hel
Quantity: 22
CH-47F *Chinook* Hvy tpt hel
Quantity: 15
(US) Boeing
Combined value: US$3bn

2016 P-8I *Neptune* – ASW ac
Quantity: 4   **Value:** US$1bn
(US) Boeing

2017 M777A2 – 155mm Arty
Quantity: 145   **Value:** US$542.1m
(US) BAE Land Systems and Armaments

2018 C-17A *Globemaster* III – Hvy tpt hel
Quantity: 1   **Value:** US$262m
(US) Boeing

2018 S-400 (SA-21 *Growler*) – SAM
Quantity: 80   **Value:** US$5.4bn
(RUS) Almaz-Antey

strengthen defence R&D. Plans included intellectual-property reform and the creation of a new agency called Defense Science and Technology Planning and Evaluation, to focus on emerging technologies. The plan also contained measures to support arms exports, also via a new agency called the Defense Industry Promotion Association.

CHINA

President Xi Jinping continues to reform Chinese governance. This includes his ambitious plan to modernise the People's Liberation Army (PLA) by 2035 and complete its transformation into 'world-class forces' capable of winning wars by 2049. These major policy projects have attracted significant attention in China and internationally, drawing concern not only for the return of highly centralised decision-making in Beijing in the hands of Xi, but also for the expanding government-led military outreach that has led to an escalation of regional tensions.

Centralised control

The primacy of the Communist Party of China (CCP), and its leadership role in government, the armed forces and society, was made clear at the 19th Party Congress in October 2017. Furthermore, the president's theory – 'Xi Jinping Thought on Socialism with Chinese Characteristics for a New Era' – was written into the Party's constitution, cementing Xi's power in the manner of the precedents set by his predecessors Mao Zedong and Deng Xiaoping. Furthermore, at the 13th National People's Congress (NPC) in March 2018, a constitutional amendment was approved, abolishing term limits for the presidency. Under Xi, the distinctions between party and state have become increasingly blurred, moving away from Deng's vision whereby the two were separate, and each had distinct powers.

The 19th Party Congress visibly illustrated the Party's expanding control over the PLA, and the recentralisation of decision-making power into Xi and his allies' hands within a slimmed-down Central Military Commission (CMC). Before the 19th Party Congress, the CMC had a chairman (Xi), two vice-chairmen and seven members. At its close, as well as Xi as chairman, the CMC comprised two vice-chairmen and four members. All are close allies of Xi, with personal ties to him. The signal was that Xi would continue to strictly control military reform, to him a personal project.

The PLA has undergone further organisational change in 2018. A key message has been that the PLA serves the Party, not the other way round. As part of this, Xi has extended his anti-graft campaign – which previously only targeted high-level PLA officials – to include lower-ranking officials. During Xi's first term as president, more than 13,000 PLA officers, including 100 generals, were targeted in the anti-corruption campaign by the Party's Central Commission for Discipline Inspection and the State's National Supervision Commission. This has earned Xi both respect for ridding branches of the armed forces of corrupt 'tigers' (high-level officials) and 'flies' (rank-and-file cadres), but also criticism for his use of the campaign to remove political opponents and promote his allies to positions of power.

However, control of the PLA by the Party and Xi has not gone unchallenged. Years of insufficient care have led to discontent among PLA veterans, and since 2016 – when there was a large-scale protest in Beijing in front of the defence ministry – veterans have periodically staged public protests in Beijing over unpaid demobilisation benefits, healthcare and pensions. These protests have spread beyond Beijing despite the CCP's creation of the Ministry of Veterans Affairs in March 2018 to deal with their concerns. For instance, a group of over 1,000 PLA veterans staged a protest in Zhenjiang, Jiangsu province, in June 2018. While the leadership of Xi regarding the PLA and political leadership may be publicly projected as strong, these protests nonetheless raise questions. Indeed, following a speech to PLA chiefs at the 2018 Party leaders' summer retreat at Beidaihe, Hebei province, Xi once again called for 'absolute loyalty' and 'strengthening the party's leadership in the army' in order to make China and the PLA powerful. At public appearances in 2018, Xi's consistent calls for unwavering PLA loyalty to the Party may in fact betray some concern over the strength of this.

While Xi tries to strengthen control of the PLA, he is using what the 2015 defence white paper labelled as China's 'strategic opportunity' of a favourable external environment to modernise the PLA and bolster the armed forces' power-projection capability. The PLA Navy and PLA Air Force (PLAAF) in particular continue to modernise their equipment inventories, and the armed forces have started to integrate new technologies, such as uninhabited aerial vehicles (UAVs), while China continues to develop its capabilities and innovation in the fields of cyber, space and electronic warfare.

In 2017 and 2018, China demonstrated a more assertive posture in relation to Taiwan and in the East China Sea. In May 2018, the PLAAF flew H-6K bombers and Su-35 *Flanker* E combat aircraft around Taiwan. These 'training flights', as the PLA put it, were an attempt to discourage Taipei from making any moves towards independence. In September 2018, Japan's then defence minister Itsunori Onodera warned of China's unilateral escalation of military activities in the sea and airspace around Japan. In the South China Sea, China's militarisation of the islands and features it occupies in the Spratlys continues.

Further afield, China has expanded the reach of its international infrastructure-development project, the Belt and Road Initiative. However, regional and international fears have yet to be realised over dual-use ports along the 'maritime silk route' that China has built. In addition to its military-logistics base in Djibouti, China announced in August 2018 that it is fully funding and building a training camp in Afghanistan that will be used to improve the counter-terrorism capabilities of both Afghan troops and the PLA. Alongside numerous and increasingly complex training exercises in China, the region and internationally – and continuing deployment on UN operations – this Afghanistan mission will provide the PLA with valuable, albeit non-combat, operational experience.

Beijing is simultaneously modernising its armed forces, expanding its global reach and engaging in domestic reforms. Maintaining this pace and breadth may prove a challenge, and if the veterans' protests are indicative of morale and cohesion issues within the force and illustrate concerns over the extent of the Party's influence over the PLA, they may influence Xi's ability to deliver on the two deadlines he has set for China's military progress.

South China Sea

In 2015, Xi promised then US president Barack Obama that China would not militarise its reclaimed features in the Spratly Islands. Events since that date would seem to indicate otherwise.

It is true that China's large-scale dredging and reclamation of land appears to have halted, at least for now. However, between 2013 and 2015, China reclaimed 17 times more land than the combined amount reclaimed over the past 40 years by the four other regional Spratly Island claimants (Malaysia, the Philippines, Taiwan and Vietnam). By 2016, China had reclaimed approximately 12.95 square kilometres of land. Between 2016 and 2018, the PLA instead intensified its efforts to fortify these features by building infrastructure and a range of military facilities.

The three largest of the Spratly Islands (Fiery Cross Reef, Mischief Reef and Subi Reef) now host 3-km-long runways, hangars for combat aircraft, ammunition bunkers, barracks, large berthing facilities, anti-aircraft guns and close-in weapons systems. The seven Chinese-reclaimed Spratly Islands today house over 40 varying radar facilities that represent a significant enhancement of China's capabilities in the area relating not just to command and control but also intelligence, surveillance and reconnaissance. In April 2018, reports emerged that China had deployed jamming equipment to Mischief Reef in the Spratlys.

While surface-to-air missiles and anti-ship cruise missiles (ASCMs) have not yet been installed in the Spratlys, further north, in the Paracel Islands group, China has deployed HQ-9 air-defence systems, probably YJ-62 ASCMs, as well as J-11B combat aircraft on Woody Island, the latter two possibly as short-term deployments. In May 2018, an H-6K bomber landed on Woody Island, the first time that one of these bombers had landed on one of China's South China Sea islands.

While strategic and regional messaging might be key to Beijing's rationale, and the capability of the deployed equipment has yet to be tested in combat, Beijing has nonetheless changed the power balance in the South China Sea. The calculus involved in any decision by the US or its allies on possible military action in the South China Sea has become more complex, and potentially with higher risk. So far, Washington has responded by continuing to conduct freedom-of-navigation naval operations and overflights. In May 2018, the US disinvited China from the 2018 RIMPAC exercise, citing as the reason China's militarisation of the South China Sea. Meanwhile, the resurrected 'Quad' regional grouping (which includes Australia, India, Japan and the US) has yet to take shape, with New Delhi denying that the grouping has any military or defence function.

While the US considers its options, China has succeeded in dividing Association of Southeast Asian Nations (ASEAN) member states and promoting its strategy of bilateral multilateralism. Whether or not

Map 7 Chinese military facilities in the South China Sea

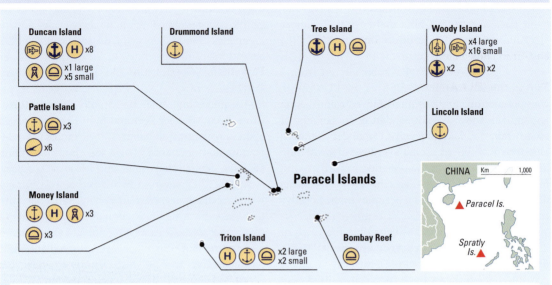

China's land reclamation in the Spratlys and Paracels seems to have stopped in recent years, and the focus has instead turned to building up permanent infrastructure. All the Chinese-controlled features in the Spratlys have what appear to be permanent weapons emplacements but this is not the case in the Paracels, though weapons have appeared there occasionally. This might be due to the proximity of the Paracels to Hainan, making them less vulnerable. In the Spratlys, a variety of radars and radomes now seem to be part of the permanent infrastructure, indicating the extent of Chinese command-and-control and ISR capabilities in the South China Sea. The ports in the Spratly Islands, including deep-water berths, could in the future support a wide range of naval vessels. Lastly, 3 km runways, aircraft hangars and weapons-storage facilities on Woody Island in the Paracels and Subi, Fiery Cross and Mischief reefs in the Spratlys will enable greater reach for Chinese airpower.

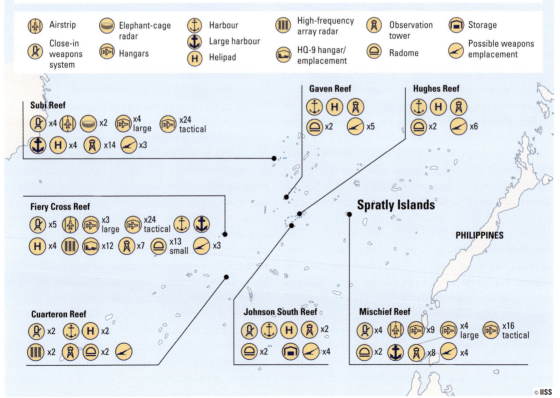

the US and its allies in the Indo-Pacific can agree on how to counter China in the near future, it seems that Beijing will continue to slowly change the strategic environment of the South China Sea at sea, in the air and on reclaimed land.

PLA Army (PLAA)

The process of reorganisation and rebasing begun in 2017 is mostly complete, although some brigade moves may yet take place, largely in the Northern and Western Theatre Commands. However, the distinction between the areas of responsibility of the Tibet Military Command and the Western Theatre Command's 77th Group Army now seems to have become blurred, with the latter beginning to rebase part of its manoeuvre force within Tibet itself.

The focus of the PLAA now appears to be on internal restructuring within the new combined arms brigades and training. The first reorganised light combined arms infantry unit, formed in 2014 and now part of the 78th Group Army in the Northern Theatre Command, was unveiled publicly in 2018. Utilising 4×4 vehicles from the Dongfeng Mengshi family as personnel carriers, and truck- and jeep-mounted howitzers and mortars for fire support, this formation – a battalion of the 48th Combined Arms Brigade – is a template for the rest of the PLAA's light combined arms units. The two newly redesignated air-assault brigades in the Eastern and Southern theatre commands, the 121st from the 75th Group Army and the 161st from the 83rd Group Army, are also now working up their capabilities and have begun exercising in their new role.

For the heavy and medium combined arms brigades, progress in modernising the PLAA's armoured-fighting-vehicle fleet is still only incremental; a limiting factor is that the army is a relatively low priority for re-equipment. The ZTZ-99 main battle tank, although in production for nearly two decades, continues to equip less than a quarter of the new heavy combined arms brigades. The most advanced variant of the ZTZ-99, the ZTZ-99A, appears to remain restricted to the two formations already equipped with it prior to the reorganisation (the 112th Mechanised Division and 62nd Combined Arms Brigade).

More progress seems to have been made with the army's combat-support equipment, including artillery, engineering and air-defence systems. The indigenous HQ-16 air-defence system, which analysts consider to be roughly analogous to Russia's *Buk*, is now in service with nine of the group armies, as well as with units in Tibet and Shanghai. This gives the PLAA its first widespread medium-range air-defence capability.

PLA Rocket Force (PLARF)

The PLARF remains organised in a series of corps-leader-grade 'bases', now numbering nine in total. Six of them (bases 61–66) command the force's operational missile brigades, while the other three handle warhead storage and transport (67 Base), specialist engineering (68 Base) and test and training (69 Base). The multiple new missile brigades formed during 2017 are now beginning to take shape, with some resultant relocation of units and changes to equipment and missions. In 62 Base, a combination of rebasing of existing units and the formation of two new brigades is likely to result in an additional brigade of DF-21D medium-range ballistic missiles (MRBMs) and a first brigade of DF-26 intermediate-range ballistic missiles being formed in southern China. Both of these missile types have anti-ship capabilities and when the brigades reach operational capability will add to the PLARF's ability to hold at risk possible targets in the South China Sea and Indian Ocean. In northern China, the new brigade in 65 Base will also most probably equip with the DF-21D, since it is currently co-located in Dalian, Liaoning province, with an existing DF-21D formation. This would result in a doubling of the PLARF's anti-ship ballistic-missile brigades, when compared to its roster before the reorganisation began.

The two new brigades formed in 64 and 66 bases are both likely to work up as road-mobile intercontinental-ballistic-missile (ICBM) units; one is most probably charged with bringing the still-developmental DF-41 (CH-SS-X-20) ICBM into service, while the other will probably equip with either the DF-31A(G) ICBM or additional DF-41s. Both of these missiles are believed to be capable of deploying multiple independently targetable re-entry vehicles. The new brigades would mark the first expansion of the PLARF's road-mobile ICBM fleet in nearly a decade.

In late 2017, media reports described two test firings of a new developmental short-range ballistic missile or MRBM, reportedly with a hypersonic glide-vehicle payload. It is reported that this missile may have the PLA designation DF-17, but there is limited further information available on the missile; its connections, if any, to existing PLARF designs; and its intended mission.

PLA Navy (PLAN) and China Coast Guard (CCG)

In April 2018, China deployed to the South China Sea its largest assembly of naval power in modern times. Led by the aircraft carrier *Liaoning*, what amounted to a fleet review consisted of nearly 50 vessels and sent a significant message. It underscored the dramatic progress in the capabilities of the PLAN, not least in its potential for blue-water operations.

The PLAN has taken further steps in developing its aircraft-carrier capability. In June 2018, China announced that the *Liaoning* had reached initial operating capability, and three months later said that it had carried out night-flying operations. This provides further evidence that China may be on the cusp of a real, if still limited, operational carrier capability.

In addition, a second aircraft carrier has begun sea trials and could be accepted into service as early as 2019. Built in China, this second ship is a modified version of the *Liaoning*. There were also increasing indicators that work is under way on a third, larger vessel that may be fitted with some form of catapult and arrester gear.

Shipyard output seems to be focusing even more than before on high-capability large surface combatants, adding to the sense that Chinese naval-capability development may be entering a new phase. In July 2018, there were simultaneous launches of two of the new Type-055 cruisers. This meant that four had been launched in just over a year, while at least four more are under construction. The first of the Type-055s began sea trials in August 2018.

It has been estimated that the Type-055s displace between 10,000 and 13,000 tonnes and will enhance the navy's capabilities in task-group operations and independent blue-water deployments. They are seen as most analogous to the United States' *Ticonderoga*-class cruisers, albeit perhaps slightly larger. The *Ticonderoga*s act as air-defence command ships for US Navy carrier strike groups; they have a 122-cell vertical-launch system, compared to 112 cells for the Type-055s. A stretched version of the Type-052D destroyer was observed with a modified flight deck, possibly to accommodate the new Harbin Z-20 helicopter, perhaps in an anti-submarine role.

The PLAN still has areas of relative weakness, notably in anti-submarine warfare and amphibious operations, which continue to constrain its blue-water aspirations. But it also continues to make strides in addressing these deficiencies.

Shipyards continue to build smaller surface combatants too, particularly Type-054A frigates and Type-056A corvettes, and in September the PLAN commissioned its fifth Type-071 large amphibious landing ship. A first Type-075 amphibious assault vessel is under construction in Shanghai.

China is also transforming its marine corps. From a force a few years ago of two brigades and approximately 10,000 personnel, the US Department of Defense estimates that by 2020 it will consist of some seven brigades and 30,000 personnel, with a much wider scope of missions.

The PLAN's four Type-094 *Jin*-class ballistic-missile submarines appear now to be operational. However, it remains unclear whether this means that China is able to deliver an effective deterrent capability. Broader submarine-modernisation efforts continue, and two Type-039B *Yuan* II-class conventionally powered submarines may have commissioned in 2018.

In July, administrative control of China's coastguard was transferred from the civilian State Oceanic Administration to the armed forces under the People's Armed Police. The potential impact of this move remained uncertain, beyond clarifying and streamlining a chain of command widely assumed to already exist.

China's consolidation of its infrastructure on the disputed features it has developed in the South China Sea, plus the ongoing enhancement of its naval capabilities, continued to strengthen its ability to exert influence and potentially exercise control there. During 2018, the incremental progress of these developments reached the point at which the US took the decision to disinvite the PLAN from the US-led *Rim of the Pacific* exercise. This and a number of other friction points between the two navies during 2018, including a significantly close encounter between the two nations' warships during a US freedom-of-navigation operation in September, portended challenges for both nations' navies in 2019 and highlighted the limits of existing agreements on managing incidents at sea.

PLA Air Force (PLAAF)

The capabilities and institutional influence of the PLAAF have advanced significantly in recent years; the ground forces were traditionally the dominant service. General Xu Qiliang, as vice-chairman of the CMC, is now the most senior member of the PLA armed services; a career air-force officer, he was formerly the PLAAF commander. Another PLAAF officer, General Yi Xiaoguang, is the commander of the Central Theatre Command, responsible for the security of Beijing and the surrounding area. These appointments are emblematic of the air force's progress; they would have been nearly unthinkable, say analysts, just a decade ago. Change has been under way since the late 1990s, but a major push came when the PLAAF received its first service-specific strategy in 2004, instructing it to 'integrate air and space and be simultaneously prepared for offensive and defensive operations'. For China, this is not simply a matter of improving hardware and weapons systems. There has been a simultaneous drive to remake the PLA as an organisation as well as its people, their mindset, their training and their roles. This has affected not only the PLAAF, but also the PLAN and its naval aviation branch (PLANAF).

The training and exercise regimen of both the air force and naval aviation have seen considerable change. The PLAAF now has a series of exercises, the 'Four Key Brands', which enable it to test operational capability as well as assess progress towards its modernisation goals. These exercises exemplify a move away from scripted drills toward a focus on what China terms 'back to back' exercises, where neither side in the exercise has prior knowledge of the other's plans. By doing this, the PLA is attempting to learn from Western armed forces and focus on preparing its next generation of pilots for more realistic – i.e., unscripted – combat in a complex electromagnetic environment.

The PLAAF has also started expanding the scope and scale of its missions, and there is greater emphasis on operations over water. Less than 30 years ago, PLAAF training manuals included the warning that these operations included challenges such as the 'weather changes rapidly' and 'the horizon is difficult to detect'. PLAAF aircraft first flew to the centre line of the Taiwan Strait in 1998 and over the Miyako Strait for the first time in May 2015. Since then, however, there have been multiple flights into the Pacific, some circumnavigating Taiwan, comprising many aircraft types. As it sorties farther from the mainland and conducts patrols more frequently, the PLAAF is improving pilot training and experience, and increasing its interaction with the PLAN's surface and aviation assets. At the same time, the PLANAF is developing its capabilities in carrier operations. Overall, the trend for the PLA's aviation forces is for new aircraft, better pilots, improved training and more interoperability.

Nonetheless, significant challenges remain. One relates to the human side of military capability. More progress needs to be made in ensuring that senior and more conservative leaders trust new ideas and younger troops. Recruiting, training and retaining high-quality personnel is a challenge for any armed force, and one that the PLA is facing as it struggles to build an NCO corps and attract more college graduates.

Another challenge relates to 'jointness'. One of the core objectives of the PLA's most recent round of reforms, this relates to the employment of forces from two or more service branches such that they can together conduct coordinated operations. This is a major change for the PLA, which has long been ground-centric, with organisationally discrete institutions. Indeed, US analysts say both the PLAAF and PLANAF have retained a full suite of aviation capacities because they have not been able to draw on the other's capabilities. This prevents them from realising economies of scale that would result from each maintaining a limited number of distinct capabilities. Interaction among units was traditionally limited in the absence of a common higher-echelon command: regiments within the same corps rarely trained or exercised together because of strict command-and-control relationships. This is slowly beginning to change and there is evidence, albeit limited in comparison to Western experiences, that the PLAAF and PLANAF are looking to develop a level of jointness through common training.

The PLA is also engaged in a concerted effort to produce strategically effective aviation forces. Longer-duration missions, further from the mainland, and increased integration among and between PLAAF and PLAN aviation will in future become more commonplace. This effort is taking place during a time Beijing terms a 'strategic opportunity'. This means that the Communist Party of China has decided that the risks required to implement these changes are worth bearing now, because the risk of major conflict with a large power is relatively low. Consequently, Beijing hopes that when this period of strategic opportunity ends, its future force will be ready to compete with peer competitors.

Equipment progress

The Chengdu J-20 combat aircraft remains on track to be introduced into front-line service with the PLAAF around 2020. An operational test-and-evaluation unit is now flying with the type and initial production-standard J-20A aircraft are being delivered, so far at a modest rate. The J-20A will be the first Chinese combat aircraft designed from the outset with low-observable characteristics to enter the PLAAF inventory.

The PLAAF has also stood up its first unit equipped with the Sukhoi Su-35 *Flanker* E. All 24 Su-35s in the initial order were expected to be delivered by the end of 2018 or early 2019. The deal included acquisition of the export version of the Russian R-77-1 (AA-12B *Adder*) active-radar-guided medium-range air-to-air missile, an upgrade of the basic R-77. Delivery of this missile to the PLAAF has already begun. However, it is not clear whether the PLAAF will buy additional Su-35 aircraft, or if its operational experience with the type will lead it to favour its own defence industry's continuing development of a single-seat *Flanker*, the J-11D.

Development work on the successor to the H-6 medium bomber, the H-20, continues. State-owned media noted in October 2018 that the project was making 'significant progress'. The H-20 is assumed to be a low-observable – possibly tailless – design, which could enter service from the latter half of the 2020s. Xian, a subsidiary of the Aviation Industry Corporation of China (AVIC), continues to build upgraded variants of the H-6 and is involved with the H-20 programme.

The H-20 is a key element of the PLAAF's equipment recapitalisation and part of its goal to become a 'strategic air force'. This likely includes a nuclear role – the current bomber, the H-6K, is assessed as not having a nuclear role – as well as other tasks. Indeed, the shift emphasises the PLAAF's ability to conduct defensive and offensive air operations beyond the Chinese mainland, as well as to carry out large-scale air operations in concert with ground or maritime forces. Restructuring tactical aviation from a regimental- to a brigade-based organisation is a part of this ambition.

Production of Xian's Y-20 heavy transport aircraft continues, and the first regiment is forming with this type. The Y-20 will also likely be the basis for a tanker aircraft that will eventually replace the H-6 in this role. There are also increasing numbers of special-mission aircraft within the PLAAF inventory. For example, electronic-warfare versions of the JH-7 fighter/ground-attack aircraft appear to have been fielded at unit level, while an escort jammer variant of the J-16, the J-16D, is also in test.

UAVs are increasingly joining the inventory. These will likely take on electronic-warfare roles alongside other intelligence, surveillance and reconnaissance tasks. The PLAAF continues to acquire UAVs with the potential to deliver capabilities from the tactical to theatre level.

DEFENCE ECONOMICS

According to Beijing, China's 2018 defence budget was RMB1.11 trillion (US$168 billion) – an increase of 8.1% on the 2017 figure of RMB1.02trn (US$151bn). Although this percentage increase was greater than in 2017, when the budget was 7% higher than that in 2016, growth is still in single digits. By contrast, between 2011 and 2016, the defence budget grew by more than 10% each year. But 2017 and 2018 figures indicate that single-digit growth is the new normal, placed within the context of China's overall slow economic growth. Nonetheless, despite this slowdown, which it should be remembered is relative – China's GDP still grew by 6.6% in 2018, down from an average of 10% growth annually between 2000 and 2009 – Chinese authorities have also engaged in reforms intended to further develop defence-industrial capabilities.

Improving China's defence sector is a priority for Xi for two principal reasons: firstly, so it can develop advanced weapons systems for the PLA, and secondly, to help transition China's economic structure from low-end processing to high-end manufacturing. These efforts have been focused in three areas: civil–military integration (CMI); innovation; and industrial rationalisation. China's defence industry has already made significant strides. IISS assessments indicate that in 2016, defence-related revenue for eight of the ten Chinese state-owned enterprises (SOEs) involved in defence production would place seven of these in the top 20 of the world's most profitable defence firms. Three of these – China South Industries Group Corporation (CSGC), China Aviation Industry Corporation (AVIC) and China North Industries Group Corporation (NORINCO) – appear in the top ten.

Civil–military integration

Xi has often stressed the importance of CMI, also termed civil–military fusion. It was made a national priority in 2015. On 2 March 2018, Xi chaired the first plenary meeting (and third overall) of the Central Commission for Integrated Civilian–Military

Development (CCIMCD), which was set up in January 2017. At the March meeting, Xi emphasised the need for a national civil–military fusion and development strategy and to further develop CMI. These support China's goals of having by 2049 world-class military forces and achieving a modern socialist country ('the Chinese Dream and the dream of building a powerful military', as Xi put it to the 19th Party Congress in October 2017). The meeting approved measures including strategic-development guidelines for CMI, the 2018 plan of action for the CCIMCD, a programme to develop CMI pilot zones focused on innovation and a list of the prospective pilot zones.

The whole party–state system has been mobilised to deliver Xi's instructions. For instance, the Office of CCIMCD, which is responsible for routine work, has organised workshops to promote civil–military fusion, review progress made so far in these areas and fix any problems identified. As part of this, central-government officials have been dispatched to different locations across China as part of their investigations. All major state-owned enterprises are required to select areas to take part in pilot CMI reform programmes, and some military officials are supposed to work for periods in their relevant civil-sector industries.

Innovation

The CMI policy is strongly connected to efforts in China to boost defence-industrial innovation. Priorities for 2018 included the continued overhaul of China's defence science-and-technology (S&T) research institutes and academies. Under way since 2017, this programme aims to change the ownership structure of wholly state-owned defence S&T research institutes and academies (those manufacturing sub-systems or even final assembly) so that they can be listed on the stock market. This effort started in the early 2000s, though the focus at that time was on those firms manufacturing spare parts; it is estimated that at least US$30bn was raised from the stock market. Now the focus is shifting to research institutes and academies.

In the plan, 41 defence-research institutes were identified for ownership reform, covering ordnance, electronics, aerospace, shipbuilding, aviation and the nuclear sector. In May 2018, the Southwest Automation Institute (or 58th Institute) of China South Industries Group Company Ltd was approved as the first out of the 41 institutes to complete the change. Located in Mianyang City, Sichuan province, this

China's innovation pilot zones
- ChengDeMian (Chengdu-Deyang-Mianyang), Sichuan Province
- Chongqiang
- Dalian, Liaoning Province
- Lanzhou, Gansu Province
- Luoyang, Henan Province
- Ningbo, Zhoushan, Hangzhou and Shaoxing, Zhejiang Province
- Ningde, Fujian Province
- Qingdao West Coast New Area, Shandong Province
- Shenzhen, Guangdong Province
- Wuhan, Hubei Province
- Xian, Shaanxi Province
- Zhongguancun, Beijing

town is well known as a science and manufacturing centre. Its achievements include the production of intelligent munitions, digital manufacturing and digital machine-tool production, among other areas; its total assets reportedly amount to RMB1bn (about US$154 million).

Analysts think that the 58th Institute case is widely reported so that its transformation can be a model for others to follow. The goal was to similarly overhaul the remaining 40 institutes by the end of 2018 and, by 2020, convert the majority of defence S&T research institutes into corporations. However, not all defence-research institutes and academies are going to be overhauled. Institutes responsible for basic research will reportedly remain unchanged but those for technological development and engineering will be overhauled.

However, converting these organisations is a challenging task, involving changes to areas ranging from salaries and employee welfare to tax incentives, debt arrangement, asset liquidation, the CCP's role in management, labour unions, and price policies for weapons and equipment.

The March 2018 CCIMCD meeting approved the first batch of 15 CMI innovation pilot zones.

These zones can be classified as one of five types: areas with traditional heavy defence industries, though with emerging numbers of private defence subcontractors – Sichuan and Shaanxi provinces being typical cases; areas with the potential to develop disruptive technologies – such as Shenzhen, which is emerging as a tech city; areas with good infrastructure, suitable as incubators for new industries – Ningbo and Hangzhou are seen as ideal examples; areas with a heavy military presence that requires social support, such as Qingdao and Dalian – where military logistics heavily rely on local support; and areas with dual-use heavy industries, such as Ningde and Zhoushan, which are identified as potential military and civilian ports with expansion potential.

The idea of innovation pilot zones dates back to 2016, when the National Development and Reform Commission set out a plan to have ten such zones. In the end, with motivations perhaps including the chance of gaining central-government funding as well as Xi's favour, at least 26 applications and proposals were reportedly submitted by ministries, provinces and major cities. Xi was reported to have set out instructions emphasising 'institutional innovation', creating a new model that could be imitated elsewhere to help break obstacles to CMI.

In order to develop China's capabilities in sophisticated integrated circuits, advanced computing and biotechnologies, Beijing announced in January 2018 that it would set up national industrial innovation centres and issued documentation. In April, a National Information Optoelectronics Innovation Center (NIOIC) was established at a technology centre in Wuhan, Hubei province, run by FiberHome Technologies, a state-owned enterprise under the supervision of the State-Owned Assets Supervision and Administration Commission. The NIOIC is also home to the national laboratory for fibre-optic and cyber-communications technology and the national engineering centre for fibre-optic-communications technology, among others. It has reportedly been tasked to develop indigenous advanced integrated circuit chips, amid trade disputes with the US focused on technological competition, so that defence and cyber security can be assured and the government's 'Made in China 2025' programme, to improve China's domestic high-tech manufacturing capacity, can be fully supported. Meanwhile, the State Administration for Science, Technology and Industry (SASTIND) runs the National Defense Technology Innovation Centre, designed to implement an innovation-driven technology-development strategy. In 2018, two new centres were approved: the Defense S&T Industry Aviation Engine Innovation Centre, under the Aero Engine Corporation of China, and the Maritime Defense Technology Innovation Centre, under the China Shipbuilding Industry Corporation. It is reported that 11 centres will eventually be approved.

Industrial rationalisation

Over the past decade, China's defence industry has been organised under ten state-owned conglomerates. This system too is now being challenged and in January 2018 the government announced that China Nuclear Engineering and Construction Group Corporation would be merged with China National Nuclear Corporation.

Reports indicated in March that approval has also been given in principle for a merger between China's two major shipbuilding companies – the China State Shipbuilding Corporation and China Shipbuilding Industries Corporation (CSIC). It is estimated that after the merger, total sales revenue will reach RMB$508bn (US$77bn), a figure exceeding the total revenue of South Korea's three major shipbuilders: Hyundai Heavy Industries, Daewoo Shipbuilding and Marine Engineering Co. Ltd, and Samsung Heavy Industry. There has been no formal announcement, however, which analysts assess could be related to ongoing investigations into allegations of corruption. Nonetheless, reports of the potential merger reflect Xi's instruction that China's state-owned enterprises become bigger and stronger in order to compete globally.

The Chinese government is also now encouraging private-sector involvement in defence S&T. There have been instances of this in the aerospace sector, though some of the firms are subsidiaries of state-owned aerospace conglomerates, such as Beijing OneSpace Technology Co. Ltd. OneSpace, reportedly with support from SASTIND, launched China's first private rocket in May 2018 on a mission to collect data for the Aviation Industry Corporation of China. Another example is LandSpace Technology Corporation, founded in 2015, which announced in July the completion of its ZQ-2 rocket system. Ground tests of the ZQ-2 are expected to be completed in 2019, with a launch following in 2020. In January 2017, LandSpace obtained the first private commercial launch contract for a foreign customer, launching two satellites for Danish firm GOMSpace aboard a LandSpace-1 rocket in February 2018. A third example is ExPace Technology Corporation. This subsidiary of the China Aerospace Science and Industry Corporation is also known as the CASIC Rocket Technology Company; it serves as its commercial rocket division and focuses on small satellite launches to low-Earth orbit. Established in February 2016 in Wuhan, ExPace is developing its *Kuaizhou* rockets for different payloads and looking into fast launches of solid-fuel rockets.

JAPAN

Japan's evolving defence posture remains driven by a combination of international and domestic pressures. Japanese concerns over North Korea's provocations were exacerbated in 2017 by a series of missile tests, while China's military modernisation and growing maritime activities in the East and South China seas continue to worry Tokyo. Meanwhile, the US presidency of Donald Trump has proven unsettling. On the one hand, the US administration has pledged with its Japanese ally 'maximum pressure' on North Korea and commitment to the defence of Japan's Senkaku/Diaoyu Islands, but on the other hand it is rapidly seeking rapprochement with North Korea and demanding that Japan pay more for its own defence and for the benefits of the alliance. Consequently, the Japan Self-Defense Forces (JSDF) have continued to augment their capabilities, mainly in the service of the US–Japan alliance, but seeking a degree of autonomy to hedge against abandonment by the US. At the same time, Prime Minister Shinzo Abe has faced domestic challenges to his leadership and security policy, despite in October 2017 winning for the governing Liberal Democratic Party (LDP) a fifth consecutive electoral victory since 2012.

Japan's principal new commitment to the US–Japan alliance has been the formal decision in December 2017 to strengthen its ballistic-missile-defence (BMD) capabilities with the purchase from the US of two *Aegis* Ashore units. These should bolster the JSDF's ability to intercept ballistic missiles; may enhance Japan's defence against cruise missiles if it procures the SM-6 interceptor; and, just as importantly, responds to Trump's calls for Japan to procure more US equipment as a quid pro quo for US security pledges. The *Aegis* Ashore procurement has provoked some controversy in Japan, with local authorities voicing opposition. Furthermore, only one unit will likely deploy by 2023 and the estimated cost has doubled to around US$3.6 billion.

In the meantime, Japan is deepening cooperation with the US armed forces. The Japan Maritime Self-Defense Force (JMSDF) was revealed in April 2018 as having refuelled US destroyers on BMD duties 17 times in 2017. This was accomplished using the Acquisition and Cross-Servicing Agreement and the expanded definitions of Japanese support for the US in contingencies under new security legislation passed in 2015. Then defence minister Itsunori Onodera suggested in August 2017 that collective self-defence legislation could be used by the JMSDF to intercept North Korean missiles targeted at Guam, even if Japan was not itself directly threatened. Japan Air Self-Defense Force (JASDF) fighter aircraft carried out drills that same month with US B-1 and B-52 bombers in the vicinity of the Sea of Japan as an indirect demonstration to North Korea of US–Japan interoperability and solidarity. The Abe administration has furthermore proved resolute in pushing ahead with plans to relocate the US Marine Corps Air Station at Futenma to Henoko, within Okinawa Prefecture, continuing with land-reclamation works at the new site despite legal action and protests from the prefectural government.

The Japan Ministry of Defense (JMoD) has in the past three years secured budget increases that have enabled the JSDF to expand existing capabilities and to move into new areas. The JASDF deployed the first of its F-35A combat aircraft at Misawa in northern Japan in January 2018 and was allocated a budget in March for investigating the procurement of air-launched cruise missiles. Japan's apparent intent is to utilise its *Aegis* destroyers, *Aegis* Ashore, F-35As, cruise missiles and uninhabited aerial vehicles to create an integrated system with defensive and potentially offensive aspects to complement US power projection, but also compensate for any US reluctance to defend Japan in the future. The budget also included a sum for research into hypersonic systems and related propulsion.

The JMSDF launched its seventh *Aegis* destroyer in July 2017. Onodera reported in March 2018 that the JMoD was actively studying the conversion of the *Izumo*-class vessels to enable the operation of F-35Bs, confirming long-held speculation that these were not only de facto helicopter carriers but designed to become eventually fully fledged fixed-wing aircraft carriers. Japan has long called these vessels 'helicopter-carrying destroyers'. Though in the post-war period Japan has denied itself the procurement of carriers as an offensive capability, the conversion project was justified by referring to a 'defensive carrier' that was focused on the protection of Japan's outlying islands.

In March 2018, the Japan Ground Self-Defense Force (JGSDF) established the Amphibious Rapid Deployment Brigade (ARDB). This proto-marine force will focus on the defence of outlying islands and be equipped with AAV7 amphibious vehicles and *Osprey* aircraft. In addition, the JGSDF is planning to deploy surface-to-ship guided missiles in Japan's southwest islands to ensure that if necessary the straits between Okinawa Prefecture and Taiwan can be closed to Chinese warships. As part of a reorganisation, a single headquarters has been set up to coordinate inter-regional JGSDF action, and lighter and more deployable forces are being created, particularly in the Western and Central armies.

New National Defence Programme Guidelines were due by the end of 2018 and were likely to promote JSDF 'cross-domain' capabilities, reinforced by cyberspace and space capabilities. However, Tokyo's moves to strengthen the US–Japan alliance and its capabilities face some domestic opposition. Defence-procurement costs are seen to be escalating: in 2018, these reportedly increased for Japan's indigenous C-2 transport programme, along with F-35A unit costs and the rising cost of *Aegis* Ashore, which could constrain Japan's scope to acquire new systems such as a successor to the F-2 fighter.

Abe's leadership and plans for security-policy reforms have also been questioned due to his entanglement in personal financial scandals and internal competition for the LDP presidency election that took place in September 2018. This election saw Abe re-elected as LDP leader, allowing him to serve another term in which he would become Japan's longest-serving prime minister. Additionally, public trust in the JMoD was tarnished by revelations that the JGSDF concealed operations logs for the South Sudan peacekeeping operation. This was in order to cover up the deteriorating local security situation and risk of combat, but the scandal led to the eventual resignation of Onodera's predecessor Tomomi Inada. Abe survived these challenges and has focused the next stage of his premiership on formal revision of the constitution and the so-called 'peace clause' of Article 9; this is the final, long-term goal of his political career and is seen as essential by Abe to free Japan from past constraints on security policy. Abe has proposed revisions that leave intact the current clauses of Article 9 but add a further clause that the 'JSDF is maintained as an armed organisation to take necessary self-defence measures'. Abe's supporters argue this is a moderate proposal simply acknowledging the reality of the JSDF's existence. But critics respond that the lack of specificity in defining 'self-defence measures' could lead to Japan's exercise of force beyond the previous interpretation of the minimum necessary for self-defence.

THAILAND

The Royal Thai Armed Forces (RTARF) have always exercised important domestic political and internal-security roles alongside their responsibility for external defence. The 22 May 2014 coup took place after Thailand had been wracked for months by violent political conflict between factions supporting and opposing the elected civilian government led by Yingluck Shinawatra, the sister of former prime minister Thaksin Shinawatra. (Thaksin's populist administration had itself been overthrown by an earlier coup in 2006.) Since May 2014, the armed forces, acting through the National Council for Peace and Order, have closely supervised both the government and law enforcement on a day-to-day basis. The armed forces – and particularly the Royal Thai Army (RTA), which remains the dominant service – have also attempted to plot a course for the country through a wide-ranging, 20-year National Strategy. This plan, which focuses on security as well as political, economic, social and environmental aspects, was unanimously approved in July 2018 by the military-dominated National Legislative Assembly. According to Thailand's 2017 constitution, the policies of future elected governments must conform to the National Strategy. The military government has several times postponed the general election, which will allow a return to democratic rule; it was next scheduled to be held between late February and early May 2019. Meanwhile, Prime Minister Prayut Chan-o-cha has indicated his interest in continuing 'political work' and it is widely rumoured that he may seek to lead a political party in order to continue in his present role after the 2019 election.

Internal and external security

Maintaining internal security in Thailand's three southernmost provinces (Narrathiwat, Patani and Yala) remains an important operational task for the RTARF, particularly for the army and the marine corps. Forces are deployed there to tackle an insurgent campaign by ethnic-Malay separatists – largely by groups affiliated with the Barisan Revolusi Nasional–Coordinate – which re-ignited in 2004. A tentative peace process has been under way since 2015 and achieved an initial result with the announcement in February 2018 that a pilot violence-free 'safety zone' would be established later in the year. Violence in the region has decreased because of the peace process, the government's security measures and a rehabilitation

Asia

▲ Map 8 **Thailand: principal military bases**

scheme for insurgents. Indeed, the annual death toll from the conflict of 235 in 2017 was the lowest since 2004.

The RTA's 4th Army Region is headquartered further north in the Kra peninsula at Nakhon Si Thammarat. It includes two infantry divisions and a 'development' division, totalling around 35,000 troops. Along with the navy-controlled Royal Thai Marine Corps, the 4th Army Region provides forces for operations in the troubled provinces. However, many front-line duties are carried out by black-uniformed army auxiliaries known as Thahan Pran ('hunter-soldiers', often referred to as 'rangers'), who operate closely with paramilitary Border Patrol Police units. The headquarters of the multi-agency Internal Security Operations Command Area 4 at Fort Sirindhorn in Yarang District, Patani province, directs operations by all security forces in the region.

Though the main priority for the RTARF is to ensure national unity and internal security, the armed forces are nevertheless well funded, equipped and trained to deter and defend Thailand against state adversaries. Over the last 40 years, a series of threats have arisen from Thailand's immediate neighbours. Border security was a priority during the 1980s, after the Soviet-supported Vietnamese invasion of Cambodia forced Khmer Rouge and other Cambodian forces opposed to Hanoi's occupation across the border, as well as the refugee populations they controlled. Thailand was one of the nations that supported Cambodian opposition groups and there were frequent clashes between Thai and Vietnamese troops, with protracted fighting in early 1987 near Chong Bok, where the borders of Cambodia, Laos and Thailand intersect. In late 1987 and early 1988, there were border clashes between Thai- and Vietnamese-supported Laotian forces over disputed territory. Sporadic security challenges to Thailand's borders continued after the end of the Cold War and the Cambodian peace settlement of 1991. There was a major border clash with Myanmar in 2001, and in 2010–12 fighting between Myanmar government forces and ethnic-minority rebels spilled across the border into Thailand. In 2008–11, there were a series of confrontations and exchanges of fire with Cambodian forces over disputed border territory around the Preah Vihear temple.

Unlike some of its fellow members of the Association of Southeast Asian Nations (ASEAN), notably Malaysia, the Philippines and Vietnam, Thailand is not a territorial claimant in the South China Sea and does not perceive a direct threat from China's growing power and maritime assertiveness. Indeed, Thailand's relations with China have warmed during the current decade, influenced by historical ties, current economic links and Thailand's foreign-policy recalibration following the adverse Western reaction to the 2014 coup. Nevertheless, Thailand has substantial maritime interests due to its long coastline, the economic importance of marine resources (especially natural gas) within its exclusive economic zone, its large fishing fleet, its heavy economic dependence on international trade and its increasingly important coastal industrial development. These all provide important reasons for developing the country's navy.

Foreign-defence relations

Since the 1950s, defence and security relations with the United States have strongly influenced Thailand's defence policy, doctrine and equipment procurement. The basis for the relationship lies in Thailand's importance as a relatively stable, pro-Western bastion during the Cold War: at that time, it needed external support in the face of both external and domestic communist threats. Thailand was a signatory to the 1954 Manila Pact, which, among other things, established the Southeast Asia Treaty Organisation (SEATO). SEATO dissolved in 1977, but the Manila Pact remains in force, as does the so-called Rusk–Thanat communiqué of 1962, under which the US promised to assist Thailand if it faced aggression from neighbouring countries. Together with Thailand's post-2003 status as a Major Non-NATO Ally, these agreements provide the foundation for US–Thai security relations. Building on support in earlier decades, Thailand allowed the US to use the naval air base at U-Tapao as a staging post for flights supporting operations in Afghanistan and Iraq.

Thailand's armed forces have benefited from substantial infusions of US defence equipment, logistic and infrastructural support, and training, managed by the Bangkok-based Joint US Military Advisory Group Thailand. However, the coups of 2006 and 2014 undermined bilateral security relations as well as political ties. Subsequent US restrictions on the supply of military equipment notably provided an important reason for Thailand to diversify its defence procurement. Nevertheless, US–Thai engagement through military exercises has endured. Indeed, the annual *Cobra Gold* exercise organised in Thailand by the US Pacific (now Indo-Pacific) Command and RTARF remains the largest multilateral exercise in the Asia-Pacific region. Other annual exercises involving Thai and US forces are the *CARAT Thailand* (naval interoperability), *Guardian Sea* (anti-submarine warfare), *Hanuman Guardian* (army) and *Cope Tiger* (air force) series.

Thailand also maintains good defence relations with several other regional US allies or security partners, including Australia, where exercise cooperation includes the *Chapel Gold* (jungle warfare), *AusThai* (naval), *Pitch Black* (multinational air combat) and *Kakadu* (multinational naval) exercise. Thailand cooperates with fellow ASEAN members through the ASEAN Defence Ministers' Meeting (ADMM) and ADMM–Plus (also involving eight of ASEAN's Dialogue Partners), though its strongest bilateral defence cooperation in Southeast Asia is with Singapore. The Singapore Armed Forces (SAF) have conducted extensive training activities in Thailand since the 1970s, and the Republic of Singapore Air Force organises the *Cope Tiger* air-force exercise with its Thai and US counterparts. In November 2017, Singapore's Ministry of Defence said that bilateral defence cooperation with Thailand would be strengthened, with particular emphasis on closer naval cooperation, counter-terrorism and cyber security. Thailand's defence relations with Japan have intensified since June 2016, when the two nations' defence ministers agreed on a range of exchanges, including bilateral army staff talks and the dispatch of RTA observers to a disaster-relief exercise in Japan.

Thailand's alliance with the US has not prevented it from developing defence relations with China, which have deepened since 2014. In 2015, the navy selected China to supply submarines as the basis for re-establishing a sub-surface capability; in May 2017, Thailand ordered one S26T boat (an export variant of China's *Yuan* class), with delivery by 2023 scheduled. The contract is reported to include some weapons systems, spare parts and technology transfer (understood to include developing the Royal Thai Navy's Sattahip dockyard such that it can support submarine operations and construction of a similar facility on the southwest coast to support submarine operations in the Andaman Sea). Orders for another two submarines are expected in 2021–22. Thailand has also purchased Chinese-made armoured vehicles: 28 VT-4 (MBT-3000) main battle tanks (MBTs) were delivered by the end of 2017. Plans to purchase ten more VT-4s along with 34 VN-1 (ZBL-08) wheeled armoured personnel carriers (APCs) were approved in April 2017. At this time, Deputy Prime Minister Prawit Wongsuwan confirmed that an order of a further 11 VT-4s was planned, so that they could equip a full battalion. In January 2018, Army Commander-in-Chief General Chalermchai Sitthisart confirmed plans to collaborate with China in establishing a military-vehicle maintenance, repair and overhaul facility in Thailand. Since 2015, the two countries have also organised *Falcon Strike*, a bilateral air-force exercise series in Thailand, which was held for the third time in September 2018.

Defence economics

Thailand's defence spending is the third largest in Southeast Asia (after Singapore and Indonesia), and the armed forces' political role has helped to ensure that the defence sector not only continues to receive substantial funding but that there are significant annual increases in the military budget. The defence budget for the 2019 fiscal year (starting in October 2018) of US$7.06 billion represents a 4.2% increase over the previous year. It comprises 7.6% of government spending and approximately 1.4% of GDP. About half the budget is allocated to the army; the remainder is more or less evenly divided between the navy and air force, with a small proportion supporting the defence ministry and armed-forces headquarters. It is thought that around two-thirds of the defence budget is used to meet routine personnel, maintenance and operational costs, including the substantial sums associated with internal-security operations in southern Thailand. The remainder of the defence budget is used for procurement and infrastructural projects. The 'Vision 2026' defence-modernisation plan, approved by Thailand's Defence Council in October 2017, outlines the armed forces' capability improvements over the next decade, recognising that the extent of modernisation will depend on the country's overall economic progress and the allocation of resources to the defence sector. The plan also states the objective of increasing the defence budget to 2% of GDP within the next several years.

Industry and procurement

In its Defence Industry Masterplan, the government emphasises the importance of expanding Thailand's presently limited defence industry as an important component of developing the country's military capability, while ensuring that defence spending benefits the national economy. The Masterplan sees technology transfers from foreign defence-equipment suppliers – possibly mandated in the future through a more explicit offset policy – as playing a central role in defence-industrial development, which the government intends to concentrate particularly in Thailand's Eastern Economic Corridor (EEC). The naval dockyard at Sattahip in Chonburi province and the nearby naval air base at U-Tapao are viewed respectively as future hubs for the naval and military-aerospace industry. In November 2017, the government identified the defence industry as the 11th key industry targeted to expand in the EEC. Moreover, legislative changes will allow local defence-industrial enterprises – which are mainly owned and operated by the armed forces – to more easily collaborate with foreign defence companies. Already, the Royal Thai Navy's Bangkok Dock company is building modified *River*-class offshore patrol vessels (OPVs) with the United Kingdom's BAE Systems, and the RTA's Weapon Production Centre is assembling ATMOS 2000 self-propelled howitzers in collaboration with Israel's Elbit Systems. In the aerospace sector, the private Thai company Avia Satcom, in which Saab has a 37% equity stake, has developed tactical data links for *Gripen* combat aircraft.

In the past, Thailand's military capability has not been helped by the diversity of equipment operated by the RTARF and by its uncoordinated procurement system, with each service having responsibility for its own equipment programmes. However, the present government is making serious efforts to reform defence procurement, particularly through an expanded role for the defence ministry's Defence Technology Institute. Under legislation that was expected to come into effect by early 2019, this will become the Defence Technology Agency (DTA). The DTA will act as a central procurement agency for the armed forces, as well as overseeing the development of Thailand's defence industry.

Thailand's armed forces have benefited from limited re-equipment programmes during the present decade, but there are still major outstanding requirements.

Army

Following contracts with Ukraine's Ukroboronprom, the army has taken delivery of more than 200 BTR-3E1 APCs and 49 T-84 *Oplot* MBTs. Delays in fulfilling that contract probably provide an additional reason for the RTA's increased interest in China as a source of armoured vehicles. Given an overall requirement for 150 new MBTs to replace US-made M48s and M60s, further orders for Chinese tanks are possible. Since 2015, the army has been bringing into service 12 locally produced Elbit Systems ATMOS 2000 howitzers, with the Marine Corps taking another six. Twenty-six more may be ordered for the army, with possibly ten units for the Marine Corps. The army has also purchased Oerlikon *Skyguard* 3 air-defence fire-control systems, as part of a package with eight 35 mm Oerlikon GDF-007 Twin Guns and ammunition. The already diverse inventory of the army's aviation component has received more helicopters from Russia (Mi-17V5s), the US (UH-60Ms), Italy (AW139s) and the European Airbus company (EC145s and UH-72As). Reports suggest that the RTA may buy additional Mi-17V5s. The army also reportedly has a requirement for additional fixed-wing transport aircraft.

Air Force

The most important procurement by the Royal Thai Air Force (RTAF) over the last ten years involved the acquisition of 12 JAS 39 *Gripen* multi-role combat aircraft, two Saab 340 *Erieye* airborne early-warning (AEW) aircraft and a national air command-and-control system (ACCS), based on Saab's 9AIR C4I product, together with data links. This effected a step change in the potential combat-effectiveness of the RTAF, by providing the basis for an integrated and potentially highly effective air-defence capability. According to Saab, the company provided access to the source codes for the *Gripen* so that the RTAF could 'develop, upgrade, modify or add equipment, sensors and weapon systems in the future by themselves'. There is now a requirement for an additional six *Gripen* aircraft. In September 2018, Saab announced that it had been contracted to upgrade Thailand's ACCS with 'new hardware and software enhancements'. The next-most-important air-force procurement has involved 12 T-50TH *Golden Eagle* armed lead-in training aircraft from South Korea, with deliveries under way from January 2018.

Navy

Much media coverage of Royal Thai Navy (RTN) procurement has justifiably focused on its submarine programme, which is significant not just in terms of Thailand's prospective acquisition of a new capability, but also because of its opportunity costs for the service. Nevertheless, a significant surface-ship procurement programme is also under way, involving a DW 3000F frigate modelled on the South Korean *Gwanggaeto* class. The ship began sea trials in December 2017 and was scheduled for delivery during 2018. However, funding constraints seem at least temporarily to have stymied plans for a second DW 3000F frigate. In addition, a second *Krabi*-class OPV (one of the modified *River*-class vessels) is under construction at Sattahip; the navy is expected to order more ships in the same class. While the procurement of new vessels has been limited, during the present decade the RTN has upgraded important surface units, notably its two Chinese-built Type-25T *Naresuan*-class frigates (commissioned in 1994–95), which Saab equipped with new combat-management systems, fire-control radars and data links allowing direct communication with the RTAF's *Erieye* AEW platforms.

Afghanistan AFG

New Afghan Afghani Afs		2017	2018	2019
GDP	Afs	1.38tr	1.45tr	
	US$	20.2bn	20.4bn	
per capita	US$	570	565	
Growth	%	2.7	2.3	
Inflation	%	5.0	3.0	
Def bdgt [a]	Afs	148bn	147bn	
	US$	2.17bn	2.06bn	
US$1=Afs		68.08	71.27	

[a] Security expenditure. Includes expenditure on Ministry of Defence, Ministry of Interior, Ministry of Foreign Affairs, National Security Council and the General Directorate of National Security. Also includes donor funding.

Population 34,940,837

Ethnic groups: Pashtun 38%; Tajik 25%; Hazara 19%; Uzbek 12%; Aimaq 4%; Baluchi 0.5%

Age	0–14	15–19	20–24	25–29	30–64	65 plus
Male	20.8%	5.8%	5.3%	4.3%	13.3%	1.2%
Female	20.1%	5.6%	5.2%	4.1%	12.9%	1.4%

Capabilities

The Afghan National Defence and Security Forces (ANDSF) are optimised for counter-insurgency and counter-terrorist operations against the Taliban and other groups. Although ANDSF casualties are no longer reported by the US and NATO, credible media reports suggested that already high losses due to casualties and desertion further increased in 2018. These losses have operational effect. Overall, the ANDSF had a personnel shortage of 12%, struggling to retain key specialists including pilots, aircraft mechanics, technical specialists and special-operations forces. Army and police SOF are well regarded by NATO and bear the brunt of offensive operations and intelligence-led strike operations against insurgent networks. NATO advisers remain embedded in the defence and interior ministries, although the ANDSF are now responsible for the majority of training, albeit with NATO support. The additional US forces authorised to support the new US Afghan strategy reached full strength in the middle of 2018 and the UK announced a significant increase in its troop numbers. Indigenous logistic support is slowly improving but remains a source of weakness. Efforts are also under way to improve leadership, intelligence, logistics and coordination between different service arms. The ANDSF Road Map contains ambitious plans to improve capability but depends on continued international support. Air-force modernisation continues, but maintenance difficulties reduce aircraft availability. Afghan forces' logistics are optimised for internal deployments, but their effectiveness is limited by a shortage of sufficiently educated and trained personnel. Afghan forces depend greatly on imported military equipment.

ACTIVE 174,300 (Army 167,000 Air Force 7,300)
Paramilitary 148,700

ORGANISATIONS BY SERVICE

Afghan National Army (ANA) 167,00

5 regional comd

FORCES BY ROLE
SPECIAL FORCES
1 spec ops div (1 (National Mission) SF bde (1 SF gp; 1 mech inf bn (2 mech inf coy)); 2 cdo bde (1 mech inf coy, 4 cdo bn); 1 (1st MSF) mech bde (2 mech inf bn); 1 (2nd MSF) mech bde (3 mech inf bn))

MANOEUVRE
Light
1 (201st) corps (3 inf bde (4 inf bn, 1 sy coy, 1 cbt spt bn, 1 CSS bn), 1 inf bde (3 inf bn, 1 sy coy, 1 cbt spt bn, 1 CSS bn), 1 engr bn, 1 int bn, 2 MP coy, 1 sigs bn)
1 (203rd) corps (2 inf bde (5 inf bn, 1 sy coy, 1 cbt spt bn, 1 CSS bn), 2 inf bde (4 inf bn, 1 sy coy, 1 cbt spt bn, 1 CSS bn), 1 engr bn, 1 int bn, 2 MP coy, 1 sigs bn)
1 (205th) corps (4 inf bde (4 inf bn, 1 sy coy, 1 cbt spt bn, 1 CSS bn), 1 engr bn, 1 int bn, 2 MP coy, 1 sigs bn)
1 (207th) corps (3 inf bde (4 inf bn, 1 sy coy, 1 cbt spt bn, 1 CSS bn), 1 engr bn, 1 int bn, 2 MP coy, 1 sigs bn)
1 (209th) corps (1 div HQ; 3 inf bde (4 inf bn, 1 sy coy, 1 cbt spt bn, 1 CSS bn), 1 engr bn, 1 int bn, 2 MP coy, 1 sigs bn)
1 (215th) corps (3 inf bde (4 inf bn, 1 sy coy, 1 cbt spt bn, 1 CSS bn), 1 inf bde (2 inf bn, 1 cbt spt bn, 1 CSS bn), 1 engr bn, 1 int bn, 2 MP coy, 1 sigs bn)
1 (111st Capital) div (1 inf bde (1 tk bn, 1 mech inf bn, 2 inf bn, 1 sy coy, 1 cbt spt bn, 1 CSS bn), 1 inf bde (4 inf bn, 1 sy coy, 1 cbt spt bn, 1 CSS bn), 1 int bn)

EQUIPMENT BY TYPE
ARMOURED FIGHTING VEHICLES
MBT 20 T-55/T-62 (24 more in store†)
APC 996
    APC (T) 173 M113A2†
    APC (W) 623 MSFV (inc variants)
    PPV 200 *Maxxpro*
ENGINEERING & MAINTENANCE VEHICLES
ARV 20 *Maxxpro* ARV
MW *Bozena*
ARTILLERY 775
TOWED 109: **122mm** 85 D-30†; **155mm** 24 M114A1†
MOR 82mm 666: 521 2B14†; 105 M-69†; 40 M252†

Afghan Air Force (AAF) 7,300

Including Special Mission Wing

EQUIPMENT BY TYPE
AIRCRAFT 19 combat capable
TPT 47: **Medium** 4 C-130H *Hercules*; **Light** 42: 24 Cessna 208B; 18 PC-12 (Special Mission Wing); **PAX** 1 B-727 (2 more in store)
TRG 19 EMB-314 *Super Tucano** (of which 7 in the US for trg)
HELICOPTERS
ATK 4 Mi-35 *Hind*
MRH 101: 3 *Cheetal*; 25 MD-530F (11 armed); 73 Mi-17 *Hip* H (incl 28 Special Mission Wing hel)
TPT • Medium 16 UH-60A+ *Black Hawk*
BOMBS
Laser-guided GBU-58 *Paveway* II

Paramilitary 148,700

Afghan National Police 148,700

Under control of Interior Ministry. Includes Afghan Uniformed Police (AUP), Afghan National Civil Order Police (ANCOP), Afghan Border Police (ABP), Police Special Forces (GDPSU) and Afghan Anti-Crime Police (AACP)

FOREIGN FORCES

All *Operation Resolute Support* unless otherwise specified
Albania 136
Armenia 121
Australia 300; 1 SF unit; 1 sy unit; 1 sigs unit
Austria 17
Azerbaijan 120
Belgium 78
Bosnia-Herzegovina 63
Bulgaria 158
Croatia 123
Czech Republic 281; 1 sy coy; 1 MP unit
Denmark 160
Estonia 40
Finland 29
Georgia 870; 1 lt inf bn
Germany 1,300; 1 bde HQ; 1 recce bn; 1 hel flt with CH-53G *Stallion*; 1 ISR UAV flt with *Heron* UAV
Greece 5
Hungary 111
India Indo-Tibetan Border Police 335 (facilities protection)
Italy 800; 1 mech inf bde HQ; 1 mech inf regt(-); 1 hel regt(-) with AW129 *Mangusta*; NH90; RQ-7
Latvia 36
Lithuania 50
Luxembourg 2
Macedonia (FYROM) 44
Mongolia 120
Montenegro 20
Netherlands 160
New Zealand 13
Norway 70
Poland 315 • UNAMA 1 obs
Portugal 195
Romania 742; 1 inf bn
Slovakia 36
Slovenia 8
Spain 40
Sweden 29
Turkey 506; 1 mot inf bn(-)
Ukraine 11
United Kingdom 1,100; 1 inf bn(+); 1 hel flt with 3 SA330 *Puma* HC2
United States 8,475; 1 div HQ; 1 ARNG div HQ (fwd); 1 spec ops bn; 3 inf bde(-); 1 inf bn; 1 ARNG inf bn; 1 mne regt(-); 1 arty bty with M777A2; 1 ARNG MRL bty with M142 HIMARS; 1 EOD bn; 1 cbt avn bde with AH-64E *Apache*; CH-47F *Chinook*; UH-60L *Black Hawk*; 1 FGA sqn with F-16C *Fighting Falcon*; 1 atk sqn with 12 A-10C *Thunderbolt II*; 1 ISR gp with MC-12W *Liberty*; 1 ISR unit with RC-12X *Guardrail*; 1 EW sqn with EC-130H *Compass Call*, 1 tpt sqn with C-130J-30 *Hercules*, 1 CSAR sqn with HH-60G *Pave Hawk*; 1 CISR UAV sqn with MQ-9A *Reaper*; 1 ISR UAV unit with RQ-21A *Blackjack* • Operation *Freedom's Sentinel* 8,000

Australia AUS

Australian Dollar A$		2017	2018	2019
GDP	A$	1.80tr	1.89tr	
	US$	1.38tr	1.43tr	
per capita	US$	55,693	56,698	
Growth	%	2.2	3.2	
Inflation	%	2.0	2.2	
Def bdgt	A$	31.9bn	35.2bn	35.5bn
	US$	24.4bn	26.6bn	
US$1=A$		1.30	1.32	
Population	23,470,145			

Age	0–14	15–19	20–24	25–29	30–64	65 plus
Male	9.1%	3.1%	3.4%	3.7%	23.3%	7.6%
Female	8.6%	3.0%	3.2%	3.5%	22.7%	8.8%

Capabilities

The Australian Defence Force (ADF) is capable, well trained and well equipped, with strong doctrine, logistic support and C4ISR. It also has considerable recent operational experience. In March 2016, the government published Australia's third defence white paper in seven years. This identified China's growing regional role, regional military modernisation and inter-state rivalry as among the influences shaping defence policy. The defence of Australia, securing maritime Southeast Asia and the Pacific, and contributing to stability and the 'rules-based order' across the wider Indo-Pacific region are the country's three main 'defence objectives'. The country's primary ally is the US, but it is also forging closer defence ties with India, Japan and South Korea, while remaining committed to the Five Power Defence Arrangements and close defence relations with New Zealand. The armed forces have considerable operational experience and have played an active part in operations in Afghanistan as well as in the coalition fighting ISIS in Iraq and Syria. Strategic air and sealift platforms give the ADF considerable capability to move and sustain deployments overseas. Australia is significantly modernising its navy and locally building submarines, destroyers and frigates based on European designs. Combat-air and maritime-patrol capabilities are also being boosted. Australia imports most of its significant defence equipment but possesses a growing defence industry. Its largest naval shipbuilders are ASC Shipbuilding and Austal, whose US subsidiary, Austal USA, builds vessels for the US Navy.

ACTIVE 57,050 (Army 29,000 Navy 13,650 Air 14,400)

RESERVE 21,050 (Army 13,200 Navy 2,800 Air 5,050)

Integrated units are formed from a mix of reserve and regular personnel. All ADF operations are now controlled by Headquarters Joint Operations Command (HQJOC)

ORGANISATIONS BY SERVICE

Space
EQUIPMENT BY TYPE
SATELLITES • COMMUNICATIONS 1 *Optus* C1 (dual use for civil/mil comms)

Army 29,000

Forces Command
FORCES BY ROLE
COMMAND
1 (1st) div HQ (1 sigs regt)
MANOEUVRE
Mechanised
1 (1st) mech inf bde (1 armd cav regt, 1 mech inf bn, 1 lt mech inf bn, 1 arty regt, 1 cbt engr regt, 1 sigs regt, 1 CSS bn)
2 (3rd & 7th) mech inf bde (1 armd cav regt, 2 mech inf bn, 1 arty regt, 1 cbt engr regt, 1 sigs regt, 1 CSS bn)
Amphibious
1 (2nd RAR) amph bn
Aviation
1 (16th) avn bde (1 regt (2 ISR hel sqn), 1 regt (3 tpt hel sqn), 1 regt (2 spec ops hel sqn, 1 avn sqn))
COMBAT SUPPORT
1 (6th) cbt spt bde (1 STA regt (1 STA bty, 1 UAV bty, 1 CSS bty), 1 AD/FAC regt (integrated), 1 engr regt (2 construction sqn, 1 EOD sqn), 1 EW regt, 1 int bn)
COMBAT SERVICE SUPPORT
1 (17th) CSS bde (3 log bn, 3 med bn, 1 MP bn)

Special Operations Command
FORCES BY ROLE
SPECIAL FORCES
1 (SAS) SF regt
1 (SF Engr) SF regt
2 cdo regt
COMBAT SUPPORT
3 sigs sqn (incl 1 reserve sqn)
COMBAT SERVICE SUPPORT
1 CSS sqn

Reserve Organisations 13,200 reservists

Force Command
FORCES BY ROLE
COMMAND
1 (2nd) div HQ
MANOEUVRE
Reconnaissance
3 (regional force) surv unit (integrated)
Light
1 (4th) inf bde (1 recce regt, 2 inf bn, 1 engr regt, 1 spt bn)
1 (5th) inf bde (1 recce bn, 4 inf bn, 1 engr regt, 2 spt bn)
1 (9th) inf bde (1 recce sqn, 2 inf bn, 1 spt bn)
1 (11th) inf bde (1 recce regt, 3 inf bn, 1 engr regt, 1 spt bn)
1 (13th) inf bde (1 recce sqn, 2 inf bn, 1 spt bn)
COMBAT SUPPORT
1 arty regt
1 sigs regt
COMBAT SERVICE SUPPORT
1 trg bde

EQUIPMENT BY TYPE
ARMOURED FIGHTING VEHICLES
MBT 59 M1A1 *Abrams*
IFV 253 ASLAV-25 (all variants)
APC • APC (T) 431 M113AS4
AUV 1,042: 1,020 *Bushmaster* IMV; 22 *Hawkei*
ENGINEERING & MAINTENANCE VEHICLES
ARV 45: 15 ASLAV-F; 17 ASLAV-R; 19 M88A2
VLB 5 *Biber*
MW 20: 12 *Husky*; 8 MV-10
ANTI-TANK/ANTI-INFRASTRUCTURE
MSL • MANPATS FGM-148 *Javelin*
RCL • 84mm *Carl Gustav*
ARTILLERY 239
TOWED 155mm 54 M777A2
MOR 81mm 185
AMPHIBIOUS 15 LCM-8 (capacity either 1 MBT or 200 troops)
HELICOPTERS
ATK 22 *Tiger*
TPT 82: **Heavy** 10 CH-47F *Chinook*; **Medium** 72: 38 NH90 TTH (MRH90 TTH); 34 S-70A *Black Hawk*
UNMANNED AERIAL VEHICLES
ISR • **Medium** 15 RQ-7B *Shadow* 200
AIR DEFENCE • SAM • **Point-defence** RBS-70

Navy 13,660
Fleet Comd HQ located at Sydney. Naval Strategic Comd HQ located at Canberra
EQUIPMENT BY TYPE
SUBMARINES • TACTICAL • SSK 6 *Collins* with 6 single 533mm TT with Mk48 *Sea Arrow* ADCAP HWT/UGM-84C *Harpoon* AShM
PRINCIPAL SURFACE COMBATANTS 13
DESTROYERS • DDGHM
2 *Hobart* with *Aegis* Baseline 7.1 C2, 2 quad lnchr with RGM-84D *Harpoon* AShM, 6 8-cell Mk41 VLS with SM-2 Block IIIB SAM/RIM-162A ESSM SAM, 2 twin 324mm ASTT with MU90 LWT, 1 *Phalanx* CIWS, 1 127mm gun (capacity 1 MH-60R *Seahawk*)
FRIGATES • FFGHM 11
3 *Adelaide* (Mod) with 1 Mk13 GMLS with RGM-84L *Harpoon* Block II AShM/SM-2 Block IIIA SAM, 1 8-cell Mk41 VLS with RIM-162B ESSM SAM, 2 triple Mk32 324mm ASTT with MU90 LWT, 1 *Phalanx* Block 1B CIWS, 1 76mm gun (capacity 2 MH-60R *Seahawk* ASW hel)
8 *Anzac* (GER MEKO 200) with 2 quad Mk141 lnchr with RGM-84L *Harpoon* Block II AShM, 1 8-cell Mk41 VLS with RIM-162B ESSM SAM, 2 triple 324mm ASTT with MU90 LWT, 1 127mm gun (capacity 2 MH-60R *Seahawk* ASW hel)

PATROL AND COASTAL COMBATANTS 15
  PCO 15: 13 *Armidale* (*Bay* mod); 2 *Cape* (leased)
MINE WARFARE • MINE COUNTERMEASURES •
MHO 4 *Huon* (2 *Huon* in reserve)
AMPHIBIOUS
  PRINCIPAL AMPHIBIOUS SHIPS 3
    LHD 2 *Canberra* (capacity 8 hel; 4 LCM; 100 veh; 1,000 troops)
    LSD 1 *Choules* (ex-UK *Bay*) (capacity 1 med hel; 2 LCVP; 24 MBT; 350 troops)
  LANDING CRAFT 17
    LCM 12 LCM-1E
    LCVP 5
LOGISTICS AND SUPPORT 14
  AGHS 2 *Leeuwin* with 1 hel landing platform
  AGS 4 *Paluma*
  AORH 1 *Success*
  AOR 1 *Sirius*
The following vessels are operated by a private company, DMS Maritime:
  ASR 2: 1 *Besant*; 1 *Stoker*
  AX 2: 1 *Seahorse Horizon*; 1 *Seahorse Standard*
  AXL 1 *Seahorse Mercator*
  AXS 1 *Young Endeavour*

Naval Aviation 1,350

FORCES BY ROLE
ANTI SUBMARINE WARFARE
  1 sqn with NH90 (MRH90)
  1 sqn with MH-60R *Seahawk*
TRAINING
  1 OCU sqn with MH-60R *Seahawk*
  1 sqn with Bell 429; H135
EQUIPMENT BY TYPE
HELICOPTERS
  ASW 24 MH-60R *Seahawk*
  TPT 25: **Medium** 6 NH90 (MRH90); **Light** 19: 4 Bell 429; 15 H135

Clearance Diving Branch

FORCES BY ROLE
SPECIAL FORCES
  2 diving unit

Air Force 14,400

FORCES BY ROLE
FIGHTER/GROUND ATTACK
  3 sqn with F/A-18A/B *Hornet*
  1 sqn with F/A-18F *Super Hornet*
  1 sqn (forming) with F-35A *Lightning* II
ANTI SUBMARINE WARFARE
  1 sqn with AP-3C *Orion*
  1 sqn (forming) with P-8A *Poseidon*
ELECTRONIC WARFARE
  1 sqn with EA-18G *Growler*
ISR
  1 (FAC) sqn with PC-9/A(F)
AIRBORNE EARLY WARNING & CONTROL
  1 sqn with B-737-700 *Wedgetail* (E-7A)
TANKER/TRANSPORT
  1 sqn with A330 MRTT (KC-30A)
TRANSPORT
  1 VIP sqn with B-737BBJ; CL-604 *Challenger*
  1 sqn with Beech 350 *King Air*
  1 sqn with C-17A *Globemaster* III
  1 sqn with C-27J *Spartan*
  1 sqn with C-130J-30 *Hercules*
TRAINING
  1 OCU with F/A-18A/B *Hornet*
  1 sqn with Beech 350 *King Air*
  2 (LIFT) sqn with *Hawk* MK127*
EQUIPMENT BY TYPE
AIRCRAFT 172 combat capable
  FGA 105: 55 F/A-18A *Hornet*; 16 F/A-18B *Hornet*; 24 F/A-18F *Super Hornet*; 10 F-35A *Lightning* II (in test)
  ASW 22: 15 AP-3C *Orion*; 7 P-8A *Poseidon*
  EW 12 EA-18G *Growler**
  AEW&C 6 B-737-700 *Wedgetail* (E-7A)
  TKR/TPT 5 A330 MRTT (KC-30A)
  TPT 51: **Heavy** 8 C-17A *Globemaster* III; **Medium** 22: 10 C-27J *Spartan*; 12 C-130J-30 *Hercules*; **Light** 16 Beech 350 *King Air*; **PAX** 5: 2 B-737BBJ (VIP); 3 CL-604 *Challenger* (VIP)
  TRG 107: 33 *Hawk* Mk127*; 62 PC-9/A (incl 4 PC-9/A(F) for tgt marking); 12 PC-21
AIR-LAUNCHED MISSILES
  AAM • IIR AIM-9X *Sidewinder* II; ASRAAM; **ARH** AIM-120B/C-5/C-7 AMRAAM
  AShM AGM-84A *Harpoon*
  LACM Conventional AGM-158 JASSM
BOMBS
  Laser-guided *Paveway* II/IV; Laser JDAM
  INS/GPS-guided AGM-154C JSOW; JDAM; JDAM-ER

Cyber

Australia's Chief of Defence Force announced in January 2018 the establishment of a new Defence SIGINT and Cyber Command, marking the latest organisational change in Australia's developing cyber capabilities. Australia's Cyber Security Strategy was launched in April 2016. During the launch, the government publicly announced Australia's offensive cyber capabilities, to respond to cyber intrusions against Australian networks. This capability is housed in the Australian Signals Directorate (ASD). The Defence SIGINT and Cyber Command will contain personnel from the joint SIGINT unit and the Joint Cyber Unit alongside civilians from the ASD. Command of the Defence SIGINT and Cyber Command runs from CDF through the Joint Capabilities (Information Warfare) Division. This division was formed in mid-2017, consisting of four branches: Information Warfare Capability; C4 and Battle Management Capability; the Capability Support Directorate; and the Joint Cyber Unit. It will be responsible for offensive and defensive cyber operations. The 2016 Defence White Paper acknowledged the growing challenge from cyber threats and the need to continue developing Australia's capabilities to protect systems and networks. The Australian Cyber Security Centre (ACSC) is Australia's lead organisation for cyber security. Opened in November

2014, the ACSC in July 2018 became part of the ASD, which became a statutory agency. Australian government cyber-security expertise from CERT Australia and the Digital Transformation Agency also moved into the ACSC.

DEPLOYMENT

AFGHANISTAN: NATO • ISAF *Operation Resolute Support* (*Highroad*) 270; 1 SF unit; 1 sy unit; 1 sigs unit

ARABIAN SEA: Combined Maritime Forces • CTF-150 (*Operation Manitou*) 1 FFGHM

EGYPT: MFO (*Operation Mazurka*) 27

IRAQ: *Operation Inherent Resolve* (*Okra*) 380; 1 SF gp; 1 trg unit

MALAYSIA: 120; 1 inf coy (on 3-month rotational tours); 2 AP-3C *Orion* (on rotation)

MIDDLE EAST: UN • UNTSO (*Operation Paladin*) 12 obs

PHILIPPINES: *Operation Augury* 100 (trg team)

SOUTH SUDAN: UN • UNMISS (*Operation Aslan*) 23; 1 obs

UNITED ARAB EMIRATES: *Operation Accordion* 500: 1 tpt det with 2 C-130J-30 Hercules; Operation Inherent Resolve (Okra) 150; 1 B-737-700 Wedgetail (E-7A); 1 A330 MRTT (KC-30A)

FOREIGN FORCES

New Zealand 9 (air navigation trg)

Singapore 230: 1 trg sqn at Pearce with PC-21 trg ac; 1 trg sqn at Oakey with 12 AS332 *Super Puma*; AS532 *Cougar*

United States US Pacific Command: 1,500; 1 SEWS at Pine Gap; 1 comms facility at NW Cape; 1 SIGINT stn at Pine Gap • US Strategic Command: 1 detection and tracking radar at Naval Communication Station Harold E. Holt

Bangladesh BGD

Bangladeshi Taka Tk		2017	2018	2019
GDP	Tk	21.1tr	23.9tr	
	US$	262bn	286bn	
per capita	US$	1,603	1,736	
Growth	%	7.4	7.3	
Inflation	%	5.6	6.0	
Def bdgt	Tk	236bn	264bn	291bn
	US$	2.93bn	3.16bn	
FMA (US)	US$	2m	0m	
US$1=Tk		80.63	83.62	

Population 159,453,001

Religious groups: Muslim 90%; Hindu 9%; Buddhist 1%

Age	0–14	15–19	20–24	25–29	30–64	65 plus
Male	13.9%	5.0%	4.7%	4.1%	18.6%	3.0%
Female	13.4%	4.8%	4.7%	4.4%	20.1%	3.4%

Capabilities

Bangladesh has limited military capability that is optimised for border and domestic security. A wide-ranging defence modernisation plan is under way, called Forces 2030. Counter-terrorism operations increased following a July 2016 attack and it is mounting coordinated patrols of the Bay of Bengal with India. In the recent past, Bangladesh has relied on Chinese and Russian aid and credit to overcome its limited procurement funding. It has increased defence collaboration with India. The country has a long record of UN peacekeeping deployments, with UN payments reportedly providing an important income source. In Autumn 2017, the army deployed to the country's eastern border to provide humanitarian assistance to Rohingya refugees fleeing Myanmar. A major naval-recapitalisation and -expansion programme is under way to better protect the country's large EEZ, including procurement of Chinese corvettes. A requirement for modern howitzers and light armoured vehicles for peacekeeping missions has been announced. Substantial efforts have been made to strengthen the nascent shipbuilding industry and work has begun on a new submarine-support facility. The armed forces reportedly retain extensive business interests, in real estate, banks and other businesses.

ACTIVE 157,050 (Army 126,150 Navy 16,900 Air 14,000) Paramilitary 63,900

ORGANISATIONS BY SERVICE

Army 126,150

FORCES BY ROLE
COMMAND
  9 inf div HQ
SPECIAL FORCES
  1 cdo bn
MANOEUVRE
  Armoured
  1 armd bde
  3 indep armd regt
  Light
  23 inf bde
  1 (composite) bde
COMBAT SUPPORT
  9 arty bde
  1 engr bde
  1 sigs bde
AVIATION
  1 avn regt (1 avn sqn; 1 hel sqn)
AIR DEFENCE
  1 AD bde

EQUIPMENT BY TYPE
ARMOURED FIGHTING VEHICLES
  MBT 276: 174 Type-59; 58 Type-69/Type-69G; 44 Type-90-II (MBT-2000)
  LT TK 8 Type-62
  RECCE 8+ BOV M11
  APC 481
    APC (T) 134 MT-LB
    APC (W) 347: 330 BTR-80; 17 *Cobra*
ENGINEERING & MAINTENANCE VEHICLES
  AEV MT-LB
  ARV 3+: T-54/T-55; Type-84; 3 Type-654
  VLB MTU
ANTI-TANK/ANTI-INFRASTRUCTURE
  MSL • MANPATS 9K115-2 *Metis* M1 (AT-13 *Saxhorn*-2)
  RCL 106mm 238 M40A1

ARTILLERY 853+
SP 155mm 12 NORA B-52
TOWED 363+: 105mm 170 Model 56 pack howitzer; 122mm 131: 57 Type-54/54-1 (M-30); 20 Type-83; 54 Type-96 (D-30), 130mm 62 Type-59-1 (M-46)
MRL 122mm 6 (PRC)
MOR 472: 81mm 11 M29A1; 82mm 366 Type-53/type-87/M-31 (M-1937); 120mm 95 AM-50/UBM 52
AMPHIBIOUS • LANDING CRAFT 3: 1 LCT; 2 LCVP
AIRCRAFT • TPT • Light 7: 1 C295; 5 Cessna 152; 1 PA-31T *Cheyenne*
HELICOPTERS
MRH 2 AS365N3 *Dauphin*
TPT 6: Medium 3 Mi-171Sh Light 3 Bell 206L-4 *Long Ranger*
AIR DEFENCE
SAM
Short-range FM-90
Point-defence QW-2; HN-5A (being replaced by QW-2)
GUNS • TOWED 166: 37mm 132 Type-65/74; 57mm 34 Type-59 (S-60)

Navy 16,900
EQUIPMENT BY TYPE
SUBMARINES • TACTICAL • SSK 2 *Nabajatra* (ex-PRC *Ming* Type-035G) with 8 single 533mm TT
PRINCIPAL SURFACE COMBATANTS • FRIGATES 4
FFGHM 1 *Bangabandhu* (ROK modified *Ulsan*) with 2 twin lnchr with *Otomat* Mk2 AShM, 1 octuple HHQ-7 SAM, 2 triple 324mm TT with A244 LWT, 1 76mm gun (capacity: 1 AW109E hel)
FFG 3:
2 *Abu Bakr* (ex-PRC *Jianghu* III) with 2 twin lnchr with C-802A AShM, 2 RBU 1200 A/S mor, 2 twin 100mm gun
1 *Osman* (ex-PRC *Jianghu* I) with 2 quad lnchr with C-802 (CH-SS-N-8 *Saccade*) AShM, 2 RBU 1200 A/S mor, 2 twin 100mm gun
PATROL AND COASTAL COMBATANTS 52
CORVETTES 8
FSGM 2 *Shadhinota* (PRC C13B) with 2 twin lnchr with C-802 (CH-SS-N-8 *Saccade*) AShM, 1 octuple FL-3000N lnchr with HHQ-10 SAM, 1 76mm gun, 1 hel landing platform
FSG 4:
2 *Durjoy* with 2 twin lnchr with C-704 AShM, 1 76mm gun
2 *Bijoy* (ex-UK *Castle*) with 2 twin lnchr with C-704 AShM, 1 76mm gun, 1 hel landing platform
FS 2 *Durjoy* with 2 triple 324mm ASTT, 1 76mm gun
PSOH 2 *Somudra Joy* (ex-USCG *Hero*) with 1 76mm gun, hel landing platform
PCFG 4 *Durdarsha* (ex-PRC *Huangfeng*) with 4 single lnchr with HY-2 (CH-SS-N-2 *Safflower*) AShM
PCO 6: 1 *Madhumati* (*Sea Dragon*) with 1 57mm gun; 5 *Kapatakhaya* (ex-UK *Island*)
PCC 8:
2 *Meghna* with 1 57mm gun (fishery protection)
1 *Nirbhoy* (ex-PRC *Hainan*) with 4 RBU 1200 A/S mor; 2 twin 57mm gun
5 *Padma*
PBFG 5 *Durbar* (PRC *Hegu*) with 2 single lnchr with SY-1 AShM
PBFT 4 *Huchuan* (PRC) with 2 single 533mm TT each with YU-1 Type-53 HWT
PBF 4 *Titas* (ROK *Sea Dolphin*)
PB 11: 1 *Barkat* (ex-PRC *Shanghai* III); 2 *Karnaphuli*; 1 *Salam* (ex-PRC *Huangfen*); 7 *Shaheed Daulat* (PRC *Shanghai* II)
MINE WARFARE • MINE COUNTERMEASURES 5
MSO 5: 1 *Sagar*; 4 *Shapla* (ex-UK *River*)
AMPHIBIOUS
LANDING SHIPS • LSL 1
LANDING CRAFT 14
LCT 2
LCU 4 (of which 2†)
LCVP 3†
LCM 5 *Darshak* (*Yuchin*)
LOGISTICS AND SUPPORT 9
AG 1
AGHS 2: 1 *Agradoot*; 1 *Anushandhan*
AOR 2 (coastal)
AOT 1 *Khan Jahangir Ali*
AR 1†
ATF 1†
AX 1 *Shaheed Ruhul Amin*

Naval Aviation
EQUIPMENT BY TYPE
AIRCRAFT • TPT • Light 2 Do-228NG (MP)
HELICOPTERS • TPT • Light 2 AW109E *Power*

Special Warfare and Diving Command 300

Air Force 14,000
FORCES BY ROLE
FIGHTER
1 sqn with MiG-29B/UB *Fulcrum*
FIGHTER/GROUND ATTACK
1 sqn with F-7MB/FT-7B *Airguard*
1 sqn with F-7BG/FT-7BG *Airguard*
1 sqn with F-7BGI/FT-7BGI *Airguard*
GROUND ATTACK
1 sqn with Yak-130 *Mitten**
TRANSPORT
1 sqn with An-32 *Cline*
1 sqn with C-130B *Hercules*
1 sqn with L-410UVP
TRAINING
1 sqn with K-8W *Karakorum**; L-39ZA *Albatros**
1 sqn with PT-6
TRANSPORT HELICOPTER
1 sqn with AW139; Mi-17 *Hip* H; Mi-17-1V *Hip* H; Mi-171Sh
1 sqn with Mi-17 *Hip* H; Mi-17-1V *Hip* H; Mi-171Sh

1 sqn with Bell 212
1 trg sqn with Bell 206L *Long Ranger*; AW119 *Koala*

EQUIPMENT BY TYPE
AIRCRAFT 81 combat capable
  FTR 53: 9 F-7MB *Airguard*; 11 F-7BG *Airguard*; 12 F-7BGI *Airguard*; 5 FT-7B *Airguard*; 4 FT-7BG *Airguard*; 4 FT-7BGI *Airguard*; 6 MiG-29 *Fulcrum*; 2 MiG-29UB *Fulcrum*
  TPT 11: **Medium** 4 C-130B *Hercules*; **Light** 7: 3 An-32 *Cline*†; 3 L-410UVP; 1 C295W
  TRG 38: 8 K-8W *Karakorum**; 7 L-39ZA *Albatros**; 10 PT-6; 13 Yak-130 *Mitten**
HELICOPTERS
  MRH 16: 2 AW139 (SAR); 12 Mi-17 *Hip* H; 2 Mi-17-1V *Hip* H (VIP)
  TPT 15: **Medium** 7 Mi-171Sh; **Light** 8: 2 Bell 206L *Long Ranger*; 4 Bell 212; 2 AW119 *Koala*
AIR-LAUNCHED MISSILES
  AAM • **IR** R-3 (AA-2 *Atoll*)‡; R-73 (AA-11 *Archer*); PL-5; PL-7; **SARH** R-27R (AA-10A *Alamo*)

Paramilitary 63,900

Ansars 20,000+
Security Guards

Rapid Action Battalions 5,000
Ministry of Home Affairs
FORCES BY ROLE
MANOEUVRE
  Other
    14 paramilitary bn

Border Guard Bangladesh 38,000
FORCES BY ROLE
MANOEUVRE
  Amphibious
    1 rvn coy
  Other
    54 paramilitary bn

Coast Guard 900
EQUIPMENT BY TYPE
PATROL AND COASTAL COMBATANTS 13
  PSO 4 *Syed Nazrul* (ex-ITA *Minerva*) with 1 hel landing platform
  PB 4: 1 *Ruposhi Bangla*; 1 *Shaheed Daulat*; 2 *Shetgang*
  PBR 5 *Pabna*

DEPLOYMENT

CENTRAL AFRICAN REPUBLIC: UN • MINUSCA 1,010; 9 obs; 1 cdo coy; 1 inf bn; 1 med coy
CYPRUS: UN • UNFICYP 2
DEMOCRATIC REPUBLIC OF THE CONGO: UN • MONUSCO 1,710; 5 obs; 1 inf bn; 1 engr coy; 1 avn coy; 2 hel coy
LEBANON: UN • UNIFIL 116; 1 FSG
MALI: UN • MINUSMA 1,415; 3 obs; 1 inf bn; 1 engr coy; 2 sigs coy; 1 tpt coy
SOMALIA: UN • UNSOM 1 obs
SOUTH SUDAN: UN • UNMISS 1,601; 7 obs; 1 inf bn; 2 rvn coy; 2 engr coy
SUDAN: UN • UNAMID 356; 3 obs; 2 inf coy
WESTERN SAHARA: UN • MINURSO 29; 7 obs; 1 fd hospital

Brunei BRN

Brunei Dollar B$		2017	2018	2019
GDP	B$	16.7bn	19.7bn	
	US$	12.1bn	14.7bn	
per capita	US$	28,278	33,824	
Growth	%	1.3	2.3	
Inflation	%	-0.2	0.4	
Def bdgt	B$	452m	493m	
	US$	327m	367n	
US$1=B$		1.38	1.34	

Population	450,565

Ethnic groups: Malay 65.7%; Chinese 10.3%; indigenous 3.4%; other or unspecified 23.6%

Age	0–14	15–19	20–24	25–29	30–64	65 plus
Male	11.8%	4.0%	4.4%	4.5%	22.1%	2.5%
Female	11.1%	3.9%	4.5%	4.8%	23.8%	2.7%

Capabilities

The Royal Brunei Armed Forces are professional and well trained. The 2011 defence white paper set out missions such as ensuring territorial integrity and upholding the constitution. C4ISR capabilities are being improved to offset the forces' relatively small size, and the white paper advocates pursuing procurement to strengthen airspace control, hardening C4 systems against cyber attack and protecting national communications infrastructure. Brunei plans to develop a fully mechanised battalion and stated in the white paper that it would examine potential replacements for its *Scorpion* light tanks. There is a long-established relationship with the UK, for whom Brunei has hosted a garrison since 1962 and a jungle-warfare school since 1972. Brunei is a member of ASEAN and has a close relationship with Singapore, for whom it hosts a permanent training base. The 2011 white paper advocates participation in regional exercises, with an emphasis on command and control, humanitarian assistance and disaster response, and maritime patrol. Brunei does not have the ability to deploy abroad without assistance, but has maintained a small deployment to UNIFIL in Lebanon since 2008. Brunei has no domestic defence industry and imports its military equipment. In 2010, the Centre of Science and Technology Research and Development was established to lead on defence-technology research, manage defence procurements, and provide engineering and support services to the armed forces.

ACTIVE 7,200 (Army 4,900 Navy 1,200 Air 1,100)
Paramilitary 400-500

RESERVE 700 (Army 700)

ORGANISATIONS BY SERVICE

Army 4,900
FORCES BY ROLE
MANOEUVRE
  Light
  3 inf bn
COMBAT SUPPORT
  1 cbt spt bn (1 armd recce sqn, 1 engr sqn)

Reserves 700
FORCES BY ROLE
MANOEUVRE
  Light
  1 inf bn

EQUIPMENT BY TYPE
ARMOURED FIGHTING VEHICLES
  LT TK 20 FV101 *Scorpion* (incl FV105 *Sultan* CP)
  APC • APC (W) 45 VAB
ENGINEERING & MAINTENANCE VEHICLES
  ARV 2 *Samson*
ARTILLERY • MOR 81mm 24

Navy 1,200
FORCES BY ROLE
SPECIAL FORCES
  1 SF sqn
EQUIPMENT BY TYPE
PATROL AND COASTAL COMBATANTS 9
  CORVETTES • FSG 4 *Darussalam* with 2 twin lnchr with MM40 *Exocet* Block 2 AShM, 1 57mm gun, 1 hel landing platform
  PCC 4 *Ijtihad*
  PBF 1 *Mustaed*
AMPHIBIOUS • LANDING CRAFT • LCU 4: 2 *Teraban*; 2 *Cheverton Loadmaster*

Air Force 1,100
FORCES BY ROLE
MARITIME PATROL
  1 sqn with CN235M
TRAINING
  1 sqn with PC-7; Bell 206B *Jet Ranger* II
TRANSPORT HELICOPTER
  1 sqn with Bell 214 (SAR)
  1 sqn with Bo-105
  1 sqn with S-70i *Black Hawk*
AIR DEFENCE
  1 sqn with *Rapier*
  1 sqn with *Mistral*
EQUIPMENT BY TYPE
AIRCRAFT
  MP 1 CN235M
  TRG 4 PC-7
HELICOPTERS
  TPT 21: **Medium** 13: 1 Bell 214 (SAR); 12 S-70i *Black Hawk*; **Light** 8: 2 Bell 206B *Jet Ranger* II; 6 Bo-105 (armed, 81mm rockets)
AIR DEFENCE • SAM • Point-defence *Rapier*; *Mistral*

Paramilitary 400–500

Gurkha Reserve Unit 400–500
FORCES BY ROLE
MANOEUVRE
  Light
  2 inf bn(-)

DEPLOYMENT
LEBANON: UN • UNIFIL 30
PHILIPPINES: IMT 9

FOREIGN FORCES
Singapore 1 trg camp with infantry units on rotation; 1 trg school; 1 hel det with AS332 *Super Puma*
United Kingdom 1,000; 1 Gurkha bn; 1 jungle trg centre; 1 hel flt with 3 Bell 212

Cambodia CAM

Cambodian Riel r		2017	2018	2019
GDP	r	89.7tr	99.1tr	
	US$	22.1bn	24.1bn	
per capita	US$	1,379	1,485	
Growth	%	6.9	7.0	
Inflation	%	2.9	3.3	
Def bdgt [a]	r	ε3.20tr	ε3.90tr	
	US$	ε788m	ε951m	
US$1=r		4,059.21	4,103.84	

[a] Defence and security budget

Population 16,449,519
Ethnic groups: Khmer 90%; Vietnamese 5%; Chinese 1%

Age	0–14	15–19	20–24	25–29	30–64	65 plus
Male	15.5%	4.4%	4.4%	5.1%	17.5%	1.6%
Female	15.2%	4.4%	4.6%	5.2%	19.2%	2.7%

Capabilities

Despite their name, which reflects Cambodia's formal status as a constitutional monarchy, the Royal Cambodian Armed Forces (RCAF) are essentially the modern manifestation of the armed forces of the former People's Republic of Kampuchea, established in 1979 following Vietnam's invasion. Cambodia faces no direct external military threats, besides border clashes with Thailand. Security concerns regard mainly transnational threats generating instability such as drug trafficking. Cambodia's most important international links are with the Chinese and Vietnamese armed forces. China and Cambodia have developed training ties in recent years, and exercises have grown in scale. Skirmishes on the border with Thailand since 2008 provided little indication of capacity for high-intensity combat. Cambodia lacks resources for personnel training, which is partly financed by Chinese military assistance. The RCAF has an excessive number of senior officers, while many formations and units appear to be of only nominal status. Cambodia has contributed personnel to UN peacekeeping missions, including MINUSCA and MINUSMA. Despite increased defence spending in recent years, the armed forces rely largely on equipment donations and second-hand procurements, including from China and South Korea. Cambodia has no domestic defence industry, with no ability to design and manufacture modern equipment for its armed forces.

ACTIVE 124,300 (Army 75,000 Navy 2,800 Air 1,500 Provincial Forces 45,000) **Paramilitary 67,000**

Conscript liability 18 months service authorised but not implemented since 1993

ORGANISATIONS BY SERVICE

Army ε75,000

6 Military Regions (incl 1 special zone for capital)

FORCES BY ROLE
SPECIAL FORCES
  1 (911th) AB/SF Bde
MANOEUVRE
  Light
  2 (2nd & 3rd Intervention) inf div (3 inf bde)
  5 (Intervention) indep inf bde
  8 indep inf bde
  Other
  1 (70th) sy bde (4 sy bn)
  17 (border) sy bn
COMBAT SUPPORT
  2 arty bn
  4 fd engr regt
COMBAT SERVICE SUPPORT
  1 (construction) engr regt
  2 tpt bde
AIR DEFENCE
  1 AD bn
EQUIPMENT BY TYPE
ARMOURED FIGHTING VEHICLES
  MBT 200+: 50 Type-59; 150+ T-54/T-55
  LT TK 20+: Type-62; 20 Type-63
  RECCE 4+ BRDM-2
  IFV 70 BMP-1
  APC 230+
    APC (T) M113
    APC (W) 230: 200 BTR-60/BTR-152; 30 OT-64
ENGINEERING & MAINTENANCE VEHICLES
  ARV T-54/T-55
  MW *Bozena*; RA-140 DS
ANTI-TANK/ANTI-INFRASTRUCTURE
  RCL 82mm B-10; **107mm** B-11
ARTILLERY 433+
  TOWED 400+: **76mm** ZIS-3 (M-1942)/**122mm** D-30/**122mm** M-30 (M-1938)/**130mm** Type-59-I
  MRL 33+: **107mm** Type-63; **122mm** 13: 8 BM-21; 5 RM-70; **132mm** BM-13-16 (BM-13); **140mm** 20 BM-14-16 (BM-14)
  MOR 82mm M-37; **120mm** M-43; **160mm** M-160
AIR DEFENCE
  SAM • Point-defence FN-6; FN-16 (reported)
  GUNS • TOWED 14.5mm ZPU-1/ZPU-2/ZPU-4; **37mm** M-1939; **57mm** S-60

Navy ε2,800 (incl 1,500 Naval Infantry)

EQUIPMENT BY TYPE
PATROL AND COASTAL COMBATANTS 14
  PBF 3 *Stenka*
  PB 9: 4 (PRC 46m); 3 (PRC 20m); 2 *Shershen*
  PBR 2 *Kaoh Chhlam*
AMPHIBIOUS • LANDING CRAFT
  LCU 1
LOGISTICS AND SUPPORT • AFDL 1

Naval Infantry 1,500

FORCES BY ROLE
MANOEUVRE
  Light
  1 (31st) nav inf bde
COMBAT SUPPORT
  1 arty bn

Air Force 1,500

FORCES BY ROLE
ISR/TRAINING
  1 sqn with P-92 *Echo* (L-39 *Albatros** in store)
TRANSPORT
  1 VIP sqn (reporting to Council of Ministers) with An-24RV *Coke*; AS350 *Ecureuil*; AS355F2 *Ecureuil* II
  1 sqn with BN-2 *Islander*; Y-12 (II)
TRANSPORT HELICOPTER
  1 sqn with Mi-17 *Hip* H; Mi-8 *Hip*; Z-9; (Mi-26 *Halo* in store)
EQUIPMENT BY TYPE
AIRCRAFT
  TPT • Light 12: 2 An-24RV *Coke*; 1 BN-2 *Islander*; 2 MA60; 5 P-92 *Echo* (pilot trg/recce); 2 Y-12 (II)
  TRG (5 L-39 *Albatros** in store)
HELICOPTERS
  MRH 14: 3 Mi-17 *Hip* H; 11 Z-9
  TPT 8: **Heavy** (2 Mi-26 *Halo* in store); **Medium** 4 Mi-8 *Hip*; **Light** 4: 2 AS350 *Ecureuil*; 2 AS355F2 *Ecureuil* II

Provincial Forces 45,000+

Reports of at least 1 inf regt per province, with varying numbers of inf bn (with lt wpn)

Paramilitary

Police 67,000 (including gendarmerie)

DEPLOYMENT

CENTRAL AFRICAN REPUBLIC: UN • MINUSCA 221; 6 obs; 1 engr coy

LEBANON: UN • UNIFIL 184; 1 engr coy

MALI: UN • MINUSMA 303: 2 engr coy; 1 EOD coy

SOUTH SUDAN: UN • UNMISS 79; 6 obs; 1 MP unit

SUDAN: UN • UNAMID 1 obs

China, People's Republic of PRC

Chinese Yuan Renminbi Y		2017	2018	2019
GDP	Y	81.2tr	88.6tr	
	US$	12.0tr	13.5tr	
per capita	US$	8,643	9,633	
Growth	%	6.9	6.6	
Inflation	%	1.6	2.2	
Def exp [a]	Y	1.41tr	n.k	
	US$	209bn	n.k	
Def bdgt [b]	Y	1.02tr	1.11tr	
	US$	151bn	168bn	
US$1=Y		6.76	6.58	

[a] official defence budget & other military-related expenditure
[b] official defence budget

Population 1,392,508,664

Ethnic groups: Han 91.5%; Zhuang 1.3%; Hui 0.8%; Manchu 0.8%; Uighur 0.7%; Tibetan 0.5%; other or unspecified 4.4%

Age	0–14	15–19	20–24	25–29	30–64	65 plus
Male	9.2%	3.0%	3.6%	4.3%	25.8%	5.4%
Female	7.9%	2.6%	3.2%	4.1%	24.9%	5.9%

Capabilities

China's People's Liberation Army (PLA) remains the world's largest armed force, with an increasingly modern, advanced equipment inventory. Its operational effectiveness, however, remains hampered by training and doctrine issues. China's most recent, 2015 defence white paper outlined the importance of power-projection capabilities, emphasising the requirements for offensive and defensive air operations and 'open seas protection'. A major restructuring process is now mostly in effect and will probably be complete by 2020. The establishment of the Strategic Support Force underscores the importance placed upon the further development of China's cyber, space and information-dominance capabilities. China does not maintain any formal alliances, but it does have a number of key defence relationships with regional states and through its membership of the SCO. It also boosted defence ties in Africa in 2018. Improving readiness for combat operations is a key objective of the current reforms; the PLA currently lacks any significant recent combat experience and its training has traditionally suffered from over-scripted and unrealistic exercises. Though these weaknesses are acknowledged and possibly being addressed, it is unclear how effective the newly established structures will be at generating and controlling high-intensity combined-arms capabilities. In the short term, changes to roles and requirements for officers may have had a detrimental effect on morale within the PLA, as well as on its overall level of readiness. The requirement for out-of-area operations is relatively new for the PLA; the navy is the only service to have experience in extended deployments, assisted by its new support base in Djibouti. Major platform inventories in all the services comprise a heterogeneous mix of modern, older and obsolescent designs. The reduction in overall force size as part of the restructuring process has seen some older equipment designs finally withdrawn from service. China has an extensive defence-industrial base, capable of indigenously producing advanced equipment across all domains, although questions persist over quality and reliability.

ACTIVE 2,035,000 (Ground Forces 975,000 Navy 250,000 Air Force 395,000 Strategic Missile Forces 120,000 Strategic Support Force 145,000 Other 150,000) **Paramilitary 660,000**

Conscript liability Selective conscription; all services 24 months

RESERVE ε510,000

ORGANISATIONS BY SERVICE

Strategic Missile Forces 120,000+

People's Liberation Army Rocket Force

The People's Liberation Army Rocket Force (formerly the Second Artillery Force) organises and commands its own troops to launch nuclear counter-attacks with strategic missiles and to conduct operations with conventional missiles. Organised as launch bdes subordinate to 6 army-level msl bases. Org varies by msl type

FORCES BY ROLE
SURFACE-TO-SURFACE MISSILE
  1 ICBM bde with DF-4
  2 ICBM bde with DF-5A
  1 ICBM bde with DF-5B
  1 ICBM bde with DF-31
  2 ICBM bde with DF-31A/A(G)
  2 IRBM bde with DF-26
  2 MRBM bde with DF-16
  6 MRBM bde with DF-21A/E
  2 MRBM bde with DF-21C
  2 MRBM bde with DF-21D
  4 SRBM bde with DF-11A
  2 SRBM bde with DF-15B
  2 GLCM bde with CJ-10/CJ-10A
  5+ SSM bde (forming)

EQUIPMENT BY TYPE
SURFACE-TO-SURFACE MISSILE LAUNCHERS
  ICBM • Nuclear 70: ε10 DF-4 (CH-SS-3); ε20 DF-5A/B (CH-SS-4 Mod 2/3); ε8 DF-31 (CH-SS-10 Mod 1); ε24 DF-31A (CH-SS-10 Mod 2); ε8 DF-31A(G) (CH-SS-10 Mod 3)
  IRBM • Dual-capable ε30 DF-26
  MRBM 158: **Nuclear** ε80 DF-21A/DF-21E (CH-SS-5 Mod 2/6); **Conventional** 78: ε24 DF-16 (CH-SS-11 Mod 1/2); ε24 DF-21C (CH-SS-5 Mod 4); ε30 DF-21D (CH-SS-5 Mod 5 – ASBM)
  SRBM • Conventional 189: ε108 DF-11A (CH-SS-7 Mod 2); ε81 DF-15B (CH-SS-6 Mod 3)
  GLCM • Conventional ε54 CJ-10/CJ-10A

Navy
EQUIPMENT BY TYPE
SUBMARINES • STRATEGIC • SSBN 4:
  4 *Jin* (Type-094) with up to 12 JL-2 (CH-SS-N-14) strategic SLBM, 6 single 533mm TT with Yu-6 HWT

Defensive
EQUIPMENT BY TYPE
RADAR • STRATEGIC: 4+ large phased array radars; some detection and tracking radars

Space
EQUIPMENT BY TYPE
SATELLITES 103
  COMMUNICATIONS 6 *Zhongxing* (dual-use telecom satellites for civ/mil comms)
  NAVIGATION/POSITIONING/TIMING 33: 3 *Beidou*-2(M); 6 *Beidou*-2(G); 6 *Beidou*-2(IGSO); 1 *Beidou*-3(G); 16 *Beidou*-3(M); 1 *Beidou*-3 (ISGO)
  ISR 49: 2 *Haiyang* (remote sensing); 46 *Yaogan Weixing* (remote sensing); 1 *Ziyuan* (ZY-2 – remote sensing)
  ELINT/SIGINT 15: 8 *Shijian* 6 (4 pairs – reported ELINT/SIGINT role); 7 *Shijian* 11 (reported ELINT/SIGINT role)

Ground Forces ε975,000
In late 2015, a single, separate headquarters was established for the People's Liberation Army (PLA) ground forces, in place of the four general departments

FORCES BY ROLE
COMMAND
  13 (Group) army HQ
SPECIAL FORCES
  15 spec ops bde
MANOEUVRE
  Armoured
  27 (cbd arms) armd bde
  1 hy mech inf div (1 armd regt, 2 mech inf regt, 1 arty regt, 1 AD regt)
  Mechanised
  1 (high alt) mech inf div (1 armd regt, 2 mech inf regt, 1 arty regt, 1 AD regt)
  23 (cbd arms) mech inf bde
  Light
  3 (high alt) mot inf div (1 armd regt, 2 mot inf regt, 1 arty regt, 1 AD regt)
  24 (cbd arms) inf bde
  Air Manoeuvre
  2 air aslt bde
  Amphibious
  6 amph aslt bde
  Other
  1 (OPFOR) mech inf bde
  1 mech gd div (1 armd regt, 2 mech inf regt, 1 arty regt, 1 AD regt)
  1 sy gd div (4 sy regt)
  16 (border) sy bde
  15 (border) sy regt
  1 (border) sy gp
COMBAT SUPPORT
  15 arty bde
  13 engr/NBC bde
  2 engr regt
COMBAT SERVICE SUPPORT
  13 spt bde
COASTAL DEFENCE
  19 coastal arty/AShM bde
AVIATION
  1 mixed avn bde
HELICOPTER
  12 hel bde

TRAINING
  4 hel trg regt
AIR DEFENCE
  15 AD bde

Reserves
The People's Liberation Army Reserve Force is being restructured, and the army component reduced. As a result some of the units below may have been re-roled or disbanded

FORCES BY ROLE
MANOEUVRE
  Armoured
  2 armd regt
  Light
  18 inf div
  4 inf bde
  3 indep inf regt
COMBAT SUPPORT
  3 arty div
  7 arty bde
  15 engr regt
  1 ptn br bde
  3 ptn br regt
  10 chem regt
  10 sigs regt
COMBAT SERVICE SUPPORT
  9 log bde
  1 log regt
AIR DEFENCE
  17 AD div
  8 AD bde
  8 AD regt

EQUIPMENT BY TYPE
ARMOURED FIGHTING VEHICLES
  MBT 5,800: 600 ZTZ-59; 650 ZTZ-59-II; 600 ZTZ-59D; 200 ZTZ-79; 300 ZTZ-88A/B; 1,000 ZTZ-96; 1,500 ZTZ-96A; 600 ZTZ-99; 250 ZTZ-99A; 100 ZTQ-15
  LT TK 450: 250 ZTD-05; 100 ZTQ-62; 100 ZTS-63A
  ASLT 600 ZTL-11
  IFV 5,000: 400 ZBD-04; 1,000 ZBD-04A; 1,200 ZBL-08; 600 ZBD-86; 650 ZBD-86A; 550 ZSL-92; 600 ZSL-92B
  APC 3,950
    APC (T) 2,700: 750 ZSD-63; 200 ZSD-63C; 1,750 ZSD-89
    APC (W) 1,250: 700 ZSL-92A; 500 ZSL-10; 50 ZSL-93
  AAV 300+ ZBD-05
  AUV Dongfeng Mengshi; *Tiger* 4×4
ENGINEERING & MAINTENANCE VEHICLES
  ARV Type-73; Type-84; Type-85; Type-97; Type-654
  VLB KMM; MTU; TMM; Type-84A
  MW Type-74; Type-79; Type-81-II; Type-84
ANTI-TANK/ANTI-INFRASTRUCTURE
  MSL
    SP 1,000: 450 HJ-8 (veh mounted); 100 HJ-10; 450 ZSL-02B
    MANPATS HJ-73D; HJ-8A/C/E; HJ-11
  RCL 3,966: **75mm** PF-56; **82mm** PF-65 (B-10); PF-78; **105mm** PF-75; **120mm** PF-98

GUNS 1,788
  SP 480: 100mm 250 PTL-02; 120mm 230 PTZ-89
  TOWED • 100mm 1,308 PT-73 (T-12)/PT-86
ARTILLERY 8,954+
  SP 2,120: 122mm 1,650: 500 PLZ-89; 350 PLZ-07A; 150 PLZ-07B; 300 PCL-09; 350 PLL-09; 152mm 150 PLZ-83A/B; 155mm 320 PLZ-05; (400 in store: 122mm 200 PLZ-89; 152mm 200 PLZ-83A)
  TOWED 1,234: 122mm 500 PL-96 (D-30); 130mm 234 PL-59 (M-46)/PL-59-I; 152mm 500 PL-66 (D-20); (4,400 in store: 122mm 2,800 PL-54-1 (M-1938)/PL-83/PL-60 (D-74)/PL-96 (D-30); 152mm 1,600 PL-54 (D-1)/PL-66 (D-20))
  GUN/MOR 120mm 1,250: 450 PLL-05; 800 PPZ-10
  MRL 1,550+ 107mm PH-63; 122mm 1,375: 550 PHL-81/PHL-90; 350 PHL-11; 375 PHZ-89; 100 PHZ-11; 300mm 175 PHL-03; (700 in store: 122mm 700 PHL-81)
  MOR 2,800: 82mm PP-53 (M-37)/PP-67/PP-82/PP-87; SP 82mm PCP-001; 100mm PP-89
COASTAL DEFENCE
  AShM HY-1 (CH-SSC-2 Silkworm); HY-2 (CH-SSC-3 Seersucker); HY-4 (CH-SSC-7 Sadsack); YJ-62
PATROL AND COASTAL COMBATANTS 25
  PB 25: 9 Huzong; 16 Shenyang
AMPHIBIOUS • LANDING CRAFT • LCM 205: 3+ Yugong; 50+ Yunnan II; 100+ Yupen; 2+ Yutu; 50 Yuwei
LOGISTICS AND SUPPORT 22
  AK 6+ Leizhuang
  AKR 1 Yunsong (capacity 1 MBT; 1 med hel)
  ARC 1
  AOT 11: 1 Fuzhong; 8 Fubing; 2 Fulei
  ATF 2 Huntao
  AX 1 Haixun III
AIRCRAFT • TPT 9: Medium 5: 4 Y-8; 1 Y-9; Light 4 Y-7
HELICOPTERS
  ATK 270+: 150 WZ-10; 120+ WZ-19
  MRH 351: 22 Mi-17 Hip H; 3 Mi-17-1V Hip H; 38 Mi-17V-5 Hip H; 25 Mi-17V-7 Hip H; 8 SA342L Gazelle; 21 Z-9A; 31 Z-9W; 10 Z-9WA; 193 Z-9WZ
  TPT 382: Heavy 105: 9 Z-8A; 96 Z-8B; Medium 209: 50 Mi-8T Hip; 140 Mi-171; 19 S-70C2 (S-70C) Black Hawk; Light 68: 53 AS350 Ecureuil; 15 H120 Colibri
UNMANNED AERIAL VEHICLES
  ISR • Heavy BZK-005; BZK-009 (reported); Medium BZK-006 (incl variants); BZK-007; BZK-008; Light Harpy (anti-radiation)
AIR DEFENCE
  SAM
    Medium-range 168+: 150+ HQ-16A; 18 HQ-17
    Short-range 254: 24 9K331 Tor-M1 (SA-15 Gauntlet); 30 HQ-6D; 200 HQ-7A/B
    Point-defence HN-5A/-5B; FN-6; QW-1; QW-2
  GUNS 7,396+
    SP 396: 25mm 270 PGZ-04A; 35mm 120 PGZ-07; 37mm 6 PGZ-88
    TOWED 7,000+: 25mm PG-87; 35mm PG-99 (GDF-002); 37mm PG-55 (M-1939)/PG-65/PG-74; 57mm PG-59 (S-60); 100mm PG-59 (KS-19)
AIR-LAUNCHED MISSILES
  AAM • IR TY-90
  ASM AKD-8; AKD-9; AKD-10

Navy ε250,000

The PLA Navy is organised into five service arms: submarine, surface, naval aviation, coastal defence and marine corps, as well as other specialised units. There are three fleets, one each in the Northern, Eastern and Southern theatre commands

EQUIPMENT BY TYPE
SUBMARINES 59
STRATEGIC • SSBN 4:
  4 Jin (Type-094) with up to 12 JL-2 (CH-SS-N-14) strategic SLBM, 6 single 533mm TT with Yu-6 HWT
TACTICAL 55
  SSN 6:
    2 Shang I (Type-093) with 6 single 533mm TT with Yu-3 HWT/Yu-6 HWT/YJ-82 (CH-SS-N-7) AShM or YJ-18 (CH-SS-N-13) AShM
    4 Shang II (Type-093A) with 6 single 533mm TT with Yu-3 HWT/Yu-6 HWT/YJ-82 (CH-SS-N-7) AShM or YJ-18 (CH-SS-N-13) AShM
    (3 Han (Type-091) in reserve with 6 single 533mm TT with Yu-3 HWT/YJ-82 (CH-SS-N-7) AShM)
  SSK 48:
    2 Kilo (Project 877) with 6 single 533mm TT with TEST-71ME HWT/53-65KE HWT
    2 Improved Kilo (Project 636) with 6 single 533mm TT with TEST-71ME HWT/53-65KE HWT
    8 Improved Kilo (Project 636M) with 6 single 533mm TT with TEST-71ME HWT/53-65KE HWT/3M54E Klub-S (SS-N-27B Sizzler) AShM
    8 Ming (4 Type-035(G), 4 Type-035B) with 8 single 533mm TT with Yu-3 HWT/Yu-4 HWT
    12 Song (Type-039(G)) with 6 single 533mm TT with Yu-3 HWT/Yu-6 HWT/YJ-82 (CH-SS-N-7) AShM or YJ-18 (CH-SS-N-13) AShM
    4 Yuan (Type-039A) with 6 533mm TT with Yu-3 HWT/Yu-6 HWT/YJ-82 (CH-SS-N-7) AShM or YJ-18 (CH-SS-N-13) AShM
    12 Yuan II (Type-039B) with 6 533mm TT with Yu-3 HWT/Yu-6 HWT/YJ-82 (CH-SS-N-7) AShM or YJ-18 (CH-SS-N-13) AShM
    (8 Ming (Type-035(G)) in reserve with 8 single 533mm TT with Yu-3 HWT/Yu-4 HWT)
  SSB 1 Qing (Type-032) (SLBM trials)
PRINCIPAL SURFACE COMBATANTS 87
  AIRCRAFT CARRIERS • CV 1
    1 Liaoning (RUS Kuznetsov) with 4 18-cell GMLS with HHQ-10 SAM, 2 RBU 6000 Smerch 2 A/S mor, 3 H/PJ-11 CIWS (capacity 18–24 J-15 ac; 17 Ka-28/Ka-31/Z-8S/Z-8JH/Z-8AEW hel)
  DESTROYERS 27
    DDGHM 25:
      2 Hangzhou (RUS Sovremenny I (Project 956E)) with 2 quad lnchr with 3M80/3M82 Moskit (SS-N-22A/B Sunburn) AShM, 2 3K90 Uragan (SA-N-7 Gadfly) SAM, 2 twin 533mm ASTT, 2 RBU 1000 Smerch 3 A/S mor, 4 AK630 CIWS, 2 twin 130mm gun (capacity 1 Z-9C/Ka-28 Helix A hel) (of which 1 in refit)
      2 Hangzhou (RUS Sovremenny II (Project 956EM)) with 2 quad lnchr with 3M80/3M82 Moskit (SS-N-22A/B

Sunburn) AShM, 2 *Yezh* (SA-N-12 *Grizzly*) SAM, 2 twin 533mm ASTT, 2 RBU 1000 *Smerch* 3 A/S mor, 2 *Kortik* CIWS with 9M311E (SA-N-11 *Grison*) SAM, 1 twin 130mm gun (capacity 1 Z-9C/Ka-28 *Helix* A hel)

1 *Luhai* (Type-051B) with 2 quad lnchr with YJ-12A AShM, 1 32-cell VLS with HHQ-16 SAM/Yu-8 A/S msl,2 triple 324mm ASTT with Yu-7 LWT, 1 twin 100mm gun (capacity 2 Z-9C/Ka-28 *Helix* A hel)

2 *Luhu* (Type-052) with 4 quad lnchr with YJ-83 AShM, 1 octuple lnchr with HHQ-7 SAM, 2 triple 324mm ASTT with Yu-7 LWT, 2 FQF 2500 A/S mor, 2 H/PJ-12 CIWS, 1 twin 100mm gun (capacity 2 Z-9C hel)

2 *Luyang* (Type-052B) with 4 quad lnchr with YJ-83 AShM, 2 single lnchr with *Yezh* (SA-N-12 *Grizzly*) SAM, 2 triple 324mm TT with Yu-7 LWT, 2 H/PJ-12 CIWS, 1 100mm gun (capacity 1 Ka-28 *Helix* A hel)

6 *Luyang* II (Type-052C) with 2 quad lnchr with YJ-62 AShM, 8 sextuple VLS with HHQ-9 SAM, 2 triple 324mm TT with Yu-7 LWT, 2 H/PJ-12 CIWS, 1 100mm gun (capacity 2 Ka-28 *Helix* A hel)

10 *Luyang* III (Type-052D) with 8 octuple VLS with YJ-18A (CH-SS-N-13) AShM/HHQ-9ER SAM/ Yu-8 A/S msl, 1 24-cell GMLS with HHQ-10 SAM, 2 triple 324mm TT with Yu-7 LWT, 1 H/PJ-12 CIWS (1 with H/PJ-11 CIWS), 1 130mm gun (capacity 2 Ka-28 *Helix* A hel)

DDGM 2:

2 *Luzhou* (Type-051C) with 2 quad lnchr with YJ-83 AShM; 6 sextuple VLS with S-300FM (SA-N-20 *Grumble*) SAM, 2 H/PJ-12 CIWS, 1 100mm gun, 1 hel landing platform

FRIGATES 59

FFGHM 40:

2 *Jiangkai* (Type-054) with 2 quad lnchr with YJ-83 AShM, 1 octuple lnchr with HHQ-7 SAM, 2 triple 324mm TT with Yu-7 LWT, 2 RBU 1200 A/S mor, 4 AK630 CIWS, 1 100mm gun (capacity 1 Ka-28 *Helix* A/Z-9C hel)

16 *Jiangkai* II (Type-054A) with 2 quad lnchr with YJ-83 AShM, 1 32-cell VLS with Yu-8 A/S msl/ HHQ-16 SAM, 2 triple 324mm TT with Yu-7 LWT, 2 FQF 2300 A/S mor, 2 H/PJ-12 CIWS, 1 76mm gun (capacity 1 Ka-28 *Helix* A/Z-9C hel)

12 *Jiangkai* II (Type-054A) with 2 quad lnchr with YJ-83 AShM, 1 32-cell VLS with Yu-8 A/S msl/ HHQ-16 SAM, 2 triple 324mm TT with Yu-7 LWT, 2 FQF 2300 A/S mor, 2 H/PJ-11 CIWS, 1 76mm gun (capacity 1 Ka-28 *Helix* A/Z-9C hel)

7 *Jiangwei* II (Type-053H3) with 2 quad lnchr with YJ-83 AShM, 1 octuple lnchr with HHQ-7 SAM, 2 RBU 1200 A/S mor, 1 twin 100mm gun (capacity 2 Z-9C hel)

3 *Jiangwei* II (Type-053H3) with 2 quad lnchr with YJ-83 AShM, 1 8-cell GMLS with HHQ-10 SAM, 2 RBU 1200 A/S mor, 1 twin 100mm gun (capacity 2 Z-9C hel)

FFGM 4:

2 *Luda* IV (Type-051DT) with 4 quad lnchr with YJ-83 AShM, 1 octuple lnchr with HHQ-7 SAM, 2 FQF 2500 A/S mor, 2 130mm gun, 3 twin 57mm gun

2 *Luda* IV (Type-051G) with 4 quad lnchr with YJ-83 AShM, 1 octuple lnchr with HHQ-7 SAM, 2 FQF 2500 A/S mor, 2 triple 324mm ASTT, 2 twin 100mm gun

FFG 15:

6 *Jianghu* I (Type-053H1) with 2 twin lnchr with HY-2 (CH-SS-N-2) AShM, 2 RBU 1200 A/S mor, 1 twin 100mm gun (capacity 1 Z-9C hel)

1 *Jianghu* III (Type-053H2) with 2 quad lnchr with YJ-83 AShM, 2 RBU 1200, 2 twin 100mm gun

6 *Jianghu* I Upgrade (Type-053H1G) with 2 quad lnchr with YJ-83 AShM, 2 RBU 1200, 2 twin 100mm gun

2 *Luda* I (Type-051) with 2 triple lnchr with HY-2 (CH-SS-N-2) AShM, 2 triple 324mm ASTT, 2 FQF 2500 A/S mor, 2 twin 130mm gun (minelaying capability)

PATROL AND COASTAL COMBATANTS ε205

CORVETTES • FSGM 41:

21 *Jiangdao* I (Type-056) with 2 twin lnchr with YJ-83 AShM, 1 8-cell GMLS with HHQ-10 SAM, 2 triple 324mm ASTT with Yu-7 LWT, 1 76mm gun, 1 hel landing platform

20 *Jiangdao* II (Type-056A) with 2 twin lnchr with YJ-83 AShM, 1 8-cell GMLS with HHQ-10 SAM, 2 triple 324mm ASTT with Yu-7 LWT, 1 76mm gun, 1 hel landing platform

PCFG ε60 *Houbei* (Type-022) with 2 quad lnchr with YJ-83 AShM, 1 H/PJ-13 CIWS

PCG 26

6 *Houjian* (Type-037-II) with 2 triple lnchr with YJ-8 (CH-SS-N-4) AShM, 1 76mm gun

20 *Houxin* (Type-037-IG) with 2 twin lnchr with YJ-8 (CH-SS-N-4) AShM

PCC 48

2 *Haijiu* (Type-037-I) with 4 RBU 1200 A/S mor, 1 twin 57mm gun

30 *Hainan* (Type-037) with ε4 RBU 1200 A/S mor, 2 twin 57mm gun

16 *Haiqing* (Type-037-IS) with 2 FQF-3200 A/S mor

PB ε30 *Shanghai* III (Type-062-1)

MINE WARFARE 42

MINE COUNTERMEASURES 50

MCO 16: 4 *Wochi* (Type-081); 6 *Wochi* mod (Type-081A); 6 *Wozang* (Type-082II)

MSC 16: 4 *Wosao* I (Type-082); 12 *Wosao* II (Type-082-II)

MSD 18 *Wonang* (Type-529) (operated by *Wozang* MCO)

AMPHIBIOUS

PRINCIPAL AMPHIBIOUS SHIPS • LPD 5 *Yuzhao* (Type-071) with 4 AK630 CIWS, 1 76mm gun (capacity 4 *Yuyi* LCAC plus supporting vehicles; 800 troops; 60 armoured vehs; 4 hel)

LANDING SHIPS 49

LSM 21:

1 *Yudeng* (Type-073-II) (capacity 5 tk or 500 troops)

10 *Yuhai* (Type-074) (capacity 2 tk; 250 troops)

10 *Yunshu* (Type-073A) (capacity 6 tk)

LST 28:

4 *Yukan* (Type-072-IIG) (capacity 2 LCVP; 10 tk; 200 troops)

9 *Yuting* I (Type-072-II/III) (capacity 10 tk; 250 troops; 2 hel)
9 *Yuting* II (Type-072A) (capacity 4 LCVP; 10 tk; 250 troops)
6 *Yuting* II (Type-072B) (capacity 4 LCVP; 10 tk; 250 troops)

LANDING CRAFT 63
  LCM ε30 *Yunnan*
  LCU 11 *Yubei* (Type-074A) (capacity 10 tanks or 150 troops)
  LCAC 14: 10 *Yuyi*; 4 *Zubr*
  UCAC 12 *Payi* (Type-724)

LOGISTICS AND SUPPORT 145
  ABU 1 Type-744A
  AFS 3: 2 *Dayun* (Type-904); 1 *Danyao* I (Type-904A)
  AFSH 2 *Danyao* II (Type-904B)
  AG 7: 6 *Kanhai*; 1 *Kanwu*
  AGB 2 *Yanrao* (Type-272) with 1 hel landing platform
  AGE 7: 2 *Dahua* (Type-909) with 1 hel landing platform (weapons test platform); 1 *Kantan*; 2 *Shupang* (Type-636); 1 *Yanqian* (Type-904I); 1 *Yuting* I (naval rail gun test ship)
  AGI 15: 1 *Dadie*; 1 *Dongdiao* (Type-815) with 1 hel landing platform; 5 *Dongdiao* (Type-815A) with 1 hel landing platform; 8 FT-14
  AGM 4 *Yuan Wang* (Type-718) (space and missile tracking)
  AGOR 2 *Dahua*
  AGS 4 *Shupang* (Type-636A) with 1 hel landing platform
  AH 8: 5 *Ankang*; 1 *Anwei* (Type-920); 2 *Qiongsha* (hospital conversion)
  AOEH 1 *Fuyu* (Type-901) with 2 H/PJ-13 CIWS
  AOR 1 *Fuqing* (Type-905) with 1 hel landing platform
  AORH 9: 2 *Fuchi* (Type-903); 6 *Fuchi* mod (Type-903A); 1 *Fusu*
  AOT 22: 4 *Fubai*; 16 *Fujian* (Type-632); 2 *Fuxiao*
  AP 4: 2 *Daguan*; 2 *Darong*
  ARC 2 *Youlan*
  ARS 14: 1 *Dadao*; 1 *Dadong*; 1 *Dalang* II (Type-922III); 3 *Dalang* III (Type-922IIIA); 3 *Dasan*; 2 *Dazhou*; 3 *Hai Jiu* 101 with 1 hel landing platform
  ASR 6: 3 *Dalao* (Type-926); 3 *Dajiang* (Type-925) (capacity 2 Z-8)
  ATF 14: ε11 *Hujiu*; 3 *Tuqiang*
  AWT 8: 4 *Fujian*; 3 *Fushi*; 1 *Jinyou*
  AX 4:
    1 *Dashi* (Type-0891A) with 2 hel landing platforms
    1 *Daxin* with 2 FQF 1200 A/S mor, 2 Type-69 CIWS, 1 57mm gun, 1 hel landing platform
    1 *Qi Ji Guang* (Type-927) with 1 76mm gun, 1 hel landing platform
    1 *Yudao*
  ESD 1 *Donghaidao*
COASTAL DEFENCE • **AShM** 72 YJ-12/YJ-62 (3 regt)

Naval Aviation 26,000
FORCES BY ROLE
Naval aviation fighter/ground-attack units adopted brigade structure in 2017
BOMBER
  2 regt with H-6DU/G/J

FIGHTER/GROUND ATTACK
  1 bde with J-10A/S *Firebird*; Su-30MK2 *Flanker* G
  1 bde with J-11B/BS *Flanker* L
  1 bde with J-11B/BS *Flanker* L; JH-7A *Flounder*
  1 bde with J-8F *Finback*; JH-7A *Flounder*
  1 regt with J-15 *Flanker*
GROUND ATTACK
  1 bde with JH-7 *Flounder*
ASW/AEW
  3 regt with Y-8J; KJ-200; KJ-500; KQ-200
ELINT/ISR/AEW
  1 regt with Y-8JB/X; Y-9JZ
TRANSPORT
  1 regt with Y-7H; Y-8C; CRJ-200/700
TRAINING
  1 regt with CJ-6A
  1 regt with HY-7
  2 regt with JL-8
  1 regt with JL-9G
  1 regt with JL-9
  1 regt with JL-10
  1 regt with Z-9C
HELICOPTER
  1 regt with Ka-27PS; Ka-28; Ka-31
  1 regt with SH-5; AS365N; Z-9C/D; Z-8J/JH
  1 regt with Y-7G; Z-8; Z-8J; Z-8S; Z-9C/D
AIR DEFENCE
  2 SAM bde with HQ-9

EQUIPMENT BY TYPE
AIRCRAFT 385 combat capable
  BBR 31: 27 H-6G; 4 H-6J
  FTR 24 J-8F *Finback*
  FGA 139: 16 J-10A *Firebird*; 7 J-10S *Firebird*; 72 J-11B/BS *Flanker* L; 20 J-15 *Flanker*; 24 Su-30MK2 *Flanker* G
  ATK 120: 48 JH-7; 72 JH-7A *Flounder*
  ASW 8+: 3 SH-5; 5+ KQ-200
  ELINT 13: 4 Y-8JB *High New* 2; 3 Y-8X; 6 Y-9JZ
  AEW&C 16: 6 KJ-200 *Moth*; 6 KJ-500; 4 Y-8J *Mask*
  TKR 5 H-6DU
  TPT 38: **Medium** 6 Y-8C; **Light** 28: 20 Y-5; 2 Y-7G; 6 Y-7H; **PAX** 4: 2 CRJ-200; 2 CRJ-700
  TRG 118: 38 CJ-6; 12 HY-7; 16 JL-8*; 28 JL-9*; 12 JL-9G*; 12 JL-10*
HELICOPTERS
  ASW 28: 14 Ka-28 *Helix* A; 14 Z-9C
  AEW 10+: 9 Ka-31; 1+ Z-18 AEW
  MRH 18: 7 AS365N; 11 Z-9D
  SAR 11: 3 Ka-27PS; 4 Z-8JH; 2 Z-8S; 2 Z-9S
  TPT 38: **Heavy** 30: 8 SA321 *Super Frelon*; 9 Z-8; 13 Z-8J; **Medium** 8 Mi-8 *Hip*
UNMANNED AERIAL VEHICLES
  ISR Heavy BZK-005; **Medium** BZK-007
AIR DEFENCE
  SAM • **Long-range** 32 HQ-9
AIR-LAUNCHED MISSILES
  AAM • **IR** PL-5; PL-8; PL-9; R-73 (AA-11 *Archer*); **IR/SARH** R-27 (AA-10 *Alamo*); **SARH** PL-11; **ARH** R-77 (AA-12A *Adder*); PL-12
  ASM KD-88
  AShM Kh-31A (AS-17B *Krypton*); YJ-12; YJ-61; YJ-8K; YJ-83K; YJ-9
  ARM Kh-31P (AS-17A *Krypton*); YJ-91

BOMBS
  Laser-guided: LS-500J
  TV-guided: KAB-500KR; KAB-1500KR

Marines ε25,000
FORCES BY ROLE
SPECIAL FORCES
  1 spec ops bde
MANOEUVRE
  Mechanised
    1 mne bde
  Light
    3 mne bde
  Amphibious
    2 mne bde
EQUIPMENT BY TYPE
ARMOURED FIGHTING VEHICLES
  MBT some ZTQ-15
  LT TK 73 ZTD-05
  ASLT 30 ZTL-11
  IFV 60 ZBL-08
  AAV 152 ZBD-05
ANTI-TANK/ANTI-INFRASTRUCTURE
  MSL • MANPATS HJ-73; HJ-8
  RCL 120mm Type-98
ARTILLERY 40+
  SP 122mm 40+: 20+ PLZ-07; 20+ PLZ-89
  MRL 107mm PH-63
  MOR 82mm
AIR DEFENCE • SAM • Point-defence HN-5

Air Force 395,000
FORCES BY ROLE
Fighter/ground-attack units adopted bde structure in 2017
BOMBER
  1 regt with H-6M
  2 regt with H-6H
  5 regt with H-6K
FIGHTER
  5 bde with J-7 *Fishcan*
  5 bde with J-7E *Fishcan*
  3 bde with J-7G *Fishcan*
  4 bde with J-8F/H *Finback*
  2 bde with J-11A/Su-27SK/Su-27UBK *Flanker*
  4 bde with J-11A/J-11B/Su-27UBK *Flanker*
  3 bde with J-11B/BS *Flanker* L
FIGHTER/GROUND ATTACK
  8 bde with J-10A/J-10S *Firebird*
  2 bde with J-10B/S *Firebird*
  1 bde with J-10B/C/S *Firebird*
  2 bde with J-10C/S *Firebird*
  1 bde with Su-35 *Flanker*; Su-30MKK *Flanker*
  3 bde with J-16 *Flanker*
  3 bde with Su-30MKK *Flanker*
GROUND ATTACK
  6 bde with JH-7A *Flounder*
ELECTRONIC WARFARE
  2 regt with Y-8CB/G/XZ
ISR
  1 regt with JZ-8F *Finback**
  1 bde with JZ-8F *Finback**
  1 regt with Y-8H1
AIRBORNE EARLY WARNING & CONTROL
  1 regt with KJ-200 *Moth*; KJ-500; KJ-2000; Y-8T
COMBAT SEARCH & RESCUE
  4 bde with Y-5; Mi-171E; Z-8
  1 regt with Y-5; Mi-171E; Z-8
TANKER
  1 bde with H-6U
TRANSPORT
  1 (VIP) regt with B-737; CRJ-200/700
  1 (VIP) regt with B-737; Tu-154M; Tu-154M/D
  1 regt with Il-76MD/TD *Candid*
  1 regt with Il-76MD *Candid*; Il-78 *Midas*
  1 regt with Mi-17V-5; Y-7
  1 regt with Y-5/Y-7/Z-9
  1 regt with Y-5/Y-7
  3 regt with Y-7
  1 regt with Y-8
  1 regt with Y-8; Y-9
TRAINING
  5 bde with CJ-6/6A/6B; Y-5
  8 bde with J-7; JJ-7A
  13 bde with JL-8; JL-9
TRANSPORT HELICOPTER
  1 regt with AS332 *Super Puma*; H225 (VIP)
ISR UAV
  2 bde with GJ-1
AIR DEFENCE
  1 SAM div
  21 SAM bde
EQUIPMENT BY TYPE
AIRCRAFT 2,413 combat capable
  BBR 172: ε12 H-6 (trg role); ε60 H-6H/M; ε100 H-6K
  FTR 759: 200 J-7 *Fishcan*; 192 J-7E *Fishcan*; 120 J-7G *Fishcan*; 50 J-8F *Finback*; 50 J-8H *Finback*; 95 J-11; 20 Su-27SK *Flanker*; 32 Su-27UBK *Flanker*
  FGA 702+: 78 J-10 *Firebird*; 142 J-10A *Firebird*; 55+ J-10B *Firebird*; 80+ J-10C *Firebird*; 48 J-10S *Firebird*; 130 J-11B/BS *Flanker* L; 60+ J-16 *Flanker*; 12+ J-20A (in test); 73 Su-30MKK *Flanker*; 24 Su-35 *Flanker*
  ATK 140 JH-7A *Flounder*
  EW 14: 4 Y-8CB *High New* 1; 6 Y-8G *High New* 3; 2 Y-8XZ *High New* 7; 2 Y-9XZ
  ELINT 4 Tu-154M/D *Careless*
  ISR 51: 24 JZ-6 *Finback**; 24 JZ-8F *Finback**; 3 Y-8H1
  AEW&C 13: 4 KJ-200 *Moth*; 5 KJ-500; 4 KJ-2000
  C2 5: 2 B-737; 3 Y-8T *High New* 4
  TKR 13: 10 H-6U; 3 Il-78 *Midas*
  TPT 335+ **Heavy** 27: 20 Il-76MD/TD *Candid*; 7 Y-20; **Medium** 42+: 30 Y-8C; 12+ Y-9; **Light** 239: 170 Y-5; 41 Y-7/Y-7H; 20 Y-11; 8 Y-12; **PAX** 27: 9 B-737 (VIP); 5 CRJ-200; 5 CRJ-700; 8 Tu-154M *Careless*
  TRG 1,004+: 400 CJ-6/-6A/-6B; 12+ HY-7; 50 JJ-7*; 150 JJ-7A*; 350 JL-8*; 30 JL-9*; 12+ JL-10*
HELICOPTERS
  MRH 22: 20 Z-9; 2 Mi-17V-5 *Hip* H
  TPT 31+: **Heavy** 18+ Z-8; **Medium** 13+: 6+ AS332 *Super Puma* (VIP); 3 H225 (VIP); 4+ Mi-171
UNMANNED AERIAL VEHICLES
  CISR • **Heavy** 12+ GJ-1; GJ-2
  ISR • **Heavy** 7+ EA-03

AIR DEFENCE
SAM 754+
  Long-range 356+: 180+ HQ-9/-9B; 32 S-300PMU (SA-10 *Grumble*); 64 S-300PMU1 (SA-20 *Gargoyle*); 64 S-300PMU2 (SA-20 *Gargoyle*); 16 S-400 (SA-21B *Growler*)
  Medium-range 320+: 120+ HQ-2/-2A/-2B; 150 HQ-12 (KS-1A); 50+ HQ-22
  Short-range 78+: 24+ HQ-6A; 24 HQ-6D; ε30 HQ-7
GUNS 16,000 **100mm/85mm**
AIR-LAUNCHED MISSILES
  AAM • **IR** PL-5B/C; PL-8; R-73 (AA-11 *Archer*); **IIR** PL-10; **IR/SARH** R-27 (AA-10 *Alamo*); **SARH** PL-11; **ARH** PL-12; PL-15 (entering service); R-77 (AA-12A *Adder*); R-77-1 (RVV-SD) (AA-12B *Adder*)
  ASM AKD-9; AKD-10; KD-88; Kh-29 (AS-14 *Kedge*); Kh-59M (AS-18 *Kazoo*)
  AShM Kh-31A (AS-17B *Krypton*)
  ARM Kh-31P (AS-17A *Krypton*); YJ-91 (Domestically produced Kh-31P variant)
  ALCM • **Conventional** CJ-20; YJ(KD)-63
BOMBS
  Laser-guided: LS-500J; LT-2
  TV-guided: KAB-500KR; KAB-1500KR

Airborne Corps
FORCES BY ROLE
SPECIAL FORCES
  1 spec ops bde
MANOEUVRE
  Air Manoeuvre
  6 AB bde
  Aviation
  1 hel regt
COMBAT SERVICE SUPPORT
  1 spt bde
TRANSPORT
  1 bde with Y-7; Y-8
EQUIPMENT BY TYPE
ARMOURED FIGHTING VEHICLES
  ABCV 180 ZBD-03
  APC • **APC (T)** 4 ZZZ-03 (CP)
ANTI-TANK/ANTI-INFRASTRUCTURE
  SP some HJ-9
ARTILLERY 162+
  TOWED 122mm ε54 PL-96 (D-30)
  MRL 107mm ε54 PH-63
  MOR 54+: **82mm** some; **100mm** 54
AIRCRAFT • **TPT** 20: **Medium** 6 Y-8; **Light** 14: 2 Y-7; 12 Y-12D
HELICOPTERS
  ATK 8 WZ-10K
  CSAR 8 Z-8KA
  MRH 12 Z-9WZ
AIR DEFENCE
  SAM • **Point-defence** QW-1
  GUNS • **TOWED 25mm** 54 PG-87

Strategic Support Force ε175,000
At the end of 2015, a new Strategic Support Force was established by drawing upon capabilities previously exercised by the PLA's 3rd and 4th departments and other central functions. It reports to the Central Military Commission and is believed to be responsible for the PLA's space and cyber capabilities

Theatre Commands
In early 2016, the previous seven military regions were consolidated into five new theatre commands

Eastern Theatre Command

Eastern Theatre Ground Forces
71st Group Army
(1 spec ops bde, 3 armd bde, 2 mech inf bde, 1 inf bde, 1 arty bde, 1 engr/NBC bde regt, 1 spt bde, 1 hel bde, 1 AD bde)
72nd Group Army
(1 spec ops bde, 1 armd bde, 1 mech inf bde, 2 inf bde, 2 amph bde, 1 arty bde, 1 engr/NBC bde, 1 spt bde, 1 hel bde, 1 AD bde)
73rd Group Army
(1 spec ops bde, 1 armd bde, 1 mech inf bde, 2 inf bde, 2 amph bde, 1 arty bde, 1 engr/NBC bde, 1 spt bde, 1 hel bde, 1 AD bde)

Eastern Theatre Navy
Coastal defence from south of Lianyungang to Dongshan (approx. 35°10′N to 23°30′N), and to seaward; HQ at Ningbo; support bases at Fujian, Zhoushan, Ningbo
17 **SSK**; 10 **DDGHM**; 18 **FFGHM**; 6 **FFG**; 19 **FSGM**; ε30 **PCFG/PCG**; ε22 **MCMV**; 2 **LPD**; ε22 **LST/M**

Eastern Theatre Navy Aviation
1st Naval Aviation Division
(1 bbr regt with H-6DU/G; 1 ASW regt with KQ-200; 1 hel regt with Ka-27PS; Ka-28; Ka-31)
Other Forces
(1 FGA bde with JH-7; 1 FGA bde with Su-30MK2; J-10A)

Eastern Theatre Air Force
10th Bomber Division
(1 bbr regt with H-6H; 1 bbr regt with H-6K; 1 bbr regt with H-6M)
26th Special Mission Division
(1 AEW&C regt with KJ-200/KJ-500/Y-8T; 1 AEW&C regt with KJ-2000/Y-8T)
Fuzhou Base
(1 ftr bde with J-7E; 1 ftr bde with J-11A/B; 1 FGA bde with J-16; 1 FGA bde with Su-30MKK; 2 SAM bde)
Shanghai Base
(1 ftr bde with J-7E; 1 ftr bde with J-8F; 1 ftr bde with J-11B; 1 FGA bde with J-10A; 1 FGA bde with J-16; 1 FGA bde with Su-30MKK; 2 atk bde with JH-7A; 1 trg bde with J-7/JJ-7A; 2 SAM bde)
Other Forces
(1 ISR bde with JZ-8F; 1 CSAR bde; 1 Flight Instructor Training Base with CJ-6; JL-8; JL-9; JL-10)

Other Forces
Marines
(2 mne bde)

Southern Theatre Command
Southern Theatre Ground Forces
74th Group Army
(1 spec ops bde, 1 armd bde, 1 mech inf bde, 2 inf bde, 2 amph bde, 1 arty bde, 1 engr/NBC bde, 1 spt bde, 1 hel bde, 1 AD bde)
75th Group Army
(1 spec ops bde, 4 armd bde, 1 mech inf bde, 1 inf bde, 1 air aslt bde, 1 arty bde, 1 engr/NBC bde, 1 spt bde, 1 AD bde)
Other Forces
(1 (composite) inf bde (Hong Kong); 1 hel sqn (Hong Kong), 1 AD bn (Hong Kong))

Southern Theatre Navy
Coastal defence from Dongshan (approx. 23°30′N) to VNM border, and to seaward (including Paracel and Spratly islands); HQ at Zhanjiang; support bases at Yulin, Guangzhou
4 **SSBN**; 2 **SSN**; 16 **SSK**; 10 **DDGHM**; 12 **FFGHM**; 2 **FFGM**; 7 **FFG**; 14 **FSGM**; ε38 **PCFG/PCG**; ε16 **MCMV**; 3 **LPD**; ε21 **LST/M**

Southern Theatre Navy Aviation
3rd Naval Aviation Division
(1 ASW/AEW&C regt with KJ-500; KQ-200; 1 bbr regt with H-6DU/G/J; 1 tpt/hel regt with Y-7G; Z-8; Z-8J; Z-8S; Z-9C/D)
Other Forces
(1 FGA bde with J-11B; 1 FGA bde with J-11B; JH-7A; 1 SAM bde)

Southern Theatre Air Force
8th Bomber Division
(2 bbr regt with H-6K)
20th Special Mission Division
(3 EW regt with Y-8CB/G/XZ)
Kunming Base
(1 FGA bde with J-10A; 1 FGA bde with J-10C; 1 trg bde with JJ-7A; 1 SAM bde)
Nanning Base
(2 FGA bde with J-10A; 1 FGA bde with J-10B/C; 1 FGA bde with Su-35; 1 FGA bde with J-7; 1 FGA bde with Su-30MKK; 1 atk bde with JH-7A; 2 trg bde with J-7/JJ-7A; 1 SAM bde)
Other Forces
(1 tkr bde with H-6U; 1 CSAR bde)

Other Forces
Marines
(2 mne bde)

Western Theatre Command
Western Theatre Ground Forces
76th Group Army
(1 spec ops bde, 4 armd bde, 2 inf bde, 1 arty bde, 1 engr/NBC bde, 1 spt bde, 1 hel bde, 1 AD bde)
77th Group Army
(1 spec ops bde, 1 armd bde, 2 mech inf bde; 3 inf bde, 1 arty bde, 1 engr/NBC bde, 1 spt bde, 1 hel bde, 1 AD bde)
Xinjiang Military District
(1 spec ops bde, 1 (high alt) mech div, 3 (high alt) mot div, 1 arty bde, 1 AD bde, 1 engr regt, 1 EW regt, 1 hel bde)
Xizang Military District
(1 spec ops bde; 1 (high alt) mech inf bde; 2 mtn inf bde; 1 arty bde, 1 AD bde, 1 engr bde, 1 EW regt, 1 hel bde)

Western Theatre Air Force
4th Transport Division
(1 tpt regt with Y-8/Y-9; 1 tpt regt with Y-7; 1 tpt regt with Mi-17V-5/Y-7/Y-20)
Lanzhou Base
(1 ftr bde with J-11AB; 1 ftr bde with J-7; 1 ftr bde with J-7E; 1 FGA bde with J-16; 1 SAM bde)
Urumqi Base
(1 ftr bde with J-8H; 1 ftr bde with J-11B; 1 atk bde with JH-7A; 2 SAM bde)
Lhasa Base
(1 SAM bde)
Xi'an Flying Academy
(1 trg bde with JJ-7A; 1 trg bde with JL-9; 2 trg bde with JL-8; 1 trg bde with Y-7; Y-8)
Other Forces
(1 surv regt with Y-8H1; 1 CSAR regt)

Northern Theatre Command
Northern Theatre Ground Forces
78th Group Army
(1 spec ops bde, 4 armd bde, 1 mech inf bde, 1 inf bde, 1 arty bde, 1 engr/NBC bde, 1 spt bde, 1 hel bde, 1 AD bde)
79th Group Army
(1 spec ops bde, 2 armd bde, 3 mech inf bde, 1 inf bde, 1 arty bde, 1 engr/NBC bde, 1 spt bde, 1 hel bde, 1 AD bde)
80th Group Army
(1 spec ops bde, 1 armd bde; 1 mech inf bde, 4 inf bde, 1 arty bde, 1 engr/NBC bde, 1 spt bde, 1 hel bde, 1 AD bde)

Northern Theatre Navy
Coastal defence from the DPRK border (Yalu River) to south of Lianyungang (approx 35°10′N), and to seaward; HQ at Qingdao; support bases at Lushun, Qingdao.
4 **SSN**; 15 **SSK**; 1 **CV**; 5 **DDGHM**; 2 **DDGM**; 10 **FFGHM**; 2 **FFGM**; 4 **FFG**; 8 **FSGM**; ε18 **PCFG/PCG**; ε12 **MCMV**; ε7 **LST/M**

Northern Theatre Navy Aviation
2nd Naval Air Division
(2 EW/ISR/AEW regt with Y-8J/JB/W/X; Y-9JZ; 1 MP/hel regt with SH-5; AS365N; Ka-28; SA321; Z-8J/JH; Z-9C/D)

Other Forces
(1 ftr regt with J-15; 1 FGA bde with JH-7A; J-8F; 1 tpt regt with Y-7H/Y-8C/CRJ-200/CRJ-700; 1 trg regt with CJ-6A; 2 trg regt with JL-8; 1 trg regt with HY-7; 1 trg regt with JL-9G; 1 trg regt with JL-9; 1 trg regt with JL-10)

Northern Theatre Air Force
16th Special Mission Division
(1 EW regt with Y-8/Y-8CB/Y-8G; 1 ISR regt with JZ-8F; 1 tpt regt with Y-5/Y-7)
Dalian Base
(2 ftr bde with J-7H; 1 ftr bde with J-8F; 2 ftr bde with J-11B; 2 FGA bde with J-7E; 1 FGA bde with J-10A; 1 FGA bde with J-10B; 1 atk bde with JH-7A; 1 trg bde with JJ-7A; 3 SAM bde)
Jinan Base
(1 atk bde with JH-7A; 1 FGA bde with J-10A; 1 ftr bde with J-8F/H; 1 ftr bde with J-7G; 2 SAM bde)
Harbin Flying Academy
(1 trg bde with CJ-6; Y-5; 1 trg bde with H-6; HY-7; 2 trg bde with JL-8; 1 trg bde with JL-9)
Other Forces
(1 CSAR bde)

Other Forces
Marines
(2 mne bde)

Central Theatre Command
Central Theatre Ground Forces
81st Group Army
(1 spec ops bde, 2 armd bde, 2 mech inf bde, 1 (OPFOR) mech inf bde, 1 inf bde, 1 arty bde, 1 engr/NBC bde, 1 spt bde, 1 avn bde, 1 AD bde)
82nd Group Army
(1 spec ops bde, 2 armd bde, 2 mech bde, 2 inf bde, 1 arty bde, 1 engr/NBC bde, 1 spt bde, 1 hel bde, 1 AD bde)
83rd Group Army
(1 spec ops bde, 1 armd bde, 5 mech inf bde, 1 air aslt bde, 1 arty bde, 1 engr/NBC bde, 1 spt bde, 1 AD bde)
Other Forces
(1 hy mech inf div, 2 (Beijing) gd div)

Central Theatre Air Force
13th Transport Division
(1 tpt regt with Y-8C; 1 tpt regt with Il-76MD/TD; 1 tpt regt with Il-76MD; Il-78)
34th VIP Transport Division
(1 tpt regt with B-737; CRJ200/700; 1 tpt regt with B-737; Tu-154M; Tu-154M/D; 1 tpt regt with Y-7; 1 hel regt with AS332; H225)
36th Bomber Division
(2 bbr regt with H-6K; 1 bbr regt with H-6H)
Datong Base
(1 ftr bde with J-7; 1 ftr bde with J-11A/B; 2 FGA bde with J-7E/G; 2 FGA bde with J-10A; 1 FGA bde with J-10C; 1 SAM div; 4 SAM bde)
Wuhan Base
(2 ftr bde with J-7; 1 ftr bde with Su-27SK/J-11A; 1 FGA bde with J-10B; 1 trg bde with J-7/JJ-7A; 2 SAM bde)

Shijiazhuang Flying Academy
(4 trg bde with JL-8)
Airborne Corps
(6 AB bde)
Other Forces
(1 CSAR bde)

Paramilitary 660,000+ active

People's Armed Police ε660,000
In 2018 the People's Armed Police (PAP) divested its border defence, firefighting, gold, forest, hydropower and security-guard units. In addition to the forces listed below, PAP also has 32 regional commands, each with one or more mobile units

FORCES BY ROLE
MANOEUVRE
Other
1 (1st Mobile) paramilitary corps (3 SF regt; 9 (mobile) paramilitary units; 1 engr/CBRN unit; 1 hel unit)
1 (2nd Mobile) paramilitary corps (2 SF unit; 9 (mobile) paramilitary units; 1 engr/CBRN unit; 1 hel unit)

China Coast Guard (CCG)
In 2018 the CCG was moved from the authority of the SOA to that of the People's Armed Police

EQUIPMENT BY TYPE
PATROL AND COASTAL COMBATANTS 422
  PSOH 41:
    2 *Zhaotou* with 1 76mm gun (capacity 2 med hel)
    6 *Zhaoduan* (Type-054 mod) with 1 76mm gun (capacity 1 med hel)
    3 *Jiangwei* I (Type-053H2G) (capacity 1 med hel) (ex-PLAN)
    4 *Shuoshi* II (capacity 1 med hel)
    2 *Shucha* I (capacity 1 med hel)
    10 *Shucha* II (capacity 1 med hel)
    12 *Zhaoyu* (capacity 1 med hel)
    1 *Zhoachang* (capacity 1 med hel)
    1 *Zhongyang* (capacity 1 med hel)
  PSO 45:
    9 *Zhaojun* (Type-718B) with 1 76mm gun, 1 hel landing platform
    1 *Dalang* I (Type-922) (ex-PLAN) 1 *Haixun* II with 1 hel landing platform
    1 *Hai Yang* (Type-625C) (ex-PLAN)
    1 *Jianghu* I (Type-053H) (ex-PLAN)
    1 *Kanjie* (Type-636A) with 1 hel landing platform (ex-PLAN)
    6 *Shusheng* with 1 hel landing platform
    3 *Shuwu*
    3 *Tuzhong* (ex-PLAN)
    1 *Wolei* (Type-918) (ex-PLAN)
    1 *Xiang Yang Hong* 9 (ex-PLAN)
    4 *Zhaolai* with 1 hel landing platform
    14 *Zhaotim*
  PCO 33: 4 *Zhaogao* (Type-056 mod) with 1 hel landing platform; 1 *Shuke* I; 4 *Shuke* II; 14 *Shuke* III; 3 *Shuyou*; 4 *Zhaodai*; 3 *Zhaoming*

PCC 103: 25+ Type-618B-II; 45 *Hailin* I/II; 1 *Shuzao* II; 14 *Shuzao* III; 9 *Zhongeng*; 2 *Zhongmei*; 7 *Zhongsui*
PB/PBF ε200
AMPHIBIOUS • LST 2 *Yuting* I (Type-072-II) (Ex-PLAN; used as hospital vessels and island supply)
LOGISTICS AND SUPPORT 28
AG 7: 5+ *Kaobo*; 2 *Shutu*
AGB 1 *Yanbing* (Type-071) (ex-PLAN)
AGOR 9: 4 *Haijian*; 3 *Shuguang* 04 (ex-PLAN); 2 *Xiang Yang Hong* 9
ATF 11
AIRCRAFT
MP 1+ MA60H
TPT • Light Y-12 (MP role)
HELICOPTERS
TPT • Light Z-9

Maritime Militia

Made up of full- and part-time personnel. Reports to PLA command and trains to assist PLAN and CCG in a variety of military roles. These include ISR, maritime law enforcement, island supply, troop transport and supporting sovereignty claims. The Maritime Militia operates a variety of civilian vessels including fishing boats and oil tankers.

Cyber

The PLA has devoted much attention to information warfare over the past decade, in terms of both battlefield electronic warfare (EW) and wider cyber-warfare capabilities. The main doctrine is the 'Integrated Network Electronic Warfare' (INEW) document, which guides PLA computer-network operations. PLA thinking appears to have moved beyond INEW, towards a new concept of 'information confrontation' (*xinxi duikang*), which aims to integrate both electronic and non-electronic aspects of information warfare within a single command authority. PLA thinking sees warfare under informationised conditions as characterised by opposing sides using complete systems of ground, naval, air, space and electromagnetic forces. Since 2008, major PLA military exercises have had cyber and information-operations components that have been both offensive and defensive in nature. The PLA reorganised in 2015 and established three new support branches including the Strategic Support Force (SSF). Although precise responsibilities remain unclear, the SSF reportedly has three sections: the first dealing with intelligence and military operations in cyberspace (defensive and offensive); the second responsible for military space operations (surveillance and satellite); and the third in charge of defensive and offensive EW and electronic intelligence. In March 2017, China released an International Strategy for Cooperation in Cyberspace, which stated that the PLA will play an 'important role' in cyberspace. The strategy also stated that the country would 'expedite the development of a cyber force and enhance capabilities in terms of situational awareness, cyber defense, supporting state activities and participating in international cooperation, to prevent major cyber crisis, safeguard cyber security and maintain national security and social stability'. In 2017, China also announced the establishment of a Central Commission for Integrated Military and Civilian Development, which seeks to integrate civilian technologies, including in the fields of information and communications technologies and artificial intelligence, into the PLA. China is investing heavily in quantum technology and announced in September 2017 that it would build the largest quantum-research facility in the world to support technology developments that can be used by the armed forces, including codebreaking capabilities and covert navigational capacities for submarines.

DEPLOYMENT

DEMOCRATIC REPUBLIC OF THE CONGO: UN • MONUSCO 223; 9 obs; 1 engr coy; 1 fd hospital

DJIBOUTI: 240; 1 mne coy(-); 1 med unit; 2 ZTL-11; 8 ZBL-08; 1 LPD; 1 ESD

GULF OF ADEN: 1 DDGHM; 1 FFGHM; 1 AORH

LEBANON: UN • UNIFIL 418; 2 engr coy; 1 med coy

MALI: UN • MINUSMA 403; 1 sy coy; 1 engr coy; 1 fd hospital

MIDDLE EAST: UN • UNTSO 5 obs

SOUTH SUDAN: UN • UNMISS 1,040; 5 obs; 1 inf bn; 1 engr coy; 1 fd hospital

SUDAN: UN • UNAMID 374; 1 engr coy

WESTERN SAHARA: UN • MINURSO 11 obs

Fiji FJI

Fijian Dollar F$		2017	2018	2019
GDP	F$	10.1bn	10.7bn	
	US$	4.89bn	5.22bn	
per capita	US$	5,528	5,877	
Growth	%	3.0	3.2	
Inflation	%	3.4	3.9	
Def bdgt	F$	105m	102m	
	US$	51.0m	49.7m	
US$1=F$		2.06	2.05	

Population 926,276

Ethnic groups: Fijian 51%; Indian 44%; European/other 5%

Age	0–14	15–19	20–24	25–29	30–64	65 plus
Male	14.0%	4.0%	4.2%	4.0%	21.5%	3.1%
Female	13.4%	3.8%	4.0%	3.8%	20.5%	3.7%

Capabilities

The Republic of Fiji Military Forces (RFMF) are an infantry-dominated defence force with a small naval element. The RFMF has intervened heavily in Fiji's domestic politics, and between a third coup in 2006 and 2014, democracy was effectively suspended. The RFMF is constructing a deployable force headquarters, which will administer all peacekeeping and HADR forces. International peacekeeping operations are an important revenue source for the government. Fiji's principal allies are Australia and New Zealand, with whom the RFMF regularly conducts training and maritime patrols. In 2016, the RFMF announced that it planned to recruit more women for peacekeeping missions, while in early 2018 the navy began recruiting its first-ever women sailors. The RFMF has recently instituted a Regimental Sergeant Major's course to improve the quality of senior NCOs and to raise standards across the rest of the force. Previously, personnel were sent overseas to receive this level of training. The 2017–18 Defence Budget identified a requirement to put the navy's patrol vessels through a life-extension programme. Fiji has no significant defence industry and is only able to carry out basic equipment maintenance domestically. Significant upgrade and maintenance work is usually conducted in Australia.

ACTIVE 3,500 (Army 3,200 Navy 300)

RESERVE ε6,000
(to age 45)

ORGANISATIONS BY SERVICE

Army 3,200 (incl 300 recalled reserves)
FORCES BY ROLE
SPECIAL FORCES
　1 spec ops coy
MANOEUVRE
　Light
　3 inf bn
COMBAT SUPPORT
　1 arty bty
　1 engr bn
COMBAT SUPPORT
　1 log bn

Reserves 6,000
FORCES BY ROLE
MANOEUVRE
　Light
　3 inf bn
EQUIPMENT BY TYPE
ARMOURED FIGHTING VEHICLES
　AUV 10 *Bushmaster* IMV
ARTILLERY 16
　TOWED 85mm 4 25-pdr (ceremonial)
　MOR 81mm 12

Navy 300
EQUIPMENT BY TYPE
PATROL AND COASTAL COMBATANTS • PB 5: 3 *Kula* (AUS *Pacific*); 2 *Levuka*

DEPLOYMENT

EGYPT: MFO 170; elm 1 inf bn
IRAQ: UN • UNAMI 165; 2 sy unit
LEBANON: UN • UNIFIL 136; 1 inf coy
MIDDLE EAST: UN • UNTSO 2 obs
SOUTH SUDAN: UN • UNMISS 2
SYRIA/ISRAEL: UN • UNDOF 290; 1 inf bn(-); elm 1 log bn

India IND

Indian Rupee Rs		2017	2018	2019
GDP	Rs	168tr	188tr	
	US$	2.60tr	2.69tr	
per capita	US$	1,976	2,016	
Growth	%	6.7	7.3	
Inflation	%	3.6	4.7	
Def bdgt [a]	Rs	3.74tr	4.04tr	
	US$	58.0bn	57.9bn	
US$1=Rs		64.45	69.87	

[a] Includes defence civil estimates, which include military pensions

| Population | 1,296,834,042 |

Religious groups: Hindu 80%; Muslim 14%; Christian 2%; Sikh 2%

Age	0–14	15–19	20–24	25–29	30–64	65 plus
Male	14.3%	4.8%	4.7%	4.3%	20.8%	3.0%
Female	12.7%	4.2%	4.1%	3.9%	19.8%	3.4%

Capabilities

India continues its military modernisation, though progress in some areas remains slow. The armed forces are orientated against both China and Pakistan. Large numbers of paramilitary forces remain employed in the internal-security role, while the army has a major role in internal security in Jammu and Kashmir and in manning front-line positions along the disputed borders with Pakistan. An Indian Joint Armed Forces Doctrine was issued in 2017. Much is consistent with similar US and NATO doctrines. It also sets out joint doctrine for Indian nuclear command and control, and sees an 'emerging triad' of space, cyber and special-operations capabilities complementing conventional land, sea and air capabilities. A defence space agency, defence cyber agency and special-operations division are to be formed. Defence cooperation with the US continues to grow, with an increasing level of exercising and sales of US equipment. It is also showing great interest in Russian equipment including an order for the S-400 missile-defence system. Indian personnel participate in numerous bilateral and multilateral exercises, and the country is one of the top troop contributors to UN peacekeeping operations. However, the overall capability of the conventional forces is limited by inadequate logistics, maintenance and shortages of ammunition and spare parts. India continues to modernise its conventional military capabilities and its nuclear forces, particularly its delivery systems, but many equipment projects have experienced significant delays and cost overruns, particularly indigenous systems. The government's 'Make in India' policy aims to strengthen the defence-industrial base. Apart from nuclear weapons and missiles, its indigenous defence industry is often slower to field new capabilities than foreign suppliers.

ACTIVE 1,444,500 (Army 1,237,000 Navy 67,700 Air 127,200 Coast Guard 12,600) **Paramilitary 1,585,950**

RESERVE 1,155,000 (Army 960,000 Navy 55,000 Air 140,000) **Paramilitary 941,000**

Army first-line reserves (300,000) within 5 years of full-time service, further 500,000 have commitment to age 50

ORGANISATIONS BY SERVICE

Strategic Forces Command

Strategic Forces Command (SFC) is a tri-service command established in 2003. The commander-in-chief of SFC, a senior three-star military officer, manages and administers all strategic forces through separate army and air-force chains of command

FORCES BY ROLE
SURFACE-TO-SURFACE MISSILE
  1 SRBM gp with *Agni* I
  1 MRBM gp with *Agni* II
  1 IRBM gp (reported forming) with *Agni* III
  2 SRBM gp with SS-250 *Prithvi* II
EQUIPMENT BY TYPE
SURFACE-TO-SURFACE MISSILE LAUNCHERS 54
  ICBM • Nuclear *Agni* V (in test)
  IRBM • Nuclear *Agni* III (entering service); *Agni* IV (in test)
  MRBM • Nuclear ε12 *Agni* II
  SRBM • Nuclear 42: ε12 *Agni* I; ε30 SS-250 *Prithvi* II; some SS-350 *Dhanush* (naval testbed)
SUBMARINES • STRATEGIC • SSBN 1 *Arihant* with 4 1-cell VLS with K-15 *Sagarika* SLBM, 6 533mm TT
AIR-LAUNCHED MISSILES
  ALCM • Nuclear *Nirbhay* (likely nuclear capable; in development)
Some Indian Air Force assets (such as *Mirage* 2000H or Su-30MKI) may be tasked with a strategic role

Space

EQUIPMENT BY TYPE
SATELLITES 12
  NAVIGATION, POSITONING, TIMING: 7 IRNSS
  COMMUNICATIONS: 2 GSAT
  ISR 3: 1 *Cartosat* 2C; 2 RISAT

Army 1,237,000

6 Regional Comd HQ (Northern, Western, Central, Southern, Eastern, Southwestern), 1 Training Comd (ARTRAC)
FORCES BY ROLE
COMMAND
  4 (strike) corps HQ
  10 (holding) corps HQ
SPECIAL FORCES
  8 SF bn
MANOEUVRE
  Armoured
  3 armd div (2–3 armd bde, 1 arty bde (2 arty regt))
  8 indep armd bde
  Mechanised
  6 (RAPID) mech inf div (1 armd bde, 2 mech inf bde, 1 arty bde)
  2 indep mech bde
  Light
  15 inf div (2–5 inf bde, 1 arty bde)
  1 inf div (forming)
  7 indep inf bde
  12 mtn div (3-4 mtn inf bde, 3–4 arty regt)
  2 indep mtn bde
  Air Manoeuvre
  1 para bde
SURFACE-TO-SURFACE MISSILE
  1 SRBM gp with *Agni* I
  1 MRBM gp with *Agni* II
  1 IRBM gp (reported forming) with *Agni* III
  2 SRBM gp with SS-250 *Prithvi* II
  3 GLCM regt with PJ-10 *Brahmos*
COMBAT SUPPORT
  3 arty div (2 arty bde, 1 MRL bde)
  2 indep arty bde
  4 engr bde
HELICOPTER
  14 hel sqn
AIR DEFENCE
  8 AD bde

Reserve Organisations

Reserves 300,000 reservists (first-line reserve within 5 years full-time service); **500,000 reservists** (commitment until age 50) (total 800,000)

Territorial Army 160,000 reservists (only 40,000 regular establishment)
FORCES BY ROLE
MANOEUVRE
  Light
  42 inf bn
COMBAT SUPPORT
  6 (Railway) engr regt
  2 engr regt
  1 sigs regt
COMBAT SERVICE SUPPORT
  6 ecological bn
EQUIPMENT BY TYPE
ARMOURED FIGHTING VEHICLES
  MBT 3,565+: 122 *Arjun*; 2,418 T-72M1; 1,025+ T-90S (ε1,100 various models in store)
  RECCE *Ferret* (used for internal-security duties along with some indigenously built armd cars)
  IFV 3,100: 700 BMP-1; 2,400 BMP-2 *Sarath* (incl some BMP-2K CP)
  APC 336+
    APC (W) 157+ OT-64
    PPV 179: 165 *Casspir*; 14+ *Yukthirath* MPV
ENGINEERING & MAINTENANCE VEHICLES
  AEV BMP-2; FV180
  ARV 730+: T-54/T-55; 156 VT-72B; 222 WZT-2; 352 WZT-3
  VLB AM-50; BLG-60; BLG T-72; *Kartik*; MTU-20; MT-55; *Sarvatra*
  MW 24 910 MCV-2
ANTI-TANK/ANTI-INFRASTRUCTURE
  MSL
    SP 110 9P148 *Konkurs* (AT-5 *Spandrel*)
    MANPATS 9K113 *Konkurs* (AT-5 *Spandrel*); *Milan* 2
  RCL 3,000+: **84mm** *Carl Gustav*; **106mm** 3,000+ M40A1 (10 per inf bn)

ARTILLERY 9,719+
  SP 155mm 10 K9 *Varja*
  TOWED 2,975+: **105mm** 1,350+: 600+ IFG Mk1/Mk2/Mk3 (being replaced); up to 700 LFG; 50 M-56; **122mm** 520 D-30; **130mm** ε600 M-46 (500 in store) **155mm** 505: ε300 FH-77B; ε200 M-46 (mod); 5 M777A2
  MRL 214: **122mm** ε150 BM-21/LRAR **214mm** 36 *Pinaka* (non-operational) **300mm** 28 9A52 *Smerch*
  MOR 6,520+: **81mm** 5,000+ E1; **120mm** ε1,500 AM-50/E1; **SP 120mm** E1; **160mm** 20 M-58 Tampella
SURFACE-TO-SURFACE MISSILE LAUNCHERS
  IRBM • Nuclear some *Agni*-III (entering service)
  MRBM • Nuclear ε12 *Agni*-II
  SRBM • Nuclear 42: ε12 *Agni*-I; ε30 250 *Prithvi* II
  GLCM • Conventional 15 PJ-10 *Brahmos*
AMPHIBIOUS 2 LCVP
HELICOPTERS
  MRH 275+: 80 *Dhruv*; 12 *Lancer*; 3+ *Rudra*; 120 SA315B *Lama* (*Cheetah*); 60 SA316B *Alouette* III (*Chetak*)
UNMANNED AERIAL VEHICLES
  ISR • Medium 25: 13 *Nishant*; 12 *Searcher* Mk I/II
AIR DEFENCE
  SAM • Medium-range *Akash* • **Short-range** 180 2K12 *Kub* (SA-6 *Gainful*) • **Point-defence** 500+: 50+ 9K33 *Osa* (SA-8B *Gecko*); 200 9K31 *Strela*-1 (SA-9 *Gaskin*); 250 9K35 *Strela*-10 (SA-13 *Gopher*); 9K310 *Igla*-1 (SA-16 *Gimlet*); 9K38 *Igla* (SA-18 *Grouse*)
  GUNS 2,395+
    SP 155+: **23mm** 75 ZSU-23-4; ZU-23-2 (truck-mounted); **30mm** 20-80 2S6 *Tunguska*
    TOWED 2,240+: **20mm** Oerlikon (reported); **23mm** 320 ZU-23-2; **40mm** 1,920 L40/70

Navy 67,700 (incl 7,000 Naval Avn and 1,200 Marines)

Fleet HQ New Delhi. Commands located at Mumbai, Vishakhapatnam, Kochi & Port Blair

EQUIPMENT BY TYPE
SUBMARINES 16
  STRATEGIC • SSBN 1 *Arihant* with 4 1-cell VLS with K-15 *Sagarika* SLBM, 6 533mm TT
  TACTICAL 15
    SSN 1 *Chakra* (ex-RUS *Akula* II) with 4 single 533mm TT with 3M14E *Klub-S* (SS-N-30) LACM/3M54E *Klub-S* (SS-N-27 *Sizzler*) AShM, 4 single 650mm TT with T-65 HWT (RUS lease agreement; damaged in 2017, awaiting repair)
    SSK 14:
      4 *Shishumar* (GER T-209/1500) with 8 single 533mm TT with AEG SUT mod 1 HWT
      2 *Sindhughosh* (FSU *Kilo*) with 6 single 533mm TT with 53-65KE HWT/TEST-71ME HWT/SET-65E HWT
      7 *Sindhughosh* (FSU *Kilo*) with 6 single 533mm TT with 53-65KE HWT/TEST-71ME HWT/SET-65E HWT/3M54E *Klub* (SS-N-27 *Sizzler*) AShM
      1 *Kalvari* (FRA *Scorpène*) with 6 533mm TT with 5M39 *Exocet* Block 2 AShM/5UT HWT
PRINCIPAL SURFACE COMBATANTS 28
  AIRCRAFT CARRIERS 1
    CV 1 *Vikramaditya* (ex-FSU *Kiev* mod) with 3 octuple VLS with *Barak*-1 SAM, 4 AK630 CIWS (capacity: 12 MiG-29K/KUB *Fulcrum* FGA ac; 6 Ka-28 *Helix* A ASW hel/Ka-31 *Helix* B AEW hel)
  DESTROYERS 14
    DDGHM 9:
      3 *Delhi* with 4 quad lnchr with 3M24E *Uran*-E (SS-N-25 *Switchblade*) AShM, 2 single lnchr with 3K90 *Uragan* (SA-N-7 *Gadfly*) SAM, 4 octuple VLS with *Barak*-1 SAM, 5 single 533mm ASTT, 2 RBU 6000 A/S mor; 2 AK630 CIWS, 1 100mm gun (capacity either 2 *Dhruv* hel/*Sea King* Mk42A ASW hel)
      3 *Kolkata* with 2 octuple VLS with *Brahmos* AShM; 4 octuple VLS fitted for *Barak*-8 SAM; 2 twin 533mm TT with SET-65E HWT, 2 RBU 6000 *Smerch* 2 A/S mor, 4 AK630 CIWS, 1 76mm gun (capacity 2 *Dhruv*/*Sea King* Mk42B hel)
      3 *Shivalik* with 1 octuple VLS with 3M54E *Klub-N* (SS-N-27 *Sizzler*) AShM/*Brahmos* AShM, 4 octuple VLS with *Barak*-1 SAM, 1 single lnchr with 3K90 *Uragan* (SA-N-7 *Gadfly*) SAM, 2 triple 324mm ASTT, 2 RBU 6000 *Smerch* 2 A/S mor, 2 AK630 CIWS, 1 76mm gun (capacity 1 *Sea King* Mk42B ASW hel)
    DDGM 5:
      2 *Rajput* (FSU *Kashin*) with 2 twin lnchr with P-15M *Termit* (SS-N-2C *Styx*) AShM, 2 twin lnchr with M-1 *Volna* (SA-N-1 *Goa*) SAM, 5 single 533mm ASTT with *Varanustra* HWT, 2 RBU 6000 *Smerch* 2 A/S mor, 2 AK630 CIWS, 1 76mm gun (capacity Ka-28 *Helix* A hel)
      1 *Rajput* (FSU *Kashin*) with 2 twin lnchr with *Brahmos* AShM, 2 single lnchr with P-15M *Termit* (SS-N-2C *Styx*) AShM, 2 twin lnchr with M-1 *Volna* (SA-N-1 *Goa*) SAM, 5 single 533mm ASTT with SET-65E HWT, 2 RBU 6000 *Smerch* 2 A/S mor, 4 AK630 CIWS, 1 76mm gun (capacity 1 Ka-28 *Helix* A hel)
      2 *Rajput* (FSU *Kashin*) with 1 octuple VLS with *Brahmos* AShM, 2 twin lnchr with P-15M *Termit* (SS-N-2C *Styx*) AShM, 2 octuple VLS with *Barak* SAM. 1 twin lnchr with M-1 *Volna* (SA-N-1 *Goa*) SAM, 5 single 533mm ASTT with SET-65E HWT, 2 RBU 6000 *Smerch* 2 A/S mor, 4 AK630 CIWS, 1 76mm gun (capacity 1 Ka-28 *Helix* A hel)
  FRIGATES 13
    FFGHM 10:
      3 *Brahmaputra* with 4 quad lnchr with 3M24E *Uran*-E (SS-N-25 *Switchblade*) AShM, 3 octuple VLS with *Barak*-1 SAM, 2 triple 324mm ASTT with A244 LWT, 4 AK630 CIWS, 1 76mm gun (capacity 2 SA316B *Alouette* III (*Chetak*)/*Sea King* Mk42 ASW hel) (of which 1 non-operational)
      1 *Godavari* with 4 single lnchr with P-15M *Termit* (SS-N-2D *Styx*) AShM, 1 octuple VLS with *Barak*-1 SAM, 2 triple 324mm ASTT with A244 LWT, 4 AK630 CIWS, 1 76mm gun (capacity 2 SA316B *Alouette* III (*Chetak*)/*Sea King* Mk42 ASW hel)
      3 *Talwar* I with 1 octuple VLS with 3M54E *Klub-N* (SS-N-27 *Sizzler*) AShM, 1 single lnchr with 3K90 *Uragan* (SA-N-7 *Gadfly*) SAM, 2 twin 533mm ASTT with SET-65E HWT, 2 RBU 6000 *Smerch* 2

A/S mor, 2 *Kashtan* (CADS-N-1) CIWS, 1 100mm gun (capacity 1 *Dhruv*/Ka-28 *Helix* A ASW hel)

3 *Talwar* II with 1 octuple VLS with *Brahmos* AShM, 1 single lnchr with 3K90 *Uragan* (SA-N-7 *Gadfly*) SAM, 2 twin 533mm ASTT with SET-65E HWT, 2 RBU 6000 *Smerch* 2 A/S mor, 2 AK630 CIWS, 1 100mm gun (capacity 1 *Dhruv*/Ka-28 *Helix* A ASW hel)

FFH 3:

3 *Kamorta* with 2 twin 533mm TT, 2 RBU 6000 *Smerch* 2 A/S mor, 2 AK630 CIWS, 1 76mm gun (capacity 1 *Dhruv*/Ka-28 *Helix* A ASW hel)

PATROL AND COASTAL COMBATANTS 106

CORVETTES • FSGM 8:

4 *Khukri* with 2 twin lnchr with P-15M *Termit* (SS-N-2C *Styx*) AShM, 2 twin lnchr (manual aiming) with 9K32M *Strela*-2M (SA-N-5 *Grail*) SAM, 2 AK630 CIWS, 1 76mm gun, 1 hel landing platform (for *Dhruv*/SA316 *Alouette* III (*Chetak*))

4 *Kora* with 4 quad lnchr with 3M24E *Uran*-E (SS-N-25 *Switchblade*) AShM, 1 quad lnchr (manual aiming) with 9K32M *Strela*-2M (SA-N-5 *Grail*) SAM, 2 AK630 CIWS, 1 76mm gun, 1 hel landing platform (for *Dhruv*/SA316 *Alouette* III (*Chetak*))

PSOH 10: 4 *Saryu* with 2 AK630 CIWS, 1 76mm gun (capacity 1 *Dhruv*); 6 *Sukanya* with 4 RBU 2500 A/S mor (capacity 1 SA316 *Alouette* III (*Chetak*))

PCFGM 8

6 *Veer* (FSU *Tarantul*) with 4 single lnchr with P-15M *Termit* (SS-N-2D *Styx*) AShM, 2 quad lnchr (manual aiming) with 9K32M *Strela*-2M (SA-N-5 *Grail*), 2 AK630 CIWS, 1 76mm gun

2 *Prabal* (mod *Veer*) each with 4 quad lnchr with 3M24E *Uran*-E (SS-N-25 *Switchblade*) AShM, 1 quad lnchr (manual aiming) with 9K32M *Strela*-2M (SA-N-5 *Grail*) SAM, 2 AK630 CIWS, 1 76mm gun

PCMT 3 *Abhay* (FSU *Pauk* II) with 1 quad lnchr (manual aiming) with 9K32M *Strela*-2M (SA-N-5 *Grail*) SAM, 2 twin 533mm ASTT, 2 RBU 1200 A/S mor, 1 76mm gun

PCC 15: 4 *Bangaram*; 10 *Car Nicobar*; 1 *Trinkat* (SDB Mk5)

PCF 4 *Tarmugli* (*Car Nicobar* mod)

PBF 58: 9 Immediate Support Vessel (Rodman 78); 13 Immediate Support Vessel (Craftway); 15 Plascoa 1300 (SPB); 5 *Super Dvora*; 16 Solas Marine Interceptor (additional vessels in build)

MINE WARFARE • MINE COUNTERMEASURES 1

MSO 1 *Pondicherry* (FSU *Natya*) with 2 RBU 1200 A/S mor

AMPHIBIOUS

PRINCIPAL AMPHIBIOUS VESSELS 1

LPD 1 *Jalashwa* (ex-US *Austin*) with 1 *Phalanx* CIWS (capacity up to 6 med spt hel; either 9 LCM or 4 LCM and 2 LCAC; 4 LCVP; 930 troops)

LANDING SHIPS 8

LSM 3 *Kumbhir* (FSU *Polnocny* C) (capacity 5 MBT or 5 APC; 160 troops)

LST 5:

2 *Magar* (capacity 15 MBT or 8 APC or 10 trucks; 500 troops)

3 *Magar* mod (capacity 11 MBT or 8 APC or 10 trucks; 500 troops)

LANDING CRAFT 12

LCM 4 LCM 8 (for use in *Jalashwa*)

LCT 8: 4 LCU Mk-IV (capacity 1 *Arjun* MBT/2 T-90 MBT/4 IFV/160 troops); 4 LCU Mk-3 (capacity 2 APC; 120 troops)

LOGISTICS AND SUPPORT 40

AFD 2: 1 FDN-1; 1 FDN-2

AGOR 1 *Sagardhwani* with 1 hel landing platform

AGHS 8: 1 *Makar*; 7 *Sandhayak*

AO 2 GSL 1,000T Fuel Barge

AOL 10: 1 *Ambika*; 2 *Poshak* II; 7 *Purak*

AOR 1 *Jyoti* with 1 hel landing platform

AORH 3: 1 *Aditya* (based on *Deepak* (1967) Bremer Vulkan design); 2 *Deepak* with 4 AK630 CIWS

AP 3 *Nicobar* with 1 hel landing platform

ASR 1

ATF 1

AWT 3 *Ambuda* II

AX 1 *Tir*

AXS 4: 2 *Mhadei*; 2 *Tarangini*

Naval Aviation 7,000

FORCES BY ROLE

FIGHTER/GROUND ATTACK

2 sqn with MiG-29K/KUB *Fulcrum*

ANTI-SUBMARINE WARFARE

1 sqn with Ka-28 *Helix* A

1 sqn with *Sea King* Mk42B

MARITIME PATROL

2 sqn with BN-2 *Islander*; Do-228-101; Il-38SD *May*

1 sqn with P-8I *Neptune*

AIRBORNE EARLY WARNING & CONTROL

1 sqn with Ka-31 *Helix* B

SEARCH & RESCUE

1 sqn with SA316B *Alouette* III (*Chetak*); *Sea King* Mk42C

1 sqn with *Dhruv*

TRANSPORT

1 sqn with HS-748M (HAL-748M)

TRAINING

1 sqn with Do-228

1 sqn with HJT-16 *Kiran* MkI/II, *Hawk* Mk132

1 hel sqn with *Sea King* Mk42B

TRANSPORT HELICOPTER

1 sqn with UH-3H *Sea King*

ISR UAV

1 sqn with *Heron*; *Searcher* MkII

EQUIPMENT BY TYPE

AIRCRAFT 75 combat capable

FTR 45 MiG-29K/KUB *Fulcrum*

ASW 13: 5 Il-38SD *May*; 8 P-8I *Neptune*

MP 13 Do-228-101

TPT 37:

Light 27: 17 BN-2 *Islander*; 10 Do-228

PAX 10 HS-748M (HAL-748M)

TRG 29: 6 HJT-16 *Kiran* MkI; 6 HJT-16 *Kiran* MkII; 17 *Hawk* Mk132*

HELICOPTERS

ASW 30: 12 Ka-28 *Helix* A; 18 *Sea King* Mk42B

MRH 58: 10 *Dhruv*; 25 SA316B *Alouette* III (*Chetak*); 23 SA319 *Alouette* III
AEW 11 Ka-31 *Helix* B
TPT • Medium 11: 5 *Sea King* Mk42C; up to 6 UH-3H *Sea King*

UNMANNED AERIAL VEHICLES
ISR 10: **Heavy** 4 *Heron;* **Medium** 6 *Searcher* Mk II
AIR-LAUNCHED MISSILES
AAM • IR R-550 *Magic/Magic 2*; R-73 (AA-11 *Archer*) **IR/SARH** R-27 (AA-10 *Alamo*); **ARH**: R-77 (AA-12A *Adder*)
AShM AGM-84 *Harpoon* (on P-8I ac); Kh-35 (AS-20 *Kayak*; on *May* ac); *Sea Eagle* (service status unclear)

Marines ε1,200 (Additional 1,000 for SPB duties)

After the Mumbai attacks, the Sagar Prahari Bal (SPB), with 80 PBF, was established to protect critical maritime infrastructure

FORCES BY ROLE
SPECIAL FORCES
1 (marine) cdo force
MANOEUVRE
Amphibious
1 amph bde

Air Force 127,200

5 regional air comds: Western (New Delhi), Southwestern (Gandhinagar), Eastern (Shillong), Central (Allahabad), Southern (Trivandrum). 2 support comds: Maintenance (Nagpur) and Training (Bangalore)

FORCES BY ROLE
FIGHTER
3 sqn with MiG-29 *Fulcrum*; MiG-29UB *Fulcrum*
FIGHTER/GROUND ATTACK
4 sqn with *Jaguar* IB/IS
6 sqn with MiG-21 *Bison*
3 sqn with MiG-27ML/MiG-23UB *Flogger*
3 sqn with *Mirage* 2000E/ED/I/IT (2000H/TH – secondary ECM role)
11 sqn with Su-30MKI *Flanker*
ANTI SURFACE WARFARE
1 sqn with *Jaguar* IM
ISR
1 unit with Gulfstream IV SRA-4
AIRBORNE EARLY WARNING & CONTROL
1 sqn with Il-76TD *Phalcon*
TANKER
1 sqn with Il-78 *Midas*
TRANSPORT
1 sqn with C-130J-30 *Hercules*
1 sqn with C-17A *Globemaster* III
5 sqn with An-32/An-32RE *Cline*
1 (comms) sqn with B-737; B-737BBJ; EMB-135BJ
4 sqn with Do-228; HS-748
1 sqn with Il-76MD *Candid*
1 flt with HS-748
TRAINING
1 OCU sqn with Su-30MKI *Flanker*
1 sqn (forming) with *Tejas*

Some units with An-32; Do-228; *Hawk* Mk 132*; HJT-16 *Kiran* MkI/II; *Jaguar* IS/IM; MiG-21bis; MiG-21FL; MiG-21M/MF; MiG-27ML; PC-7 *Turbo Trainer* MkII; SA316B *Alouette* III (*Chetak*)
ATTACK HELICOPTER
2 sqn with Mi-25 *Hind*; Mi-35 *Hind*
TRANSPORT HELICOPTER
5 sqn with *Dhruv*
7 sqn with Mi-17/Mi-17-1V *Hip* H
12 sqn with Mi-17V-5 *Hip* H
2 sqn with SA316B *Alouette* III (*Chetak*)
1 flt with Mi-26 *Halo*
2 flt with SA315B *Lama* (*Cheetah*)
2 flt with SA316B *Alouette* III (*Chetak*)
ISR UAV
5 sqn with *Heron; Searcher* MkII
AIR DEFENCE
25 sqn with S-125 *Pechora* (SA-3B *Goa*)
6 sqn with 9K33 *Osa-AK* (SA-8B *Gecko*)
2 sqn with *Akash*
10 flt with 9K38 *Igla-1* (SA-18 *Grouse*)

EQUIPMENT BY TYPE
AIRCRAFT 814 combat capable
FTR 62: 55 MiG-29 *Fulcrum* (incl 12+ MiG-29UPG); 7 MiG-29UB *Fulcrum*
FGA 534: 114 MiG-21 *Bison*; 39 MiG-21U/UM *Mongol*; 60 MiG-27ML *Flogger*; 20 MiG-23UB *Flogger*; 40 *Mirage* 2000E/I (2000H); 10 *Mirage* 2000ED/IT (2000TH); 242 Su-30MKI *Flanker*; 9 *Tejas*
ATK 115: 28 *Jaguar* IB; 79 *Jaguar* IS; 8 *Jaguar* IM
ISR 3 Gulfstream IV SRA-4
AEW&C 4: 1 EMB-145AEW *Netra* (2 more in test); 3 Il-76TD *Phalcon*
TKR 6 Il-78 *Midas*
TPT 242: **Heavy** 27: 10 C-17A *Globemaster* III; 17 Il-76MD *Candid*; **Medium** 10 C-130J-30 *Hercules*; **Light** 141: 57 An-32; 45 An-32RE *Cline*; 35 Do-228; 4 EMB-135BJ; **PAX** 64: 1 B-707; 4 B-737; 3 B-737BBJ; 56 HS-748
TRG 311: 103 *Hawk* Mk132*; 91 HJT-16 *Kiran* MkI/IA; 42 HJT-16 *Kiran* MkII; 75 PC-7 *Turbo Trainer* MkII
HELICOPTERS
ATK 19 Mi-25/Mi-35 *Hind*
MRH 390: 60 *Dhruv*; 35 Mi-17 *Hip* H; 45 Mi-17-1V *Hip* H; 149 Mi-17V-5 *Hip* H; 59 SA315B *Lama* (*Cheetah*); 39 SA316B *Alouette* III (*Chetak*); 3+ *Rudra*
TPT • Heavy 1+ Mi-26 *Halo*
UNMANNED AERIAL VEHICLES
ISR • Heavy 9 *Heron*; **Medium** some *Searcher* MkII
AIR DEFENCE • SAM
Medium-range *Akash*
Short-range S-125 *Pechora* (SA-3B *Goa*)
Point-defence 9K33 *Osa-AK* (SA-8B *Gecko*); 9K38 *Igla* (SA-18 *Grouse*)
AIR-LAUNCHED MISSILES
AAM • IR R-60 (AA-8 *Aphid*); R-73 (AA-11 *Archer*) R-550 *Magic*; **IIR** *Mica* IR; **IR/SARH** R-27 (AA-10 *Alamo*); **SARH** Super 530D **ARH** R-77 (AA-12A *Adder*); *Mica* RF
AShM AGM-84 *Harpoon*; AM39 *Exocet*; Kh-31A (AS-17B *Krypton*); *Sea Eagle*†

ASM Kh-29 (AS-14 *Kedge*); Kh-59 (AS-13 *Kingbolt*); Kh-59M (AS-18 *Kazoo*); AS-30; Kh-23 (AS-7 *Kerry*)‡; *Popeye* II (*Crystal Maze*)
ARM Kh-25MP (AS-12 *Kegler*); Kh-31P (AS-17A *Krypton*)
ALCM • Nuclear *Nirbhay* (likely nuclear capable; in development)
BOMBS • Laser-guided *Paveway* II

Coast Guard 12,600

EQUIPMENT BY TYPE
PATROL AND COASTAL COMBATANTS 115
  PSOH 16: 2 *Sankalp* (capacity 1 *Chetak/Dhruv* hel); 4 *Samar* with 1 76mm gun (capacity 1 *Chetak/Dhruv* hel); 6 *Samarth*; 1 *Vikram* (capacity 1 *Dhruv* hel); 3 *Vishwast* (capacity 1 *Dhruv* hel)
  PSO 3 *Samudra Prahari* with 1 hel landing platform
  PCO 1 *Vikram* with 1 hel landing platform
  PCC 40: 20 *Aadesh*; 8 *Rajshree*; 5 *Rani Abbakka*; 7 *Sarojini Naidu*
  PBF 55: 6 C-154; 2 C-141; 11 C-143; 39 C-401
  PB 1 *Priyadarshini*
AMPHIBIOUS
  UCAC 18: 6 H-181 (*Griffon* 8000TD); 12 H-187 (*Griffon* 8000TD)
AIRCRAFT • TPT • Light 23 Do-228
HELICOPTERS • MRH 21: 4 *Dhruv*; 17 SA316B *Alouette* III (*Chetak*)

Paramilitary 1,585,950

Rashtriya Rifles 65,000
Ministry of Defence. 15 sector HQ
FORCES BY ROLE
MANOEUVRE
  Other
  65 paramilitary bn

Assam Rifles 63,750
Ministry of Home Affairs. Security within northeastern states, mainly army-officered; better trained than BSF
FORCES BY ROLE
Equipped to roughly same standard as an army inf bn
COMMAND
  7 HQ
MANOEUVRE
  Other
  46 paramilitary bn
EQUIPMENT BY TYPE
ARTILLERY • MOR 81mm 252

Border Security Force 257,350
Ministry of Home Affairs
FORCES BY ROLE
MANOEUVRE
  Other
  186 paramilitary bn
EQUIPMENT BY TYPE
Small arms, lt arty, some anti-tank weapons
ARTILLERY • MOR 81mm 942+
AIRCRAFT • TPT some (air spt)
HELICOPTERS • MRH 2 Mi-17V-5 *Hip*

Central Industrial Security Force 144,400 (lightly armed security guards)
Ministry of Home Affairs. Guards public-sector locations

Central Reserve Police Force 313,650
Ministry of Home Affairs. Internal-security duties, only lightly armed, deployable throughout the country
FORCES BY ROLE
MANOEUVRE
  Other
  236 paramilitary bn
  10 (rapid action force) paramilitary bn
  10 (CoBRA) paramilitary bn
  6 (Mahila) paramilitary bn (female)
  2 sy gp
COMBAT SUPPORT
  5 sigs bn

Defence Security Corps 31,000
Provides security at Defence Ministry sites

Indo-Tibetan Border Police 89,450
Ministry of Home Affairs. Tibetan border security SF/guerrilla-warfare and high-altitude-warfare specialists
FORCES BY ROLE
MANOEUVRE
  Other
  56 paramilitary bn

National Security Guards 12,000
Anti-terrorism contingency deployment force, comprising elements of the armed forces, CRPF and Border Security Force

Railway Protection Forces 70,000

Sashastra Seema Bal 76,350
Guards the borders with Nepal and Bhutan

Special Frontier Force 10,000
Mainly ethnic Tibetans

Special Protection Group 3,000
Protection of ministers and senior officials

State Armed Police 450,000
For duty primarily in home state only, but can be moved to other states. Some bn with GPMG and army-standard infantry weapons and equipment
FORCES BY ROLE
MANOEUVRE
  Other
  144 (India Reserve Police) paramilitary bn

Reserve Organisations

Civil Defence 500,000 reservists
Operate in 225 categorised towns in 32 states. Some units for NBC defence

Home Guard 441,000 reservists (547,000 authorised str)

In all states except Arunachal Pradesh and Kerala; men on reserve lists, no trg. Not armed in peacetime. Used for civil defence, rescue and firefighting provision in wartime; 6 bn (created to protect tea plantations in Assam)

Cyber

The Defence Information Assurance and Research Agency (DIARA) is mandated to deal with cyber-security-related issues for the armed forces. All services have their own cyber-security policies and CERT teams, and headquarters maintain information-security policies. The Indian Army raised the Army Cyber Security Establishment in 2005 and set up the Cyber Security Laboratory at the Military College of Telecommunication Engineering (under the Corps of Signals) in April 2010. The Department for Defence Production in 2018 produced a cyber-security framework so that defence organisations can work towards more common conceptions of their cyber posture, and their cyber-security requirements. The services have their own cyber groups, and further meetings took place in 2018 regarding the long-discussed proposal to establish a tri-service command for cyberspace.

DEPLOYMENT

AFGHANISTAN: 335 (Indo-Tibetan Border Police paramilitary: facilities protection)

DEMOCRATIC REPUBLIC OF THE CONGO: UN • MONUSCO 2,625; 22 obs; 3 inf bn; 1 fd hospital

LEBANON: UN • UNIFIL 900; 1 inf bn; 1 med coy

MIDDLE EAST: UN • UNTSO 2 obs

SOMALIA: UN • UNSOM 1 obs

SOUTH SUDAN: UN • UNMISS 2,351; 18 obs; 2 inf bn; 1 engr coy; 2 fd hospital

SUDAN: UN • UNISFA 2; 2 obs

SYRIA/ISRAEL: UN • UNDOF 194; 1 log bn(-)

WESTERN SAHARA: UN • MINURSO 3 obs

FOREIGN FORCES

Total numbers for UNMOGIP mission in India and Pakistan
Chile 2 obs
Croatia 9 obs
Italy 2 obs
Korea, Republic of 7 obs
Philippines 6 obs
Romania 2 obs
Sweden 5 obs
Switzerland 3 obs
Thailand 4 obs
Uruguay 3 obs

Indonesia IDN

Indonesian Rupiah Rp		2017	2018	2019
GDP	Rp	13589tr	14778tr	
	US$	1.02tr	1.01tr	
per capita	US$	3,876	3,789	
Growth	%	5.1	5.1	
Inflation	%	3.8	3.4	
Def bdgt	Rp	115tr	108tr	107tr
	US$	8.60bn	7.32bn	
FMA (US)	US$	14m	0m	
US$1=Rp		13382.56	14700.39	

Population	262,787,403

Ethnic groups: Jawa 40.2%; Sunda, Priangan 15.5%; Banjar, Melayu Banjar 4%; other or unspecified 40.5%

Age	0–14	15–19	20–24	25–29	30–64	65 plus
Male	12.5%	4.4%	4.2%	3,9%	21.8%	3.2%
Female	12.1%	4.2%	4.1%	3.8%	21.7%	4.1%

Capabilities

Indonesia's TNI is the largest armed force in Southeast Asia. It has traditionally been concerned primarily with internal security and counter-insurgency. All three services are based on regional commands. The army remains the dominant service and is deployed operationally in West Papua, central Sulawesi and elsewhere. A modernisation plan adopted in 2010 called for the establishment by 2024 of a 'Minimum Essential Force' including strengthened naval and air capabilities. The 2015 defence white paper outlined Indonesia's 'Global Maritime Fulcrum' policy and advocated building up maritime, satellite and UAV capabilities. In 2018, Indonesia expanded its forces in the eastern areas of the country and stood up a long-expected third naval fleet command and a third air-force command to organise existing units in that area. Indonesia also created a new army reserve division and a third marines group, both to be stationed in the east. An ASEAN member, Indonesia has no formal defence alliances but there are defence-cooperation agreements with other states. It also maintains good relations with China, which has supplied some military equipment. The armed forces have contributed to UN and other international peace-keeping operations. Indonesia regularly exercises with Australian and US armed forces and those of Southeast Asian states. Indonesia's inventory comprises equipment from diverse international sources, and the country uses technology-transfer agreements to develop its national defence industry. The 2015 white paper advocated the creation of a strong, independent defence industry, with emphasis on the maritime sector. Indonesia has a number of public and private defence companies that provide services and equipment across the domains.

ACTIVE 395,500 (Army 300,400 Navy 65,000 Air 30,100) **Paramilitary 280,000**

Conscription liability 24 months selective conscription authorised (not required by law)

RESERVE 400,000

Army cadre units; numerical str n.k., obligation to age 45 for officers

ORGANISATIONS BY SERVICE

Army ε300,400

Mil Area Commands (KODAM)
14 comd (I, II, III, IV, V, VI, VII, IX, XII, XVI, XVII, XVIII, Jaya & Iskandar Muda)

FORCES BY ROLE
MANOEUVRE
  Mechanised
    3 armd cav bn
    5 cav bn
  Light
    1 inf bde (1 cav bn, 3 inf bn)
    3 inf bde (2 cdo bn, 1 inf bn)
    1 inf bde (1 cdo bn, 2 inf bn)
    3 inf bde (3 inf bn)
    32 indep inf bn
    16 cdo bn
COMBAT SUPPORT
  12 fd arty bn
  7 cbt engr bn
COMBAT SERVICE SUPPORT
  4 construction bn
AVIATION
  1 composite avn sqn
HELICOPTER
  1 hel sqn with Bo-105; Bell 205A; Bell 412; AH-64E *Apache Guardian*
  1 hel sqn Mi-35P *Hind*; Mi-17V-5 *Hip* H
AIR DEFENCE
  1 AD regt (2 ADA bn, 1 SAM unit)
  6 ADA bn
  3 SAM unit

Special Forces Command (KOPASSUS)
FORCES BY ROLE
SPECIAL FORCES
  3 SF gp (total: 2 cdo/para unit, 1 CT unit, 1 int unit)

Strategic Reserve Command (KOSTRAD)
FORCES BY ROLE
COMMAND
  3 div HQ
MANOEUVRE
  Armoured
    2 armd bn
  Mechanised
    1 mech inf bde (3 mech inf bn)
  Light
    1 inf bde (3 cdo bn)
    1 inf bde (2 cdo bn)
    1 inf bde (2 inf bn)
  Air Manoeuvre
    3 AB bde (3 AB bn)
COMBAT SUPPORT
  2 fd arty regt (1 SP arty bn; 2 arty bn)
  1 arty bn 2 cbt engr bn
AIR DEFENCE
  2 AD bn

EQUIPMENT BY TYPE
ARMOURED FIGHTING VEHICLES
  MBT 79: 42 *Leopard* 2A4; 37 *Leopard* 2RI
  LT TK 350: 275 AMX-13 (partially upgraded); 15 PT-76; 60 *Scorpion* 90
  RECCE 142: 55 *Ferret* (13 upgraded); 69 *Saladin* (16 upgraded); 18 VBL
  IFV 64: 22 *Black Fox*; 42 *Marder* 1A3
  APC 634+
    APC (T) 267: 75 AMX-VCI; 34 BTR-50PK; 15 FV4333 *Stormer*; 143 M113A1-B
    APC (W) 367+: ε150 *Anoa*; some *Barracuda*; 40 BTR-40; 45 FV603 *Saracen* (14 upgraded); 100 LAV-150 *Commando*; 32 VAB-VTT
    PPV some *Casspir*
  AUV 39: 14 APR-1; 3 *Bushmaster*; 22 *Commando Ranger*;
ENGINEERING & MAINTENANCE VEHICLES
  AEV 4: 3 *Leopard* 2; 1 M113A1-B-GN
  ARV 15+: 2 AMX-13; 6 AMX-VCI; 3 BREM-2; 4 BPz-3 *Buffel*; *Stormer*; T-54/T-55
  VLB 16: 10 AMX-13; 4 *Leguan*; 2 *Stormer*
ANTI-TANK/ANTI-INFRASTRUCTURE
  MSL • MANPATS SS.11; *Milan*; 9K11 *Malyutka* (AT-3 *Sagger*)
  RCL 90mm M67; **106mm** M40A1
  RL 89mm LRAC
ARTILLERY 1,198+
  SP 74: **105mm** 20 AMX Mk61; **155mm** 54: 36 CAESAR; 18 M109A4
  TOWED 133+: **105mm** 110+: some KH-178; 60 M101; 50 M-56; **155mm** 23: 5 FH-88; 18 KH-179
  MRL 127mm 36 ASTROS II Mk6
  MOR 955: **81mm** 800; **120mm** 155: 75 Brandt; 80 UBM 52
AMPHIBIOUS • LCU 17: 1 ADRI XXXII; 4 ADRI XXXIII; 1 ADRI XXXIX; 1 ADRI XL; 3 ADRI XLI; 2 ADRI XLIV; 2 ADRI XLVI; 2 ADRI XLVIII; 1 ADRI L
AIRCRAFT • TPT • Light 9: 1 BN-2A *Islander*; 6 C-212 *Aviocar* (NC-212); 2 *Turbo Commander* 680
HELICOPTERS
  ATK 14: 6 Mi-35P *Hind*; 8 AH-64E *Apache Guardian*
  MRH 40: 6 H125M *Fennec*; 17 Bell 412 *Twin Huey* (NB-412); 17 Mi-17V-5 *Hip* H
  TPT • Light 29: 7 Bell 205A; 20 Bo-105 (NBo-105); 2 H120 *Colibri*
  TRG 12 Hughes 300C
AIR DEFENCE
  SAM • Point-defence 95+: 2 *Kobra* (with 125 GROM-2 msl); TD-2000B (*Giant Bow* II); 51 *Rapier*; 42 RBS-70; QW-3
  GUNS • TOWED 411: **20mm** 121 Rh 202; **23mm** *Giant Bow*; **40mm** 90 L/70; **57mm** 200 S-60
AIR-LAUNCHED MISSILES
  ASM AGM-114 *Hellfire*

Navy ε65,000 (including Marines and Aviation)
Three fleets: East (Sorong), Central (Surabaya) and West (Jakarta). Two Forward Operating Bases at Kupang (West Timor) and Tahuna (North Sulawesi)

EQUIPMENT BY TYPE
SUBMARINES • TACTICAL • SSK 4:
  2 *Cakra* (Type-209/1300) with 8 single 533mm TT with SUT HWT
  2 *Nagapasa* (Type-209/1400) with 8 single 533mm TT with *Black Shark* HWT
PRINCIPAL SURFACE COMBATANTS 13
  FRIGATES 13
    FFGHM 5:
      1 *Ahmad Yani* (ex-NLD *Van Speijk*) with 2 twin-cell VLS with 3M55E *Yakhont* (SS-N-26 *Strobile*) AShM; 2 SIMBAD twin lnchr (manual) with *Mistral* SAM, 2 triple 324mm ASTT with Mk46 LWT, 1 76mm gun (capacity 1 Bo-105 (NBo-105) hel)
      2 *Ahmad Yani* (ex-NLD *Van Speijk*) with 2 twin lnchr with C-802 (CH-SS-N-8 *Saccade*) AShM, 2 SIMBAD twin lnchr (manual) with *Mistral* SAM, 2 triple 324mm ASTT with Mk46 LWT, 1 76mm gun (capacity 1 Bo-105 (NBo-105) hel)
      2 *R.E. Martadinata* (SIGMA 10514) with 2 quad lnchr with MM40 *Exocet* Block 3 AShM, 2 6-cell VLS with VL-*MICA* SAM, 2 triple 324mm ASTT with A244/S LWT, 1 *Millennium* CIWS, 1 76mm gun (1 med hel)
    FFGM
      4 *Diponegoro* (SIGMA 9113) with 2 twin lnchr with MM40 *Exocet* Block 2 AShM, 2 quad *Tetral* lnchr with *Mistral* SAM, 2 triple 324mm ASTT with MU90 LWT, 1 76mm gun, 1 hel landing platform
    FFG
      1 *Hajar Dewantara* (trg role) with 2 twin lnchr with MM38 *Exocet* AShM, 2 single 533mm ASTT with SUT HWT, 1 57mm gun (capacity 1 Bo-105 (NBo-105) hel)
    FFHM 3:
      3 *Ahmad Yani* (ex-NLD *Van Speijk*) with 2 SIMBAD twin lnchr (manual) with *Mistral* SAM, 2 triple 324mm ASTT with Mk46 LWT, 1 76mm gun (capacity 1 Bo-105 (NBo-105) hel)
PATROL AND COASTAL COMBATANTS 116
  CORVETTES 20
    FSGM 3 *Bung Tomo* with 2 quad lnchr with MM40 *Exocet* Block 2 AShM, 1 18-cell VLS with *Sea Wolf* SAM, 2 triple 324mm ASTT, 1 76mm gun (capacity: 1 Bo-105 hel)
    FSGH 1 *Nala* with 2 twin lnchr with MM38 *Exocet* AShM, 1 twin 375mm A/S mor, 1 120mm gun (capacity 1 lt hel)
    FSG 2 *Fatahillah* with 2 twin lnchr with MM38 *Exocet* AShM, 2 triple B515 *ILAS*-3/Mk32 324mm ASTT with A244/Mk46 LWT, 1 twin 375mm A/S mor, 1 120mm gun
    FS 14 *Kapitan Pattimura* (GDR *Parchim* I) with 4 single 400mm ASTT, 2 RBU 6000 *Smerch* 2 A/S mor, 1 twin 57mm gun
    PCFG 3 *Mandau* with 4 single lnchr with MM38 *Exocet* AShM, 1 57mm gun
    PCG 5:
      3 *Sampari* (KCR-60M) with 2 twin lnchr for C-705 AShM
      2 *Todak* with 2 single lnchr with C-802 (CH-SS-N-8 *Saccade*), 1 57mm gun
    PCT 2 *Andau* with 2 single 533mm TT, 1 57mm gun
    PCC 11: 4 *Kakap* with 1 hel landing platform; 2 *Pandrong*; 3 *Pari* with 1 57mm gun; 2 *Todak* with 1 57mm gun
    PBG 8:
      2 *Clurit* with 2 single lnchr with C-705 AShM, 1 AK630 CIWS
      6 *Clurit* with 2 single lnchr with C-705 AShM
    PBF 4 Combat Boat AL D-18
    PB 63: 2 *Badau* (ex-BRN *Waspada*); 9 *Boa*; 1 *Cucut* (ex-SGP *Jupiter*); 4 *Kobra*; 1 *Krait*; 8 *Sibarau*; 22 *Sinabang* (KAL 28); 4 *Tarihu*; 7 *Tatihu* (PC-40); 5 *Viper*
MINE WARFARE • MINE COUNTERMEASURES 8
  MCO 2 *Pulau Rengat*
  MSC 6 *Pulau Rote* (ex-GDR *Wolgast*)
AMPHIBIOUS
  PRINCIPAL AMPHIBIOUS VESSELS • LPD 5:
    1 *Dr Soeharso* (ex-*Tanjung Dalpele*; capacity 2 LCU/LCVP; 13 tanks; 500 troops; 2 AS332L *Super Puma*) (used in AH role)
    4 *Makassar* (capacity 2 LCU or 4 LCVP; 13 tanks; 500 troops; 2 AS332L *Super Puma*)
  LANDING SHIPS • LST 19
    1 *Teluk Amboina* (capacity 16 tanks; 800 troops)
    1 *Teluk Bintuni* (capacity 10 MBT)
    10 *Teluk Gilimanuk* (ex-GDR *Frosch*)
    2 *Teluk Langsa* (capacity 16 tanks; 200 troops)
    5 *Teluk Semangka* (capacity 17 tanks; 200 troops)
  LANDING CRAFT 55
    LCM 20
    LCU 5
    LCVP 30
LOGISTICS AND SUPPORT 26
  AGF 1 *Multatuli* with 1 hel landing platform
  AGOR 2 *Rigel*
  AGOS 1 *Leuser*
  AGHS 1
  AGS 3 *Pulau Rote* (ex-GDR *Wolgast*)
  AKSL 4
  AORLH 1 *Arun* (ex-UK *Rover*) (damaged at sea 2018, in repair)
  AOR 1 *Tarakan* with 1 hel landing platform
  AOT 3: 2 *Khobi*; 1 *Sorong*
  AP 4: 1 *Tanjung Kambani* (troop transport) with 1 hel landing platform; 1 *Tanjung Nusanive* (troop transport); 2 *Karang Pilang* (troop transport)
  ATF 1
  AXS 3

Naval Aviation ε1,000
EQUIPMENT BY TYPE
AIRCRAFT
  MP 27: 3 C212-200; 4 CN235 MPA; 14 N-22B *Searchmaster* B; 6 N-22SL *Searchmaster* L
  TPT • Light 33: 1 Beech 350i *King Air* (VIP transport); 8 Beech G36 *Bonanza*; 2 Beech G38 *Baron*; 17 C-212-200 *Aviocar*; 3 TB-9 *Tampico*; 2 TB-10
HELICOPTERS
  ASW 4 AS565MBe *Panther*
  MRH 4 Bell 412 (NB-412) *Twin Huey*

CSAR 4 H225M *Caracal*
TPT 15: **Medium** 3 AS332L *Super Puma* (NAS322L);
Light 12: 3 H120 *Colibri*; 9 Bo-105 (NBo-105)

Marines ε20,000
FORCES BY ROLE
SPECIAL FORCES
1 SF bn
MANOEUVRE
Amphibious
2 mne gp (1 cav regt, 3 mne bn, 1 arty regt, 1 cbt spt regt, 1 CSS regt)
1 mne gp (forming)
1 mne bde (3 mne bn)
EQUIPMENT BY TYPE
ARMOURED FIGHTING VEHICLES
  LT TK 65: 10 AMX-10 PAC 90; 55 PT-76†
  RECCE 21 BRDM-2
  IFV 114: 24 AMX-10P; 22 BMP-2; 54 BMP-3F; 2 BTR-4; 12 BTR-80A
  APC 103: • **APC (T)** 100 BTR-50P; **APC (W)** 3 BTR-4M
  AAV 10 LVTP-7A1
ARTILLERY 71+
  TOWED 50: **105mm** 22 LG1 MK II; **122mm** 28 M-38
  MRL 122mm 21: 4 PHL-90B; 9 RM-70; 8 RM-70 *Vampir*
  MOR 81mm
AIR DEFENCE • **GUNS** • **40mm** 5 L/60/L/70; **57mm** S-60

Air Force 30,100
3 operational comd (East, Central and West) plus trg comd
FORCES BY ROLE
FIGHTER
  1 sqn with F-5E/F *Tiger* II
  1 sqn with F-16A/B/C/D *Fighting Falcon*
FIGHTER/GROUND ATTACK
  1 sqn with F-16C/D *Fighting Falcon*
  1 sqn with Su-27SK/SKM *Flanker*; Su-30MK/MK2 *Flanker*
  2 sqn with *Hawk* Mk109*/Mk209*
  1 sqn with T-50i *Golden Eagle**
GROUND ATTACK
  1 sqn with EMB-314 (A-29) *Super Tucano**
MARITIME PATROL
  1 sqn with B-737-200; CN235M-220 MPA
TANKER/TRANSPORT
  1 sqn with C-130B/KC-130B *Hercules*
TRANSPORT
  1 VIP sqn with B-737-200; C-130H/H-30 *Hercules*; L-100-30; F-27-400M *Troopship*; F-28-1000/3000; AS332L *Super Puma* (NAS332L); SA330SM *Puma* (NAS300SM)
  1 sqn with C-130H/H-30 *Hercules*; L-100-30
  1 sqn with C-212 *Aviocar* (NC-212)
  1 sqn with CN235M-110; C295M
TRAINING
  1 sqn with Grob 120TP
  1 sqn with KT-1B
  1 sqn with SF-260M; SF-260W *Warrior*
TRANSPORT HELICOPTER
  2 sqn with H225M; AS332L *Super Puma* (NAS332L); SA330J/L *Puma* (NAS330J/L); H120 *Colibri*

EQUIPMENT BY TYPE
Only 45% of ac op
AIRCRAFT 109 combat capable
  FTR 9: 7 F-16A *Fighting Falcon*; 2 F-16B *Fighting Falcon* (8 F-5E *Tiger* II; 4 F-5F *Tiger* II non-operational)
  FGA 40: 19 F-16C *Fighting Falcon*; 5 F-16D *Fighting Falcon*; 2 Su-27SK; 3 Su-27SKM; 2 Su-30MK; 9 Su-30MK2
  MP 6: 3 B-737-200; 3 CN235M-220 MPA
  TKR 1 KC-130B *Hercules*
  TPT 49: **Medium** 16: 4 C-130B *Hercules*; 4 C-130H *Hercules*; 6 C-130H-30 *Hercules*; 2 L-100-30; **Light** 24: 9 C295; 9 C-212 *Aviocar* (NC-212); 5 CN235-110; 1 F-27-400M *Troopship*; **PAX** 9: 1 B-737-200; 3 B-737-400; 1 B-737-500; 1 B-737-800BBJ; 1 F-28-1000; 2 F-28-3000
  TRG 121: 15 EMB-314 (A-29) *Super Tucano**; 30 Grob 120TP; 7 *Hawk* Mk109*; 23 *Hawk* Mk209*; 14 KT-1B; 10 SF-260M; 7 SF-260W *Warrior*; 15 T-50i *Golden Eagle**
HELICOPTERS
  TPT 36: **Heavy** 6 H225M (CSAR); **Medium** 18: 9 AS332 *Super Puma* (NAS332L) (VIP/CSAR); 1 SA330SM *Puma* (NAS330SM) (VIP); 4 SA330J *Puma* (NAS330J); 4 SA330L *Puma* (NAS330L); **Light** 12 H120 *Colibri*
AIR-LAUNCHED MISSILES
  AAM • **IR** AIM-9P *Sidewinder*; R-73 (AA-11 *Archer*); **IR/SARH** R-27 (AA-10 *Alamo*)
  ARH R-77 (AA-12A *Adder*)
  ASM AGM-65G *Maverick*
  ARM Kh-31P (AS-17A *Krypton*)

Special Forces (Paskhasau)
FORCES BY ROLE
SPECIAL FORCES
  3 (PASKHASAU) SF wg (total: 6 spec ops sqn)
  4 indep SF coy
EQUIPMENT BY TYPE
AIR DEFENCE
  SAM • **Point** QW-3
  GUNS • **TOWED 35mm** 6 Oerlikon *Skyshield*

Paramilitary 280,000+

Police ε280,000 (including 14,000 police 'mobile bde' (BRIMOB) org in 56 coy, incl CT unit (Gegana))
EQUIPMENT BY TYPE
ARMOURED FIGHTING VEHICLES
  APC (W) 34 *Tactica*
AIRCRAFT • **TPT** • **Light** 5: 2 Beech 18; 2 C-212 *Aviocar* (NC-212); 1 *Turbo Commander* 680
HELICOPTERS • **TPT** • **Light** 22: 3 Bell 206 *Jet Ranger*; 19 Bo-105 (NBo-105)

KPLP (Coast and Seaward Defence Command)
Responsible to Military Sea Communications Agency
EQUIPMENT BY TYPE
PATROL AND COASTAL COMBATANTS 31
  PCO 4: 2 *Arda Dedali*; 2 *Trisula*
  PB 27: 4 *Golok* (SAR); 5 *Kujang*; 3 *Rantos*; 15 (various)
LOGISTICS AND SUPPORT • **ABU** 1 *Jadayat*

Bakamla (Maritime Security Agency)
EQUIPMENT BY TYPE
PATROL AND COASTAL COMBATANTS 7
 PSO 1 *Tanjung Datu* with 1 hel landing platform
 PB 6 *Bintang Laut* (KCR-40 mod)

Reserve Organisations

Kamra People's Security ε40,000
Report for 3 weeks' basic training each year; part-time police auxiliary.

DEPLOYMENT

CENTRAL AFRICAN REPUBLIC: UN • MINUSCA 208; 4 obs; 1 engr coy

DEMOCRATIC REPUBLIC OF THE CONGO: UN • MONUSCO 180; 9 obs; 1 engr coy

LEBANON: UN • UNIFIL 1,295; 1 inf bn; 1 MP coy; 1 FSGHM

MALI: UN • MINUSMA 9; 1 obs

PHILIPPINES: IMT 9

SOUTH SUDAN: UN • UNMISS 2; 3 obs

SUDAN: UN • UNAMID 800; 4 obs; 1 inf bn
UN • UNISFA 2 obs

WESTERN SAHARA: UN • MINURSO 3 obs

Japan JPN

Japanese Yen ¥		2017	2018	2019
GDP	¥	547tr	557tr	
	US$	4.87tr	5.07tr	
per capita	US$	38,449	40,106	
Growth	%	1.7	1.1	
Inflation	%	0.5	1.2	
Def bdgt	¥	5.13tr	5.19tr	5.29tr
	US$	45.7bn	47.3bn	
US$1=¥		112.17	109.85	

Population 126,168,156

Ethnic groups: Korean <1%

Age	0–14	15–19	20–24	25–29	30–64	65 plus
Male	6.5%	2.5%	2.6%	2.4%	22.0%	12.4%
Female	6.2%	2.2%	2.3%	2.4%	22.4%	16.0%

Capabilities

Japan's concerns over its regional security environment have heightened, as evidenced in its 2018 defence white paper. These principally relate to an emerging security challenge from China and an established concern over North Korea. This has stimulated defence-budget increases and defence-policy and legislative reforms to enable Japan to play a more active international security role. While the offensive capacity of the Japan Self-Defense Force (JSDF) remains weak, the navy has strengths in anti-submarine warfare and air defence. In 2018, a Ground Component Command was created to oversee the Ground Self-Defense Force, previously organised into five regional commands. An Amphibious Rapid Deployment Brigade was also created, tasked mainly with the defence of remote islands. Japan's alliance with the US remains the cornerstone of its defence policy, reflected by the continued US basing, the widespread use of US equipment across all three services and regular training with US forces. The JSDF trains regularly, including in US-led international exercises. However, personnel recruitment and retention are an issue in the context of an ageing population. Due to their defensive mandate, JSDF deployments are mostly for peacekeeping purposes. The ongoing military-procurement drive has focused for the first time on power projection, mobility and ISR, with the first domestically produced F-35 combat aircraft rolled out in mid-2017. Japan has expressed a desire to boost its ballistic-missile-defence capability by purchasing the *Aegis* Ashore system. Budget documents also note research on a hypersonic glide body and new anti-ship missiles. Japan has an advanced defence-industrial base, which produces modern equipment for the JSDF.

ACTIVE 247,150 (Ground Self-Defense Force 150,850 Maritime Self-Defense Force 45,350 Air Self-Defense Force 46,950 Central Staff 4,000) **Paramilitary 14,000**

RESERVE 56,000 (General Reserve Army (GSDF) 46,000 Ready Reserve Army (GSDF) 8,100 Navy 1,100 Air 800)

ORGANISATIONS BY SERVICE

Space
EQUIPMENT BY TYPE
SATELLITES 11
 COMMUNICATIONS 2: 1 *Kirameki*-1; 1 *Kirameki*-2
 ISR 9 IGS

Ground Self-Defense Force 150,850
FORCES BY ROLE
COMMAND
 5 army HQ (regional comd)
SPECIAL FORCES
 1 spec ops unit (bn)
MANOEUVRE
 Armoured
 1 (7th) armd div (1 armd recce sqn, 3 tk regt, 1 armd inf regt, 1 hel sqn, 1 SP arty regt, 1 AD regt, 1 cbt engr bn, 1 sigs bn, 1 NBC bn, 1 log regt)
 1 indep tk bn
 Mechanised
 1 (2nd) inf div (1 armd recce sqn, 1 tk regt, 3 inf regt, 1 hel sqn, 1 SP arty regt, 1 AT coy, 1 ADA bn, 1 cbt engr bn, 1 sigs bn, 1 NBC bn, 1 log regt)
 1 (4th) inf div (1 armd recce sqn, 3 inf regt, 1 inf coy, 1 hel sqn, 1 fd arty regt, 1 AT coy, 1 SAM bn, 1 cbt engr bn, 1 sigs bn, 1 NBC bn, 1 log regt)
 1 (9th) inf div (1 armd recce sqn, 1 tk bn, 3 inf regt, 1 hel sqn, 1 fd arty regt, 1 SAM bn, 1 cbt engr bn, 1 sigs bn, 1 NBC bn, 1 log regt)
 2 (5th & 11th) inf bde (1 armd recce sqn, 1 tk bn, 3 inf regt, 1 hel sqn, 1 SP arty bn, 1 SAM coy, 1 cbt engr coy, 1 sigs coy, 1 NBC coy, 1 log bn)

Light
2 (1st & 3rd) inf div (1 recce sqn, 1 tk bn, 3 inf regt, 1 hel sqn, 1 fd arty bn, 1 SAM bn, 1 cbt engr bn, 1 sigs bn, 1 NBC bn, 1 log regt)
2 (6th & 10th) inf div (1 recce sqn, 1 tk bn, 3 inf regt, 1 hel sqn, 1 fd arty regt, 1 SAM bn, 1 cbt engr bn, 1 sigs bn, 1 NBC bn, 1 log regt)
1 (8th) inf div (1 recce sqn, 3 inf regt, 1 hel sqn, 1 SAM bn, 1 cbt engr bn, 1 sigs bn, 1 NBC bn, 1 log regt)
1 (13th) inf bde (1 recce sqn, 1 tk coy, 3 inf regt, 1 hel sqn, 1 fd arty bn, 1 SAM coy, 1 cbt engr coy, 1 NBC coy, 1 sigs coy, 1 log bn)
1 (14th) inf bde (1 recce sqn, 1 lt armd coy, 2 inf regt, 1 hel sqn, 1 SAM coy, 1 cbt engr coy, 1 NBC coy, 1 sigs coy, 1 log bn)
1 (15th) inf bde (1 recce sqn, 1 inf regt, 1 avn sqn, 1 AD regt, 1 cbt engr coy, 1 NBC coy, 1 sigs coy, 1 log bn)

Air Manoeuvre
1 (1st) AB bde (3 AB bn, 1 fd arty bn, 1 cbt engr coy, 1 sigs coy, 1 log bn)
1 (12th) air mob inf bde (1 recce sqn, 3 inf regt, 1 avn sqn, 1 fd arty bn, 1 SAM coy, 1 cbt engr coy, 1 NBC coy, 1 sigs coy, 1 log bn)

Amphibious
1 amph bde(-) (1 amph regt)

COMBAT SUPPORT
1 arty bde (2 SP arty regt; 3 AShM regt)
1 (Western Army) fd arty regt
2 arty unit (1 MRL bn; 1 AShM regt)
1 (Central Army) fd arty bn
4 engr bde
1 engr unit
1 EW bn
5 int bn
1 MP bde
1 sigs bde

COMBAT SERVICE SUPPORT
5 log unit (bde)
5 trg bde

HELICOPTER
1 hel bde (5 tpt hel sqn; 1 VIP tpt hel bn)
5 hel gp (1 atk hel bn, 1 hel bn)

AIR DEFENCE
2 SAM bde (2 SAM gp)
2 SAM gp

EQUIPMENT BY TYPE
ARMOURED FIGHTING VEHICLES
MBT 667: 76 Type-10; 250 Type-74; 341 Type-90
ASLT 36 Type-16 MCV
RECCE 111 Type-87
IFV 68 Type-89
APC 795
APC (T) 226 Type-73
APC (W) 569: 204 Type-82; 365 Type-96
AAV 4 AAV-7
AUV 8 Bushmaster
ENGINEERING & MAINTENANCE VEHICLES
ARV 70: 4 Type-11; 36 Type-78; 30 Type-90
VLB 22 Type-91
NBC VEHICLES 57: 41 Chemical Reconnaissance Vehicle; 16 NBC Reconnaissance Vehicle

ANTI-TANK/ANTI-INFRASTRUCTURE
MSL
SP 37 Type-96 MPMS
MANPATS Type-79 *Jyu*-MAT; Type-87 *Chu*-MAT; Type-01 LMAT
RCL • 84mm *Carl Gustav*
ARTILLERY 1,716
SP 172: **155mm** 105 Type-99; **203mm** 67 M110A2
TOWED **155mm** 340 FH-70
MRL **227mm** 99 M270 MLRS
MOR 1,105: **81mm** 652 L16 **120mm** 429; SP **120mm** 24 Type-96
COASTAL DEFENCE • AShM 104: 22 Type-12; 82 Type-88
AIRCRAFT • TPT • Light 7 Beech 350 *King Air* (LR-2)
HELICOPTERS
ATK 103: 59 AH-1S *Cobra*; 11 AH-64D *Apache*; 33 OH-1
ISR 44 OH-6D
TPT 272: **Heavy** 69: 24 CH-47D *Chinook* (CH-47J); 45 CH-47JA *Chinook*; **Medium** 42: 3 H225 *Super Puma* MkII+ (VIP); 39 UH-60L *Black Hawk* (UH-60JA); **Light** 161: 131 Bell 205 (UH-1J); 30 Enstrom 480B (TH-480B)
AIR DEFENCE
SAM
Medium-range 163: 43 Type-03 *Chu*-SAM; 120 MIM-23B I-*Hawk*
Short-range 5 Type-11 *Tan*-SAM
Point-defence 159+: 46 Type-81 *Tan*-SAM; 113 Type-93 *Kin*-SAM; Type-91 *Kei*-SAM
GUNS • SP **35mm** 52 Type-87

Maritime Self-Defense Force 45,350

Surface units organised into 4 Escort Flotillas with a mix of 8 warships each. Bases at Yokosuka, Kure, Sasebo, Maizuru, Ominato. SSK organised into two flotillas with bases at Kure and Yokosuka

EQUIPMENT BY TYPE
SUBMARINES • TACTICAL • SSK 20:
2 *Oyashio* (trg role) with 6 single 533mm TT with T-89 HWT/UGM-84C *Harpoon* AShM
9 *Oyashio* with 6 single 533mm TT with T-89 HWT/UGM-84C *Harpoon* AShM
9 *Soryu* (AIP fitted) with 6 single 533mm TT with T-89 HWT/UGM-84C *Harpoon* AShM
PRINCIPAL SURFACE COMBATANTS 49
AIRCRAFT CARRIERS • CVH 4:
2 *Hyuga* with 1 16-cell Mk41 VLS with ASROC/RIM-162B ESSM SAM, 2 triple 324mm ASTT with Mk46/Type-97 LWT, 2 *Phalanx* Block 1B CIWS (normal ac capacity 3 SH-60 *Seahawk* ASW hel; plus additional ac embarkation up to 7 SH-60 *Seahawk* or 7 MCH-101)
2 *Izumo* with 2 11-cell SeaRAM lnchr with RIM-116 SAM, 2 *Phalanx* Block 1B CIWS (normal ac capacity 7 SH-60 *Seahawk* ASW hel; plus additional ac embarkation up to 5 SH-60 *Seahawk*/MCH-101 hel)
CRUISERS • CGHM 2:
1 *Atago* with *Aegis* Baseline 7 C2, 2 quad lnchr with SSM-1B AShM, 1 64-cell Mk41 VLS with ASROC A/S

msl/SM-2 Block IIIA/B SAM/SM-3 Block IA SAM, 1 32-cell Mk41 VLS with ASROC A/S msl/SM-2 Block IIIA/B SAM/SM-3 Block IA SAM, 2 triple 324mm ASTT with Mk46 LWT, 2 *Phalanx* Block 1B CIWS, 1 127mm gun (capacity 1 SH-60 *Seahawk* ASW hel)

1 *Atago* with *Aegis* Baseline 9 C2, 2 quad lnchr with SSM-1B AShM, 1 64-cell Mk41 VLS with ASROC A/S msl/SM-2 Block IIIA/B SAM/SM-3 Block IA/IB SAM, 1 32-cell Mk41 VLS with ASROC A/S msl/SM-2 Block IIIA/B SAM/SM-3 Block IA/IB SAM, 2 triple 324mm ASTT with Mk46 LWT, 2 *Phalanx* Block 1B CIWS, 1 127mm gun (capacity 1 SH-60 *Seahawk* ASW hel)

DESTROYERS 33
DDGHM 27:
8 *Asagiri* with 2 quad Mk141 lnchr with RGM-84C *Harpoon* AShM, 1 octuple Mk29 lnchr with *Sea Sparrow* SAM, 2 triple 324mm ASTT with Mk46 LWT, 1 octuple Mk112 lnchr with ASROC, 2 *Phalanx* CIWS, 1 76mm gun (capacity 1 SH-60 *Seahawk* ASW hel)

4 *Akizuki* with 2 quad lnchr with SSM-1B AShM, 1 32-cell Mk41 VLS with ASROC/RIM-162B ESSM SAM, 2 triple 324mm ASTT with Type-97 LWT, 2 *Phalanx* CIWS, 1 127mm gun (capacity 1 SH-60 *Seahawk* ASW hel)

1 *Asahi* (*Akizuki* mod) with 2 quad lnchr with SSM-1B AShM, 8 4-cell Mk41 VLS with RIM-162B ESSM SAM/Type-07 A/S msl, 2 triple HOS-303 324mm ASTT with Type-12 LWT, 2 Mk 15 *Phalanx* Block 1B CIWS, 1 127mm gun (capacity 1 SH-60 *Seahawk* ASW hel)

9 *Murasame* with 2 quad lnchr with SSM-1B AShM, 1 16-cell Mk48 VLS with RIM-162C ESSM SAM, 2 triple 324mm TT with Mk46 LWT, 1 16-cell Mk41 VLS with ASROC, 2 *Phalanx* CIWS, 2 76mm gun (capacity 1 SH-60 *Seahawk* ASW hel)

5 *Takanami* (improved *Murasame*) with 2 quad lnchr with SSM-1B AShM, 1 32-cell Mk41 VLS with ASROC/RIM-7M/RIM-162B ESSM SAM, 2 triple 324mm TT with Mk46 LWT, 2 *Phalanx* CIWS, 1 127mm gun (capacity 1 SH-60 *Seahawk* ASW hel)

DDGM 6:
2 *Hatakaze* with 2 quad Mk141 lnchr with RGM-84C *Harpoon* AShM, 1 Mk13 GMLS with SM-1 MR SAM, 2 triple 324mm ASTT with Mk46 LWT, 1 octuple Mk112 lnchr with ASROC, 2 *Phalanx* CIWS, 2 127mm gun, 1 hel landing platform

4 *Kongou* with *Aegis* Baseline 4/5 C2, 2 quad Mk141 lnchr with RGM-84C *Harpoon* AShM, 1 29-cell Mk41 VLS with SM-2/3 SAM/ASROC, 1 61-cell Mk41 VLS with SM-2/3 SAM/ASROC, 2 triple 324mm ASTT, 2 *Phalanx* Block 1B CIWS, 1 127mm gun

FRIGATES 10
FFGHM 4 *Hatsuyuki* with 2 quad Mk141 lnchr with RGM-84C *Harpoon* AShM, 1 octuple Mk29 lnchr with RIM-7F/M *Sea Sparrow* SAM, 2 triple ASTT with Mk46 LWT, 1 octuple Mk112 lnchr with ASROC, 2 *Phalanx* CIWS, 1 76mm gun (capacity 1 SH-60 *Seahawk* ASW hel) (of which 2 in trg role)

FFG 6 *Abukuma* with 2 quad Mk141 lnchr with RGM-84C *Harpoon* AShM, 2 triple ASTT with Mk 46 LWT, 1 octuple Mk112 lnchr with ASROC, 1 *Phalanx* CIWS, 1 76mm gun

PATROL AND COASTAL COMBATANTS 6
PBFG 6 *Hayabusa* with 4 SSM-1B AShM, 1 76mm gun

MINE WARFARE • MINE COUNTERMEASURES 27
MCCS 5:
1 *Ieshima*
1 *Uraga* with 1 76mm gun, 1 hel landing platform (for MCH-101 hel)
1 *Uraga* with 1 hel landing platform (for MCH-101)
2 *Uwajima*

MSC 19: 3 *Hirashima*; 12 *Sugashima*; 1 *Uwajima*; 3 *Enoshima*
MSO 3: 2 *Awaji*; 1 *Yaeyama*

AMPHIBIOUS
PRINCIPAL AMPHIBIOUS SHIPS • LHD 3 *Osumi* with 2 *Phalanx* CIWS (capacity for 2 CH-47 hel) (capacity 10 Type-90 MBT; 2 LCAC(L) ACV; 330 troops)
LANDING CRAFT 8
LCM 2 LCU-2001
LCAC 6 LCAC(L) (capacity either 1 MBT or 60 troops)

LOGISTICS AND SUPPORT 21
AGBH 1 *Shirase* (capacity 2 AW101 *Merlin* hel)
AGEH 1 *Asuka* with 1 8-cell VLS (wpn trials) (capacity 1 SH-60 *Seahawk* hel)
AGOS 2 *Hibiki* with 1 hel landing platform
AGS 3: 1 *Futami*; 1 *Nichinan*; 1 *Shonan*
AOE 5: 2 *Mashu* (capacity 1 med hel); 3 *Towada* with 1 hel landing platform
ARC 1 *Muroto*
ASR 2: 1 *Chihaya* with 1 hel landing platform; 1 *Chiyoda II* with 1 hel landing platform
AX 6:
1 *Kashima* with 2 triple 324mm ASTT, 1 76mm gun, 1 hel landing platform
1 *Kurobe* with 1 76mm gun (trg spt ship)
3 *Shimayuki* with 2 quad lnchr with RGM-84 *Harpoon* AShM, 1 octuple Mk29 lnchr with RIM-7M *Sea Sparrow* SAM, 1 octuple Mk112 lnchr with ASROC, 2 triple 324mm ASTT with Mk46 LWT, 2 *Phalanx* CIWS, 1 76mm gun
1 *Tenryu* (trg spt ship); with 1 76mm gun (capacity: 1 med hel)

Naval Aviation ε9,800
7 Air Groups
FORCES BY ROLE
ANTI SUBMARINE/SURFACE WARFARE
5 sqn with SH-60B (SH-60J)/SH-60K *Seahawk*
MARITIME PATROL
1 sqn with P-1; P-3C *Orion*
3 sqn with P-3C *Orion*
ELECTRONIC WARFARE
1 sqn with EP-3 *Orion*
MINE COUNTERMEASURES
1 sqn with MCH-101
SEARCH & RESCUE
1 sqn with *Shin Meiwa* US-1A/US-2
2 sqn with UH-60J *Black Hawk*

TRANSPORT
1 sqn with AW101 *Merlin* (CH-101); Beech 90 *King Air* (LC-90); KC-130R *Hercules*
TRAINING
1 sqn with Beech 90 *King Air* (TC-90)
1 sqn with P-3C *Orion*
1 sqn with T-5J
1 hel sqn with H135 (TH-135); OH-6DA; SH-60B (SH-60J) *Seahawk*
EQUIPMENT BY TYPE
AIRCRAFT 78 combat capable
ASW 78: 16 P-1; 62 P-3C *Orion*
ELINT 5 EP-3C *Orion*
SAR 5: 1 *Shin Meiwa* US-1A; 4 *Shin Meiwa* US-2
TPT 27: **Medium** 6 C-130R *Hercules*; **Light** 21: 5 Beech 90 *King* Air (LC-90); 16 Beech 90 *King Air* (TC-90)
TRG 30 T-5J
HELICOPTERS
ASW 87: 35 SH-60B *Seahawk* (SH-60J); 52 SH-60K *Seahawk*
MCM 10 MCH-101
SAR 15 UH-60J *Black Hawk*
TPT 18: **Medium** 3 AW101 *Merlin* (CH-101); **Light** 15 H135 (TH-135)

Air Self-Defense Force 46,950

7 cbt wg
FORCES BY ROLE
FIGHTER
7 sqn with F-15J *Eagle*
2 sqn with F-4EJ (F-4E) *Phantom* II
3 sqn with Mitsubishi F-2
1 sqn (forming) with F-35A *Lightning* II
ELECTRONIC WARFARE
2 sqn with Kawasaki EC-1; YS-11E
ISR
1 sqn with RF-4EJ (RF-4E) *Phantom* II*
AIRBORNE EARLY WARNING & CONTROL
2 sqn with E-2C *Hawkeye*
1 sqn with E-767
SEARCH & RESCUE
1 wg with U-125A *Peace Krypton*; UH-60J *Black Hawk*
TANKER
1 sqn with KC-767J
TRANSPORT
1 (VIP) sqn with B-747-400
2 sqn with C-1; C-2
1 sqn with C-130H *Hercules*
Some (liaison) sqn with Gulfstream IV (U-4); T-4*
TRAINING
1 (aggressor) sqn with F-15J *Eagle*
TEST
1 wg with F-15J *Eagle*; T-4*
TRANSPORT HELICOPTER
4 flt with CH-47JA *Chinook*
EQUIPMENT BY TYPE
AIRCRAFT 547 combat capable
FTR 189: 147 F-15J *Eagle*; 42 F-15DJ *Eagle*
FGA 148: 58 F-2A; 30 F-2B; 51 F-4E *Phantom* II (F-4EJ); 9 F-35A *Lightning* II (in test)

EW 3: 1 Kawasaki EC-1; 2 YS-11EA
ISR 17: 13 RF-4E *Phantom* II* (RF-4J); 4 YS-11EB
AEW&C 17: 13 E-2C *Hawkeye*; 4 E-767
SAR 26 U-125A *Peace Krypton*
TKR 6: 2 KC-130H *Hercules*; 4 KC-767J
TPT 59: **Medium** 19: 13 C-130H *Hercules*; 6 C-2; **PAX** 40: 2 B-747-400; 1 B-777-300ER (VIP); 13 Beech T-400; 19 C-1; 5 Gulfstream IV (U-4)
TRG 246: 197 T-4*; 49 T-7
HELICOPTERS
SAR 35 UH-60J *Black Hawk*
TPT • **Heavy** 15 CH-47JA *Chinook*
AIR-LAUNCHED MISSILES
AAM • IR AAM-3 (Type-90); AIM-9 *Sidewinder*; IIR AAM-5 (Type-04); SARH AIM-7 *Sparrow*; ARH AAM-4 (Type-99); AIM-120C5/C7 AMRAAM (limited numbers)
ASM ASM-1 (Type-80); ASM-2 (Type-93)

Air Defence

Ac control and warning. 4 wg; 28 radar sites
FORCES BY ROLE
AIR DEFENCE
6 SAM gp (total: 24 SAM bty with MIM-104D/F *Patriot* PAC-2/3)
1 AD gp with Type-81 *Tan-SAM*; M167 *Vulcan*
EQUIPMENT BY TYPE
AIR DEFENCE
SAM
Long-range 120 MIM-104D/F *Patriot* PAC-2 GEM/PAC-3
Point-defence Type-81 *Tan-SAM*
GUNS • TOWED 20mm M167 *Vulcan*

Paramilitary 14,000

Coast Guard 14,000

Ministry of Land, Transport, Infrastructure and Tourism (no cbt role)
EQUIPMENT BY TYPE
PATROL AND COASTAL COMBATANTS 367
PSOH 14: 2 *Mizuho* (capacity 2 hels); 2 *Shikishima* (capacity 2 hels); 1 *Soya* (capacity 1 hel) (icebreaking capability); 9 *Tsugaru* (*Soya* mod) (capacity 1 hel)
PSO 43:
3 *Hida* with 1 hel landing platform
1 *Izu* with 1 hel landing platform
9 *Hateruma* with 1 hel landing platform
6 *Iwami*
1 *Kojima* (trg) with 1 hel landing platform
2 *Kunigami* with 1 hel landing platform
1 *Miura* with 1 hel landing platform
6 *Ojika* with 1 hel landing platform
14 *Taketomi* with 1 hel landing platform
PCO 16: 3 *Aso*; 6 *Katori*; 7 *Teshio*
PCC 26: 4 *Amami*; 22 *Tokara*
PBF 47: 20 *Hayagumo*; 5 *Mihashi*; 14 *Raizan*; 2 *Takatsuki*; 6 *Tsuruugi*
PB 54: 4 *Asogiri*; 4 *Hamagumo*; 11 *Hayanami*; 12 *Katonami*; 1 *Matsunami*; 4 *Murakumo*; 2 *Natsugiri*; 6 *Shimoji*; 10 *Yodo*
PBI 167: 2 *Hakubai*; 1 *Hayagiku*; 164 *Himegiku*

LOGISTICS AND SUPPORT 16
  ABU 1 *Teshio*
  AGS 12: 6 *Hamashio*; 1 *Jinbei*; 2 *Meiyo*; 1 *Shoyo*; 1 *Takuyo*; 1 *Tenyo*
  AX 3
  AIRCRAFT
    MP 2 *Falcon* 900 MPAT
    SAR 4 Saab 340B
    TPT 25: **Light** 23: 5 Cessna 172; 9 Beech 350 *King Air* (LR-2); 9 DHC *Dash-7* (Bombardier 300) (MP); **PAX** 2 Gulfstream V (MP)
  HELICOPTERS
    MRH 5 Bell 412 *Twin Huey*
    SAR 11 S-76D
    TPT 36: **Medium** 8: 3 AS332 *Super Puma*; 5 H225 *Super Puma*; **Light** 28: 18 AW139; 3 Bell 206B *Jet Ranger* II; 4 Bell 505 *Jet Ranger* X; 3 S-76C

Cyber

In 2014, an 'Office of Cyber' was established in the C4 Systems Planning Division, Joint Staff Office (JSO) of the Japan Ministry of Defense to consolidate the cyber-planning functions of the JSO and to create a more systematic structure for responding to cyber attacks. The National Defense Program Guidelines for FY2014 and beyond stated that 'Japan will build up persistent ISR [intelligence, surveillance and reconnaissance] capabilities to prevent any acts that could impede efficient action by the SDF'. The 2014 Mid-Term Defense Program (FY2014–18) said that the Self-Defense Forces would develop specialist training for cyber personnel. The document also said that 'through its efforts to secure response capabilities in cyberspace where attackers have an overwhelming advantage, the SDF may consider the acquisition of capabilities to prevent them from using cyberspace'. A Cyber Defense Group, which integrates the cyber-warfare functions of the three armed services, was launched in March 2014 to respond to cyber threats. The group monitors defence-ministry and SDF networks and provides responses to cyber attacks. A revised Cybersecurity Strategy was developed in mid-2018.

DEPLOYMENT

ARABIAN SEA & GULF OF ADEN: Combined Maritime Forces • CTF-151: 2 DDGHM

DJIBOUTI: 170; 2 P-3C *Orion*

SOUTH SUDAN: UN • UNMISS 4

FOREIGN FORCES

United States
US Pacific Command: 53,900
  Army 2,700; 1 corps HQ (fwd); 1 SF gp; 1 avn bn; 1 SAM bn
  Navy 20,250; 1 CVN; 3 CGHM; 2 DDGHM; 8 DDGM (2 non-op); 1 LCC; 4 MCO; 1 LHD; 1 LPD; 2 LSD; 3 FGA sqn with 10 F/A-18E *Super Hornet*; 1 FGA sqn with 10 F/A-18F *Super Hornet*; 2 ASW aqn with 6 P-8A *Poseidon*; 1 ASW flt with 2 P-3C *Orion*; 2 EW sqn with 5 EA-18G *Growler*; 1 AEW&C sqn with 5 E-2D *Hawkeye*; 2 ASW hel sqn with 12 MH-60R *Seahawk*; 1 tpt hel sqn with MH-60S *Knight Hawk*; 1 base at Sasebo; 1 base at Yokosuka
  USAF: 12,50; 1 HQ (5th Air Force) at Okinawa–Kadena AB; 1 ftr wg at Misawa AB (2 ftr sqn with 22 F-16C/D *Fighting Falcon*); 1 ftr wg at Okinawa–Kadena AB (2 ftr sqn with 27 F-15C/D *Eagle*; 1 FGA sqn with 14 F-22A *Raptor*; 1 tkr sqn with 15 KC-135R *Stratotanker*; 1 AEW sqn with 2 E-3B *Sentry*; 1 CSAR sqn with 10 HH-60G *Pave Hawk*); 1 tpt wg at Yokota AB with 10 C-130J-30 *Hercules*; 2 Beech 1900C (C-12J); 1 spec ops gp at Okinawa–Kadena AB with (1 sqn with 5 MC-130H *Combat Talon*; 1 sqn with 5 MC-130J *Commando* II; 1 unit with 5 CV-22A *Osprey*); 1 ISR sqn with RC-135 *Rivet Joint*; 1 ISR UAV flt with 5 RQ-4A *Global Hawk*
  USMC 18,800; 1 mne div; 1 mne regt HQ; 1 arty regt HQ; 1 recce bn; 1 mne bn; 1 amph aslt bn; 1 arty bn; 2 FGA sqn at Iwakuni with 12 F/A-18D *Hornet*; 1 FGA sqn at Iwakuni with 12 F-35B *Lightning* II; 1 tkr sqn at Iwakuni with 15 KC-130J *Hercules*; 2 tpt sqn at Futenma with 12 MV-22B *Osprey*
  US Strategic Command: 1 AN/TPY-2 X-band radar at Shariki; 1 AN/TPY-2 X-band radar at Kyogamisaki

Korea, Democratic People's Republic of DPRK

North Korean Won	2017	2018	2019
GDP	US$		
per capita	US$		
Def exp	won		
	US$		

US$1=won

*definitive economic data not available

Population	25,381,085					
Age	0–14	15–19	20–24	25–29	30–64	65 plus
Male	10.5%	3.8%	4.0%	4.1%	23.0%	3.3%
Female	10.1%	3.7%	3.9%	3.9%	23.5%	6.2%

Capabilities

Renewed diplomacy reduced tensions on the Korean Peninsula in 2018, though the prospect of limiting Pyongyang's nuclear ambitions remains uncertain. Aware of the qualitative inferiority of its conventional forces, North Korea has invested in asymmetric capabilities, particularly the development of nuclear weapons and ballistic-missile delivery systems. Throughout 2017, several new nuclear-capable road-mobile ballistic-missile designs were revealed and successfully tested. North Korea remains diplomatically isolated. While foreign defence cooperation is restricted by international pressure and sanctions, Pyongyang has nonetheless often found ways to develop military ties. Official conscription for both men and women is often extended, sometimes indefinitely. Training is focused on fighting a short intensive war on the peninsula, but the armed forces' overall effectiveness in a modern conflict against technologically superior opposition is unclear. Internal exercises are conducted regularly, but those shown are staged and are not necessarily representative of wider operational capability. North Korea's conventional forces remain reliant on increasingly obsolete equipment, with older Soviet-era and Chinese-origin equipment supplemented by a number of indigenous designs and upgrades. Overall effectiveness and serviceability of some equipment remains in doubt but there is local maintenance, repair and overhaul capacity. Local defence-industrial capacity includes the manufacture of light arms, armoured vehicles, artillery and missile systems. North Korea has exported arms in the past. It is unclear whether the country would have had the capability to indigenously develop some of the technical advances it has demonstrated, including in rocket propulsion.

ACTIVE 1,280,000 (Army 1,100,000 Navy 60,000 Air 110,000 Strategic Forces 10,000) **Paramilitary 189,000**

Conscript liability Army 5–12 years, Navy 5–10 years, Air Force 3–4 years, followed by compulsory part-time service to age 40. Thereafter service in the Worker/Peasant Red Guard to age 60

RESERVE ε600,000 (Armed Forces ε600,000), **Paramilitary 5,700,000**

Reservists are assigned to units (see also Paramilitary)

ORGANISATIONS BY SERVICE

Strategic Forces ε10,000

North Korea's ballistic missiles and obsolete H-5 (Il-28) bombers could be used to deliver nuclear warheads or bombs. At present, however, there is no conclusive evidence to verify that North Korea has successfully produced a warhead or bomb capable of being delivered by these systems

EQUIPMENT BY TYPE (ε)
SURFACE-TO-SURFACE MISSILE LAUNCHERS
　ICBM 6+: *Hwasong*-13/*Hwasong*-13 mod/*Hwasong*-14 (in test); *Hwasong*-15 (in test)
　IRBM *Hwasong*-12 (in test)
　MRBM ε10 *Nodong* mod 1/mod 2 (ε90+ msl); some *Scud*-ER; *Bukkeukseong*-2 (in test); *Hwasong*-10 (*Musudan*) (in test)
　SBRM 30+ *Hwasong*-5 (SS-1C *Scud*-B)/*Hwasong*-6 (SS-1D *Scud*-C) (ε200+ msl); some *Scud* (mod) (in test)

Army ε1,100,000

FORCES BY ROLE
COMMAND
　2 mech corps HQ
　10 inf corps HQ
　1 (Capital Defence) corps HQ
MANOEUVRE
　Armoured
　　1 armd div
　　15 armd bde
　Mechanised
　　4 mech div
　Light
　　27 inf div
　　14 inf bde
COMBAT SUPPORT
　1 arty div
　21 arty bde
　9 MRL bde
　5–8 engr river crossing/amphibious regt
　1 engr river crossing bde

Special Purpose Forces Command 88,000
FORCES BY ROLE
SPECIAL FORCES
　8 (Reconnaissance General Bureau) SF bn
MANOEUVRE
　Reconnaissance
　　17 recce bn
　Light
　　9 lt inf bde
　　6 sniper bde
　Air Manoeuvre
　　3 AB bde
　　1 AB bn
　　2 sniper bde
　Amphibious
　　2 sniper bde

Reserves 600,000
FORCES BY ROLE
MANOEUVRE
　Light
　　40 inf div
　　18 inf bde

EQUIPMENT BY TYPE (ε)
ARMOURED FIGHTING VEHICLES
　MBT 3,500+ T-34/T-54/T-55/T-62/Type-59/*Chonma*/*Pokpoong*
　LT TK 560+: 560 PT-76; M-1985
　IFV 32 BTR-80A
　APC 2,500+
　　APC (T) BTR-50; Type-531 (Type-63); VTT-323
　　APC (W) 2,500 BTR-40/BTR-60/M-1992/1/BTR-152/M-2010 (6×6)/M-2010 (8×8)
ANTI-TANK/ANTI-INFRASTRUCTURE
　MSL
　　SP 9K11 *Malyutka* (AT-3 *Sagger*); M-2010 ATGM
　　MANPATS 2K15 *Shmel* (AT-1 *Snapper*); 9K111 *Fagot* (AT-4 *Spigot*); 9K113 *Konkurs* (AT-5 *Spandrel*)
　RCL 82mm 1,700 B-10
ARTILLERY 21,100+
　SP/TOWED 8,500:
　　SP 122mm M-1977; M-1981; M-1985; M-1991; **130mm** M-1975; M-1981; M-1991; **152mm** M-1974; M-1977; M-2018; **170mm** M-1978; M-1989
　　TOWED 122mm D-30; D-74; M-1931/37; **130mm** M-46; **152mm** M-1937; M-1938; M-1943
　GUN/MOR 120mm (reported)
　MRL 5,100: **107mm** Type-63; VTT-323 107mm; **122mm** BM-11; M-1977 (BM-21); M-1985; M-1992; M-1993; VTT-323 122mm; **200mm** BMD-20; **240mm** BM-24; M-1985; M-1989; M-1991; **300mm** some
　MOR 7,500: **82mm** M-37; **120mm** M-43; **160mm** M-43
SURFACE-TO-SURFACE MISSILE LAUNCHERS
　SBRM 24 FROG-3/5/7; *some Toksa* (SS-21B *Scarab* mod)
AIR DEFENCE
　SAM • **Point-defence** 9K35 *Strela*-10 (SA-13 *Gopher*); 9K310 *Igla*-1 (SA-16 *Gimlet*); 9K32 *Strela*-2 (SA-7 *Grail*)‡
　GUNS 11,000
　　SP 14.5mm M-1984; **23mm** M-1992; **37mm** M-1992; **57mm** M-1985

TOWED 11,000: **14.5mm** ZPU-1/ZPU-2/ZPU-4; **23mm** ZU-23; **37mm** M-1939; **57mm** S-60; **85mm** M-1939 *KS-12*; **100mm** KS-19

Navy ε60,000
EQUIPMENT BY TYPE
SUBMARINES • TACTICAL 73
  SSB 1 *Gorae* with 1 *Bukkeukseong*-1 SLBM (SLBM trials)
  SSK 20 PRC Type-033/FSU *Romeo*† with 8 single 533mm TT with SAET-60 HWT
  SSC 32+:
    ε30 *Sang-O* some with 2 single 533mm TT with 53–65 HWT
    2+ *Sang-O* II with 4 single 533mm TT with 53–65 HWT
  SSW ε20† (some *Yugo* some with 2 single 406mm TT; some *Yeono* some with 2 single 533mm TT)
PRINCIPAL SURFACE COMBATANTS 2
  FRIGATES • FFG 2:
    1 *Najin* with 2 single lnchr with P-15 *Termit* (SS-N-2 *Styx*) AShM, 2 RBU 1200 A/S mor, 2 100mm gun, 2 twin 57mm gun
    1 *Najin* with 2 twin lnchr with *Kumsong*-3 mod (KN-SS-N-2 *Stormpetrel*) AShM, 2 RBU 1200 A/S mor, 2 100mm gun, 2 twin 57mm gun (operational status unclear)
PATROL AND COASTAL COMBATANTS 383+
  CORVETTES • FS 5
    4 *Sariwon* with 2 twin 57mm gun
    1 *Tral* with 1 85mm gun
  PCG 10:
    10 *Soju* (FSU *Osa* I (Project 205) mod) with 4 single lnchr with P-15 *Termit* (SS-N-2 *Styx*) AShM
  PCC 18:
    6 *Hainan* with 4 RBU 1200 A/S mor, 2 twin 57mm gun
    7 *Taechong* I with 2 RBU 1200 A/S mor, 1 85mm gun, 1 twin 57mm gun
    5 *Taechong* II with 2 RBU 1200 A/S mor, 1 100mm gun, 1 twin 57mm gun
  PBFG 25+:
    4 *Huangfeng* (Type-021) with 4 single lnchr with P-15 *Termit* (SS-N-2) AShM, 2 twin AK230 CIWS
    6 *Komar* with 2 single lnchr with P-15 *Termit* (SS-N-2) AShM
    8 *Osa* I with 4 single lnchr with P-15 *Termit* (SS-N-2 *Styx*) AShM, 2 twin AK230 CIWS
    6 *Sohung* (Komard mod) with 2 single lnchr with P-15 *Termit* (SS-N-2) AShM
    1+ *Nongo* with 2 twin lnchr with *Kumsong*-3 mod (KN-SS-N-2 *Stormpetrel*) AShM, 2 30mm CIWS (operational status unknown)
  PBF 229:
    54 *Chong-Jin* with 1 85mm gun
    142 *Ku Song/Sin Hung/Sin Hung* (mod)
    33 *Sinpo*
  PB 96:
    59 *Chaho*
    6 *Chong-Ju* with 2 RBU 1200 A/S mor, 1 85mm gun
    13 *Shanghai* II
    18 SO-1 with 4 RBU 1200 A/S mor, 2 twin 57mm gun

MINE WARFARE • MINE COUNTERMEASURES 24
  MSC 24: 19 *Yukto* I; 5 *Yukto* II
AMPHIBIOUS
  LANDING SHIPS • LSM 10 *Hantae* (capacity 3 tanks; 350 troops)
  LANDING CRAFT 257
    LCPL 96 *Nampo* (capacity 35 troops)
    LCM 25
    UCAC 136 *Kongbang* (capacity 50 troops)
LOGISTICS AND SUPPORT 23:
  AGI 14 (converted fishing vessels)
  AS 8 (converted cargo ships)
  ASR 1 *Kowan*

Coastal Defence
FORCES BY ROLE
COASTAL DEFENCE
  2 AShM regt with HY-1/*Kumsong*-3 (6 sites, some mobile launchers)
EQUIPMENT BY TYPE
COASTAL DEFENCE
  ARTY 130mm M-1992; SM-4-1
  AShM HY-1; *Kumsong*-3
  ARTILLERY • TOWED 122mm M-1931/37; **152mm** M-1937

Air Force 110,000
4 air divs. 1st, 2nd and 3rd Air Divs (cbt) responsible for N, E and S air-defence sectors respectively; 8th Air Div (trg) responsible for NE sector. The AF controls the national airline
FORCES BY ROLE
BOMBER
  3 lt regt with H-5; Il-28 *Beagle*
FIGHTER
  1 regt with MiG-15 *Fagot*
  6 regt with J-5; MiG-17 *Fresco*
  4 regt with J-6; MiG-19 *Farmer*
  5 regt with J-7; MiG-21F-13/PFM *Fishbed*
  1 regt with MiG-21bis *Fishbed*
  1 regt with MiG-23ML/P *Flogger*
  1 regt with MiG-29A/S/UB *Fulcrum*
GROUND ATTACK
  1 regt with Su-25/Su-25UBK *Frogfoot*
TRANSPORT
  Some regt with An-2 *Colt*/Y-5 (to infiltrate 2 air-force sniper brigades deep into ROK rear areas); An-24 *Coke*; Il-18 *Coot*; Il-62M *Classic*; Tu-134 *Crusty*; Tu-154 *Careless*
TRAINING
  Some regt with CJ-6; FT-2; MiG-21U/UM
TRANSPORT HELICOPTER
  Some regt with Hughes 500D/E; Mi-8 *Hip*; Mi-17 *Hip* H; Mil-26 *Halo*; PZL Mi-2 *Hoplite*; Z-5
AIR DEFENCE
  19 bde with S-125 *Pechora* (SA-3 *Goa*); S-75 *Dvina* (SA-2 *Guideline*); S-200 *Angara* (SA-5 *Gammon*); 9K36 *Strela*-3 (SA-14 *Gremlin*); 9K310 *Igla*-1 (SA-16 *Gimlet*); 9K32 *Strela*-2 (SA-7 *Grail*)‡; *Pongae*-5

EQUIPMENT BY TYPE
AIRCRAFT 545 combat capable
  BBR 80 Il-28 *Beagle*/H-5†
  FTR 401+: MiG-15 *Fagot*; 107 MiG-17 *Fresco*/J-5; 100 MiG-19 *Farmer*/J-6; 120 MiG-21F-13 *Fishbed*/J-7; MiG-21PFM *Fishbed*; 46 MiG-23ML *Flogger;* 10 MiG-23P *Flogger;* 18+ MiG-29A/S/UB *Fulcrum*
  FGA 30 MiG-21bis *Fishbed* (18 Su-7 *Fitter* in store)
  ATK 34 Su-25/Su-25UBK *Frogfoot*
  TPT 217+: **Heavy** some Il-76 (operated by state airline); **Light** 208: 6 An-24 *Coke*; 2 Tu-134 *Crusty*; ε200 An-2 *Colt*/Y-5; **PAX** 9: 2 Il-18 *Coot*; 2 Il-62M *Classic*; 4 Tu-154 *Careless*; 1 Tu-204-300
  TRG 215+: 180 CJ-6; 35 FT-2; some MiG-21U/UM
HELICOPTERS
  MRH 80 Hughes 500D/E†
  TPT 206: **Heavy** 4 Mi-26 *Halo*; **Medium** 63: 15 Mi-8 *Hip*/Mi-17 *Hip* H; 48 Mi-4 *Hound*/Z-5; **Light** 139 PZL Mi-2 *Hoplite*
UNMANNED AERIAL VEHICLES
  ISR • Medium some (unidentified indigenous type); **Light** *Pchela*-1 (*Shmel*) (reported)
AIR DEFENCE • SAM
  Long-range 38 S-200 *Angara* (SA-5 *Gammon*)
  Medium-range 179+: some *Pongae*-5 (status unknown); 179+ S-75 *Dvina* (SA-2 *Guideline*)
  Short-range 133 S-125 *Pechora* (SA-3 *Goa*)
  Point-defence 9K32 *Strela*-2 (SA-7 *Grail*)‡; 9K36 *Strela*-3 (SA-14 *Gremlin*); 9K310 *Igla*-1 (SA-16 *Gimlet*)
AIR-LAUNCHED MISSILES
  AAM • IR R-3 (AA-2 *Atoll*)‡; R-60 (AA-8 *Aphid);* R-73 (AA-11 *Archer);* PL-5; PL-7; **SARH** R-23/24 (AA-7 *Apex*); R-27R/ER (AA-10 A/C *Alamo*)
  ASM Kh-23 (AS-7 *Kerry*)‡; Kh-25 (AS-10 *Karen*)

Paramilitary 189,000 active

Security Troops 189,000 (incl border guards, public-safety personnel)
Ministry of Public Security

Worker/Peasant Red Guard ε5,700,000 reservists
Org on a province/town/village basis; comd structure is bde–bn–coy–pl; small arms with some mor and AD guns (but many units unarmed)

Cyber
Since the 1970s, the North Korean military (the Korean People's Army, KPA) maintained a modest electronic warfare (EW) capability. As a result of strategic reviews following *Operation Desert Storm*, the KPA established an information-warfare capability under the concept of 'electronic intelligence warfare'. The two key organisations are the Reconnaissance General Bureau (RGB), which conducts covert operations in peacetime, and the General Staff Department (GSD), which is responsible for cyber operations in support of conventional military efforts. The General Staff Department is responsible for operational command and oversees cyber, EW and psychological operations. This includes the Electronic Warfare Bureau, which was reportedly established in the mid-1980s. Specialists assess North Korea as conceiving of cyber capabilities as useful tools for 'coercive diplomacy' and 'disruptive actions' in the South in the case of war. North Korea has launched distributed-denial-of-service attacks on South Korean institutions and pursues cyber infiltration against military and other government agencies. The attack on Sony Pictures in 2014 was attributed to North Korea. North Korea was also publicly identified as the source of the 2017 WannaCry ransomware attack whose aim appeared to be to raise money for the state. South Korea estimates that North Korea has a nearly 7,000-strong unit of cyber-warfare specialists, some of whom are deployed overseas and tasked with raising revenue for the state through various forms of cyber criminality.

Korea, Republic of ROK

South Korean Won		2017	2018	2019
GDP	won	1,741tr	1,822tr	
	US$	1.54tr	1.66tr	
per capita	US$	29,938	32,046	
Growth	%	3.1	2.8	
Inflation	%	1.9	1.5	
Def bdgt	won	40.6tr	43.2tr	46.7tr
	US$	35.9bn	39.2bn	
US$1=won		1,130.42	1,100.67	

Population 51,418,097

Age	0–14	15–19	20–24	25–29	30–64	65 plus
Male	6.7%	2.8%	3.6%	3.6%	27.1%	6.2%
Female	6.3%	2.6%	3.2%	3.1%	26.3%	8.3%

Capabilities
South Korea's defence policy remains focused on its difficult relationship with North Korea, notwithstanding recent diplomatic re-engagement. Seoul has looked to recapitalise conventional military capabilities to ensure a qualitative edge over Pyongyang. It also has prioritised acquiring new capabilities for a three-axis approach of 'Kill Chain', 'Korea Air and Missile Defence' and 'Korea Massive Punishment and Retaliation'. The Defence Reform 2.0 project announced in 2018 sets out ambitions to modernise and restructure the armed forces, placing emphasis on new technologies. The established alliance with the US is a major element of defence strategy, though the planned transfer of wartime operational control of forces to Seoul is now 'conditions based' with no firm date set. A large number of US military personnel and equipment remained stationed in South Korea; the US THAAD missile-defence system was deployed in 2017 in light of concerns over North Korea's missile capabilities. South Korea's forces remain some of the best equipped and trained in the region. South Korea has demonstrated the capacity to support small international deployments, including contributions to UN missions and counter-piracy operations in the Arabian Sea. The inventory increasingly comprises modern systems. South Korea has developed a broad range of domestic defence industries, which are capable of supplying the majority of military requirements. However, there is still reliance on the US in areas such as front-line combat aircraft. Local defence industries are finding growing export success, particularly with the T-50 jet trainer and K-9 self-propelled howitzer.

ACTIVE 625,000 (Army 490,000 Navy 70,000 Air 65,000) **Paramilitary 9,000**

Conscript liability Service period reducing from Oct 2018, by three months for the army and marines (now 18 months), and the navy (now 20 months); and by two months for the air force (now 22 months).

RESERVE 3,100,000

Reserve obligation of three days per year. First Combat Forces (Mobilisation Reserve Forces) or Regional Combat Forces (Homeland Defence Forces) to age 33

Reserve Paramilitary 3,000,000
Being reorganised

ORGANISATIONS BY SERVICE

Army 490,000
FORCES BY ROLE
COMMAND
 2 army HQ
 8 corps HQ
 1 (Capital Defence) comd HQ
SPECIAL FORCES
 1 (Special Warfare) SF comd
 6 SF bde
 1 indep SF bn
 2 cdo bde
 6 cdo regt
 2 indep cdo bn
MANOEUVRE
 Armoured
  5 armd bde
  3 mech inf div (1 recce bn, 1 armd bde, 2 armd inf bde, 1 fd arty bde, 1 engr bn)
 Mechanised
  3 mech inf div (1 recce bn, 1 armd bde, 2 mech inf bde, 1 fd arty bde, 1 engr bn)
 Light
  16 inf div (1 recce bn, 1 tk bn, 3 inf regt, 1 arty regt (4 arty bn), 1 engr bn)
  2 indep inf bde
 Air Manoeuvre
  1 air aslt bde
 Other
  5 sy regt
SURFACE-TO-SURFACE MISSILE
 3 SSM bn
COMBAT SUPPORT
 6 engr bde
 5 engr gp
 1 CBRN defence bde
 8 sigs bde
COMBAT SERVICE SUPPORT
 4 log spt comd
HELICOPTER
 1 (army avn) comd
AIR DEFENCE
 1 ADA bde
 5 ADA bn

Reserves
FORCES BY ROLE
COMMAND
 1 army HQ
MANOEUVRE
 Light
  24 inf div
EQUIPMENT BY TYPE
ARMOURED FIGHTING VEHICLES
 MBT 2,514: 1,000 K1; 484 K1A1; 100 K2; 253 M48; 597 M48A5; 80 T-80U; (400 M47 in store)
 IFV 540: ε500 K21; 40 BMP-3
 APC 2,790
  APC (T) 2,560: 300 Bv 206; 1,700 KIFV; 420 M113; 140 M577 (CP)
  APC (W) 220; 20 BTR-80; 200 KM-900/-901 (Fiat 6614)
 PPV 10 *MaxxPro*
ENGINEERING & MAINTENANCE VEHICLES
 AEV 207 M9
 ARV 238+: 200 K1; K21 ARV; K288A1; M47; 38 M88A1
 VLB 56 K1
ANTI-TANK/ANTI-INFRASTRUCTURE
 MSL
  SP *Hyeongung*
  MANPATS 9K115 *Metis* (AT-7 *Saxhorn*); *Hyeongung*; TOW-2A
 RCL 57mm; **75mm**; **90mm** M67; **106mm** M40A2
 GUNS 58
  SP 90mm 50 M36
  TOWED 76mm 8 M18 *Hellcat* (AT gun)
ARTILLERY 11,067+
 SP 1,353+: **155mm** 1,340: ε300 K9 *Thunder*; 1,040 M109A2 (K55/K55A1); **175mm** some M107; **203mm** 13 M110
 TOWED 3,500+: **105mm** 1,700 M101/KH-178; **155mm/203mm** 1,800+ KH-179/M114/M115
 MRL 214+: **130mm** 156 K136 *Kooryong*; **227mm** 58: 48 M270 MLRS; 10 M270A1 MLRS; **239mm** some *Chunmoo*
 MOR 6,000: **81mm** KM29 (M29); **107mm** M30
SURFACE-TO-SURFACE MISSILE LAUNCHERS
 SRBM • Conventional 30 *Hyonmu* IIA/IIB; MGM-140A/B ATACMS (launched from M270/M270A1 MLRS)
 GLCM • Conventional *Hyonmu* III
HELICOPTERS
 ATK 96: 60 AH-1F/J *Cobra*; 36 AH-64E *Apache*
 MRH 175: 130 Hughes 500D; 45 MD-500
 TPT 324: **Heavy** 37: 31 CH-47D *Chinook*; 6 MH-47E *Chinook*; **Medium** 175: 88 KUH-1 *Surion*; 87 UH-60P *Black Hawk*; **Light** 112: ε100 Bell 205 (UH-1H *Iroquois*); 12 Bo-105
AIR DEFENCE
 SAM • Point-defence *Chun Ma* (*Pegasus*); FIM-92 *Stinger*; *Javelin*; *Mistral*; 9K310 Igla-1 (SA-16 *Gimlet*)
 GUNS 330+
  SP 170: **20mm** ε150 KIFV *Vulcan* SPAAG; **30mm** 20 BIHO *Flying Tiger*
  TOWED 160: **20mm** 60 M167 *Vulcan*; **35mm** 20 GDF-003; **40mm** 80 L/60/L/70; M1
AIR-LAUNCHED MISSILES
 ASM AGM-114R1 *Hellfire*

Navy 70,000 (incl marines)

Three separate fleet elements: 1st Fleet Donghae (East Sea/Sea of Japan); 2nd Fleet Pyeongtaek (West Sea/Yellow Sea); 3rd Fleet Busan (South Sea/Korea Strait); independent submarine command; three additional flotillas (incl SF, mine warfare, amphibious and spt elements) and 1 Naval Air Wing (3 gp plus spt gp)

EQUIPMENT BY TYPE
SUBMARINES • TACTICAL 22
  SSK 16:
    6 *Chang Bogo* I (GER Type-209/1200; KSS-1) with 8 single 533mm TT with SUT HWT/K731 *White Shark* HWT
    3 *Chang Bogo* I (GER Type-209/1200; KSS-1) with 8 single 533mm TT with SUT HWT/K731 *White Shark* HWT/UGM-84 *Harpoon* AShM
    7 *Chang Bogo* II (GER Type-214; KSS-2; AIP fitted) with 8 single 533mm TT with SUT HWT/K731 *White Shark* HWT/*Hae Sung* I AShM/*Hae Sung* III LACM
  SSC 6 *Cosmos*
PRINCIPAL SURFACE COMBATANTS 26
  CRUISERS • CGHM 3:
    3 *Sejong* (KDD-III) with *Aegis* Baseline 7 C2, 6 8-cell K-VLS with *Hae Sung* II LACM/*Red Shark* A/S msl, 4 quad lnchr with *Hae Sung* I AShM, 10 8-cell Mk41 VLS with SM-2 Block IIIA/B SAM (6 fwd, 4 aft), 1 21-cell Mk49 GMLS with RIM-116 RAM SAM, 2 triple Mk32 324mm ASTT with K745 LWT, 1 *Goalkeeper* CIWS, 1 127mm gun (capacity 2 *Lynx* Mk99/AW159 *Wildcat* hels)
  DESTROYERS • DDGHM 6:
    6 *Chungmugong Yi Sun-Sin* (KDD-II) with 2 8-cell K-VLS with *Hae Sung* II LACM/*Red Shark* A/S msl, 2 Mk141 lnchr with RGM-84C *Harpoon* AShM/*Hae Sung* I AShM, 4 8-cell Mk41 VLS with SM-2 Block IIIA/B SAM, 1 21-cell Mk49 GMLS with RIM-116 RAM SAM, 2 triple Mk32 324mm ASTT with Mk46 LWT, 1 *Goalkeeper* CIWS, 1 127mm gun (capacity 1 *Lynx* Mk99/AW159 *Wildcat* hel)
  FRIGATES 17
    FFGHM 10:
      3 *Gwanggaeto Daewang* (KDD-I) with 2 quad Mk141 lnchr with RGM-84 *Harpoon* AShM, 2 8-cell Mk48 VLS with RIM-7P *Sea Sparrow* SAM, 2 triple Mk32 324mm ASTT with Mk46 LWT, 2 *Goalkeeper* CIWS, 1 127mm gun (capacity 1 *Lynx* Mk99/AW159 *Wildcat* hel)
      6 *Incheon* with 2 quad lnchr with *Hae Sung* I AShM/TSLM LACM, 1 21-cell Mk49 lnchr with RIM-116 SAM, 2 triple 324mm ASTT with K745 *Blue Shark* LWT, 1 Mk15 1B *Phalanx* CIWS, 1 127 mm gun (capacity 1 *Lynx* Mk99/AW159 *Wildcat* hel)
      1 *Daegu* (*Incheon* Batch II) with 2 8-cell K-VLS with *Hae Sung* II LACM/TSLM LACM/K-SAAM SAM/*Red Shark* A/S msl, 2 quad lnchr with TSLM LACM/*Hae Sung* I AShM, 2 KMk. 32 triple 324mm ASTT with K745 *Blue Shark* LWT, 1 Mk 15 *Phalanx* Block 1B CIWS, 1 127mm gun (capacity 1 *Lynx* Mk99/AW159 *Wildcat* hel)
    FFG 7 *Ulsan* with 2 quad Mk141 lnchr with RGM-84C *Harpoon* AShM, 2 triple Mk32 324mm ASTT with Mk46 LWT, 2 76mm gun
PATROL AND COASTAL COMBATANTS ε101
  CORVETTES • FSG 32:
    18 *Gumdoksuri* with 2 twin lnchr with *Hae Sung* I AShM, 1 76mm gun
    8 *Po Hang* (Flight IV) with 2 twin lnchr with RGM-84 *Harpoon* AShM, 2 triple 324mm ASTT with Mk46 LWT, 2 76mm gun
    6 *Po Hang* (Flight V) with 2 twin lnchr with *Hae Sung* I AShM, 2 KMk. 32 triple 324mm ASTT with K745 *Blue Shark* LWT, 2 76mm gun
  PCF 1 *Chamsuri* II with 1 12-cell 130mm MRL, 1 76mm gun
  PBF ε68 *Sea Dolphin*
MINE WARFARE 10
  MINE COUNTERMEASURES 9
    MHO 6 *Kan Kyeong*
    MSO 3 *Yang Yang*
  MINELAYERS • ML 1 *Won San* with 2 triple Mk32 324mm ASTT, 1 76mm gun, 1 hel landing platform
AMPHIBIOUS
  PRINCIPAL AMPHIBIOUS SHIPS 5
    LHD
      1 *Dokdo* with 1 Mk49 GMLS with RIM-116 SAM, 2 *Goalkeeper* CIWS (capacity 2 LCAC; 10 tanks; 700 troops; 10 UH-60 hel)
    LPD 4:
      4 *Cheonwangbong* (LST-II) (capacity 3 LCM; 2 MBT; 8 AFV; 300 troops; 2 med hel)
  LANDING SHIPS • LST 4 *Go Jun Bong* with 1 hel landing platform (capacity 20 tanks; 300 troops)
  LANDING CRAFT 22
    LCAC 5: 3 *Tsaplya* (capacity 1 MBT; 130 troops); 2 LSF-II (capacity 150 troops or 1 MBT & 24 troops)
    LCM 10 LCM-8
    LCT 3 *Mulgae* II
    LCU 4 *Mulgae* I
LOGISTICS AND SUPPORT 7
  AG 1 *Sunjin* (trials spt)
  AORH 3 *Chun Jee*
  ARS 1 *Cheong Hae Jin*
  ASR 1 *Tongyeong*
  AX 1 MTB

Naval Aviation
EQUIPMENT BY TYPE
AIRCRAFT 16 combat capable
  ASW 16: 8 P-3C *Orion*; 8 P-3CK *Orion*
  TPT • Light 5 Cessna F406 *Caravan* II
HELICOPTERS
  ASW 31: 11 *Lynx* Mk99; 12 *Lynx* Mk99A; 8 AW159 *Wildcat*
  MRH 3 SA319B *Alouette* III
  TPT 15: **Medium** 8 UH-60P *Black Hawk* **Light** 7 Bell 205 (UH-1H *Iroquois*)

Marines 29,000
FORCES BY ROLE
SPECIAL FORCES
  1 SF regt

MANOEUVRE
Amphibious
2 mne div (1 recce bn, 1 tk bn, 3 mne regt, 1 amph bn, 1 arty regt, 1 engr bn)
1 mne bde
COMBAT SUPPORT
Some cbt spt unit
EQUIPMENT BY TYPE
ARMOURED FIGHTING VEHICLES
MBT 100: 50 K1A1; 50 M48
AAV 166 AAV-7A1
ANTI-TANK/ANTI-INFRASTUCTURE
MSL • SP *Spike* NLOS
ARTILLERY • TOWED 105mm; 155mm
COASTAL DEFENCE • AShM RGM-84A *Harpoon* (truck mounted)
HELICOPTERS • TPT • Medium 1 MUH-1 *Surion*

Naval Special Warfare Flotilla

Air Force 65,000
4 Comd (Ops, Southern Combat, Logs, Trg)
FORCES BY ROLE
FIGHTER/GROUND ATTACK
2 sqn with F-4E *Phantom* II
6 sqn with F-5E/F *Tiger* II
3 sqn with F-15K *Eagle*
10 sqn with F-16C/D *Fighting Falcon* (KF-16C/D)
2 sqn with FA-50 *Fighting Eagle*
ISR
1 wg with KO-1
SIGINT
1 sqn with Hawker 800RA/XP
SEARCH & RESCUE
2 sqn with AS332L *Super Puma*; Bell 412EP; HH-47D *Chinook*; HH-60P *Black Hawk*; Ka-32 *Helix* C
TRANSPORT
1 VIP sqn with B-737-300; B-747; CN235-220; S-92A *Superhawk*; VH-60P *Black Hawk* (VIP)
3 sqn (incl 1 Spec Ops) with C-130H/H-30/J-30 *Hercules*
2 sqn with CN235M-100/220
TRAINING
2 sqn with F-5E/F *Tiger* II
1 sqn with F-16C/D *Fighting Falcon*
4 sqn with KT-1
1 sqn with Il-103
3 sqn with T-50/TA-50 *Golden Eagle**
TRANSPORT HELICOPTER
1 sqn with UH-60P *Black Hawk* (Spec Ops)
AIR DEFENCE
3 AD bde (total: 3 SAM bn with MIM-23B I-*Hawk*/*Cheongung*; 2 SAM bn with MIM-104E *Patriot* PAC-2 GEM-T)
EQUIPMENT BY TYPE
AIRCRAFT 590 combat capable
FTR 174: 142 F-5E *Tiger* II; 32 F-5F *Tiger* II
FGA 336: 60 F-4E *Phantom* II; 59 F-15K *Eagle*; 118 F-16C *Fighting Falcon* (KF-16C); 45 F-16D *Fighting Falcon* (KF-16D); 4 F-35A *Lightning* II (in test); 50 FA-50 *Fighting Eagle*
AEW&C 4 B-737 AEW
ISR 24: 4 Hawker 800RA; 20 KO-1
SIGINT 6: 4 Hawker 800SIG; 2 *Falcon* 2000 (COMINT/SIGINT)
TPT 38: **Medium** 16: 8 C-130H *Hercules*; 4 C-130H-30 *Hercules*; 4 C-130J-30 *Hercules*; **Light** 20: 12 CN235M-100; 8 CN235M-220 (incl 2 VIP); **PAX** 2: 1 B-737-300; 1 B-747
TRG 183: 83 KT-1; 49 T-50 *Golden Eagle**; 9 T-50B *Black Eagle** (aerobatics); 22 TA-50 *Golden Eagle**; ε20 KT-100
HELICOPTERS
SAR 16: 5 HH-47D *Chinook*; 11 HH-60P *Black Hawk*
MRH 3 Bell 412EP
TPT • **Medium** 30: 2 AS332L *Super Puma*; 8 Ka-32 *Helix* C; 3 S-92A *Super Hawk*; 7 UH-60P *Black Hawk*; 10 VH-60P *Black Hawk* (VIP)
UNMANNED AERIAL VEHICLES • ISR 103+: **Medium** 3+: some *Night Intruder*; 3 *Searcher* **Light** 100 *Harpy* (anti-radiation)
AIR DEFENCE • SAM 206
Long-range 48 MIM-104E *Patriot* PAC-2 GEM-T
Medium-range *Cheongung* (KM-SAM); 158 MIM-23B I-*Hawk*
AIR-LAUNCHED MISSILES
AAM • **IR** AIM-9 *Sidewinder*; **IIR** AIM-9X *Sidewinder* II; **SARH** AIM-7 *Sparrow*; **ARH** AIM-120B/C-5/7 AMRAAM
ASM AGM-65A *Maverick*; AGM-130
AShM AGM-84L *Harpoon* Block II; AGM-142 *Popeye*
ARM AGM-88 HARM
ALCM AGM-84H SLAM-ER; KEPD-350 *Taurus*
BOMBS • Laser-guided *Paveway* II

Paramilitary 9,000 active

Civilian Defence Corps 3,000,000 reservists (to age 50)

Coast Guard 9,000
Part of the Ministry of Maritime Affairs and Fisheries. Five regional headquarters and 17 coastguard stations
EQUIPMENT BY TYPE
PATROL AND COASTAL COMBATANTS 81
PSOH 15: 1 *Lee Cheong-ho* with 1 76mm gun; 1 *Sambongho*; 13 *Tae Pung Yang* with 1 med hel
PSO 21: 3 *Han Kang* with 1 76mm gun, 1 hel landing platform; 5 *Han Kang* II with 1 76mm gun, 1 hel landing pllatform; 12 *Jaemin* with 1 hel landing platform; 1 *Sumjinkang*
PCO 15 *Tae Geuk*
PCC 26: 4 *Bukhansan*; 6 (430 tonne); 14 *Hae Uri*; 2 *Hae Uri* II
PB ε4 (various)
AMPHIBIOUS
LANDING CRAFT • UCAC 8: 1 BHT-150; 4 *Griffon* 470TD; 3 *Griffon* 8000TD
AIRCRAFT
MP 5: 1 C-212-400 MP; 4 CN235-110 MPA
TPT • **PAX** 1 CL-604

HELICOPTERS
    MRH 7: 5 AS565MB *Panther*; 1 AW139; 1 Bell 412SP
    SAR 1 S-92
    TPT • Medium 8 Ka-32 *Helix* C

Cyber

Defense Cyber Command was established in the Ministry of National Defense in February 2015, but reports in 2018 indicated that it would be renamed as the Cyber Operations Command in light of the mid-2018 Defense Reform 2.0 initiative, and the findings of a Defense Cybersecurity Development Plan. The group will no longer be concerned with 'cyber psychological operations', reports said. A Korea–US National Cyber Defense Cooperation Working Group shares information and enhances cooperation including over policy, strategy, doctrine and training. There are also trilateral meetings with Japan and the US on cyber issues. In 2015, a unit responsible for overseeing cyber operations was established within the Joint Chiefs of Staff (JCS). The renamed Cyber Operations Command will reportedly be under the control of the chairman of the JCS, with the JCS in charge of 'operational plans to cope with cyberattacks'. The defence ministry is preparing a National Defense Cybersecurity Strategy, and announced in April 2017 that it would allocate US$218 million for cyber capabilities in 2018–22.

DEPLOYMENT

ARABIAN SEA & GULF OF ADEN: Combined Maritime Forces • CTF-151: 1 DDGHM

INDIA/PAKISTAN: UN • UNMOGIP 7 obs

LEBANON: UN • UNIFIL 335; 1 mech inf coy; 1 engr coy; 1 sigs coy; 1 maint coy

SOUTH SUDAN: UN • UNMISS 273; 2 obs; 1 engr coy

SUDAN: UN • UNAMID 2

UNITED ARAB EMIRATES: 139 (trg activities at UAE Spec Ops School)

WESTERN SAHARA: UN • MINURSO 4 obs

FOREIGN FORCES

Sweden NNSC: 5 obs
Switzerland NNSC: 5 obs
United States US Pacific Command: 28,500
    Army 19,200; 1 HQ (8th Army) at Yongsan; 1 div HQ at Ujieongbu; 1 armd bde with M1A2 SEPv2 *Abrams*; M2A2/M3A3 *Bradley*; M109A6; 1 (cbt avn) hel bde with AH-64 *Apache*; CH-47 *Chinook*; UH-60 *Black Hawk*; 1 MRL bde with M270A1 MLRS; 1 AD bde with MIM-104 *Patriot*/FIM-92A *Avenger*; 1 SAM bty with THAAD; 1 (APS) armd bde eqpt set
    Navy 250
    USAF 8,800; 1 HQ (7th Air Force) at Osan AB; 1 ftr wg at Kunsan AB (2 ftr sqn with 20 F-16C/D *Fighting Falcon*); 1 ftr wg at Osan AB (1 ftr sqn with 20 F-16C/D *Fighting Falcon*, 1 atk sqn with 24 A-10C *Thunderbolt* II); 1 ISR sqn at Osan AB with U-2S
    USMC 250

Laos LAO

New Lao Kip		2017	2018	2019
GDP	kip	140tr	152tr	
	US$	17.0bn	18.2bn	
per capita	US$	2,541	2,690	
Growth	%	6.9	6.8	
Inflation	%	0.8	0.9	
Def exp	kip	n.k.	n.k.	
	US$	n.k.	n.k.	
US$1=kip		8245.79	8324.69	

Population   7,234,171

Ethnic groups: Lao 55%; Khmou 11%; Hmong 8%

Age	0–14	15–19	20–24	25–29	30–64	65 plus
Male	16.3%	5.5%	4.9%	4.6%	16.5%	1.8%
Female	15.9%	5.5%	5.0%	4.7%	17.1%	2.2%

Capabilities

The Lao People's Armed Forces (LAPF) have considerable military experience from the Second Indo-China War and the 1988 border war with Thailand. They are closely linked to the ruling Communist Party and their primary role is internal security. A lack of financial resources has limited defence spending and military procurement for two decades. Contacts continue with the Chinese and Vietnamese armed forces, while there is strong defence cooperation with Russia. Laos also participates in ADMM–Plus military exercises, and in 2014–15 was co-chair with Japan of the ADMM–Plus expert working group on HADR. Training support is provided by friendly countries such as Russia and Vietnam. The LAPF have participated in regional exercises with neighbouring countries but have made no international deployments and have little capacity for sustained operations. In 2017, Russia and Laos signed a military-technical agreement to strengthen existing armaments cooperation. Laos still operates Soviet-era military equipment, and relies on Russian technical assistance. The country lacks a traditional defence industrial base and maintenance capacity is limited, reflected in a support contract for a Russian firm to maintain the air force's Mi-17 helicopters.

ACTIVE 29,100 (Army 25,600 Air 3,500) **Paramilitary 100,000**

Conscript liability 18 months minimum

ORGANISATIONS BY SERVICE

Space
EQUIPMENT BY TYPE
SATELLITES • **ISR** 1 LaoSat-1

Army 25,600
FORCES BY ROLE
4 mil regions
MANOEUVRE
    Armoured
    1 armd bn

Light
 5 inf div
 7 indep inf regt
 65 indep inf coy
COMBAT SUPPORT
 5 arty bn
 1 engr regt
 2 (construction) engr regt
AIR DEFENCE
 9 ADA bn
EQUIPMENT BY TYPE
ARMOURED FIGHTING VEHICLES
 MBT 25: 15 T-54/T-55; 10 T-34/85
 LT TK 10 PT-76
 APC • APC (W) 50: 30 BTR-40/BTR-60; 20 BTR-152
 AUV ZYZ-8002 (CS/VN3)
ENGINEERING & MAINTENANCE VEHICLES
 ARV T-54/T-55
 VLB MTU
ANTI-TANK/ANTI-INFRASTRUCTURE • RCL 57mm M18/A1; **75mm** M20; **106mm** M40; **107mm** B-11
ARTILLERY 62+
 TOWED 62: **105mm** 20 M101; **122mm** 20 D-30/M-30 M-1938; **130mm** 10 M-46; **155mm** 12 M114
 MOR 81mm; 82mm; 107mm M-1938/M2A1; **120mm** M-43
AIR DEFENCE
 SAM • Point-defence 9K32 *Strela*-2 (SA-7 *Grail*)‡; 9K310 *Igla*-1 (SA-16 *Gimlet*)
 GUNS
  SP 23mm ZSU-23-4
  TOWED 14.5mm ZPU-1/ZPU-4; **23mm** ZU-23; **37mm** M-1939; **57mm** S-60

Army Marine Section ε600
EQUIPMENT BY TYPE
PATROL AND COASTAL COMBATANTS • PBR some
AMPHIBIOUS LCM some

Air Force 3,500
FORCES BY ROLE
TRANSPORT
 1 regt with MA60; MA600; Mi-17 *Hip* H
EQUIPMENT BY TYPE
AIRCRAFT
 TPT • Light 5: 1 An-74TK *Coaler*; 2 MA60; 2 MA600
HELICOPTERS
 MRH 15: 6 Mi-17 *Hip* H; 5 Mi-17V-5 *Hip*; 4 Z-9A
 TPT 4: **Medium** 1 Ka-32T *Helix* C; **Light** 3 SA360 *Dauphin*

Paramilitary

Militia Self-Defence Forces 100,000+
Village 'home guard' or local defence

Malaysia MYS

Malaysian Ringgit RM		2017	2018	2019
GDP	RM	1.35tr	1.42tr	
	US$	312bn	347bn	
per capita	US$	9,755	10,704	
Growth	%	5.9	4.7	
Inflation	%	3.8	1.0	
Def bdgt	RM	15.1bn	15.9bn	
	US$	3.48bn	3.87bn	
US$1=RM		4.33	4.10	

Population 31,809,660

Ethnic groups: Malay 50.1%; Chinese 22.5%; Indian 6.5%; other or unspecified 20.9%

Age	0–14	15–19	20–24	25–29	30–64	65 plus
Male	14.1%	4.4%	4.1%	3.8%	21.2%	3.0%
Female	13.3%	4.2%	4.0%	3.8%	20.6%	3.3%

Capabilities

Substantial modernisation programmes over the past 30 years have developed the Malaysian armed forces' capacity for external defence. However, the 2013 armed intrusion at Lahad Datu in Sabah state, the aftermath of the March 2014 disappearance of Malaysia Airlines flight MH370 and Chinese naval intrusions into Malaysia's EEZ in 2015–16 revealed capability shortcomings, particularly in air and maritime surveillance. Addressing these capability gaps is a high priority, but budgetary constraints have slowed equipment procurement and infrastructural improvements. Malaysian forces regularly participate in ADMM-Plus, Five Power Defence Arrangements and other exercises with regional and international partners, including the US. Malaysia has invested in synthetic military training aids. In 2017, Malaysia began trilateral joint maritime patrols and joint Sulu Sea air patrols with Indonesia and the Philippines. The majority of Malaysia's military equipment is ageing and in several cases non-operational. However, some modest investments in new equipment have been made. For example, 22 Squadron was established in 2015 to operate Malaysia's new A400M transport aircraft. In recent decades, Malaysia has maintained a small defence industry providing maintenance, repair and overhaul services. Several companies now licence-build several major equipment types, such as *Gowind*-class frigates, though they have yet to export these.

ACTIVE 113,000 (Army 80,000 Navy 18,000 Air 15,000) Paramilitary 22,500

RESERVE 51,600 (Army 50,000, Navy 1,000 Air Force 600) Paramilitary 244,700

ORGANISATIONS BY SERVICE

Army 80,000 (to be 60–70,000)
2 mil region, 4 area comd (div)
FORCES BY ROLE
SPECIAL FORCES
 1 SF bde (3 SF bn)
MANOEUVRE
 Armoured
  1 tk regt (5 armd bn)

Mechanised
5 armd regt
1 mech inf bde (4 mech bn, 1 cbt engr sqn)
Light
5 inf bde (3 inf bn, 1 arty regt)
2 inf bde (3 inf bn)
1 inf bde (2 inf bn, 1 arty regt)
1 inf bde (2 inf bn)
Air Manoeuvre
1 (Rapid Deployment Force) AB bde (1 lt tk sqn, 4 AB bn, 1 lt arty regt, 1 engr sqn)
Other
1 (border) sy bde (5 bn)
1 (border) sy bde (forming)
COMBAT SUPPORT
9 arty regt
1 STA regt
1 MRL regt
1 cbt engr sqn
3 fd engr regt (total: 7 cbt engr sqn, 3 engr spt sqn)
1 construction regt
1 int unit
4 MP regt
1 sigs regt
HELICOPTER
1 hel sqn
1 tpt sqn with S-61A-4 *Nuri* (forming)
AIR DEFENCE
3 ADA regt
EQUIPMENT BY TYPE
ARMOURED FIGHTING VEHICLES
MBT 48 PT-91M *Twardy*
LT TK 21 *Scorpion*-90
RECCE 214: 130 AML-60/90; 74 SIBMAS (some†); 10 VBL
IFV 136: 31 ACV300 *Adnan* (25mm *Bushmaster*); 13 ACV300 *Adnan* AGL; 46 AV8 *Gempita* IFV25; 46 AV8 *Gempita* IFV30 (incl 10 with *Ingwe* ATGM)
APC 832
  APC (T) 265: 149 ACV300 *Adnan* (incl 69 variants); 13 FV4333 *Stormer* (upgraded); 63 K200A; 40 K200A1
  APC (W) 538: 32 *Anoa*; 26 AV8 *Gempita* APC (incl 13 CP; 3 sigs); 300 *Condor* (incl variants); 150 LAV-150 *Commando*; 30 M3 Panhard
  PPV 29: 9 IAG *Guardian*; 20 *Lipanbara*
ENGINEERING & MAINTENANCE VEHICLES
AEV 3 MID-M
ARV 47+: *Condor*; 15 ACV300; 4 K288A1; 22 SIBMAS; 6 WZT-4
VLB 5+: *Leguan*; 5 PMCz-90
NBC VEHICLES K216A1
ANTI-TANK/ANTI-INFRASTRUCTURE • MSL
SP 8 ACV300 *Baktar Shikan*
  MANPATS 9K115 *Metis* (AT-7 *Saxhorn*); 9K115-2 *Metis-M* (AT-13 *Saxhorn 2*); *Eryx*; *Baktar Shihan* (HJ-8); SS.11
RCL 260: 84mm 236 *Carl Gustav*; 106mm 24 M40
ARTILLERY 424
  TOWED 134: 105mm 100 Model 56 pack howitzer; 155mm 34: 12 FH-70; 22 G-5
  MRL 36 ASTROS II (equipped with 127mm SS-30)

MOR 254: 81mm 232; SP 81mm 14: 4 K281A1; 10 ACV300-S; SP 120mm 8 ACV-S
AMPHIBIOUS • LANDING CRAFT
LCA 165 Damen Assault Craft 540 (capacity 10 troops)
HELICOPTERS • TPT 12: Medium 2 S-61A-4 *Nuri*; Light 10 AW109
AIR DEFENCE
SAM • Point-defence 15+: 15 *Jernas* (*Rapier* 2000); *Anza*; HY-6 (FN-6); 9K38 *Igla* (SA-18 *Grouse*); *Starstreak*; QW-1 *Vanguard*;
GUNS 52+
  SP 20mm K263
  TOWED 52: 35mm 16 GDF-005; 40mm 36 L40/70

Reserves

Territorial Army
Some paramilitary forces to be incorporated into a re-organised territorial organisation
FORCES BY ROLE
MANOEUVRE
Mechanised
4 armd sqn
Light
16 inf regt (3 inf bn)
Other
5 (highway) sy bn
COMBAT SUPPORT
5 arty bty
2 fd engr regt
1 int unit
3 sigs sqn
COMBAT SUPPORT
4 med coy
5 tpt coy

Navy 18,000

3 Regional Commands: Kuantan (East Coast), Kinabalu (Borneo) and Langkawi (West Coast)
EQUIPMENT BY TYPE
SUBMARINES • TACTICAL • SSK 2 *Tunku Abdul Rahman* (FRA *Scorpène*) with 6 single 533mm TT with WASS *Black Shark* HWT/SM39 *Exocet* AShM
PRINCIPAL SURFACE COMBATANTS 10
FRIGATES 10
  FFGHM 2:
    2 *Lekiu* with 2 quad lnchr with MM40 *Exocet* Block 2 AShM, 1 16-cell VLS with *Sea Wolf* SAM, 2 B515 ILAS-3 triple 324mm ASTT with A244/S LWT, 1 57mm gun (capacity 1 *Super Lynx* hel)
  FFG 2:
    2 *Kasturi* with 2 quad lnchr with MM40 *Exocet* Block 2 AShM, 2 B515 ILAS-3 triple 324mm ASTT with A244/S LWT, 1 100mm gun, 1 57mm gun, 1 hel landing platform
  FF 6:
    6 *Kedah* (GER MEKO) with 1 76mm gun, 1 hel landing platform (fitted for MM40 *Exocet* AShM & RAM CIWS)

PATROL AND COASTAL COMBATANTS 37
  CORVETTES • FSGM 4 *Laksamana* with 3 twin lnchr with Mk 2 *Otomat* AShM, 1 *Albatros* quad lnchr with *Aspide* SAM, 1 76mm gun
  PCFG 4 *Perdana* (FRA *Combattante* II) with 2 single lnchr with MM38 *Exocet* AShM, 1 57mm gun
  PBG 4 *Handalan* (SWE *Spica*-M) with 2 twin lnchr with MM38 *Exocet* AShM , 1 57mm gun
  PBF 17 *Tempur* (SWE CB90)
  PB 8: 6 *Jerong* (Lurssen 45) with 1 57mm gun; 2 *Sri Perlis*
MINE WARFARE • MINE COUNTERMEASURES 4
  MCO 4 *Mahamiru* (ITA *Lerici*)
LOGISTICS AND SUPPORT 13
  AFS 2: 1 *Mahawangsa* with 2 57mm guns, 1 hel landing platform; 1 *Sri Indera Sakti* with 1 57mm gun, 1 hel landing platform
  AG 2 *Bunga Mas Lima* with 1 hel landing platform
  AGS 1 *Perantau*
  AP 2 *Sri Gaya*
  ASR 1 *Mega Bakti*
  ATF 1
  AX 3: 1 *Hang Tuah* with 1 57mm gun, 1 hel landing platform; 2 *Gagah Samudera* with 1 hel landing platform
  AXS 1

Naval Aviation 160

EQUIPMENT BY TYPE
HELICOPTERS
  ASW 6 *Super Lynx* 300
  MRH 6 AS555 *Fennec*
AIR-LAUNCHED MISSILES • AShM *Sea Skua*

Special Forces

FORCES BY ROLE
SPECIAL FORCES
  1 (mne cdo) SF unit

Air Force 15,000

1 air op HQ, 2 air div, 1 trg and log comd, 1 Intergrated Area Def Systems HQ
FORCES BY ROLE
FIGHTER
  2 sqn with MiG-29/MiG-29UB *Fulcrum*
FIGHTER/GROUND ATTACK
  1 sqn with F/A-18D *Hornet*
  1 sqn with Su-30MKM *Flanker*
  2 sqn with *Hawk* Mk108*/Mk208*
FIGHTER/GROUND ATTACK/ISR
  1 sqn with F-5E/F *Tiger* II; RF-5E *Tigereye**
MARITIME PATROL
  1 sqn with Beech 200T
TANKER/TRANSPORT
  2 sqn with KC-130H *Hercules*; C-130H *Hercules*; C-130H-30 *Hercules*; Cessna 402B
TRANSPORT
  1 sqn with A400M *Atlas*
  1 (VIP) sqn with A319CT; AW109; B-737-700 BBJ; BD700 *Global Express*; F-28 *Fellowship*; *Falcon* 900
  1 sqn with CN235
TRAINING
  1 unit with PC-7; SA316 *Alouette* III
TRANSPORT HELICOPTER
  4 (tpt/SAR) sqn with H225M *Super Cougar*; S-61A-4 *Nuri*; S-61N; S-70A *Black Hawk*
AIR DEFENCE
  1 sqn with *Starburst*
SPECIAL FORCES
  1 (Air Force Commando) unit (airfield defence/SAR)
EQUIPMENT BY TYPE
AIRCRAFT 66 combat capable
  FTR 21: 8 F-5E *Tiger* II; 3 F-5F *Tiger* II; 8 MiG-29 *Fulcrum* (MiG-29N); 2 MiG-29UB *Fulcrum* (MIG-29NUB)
  FGA 26: 8 F/A-18D *Hornet*; 18 Su-30MKM
  ISR 5: 3 Beech 200T; 2 RF-5E *Tigereye**
  TKR 4 KC-130H *Hercules*
  TKR/TPT 4 A400M *Atlas*
  TPT 33: **Medium** 10: 2 C-130H *Hercules*; 8 C-130H-30 *Hercules*; **Light** 18: 9 CN235M-220 (incl 1 VIP); 9 Cessna 402B (2 modified for aerial survey); **PAX** 5: 1 A319CT; 1 B-737-700 BBJ; 1 BD700 *Global Express*; 1 F-28 *Fellowship*; 1 *Falcon* 900
  TRG 78: 5 *Hawk* Mk108*; 12 *Hawk* Mk208*; 7 MB-339C; 7 MD3-160 *Aero Tiga*; 30 PC-7; 17 PC-7 Mk II *Turbo Trainer*
HELICOPTERS
  MRH 17 SA316 *Alouette* III
  TPT 42: **Heavy** 12 H225M *Super Cougar*; **Medium** 29: 25 S-61A-4 *Nuri*; 2 S-61N; 2 S-70A *Black Hawk*; **Light** 1 AW109
UNMANNED AERIAL VEHICLES
  ISR • Medium *Aludra*
AIR DEFENCE • SAM • Point-defence *Starburst*
AIR-LAUNCHED MISSILES
  AAM • IR AIM-9 *Sidewinder*; R-73 (AA-11 *Archer*); **IIR** AIM-9X *Sidewinder* II; **IR/SARH** R-27 (AA-10 *Alamo*); **SARH** AIM-7 *Sparrow*; **ARH** AIM-120C AMRAAM; R-77 (AA-12A *Adder*)
  ASM AGM-65 *Maverick*; Kh-29T (AS-14B *Kedge*); Kh-29L (AS-14A *Kedge*); Kh-31P (AS-17A *Krypton*); Kh-59M (AS-18 *Kazoo*)
  ARM Kh-31P (AS-17A *Krypton*);
  AShM AGM-84D *Harpoon*; Kh-31A (AS-17B *Krypton*)
BOMBS
  Electro-optical guided KAB-500KR; KAB-500OD
  Laser-guided *Paveway* II

Paramilitary ε22,500

Police–General Ops Force 18,000

FORCES BY ROLE
COMMAND
  5 bde HQ
SPECIAL FORCES
  1 spec ops bn
MANOEUVRE
  Other
  19 paramilitary bn
  2 (Aboriginal) paramilitary bn
  4 indep paramilitary coy

EQUIPMENT BY TYPE
ARMOURED FIGHTING VEHICLES
RECCE 192: ε100 S52 *Shorland*; 92 F V 701 *Ferret* (60 mod)
APC • APC (W) 140 AT105 *Saxon*
AUV ε30 SB-301

Malaysian Maritime Enforcement Agency (MMEA) ε4,500

Controls 5 Maritime Regions (Northern Peninsula; Southern Peninsula; Eastern Peninsula; Sarawak; Sabah), subdivided into a further 18 Maritime Districts. Supported by one provisional MMEA Air Unit

EQUIPMENT BY TYPE
PATROL AND COASTAL COMBATANTS 130
PSO 4: 1 *Arau* (ex-JPN *Nojima*) with 1 hel landing platform; 2 *Langkawi* with 1 57mm gun, 1 hel landing platform; 1 *Pekan* (ex-JPN *Ojika*) with 1 hel landing platform
PCC 3 *Bagan Datuk*
PBF 57: 18 *Penggalang 17* (TUR MRTP 16); 2 *Penggalang 18*; 6 *Penyelamat 20*; 16 *Penggalang 16*; 15 *Tugau*
PB 66: 15 *Gagah*; 4 *Malawali*; 2 *Nusa*; 3 *Nusa 28*; 1 *Peninjau*; 7 *Ramunia*; 2 *Rhu*; 4 *Semilang*; 6 *Sipadan* (ex-*Kris/Sabah*); 8 *Icarus 1650*; 10 *Pengawal*; 4 *Penyelamat*; 2 *Perwira*; 1 *Sugut*
LOGISTICS AND SUPPORT • AX 1 *Marlin*
AIRCRAFT • MP 2 Bombardier 415MP
HELICOPTERS
SAR 3 AW139
MRH 3 AS365 *Dauphin*

Area Security Units 3,500 reservists
(Auxiliary General Ops Force)
FORCES BY ROLE
MANOEUVRE
Other
89 paramilitary unit

Border Scouts 1,200 reservists
in Sabah, Sarawak

People's Volunteer Corps 240,000 reservists (some 17,500 armed)
RELA

DEPLOYMENT
DEMOCRATIC REPUBLIC OF THE CONGO: UN • MONUSCO 2; 4 obs
LEBANON: UN • UNIFIL 829; 1 mech inf bn
PHILIPPINES: IMT 16
SUDAN: UN • UNAMID 3; 1 obs; UN • UNISFA 1 obs
WESTERN SAHARA: UN • MINURSO 5 obs

FOREIGN FORCES
Australia 130; 1 inf coy (on 3-month rotational tours); 1 AP-3C *Orion* on occasion

Mongolia MNG

Mongolian Tugrik t		2017	2018	2019
GDP	t	27.2tr	31.2tr	
	US$	11.1bn	12.7bn	
per capita	US$	3,640	4,098	
Growth	%	5.1	6.2	
Inflation	%	4.6	7.6	
Def bdgt	t	207bn	257bn	261bn
	US$	84.8m	105m	
FMA (US)	US$	2.6m	0m	
US$1=t		2439.79	2452.15	

Population 3,103,428
Ethnic groups: Khalkh 81.9%; Kazakh 3.8%; Dorvod 2.7%; other or unspecified 11.6%

Age	0–14	15–19	20–24	25–29	30–64	65 plus
Male	13.8%	3.8%	4.1%	4.9%	20.5%	1.8%
Female	13.2%	3.7%	4.0%	5.0%	22.5%	2.6%

Capabilities

Mongolia's latest defence-policy document, from 2015, stresses the importance of peacekeeping and anti-terrorist capabilities. The country has no formal military alliances, but pursues defence ties and bilateral training with multiple regional powers and others including India, Turkey and the US. Mongolia is also seeking to develop its security relationship with China. Mongolia hosts the annual *Khaan Quest* multinational peacekeeping-training exercises. The country's main exercise partners are India and Russia, with each country running regular bilateral exercises. Mongolia's most significant deployments are to the UN peacekeeping mission in South Sudan and Afghanistan. The armed forces remain reliant on Soviet-era equipment, although this has been supplemented by deliveries of second-hand Russian weapons. Barring maintenance facilities, there is no significant defence-industrial base, and Mongolia relies on imports from Russia to equip its armed forces.

ACTIVE 9,700 (Army 8,900 Air 800) Paramilitary 7,500
Conscript liability 12 months for males aged 18–25
RESERVE 137,000 (Army 137,000)

ORGANISATIONS BY SERVICE

Army 5,600; 3,300 conscript (total 8,900)
FORCES BY ROLE
MANOEUVRE
Mechanised
1 MR bde
Light
1 (rapid deployment) lt inf bn (2nd bn to form)
Air Manoeuvre
1 AB bn
COMBAT SUPPORT
1 arty regt

EQUIPMENT BY TYPE
ARMOURED FIGHTING VEHICLES
  MBT 420: 370 T-54/T-55; 50 T-72A
  RECCE 120 BRDM-2
  IFV 310 BMP-1
  APC • APC (W) 210: 150 BTR-60; 40 BTR-70M; 20 BTR-80
ENGINEERING & MAINTENANCE VEHICLES
  ARV T-54/T-55
ANTI-TANK/ANTI-INFRASTRUCTURE
  GUNS • TOWED 200: **85mm** D-44/D-48; **100mm** M-1944/MT-12
ARTILLERY 570
  TOWED ε300: **122mm** D-30/M-30 (M-1938); **130mm** M-46; **152mm** ML-20 (M-1937)
  MRL **122mm** 130 BM-21
  MOR 140: **120mm**; **160mm**; **82mm**
AIR DEFENCE
  SAM Medium-range 2+ S-125 *Pechora*-2M (SA-26)
  GUNS • TOWED **23mm** ZU-23-2

Air Force 800
FORCES BY ROLE
TRANSPORT
  1 sqn with An-24 *Coke*; An-26 *Curl*
ATTACK/TRANSPORT HELICOPTER
  1 sqn with Mi-8 *Hip*; Mi-171
AIR DEFENCE
  2 regt with S-60/ZPU-4/ZU-23
EQUIPMENT BY TYPE
AIRCRAFT • TPT • **Light** 3: 2 An-24 *Coke*; 1 An-26 *Curl*
HELICOPTERS
  TPT • **Medium** 12: 10 Mi-8 *Hip*; 2 Mi-171
AIR DEFENCE • GUNS • TOWED 150: **14.5mm** ZPU-4; **23mm** ZU-23; **57mm** S-60

Paramilitary 7,500 active

Border Guard 1,300; 4,700 conscript (total 6,000)

Internal Security Troops 400; 800 conscript (total 1,200)
FORCES BY ROLE
MANOEUVRE
  Other
    4 gd unit

Construction Troops 300

DEPLOYMENT
AFGHANISTAN: NATO • *Operation Resolute Support* 120
DEMOCRATIC REPUBLIC OF THE CONGO: UN • MONUSCO 2 obs
SOUTH SUDAN: UN • UNMISS 867; 7 obs; 1 inf bn
SUDAN: UN • UNAMID 2; **UN** • UNISFA 1; 2 obs
WESTERN SAHARA: UN • MINURSO 4 obs

Myanmar MMR

Myanmar Kyat K		2017	2018	2019
GDP	K	91.3tr	97.7tr	
	US$	67.3bn	71.5bn	
per capita	US$	1,278	1,354	
Growth	%	6.8	6.4	
Inflation	%	4.0	6.0	
Def bdgt	K	2.92tr	2.66tr	
	US$	2.15bn	1.95bn	
US$1=K		1356.68	1365.23	

Population 55,622,506

Ethnic groups: Burman 68%; Shan 9%; Karen 7%; Rakhine 4%; Chinese 3+%; Other Chin, Kachin, Kayan, Lahu, Mon, Palaung, Pao, Wa, 9%

Age	0–14	15–19	20–24	25–29	30–64	65 plus
Male	13.6%	4.4%	4.4%	4.0%	20.4%	2.5%
Female	13.0%	4.3%	4.4%	4.2%	21.6%	3.2%

Capabilities

Since the country's independence struggle in the 1940s, Myanmar's large, army-dominated Tatmadaw (armed forces) has been intimately involved in domestic politics. Even though the National League for Democracy (NLD) won the November 2015 election, the armed forces remain politically powerful. A defence white paper published in 2016 placed as a key priority ending conflicts with domestic armed groups. It also gives a 'state-building' role to the Tatmadaw, legitimising continued intervention in the country's politics. In its counter-insurgency operations, the Tatmadaw has been accused by international organisations of human-rights abuses, and concerns have increased after military actions against the Rohingya minority in 2017. China and Russia are key defence-cooperation partners, including bilateral military exercises and the provision of weapons. In 2016, Myanmar and Russia signed a broad cooperation agreement including military training. Due to long-running domestic conflicts, the Tatmadaw has experience with counter-insurgency operations and jungle warfare. Although there have been small deployments to UN missions, the Tatmadaw remains essentially an internally focused force. Since the 1990s, the armed forces have attempted to develop limited conventional-warfare capabilities, and have brought into service new armoured vehicles, air-defence weapons, artillery, combat aircraft and ships procured mainly from China and Russia. There is limited defence-industrial capacity. The Aircraft Production and Maintenance Base has assembled Chinese K-8 trainer aircraft and Myanmar allegedly aims to negotiate license-production for the Chinese JF-17 combat aircraft. Myanmar also has growing shipbuilding capabilities, notably through the Naval Dockyard in Yangon, which launched patrol and utility vessels in 2018.

ACTIVE 406,000 (Army 375,000 Navy 16,000 Air 15,000) **Paramilitary 107,000**

Conscript liability 24–36 months

ORGANISATIONS BY SERVICE

Army ε375,000

14 military regions, 7 regional op comd

FORCES BY ROLE
COMMAND
20 div HQ (military op comd)
10 inf div HQ
34+ bde HQ (tactical op comd)
MANOEUVRE
Armoured
10 armd bn
Light
100 inf bn (coy)
337 inf bn (coy) (regional comd)
COMBAT SUPPORT
7 arty bn
37 indep arty coy
6 cbt engr bn
54 fd engr bn
40 int coy
45 sigs bn
AIR DEFENCE
7 AD bn
EQUIPMENT BY TYPE
ARMOURED FIGHTING VEHICLES
  MBT 185+: 10 T-55; 50 T-72S; 25+ Type-59D; 100 Type-69-II
  LT TK 105 Type-63 (ε60 serviceable)
  ASLT 24 PTL-02 mod
  RECCE 87+: 12+ EE-9 *Cascavel*; 45 *Ferret*; 30 Mazda; MAV-1
  IFV 10+ BTR-3U
  APC 431+
    APC (T) 331: 26 MT-LB; 250 Type-85; 55 Type-90
    APC (W) 90+: 20 Hino; 40 Humber *Pig*; 30+ Type-92
    PPV 10 MPV
ENGINEERING & MAINTENANCE VEHICLES
  ARV Type-72
  VLB MT-55A
ANTI-TANK/ANTI-INFRASTRUCTURE
  RCL 84mm *Carl Gustav*; **106mm** M40A1
  GUNS • TOWED 60: **57mm** 6-pdr; **76mm** 17-pdr
ARTILLERY 422+
  SP 155mm 42: 30 NORA B-52; 12 SH-1
  TOWED 264+: **105mm** 132: 36 M-56; 96 M101; **122mm** 100 D-30; **130mm** 16 M-46; **140mm**; **155mm** 16 Soltam M-845P
  MRL 36+: **107mm** 30 Type-63; **122mm** BM-21 *Grad* (reported); Type-81; **240mm** 6+ M-1985 mod
  MOR 80+: **82mm** Type-53 (M-37); **120mm** 80+: 80 Soltam; Type-53 (M-1943)
SURFACE-TO-SURFACE MISSILE LAUNCHERS
  SRBM • Conventional some *Hwasong*-6 (reported)
AIR DEFENCE
  SAM
    Medium-range 4+: 4 KS-1A (HQ-12); S-125 *Pechora*-2M (SA-26); 2K12 *Kvadrat*-M (SA-6 *Gainful*)
    Point-defence Some 2K22 *Tunguska* (SA-19 *Grison*); HN-5 *Hong Nu/Red Cherry* (reported); 9K310 *Igla*-1 (SA-16 *Gimlet*)
  GUNS 46 **SP 57mm** 12 Type-80
  TOWED 34: **37mm** 24 Type-74; **40mm** 10 M1

Navy ε16,000
EQUIPMENT BY TYPE
PRINCIPAL SURFACE COMBATANTS • FRIGATES 5
  FFGHM 2 *Kyansitthar* with 2 twin lnchr with C-802 (CH-SS-N-8 *Saccade*) AShM, 1 sextuple lnchr with MANPAD SAM, 4 AK630 CIWS, 1 76mm gun (capacity 1 med hel)
  FFG 3:
    1 *Aung Zeya* with 2 quad lnchr with DPRK AShM (possibly Kh-35 derivative), 4 AK630 CIWS, 1 76mm gun, 1 hel landing platform
    2 *Mahar Bandoola* (PRC Type-053H1) with 2 quad lnchr with C-802 (CH-SS-N-8 *Saccade*) AShM, 2 RBU 1200 A/S mor, 2 twin 100mm gun
PATROL AND COASTAL COMBATANTS 77
  CORVETTES 3
    FSGHM 1 *Tabinshwethi* (*Anawrahta* mod) with 2 twin lnchr with C-802 (CH-SS-N-8 *Saccade*), 1 sextuple lnchr with unknown MANPADs, 2 RBU 1200 A/S mor, 2 AK630 CIWS, 1 76mm gun (capacity 1 med hel)
    FSG 2 *Anawrahta* with 2 twin lnchr with C-802 (CH-SS-N-8 *Saccade*) AShM, 2 RDC-32 A/S mor, 1 76mm gun, 1 hel landing platform
  PSOH 1 *Inlay* with 1 twin 57mm gun
  PCG 7: 6 *Houxin* with 2 twin lnchr with C-801 (CH-SS-N-4 *Sardine*) AShM; 1 FAC(M) mod with 2 twin lnchr with C-802 (CH-SS-N-8 *Saccade*) AShM, 1 AK630 CIWS
  PCO 2 *Indaw*
  PCC 11: 2 *Admirable* (ex-US); 9 *Hainan* with 4 RBU 1200 A/S mor, 2 twin 57mm gun
  PBG 4 *Myanmar* with 2 single lnchr with C-801 (CH-SS-N-4 *Sardine*) AShM
  PBF 3: 1 Type-201; 2 *Super Dvora* Mk III
  PB 32: 3 PB-90; 6 PGM 401; 6 PGM 412; 14 *Myanmar*; 3 *Swift*
  PBR 14: 4 *Sagu*; 9 Y-301†; 1 Y-301 (Imp)
AMPHIBIOUS • LANDING CRAFT 15
  LCU 5; **LCM** 10
LOGISTICS AND SUPPORT 13
  ABU 1
  AGHS 2: 1 *Innya*; 1 (near shore)
  AGS 1
  AH 2
  AK 1
  AKSL 5
  AP 1 *Chindwin*

Naval Infantry 800
FORCES BY ROLE
MANOEUVRE
  Light
  1 inf bn

Air Force ε15,000
FORCES BY ROLE
FIGHTER
  4 sqn with F-7 *Airguard*; FT-7; MiG-29B *Fulcrum*; MiG-29SM *Fulcrum*; MiG-29UB *Fulcrum*
GROUND ATTACK
  2 sqn with A-5M *Fantan*
TRANSPORT
  1 sqn with An-12 *Cub*; F-27 *Friendship*; FH-227; PC-6A/B *Turbo Porter*

TRAINING
2 sqn with G-4 *Super Galeb**; PC-7 *Turbo Trainer**; PC-9*
1 (trg/liaison) sqn with Cessna 550 *Citation* II; Cessna 180 *Skywagon*; K-8 *Karakorum**

TRANSPORT HELICOPTER
4 sqn with Bell 205; Bell 206 *Jet Ranger*; Mi-17 *Hip* H; Mi-35P *Hind*; PZL Mi-2 *Hoplite*; PZL W-3 *Sokol*; SA316 *Alouette* III

EQUIPMENT BY TYPE
AIRCRAFT 153 combat capable
  FTR 63: 21 F-7 *Airguard*; 10 FT-7; 11 MiG-29 *Fulcrum*; 6 MiG-29SE *Fulcrum*; 10 MiG-29SM *Fulcrum*; 5 MiG-29UB *Fulcrum*
  FGA 6 JF-17 *Thunder* (FC-1 Block 2)
  ATK 22 A-5M *Fantan*
  TPT 20: **Medium** 5: 4 Y-8D; 1 Y-8F-200W **Light** 16: 3 Beech 1900D; 4 Cessna 180 *Skywagon*; 1 Cessna 550 *Citation* II; 3 F-27 *Friendship*; 5 PC-6A/B *Turbo Porter*; **PAX** 1+ FH-227
  TRG 82: 11 G-4 *Super Galeb**; 20 Grob G120; 24+ K-8 *Karakorum**; 12 PC-7 *Turbo Trainer**; 9 PC-9*; 6 Yak-130 *Mitten**
HELICOPTERS
  ATK 10 Mi-35P *Hind*
  MRH 23: 3 AS365; 11 Mi-17 *Hip* H; 9 SA316 *Alouette* III
  TPT 45: **Medium** 10 PZL W-3 *Sokol*; **Light** 35: 12 Bell 205; 6 Bell 206 *Jet Ranger*; 17 PZL Mi-2 *Hoplite*
UNMANNED AERIAL VEHICLES
  CISR • **Heavy** 4 CH-3
AIR-LAUNCHED MISSILES • **AAM** • **IR** PL-5; R-73 (AA-11 *Archer*); **IR/SARH** R-27 (AA-10 *Alamo*)

Paramilitary 107,000

People's Police Force 72,000

People's Militia 35,000

DEPLOYMENT
SOUTH SUDAN: UN • UNMISS 1; 1 obs

Nepal NPL

Nepalese Rupee NR		2017	2018	2019
GDP	NR	2.64tr	3.01tr	
	US$	24.9bn	28.8bn	
per capita	US$	848	971	
Growth	%	7.9	6.3	
Inflation	%	4.5	4.2	
Def bdgt	NR	35.7bn	45.0bn	44.9bn
	US$	336m	431m	
FMA (US)	US$	1.7m	0m	
US$1=NR		106.21	104.37	

Population   29,717,587
Religious groups: Hindu 90%; Buddhist 5%; Muslim 3%

Age	0–14	15–19	20–24	25–29	30–64	65 plus
Male	15.4%	5.5%	5.4%	4.2%	15.7%	2.6%
Female	14.1%	5.2%	5.4%	4.8%	18.9%	2.7%

Capabilities

The principal role of Nepal's armed forces is maintaining territorial integrity, but they have also traditionally focused on internal security and humanitarian relief. Nepal has a policy of providing contingents to UN peacekeeping operations in the Middle East and Africa. Training support is provided by several countries, including China, India and the US. Following a 2006 peace accord with the Maoist People's Liberation Army, Maoist personnel underwent a process of demobilisation or integration into the armed forces. Gurkhas continue to be recruited by the British and Indian armed forces and the Singaporean police. The small air wing provides a limited transport and support capacity but mobility remains a challenge, in part because of the country's topography. This deficit was highlighted by Nepal's dependence on foreign-military logistical and medical assistance following the earthquake in April 2015. This dependence remains. Nepal's logistic capability appears to be sufficient for internal-security operations, including countering IEDs, however its contingents on UN peacekeeping operations appear to largely depend on contracted logistic support. Modernisation plans include a very limited increase in the size of its air force. Barring maintenance capacities there is no defence-industrial base, and Nepal is dependent on foreign suppliers for modern equipment.

ACTIVE 96,600 (Army 96,600) Paramilitary 15,000

ORGANISATIONS BY SERVICE

Army 96,600
FORCES BY ROLE
COMMAND
  6 inf div HQ
  1 (valley) comd
SPECIAL FORCES
  1 bde (1 SF bn, 1 AB bn, 1 cdo bn, 1 ranger bn, 1 mech inf bn)
MANOEUVRE
  Light
  16 inf bde (total: 62 inf bn; 32 indep inf coy)
COMBAT SUPPORT
  4 arty regt
  5 engr bn
AIR DEFENCE
  2 AD regt
  4 indep AD coy

EQUIPMENT BY TYPE
ARMOURED FIGHTING VEHICLES
  RECCE 40 *Ferret*
  APC 253
    APC (W) 13: 8 OT-64C; 5 WZ-551
    PPV 240: 90 *Casspir*; 150 MPV
ARTILLERY 92+
  TOWED 105mm 22: 8 L118 Light Gun; 14 pack howitzer (6 non-operational)
  MOR 70+: **81mm; 120mm** 70 M-43 (est 12 op)
AIR DEFENCE • GUNS • TOWED 32+: **14.5mm** 30 Type-56 (ZPU-4); **37mm** (PRC); **40mm** 2 L/60

Air Wing 320
EQUIPMENT BY TYPE†
AIRCRAFT • TPT 2: **Light** 2: 1 BN-2T *Islander*; 1 M-28 *Skytruck*

HELICOPTERS
MRH 12: 2 *Dhruv*; 2 *Lancer*; 3 Mi-17-1V *Hip* H; 2 Mi-17V-5 *Hip*; 1 SA315B *Lama (Cheetah)*; 2 SA316B *Alouette* III
TPT 3: **Medium** 1 SA330J *Puma*; **Light** 2 AS350B2 *Ecureuil*

Paramilitary 15,000

Armed Police Force 15,000
Ministry of Home Affairs

DEPLOYMENT

CENTRAL AFRICAN REPUBLIC: UN • MINUSCA 340; 4 obs; 1 MP coy

DEMOCRATIC REPUBLIC OF THE CONGO: UN • MONUSCO 884; 10 obs; 1 inf bn; 1 engr coy

IRAQ: UN • UNAMI 77; 1 sy unit

LEBANON: UN • UNIFIL 871; 1 mech inf bn

LIBYA: UN • UNISMIL 229; 1 obs; 2 sy coy

MALI: UN • MINUSMA 153; 3 obs; 1 EOD coy

MIDDLE EAST: UN • UNTSO 4 obs

SOUTH SUDAN: UN • UNMISS 1,745; 13 obs; 2 inf bn

SUDAN: UN • UNAMID 359; 7 obs; 2 inf coy; **UN** • UNISFA 5; 1 obs

SYRIA/ISRAEL: UN • UNDOF 333; 2 mech inf coy

WESTERN SAHARA: UN • MINURSO 5 obs

FOREIGN FORCES
United Kingdom 60 (Gurkha trg org)

New Zealand NZL

New Zealand Dollar NZ$		2017	2018	2019
GDP	NZ$	283bn	296bn	
	US$	201bn	206bn	
per capita	US$	41,572	41,616	
Growth	%	3.0	3.1	
Inflation	%	1.9	1.4	
Def bdgt	NZ$	3.31bn	3.40bn	3.75bn
	US$	2.35bn	2.37bn	
US$1=NZ$		1.41	1.44	
Population	4,545,627			

Age	0–14	15–19	20–24	25–29	30–64	65 plus
Male	10.1%	3.3%	3.4%	3.4%	22.3%	7.2%
Female	9.6%	3.2%	3.2%	3.4%	22.5%	8.4%

Capabilities

New Zealand has a strong military tradition. The New Zealand Defence Force (NZDF) is well trained and has operational experience. The June 2016 defence white paper foresaw a range of challenges likely to affect the country's security in the period to 2040, including rising tension in the South and East China seas. In response, among other areas, defence policy will emphasise awareness of and capacity to respond to activity in the maritime domain. The white paper indicated investment in improved maritime air-surveillance capability, new cyber-support capability for deployed operations and additional intelligence personnel, but said that until 2030 defence spending was expected to remain pegged at around 1% of GDP. There are also plans to expand army personnel strength over the next decade. New Zealand's closest defence partner is Australia but the country has revived defence relations with the US. The 2016 Defence Capability Plan outlined procurements needed to achieve the white paper's vision, including deliveries of new frigates in the late 2020s and P-8A *Poseidon* maritime-patrol aircraft in the 2020s. However, the decommissioning of HMNZS *Endeavour* in 2017 meant New Zealand lost its at-sea-replenishment capability, which will not return until HMNZS *Aotearoa* enters service in 2021. New Zealand has a small defence industry consisting of numerous private companies and subsidiaries of larger North American and European companies. These companies are able to provide some maintenance, repair and overhaul capability but significant work, such as the ANZAC frigate upgrade, is contracted to foreign companies.

ACTIVE 9,000 (Army 4,500 Navy 2,050 Air 2,450)

RESERVE 2,300 (Army 1,650 Navy 450 Air Force 200)

ORGANISATIONS BY SERVICE

Army 4,500
FORCES BY ROLE
SPECIAL FORCES
  1 SF regt
MANOEUVRE
  Light
  1 inf bde (1 armd recce regt, 2 lt inf bn, 1 arty regt (2 arty bty), 1 engr regt(-), 1 MP coy, 1 sigs regt, 2 log bn, 1 med bn)
EQUIPMENT BY TYPE
ARMOURED FIGHTING VEHICLES
  IFV 93 NZLAV-25
ENGINEERING & MAINTENANCE VEHICLES
  AEV 7 NZLAV
  ARV 3 LAV-R
ANTI-TANK/ANTI-INFRASTRUCTURE
  MSL • **MANPATS** FGM-148 *Javelin*
  RCL 84mm *Carl Gustav*
ARTILLERY 60
  TOWED 105mm 24 L118 Light Gun
  MOR 81mm 36

Reserves

Territorial Force 1,650 reservists
Responsible for providing trained individuals for augmenting deployed forces
FORCES BY ROLE
COMBAT SERVICE SUPPORT
  3 (Territorial Force Regional) trg regt

Navy 2,050

Fleet based in Auckland. Fleet HQ at Wellington

EQUIPMENT BY TYPE
PRINCIPAL SURFACE COMBATANTS • FRIGATES • FFHM 2:

2 *Anzac* (GER MEKO 200) with 1 octuple Mk41 VLS with RIM-7M *Sea Sparrow* SAM, 2 triple Mk32 324mm TT with Mk46 mod 5 LWT, 1 Mk15 *Phalanx* Block 1B CIWS, 1 127mm gun (capacity 1 SH-2G(I) *Super Seasprite* ASW hel)

PATROL AND COASTAL COMBATANTS 6

PSOH 2 *Otago* (capacity 1 SH-2G(I) *Super Seasprite* ASW hel) (ice-strengthened hull)

PCC 4 *Lake*

AMPHIBIOUS • LANDING CRAFT • LCM 2

LOGISTICS AND SUPPORT • 1

AKRH 1 *Canterbury* (capacity 4 NH90 tpt hel; 1 SH-2G(I) *Super Seasprite* ASW hel; 2 LCM; 16 NZLAV; 14 NZLAV; 20 trucks; 250 troops)

Air Force 2,450

FORCES BY ROLE
MARITIME PATROL

1 sqn with P-3K2 *Orion*

TRANSPORT

1 sqn with B-757-200 (upgraded); C-130H *Hercules* (upgraded)

ANTI-SUBMARINE/SURFACE WARFARE

1 (RNZAF/RNZN) sqn with SH-2G(I) *Super Seasprite*

TRAINING

1 sqn with T-6C *Texan* II

1 sqn with Beech 200 *King Air* (leased)

TRANSPORT HELICOPTER

1 sqn with AW109; NH90

EQUIPMENT BY TYPE

AIRCRAFT 6 combat capable

ASW 6 P-3K2 *Orion*

TPT 11: **Medium** 5 C-130H *Hercules* (upgraded); **Light** 4 Beech 200 *King Air* (leased); **PAX** 2 B-757-200 (upgraded)

TRG 11 T-6C *Texan* II

HELICOPTERS

ASW 8 SH-2G(I) *Super Seasprite*

TPT 13: **Medium** 8 NH90; **Light** 5 AW109

AIR-LAUNCHED MISSILES • AShM AGM-119 *Penguin* Mk2 mod7

DEPLOYMENT

AFGHANISTAN: NATO • *Operation Resolute Support* 13

EGYPT: MFO 26; 1 trg unit; 1 tpt unit

IRAQ: *Operation Inherent Resolve* 143; 1 trg unit

MIDDLE EAST: UN • UNTSO 7 obs

SOUTH SUDAN: UN • UNMISS 2; 3 obs

Pakistan PAK

Pakistani Rupee Rs		2017	2018	2019
GDP	Rs	32.0tr	34.4tr	
	US$	305bn	307bn	
per capita	US$	1,546	1,527	
Growth	%	5.4	5.8	
Inflation	%	4.1	3.9	
Def bdgt [a]	Rs	1.02tr	1.26tr	1.36tr
	US$	9.75bn	11.2bn	
FMA (US)	US$	242m	100m	
US$1=Rs		104.81	112.08	

[a] Includes defence allocations to the Public Sector Development Programme (PSDP), including funding to the Defence Division and the Defence Production Division

Population 207,862,518

Religious groups: Hindu less than 3%

Age	0–14	15–19	20–24	25–29	30–64	65 plus
Male	15.8%	5.5%	5.3%	4.9%	17.7%	2.1%
Female	15.0%	5.1%	5.0%	4.6%	16.6%	2.4%

Capabilities

The armed forces have considerable domestic political influence, including a strong voice on security policy. Pakistan's nuclear and conventional forces have traditionally been oriented and structured against a prospective threat from India. Since 2008, however, counter-insurgency and counter-terrorism have been of increasing importance and are now the forces' main effort. While an army-led counter-terrorism operation has improved domestic security, terrorist attacks continue. The armed forces have a major role in disaster relief and are well practised in such operations. China is Pakistan's main defence partner, with all three services employing a large amount of Chinese equipment. Military cooperation with the US is limited by sanctions aiming to improve cooperation on counter-terrorism. Recruitment is good, retention is high and the forces are well trained. The army and air force have considerable operational experience from a decade of counter-insurgency operations in Pakistan's tribal areas. Major investment in military nuclear programmes continue, including the commissioning of a VLF submarine-communications facility and the continued development of a submarine-launched cruise missile. The air force is modernising its inventory while improving its precision-strike and ISR capabilities. Recent and likely future naval investment in Chinese-supplied frigates, missile craft and submarines would improve sea-denial capabilities. The indigenous defence industry exports defence equipment, weapons and ammunition. There is considerable defence-industrial collaboration with China, notably through the co-development of the JF-17 combat aircraft.

ACTIVE 653,800 (Army 560,000 Navy 23,800 Air 70,000) **Paramilitary 282,000**

ORGANISATIONS BY SERVICE

Strategic Forces

Operational control rests with the National Command Authority. The Strategic Plans Directorate (SPD) manages and commands all of Pakistan's military nuclear capability.

The SPD also commands a reportedly 25,000-strong military security force responsible for guarding military nuclear infrastructure

Army Strategic Forces Command 12,000–15,000

Commands all land-based strategic nuclear forces

EQUIPMENT BY TYPE
SURFACE-TO-SURFACE MISSILE LAUNCHERS 60+
MRBM • Nuclear ε30 *Ghauri/Ghauri* II (*Hatf*-5)/ *Shaheen*-2 (*Hatf*-6 – in test); *Shaheen*-3 (in test)
SRBM • Nuclear 30+: ε30 *Ghaznavi* (*Hatf*-3 – PRC M-11)/*Shaheen*-1 (*Hatf*-4); some *Abdali* (*Hatf*-2); some *Nasr* (*Hatf*-9)
GLCM • Nuclear *Babur* (*Hatf*-7); *Ra'ad* (*Hatf*-8 – in test)

Air Force

1–2 sqn of F-16A/B or *Mirage* 5 may be assigned a nuclear-strike role

Army 560,000

FORCES BY ROLE
COMMAND
9 corps HQ
1 (area) comd
SPECIAL FORCES
2 SF gp (total: 4 SF bn)
MANOEUVRE
Armoured
2 armd div
7 indep armd bde
Mechanised
2 mech inf div
1 indep mech bde
Light
18 inf div
5 indep inf bde
Other
1 sy div (1 more div forming)
COMBAT SUPPORT
1 arty div
14 arty bde
7 engr bde
AVIATION
1 VIP avn sqn
4 avn sqn
HELICOPTER
3 atk hel sqn
2 ISR hel sqn
2 SAR hel sqn
2 tpt hel sqn
1 spec ops hel sqn
AIR DEFENCE
1 AD comd (3 AD gp (total: 8 AD bn))
EQUIPMENT BY TYPE
ARMOURED FIGHTING VEHICLES
MBT 2,496+: 300 *Al-Khalid* (MBT 2000); ε50 *Al-Khalid* I; 320 T-80UD; 51 T-54/T-55; 1,100 Type-59/*Al-Zarrar*; 400 Type-69; 275+ Type-85 (270 M48A5 in store)
APC 1,605
APC (T) 1,260: 1,160 M113/*Talha*; ε100 Type-63

APC (W) 120 BTR-70/BTR-80
PPV 225 *Maxxpro*
AUV 10 *Dingo* 2 **ENGINEERING & MAINTENANCE VEHICLES**
ARV 117+: 65 Type-653; *Al-Hadeed*; 52 M88A1; T-54/T-55
VLB M47M; M48/60
MW *Aardvark* Mk II
ANTI-TANK/ANTI-INFRASTRUCTURE
MSL
SP M901 TOW
MANPATS HJ-8; TOW
RCL 75mm Type-52; **106mm** M40A1 **RL 89mm** M20
GUNS 85mm 200 Type-56 (D-44)
ARTILLERY 4,472+
SP 375: **155mm** 315: 200 M109A2; ε115 M109A5 **203mm** 60 M110/M110A2
TOWED 1,659: **105mm** 329: 216 M101; 113 M-56; **122mm** 570: 80 D-30 (PRC); 490 Type-54 (M-1938); **130mm** 410 Type-59-I; **155mm** 322: 144 M114; 148 M198; ε30 *Panter*; **203mm** 28 M115
MRL 88+: **107mm** Type-81; **122mm** 52+: 52 *Azar* (Type-83); some KRL-122; **300mm** 36 A100
MOR 2,350+: **81mm**; **120mm** AM-50
SURFACE-TO-SURFACE MISSILE LAUNCHERS
MRBM • Nuclear ε30 *Ghauri/Ghauri* II (*Hatf*-5); some *Shaheen*-2 (*Hatf*-6 – in test); *Shaheen*-3 (in test)
SRBM 135+: **Nuclear** 30+: ε30 *Ghaznavi* (*Hatf*-3 – PRC M-11)/*Shaheen*-1 (*Hatf*-4); some *Abdali* (*Hatf*-2); some *Nasr* (*Hatf*-9); **Conventional** 105 *Hatf*-1
GLCM • Nuclear some *Babur* (*Hatf*-7)
AIRCRAFT
TPT • Light 14: 1 Beech 200 *King Air*; 1 Beech 350 *King Air*; 3 Cessna 208B; 1 Cessna 421; 1 Cessna 550 *Citation*; 1 Cessna 560 *Citation*; 2 *Turbo Commander* 690; 4 Y-12(II)
TRG 87 MFI-17B *Mushshak*
HELICOPTERS
ATK 42: 38 AH-1F/S *Cobra* with TOW; 4 Mi-35M *Hind* (1 Mi-24 *Hind* in store)
MRH 115+: 10 H125M *Fennec*; 7 AW139; 26 Bell 412EP *Twin Huey*; 38+ Mi-17 *Hip* H; 2 Mi-171E *Hip*; 12 SA315B *Lama*; 20 SA319 *Alouette* III
TPT 76: **Medium** 36: 31 SA330 *Puma*; 4 Mi-171; 1 Mi-172; **Light** 40: 17 H125 *Ecureuil* (SAR); 5 Bell 205 (UH-1H *Iroquois*); 5 Bell 205A-1 (AB-205A-1); 13 Bell 206B *Jet Ranger* II
TRG 10 Hughes 300C
UNMANNED AERIAL VEHICLES
ISR • Light *Bravo*; *Jasoos*; *Vector*
AIR DEFENCE
SAM
Medium-range LY-80
Short-range FM-90
Point-defence M113 with RBS-70; *Anza* Mk1/Mk2; FIM-92 *Stinger*; HN-5A; *Mistral*; RBS-70
GUNS • TOWED 1,933: **14.5mm** 981; **35mm** 248 GDF-002/GDF-005 (with 134 *Skyguard* radar units); **37mm** 310 Type-55 (M-1939)/Type-65; **40mm** 50 L/60; **57mm** 144 Type-59 (S-60); **85mm** 200 Type-72 (M-1939) KS-12

Navy 23,800 (incl ε3,200 Marines and ε2,000 Maritime Security Agency (see Paramilitary))
EQUIPMENT BY TYPE
SUBMARINES • TACTICAL 8
  SSK 5:
    2 *Hashmat* (FRA *Agosta* 70) with 4 single 533mm ASTT with F17P HWT/UGM-84 *Harpoon* AShM
    3 *Khalid* (FRA *Agosta* 90B – 2 with AIP) with 4 single 533mm ASTT with DM2A4 HWT/SM39 *Exocet* AShM
  SSI 3 MG110 (SF delivery) each with 2 single 533mm TT
PRINCIPAL SURFACE COMBATANTS • FRIGATES 9
  FFGHM 4 *Sword* (F-22P) with 2 quad lnchr with C-802A AShM, 1 octuple lnchr with HHQ-7 SAM, 2 triple 324mm ASTT with ET-52C LWT, 2 sextuple RDC-32 A/S mor, 1 Type 730B CIWS, 1 76mm gun (capacity 1 Z-9C *Haitun* hel)
  FFGH 3:
    1 *Alamgir* (ex-US *Oliver Hazard Perry*) with 2 quad lnchr with RGM-84 *Harpoon* AShM, 2 triple 324mm ASTT with Mk46 LWT, 1 Mk 15 *Phalanx* CIWS, 1 76mm gun
    1 *Tariq* (ex-UK *Amazon*) with 2 quad Mk141 lnchr with RGM-84 *Harpoon* AShM, 2 triple 324mm ASTT with Mk 46 LWT, 1 Mk 15 *Phalanx* Block 1B CIWS, 1 114mm gun (capacity 1 hel)
    1 *Tariq* (ex-UK *Amazon*) with 2 quad Mk141 lnchr with RGM-84 *Harpoon* AShM, 1 Mk 15 *Phalanx* Block 1B CIWS, 1 114mm gun (capacity 1 hel)
  FFHM 2 *Tariq* (ex-UK *Amazon*) with 1 sextuple lnchr with LY-60N SAM, 2 single 400mm TT with Typ 45 LWT, 1 Mk 15 *Phalanx* Block 1B CIWS, 1 114mm gun (capacity 1 hel)
PATROL AND COASTAL COMBATANTS 17
  PCG 3:
    2 *Azmat* (FAC(M)) with 2 quad lnchr with C-802A AShM, 1 AK630 CIWS
    1 *Azmat* (FAC(M)) with 2 triple lnchr with C-602 AShM, 1 AK630 CIWS
  PBFG 2 *Zarrar* (33) with 4 single lnchr each with RGM-84 *Harpoon* AShM
  PBG 4:
    2 *Jalalat* with 2 twin lnchr with C-802 (CH-SS-N-8 *Saccade*) AShM
    2 *Jurrat* with 2 twin lnchr with C-802 (CH-SS-N-8 *Saccade*) AShM
  PBF 2 *Kaan* 15
  PB 6: 1 *Larkana*; 1 *Rajshahi*; 4 M16 Fast Assault Boat
MINE WARFARE • MINE COUNTERMEASURES
  MCC 3 *Munsif* (FRA *Eridan*)
AMPHIBIOUS • LANDING CRAFT 8
  LCM 2
  LCAC 2 *Griffon* 8100TD
  UCAC 4 *Griffon* 2000
LOGISTICS AND SUPPORT 8
  AGS 1 *Behr Paima*
  AOL 2 *Madagar*
  AOR 1 *Moawin* II (Fleet Tanker) with 1 hel landing platform
  AORH 1 *Fuqing* with 1 *Phalanx* CIWS (capacity 1 SA319 *Alouette* III hel)
  AOT 2 *Gwadar*
  AXS 1

Marines ε3,200
FORCES BY ROLE
SPECIAL FORCES
  1 cdo gp
MANOEUVRE
  Amphibious
  3 mne bn
AIR DEFENCE
  1 AD bn

Naval Aviation
EQUIPMENT BY TYPE
AIRCRAFT 8 combat capable
  ASW 8: 7 P-3B/C *Orion*; 1 ATR-72-500
  MP 6 F-27-200 MPA
  TPT 3: **Light** 2 ATR-72-500; **PAX** 1 Hawker 850XP
HELICOPTERS
  ASW 11: 4 *Sea King* Mk45; 7 Z-9C *Haitun*
  MRH 6 SA319P *Alouette* III
AIR-LAUNCHED MISSILES • AShM AM39 *Exocet*

Air Force 70,000
3 regional comds: Northern (Peshawar), Central (Sargodha), Southern (Masroor). The Composite Air Tpt Wg, Combat Cadres School and PAF Academy are Direct Reporting Units
FORCES BY ROLE
FIGHTER
  3 sqn with F-7PG/FT-7PG *Airguard*
  1 sqn with F-16A/B MLU *Fighting Falcon*
  1 sqn with F-16A/B ADF *Fighting Falcon*
  1 sqn with *Mirage* IIID/E (IIIOD/EP)
FIGHTER/GROUND ATTACK
  2 sqn with JF-17 *Thunder*
  2 sqn with JF-17 *Thunder* Block II
  1 sqn with F-16C/D Block 52 *Fighting Falcon*
  3 sqn with *Mirage* 5 (5PA)
ANTI-SURFACE WARFARE
  1 sqn with *Mirage* 5PA2/5PA3 with AM-39 *Exocet* AShM
ELECTRONIC WARFARE/ELINT
  1 sqn with *Falcon* 20F
AIRBORNE EARLY WARNING & CONTROL
  1 sqn with Saab 2000; Saab 2000 *Erieye*
  1 sqn with ZDK-03
SEARCH & RESCUE
  1 sqn with Mi-171Sh (SAR/liaison)
  6 sqn with SA316 *Alouette* III
  1 sqn with AW139
TANKER
  1 sqn with Il-78 *Midas*
TRANSPORT
  1 sqn with C-130B/E *Hercules*; CN235M-220; L-100-20
  1 VIP sqn with B-707; Cessna 560XL *Citation Excel*; CN235M-220; F-27-200 *Friendship*; *Falcon* 20E; Gulfstream IVSP
  1 (comms) sqn with EMB-500 *Phenom* 100; Y-12 (II)
TRAINING
  1 OCU sqn with F-7P/FT-7P *Skybolt*
  1 OCU sqn with *Mirage* III/*Mirage* 5
  1 OCU sqn with F-16A/B MLU *Fighting Falcon*

2 sqn with K-8 *Karakorum**
2 sqn with MFI-17
2 sqn with T-37C *Tweet*

AIR DEFENCE
1 bty with HQ-2 (SA-2 *Guideline*); 9K310 *Igla*-1 (SA-16 *Gimlet*)
6 bty with *Crotale*
10 bty with SPADA 2000

EQUIPMENT BY TYPE
AIRCRAFT 425 combat capable
  FTR 153: 46 F-7PG *Airguard*; 20 F-7P *Skybolt*; 24 F-16A MLU *Fighting Falcon*; 21 F-16B MLU *Fighting Falcon*; 9 F-16A ADF *Fighting Falcon*; 4 F-16B ADF *Fighting Falcon*; 21 FT-7; 6 F-7PG; 2 *Mirage* IIIB
  FGA 224: 12 F-16C Block 52 *Fighting Falcon*; 6 F-16D Block 52 *Fighting Falcon*; 49 JF-17 *Thunder* (FC-1 Block 1); 36 JF-17 *Thunder* (FC-1 Block 2); 7 *Mirage* IIID (*Mirage* IIIOD); 63 *Mirage* IIIE (IIIEP); 39 *Mirage* 5 (5PA)/5PA2; 2 *Mirage* 5D (5DPA)/5DPA2; 10 *Mirage* 5PA3 (ASuW)
  ISR 10 *Mirage* IIIR* (*Mirage* IIIRP)
  ELINT 2 *Falcon* 20F
  AEW&C 7: 3 Saab 2000 *Erieye*; 4 ZDK-03
  TKR 4 Il-78 *Midas*
  TPT 35: **Medium** 16: 5 C-130B *Hercules*; 10 C-130E *Hercules*; 1 L-100-20; **Light** 14: 2 Cessna 208B; 1 Cessna 560XL *Citation Excel*; 4 CN235M-220; 4 EMB-500 *Phenom* 100; 1 F-27-200 *Friendship*; 2 Y-12 (II); **PAX** 5: 1 B-707; 1 *Falcon* 20E; 2 Gulfstream IVSP; 1 Saab 2000
  TRG 142: 38 K-8 *Karakorum**; 80 MFI-17B *Mushshak*; 24 T-37C *Tweet*
HELICOPTERS
  MRH 19: 15 SA316 *Alouette* III; 4 AW139
  TPT • **Medium** 4 Mi-171Sh
UNMANNED AERIAL VEHICLES
  CISR • **Heavy** CH-3 (*Burraq*)
  ISR • **Medium** *Falco*
AIR DEFENCE • **SAM** 190+
  Medium-range 6 HQ-2 (SA-2 *Guideline*)
  Short-range 184: 144 *Crotale*; ε40 SPADA 2000
  Point-defence 9K310 *Igla*-1 (SA-16 *Gimlet*)
AIR-LAUNCHED MISSILES
  AAM • **IR** AIM-9L/P *Sidewinder*; *U-Darter*; PL-5; **SARH** *Super* 530; **ARH** PL-12; AIM-120C AMRAAM
  ASM AGM-65 *Maverick*; *Raptor* II
  AShM AM39 *Exocet*
  ARM MAR-1
  ALCM • **Nuclear** *Ra'ad* (in test)
BOMBS
  INS/SAT-guided FT-6 (REK)
  Laser-guided *Paveway* II

Paramilitary 282,000 active

Pakistan Coast Guards
Ministry of Interior
EQUIPMENT BY TYPE
PATROL AND COASTAL COMBATANTS 5
  PBF 4
  PB 1

Frontier Corps 70,000
Ministry of Interior
FORCES BY ROLE
MANOEUVRE
  Reconnaissance
  1 armd recce sqn
  Other
  11 paramilitary regt (total: 40 paramilitary bn)
EQUIPMENT BY TYPE
ARMOURED FIGHTING VEHICLES
  APC (W) 45 UR-416

Maritime Security Agency ε2,000
FORCES BY ROLE
MARITIME PATROL
1 sqn with BN-2T *Defender*
EQUIPMENT BY TYPE
PATROL AND COASTAL COMBATANTS 19
  PSO 1 *Kashmir*
  PCC 10: 4 *Barkat*; 4 *Hingol*; 2 *Sabqat* (ex-US *Island*)
  PBF 5
  PB 3 *Guns*
AIRCRAFT • **TPT** • **Light** 3 BN-2T *Defender*

National Guard 185,000
Incl Janbaz Force; Mujahid Force; National Cadet Corps; Women Guards

Pakistan Rangers 25,000
Ministry of Interior

DEPLOYMENT

ARABIAN SEA: Combined Maritime Forces • 1 FFGH

CENTRAL AFRICAN REPUBLIC: UN • MINUSCA 1,259; 10 obs; 1 inf bn; 1 engr coy; 1 hel sqn

CYPRUS: UN • UNFICYP 1

DEMOCRATIC REPUBLIC OF THE CONGO: UN • MONUSCO 2,758; 18 obs; 4 inf bn; 1 hel sqn

MALI: UN • MINUSMA 3

SOMALIA: UN • UNSOM 1 obs; UN • UNSOS 1 obs

SOUTH SUDAN: UN • UNMISS 4; 2 obs

SUDAN: UN • UNAMID 1,170; 6 obs; 1 inf bn, 1 engr pl; 1 med pl

WESTERN SAHARA: UN • MINURSO 14 obs

FOREIGN FORCES

Figures represent total numbers for UNMOGIP mission in India and Pakistan
Chile 2 obs
Croatia 9 obs
Italy 2 obs
Korea, Republic of 7 obs
Philippines 6 obs
Romania 2 obs
Sweden 5 obs

Switzerland 3 obs
Thailand 4 obs
Uruguay 3 obs

Papua New Guinea PNG

Papua New Guinea Kina K		2017	2018	2019
GDP	K	63.8bn	68.5bn	
	US$	19.8bn	20.8bn	
per capita	US$	2,402	2,465	
Growth	%	2.5	-1.1	
Inflation	%	5.4	4.2	
Def bdgt	K	229m	209m	
	US$	71.1m	63.2m	
US$1=K		3.20	3.30	
Population	7,027,332			

Age	0–14	15–19	20–24	25–29	30–64	65 plus
Male	16.8%	5.3%	4.8%	4.1%	17.8%	2.2%
Female	16.2%	5.1%	4.7%	4.1%	16.8%	2.2%

Capabilities

Since independence in 1975, the Papua New Guinea Defence Force (PNGDF) has suffered from underfunding and lack of capacity to perform its core roles. A reform programme reduced personnel strength from around 4,000 to 2,100 between 2002 and 2007. However, during the current decade, the government has made efforts to revive defence capability. A 2013 defence white paper identified the PNGDF's core roles, including defending the state and civil-emergency assistance, but noted that 'defence capabilities have deteriorated to the extent that we have alarming gaps in our land, air and maritime borders'. The white paper called for strengthening defence capability on an ambitious scale, with long-term plans calling for a 'division-sized force' of 10,000 personnel by 2030. The PNGDF continues to receive substantial external military assistance from Australia but also from China. In late 2018, plans to build a joint US–Australia–Papua New Guinea naval base at Lombrum were announced. The PNGDF is not able to deploy outside of the country without outside assistance and there have only been small PNGDF deployments to UN peacekeeping missions. The PNGDF will receive four of the 21 *Guardian*-class patrol boats that Australia is donating to small Pacific Ocean nations, which will replace the four *Pacific*-class boats Australia donated in the 1980s. Papua New Guinea has no significant defence industry, though there is some local maintenance capacity.

ACTIVE 3,600 (Army 3,300 Maritime Element 200 Air 100)

ORGANISATIONS BY SERVICE

Army ε3,300
FORCES BY ROLE
SPECIAL FORCES
  1 spec ops unit
MANOEUVRE
  Light
    2 inf bn

COMBAT SUPPORT
  1 engr bn
  1 EOD unit
  1 sigs sqn
EQUIPMENT BY TYPE
ARTILLERY • MOR 3+: 81mm Some; 120mm 3

Maritime Element ε200
1 HQ located at Port Moresby
EQUIPMENT BY TYPE
PATROL AND COASTAL COMBATANTS • PB 4 *Rabaul* (*Pacific*)
AMPHIBIOUS • LANDING SHIPS • LCT 3 *Salamaua* (ex-AUS *Balikpapan*) (of which 1 in trg role)

Air Force ε100
FORCES BY ROLE
TRANSPORT
  1 sqn with CN235M-100; IAI-201 *Arava*
TRANSPORT HELICOPTER
  1 sqn with Bell 205 (UH-1H *Iroquois*)†
EQUIPMENT BY TYPE
AIRCRAFT • TPT • Light 3: 1 CN235M-100 (1 more in store); 2 IAI-201 *Arava*
HELICOPTERS • TPT • Light 3: 2 Bell 412 (leased); 1 Bell 212 (leased) (2 Bell 205 (UH-1H *Iroquois*) non-operational)

DEPLOYMENT

SUDAN: UN • UNAMID 2 obs

Philippines PHL

Philippine Peso P		2017	2018	2019
GDP	P	15.8tr	17.6tr	
	US$	314bn	332bn	
per capita	US$	2,989	3,099	
Growth	%	6.7	6.5	
Inflation	%	2.9	4.9	
Def bdgt [a]	P	137bn	148bn	188bn
	US$	2.73bn	2.79bn	
FMA (US)	US$	40m	0m	
US$1=P		50.40	53.00	
[a] Excludes military pensions				
Population	105,893,381			

Age	0–14	15–19	20–24	25–29	30–64	65 plus
Male	16.9%	5.1%	4.7%	4.2%	17.4%	1.9%
Female	16.2%	4.9%	4.5%	4.0%	17.5%	2.7%

Capabilities

Despite modest increases in defence funding in recent years, mainly in response to rising tensions in the South China Sea, the capabilities and procurement plans of the Armed Forces of the Philippines (AFP) remain limited. The Philippines would still struggle to provide more than a token national capability to defend its maritime claims. Organisational changes include the establishment in 2018 of an AFP Special Operations Command to command all special-forces units. Military leaders said this resulted from lessons learned in the Zamboanga City attack in 2013 and the Marawi siege in 2017. Lessons learned after Marawi will also likely lead to renewed focus on the capabilities and tactics needed for urban operations. Although President Duterte announced in 2016 a 'separation' from the US and the pursuit of closer relations with China, he described the US as an important security ally, especially in support of counter-terrorism, in September 2017. The Philippines is an ASEAN member. In 2017 it began trilateral joint maritime patrols and joint Sulu Sea patrols with Indonesia and Malaysia to counter regional terrorist activity. The armed forces continue to be deployed on internal-security duties in the south, where Manila faces continuing challenges from insurgent groups. The second phase (2018–22) of the 'second horizon' AFP modernisation programme was approved in 2018. Plans include new artillery systems, multi-role fighters, radars, transport aircraft and frigates. Feasibility studies are under way for the creation of a defence-industry zone in Limay, Bataan, to better enable technology transfer. The Philippine Aerospace Development Corporation has assembled a variety of small helicopters and aircraft for the AFP, as well as providing maintenance, repair and overhaul services for military aircraft.

ACTIVE 142,350 (Army 101,000 Navy 23,750 Air 17,600) Paramilitary 11,100

RESERVE 131,000 (Army 100,000 Navy 15,000 Air 16,000) Paramilitary 50,000 (to age 49)

ORGANISATIONS BY SERVICE

Army 101,000

5 Area Unified Comd (joint service), 1 National Capital Region Comd

FORCES BY ROLE
SPECIAL FORCES
  1 spec ops comd (1 ranger regt, 1 SF regt, 1 CT regt)
MANOEUVRE
  Mechanised
  1 mech inf div (2 mech bde (total: 3 lt armd sqn; 7 armd cav tp; 4 mech inf bn; 1 cbt engr coy; 1 avn bn; 1 cbt engr coy, 1 sigs coy))
  Light
  1 div (4 inf bde; 1 arty bn, 1 int bn, 1 sigs bn)
  9 div (3 inf bde; 1 arty bn, 1 int bn, 1 sigs bn)
  Other
  1 (Presidential) gd gp
COMBAT SUPPORT
  1 arty regt HQ
  5 engr bde

EQUIPMENT BY TYPE
ARMOURED FIGHTING VEHICLES
  LT TK 7 FV101 *Scorpion*
  IFV 54: 2 YPR-765; 34 M113A1 FSV; 18 M113A2 FSV
  APC 387
    APC (T) 168: 6 ACV300; 42 M113A1; 120 M113A2
    APC (W) 219: 73 LAV-150 *Commando*; 146 *Simba*
ENGINEERING & MAINTENANCE VEHICLES
  ARV ACV-300; *Samson*; M578; 4 M113 ARV
ANTI-TANK-ANTI-INFRASTRUCTURE • RCL 75mm M20; **90mm** M67; **106mm** M40A1

ARTILLERY 260+ TOWED 220: **105mm** 204 M101/M102/Model 56 pack howitzer; **155mm** 16: 10 M114/M-68; 6 Soltam M-71
MOR 40+: **81mm** M29; **107mm** 40 M30
AIRCRAFT
  TPT • Light 4: 1 Beech 80 *Queen Air*; 1 Cessna 170; 1 Cessna 172; 1 Cessna P206A
UNMANNED AERIAL VEHICLES • ISR • Medium *Blue Horizon*

Navy 23,750

EQUIPMENT BY TYPE
PATROL AND COASTAL COMBATANTS 69
  PSOH 3 *Gregorio del Pilar* (ex-US *Hamilton*) with 1 76mm gun (capacity 1 Bo 105)
  PCF 1 *General Mariano Alvares* (ex-US *Cyclone*)
  PCO 10:
    3 *Emilio Jacinto* (ex-UK *Peacock*) with 1 76mm gun
    5 *Miguel Malvar* (ex-US) with 1 76mm gun
    2 *Rizal* (ex-US *Auk*) with 2 76mm gun
  PBFG 3 MPAC Mk3 with 1 *Typhoon* MLS-ER quad lnchr with *Spike*-ER SSM
  PBF 16: 2 *Conrado Yap* (ex-ROK *Sea Hawk*); 5 *Tomas Batilo* (ex-ROK *Chamsuri*); 6 MPAC Mk1/2
  PB 30: 22 *Jose Andrada*; 2 *Kagitingan*; 2 *Point* (ex-US); 4 *Swift* Mk3 (ex-US)
  PBR 6 Silver Ships
AMPHIBIOUS
  PRINCIPAL AMPHIBIOUS SHIPS 2
    LPD 2 *Tarlac* (IDN *Makassar*) (capacity 2 LCU; 2 hels; 13 tanks; 500 troops)
  LANDING SHIPS • LST 4:
    2 *Bacolod City* (US *Besson*) with 1 hel landing platform (capacity 32 tanks; 150 troops)
    2 LST-1/542 (ex-US) (capacity 16 tanks; 200 troops)
  LANDING CRAFT 11
    LCM 2: 1 *Manobo*; 1 *Tagbanua* (capacity 100 tons; 200 troops)
    LCT 5 *Ivatan* (ex-AUS *Balikpapan*)
    LCU 4: 3 LCU Mk 6 (ex-US); 1 *Mulgae* I (ex-RoK)
LOGISTICS AND SUPPORT 6
  AGOR 1 *Gregorio Velasquez* (ex-US *Melville*)
  AOL 1
  AO 1 *Lake Caliraya*
  AP 1
  AWT 2

Naval Aviation

EQUIPMENT BY TYPE
AIRCRAFT • TPT • Light 11: 4 BN-2A *Defender*; 2 Cessna 177 *Cardinal*; 5 Beech 90 *King Air* (TC-90) (leased)
HELICOPTERS • TPT 13: **Medium** 4 Mi-171Sh; **Light** 9: 3 AW109; 2 AW109E; 4 Bo-105

Marines 8,300

FORCES BY ROLE
SPECIAL FORCES
  1 (force recon) spec ops bn
MANOEUVRE
  Amphibious
  4 mne bde (total: 12 mne bn)

COMBAT SUPPORT
1 CSS bde (6 CSS bn)

EQUIPMENT BY TYPE
ARMOURED FIGHTING VEHICLES
  APC • **APC (W)** 42: 19 LAV-150 *Commando*; 23 LAV-300
  AAV 59: 4 LVTH-6†; 55 LVTP-7
ARTILLERY 37+
  TOWED 37: **105mm** 31: 23 M101; 8 M-26; **155mm** 6 Soltam M-71
  MOR 107mm M30

Naval Special Operations Group
FORCES BY ROLE
SPECIAL FORCES
  1 SEAL unit
  1 diving unit
  10 naval spec ops unit
  1 special boat unit
COMBAT SUPPORT
  1 EOD unit

Air Force 17,600
FORCES BY ROLE
FIGHTER
  1 sqn with FA-50PH *Fighting Eagle**
GROUND ATTACK
  1 sqn with OV-10A/C *Bronco**
ISR
  1 sqn with *Turbo Commander* 690A
SEARCH & RESCUE
  4 (SAR/Comms) sqn with Bell 205 (UH-1M *Iroquois*); AUH-76
TRANSPORT
  1 sqn with C-130B/H/T *Hercules*; L-100-20
  1 sqn with N-22B *Nomad*; N-22SL *Searchmaster*; C-212 *Aviocar* (NC-212i)
  1 sqn with F-27-200 MPA; F-27-500 *Friendship*
  1 VIP sqn with F-28 *Fellowship*
TRAINING
  1 sqn with SF-260F/TP
  1 sqn with T-41B/D/K *Mescalero*
  1 sqn with S-211*
ATTACK HELICOPTER
  1 sqn with MD-520MG
TRANSPORT HELICOPTER
  1 sqn with AUH-76
  1 sqn with W-3 *Sokol*
  4 sqn with Bell 205 (UH-1H *Iroquois*)
  1 (VIP) sqn with Bell 412EP *Twin Huey*; S-70A *Black Hawk* (S-70A-5)

EQUIPMENT BY TYPE
AIRCRAFT 34 combat capable
  FGA 12 FA-50PH *Fighting Eagle*
  MP 3: 1 C-130T MP mod; 1 F-27-200 MPA; 1 N-22SL *Searchmaster*
  ISR 12: 2 Cessna 208B *Grand Caravan*; 10 OV-10A/C *Bronco**
  TPT 15: **Medium** 4: 1 C-130B *Hercules*; 2 C-130H *Hercules*; 1 C-130T *Hercules* **Light** 8: 3 C295; 1 F-27-500 *Friendship*; 1 N-22B *Nomad*; 1 *Turbo Commander* 690A; 2 C-212 *Aviocar* (NC-212i); **PAX** 1 F-28 *Fellowship* (VIP)
  TRG 39: 12 S-211*; 7 SF-260F; 10 SF-260TP; 10 T-41B/D/K *Mescalero*
HELICOPTERS
  MRH 32: 8 W-3 *Sokol*; 3 AUH-76; 8 Bell 412EP *Twin Huey*; 2 Bell 412HP *Twin Huey*; 11 MD-520MG
  TPT 34: **Medium** 1 S-70A *Black Hawk* (S-70A-5); **Light** 33: 2 AW109E; 11 Bell 205 (UH-1D); 20 Bell 205 (UH-1H *Iroquois*) (25 more non-operational)
UNMANNED AERIAL VEHICLES
  ISR • **Medium** 2 *Blue Horizon* II
AIR-LAUNCHED MISSILES
  AAM • **IR** AIM-9 *Sidewinder*
  ASM AGM-65D *Maverick*

Paramilitary 11,100

Coast Guard 11,100
EQUIPMENT BY TYPE
Rodman 38 and Rodman 101 owned by Bureau of Fisheries and Aquatic Resources
PATROL AND COASTAL COMBATANTS 84
  PCO 5: 4 *San Juan* with 1 hel landing platform; 1 *Balsam*
  PCC 2 *Tirad*
  PB 66: 2 *Boracay* (FPB 72 Mk II); 3 *De Haviland*; 4 *Ilocos Norte*; 1 *Palawan*; 12 PCF 50 (US *Swift* Mk1/2); 10 PCF 46; 10 PCF 65 (US *Swift* Mk3); 4 Rodman 38; 10 Rodman 101; 10 *Parola* (MRRV)
  PBR 11
LOGISTICS AND SUPPORT • **ABU** 1 *Corregidor*
AIRCRAFT • **TPT** • **Light** 2 BN-2 *Islander*
HELICOPTERS • **TPT** • **Light** 2 Bo-105

Citizen Armed Force Geographical Units
50,000 reservists
FORCES BY ROLE
MANOEUVRE
  Other 56 militia bn (part-time units which can be called up for extended periods)

DEPLOYMENT
CENTRAL AFRICAN REPUBLIC: UN • MINUSCA 2 obs
INDIA/PAKISTAN: UN • UNMOGIP 6 obs
SOUTH SUDAN: UN • UNMISS 2 obs

FOREIGN FORCES
Australia *Operation Augury* 100
Brunei IMT 9
Indonesia IMT 9
Malaysia IMT 16
United States US Pacific Command: *Operation Pacific Eagle - Philippines* 250

Singapore SGP

Singapore Dollar S$		2017	2018	2019
GDP	S$	447bn	466bn	
	US$	324bn	347bn	
per capita	US$	57,713	61,230	
Growth	%	3.6	2.9	
Inflation	%	0.6	1.0	
Def bdgt	S$	14.2bn	14.8bn	
	US$	10.3bn	11.0bn	
US$1=S$		1.38	1.34	

Population 5,995,991

Ethnic groups: Chinese 74.1%; Malay 13.4%; Indian 9.2%; other or unspecified 3.3%

Age	0–14	15–19	20–24	25–29	30–64	65 plus
Male	6.5%	3.2%	4.6%	5.3%	24.6%	4.6%
Female	6.2%	3.2%	5.0%	5.6%	25.6%	5.4%

Capabilities

The Singapore Armed Forces (SAF) are the best equipped in Southeast Asia. They are organised essentially along Israeli lines, with the air force and navy staffed mainly by professional personnel while, apart from a small core of regulars, the much larger army is based on conscripts and reservists. Although there are no publicly available defence-policy documents, it is widely presumed that the SAF's primary role is to deter attacks on the city state or interference with its vital interests – particularly its sea lines of communication – by potential regional adversaries. There is now an additional focus on counter-terrorist operations. The defence budget has increased to the extent that Singapore outspends all its Southeast Asian counterparts. With an ageing population and declining conscript cohort, there is a significant personnel challenge, which the defence ministry is looking to address by lean staffing and increased use of technology. There is routine overseas training, and plans have been announced to further improve domestic training areas. The SAF also engages extensively in bilateral and multilateral exercises with regional and international partners. Singaporean forces have gradually become more involved in multinational operations, including the US-led air offensive against ISIS. While such deployments have provided some operational experience, and training standards and operational readiness are high, the army's reliance on conscripts and reservists limits its capacity for sustained operations abroad. Equipment modernisation continues, with Littoral-Mission Vessels commissioned and progress on the procurement of armoured vehicles and surface-to-air missiles. There is a small but sophisticated defence industry. ST Engineering group manufactures several types of armoured vehicles and corvettes for the SAF.

ACTIVE 72,500 (Army 50,000 Navy 9,000 Air 13,500)
Paramilitary 8,400
Conscription liability 22–24 months

RESERVE 312,500 (Army 300,000 Navy 5,000 Air 7,500)
Annual trg to age 40 for army other ranks, 50 for officers

ORGANISATIONS BY SERVICE

Army 15,000; 35,000 conscript (total 50,000)
FORCES BY ROLE
COMMAND
  3 (combined arms) div HQ
  1 (rapid reaction) div HQ
  3 armd bde HQ
  9 inf bde HQ
  1 air mob bde HQ
  1 amph bde HQ
SPECIAL FORCES
  1 cdo bn
MANOEUVRE
  Reconnaissance
  3 lt armd/recce bn
  Armoured
  1 armd bn
  Mechanised
  6 mech inf bn
  Light
  2 (gds) inf bn
  Other
  2 sy bn
COMBAT SUPPORT
  2 arty bn
  1 STA bn
  2 engr bn
  1 EOD bn
  1 ptn br bn
  1 int bn
  2 ISR bn
  1 CBRN bn
  3 sigs bn
COMBAT SERVICE SUPPORT
  3 med bn
  2 tpt bn
  3 spt bn

Reserves
Activated units form part of divisions and brigades listed above; 1 op reserve div with additional inf bde; People's Defence Force Comd (homeland defence) with 12 inf bn
FORCES BY ROLE
SPECIAL FORCES
  1 cdo bn
MANOEUVRE
  Reconnaissance
  6 lt armd/recce bn
  Mechanised
  6 mech inf bn
  Light
  ε56 inf bn
COMBAT SUPPORT
  ε12 arty bn
  ε8 engr bn
EQUIPMENT BY TYPE
ARMOURED FIGHTING VEHICLES
  MBT 96 *Leopard* 2SG (80–100 *Tempest* (upgraded *Centurion*) reported in store)
  LT TK 372: 22 AMX-10 PAC 90; ε350 AMX-13 SM1

IFV 572+: 22 AMX-10P; 250 *Bionix* IFV-25; 250 *Bionix* IFV-40/50; 50+ M113A1/A2 (some with 40mm AGL, some with 25mm gun)
APC 1,576+
  APC (T) 1,100+: 700+ M113A1/A2; 400+ ATTC *Bronco*
  APC (W) 415: 250 LAV-150 *Commando*/V-200 *Commando*; 135 *Terrex* ICV; 30 V-100 *Commando*
  PPV 61+: 6+ *Belrex*; 15 *MaxxPro Dash*; 40 *Peacekeeper*
ENGINEERING & MAINTENANCE VEHICLES
  AEV 94: 18 CET; 54 FV180; 14 *Kodiak*; 8 M728
  ARV *Bionix*; *Büffel*; LAV-150; LAV-300
  VLB 72+: *Bionix*; LAB 30; *Leguan*; M2; 60 M3; 12 M60
  MW 910-MCV-2; *Trailblazer*
ANTI-TANK/ANTI-INFRASTRUCTURE
  MSL • MANPATS Milan; *Spike*-SR; *Spike*-MR
  RCL 90+: **84mm** Carl Gustav; **106mm** 90 M40A1
ARTILLERY 798+
  SP 155mm 54 SSPH-1 *Primus*
  TOWED 88: **105mm** (37 LG1 in store); **155mm** 88: 18 FH-2000; ε18 *Pegasus*; 52 FH-88
  MRL 227mm 18 M142 HIMARS
  MOR 638+
    SP 90+: **81mm**; **120mm** 90: 40 on *Bronco*; 50 on M113
    TOWED 548: **81mm** 500 **120mm** 36 M-65; **160mm** 12 M-58 Tampella
UNMANNED AERIAL VEHICLES • ISR • Light *Skylark*

Navy 3,000; 1,000 conscript; ε5,000 active reservists (total 9,000)
EQUIPMENT BY TYPE
SUBMARINES • TACTICAL • SSK 4:
  2 *Challenger* (ex-SWE *Sjoormen*) with 2 single 400mm TT, 4 single 533mm TT
  2 *Archer* (ex-SWE *Västergötland*) (AIP fitted) with 3 single 400mm TT, 6 single 533mm TT for WASS *Black Shark* HWT
PRINCIPAL SURFACE COMBATANTS 6:
  FRIGATES • FFGHM 6 *Formidable* with 2 quad lnchr with RGM-84 *Harpoon* AShM, 4 octuple VLS with *Aster* 15 SAM, 2 triple B515 324mm ASTT with A244 LWT, 1 76mm gun (capacity 1 S-70B *Sea Hawk* hel)
PATROL AND COASTAL COMBATANTS 26
  CORVETTES 11
    FSGM 6 *Victory* with 2 quad Mk140 lnchr with RGM-84C *Harpoon* AShM, 2 octuple lnchr with *Barak* SAM, 2 triple B515 324mm ASTT with A244S LWT, 1 76mm gun
    FSM 5 *Independence* (Littoral Mission Vessel) with 1 12-cell CLA VLS with VL-*MICA*, 1 76mm gun, 1 hel landing platform
  PCO 7 *Fearless* with 1 76mm gun (can be fitted with 2 sextuple *Sadral* lnchr with *Mistral* SAM)
  PBF 8: 2 SMC Type 1; 6 SMC Type 2
MINE WARFARE • MINE COUNTERMEASURES
  MCC 4 *Bedok*
AMPHIBIOUS
  PRINCIPAL AMPHIBIOUS SHIPS • LPD 4 *Endurance* with 2 twin lnchr with *Mistral* SAM, 1 76mm gun (capacity 2 hel; 4 LCVP; 18 MBT; 350 troops)
  LANDING CRAFT 23
    LCVP 23: ε17 FCEP; 6 FCU
LOGISTICS AND SUPPORT 2
  ASR 1 *Swift Rescue*
  AX 1

Naval Diving Unit
FORCES BY ROLE
SPECIAL FORCES
  1 SF gp
  1 (diving) SF gp
COMBAT SUPPORT
  1 EOD gp

Air Force 13,500 (incl 3,000 conscript)
5 comds
FORCES BY ROLE
FIGHTER/GROUND ATTACK
  2 sqn with F-15SG *Eagle*
  3 sqn with F-16C/D *Fighting Falcon* (some used for ISR with pods)
ANTI-SUBMARINE WARFARE
  1 sqn with S-70B *Seahawk*
MARITIME PATROL/TRANSPORT
  1 sqn with F-50
AIRBORNE EARLY WARNING & CONTROL
  1 sqn with G550-AEW
TANKER
  1 sqn with KC-135R *Stratotanker*; A330 MRTT
TANKER/TRANSPORT
  1 sqn with KC-130B/H *Hercules*; C-130H *Hercules*
TRAINING
  1 (FRA-based) sqn with M-346 *Master*
  4 (US-based) units with AH-64D *Apache*; CH-47D *Chinook*; F-15SG: F-16C/D
  1 (AUS-based) sqn with PC-21
  1 hel sqn with H120 *Colibri*
ATTACK HELICOPTER
  1 sqn with AH-64D *Apache*
TRANSPORT HELICOPTER
  1 sqn with CH-47SD *Super D Chinook*
  2 sqn with AS332M *Super Puma*; AS532UL *Cougar*
ISR UAV 1 sqn with *Hermes* 450
  2 sqn with *Heron* 1
AIR DEFENCE
  1 AD bn with *Mistral* opcon Army
  3 AD bn with RBS-70; 9K38 *Igla* (SA-18 *Grouse*) opcon Army
  1 ADA sqn with Oerlikon
  1 AD sqn with MIM-23 *Hawk*; SAMP/T
  1 AD sqn with *Spyder*
  1 radar sqn with radar (mobile)
  1 radar sqn with LORADS
MANOEUVRE
  Other
  4 (field def) sy sqn
EQUIPMENT BY TYPE
AIRCRAFT 105 combat capable
  FGA 100: 40 F-15SG *Eagle*; 20 F-16C Block 52 *Fighting Falcon*; 20 F-16D Block 52 *Fighting Falcon*; 20 F-16D Block 52+ *Fighting Falcon* (incl reserves)
  ATK (4 A-4SU *Super Skyhawk*; 10 TA-4SU *Super Skyhawk* in store)
  MP 5 F-50 *Maritime Enforcer**
  AEW&C 4 G550-AEW
  TKR 5: 1 KC-130H *Hercules*; 4 KC-135R *Stratotanker*
  TKR/TPT 5: 1 A330 MRTT; 4 KC-130B *Hercules*

TPT 9: **Medium** 5 C-130H *Hercules* (2 ELINT); **PAX** 4 F-50
TRG 31: 12 M-346 *Master*; 19 PC-21
HELICOPTERS
 ATK 19 AH-64D *Apache*
 ASW 8 S-70B *Seahawk*
 TPT 51: **Heavy** 16: 6 CH-47D *Chinook*; 10 CH-47SD *Super D Chinook*; **Medium** 30: 18 AS332M *Super Puma* (incl 5 SAR); 12 AS532UL *Cougar*; **Light** 5 H120 *Colibri* (leased)
UNMANNED AERIAL VEHICLES
 ISR 17+: **Heavy** 8+ *Heron* 1; **Medium** 9+ *Hermes* 450
AIR DEFENCE
 SAM
  Long-range 4+ SAMP/T
  Medium-range MIM-23 *Hawk*
  Short-range *Spyder*-SR
  Point-defence 9K38 *Igla* (SA-18 *Grouse*) (some on V-200/M113); *Mistral*; RBS-70
 GUNS 34
  SP 20mm GAI-C01
  TOWED 34 **20mm** GAI-C01; **35mm** 34 GDF (with 25 *Super-Fledermaus* fire control radar)
AIR-LAUNCHED MISSILES
 AAM • IR AIM-9N/P *Sidewinder*; *Python* 4 (reported); IIR AIM-9X *Sidewinder* II; SARH AIM-7P *Sparrow*; ARH (AIM-120C5/7 AMRAAM in store in US)
 ASM: AGM-65B/G *Maverick*; AGM-114 *Hellfire*; AGM-154A/C JSOW
 AShM AGM-84 *Harpoon*; AM39 *Exocet*
 ARM AGM-45 *Shrike*
BOMBS
 INS/GPS guided GBU-31 JDAM
 Laser-guided *Paveway* II

Paramilitary 8,400 active

Civil Defence Force 5,600 (incl conscripts); 500 auxiliaries (total 6,100)

Singapore Police Coast Guard 1,000
EQUIPMENT BY TYPE
PATROL AND COASTAL COMBATANTS 102
 PBF 81: 25 *Angler Ray*; 2 *Atlantic Ray*; 1 *Marlin*; 11 *Sailfish*; 10 *Shark*; 32 other
 PB 21: 19 *Amberjack*; 2 *Manta Ray*

Singapore Gurkha Contingent 1,800
Under the Police
FORCES BY ROLE
MANOEUVRE
 Other
  6 paramilitary coy

Cyber

The Singapore Ministry of Defence (MINDEF) has long identified the potential damage that could be caused by cyber attacks, with this concern perhaps more acute following its adoption of the Integrated Knowledge-based Command-and-Control doctrine, designed to aid the transition of Singapore's armed forces to a 'third-generation' force. Singapore's Defence Cyber Organisation (DCO) consists of four formations and is responsible for overseeing cyber policy, training and defending military networks. Meanwhile, under the DCO, the Cyber Security Division is the first responder to cyber attacks; the Plans and Policy Directorate oversees cyber capability development; and the Cyber Security Inspectorate conducts vulnerability assessment. The Singapore Armed Forces (SAF) Cyber Defence Group (CDG) was created under the SAF C4 Command (itself created in 2017) to provide round-the-clock cyber defence of SAF networks. According to MINDEF, 'The CDG consists of dedicated cyber defence units that are responsible for cybersecurity monitoring, incident response and audits of SAF networks.' The SAF has created new cyber-defence positions for national servicemen (NSF) and regular personnel. A Cyber NSF scheme was launched in February 2018 to help the armed forces benefit from cyber skills in the forces. When fully established, MINDEF says that the DCO will have about 2,600 personnel, supported by specialists in the Defence Science and Technology Agency and the Defence Science Organisation.

DEPLOYMENT

AUSTRALIA: 2 trg schools – 1 with 12 AS332 *Super Puma*/AS532 *Cougar* (flying trg) located at Oakey; 1 with PC-21 (flying trg) located at Pearce. Army: prepositioned AFVs and heavy equipment at Shoalwater Bay training area

BRUNEI: 1 trg camp with inf units on rotation; 1 hel det with AS332 *Super Puma*

FRANCE: 200: 1 trg sqn with 12 M-346 *Master*

KUWAIT: Operation Inherent Resolve 11

TAIWAN: 3 trg camp (incl inf and arty)

THAILAND: 1 trg camp (arty, cbt engr)

UNITED STATES: Trg units with F-16C/D; 12 F-15SG; AH-64D *Apache*; 6+ CH-47D *Chinook*

FOREIGN FORCES

United States US Pacific Command: 200; 1 naval spt facility at Changi naval base; 1 USAF log spt sqn at Paya Lebar air base

Sri Lanka LKA

Sri Lankan Rupee Rs		2017	2018	2019
GDP	Rs	13.3tr	14.5tr	
	US$	87.3bn	92.5bn	
per capita	US$	4,073	4,265	
Growth	%	3.3	3.7	
Inflation	%	6.5	4.8	
Def bdgt	Rs	284bn	273bn	
	US$	1.86bn	1.74bn	
FMA (US)	US$	0.5m	0m	
US$1=Rs		152.46	157.04	

Population	22,576,592					
Age	0–14	15–19	20–24	25–29	30–64	65 plus
Male	12.1%	3.8%	3.6%	3.6%	21.5%	4.2%
Female	11.6%	3.7%	3.5%	3.7%	23.0%	5.8%

Capabilities

Since the defeat of the Tamil Tigers, the armed forces have reoriented to a peacetime internal-security role. Military support has been provided by China, in an indication of a growing military-to-military relationship. The US has eased its long-standing military trade restrictions. Japan has stated an intention to increase maritime cooperation with the country. Sri Lanka has little capacity for force projection beyond its national territory but has sent small numbers of troops on UN missions. Colombo is developing a national cyber-security centre. The navy's littoral capability, based on fast-attack and patrol boats, has been strengthened with the acquisition of offshore patrol vessels, while the US has gifted a former US coastguard cutter and China has announced that it is gifting a frigate. The army is reducing in size and there appears to have been little spending on new equipment since the end of the civil war, although Sri Lanka is looking to begin a series of procurements to fill key capability gaps. It was reported in 2018 that some naval units would relocate to a new port at Hambantota, leased by China. Beyond maintenance facilities and limited fabrication, such as at Sri Lanka's shipyards, there is no defence-industrial base.

ACTIVE 255,000 (Army 177,000 Navy 50,000 Air 28,000) Paramilitary 62,200

RESERVE 5,500 (Army 1,100 Navy 2,400 Air Force 2,000) Paramilitary 30,400

ORGANISATIONS BY SERVICE

Army 113,000; 64,00 active reservists (recalled) (total 177,000)

Regt are bn sized
FORCES BY ROLE
COMMAND
  7 region HQ
  21 div HQ
SPECIAL FORCES
  1 indep SF bde
MANOEUVRE
  Reconnaissance
  3 armd recce regt
  Armoured
  1 armd bde(-)
  Mechanised
  1 mech inf bde
  Light
  60 inf bde
  1 cdo bde
  Air Manoeuvre
  1 air mob bde
COMBAT SUPPORT
  7 arty regt
  1 MRL regt
  8 engr regt
  6 sigs regt
EQUIPMENT BY TYPE
ARMOURED FIGHTING VEHICLES
  MBT 62 T-55A/T-55AM2
  RECCE 15 *Saladin*
  IFV 62+: 13 BMP-1; 49 BMP-2; WZ-551 20mm
  APC 211+
  APC (T) 30+: some Type-63; 30 Type-85; some Type-89
  APC (W) 181: 25 BTR-80/BTR-80A; 31 *Buffel*; 20 WZ-551; 105 *Unicorn*
ENGINEERING & MAINTENANCE VEHICLES
  ARV 16 VT-55
  VLB 2 MT-55
ANTI-TANK/ANTI-INFRASTRUCTURE
  MANPATS HJ-8
  RCL 40: **105mm** ε10 M-65; **106mm** ε30 M40
  GUNS **85mm** 8 Type-56 (D-44)
ARTILLERY 908
  TOWED 96: **122mm** 20; **130mm** 30 Type-59-I; **152mm** 46 Type-66 (D-20)
  MRL **122mm** 28: 6 KRL-122; 22 RM-70
  MOR 784: **81mm** 520; **82mm** 209; **120mm** 55 M-43
UNMANNED AERIAL VEHICLES
  ISR • Medium 1 *Seeker*

Navy ε37,000; ε13,000 active reserves (total 50,000)

Seven naval areas
EQUIPMENT BY TYPE
PATROL AND COASTAL COMBATANTS 128
  PSOH 3: 1 *Sayura* (IND *Vigraha*); 2 *Sayurala* (IND *Samarth*)
  PCG 2 *Nandimithra* (ISR *Sa'ar* 4) with 3 single lnchr with *Gabriel II* AShM, 1 76mm gun
  PCO 2: 1 *Samudura* (ex-US *Reliance*); 1 *Sagara* (IND *Vikram*) with 1 hel landing platform
  PCC 1 *Jayasagara*
  PBF 74: 26 *Colombo*; 6 *Shaldag*; 4 *Super Dvora* Mk II; 6 *Super Dvora* Mk III; 5 *Trinity Marine*; 27 *Wave Rider*
  PB 20: 4 *Cheverton*; 2 *Mihikatha* (ex-AUS *Bay*); 2 *Prathapa* (PRC mod *Haizhui*); 3 *Ranajaya* (PRC *Haizhui*); 1 *Ranarisi* (PRC mod *Shanghai* II); 5 *Weeraya* (PRC *Shanghai* II); 3 (various)
  PBR 26
AMPHIBIOUS
  LANDING SHIPS • LSM 1 *Shakthi* (PRC *Yuhai*) (capacity 2 tanks; 250 troops)
  LANDING CRAFT 8
    LCM 2
    LCP 3 *Hansaya*
    LCU 2 *Yunnan*
    UCAC 1 M 10 (capacity 56 troops)
LOGISTICS AND SUPPORT 3: 2 AP; 1 AX

Marines ε500

FORCES BY ROLE
MANOEUVRE
  Amphibious
  1 mne bn

Special Boat Service ε100

Reserve Organisations

Sri Lanka Volunteer Naval Force (SLVNF) 13,000 active reservists

Air Force 28,000 (incl SLAF Regt)
FORCES BY ROLE
FIGHTER
 1 sqn with F-7BS/G; FT-7
FIGHTER/GROUND ATTACK
 1 sqn with *Kfir* C-2/C-7/TC-2
 1 sqn with K-8 *Karakorum**
TRANSPORT
 1 sqn with An-32B *Cline*; C-130K *Hercules*; Cessna 421C *Golden Eagle*
 1 sqn with Beech B200 *King Air*; Y-12 (II)
TRAINING
 1 wg with PT-6, Cessna 150L
ATTACK HELICOPTER
 1 sqn with Mi-24V *Hind* E; Mi-35P *Hind*
TRANSPORT HELICOPTER
 1 sqn with Mi-17 *Hip* H; Mi-171Sh
 1 sqn with Bell 206A/B (incl basic trg), Bell 212
 1 (VIP) sqn with Bell 212; Bell 412 *Twin Huey*
ISR UAV
 1 sqn with *Blue Horizon* II
 1 sqn with *Searcher* MkII
MANOEUVRE
 Other
 1 (SLAF) sy regt
EQUIPMENT BY TYPE
AIRCRAFT 13 combat capable
 FTR 5: 3 F-7GS; 2 FT-7 (3 F-7BS; 1 F-7GS non-operational)
 FGA 1 *Kfir* C-2 (2 *Kfir* C-2; 1 *Kfir* C-7; 2 *Kfir* TC-2; 6 MiG-27M *Flogger* J2; 1 MiG-23UB *Flogger* C non-operational)
 TPT 21: **Medium** 2 C-130K *Hercules*; **Light** 19: 3 An-32B *Cline*; 6 Cessna 150L; 1 Cessna 421C *Golden Eagle*; 7 Y-12 (II); 2 Y-12 (IV)
 TRG 14: 7 K-8 *Karakoram**; 7 PT-6
HELICOPTERS
 ATK 11: 6 Mi-24P *Hind*; 3 Mi-24V *Hind* E; 2 Mi-35V *Hind*
 MRH 18: 6 Bell 412 *Twin Huey* (VIP); 2 Bell 412EP (VIP); 10 Mi-17 *Hip* H
 TPT 16: **Medium** 4 Mi-171Sh; **Light** 12: 2 Bell 206A *Jet Ranger*; 2 Bell 206B *Jet Ranger*; 8 Bell 212
UNMANNED AERIAL VEHICLES
 ISR • Medium 2+: some *Blue Horizon* II; 2 *Searcher* MkII
AIR DEFENCE • GUNS • TOWED 27: **40mm** 24 L/40; **94mm** 3 (3.7in)
AIR-LAUNCHED MISSILES
 AAM • IR PL-5E

Paramilitary ε62,200

Home Guard 13,000

National Guard ε15,000

Police Force 30,200; 1,000 (women) (total 31,200) 30,400 reservists

Ministry of Defence Special Task Force 3,000
Anti-guerrilla unit

Coast Guard n/k
Ministry of Defence

EQUIPMENT BY TYPE
PATROL AND COASTAL COMBATANTS 17
 PCO 1 *Suraksha* (ex-IND *Vikram*) with 1 hel landing platform
 PBF 11: 2 *Dvora*; 4 *Super Dvora* Mk I; 3 *Killer* (ROK); 2 (Inshore Patrol Craft)
 PB 4: 2 Simonneau Type-508; 2 *Samudra Raksha*
 PBR 1

DEPLOYMENT

CENTRAL AFRICAN REPUBLIC: UN • MINUSCA 115; 6 obs; 1 hel sqn

LEBANON: UN • UNIFIL 150; 1 inf coy

MALI: UN • MINUSMA 200; 7 obs; 1 sy coy

SOUTH SUDAN: UN • UNMISS 172; 2 obs; 1 fd hospital; 1 hel sqn

SUDAN: UN • UNISFA 2; 5 obs

WESTERN SAHARA: UN • MINURSO 4 obs

Taiwan (Republic of China) ROC

New Taiwan Dollar NT$		2017	2018	2019
GDP	NT$	17.4tr	18.1tr	
	US$	573bn	603bn	
per capita	US$	24,292	25,534	
Growth	%	2.9	2.7	
Inflation	%	1.1	1.5	
Def bdgt	NT$	319bn	332bn	346bn
	US$	10.5bn	11.0bn	
US$1=NT$		30.44	30.05	

Population	23,545,963

Ethnic groups: Taiwanese 84%; mainland Chinese 14%

Age	0–14	15–19	20–24	25–29	30–64	65 plus
Male	6.5%	2.9%	3.5%	3.5%	26.5%	6.6%
Female	6.2%	2.8%	3.3%	3.4%	27.1%	7.8%

Capabilities

Taiwan's relationship with China and its attempts to sustain a credible military capability dominate its security policy. The latest Quadrennial Defense Review, published in March 2017, highlighted the continued challenge from Beijing. Taiwan's current focus is therefore on air defence and deterrence in coastal areas, on both sides of the island. The armed forces are well trained and exercise regularly. Demographic pressure has influenced plans for force reductions and a shift towards an all-volunteer force. Taiwan's main alliance partnership is with the US. The Taiwan Relations Act from 1979 states that 'the United States shall provide Taiwan with arms of a defensive character'. Despite persistent US refusal to sanction the transfer of new combat aircraft, Taiwan has obtained US assistance to modernise its current fleet of F-16s to F-16V standard. Nevertheless, Taipei maintains an interest in the F-35. Due to the lack of potential foreign equipment suppliers, Taiwan is modernising its existing holdings and developing its domestic defence-industry capabilities through increased funding and the development of new weapons programmes. Taiwan's defence-industrial base has strengths in aerospace, shipbuilding and missiles.

An indigenous-submarine programme was officially launched in 2017, with the aim to locally build eight boats. The National Chung-Shan Institute of Science and Technology is in charge of most defence R&D.

ACTIVE 163,000 (Army 88,000 Navy 40,000 Air 35,000) **Paramilitary 11,450**

Conscript liability
(19–40 years) 12 months for those born before 1993; four months for those born after 1994 (alternative service available). Conscription officially ended in January 2018 and it was planned that the last conscripts would demobilise by the end of 2018

RESERVE 1,657,000 (Army 1,500,000 Navy 67,000 Air Force 90,000)
Some obligation to age 30

ORGANISATIONS BY SERVICE

Army 88,000 (incl ε5,000 MP)
FORCES BY ROLE
COMMAND
  3 corps HQ
  5 defence comd HQ
SPECIAL FORCES/HELICOPTER
  1 SF/hel comd (2 spec ops gp, 2 hel bde)
MANOEUVRE
  Armoured
  4 armd bde
  Mechanised
  3 mech inf bde
  Light
  6 inf bde
COMBAT SUPPORT
  3 arty gp
  3 engr gp
  3 CBRN gp
  3 sigs gp
COASTAL DEFENCE
  1 AShM bn

Reserves
FORCES BY ROLE
MANOEUVRE
  Light
  21 inf bde
EQUIPMENT BY TYPE
ARMOURED FIGHTING VEHICLES
  MBT 565: 200 M60A3; 100 M48A5; 265 M48H *Brave Tiger*
  LT TK 625 M41/Type-64 (230 M24 *Chaffee* (90mm gun) in store)
  IFV 225 CM-25 (M113 with 20–30mm cannon)
  APC 1,220
    APC (T) 650 M113
    APC (W) 570: ε270 CM-32 *Yunpao*; 300 LAV-150 *Commando*
ENGINEERING & MAINTENANCE VEHICLES
  AEV 18 M9
  ARV CM-27/A1; 37 M88A1
  VLB 22 M3; M48A5

NBC VEHICLES 48+: BIDS; 48 K216A1; KM453
ANTI-TANK/ANTI-INFRASTRUCTURE
  MSL
    SP TOW
    MANPATS FGM-148 *Javelin*; TOW
  RCL 500+: **90mm** M67; **106mm** 500+: 500 M40A1; Type-51
ARTILLERY 2,200
  SP 488: **105mm** 100 M108; **155mm** 318: 225 M109A2/A5; 48 M44T; 45 T-69; **203mm** 70 M110
  TOWED 1,060+: **105mm** 650 T-64 (M101); **155mm** 340+: 90 M59; 250 T-65 (M114); M44; XT-69; **203mm** 70 M115
  MRL 330: **117mm** 120 *Kung Feng* VI; **126mm** 210: 60 *Kung Feng* III/*Kung Feng* IV; 150 RT 2000 *Thunder* (KF towed and SP)
  MOR 322+
    SP 162+: **81mm** 72+: M29; 72 M125; **107mm** 90 M106A2
    TOWED 81mm 160 M29; T-75; **107mm** M30; **120mm** K5; XT-86
COASTAL DEFENCE
  ARTY 54: **127mm** ε50 US Mk32 (reported); **240mm** 4 M1
  AShM *Ching Feng*
HELICOPTERS
  ATK 96: 67 AH-1W *Cobra*; 29 AH-64E *Apache*
  MRH 38 OH-58D *Kiowa Warrior*
  TPT 110: **Heavy** 8 CH-47SD *Super D Chinook*; **Medium** 26 UH-60M *Black Hawk*; **Light** 76 Bell 205 (UH-1H *Iroquois*)
  TRG 29 TH-67 *Creek*
UNMANNED AERIAL VEHICLES
  ISR • Light *Mastiff* III
AIR DEFENCE
  SAM • Point-defence 76: 74 M1097 *Avenger*; 2 M48 *Chaparral*; FIM-92 *Stinger*
  GUNS 400
    SP 40mm M42
    TOWED 20: **35mm** 20 GDF-001 (30 systems with 20 guns) **40mm** L/70

Navy 40,000
EQUIPMENT BY TYPE
SUBMARINES • TACTICAL • SSK 4:
  2 *Hai Lung* with 6 single 533mm TT with SUT HWT/UGM-84L *Harpoon* Block II AShM
  2 *Hai Shih*† (ex-US *Guppy* II – trg role) with 10 single 533mm TT (6 fwd, 4 aft) with SUT HWT
PRINCIPAL SURFACE COMBATANTS 26
  CRUISERS • CGHM 4 *Keelung* (ex-US *Kidd*) with 2 quad lnchr with RGM-84L *Harpoon* Block II AShM, 2 twin Mk26 GMLS with RIM-66K-2 SM-2MR Block IIIA SAM, 2 triple Mk32 324mm ASTT with Mk46 LWT, 2 Mk 15 *Phalanx* Block 1B CIWS, 2 127mm gun (capacity 1 S-70 ASW hel)
  FRIGATES 22
    FFGHM 21:
      8 *Cheng Kung* (US *Oliver Hazard Perry* mod) with 2 quad lnchr with *Hsiung Feng* II/III AShM, 1 Mk13 GMLS with SM-1MR SAM, 2 triple 324mm ASTT with Mk 46 LWT, 1 Mk 15 *Phalanx* Block 1B CIWS, 1 76mm gun (capacity 2 S-70C ASW hel)
      2 *Meng Chuan* (ex-US *Oliver Hazard Perry*) with 1 Mk13 GMLS with RGM-84 *Harpoon* AShM/SM-

1MR SAM, 2 triple 324mm ASTT with Mk 46 LWT, 1 Mk 15 *Phalanx* Block 1B CIWS, 1 76mm gun (capacity 2 S-70C ASW hel)

5 *Chin Yang* (ex-US *Knox*) with 1 octuple Mk16 lnchr with ASROC/RGM-84C *Harpoon* AShM, 2 triple lnchr with SM-1MR SAM, 2 twin lnchr with SM-1MR SAM, 2 twin 324mm ASTT with Mk 46 LWT, 1 Mk 15 *Phalanx* Block 1B CIWS, 1 127mm gun (capacity 1 MD-500 hel)

6 *Kang Ding* with 2 quad lnchr with *Hsiung Feng* II AShM, 1 quad lnchr with *Sea Chaparral* SAM, 2 Mk32 triple 324mm ASTT with Mk 46 LWT, 1 Mk 15 *Phalanx* Block 1B CIWS, 1 76mm gun (capacity 1 S-70C ASW hel)

FFGH • 1 *Chin Yang* (ex-US *Knox*) with 1 octuple Mk112 lnchr with ASROC/RGM-84C *Harpoon* AShM, 2 twin 324mm ASTT with Mk 46 LWT, 1 Mk 15 *Phalanx* Block 1B CIWS, 1 127mm gun (capacity 1 MD-500 hel)

PATROL AND COASTAL COMBATANTS 44

CORVETTES • **FSG** 1 *Tuo Jiang* (*Hsun Hai*) with 4 twin lnchr with *Hsiung Feng* II AShM, 4 twin lnchr with *Hisung Feng* III AShM, 2 triple 324mm TT, 1 Mk 15 *Phalanx* Block 1B CIWS; 1 76mm gun

PCG 11:

1 *Jin Chiang* with 1 quad lnchr with *Hsiung Feng* II AShM

4 *Jin Chiang* with 2 twin lnchr with *Hsiung Feng* II AShM, 1 76mm gun

6 *Jin Chiang* with 1 quad lnchr with *Hsiung Feng* III AShM, 1 76mm gun

PCC 1 *Jin Chiang* (test platform)

PBG 31 *Kwang Hua* with 2 twin lnchr with *Hsiung Feng* II AShM

MINE WARFARE • **MINE COUNTERMEASURES** 9

MHC 6: 4 *Yung Feng*; 2 *Yung Jin* (ex-US *Osprey*)

MSO 3 *Yung Yang* (ex-US *Aggressive*)

COMMAND SHIPS • **LCC** 1 *Kao Hsiung*

AMPHIBIOUS

PRINCIPAL AMPHIBIOUS SHIPS • **LSD** 1 *Shiu Hai* (ex-US *Anchorage*) with 2 Mk 15 *Phalanx* CIWS, 1 hel landing platform (capacity either 2 LCU or 18 LCM; 360 troops)

LANDING SHIPS

LST 8:

6 *Chung Hai* (capacity 16 tanks; 200 troops)

2 *Chung Ho* (ex-US *Newport*) with 1 Mk 15 *Phalanx* CIWS , 1 hel landing platform (capacity 3 LCVP, 23 AFVs, 400 troops)

LANDING CRAFT 47

LCM ε35 (various)

LCU 12 LCU 1610 (capacity 2 M60A3 or 400 troops) (minelaying capability)

LOGISTICS AND SUPPORT 12

AGOR 1 *Ta Kuan*

AOEH 1 *Panshih* with 1 quad lnchr with *Sea Chaparral* SAM, 2 Mk 15 *Phalanx* CIWS (capacity 3 med hel)

AOE 1 *Wu Yi* with 1 quad lnchr with *Sea Chaparra*l SAM, 1 hel landing platform

ARS 2: 1 *Da Hu* (ex-US *Diver*); 1 *Da Juen* (ex-US *Bolster*)

ATF 7 *Ta Tung* (ex-US *Cherokee*)

Marines 10,000

FORCES BY ROLE

MANOEUVRE

Amphibious

3 mne bde

COMBAT SUPPORT

Some cbt spt unit

EQUIPMENT BY TYPE

ARMOURED FIGHTING VEHICLES

AAV 202: 52 AAV-7A1; 150 LVTP-5A1

ENGINEERING & MAINTENANCE VEHICLES

ARV 2 AAVR-7

ANIT-TANK/ANTI-INFRASTRUCTURE

RCL 106mm

ARTILLERY • **TOWED** 105mm; 155mm

Naval Aviation

FORCES BY ROLE

ANTI SUBMARINE WARFARE

2 sqn with S-70C *Seahawk* (S-70C *Defender*)

1 sqn with MD-500 *Defender*

ISR UAV

1 bn with *Chung Shyang* II

EQUIPMENT BY TYPE

HELICOPTERS

ASW 20 S-70C *Seahawk* (S-70C *Defender*)

MRH 10 MD-500 *Defender*

UNMANNED AERIAL VEHICLES • **ISR** • **Medium** ε29 *Chung Shyang* II

Air Force 35,000

FORCES BY ROLE

FIGHTER

3 sqn with *Mirage* 2000-5E/D (2000-5EI/DI)

FIGHTER/GROUND ATTACK

3 sqn with F-5E/F *Tiger* II

6 sqn with F-16A/B *Fighting Falcon*

5 sqn with F-CK-1A/B/C/D *Ching Kuo*

ANTI-SUBMARINE WARFARE

1 sqn with P-3C *Orion*

ELECTRONIC WARFARE

1 sqn with C-130HE *Tien Gian*

ISR

1 sqn with RF-5E *Tigereye*

AIRBORNE EARLY WARNING & CONTROL

1 sqn with E-2T *Hawkeye*

SEARCH & RESCUE

1 sqn with H225; S-70C *Black Hawk*

TRANSPORT

2 sqn with C-130H *Hercules*

1 (VIP) sqn with B-727-100; B-737-800; Beech 1900; F-50; S-70C *Black Hawk*

TRAINING

1 sqn with AT-3A/B *Tzu-Chung**

1 sqn with Beech 1900

1 (basic) sqn with T-34C *Turbo Mentor*

EQUIPMENT BY TYPE

AIRCRAFT 479 combat capable

FTR 285: 87 F-5E/F *Tiger* II (some in store); 143 F-16A/B *Fighting Falcon*; 9 *Mirage* 2000-5D (2000-5DI); 46 *Mirage* 2000-5E (2000-5EI)

FGA 127 F-CK-1C/D *Ching Kuo*
ASW 12 P-3C *Orion*
EW 1 C-130HE *Tien Gian*
ISR 7 RF-5E *Tigereye*
AEW&C 6 E-2T *Hawkeye*
TPT 33: **Medium** 19 C-130H *Hercules*; **Light** 10 Beech 1900; **PAX** 4: 1 B-737-800; 3 F-50
TRG 97: 55 AT-3A/B *Tzu-Chung*; 42 T-34C *Turbo Mentor*
HELICOPTERS
TPT • Medium 19: 3 H225; 16 S-70C *Black Hawk*; 8 UH-60M *Black Hawk*
AIR DEFENCE
SAM • Point-defence *Antelope*
AIR-LAUNCHED MISSILES
AAM • IR AIM-9J/P *Sidewinder*; R-550 *Magic* 2; *Shafrir*; *Sky Sword* I; **IR/ARH** *Mica*; **ARH** AIM-120C AMRAAM; *Sky Sword* II
ASM AGM-65A *Maverick*
AShM AGM-84 *Harpoon*
ARM *Sky Sword* IIA
LACM Conventional *Wan Chien*
BOMBS • Laser-guided *Paveway* II

Air Defence and Missile Command
FORCES BY ROLE
SURFACE-TO-SURFACE MISSILE
 3 SSM bty with *Hsiung Feng* IIE
AIR DEFENCE
 2 AD/SAM gp (total: 13 bty with MIM-23 *Hawk*; 4 bty with MIM-104F *Patriot* PAC-3; 6 bty with *Tien Kung* I *Sky Bow*/*Tien Kung* II *Sky Bow*)
EQUIPMENT BY TYPE
SURFACE-TO-SURFACE MISSILE LAUNCHERS
 GLCM • Conventional ε12 *Hsiung Feng* IIE
AIR DEFENCE • SAM • Medium-range 600+: 100 MIM-23 *Hawk*; ε500 *Tien Kung* I *Sky Bow*/*Tien Kung* II *Sky Bow*
MISSILE DEFENCE • Medium-range 24+ MIM-104F *Patriot* PAC-3

Paramilitary 11,450

Coast Guard 11,450
EQUIPMENT BY TYPE
PATROL AND COASTAL COMBATANTS 161
 PSOH 4: 2 *Tainan*; 2 *Yilan*
 PSO 6: 4 *Miaoli* with 1 hel landing platform; 2 *Ho Hsing*
 PCO 13: 2 *Kinmen*; 2 *Mou Hsing*; 3 *Shun Hu* 7; 4 *Taichung*; 2 *Taipei*
 PBF ε56 (various)
 PB 82: 1 *Shun Hu* 6; ε81 (various)

Cyber

Although Taiwan has a highly developed civilian IT sector, the government has been relatively slow to exploit this advantage for national-defence purposes. However, for the past decade, Taipei has been working on its *Po Sheng* – Broad Victory – C4ISR programme, an all-hazards system with a significant defence component. The main focus of the military component of this programme is countering Chinese information-warfare and electronic-warfare (EW) attacks. The authorities responsible for cyber activity include the National Security Bureau, the defence ministry, and the Research, Development and Evaluation Commission. In 2015, a Defense Policy Paper recommended that an independent fourth service branch combining cyber and electronic-warfare capabilities should be formed. The Information, Communications and Electronic Warfare Command was established in mid-2017 and is responsible for coordinating cyber defence and directing R&D efforts in cyber and EW.

FOREIGN FORCES
Singapore 3 trg camp (incl inf and arty)

Thailand THA

Thai Baht b		2017	2018	2019
GDP	b	15.5tr	16.4tr	
	US$	455bn	490bn	
per capita	US$	6,591	7,084	
Growth	%	3.9	4.6	
Inflation	%	0.7	0.9	
Def bdgt	b	214bn	217bn	224bn
	US$	6.29bn	6.51bn	
US$1=b		33.93	33.39	

Population 68,615,858

Ethnic and religious groups: Thai 75%; Chinese 14%; Muslim 4%

Age	0–14	15–19	20–24	25–29	30–64	65 plus
Male	8.6%	3.3%	3.8%	3.7%	24.9%	4.8%
Female	8.2%	3.1%	3.7%	3.6%	26.2%	6.2%

Capabilities

Thailand has large, well-funded armed forces and its air force is one of the best equipped and trained in Southeast Asia, while the introduction into service of *Gripen* combat aircraft and Saab 340 airborne early-warning platforms has boosted Thai airpower. The Vision 2026 defence-modernisation plan, approved by the defence council in October 2017, outlines the armed forces' capability improvements over the next decade. Thailand is considered a major non-NATO ally by the US, while the country has developed deeper defence ties with China since the military coup in 2014. The armed forces regularly take part in international military exercises. A small number of personnel remain deployed on the UNAMID mission to Darfur, Sudan. The military-modernisation effort includes the development of submarines, anti-submarine warfare capabilities and a surface-ship procurement programme. The armoured vehicle fleet has been recapitalised with deliveries from Ukraine and China. The arrival of the Saab 340 AEW aircraft, along with the *Gripen* combat aircraft and a command-and-control system, has provided a step change in air capability. Under its Defence Industry Masterplan, the government indicates that expanding Thailand's presently limited defence sector can be an important way of developing military capability. The government is making efforts to reform defence procurement and offsets by expanding the role of its Defence Technology Institute. It is planned that this will change in 2019 to become the Defence Technology Agency, acting as a central procurement agency for the armed forces, as well as overseeing the development of Thailand's defence industry.

ACTIVE 360,850 (Army 245,000 Navy 69,850 Air 46,000) **Paramilitary 93,700**

Conscription liability 24 months

RESERVE 200,000 Paramilitary 45,000

ORGANISATIONS BY SERVICE

Army 130,000; ε115,000 conscript (total 245,000)
FORCES BY ROLE
COMMAND
4 (regional) army HQ
3 corps HQ
SPECIAL FORCES
1 SF div
1 SF regt
MANOEUVRE
Armoured
3 cav div (1 recce bn; 3 tk regt (3 tk bn); 1 indep tk bn; 1 sigs bn; 1 maint bn; 1 hel sqn)
Mechanised
1 mech inf div (1 recce coy; 1 recce sqn; 1 tk bn; 1 inf regt (4 inf bn); 3 inf regt; 1 engr bn; 1 sigs bn)
Light
8 inf div (1 recce sqn; 3 inf regt (3 inf bn); 1 engr bn; 1 sigs bn)
COMBAT SUPPORT
1 arty div
1 engr div
COMBAT SERVICE SUPPORT
4 economic development div
HELICOPTER
Some hel flt
ISR UAV
1 UAV bn with *Hermes* 450; *Searcher* II
AIR DEFENCE
1 ADA div (6 bn)
EQUIPMENT BY TYPE
ARMOURED FIGHTING VEHICLES
MBT 360: 53 M60A1; 125 M60A3; 105 M48A5; 49 T-84 *Oplot*; 28 VT-4; (50 Type-69 in store)
LT TK 194: 24 M41; 104 *Scorpion* (50 in store); 66 *Stingray*
RECCE 32 S52 *Shorland*
IFV 168 BTR-3E1
APC 1,140
  APC (T) 880: *Bronco*; 430 M113A1/A3; 450 Type-85
  APC (W) 160: 9 BTR-3K (CP); 6 BTR-3C (amb); 18 *Condor*; 142 LAV-150 *Commando*
  PPV 100 REVA
ENGINEERING & MAINTENANCE VEHICLES
ARV 58: 2 BREM-84 *Atlet*; 13 BTR-3BR; 22 M88A1; 6 M88A2; 10 M113; 5 Type-653; WZT-4
VLB Type-84
MW *Bozena*; *Giant Viper*
ANTI-TANK/ANTI-INFRASTRUCTURE
MSL
  SP 30+: 18+ M901A5 (TOW); 12 BTR-3RK
  MANPATS M47 *Dragon*
RCL 180: **75mm** 30 M20; **106mm** 150 M40
ARTILLERY 2,643
  SP 155mm 32: 6 ATMOS-2000; 6 CAESAR; 20 M109A5

TOWED 617: **105mm** 340: 24 LG1 MkII; 12 M-56; 200 M101/M425; 12 M102; 32 M618A2; 60 L119 Light Gun; **155mm** 277: 90 GHN-45 A1; 48 M114; 118 M198; 21 M-71
MRL 68: **122mm** 6: 6 M-130 60 PHZ-85; **302mm** 4: 1 DTI-1 (WS-1B); 3 DTI-1G (WS-32)
MOR 1,926+: **SP 81mm** 39: 18 BTR-3M1; 21 M125A3; **SP 107mm** M106A3; **SP 120mm** 20: 8 BTR-3M2; 12 M1064A3; 1,867 **81mm/107mm/120mm**
AIRCRAFT
TPT • **Light** 19: 2 Beech 200 *King Air*; 2 Beech 1900C; 1 C-212 *Aviocar*; 1 C295W; 9 Cessna A185E (U-17B); 2 ERJ-135LR; 2 *Jetstream* 41
TRG 33: 11 MX-7-235 *Star Rocket*; 22 T-41B *Mescalero*
HELICOPTERS
ATK 7 AH-1F *Cobra*
MRH 15: 8 AS550 *Fennec*; 2 AW139; 5 Mi-17V-5 *Hip H*
TPT 216: **Heavy** 5 CH-47D *Chinook*; **Medium** 12: 9 UH-60L *Black Hawk*; 3 UH-60M *Black Hawk*; **Light** 199: 93 Bell 205 (UH-1H *Iroquois*); 27 Bell 206 *Jet Ranger*; 52 Bell 212 (AB-212); 16 Enstrom 480B; 6 H145M (VIP tpt); 5 UH-72A *Lakota*
TRG 53 Hughes 300C
UNMANNED AERIAL VEHICLES
ISR • **Medium** 4 *Hermes* 450; *Searcher*; *Searcher* II
AIR DEFENCE
SAM
  Short-range *Aspide*
  Point-defence 8+: 8 *Starstreak*; 9K338 *Igla-S* (SA-24 *Grinch*)
GUNS 184
  SP 54: **20mm** 24 M163 *Vulcan*; **40mm** 30 M1/M42 SP
  TOWED 138: **20mm** 24 M167 *Vulcan*; **35mm** 8 GDF-007 with Skyguard 3; **37mm** 52 Type-74; **40mm** 48 L/70; **57mm** ε6 Type-59 (S-60) (18+ more non-operational)

Reserves
FORCES BY ROLE
COMMAND
1 inf div HQ

Navy 44,000 (incl Naval Aviation, Marines, Coastal Defence); 25,850 conscript (total 69,850)
EQUIPMENT BY TYPE
PRINCIPAL SURFACE COMBATANTS 9
  AIRCRAFT CARRIERS • CVH 1:
    1 *Chakri Naruebet* with 2 sextuple *Sadral* lnchr with *Mistral* SAM (capacity 6 S-70B *Seahawk* ASW hel)
  FRIGATES 8
  FFGHM 2:
    2 *Naresuan* with 2 quad Mk141 lnchr with RGM-84 *Harpoon* AShM, 1 8 cell Mk41 Mod 30 VLS with RIM-162B ESSM SAM, 2 triple Mk32 324mm TT with Mk46 LWT, 1 127mm gun (capacity 1 *Super Lynx* 300 hel)
  FFG 4:
    2 *Chao Phraya* (trg role) with 4 twin lnchr with C-802A AShM, 2 RBU 1200 A/S mor, 2 twin 100mm gun
    2 *Chao Phraya* with 4 twin lnchr with C-802A AShM, 2 RBU 1200 A/S mor, 1 twin 100mm gun, 1 hel landing platform

FF 2:
  1 *Makut Rajakumarn* with 2 triple 324mm ASTT, 2 114mm gun
  1 *Pin Klao* (ex-US Cannon) (trg role) with 6 single 324mm ASTT, 3 76mm gun

PATROL AND COASTAL COMBATANTS 82
  CORVETTES 7
    FSGM 2 *Rattanakosin* with 2 twin Mk140 lnchr with RGM-84 *Harpoon* AShM, 1 octuple *Albatros* lnchr with *Aspide* SAM, 2 triple Mk32 324mm ASTT with *Stingray* LWT, 1 76mm gun
    FS 5:
      3 *Khamronsin* with 2 triple 324mm ASTT with *Stingray* LWT, 1 76mm gun
      2 *Tapi* with 2 triple 324mm ASTT with Mk46 LWT, 1 76mm gun
  PSO 1 *Krabi* (UK *River* mod) with 1 76mm gun
  PCFG 6:
    3 *Prabparapak* with 2 single lnchr with *Gabriel* I AShM, 1 triple lnchr with *Gabriel* I AShM, 1 57mm gun
    3 *Ratcharit* with 2 twin lnchr with MM38 *Exocet* AShM, 1 76mm gun
  PCOH 2 *Pattani* (1 in trg role) with 1 76mm gun
  PCO 4: 3 *Hua Hin* with 1 76mm gun; 1 M58 Patrol Gun Boat with 1 76mm gun
  PCC 9: 3 *Chon Buri* with 2 76mm gun; 6 *Sattahip* with 1 76mm gun
  PBF 4 M18 Fast Assault Craft (capacity 18 troops)
  PB 49: 1 T-11 (US PGM-71); 3 T-81; 9 T-91; 3 M36 Patrol Boat; 13 T-213; 1 T-227; 13 M21 Patrol Boat; 3 T-991; 3 T-994

MINE WARFARE • MINE COUNTERMEASURES 17
  MCCS 1 *Thalang*
  MCO 2 *Lat Ya*
  MCC 2 *Bang Rachan*
  MSR 12: 7 T1; 5 T6

AMPHIBIOUS
  PRINCIPAL AMPHIBIOUS SHIPS 1
    LPD 1 *Anthong* (SGP *Endurance*) with 1 76mm gun (capacity 2 hel; 19 MBT; 500 troops)
  LANDING SHIPS 2
    LST 2 *Sichang* with 2 hel landing platform (capacity 14 MBT; 300 troops)
  LANDING CRAFT 14
    LCU 9: 3 *Man Nok*; 2 *Mataphun* (capacity either 3–4 MBT or 250 troops); 4 *Thong Kaeo*
    LCM 2
    UCAC 3 *Griffon* 1000TD

LOGISTICS AND SUPPORT 13
  ABU 1 *Suriya*
  AGOR 1 *Sok*
  AGS 2
  AOL 6: 1 *Matra* with 1 hel landing platform; 3 *Proet*; 1 *Prong*; 1 *Samui*
  AOR 1 *Chula*
  AORH 1 *Similan* (capacity 1 hel)
  AWT 1

Naval Aviation 1,200
EQUIPMENT BY TYPE
AIRCRAFT 3 combat capable

  ASW 2 P-3A *Orion* (P-3T)
  ISR 9 *Sentry* O-2-337
  MP 1 F-27-200 MPA*
  TPT • Light 15: 7 Do-228-212; 2 ERJ-135LR; 2 F-27-400M *Troopship*; 3 N-24A *Searchmaster*; 1 UP-3A *Orion* (UP-3T)
HELICOPTERS
  ASW 8: 6 S-70B *Seahawk*; 2 Super Lynx 300
  MRH 2 MH-60S *Knight Hawk*
  TPT 18: **Medium** 2 Bell 214ST (AB-214ST); **Light** 16: 6 Bell 212 (AB-212); 5 H145M; 5 S-76B
AIR-LAUNCHED MISSILES • AShM AGM-84 *Harpoon*

Marines 23,000
FORCES BY ROLE
COMMAND
  1 mne div HQ
MANOEUVRE
  Reconnaissance
  1 recce bn
  Light
  2 inf regt (total: 6 bn)
  Amphibious
  1 amph aslt bn
COMBAT SUPPORT
  1 arty regt (3 fd arty bn, 1 ADA bn)
EQUIPMENT BY TYPE
ARMOURED FIGHTING VEHICLES
  IFV 14 BTR-3E1
  APC (W) 24 LAV-150 *Commando*
  AAV 33 LVTP-7
ENGINEERING & MAINTENANCE VEHICLES
  ARV 1 AAVR-7
ANTI-TANK/ANTI-INFRASTRUCTURE • MSL
  SP 10 M1045A2 HMMWV with TOW
  MANPATS M47 *Dragon*; TOW
ARTILLERY • TOWED 48: **105mm** 36 (reported); **155mm** 12 GC-45
AIR DEFENCE
  SAM Point-defence QW-18
  GUNS 12.7mm 14

Naval Special Warfare Command

Air Force ε46,000
4 air divs, one flying trg school
FORCES BY ROLE
FIGHTER
  2 sqn with F-5E/5F *Tiger* II
  3 sqn with F-16A/B *Fighting Falcon*
FIGHTER/GROUND ATTACK
  1 sqn with *Gripen* C/D
GROUND ATTACK
  1 sqn with *Alpha Jet**
  1 sqn with AU-23A *Peacemaker*
  1 sqn with L-39ZA *Albatros**; T-50TH *Golden Eagle**
ELINT/ISR
  1 sqn with DA42 MPP *Guardian*
AIRBORNE EARLY WARNING & CONTROL
  1 sqn with Saab 340B; Saab 340 *Erieye*

TRANSPORT
1 (Royal Flight) sqn with A319CJ; A340-500; B-737-800
1 sqn with ATR-72; BAe-748
1 sqn with BT-67
1 sqn with C-130H/H-30 *Hercules*

TRAINING
1 sqn with L-39ZA *Albatros**
1 sqn with CT-4A/B *Airtrainer*; T-41D *Mescalero*
1 sqn with CT-4E *Airtrainer*
1 sqn with PC-9

TRANSPORT HELICOPTER
1 sqn with Bell 205 (UH-1H *Iroquois*)
1 sqn with Bell 412 *Twin Huey*; S-92A

EQUIPMENT BY TYPE
AIRCRAFT 150 combat capable
  FTR 78: 1 F-5B *Freedom Fighter*; 21 F-5E *Tiger* II; 3 F-5F *Tiger* II (F-5E/F being upgraded); 38 F-16A *Fighting Falcon*; 15 F-16B *Fighting Falcon*
  FGA 11: 7 *Gripen* C; 4 *Gripen* D
  ATK 17 AU-23A *Peacemaker*
  ISR 5 DA42 MPP *Guardian*
  AEW&C 2 Saab 340 *Erieye*
  ELINT 2 Saab 340 *Erieye* (COMINT/ELINT)
  TPT 42: **Medium** 14: 6 C-130H *Hercules*; 6 C-130H-30 *Hercules*; 2 Saab 340B; **Light** 21: 3 ATR-72; 3 Beech 200 *King Air*; 8 BT-67; 1 Commander 690; 6 DA42M; **PAX** 7: 1 A319CJ; 1 A320CJ; 1 A340-500; 1 B-737-800; 3 SSJ-100-95LR (1 A310-324 in store)
  TRG 111: 16 *Alpha Jet**; 13 CT-4A *Airtrainer*; 6 CT-4B *Airtrainer*; 20 CT-4E *Airtrainer*; 26 L-39ZA *Albatros**; 21 PC-9; 7 T-41D *Mescalero*; 2 T-50TH *Golden Eagle**
HELICOPTERS
  MRH 11: 2 Bell 412 *Twin Huey*; 2 Bell 412SP *Twin Huey*; 1 Bell 412HP *Twin Huey*; 6 Bell 412EP *Twin Huey*
  CSAR 6 H225M *Super Cougar*
  TPT 20: **Medium** 3 S-92A *Super Hawk*; **Light** 17 Bell 205 (UH-1H *Iroquois*)
AIR-LAUNCHED MISSILES
  AAM • **IR** AIM-9P/S *Sidewinder*; *Python* 3; **IIR** IRIS-T;
  ARH AIM-120 AMRAAM
  ASM AGM-65 *Maverick*
  AShM RBS15F
BOMBS • **Laser-guided** *Paveway* II

Paramilitary ε93,700

Border Patrol Police 20,000

Marine Police 2,200
EQUIPMENT BY TYPE
PATROL AND COASTAL COMBATANTS 98
  PCO 1 *Srinakrin*
  PCC 2 *Hameln*
  PB 49: 2 *Chasanyabadee*; 3 *Cutlass*; 2 *Ratayapibanbancha* (*Reef Ranger*); 1 *Sriyanont*; 41 (various)
  PBR 46

National Security Volunteer Corps 45,000 – Reserves

Police Aviation 500
EQUIPMENT BY TYPE
AIRCRAFT 6 combat capable
  ATK 6 AU-23A *Peacemaker*
  TPT 16: **Light** 15: 2 CN235; 8 PC-6 *Turbo-Porter*; 3 SC-7 3M *Skyvan*; 2 Short 330UTT; **PAX** 1 F-50
HELICOPTERS
  MRH 12: 6 Bell 412 *Twin Huey*; 6 Bell 429
  TPT • **Light** 61: 27 Bell 205A; 14 Bell 206 *Jet Ranger*; 20 Bell 212 (AB-212)

Provincial Police 50,000 (incl ε500 Special Action Force)

Thahan Phran (Hunter Soldiers) 21,000
Volunteer irregular force
FORCES BY ROLE
MANOEUVRE
  Other
    22 paramilitary regt (total: 275 paramilitary coy)

DEPLOYMENT
INDIA/PAKISTAN: UN • UNMOGIP 4 obs
SOUTH SUDAN: UN • UNMISS 1; 2 obs
SUDAN: UN • UNAMID 9; 1 obs

FOREIGN FORCES
United States US Pacific Command: 300

Timor-Leste TLS

US$		2017	2018	2019
GDP	US$	2.78bn	3.16bn	
per capita	US$	2,237	2,486	
Growth	%	-4.6	0.8	
Inflation	%	0.6	1.8	
Def bdgt	US$	25.4m	26.5m	
Population	1,321,929			

Age	0–14	15–19	20–24	25–29	30–64	65 plus
Male	20.8%	5.8%	4.6%	3.8%	13.2%	1.9%
Female	19.6%	5.6%	4.5%	4.0%	14.2%	2.1%

Capabilities
The small Timor-Leste Defence Force (F-FDTL) has been afflicted by funding, personnel and morale challenges since it was established in 2001. While the F-FDTL is responsible for external defence, its parallel internal-security role has sometimes brought it into conflict with the national police force. The F-FDTL has been reconstituted but is still a long way from meeting the ambitious force-structure goals set out in the Force 2020 plan published in 2007. The origins of the F-FDTL in the Falintil national resistance force, and continuing training and doctrinal emphasis on low-intensity infantry tactics, mean that the force provides a deterrent to invasion. In 2017, Portugal and Timor-Leste signed a defence cooperation agreement up to 2022. The F-FDTL sometimes receives training from Australian and US personnel. Australia is donating

two *Guardian*-class patrol vessels as part of its Pacific Patrol Boat Replacement programme; these are due to arrive in 2023. Maintenance capacity is unclear and the country has no traditional defence industry.

ACTIVE 2,280 (Army 2,200 Naval Element 80)

ORGANISATIONS BY SERVICE

Army 2,200
Training began in January 2001 with the aim of deploying 1,500 full-time personnel and 1,500 reservists. Authorities are engaged in developing security structures with international assistance

FORCES BY ROLE
MANOEUVRE
  Light
  2 inf bn
COMBAT SUPPORT
  1 MP pl
COMBAT SERVICE SUPPORT
  1 log spt coy

Naval Element 80
EQUIPMENT BY TYPE
PATROL AND COASTAL COMBATANTS 7
  PB 7: 2 *Albatros*; 2 *Dili* (ex-ROK); 2 *Shanghai* II; 1 *Kamenassa* (ex-ROK *Chamsuri*)

Air Component
EQUIPMENT BY TYPE
AIRCRAFT • TPT • Light 1 Cessna 172

Vietnam VNM

Vietnamese Dong d		2017	2018	2019
GDP	d	5006tr	5506tr	
	US$	220bn	241bn	
per capita	US$	2,353	2,553	
Growth	%	6.8	6.6	
Inflation	%	3.5	3.8	
Def bdgt	d	ε9.93tr	ε1.10tr	ε1.23tr
	US$	ε4.37bn	ε4.83bn	
FMA (US)	US$	12m	0m	
US$1=d		22715.61	22807.26	

Population 97,040,334

Ethnic groups: Kinh 85.7%; Tay 1.9%; Thai 1.8%; Khome 1.4%; Hmong 1.3%; other or unspecified 7.1%

Age	0–14	15–19	20–24	25–29	30–64	65 plus
Male	12.2%	4.0%	4.2%	4.7%	22.5%	2.5%
Female	11.0%	3.7%	4.0%	4.5%	22.9%	3.9%

Capabilities

Vietnam has a stronger military tradition and its armed forces have more operational experience than any of its neighbours. Its defence efforts and armed forces also benefit from broad popular support, particularly in the context of tensions with China over conflicting claims in the South China Sea. Vietnam adopted a new Law on National Defence in 2018 that focused, among other areas, on information warfare. Legislation is also being discussed that seeks to increase the role of the coastguard, including the use of force to defend sovereignty. Vietnam is looking to diversify its security partnerships. Washington lifted its arms embargo on Hanoi in 2016, while New Delhi and Seoul are understood to be seeking inroads into Vietnam's defence market. The forces are conscript-based, and there is a plan to reduce their numbers in the armed forces and other institutions, such as military colleges and hospitals, by 2022. Recapitalisation efforts have focused on the navy and air force, mainly with a view to disputes in the Spratly Islands. While Hanoi cannot hope to balance China's power on its own, the recent development of a submarine capability and the procurement of additional Su-30MK2 combat aircraft and new air-defence capabilities would complicate Beijing's military options. Vietnam may also be looking to procure assets that would increase its surveillance capacities in the South China Sea, such as UAVs. Vietnam has limited but expanding defence-industrial capacities, dominated by the state-owned Viettel Military Industry and Telecoms Group.

ACTIVE 482,000 (Army 412,000 Navy 40,000 Air 30,000) **Paramilitary 40,000**

Conscript liability 2 years army and air defence, 3 years air force and navy, specialists 3 years, some ethnic minorities 2 years

RESERVES Paramilitary 5,000,000

ORGANISATIONS BY SERVICE

Space
EQUIPMENT BY TYPE
SATELLITES • ISR 1 VNREDSat

Army ε412,000
8 Mil Regions (incl capital)
FORCES BY ROLE
COMMAND
  4 corps HQ
SPECIAL FORCES
  1 SF bde (1 AB bde, 1 demolition engr regt)
MANOEUVRE
  Armoured
  6 armd bde
  3 armd regt
  Mechanised
  2 mech inf div
  Light
  23 inf div
SURFACE-TO-SURFACE MISSILE
  1 SRBM bde
COMBAT SUPPORT
  13 arty bde
  1 arty regt
  10 engr bde
  1 engr regt
  1 EW unit
  3 sigs bde
  2 sigs regt
COMBAT SERVICE SUPPORT
  9 economic construction div
  1 log regt

1 med unit
1 trg regt
AIR DEFENCE
11 AD bde

Reserve
MANOEUVRE
Light
9 inf div

EQUIPMENT BY TYPE
ARMOURED FIGHTING VEHICLES
MBT 1,270: 70 T-62; 350 Type-59; 850 T-54/T-55 (45 T-34† in store)
LT TK 620: 300 PT-76; 320 Type-62/Type-63
RECCE 100 BRDM-1/BRDM-2
IFV 300 BMP-1/BMP-2
APC 1,380+
  APC (T) 280+: Some BTR-50; 200 M113 (to be upgraded); 80 Type-63
  APC (W) 1,100 BTR-40/BTR-60/BTR-152
ANTI-TANK/ANTI-INFRASTRUCTURE
MSL • MANPATS 9K11 *Malyutka* (AT-3 *Sagger*)
RCL **75mm** Type-56; **82mm** Type-65 (B-10); **87mm** Type-51
  GUNS
  SP 100mm SU-100; **122mm** SU-122
  TOWED 100mm T-12 (arty); M-1944
ARTILLERY 3,040+
SP 30+: **122mm** 2S1 *Gvozdika*; **152mm** 30 2S3 *Akatsiya*; **175mm** M107
TOWED 2,300: **105mm** M101/M102; **122mm** D-30/Type-54 (M-1938)/Type-60 (D-74); **130mm** M-46; **152mm** D-20; **155mm** M114
MRL 710+: **107mm** 360 Type-63; **122mm** 350 BM-21 *Grad*; **140mm** BM-14
MOR **82mm**; **120mm** M-1943; **160mm** M-1943
SURFACE-TO-SURFACE MISSILE LAUNCHERS
SRBM • Coventional Scud-B/C
AIR DEFENCE
SAM • Point-defence 9K32 *Strela*-2 (SA-7 *Grail*)‡; 9K310 *Igla*-1 (SA-16 *Gimlet*); 9K38 *Igla* (SA-18 *Grouse*)
  GUNS 12,000
    SP 23mm ZSU-23-4
    TOWED 14.5mm/30mm/37mm/57mm/85mm/100mm

Navy ε40,000 (incl ε27,000 Naval Infantry)
EQUIPMENT BY TYPE
SUBMARINES • TACTICAL 8
SSK 6 *Hanoi* (RUS *Varshavyanka*) with 6 533mm TT with 3M14E *Klub*-S (SS-N-30) LACM/3M54E *Klub*-S (SS-N-27 *Sizzler*) AShM/53-65KE HWT/TEST-71ME HWT
SSI 2 *Yugo* (DPRK)
PRINCIPAL SURFACE COMBATANTS 4
  FRIGATES • FFGM 4
  2 *Dinh Tien Hoang* (RUS *Gepard* 3.9 (Project 11661E)) with 2 quad lnchr with 3M24E *Uran*-E (SS-N-25 *Switchblade*) AShM, 1 *Palma* lnchr with *Sosna*-R SAM, 2 AK630 CIWS, 1 76mm gun, 1 hel landing platform
  2 *Tran Huang Dao* (RUS *Gepard* 3.9 (Project 11661E)) with 2 quad lnchr with 3M24E *Uran*-E (SS-N-25 *Switchblade*), 1 *Palma* lnchr with *Sosna*-R SAM, 2 twin 533mm TT with SET-53M HWT, 2 AK630 CIWS, 1 76mm gun, 1 hel landing platform
PATROL AND COASTAL COMBATANTS 68
  CORVETTES 6:
  FSGM 1 BPS-500 with 2 quad lnchr with 3M24E *Uran*-E (SS-N-25 *Switchblade*) AShM, 9K32 *Strela*-2M (SA-N-5 *Grail*) SAM (manually operated), 2 twin 533mm TT, 1 RBU-1600 A/S mor, 1 AK630 CIWS, 1 76mm gun
  FS 5:
  3 *Petya* II (FSU) with 1 quintuple 406mm ASTT, 4 RBU 6000 *Smerch* 2 A/S mor, 2 twin 76mm gun
  2 *Petya* III (FSU) with 1 triple 533mm ASTT with SET-53ME HWT, 4 RBU 2500 *Smerch* 1 A/S mor, 2 twin 76mm gun
  PCFGM 12:
  4 *Tarantul* (FSU) with 2 twin lnchr with P-15 *Termit* (SS-N-2D *Styx*) AShM, 1 quad lnchr with 9K32 *Strela*-2M (SA-N-5 *Grail*) SAM (manually operated), 2 AK630 CIWS, 1 76mm gun
  8 *Tarantul* V with 4 quad lnchr with 3M24E *Uran*-E (SS-N-25 *Switchblade*) AShM; 1 quad lnchr with 9K32 *Strela*-2M (SA-N-5 *Grail*) SAM (manually operated), 2 AK630 CIWS, 1 76mm gun
  PCO 5: 1 Project FC264; 4 TT-400TP with 2 AK630 CIWS, 1 76mm gun
  PCC 6 *Svetlyak* with 1 AK630 CIWS, 1 76mm gun
  PBFG 8 *Osa* II with 4 single lnchr with P-15 *Termit* AShM
  PBFT 2 *Shershen*† (FSU) with 4 single 533mm TT
  PH 2 *Turya*† with 1 twin 57mm gun
  PHT 3 *Turya*† with 4 single 533mm TT, 1 twin 57mm gun
  PB 20: 14 *Zhuk*†; 4 *Zhuk* (mod); 2 TP-01
  PBR 4 *Stolkraft*
MINE WARFARE • MINE COUNTERMEASURES 13
  MSO 2 *Yurka*
  MSC 4 *Sonya*
  MHI 2 *Korund* (*Yevgenya*) (Project 1258)
  MSR 5 K-8
AMPHIBIOUS
  LANDING SHIPS 7
  LSM 5:
    1 *Polnochny* A (capacity 6 Lt Tk/APC; 200 troops)
    2 *Polnochny* B (capacity 6 Lt Tk/APC; 200 troops)
    2 *Nau Dinh*
  LST 2 *Tran Khanh Du* (ex-US LST 542) with 1 hel landing platform (capacity 16 Lt Tk/APC; 140 troops)
  LANDING CRAFT • LCM 12
  8 LCM 6 (capacity 1 Lt Tk or 80 troops)
  4 LCM 8 (capacity 1 MBT or 200 troops)
LOGISTICS AND SUPPORT 27
  AFD 2
  AGS 1 *Tran Dai Nia* (Damen Research Vessel 6613)
  AGSH 1
  AKSL 18
  AP 1 *Truong Sa*
  AT 2
  AWT 1
  AXS 1 *Le Quy Don*

Naval Infantry ε27,000
EQUIPMENT BY TYPE
ARMOURED FIGHTING VEHICLES
  LT TK PT-76; Type-63
  APC • APC (W) BTR-60

Coastal Defence
FORCES BY ROLE
COASTAL DEFENCE
  3 AShM bde
  1 coastal arty bde
EQUIPMENT BY TYPE
COASTAL DEFENCE • AShM 4K44 *Redut* (SSC-1B *Sepal*); 4K51 *Rubezh* (SSC-3 *Styx*); K-300P *Bastion*-P (SSC-5 *Stooge*)
ARTILLERY • MRL 160mm AccuLAR-160; **306mm** EXTRA

Navy Air Wing
FORCES BY ROLE
ASW/SAR
  1 regt with H225; Ka-28 (Ka-27PL) *Helix* A; Ka-32 *Helix* C
EQUIPMENT BY TYPE
AIRCRAFT • TPT • Light 6 DHC-6-400 *Twin Otter*
HELICOPTERS
  ASW 10 Ka-28 *Helix* A
  TPT • Medium 4: 2 H225; 2 Ka-32 *Helix* C

Air Force 30,000
3 air div, 1 tpt bde
FORCES BY ROLE
FIGHTER/GROUND ATTACK
  3 regt with Su-22M3/M4/UM *Fitter* (some ISR)
  1 regt with Su-27SK/Su-27UBK *Flanker*
  1 regt with Su-27SK/Su-27UBK *Flanker*; Su-30MK2
  2 regt with Su-30MK2
TRANSPORT
  2 regt with An-2 *Colt*; An-26 *Curl*; Bell 205 (UH-1H *Iroquois*); Mi-8 *Hip*; Mi-17 *Hip H*; M-28 *Bryza*
TRAINING
  1 regt with L-39 *Albatros*
  1 regt with Yak-52
ATTACK/TRANSPORT HELICOPTER
  2 regt with Mi-8 *Hip*; Mi-17 *Hip H*; Mi-171; Mi-24 *Hind*
AIR DEFENCE
  6 AD div HQ
  2 SAM regt with S-300PMU1 (SA-20 *Gargoyle*)
  2 SAM regt with *Spyder*-MR
  3 SAM regt with S-75 *Dvina* (SA-2 *Guideline*)
  4 SAM regt with S-135-2TM *Pechora* (SA-26)
  5 ADA regt

EQUIPMENT BY TYPE
AIRCRAFT 73 combat capable
  FGA 73: 27 Su-22M3/M4/UM *Fitter* (some ISR); 6 Su-27SK *Flanker*; 5 Su-27UBK *Flanker*; 35 Su-30MK2 *Flanker*
  TPT • Light 24: 6 An-2 *Colt*; 12 An-26 *Curl*; 3 C295M; 1 M-28 *Bryza*; 2 C-212 *Aviocar* (NC-212i)
  TRG 47: 17 L-39 *Albatros*; 30 Yak-52
HELICOPTERS
  MRH 6 Mi-17 *Hip* H
  TPT 28: Medium 17: 14 Mi-8 *Hip*; 3 Mi-171; **Light** 11 Bell 205 (UH-1H *Iroquois*)
AIR DEFENCE
  SAM 12+:
    Long-range 12 S-300PMU1 (SA-20 *Gargoyle*)
    Medium-range S-75 *Dvina* (SA-2 *Guideline*); S-125-2TM *Pechora* (SA-26), *Spyder*-MR
    Short-range 2K12 *Kub* (SA-6 *Gainful*);
    Point-defence 9K32 *Strela*-2 (SA-7 *Grail*)‡; 9K310 *Igla*-1 (SA-16 *Gimlet*)
  GUNS 37mm; 57mm; 85mm; 100mm; 130mm
AIR-LAUNCHED MISSILES
  AAM • IR R-60 (AA-8 *Aphid*); R-73 (AA-11 *Archer*); **IR/SARH** R-27 (AA-10 *Alamo*); **ARH** R-77 (AA-12A *Adder*)
  ASM Kh-29L/T (AS-14 *Kedge*); Kh-59M (AS-18 *Kazoo*)
  AShM Kh-31A (AS-17B *Krypton*)
  ARM Kh-28 (AS-9 *Kyle*); Kh-31P (AS-17A *Krypton*)

Paramilitary 40,000+ active

Border Defence Corps ε40,000

Coast Guard
EQUIPMENT BY TYPE
PATROL AND COASTAL COMBATANTS 69+
  PSO 4 DN2000 (Damen 9014)
  PCO 13+: 1 *Mazinger* (ex-ROK); 9 TT-400; 3+ other
  PCC 2 *Hae Uri* (ex-ROK)
  PBF 24: 22 MS-50S; 2 *Shershen*
  PB 26: 1 MS-50; 12 TT-200; 13 TT-120
LOGISTICS AND SUPPORT 5
  AFS 1
  ATF 4 Damen Salvage Tug
  AIRCRAFT • MP 3 C-212-400 MPA

Local Forces ε5,000,000 reservists
Incl People's Self-Defence Force (urban units) and People's Militia (rural units); comprises static and mobile cbt units, log spt and village protection pl; some arty, mor and AD guns; acts as reserve

DEPLOYMENT

CENTRAL AFRICAN REPUBLIC: UN • MINUSCA 4; 1 obs
SOUTH SUDAN: UN • UNMISS 1; 2 obs

Arms procurements and deliveries – Asia

Selected events in 2018

- In May, Indonesian state-owned insurance company PT Askrindo and the National Association of Private Defense Industries (Pinhantanas) signed an agreement to allow the former to supply private Indonesian defence SMEs with credit, guarantees and insurance. The agreement was backed by the defence ministry, which is trying to expand the country's defence-industrial base.

- In June, Australia announced that it had selected BAE Systems' Global Combat Ship design for its Future Frigate programme. Nine *Hunter*-class frigates, as they will be known in Australian service, will replace the *Anzac* class, starting in the late 2020s. The ships will be fitted with a locally designed and built CEAFAR2 phased-array radar and will have the *Aegis* combat-management system. Design and construction is expected to cost AU$35bn (US$27.64bn).

- Vietnam passed an amendment in June strengthening the government's drive to further reduce the number of army-owned businesses from 88 to 16. The defence ministry hopes that at the end of the reform process, the armed forces will only control businesses focused on security and defence.

- China's first indigenously built aircraft carrier, the Type-002, began sea trials in May and could enter service in 2019. The first Type-055 (*Renhai*) cruiser began sea trials in August.

- As part of the Defense Reform 2.0 plan, announced in August, South Korea launched a Defense Business Innovation Plan, which aims to simplify and speed up the process of meeting equipment requirements, as well as address the shrinking defence-industrial workforce.

- Indonesia began negotiations with South Korea in October to reduce its share of the KF-X fighter programme due to economic constraints. Since joining the programme in 2016, Indonesia has reportedly struggled to keep up with payments. Indonesia is currently committed to 20% of the KF-X development cost, which is expected to be approximately US$1.9bn. The first prototype is expected to be completed in 2021.

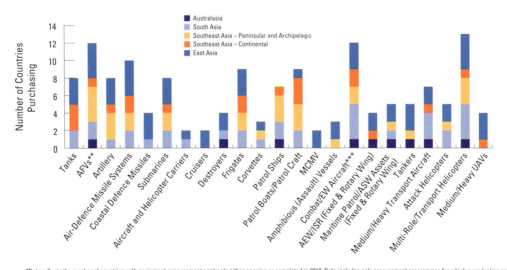

Figure 19 **Asia: selected ongoing or completed procurement priorities in 2018**

*Data reflects the number of countries with equipment-procurement contracts either ongoing or completed in 2018. Data includes only procurement programmes for which a production contract has been signed. The data does not include upgrade programmes.
**Armoured fighting vehicles not including main battle tanks ***Includes combat-capable training aircraft

© IISS

Table 14 Republic of Korea: naval platform procurement programmes, by contract date

Class	Type	Quantity	Value (US$)	Prime contractor	Contract date
Incheon (FFG-I)	FFGHM	1	127.04m	HHI	2008
Chang Bogo II (Type-214)	SSK	6	3.5bn	DSME & HHI	2009
Incheon (FFG-I)	FFGHM	2	n.k.	HHI	2010
Incheon (FFG-I)	FFGHM	2	294.65m	STX Offshore and Shipbuilding	2010
Nampo (MLS-II)	ML	1	n.k.	HHI	c.2012
KSS-III Batch I	SSG	1	2.06bn	DSME	2012
Incheon (FFG-I)	FFGHM	1	n.k.	STX Offshore and Shipbuilding	2013
Daegu (FFG-II)	FFGHM	1	294.65m	DSME	2013
Chamsuri II (PKMR)	PCF	1	58.03m	HHIC	2014
Marado (Dokdo Mod)	LHD	1	396.5m	HHIC	2014
Cheonwangbong (LST-II)	LPD	1	142.46m	HHI	2014
KDD-III Batch II	CGHM	Design Work	15.9m	HHI	2016
Chamsuri II (PKMR)	PCF	3	173.33m	HHIC	2016
Daegu (FFG-II)	FFGHM	1	295.99m	DSME	2016
FFG-III	FFGHM	Design Work	n.k.	HHI	2016
Daegu (FFG-II)	FFGHM	2	609.41m	HHI	2016
LSF-II	LCAC	2	132.68m	HHIC	2016
Chamsuri II (PKMR)	PCF	4	234.83m	HHIC	2017
LCU	LST	3	29.43m	HHIC	2017
Cheonwangbong (LST-II)	LPD	1	n.k.	HHI	c.2017
Daegu (FFG-II)	FFGHM	2	555.21m	DSME	2018

DSME – Daewoo Shipbuilding & Marine Engineering; HHI – Hyundai Heavy Industries; HHIC – Hanjin Heavy Industries & Construction

Table 15 Japan FY2019 defence-budget request: top ten new equipment acquisition programmes by value

Equipment	Type	Quantity	Value (JPY)	Value (US$)	Prime contractor(s)
Aegis Ashore	BMD SAM system	2 systems	234.3bn	2.13bn	Lockheed Martin (US)
30FF	FFGHM	2	99.5bn	906m	MHI and MES (JPN)
F-35A *Lightning* II	FGA ac	6	91.6bn	834m	Lockheed Martin (US) MHI (JPN)
SM-3 Block IIA; SM-3 Block IB	Ship-launched SAM	n.k.	81.8bn	745m	Raytheon (US)
Soryu class	SSK	1	71.1bn	647m	MHI (JPN)
E-2D *Hawkeye*	AEW&C ac	2	54.4bn	495m	Northrop Grumman (US)
C-2	Hvy Tpt ac	2	45.7bn	416m	KHI (JPN)
Type-16	Wheeled Assault Gun	22	16.4bn	149m	MHI (JPN)
Type-03	Medium-Range SAM system	1 company	13.8bn	126m	MHI (JPN)
Type-12	Coastal anti-ship missiles	1 set	13.2bn	120m	MHI (JPN)

KHI – Kawasaki Heavy Industries; MES – Mitsui Engineering & Shipbuilding; MHI – Mitsubishi Heavy Industries

Figure 20 Rosoboronexport/Heavy Vehicles Factory: T-90S *Bhishma*

In 2000, India embarked on a plan to both modernise its tank fleet and develop an indigenous main battle tank (MBT) production capability. The plans encompassed India's plan for an indigenous design, *Arjun*, that began in the 1970s, as well as Russia's T-90S MBT. Contracts were signed with Russia in 2001 for 124 complete tanks and 186 tanks to be supplied in kit form. After this, a deal was signed with Rosoboronexport for transfer-of-technology and subsequent license production of 300 T-90S in India, with deliveries to the Indian Army to take place from 2006 to 2010.

However, deliveries from the Heavy Vehicles Factory (HVF) in Tamil Nadu did not begin until 2009. According to a 2014 report by the Indian Comptroller and Auditor General, the primary cause of delay was a Russian failure in the technology-transfer process and decision-making delays in the Indian defence ministry about next steps. Many of the documents relating to technology transfer were delivered on time but only in Russian; translation of these documents took six years to complete. Other documents were not delivered, such as those pertaining to construction of the main gun barrel. Until HVF used its plans for the similar main gun on the T-72, the company was spending significant sums importing the parts directly from Russia.

The comptroller estimated that 62% of the total cost of the 225 T-90S tanks manufactured by March 2013 was spent on importing parts. The defence ministry made up for the shortfall in local production by ordering a batch of 347 complete and kit-form T-90s in 2007. Deliveries were completed several years later. It is possible that India's T-90 production line will run into the 2020s, but production will have to pick up pace, or be supplemented by more imports, if plans remain to replace the approximately 1,900 T-72M1 *Ajeya* tanks.

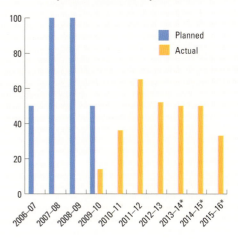

HVF licensed builds of 300 T-90S: planned and actual production

*Estimate based on achieved production rate

Prime contractor (for Indian production)
Ordnance Factory Board (IND)

Selected subcontractors
Rosoboronexport (RUS)
Bharat Electronics Limited (IND)
Engine Factory Avadi (IND)
Field Gun Factory (IND)
Gun Carriage Factory (IND)
Heavy Vehicles Factory (IND)
Opto Electronics Factory (IND)
Ordnance Factory Kanpur (IND)
Ordnance Factory Medak (IND)
Ordnance Factory Muradnagar (IND)

Indian T-90S contracts, by date

Contract Date	Quantity	Value (INR Crore)	Value (US$)	Prime contractor	Notes
Feb 2001	124	1,774	371.94m	ROE	Complete MBT
Feb 2001	186	2,312	484.74m	ROE	86 SCK and 100 CKD
Feb 2004	-	96	21.37m	OFB	Production-line set-up
Nov 2004	300	5,084*	1.13bn*	OFB	All indigenous build
Nov 2007	347	4,913	1.22bn	ROE	124 complete MBTs and 223 SCK
Sep 2011	-	971	202.62m	OFB	Production-line capacity augmentation
Dec 2013	236	6,000	991.7m	OFB	Indigenous build
Nov 2016	464	13,448	2bn	OFB	Reportedly T-90MS (T-90S upgrade)
Total	**1,657**	**34,598**	**6.43bn**		

*Estimate based on cost of 225 of the 300 built by 2013
Crore = ten million rupees; SCK = semi-completed kits; CKD = complete knock-down kits; OFB = Ordnance Factory Board; ROE = Rosoboronexport

Chapter Seven
Middle East and North Africa

- The Daesh mini-state has been largely dismantled, apart from limited territory in Southeast Syria. However, there are fears that the group is reverting to insurgent tactics. The US is demanding that Iranian forces withdraw from Syria and plans to continue supporting the Syrian Democratic Forces with SOF and air power.
- UK military commitment to the region was demonstrated by Exercise *Saif Sareea* in Oman and the plan to establish a training base there. This is the second recent enhancement to the UK's regional presence, coming just after the official opening in 2018 of a permanent presence in Bahrain.
- Gulf Arab navies are undertaking significant development programmes to equip themselves for a more challenging and complex regional maritime environment.
- Israel has been enforcing a red line around the transfer of advanced military technology from Iran to Hizbullah and also conducting a campaign of air and missile strikes against Iranian forces in Syria. However, following the 17 September shootdown by Syria of a Russian IL-20 surveillance aircraft, Russia's supply of S-300 missiles to Syrian forces will complicate Israel's plans and calculations.
- Delivery of Russian combat helicopters to Algeria and MiG-29M2 multi-role fighters to Egypt continued in 2018, while Israel and Saudi Arabia were the recipients of more F-35s and F-15s respectively.
- Regional defence spending is falling, for those countries where data is available. This includes US Foreign Military Financing to Egypt and Israel.

Saudi Arabia, real-terms defence spending, 2009–18 (US$bn, constant 2010)*

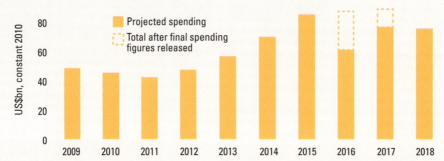

*Note: Saudi authorities in recent years have later revised defence-spending totals upwards when the government releases its actual spending figures. As such, it is possible that the R311bn announced for 2018 might be an underestimate.

Active military personnel – top 10
(25,000 per unit)

Iran 523,000	Syria 139,000
Egypt 438,500	Algeria 130,000
Saudi Arabia 227,000	Jordan 100,500
Morocco 195,800	Iraq 64,000
Israel 169,500	United Arab Emirates 63,000

Regional defence policy and economics 322 ▶

Armed forces data section 332 ▶

Arms procurements and deliveries 377 ▶

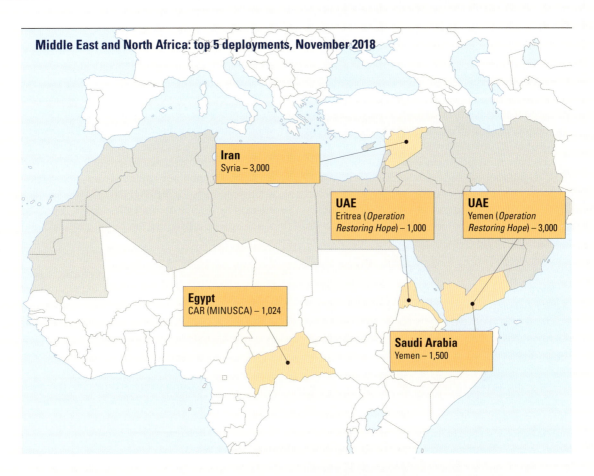

Middle East and North Africa

Conflict and regional rivalries continue to shape the posture of key actors in the Middle East, as well as motivate interventions and drive defence planning and acquisition.

Regional security debates remained dominated by the potential for escalation between the United States, Israel and Saudi Arabia on the one hand and Iran and its allies on the other. While the US sought to organise its Arab allies in a coalition called the Middle East Strategic Alliance (MESA), the venture faced significant obstacles, notably rifts between Arab states themselves. Another troubled coalition was the Saudi-led Islamic Military Counter Terrorism Coalition. Its official launch in November 2017 was followed by little activity, reflecting the lack of political commitment of the member nations to the initiative.

The US withdrawal from the Joint Comprehensive Plan of Action (JCPOA) and its imposition of severe sanctions to curtail Iran's oil exports – the country's main source of foreign currency – complicated Iran's defence-modernisation plans. Tehran had approached China and Russia with a view to modernising its air force and air defences, and to acquire naval- and land-weapons systems, but shrinking revenues threatened these plans. Beijing and Moscow, themselves facing US pressure on other issues, seemed willing to accommodate Tehran. Both denounced the US withdrawal from the JCPOA and indicated that they would continue to offer to Iran the economic benefits promised under the deal. They also continued high-profile engagement with Tehran. Iran played an increasingly important role in the Shanghai Cooperation Organisation, and Tehran organised a well-attended meeting on the security of South and Central Asia. One key question was whether China and Russia would fulfil Tehran's ambitious defence-procurement plans. Meanwhile, an agreement looked to have ended decades of tension in the Caspian Sea.

The rivalry between Saudi Arabia and the United Arab Emirates on one side and Qatar on the other has led to scrutiny of these countries' weapons procurements, and the broader diplomatic factors that might underpin some of these. Saudi Arabia has pursued ambitious defence projects, ranging from the acquisition of new platforms to setting in motion its defence-industrialisation plans under the recently established Saudi Arabian Military Industries. The place of weapons procurements in Riyadh's international strategy was made clear during a visit to the White House by Saudi Crown Prince Muhammad bin Salman in May 2018, with US President Donald Trump holding signs showing Saudi Arabia's recent arms deals with the US. Qatar is also seeking to secure important defence partnerships. In recent years, it has embarked on ambitious aircraft-acquisition plans, including contracts for Eurofighter *Typhoon*s (a letter of intent was signed in September 2017), F-15QAs (this sale was approved by the US in 2016) and the 2015 deal for *Rafale*s.

Several crises highlighted the close link between defence sales and politics. Over the past year, Saudi Arabia faced deteriorating relations with countries from which it bought weaponry. Some of these countries had implemented measures restricting sales based on criteria that included, for Sweden, a 'democracy' clause. Spain briefly suspended the sale of ammunition and bombs over the conduct of the Yemen war, and Riyadh expressed displeasure after the German foreign minister spoke of concern about its regional policies.

Syria's many wars

In 2018, the Syrian conflict entered a new phase. International powers and regional players, as well as a multitude of Syrian, militia and jihadi actors, are now involved. At the beginning of the year, Iran, Russia, Turkey and the US all maintained a military presence in the country, seeking to shape the battlefield, protect their partners and erode – if only tentatively at present – the position of adversaries, and ultimately strengthen their position for a putative endgame.

This made for a volatile landscape, with multiple military engagements taking place and a risk of broader escalation. Indeed, three distinct wars and a mini-intervention are unfolding in the country simultaneously. Firstly, the last stage of the war between the now near-victorious regime of Syrian President Bashar al-Assad and the remnants of the rebellion threaten to cause yet more suffering for the Syrian population, with the battle for heavily populated Idlib in sight. With the last rebel pockets falling in the south, around Damascus and in Homs, the regime proceeded in 2018 to consolidate its authority, forcing former rebels and others who had fled conscription to join its ranks. Reflecting the pressure that the regime's army is under after seven years of war, it was reported that amnesties were in place for those avoiding the draft, though many Syrian youths still attempt to avoid service. A new framework to bring the various militias under government control was put in place with Russian encouragement, and Moscow also undertook to reorganise elements of the Syrian armed forces, reportedly including not just the 'Tiger Force' but also some division-level formations.

Idlib became the focus of intense diplomacy in mid- to late 2018. It was surrounded by regime and allied militia forces intent on seizing the enclave, vulnerable to Russian air attacks, and controlled by a mix of mainstream rebel and jihadi groups. Though the regime would likely be able to capture Idlib with assistance from Russia, it would in all probability be a costly operation. While the US remained principally concerned by the strength of the al-Qaeda offshoot in Idlib, the dilemma was most significant for Turkey. Ankara was aware that its territory would likely become the destination for new waves of refugees and be targeted by jihadi groups. Ultimately, cost calculations in Ankara and Moscow led to an arrangement to create a buffer zone between rebels in the province and government forces that was still being negotiated at the time of writing. But Turkey was entangled in another conflict in Syria. In early 2018, Ankara launched an intervention to capture the northwest province of Afrin and expel Kurdish forces out of concern that they would support an insurgency inside Turkish territory. Though progress was slow at first, *Operation Olive Branch* saw Turkish forces take over the whole region in just over two months, although Turkish troops, backed by Syrian militias, then faced an active Kurdish insurgency and were criticised for some actions by human-rights organisations. Meanwhile, in Syria's northeast, the coalition against Islamic State, also known as ISIS or ISIL, proceeded to destroy the remaining military infrastructure of the jihadi group along the Euphrates River Valley. However, ISIS reverted to its previous insurgent behaviour, taking advantage of the absence of a state presence to harass local forces and populations.

The US posture has changed over the year, reflecting the new focus of the Trump administration on containing and eventually forcing out Iran from Syria. The Trump administration argued that a US presence was essential to ensure the enduring defeat of ISIS and to disrupt Iran's territorial reach and operational freedom of action. The US armed forces have built more than a dozen operating bases across the large territory from the Iraqi border to northwest Syria and along the Euphrates River, and solidified the military partnership with Kurdish armed groups. The degree of US involvement became clear when US troops, backed by substantial air assets, confronted a mix of Syrian militia forces and (it was reported) Russian private military contractors in Deir ez-Zor in February 2018; scores of Russians and Syrians were reported to have died.

Reducing Iran's footprint is also Israel's priority. Israel has resigned itself to the return of Assad regime forces to southern Syria, but has sought Russian help to prevent Iranian and allied elements from deploying close to its borders. Significantly, Israeli military officials disclosed that Israel had conducted over 200 attacks across Syria in recent years, revealing the extent of Israeli intelligence penetration and military activities in Syria. The targets included weapons-storage facilities, missile-manufacturing plants and key individuals. The damage to Iran's military infrastructure in Syria seemed severe and costly, though not irreparable given the commitment that Iran seems to have to developing its presence in Syria.

Active military operations by so many powers in such a small space has always meant that there was a risk of accidents taking place; this is one reason why Russia and the US established 'deconfliction' procedures as far back as 2016, including a command-level hotline. In September, Syria's air defences mistakenly shot down a Russian surveillance aircraft shortly after an Israeli airstrike. Russia shortly afterwards transferred to Syria an S-300 air-defence system, potentially complicating Israel's operational freedom in Syria.

Yemen

The humanitarian toll from the war in Yemen means that not only does the war remain in the headlines, but there has been mounting criticism in Western states of their governments' support for the Saudi-led coalition. After two years of relatively static front lines, a series of advances on the southwest coast by UAE-backed forces signalled a new phase. UAE forces and allied Yemeni factions (notably from forces loyal to former president Ali Abdullah Saleh, killed in December 2017 by his erstwhile Houthi allies) moved to capture the port city of Hudaydah. Seizing the city would disrupt Houthi tax revenues and weaken their hold over Sana'a and central Yemen. UN agencies and many countries criticised the move, arguing it would only exacerbate the ongoing humanitarian crisis. Temporary ceasefires were agreed and ideas tabled for the management of the port by the UN, but the lack of political progress inevitably led to a resumption of the fighting. The security situation in Aden, Taizz and elsewhere remained troubled, illustrating the difficulty facing the coalition and its local Yemeni allies in generating political stability and in reconstruction tasks.

This occurred as criticism of the Saudi-led coalition rose in Washington and elsewhere. Several coalition airstrikes hit civilian targets, including hospitals and a school bus. While the Saudis eventually accepted responsibility for this attack, it changed the tone of the debate over the war, not least in the US Congress. A non-binding resolution (invoking the War Powers Act), was passed by the US Senate in December. If enacted, it would remove US forces engaged in hostilities in Yemen (bar those on counter-terror missions), though it was likely to be vetoed by the White House. In November, the US had ceased refuelling coalition aircraft.

For Riyadh, the war presents a challenge of how, and whether, it is possible to declare victory. Withdrawal, however, is unthinkable, not least because the Houthis still fire missiles at Saudi Arabia and anti-ship missiles at Saudi oil tankers in the Bab el-Mandeb Strait. Riyadh saw the latter as an Iranian pressure tactic, as Iran faced a cut in oil exports.

In parallel, the US and its allies continued their fight against al-Qaeda in the Arabian Peninsula. The number of special-forces operations and UAV attacks increased, with some operations mounted in cooperation with UAE forces, as well as local partners.

DEFENCE ECONOMICS

According to the International Monetary Fund (IMF), growth recovered in 2017–18 in the Middle East and North Africa, which in the IMF's definition includes Afghanistan and Pakistan. Oil-exporting states saw their GDP rise from 1.2% in 2017 to 1.4% in 2018, while GDP grew in oil-importing states from 4.1% to 4.5%. Notably, Kuwait, Oman and Saudi Arabia, which were all in recession in 2017, registered growth in 2018. However, the Iranian economy contracted by 1.5% in 2018 and the IMF forecast that recession would continue in 2019.

In oil-exporting countries, this limited rebound was explained by the recovery in energy prices. According to the World Bank, the average price of crude oil rose from US$50.8 per barrel in 2015 to just over US$80 per barrel in October 2018. This price was above, or close to, most of the Gulf Cooperation Council (GCC) states' fiscal break-even prices. Governments in the region nonetheless continued to implement fiscal-consolidation measures. For instance, Saudi Arabia and the United Arab Emirates (UAE) both introduced a 5% value-added tax (VAT) in 2018, while Bahrain may introduce VAT in early 2019.

Iran, however, did not benefit from the rebound in oil prices as much as its neighbours. The US announcement that it would reinstate sanctions on Iran weakened the rial against the dollar. As a result, inflation picked up again; it was estimated by the IMF to be 29.6% in 2018. US sanctions include an embargo on Iranian oil that took effect in November 2018, depriving Tehran of a key source of revenue. Iranian oil income as a share of total government revenue was estimated by the World Bank in 2016 at just above 33%. US sanctions will also restrict Iranian access to financing and investment from abroad. For instance, despite European Union statements that it would shield its member states' companies from US

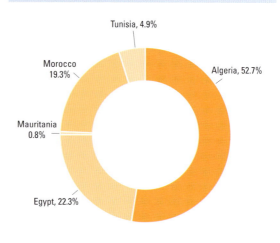

▼ Figure 21 **North Africa defence expenditure 2017: sub-regional breakdown**

Tunisia, 4.9%
Morocco 19.3%
Algeria, 52.7%
Mauritania 0.8%
Egypt, 22.3%

Note: analysis excludes Libya

© IISS

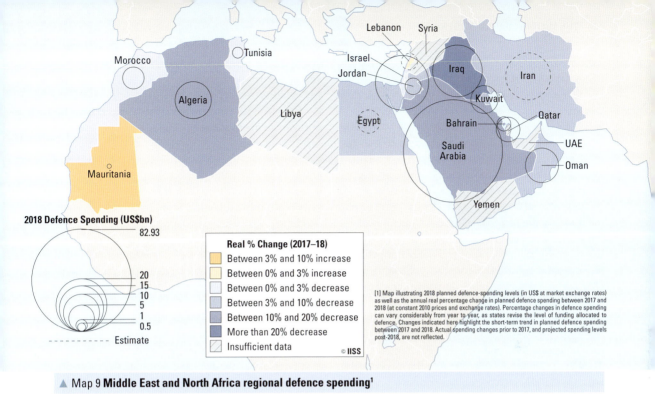

▲ Map 9 **Middle East and North Africa regional defence spending**[1]

sanctions, European airlines had by late 2018 already withdrawn from Iran, as had Total, one of the world's largest oil firms.

Among oil-importing states, growth was stronger in North Africa than in the Levant. In Lebanon (which registered 1.0% real GDP growth in 2018) and Jordan (2.3% in 2018), the effects of regional conflicts and political uncertainty negatively affected growth. However, Egypt's financial situation has improved in recent years, with real GDP growth reaching 5.3% in 2018 (4.2% in 2017). Inflation slowed from 23.5% in 2017 to 20.9% in 2018 and is forecast to fall further to 14% in 2019, according to the IMF. Egypt's budget deficit also narrowed in 2018 through the implementation of austerity measures, including the increase in VAT and cuts in energy subsidies, and the country's foreign reserves are being rebuilt.

Defence spending and procurement

Defence spending in the Middle East and North Africa is falling, for those countries where data is available, from US$191 billion in 2017 to US$181bn in 2018, in current terms. This includes US Foreign Military Financing for Egypt and Israel. This decline was largely driven by the announcement at the start of 2018 of Saudi Arabia's defence and security budget. That said, Saudi authorities in recent years have later revised defence-spending totals upwards when the government releases its actual spending figures. For instance, Saudi Arabia's defence and security budget was first declared to be R288bn (US$76.8bn) for 2017, but then was revised upwards to R334bn (US$89.1bn). As such, it is possible that the R311bn (US$82.9bn) announced for 2018 might be an underestimate, only temporarily reducing the region's military-expenditure totals. Fluctuating exchange rates also contributed to the overall regional decline. For instance, Algeria projected a stable defence budget at D1.12 trillion for both 2017 and 2018, but this in fact meant a decrease in US-dollar terms, from US$10.1bn to US$9.9bn. Similarly, the weakened Iranian rial meant Tehran's defence spending declined (when

▼ Figure 22 **Saudi Arabia defence expenditure** as % of GDP

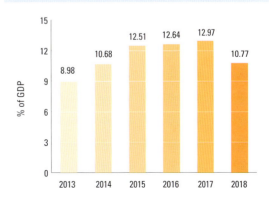

converted into dollars), from US$21.0bn in 2017 to US$19.6bn in 2018.

Meanwhile, other countries are just spending less on defence. In Iraq, for example, total defence and security spending declined by 10% in nominal terms, from D22.8trn (US$19.5bn) in 2017 to D20.4trn (US$17.3bn) in 2018. This reduction can be explained, in part, by the end of the military campaign against the Islamic State, also known as ISIS or ISIL.

Regional defence-spending totals are further distorted by the fact that reliable data is unavailable for some countries, such as those in conflict (e.g., Libya and Syria) or countries with large budgets who do not publish budget figures (e.g., Qatar and the UAE). In the latter countries, in particular Qatar, the list of procurement announcements in recent years suggests that there has been no reduction in defence expenditure. Furthermore, Qatar and the UAE have each extended their conscription requirements (from three to 12 months and 12 to 16 months respectively), which will likely increase military outlays.

Qatar's recent procurements have focused on combat aircraft. Having signed a deal for 36 Boeing F-15 *Eagle*s in December 2017 and 24 Eurofighter *Typhoon*s that same month, Doha exercised an option for an additional 12 Dassault *Rafale*s in March 2018, following the 2015 deal with France for a first batch of 24. Once these contracts are complete, Qatar will have 96 combat aircraft to replace its current fleet of 12 *Mirage* 2000s. Qatar is not the only country in the region looking to modernise its combat-aircraft fleet. In June 2018, Bahrain signed a contract with Lockheed Martin for 16 F-16V Block 70 *Fighting Falcon*s, while Kuwait signed with Boeing for 28 F/A-18E/F *Super Hornet*s. Kuwait had already signed a contract with Italy in April 2016 for 28 *Typhoon*s.

Saudi Arabia has embarked on a naval-modernisation programme. Key contracts signed in 2018 included *Avante* 2200 frigates from Spain's Navantia, to be delivered by 2022; HSI 32 fast patrol boats and *Combattante* FS56 guided-missile patrol craft from France's CMN; and Littoral Combat Ships from the United States' Lockheed Martin. These procurements are expected to contribute to the Saudi Naval Expansion Programme (SNEP II), which aims to modernise the Kingdom's Eastern Fleet.

Defence industry and markets

Opposition in Europe to arms sales to state parties to the Yemen conflict complicated Navantia's frigate contract with Saudi Arabia. After halting the sale of laser-guided bombs to Saudi Arabia, the Spanish authorities backtracked on this decision to try and ensure, reports said, that the frigate deal was not jeopardised. This reflects the complexities for European governments of selling weapons systems to Middle Eastern states. Similarly, although Sweden had introduced export-control regulations banning arms sales to non-democracies, Saab pursued follow-on orders for the *GlobalEye* advanced airborne early-warning and control aircraft sale to the UAE, and in late 2017 established a centre in Abu Dhabi to develop and produce sensor systems. Germany and Finland faced similar internal contradictions, with continued arms exports to the region despite political announcements to the contrary.

Riyadh's contract for Spanish frigates highlighted the established trend in the Middle East whereby weapons procurements are supposed to also help develop local production capacities. Launched in May 2017, Saudi Arabian Military Industries (SAMI) is at the forefront of procurement decisions in the Kingdom, with a mission to increase technology transfers. The agreement for *Avante* 2200 frigates is expected to generate 6,000 jobs over five years in Saudi Arabia, while a contract signed by Boeing and SAMI to develop a joint venture for military-helicopter maintenance is also expected to create 6,000 jobs. The new procurement system in Saudi Arabia has, however, disrupted traditional negotiating channels for arms suppliers, as exemplified by the demise of France's ODAS, an arms-brokering company established in 1974. Paris and Riyadh agreed to dismantle it and open up new channels.

Saudi Arabia's procurement reforms were modelled after the UAE's, which has had success in developing its local defence-industrial base, including the creation of the Emirates Defence Industries Company (EDIC) in 2014. EDIC is headed by Luc Vigneron, former CEO of Thales, while SAMI's CEO is Andreas Schwer, former CEO of Rheinmetall. Qatar launched its own defence-procurement body, Barzan Holdings, during the DIMDEX arms fair in March 2018. The organisation is intended to lead on defence procurement in Qatar and ensure that contracts include technology transfers benefiting Qatar's economy. Barzan Holdings rapidly signed a series of agreements with major foreign defence companies, including, among others, with Raytheon on a new cyber academy; a joint venture with Kongsberg on defence technology, digitisation and the maritime industry; a joint venture with Rheinmetall (Rheinmetall Barzan Advanced Technologies); a joint venture with Turkey's Aselsan to produce reconnaissance and surveillance systems; and a letter of intent with Fincantieri for cooperation on coastal-defence surveillance. The vast array of suppliers and agreements reinforces the view that Qatar's defence-procurement and defence-industrial strategy are motivated by diplomatic factors as well as military imperatives.

IRAQ: REBUILDING THE ARMED FORCES

Fifteen years after the invasion of Iraq in 2003, and after multiple attempts at their effective reconstitution, Iraq's security forces are still struggling to regain the necessary capabilities to take full responsibility for national security. The ostensible defeat in Iraq of the Islamic State, also known as ISIS or ISIL, may give Baghdad a period of comparative stability, allowing for reflection on the lessons of the counter-ISIS campaign and time to plan for the development of its armed forces and defence institutions. At least in the near term, NATO- and US-led capacity-building efforts continue, aimed at helping to produce Iraqi armed forces of enduring and self-sustaining effectiveness. Nonetheless, the September 2018 report by the lead inspector-general for *Operation Inherent Resolve* contained a stark assessment by the Pentagon: it would take 'years, if not decades' until Iraq is able to secure 'enduring defeat' of ISIS.

In 2011, the Iraqi armed forces were 'ready, capable, and proven', according to the architects of their reconstruction. Work had been under way for eight years at that point. However, three years later, the new forces collapsed catastrophically in the face of ISIS. In early 2014, operating principally from within Syria, ISIS had entered western Iraq and taken control of much of Anbar province. In June, they moved into northern Iraq and advanced on Mosul. Within a week, Iraq's second city had been captured. Four divisions of Iraqi troops had been routed by, some estimated, 1,500 ISIS fighters, while 500,000 civilians had been displaced and the insurgents had advanced to within 150 kilometres of Baghdad.

First steps

In May 2003, the Coalition Provisional Authority (CPA) that governed Iraq in the aftermath of the Second Gulf War issued two orders. The first removed the top tiers of all ministries of state, in an act of 'de-Ba'athification'. The second dissolved the Iraqi Ministry of Defence and disbanded the Iraqi armed forces: army, air force, navy, air-defence force, republican guard, special republican guard, and various other forces and paramilitaries. The effect of this was to remove the executive and leadership of Iraq's defence and security institutions, and some 500,000 military personnel, from their duties.

By August 2003, a US-led Coalition Military Assistance Training Team (CMATT) was training a modest volunteer 'New Iraqi Army', consisting of an initial nine battalions of a prospective three-infantry-division force, to be formed within two years; a coastal-defence force; and, later, a military-aviation arm. In March 2004, CPA order number 67 formed the Iraqi Armed Forces, including air- and coastal-defence forces, and established a new ministry of defence. Almost immediately, these forces faced developmental challenges that would persist in one form or another for the next ten years: short-term goals (shaped if not imposed from outside the country); concurrent capacity-building and fighting; and a variable purpose of counter-insurgency operations and national defence against external threats.

Building a force under fire

By April 2004, the evolving Iraqi armed forces were failing to tackle a rising Sunni insurgency that was taking hold across the country. The CMATT timetable for training the whole force – which was still well under its intended strength – had already been compressed from two years to one, and the armed forces found themselves refocused on internal-security tasks.

During 2004–09, the large-scale creation of new armed forces took place alongside a nationwide counter-insurgency campaign. The supposed advantages of cumulative, experiential improvement were, however, less evident than continuous, short-term operational expediency and competing and often overwhelming demands placed on senior decision-makers and military leaders.

While the armed forces helped ensure that elections could be held at the end of January 2005, the force remained fragile. It had been increased in ambition, by this time expanding to an authorised strength of ten divisions, but it was judged that only 40,000 troops were combat ready and that absenteeism ran at some 40% of declared strength. Even embedding coalition 'military transition teams' across the army down to brigade level from the spring of that year failed to generate the necessary rate of improvement.

In 2008, the further-expanded Iraqi armed forces enjoyed some notable successes, such as the first 'independent' division-level operation to resecure Basra in March. However, more generally, Iraqi military achievements, capacity and self-reliance tended during this period to be exaggerated.

Although levels of violence in Iraq had decreased significantly by 2010–11, the withdrawal of US combat troops by the end of 2011 was premature. Senior Iraqi military leaders were reported at the time to be expecting US support to remain in place for a further decade.

The 2014 collapse

The failure of defence executive, institutional, managerial and support functions to develop adequately since 2003 came into sharp focus in 2014. Across the armed forces, combat capabilities had attracted greater attention and resources than combat support or service support. While the army had most of its main battle tanks, less than half of its artillery and logistical requirements had been met, with the US covering the shortfall. Priority also tended to be afforded to operational needs rather than to the higher management of defence. Imbalanced capability and the defence ministry's lack of expertise or experience meant the forces were less robust and resilient than their scale suggested. Gradually escalating insecurity and diminishing morale were exacerbated by suspicions of corruption and political and ethnic sectarianism.

But it was their precipitate collapse in northern Iraq in June 2014 and their powerlessness to prevent ISIS's march south towards Baghdad that demonstrated unequivocally the Iraqi armed forces' inability to secure their borders and, once breached, to defend the country.

Failure has been attributed to a range of factors. There were evident shortcomings at the tactical level. In the defence of Mosul, some military commanders underperformed and low morale saw troops flee in large numbers rather than fight. While these may be proximate causes, the extent and magnitude of the collapse resulted from a lack of requisite fighting power. Physically, the armed forces were not capable of conducting autonomous medium- or high-intensity operations. Even at the point when the US had left the country two years earlier, so-called independent Iraqi operations were still reliant on US airpower, intelligence and sustainment. It has been argued that the reconstruction of the armed forces and wider security-sector reform were incomplete and that – once unsupported – decline was always more likely than continuing growth. It has also been asserted that because the Iraqi armed forces were rebuilt to a Western design (assuming all-arms cooperation, with systematic logistics and sustainment) and based upon Western doctrine and concepts (such as mission command and delegated authority), which were not integral to Iraqi military culture, such developments were unlikely to be self-perpetuating.

Fundamental to the armed forces' decline and eventual collapse in 2014 was the political malaise under the regime of then-prime minister Nouri al-Maliki. Firstly, endemic corruption undermined significant aspects of military capability: ghost soldiers, salaried but not recruited, concealed large-scale undermanning; funds for combat supplies and equipment sustainment were redirected, so that the actual capability of units was much less than it should have been, or appeared to be. Secondly, command of the armed forces, and their deployment and employment, became increasingly sectarian. Shia loyalists replaced Sunni and Kurdish professionals in positions of authority, and the armed forces became instrumental in political control. Their legitimacy, as well as their effectiveness in terms of defence and security, was duly eroded.

Present day

The rebuilding of Iraq's armed forces since 2014 has again proceeded with international support. However, defence capacity-building in Iraq today has a substantial security-sector reform component, suggesting that past shortcomings in this area may now receive the attention they deserve. However, challenges remain relating to the type of force Iraq needs for a conventional military role. While the force needs to consider the transition to performing new roles, day-to-day internal-security taskings continue: a 2018 report by the US Department of Defense assessed that ISIS had transitioned into a 'clandestine insurgency' in Iraq.

Some of the tactics employed by Iraq's armed forces in the battle for Mosul in 2017 demonstrated impressive adaptability under fire, such as when armoured plant machinery was used in street-to-street fighting to counter flanking vehicle-borne improvised-explosive-device (IED) attacks, allowing the main force to proceed. Yet significant challenges remain not just in shaping the strategic direction of the armed forces, but also in terms of their organisation.

For instance, the future of the Shia-dominated Popular Mobilisation Units, the set of paramilitary forces that were greatly empowered during the drive to oust ISIS from Iraq, is unclear. These groups and their leaders are viewed in the region as proxies for Iranian influence. Reports persist that the units are positioning for a more formal political role in Iraq, which might complicate any move to disarm or totally integrate them into the Iraqi armed forces. Questions also continue over the status of Kurdish forces in Iraq's north. These troops were integral to holding back the advance of ISIS in the north and then, after coalition training and military assistance, taking part in combat operations in coordination with the main offensive by coalition troops and the Iraqi security forces.

The overall aim is to produce non-sectarian, politically neutral Iraqi armed forces. The army-linked, elite Counter Terrorism Service (CTS) reportedly 'enjoys legal autonomy' but may provide a model for some aspects of 'force health' that are vital for the future of the armed forces. For example, their relative success in recruiting and retention likely results from their combat record in standing their ground against the ISIS advance and then being in the vanguard of the campaign to recapture Mosul in 2017. The stress on developing unit cohesion within the basic and special-to-arm training process could be a lesson, as could the reported practice within the CTS of randomly assigning personnel to special-operations battalions across Iraq. A challenge for the CTS and its Western training partners will be in diffusing such lessons across the wider force, so that the CTS becomes a model for other elements and is not alone in attracting the best recruits.

Overall, the challenges for the Iraqi armed forces remain stark. New military systems have been introduced in recent years, ranging from M1A1 main battle tanks to F-16 combat aircraft, but according to the US,

> systemic weaknesses remain, many of which are the same deficiencies that enabled the rise of ISIS in 2014. The ISF continues to suffer from poor management of intelligence; corruption and 'ghost soldiers'; overlapping command arrangements with conflicting chains of command; micromanagement; and inefficient and inadequate systems for planning and transmitting orders.

Deficiencies in intelligence mean that the Iraqi forces remain 'years, if not decades' away from ending reliance on coalition support in this area. Foreign troops remain engaged on military-assistance tasks, including some 5,000 US personnel. In mid-2018, NATO committed at its Brussels Summit to build on its years of assistance to post-Saddam Iraq by launching a Canadian-led training and capacity-building mission, which began operations in late 2018. It is likely, given the factors identified by the *Operation Inherent Resolve* inspector-general, that Iraq's armed forces will continue to require military and security assistance for some time yet.

GULF REGION: TRAINING AND SUSTAINABILITY

In March 2015, a Saudi-led coalition intervened in Yemen under a United Nations mandate to support President Abd Rabbo Mansour Hadi. Much of the coalition's military activity has been conducted from the air, but the armed forces of the United Arab Emirates have conducted conventional and hybrid operations over complex terrain and with extended supply lines. The Saudi land forces, meanwhile, are securing their border with Yemen over extended internal supply lines, while maritime and air-defence forces have also been engaged. Neither Saudi Arabia nor the UAE seemed prepared for this type of conflict in that neither had a defence policy based on a clearly defined threat – at least one that was publicly accessible – and certainly not one that discussed a regional intervention. As a result, the equipment, training, doctrine and logistics priorities that might be associated with tasks such as intervention operations were, analysts understand, not in place. Equipment inventories and training programmes were geared more towards conventional war fighting, while exercises tended to be short and culminate in a set-piece and heavily rehearsed final 'serial'. The composition of some of the region's armed forces is also significant: the Saudi armed forces comprise Saudi nationals, but the armed forces of the UAE and Qatar, for example, are not only smaller but in the main also have larger numbers of serving non-nationals, usually in the ranks, alongside Emirati or Qatari officers.

United Arab Emirates

While operations in Yemen are overall conducted by the Saudi-led coalition, some analysts argue that the UAE's armed forces are those that have been engaged in many of the ground operations, while also demonstrating maturity in the air environment. For the UAE, the ability to mount and maintain these missions derives from its early investment in developing military experience, and in particular human capital, through the deployment of Emirati military units to Afghanistan, Kosovo and Somalia; long-standing training courses (including training aimed at improving air–ground integration); and a number of programmes that engaged foreign advisers. Notably, these programmes included the engagement in 2009 of former Australian Special Forces commander Major-General Mike Hindmarsh as an adviser and commander of the Presidential Guard and, more recently, appointing retired US Army Lieutenant-Colonel Stephen Toumajan as a UAE major-general to run the Joint Aviation Command (JAC).

It is understood that there are now substantial numbers of retired expatriate advisers, instructors and aviators in both of these Emirati organisations, whose presence is creating small and growing pockets of expertise. In addition, the formation of the Emirates Defence Industries Corporation (EDIC) as an 'umbrella' organisation (both for the manufacture and support of defence equipment) has the potential to be a further step towards the generation of a defence sector able to support modern operational armed forces. There is a growing capacity for logistics support and sustainability through defence firms such as AMMROC, EDIC MRO Land, and Global Aviation Logistics, but political factors and a lack of institutional experience can act as a brake. For instance, it is unclear whether the armed forces have developed the ability to act as a truly 'intelligent customer', such that the organisation clearly understands the work it may actually require of the contractor and is able to critically review the contractor's performance. Analysts also consider that there may be inexperience in output-based contracting, where the focus is on the actual delivery of a service or capability (such as the number of hours a maintained aircraft is able to remain operational before its next service), as opposed to the physical aspects of a support contract (such as the hours spent on servicing), as well as inexperience in managing large fleets, particularly when they are as diverse as the JAC's aviation inventory.

A defence-planning reform programme is under way in the UAE, driven by consultants and supported by former service personnel from other countries. Among other things, it is intended to engender an intelligence-driven and capability-based culture. Progress is reportedly slow, partly due to bureaucratic factors but also because the experience to run a ministry of defence cannot be created overnight. There is also the regular distraction (or attraction) of cutting-edge capabilities, which sometimes overshadows the need to get the best from the people and equipment already in service. While there may be a strong case for obtaining the support of individuals and organisations with current operational skills in order to improve support functions, this tends to be less eye-catching.

Saudi Arabia

Saudi Arabia has experienced a different set of challenges. With the exception, analysts assert, of pockets of good practice in the Royal Saudi Air Force (RSAF) through extended training and engagement with the United Kingdom and the United States, the lack of investment in people and support capabilities has probably been the main overall lesson from current operations. Although the Saudi focus on the air domain in Yemen may indicate confidence that airpower will lead to the defeat of the Houthis, it may equally indicate a lack of confidence in land forces. The land forces had a previous encounter with Houthi forces in 2009 but it is unclear what, if any, lessons were learned. On the surface, an investment equivalent to that made by the UAE in its deployments has been absent. At the pilot level, there are skilled operators, reflecting that the RSAF has trained to positive effect with UK, US and NATO member states' air forces, but as far as can be observed there is little depth in essential supporting capabilities.

However, analysts consider that realisation of these limitations has led to an ambitious defence-reform programme that is intended to have training and sustainability at its core. The programme – led by a transformation management office (TMO) comprising hand-picked and experienced Saudi nationals, alongside consultants – is intended to ensure that human resources and a strong central ministry of defence are at the heart of the reform programme. The initiative to create the post of Assistant Minister of Defence for Executive Affairs is intended to bring private-sector experience and rigour to the development of the defence ministry's enabling functions. Khalid al-Bayari, formerly CEO of Saudi Telecom Company, was appointed to the post in February 2018. Work has simultaneously been under way to identify the personnel best suited to this new structure; more than 500 officers went through an assessment centre and are expected to move to new posts in the coming months. In parallel, the TMO is involved in some 300 initiatives, spread over the next ten years, including extensive training reform and improved readiness and cost-effectiveness. Here, lessons might be derived from the UAE programme, where analysts considered that the experience of expatriate military professionals could provide insights and benefits that complement the work of consultants.

Other states

Meanwhile, the past three years have seen significant investment by Qatar in new defence equipment. At least on the surface, this investment seems to give little thought to integration or support. At a time when many other nations are looking to rationalise equipment and introduce more multi-role platforms to ease support demands, Qatar is broadening its inventory. By contrast, observers understand that expenditure on training amounts to handfuls of individual and group hires, often of retired expatriate military personnel. These personnel work in silos directed by senior officers, few of whom have experience in front-line units or on operations.

By comparison, the authorities in Oman have quietly created a solid base from which to grow their military capability. Working substantially with a single partner through a government-to-government arrangement, as Muscat has done with the UK, may not suit other countries, but the durability of the Oman–UK relationship should not be underestimated: it may be possible to buy the time of advisers and trainers, but commitment to defence reform is required over the long term. Operations in Yemen have highlighted the importance of human capital and logistics: well-trained and experienced people are central to progress, with the ability to sustain both forces and equipment close behind. Improving this may well require carefully selected advisers sharing their experience, but it also requires an open-minded client with the patience to listen, learn, accrue experience and drive change.

Algeria ALG

Algerian Dinar D		2017	2018	2019
GDP	D	18.6tr	21.2tr	
	US$	168bn	188bn	
per capita	US$	4,034	4,450	
Growth	%	1.4	2.5	
Inflation	%	5.6	6.5	
Def bdgt	D	1.12tr	1.12tr	
	US$	10.1bn	9.93bn	
US$1=D		110.97	112.64	

Population   41,657,488

Age	0–14	15–19	20–24	25–29	30–64	65 plus
Male	15.1%	3.5%	4.0%	4.4%	20.9%	2.7%
Female	14.4%	3.4%	3.8%	4.2%	20.5%	3.1%

Capabilities

The armed forces are among the most capable and best equipped in North Africa. Territorial integrity, internal security and regional stability are the primary roles of the armed forces. Algeria is part of the African Union's North African Regional Capability Standby Force, hosting the force's logistics base in Algiers. Algeria discusses with its neighbours regional security challenges like counter-terrorism, and has particularly close security cooperation with Tunisia. The conscript-based force exercises regularly, with training appearing to be of a relatively good standard. There is an ongoing attempt to make the armed forces more professional, which was reflected in the reduction of conscription liability from 18 to 12 months in 2014. The armed forces' logistics capabilities appear sufficient to support internal deployments. The army and air force's inventories consist of a core of modern, primarily Russian-sourced equipment, though China has also supplied equipment, including self-propelled artillery. Algiers has expressed interest in acquiring more fixed-wing combat aircraft and the navy is investing in its submarine fleet. Local industry, and the services, are capable of equipment maintenance. However, while Algeria is largely dependent on foreign suppliers for new equipment, it has in recent years made significant investments towards developing a domestic defence industry. This has led to a number of joint ventures with foreign partners, such as with Italy's Leonardo over the licensed production of helicopters.

ACTIVE 130,000 (Army 110,000 Navy 6,000 Air 14,000) **Paramilitary 187,200**
Conscript liability 12 months

RESERVE 150,000 (Army 150,000) to age 50

ORGANISATIONS BY SERVICE

Army 35,000; 75,000 conscript (total 110,000)
FORCES BY ROLE
6 Mil Regions
MANOEUVRE
 Armoured
 2 (1st & 8th) armd div (3 tk regt; 1 mech regt, 1 arty gp)
 1 indep armd bde
 Mechanised
 2 (12th & 40th) mech div (1 tk regt; 3 mech regt, 1 arty gp)
 3 indep mech bde
 Light
 2 indep mot bde
 Air Manoeuvre
 1 AB div (4 para regt; 1 SF regt)
COMBAT SUPPORT
 2 arty bn
 1 AT regt
 4 engr bn
AIR DEFENCE
 7 AD bn
EQUIPMENT BY TYPE
ARMOURED FIGHTING VEHICLES
 MBT 1,467: 270 T-54/T-55; 300 T-62; 325 T-72M1/M1M; 572 T-90SA
 RECCE 134: 44 AML-60; 26 BRDM-2; 64 BRDM-2M with 9M133 *Kornet* (AT-14 *Spriggan*)
 IFV 1,089: 285 BMP-1; 304 BMP-2; 400 BMP-2M with 9M133 *Kornet* (AT-14 *Spriggan*); 100 BMP-3
 APC 807+
  APC (T) VP-6
  APC (W) 805+: 250 BTR-60; 150 BTR-80; 150 OT-64; 55 M3 Panhard; 100+ *Fuchs 2*; 100 *Fahd*
  PPV 2 *Marauder*
  AUV Nimr *Ajban*
ENGINEERING & MAINTENANCE VEHICLES
 AEV IMR-2
 ARV BREM-1
 MW UR-77
ANTI-TANK/ANTI-INFRASTRUCTURE
 SP 28 9P163-3 *Kornet*-EM (AT-14 *Spriggan*)
 MSL • MANPATS 9K11 *Malyutka* (AT-3 *Sagger*); 9K111 *Fagot* (AT-4 *Spigot*); 9K111-1 *Konkurs* (AT-5 *Spandrel*); 9K115-2 *Metis*-M1 (AT-13 *Saxhorn*-2); 9K135 *Kornet*-E (AT-14 *Spriggan*); Milan
 RCL 180: 82mm 120 B-10; 107mm 60 B-11
 GUNS 250: 57mm 160 ZIS-2 (M-1943); 85mm 80 D-44; 100mm 10 T-12
ARTILLERY 1,098
 SP 224: 122mm 140 2S1 *Gvozdika*; 152mm 30 2S3 *Akatsiya*; 155mm ε54 PLZ-45
 TOWED 393: 122mm 345: 160 D-30; 25 D-74; 100 M-1931/37; 60 M-30; 130mm 10 M-46; 152mm 20 M-1937 (ML-20); 155mm 18 Type-88 (PLL-01)
 MRL 151: 122mm 51: 48 BM-21 *Grad*; 3+ SR5; 140mm 48 BM-14; 220mm 4 TOS-1A; 240mm 30 BM-24; 300mm 18 9A52 *Smerch*
 MOR 330: 82mm 150 M-37; 120mm 120 M-1943; 160mm 60 M-1943
SURFACE-TO-SURFACE MISSILE LAUNCHERS
 SRBM 4 *Iskander*-E
AIR DEFENCE
 SAM 106+
  Short-range 38 96K6 *Pantsir*-S1 (SA-22 *Greyhound*); *Pantsir*-SM
  Point-defence 68+: ε48 9K33M *Osa* (SA-8B *Gecko*); ε20 9K31 *Strela*-1 (SA-9 *Gaskin*); 9K32 *Strela*-2 (SA-7A/B *Grail*)‡; QW-2
 GUNS ε830
  SP 23mm ε225 ZSU-23-4

TOWED ε605: **14.5mm** 100: 60 ZPU-2; 40 ZPU-4; **23mm** 100 ZU-23; **37mm** ε150 M-1939; **57mm** 75 S-60; **85mm** 20 M-1939 (KS-12); **100mm** 150 KS-19; **130mm** 10 KS-30

Navy ε6,000
EQUIPMENT BY TYPE
SUBMARINES • TACTICAL • SSK 4:
  2 *Kilo* (FSU *Paltus*) with 6 single 533mm TT with Test-71ME HWT/3M54E *Klub*-S (SS-N-27 *Sizzler*) AShM
  2 Improved *Kilo* (RUS *Varshavyanka*) with 6 single 533mm TT with Test-71ME HWT/3M54E *Klub*-S (SS-N-27 *Sizzler*) AShM
PRINCIPAL SURFACE COMBATANTS • FRIGATES 8
  FFGHM 5:
    3 *Adhafer* (C28A) with 2 quad lnchr with C-802A AShM, 1 FM-90 lnchr with HHQ-7 SAM, 2 triple 324mm ASTT, 2 Type-730B CIWS, 1 76mm gun (capacity 1 hel)
    2 *Erradii* (MEKO 200AN) with 2 octuple lnchrs with RBS15 Mk3 AShM, 4 8-cell VLS with *Umkhonto*-IR SAM, 2 twin 324mm TT with MU90 LWT, 1 127mm gun (capacity 1 *Super Lynx* 300)
  FF 3 *Mourad Rais* (FSU *Koni*) with 2 twin 533mm TT, 2 RBU 6000 *Smerch* 2 A/S mor, 2 twin 76mm gun
PATROL AND COASTAL COMBATANTS 25
  CORVETTES 7
    FSGM 3 *Rais Hamidou* (FSU *Nanuchka* II) with up to 4 twin lnchr with 3M24E *Uran*-E (SS-N-25 *Switchblade*) AShM, 1 twin lnchr with 9M33 *Osa*-M (SA-N-4 *Gecko*) SAM, 1 AK630 CIWS, 1 twin 57mm gun
    FSG 4:
      3 *Djebel Chenoua* with 2 twin lnchr with C-802 (CH-SS-N-8 *Saccade*) AShM, 1 AK630 CIWS, 1 76mm gun
      1 *Rais Hassen Barbier* (*Djebel Chenoua* mod) with 2 twin lnchr with C-802 (CH-SS-N-8 *Saccade*) AShM, 1 Type-730 CIWS, 1 76mm gun
  PBFG 9 *Osa* II (3†) with 4 single lnchr with P-15 *Termit* (SS-N-2B *Styx*) AShM
  PB 9 *Kebir* with 1 76mm gun
MINE WARFARE • MINE COUNTERMEASURES 1
  MCC 1 *El-Kasseh* (ITA *Gaeta* mod)
AMPHIBIOUS 7
  PRINCIPAL AMPHIBIOUS SHIPS • LHD 1 *Kalaat Beni Abbes* with 1 8-cell A50 VLS with *Aster*-15 SAM, 1 76mm gun (capacity 5 med hel; 3 LCVP; 15 MBT; 350 troops)
  LANDING SHIPS 3:
    LSM 1 *Polnochny* B with 1 twin AK230 CIWS (capacity 6 MBT; 180 troops)
    LST 2 *Kalaat beni Hammad* (capacity 7 MBT; 240 troops) with 1 med hel landing platform
  LANDING CRAFT • LCVP 3
LOGISTICS AND SUPPORT 3
  AGS 1 *El Idrissi*
  AX 1 *Daxin* with 2 twin AK230 CIWS, 1 76mm gun, 1 hel landing platform
  AXS 1 *El Mellah*

Naval Infantry
FORCES BY ROLE
MANOEUVRE
  Amphibious
  1 naval inf bn

Naval Aviation
EQUIPMENT BY TYPE
HELICOPTERS
  MRH 9: 3 AW139 (SAR); 6 *Super Lynx* 300
  SAR 9: 5 AW101 SAR; 4 *Super Lynx* Mk130

Coastal Defence
EQUIPMENT BY TYPE
COASTAL DEFENCE
  AShM 4K51 *Rubezh* (SSC-3 *Styx*)

Coast Guard ε500
EQUIPMENT BY TYPE
PATROL AND COASTAL COMBATANTS 55
  PBF 6 *Baglietto* 20
  PB 49: 6 *Baglietto Mangusta*; 12 *Jebel Antar*; 21 *Deneb*; 4 *El Mounkid*; 6 *Kebir* with 1 76mm gun
LOGISTICS AND SUPPORT 9
  AR 1 *El Mourafek*
  ARS 3 *El Moundjid*
  AXL 5 *El Mouderrib* (PRC *Chui-E*) (2 more in reserve†)

Air Force 14,000
FORCES BY ROLE
FIGHTER
  1 sqn with MiG-25PDS/RU *Foxbat*
  4 sqn with MiG-29C/UB *Fulcrum*
FIGHTER/GROUND ATTACK
  3 sqn with Su-30MKA *Flanker*
GROUND ATTACK
  2 sqn with Su-24M/MK *Fencer D*
ELINT
  1 sqn with Beech 1900D
MARITIME PATROL
  2 sqn with Beech 200T/300 *King Air*
ISR
  1 sqn with Su-24MR *Fencer* E*; MiG-25RBSh *Foxbat* D*
TANKER
  1 sqn with Il-78 *Midas*
TRANSPORT
  1 sqn with C-130H/H-30 *Hercules*; L-100-30
  1 sqn with C-295M
  1 sqn with Gulfstream IV-SP; Gulfstream V
  1 sqn with Il-76MD/TD *Candid*
TRAINING
  2 sqn with Z-142
  1 sqn with Yak-130 *Mitten**
  2 sqn with L-39C/ZA *Albatros*
  1 hel sqn with PZL Mi-2 *Hoplite*
ATTACK HELICOPTER
  3 sqn with Mi-24 *Hind* (one re-equipping with Mi-28NE *Havoc*)

TRANSPORT HELICOPTER
1 sqn with AS355 *Ecureuil*
5 sqn with Mi-8 *Hip*; Mi-17 *Hip* H
1 sqn with Ka-27PS *Helix* D; Ka-32T *Helix*
ISR UAV
1 sqn with *Seeker* II
AIR DEFENCE
3 ADA bde
3 SAM regt with S-125 *Neva* (SA-3 *Goa*); 2K12 *Kub* (SA-6 *Gainful*); S-300PMU2 (SA-20 *Gargoyle*)

EQUIPMENT BY TYPE
AIRCRAFT 135 combat capable
  FTR 34: 11 MiG-25PDS/RU *Foxbat*; 23 MiG-29C/UB *Fulcrum*
  FGA 44 Su-30MKA
  ATK 33 Su-24M/MK *Fencer* D
  ISR 8: 4 MiG-25RBSh *Foxbat* D*; 4 Su-24MR *Fencer* E*
  TKR 6 Il-78 *Midas*
  TPT 65: **Heavy** 11: 3 Il-76MD *Candid* B; 8 Il-76TD *Candid*; **Medium** 16: 8 C-130H *Hercules*; 6 C-130H-30 *Hercules*; 2 L-100-30; **Light** 32: 3 Beech C90B *King Air*; 5 Beech 200T *King Air*; 6 Beech 300 *King Air*; 12 Beech 1900D (electronic surv); 5 C-295M; 1 F-27 *Friendship*; **PAX** 6: 1 A340; 4 Gulfstream IV-SP; 1 Gulfstream V
  TRG 99: 36 L-39ZA *Albatros*; 7 L-39C *Albatros*; 16 Yak-130 *Mitten**; 40 Z-142
HELICOPTERS
  ATK 39: 31 Mi-24 *Hind*; 6+ Mi-28NE *Havoc*; 2+ Mi-28UB *Havoc*
  SAR 3 Ka-27PS *Helix* D
  MRH 85: 8 AW139 (SAR); 3 Bell 412EP; 74 Mi-8 *Hip* (med tpt)/Mi-17 *Hip* H
  TPT 48: **Heavy** 8 Mi-26T2 *Halo*; **Medium** 4 Ka-32T *Helix*; **Light** 44: 8 AW119KE *Koala*; 8 AS355 *Ecureuil*; 28 PZL Mi-2 *Hoplite*
UNMANNED AERIAL VEHICLES
  CISR • Heavy CH-3; CH-4
  ISR • Medium *Seeker* II
AIR DEFENCE
  Long-range S-300PMU2 (SA-20 *Gargoyle*)
  Medium-range 9K317 *Buk*-M2E (SA-17 *Grizzly*); S-125 *Pechora*-M (SA-3 *Goa*)
  Short-range 2K12 *Kvadrat* (SA-6 *Gainful*)
  GUNS 725 100mm/130mm/85mm
AIR-LAUNCHED MISSILES
  AAM • IR R-60 (AA-8 *Aphid*); R-73 (A-11 *Archer*); **IR/SARH** R-40/46 (AA-6 *Acrid*); R-23/24 (AA-7 *Apex*); R-27 (AA-10 *Alamo*); **ARH** R-77 (AA-12A *Adder*);
  ASM Kh-25 (AS-10 *Karen*); Kh-29 (AS-14 *Kedge*); Kh-59ME (AS-18 *Kazoo*); ZT-35 *Ingwe*; 9M120 *Ataka* (AT-9 *Spiral*-2)
  AShM Kh-31A (AS-17B *Krypton*)
  ARM Kh-25MP (AS-12A *Kegler*); Kh-31P (AS-17A *Krypton*)

Paramilitary ε187,200

Gendarmerie 20,000
Ministry of Defence control; 6 regions

EQUIPMENT BY TYPE
ARMOURED FIGHTING VEHICLES
  RECCE AML-60
  APC • APC (W) 210: 100 TH-390 *Fahd*; 110 Panhard M3
HELICOPTERS • TPT • Light 12+: 12 AW109; Some PZL Mi-2 *Hoplite*

National Security Forces 16,000
Directorate of National Security. Small arms

Republican Guard 1,200
EQUIPMENT BY TYPE
ARMOURED FIGHTING VEHICLES
  RECCE AML-60
  APC • APC (T) M3 half-track

Legitimate Defence Groups ε150,000
Self-defence militia, communal guards (60,000)

DEPLOYMENT

DEMOCRATIC REPUBLIC OF THE CONGO: UN • MONUSCO 3 obs

Bahrain BHR

Bahraini Dinar D		2017	2018	2019
GDP	D	13.3bn	14.8bn	
	US$	35.3bn	39.3bn	
per capita	US$	24,326	26,532	
Growth	%	3.8	3.2	
Inflation	%	1.4	3.0	
Def bdgt [a]	D	557m	557m	
	US$	1.48bn	1.48bn	
US$1=D		0.38	0.38	

[a] Excludes funds allocated to the Ministry of the Interior

Population	1,442,659

Ethnic groups: Nationals 46%; Asian 45.5%; African 1.5%; other or unspecified 7%

Age	0–14	15–19	20–24	25–29	30–64	65 plus
Male	9.6%	3.7%	5.0%	6.2%	34.4%	1.5%
Female	9.3%	3.2%	3.6%	3.9%	18.0%	1.5%

Capabilities

Bahrain's armed forces are capable and well equipped. The country occupies a critical and challenging strategic position between regional rivals Iran and Saudi Arabia. The principal roles of the armed forces are territorial defence and internal-security support. Bahrain is a member of the GCC. Its most critical security relationship is with Saudi Arabia, but it also has a strong defence relationship with the US. The US 5th Fleet is headquartered in Bahrain, as is the combined maritime forces headquarters. In 2018, the UK reopened a permanent naval facility in Bahrain. Military service is voluntary and personnel are relatively well trained. Despite their small size, the armed forces have carried out a number of limited expeditionary deployments to support coalition operations, including in support of the Saudi-led intervention in Yemen. For a period in 2017–18, Bahrain commanded Combined Task Force 151, focused on countering piracy and other armed criminality at sea – the first time a GCC nation had assumed command of a CTF outside the Arabian Gulf. In a major enhancement to Bahrain's air mobility, it has bought ex-UK C-130J transport aircraft. As part of a major air-force modernisation, Bahrain intends to buy F-16V fighters and to upgrade its existing F-16C/Ds to that configuration. The armed forces have their own maintenance support, but Bahrain has little in the way of a defence-industrial base beyond the limited naval-ship maintenance support provided by the Arab Shipbuilding and Repair Yard.

ACTIVE 8,200 (Army 6,000 Navy 700 Air 1,500)
Paramilitary 11,260

ORGANISATIONS BY SERVICE

Army 6,000
FORCES BY ROLE
SPECIAL FORCES
  1 SF bn
MANOEUVRE
  Armoured
  1 armd bde(-) (1 recce bn, 2 armd bn)
  Mechanised
  1 inf bde (2 mech bn, 1 mot bn)
  Light
  1 (Amiri) gd bn
COMBAT SUPPORT
  1 arty bde (1 hvy arty bty, 2 med arty bty, 1 lt arty bty, 1 MRL bty)
  1 engr coy
COMBAT SERVICE SUPPORT
  1 log coy
  1 tpt coy
  1 med coy
AIR DEFENCE
  1 AD bn (1 ADA bty, 2 SAM bty)
EQUIPMENT BY TYPE
ARMOURED FIGHTING VEHICLES
  MBT 180 M60A3
  RECCE 22 AML-90
  IFV 67: 25 YPR-765 PRI; 42 AIFV-B-C25
  APC 203+
    APC (T) 203: 200 M113A2; 3 AIFV-B
    APC (W) Arma 6×6
  AUV M-ATV
ENGINEERING & MAINTENANCE VEHICLES
  ARV 53 Fahd 240
ANTI-TANK/ANTI-INFRASTRUCTURE
  MSL
    SP 5 AIFV-B-Milan; HMMWV with BGM-71A TOW
    MANPATS BGM-71A TOW; Kornet-EM
  RCL 31: **106mm** 25 M40A1; **120mm** 6 MOBAT
ARTILLERY 161
  SP 82: **155mm** 20 M109A5; **203mm** 62 M110A2
  TOWED 36: **105mm** 8 L118 Light Gun; **155mm** 28 M198
  MRL 13: **122mm** 4 SR5; **227mm** 9 M270 MLRS
  MOR 30: **81mm** 18: 12 L16; 6 EIMOS; **SP 120mm** 12 M113A2

SURFACE-TO-SURFACE MISSILE LAUNCHERS
  SRBM • **Conventional** MGM-140A ATACMS (launched from M270 MLRS)
AIR DEFENCE
  SAM
    Medium-range 6 MIM-23B I-Hawk
    Short-range 7 Crotale
    Point-defence FIM-92 Stinger; RBS-70
  GUNS 24: **35mm** 12 Oerlikon; **40mm** 12 L/70

Navy 700
EQUIPMENT BY TYPE
PRINCIPAL SURFACE COMBATANTS 1
  FRIGATES • **FFGHM** 1 Sabha (ex-US Oliver Hazard Perry) with 1 Mk13 GMLS with SM-1MR SAM/RGM-84C Harpoon AShM, 2 triple 324mm Mk32 ASTT with Mk46 LWT, 1 Phalanx Block 1B CIWS, 1 76mm gun (capacity 1 Bo-105 hel)
PATROL AND COASTAL COMBATANTS 12
  CORVETTES • **FSG** 2 Al Manama (GER Lurssen 62m) with 2 twin lnchr with MM40 Exocet AShM, 2 76mm guns, 1 hel landing platform
  PCFG 4 Ahmed el Fateh (GER Lurssen 45m) with 2 twin lnchr with MM40 Exocet AShM, 1 76mm gun
  PB 4: 2 Al Jarim (US Swift FPB-20); 2 Al Riffa (GER Lurssen 38m)
  PBF 2 Mk V SOC
AMPHIBIOUS • LANDING CRAFT 9
  LCM 7: 1 Loadmaster; 4 Mashtan; 2 Dinar (ADSB 42m)
  LCVP 2 Sea Keeper

Naval Aviation
EQUIPMENT BY TYPE
HELICOPTERS • **TPT** • **Light** 2 Bo-105

Air Force 1,500
FORCES BY ROLE
FIGHTER
  2 sqn with F-16C/D Fighting Falcon
FIGHTER/GROUND ATTACK
  1 sqn with F-5E/F Tiger II
TRANSPORT
  1 (Royal) flt with B-727; B-747; BAe-146; Gulfstream II; Gulfstream IV; Gulfstream 450; Gulfstream 550; S-92A
TRAINING
  1 sqn with Hawk Mk129*
  1 sqn with T-67M Firefly
ATTACK HELICOPTER
  2 sqn with AH-1E/F Cobra; TAH-1P Cobra
TRANSPORT HELICOPTER
  1 sqn with Bell 212 (AB-212)
  1 sqn with UH-60M Black Hawk
  1 (VIP) sqn with Bo-105; S-70A Black Hawk; UH-60L Black Hawk
EQUIPMENT BY TYPE
AIRCRAFT 38 combat capable
  FTR 12: 8 F-5E Tiger II; 4 F-5F Tiger II
  FGA 20: 16 F-16C Block 40 Fighting Falcon; 4 F-16D Block 40 Fighting Falcon

TPT 11: **Medium** 1 C-130J *Hercules*; **PAX** 10: 1 B-727; 2 B-747; 1 Gulfstream II; 1 Gulfstream IV; 1 Gulfstream 450; 1 Gulfstream 550; 3 BAe-146
TRG 9: 6 *Hawk* Mk129*; 3 T-67M *Firefly*
HELICOPTERS
ATK 28: 16 AH-1E *Cobra*; 12 AH-1F *Cobra*
TPT 27: **Medium** 13: 3 S-70A *Black Hawk*; 1 S-92A (VIP); 1 UH-60L *Black Hawk*; 8 UH-60M *Black Hawk*; **Light** 14: 11 Bell 212 (AB-212); 3 Bo-105
TRG 6 TAH-1P *Cobra*
AIR-LAUNCHED MISSILES
AAM • **IR** AIM-9P *Sidewinder*; **SARH** AIM-7 *Sparrow*; **ARH** AIM-120B/C AMRAAM
ASM AGM-65D/G *Maverick*; some TOW
BOMBS
Laser-guided GBU-10/12 *Paveway* II

Paramilitary ε11,260

Police 9,000

Ministry of Interior

EQUIPMENT BY TYPE
ARMOURED FIGHTING VEHICLES
  RECCE 8 S52 *Shorland*
  APC • **APC (W)** Otokar ISV; *Cobra*
HELICOPTERS
  MRH 2 Bell 412 *Twin Huey*
  ISR 2 Hughes 500
  TPT • **Light** 1 Bo-105

National Guard ε2,000

FORCES BY ROLE
MANOEUVRE
  Other
    3 paramilitary bn
EQUIPMENT BY TYPE
ARMOURED FIGHTING VEHICLES
  APC • **APC (W)** *Arma* 6×6; *Cobra*

Coast Guard ε260

Ministry of Interior
PATROL AND COASTAL COMBATANTS 52
  PBF 23: 2 Ares 18; 4 *Jaris*; 6 *Saham*; 6 *Fajr*; 5 *Jarada*
  PB 29: 6 *Haris*; 1 *Al Muharraq*; 10 *Deraa* (of which 4 Halmatic 20, 2 *Souter* 20, 4 Rodman 20); 10 *Saif* (of which 4 *Fairey Sword*, 6 *Halmatic* 160); 2 *Hawar*
AMPHIBIOUS • **LANDING CRAFT** • **LCU** 1 *Loadmaster* II

DEPLOYMENT

SAUDI ARABIA: *Operation Restoring Hope* 250; 1 SF gp; 1 arty gp; 6 F-16C *Fighting Falcon*

FOREIGN FORCES

United Kingdom Air Force 160: 1 naval base
United States US Central Command 5,000; 1 HQ (5th Fleet); 1 AD bty with MIM-104E/F *Patriot* PAC-2/3

Egypt EGY

Egyptian Pound E£		2017	2018	2019
GDP	E£	3.47tr	4.36tr	
	US$	237bn	249bn	
per capita	US$	2,495	2572	
Growth	%	4.2	5.3	
Inflation	%	23.5	20.9	
Def bdgt	E£	47.1bn	51.6bn	59.0bn
	US$	3.21bn	2.90bn	
FMA (US)	US$	1.23bn	1.3bn	1.3bn
US$1=E£		14.67	17.78	

Population	99,413,317					
Age	0–14	15–19	20–24	25–29	30–64	65 plus
Male	17.3%	4.7%	4.9%	4.8%	17.3%	2.1%
Female	16.1%	4.4%	4.6%	4.6%	17.0%	2.2%

Capabilities

Egypt's armed forces are the largest in the region and are principally focused on territorial integrity and internal security, including combating ISIS-affiliated groups in northern Sinai. Egypt and the US maintain a strong strategic partnership, which has seen significant US equipment deliveries and ongoing Foreign Military Aid payments. Defence relations with Russia have developed, particularly regarding procurements. Operational experience will have been bolstered by counter-insurgency operations in the Sinai and contributions to several UN deployments. Training is supplemented by regular involvement in a number of multinational exercises. Egypt has a developing capacity to deploy independently beyond its borders. It contributes to UN missions, has intervened militarily in Libya and sent combat aircraft to support the Saudi-led coalition in Yemen. The navy's two new *Mistral*-class amphibious ships will bolster the capacity to deploy regionally. The armed forces' inventory primarily comprise obsolete Soviet-era systems and newer Western equipment. However, the armed forces are undertaking an extensive equipment-recapitalisation programme, which is seeing the delivery of Russian multi-role fighters, attack helicopters and SAM systems. Combat aircraft have also been sourced from France and armed UAVs from China. Naval recapitalisation includes German-built submarines and French-designed frigates. Egypt has an established domestic defence industry, supplying equipment for both the armed forces and export markets, ranging from small arms to armoured vehicles. There is a history of licensed and co-production with foreign companies, including the local assembly of M1A1 main battle tanks from US-supplied kits and the production of frigates with French assistance.

ACTIVE 438,500 (Army 310,000 Navy 18,500 Air 30,000 Air Defence Command 80,000) **Paramilitary 397,000**
Conscription liability 12–36 months (followed by refresher training over a period of up to 9 years)

RESERVE 479,000 (Army 375,000 Navy 14,000 Air 20,000 Air Defence Command 70,000)

ORGANISATIONS BY SERVICE

Army 90,000–120,000; 190,000–220,000 conscript (total 310,000)

FORCES BY ROLE
SPECIAL FORCES
5 cdo gp
1 counter-terrorist unit
MANOEUVRE
Armoured
4 armd div (2 armd bde, 1 mech bde, 1 arty bde)
4 indep armd bde
1 Republican Guard bde
Mechanised
8 mech div (1 armd bde, 2 mech bde, 1 arty bde)
4 indep mech bde
Light
1 inf div
2 indep inf bde
Air Manoeuvre
2 air mob bde
1 para bde
SURFACE-TO-SURFACE MISSILE
1 SRBM bde with FROG-7
1 SRBM bde with *Scud*-B
COMBAT SUPPORT
15 arty bde
6 engr bde (3 engr bn)
2 spec ops engr bn
6 salvage engr bn
24 MP bn
18 sigs bn
COMBAT SERVICE SUPPORT
36 log bn
27 med bn
EQUIPMENT BY TYPE
ARMOURED FIGHTING VEHICLES
MBT 2,480: 1,130 M1A1 *Abrams*; 300 M60A1; 850 M60A3; 200 T-62 (840 T-54/T-55; 300 T-62 all in store)
RECCE 412: 300 BRDM-2; 112 *Commando Scout*
IFV 405+: 390 YPR-765 25mm; 15+ BMP-1 (205 BMP-1 in store)
APC 4,701+
 APC (T) 2,700: 2,000 M113A2/YPR-765 (incl variants); 500 BTR-50; 200 OT-62
 APC (W) 1,560: 250 BMR-600P; 250 BTR-60; 410 *Fahd-30*/TH 390 *Fahd*; 650 *Walid*
 PPV 441+: 92 *Caiman*; some REVA III; some REVA V LWB; 349 RG-33L (incl 89 amb)
 AUV 95+: *Panthera* T6; 95+ *Sherpa Light Scout*
ENGINEERING & MAINTENANCE VEHICLES
ARV 367+: *Fahd* 240; BMR 3560.55; 12 *Maxxpro* ARV; 220 M88A1; 90 M88A2; M113 ARV; 45 M578; T-54/55 ARV
VLB KMM; MTU; MTU-20
MW *Aardvark* JFSU Mk4
ANTI-TANK/ANTI-INFRASTRUCTURE • MSL
SP 352+: 52 M901, 300 YPR-765 PRAT; HMMWV with TOW-2
MANPATS 9K11 *Malyutka* (AT-3 *Sagger*) (incl BRDM-2); HJ-73; *Milan*; TOW-2
ARTILLERY 4,468
SP 492+: **122mm** 124+: 124 SP 122; D-30 mod; **130mm** M-46 mod; **155mm** 368: 164 M109A2; 204 M109A5
TOWED 962: **122mm** 526: 190 D-30M; 36 M-1931/37; 300 M-30; **130mm** 420 M-46; **155mm** 16 GH-52

MRL 450: **122mm** 356: 96 BM-11; 60 BM-21; 50 *Sakr*-10; 50 *Sakr*-18; 100 *Sakr*-36; **130mm** 36 K136 *Kooryong*; **140mm** 32 BM-14; **227mm** 26 M270 MLRS; **240mm** (48 BM-24 in store)
MOR 2,564: **81mm** 50 M125A2; **82mm** 500; **SP 107mm** 100: 65 M106A1; 35 M106A2; **120mm** 1,848: 1,800 M-1943; 48 Brandt; **SP 120mm** 36 M1064A3; **160mm** 30 M-160
SURFACE-TO-SURFACE MISSILE LAUNCHERS
SRBM • **Conventional** 42+: 9 FROG-7; 24 *Sakr*-80; 9 *Scud*-B
UNMANNED AERIAL VEHICLES
ISR • **Medium** R4E-50 *Skyeye*; ASN-209
AIR DEFENCE
SAM
 Point-defence 141+: 50 M1097 *Avenger*; 26 M48 *Chaparral*; 45 *Sinai*-23 with *Ayn al-Saqr*; 20 9K31 *Strela*-1 (SA-9 *Gaskin*); *Ayn al-Saqr*; 9K32 *Strela*-2 (SA-7 *Grail*)‡; FIM-92 *Stinger*; 9K38 *Igla* (SA-18 *Grouse*)
GUNS
 SP 160: **23mm** 120 ZSU-23-4; **57mm** 40 ZSU-57-2
 TOWED 700: **14.5mm** 300 ZPU-4; **23mm** 200 ZU-23-2; **57mm** 200 S-60

Navy ε8,500 (incl 2,000 Coast Guard); 10,000 conscript (total 18,500)

EQUIPMENT BY TYPE
SUBMARINES • TACTICAL • SSK 6
4 *Romeo*† (PRC Type-033) with 8 single 533mm TT with UGM-84C *Harpoon* AShM/Mk37 HWT (being replaced by Type-209/1400)
2 Type-209/1400 with 8 single 533mm TT with UGM-84L *Harpoon* Block II AShM/DM2A4/*SeaHake* Mod 4 HWT
PRINCIPAL SURFACE COMBATANTS 9
 DESTROYERS • DDGHM 1 *Tahya Misr* (FRA *Aquitaine*) with 2 quad lnchr with MM40 *Exocet* Block 3 AShM, 2 octuple A43 VLS with *Aster* 15 SAM, 2 twin B515 324mm ASTT with MU90 LWT, 1 76mm gun (capacity 1 med hel)
 FRIGATES 9
  FFGHM 5:
   4 *Alexandria* (ex-US *Oliver Hazard Perry*) with 1 Mk13 GMLS with RGM-84C *Harpoon* AShM/SM-1MP SAM, 2 triple 324mm ASTT with Mk 46 LWT, 1 Mk 15 *Phalanx* CIWS, 1 76mm gun (capacity 2 SH-2G *Super Seasprite* ASW hel)
   1 *El Fateh* (*Gowind* 2500) with 2 quad lnchrs with MM40 *Exocet* Block 3 AShM, 1 16-cell VLS with VL-MICA SAM, 2 triple 324mm ASTT with MU90 LWT, 1 76mm gun (capacity 1 med hel)
  FFGH 2 *Damyat* (ex-US *Knox*) with 1 octuple Mk16 GMLS with RGM-84C *Harpoon* AShM/ASROC, 2 twin 324mm Mk 32 TT with Mk 46 LWT, 1 Mk 15 *Phalanx* CIWS, 1 127mm gun (capacity 1 SH-2G *Super Seasprite* ASW hel)
  FFG 2 *Najim Al Zaffer* (PRC *Jianghu* I) with 2 twin lnchr with HY-2 (CH-SS-N-2 *Safflower*) AShM, 4 RBU 1200 A/S mor, 2 twin 57mm guns
PATROL AND COASTAL COMBATANTS 61
 CORVETTES 7
  FSGM 6:
   2 *Abu Qir* (ESP *Descubierta* – 1†) with 2 quad Mk141 lnchr with RGM-84C *Harpoon* AShM, 1 octuple *Albatros* lnchr with *Aspide* SAM, 2 triple Mk32

324mm ASTT with *Sting Ray* LWT, 1 twin 375mm A/S mor, 1 76mm gun
4 *Ezzat* (US *Ambassador* IV) with 2 quad lnchr with RGM-84L *Harpoon* Block II AShM, 1 21-cell Mk49 lnchr with RAM Block 1A SAM, 1 Mk15 Mod 21 Block 1B *Phalanx* CIWS 1 76mm gun
FS 1 *Shabab Misr* (ex-RoK *Po Hang*) with 2 76mm guns
PCFG 12:
1 *Molnya* (RUS *Tarantul* IV) with 2 twin lnchr with 3M80E *Moskit* (SS-N-22 *Sunburn*), 2 AK630 CIWS, 1 76mm gun
6 *Ramadan* with 4 single lnchr with *Otomat* MkII AShM, 1 76mm gun
5 *Tiger* with 2 twin lnchr with MM38 *Exocet* AShM, 1 76mm gun
PCC 5:
5 *Al-Nour* (ex-PRC *Hainan* – 3 more in reserve†) with 2 triple 324mm TT, 4 RBU 1200 A/S mor, 2 twin 57mm guns
PBFG 17:
4 *Hegu* (PRC – *Komar* type) with 2 single lnchr with SY-1 AShM (2 additional vessels in reserve)
5 *October* (FSU *Komar* – 1†) with 2 single lnchr with *Otomat* MkII AShM (1 additional vessel in reserve)
8 *Osa* I (ex-YUG – 3†) with 1 9K32 *Strela*-2 (SA-N-5 *Grail*) SAM (manual aiming), 4 single lnchr with P-15 *Termit* (SS-N-2A *Styx*) AShM
PBFM 4:
4 *Shershen* (FSU) with 1 9K32 *Strela*-2 (SA-N-5 *Grail*) SAM (manual aiming), 1 12-tube BM-24 MRL
PBF 10:
6 *Kaan* 20 (TUR MRTP 20)
4 *Osa* II (ex-FIN)
PB 6:
4 *Shanghai* II (PRC)
2 *Shershen* (FSU – 1†) with 4 single 533mm TT, 1 8-tube BM-21 MRL
MINE WARFARE • MINE COUNTERMEASURES 14
MHC 5: 2 *Al Siddiq* (ex-US *Osprey*); 3 *Dat Assawari* (US Swiftships)
MSI 2 *Safaga* (US Swiftships)
MSO 7: 3 *Assiout* (FSU T-43 class); 4 *Aswan* (FSU *Yurka*)
AMPHIBIOUS 20
PRINCIPAL AMPHIBIOUS SHIPS • LHD 2 *Gamal Abdel Nasser* (FRA *Mistral*) (capacity 16 med hel; 2 LCT or 4 LCM; 13 MBTs; 50 AFVs; 450 troops)
LANDING SHIPS • LSM 3 *Polnochny* A (FSU) (capacity 6 MBT; 180 troops)
LANDING CRAFT 15:
LCM 13: 4 CTM NG; 9 *Vydra* (FSU) (capacity either 3 MBT or 200 troops)
LCT 2 EDA-R
LOGISTICS AND SUPPORT 24
AOT 7 *Ayeda* (FSU *Toplivo* – 1 additional in reserve)
AE 1 *Halaib* (ex-GER *Westerwald*-class)
AKR 3 *Al Hurreya*
AR 1 *Shaledin* (ex-GER *Luneberg*-class)
ARS 2 *Al Areesh*
ATF 5 *Al Maks*† (FSU *Okhtensky*)
AX 5: 1 *El Fateh*† (ex-UK 'Z' class); 1 *El Horriya* (also used as the presidential yacht); 1 *Al Kousser*; 1 *Intishat*; 1 other

Coastal Defence
Army tps, Navy control
EQUIPMENT BY TYPE
COASTAL DEFENCE
ARTY 100mm; **130mm** SM-4-1; **152mm**
AShM 4K87 (SS-C-2B *Samlet*); *Otomat* MkII

Naval Aviation
All aircraft operated by Air Force
AIRCRAFT • TPT • Light 4 Beech 1900C (maritime surveillance)
HELICOPTERS
ASW 10 SH-2G *Super Seasprite* with Mk 46 LWT
MRH 5 SA342L *Gazelle*
UNMANNED AERIAL VEHICLES
ISR • Light 2 S-100 *Camcopter*

Coast Guard 2,000
EQUIPMENT BY TYPE
PATROL AND COASTAL COMBATANTS 79
PBF 14: 6 *Crestitalia*; 5 *Swift Protector*; 3 *Peterson*
PB 65: 5 *Nisr*; 12 *Sea Spectre* MkIII; 15 *Swiftships*; 21 *Timsah*; 3 Type-83; 9 *Peterson*

Air Force 30,000 (incl 10,000 conscript)
FORCES BY ROLE
FIGHTER
1 sqn with F-16A/B *Fighting Falcon*
8 sqn with F-16C/D *Fighting Falcon*
1 sqn with J-7
3 sqn with MiG-21 *Fishbed*/MiG-21U *Mongol* A
2 sqn with *Mirage* 5D/E
1 sqn with *Mirage* 2000B/C
FIGHTER/GROUND ATTACK
1 sqn with *Mirage* 5E2
1 sqn (forming) with *Rafale* DM
1 sqn (forming) with MiG-29M/M2 *Fulcrum*
ANTI-SUBMARINE WARFARE
1 sqn with SH-2G *Super Seasprite*
MARITIME PATROL
1 sqn with Beech 1900C
ELECTRONIC WARFARE
1 sqn with Beech 1900 (ELINT); *Commando* Mk2E (ECM)
ELECTRONIC WARFARE/TRANSPORT
1 sqn with C-130H/VC-130H *Hercules*
AIRBORNE EARLY WARNING
1 sqn with E-2C *Hawkeye*
SEARCH & RESCUE
1 unit with AW139
TRANSPORT
1 sqn with An-74TK-200A
1 sqn with C-130H/C-130H-30 *Hercules*
1 sqn with C295M
1 sqn with DHC-5D *Buffalo*
1 sqn with B-707-366C; B-737-100; Beech 200 *Super King Air*; *Falcon* 20; Gulfstream III; Gulfstream IV; Gulfstream IV-SP
TRAINING
1 sqn with *Alpha Jet**
1 sqn with DHC-5 *Buffalo*

3 sqn with EMB-312 *Tucano*
1 sqn with Grob 115EG
ε6 sqn with K-8 *Karakorum**
1 sqn with L-39 *Albatros*; L-59E *Albatros**
ATTACK HELICOPTER
2 sqn with AH-64D *Apache*
1 sqn with Ka-52A *Hokum* B
2 sqn with SA-342K *Gazelle* (with HOT)
1 sqn with SA-342L *Gazelle*
TRANSPORT HELICOPTER
1 sqn with CH-47C/D *Chinook* 1 sqn with Mi-8
1 sqn with Mi-8/Mi-17-V1 *Hip*
1 sqn with S-70 *Black Hawk*; UH-60A/L *Black Hawk*
UAV
Some sqn with R4E-50 *Skyeye*; *Wing Loong* (GJ-1)
EQUIPMENT BY TYPE
AIRCRAFT 578 combat capable
FTR 62: 26 F-16A *Fighting Falcon*; 6 F-16B *Fighting Falcon*; ε30 J-7
FGA 313: 139 F-16C *Fighting Falcon*; 37 F-16D *Fighting Falcon*; 3 *Mirage* 2000B; 15 *Mirage* 2000C; 36 *Mirage* 5D/E; 12 *Mirage* 5E2; ε40 MiG-21 *Fishbed*/MiG-21U *Mongol* A; ε14 MiG-29M/M2 *Fulcrum*; 9 *Rafale* DM; 8 *Rafale* EM
ELINT 2 VC-130H *Hercules*
ISR 12: ε6 AT-802 *Air Tractor**; 6 *Mirage* 5R (5SDR)*
AEW&C 7 E-2C *Hawkeye*
TPT 80: **Medium** 24: 21 C-130H *Hercules*; 3 C-130H-30 *Hercules*; **Light** 45: 3 An-74TK-200A; 1 Beech 200 *King Air*; 4 Beech 1900 (ELINT); 4 Beech 1900C; 24 C295M; 9 DHC-5D *Buffalo* (being withdrawn) **PAX** 11: 1 B-707-366C; 3 *Falcon* 20; 2 Gulfstream III; 1 Gulfstream IV; 4 Gulfstream IV-SP
TRG 329: 36 *Alpha Jet**; 54 EMB-312 *Tucano*; 74 Grob 115EG; 120 K-8 *Karakorum**; 10 L-39 *Albatros*; 35 L-59E*
HELICOPTERS
ATK 57+: 45 AH-64D *Apache*; 12+ Ka-52A *Hokum* B
ASW 10 SH-2G *Super Seasprite* (opcon Navy)
ELINT 4 *Commando* Mk2E (ECM)
MRH 72: 2 AW139 (SAR); 65 SA342K *Gazelle* (some with HOT); 5 SA342L *Gazelle* (opcon Navy)
TPT 96: **Heavy** 19: 3 CH-47C *Chinook*; 16 CH-47D *Chinook*; **Medium** 77: 2 AS-61; 24 *Commando* (of which 3 VIP); 40 Mi-8T *Hip*; 3 Mi-17-1V *Hip*; 4 S-70 *Black Hawk* (VIP); 4 UH-60L *Black Hawk* (VIP)
TRG 17 UH-12E
UNMANNED AERIAL VEHICLES
CISR • **Heavy** 4+ *Wing Loong* (GJ-1)
ISR • **Medium** R4E-50 *Skyeye*
AIR LAUNCHED MISSILES
AAM • **IR** R-3 (AA-2 *Atoll*)‡; AIM-9M/P *Sidewinder*; R-550 *Magic*; 9M39 Igla-V; **IIR** *Mica* IR; **ARH** *Mica* RF; **SARH** AIM-7E/F/M *Sparrow*; R-530
ASM AGM-65A/D/F/G *Maverick*; AGM-114F/K *Hellfire*; AS-30L; HOT; AKD-10 (LJ-7); 9M120 *Ataka* (AT-9 *Spiral*-2)
AShM AGM-84L *Harpoon* Block II; AM39 *Exocet*;
ARM *Armat*; Kh-25MP (AS-12 *Kegler*)
BOMBS
Laser-guided GBU-10/12 *Paveway* II

Air Defence Command 80,000 conscript; 70,000 reservists (total 150,000)

FORCES BY ROLE
AIR DEFENCE
5 AD div (geographically based) (total: 12 SAM bty with M48 *Chaparral*, 12 radar bn, 12 ADA bde (total: 100 ADA bn), 12 SAM bty with MIM-23B I-*Hawk*, 14 SAM bty with *Crotale*, 18 AD bn with RIM-7M *Sea Sparrow* with *Skyguard*/GDF-003 with *Skyguard*, 110 SAM bn with S-125 *Pechora*-M (SA-3A *Goa*); 2K12 *Kub* (SA-6 *Gainful*); S-75M *Volkhov* (SA-2 *Guideline*))

EQUIPMENT BY TYPE
AIR DEFENCE
SAM 812+
Long-range S-300V4 (SA-23)
Medium-range 612+: 40+ *Buk*-M1-2/M2E (SA-11/SA-17); 78+ MIM-23B I-*Hawk*; 282 S-75M *Volkhov* (SA-2 *Guideline*); 212+ S-125 *Pechora*-M (SA-3A *Goa*)
Short-range 150+: 56+ 2K12 *Kub* (SA-6 *Gainful*); 10 9K331M *Tor*-M1 (SA-15 *Gauntlet*); 24+ *Crotale*; 80 RIM-7M *Sea Sparrow* with *Skyguard*
Point-defence 50+ M48 *Chaparral*
GUNS 1,646+
SP • **23mm** 266+: 36+ *Sinai*-23 with *Ayn al-Saqr* MANPAD; 230 ZSU-23-4 *Shilka*
TOWED 1,380: **35mm** 80 GDF-003 with *Skyguard*; **57mm** 600 S-60; **85mm** 400 M-1939 (KS-12); **100mm** 300 KS-19

Paramilitary ε397,000 active

Central Security Forces ε325,000
Ministry of Interior; includes conscripts
ARMOURED FIGHTING VEHICLES
APC • APC (W) *Walid*
AUV *Sherpa Light Scout*

National Guard ε60,000
Lt wpns only
FORCES BY ROLE
MANOEUVRE
Other
8 paramilitary bde (cadre) (3 paramilitary bn)
EQUIPMENT BY TYPE
ARMOURED FIGHTING VEHICLES APC • APC (W) 250 *Walid*

Border Guard Forces ε12,000
Ministry of Interior; lt wpns only
FORCES BY ROLE
MANOEUVRE
Other
18 Border Guard regt

DEPLOYMENT

CENTRAL AFRICAN REPUBLIC: UN • MINUSCA 1,015; 9 obs; 1 inf bn; 1 tpt coy

DEMOCRATIC REPUBLIC OF THE CONGO: UN • MONUSCO 155; 16 obs; 1 SF coy

LIBERIA: UN • UNMIL 2 obs

MALI: UN • MINUSMA 327; 3 obs; 2 sy coy; 1 MP coy

SAUDI ARABIA: *Operation Restoring Hope* 6 F-16C *Fighting Falcon*

SOUTH SUDAN: UN • UNMISS 1; 2 obs

SUDAN: UN • UNAMID 854; 20 obs; 1 inf bn

WESTERN SAHARA: UN • MINURSO 18 obs

FOREIGN FORCES

Australia MFO (*Operation Mazurka*) 27
Canada MFO 68
Colombia MFO 275; 1 inf bn
Czech Republic MFO 18; 1 C295M
Fiji MFO 170; elm 1 inf bn
France MFO 1
Italy MFO 78; 3 PB
New Zealand MFO 26; 1 trg unit; 1 tpt unit
Norway MFO 3
United Kingdom MFO 2
United States MFO 454; elm 1 ARNG recce bn; 1 ARNG spt bn (1 EOD coy, 1 medical coy, 1 hel coy)
Uruguay MFO 41 1 engr/tpt unit

Iran IRN

Iranian Rial r		2017	2018	2019
GDP	r	14807tr	20218tr	
	US$	431bn	430bn	
per capita	US$	5,290	5,222	
Growth	%	3.7	-1.5	
Inflation	%	9.6	29.6	
Def bdgt	r	720tr	921tr	
	US$	21.0bn	19.6bn	
US$1=r		34378.43	47009.15	

Population 83,024,745

Ethnic groups: Persian 51%; Azeri 24%; Gilaki/Mazandarani 8%; Kurdish 7%; Arab 3%; Lur 2%; Baloch 2%; Turkman 2%

Age	0–14	15–19	20–24	25–29	30–64	65 plus
Male	12.4%	3.5%	3.7%	5.2%	23.4%	2.5%
Female	11.8%	3.3%	3.6%	4.9%	22.7%	2.9%

Capabilities

Iran is a major regional military power, due to a combination of asymmetric and other strategies, despite significant handicaps to its conventional capabilities because of international sanctions and restrictions on arms imports. Iran's armed forces consist of the regular armed forces, with a mix of ageing combat equipment, and the Islamic Revolutionary Guard Corps (IRGC), with a focus on asymmetric capabilities. Chiefly through the IRGC, Iran exerts significant military influence via a range of regional allies and proxies, in effect a form of expeditionary capability. It has also developed a ballistic-missile inventory. Iran has been largely isolated since 1979 though it has a key relationship with Syria and ties with Russia, including for defence sales. It has developed significant influence in weaker regional states like Lebanon, Iraq and Yemen through a network of non-state groups, such as Hizbullah and Houthi forces. The armed forces are numerous by regional standards and its personnel are reasonably well trained, with some benefiting from operational experience. The IRGC's Quds Force is a principal element of Iran's military power abroad, while elements of the Basij militia also play a foreign role. The regular navy has limited power-projection capabilities, while the IRGC navy is responsible for maritime security close to home. The armed forces struggle with an ageing inventory of primary combat equipment that ingenuity and asymmetric-warfare techniques can only partially offset. China and Russia are potentially major suppliers. Tehran procured from Russia what is believed to be the S-300PMU2 (SA-20 *Gargoyle*) long-range SAM system. In regional terms, Iran has a well-developed defence-industrial base, which has displayed the capacity to support and sustain equipment. Key sectors continue to develop, including missiles and guided weapons, but the defence industry is still incapable of meeting the need for modern weapons systems.

ACTIVE 523,000 (Army 350,000 Islamic Revolutionary Guard Corps 125,000 Navy 18,000 Air 30,000) **Paramilitary 40,000**

Armed Forces General Staff coordinates two parallel organisations: the regular armed forces and the Islamic Revolutionary Guard Corps

Conscript liability 18–21 months (reported, with variations depending on location in which service is performed)

RESERVE 350,000 (Army 350,000, ex-service volunteers)

ORGANISATIONS BY SERVICE

Army 130,000; 220,000 conscript (total 350,000)

FORCES BY ROLE
5 corps-level regional HQ
COMMAND
  1 cdo div HQ
  4 armd div HQ
  2 mech div HQ
  4 inf div HQ
SPECIAL FORCES
  1 cdo div (3 cdo bde)
  6 cdo bde
  1 SF bde
MANOEUVRE
  Armoured
  8 armd bde
  Mechanised
  14 mech bde
  Light
  12 inf bde
  Air Manoeuvre
  1 AB bde
  Aviation
  Some avn gp
COMBAT SUPPORT
  5 arty gp
EQUIPMENT BY TYPE

Totals incl those held by IRGC Ground Forces. Some equipment serviceability in doubt

ARMOURED FIGHTING VEHICLES
MBT 1,513+: 480 T-72S; 150 M60A1; 75+ T-62; 100 *Chieftain* Mk3/Mk5; 540 T-54/T-55/Type-59/*Safir*-74; 168 M47/M48; *Zulfiqar*
LT TK 80+: 80 *Scorpion*; *Towsan*
RECCE 35 EE-9 *Cascavel*
IFV 610+: 210 BMP-1; 400 BMP-2 with 9K111 *Fagot* (AT-4 *Spigot*); BMT-2 *Cobra*
APC 640+
   APC (T) 340: 140 *Boragh* with 9K111 *Fagot* (AT-4 *Spigot*); 200 M113
   APC (W) 300+: 300 BTR-50/BTR-60; *Rakhsh*

ENGINEERING & MAINTENANCE VEHICLES
ARV 20+: BREM-1 reported; 20 *Chieftain* ARV; M578; T-54/55 ARV reported
VLB 15: 15 *Chieftain* AVLB
MW *Taftan* 1

ANTI-TANK/ANTI-INFRASTRUCTURE
MSL • MANPATS 9K11 *Malyutka* (AT-3 *Sagger*/I-*Raad*); 9K111 *Fagot* (AT-4 *Spigot*); 9K111-1 *Konkurs* (AT-5 *Spandrel*/*Towsan*-1); *Saeqhe* 1; *Saeqhe* 2; *Toophan*; *Toophan* 2
RCL 200+: **75mm** M20; **82mm** B-10; **106mm** ε200 M40; **107mm** B-11

ARTILLERY 6,798+
SP 292+: **122mm** 60+: 60 2S1 *Gvozdika*; *Raad*-1 (*Thunder* 1); **155mm** 150+: 150 M109A1; *Raad*-2 (*Thunder* 2); **170mm** 30 M-1978; **175mm** 22 M107; **203mm** 30 M110
TOWED 2,030+; **105mm** 150: 130 M101A1; 20 M-56; **122mm** 640: 540 D-30; 100 Type-54 (M-30); **130mm** 985 M-46; **152mm** 30 D-20; **155mm** 205: 120 GHN-45; 70 M114; 15 Type-88 WAC-21; **203mm** 20 M115
MRL 1,476+: **107mm** 1,300: 700 Type-63; 600 HASEB *Fadjr* 1; **122mm** 157: 7 BM-11; 100 BM-21 *Grad*; 50 *Arash*/*Hadid*/*Noor*; **240mm** 19+: ε10 *Fadjr* 3; 9 M-1985; **330mm** *Fadjr* 5
MOR 3,000: **81mm**; **82mm**; **107mm** M30; **120mm** M-65

SURFACE-TO-SURFACE MISSILE LAUNCHERS
SRBM • Conventional ε30 CH-SS-8 (175 msl); *Shahin*-1/*Shahin*-2; *Nazeat*; *Oghab*

AIRCRAFT • TPT 17 **Light** 16: 10 Cessna 185; 2 F-27 *Friendship*; 4 *Turbo Commander* 690; **PAX** 1 *Falcon* 20

HELICOPTERS
ATK 50 AH-1J *Cobra*
TPT 167: **Heavy** ε20 CH-47C *Chinook*; **Medium** 69: 49 Bell 214; 20 Mi-171; **Light** 78: 68 Bell 205A (AB-205A); 10 Bell 206 *Jet Ranger* (AB-206)

UNMANNED AERIAL VEHICLES
HELICOPTERS
CISR • Medium *Shahed* 129
ISR • Medium *Mohajer* 3/4; **Light** *Mohajer* 2; *Ababil*

AIR DEFENCE
SAM
  Short-range FM-80
  Point-defence 9K36 *Strela*-3 (SA-14 *Gremlin*); 9K32 *Strela*-2 (SA-7 *Grail*)‡; *Misaq* 1 (QW-1 *Vanguard*); *Misaq* 2 (QW-18); 9K338 *Igla*-S (SA-24 *Grinch*) (reported); HN-5A
GUNS 1,122
  SP 180: **23mm** 100 ZSU-23-4; **57mm** 80 ZSU-57-2
  TOWED 942+: **14.5mm** ZPU-2; ZPU-4; **23mm** 300 ZU-23-2; **35mm** 92 GDF-002; **37mm** M-1939; **40mm** 50 L/70; **57mm** 200 S-60; **85mm** 300 M-1939

Islamic Revolutionary Guard Corps 125,000+

Islamic Revolutionary Guard Corps Ground Forces 100,000+
Controls Basij paramilitary forces. Lightly manned in peacetime. Primary role: internal security; secondary role: external defence, in conjunction with regular armed forces

FORCES BY ROLE
COMMAND
  31 provincial corps HQ (2 in Tehran)
SPECIAL FORCES
  3 spec ops div
MANOEUVRE
  Armoured
  2 armd div
  3 armd bde
  Light
  8+ inf div
  5+ inf bde
  Air Manoeuvre
  1 AB bde

Islamic Revolutionary Guard Corps Naval Forces 20,000+ (incl 5,000 Marines)
FORCES BY ROLE
COMBAT SUPPORT
  Some arty bty
  Some AShM bty with HY-2 (CH-SSC-3 *Seersucker*) AShM

EQUIPMENT BY TYPE
In addition to the vessels listed, the IRGC operates a substantial number of patrol boats with a full-load displacement below 10 tonnes, including ε40 *Boghammar*-class vessels and small *Bavar*-class wing-in-ground effect air vehicles

PATROL AND COASTAL COMBATANTS 126
  PBFG 56:
    5 C14 with 2 twin lnchr with C-701 (*Kosar*)/C-704 (*Nasr*) AShM
    10 Mk13 with 2 single lnchr with C-704 (*Nasr*) AShM, 2 single 324mm TT
    10 *Thondor* (PRC *Houdong*) with 2 twin lnchr with C-802A (*Ghader*) AShM, 2 twin AK230 CIWS
    25 *Peykaap* II (IPS-16 mod) with 2 single lnchr with C-701 (*Kosar*) AShM/C-704 (*Nasr*), 2 single 324mm TT
    6 *Zolfaghar* (*Peykaap* III/IPS-16 mod) with 2 single lnchr with C-701 (*Kosar*)/C-704 (*Nasr*) AShM
  PBFT 15 *Peykaap* I (IPS -16) with 2 single 324mm TT
  PBF 35: 15 *Kashdom* II; 10 *Tir* (IPS-18); ε10 *Pashe* (MIG-G-1900)
  PB ε20 *Ghaem*
AMPHIBIOUS
  LANDING SHIPS • LST 3 *Hormuz* 24 (*Hejaz* design for commercial use)
  LANDING CRAFT • LCT 2 *Hormuz* 21 (minelaying capacity)
LOGISTICS AND SUPPORT • AP 3 *Naser*
COASTAL DEFENCE • AShM C-701 (*Kosar*); C-704 (*Nasr*); C-802; HY-2 (CH-SSC-3 *Seersucker*)

HELICOPTERS
    MRH 5 Mi-171 *Hip*
    TPT • Light some Bell 206 (AB-206) *Jet Ranger*

Islamic Revolutionary Guard Corps Marines 5,000+

FORCES BY ROLE
MANOEUVRE
    Amphibious
    1 marine bde

Islamic Revolutionary Guard Corps Aerospace Force

Controls Iran's strategic-missile force
FORCES BY ROLE
MISSILE
    ε1 bde with *Shahab-1/-2*; *Qiam-1*
    ε1 bn with *Shahab-3*
EQUIPMENT BY TYPE
SURFACE-TO-SURFACE MISSILE LAUNCHERS
    MRBM • Conventional up to 50: *Shahab-3* (mobile & silo); some *Ghadr-1* (in test); some *Emad-1* (in test); some *Sajjil-2* (in devt); some *Khorramshahr* (in devt)
    SRBM • Conventional up to 100: some *Fateh 110*; Some *Khalij Fars* (*Fateh* 110 mod ASBM); some *Shahab-1/-2*; some *Qiam-1*; some *Zelzal*
UNMANNED AERIAL VEHICLES
    CISR • Medium
    Shahed 129

Navy 18,000

HQ at Bandar Abbas
EQUIPMENT BY TYPE
In addition to the vessels listed, the Iranian Navy operates a substantial number of patrol boats with a full-load displacement below 10 tonnes
SUBMARINES 21
    TACTICAL 21
        SSK 3 *Taregh* (RUS *Paltus* Project-877EKM) with 6 single 533mm TT
        SSC 1 *Fateh* (in trials)
        SSW 17: 16 *Qadir* with 2 single 533mm TT with *Valfajar* HWT (additional vessels in build); 1 *Nahang*
PATROL AND COASTAL COMBATANTS 67
    CORVETTES 6
        FSGM 1 *Jamaran* (UK Vosper Mk 5 derivative – 1 more undergoing sea trials) with 2 twin lnchr with C-802 (*Noor*) (CH-SS-N-8 *Saccade*) AShM, 2 single lnchr with SM-1 SAM, 2 triple 324mm Mk32 ASTT, 1 76mm gun, 1 hel landing platform
        FSG 5:
        3 *Alvand* (UK Vosper Mk 5) with 2 twin lnchr with C-802 (CH-SS-N-8 *Saccade*) AShM, 2 triple Mk32 324mm ASTT, 1 114mm gun
        2 *Bayandor* (US PF-103) with 2 twin lnchr with C-802 (CH-SS-N-8 *Saccade*) AShM, 2 triple 324mm Mk32 ASTT, 1 76mm gun
    PCFG 13 *Kaman* (FRA *Combattante* II) with 1–2 twin lnchr with C-802 (*Noor*) (CH-SS-N-8 *Saccade*) AShM, 1 76mm gun

    PBG 9:
        3 *Hendijan* with 2 twin lnchr with C-802 (*Noor*) (CH-SS-N-8 *Saccade*) AShM
        3 *Kayvan* with 2 single lnchr with C-704 (*Nasr*) AShM
        3 *Parvin* with 2 single lnchr with C-704 (*Nasr*) AShM
    PBFT 3 *Kajami* (semi-submersible) with 2 324mm TT
    PBF 1 MIL55
    PB 34: 9 C14; 9 *Hendijan*; 6 MkII; 10 MkIII
AMPHIBIOUS
    LANDING SHIPS 12
        LSM 3 *Farsi* (ROK) (capacity 9 tanks; 140 troops)
        LST 3 *Hengam* with 1 hel landing platform (capacity 9 tanks; 225 troops)
        LSL 6 *Fouque*
    LANDING CRAFT 11
        LCT 2
        LCU 1 *Liyan* 110
        UCAC 8: 2 *Wellington* Mk 4; 4 *Wellington* Mk 5; 2 *Tondar* (UK *Winchester*)
LOGISTICS AND SUPPORT 18
    AE 2 *Delvar*
    AFD 2 *Dolphin*
    AG 1 *Hamzah* with 2 single lnchr with C-802 (*Noor*) (CH-SS-N-8 *Saccade*) AShM
    AK 3 *Delvar*
    AORH 3: 2 *Bandar Abbas*; 1 *Kharg* with 1 76mm gun
    AWT 5: 4 *Kangan*; 1 *Delvar*
    AX 2 *Kialas*
COASTAL DEFENCE • AShM C-701 (*Kosar*); C-704 (*Nasr*); C-802 (*Noor*); C-802A (*Ghader*); *Ra'ad* (reported)

Marines 2,600

FORCES BY ROLE
MANOEUVRE
    Amphibious
    2 marine bde

Naval Aviation 2,600

EQUIPMENT BY TYPE
AIRCRAFT
    TPT 16: **Light** 13: 5 Do-228; 4 F-27 *Friendship*; 4 Turbo Commander 680; **PAX** 3 Falcon 20 (ELINT)
HELICOPTERS
    ASW ε10 SH-3D *Sea King*
    MCM 3 RH-53D *Sea Stallion*
    TPT • Light 17: 5 Bell 205A (AB-205A); 2 Bell 206 *Jet Ranger* (AB-206); 10 Bell 212 (AB-212)

Air Force 30,000 (incl 12,000 Air Defence)

FORCES BY ROLE
Serviceability probably about 60% for US ac types and about 80% for PRC/Russian ac. Includes IRGC AF equipment
FIGHTER
    1 sqn with F-7M *Airguard*; JJ-7*
    2 sqn with F-14 *Tomcat*
    2 sqn with MiG-29A/UB *Fulcrum*
FIGHTER/GROUND ATTACK
    1 sqn with *Mirage* F-1E; F-5E/F *Tiger* II
    5 sqn with F-4D/E *Phantom* II
    3 sqn with F-5E/F *Tiger* II

1 sqn (forming) with Su-22M4 *Fitter K*; Su-22UM-3K *Fitter G*
GROUND ATTACK
1 sqn with Su-24MK *Fencer D*
MARITIME PATROL
1 sqn with P-3F *Orion**
ISR
1 (det) sqn with RF-4E *Phantom II**
SEARCH & RESCUE
Some flt with Bell 214C (AB-214C)
TANKER/TRANSPORT
1 sqn with B-707; B-747; B-747F
TRANSPORT
1 sqn with B-707; *Falcon* 50; L-1329 *Jetstar*; Bell 412
2 sqn with C-130E/H *Hercules*
1 sqn with F-27 *Friendship*; *Falcon* 20
1 sqn with Il-76 *Candid*; An-140 (Iran-140 *Faraz*)
TRAINING
1 sqn with Beech F33A/C *Bonanza*
1 sqn with F-5B *Freedom Fighter*
1 sqn with PC-6
1 sqn with PC-7 *Turbo Trainer*
Some units with EMB-312 *Tucano*; MFI-17 *Mushshak*; TB-21 *Trinidad*; TB-200 *Tobago*
TRANSPORT HELICOPTER
1 sqn with CH-47 *Chinook*
Some units with Bell 206A *Jet Ranger* (AB-206A); *Shabaviz* 2-75; *Shabaviz* 2061
AIR DEFENCE
16 bn with MIM-23B I-*Hawk*/*Shahin*
4 bn with S-300PMU2 (SA-20 *Gargoyle*)
5 sqn with FM-80 (*Crotale*); *Rapier*; *Tigercat*; S-75M *Volkhov* (SA-2 *Guideline*); S-200 *Angara* (SA-5 *Gammon*); FIM-92A *Stinger*; 9K32 *Strela*-2 (SA-7 *Grail*)‡; 9K331 *Tor*-M1 (SA-15 *Gauntlet*)
EQUIPMENT BY TYPE
AIRCRAFT 336 combat capable
 FTR 184+: 20 F-5B *Freedom Fighter*; 55+ F-5E/F *Tiger II*
 24 F-7M *Airguard*; 43 F-14 *Tomcat*; 36 MiG-29A/U/UB *Fulcrum*; up to 6 *Azarakhsh* (reported)
 FGA 89: 64 F-4D/E *Phantom II*; 10 *Mirage* F-1E; up to 6 *Saegheh* (reported); up to 7 Su-22M4 *Fitter K*; 3+ Su-22UM-3K *Fitter G*
 ATK 39: 29 Su-24MK *Fencer D*; 7 Su-25K *Frogfoot* (status unknown); 3 Su-25UBK *Frogfoot* (status unknown)
 ASW 3 P-3F *Orion*
 ISR: 6+ RF-4E *Phantom II**
 TKR/TPT 3: ε1 B-707; ε2 B-747
 TPT 117: **Heavy** 12 Il-76 *Candid*; **Medium** ε19 C-130E/H *Hercules*; **Light** 75: 11 An-74TK-200; 5 An-140 (Iran-140 *Faraz*); 10 F-27 *Friendship*; 1 L-1329 *Jetstar*; 10 PC-6B *Turbo Porter*; 8 TB-21 *Trinidad*; 4 TB-200 *Tobago*; 3 *Turbo Commander* 680; 14 Y-7; 9 Y-12; **PAX** 11: 2 B-707; 1 B-747; 4 B-747F; 1 *Falcon* 20; 3 *Falcon* 50
 TRG 141: 25 Beech F33A/C *Bonanza*; 15 EMB-312 *Tucano*; 14 JJ-7*; 25 MFI-17 *Mushshak*; 12 *Parastu*; 15 PC-6; 35 PC-7 *Turbo Trainer*
HELICOPTERS
 MRH 2 Bell 412
 TPT 34+: **Heavy** 2+ CH-47 *Chinook*; **Medium** 30 Bell 214C (AB-214C); **Light** 2+: 2 Bell 206A *Jet Ranger* (AB-206A);

some *Shabaviz* 2-75 (indigenous versions in production); some *Shabaviz* 2061
AIR DEFENCE
 SAM 514+:
  Long-range 10 S-200 *Angara* (SA-5 *Gammon*); 32 S-300PMU2 (SA-20 *Gargoyle*)
  Medium-range 195+: 150+ MIM-23B I-*Hawk*/*Shahin*; 45 S-75 *Dvina* (SA-2 *Guideline*);
  Short-range 279: 250 FM-80 (*Crotale*); 29 9K331 *Tor*-M1 (SA-15 *Gauntlet*)
  Point-defence 30+: 30 *Rapier*; FIM-92 *Stinger*; 9K32 *Strela*-2 (SA-7 *Grail*)‡
 GUNS • TOWED 23mm ZU-23-2; **35mm** GDF-002
AIR-LAUNCHED MISSILES
 AAM • IR PL-2A‡; PL-7; R-60 (AA-8 *Aphid*); R-73 (AA-11 *Archer*); AIM-9J *Sidewinder*; **IR/SARH** R-27 (AA-10 *Alamo*); **SARH** AIM-7E-2 *Sparrow*; **ARH** AIM-54 *Phoenix*†
 ASM AGM-65A *Maverick*; Kh-25 (AS-10 *Karen*); Kh-25ML (AS-10 *Karen*); Kh-29 (AS-14 *Kedge*)
 AShM C-801K
 ARM Kh-58 (AS-11 *Kilter*)
BOMBS
 Electro-optical guided GBU-87/B *Qassed*

Air Defence Command

Established to coordinate army, air-force and IRGC air-defence assets. Precise composition unclear

Paramilitary 40,000–60,000

Law-Enforcement Forces 40,000–60,000 (border and security troops); 450,000 on mobilisation (incl conscripts)

Part of armed forces in wartime
EQUIPMENT BY TYPE
PATROL AND COASTAL COMBATANTS • PB ε90
AIRCRAFT • TPT • Light 2+: 2 An-140; some Cessna 185/Cessna 310
HELICOPTERS • TPT • Light ε24 AB-205 (Bell 205)/AB-206 (Bell 206) *Jet Ranger*

Basij Resistance Force ε600,000 on mobilisation

Paramilitary militia with claimed membership of 12.6 million; ε600,000 combat capable
FORCES BY ROLE
MANOEUVRE
 Other
 2,500 militia bn(-) (claimed, limited permanent membership)

Cyber

Iran has a well-developed capacity for cyber operations. It has a well-educated and computer-literate young population. The Stuxnet incident in 2010 is reported to have been a turning point in Iran's approach to cyber capabilities. In 2011–12, Tehran established a Joint Chiefs of Staff Cyber Command with emphasis on thwarting attacks against Iranian nuclear facilities and coordinating national cyber warfare and information security. In September 2015,

Ayatollah Ali Khamenei appointed members to a Supreme Council for Cyberspace, reportedly a policymaking and supervisory body. The IRGC has its own Cyber Defence Command; IRGC civilian business interests will aid its activities in this area. The precise relationship of groups such as the 'Iranian Cyber Army' to regime and military organisations is unclear, but the former has launched hacking attacks against a number of foreign organisations. There are continued reports of increasing investment in cyber capabilities, used not only for propaganda and intelligence exploitation but also as a means for Iran to attempt to offset its conventional military weakness vis-à-vis its neighbours and the US, and to exfiltrate commercial data. On 23 March 2018, the US Department of Justice indicted nine Iranian employees of the Tehran-based Mabna Institute for a multi-year cyber-espionage campaign against US universities, which they allegedly carried out on behalf of the IRGC.

DEPLOYMENT

GULF OF ADEN AND SOMALI BASIN: Navy: 1 FSG; 1 AORH

SUDAN: UN • UNAMID 1; 3 obs

SYRIA: 3,000

Iraq IRQ

Iraqi Dinar D		2017	2018	2019
GDP	D	227tr	273tr	
	US$	192bn	231bn	
per capita	US$	4,950	5,793	
Growth	%	-2.1	1.5	
Inflation	%	0.1	2.0	
Def bdgt [a]	D	22.8tr	204tr	
	US$	19.3bn	17.3bn	
FMA (US$)	US$	250m	0m	
US$1=D		1182.00	1182.00	

[a] Defence and security budget

Population 40,194,216

Ethnic and religious groups: Arab 75–80%, of which Shia Muslim 55%, Sunni Muslim 45%; Kurdish 20–25%

Age	0–14	15–19	20–24	25–29	30–64	65 plus
Male	19.9%	5.4%	4.5%	3.9%	15.3%	1.6%
Female	19.1%	5.2%	4.4%	3.8%	15.1%	2.0%

Capabilities

The armed forces' capabilities and morale have improved since the collapse of several divisions in the face of the ISIS advance in the north in 2014. The recapture of Mosul demonstrated incremental growth in capability, in terms of combat power and tactics, as the Iraqi armed forces adapted to fight ISIS in urban areas. The future of the Kurdish Peshmerga forces and the Popular Mobilisation Forces militias, particularly questions over their integration into a national-security framework, remains an issue for Baghdad. The government's most critical security relationship is with the US, and other participants in the international counter-ISIS coalition. The level of attrition among Iraqi forces has caused concern, particularly among the well-regarded Counter-Terrorism Service, which is often used as a spearhead force. The US has been engaged in a training effort, not least in regenerating air-force capabilities. NATO announced a new training mission, starting in late 2018. A key focus is adapting Iraqi forces to address a developing ISIS insurgency beyond the urban areas. Iraqi forces appear to have improved their ability to conduct complex operations, including at range within the country. However, there has been a reliance on US air support and coalition ISR assistance, suggesting continuing capability limitations in this area. Significant logistical shortcomings remain, including logistics support and intelligence integration. The inventory comprises Soviet-era and Russian equipment combined with newer European- and US-sourced platforms. A major enhancement has been the delivery and integration of F-16 combat aircraft. The long-standing ambition to purchase attack helicopters has been fulfilled. Barring military maintenance facilities, the Iraqi defence industry has only a limited ability to manufacture light weapons and ammunition.

ACTIVE 64,000 (Army 54,000 Navy 3,000 Air 4,000 Air Defence 3,000) **Paramilitary 145,000**

ORGANISATIONS BY SERVICE

Army 54,000

Due to ongoing conflict with ISIS insurgents, there have been significant personnel and equipment losses in the Iraqi Army. Many formations are now under-strength. Military capability has been bolstered by the activity of Shia militias and Kurdish Peshmerga forces

FORCES BY ROLE
SPECIAL FORCES
  3 SF bde
  1 ranger bn
MANOEUVRE
  Armoured
  1 (9th) armd div (2 armd bde, 2 mech bde, 1 engr bn, 1 sigs regt, 1 log bde)
  Mechanised
  3 (5th, 8th & 10th) mech div (4 mech inf bde, 1 engr bn, 1 sigs regt, 1 log bde)
  1 (7th) mech div (2 mech inf bde, 1 inf bde, 1 engr bn, 1 sigs regt, 1 log bde)
  Light
  1 (6th) mot div (3 mot inf bde, 1 inf bde, 1 engr bn, 1 sigs regt, 1 log bde)
  1 (14th) mot div (2 mot inf bde, 3 inf bde, 1 engr bn, 1 sigs regt, 1 log bde)
  1 (1st) inf div (2 inf bde)
  1 (11th) inf div (3 lt inf bde, 1 engr bn, 1 sigs regt, 1 log bde)
  1 (15th) inf div (5 inf bde)
  1 (16th) inf div (2 inf bde)
  1 (17th Cdo) inf div (4 inf bde, 1 engr bn, 1 sigs regt, 1 log bde)
  1 inf bde
  Other
  1 (PM SF) sy div (3 inf bde)
HELICOPTER
  1 atk hel sqn with Mi-28NE *Havoc*
  1 atk hel sqn with Mi-35M *Hind*

1 sqn with Bell 205 (UH-1H *Huey* II)
3 atk hel sqn with Bell T407; H135M
3 sqn with Mi-17 *Hip* H; Mi-171Sh
1 ISR sqn with SA342M *Gazelle*
2 trg sqn with Bell 206; OH-58C *Kiowa*
1 trg sqn with Bell 205 (UH-1H *Huey* II)
1 trg sqn with Mi-17 *Hip*

EQUIPMENT BY TYPE
ARMOURED FIGHTING VEHICLES
  MBT 393+: ε100 M1A1 *Abrams*; 168+ T-72M/M1; ε50 T-55; 75 T-90S
  RECCE 453: ε400 *Akrep*; 18 BRDM 2; 35 EE-9 *Cascavel*;
  IFV 240+: ε80 BMP-1; some BMP-3; ε60 BTR-4 (inc variants); 100 BTR-80A
  APC 2,092+
    APC (T) 900: ε500 M113A2/*Talha*; ε400 MT-LB
    PPV 1,192+: 12 *Barracuda*; 250 *Caiman*; ε500 *Dzik-3*; ε400 ILAV *Badger*; *Mamba*; 30 *Maxxpro*
    AUV M-ATV
ENGINEERING & MAINTENANCE VEHICLES
  ARV 222+: 180 BREM; 35+ M88A1/2; 7 *Maxxpro* ARV; T-54/55 ARV; Type-653; VT-55A
NBC VEHICLES 20 *Fuchs* NBC
ANTI-TANK/ANTI-INFRASTRUCTURE
  MSL • **MANPATS** 9K135 *Kornet* (AT-14 *Spriggan*) (reported)
ARTILLERY 1,085+
  SP 72+: **152mm** 18+ Type-83; **155mm** 30: 6 M109A1; 24 M109A5
  TOWED 60+: **130mm** M-46/Type-59; **152mm** D-20; Type-83; **155mm** ε60 M198
  MRL 3+: **122mm** some BM-21 *Grad*; **220mm** 3+ TOS-1A
  MOR 950+: **81mm** ε500 M252; **120mm** ε450 M120; **240mm** M-240
HELICOPTERS
  ATK 28: 11 Mi-28NE *Havoc*; 4 Mi-28UB *Havoc*; 13 Mi-35M *Hind*
  MRH 63+: 4+ SA342 *Gazelle*; 17 Bell IA407; 23 H135M; ε19 Mi-17 *Hip* H/Mi-171Sh
  ISR 10 OH-58C *Kiowa*
  TPT • **Light** 44: 16 Bell 205 (UH-1H *Huey* II); 10 Bell 206B3 *Jet Ranger*; ε18 Bell T407
UNMANNED AERIAL VEHICLES • **CISR Heavy** CH-4
AIR-LAUNCHED MISSILES • **ASM** 9K114 *Shturm* (AT-6 *Spiral*); AR-1; *Ingwe*

Navy 3,000
EQUIPMENT BY TYPE
PATROL AND COASTAL COMBATANTS 32
  PCO 2 *Al Basra* (US *River Hawk*)
  PCC 4 *Fateh* (ITA *Diciotti*)
  PB 20: 12 Swiftships 35; 5 *Predator* (PRC 27m); 3 *Al Faw*
  PBR 6: 2 Type-200; 4 Type-2010

Marines 1,000
FORCES BY ROLE
MANOEUVRE
  Amphibious
    2 mne bn

Air Force ε4,000
FORCES BY ROLE
FIGHTER/GROUND ATTACK
  1 sqn with F-16C/D *Fighting Falcon*
GROUND ATTACK
  1 sqn with Su-25/Su-25K/Su-25UBK *Frogfoot*
  1 sqn with L-159A; L-159T1
ISR
  1 sqn with CH-2000 *Sama*; SB7L-360 *Seeker*
  1 sqn with Cessna 208B *Grand Caravan*; Cessna AC-208B *Combat Caravan*
  1 sqn with Beech 350 *King Air*
TRANSPORT
  1 sqn with An-32B *Cline*
  1 sqn with C-130E/J-30 *Hercules*
TRAINING
  1 sqn with Cessna 172, Cessna 208B
  1 sqn with *Lasta*-95
  1 sqn with T-6A
  1 sqn with T-50IQ *Golden Eagle**
EQUIPMENT BY TYPE
AIRCRAFT 65 combat capable
  FGA 21: 18 F-16C *Fighting Falcon*; 3 F-16D *Fighting Falcon*;
  ATK 30: 10 L-159A; 1 L-159T1; ε19 Su-25/Su-25K/Su-25UBK *Frogfoot*
  ISR 10: 2 Cessna AC-208B *Combat Caravan**; 2 SB7L-360 *Seeker*; 6 Beech 350ER *King Air*
  TPT 29: **Medium** 15: 3 C-130E *Hercules*; 6 C-130J-30 *Hercules*; 6 An-32B *Cline* (of which 2 combat capable); **Light** 14: 1 Beech 350 *King Air*; 5 Cessna 208B *Grand Caravan*; 8 Cessna 172
  TRG 45+: 8 CH-2000 *Sama*; 10+ *Lasta*-95; 15 T-6A; 12 T-50IQ *Golden Eagle**
AIR-LAUNCHED MISSILES
  AAM • **IR** AIM-9L *Sidewinder*; AIM-9M *Sidewinder*
  ASM AGM-114 *Hellfire*
BOMBS
  Laser-Guided GBU-12 *Paveway* II
  INS/GPS-guided FT-9

Air Defence Command ε3,000
FORCES BY ROLE
AIR DEFENCE
  1 bn with 96K6 *Pantsir*-S1 (SA-22 *Greyhound*)
  1 bn with M1097 *Avenger*
  1 bn with 9K338 *Igla*-S (SA-24 *Grinch*)
  1 bn with ZU-23-2; S-60
EQUIPMENT BY TYPE
AIR DEFENCE
  SAM
    Short-range 24 96K6 *Pantsir*-S1 (SA-22 *Greyhound*)
    Point-defence M1097 *Avenger*; 9K338 *Igla*-S (SA-24 *Grinch*)
  GUNS • **TOWED 23mm** ZU-23-2; **57mm** S-60

Paramilitary ε145,000

Iraqi Federal Police ε36,000

Border Enforcement ε9,000

Militias ε100,000

Popular Mobilisation Forces include: Kata'ib Sayyid al-Shuhada Brigade; Kata'ib Hizbullah; Badr Brigades; Peace Brigades and Imam Ali Battalions

FOREIGN FORCES

Australia Operation Inherent Resolve (Okra) 380
Belgium Operation Inherent Resolve (Valiant Phoenix) 30
Canada Operation Inherent Resolve (Impact) 370; 1 SF gp; 1 med unit; 1 hel flt with 4 Bell 412 (CH-146 Griffon)
Czech Republic Operation Inherent Resolve 30
Denmark Operation Inherent Resolve 190; 1 SF gp; 1 trg team
Estonia Operation Inherent Resolve 7
Fiji UNAMI 165; 2 sy unit
Finland Operation Inherent Resolve 100; 1 trg unit
France Operation Inherent Resolve (Chammal) 500; 1 SF gp; 1 trg unit; 1 SP arty bty with 4 CAESAR
Germany Operation Inherent Resolve 110; some trg unit
Hungary Operation Inherent Resolve 164
Italy Operation Inherent Resolve (Prima Parthica) 845; 1 inf regt; 1 trg unit; 1 hel sqn with 4 NH90
Latvia Operation Inherent Resolve 6
Nepal UNAMI 77; 1 sy unit
Netherlands Operation Inherent Resolve 150; 3 trg units
New Zealand Operation Inherent Resolve 143; 1 trg unit
Norway Operation Inherent Resolve 60; 1 trg unit
Poland Operation Inherent Resolve 130
Portugal Operation Inherent Resolve 34
Romania Operation Inherent Resolve 50
Slovenia Operation Inherent Resolve 6
Spain Operation Inherent Resolve 350; 2 trg units
Sweden Operation Inherent Resolve 66
Turkey Army 2,000; 1 armd BG
United Kingdom Operation Inherent Resolve (Shader) 400; 2 inf bn(-); 1 engr sqn(-)
United States Operation Inherent Resolve 5,000; 1 mtn div HQ; 1 cav bde(-); 1 EOD pl; 1 atk hel sqn with AH-64D Apache

Israel ISR

New Israeli Shekel NS		2017	2018	2019
GDP	NS	1.26tr	1.31tr	
	US$	351bn	366bn	
per capita	US$	40,273	41,180	
Growth	%	3.3	3.6	
Inflation	%	0.2	0.9	
Def bdgt	NS	68.0bn	66.3bn	
	US$	18.9bn	18.5bn	
FMA (US)	US$	3.2bn	3.1bn	3.3bn
US$1=NS		3.60	3.58	

Population	8,424,904					
Age	0–14	15–19	20–24	25–29	30–64	65 plus
Male	13.9%	4.1%	3.8%	3.6%	19.5%	5.2%
Female	13.3%	4.0%	3.6%	3.5%	19.0%	6.4%

Capabilities

The Israel Defense Forces (IDF) are organised for territorial defence, short-term interventions in neighbouring states and limited regional power projection. Israel is widely believed to possess a nuclear-weapons capability. The IDF began a five-year defence programme (Plan Gideon) in 2015, focusing resources on its regular front-line combat formations. Many reserve units have been disbanded and older equipment retired from service. The US remains Israel's key defence partner, as well as a significant source of funding, and is instrumental in several of the IDF's equipment programmes, particularly in missile defence and combat aviation. Israel also maintains discreet ties with a number of Arab states. Personnel quality and training are generally high, despite the IDF's continuing reliance on national service. Ground-forces training is being overhauled, with new training centres under construction. The IDF has no requirement for out-of-area deployments and its logistics capabilities are limited to sustaining operations within Israel itself or in immediate neighbouring territories. The largely asymmetric nature of the threats faced by the IDF in recent years has focused modernisation efforts on force-protection, missile-defence and precision-strike capabilities. Israel maintains a broad defence-industrial base, with world-class capabilities in several areas, notably armoured vehicles, unmanned systems, guided weapons and cyber security.

ACTIVE 169,500 (Army 126,000 Navy 9,500 Air 34,000) **Paramilitary 8,000**

Conscript liability Officers 48 months, other ranks 32 months, women 24 months (Jews and Druze only; Christians, Circassians and Muslims may volunteer)

RESERVE 465,000 (Army 400,000 Navy 10,000 Air 55,000)

Annual trg as cbt reservists to age 40 (some specialists to age 54) for male other ranks, 38 (or marriage/pregnancy) for women

ORGANISATIONS BY SERVICE

Strategic Forces

Israel is widely believed to have a nuclear capability – delivery means include F-15I and F-16I ac, *Jericho* 2 IRBM and, reportedly, *Dolphin/Tanin*-class SSKs with LACM

FORCES BY ROLE
SURFACE-TO-SURFACE MISSILE
3 IRBM sqn with *Jericho* 2
EQUIPMENT BY TYPE
SURFACE-TO-SURFACE MISSILE LAUNCHERS
IRBM • Nuclear: ε24 *Jericho* 2

Strategic Defences
FORCES BY ROLE
AIR DEFENCE
3 bty with *Arrow* 2 ATBM with *Green Pine/Super Green Pine* radar and *Citrus Tree* command post
10 bty with *Iron Dome* (incl reserve bty)
6 bty with MIM-104C *Patriot* PAC-2
2 bty with *David's Sling*

Space
EQUIPMENT BY TYPE
SATELLITES 9
COMMUNICATIONS 3 *Amos*
ISR 6: 1 EROS; 4 *Ofeq* (7, 9, 10 & 11); 1 TecSAR-1 (*Polaris*)

Army 26,000; 100,000 conscript (total 126,000)
Organisation and structure of formations may vary according to op situations. Equipment includes that required for reserve forces on mobilisation
FORCES BY ROLE
COMMAND
3 (regional comd) corps HQ
2 armd div HQ
5 (territorial) inf div HQ
1 (home defence) comd HQ
SPECIAL FORCES
3 SF bn
1 spec ops bde (4 spec ops unit)
MANOEUVRE
Reconnaissance
1 indep recce bn
Armoured
3 armd bde (1 armd recce coy, 3 armd bn, 1 AT coy, 1 cbt engr bn)
Mechanised
3 mech inf bde (3 mech inf bn, 1 cbt spt bn, 1 sigs coy)
1 mech inf bde (5 mech inf bn)
1 indep mech inf bn
Light
2 indep inf bn
Air Manoeuvre
1 para bde (3 para bn, 1 cbt spt bn, 1 sigs coy)
Other
1 armd trg bde (3 armd bn)
COMBAT SUPPORT
3 arty bde
3 engr bn
1 EOD coy
1 CBRN bn
1 int bde (3 int bn)
1 SIGINT unit
2 MP bn

Reserves 400,000+ on mobilisation
FORCES BY ROLE
COMMAND
3 armd div HQ
1 AB div HQ
MANOEUVRE
Armoured
9 armd bde
Mechanised
8 mech inf bde
Light
16 (territorial/regional) inf bde
Air Manoeuvre
4 para bde
Mountain
1 mtn inf bn
COMBAT SUPPORT
5 arty bde
COMBAT SERVICE SUPPORT
6 log unit
EQUIPMENT BY TYPE
ARMOURED FIGHTING VEHICLES
MBT 490: ε160 *Merkava* MkIII; ε330 *Merkava* MkIV; ε370 *Merkava* MkII; ε570 *Merkava* MkIII; ε180 *Merkava* MkIV all in store)
RECCE ε300 RBY-1 RAMTA
APC • APC (T) 1,300: ε200 *Namer*; ε200 *Achzarit* (modified T-55 chassis); 500 M113A2; ε400 *Nagmachon* (*Centurion* chassis); *Nakpadon* (5,000 M113A1/A2 in store)
AUV 100 *Ze'ev*
ENGINEERING & MAINTENANCE VEHICLES
AEV D9R; *Namer*; *Puma*
ARV *Centurion* Mk2; *Eyal*; *Nemmera*; M88A1; M113 ARV
VLB *Alligator* MAB; M48/60; MTU
NBC VEHICLES ε8 TPz-1 *Fuchs* NBC
ANTI-TANK/ANTI-INFRASTRUCTURE • MSL
SP M113 with *Spike*; *Tamuz* (*Spike* NLOS)
MANPATS IMI MAPATS; *Spike* MR/LR/ER
ARTILLERY 530
SP 250: **155mm** 250 M109A5 (**155mm** 148 Soltam L-33; 30 M109A1; 50 M-50; **175mm** 36 M107; **203mm** 36 M110 all in store)
TOWED (**122mm** 5 D-30; **130mm** 100 M-46; **155mm** 171: 40 M-46 mod; 50 M-68/M-71; 81 M-839P/M-845P all in store)
MRL 30: **227mm** 30 M270 MLRS; **306mm** IMI *Lynx* (**122mm** 58 BM-21 *Grad*; **160mm** 50 LAR-160; **227mm** 18 M270 MLRS; **240mm** 36 BM-24; **290mm** 20 LAR-290 all in store)
MOR 250: **81mm** 250 (**81mm** 1,100; **120mm** 650; **160mm** 18 Soltam M-66 all in store)
SURFACE-TO-SURFACE MISSILE LAUNCHERS
IRBM • Nuclear ε24 *Jericho* 2
SRBM • Dual-capable (7 *Lance* in store)
AIR DEFENCE • SAM • Point-defence 20 *Machbet*; FIM-92 *Stinger*

Navy 7,000; 2,500 conscript (total 9,500)
EQUIPMENT BY TYPE
SUBMARINES • TACTICAL
  SSK 5:
    3 *Dolphin* (GER HDW design) with 6 single 533mm TT with UGM-84C *Harpoon* AShM/DM2A3/4 HWT/*Kaved* HWT, 4 single 650mm TT
    2 *Tanin* (GER HDW design with AIP) with 6 single 533mm TT with UGM-84C *Harpoon* AShM/DM2A3/4 HWT/*Kaved* HWT, 4 single 650mm TT
PATROL AND COASTAL COMBATANTS 45
  CORVETTES • FSGHM 3:
    2 *Eilat* (*Sa'ar* 5) with 2 quad lnchr with RGM-84 *Harpoon* AShM/*Gabriel* AShM, 1 32-cell VLS with *Barak*-1 SAM (being upgraded to *Barak*-8), 2 triple 324mm TT with Mk 46 LWT, 1 Mk 15 *Phalanx* CIWS (capacity 1 AS565SA *Panther* ASW hel)
    1 *Eilat* (*Sa'ar* 5) with 2 quad lnchr with RGM-84 *Harpoon* AShM/*Gabriel* AShM, 1 32-cell VLS with *Barak*-8 SAM, 2 triple 324mm TT with Mk 46 LWT, 1 Mk 15 *Phalanx* CIWS (capacity 1 AS565SA *Panther* ASW hel)
  PCGM 8 *Hetz* (*Sa'ar* 4.5) with 2 quad lnchr with RGM-84 *Harpoon* AShM (can also be fitted with up to 6 single lnchr with *Gabriel* II AShM), 2 8-cell Mk56 VLS with *Barak*-1 SAM, (can be fitted with 2 triple 324mm Mk32 TT with Mk46 LWT), 1 Mk 15 *Phalanx* CWIS, 1 76mm gun
  PBF 34: 5 *Shaldag* with 1 *Typhoon* CIWS; 3 *Stingray*; 9 *Super Dvora* Mk I (SSM & TT may be fitted); 4 *Super Dvora* Mk II (SSM & TT may be fitted); 6 *Super Dvora* Mk II-I (SSM & TT may be fitted); 4 *Super Dvora* Mk III (SSM & TT may be fitted); 3 *Super Dvora* Mk III with 1 *Typhoon* CIWS (SSM may be fitted)
AMPHIBIOUS • LANDING CRAFT • LCVP 2 *Manta*
LOGISTICS AND SUPPORT 3
  AG 2 *Bat Yam* (ex-GER Type-745)
  AX 1 *Queshet*

Naval Commandos ε300
FORCES BY ROLE
SPECIAL FORCES
  1 cdo unit

Air Force 34,000
Responsible for Air and Space Coordination
FORCES BY ROLE
FIGHTER & FIGHTER/GROUND ATTACK
  1 sqn with F-15A/B/D *Eagle*
  1 sqn with F-15B/C/D *Eagle*
  1 sqn with F-15I *Ra'am*
  6 sqn with F-16C/D *Fighting Falcon*
  4 sqn with F-16I *Sufa*
  1 sqn with F-35I *Adir*
ANTI-SUBMARINE WARFARE
  1 sqn with AS565SA *Panther* (missions flown by IAF but with non-rated aircrew)
ELECTRONIC WARFARE
  2 sqn with RC-12D *Guardrail*; Beech A36 *Bonanza* (*Hofit*); Beech 200 *King Air*; Beech 200T *King Air*; Beech 200CT *King Air*

AIRBORNE EARLY WARNING & CONTROL
  1 sqn with Gulfstream G550 *Eitam*; Gulfstream G550 *Shavit*
TANKER/TRANSPORT
  1 sqn with C-130E/H *Hercules*; KC-130H *Hercules*
  1 sqn with C-130J-30 *Hercules*
  1 sqn with KC-707
TRAINING
  1 OPFOR sqn with F-16C/D *Fighting Falcon*
  1 sqn with M-346 *Master* (*Lavi*)
ATTACK HELICOPTER
  1 sqn with AH-64A *Apache*
  1 sqn with AH-64D *Apache*
TRANSPORT HELICOPTER
  2 sqn with CH-53D *Sea Stallion*
  2 sqn with S-70A *Black Hawk*; UH-60A *Black Hawk*
  1 medevac unit with CH-53D *Sea Stallion*
UAV
  1 ISR sqn with *Hermes* 450
  1 ISR sqn with *Heron* (*Shoval*); *Heron* TP (*Eitan*)
  1 ISR sqn with *Heron* (*Shoval*) (MP role)
AIR DEFENCE
  3 bty with *Arrow* 2
  10 bty with *Iron Dome*
  6 bty with MIM-104C *Patriot* PAC-2
  2 bty with *David's Sling*
SPECIAL FORCES
  1 SF unit
  1 spec ops unit
EQUIPMENT BY TYPE
AIRCRAFT 352 combat capable
  FTR 58: 16 F-15A *Eagle*; 6 F-15B *Eagle*; 17 F-15C *Eagle*; 19 F-15D *Eagle*
  FGA 264: 25 F-15I *Ra'am*; 78 F-16C *Fighting Falcon*; 49 F-16D *Fighting Falcon*; 98 F-16I *Sufa*; 14 F-35I *Adir*
  ISR 6 RC-12D *Guardrail*
  ELINT 4: 1 EC-707; 3 Gulfstream G550 *Shavit*
  AEW 4: 2 B-707 *Phalcon*; 2 Gulfstream G550 *Eitam* (1 more on order)
  TKR/TPT 11: 4 KC-130H *Hercules*; 7 KC-707
  TPT 62: **Medium** 15: 5 C-130E *Hercules*; 6 C-130H *Hercules*; 4 C-130J-30 *Hercules*; **Light** 47: 3 AT-802 *Air Tractor*; 9 Beech 200 *King Air*; 8 Beech 200T *King Air*; 5 Beech 200CT *King Air*; 22 Beech A36 *Bonanza* (*Hofit*)
  TRG 67: 17 Grob G-120; 30 M-346 *Master* (*Lavi*)*; 20 T-6A
HELICOPTERS
  ATK 43: 26 AH-64A *Apache*; 17 AH-64D *Apache* (*Sarat*)
  ASW 7 AS565SA *Panther* (missions flown by IAF but with non-rated aircrew)
  ISR 12 OH-58B *Kiowa*
  TPT 81: **Heavy** 26 CH-53D *Sea Stallion*; **Medium** 49: 39 S-70A *Black Hawk*; 10 UH-60A *Black Hawk*; **Light** 6 Bell 206 *Jet Ranger*
UNMANNED AERIAL VEHICLES
  ISR 3+: **Heavy** 3+: *Heron* (*Shoval*); 3 *Heron* TP (*Eitan*); RQ-5A *Hunter*; **Medium** *Hermes* 450; *Hermes* 900 (22+ *Searcher* MkII in store); **Light** *Harpy* (anti-radiation UAV)
AIR DEFENCE
  SAM 54+:
    Long-range MIM-104C *Patriot* PAC-2; **Medium-range** 24 *Arrow* 2; some *David's Sling*; **Short-range** ε30 *Iron Dome*

GUNS 920
  SP 165: **20mm** 105 M163 *Machbet Vulcan*; **23mm** 60 ZSU-23-4
  TOWED 755: **23mm** 150 ZU-23-2; **20mm/37mm** 455 M167 *Vulcan* towed 20mm/M-1939 towed 37mm/TCM-20 towed 20mm; **40mm** 150 L/70
AIR-LAUNCHED MISSILES
  AAM • IR AIM-9 *Sidewinder*; *Python* 4; IIR *Python* 5; ARH AIM-120C AMRAAM
  ASM AGM-114 *Hellfire*; AGM-62B *Walleye*; AGM-65 *Maverick*; *Delilah* AL; *Popeye* I/*Popeye* II; *Spike* NLOS
BOMBS
  IIR guided *Opher*
  Laser-guided *Griffin*; *Lizard*; *Paveway* II
  INS/GPS guided GBU-31 JDAM; GBU-39 Small Diameter Bomb (*Barad Had*); *Spice*

Airfield Defence 3,000 active (15,000 reservists)

Paramilitary ε8,000

Border Police ε8,000

Cyber

Israel has a substantial capacity for cyber operations. In early 2012, the National Cyber Bureau was created in the prime minister's office to develop technology, human resources and international collaboration. It is reported that the IDF's 'Unit 8200' is responsible for ELINT and some cyber operations. In 2012, according to the IDF, the C4I Directorate and Unit 8200 were combined into a new task force, charged with 'developing offensive capabilities and operations'. Specialist training courses exist, including the four-month *Cyber Shield* activity. In April 2016, the National Cyber Defense Authority was created, consolidating cyber defences into one body. Although the IDF's Gideon plan called for a Joint Cyber Command, in January 2017 the IDF announced it would not take this step. The cyber-defence unit of the C4I Directorate and Unit 8200 work together in tackling cyber threats. Civil agencies reportedly have responsibility for cyber threats against critical national infrastructure.

FOREIGN FORCES

UNTSO unless specified. UNTSO figures represent total numbers for mission.
Argentina 3 obs
Australia 12 obs
Austria 4 obs
Belgium 1 obs
Bhutan 4 obs • UNDOF 3
Canada 4 obs
Chile 3 obs
China 5 obs
Czech Republic UNDOF 3
Denmark 11 obs
Estonia 3 obs
Fiji 2 obs • UNDOF 290; 1 inf bn(-); elm 1 log bn
Finland 18 obs
Ghana UNDOF 12
India 2 obs • UNDOF 194; 1 log bn(-)
Ireland 13 obs • UNDOF 126; 1 inf coy
Nepal 4 obs • UNDOF 333; 2 mech inf coy
Netherlands 13 obs • UNDOF 2
New Zealand 7 obs
Norway 14 obs
Russia 5 obs
Serbia 1 obs
Slovakia 2 obs
Slovenia 3 obs
Sweden 6 obs
Switzerland 12 obs
United States 2 obs • US Strategic Command; 1 AN/TPY-2 X-band radar at Mount Keren

Jordan JOR

Jordanian Dinar D		2017	2018	2019
GDP	D	28.4bn	29.7bn	
	US$	40.1bn	41.9bn	
per capita	US$	4,136	4,228	
Growth	%	2.0	2.3	
Inflation	%	3.3	4.5	
Def bdgt [a]	D	1.16bn	1.16bn	
	US$	1.63bn	1.63bn	
FMA (US)	US$	470m	350m	350m
US$1=D		0.71	0.71	

[a] Excludes expenditure on public order and safety

Population 10,458,413
Ethnic groups: Palestinian ε50–60%

Age	0–14	15–19	20–24	25–29	30–64	65 plus
Male	17.5%	5.5%	5.2%	4.7%	18.1%	1.7%
Female	16.6%	4.9%	4.4%	3.9%	15.6%	1.8%

Capabilities

The Jordanian armed forces (JAF) are structured to provide border security and an armoured response to conventional threats. Their well-regarded operational capability belies their moderate size and ageing equipment inventory. There is no recent public statement of defence policy, although the ongoing civil war in Syria is a clear concern. The armed forces have undergone budget-led restructuring, with the disbandment of the joint Special Operations Command and the 3rd Armoured Division. Jordan is a major non-NATO ally of the US with whom it maintains a close defence relationship. The country has developed a bespoke special-forces training centre and has hosted training for numerous state and non-state military forces. Personnel are well trained, particularly aircrew and special forces, who are highly regarded internationally. Jordanian forces are able to independently deploy regionally and have participated in ISAF operations in Afghanistan and in coalition air operations over Syria and Yemen. In contrast to the GCC states, the Jordanian inventory largely comprises older systems. Although the state-owned King Abdullah II Design and Development Bureau (KADDB) has demonstrated a vehicle-upgrade capacity, the army has largely recapitalised its armoured-vehicle fleet with second-hand armour from European countries. KADDB produces some light armoured vehicles for domestic use, but the company currently has little export profile.

ACTIVE 100,500 (Army 86,000 Navy 500 Air 14,000)
Paramilitary 15,000

RESERVE 65,000 (Army 60,000 Joint 5,000)

ORGANISATIONS BY SERVICE

Army 86,000
FORCES BY ROLE
SPECIAL FORCES
  1 (Royal Guard) SF gp (1 SF regt, 1 SF bn, 1 CT bn)
  1 (AB) SF bde (3 SF bn)
MANOEUVRE
  Armoured
  3 armd bde
  Mechanised
  5 mech bde
  Light
  3 lt inf bde
  Air Manoeuvre
  1 (QRF) AB bde (1 SF bn, 2 AB bn)
COMBAT SUPPORT
  3 arty bde
  3 AD bde
  1 MRL bn
EQUIPMENT BY TYPE
ARMOURED FIGHTING VEHICLES
  MBT 282: ε100 FV4034 *Challenger* 1 (*Al Hussein*) (being withdrawn); 182 M60 *Phoenix* (274 FV4030/2 *Khalid* in store)
  LT TK (19 FV101 *Scorpion* in store)
  ASLT 141 B1 *Centauro*
  RECCE 103 FV107 *Scimitar*
  IFV 751: 13 AIFV-B-C25; 31 BMP-2; 50 *Marder* 1A3; 321 *Ratel*-20; 336 YPR-765 PRI
  APC 879+
    APC (T) 729: 370 M113A1/A2 Mk1J; 269 M577A2 (CP); 87 YPR-765 PRCO (CP); 3 AIFV-B
    PPV 150: 25 *Marauder*; 25 *Matador*; 100 *MaxxPro*
  AUV 35 *Cougar*
ENGINEERING & MAINTENANCE VEHICLES
  ARV 155+: *Al Monjed*; 55 *Chieftain* ARV; *Centurion* Mk2; 20 M47; 32 M88A1; 30 M578; 18 YPR-806
  MW 12 *Aardvark* Mk2
ANTI-TANK/ANTI-INFRASTRUCTURE • MSL
  SP 115: 70 M901; 45 AIFV-B-*Milan*
  MANPATS FGM-148 *Javelin*; TOW/TOW-2A; 9K135 *Kornet* (AT-14 *Spriggan*)
ARTILLERY 1,429+
  SP 554: **105mm** 48: 30 M52; 18 MOBAT; **155mm** 358 M109A1/A2; **203mm** 148 M110A2
  TOWED 82: **105mm** 54 M102; **155mm** 28: 10 M1/M59; 18 M114; **203mm** (4 M115 in store)
  MRL 16+: **227mm** 12 M142 HIMARS; **273mm** 4+ WM-80
  MOR 777: **81mm** 359; **SP 81mm** 50; **107mm** 50 M30; **120mm** 300 Brandt **SP 120mm** 18 *Agrab* Mk2

AIR DEFENCE
  SAM • Point-defence 140+: 92 9K35 *Strela*-10 (SA-13 *Gopher*); 48 9K33 *Osa*-M (SA-8 *Gecko*); 9K36 *Strela*-3 (SA-14 *Gremlin*); 9K310 *Igla*-1 (SA-16 *Gimlet*); 9K38 *Igla* (SA-18 *Grouse*)
  GUNS • SP 200: **20mm** 100 M163 *Vulcan*; **23mm** 40 ZSU-23-4; **35mm** 60 *Cheetah* (*Gepard*)

Navy ε500
EQUIPMENT BY TYPE
PATROL AND COASTAL COMBATANTS 7
  PB 7: 3 *Al Hussein* (UK Vosper 30m); 4 *Abdullah* (US *Dauntless*)

Marines
FORCES BY ROLE
MANOEUVRE
  Amphibious
  1 mne unit

Air Force 14,000
FORCES BY ROLE
FIGHTER/GROUND ATTACK
  2 sqn with F-16AM/BM *Fighting Falcon*
GROUND ATTACK
  1 sqn with AC-235
ISR
  1 sqn with AT-802U *Air Tractor*; Cessna 208B
TRANSPORT
  1 sqn with C-130E/H *Hercules*
  1 unit with Il-76MF *Candid*
TRAINING
  1 OCU with F-16AM/BM *Fighting Falcon*
  1 OCU with *Hawk* Mk63
  1 sqn with PC-21
  1 sqn with Grob 120TP
  1 hel sqn with R-44 *Raven* II
ATTACK HELICOPTER
  2 sqn with AH-1F *Cobra* (with TOW)
TRANSPORT HELICOPTER
  1 sqn with AS332M *Super Puma*
  1 sqn with Bell 205 (UH-1H *Iroquois*); UH-60A *Black Hawk*
  1 sqn with H135M (Tpt/SAR)
  1 sqn with MD-530F
  1 sqn with UH-60L *Black Hawk*
  1 sqn with Mi-26T2 *Halo* (forming)
  1 (Royal) flt with S-70A *Black Hawk*; UH-60L/M *Black Hawk*; AW139
ISR UAV
  1 sqn with CH-4B; S-100 *Camcopter*
AIR DEFENCE
  2 bde with MIM-104C *Patriot* PAC-2; MIM-23B Phase III I-*Hawk*
EQUIPMENT BY TYPE
AIRCRAFT 59 combat capable
  FGA 47: 33 F-16AM *Fighting Falcon*; 14 F-16BM *Fighting Falcon*
  ATK 2 AC235
  ISR 10 AT-802U *Air Tractor**

TPT 12: **Heavy** 2 Il-76MF *Candid*; **Medium** 3 C-130E *Hercules* (1 C-130B *Hercules*; 4 C-130H *Hercules* in store); **Light** 7: 5 Cessna 208B; 2 M-28 *Skytruck* (2 C295M in store, offered for sale)
TRG 24: up to 16 Grob 120TP; 8 PC-21 (12 *Hawk* Mk63* in store, offered for sale)
HELICOPTERS
ATK 12 AH-1F *Cobra* (17 more in store, offered for sale)
MRH 14: 3 AW139; 11 H135M (Tpt/SAR) (6 MD-530F in store)
TPT 48: **Heavy** 1 Mi-26T2 *Halo*; **Medium** 35: 10 AS332M *Super Puma* (being WFU); 25 S-70A/UH-60A/UH-60L/VH-60M *Black Hawk*; **Light** 12 R-44 *Raven* II (13 Bell 205 (UH-1H *Iroquois*) in store, offered for sale)
UNMANNED AERIAL VEHICLES
CISR • **Heavy** some CH-4B
ISR • **Light** up to 10 S-100 *Camcopter*
AIR DEFENCE • SAM 64:
Long-range 40 MIM-104C *Patriot* PAC-2
Medium-range 24 MIM-23B Phase III I-*Hawk*
AIR-LAUNCHED MISSILES
AAM • **IR** AIM-9J/N/P *Sidewinder*; **SARH** AIM-7 *Sparrow*; **ARH** AIM-120C AMRAAM
ASM AGM-65D/G *Maverick*; BGM-71 TOW
BOMBS
Laser-guided GBU-10/12 *Paveway* II

Paramilitary ε15,000 active

Gendarmerie ε15,000 active
3 regional comd
FORCES BY ROLE
SPECIAL FORCES
2 SF unit
MANOEUVRE
Other
10 sy bn
EQUIPMENT BY TYPE
ARMOURED FIGHTING VEHICLES
APC • **APC (W)** 25+: AT105 *Saxon* (reported); 25+ EE-11 *Urutu*
AUV AB2 *Al-Jawad*

DEPLOYMENT

CENTRAL AFRICAN REPUBLIC: UN • MINUSCA 7; 3 obs
DEMOCRATIC REPUBLIC OF THE CONGO: UN • MONUSCO 4; 6 obs
MALI: UN • MINUSMA 61; 1 obs
SAUDI ARABIA: *Operation Restoring Hope* 6 F-16C *Fighting Falcon*
SOUTH SUDAN: UN • UNMISS 4
SUDAN: UN • UNAMID 11; 5 obs
WESTERN SAHARA: UN • MINURSO 2 obs

FOREIGN FORCES

Belgium *Operation Inherent Resolve* (*Desert Falcon*) 30
France *Operation Inherent Resolve* (*Chammal*) 8 *Rafale* F3; 1 *Atlantique* 2
Germany *Operation Inherent Resolve* 300; 4 *Tornado* ECR; 1 A310 MRTT
Netherlands *Operation Inherent Resolve* 150; 6 F-16AM *Fighting Falcon*
Norway *Operation Inherent Resolve* 60
United States Central Command: *Operation Inherent Resolve* 2,300; 1 FGA sqn with 12 F-15E *Strike Eagle*; 1 CISR sqn with 12 MQ-9A *Reaper*

Kuwait KWT

Kuwaiti Dinar D		2017	2018	2019
GDP	D	36.4bn	43.6bn	
	US$	121bn	145bn	
per capita	US$	27,394	31,916	
Growth	%	-3.3	2.3	
Inflation	%	1.5	0.8	
Def bdgt	D	1.75bn	1.87bn	
	US$	5.79bn	6.18bn	
US$1=D		0.30	0.30	

Population	2,916,467

Ethnic groups: Nationals 35.5%; other non-Arab Asian countries 37.7%; other Arab countries 17.5%; other or unspecified 9.3%

Age	0–14	15–19	20–24	25–29	30–64	65 plus
Male	12.9%	3.2%	5.1%	7.2%	28.7%	1.2%
Female	11.9%	3.0%	3.8%	4.3%	17.3%	1.5%

Capabilities

Kuwait's small but capable armed forces have benefited considerably from the significant presence on Kuwaiti territory of sizeable US forces. The primary responsibility is territorial defence, through a strategy of sufficient readiness to provide a holding force until the mobilisation of friendly forces. The National Guard, under its Strategic Vision 2020 plan, intends to boost readiness and equipment capability. Kuwait is a member of the GCC and has a bilateral defence-cooperation agreement with the US, which provides for a range of joint activities and mentoring, and the stationing and pre-positioning of significant numbers of US personnel and supplies of equipment. Since 2004, Kuwait has been designated a US major non-NATO ally. Kuwait operates a system of voluntary military service but suffers from a limited population pool. Contributions of air and ground assets have been made to the Saudi-led coalition in Yemen, but otherwise the country has limited deployment ambitions. There is limited logistic-support capacity, although heavy-airlift and airborne-tanking assets grant a limited airborne-expeditionary capability. The equipment inventory includes a range of modern European- and US-sourced platforms, including advanced air-defence-missile batteries. Kuwait is recapitalising its combat-aircraft fleet with the F/A-18E/F *Super Hornet* and Eurofighter *Typhoon*, which together will significantly enhance its air-combat capabilities. There are also indications that it wants to upgrade its fleet of main battle tanks and seek additional attack helicopters, and possibly new missile-armed multi-mission fast attack craft for the navy. Kuwait lacks a domestic defence-industrial base and is reliant on imports, albeit with offset requirements to help stimulate the country's wider industrial sector.

ACTIVE 17,500 (Army 13,000 Navy 2,000 Air 2,500)
Paramilitary 7,100
Conscript liability 12 months

RESERVE 23,700 (Joint 23,700)
Reserve obligation to age 40; 1 month annual trg

ORGANISATIONS BY SERVICE

Army 13,000
FORCES BY ROLE
SPECIAL FORCES
  1 SF unit
MANOEUVRE
  Reconnaissance
  1 mech/recce bde
  Armoured
  3 armd bde
  Mechanised
  2 mech inf bde
  Light
  1 cdo bn
  Other
  1 (Amiri) gd bde
COMBAT SUPPORT
  1 arty bde
  1 engr bde
  1 MP bn
COMBAT SERVICE SUPPORT
  1 log gp
  1 fd hospital

Reserve
FORCES BY ROLE
MANOEUVRE
  Mechanised
  1 bde
EQUIPMENT BY TYPE
ARMOURED FIGHTING VEHICLES
  MBT 293: 218 M1A2 *Abrams*; 75 M-84 (75 more in store)
  IFV 492: 76 BMP-2; 180 BMP-3; 236 *Desert Warrior*† (incl variants)
  APC 260
    APC (T) 260: 230 M113A2; 30 M577 (CP)
    APC (W) (40 TH 390 *Fahd* in store)
ENGINEERING & MAINTENANCE VEHICLES
  ARV 24+: 24 M88A1/2; Type-653A; *Warrior*
  MW *Aardvark* Mk2
NBC VEHICLES 11 TPz-1 *Fuchs* NBC
ARTY 211
  SP 155mm 106: 37 M109A3; 18 Mk F3; 51 PLZ-45 (18 AU-F-1 in store)
  MRL 300mm 27 9A52 *Smerch*
  MOR 78: **81mm** 60; **107mm** 6 M30; **120mm** ε12 RT-F1
ANTI-TANK/ANTI-INFRASTRUCTURE
  MSL
    SP 74: 66 HMMWV TOW; 8 M901
    MANPATS TOW-2; M47 *Dragon*
  RCL 84mm *Carl Gustav*

AIR DEFENCE
  SAM
    Short-range 12 *Aspide*
    Point-defence *Starburst*; FIM-92 *Stinger*
  GUNS • TOWED 35mm 12+ Oerlikon

Navy ε2,000 (incl 500 Coast Guard)
EQUIPMENT BY TYPE
PATROL AND COASTAL COMBATANTS 20
  PCFG 2:
    1 *Al Sanbouk* (GER Lurssen TNC-45) with 2 twin lnchr with MM40 *Exocet* AShM, 1 76mm gun
    1 *Istiqlal* (GER Lurssen FPB-57) with 2 twin lnchr with MM40 *Exocet* AShM, 1 76mm gun
  PBF 10 *Al Nokatha* (US Mk V *Pegasus*)
  PBG 8 *Um Almaradim* (FRA P-37 BRL) with 2 twin lnchr with *Sea Skua* AShM
AMPHIBIOUS LANDING CRAFT 6
  LCM 1 *Abhan* (ADSB 42m)
  LCVP 5 ADSB 16m
LOGISTICS AND SUPPORT • AG 1 *Sawahil* with 1 hel landing platform

Air Force 2,500
FORCES BY ROLE
FIGHTER/GROUND ATTACK
  2 sqn with F/A-18C/D *Hornet*
TRANSPORT
  1 sqn with C-17A *Globemaster* III; KC-130J *Hercules*; L-100-30
TRAINING
  1 unit with EMB-312 *Tucano**; *Hawk* Mk64*
ATTACK HELICOPTER
  1 sqn with AH-64D *Apache*
  1 atk/trg sqn with SA342 *Gazelle* with HOT
TRANSPORT HELICOPTER
  1 sqn with AS532 *Cougar*; SA330 *Puma*; S-92
EQUIPMENT BY TYPE
AIRCRAFT 66 combat capable
  FGA 39: 31 F/A-18C *Hornet*; 8 F/A-18D *Hornet*
  TKR 3 KC-130J *Hercules*
  TPT 5: **Heavy** 2 C-17A *Globemaster* III; **Medium** 3 L-100-30
  TRG 27: 11 *Hawk* Mk64*; 16 EMB-312 *Tucano**
HELICOPTERS
  ATK 16 AH-64D *Apache*
  MRH 13 SA342 *Gazelle* with HOT
  TPT • Medium 13: 3 AS532 *Cougar*; 7 SA330 *Puma*; 3 S-92
AIR-LAUNCHED MISSILES
  AAM • IR AIM-9L *Sidewinder*; R-550 *Magic*; **SARH** AIM-7F *Sparrow*; **ARH** AIM-120C7 AMRAAM
  ASM AGM-65G *Maverick*; AGM-114K *Hellfire*; HOT
  AShM AGM-84D *Harpoon* Block IC

Air Defence Command
FORCES BY ROLE
AIR DEFENCE
  1 SAM bde (7 SAM bty with MIM-104D *Patriot* PAC-2 GEM)
  1 SAM bde (6 SAM bty with *Skyguard/Aspide*)

EQUIPMENT BY TYPE
AIR DEFENCE • SAM 52:
Long-range 40 MIM-104D *Patriot* PAC-2 GEM
Short-range 12 *Skyguard/Aspide*

Paramilitary ε7,100 active

National Guard ε6,600 active
FORCES BY ROLE
SPECIAL FORCES
 1 SF bn
MANOEUVRE
 Reconnaissance
 1 armd car bn
 Other
 3 security bn
COMBAT SUPPORT
 1 MP bn
EQUIPMENT BY TYPE
ARMOURED FIGHTING VEHICLES
 RECCE 20 VBL
 IFV 70 *Pandur* (incl variants)
 APC • APC (W) 27+: 5+ *Desert Chameleon*; 22 S600 (incl variants)
ENGINEERING & MAINTENANCE VEHICLES
 ARV *Pandur*

Coast Guard 500
EQUIPMENT BY TYPE
PATROL AND COASTAL COMBATANTS 32
 PBF 12 *Manta*
 PB 20: 3 *Al Shaheed*; 4 *Inttisar* (Austal 31.5m); 3 *Kassir* (Austal 22m); 10 *Subahi*
AMPHIBIOUS • LANDING CRAFT • LCU 4: 2 *Al Tahaddy*; 1 *Saffar*; 1 other
LOGISTICS AND SUPPORT • AG 1 *Sawahil*

DEPLOYMENT

SAUDI ARABIA: Operation Restoring Hope 4 F/A-18A *Hornet*

FOREIGN FORCES

Canada Operation Inherent Resolve (*Impact*) 1 A310 MRTT (C-150T); 2 C-130J-30 *Hercules* (CC-130J)
Denmark Operation Inherent Resolve 20
Italy Operation Inherent Resolve (*Prima Parthica*) 255; 4 AMX; 2 MQ-9A *Reaper*; 1 KC-767A
Singapore Operation Inherent Resolve 11
United Kingdom Operation Inherent Resolve (*Shader*) 50; 1 CISR UAV sqn with 8 MQ-9A *Reaper*
United States Central Command: 14,000; 1 ARNG armd bde; 1 ARNG cbt avn bde; 1 spt bde; 2 AD bty with MIM-104E/F *Patriot* PAC-2/3; 1 FGA sqn with 12 F-16C *Fighting Falcon*; 1 CISR UAV sqn with MQ-9A *Reaper*; 1 (APS) armd bde eqpt set; 1 (APS) inf bde eqpt set

Lebanon LBN

Lebanese Pound LP		2017	2018	2019
GDP	LP	81.7tr	85.5tr	
	US$	54.2bn	56.7bn	
per capita	US$	12,013	12,454	
Growth	%	1.5	1.0	
Inflation	%	4.5	6.5	
Def bdgt	LP	2.81tr	3.20tr	
	US$	1.87bn	2.12bn	
FMA (US)	US$	80m	0m	50m
US$1=LP		1507.51	1507.51	

Population	6,100,075

Ethnic and religious groups: Christian 30%; Druze 6%; Armenian 4%; excl ε300,000 Syrians and ε350,000 Palestinian refugees

Age	0–14	15–19	20–24	25–29	30–64	65 plus
Male	11.9%	4.1%	4.1%	4.3%	22.6%	3.0%
Female	11.4%	3.9%	3.9%	4.2%	22.5%	4.0%

Capabilities

The Lebanese Armed Forces (LAF) are focused on internal and border security. However, the LAF's ability to fulfil its missions remains under strain from Hizbullah's position in national politics and from the spillover effects of the Syrian conflict. Publication of a new National Defence Strategy continues to be delayed by political divisions. Training and material support are received from the US, as well as from France, Italy and the UK. Previous material support from Saudi Arabia was curtailed for political reasons. Personnel quality and capability is relatively high for the region and US special-operations personnel continue to provide operational advice and assistance. LAF operations against ISIS have demonstrated improved capability. The LAF has no requirement for extra-territorial deployment and minimal capability to do so. It remains dependent on foreign support to replace and modernise its ageing equipment inventory. Barring some light maintenance facilities in the services, Lebanon has no significant domestic defence industry.

ACTIVE 60,000 (Army 56,600 Navy 1,800 Air 1,600)
Paramilitary 20,000

ORGANISATIONS BY SERVICE

Army 56,600
FORCES BY ROLE
5 regional comd (Beirut, Bekaa Valley, Mount Lebanon, North, South)
SPECIAL FORCES
 1 cdo regt
MANOEUVRE
 Armoured
 1 armd regt
 Mechanised
 11 mech inf bde
 Air Manoeuvre
 1 AB regt

Amphibious
1 mne cdo regt
Other
1 Presidential Guard bde
6 intervention regt 4 border sy regt
COMBAT SUPPORT
2 arty regt
1 cbt spt bde (1 engr regt, 1 AT regt, 1 sigs regt; 1 log bn)
1 MP gp
COMBAT SERVICE SUPPORT
1 log bde
1 med gp
1 construction regt
EQUIPMENT BY TYPE
MBT 334: 92 M48A1/A5; 10 M60A2; 185 T-54; 47 T-55
RECCE 55 AML
IFV 48: 16 AIFV-B-C25; 32 M2A2 *Bradley*
APC 1,378
  APC (T) 1,274 M113A1/A2 (incl variants)
  APC (W) 96: 86 VAB VCT; 10 VBPT-MR *Guarani*
  PPV 8 *Maxxpro*
ENGINEERING & MAINTENANCE VEHICLES
  ARV M113 ARV; T-54/55 ARV reported
  VLB MTU-72 reported
  MW *Bozena*
ARTILLERY 611
  SP 155mm 12 M109A2
  TOWED 313: **105mm** 13 M101A1; **122mm** 35: 9 D-30; 26 M-30; **130mm** 15 M-46; **155mm** 250: 18 M114A1; 218 M198; 14 Model-50
  MRL 122mm 11 BM-21
  MOR 275: **81mm** 134; **82mm** 112; **120mm** 29 Brandt
ANTI-TANK/ANTI-INFRASTRUCTURE
  MSL
    SP 15 VAB with HOT
    MANPATS *Milan*; TOW
  RCL 106mm 113 M40A1
UNMANNED AERIAL VEHICLES
  ISR • Medium 8 *Mohajer* 4
AIR DEFENCE
  SAM • Point-defence 9K32 *Strela*-2/2M (SA-7A *Grail*/SA-7B *Grail*)‡
  GUNS • TOWED 77: **20mm** 20; **23mm** 57 ZU-23-2

Navy 1,800
EQUIPMENT BY TYPE
PATROL AND COASTAL COMBATANTS 13
  PCC 1 *Trablous*
  PB 11: 1 *Aamchit* (ex-GER *Bremen*); 1 *Al Kalamoun* (ex-FRA *Avel Gwarlarn*); 7 *Tripoli* (ex-UK *Attacker/Tracker* Mk 2); 1 *Naquora* (ex-GER *Bremen*); 1 *Tabarja* (ex-GER *Bergen*)
  PBF 1
AMPHIBIOUS
  LANDING CRAFT • LCT 2 *Sour* (ex-FRA EDIC – capacity 8 APC; 96 troops)

Air Force 1,600
4 air bases
FORCES BY ROLE
GROUND ATTACK
  1 sqn with Cessna AC-208 *Combat Caravan**
  1 sqn with EMB-314 *Super Tucano**
ATTACK HELICOPTER
  1 sqn with SA342L *Gazelle*
TRANSPORT HELICOPTER
  4 sqn with Bell 205 (UH-1H)
  1 sqn with SA330/IAR330SM *Puma*
  1 trg sqn with R-44 *Raven* II
EQUIPMENT BY TYPE
AIRCRAFT 9 combat capable
  ISR 3 Cessna AC-208 *Combat Caravan**
  TRG 9: 3 *Bulldog*; 6 EMB-314 *Super Tucano**
HELICOPTERS
  MRH 9: 1 AW139; 8 SA342L *Gazelle* (5 SA342L *Gazelle*; 5 SA316 *Alouette* III; 1 SA318 *Alouette* II all non-operational)
  TPT 38: **Medium** 13: 3 S-61N (fire fighting); 10 SA330/IAR330 *Puma*; **Light** 25: 18 Bell 205 (UH-1H *Huey*); 3 Bell 205 (UH-1H *Huey* II); 4 R-44 *Raven* II (basic trg) (11 Bell 205; 7 Bell 212 all non-operational)
AIR LAUNCHED MISSILES
  ASM AGM-114 *Hellfire*

Paramilitary ε20,000 active

Internal Security Force ε20,000
Ministry of Interior
FORCES BY ROLE
Other Combat Forces
  1 (police) judicial unit
  1 regional sy coy
  1 (Beirut Gendarmerie) sy coy
EQUIPMENT BY TYPE
ARMOURED FIGHTING VEHICLES
  APC • APC (W) 60 V-200 *Chaimite*

Customs
EQUIPMENT BY TYPE
PATROL AND COASTAL COMBATANTS 7
  PB 7: 5 *Aztec*; 2 *Tracker*

FOREIGN FORCES
Unless specified, figures refer to UNTSO and represent total numbers for the mission
Argentina 3 obs
Armenia UNIFIL 33
Australia 12 obs
Austria 4 obs • UNIFIL 182: 1 log coy
Bangladesh UNIFIL 116: 1 FSG
Belarus UNIFIL 5
Belgium 1 obs
Bhutan 4 obs
Brazil UNIFIL 222: 1 FFGHM
Brunei UNIFIL 30

Cambodia UNIFIL 184: 1 engr coy
Canada 4 obs (*Operation Jade*)
Chile 3 obs
China, People's Republic of 5 obs • UNIFIL 418: 2 engr coy; 1 med coy
Colombia UNIFIL 1
Croatia UNIFIL 1
Cyprus UNIFIL 2
Denmark 11 obs
El Salvador UNIFIL 52: 1 inf pl
Estonia 3 obs • UNIFIL 38
Fiji 2 obs • UNIFIL 136; 1 inf coy
Finland 18 obs • UNIFIL 300; elm 1 mech inf bn; 1 maint coy
France UNIFIL 669: 1 mech inf bn(-); VBL; VBCI; VAB; *Mistral*
Germany UNIFIL 112: 1 FFGM
Ghana UNIFIL 870: 1 mech inf bn
Greece UNIFIL 148: 1 FFGHM
Guatemala UNIFIL 2
Hungary UNIFIL 10
India 2 obs • UNIFIL 900: 1 inf bn; 1 med coy
Indonesia UNIFIL 1,295: 1 inf bn; 1 MP coy; 1 FSGHM
Ireland 13 obs • UNIFIL 353: elm 1 mech inf bn
Italy UNIFIL 1,043: 1 mech bde HQ; 1 mech inf bn; 1 engr coy; 1 sigs coy; 1 hel bn
Kenya UNIFIL 1
Korea, Republic of UNIFIL 335: 1 mech inf coy; 1 engr coy; 1 sigs coy; 1 maint coy
Macedonia (FYROM) UNIFIL 2
Malaysia UNIFIL 829: 1 mech inf bn
Nepal 4 obs • UNIFIL 871: 1 mech inf bn
Netherlands 13 obs • UNIFIL 1
New Zealand 7 obs
Nigeria UNIFIL 1
Norway 14 obs
Qatar UNIFIL 2
Russia 5 obs
Serbia 1 obs • UNIFIL 177; 1 mech inf coy
Sierra Leone UNIFIL 3
Slovakia 2 obs
Slovenia 3 obs • UNIFIL 18
Spain UNIFIL 630: 1 mech bde HQ; 1 mech inf bn(-); 1 engr coy; 1 sigs coy
Sri Lanka UNIFIL 150: 1 inf coy
Sweden 6 obs
Switzerland 12 obs
Tanzania UNIFIL 159: 1 MP coy
Turkey UNIFIL 86: 1 PCFG
United States 2 obs

Libya LBY

Libyan Dinar D		2017	2018	2019
GDP	D	42.3bn	59.9bn	
	US$	30.6bn	43.2bn	
per capita	US$	4,740	6,639	
Growth	%	64.0	10.9	
Inflation	%	28.5	28.1	
Def exp	D	n.k.	n.k.	
	US$	n.k.	n.k.	
US$1=D		1.39	1.39	
Population	6,754,507			

Age	0–14	15–19	20–24	25–29	30–64	65 plus
Male	13.1%	4.3%	4.3%	4.6%	23.2%	2.2%
Female	12.5%	4.1%	4.1%	4.2%	21.2%	2.3%

Capabilities

Armed groups in Libya are composed of a mix of semi-regular military units, tribal militias and armed civilians based around General Haftar's Libyan National Army (LNA) in the eastern part of the country and Prime Minister Fayez al-Sarraj's internationally recognised Government of National Accord (GNA) in the west. Both the GNA's and LNA's affiliated forces have relatively low levels of training. The presence in these formations of units from the former Gadhafi-era army has bolstered their military capability. Meanwhile, the GNA-affiliated forces have since 2016 benefited from several military advisory and training programmes, including EUNAVFOR–MED maritime-security training for the Libyan Navy and Coast Guard. LNA troops have combat experience from fighting ISIS in the eastern coastal region and they have allegedly received training and combat support from external actors in the region. Both organisations' equipment is mainly of Russian or Soviet origin, including items from the former Libyan armed forces, and suffers from varying degrees of obsolescence. However, the lack of high-technology platforms has allowed both forces to maintain minimum operational standards. The country has no domestic defence-industrial capability.

Forces loyal to the Government of National Accord (Tripoli-based)

ACTIVE n.k.

ORGANISATIONS BY SERVICE

Ground Forces n.k.
EQUIPMENT BY TYPE
ARMOURED FIGHTING VEHICLES
  MBT T-55; T-72
  IFV BMP-2
  APC • APC (T) 4K-7FA *Steyr*
  AUV Nimr *Ajban*
ENGINEERING & MAINTENANCE VEHICLES
  ARV *Centurion* 105 AVRE
ANTI-TANK/ANTI-INFRASTRUCTURE
  MSL • SP 9P157-2 *Khrizantema*-S (AT-15 *Springer*)
ARTILLERY
  SP 155mm *Palmaria*
  TOWED 122mm D-30

Navy n.k.

A number of intact naval vessels remain in Tripoli, although serviceability is questionable

EQUIPMENT BY TYPE
PRINCIPAL SURFACE COMBATANTS 1
  FRIGATES • FFGM 1 *Al Hani* (FSU *Koni*) (in Italy for refit since 2013) with 2 twin lnchr with P-15 *Termit*-M (SS-N-2C *Styx*) AShM, 1 twin lnchr with 9K33 *Osa*-M (SA-N-4 *Gecko*) SAM, 2 twin 406mm ASTT with USET-95 Type-40 LWT, 1 RBU 6000 *Smerch* 2 A/S mor, 2 twin 76mm gun†
PATROL AND COASTAL COMBATANTS 3+
  PBFG 1 *Sharaba* (FRA *Combattante* II) with 4 single lnchr with *Otomat* Mk2 AShM, 1 76mm gun†
  PB 2+ PV30
AMPHIBIOUS
  LANDING SHIPS • LST 1 *Ibn Harissa* with 3 twin 40mm DARDO CIWS† (capacity 1 hel; 11 MBT; 240 troops)
LOGISTICS AND SUPPORT 2
  AFD 1
  ARS 1 *Al Munjed* (YUG *Spasilac*)†

Air Force n.k.

EQUIPMENT BY TYPE
AIRCRAFT 14+ combat capable
  FGA 2 MiG-23BN
  ATK 1 J-21 *Jastreb*†
  TRG 11+: 3 G-2 *Galeb**; up to 8 L-39ZO*; some SF-260
HELICOPTERS
  ATK Mi-24 *Hind*
  TPT • Medium Mi-17 *Hip*
AIR-LAUNCHED MISSILES • AAM • IR R-3 (AA-2 *Atoll*)‡; R-60 (AA-8 *Aphid*); R-24 (AA-7 *Apex*)

Paramilitary n.k.

Coast Guard n.k.
EQUIPMENT BY TYPE
PATROL AND COASTAL COMBATANTS 7+
  PCC Damen Stan 2909 (YTB armed with with 14.5mm ZSU-2 AD GUNS and 122mm MRL)
  PBF 4 *Bigliani*
  PB 3: 1 *Burdi* (Damen Stan 1605); 1 *Hamelin*; 1 *Ikrimah* (FRA RPB 20)

TERRITORY WHERE THE RECOGNISED AUTHORITY DOES NOT EXERCISE EFFECTIVE CONTROL

Data here represents the de facto situation. This does not imply international recognition

ACTIVE n.k.

ORGANISATIONS BY SERVICE

Libyan National Army n.k.

EQUIPMENT BY TYPE
ARMOURED FIGHTING VEHICLES
  MBT T-55; T-72
  RECCE BRDM-2; EE-9 *Cascavel*
  IFV BMP-1; *Ratel*-20
  APC
    APC (T) M113
    APC (W) BTR-60PB; Nimr *Jais*; *Puma*
    PPV *Al-Wahsh*; *Caiman*; Streit *Spartan*; Streit *Typhoon*
  AUV *Panthera* T6; *Panthera* F9
ANTI-TANK/ANTI-INFRASTRUCTURE
  MSL
    SP 10 9P157-2 *Khryzantema*-S (status unknown)
    MANPATS 9K11 *Malyutka* (AT-3 *Sagger*); 9K111 *Fagot* (AT-4 *Spigot*); 9K111-1 *Konkurs* (AT-5 *Spandrel*); *Milan*
  RCL some: **106mm** M40A1; **84mm** *Carl Gustav*
ARTILLERY
  SP 122mm 2S1 *Gvodzika*
  TOWED 122mm D-30
  MRL 107mm Type-63; **122mm** BM-21 *Grad*
  MOR M106
AIR DEFENCE
  SAM
    Short-range 2K12 *Kvadrat* (SA-6 *Gainful*)
    Point-defence 9K338 *Igla*-S (SA-24 *Grinch*)
  GUNS • SP 14.5mm ZPU-2 (on tch); **23mm** ZSU-23-4 *Shilka*; ZU-23-2 (on tch)

Navy n.k.
EQUIPMENT BY TYPE
PATROL AND COASTAL COMBATANTS 7+
  PB: 7+: 1 *Burdi* (Damen Stan 1605) with 1 23mm gun; 1 *Burdi* (Damen Stan 1605) with 1 76mm gun; 1 *Burdi* (Damen Stan 1605); 2 *Ikrimah* (FRA RPB20); 1 *Hamelin*; 1+ PV30
LOGISTICS AND SUPPORT 1
  AFD 1

Air Force n.k.
EQUIPMENT BY TYPE
AIRCRAFT 5+ combat capable
  FTR MiG-23 *Flogger*
  FGA 5+: 3+ MiG-21bis/MF *Fishbed*; 1 *Mirage* F-1ED; 1 Su-22UM-3K *Fitter*
  TRG 1+ MiG-21UM *Mongol* B
HELICOPTERS
  ATK Mi-24/35 *Hind*
  TPT Medium Mi-8/Mi-17 *Hip*
AIR-LAUNCHED MISSILES • AAM • IR R-3 (AA-2 *Atoll*)‡; R-60 (AA-8 *Aphid*)

FOREIGN FORCES

Germany UNSMIL 2 obs
Italy MIASIT 375
Nepal UNSMIL 230; 1 obs; 2 sy coy
United Arab Emirates 6 AT-802; 2 UH-60M; 2 *Wing Loong* I (GJ-1) UAV
United Kingdom UNSMIL 1 obs
United States UNSMIL 1 obs

Mauritania MRT

Mauritanian Ouguiya OM		2017	2018	2019
GDP	OM	1.76tr	1.86tr	
	US$	4.94bn	5.20bn	
per capita	US$	1,271	1,310	
Growth	%	3.5	2.5	
Inflation	%	2.3	3.8	
Def bdgt	OM	51.6bn	56.8bn	
	US$	145m	158m	
US$1=OM			356.57	358.65

Population	3,840,429					
Age	0–14	15–19	20–24	25–29	30–64	65 plus
Male	19.2%	5.2%	4.5%	3.9%	13.8%	1.6%
Female	19.0%	5.3%	4.8%	4.3%	16.3%	2.2%

Capabilities

The country's small and modestly equipped armed forces are tasked with maintaining territorial integrity and internal security. In light of the regional threat from extremist Islamist groups, border security is also a key role for the armed forces, which are accustomed to counter-insurgency operations in the desert. The country is a member of the G5 Sahel group. Mauritania's armed forces take part in the US-led special-operations *Flintlock* training exercise. The country also benefits from training with French armed forces. Deployment capabilities are limited to neighbouring countries without external support, but the armed forces have demonstrated mobility and sustainability in desert regions. Mauritania has a limited and ageing equipment inventory, which hampers operational capability. Despite some recent acquisitions, including small ISR aircraft, aviation resources are insufficient considering the size of the country. Naval equipment is geared toward coastal-surveillance missions but there are plans to increase amphibious capabilities. There is no domestic defence industry.

ACTIVE 15,850 (Army 15,000 Navy 600 Air 250)
Paramilitary 5,000
Conscript liability 24 months

ORGANISATIONS BY SERVICE

Army 15,000
FORCES BY ROLE
6 mil regions
MANOEUVRE
  Reconnaissance
  1 armd recce sqn
  Armoured
  1 armd bn
  Light
  7 mot inf bn
  8 (garrison) inf bn
  Air Manoeuvre
  1 cdo/para bn
  Other
  2 (camel corps) bn
  1 gd bn

COMBAT SUPPORT
3 arty bn
4 ADA bty
1 engr coy
EQUIPMENT BY TYPE
ARMOURED FIGHTING VEHICLES
  MBT 35 T-54/T-55
  RECCE 70: 20 AML-60; 40 AML-90; 10 *Saladin*
  APC • APC (W) 37: 12 *Cobra*; 5 FV603 *Saracen*; ε20 Panhard M3
ENGINEERING & MAINTENANCE VEHICLES
  ARV T-54/55 ARV reported
ANTI-TANK/ANTI-INFRASTRUCTURE
  MSL • MANPATS *Milan*
  RCL • 106mm ε90 M40A1
ARTILLERY 180
  TOWED 80: **105mm** 36 HM-2/M101A1; **122mm** 44: 20 D-30; 24 D-74
  MRL 10: **107mm** 4 Type-63; **122mm** 6 Type-81
  MOR 90: **81mm** 60; **120mm** 30 Brandt
AIR DEFENCE
  SAM • Point-defence ε4 SA-9 *Gaskin* (reported); 9K32 *Strela*-2 (SA-7 *Grail*)‡
  GUNS • TOWED 82: **14.5mm** 28: 16 ZPU-2; 12 ZPU-4; **23mm** 20 ZU-23-2; **37mm** 10 M-1939; **57mm** 12 S-60; **100mm** 12 KS-19

Navy ε600
EQUIPMENT BY TYPE
PATROL AND COASTAL COMBATANTS 17
  PCO 1 *Voum-Legleita*
  PCC 7: 1 *Aboubekr Ben Amer* (FRA OPV 54); 1 *Arguin*; 2 *Conejera*; 1 *Limam El Hidrami* (PRC); 2 *Timbédra* (PRC Huangpu Mod)
  PB 9: 1 *El Nasr*† (FRA *Patra*); 4 *Mandovi*; 2 *Saeta*-12; 2 *Megsem Bakkar* (FRA RPB20 – for SAR duties)

Air Force 250
EQUIPMENT BY TYPE
AIRCRAFT 4 combat capable
  ISR 2 Cessna 208B *Grand Caravan*
  TPT 8: **Light** 7: 2 BN-2 *Defender*; 1 C-212; 2 PA-31T *Cheyenne* II; 2 Y-12(II); **PAX** 1 BT-67 (with sensor turret)
  TRG 11: 3 EMB-312 *Tucano*; 4 EMB-314 *Super Tucano**; 4 SF-260E
HELICOPTERS • MRH 3: 1 SA313B *Alouette* II; 2 Z-9

Paramilitary ε5,000 active

Gendarmerie ε3,000
Ministry of Interior
FORCES BY ROLE
MANOEUVRE
  Other
  6 regional sy coy
EQUIPMENT BY TYPE
ARMOURED FIGHTING VEHICLES
  APC • APC (W) 12 *Cobra*
PATROL AND COASTAL COMBATANTS • 2 Rodman 55M

National Guard 2,000
Ministry of Interior

Customs
EQUIPMENT BY TYPE
PATROL AND COASTAL COMBATANTS • PB 2: 1 *Dah Ould Bah* (FRA *Amgram* 14); 1 *Yaboub Ould Rajel* (FRA RPB18)

DEPLOYMENT
CENTRAL AFRICAN REPUBLIC: UN • MINUSCA 744; 9 obs; 1 inf bn
MALI: UN • MINUSMA 8
SOMALIA: UN • UNSOS 1 obs

Morocco MOR

Moroccan Dirham D		2017	2018	2019
GDP	D	1.06tr	1.11tr	
	US$	109bn	118bn	
per capita	US$	3,137	3,355	
Growth	%	4.1	3.2	
Inflation	%	0.8	2.4	
Def bdgt	D	33.8bn	34.3bn	
	US$	3.49bn	3.63bn	
FMA (US)	US$	10m	0m	
US$1=D		9.70	9.43	
Population	34,314,130			

Age	0–14	15–19	20–24	25–29	30–64	65 plus
Male	12.9%	4.2%	4.2%	4.0%	20.6%	3.2%
Female	12.5%	4.2%	4.2%	4.2%	22.0%	3.8%

Capabilities

Regional security challenges rank highly for Morocco's armed forces, who have gained experience in operations in Western Sahara. Despite the UN-brokered 1991 ceasefire between Morocco and the Polisario Front, the conflict in Western Sahara remains unresolved. Morocco maintains long-standing defence ties with France and the US, receiving military training and equipment from both. There is also close cooperation with NATO, and in 2016 Morocco was granted access to the Alliance's Interoperability Platform in order to strengthen the defence and security sectors and bring the armed forces to NATO standards. In 2017, Morocco rejoined the African Union. The armed forces have also gained experience from UN peacekeeping deployments and a number of multinational exercises. It was announced in late 2018 that conscription would be reintroduced. The armed forces have some capacity to deploy independently within the region, as well as to UN peacekeeping missions in sub-Saharan Africa. Morocco has also deployed overseas in a combat role, contributing F-16 aircraft to the Saudi-led coalition intervention in Yemen. The inventory primarily comprises ageing French and US equipment. However, there are plans to re-equip all the services and to invest significantly in the navy. Morocco has also launched two Earth-observation satellites, aboard European rockets, which can meet some surveillance requirements. Morocco does not yet have an established domestic defence industry and relies on imports and donations for major defence equipment. However, its relative stability has attracted Western defence companies, such as Airbus, Safran and Thales, to establish aerospace manufacturing and servicing facilities in the country.

ACTIVE 195,800 (Army 175,000 Navy 7,800 Air 13,000) **Paramilitary 50,000**
Conscript liability 12 months for men and women aged 19–25 (agreed in late 2018)

RESERVE 150,000 (Army 150,000)
Reserve obligation to age 50

ORGANISATIONS BY SERVICE

Space
EQUIPMENT BY TYPE
SATELLITES 2
  ISR 2 *Mohammed VI*

Army ε75,000; 100,000 conscript (total 175,000)
FORCES BY ROLE
2 comd (Northern Zone, Southern Zone)
MANOEUVRE
  Armoured
  1 armd bde
  11 armd bn
  Mechanised
  3 mech inf bde
  Mechanised/Light
  8 mech/mot inf regt (2–3 bn)
  Light
  1 lt sy bde
  3 (camel corps) mot inf bn
  35 lt inf bn
  4 cdo unit
  Air Manoeuvre
  2 para bde
  2 AB bn
  Mountain
  1 mtn inf bn
COMBAT SUPPORT
  11 arty bn
  7 engr bn
AIR DEFENCE
  1 AD bn

Royal Guard 1,500
FORCES BY ROLE
MANOEUVRE
  Other
  1 gd bn
  2 cav sqn
EQUIPMENT BY TYPE
ARMOURED FIGHTING VEHICLES
  MBT 602: 222 M1A1SA *Abrams*; 220 M60A1 *Patton*; 120 M60A3 *Patton*; 40 T-72B (ε200 M48A5 *Patton* in store)
  LT TK 116: 5 AMX-13; 111 SK-105 *Kuerassier*
  ASLT 80 AMX-10RC

RECCE 284: 38 AML-60-7; 190 AML-90; 40 EBR-75; 16 *Eland*
IFV 115: 10 AMX-10P; 30 *Ratel* Mk3-20; 30 *Ratel* Mk3-90; 45 VAB VCI
APC 1,225
    APC (T) 905: 400 M113A1/A2; 419 M113A3; 86 M577A2 (CP)
    APC (W) 320 VAB VTT
ENGINEERING & MAINTENANCE VEHICLES
    ARV 48+: 10 *Greif*; 18 M88A1; M578; 20 VAB-ECH
ANTI-TANK/ANTI-INFRASTRUCTURE
    MSL
        SP 80 M901
        MANPATS 9K11 *Malyutka* (AT-3 *Sagger*); M47 *Dragon*; *Milan*; TOW
    RCL 106mm 350 M40A1
    GUNS • SP 36: **90mm** 28 M56; **100mm** 8 SU-100
ARTILLERY 2,306
    SP 357: **105mm** 5 AMX Mk 61; **155mm** 292: 84 M109A1/A1B; 43 M109A2; 4 M109A3; 1 M109A4; 70 M109A5; 90 Mk F3; **203mm** 60 M110
    TOWED 118: **105mm** 50: 30 L118 Light Gun; 20 M101; **130mm** 18 M-46; **155mm** 50: 30 FH-70; 20 M114
    MRL 122mm 35 BM-21 *Grad*
    MOR 1,796: **81mm** 1,100 Expal model LN; **SP 107mm** 36 M106A2; **120mm** 550 Brandt; **SP 120mm** 110: 20 (VAB APC); 90 M1064A3
UNMANNED AERIAL VEHICLES
    ISR • Medium R4E-50 *Skyeye*
AIR DEFENCE
    SAM
        Point-defence 49+: 12 2K22M *Tunguska*-M (SA-19 *Grison*); 37 M48 *Chaparral*; 9K32 *Strela*-2 (SA-7 *Grail*)‡
    GUNS 407
        SP 20mm 60 M163 *Vulcan*
        TOWED 347: **14.5mm** 200: 150–180 ZPU-2; 20 ZPU-4; **20mm** 40 M167 *Vulcan*; **23mm** 75–90 ZU-23-2; **100mm** 17 KS-19

Navy 7,800 (incl 1,500 Marines)
EQUIPMENT BY TYPE
PRINCIPAL SURFACE COMBATANTS 6
    DESTROYERS 1
        DDGHM 1 *Mohammed* VI-class (FRA FREMM) with 2 quad lnchr with MM40 *Exocet* Block 3 AShM, 2 octuple A43 VLS with *Aster* 15 SAM, 2 triple B515 324mm ASTT with MU90 LWT, 1 76mm gun (capacity 1 AS565SA *Panther*)
    FRIGATES 5
        FFGHM 3 *Tarik ben Ziyad* (NLD SIGMA 9813/10513) with 4 single lnchr with MM40 *Exocet* Block 2/3 AShM, 2 6-cell VLS with VL-MICA SAM, 2 triple 324mm ASTT with MU90 LWT, 1 76mm gun (capacity 1 AS565SA *Panther*)
        FFGH 2 *Mohammed V* (FRA *Floreal*) with 2 single lnchr with MM38 *Exocet* AShM, 1 76mm gun (can be fitted with *Simbad* SAM) (capacity 1 AS565SA *Panther*)
PATROL AND COASTAL COMBATANTS 50
    CORVETTES • FSGM 1
        1 *Lt Col Errhamani* (ESP *Descubierto*) with 2 twin lnchr with MM38 *Exocet* AShM, 1 octuple *Albatros* lnchr with *Aspide* SAM, 2 triple 324mm ASTT with Mk46 LWT, 1 76mm gun
    PSO 1 *Bin an Zaran* (OPV 70) with 1 76mm gun
    PCG 4 *Cdt El Khattabi* (ESP *Lazaga* 58m) with 4 single lnchr with MM38 *Exocet* AShM, 1 76mm gun
    PCO 5 *Rais Bargach* (under control of fisheries dept)
    PCC 12:
        4 *El Hahiq* (DNK *Osprey* 55, incl 2 with customs)
        6 *LV Rabhi* (ESP 58m B-200D)
        2 *Okba* (FRA PR-72) each with 1 76mm gun
    PB 27: 6 *El Wacil* (FRA P-32); 10 VCSM (RPB 20); 10 Rodman 101; 1 other (UK *Bird*)
AMPHIBIOUS 5
    LANDING SHIPS 4:
        LSM 3 *Ben Aicha* (FRA *Champlain* BATRAL) (capacity 7 tanks; 140 troops)
        LST 1 *Sidi Mohammed Ben Abdallah* (US *Newport*) (capacity 3 LCVP; 400 troops)
    LANDING CRAFT 2:
        LCM 1 CTM (FRA CTM-5)
        LCT 1 *Sidi Ifni*
LOGISTICS AND SUPPORT 9
    AG 1 Damen 3011
    AGHS 1 *Dar Al Beida* (FRA BHO2M)
    AGOR 1 *Abou Barakat Albarbari*† (ex-US *Robert D. Conrad*)
    AGS 1 Stan 1504
    AK 2
    AX 1 *Essaouira*
    AXS 2

Marines 1,500
FORCES BY ROLE
MANOEUVRE
    Amphibious
    2 naval inf bn

Naval Aviation
EQUIPMENT BY TYPE
HELICOPTERS • ASW/ASUW 3 AS565SA *Panther*

Air Force 13,000
FORCES BY ROLE
FIGHTER/GROUND ATTACK
    2 sqn with F-5E/F-5F *Tiger* II
    3 sqn with F-16C/D *Fighting Falcon*
    1 sqn with *Mirage* F-1C (F-1CH)
    1 sqn with *Mirage* F-1E (F-1EH)
ELECTRONIC WARFARE
    1 sqn with EC-130H *Hercules*; *Falcon* 20 (ELINT)
MARITIME PATROL
    1 flt with Do-28
TANKER/TRANSPORT
    1 sqn with C-130/KC-130H *Hercules*
TRANSPORT
    1 sqn with CN235
    1 VIP sqn with B-737BBJ; Beech 200/300 *King Air*; *Falcon* 50; Gulfstream II/III/V-SP/G550
TRAINING
    1 sqn with *Alpha Jet**
    1 sqn T-6C

ATTACK HELICOPTER
1 sqn with SA342L *Gazelle* (some with HOT)
TRANSPORT HELICOPTER
1 sqn with Bell 205A (AB-205A); Bell 206 *Jet Ranger* (AB-206); Bell 212 (AB-212)
1 sqn with CH-47D *Chinook*
1 sqn with SA330 *Puma*

EQUIPMENT BY TYPE
AIRCRAFT 90 combat capable
 FTR 22: 19 F-5E *Tiger* II; 3 F-5F *Tiger* II
 FGA 49: 15 F-16C *Fighting Falcon*; 8 F-16D *Fighting Falcon*; 15 *Mirage* F-1C (F-1CH); 11 *Mirage* F-1E (F-1EH)
 ELINT 1 EC-130H *Hercules*
 TKR/TPT 2 KC-130H *Hercules*
 TPT 47: **Medium** 17: 4 C-27J *Spartan*; 13 C-130H *Hercules*; **Light** 19: 4 Beech 100 *King Air*; 2 Beech 200 *King Air*; 1 Beech 200C *King Air*; 2 Beech 300 *King Air*; 3 Beech 350 *King Air*; 5 CN235; 2 Do-28; **PAX** 11: 1 B-737BBJ; 2 *Falcon* 20; 2 *Falcon* 20 (ELINT); 1 *Falcon* 50 (VIP); 1 Gulfstream II (VIP); 1 Gulfstream III; 1 Gulfstream V-SP; 2 Gulfstream G550
 TRG 80: 12 AS-202 *Bravo*; 19 *Alpha Jet**; 2 CAP-10; 24 T-6C *Texan*; 9 T-34C *Turbo Mentor*; 14 T-37B *Tweet*
HELICOPTERS
 MRH 19 SA342L *Gazelle* (7 with HOT, 12 with cannon)
 TPT 77: **Heavy** 10 CH-47D *Chinook*; **Medium** 24 SA330 *Puma*; **Light** 43: 25 Bell 205A (AB-205A); 11 Bell 206 *Jet Ranger* (AB-206); 3 Bell 212 (AB-212); 4 Bell 429
AIR-LAUNCHED MISSILES
 AAM • **IR** AIM-9J *Sidewinder*; R-550 *Magic*; *Mica* IR; **IIR** AIM-9X *Sidewinder* II; **SARH** R-530; **ARH** AIM-120C7 AMRAAM; *Mica* RF
 ASM AASM; AGM-65 *Maverick*; HOT
 ARM AGM-88B HARM
BOMBS
 Laser-guided *Paveway* II; GBU-54 Laser JDAM
 INS/GPS-guided GBU-31 JDAM

Paramilitary 50,000 active

Gendarmerie Royale 20,000
FORCES BY ROLE
MANOEUVRE
 Air Manoeuvre
  1 para sqn
 Other
  1 paramilitary bde
  4 (mobile) paramilitary gp
  1 coast guard unit
TRANSPORT HELICOPTER
  1 sqn
EQUIPMENT BY TYPE
PATROL AND COASTAL COMBATANTS • PB 15 *Arcor* 53
AIRCRAFT • TRG 2 R-235 *Guerrier*
HELICOPTERS
 MRH 14: 3 SA315B *Lama*; 2 SA316 *Alouette* III; 3 SA318 *Alouette* II; 6 SA342K *Gazelle*
 TPT 8: **Medium** 6 SA330 *Puma*; **Light** 2 SA360 *Dauphin*

Force Auxiliaire 30,000 (incl 5,000 Mobile Intervention Corps)

Customs/Coast Guard
EQUIPMENT BY TYPE
PATROL AND COASTAL COMBATANTS • PB 36: 4 *Erraid*; 18 *Arcor* 46; 14 (other SAR craft)

DEPLOYMENT
CENTRAL AFRICAN REPUBLIC: UN • MINUSCA 765; 2 obs; 1 inf bn
DEMOCRATIC REPUBLIC OF THE CONGO: UN • MONUSCO 527; 2 obs; 1 inf bn; 1 fd hospital

Oman OMN

Omani Rial R		2017	2018	2019
GDP	R	27.2bn	31.4bn	
	US$	70.8bn	81.7bn	
per capita	US$	17,128	19,170	
Growth	%	-0.9	1.9	
Inflation	%	1.6	1.5	
Def bdgt	R	3.34bn	3.44bn	
	US$	8.69bn	8.95bn	
US$1=R		0.38	0.38	

Population 3,494,116
Expatriates: 27%

Age	0–14	15–19	20–24	25–29	30–64	65 plus
Male	15.4%	4.4%	5.1%	5.9%	21.6%	1.7%
Female	14.7%	4.2%	4.5%	4.6%	16.0%	1.8%

Capabilities

Oman maintains small but capable armed forces, with a particular emphasis on personnel quality and training. Their principal task is ensuring territorial integrity. Oman is uniquely placed with a long coastline outside the Gulf, so it has a particular focus on maritime security. With relatively limited resources, it maintains modern but modest equipment. Oman is a member of the GCC but has not contributed any forces to the Saudi-led intervention in Yemen. It has close defence and security ties with the UK and the US, for whom it hosts forward-deployed forces. There is a particular emphasis on training, especially with the UK. In late 2018, the two countries announced the establishment of a new joint training base in Oman. Recent deployment experience beyond Oman has been limited, but the country maintains modest logistics assets, particularly in the naval domain. The country is developing the port of Duqm into a major potential logistics hub for partners. Oman is in the process of recapitalising its core inventory with the procurement of air and naval systems, including combat aircraft and patrol and high-speed support vessels. Oman has very limited indigenous defence-industrial capacity, but it has begun local production of various types of ammunition.

ACTIVE 42,600 (Army 25,000 Navy 4,200 Air 5,000 Foreign Forces 2,000 Royal Household 6,400) **Paramilitary 4,400**

ORGANISATIONS BY SERVICE

Army 25,000
FORCES BY ROLE
(Regt are bn size)
MANOEUVRE
  Armoured
  1 armd bde (2 armd regt, 1 recce regt)
  Light
  1 inf bde (5 inf regt, 1 arty regt, 1 fd engr regt, 1 engr regt, 1 sigs regt)
  1 inf bde (3 inf regt, 2 arty regt)
  1 indep inf coy (Musandam Security Force)
  Air Manoeuvre
  1 AB regt
COMBAT SERVICE SUPPORT
  1 tpt regt
AIR DEFENCE
  1 ADA regt (2 ADA bty)
EQUIPMENT BY TYPE
ARMOURED FIGHTING VEHICLES
  MBT 117: 38 *Challenger* 2; 6 M60A1 *Patton*; 73 M60A3 *Patton*
  LT TK 37 FV101 *Scorpion*
  RECCE 137: 13 FV105 *Sultan* (CP); 124 VBL
  IFV 2 *Pars* III 8×8
  APC 200
    APC (T) 10 FV4333 *Stormer*
    APC (W) 190: 175 *Piranha* (incl variants); 15 AT-105 *Saxon*
  AUV 6 FV103 *Spartan*
ENGINEERING & MAINTENANCE VEHICLES
  ARV 11: 4 *Challenger*; 2 M88A1; 2 *Piranha*; 3 *Samson*
ARTILLERY 233
  SP 155mm 24 G-6
  TOWED 108: **105mm** 42 L118 Light Gun; **122mm** 30 D-30; **130mm** 24: 12 M-46; 12 Type-59-I; **155mm** 12 FH-70
  MOR 101: **81mm** 69; **107mm** 20 M30; **120mm** 12 Brandt
ANTI-TANK/ANTI-INFRASTRUCTURE • MSL
  SP 8 VBL with TOW
  MANPATS FGM-148 *Javelin*; Milan; TOW/TOW-2A
AIR DEFENCE
  SAM • Point-defence 8 *Mistral* 2; FGM-148 *Javelin*; 9K32 *Strela*-2 (SA-7 *Grail*)‡
  GUNS 26: **23mm** 4 ZU-23-2; **35mm** 10 GDF-005 (with *Skyguard*); **40mm** 12 L/60 (Towed)

Navy 4,200
EQUIPMENT BY TYPE
PRIMARY SURFACE COMBATANTS 3
  FFGHM 3 *Al-Shamikh* with 2 twin lnchr with MM40 *Exocet* Block 3 AShM, 2 6-cell VLS with VL-*MICA* SAM, 1 76mm gun
PATROL AND COASTAL COMBATANTS 12
  CORVETTES • FSGM 2:
    2 *Qahir Al Amwaj* with 2 quad lnchr with MM40 *Exocet* AShM, 1 octuple lnchr with *Crotale* SAM, 1 76mm gun, 1 hel landing platform
  PCFG 3 *Dhofar* with 2 quad lnchr with MM40 *Exocet* AShM, 1 76mm gun
  PCO 4 *Al Ofouq* with 1 76mm gun, 1 hel landing platform
  PCC 3 *Al Bushra* (FRA P-400) with 1 76mm gun
AMPHIBIOUS 6
  LANDING SHIPS • LST 1 *Nasr el Bahr*† with 1 hel landing platform (capacity 7 tanks; 240 troops) (in refit since 2017)
  LANDING CRAFT 5: 1 **LCU**; 3 **LCM**; 1 **LCT**
LOGISTICS AND SUPPORT 8
  AGS 1 *Al Makhirah*
  AK 1 *Al Sultana*
  AP 2 *Shinas* (commercial tpt – auxiliary military role only) (capacity 56 veh; 200 tps)
  AX 1 *Al-Mabrukah*
  AXS 1 *Shabab Oman* II
  EPF 2 *Al Mubshir* (High Speed Support Vessel 72) with 1 hel landing platform (capacity 260 troops)

Air Force 5,000
FORCES BY ROLE
FIGHTER/GROUND ATTACK
  2 sqn with F-16C/D Block 50 *Fighting Falcon*
  1 sqn with *Hawk* Mk103; *Hawk* Mk203; *Hawk* Mk166
  1 sqn with *Typhoon*
MARITIME PATROL
  1 sqn with C295MPA; SC.7 3M *Skyvan*
TRANSPORT
  1 sqn with C-130H/J/J-30 *Hercules*
  1 sqn with C295M
TRAINING
  1 sqn with MFI-17B *Mushshak*; PC-9*; Bell 206 (AB-206) *Jet Ranger*
TRANSPORT HELICOPTER
  4 (med) sqn; Bell 212 (AB-212); NH-90; *Super Lynx* Mk300 (maritime/SAR)
AIR DEFENCE
  2 sqn with *Rapier*; *Blindfire*; S713 *Martello*
EQUIPMENT BY TYPE
AIRCRAFT 63 combat capable
  FGA 35: 17 F-16C Block 50 *Fighting Falcon*; 6 F-16D Block 50 *Fighting Falcon*; 12 *Typhoon*
  MP 4 C295MPA
  TPT 20: **Medium** 6: 3 C-130H *Hercules*; 2 C-130J *Hercules*; 1 C-130J-30 *Hercules* (VIP); **Light** 12: 5 C295M; 7 SC.7 3M *Skyvan* (radar-equipped, for MP); **PAX** 2 A320-300
  TRG 44: 4 *Hawk* Mk103*; 8 *Hawk* Mk166; 12 *Hawk* Mk203*; 8 MFI-17B *Mushshak*; 12 PC-9*
HELICOPTERS
  MRH 15 *Super Lynx* Mk300 (maritime/SAR)
  TPT 26+ **Medium** 20 NH90 TTH; **Light** 6: 3 Bell 206 (AB-206) *Jet Ranger*; 3 Bell 212 (AB-212)
AIR DEFENCE • SAM
  Short-range NASAMS
  Point-defence 40 *Rapier*
MSL
  AAM • IR AIM-9/M/P *Sidewinder*; **IIR** AIM-9X *Sidewinder* II; **ARH** AIM-120C7 AMRAAM
  ASM AGM-65D/G *Maverick*
  AShM AGM-84D *Harpoon*

BOMBS
Laser-guided EGBU-10 *Paveway* II; EGBU-12 *Paveway* II
INS/GPS guided GBU-31 JDAM

Royal Household 6,400
(incl HQ staff)
FORCES BY ROLE
SPECIAL FORCES
2 SF regt

Royal Guard Brigade 5,000
FORCES BY ROLE
MANOEUVRE
Other
  1 gd bde (1 armd sqn, 2 gd regt, 1 cbt spt bn)
EQUIPMENT BY TYPE
ARMOURED FIGHTING VEHICLES
  ASLT 9 *Centauro* MGS (9 VBC-90 in store)
  IFV 14 VAB VCI
  APC • APC (W) ε50 Type-92
ANTI-TANK/ANTI-INFRASTRUCTURE
  MSL • MANPATS *Milan*
ARTILLERY • MRL 122mm 6 Type-90A
AIR DEFENCE
  SAM • Point-defence 14 *Javelin*
  GUNS • SP 9: 20mm 9 VAB VDAA

Royal Yacht Squadron 150
EQUIPMENT BY TYPE
LOGISTICS AND SUPPORT 3
  AP 1 *Fulk Al Salamah* (also veh tpt) with up to 2 AS332 *Super Puma* hel

Royal Flight 250
EQUIPMENT BY TYPE
AIRCRAFT • TPT • PAX 5: 2 B-747SP; 1 DC-8-73CF; 2 Gulfstream IV
HELICOPTERS • TPT • Medium 6: 3 SA330 (AS330) *Puma*; 2 AS332F *Super Puma*; 1 AS332L *Super Puma*

Paramilitary 4,400 active

Tribal Home Guard 4,000
org in teams of ε100

Police Coast Guard 400
EQUIPMENT BY TYPE
PATROL AND COASTAL COMBATANTS 32
  PCO 2 *Haras*
  PBF 3 *Haras* (US Mk V *Pegasus*)
  PB 27: 3 Rodman 101; 1 *Haras* (SWE CG27); 3 *Haras* (SWE CG29); 14 Rodman 58; 1 D59116; 5 *Zahra*

Police Air Wing
EQUIPMENT BY TYPE
AIRCRAFT • TPT • Light 4: 1 BN-2T *Turbine Islander*; 2 CN235M; 1 Do-228
HELICOPTERS • TPT • Light 5: 2 Bell 205A; 3 Bell 214ST (AB-214ST)

FOREIGN FORCES
United Kingdom 90

Palestinian Territories PT

New Israeli Shekel NS		2017	2018	2019
GDP	US$			
per capita	US$			
Growth	%			
Inflation	%			
US$1=NS				

*definitive economic data unavailable

Population	4,635,207				
Age	0–14	15–19	20–24	25–29	30–64	65 plus
Male	20.2%	5.7%	5.1%	4.4%	13.9%	1.5%
Female	19.1%	5.5%	5.0%	4.3%	13.7%	1.7%

Capabilities
The Palestinian Territories remain effectively divided between the Palestinian Authority-run West Bank and Hamas-run Gaza. Each organisation controls their own security forces, principally the National Security Forces (NSF) in the West Bank and the Izz al-Din al-Qassam Brigades in Gaza. Both have generally proved effective at maintaining internal security in their respective territories. The Palestinian Authority has received support from the EU, Jordan and the US. NSF battalions, as well as the Presidential Guard and Civil Police, conduct US-funded internal-security training at the Jordanian International Police Training Center. A small number of Izz al-Din al-Qassam Brigades personnel are claimed by Israel to have received military training in Iran and Syria; the brigades have substantial experience in conducting asymmetric military action against Israel. None of the Palestinian security organisations conduct external military deployments, and they lack a formal military-logistics structure. Both Hamas and the Palestinian Authority lack heavy military equipment, although the former have retained a substantial arsenal of improvised rocket and mortar capabilities, as well as some man-portable guided weapons. No formal defence industry exists, although Hamas is able to acquire light or improvised weapons, either smuggled into Gaza or of local construction.

ACTIVE 0 Paramilitary n.k.
Precise personnel-strength figures for the various Palestinian groups are not known

ORGANISATIONS BY SERVICE
There is little available data on the status of the organisations mentioned below. Following internal fighting in June 2007, Gaza has been under the de facto control of Hamas, while the West Bank is controlled by the Palestinian Authority. In October 2017, both sides agreed a preliminary reconciliation deal on control of Gaza.

Paramilitary

Palestinian Authority n.k.
Presidential Security ε3,000

Special Forces ε1,200

Police ε9,000

National Security Force ε10,000
FORCES BY ROLE
MANOEUVRE
  Other
    9 paramilitary bn

Preventative Security ε4,000

Civil Defence ε1,000

The al-Aqsa Brigades n.k.
Profess loyalty to the Fatah group that dominates the Palestinian Authority

Hamas n.k.

Izz al-Din al-Qassam Brigades ε15,000–20,000
FORCES BY ROLE
COMMAND
  6 bde HQ (regional)
MANOEUVRE
  Other
    1 cdo unit (Nukhba)
    27 paramilitary bn
    100 paramilitary coy
  COMBAT SUPPORT Some engr units
  COMBAT SERVICE SUPPORT
    Some log units
EQUIPMENT BY TYPE
ANTI-TANK/ANTI-INFRASTRUCTURE • MSL •
  MANPATS 9K11 *Malyutka* (AT-3 *Sagger*) (reported)
ARTILLERY
  MRL • *Qassam* rockets (multiple calibres); **122mm** *Grad*
  MOR some (multiple calibres)

Martime Police ε600

Qatar QTR

Qatari Riyal R		2017	2018	2019
GDP	R	608bn	685bn	
	US$	167bn	188bn	
per capita	US$	61,025	67,818	
Growth	%	1.6	2.7	
Inflation	%	0.4	3.7	
Def exp	R	n.k.	n.k.	
	US$	n.k.	n.k.	
US$1=R		3.64	3.64	

Population   2,363,569

Ethnic groups: Nationals 25%; expatriates 75%, of which Indian 18%; Iranian 10%; Pakistani 18%

Age	0–14	15–19	20–24	25–29	30–64	65 plus
Male	6.4%	2.4%	6.3%	11.0%	50.5%	0.7%
Female	6.3%	1.6%	1.9%	2.7%	9.9%	0.4%

Capabilities

Qatar is attempting to transform its military capabilities and regional defence standing based on significant equipment acquisitions, with the aim of creating one of the most well-equipped forces in the region. The diplomatic crisis with several of its GCC neighbours has brought Qatar and Turkey closer together in their limited but significant defence cooperation, which includes a small Turkish military presence in-country. The crisis appears not to have affected the significant Qatar–US military relationship, including the presence of forces from the US and other Western states at Al-Udeid air base, and the key US-run coalition air-operations centre. The pressure on personnel requirements is increasing significantly due to Qatar's acquisition programme. Changes were reported to national-service liabilities in 2018, increasing terms of service and making national service voluntary for women. The speed and scale of the equipment plan suggests that Qatar will need significant foreign help to integrate and operate its new capabilities. The Italian Navy is supporting training for new Italian-built vessels and a joint Eurofighter *Typhoon* squadron is being stood up with the UK. The Qatari armed forces initially sent air and ground elements to support the Saudi-led intervention in Yemen. The country is also acquiring platforms with potentially significant power-projection capability. Qatar's ambitious across-the-board re-equipment programme includes significant purchases of combat aircraft. These procurements will, when combined, dramatically increase the size of the air force, and it is in terms of air capabilities that there are the most questions about Qatar's ability to procure the necessary infrastructure, maintenance and personnel. Coastal-defence missiles are being acquired, while an AN/FPS-132 early-warning radar is being installed. Qatar currently has a limited indigenous defence-industrial capability, including in ship repair.

ACTIVE 16,500 (Army 12,000 Navy 2,500 Air 2,000)
Paramilitary up to 5,000
Conscript liability 12 months for all men, regardless of education; voluntary conscription for women

ORGANISATIONS BY SERVICE

Space
EQUIPMENT BY TYPE
SATELLITES • COMMUNICATIONS 1 *Es'hail*-2

Army 12,000 (including Emiri Guard)
FORCES BY ROLE
SPECIAL FORCES
  1 SF coy
MANOEUVRE
  Armoured
  1 armd bde (1 tk bn, 1 mech inf bn, 1 mor sqn, 1 AT bn)
  Mechanised
  3 mech inf bn
  Light
  1 (Emiri Guard) bde (3 inf regt)
COMBAT SUPPORT
  1 fd arty bn
EQUIPMENT BY TYPE
ARMOURED FIGHTING VEHICLES
  MBT 62 Leopard 2A7+
  ASLT 48: 12 AMX-10RC; 36 Piranha II 90mm
  RECCE 44: 20 EE-9 Cascavel; 25 Fennek; 8 V-150 Chaimite; 16 VBL
  IFV 40 AMX-10P
  APC 190
    APC (T) 30 AMX-VCI
    APC (W) 160 VAB
  APC 14 Dingo 2
ENGINEERING & MAINTENANCE VEHICLES
  AEV Wisent 2
  ARV 3: 1 AMX-30D; 2 Piranha
ANTI-TANK/ANTI-INFRASTRUCTURE
  MSL
    SP 24 VAB VCAC HOT
    MANPATS Milan
  RCL 84mm Carl Gustav
ARTILLERY 115+
  SP 155mm 52: 28 Mk F3; 24 PzH 2000
  TOWED 155mm 12 G-5
  MRL 6+: **122mm** 2+ (30-tube); **127mm** 4 ASTROS II Mk3
  MOR 45: **81mm** 26 L16; **SP 81mm** 4 VAB VPM 81; **120mm** 15 Brandt
SURFACE-TO-SURFACE MISSILE LAUNCHERS
  SRBM • Conventional 2 BP-12A (CH-SS-14 mod 2)

Navy 2,500 (incl Coast Guard)
EQUIPMENT BY TYPE
PATROL AND COASTAL COMBATANTS 11
  PCFGM 4 Barzan (UK Vita) with 2 quad lnchr with MM40 Exocet Block 3 AShM, 1 sextuple lnchr with Mistral SAM, 1 Goalkeeper CIWS, 1 76mm gun
  PCFG 3 Damsah (FRA Combattante III) with 2 quad lnchr with MM40 Exocet AShM, 1 76mm gun
  PBF 3 MRTP 16
  PB 1 MRTP 34

Coast Guard
EQUIPMENT BY TYPE
PATROL AND COASTAL COMBATANTS 12
  PBF 4 DV 15
  PB 8: 4 Crestitalia MV-45; 3 Halmatic M160; 1 other

Coastal Defence
FORCES BY ROLE
COASTAL DEFENCE
  1 bty with 3 quad lnchr with MM40 Exocet AShM
EQUIPMENT BY TYPE
COASTAL DEFENCE • AShM 12 MM40 Exocet AShM

Air Force 2,000
FORCES BY ROLE
FIGHTER/GROUND ATTACK
  1 sqn with Alpha Jet*
  1 sqn with Mirage 2000ED; Mirage 2000D
  1 sqn with Rafale (forming)
TRANSPORT
  1 sqn with C-17A Globemaster III; C-130J-30 Hercules
  1 sqn with A340; B-707; B-727; Falcon 900
ATTACK HELICOPTER
  1 ASuW sqn with Commando Mk3 with Exocet
  1 sqn with SA341 Gazelle; SA342L Gazelle with HOT
TRANSPORT HELICOPTER
  1 sqn with Commando Mk2A; Commando Mk2C
  1 sqn with AW139
EQUIPMENT BY TYPE
AIRCRAFT 18 combat capable
  FGA 12: 9 Mirage 2000ED; 3 Mirage 2000D
  TPT 18: **Heavy** 8 C-17A Globemaster III; **Medium** 4 C-130J-30 Hercules; **PAX** 6: 1 A340; 2 B-707; 1 B-727; 2 Falcon 900
  TRG 27: 6 Alpha Jet*; 21 PC-21
HELICOPTERS
  ASuW 8 Commando Mk3
  MRH 34: 21 AW139 (incl 3 for medevac); 2 SA341 Gazelle; 11 SA342L Gazelle
  TPT • Medium 4: 3 Commando Mk2A; 1 Commando Mk2C
AIR DEFENCE • SAM
  Short-Range 9 Roland II
  Point-defence Mistral; Blowpipe; FIM-92 Stinger; 9K32 Strela-2 (SA-7 Grail)‡
AIR-LAUNCHED MISSILES
  AAM • IR R-550 Magic 2; **ARH** Mica RF
  ASM Apache; HOT
  AShM AM39 Exocet

Paramilitary up to 5,000 active

Internal Security Force up to 5,000

DEPLOYMENT
LEBANON: UN • UNIFIL 2

FOREIGN FORCES
Turkey 150 (trg team)
United States US Central Command: 10,000; USAF CAOC; 1 bbr sqn with 6 B-1B Lancer; 1 ISR sqn with 4 RC-135 Rivet Joint; 1 ISR sqn with 4 E-8C JSTARS; 1 tkr sqn with 24 KC-135R/T Stratotanker; 1 tpt sqn with 4 C-17A

Globemaster; 4 C-130H/J-30 *Hercules*; 2 AD bty with MIM-104E/F *Patriot* PAC-2/3 • US Strategic Command: 1 AN/TPY-2 X-band radar

Saudi Arabia SAU

Saudi Riyal R		2017	2018	2019
GDP	R	2.58tr	2.89tr	
	US$	687bn	770bn	
per capita	US$	21,096	23,187	
Growth	%	-0.9	2.2	
Inflation	%	-0.9	2.6	
Def exp	R	334bn	311bn	
	US$	89.1bn	82.9bn	
US$1=R		3.75	3.75	

Population 33,091,113

Ethnic groups: Nationals 73%, of which Bedouin up to 10%, Shia 6%; expatriates 27%, of which Asians 20%, Arabs 6%, Africans 1%, Europeans <1%

Age	0–14	15–19	20–24	25–29	30–64	65 plus
Male	13.1%	4.2%	4.0%	4.8%	28.7%	1.8%
Female	12.6%	3.9%	3.5%	4.0%	17.9%	1.5%

Capabilities

The armed forces are one of the best equipped in the region, and the kingdom has displayed an increasing willingness to use them as part of a more assertive foreign policy. Principal roles are securing territorial integrity, internal security and regional stability. Saudi Arabia's defence posture continues to emphasise the deployment of airpower. Saudi Arabia is the leading member of the GCC. However, its most critical defence relationship is with the US, which is the ultimate external guarantor of its security. In 2017, the countries agreed to establish a Strategic Joint Consultative Group, and furthered existing defence and security cooperation. Riyadh also has significant security relationships with France and the UK, though recently there has been diversification of defence relationships, including with China. Significant training support is supplied by the US and, to a lesser extent, the UK. The armed forces continue to gain combat experience from their involvement in the conflict in Yemen. However, the operation has exposed areas of comparative weakness and capability gaps, especially in the application of precision airpower, air–ground coordination and in logistics support, such as aerial refuelling. The US remains the country's main source of advanced weaponry, followed by the UK, with whom it signed a new Military and Security Cooperation Agreement in September 2017. Saudi Arabia continues its equipment recapitalisation, with orders for combat aircraft, corvettes and multi-mission surface combatants. There is a modest domestic defence-industrial base, mainly in the assembly and overhaul of land systems. Riyadh has declared an intention to spend 50% of its defence outlays locally as part of its Vision 2030 initiative and established the state-owned Saudi Arabian Military Industries to oversee local defence production.

ACTIVE 227,000 (Army 75,000 Navy 13,500 Air 20,000 Air Defence 16,000 Strategic Missile Forces 2,500 National Guard 100,000) **Paramilitary 24,500**

ORGANISATIONS BY SERVICE

Army 75,000
FORCES BY ROLE
MANOEUVRE
  Armoured
  4 armd bde (1 recce coy, 3 tk bn, 1 mech bn, 1 fd arty bn, 1 AD bn, 1 AT bn, 1 engr coy, 1 log bn, 1 maint coy, 1 med coy)
  Mechanised
  5 mech bde (1 recce coy, 1 tk bn, 3 mech bn, 1 fd arty bn, 1 AD bn, 1 AT bn, 1 engr coy, 1 log bn, 1 maint coy, 1 med coy)
  Light
  2 lt inf bde
  1 (Royal Guard) regt (3 lt inf bn)
  Air Manoeuvre
  1 AB bde (2 AB bn, 3 SF coy)
  Aviation
  1 comd (3 hel gp)
COMBAT SUPPORT
  3 arty bde
EQUIPMENT BY TYPE
  MBT 900: 140 AMX-30; 370 M1A2/A2S *Abrams*; 390 M60A3 *Patton*
  RECCE 300 AML-60/AML-90
  IFV 760: 380 AMX-10P; 380 M2A2 *Bradley*
  APC 1,340
    APC (T) 1,190 M113A4 (incl variants)
    APC (W) 150 Panhard M3 (ε40 AF-40-8-1 *Al-Fahd* in store)
  AUV 333: 73 *Aravis*; 100 *Didgori* (amb); 160 M-ATV; *Al-Shibl* 2; Terradyne *Gurkha*;
  ENGINEERING & MAINTENANCE VEHICLES
  AEV 15 M728
  ARV 278+: 8 ACV ARV; AMX-10EHC; 55 AMX-30D; *Leclerc* ARV; 122 M88A1; 90 M578
  VLB 10 AMX-30
  MW *Aardvark* Mk2
  NBC VEHICLES 10 TPz-1 *Fuchs* NBC
  ANTI-TANK/ANTI-INFRASTRUCTURE
    MSL
      SP 290+: 90+ AMX-10P (HOT); 200 VCC-1 ITOW; M-ATV with *Milan*
      MANPATS *Hyeongung*; TOW-2A
    RCL 84mm *Carl Gustav*; 90mm M67; 106mm M40A1
  ARTILLERY 761
    SP 155mm 224: 60 AU-F-1; 110 M109A1B/A2; 54 PLZ-45
    TOWED 110: 105mm (100 M101/M102 in store); 155mm 110: 50 M114; 60 M198; 203mm (8 M115 in store)
    MRL 127mm 60 ASTROS II Mk3
    MOR 367: SP 81mm 70; SP 107mm 150 M30; 120mm 147: 110 Brandt; 37 M12-1535
  HELICOPTERS
    ATK 35: 11 AH-64D *Apache*; 24 AH-64E *Apache*
    MRH 21: 6 AS365N *Dauphin* 2 (medevac); 15 Bell 406CS *Combat Scout*
    TPT • Medium 58: 12 S-70A1 *Desert Hawk*; 22 UH-60A *Black Hawk* (4 medevac); 24 UH-60L *Black Hawk*

AIR DEFENCE • SAM
Short-range Crotale
Point-defence FIM-92 Stinger

Navy 13,500
Navy HQ at Riyadh; Eastern Fleet HQ at Jubail; Western Fleet HQ at Jeddah

EQUIPMENT BY TYPE
PRINCIPAL SURFACE COMBATANTS 7
  DESTROYERS • DDGHM 3 *Al Riyadh* (FRA *La Fayette* mod) with 2 quad lnchr with MM40 *Exocet* Block 2 AShM, 2 8-cell A43 VLS with *Aster* 15 SAM, 4 single 533mm TT with F17P HWT, 1 76mm gun (capacity 1 AS365N *Dauphin* 2 hel)
  FRIGATES • FFGHM 4 *Madina* (FRA F-2000) with 2 quad lnchr with *Otomat* Mk2 AShM, 1 octuple lnchr with *Crotale* SAM, 4 single 533mm TT with F17P HWT, 1 100mm gun (capacity 1 AS365N *Dauphin* 2 hel)
PATROL AND COASTAL COMBATANTS 32
  CORVETTES • FSG 4 *Badr* (US *Tacoma*) with 2 quad Mk140 lnchr with RGM-84C *Harpoon* AShM, 2 triple 324mm ASTT with Mk 46 LWT, 1 *Phalanx* CIWS, 1 76mm gun
  PCFG 9 *Al Siddiq* (US 58m) with 2 twin Mk140 lnchr with RGM-84C *Harpoon* AShM, 1 *Phalanx* CIWS, 1 76mm gun
  PB 19: 17 (US) *Halter Marine* 24m; 2 Plascoa 2200
MINE WARFARE • MINE COUNTERMEASURES 3
  MHC 3 *Al Jawf* (UK *Sandown*)
AMPHIBIOUS • LANDING CRAFT 5
  LCM 3 LCM 6 (capacity 80 troops)
  LCU ε2 *Al Qiaq* (US LCU 1610) (capacity 120 troops)
LOGISTICS AND SUPPORT 2
  AORH 2 *Boraida* (mod FRA *Durance*) (capacity either 2 AS365F *Dauphin* 2 hel or 1 AS332C *Super Puma*)

Naval Aviation
EQUIPMENT BY TYPE
HELICOPTERS
  MRH 34: 6 AS365N *Dauphin* 2; 15 AS565; 13 Bell 406CS *Combat Scout*
  TPT • Medium 12 AS332B/F *Super Puma*
AIR-LAUNCHED MISSILES
  AShM AM39 *Exocet*; AS-15TT

Marines 3,000
FORCES BY ROLE
SPECIAL FORCES
  1 spec ops regt with (2 spec ops bn)
EQUIPMENT BY TYPE
ARMOURED FIGHTING VEHICLES
  RECCE *Bastion Patsas*
  APC • APC (W) 135 BMR-600P

Air Force 20,000
FORCES BY ROLE
FIGHTER
  4 sqn with F-15C/D *Eagle*
FIGHTER/GROUND ATTACK
  2 sqn with F-15SA *Eagle*
  3 sqn with *Typhoon*

GROUND ATTACK
  3 sqn with *Tornado* IDS; *Tornado* GR1A
AIRBORNE EARLY WARNING & CONTROL
  1 sqn with E-3A *Sentry*
  1 sqn with Saab 2000 *Erieye*
ELINT
  1 sqn with RE-3A/B; Beech 350ER *King Air*
TANKER
  1 sqn with KE-3A
TANKER/TRANSPORT
  1 sqn with KC-130H/J *Hercules*
  1 sqn with A330 MRTT
TRANSPORT
  3 sqn with C-130H *Hercules*; C-130H-30 *Hercules*; CN-235; L-100-30HS (hospital ac)
  2 sqn with Beech 350 *King Air* (forming)
TRAINING
  1 OCU sqn with F-15SA *Eagle*
  3 sqn with *Hawk* Mk65*; *Hawk* Mk65A*; *Hawk* Mk165*
  1 sqn with *Jetstream* Mk31
  1 sqn with MFI-17 *Mushshak*; SR22T
  2 sqn with PC-9; PC-21
TRANSPORT HELICOPTER
  4 sqn with AS532 *Cougar* (CSAR); Bell 212 (AB-212); Bell 412 (AB-412) *Twin Huey* (SAR)

EQUIPMENT BY TYPE
AIRCRAFT 407 combat capable
  FTR 81: 56 F-15C *Eagle*; 25 F-15D *Eagle*
  FGA 185+: up to 67 F-15S *Eagle* (being upgraded to F-15SA configuration); 47+ F-15SA *Eagle*; 71 *Typhoon*
  ATK 67 *Tornado* IDS
  ISR 14+: 12 *Tornado* GR1A*; 2+ Beech 350ER *King Air*
  AEW&C 7: 5 E-3A *Sentry*; 2 Saab 2000 *Erieye*
  ELINT 2: 1 RE-3A; 1 RE-3B
  TKR/TPT 15: 6 A330 MRTT; 7 KC-130H *Hercules*; 2 KC-130J *Hercules*
  TKR 7 KE-3A
  TPT 47+: **Medium** 36: 30 C-130H *Hercules*; 3 C-130H-30 *Hercules*; 3 L-100-30; **Light** 11+: 10+ Beech 350 *King Air*; 1 *Jetstream* Mk31
  TRG 181: 24 *Hawk* Mk65* (incl aerobatic team); 16 *Hawk* Mk65A*; 22 *Hawk* Mk165*; 20 MFI-17 *Mushshak*; 20 PC-9; 55 PC-21; 24 SR22T
HELICOPTERS
  MRH 15 Bell 412 (AB-412) *Twin Huey* (SAR)
  TPT 30: **Medium** 10 AS532 *Cougar* (CSAR); **Light** 20 Bell 212 (AB-212)
UNMANNED AERIAL VEHICLES
  CISR • Heavy some *Wing Loong* 1 (GJ-1) (reported); some CH-4
  ISR • Medium some *Falco*
AIR-LAUNCHED MISSILES
  AAM • IR AIM-9P/L *Sidewinder*; **IIR** AIM-9X *Sidewinder* II; IRIS-T; **SARH** AIM-7 *Sparrow*; AIM-7M *Sparrow*; **ARH** AIM-120C AMRAAM
  ASM AGM-65 *Maverick*; AR-1
  AShM *Sea Eagle*; AGM-48L *Harpoon* Block II
  ARM ALARM
  ALCM *Storm Shadow*
BOMBS
  Laser-guided GBU-10/12 *Paveway* II; *Paveway* IV
  INS/GPS-guided GBU-31 JDAM; FT-9

Royal Flt

EQUIPMENT BY TYPE
AIRCRAFT • **TPT** 24: **Medium** 8: 5 C-130H *Hercules*; 3 L-100-30; **Light** 3: 1 Cessna 310; 2 Learjet 35; **PAX** 13: 1 A340; 1 B-737-200; 2 B-737BBJ; 2 B-747SP; 4 BAe-125-800; 2 Gulfstream III; 1 Gulfstream IV
HELICOPTERS • **TPT** 3+: **Medium** 3: 2 AS-61; 1 S-70 *Black Hawk*; **Light** some Bell 212 (AB-212)

Air Defence Forces 16,000

FORCES BY ROLE
AIR DEFENCE
6 bn with MIM-104D/F *Patriot* PAC-2 GEM/PAC-3
17 bty with *Shahine*/AMX-30SA
16 bty with MIM-23B I-*Hawk*
73 units (static defence) with *Crotale*/*Shahine*

EQUIPMENT BY TYPE
AIR DEFENCE
  SAM
    Long-range 108 MIM-104D/F *Patriot* PAC-2 GEM/PAC-3
    Medium-range 128 MIM-23B I-*Hawk*
    Short-range 181: 40 *Crotale*; 73 *Shahine*; 68 *Crotale*/*Shahine*
    Point-defence 400+: 400 M1097 *Avenger*; Mistral
  GUNS 1,070
    SP 942: **20mm** 92 M163 *Vulcan*; **30mm** 850 AMX-30SA
    TOWED 128: **35mm** 128 GDF Oerlikon; **40mm** (150 L/70 in store)

Strategic Missile Forces 2,500

EQUIPMENT BY TYPE
MSL • **TACTICAL**
  IRBM 10+ DF-3 (CH-SS-2) (service status unclear)
  MRBM Some DF-21 (CH-SS-5 – variant unclear) (reported)

National Guard 73,000 active; 27,000 (tribal levies) (total 100,000)

FORCES BY ROLE
MANOEUVRE
  Mechanised
  5 mech bde (1 recce coy, 3 mech inf bn, 1 SP arty bn, 1 cbt engr coy, 1 sigs coy, 1 log bn)
  Light
  5 inf bde (3 combined arms bn, 1 arty bn, 1 log bn)
  3 indep lt inf bn
  Other
  1 (Special Security) sy bde (3 sy bn)
  1 (ceremonial) cav sqn
COMBAT SUPPORT
  1 MP bn

EQUIPMENT BY TYPE
ARMOURED FIGHTING VEHICLES
  ASLT 204 LAV-AG (90mm)
  IFV 640 LAV-25
  APC • **APC (W)** 806 117 LAV-A (amb); 30 LAV-AC (ammo carrier); 296 LAV-CC (CP); 73 LAV-PC; 290 V-150 *Commando* (810 in store)

ENGINEERING & MAINTENANCE VEHICLES
  AEV 58 LAV-E
  ARV 111 LAV-R; V-150 ARV
ANTI-TANK/ANTI-INFRASTRUCTURE
  MSL
    SP 182 LAV-AT
    MANPATS TOW-2A; M47 *Dragon*
  RCL • **106mm** M40A1
ARTILLERY 359+
  SP 155mm 132 CAESAR
  TOWED 108: **105mm** 50 M102; **155mm** 58 M198
  MOR 119+: **81mm** some; **120mm** 119 LAV-M
HELICOPTERS
  ATK 12 AH-64E *Apache*
  MRH 20: 8 AH-6i *Little Bird*; 12 MD530F (trg role)
  TPT • **Medium** 23 UH-60M *Black Hawk*
AIR DEFENCE
  GUNS • **TOWED** • **20mm** 30 M167 *Vulcan*
AIR-LAUNCHED MISSILES
  ASM AGM-114R *Hellfire* II

Paramilitary 24,500+ active

Border Guard 15,000

FORCES BY ROLE
Subordinate to Ministry of Interior. HQ in Riyadh. 9 subordinate regional commands
MANOEUVRE
  Other
  Some mobile def (long-range patrol/spt) units
  2 border def (patrol) units
  12 infrastructure def units
  18 harbour def units
  Some coastal def units
COMBAT SUPPORT
  Some MP units

EQUIPMENT BY TYPE
ARMOURED FIGHTING VEHICLES
  APC • **PPV** *Caprivi* Mk3
PATROL AND COASTAL COMBATANTS 23+
  PCC 9 CSB 40
  PBF 6+: 4 *Al Jouf*; 2 *Sea Guard*; some *Plascoa* FIC 1650
  PB 8: 6 Damen Stan Patrol 2606; 2 *Al Jubatel*
AMPHIBIOUS • **LANDING CRAFT** 8: 5 UCAC *Griffon* 8000; 3 other
LOGISTICS AND SUPPORT 4: 1 **AXL**; 3 AO

Facilities Security Force 9,000+

Subordinate to Ministry of Interior

General Civil Defence Administration Units

EQUIPMENT BY TYPE
HELICOPTERS • **TPT** • **Medium** 10 Boeing *Vertol* 107

Special Security Force 500

EQUIPMENT BY TYPE
ARMOURED FIGHTING VEHICLES
  APC • **APC (W)** UR-416
  AUV *Gurkha* LAPV

DEPLOYMENT

TURKEY: *Operation Inherent Resolve* 6 F-15S *Eagle*

YEMEN: *Operation Restoring Hope* 1,500; 1 armd BG; M60A3; M2A2 Bradley; M113A4; M-ATV; 2+ MIM-104D/F *Patriot* PAC-2/3

FOREIGN FORCES

Bahrain *Operation Restoring Hope* 250; 1 SF gp; 1 arty gp; 6 F-16C *Fighting Falcon*
Egypt *Operation Restoring Hope* 6 F-16C *Fighting Falcon*
Jordan *Operation Restoring Hope* 6 F-16AM *Fighting Falcon*
Kuwait *Operation Restoring Hope* 4 F/A-18A *Hornet*
Sudan *Operation Restoring Hope* 3 Su-24 *Fencer*
United Arab Emirates *Operation Restoring Hope* 12 F-16E *Fighting Falcon*
United States US Central Command: 500

Syria SYR

Syrian Pound S£		2017	2018	2019
GDP	S£			
	US$			
per capita	US$			
Growth	%			
Inflation	%			
Def exp	S£			
	US$			
US$1=S£				

*definitive economic data unavailable

Population	19,454,263					
Age	0–14	15–19	20–24	25–29	30–64	65 plus
Male	16.1%	5.2%	4.8%	4.4%	17.9%	2.0%
Female	15.3%	5.0%	4.6%	4.4%	18.0%	2.4%

Capabilities

The civil war has significantly depleted the combat capabilities of the Syrian armed forces and transformed them into an irregularly structured militia-style organisation focused on internal security. There is no published defence doctrine or white paper, the ongoing war instead dictating de facto requirements and priorities. Most formal pre-war structures and formations exist in name only, as resources have been channelled into an irregular network of military organisations that form the regime's most effective military capabilities. Russia is the regime's dominant ally and has provided essential direct combat support and assistance to Syrian military activities, as well as significant amounts of replacement equipment. Iran and Hizbullah also continue to assist in the provision and training of militias and other ground forces. Overall levels of training remain poor, but select regular and irregular military formations have gained a reasonable degree of proficiency through combat experience. The armed forces lack the requisite capabilities for external deployment, although they remain able to redeploy moderate numbers of formations and capabilities within the country. Logistics support for major internal operations away from established bases remains a challenge. The large pre-war equipment inventory has long suffered from indifferent maintenance, a situation that has deteriorated further. Front-line combat units have been re-equipping with Russian-supplied new or surplus weapons systems. Before the civil war, Syria did not have a major domestic defence industry, although it possessed facilities for the overhaul and maintenance of its existing systems. It did, however, possess some capacity in focused areas, such as ballistic missiles and chemical weapons.

ACTIVE 139,000 (Army 100,000 Navy 4,000 Air 15,000 Air Defence 20,000) **Paramilitary 100,000**

Conscript liability 30 months (there is widespread avoidance of military service)

ORGANISATIONS BY SERVICE

Army ε100,000
FORCES BY ROLE
The Syrian Arab Army combines conventional formations, special forces and auxiliary militias. The main fighting units are the 4th Armoured Division, the Republican Guard, the paratroopers and the Special Forces (including Tiger Forces); they receive the most attention and training. Much of the remainder performs static functions across regime-held areas. Many formations are under-strength, at an estimated 500–1,000 personnel in brigades and regiments.
COMMAND
 4 corps HQ
 1 (5th Assault) corps HQ
SPECIAL FORCES
 2 SF div (total: 11 SF regt; 1 tk regt)
MANOEUVRE
 Armoured
 1 (4th) armd div (1 SF regt, 2 armd bde, 2 mech bde, 1 arty regt, 1 SSM bde (3 SSM bn with *Scud*-B/C))
 5 armd div(-)
 Mechanised
 1 (Republican Guard) mech div (3 mech bde, 2 sy regt, 1 arty regt)
 3 mech div(-)
 2 indep inf bde(-)
 Amphibious
 1 mne unit
COMBAT SUPPORT
 2 arty bde
 2 AT bde
 1 SSM bde (3 SSM bn with FROG-7)
 1 SSM bde (3 SSM bn with SS-21)
EQUIPMENT BY TYPE
Attrition during the civil war has severely reduced equipment numbers for almost all types. It is unclear how much remains available for operations
ARMOURED FIGHTING VEHICLES
 MBT T-55A; T-55AM; T-55AMV; T-62; T-62M; T-72; T-72AV; T-72B; T-72B3; T-72M1; T-90
 RECCE BRDM-2
 IFV BMP-1; BMP-2; BTR-82A
 APC
  APC (T) BTR-50
  APC (W) BTR-152; BTR-60; BTR-70; BTR-80
 APC IVECO LMV

ENGINEERING & MAINTENANCE VEHICLES
  ARV BREM-1 reported; T-54/55
  VLB MTU; MTU-20
  MW UR-77
ANTI-TANK/ANTI-INFRASTRUCTURE • MSL
  SP 9P133 *Malyutka*-P (BRDM-2 with AT-3C *Sagger*); 9P148 *Konkurs* (BRDM-2 with AT-5 *Spandrel*)
  MANPATS 9K111 *Fagot* (AT-4 *Spigot*); 9K111-1 *Konkurs* (AT-5 *Spandrel*); 9K115 *Metis* (AT-7 *Saxhorn*); 9K115-2 *Metis-M* (AT-13 *Saxhorn* 2); 9K135 *Kornet* (AT-14 *Spriggan*); *Milan*
ARTILLERY
  SP 122mm 2S1 *Gvozdika*; D-30 (mounted on T34/85 chassis); **130mm** M-46 (truck–mounted); **152mm** 2S3 *Akatsiya*
  TOWED 122mm D-30; M-30 (M1938); **130mm** M-46; **152mm** D-20; ML-20 (M-1937); **180mm** S-23
  GUN/MOR 120mm 2S9 NONA-S
  MRL 107mm Type-63; **122mm** BM-21 *Grad*; **140mm** BM-14; **220mm** 9P140 *Uragan*; **300mm** 9A52 *Smerch*; **330mm** some (also improvised systems of various calibres)
  MOR 82mm some; **120mm** M-1943; **160mm** M-160; **240mm** M-240
SURFACE-TO-SURFACE MISSILE LAUNCHERS
  SRBM • **Conventional** *Scud*-B/C/D; *Scud* look-a-like; 9K79 *Tochka* (SS-21 *Scarab*); *Fateh*-110/M-600
UNMANNED AERIAL VEHICLES
  ISR • Medium *Mohajer* 3/4; **Light** *Ababil*
AIR DEFENCE
  SAM
    Medium-range 9K37 *Buk* (SA-11 *Gadfly*); 9K317 *Buk*-M2 (SA-17 *Grizzly*)
    Short-range 96K6 *Pantsir*-S1 (SA-22 *Greyhound*)
    Point-defence 9K31 *Strela*-1 (SA-9 *Gaskin*); 9K33 *Osa* (SA-8 *Gecko*); 9K35 *Strela*-10 (SA-13 *Gopher*); 9K32 *Strela*-2 (SA-7 *Grail*)‡; 9K38 *Igla* (SA-18 *Grouse*); 9K36 *Strela*-3 (SA-14 *Gremlin*); 9K338 *Igla*-S (SA-24 *Grinch*)
  GUNS
    SP 23mm ZSU-23-4; **57mm** ZSU-57-2; S-60 (on 2K12 chassis)
    TOWED 23mm ZU-23-2; **37mm** M-1939; **57mm** S-60; **100mm** KS-19

Navy ε4,000
Some personnel are likely to have been drafted into other services
EQUIPMENT BY TYPE
PATROL AND COASTAL COMBATANTS 32†:
  CORVETTES • FS 2 *Petya* III (1†) with 1 triple 533mm ASTT with SAET-60 HWT, 4 RBU 2500 *Smerch* 1† A/S mor, 2 twin 76mm gun
  PBFG 22:
    16 *Osa* I/II with 4 single lnchr with P-15M *Termit*-M (SS-N-2C *Styx*) AShM
    6 *Tir* with 2 single lnchr with C-802 (CH-SS-N-8 *Saccade*) AShM
  PB 8 *Zhuk*†
MINE WARFARE • MINE COUNTERMEASURES 7
  MHC 1 *Sonya* with 2 quad lnchr with 9K32 *Strela*-2 (SA-N-5 *Grail*)‡ SAM, 2 AK630 CIWS
  MSO 1 *Natya* with 2 quad lnchr with 9K32 *Strela*-2 (SA-N-5 *Grail*)‡ SAM

  MSI 5 *Korund* (*Yevgenya*) (Project 1258)
AMPHIBIOUS • LANDING SHIPS • LSM 3 *Polnochny* B (capacity 6 MBT; 180 troops)
LOGISTICS AND SUPPORT • AX 1 *Al Assad*

Coastal Defence
FORCES BY ROLE
COASTAL DEFENCE
  1 AShM bde with P-35 (SSC-1B *Sepal*); P-15M *Termit*-R (SSC-3 *Styx*); C-802; K-300P *Bastion* (SSC-5 *Stooge*)
EQUIPMENT BY TYPE
COASTAL DEFENCE • AShM P-35 (SSC-1B *Sepal*); P-15M *Termit*-R (SSC-3 *Styx*); C-802; K-300P *Bastion* (SSC-5 *Stooge*)

Naval Aviation
All possibly non-operational after vacating base for Russian deployment
EQUIPMENT BY TYPE
HELICOPTERS • ASW 10: 4 Ka-28 *Helix* A; 6 Mi-14 *Haze*

Air Force ε15,000(-)
FORCES BY ROLE
FIGHTER
  2 sqn with MiG-23 MF/ML/UM *Flogger*
  2 sqn with MiG-29A/U *Fulcrum*
FIGHTER/GROUND ATTACK
  4 sqn with MiG-21MF/bis *Fishbed*; MiG-21U *Mongol* A
  2 sqn with MiG-23BN/UB *Flogger*
GROUND ATTACK
  4 sqn with Su-22 *Fitter* D
  1 sqn with Su-24 *Fencer*
  1 sqn with L-39 *Albatros**
TRANSPORT
  1 sqn with An-24 *Coke*; An-26 *Curl*; Il-76 *Candid*
  1 sqn with *Falcon* 20; *Falcon* 900
  1 sqn with Tu-134B-3
  1 sqn with Yak-40 *Codling*
ATTACK HELICOPTER
  3 sqn with Mi-25 *Hind* D
  2 sqn with SA342L *Gazelle*
TRANSPORT HELICOPTER
  6 sqn with Mi-8 *Hip*/Mi-17 *Hip* H
EQUIPMENT BY TYPE
Heavy use of both fixed- and rotary-wing assets has likely reduced readiness and availability to very low levels. It is estimated that no more than 30–40% of the inventory is operational
AIRCRAFT 236 combat capable
  FTR 64: 34 MiG-23MF/ML/UM *Flogger*; 30 MiG-29A/SM/UB *Fulcrum*
  FGA 118: 68 MiG-21MF/bis *Fishbed*; 9 MiG-21U *Mongol* A; 41 MiG-23BN/UB *Flogger*;
  ATK 39: 28 Su-22 *Fitter* D; 11 Su-24 *Fencer*
  TPT 23: **Heavy** 3 Il-76 *Candid*; **Light** 13: 1 An-24 *Coke*; 6 An-26 *Curl*; 2 PA-31 *Navajo*; 4 Yak-40 *Codling*; **PAX** 7: 2 *Falcon* 20; 1 *Falcon* 900; 4 Tu-134B-3
  TRG 15 L-39 *Albatros**
HELICOPTERS
  ATK 24 Mi-25 *Hind* D

MRH 54: 26 Mi-17 *Hip* H; 28 SA342L *Gazelle*
TPT • Medium 27 Mi-8 *Hip*
AIR-LAUNCHED MISSILES
AAM • IR R-3 (AA-2 *Atoll*)‡; R-60 (AA-8 *Aphid*); R-73 (AA-11 *Archer*); IR/SARH; R-23/24 (AA-7 *Apex*); R-27 (AA-10 *Alamo*); ARH; R-77 (AA-12A *Adder*) reported
ASM Kh-25 (AS-10 *Karen*); Kh-29T/L (AS-14 *Kedge*); HOT
ARM Kh-31P (AS-17A *Krypton*)

Air Defence Command ε20,000(-)

FORCES BY ROLE
AIR DEFENCE
4 AD div with S-125 *Pechora* (SA-3 *Goa*); 2K12 *Kub* (SA-6 *Gainful*); S-75 *Dvina* (SA-2 *Guideline*)
3 AD regt with S-200 *Angara* (SA-5 *Gammon*); S-300PMU2 (SA-20 *Gargoyle*)

EQUIPMENT BY TYPE
AIR DEFENCE • SAM
Long-range S-200 *Angara* (SA-5 *Gammon*); 24 S-300PMU2 (SA-20 *Gargoyle*)
Medium-range S-75 *Dvina* (SA-2 *Guideline*)
Short-range 2K12 *Kub* (SA-6 *Gainful*); S-125 *Pechora* (SA-3 *Goa*)
Point-defence 9K32 *Strela*-2/2M (SA-7A/B *Grail*)‡

Paramilitary ε100,000

National Defence Force ε50,000
An umbrella of disparate regime militias performing a variety of roles, including territorial control

Other Militias ε50,000
Numerous military groups fighting for the Assad regime, including Afghan, Iraqi, Pakistani and sectarian organisations. Some receive significant Iranian support

FOREIGN FORCES

Hizbullah 7,000–8,000
Iran 3,000
Russia 5,000: 1 inf BG; 3 MP bn; 1 engr unit; ε10 T-72B3/T-90; ε20 BTR-82A; 12 2A65; 4 9A52 *Smerch*; TOS-1A; 9K720 *Iskander*-M; 10 Su-24M *Fencer*; 6 Su-34; 4 Su-35S; 1 Il-20M; 12 Mi-24P/Mi-35M *Hind*; 4 Mi-8AMTSh *Hip*; 1 AShM bty with 3K55 *Bastion* (SSC-5 *Stooge*); 1 SAM bty with S-400 (SA-21 *Growler*); 1 SAM bty with S-300V4 (SA-23); 1 SAM bty with *Pantsir*-S1/S2; air base at Latakia; naval facility at Tartus

TERRITORY WHERE THE GOVERNMENT DOES NOT EXERCISE EFFECTIVE CONTROL

Data here represents the de facto situation for selected armed opposition groups and their observed equipment

National Front for Liberation ε50,000
A coalition of surviving Islamist and nationalist rebel factions formed in 2018, reportedly backed by Turkey, and operating in northwestern Syria; particularly in and around Idlib.

EQUIPMENT BY TYPE
ANTI-TANK/ANTI-INFRASTRUCTURE
MSL • MANPATS 9K11 *Malyutka* (AT-3 *Sagger*); 9K111 *Fagot* (AT-4 *Spigot*); 9K113 *Konkurs* (AT-5 *Spandrel*); 9K115-2 *Metis*-M (AT-13 *Saxhorn* 2); 9K135 *Kornet* (AT-14 *Spriggan*); BGM-71 TOW; *Milan*
ARTILLERY
TOWED 122mm D-30
MRL 107mm Type-63; 122mm BM-21 *Grad*; *Grad* (6-tube tech)
MOR 82mm some
AIR DEFENCE
SAM
Point-defence MANPADS some
GUNS
SP 14.5mm ZPU-1; ZPU-2 23mm ZU-23-2; ZSU-23-4 *Shilka*

Syrian Democratic Forces ε50,000
A coalition of predominantly Kurdish rebel groups in de facto control of much of northeastern Syria. Kurdish forces from the YPG/J (People's Protection Units/Women's Protection Units) provide military leadership and main combat power, supplemented by Arab militias and tribal groups. The SDF has benefited from considerable US and coalition air support, embedded special-operations forces and weaponry.

EQUIPMENT BY TYPE
ARMOURED FIGHTING VEHICLES
MBT T-55; T-72 (reported)
IFV BMP-1
APC • PPV *Guardian*
AUV M-ATV
ANTI-TANK/ANTI-INFRASTRUCTURE
MSL • MANPATS 9K111-1 *Konkurs*
RCL 73mm SPG-9; 90mm M-79 *Osa*
ARTILLERY
MRL 122mm BM-21 *Grad*; 9K132 *Grad*-P
MOR 82mm 82-BM-37; M-1938; 120mm M-1943; improvised mortars of varying calibre
AIR DEFENCE • GUNS
SP 14.5mm ZPU-4 (tch); ZPU-2 (tch); ZPU-1 (tch); 1 ZPU-2 (tch/on T-55); 23mm ZSU-23-4 *Shilka*; ZU-23-2 (tch); 57mm S-60
TOWED 14.5mm ZPU-2; ZPU-1; 23mm ZU-23-2

Syrian National Army ε20,000
Formed in late 2017 from Syrian Arab and Turkmen rebel factions operating under Turkish command in the Aleppo governate and northwestern Syria, including Afrin province.

EQUIPMENT BY TYPE
ARMOURED FIGHTING VEHICLES
MBT T-54; T-55; T-62
IFV BMP-1
ANTI-TANK/ANTI-INFRASTRUCTURE
MSL • MANPATS BGM-71 TOW; 9K115 *Metis* (AT-7 *Saxhorn*)
RCL 73mm SPG-9; 82mm B-10

ARTILLERY
MRL **107mm** Type-63; **122mm** 9K132 *Grad*-P
MOR **82mm** 2B9 *Vasilek*; improvised mortars of varying calibre
AIR DEFENCE • GUNS
SP **14.5mm** ZPU-4 (tch); ZPU-2 (tch); ZPU-1 (tch); **23mm** ZU-23-2 (tch); **57mm** AZP S-60
TOWED **14.5mm** ZPU-1; ZPU-2; ZPU-4; **23mm** ZU-23-2

Hayat Tahrir al-Sham (HTS) ε10,000

HTS was formed by Jabhat Fateh al-Sham (formerly known as Jabhat al-Nusra) in January 2017 by absorbing other hardline groups. It is designated a terrorist organisation by the US for its links to al-Qaeda.

EQUIPMENT BY TYPE
ANTI-TANK/ANTI-INFRASTRUCTURE
MSL • MANPATS 9K11 *Malyutka* (AT-3 *Sagger*); 9K113 *Konkurs* (AT-5 *Spandrel*); 9K115-2 *Metis*-M (AT-13 *Saxhorn* 2); 9K135 *Kornet* (AT-14 *Spriggan*)
RCL **73mm** SPG-9; **106mm** M-40
ARTILLERY
MRL **107mm** Type-63
MOR **120mm** some; improvised mortars of varying calibres
AIR DEFENCE
SAM
Point-defence 9K37M *Strela*-2M (SA-7B *Grail*)‡
GUNS
SP **14.5mm** ZPU-1; ZPU-2; **23mm** ZU-23-2; **57mm** S-60

FOREIGN FORCES

France *Operation Inherent Resolve* (*Chammal*) 1 SF unit
Turkey 500+; 1 SF coy; 1 armd coy(+); 1 arty unit
United States *Operation Inherent Resolve* 2,000+; 1 ranger unit; 1 mne bn; 1 arty bty with M777A2; 1 MRL bty with M142 HIMARS

Tunisia TUN

Tunisian Dinar D			2017	2018	2019
GDP		D	96.7bn	106bn	
		US$	40.0bn	41.7bn	
per capita		US$	3,465	3,573	
Growth		%	2.0	2.4	
Inflation		%	5.3	8.1	
Def bgt		D	2.02bn	2.33bn	2.93bn
		US$	833m	915m	
FMA (US)		US$	95m	0m	40m
US$1=D			2.42	2.55	
Population		11,516,189			
Age	0–14	15–19	20–24	25–29	30–64	65 plus
Male	13.0%	3.3%	3.5%	4.0%	22.0%	3.9%
Female	12.2%	3.2%	3.5%	4.0%	23.0%	4.3%

Capabilities

Ensuring territorial sovereignty and internal security are the main tasks of the armed forces, which have limited capacities but are undergoing a modernisation process. The civil war in Libya and Islamist terrorist groups operating from there continue to pose a security concern. In the light of terrorist attacks, the armed forces are engaged in counter-terrorism operations, and have been tasked with securing sensitive industrial sites. Designated a major non-NATO ally by the US in 2015, Tunisia also benefits from defence and security cooperation with US AFRICOM and with France. The country has received training from Algeria and is a member of the Saudi-led Islamic Military Counter Terrorism Coalition. The armed forces are involved in multinational exercises, notably those led by the US. The country is also strengthening its intelligence capabilities. Overall military capability is limited by the ageing equipment inventory, although Tunisia has been the recipient of surplus US systems, including armed utility helicopters. The country has limited defence-industrial capabilities.

ACTIVE 35,800 (Army 27,000 Navy 4,800 Air 4,000)
Paramilitary 12,000
Conscript liability 12 months selective

ORGANISATIONS BY SERVICE

Army 5,000; 22,000 conscript (total 27,000)

FORCES BY ROLE
SPECIAL FORCES
1 SF bde
1 (Sahara) SF bde
MANOEUVRE
Reconnaissance
1 recce regt
Mechanised
3 mech bde (1 armd regt, 2 mech inf regt, 1 arty regt, 1 AD regt, 1 engr regt, 1 sigs regt, 1 log gp)
COMBAT SUPPORT
1 engr regt
EQUIPMENT BY TYPE
ARMOURED FIGHTING VEHICLES
MBT 84: 30 M60A1; 54 M60A3
LT TK 48 SK-105 *Kuerassier*
RECCE 60: 40 AML-90; 20 FV601 *Saladin*
APC 350
APC (T) 140 M113A1/A2
APC (W) 110 Fiat 6614
PPV 114+: 4 *Bastion* APC: *Ejder Yalcin*; 100+ *Kirpi*
ENGINEERING & MAINTENANCE VEHICLES
AEV 2 *Greif*
ARV 9: 3 *Greif*; 6 M88A1
ANTI-TANK/ANTI-INFRASTRUCTURE • MSL
SP 35 M901 ITV TOW
MANPATS *Milan*; TOW
ARTILLERY 276
TOWED 115: **105mm** 48 M101A1/A2; **155mm** 67: 12 M114A1; 55 M198
MOR 161: **81mm** 95; SP **107mm** 48 M106; **120mm** 18 Brandt
AIR DEFENCE
SAM • Point-defence 26 M48 *Chaparral*; RBS-70

GUNS 127
SP 40mm 12 M42
TOWED 115: **20mm** 100 M-55; **37mm** 15 Type-55 (M-1939)/Type-65

Navy ε4,800
EQUIPMENT BY TYPE
PATROL AND COASTAL COMBATANTS 33
PSO 2 *Jugurtha* (Damen Stan MSOPV 1400) with 1 hel landing platform
PCFG 3 *La Galite* (FRA *Combattante* III) with 2 quad lnchr with MM40 *Exocet* AShM, 1 76mm gun
PCG 3 *Bizerte* (FRA P-48) with 8 SS 12M AShM
PCFT 6 *Albatros* (GER Type-143B) with 2 single 533mm TT, 2 76mm guns
PBF 2 20m Fast Patrol Boat
PB 17: 3 *Istiklal*; 3 *Utique* (mod PRC *Haizhui* II); 5 *Joumhouria*; 6 V Series
LOGISTICS AND SUPPORT 7:
ABU 3: 2 *Tabarka* (ex-US *White Sumac*); 1 *Sisi Bou Said*
AGE 1 *Hannibal*
AGS 1 *Khaireddine* (ex-US *Wilkes*)
AWT 1 *Ain Zaghouan* (ex-ITA *Simeto*)
AX 1 *Salambo* (ex-US *Conrad*, survey)

Air Force 4,000
FORCES BY ROLE
FIGHTER/GROUND ATTACK
1 sqn with F-5E/F-5F *Tiger* II
TRANSPORT
1 sqn with C-130B/H/J-30 *Hercules*; G.222; L-410 *Turbolet*
1 liaison unit with S-208A
TRAINING
2 sqn with L-59 *Albatros**; MB-326B; SF-260
1 sqn with MB-326K; MB-326L
TRANSPORT HELICOPTER
2 sqn with AS350B *Ecureuil*; AS365 *Dauphin* 2; AB-205 (Bell 205); SA313; SA316 *Alouette* III; UH-1H *Iroquois*; UH-1N *Iroquois*
1 sqn with HH-3E
EQUIPMENT BY TYPE
AIRCRAFT 23 combat capable
FTR 11: 9 F-5E *Tiger* II; 2 F-5F *Tiger* II
ATK 3 MB-326K
ISR 12 *Maule* MX-7-180B
TPT 18: **Medium** 13: 5 C-130B *Hercules*; 1 C-130H *Hercules*; 2 C-130J-30 *Hercules*; 5 G.222; **Light** 5: 3 L-410 *Turbolet*; 2 S-208A
TRG 30: 9 L-59 *Albatros**; 4 MB-326B; 3 MB-326L; 14 SF-260
HELICOPTERS
MRH 34: 1 AS365 *Dauphin* 2; 6 SA313; 3 SA316 *Alouette* III; 24 OH-58D *Kiowa Warrior*
SAR 11 HH-3E
TPT 39: **Medium** 8 UH-60M *Black Hawk*; **Light** 31: 6 AS350B *Ecureuil*; 15 Bell 205 (AB-205); 8 Bell 205 (UH-1H *Iroquois*); 2 Bell 212 (UH-1N *Iroquois*)
AIR-LAUNCHED MISSILES
AAM • **IR** AIM-9P *Sidewinder*
ASM AGM-114R *Hellfire*

Paramilitary 12,000
National Guard 12,000
Ministry of Interior
EQUIPMENT BY TYPE
ARMOURED FIGHTING VEHICLES
ASLT 2 EE-11 *Urutu* FSV
APC 26+:
APC (W) 16 EE-11 *Urutu* (anti-riot); VAB Mk3
PPV 10 Streit *Typhoon*
AUV IVECO LMV
PATROL AND COASTAL COMBATANTS 24
PCC 6 *Rais el Blais* (ex-GDR *Kondor* I)
PBF 7: 4 *Gabes*; 3 *Patrouiller*
PB 11: 5 *Breitla* (ex-GDR *Bremse*); 4 Rodman 38; 2 *Socomena*
HELICOPTERS
MRH 8 SA318 *Alouette* II/SA319 *Alouette* III
TPT • **Light** 3 Bell 429

DEPLOYMENT
DEMOCRATIC REPUBLIC OF THE CONGO: UN • MONUSCO 11; 4 obs
MALI: UN • MINUSMA 4; 1 obs

United Arab Emirates UAE

Emirati Dirham D		2017	2018	2019
GDP	D	1.41tr	1.59tr	
	US$	383bn	433bn	
per capita	US$	37,733	41,476	
Growth	%	0.8	2.9	
Inflation	%	2.0	3.5	
Def exp	D	n.k	n.k	
	US$	n.k	n.k	
US$1=D		3.67	3.67	

Population 9,701,315

Ethnic groups: Nationals 24%; expatriates 76%, of which Indian 30%, Pakistani 20%, other Arab 12%, other Asian 10%, UK 2%, other European 1%

Age	0–14	15–19	20–24	25–29	30–64	65 plus
Male	7.5%	1.9%	2.3%	4.6%	55.1%	1.1%
Female	6.9%	1.6%	1.8%	2.7%	14.1%	0.4%

Capabilities

The UAE's armed forces are arguably the best trained and most capable among the GCC states. In recent years, there has been a growing willingness to take part in operations, including sending an F-16 detachment to Afghanistan, participating in the air campaign in Libya and joining the Saudi-led intervention in Yemen. A new defence agreement was signed with the US in May 2017 designed to deepen military cooperation. The UAE hosts a French base and is diversifying its security relationships, including with China, India and Japan. A significant part of the UAE approach to regional security, particularly around the Horn of Africa, has been engaging in capacity building and training. The UAE's involvement in the Yemen campaign has offered combat lessons, not least of all in limited amphibious operations. This operation also demonstrates the country's developing approach to the use of force and there are signs of an acceptance of military risk. In the case of Yemen, the UAE has committed air and ground forces, particularly but not exclusively the presidential guard, deployed armour and demonstrated the use of a range of air munitions, including precision-guidance kits. The country is developing regional staging posts to support the Yemen operation. The UAE has an advanced inventory of modern equipment across the domains and is taking steps to upgrade its airborne ISR capabilities. In 2016, the UAE began to receive US-manufactured THAAD ballistic-missile-defence batteries. The country continues to develop its defence-industrial base; parent company EDIC oversees a variety of subsidiaries, including in the UAV, support, munitions, guided-weapons and defence-electronic sectors. The UAE remains reliant on external providers for major weapons systems.

ACTIVE 63,000 (Army 44,000 Navy 2,500 Air 4,500 Presidential Guard 12,000)

Conscript liability 24 months for those with no secondary-school certificate, 16 months for secondary-school graduates. Women – 9 months regardless of education

ORGANISATIONS BY SERVICE

Space
EQUIPMENT BY TYPE
SATELLITES • COMMUNICATIONS 3 *Yahsat*

Army 44,000
FORCES BY ROLE
MANOEUVRE
  Armoured
    2 armd bde
  Mechanised
    2 mech bde
  Light
    1 inf bde
COMBAT SUPPORT
  1 arty bde (3 SP arty regt)
  1 engr gp
EQUIPMENT BY TYPE
ARMOURED FIGHTING VEHICLES
  MBT 385: 45 AMX-30; 340 *Leclerc*
  LT TK 76 FV101 *Scorpion*
  RECCE 73: 49 AML-90; 24 VBL
  IFV 405: 15 AMX-10P; 390 BMP-3
  APC 928
    APC (T) 136 AAPC (incl 53 engr plus other variants)
    APC (W) 185: 45 AMV 8×8 (one with BMP-3 turret); 120 EE-11 *Urutu*; 20 VAB
    PPV 607: 465 *Caiman*; 115 *Maxxpro* LWB; 27 Nimr *Hafeet*
  AUV 650 M-ATV; Nimr *Adjban*; Nimr *Jais*
ENGINEERING & MAINTENANCE VEHICLES
  AEV 53 ACV-AESV; *Wisent*-2
  ARV 143: 8 ACV-AESV Recovery; 4 AMX-30D; 85 BREM-L; 46 *Leclerc* ARV; 15 *Maxxpro* ARV
  NBC VEHICLES 32 TPz-1 *Fuchs* NBC
ANTI-TANK/ANTI-INFRASTRUCTURE
  MSL
    SP 20 HOT; Nimr *Ajban* 440A with *Kornet*-E
    MANPATS FGM-148 *Javelin*; *Milan*; TOW
  RCL 84mm *Carl Gustav*
ARTILLERY 600+
  SP 155mm 181: 78 G-6; 85 M109A3; 18 Mk F3
  TOWED 93: 105mm 73 L118 Light Gun; 130mm 20 Type-59-I
  MRL 88+: 122mm 50+: 48 Firos-25 (est 24 op); 2 *Jobaria*; Type-90 (reported); 227mm 32 M142 HIMARS; 300mm 6 9A52 *Smerch*
  MOR 251: 81mm 134: 20 Brandt; 114 L16; 120mm 21 Brandt; SP 120mm 96 RG-31 MMP *Agrab* Mk2
SURFACE-TO-SURFACE MISSILE LAUNCHERS
  SRBM • Conventional 6 *Scud*-B (up to 20 msl); MGM-140A/B ATACMS (launched from M142 HIMARS)
UNMANNED AERIAL VEHICLES
  ISR • Medium *Seeker* II
AIR DEFENCE
  SAM • Point-defence *Blowpipe*; *Mistral*
  GUNS 62
    SP 20mm 42 M3 VDAA
    TOWED 30mm 20 GCF-BM2

Navy 2,500
EQUIPMENT BY TYPE
PRINCIPAL SURFACE COMBATANTS 1
  FRIGATES • FFGH 1
    1 *Abu Dhabi* with 2 twin lnchr with MM40 *Exocet* Block 3 AShM, 1 76mm gun
PATROL AND COASTAL COMBATANTS 42
  CORVETTES 10
    FSGHM 6:
      6 *Baynunah* with 2 quad lnchr with MM40 *Exocet* Block 3 AShM, 1 8-cell Mk56 VLS with RIM-162 ESSM SAM, 1 21-cell Mk49 GMLS with RIM-116C RAM Block 2 SAM, 1 76mm gun
    FSGM 4:
      2 *Muray Jib* (GER Lurssen 62m) with 2 quad lnchr with MM40 *Exocet* Block 2 AShM, 1 octuple lnchr with *Crotale* SAM, 1 *Goalkeeper* CIWS, 1 76mm gun, 1 hel landing platform
      2 *Ganthoot* with 2 twin lnchr with MM40 *Exocet* Block 3 AShM, 2 3-cell VLS with VL-*MICA* SAM, 1 76mm gun, 1 hel landing platform
  PCFGM 2 *Mubarraz* (GER Lurssen 45m) with 2 twin lnchr with MM40 *Exocet* AShM, 1 sextuple lnchr with *Mistral* SAM, 1 76mm gun
  PCFG 6 *Ban Yas* (GER Lurssen TNC-45) with 2 twin lnchr with MM40 *Exocet* Block 3 AShM, 1 76mm gun
  PBFG 12 *Butinah* (*Ghannatha* mod) with 4 single lncher with *Marte* Mk2/N AShM
  PBF 12: 6 *Ghannatha* with 120mm mor (capacity 42 troops); 6 *Ghannatha* (capacity 42 troops)
MINE WARFARE • MINE COUNTERMEASURES 2
  MHO 2 *Al Murjan* (ex-GER *Frankenthal*-class Type-332)
AMPHIBIOUS 29
  LANDING SHIPS • LST 2 *Alquwaisat* with 1 hel landing platform
  LANDING CRAFT 17
    LCM 5: 3 *Al Feyi* (capacity 56 troops); 2 (capacity 40 troops and additional vehicles)

LCP 4 Fast Supply Vessel (multipurpose)
LCT 8: 1 *Al Shareeah* (LSV 75m) with 1 hel landing platform; 7 (various)
LOGISTICS AND SUPPORT 3:
AFS 2 *Rmah* with 4 single 533mm TT
AX 1 *Al Semeih* with 1 hel landing platform

Air Force 4,500
FORCES BY ROLE
FIGHTER/GROUND ATTACK
3 sqn with F-16E/F Block 60 *Fighting Falcon*
3 sqn with *Mirage* 2000-9DAD/EAD/RAD
AIRBORNE EARLY WARNING AND CONTROL
1 flt with Saab 340 *Erieye*
SEARCH & RESCUE
2 flt with AW109K2; AW139
TANKER
1 flt with A330 MRTT
TRANSPORT
1 sqn with C-17A *Globemaster*
1 sqn with C-130H/H-30 *Hercules*; L-100-30
1 sqn with CN235M-100
TRAINING
1 sqn with Grob 115TA
1 sqn with *Hawk* Mk102*
1 sqn with PC-7 *Turbo Trainer*
1 sqn with PC-21
TRANSPORT HELICOPTER
1 sqn with Bell 412 *Twin Huey*
EQUIPMENT BY TYPE
AIRCRAFT 156 combat capable
FGA 137: 54 F-16E Block 60 *Fighting Falcon* (*Desert Eagle*); 24 F-16F Block 60 *Fighting Falcon* (13 to remain in US for trg); 15 *Mirage* 2000-9DAD; 44 *Mirage* 2000-9EAD
ISR 7 *Mirage* 2000 RAD*
SIGINT 1 Global 6000
AEW&C 2 Saab 340 *Erieye*
TPT/TKR 3 A330 MRTT
TPT 23: **Heavy** 7 C-17 *Globemaster* III; **Medium** 6: 3 C-130H *Hercules*; 1 C-130H-30 *Hercules*; 2 L-100-30; **Light** 10: 6 CN235; 4 DHC-8 *Dash* 8 (MP)
TRG 79: 12 Grob 115TA; 12 *Hawk* Mk102*; 30 PC-7 *Turbo Trainer*; 25 PC-21
HELICOPTERS
MRH 21: 12 AW139; 9 Bell 412 *Twin Huey*
TPT • **Light** 4: 3 AW109K2; 1 Bell 407
UNMANNED AERIAL VEHCILES
CISR • **Heavy** *Wing Loong* I (GJ-1); *Wing Loong* II
ISR • **Heavy** RQ-1E *Predator* XP
AIR-LAUNCHED MISSILES
AAM • **IR** AIM-9L *Sidewinder*; R-550 *Magic*; **IIR** AIM-9X *Sidewinder* II; **IIR/ARH** *Mica*; **ARH** AIM-120B/C AMRAAM
ASM AGM-65G *Maverick*; *Hakeem* 1/2/3 (A/B)
ARM AGM-88C HARM
ALCM *Black Shaheen* (*Storm Shadow*/SCALP EG variant)
BOMBS
INS/SAT guided *Al Tariq*
Laser-guided GBU-12/58 *Paveway* II

Air Defence
FORCES BY ROLE
AIR DEFENCE
2 AD bde (3 bn with MIM-23B I-*Hawk*; MIM-104F *Patriot* PAC-3)
3 (short range) AD bn with *Crotale*; *Mistral*; *Rapier*; RB-70; *Javelin*; 9K38 *Igla* (SA-18 *Grouse*); 96K6 *Pantsir*-S1
2 SAM bty with THAAD
EQUIPMENT BY TYPE
AIR DEFENCE • SAM
Medium-range MIM-23B I-*Hawk*; MIM-104F *Patriot* PAC-3
Short-range *Crotale*; 50 96K6 *Pantsir*-S1
Point-defence RBS-70; *Rapier*; *Javelin*; 9K38 *Igla* (SA-18 *Grouse*); *Mistral*
MISSILE DEFENCE 12 THAAD

Presidential Guard Command 12,000
FORCES BY ROLE
MANOEUVRE
Reconaissance
1 recce sqn
Mechanised
1 mech bde (1 tk bn, 4 mech inf bn, 1 AT coy, 1 cbt engr coy, 1 CSS bn)
Amphibious
1 mne bn
EQUIPMENT BY TYPE
ARMOURED FIGHTING VEHICLES
MBT 50 *Leclerc*
IFV 290: 200 BMP-3; 90 BTR-3U *Guardian*
ANTI-TANK/ANTI-INFRASTRUCTURE
MSL • **SP** HMMWV with 9M133 *Kornet*

Joint Aviation Command
FORCES BY ROLE
GROUND ATTACK
1 sqn with *Archangel*; AT802 *Air Tractor*
ANTI-SURFACE/ANTI-SUBMARINE WARFARE
1 sqn with AS332F *Super Puma*; AS565 *Panther*
TRANSPORT
1 (Spec Ops) gp with AS365F *Dauphin* 2; H125M *Fennec*; AW139; Bell 407MRH; Cessna 208B *Grand Caravan*; CH-47C/F *Chinook*; DHC-6-300/400 *Twin Otter*; UH-60L/M *Black Hawk*
ATTACK HELICOPTER
1 gp with AH-64D *Apache*
EQUIPMENT BY TYPE
AIRCRAFT 37 combat capable
ATK 23 *Archangel*
ISR ε6 AT802 *Air Tractor*
TPT • **Light** 15: 2 Beech 350 *King Air*; 8 Cessna 208B *Grand Caravan*; 1 DHC-6-300 *Twin Otter*; 4 DHC-6-400 *Twin Otter*
HELICOPTERS
ATK 28 AH-64D *Apache*
ASW 7 AS332F *Super Puma* (5 in ASuW role)

MRH 47: 4 AS365F *Dauphin* 2 (VIP); 9 H125M *Fennec*; 7 AS565 *Panther*; 3 AW139 (VIP); 20 Bell 407MRH; 4 SA316 *Alouette* III
TPT 63+: **Heavy** 22 CH-47F *Chinook*; **Medium** 41+: 11 UH-60L *Black Hawk*; 29+ UH-60M *Black Hawk*
AIR-LAUNCHED MISSILES
ASM AGM-114 *Hellfire*; *Cirit* (reported); *Hydra-70*; HOT
AShM AS-15TT; AM39 *Exocet*

Paramilitary

Critical Infrastructure and Coastal Protection Agency (CICPA)
Ministry of Interior
EQUIPMENT BY TYPE
PATROL AND COASTAL COMBATANTS 113
  PSO 1 *Al Wtaid*
  PCM 1 *Arialah* (Damen Sea Axe 6711) with 1 11-cell SeaRAM GMLS with RIM-116 RAM SAM, 1 57mm gun, 1 hel landing platform
  PBF 58: 6 *Baglietto* GC23; 3 *Baglietto* 59; 15 DV-15; 34 MRTP 16
  PB 53: 2 *Protector*; 16 (US Camcraft 65); 5 (US Camcraft 77); 6 Watercraft 45; 12 *Halmatic Work*; 12 *Al Saber*

DEPLOYMENT

ERITREA: Operation Restoring Hope 1,000; 1 armd BG; *Leclerc*; BMP-3; G-6; *Agrab* Mk2; 2 FSGHM; 2 LST; 6 LCT; 4 *Archangel*; 3 AH-64D *Apache*; 2 CH-47F *Chinook*; 4 UH-60M *Black Hawk*; *Wing Loong* 1 (GJ-1) UAV; 4 MIM-104F *Patriot* PAC-3

LIBYA: 6 AT-802; 2 UH-60M; 2 *Wing Loong* 1 (GJ-1) UAV

SAUDI ARABIA: Operation Restoring Hope 12 F-16E *Fighting Falcon*

YEMEN: Operation Restoring Hope 3,000 1 bde HQ; 2 armd BG; *Leclerc*; BMP-3; Patria AMV; M-ATV; G-6; M109A3; *Agrab* Mk2; 4 AH-64D *Apache*; 2 CH-47F *Chinook*; 4 UH-60M *Black Hawk*; 96K6 *Pantsir*-S1; 4 MIM-104F *Patriot* PAC-3

FOREIGN FORCES

Australia 650; 1 tpt det with 1 B-737-700 *Wedgetail* (E-7A); 1 A330 MRTT (KC-30A); 2 C-130J-30 *Hercules*
Denmark Operation Inherent Resolve 20
France 650: 1 armd BG (1 tk coy, 1 armd inf coy; 1 aty bty); *Leclerc*; VBCI; CAESAR; 6 *Rafale*
Italy 120; 1 tpt flt with 2 C-130J *Hercules*
Korea, Republic of: 139 (trg activities at UAE Spec Ops School)
United Kingdom 200; 1 tkr/tpt flt with C-17A *Globemaster*; C-130J *Hercules*; A330 MRTT *Voyager*
United States: 5,000; 1 ftr sqn with 6 F-22A *Raptor*; 1 ISR sqn with 4 U-2; 1 AEW&C sqn with 4 E-3 *Sentry*; 1 tkr sqn with 12 KC-10A; 1 ISR UAV sqn with RQ-4 *Global Hawk*; 2 AD bty with MIM-104E/F *Patriot* PAC-2/3

Yemen, Republic of YEM

Yemeni Rial R		2017	2018	2019
GDP	R	10.0tr	14.7tr	
	US$	31.3bn	28.5bn	
per capita	US$	1,043	926	
Growth	%	-5.9	-2.6	
Inflation	%	24.7	41.8	
Def bdgt	R	n.k	n.k	
	US$	n.k	n.k	
US$1=R		320.00	514.05	

Population 28,667,230

Ethnic groups: Majority Arab, some African and South Asian

Age	0–14	15–19	20–24	25–29	30–64	65 plus
Male	20.3%	5.8%	5.0%	4.4%	14.2%	1.3%
Female	19.2%	5.6%	4.9%	4.3%	13.9%	1.5%

Capabilities

Yemen continues to be wracked by a conflict that is, according to the UN, the world's worst humanitarian crisis. There appears to be little apparent prospect that any of the competing forces will be able to gain a decisive upper hand. The government of President Hadi appears to exercise limited control over the forces nominally loyal to it, while the proxy forces supposedly allied to the government and supported by the members of the Saudi-led coalition answer to those member states rather than Yemeni military authorities. The rebel Houthi forces, who are assumed to receive material support from Iran, are largely tribal-based militias, along with some elements of the Yemeni armed forces who were loyal to the late former president Saleh. Al-Qaeda affiliates also appear active in the country. Government forces tend to be underequipped and poorly paid compared to the proxy groups supported by the Saudi-led coalition. The Houthi rebel forces gained from the training and capabilities of the former Yemeni armed forces previously loyal to former president Saleh. The Houthi rebels appear to retain most of the more capable heavy armour and armoured fighting vehicles. Opposition forces have maintained their ability to launch surface-to-surface missiles at Saudi Arabia. The Saudi-led coalition continues to provide ground and air support for the Hadi government. The conflict appears to have been sustained by a combination of large existing stockpiles of weapons and ammunition and external supplies, despite UN embargos. There is no domestic defence industry, barring some limited maintenance and workshop facilities.

ACTIVE 40,000 (Goverment forces 40,000)

ORGANISATIONS BY SERVICE

Government forces ε40,000 (incl militia)

President Hadi's government is nominally supported by parts of the Yemeni armed forces, as well as a number of militia organisations in southern and eastern Yemen. The government's ability to exercise direct control over most of these forces is extremely limited, with local leaders and state sponsors, such as Saudi Arabia and the UAE, exercising stronger influence.

FORCES BY ROLE
MANOEUVRE
　Mechanised
　　up to 20 bde(-)
EQUIPMENT BY TYPE
ARMOURED FIGHTING VEHICLES
　MBT Some M60A1; T-34†; T-54/55; T-62; T-72
　RECCE some BRDM-2
　IFV BMP-2; BTR-80A; Ratel-20
　APC
　　APC (W) BTR-60
　PPV Streit *Cougar*; Streit *Spartan*
　AUV M-ATV
ANTI-TANK/ANTI-INFRASTRUCTURE
　MSL • MANPATS 9K11 *Malyutka* (AT-3 *Sagger*); M47 *Dragon*; TOW
　GUNS • SP 100mm SU-100†
ARTILLERY • SP 122mm 2S1 *Gvozdika*
AIRCRAFT • ISR 6 AT-802 *Air Tractor**
AIR DEFENCE • **GUNS** • **TOWED 14.5mm** ZPU-4; **23mm** ZU-23-2

FOREIGN FORCES

All *Operation Restoring Hope* unless stated

Saudi Arabia 1,500: 1 armd BG; M60A3; M2A2 *Bradley*; M113A4; M-ATV; AH-64 *Apache*; 2+ MIM-104D/F *Patriot* PAC-2/3

Sudan 950; 1 mech BG; T-72AV; BTR-70M *Kobra* 2

United Arab Emirates 3,000; 1 bde HQ; 2 armd BG; *Leclerc*; BMP-3; M-ATV; G-6; M109A3; *Agrab* Mk2; 4 AH-64D *Apache*; 2 CH-47F *Chinook*; 4 UH-60M *Black Hawk*; 96K6 *Pantsir*-S1; 4 MIM-104F *Patriot* PAC-3

TERRITORY WHERE THE GOVERNMENT DOES NOT EXERCISE EFFECTIVE CONTROL

Insurgent forces 20,000 (incl Houthi and tribes)

The Houthi-run de facto administration has controlled northern Yemen since 2015 is supported by a combination of Houthi tribal militias and elements of the Yemeni armed forces loyal to former president Ali Abdullah Saleh. Following a break between the Houthis and Saleh in late 2017 that resulted in the latter's death, his former forces have become further split between those that remained affiliated with the Houthis and those who have joined Saleh's son and nephew to fight against them.

FORCES BY ROLE
MANOEUVRE
　Mechanised
　　up to 20 bde(-)
EQUIPMENT BY TYPE
ARMOURED FIGHTING VEHICLES
　MBT T-55; T-72
　IFV BMP-2; BTR-80A
　APC • APC (W) Some BTR-40; BTR-60
　AUV M-ATV
ANTI-TANK/ANTI-INFRASTRUCTURE
　MSL • MANPATS M47 *Dragon*; 9K111-1 *Konkurs* (AT-5B *Spandrel/Towsan*-1); 9K115 *Metis* (AT-7 *Saxhorn*)
SURFACE-TO-SURFACE MISSILE LAUNCHERS
　SRBM • **Conventional** (most fired or destroyed) 9K79 *Tochka* (SS-21 *Scarab*); Scud-B/*Hwasong*-5; *Borkan*-1 (possible extended-range *Scud* derivative); *Qaher*-1 (possible *Tondar*-69 derivative)
COASTAL DEFENCE • AShM some C-801/C-802 (reported)
AIR DEFENCE • **GUNS** • **TOWED 20mm** M167 *Vulcan*; **23mm** ZU-23-2

Arms procurements and deliveries – Middle East and North Africa

Significant events in 2018

- Qatar launched Barzan Holdings at its DIMDEX trade show in March. Barzan Holdings will focus on creating joint ventures (JVs) with other companies, in order to create a defence-industrial capability in Qatar. A number of JVs were announced at the show with international companies such as BMC, Kongsberg, Raytheon, Rheinmetall and Qinetiq.

- Saudi Arabian Military Industries (SAMI) and Spain's Navantia formed a JV to work on the design and construction of the five *Avante* 2200 corvettes that Saudi Arabia ordered in mid-2018. The JV will fit out the final two corvettes with Navantia's CATIZ combat-management system in Saudi Arabia.

- Qatar continued its recent series of big-ticket procurements, with contracts for Turkish armed uninhabited aerial vehicles, armoured vehicles, patrol boats, Italian NH90 helicopters and, most significantly, a US$6.43bn deal with BAE Systems for 24 *Typhoon* combat aircraft and nine *Hawk* training aircraft.

- The Israeli government loosened arms-export regulations in October. Israeli companies can now negotiate the sale of unclassified equipment with customers without government approval. However, the Defense Export Control Agency must still sign off deals. Under previous rules, companies had to acquire a marketing licence from the government before negotiating with a customer, which could take several months.

- In September, Alexandria Shipyard launched the first of three *Gowind* 2500 frigates that are being built in Egypt. Naval Group was awarded a contract in 2014 to design and build the first vessel and provide assistance, an integrated mast, and other systems and weapons for three more frigates. *Port Said* (976) is the first major warship that Egypt has built. The first of class, *El Fateh* (971), was commissioned in October 2017.

- In July, China signed cooperation agreements with Kuwait and then the UAE. These include proposed bilateral cooperation in defence technology and industry, although the specifics were not made public. The UAE has acquired armed Chinese UAVs, while Kuwait has operated Chinese howitzers since 2000.

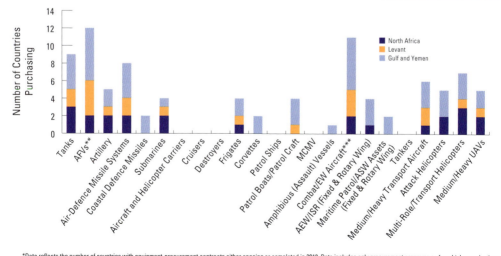

Figure 23 **Middle East and North Africa: selected ongoing or completed procurement priorities in 2018**

*Data reflects the number of countries with equipment-procurement contracts either ongoing or completed in 2018. Data includes only procurement programmes for which a production contract has been signed. The data does not include upgrade programmes.
**Armoured fighting vehicles not including main battle tanks   ***Includes combat-capable training aircraft

© IISS

Table 16 Reported Russian defence exports to Algeria: recently completed and ongoing, by contract date

Equipment	Type	Quantity	Value*	Prime contractor	Contract date	Delivery
T-90SA	MBT	185	US$1bn	UralVagonZavod	2006	2006–08
96K6 Pantsir-S1 (SA-22 Greyhound)	Short-range SP SAM	38	US$500m	KBP Instrument Design Bureau	2006	2011–13
S-300PMU2 (SA-20 Gargoyle)	Long-range SP SAM	8	US$300m	Almaz-Antey	2006	2008–09
S-300PMU2 (SA-20 Gargoyle)	Long-range SP SAM	8	US$300m	Almaz-Antey	2006	2010
Varshavyanka (Improved Kilo)	SSK	2	US$600m	Admiralty Shipyards	2006	2009
Su-30MKA (Flanker H)	FGA ac	28	US$1.5bn	United Aircraft Corporation	2006	2007–09
Yak-130 Mitten	Trg ac	16	US$300m	United Aircraft Corporation	2006	2011
S-300PMU2 (SA-20 Gargoyle)	Long-range SP SAM	8	US$400m	Almaz-Antey	2008	2012
Su-30MKA (Flanker H)	FGA ac	16	US$900m	United Aircraft Corporation	2009	2011–12
T-90SA	MBT	120	n.k.	UralVagonZavod	2011	2012–13
S-300PMU2 (SA-20 Gargoyle)	Long-range SP SAM	8	US$400m	Almaz-Antey	2011	2013–14
9K317E Buk-M2E (SA-17 Grizzly)	Medium-range SP SAM	48	n.k.	Almaz-Antey	2013	2016–ongoing
Mi-28NE Havoc	Atk Hel	42	US$2.7bn	Russian Helicopters	2013	2015–ongoing
Mi-28NE Havoc	Atk hel	42	US$2.7bn	Russian Helicopters	2013	2015–ongoing
Mi-26T2 Halo	Hvy tpt hel	6				
Mi-8AMTSh	Med tpt hel	39				
T-90SA	MBT	200	US$1bn	UralVagonZavod	2014	2015–ongoing
Tigr with Kornet-EM	SP AT Msl	28	n.k.	KBP Instrument Design Bureau	2014	2016–ongoing
Varshavyanka (Improved Kilo)	SSK	2	US$1.2bn	Admiralty Shipyards	2014	2018–ongoing
Su-30MKA (Flanker H)	FGA ac	14	US$800m	United Aircraft Corporation	2015	2017–ongoing
Mi-26T2 Halo	Hvy Tpt Hel	8	US$1bn	Russian Helicopters	2015	2017–ongoing
9M720 Iskander-E	SRBM	4	n.k.	Tekhmash	n.k.	2017
TOS-1A	220m MRL	n.k.	n.k.	Omsktransmash	n.k.	2017–18

*All contract values are from Russian media reporting and converted into US dollars

Table 17 Saudi Arabia: top ten arms orders in 2017–18, by order date

Equipment	Type	Quantity	Value (US$)	Prime contractor(s)	Order date
M1A2S Abrams	MBT	n.k.	880m	(US) General Dynamics Land Systems	2017
AH-6i Little Bird	MRH Hel	24	25.52m	(US) Boeing	Apr 2017
UH-60M Black Hawk	Med Tpt Hel	115	n.k.	(US) Sikorsky	Jun 2017
CH-47F Chinook	Hvy Tpt Hel	8	533m	(US) Boeing	Aug 2017
E-3A Sentry	AEW&C ac	5	240.2m	(US) Boeing	Oct 2017
UH-60M Black Hawk	Med Tpt Hel	17	193.85m	(US) Sikorsky	Jan 2018
Combattante FS56	PCGM	3	ε294.1m	(FRA) CMN	Jan 2018
Multi-Mission Surface Combatants (MMSC)	FFGHM	4	6bn	(US) Lockheed Martin	Mar 2018
HSI 32 (FRA CMN)	PBF	39	480m	(SAU) Zamil Offshore Services	Apr 2018
Avante 2200	FFGHM	5	2.12bn	(ESP) Navantia	Jul 2018

Table 18 Gulf Cooperation Council states: new fighter/ground-attack aircraft contracts, 2005–present

Order date	Country	Aircraft	Quantity	Value (US$)	Prime contractor	Deliveries
Dec 2005	Saudi Arabia	Eurofighter Typhoon	72	8.87bn	(UK) BAE Systems	2009–17
Dec 2011	Oman	F-16C Block 50	10	600m	(US) Lockheed Martin	2014
		F-16D Block 50	2			
Mar 2012	Saudi Arabia	F-15SA Eagle	84	11.4bn	(US) Boeing	2016–ongoing
Dec 2012	Oman	Eurofighter Typhoon	12	3.9bn*	(UK) BAE Systems	2017–18
May 2015	Qatar	Rafale	36	8.72bn	(FRA) Dassault	n.k.
Apr 2016	Kuwait	Eurofighter Typhoon	28	8.81bn	(ITA) Leonardo	2020–23
Dec 2017	Qatar	F-15QA	36	6.17bn	(US) Boeing	n.k.–2022
Jun 2018	Bahrain	F-16V Block 70	16	1.12bn	(US) Lockheed Martin	n.k.–2023
Jun 2018	Kuwait	F/A-18E Super Hornet	22	n.k.	(US) Boeing	n.k.–2021
		F/A-18F Super Hornet	6			
Sep 2018	Qatar	Eurofighter Typhoon	24	6.43bn*	(UK) BAE Systems	2022–n.k.

*Includes supply of Hawk training aircraft

Table 19 Iraq: selected procurement contracts, 2010–18

Order date	Equipment	Type	Quantity	Value (US$)	Prime contractors	Deliveries
Sep 2011	F-16C/D Block 52	FGA ac	18	ε3bn	(US) Lockheed Martin	2015–16
Oct 2012	F-16C/D Block 52	FGA ac	18	ε3bn	(US) Lockheed Martin	2016–ongoing
2012	Mi-28NE/UB Havoc	Atk hel	15	4.2bn package (reported)	(RUS) Russian Helicopters	2014–16
	Mi-35M Hind	Atk hel	28		(RUS) Russian Helicopters	2013–ongoing
	96K6 Pantsir-S1 (SA-22 Greyhound)	SAM	24		(RUS) Almaz-Antey	2014–16
	9K338 Igla-S (SA-24 Grinch)	MANPADs	n.k.		(RUS) KBM	2014–16
Dec 2013	T-50IQ Golden Eagle	Trg ac	24	2.65bn	(ROK) KAI	2017–ongoing
Aug 2014	L-159	Atk ac	12	36.13m	(CZE) Czech Government; Aero Vodochody	2015–ongoing
2015	BMP-3	IFV	500	n.k.	(RUS) Traktornyye Zavody	2018–ongoing
2016	T-90S	MBT	73	n.k.	(RUS) UralVagonZavod	2018–ongoing

Chapter Eight
Latin America and the Caribbean

- Ageing inventories and a lack of adequate funding for replacements are a limiting factor on the capabilities of many of the region's armed forces.
- Some regional armed forces remain active on internal security duties, with some nations also introducing legislation to enable these deployments.
- Latin America's defence industries saw a notable development in 2018 with the planned tie-up between Boeing and Embraer. Both firms have agreed to create new joint venture dedicated to defence sales, notably of the KC-390. Meanwhile, Saab has started building the *Gripen* facility in Brazil.
- Regional navies continue development of littoral patrol and manoeuvre capabilities, including with locally-produced patrol craft.
- Brazil's acquisition of the former-HMS *Ocean* introduces a large aviation platform with potentially more useable capability than hitherto into the region.
- Regional defence spending has bottomed out in the wake of stronger economic growth, after two years of cuts to defence spending.

Latin America and the Caribbean defence spending, 2018 – top 5, including US foreign military financing

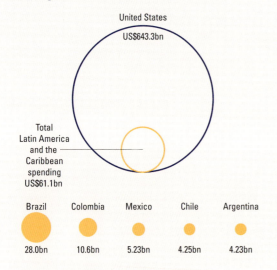

Active military personnel – top 10
(15,000 per unit)

Brazil 334,500
Colombia 293,200
Mexico 277,150
Venezuela 123,000
Peru 81,000
Chile 77,200
Argentina 74,200
Dominican Republic 56,050
Cuba 49,000
Bolivia 34,100

Tactical combat aircraft fleets, 2018
(10 per unit)

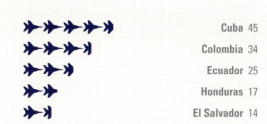

Brazil 106
Chile 74
Peru 68
Argentina 55
Venezuela 51
Cuba 45
Colombia 34
Ecuador 25
Honduras 17
El Salvador 14

Regional defence policy and economics   382 ▶
Armed forces data section   393 ▶
Arms procurements and deliveries   436 ▶

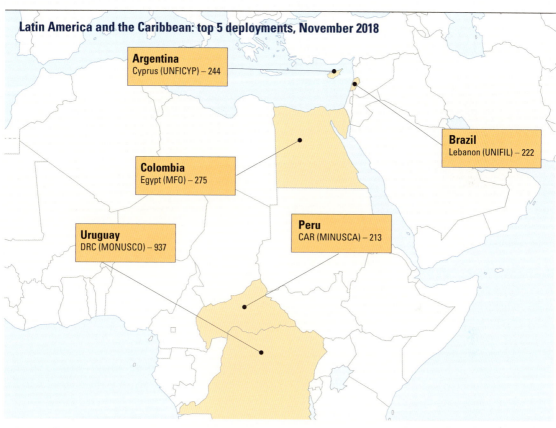

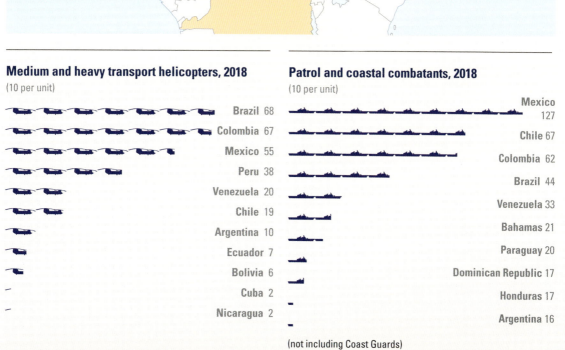

Latin America and the Caribbean

Persistent regional security challenges stemming from the threat from organised crime and drug traffickers and the need for humanitarian assistance and disaster relief (HA/DR) missions are among the issues driving developments in regional armed forces. At the same time, the effects on the region of the continuing economic crisis in Venezuela are becoming more apparent. This is principally due to its impact on Venezuela's population – the economic crisis has triggered an exodus of nationals to neighbouring countries. But it is also noticeable in the responses that it has generated in regional states, such as Brazil and Colombia, which have deployed elements of security forces as a result of the influx of Venezuelan citizens.

Reshaped domestic roles

It is noteworthy that, years after some Latin American states began to reshape military roles away from involvement in internal affairs, certain legislatures have once again focused on the military role in tasks at home, though these are now of a significantly different nature. In Brazil, the armed forces have in recent years mounted security operations, notably in urban *favela* areas, to counter organised crime. A Law and Order Guarantee (Garantia da Lei e da Ordem, or GLO) can be invoked by presidential decree, which has to establish a specific geographical area for the mission, and start and end dates, though these are flexible. The legislation has been used to enable military deployments against criminal elements in urban areas. However, the territorial restrictions on GLOs have been re-examined. In late May 2018, to allow the armed forces to intervene after striking truck drivers blocked several roads, President Michel Temer said that the GLO was valid across Brazil. The armed forces can also be deployed through a 'federal intervention', one level below a state of emergency. This mechanism was included in the 1988 constitution, but first used in February 2018, when Temer declared a federal intervention in the public security of Rio de Janeiro State.

The security challenge posed by organised crime and drug trafficking has prompted other regional states to re-examine their legislative frameworks. For example, in late 2017 the Mexican legislature approved an internal-security law, intended by the government to regulate the use of the armed forces on internal-security operations. The Mexican military has been deployed since 2006 on missions to help tackle organised crime and drug trafficking. Amid criticism that more emphasis should be placed on improving policing, President Enrique Peña Nieto said that, as well as the new law, local authorities were also obliged to strengthen institutional capacities. In November, however, the law was rejected by the Supreme Court. President-elect Andrés Manuel López Obrador discussed different approaches to tackling the country's security challenges, with a focus on preventive strategies, as well as the creation of a national guard.

Other states enacting or discussing legislative amendments include Argentina, Paraguay and Peru. In Argentina, the Macri administration announced in late July wide-ranging plans to reform the defence establishment, including legislation to modify a decree from 2006 which restricts the armed forces to tackling external state-based threats. It is understood that the plan will enable a broader assessment of threats of external origin, which would in theory allow greater latitude to deploy against non-traditional threats such as organised crime. In Paraguay, changes have been made to laws in recent years on domestic defence and security, reportedly allowing a military role in certain internal tasks without declaring a state of emergency. And in Peru, Law 30796 of June 2018 authorised the armed forces to intervene in the valley of the Apurimac, Ene and Mantaro rivers to tackle drug trafficking.

These legislative changes reflect the changing security environment in the region. Armed forces are envisaged as taking on an increasingly broad range of roles, moving away from traditional territorial-defence tasks towards tackling non-traditional challenges such as those from transnational organised crime and drug trafficking and now also including cyber threats, deployments overseas on peace-support tasks and HA/DR missions. Increasingly, multinational regional exercises also focus on these tasks. Common challenges continue to lead more defence ministries to consider the benefits from greater regional cooperation, not only through training but also in areas such as information sharing.

In Venezuela, however, the year also saw a traditional threat to the leadership, if delivered in a non-traditional way. President Nicolás Maduro survived an assassination attempt during a military parade on 4 August. It was claimed that this was engineered by a group of right-wing dissidents, who used a pair of small uninhabited aerial vehicles (UAVs) packed with explosives. Earlier in the year, arrests had been reported relating to the 2017 attack on government buildings by a police officer. After the 2018 attack, Venezuela's leadership blamed the governments of Chile, Colombia and Mexico for their potential roles in supporting what was described as a right-wing terrorist movement inside Venezuela and announced the deployment of 100,000 troops to guarantee the country's borders from a potential military intervention by its neighbours.

Regional developments

In **Colombia**, the commander of the armed forces said in June 2018 that principal defence concerns were sovereignty and territorial integrity, as well as defending against internal threats. He also noted that other key tasks were environmental protection, disaster response and exporting security – including peace-support and international training missions. Colombia hosted the international *Unitas* exercise in late 2018 and has been active in training and skill-sharing activities with other regional armed forces. However, the crisis in Venezuela continues to generate concern in Bogotá. Some reports indicate that up to one million Venezuelans have in recent years fled to Colombia. The Venezuelan situation has led to the re-examination of some of Colombia's procurement priorities, although current procurement budgets remain modest. Reports indicate that aspirations include the acquisition of air-defence systems. There are also long-standing plans to procure a replacement or complement for Colombia's ageing *Kfir* fighter-aircraft fleet (some of which were recently upgraded), as well as a surface-warship project (Plataforma Estratégica de Superficie). More broadly, reform plans continue in order to reshape the Colombian defence establishment for the post-internal-conflict environment by boosting morale, capability and transparency, and producing armed forces compatible with NATO standards.

The **Brazilian** Army deployed to the border with Venezuela in August 2018 in an effort to increase security for the local population, as well as to respond to the needs of the nearly 60,000 Venezuelans that had reportedly crossed into Brazil. Meanwhile, the Brazilian armed forces reached several significant milestones in 2018. In June, the navy commissioned the PHM *Atlantico*, formerly the United Kingdom's HMS *Ocean*. The arrival of this helicopter carrier marks the return to Brazil of a naval-aviation power-projection capability for the first time since the decommissioning of the aircraft carrier *São Paulo* (the former French Navy *Foch*) in 2017. However, the selection of a supplier for the *Tamandaré*-class corvette project, Brazil's most anticipated procurement decision, was delayed in mid-2018, causing the programme to further slip. Meanwhile, the air force continued to push for the finalisation of the test and evaluation phase of the much-anticipated KC-390 multi-role tanker transport; the air force is expected to receive its first three KC-390s in 2019.

The president of **Ecuador**, Lenín Moreno, has sought to improve significantly relations with the United States. Under the direction of Defence Minister (and retired general) Oswaldo Jarrín, the Ecuadorean armed forces have launched a reorganisation programme that includes the creation of a joint command. Jarrín has been instrumental in increasing defence and security cooperation with Washington, including supporting the temporary deployment of US air assets, such as US Customs and Border Patrol P-3 *Orion* maritime-patrol aircraft to help Ecuador monitor its large exclusive economic zone. He announced in September that the defence ministry was working on a new defence white paper. In neighbouring **Peru**, the army continues a transformation process that includes the creation of a new disaster-response brigade. The navy has launched a long-awaited programme to modernise the submarine fleet, with the first hull opened in May 2018 at the navy-run SIMA shipyards, which have also begun to build the second *Makassar*-class landing platform dock (LPD). The first LPD, BAP *Pisco*, was commissioned in June 2018.

Economic challenges in **Argentina** continue to prevent a major revamp of its armed forces. As a result, long-awaited procurement projects have been shelved or rescheduled for 2020 and onwards. Although President Mauricio Macri announced his intent to strengthen military and industrial capacity in a speech in July, the precise sums to be allocated for this process remained unclear at the time of writing.

However, capability developments in 2018 included delivery to the air force of more Beechcraft T-6C+ *Texan* II trainers; the plan is to acquire 12 airframes. This has enabled the air force's *Tucano* trainers to be repurposed for interdiction operations in the north of the country. Their employment against non-state threats reflects the shift in the country's defence policy, which until 2018 confined military activities to defending against conventional state threats.

Meanwhile, in August 2018, Argentina, Brazil, Chile, Colombia, Paraguay and Peru announced their intention to suspend indefinitely participation in the Union of South American Nations (UNASUR), a regional organisation which was created in 2008 in an effort to foster regional political, social, defence and economic cooperation. The move came after Bolivia assumed the presidency of the organisation and amid disputes with Venezuela. UNASUR's South American Defense Council had launched several multinational programmes on military education, equipment research and development, and procurement, including the joint development of a primary trainer aircraft and a tactical UAV, both of which failed to materialise.

DEFENCE ECONOMICS

After some difficult years, with a contraction of 0.6% of GDP in 2016 and only modest growth of 1.3% of GDP in 2017, Latin America and the Caribbean is seeing stronger figures, expected to reach 2% in 2018. According to the IMF, countries such as Chile (3.4%), Paraguay (4.5%), Peru (3.7%) and Uruguay (3.4%) were some of the most dynamic economies in South America in 2018.

This return to growth was enabled by both external and internal factors. Overall, the region was helped by growth in the United States, which rose from 2.5% in 2017 to 3.4% in 2018. Mexico and Central American and Caribbean countries are particularly dependent on the economic situation in the US. In 2016, Mexico exported 74% of its products to the US, with Nicaragua at 61% and Honduras at 56%. However, according to the OECD, while Mexico and Central American states have become more reliant on the US economy, South American countries have become more dependent on China's economy.

Another external factor was the recovery in commodity prices after the 2014 crash. According to the World Bank, copper prices recovered from US$5,510 per metric tonne (mt) in 2015 to over US$6,000 per mt in summer 2018. This benefited commodity exporters such as Chile, for whom copper-related exports came to 21% of its total exports in 2016, and other minerals-related exports another 20%. Peru, another metal-commodity exporter, also benefited from these rising prices.

Internally, growth was fuelled by private consumption, thanks to improved business and consumer confidence, as well as investments; this was the case in Chile and Colombia. Meanwhile, tourism grew in the Caribbean, benefiting countries such as Barbados, Belize, Jamaica and St Lucia.

However, larger countries in the region acted as a brake on the overall regional economic acceleration. Argentina, for example, has experienced difficulties since mid-2018. In the wake of the rise of interest rates in the US, Argentina saw its currency weaken sharply. Between January and September 2018, the peso lost more than 50% of its value against the US dollar. Inflation also reached record highs, up to 34.4% year-on-year in August 2018. This led Buenos Aires to implement an austerity programme, with hikes in export taxes and a reduction in the number of government ministries. Around the same time, Macri announced defence-reform plans, including a restructuring of the ministry of defence. Nonetheless, the government had to request a US$50-billion loan from the IMF. In addition, a severe drought affected Argentina's production of soya beans and corn, which had constituted 24% and 6% of its exports respectively in 2016.

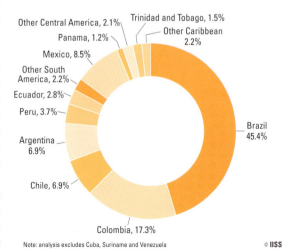

▼ Figure 24 **Latin America and the Caribbean defence spending by country and sub-region**

Note: analysis excludes Cuba, Suriname and Venezuela

© IISS

The IMF assessed that Brazil's GDP would grow from 1% in 2017 to 2.3% in 2018, rebounding after two years of recession. However, weaknesses remained, which could dampen this outlook. The Brazilian real weakened against the US dollar by 25% between September 2018 and January 2018. In May 2018, the truck drivers' strike hit the economy, hampering the shipping industry and trade, and leading to fuel shortages. Political uncertainty also dominated ahead of the presidential election in October 2018, in which right-leaning candidate Jair Bolsonaro was victorious. Most importantly, Brazil's economy, and in particular the government's room for manoeuvre, is clouded by rising debt and large deficits. These challenges, however, appear manageable when compared to Venezuela's economic crisis. The IMF has estimated an inflation rate there above 1,000,000% in 2018, and the authorities had to devaluate the currency by replacing 100,000 bolívares fuertes with one bolívar soberano.

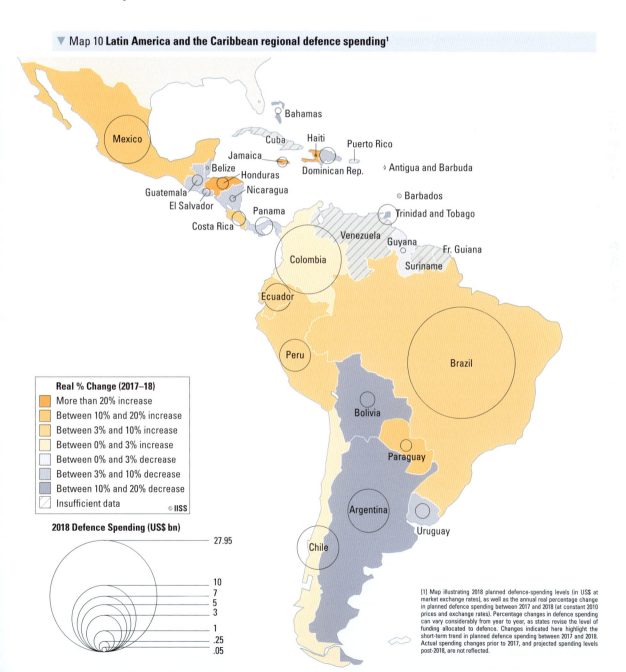

Map 10 **Latin America and the Caribbean regional defence spending**[1]

[1] Map illustrating 2018 planned defence-spending levels (in US$ at market exchange rates), as well as the annual real percentage change in planned defence spending between 2017 and 2018 (at constant 2010 prices and exchange rates). Percentage changes in defence spending can vary considerably from year to year, as states revise the level of funding allocated to defence. Changes indicated here highlight the short-term trend in planned defence spending between 2017 and 2018. Actual spending changes prior to 2017, and projected spending levels post-2018, are not reflected.

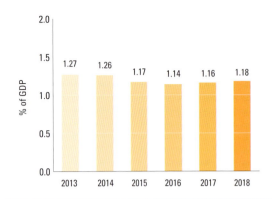

▲ Figure 25 **Latin America and the Caribbean regional defence expenditure** as % of GDP

Defence industry

A major development in the Latin American defence industry in 2018 was the planned tie-up between Boeing and Brazil's largest defence company, Embraer, which is involved in key programmes such as the delivery of *Gripen* combat aircraft to the Brazilian Air Force. It also develops the EMB-314 *Super Tucano* light-attack/training aircraft and the KC-390 transport aircraft. In 2016, Boeing and Embraer had agreed to jointly market the KC-390. However, the partnership announced in July 2018 goes beyond this. The firms have agreed to create a new joint venture dedicated to the sale of defence products, in particular the KC-390. But as the partnership deals with commercial products, it still needs to be authorised by the Brazilian authorities.

Brazil is not the only Latin American country attracting foreign interest in its defence sector. Moreover, it is not just the major Western prime contractors who see the region as a potential market. For instance, Peru's Air Force Maintenance Service has assembled the Korea Aerospace Industries KT-1P training aircraft. The final KT-1P of the 20-aircraft order was delivered in April 2017. Meanwhile, the South Korean shipbuilding firm STX agreed a partnership with Peru's SIMA shipyards to work together on the delivery of PGCP-50 maritime-patrol boats for the Peruvian Navy.

In Argentina, the major defence firm Fábrica Argentina de Aviones (FAdeA) was caught up in the country's economic challenges. The government threatened to reduce its funding if the company did not ink an export deal for its IA-63 *Pampa* III training aircraft, and lack of sales meant that the company had to lay off 500 employees over two years. However, FAdeA signed a memorandum of understanding with South Africa's Paramount Group in 2018. The opening of the African market could be an opportunity for FAdeA and might help mitigate its current difficulties.

Regional procurement

Argentina's financial problems have prevented the implementation of a planned modernisation programme that would have seen the procurement of new fighter aircraft for the air force, five ocean-patrol vessels for the navy and up to 20 medium-lift helicopters for army aviation. Nevertheless, besides T-6C+ *Texan* trainers, the air force took delivery of its first locally upgraded C-130H *Hercules* and is expected to receive the first three IA-63 *Pampa* III lead-in fighter trainers from FAdeA. The Argentinian government was also able to process the €14.2 million (US$16.8m) payment for five *Super Etendard Modernisé* naval fighters in May 2018 and expected the aircraft to be in service before the G20 summit in Buenos Aires in November–December 2018.

Bolivia received a relatively small military-assistance package from China in 2018 in the form of light vehicles and logistics equipment, including ten *Tiger* 4x4 armoured vehicles for the army. Other procurement included a light aircraft obtained from various civilian second-hand sources. The country's main investment programme in recent years has featured the procurement of a network of dual-use air-surveillance and air-traffic-control radars ordered from Thales in 2015.

The Brazilian armed forces took delivery of a significant number of armoured vehicles and artillery pieces in 2018. The army received eight ASTROS multiple-rocket launchers from AVIBRAS to complete the order for three new batteries, as well as 60 M109A5 155 mm self-propelled howitzers, while the marines received their last AAV7A1 amphibious assault vehicles. Besides the arrival in 2018 of the former UK helicopter carrier HMS *Ocean*, the navy evaluated in 2017 its first *Exocet*-equipped H225M helicopters. The country's second upgraded *Super Lynx* anti-submarine-warfare helicopter made its maiden flight in mid-2018 in the UK.

Procurement spending in Colombia remains modest, mainly due to the costs associated with the ongoing implementation of the peace process with FARC. In 2018, the armed forces took delivery of a range of logistical vehicles, including a single landing craft (ARC *Bahia Colombia*), the fifth of class; five *Defender* 380X patrol boats; and a ninth upgraded

Arpia IV helicopter. Colombia also created a new multipurpose squadron equipped with Bell 206 *Jet Ranger* helicopters and a new UAV squadron equipped with Boeing *ScanEagle* and *NightEagle* systems for the air force, while the army took delivery of a small number of locally produced TR12 *Hunter* mine-resistant ambush-protected vehicles. The air force will likely also acquire a single C-130H *Hercules* transport aircraft from surplus US Air Force stocks and announced its intention to acquire another two. Although funds remain limited in Ecuador, the government has been trying to recapitalise some of its military capabilities, particularly air mobility. A single M28 *Skytruck* light cargo plane was delivered, and it is understood that the ministry wishes to procure at least six light helicopters for the army.

CHILE

Chile's armed forces are professional and capable, if compact. Until recently, missions and planning were dominated by territorial-defence considerations, but the armed forces are also now preparing for 'missions other than war', including peacekeeping and humanitarian assistance and disaster relief (HA/DR). As part of this process, they are undertaking more exercises with regional and international partners.

Santiago's security policy is transforming from a traditional defence model to one defined by changing regional relations and new strategic priorities promoted by civilian governments. As a consequence, concepts and force structures designed to address territorial threats coexist with policy initiatives and procurement programmes associated with new tasks. At the same time, there has been a slow reduction in the defence budget and the cancellation or postponement of some procurement plans for conventional equipment. This strategic transition has continued during President Sebastián Piñera's second term in office. In his first term, in 2010–14, he proposed initiatives to modify Chile's defence policy, an aspiration to which his successor Michelle Bachelet was also committed. Chile's defence minister was elected president of the Conference of Defense Ministers of the Americas in October 2018. The defence ministry said that Chile's presidency of this group would be directed at strengthening regional cooperation in HA/DR, environmental protection, preparing for new security challenges including cyber defence, and boosting women's participation in the armed forces. In addition, Piñera, who was elected again in December 2017, is introducing substantial changes to the way Chilean defence is financed.

Security policy in transition

Following the transition to democracy in the early 1990s, Chilean defence was principally shaped by three considerations: that historical rivalries with Bolivia and Peru were still potential sources of conflict; that the armed forces retained considerable autonomy in defence affairs after political arrangements agreed during the democratic transition; and that the military-modernisation programme benefited from healthy financial resources.

These factors helped to maintain a military posture focused on external defence in the event of conventional conflict. The army was organised as a mechanised force with three motorised infantry brigades and four armoured brigades equipped with *Leopard* 1 and 2 main battle tanks and variants, the only likely role for which was the defence of the desert regions in Chile's north. The air force was conceived of as an air-superiority and strike force; it acquired 46 F-16 combat aircraft, mostly second-hand from the Netherlands but supplemented later with some new builds. The navy was designed to guarantee the protection of sea lines of communication with a surface fleet of eight principal surface combatants and to carry out interdiction operations with a submarine fleet of two Type-209/1400 and two *Scorpène*-class boats. Each of the three services operated relatively autonomously, with only a limited degree of joint organisation.

However, since the late 2000s, several factors have combined to change this model. Closer economic ties and political rapprochement with Chile's neighbours have reduced the risk of a border crisis. Chile was one of the founders of the Pacific Alliance and is an associate member of the Mercado Común del Sur (Common Market of the South, or MERCOSUR). Nonetheless, there have been disputes with neighbours, though parties have resolved to settle these through recourse to the International Court of Justice (ICJ). A long-standing maritime dispute between Chile and Peru was eventually settled only after referral to the ICJ, which in 2014 granted Lima additional maritime waters. In 2013, Bolivia took a dispute with Chile to the ICJ over its claim that it should have access to the Pacific Ocean via an 'Atacama corridor'. In October 2018, the court found that Chile 'did not undertake a legal obligation to negotiate a sovereign access to the Pacific Ocean for the Plurinational State of Bolivia'.

At the same time, successive civilian governments have strengthened their capacity to design and manage defence policy. A new organisational structure for the ministry of defence (Law 20424) was approved in 2010. This gave the civilian leadership greater influence over security-policy planning and armed-services administration by creating the offices of the under-secretary of defence and the under-secretary for the armed forces. Another outcome of the reorganisation process was that control of the paramilitary Carabineros was transferred to the Ministry of the Interior and Public Security in 2011.

As well as consolidating political control over the security establishment, recent administrations have promoted new missions for the armed forces, such as disaster relief, maritime surveillance and border security, as well as contributing to international peacekeeping missions. Indeed, while the 2010 defence white paper affirmed the need to maintain a credible deterrent capability, it also incorporated into Chile's security-policy objectives the development of non-combat activities and stronger regional cooperation.

Under this framework, the armed forces have a key role in delivering humanitarian assistance and helping to rebuild infrastructure after natural disasters. They carried out these tasks after Chile suffered severe earthquakes in 2010 and 2015, reflecting not just changing policy priorities but also that the armed forces have core capabilities vital for responding to these crises. Meanwhile, Santiago has maintained significant participation in UN missions while deepening its involvement in peacekeeping more broadly, for instance by establishing the Joint Center for Peacekeeping Operations in 2002. It contributed to MINUSTAH (Haiti) with a battalion-size unit, until the end of the operation in October 2017. Currently, Chile keeps small detachments in UNFICYP (Cyprus) and UNVMC (the mission to verify the peace process in Colombia). At the same time, it has representatives in UNMOGIP (India and Pakistan), UNTSO (Egypt, Israel, Jordan, Lebanon and Syria) and MINUSCA (Central African Republic). Chile also contributes to EUFOR *Althea*, the European Union mission responsible for maintaining security in Bosnia-Herzegovina.

An emphasis on regional security cooperation has been particularly visible in Chile's growing military ties with Argentina. Rapprochement with Buenos Aires began with the signing of a memorandum of understanding in 1995. A battalion-strength joint Cruz de Sur (Southern Cross) peacekeeping force was formed after bilateral talks in 2005 and 2006. Both nations' military units also take part in the *Solidaridad* series of biannual disaster-response drills.

▲ Map 11 **Chile: key military bases and defence-industrial facilities**

The armed forces

The armed forces are highly professional but limited in size, with just over 77,000 personnel, 46,000 of whom are in the army. Military service is mandatory, though there are usually enough volunteers to forestall compulsory notices. Only the army has a significant number of conscripts in its ranks (its non-commissioned officers are professional), while the navy and the air force are almost all professional.

There has been increased emphasis on strengthening 'jointness' and reducing the administrative and operational independence of the three services. After 2010, and the approval of Law 20424, the Joint Staff became responsible for the strategic management of the armed forces; they had traditionally held an administrative function. This decision was later accompanied by the creation of two regional joint commands (North and South). Based on this structure, the Joint Staff has acquired a greater role in directing major operations. Joint Command North, for instance, supports the police force's border-security operations through the Frontera Norte Segura (Safe Northern Border) Plan. Likewise, the Joint Staff is responsible for coordinating Chilean participation in international peacekeeping and observation missions.

Meanwhile, procurement priorities have been modified, not only in size as a result of budget reductions, but because of the broadening focus of Chile's defence policy. Investment is mainly allocated to the acquisition of multipurpose equipment capable of combat and non-combat operations.

Procurement

As a consequence, some of the capabilities required for tasks such as rapid deployment and maritime patrol have been afforded greater priority. This change is most likely to affect the army, as its structure and equipment holdings have been traditionally geared towards conventional combat operations. To date, the last significant land-system procurement by Chile was of US-origin M109A5+ self-propelled howitzers. The second batch of 12 arrived in December 2014 by means of US Foreign Military Sales.

Regular army deployments in support of disaster-relief activities have helped the development of a more flexible force, in particular by the involvement of military-engineering contingents in such tasks (and on exercises). As a part of this process, Chile has taken steps to expand its rotary-wing assets, including the acquisition of a batch of AS532AL and AS532ALe *Cougar* helicopters, the last of which was delivered in 2016. These have expanded significantly the capability of the aviation brigade, which provides air mobility for the army and plays a critical role in disaster-relief operations. Likewise, the army made significant investment in 2017 to equip its engineer battalions with new construction plant and all-terrain vehicles, improving their capabilities to manage natural disasters.

Meanwhile, the air force will have to consider how to maintain the level of platform capability that made it one of the most sophisticated air forces in the region. A significant number of its F-16 combat aircraft are approaching the limit of their operational lives, as are the air force's 1980s-vintage CASA C-101CC trainer/light-attack aircraft, and there are believed to be no immediate plans to renew or extend these capabilities. Air-force efforts have instead been directed at strengthening transport aviation, by taking into service four ex-US Marine Corps KC-130R *Hercules*, increasing to seven Chile's *Hercules* fleet. Chile's aerial-surveillance capacity is also receiving attention: three *Hermes* 900 uninhabited aerial vehicles (UAVs) are already operating as part of the Safe Northern Border Plan. A key future project will be renewing the SSOT (Sistema Satelital de la Observacion de la Tierra) intelligence, surveillance and reconnaissance satellite operated by the air force's Space Operations Group.

The Chilean Navy has bolstered its capacity for maritime-security and coastguard-related tasks. Four domestically produced *Piloto Pardo*-class offshore-patrol vessels have been acquired, two with ice-strengthened hulls. Meanwhile, the first steel was cut for a new icebreaker in 2017. This *Ice*-class vessel is due to be completed in 2022 and will provide invaluable support to expanding Chilean activities in the Antarctic. Modernisation of the navy's fleet of P-3ACH *Orion* maritime-patrol aircraft is also under way. This mid-life upgrade programme will replace, according to Lockheed Martin, elements including the 'outer wings, centre wing, horizontal stabiliser and horizontal stabiliser leading edges'.

Nonetheless, Chile's principal combat platforms are also receiving attention. The navy's three Type-23 frigates were undergoing modernisation in 2018 that involved the installation of new combat-management systems and air-defence missiles. The navy's two *Scorpène*-class submarines have also been completely overhauled, and one of the two Type-209/1400s is undergoing a similar process that will extend its service life by ten years. However, the plan to acquire a further two *Scorpène*-class boats to replace the Type-209/1400s has been postponed, while a replacement has yet to be identified for the submarine tender *Almirante José Toribio Merino Castro*, which had been taken out of service in 2015.

The navy is also developing its blue-water activities, increasing its capability to operate at distance from its bases and to participate in multinational coalitions. In 2015, the navy deployed the oiler *Almirante Montt* northwards to supply Canada's Pacific Fleet, a mission which would have given the crew valuable lessons in operations with unfamiliar vessels in distant waters. A milestone was reached in 2018 when the Chilean Navy assumed the leadership of the naval component of the RIMPAC multinational exercise taking place off Hawaii.

Defence economics

Over the past decade, Chile has consistently ranked highly in the table of Latin American defence budgets. Military expenses have traditionally been financed from three sources: firstly, annual budget allocations to the defence ministry, which have typically been used to cover salaries, operating expenses and infrastructure-construction outlays; secondly, the National Defence Provident Fund (Caja de Previsión de la Defensa Nacional, or CAPREDENA), which manages military-pension payments; and, lastly, the Copper Reserve Law (Ley Reservada del Cobre), which traditionally allocated 10% of profits from national copper exports to military procurement.

Given the difficulties in calculating the precise proportion of armed-forces funding derived from copper revenues – the government occasionally diverts some of these funds for other purposes – most estimates of Chilean defence spending tend to focus on the first two sources (the ministry's annual budget and armed-forces pensions). Together, these amounted to an average of around 1.67% of GDP between 2010 and 2014. That said, private-sector analysis of the economy in August 2018 reportedly indicated that, between 2012 and 2017, the copper law generated additional funds averaging more than US$1 billion annually for equipment acquisitions.

Salaries are the principal component of the defence-ministry budget; in 2018, these amounted to 64.2% of the total, while operating expenditure stood at 21.4%, according to the budget presented to congress in late 2017. Most of the remainder was allocated to cover a variety of financial expenses, leaving almost no room for the purchase of new weapons systems. In the past, the copper law offset this funding shortfall.

However, after attempts by previous governments, in September 2018 President Piñera announced the repeal of the copper law and the creation of a new mechanism to fund equipment acquisition. According to this new scheme, the armed forces will have two additional sources of funding apart from standard allocations to the ministry of defence. There will be a four-year budget, initially funded with US$2.6bn from remaining copper-law resources and then by new annual allocations provided by the government. A Strategic Contingency Fund will also be created, with an additional US$1bn to be used in case of a national-security crisis or natural disaster.

A share of the profits of Chile's state copper company will no longer go by law to the armed forces but will instead be transferred to the treasury in the same way as other copper revenues; the government will decide its allocation in the same way as the rest of the national budget. By repealing the copper law, Chile's civilian political leadership will gain full control over all defence funding and expenditures.

More broadly, the repeal of the copper law reflects two key changes in the Chilean political landscape. It demonstrates that the civilian government has achieved full control of defence policy, while showing an underlying change in government priorities in favour of increased investment in areas such as health and education. Indeed, recent governments sought to provide alternative uses for the funds generated by the copper law. To this end, legal changes were made that allowed copper-law revenues for disaster relief after the 2010 earthquake, during the fires in the Valparaíso region in 2014 and in early 2015 in order to finance reconstruction in flood-hit areas of the north. The bill establishing a new financing mechanism was going through the legislative process at the time of writing.

It is possible that military spending might also come under pressure as a consequence of Chile's economic situation: growth fell from 5.8% in 2010 to just 1.5% in 2017 according to the IMF. Between 2010 and 2018, the percentage of Chile's GDP devoted to the armed forces fell from 1.63% to 1.42%. The defence budget for 2018 represents a moderate increase of 3% in nominal terms in comparison to the previous year. In real terms, measured in constant (2010) US dollars, this meant an increase of 1.9% between 2017 and 2018.

The reduction in available funds for the armed forces could result in some challenges. Given its level of technical sophistication, military equipment is expensive to maintain, not to mention the costs that would be associated with new systems of similar or better capability. Consequently, the defence ministry will have to carefully manage any significant reduction in defence expenditures, in order to prevent an adverse effect on conventional defence capabilities.

Defence industry

Chile's defence industry is relatively small and dominated by public enterprises. Although they are state-owned, these firms have management independence. This has helped them adopt long-term business models, such that they are able to maintain levels of technological sophistication, relative to the rest of the region. The three key companies are FAMAE (Fábricas y Maestranzas del Ejército, manufacturing and repairing land systems), ASMAR (Astilleros y Maestranzas de la Armada, active in naval shipbuilding and repair) and ENAER (Empresa Nacional de Aeronáutica, which manufactures and maintains aircraft).

FAMAE is one of the oldest defence companies in Latin America, and has, over time, progressed from manufacturing licensed small arms to more complex activities such as the modernisation of Chile's *Leopard* 1V main battle tanks. Its defence-production capacity grew considerably in 1976 after the US imposed an arms embargo on Chile's then-military government. FAMAE's most ambitious project is the manufacture of the SLM multiple-rocket launcher, which leverages the company's prior experience with the *Rayo* programme (cancelled in 2002).

Meanwhile, maritime concern ASMAR has considerable technological expertise and a number of orders on its books. Its most important projects are the construction of the *Ice*-class icebreaker, the Type-23 modernisation project and the overhaul of the Type-209/1400 submarines. Its most significant foreign contract was for the modernisation of Ecuador's Type-209/1300 submarines, completed in 2014.

ENAER has a broad manufacturing and maintenance portfolio, spanning both civil and military aircraft. A well-known export is the T-35 *Pillan* basic trainer, which has been exported to the Dominican Republic, Ecuador and Spain, among others, while its most important domestic programme is to provide technical support to the air force's F-16 combat-aircraft fleet. The company also maintains C-130 *Hercules* transport aircraft – including for foreign customers such as Colombia. In March 2015, ENAER signed an agreement with Italy's Leonardo to provide support and produce components for C-27J *Spartan* transport aircraft and M-345 HET advanced trainers. In November 2016, ENAER signed an agreement with Airbus to develop capabilities for the maintenance and overhaul of C212, CN235 and C295 airlifters, as well as to cooperate in the production of components for space systems.

In addition to these three major state companies, Chile's defence industry includes a network of smaller private companies that specialise in the production of high-technology systems and components. Chile's defence sector has benefited from the government's long-term approach to industrial development, as well as from sustained procurement-funding levels enabled by the copper law. However, as the Chilean defence budget reduces in the face of slowing economic growth and other spending priorities, and because of changes to copper law disbursements, the risk grows that domestic contracts may come under pressure; as a result, export success will become ever more important.

MEXICO

In July 2018, Mexicans elected as president Andrés Manuel López Obrador (popularly known as AMLO) from the left-wing National Reconstruction Movement (MORENA) party. AMLO won with a landslide 53% majority. He ran on a populist campaign that focused on fighting corruption and lowering government salaries and benefits. AMLO's security proposals included the creation of a civilian-led National Guard that will blend army and marine units together with the Federal Police to create a single internal-security force. The security forces, meanwhile, remain engaged on internal-security tasks and in 2018 violence continued to pose a challenge.

Before assuming office, AMLO announced that the Mexican armed forces would remain represented in his cabinet via two distinct ministries, the Secretariá de la Defensa Nacional (SEDENA), comprising the army and air force, and the Secretariá de Marina (SEMAR), comprising the navy. These are headed by an active-duty four-star general and an admiral, who serve as (equally ranked) secretary of defence and navy respectively. While there have been reports of potential change in the political-military organisation, with a likely shift towards a single civilian-staffed defence ministry and the creation of a joint chief of staff structure, similar rumours have been heard during previous transitions. Any significant adjustment to the political-military structure will require constitutional changes, as it is currently mandated that active-duty military officers head these institutions. AMLO also announced that his administration will recruit 50,000 additional personnel to join SEDENA, SEMAR and the Federal Police.

The announcement that the 1,800-strong presidential guard would disband after AMLO takes office attracted some attention. Known as the Estado Mayor Presidencial, the guard had provided security and logistics for the office of the president since 1926. AMLO stated that his personal security would instead be guaranteed by a 20-member civilian staff. He also announced that the Presidential Air Transport (CGTAP) flight will be disbanded and sold off. This includes some 22 aircraft, including a Boeing 787-8 (delivered in 2016), four Gulfstream executive aircraft, one Beech 350i, one H225M and six AW109s.

Over the past decade, the Mexican armed forces have expanded and modernised their internal-security capabilities at the expense of their conventional capacity. Major investment is required to modernise their artillery, armour, air defence, fighter-aviation and surface-warfare capabilities.

Local production of DN-XI armoured vehicles ceased at around 150 out of a planned 1,000, though there is potential to restart the production line once the army-run defence industries finalise their move to Puebla. Most of the DN-XIs, along with around 250 *SandCats*, have been re-distributed to the newly created military police brigades. These brigades have been created by drawing personnel from infantry, cavalry and artillery units, in lieu of additional resources to significantly expand personnel levels; the Mexican Army had stood up ten of 12 of these units by 2018. The army expects to procure new 105 mm and 155 mm artillery pieces, as well as a new generation of 8x8 armoured fighting vehicles, during the 2018–24 administration.

In November 2018, the Mexican Navy was due to launch the *Reformadora*, the first of eight SIGMA 10514-class frigates, which are planned to be built at Mexican shipyards. The navy has announced plans to equip *Reformadora* with RGM-84L *Harpoon* Block II anti-ship missiles and RIM-162 ESSM and RIM-116 Block 2 missiles, as well as MH-60R *Seahawk* helicopters armed with AGM-114 *Hellfire* missiles and APKWS II guided rockets. The ship is due to enter service in 2020. Navy shipyards have also been building the seventh and eighth *Oaxaca*-class ocean-patrol vessels, ARM *Jalisco* and ARM *Estado de Mexico*, which are due to be commissioned in 2019. SEMAR expects to continue its naval construction programme under AMLO; however, the exact mix of ships to be built in the 2019–24 period remains unclear. Mexico's ongoing requirements for ocean- and coastal-patrol vessels to monitor its exclusive economic zone are likely to continue, although SEMAR has made the construction of the frigates a priority and may push for funding for at least three more by 2024.

Mexico's aviation assets were significantly modernised during the 2012–18 administration, with UH-60M *Black Hawk* and AS565MBe *Panther* helicopters arriving, as well as more Beechcraft T-6C+ *Texan* IIs and eight *King Air* 350 turboprops. Half of the *King Air*s are configured for maritime patrol and the remainder for intelligence, surveillance and reconnaissance. The procurement of further UH-60M *Black Hawk*s, mainly to begin replacement of the Mi-17 fleet, has been outlined as a priority for the 2018–24 administration. However, these requirements may be revised in early 2019, as the new administration begins to redefine its procurement priorities. The acquisition of further maritime-patrol aircraft, including a medium-altitude long-endurance (MALE) uninhabited aerial vehicle (UAV), is part of SEMAR's long-term plans.

Mexico's marines continue to expand and have now been reorganised around a brigade-level special-forces unit (UNOPES) – an amphibious marine infantry brigade, which deploys units on both the Pacific and Gulf of Mexico coasts – and 30 battalions that are in various stages of formation. Requirements for new amphibious and light armoured vehicles have been reported.

Mexico's southern radar network, known as SIVA (Sistema Integrado de Vigilancia Aérea) is augmented by a flight composed of an EMB-145AEW *Erieye* and two EMB-145RS maritime-patrol aircraft, all of which are scheduled for upgrade. Three new S45 tactical UAVs have been incorporated into the SIVA flight. An unknown number of the more capable *Hermes* 900 MALE UAVs remain assigned to the Federal Police and the National Security Investigations Centre (Centro de Investigación y Seguridad Nacional, or CISEN), an organisation that AMLO has pledged to dissolve. The repair and refurbishment of the air force's sole fighter squadron began in late 2017, and the first two F-5Es to be redelivered were operational in September 2018. The procurement of a new air-surveillance network for Mexico's northern border, based on the Thales GM400 composed of up to five radars and a command-and-control centre, was suspended due to lack of funds. Despite a US Army North/US NORTHCOM cooperation programme that led to the lease of TPS-70 radar as an emergency interim solution, SEDENA authorities have announced that the acquisition of five new radars is a priority.

Antigua and Barbuda ATG

East Caribbean Dollar EC$		2017	2018	2019
GDP	EC$	4.12bn	4.35bn	
	US$	1.52bn	1.61bn	
per capita	US$	16,702	17,477	
Growth	%	2.8	3.5	
Inflation	%	2.5	1.4	
Def bdgt [a]	EC$	16.9m	19.2m	
	US$	6.25m	7.10m	
US$1=EC$		2.70	2.70	

[a] Budget for the Ministry of Legal Affairs, Public Safety, Immigration & Labour

Population 95,882

Age	0–14	15–19	20–24	25–29	30–64	65 plus
Male	11.6%	4.1%	4.1%	3.6%	20.2%	3.6%
Female	11.3%	4.1%	4.2%	3.8%	24.6%	4.8%

Capabilities

The Antigua and Barbuda Defence Force (ABDF) focuses on internal security and disaster relief, and also contributes to regional counter-narcotics efforts. It comprises a light-infantry element, which carries out internal-security duties, and a coastguard, which is tasked with fishery protection and counter-narcotics. Antigua and Barbuda is a member of the Caribbean Community and the Caribbean Regional Security System. The country maintains defence ties with the UK and sends personnel to train in the US. The ABDF participates in US SOUTHCOM's annual *Tradewinds* disaster-relief exercise, though it has no independent capacity to deploy forces other than in its immediate neighbourhood, most recently for disaster-relief efforts in Dominica. The equipment inventory is limited to small arms and light weapons (there is a range of mainly soft-skinned vehicles), while the coastguard maintains ex-US patrol vessels and a number of smaller boats. Aside from limited maintenance facilities, there is no significant indigenous defence industry.

ACTIVE 180 (Army 130 Coast Guard 50)
(all services form combined Antigua and Barbuda Defence Force)

RESERVE 80 (Joint 80)

ORGANISATIONS BY SERVICE

Army 130
FORCES BY ROLE
MANOEUVRE
  Light
  1 inf bn HQ
  1 inf coy
COMBAT SERVICE SUPPORT
  1 spt gp (1 engr unit, 1 med unit)

Coast Guard 50
EQUIPMENT BY TYPE
PATROL AND COASTAL COMBATANTS • PB 2: 1 *Dauntless*; 1 *Swift*

Argentina ARG

Argentine Peso P		2017	2018	2019
GDP	P	10.6tr	13.6tr	
	US$	638bn	475bn	
per capita	US$	14,463	10,667	
Growth	%	2.9	-2.6	
Inflation	%	25.7	31.8	
Def bdgt	P	102bn	121bn	151bn
	US$	6.17bn	4.23bn	
US$1=P		16.56	28.67	

Population 44,694,198

Age	0–14	15–19	20–24	25–29	30–64	65 plus
Male	12.6%	4.0%	3.8%	3.8%	20.3%	5.0%
Female	11.8%	3.8%	3.7%	3.7%	20.7%	6.8%

Capabilities

Argentina's armed forces have sufficient training and equipment to fulfil internal-security tasks, although any power-projection ambition is limited by lack of funding. The armed forces principally focus on border security, surveillance and counter-narcotics operations, in part due to the increase in drug-trafficking activity in and around the country, and cooperate with Bolivia and Paraguay. Amid other defence reforms, legislation proposed in 2018 may allow greater latitude to deploy the armed forces against non-traditional threats. Military cooperation with the US centres on enhancing readiness, as well as disaster response, border security and peacekeeping. The armed forces participate in multinational exercises and bilateral peacekeeping exercises with neighbour Chile. There are limited deployment capabilities, and the equipment inventory is increasingly obsolete, with modernisation hampered by limited funding. The air force faces significant equipment-availability challenges and the navy has seen its capability decline in areas such as anti-submarine warfare, mine warfare and airborne early warning. Argentina possesses an indigenous defence-manufacturing capacity covering land, sea and air systems, although industry fortunes have dipped in recent years because of lack of investment. State-owned aviation firm FAdeA has aircraft-maintenance capabilities, but is reliant on external assistance for some manufacturing tasks.

ACTIVE 74,200 (Army 42,800 Navy 18,500 Air 12,900) **Paramilitary 31,250**

ORGANISATIONS BY SERVICE

Army 42,800
Regt and gp are usually bn-sized
FORCES BY ROLE
SPECIAL FORCES
  1 SF gp
MANOEUVRE
  Mechanised
  1 (1st) div (1 armd bde (4 tk regt, 1 mech inf regt, 1 SP arty gp, 1 cbt engr bn, 1 int coy, 1 sigs coy, 1 log coy), 1 (3rd) jungle bde (2 jungle inf regt, 1 arty gp, 1 engr bn, 1 int coy, 1 sigs coy, 1 log coy, 1 med coy); 1 (12th) jungle bde (3 jungle inf regt, 1 arty gp, 1 engr bn, 1 int

coy, 1 sigs coy, 1 log coy, 1 med coy), 2 engr bn, 1 sigs bn, 1 log coy)

1 (3rd) div (1 mech bde (1 armd recce regt, 1 tk regt, 2 mech inf regt, 1 SP arty gp, 1 cbt engr bn, 1 int coy, 1 sigs coy, 1 log coy), 1 mech bde (1 armd recce tp, 1 tk regt, 2 mech inf regt, 1 SP arty gp, 1 cbt engr bn, 1 int coy, 1 sigs coy, 1 log coy), 1 int bn, 1 sigs bn, 1 log coy)

1 (Rapid Deployment) force (1 armd bde (1 recce sqn, 3 tk regt, 1 mech inf regt, 1 SP arty gp, 1 cbt engr coy, 1 int coy, 1 sigs coy, 1 log coy), 1 mech bde (1 armd recce regt, 3 mech inf regt, 1 arty gp, 1 cbt engr coy, 1 int coy, 1 sigs coy,1 log coy), 1 AB bde (1 recce tp, 2 para regt, 1 arty gp, 1 cbt engr coy, 1 sigs coy, 1 log coy), 1 AD gp (2 AD bn))

Light

1 (2nd) mtn inf div (2 mtn inf bde (1 armd recce regt, 3 mtn inf regt, 2 arty gp, 1 cbt engr bn, 1 sigs coy, 1 log coy), 1 mtn inf bde (1 armd recce bn, 2 mtn inf regt, 1 jungle inf regt, 2 arty gp, 1 cbt engr bn, 1 sigs coy, 1 construction coy, 1 log coy), 1 AD gp, 1 sigs bn)

1 mot cav regt (presidential escort)

Air Manoeuvre

1 air aslt regt

COMBAT SUPPORT

1 arty gp (bn)
1 engr bn
1 sigs gp (1 EW bn, 1 sigs bn, 1 maint bn)
1 sigs bn
1 sigs coy

COMBAT SERVICE SUPPORT

5 maint bn

HELICOPTER

1 avn gp (bde) (1 avn bn, 1 hel bn)

EQUIPMENT BY TYPE
ARMOURED FIGHTING VEHICLES
MBT 231: 225 TAM, 6 TAM S21
LT TK 117: 107 SK-105A1 *Kuerassier*; 6 SK-105A2 *Kuerassier*; 4 *Patagón*
RECCE 47 AML-90
IFV 232: 118 VCTP (incl variants); 114 M113A2 (20mm cannon)
APC 278
  APC (T) 274: 70 M113A1-ACAV; 204 M113A2
  APC (W) 4 WZ-551B1
ENGINEERING & MAINTENANCE VEHICLES
ARV *Greif*
ANTI-TANK/ANTI-INFRASTRUCTURE
MSL • SP 3 M1025 HMMWV with TOW-2A
RCL 105mm 150 M-1968
ARTILLERY 1,108
SP 155mm 42: 23 AMX F3; 19 VCA 155 *Palmaria*
TOWED 172: 105mm 64 Model 56 pack howitzer; 155mm 108: 28 CITEFA M-77/CITEFA M-81; 80 SOFMA L-33
MRL 8: 105mm 4 SLAM *Pampero*; 127mm 4 CP-30
MOR 886: 81mm 492; SP 107mm 25 M106A2; 120mm 330 Brandt; SP 120mm 39 TAM-VCTM
AIRCRAFT
TPT • Light 14: 1 Beech 80 *Queen Air*; 3 C-212-200 *Aviocar*; 2 Cessna 208EX *Grand Caravan*; 1 Cessna 500 *Citation* (survey); 1 Cessna 550 *Citation Bravo*; 3 DA42 (to be converted to ISR role); 2 DHC-6 *Twin Otter*; 1 *Sabreliner* 75A (*Gaviao* 75A)
TRG 5 T-41 *Mescalero*
HELICOPTERS
MRH 5: 4 SA315B *Lama*; 1 Z-11
TPT 67: **Medium** 3 AS332B *Super Puma*; **Light** 64: 1 Bell 212; 25 Bell 205 (UH-1H *Iroquois* – 6 armed); 5 Bell 206B3; 13 UH-1H-II *Huey* II; 20 AB206B1
AIR DEFENCE
SAM • Point-defence RBS-70
GUNS • TOWED 229: 20mm 200 GAI-B01; 30mm 21 HS L81; 35mm 8 GDF Oerlikon (*Skyguard* fire control)

Navy 18,500

Commands: Surface Fleet, Submarines, Naval Avn, Marines

FORCES BY ROLE
SPECIAL FORCES
1 (diver) SF gp
EQUIPMENT BY TYPE
SUBMARINES • TACTICAL • SSK 2:
  1 *Salta* (GER T-209/1100) with 8 single 533mm TT with Mk 37/SST-4 HWT
  1 *Santa Cruz* (GER TR-1700) with 6 single 533mm TT with SST-4 HWT (undergoing MLU)
PRINCIPAL SURFACE COMBATANTS 11
  DESTROYERS • DDH 1 *Hercules* (UK Type-42 – utilised as a fast troop-transport ship), with 1 114mm gun (capacity 2 SH-3H *Sea King* hel)
  FRIGATES • FFGHM 10:
    4 *Almirante Brown* (GER MEKO 360) with 2 quad lnchr with MM40 *Exocet* AShM, 1 octuple *Albatros* lnchr with *Aspide* SAM, 2 triple B515 ILAS-3 324mm TT with A244 LWT, 1 127mm gun (capacity 1 AS555 *Fennec* hel)
    6 *Espora* (GER MEKO 140) with 2 twin lnchr with MM38 *Exocet* AShM, 2 triple B515 ILAS-3 324mm ASTT with A244 LWT, 1 76mm gun (capacity 1 AS555 *Fennec* hel)
PATROL AND COASTAL COMBATANTS 16
  CORVETTES • FSG 3 *Drummond* (FRA A-69) with 2 twin lnchr with MM38 *Exocet* AShM, 2 triple ILAS-3 324mm ASTT with A244 LWT, 1 100mm gun
  PSO 3:
    2 *Irigoyen* (ex-US *Cherokee*)
    1 *Teniente Olivieri* (ex-US oilfield tug)
  PCO 2:
    1 *Murature* (ex-US *King* – trg/river patrol role) with 3 105mm gun (in refit since 2016)
    1 *Sobral* (ex-US *Sotoyomo*)
  PCGT 1 *Intrepida* (GER Lurssen 45m) with 2 single lnchr with MM38 *Exocet* AShM, 2 single 533mm TT with SST-4 HWT, 1 76mm gun
  PCC 1 *Intrepida* (GER Lurssen 45m) with 1 76mm gun
  PB 6: 4 *Baradero* (*Dabur*); 2 *Punta Mogotes* (ex-US *Point*)
AMPHIBIOUS 6 LCVP
LOGISTICS AND SUPPORT 18
  ABU 3 *Red*
  AFS 4 *Puerto Argentina* (ex-RUS *Neftegaz*)

AGB 1 *Almirante Irizar* (damaged by fire in 2007; returned to service in mid-2017)
AGHS 3: 1 *Austral*; 1 *Cormoran*; 1 *Puerto Deseado* (ice-breaking capability, used for polar research)
AGOR 1 *Commodoro Rivadavia*
AK 3 *Costa Sur* (capacity 4 LCVP)
AOR 1 *Patagonia* (FRA *Durance*) with 1 hel platform
AORL 1 *Ingeniero Julio Krause*
AXS 1 *Libertad*

Naval Aviation 2,000
EQUIPMENT BY TYPE
AIRCRAFT 20 combat capable
  FGA 2 *Super Etendard* (9 more in store)
  ATK 1 AU-23 *Turbo Porter*
  ASW 7: 3 S-2T *Tracker*†; 4 P-3B *Orion*
  TPT • **Light** 7 Beech 200F/M *King Air*
  TRG 10 T-34C *Turbo Mentor**
HELICOPTERS
  ASW 2 SH-3H (ASH-3H) *Sea King*
  MRH 4 AS555 *Fennec*
  TPT • **Medium** 4 UH-3H *Sea King*
AIR-LAUNCHED MISSILES
  AAM • **IR** R-550 *Magic*
  AShM AM39 *Exocet*

Marines 2,500
FORCES BY ROLE
MANOEUVRE
  Amphibious
  1 (fleet) force (1 cdo gp, 1 (AAV) amph bn, 1 mne bn, 1 arty bn, 1 ADA bn)
  1 (fleet) force (2 mne bn, 2 navy det)
  1 force (1 mne bn)
EQUIPMENT BY TYPE
ARMOURED FIGHTING VEHICLES
  RECCE 12 ERC-90F *Sagaie*
  APC • **APC (W)** 31 VCR
  AAV 11 LVTP-7
ENGINEERING & MAINTENANCE VEHICLES
  ARV AAVR 7
ANTI-TANK/ANTI-INFRASTRUCTURE
  RCL 105mm 30 M-1974 FMK-1
ARTILLERY 89
  TOWED 19: **105mm** 13 Model 56 pack howitzer; **155mm** 6 M114
  MOR 70: **81mm** 58; **120mm** 12
AIR DEFENCE
  SAM • **Point-defence** RBS-70
  GUNS 40mm 4 Bofors 40L

Air Force 12,900
4 Major Comds – Air Operations, Personnel, Air Regions, Logistics, 8 air bde

Air Operations Command
FORCES BY ROLE
GROUND ATTACK
  2 sqn with A-4/OA-4 (A-4AR/OA-4AR) *Skyhawk*
  2 (tac air) sqn with IA-58 *Pucara*; EMB-312 *Tucano* (on loan for border surv/interdiction)
ISR
  1 sqn with Learjet 35A
SEARCH & RESCUE/TRANSPORT HELICOPTER
  2 sqn with Bell 212; Bell 212 (UH-1N); Mi-171, SA-315B *Lama*
TANKER/TRANSPORT
  1 sqn with C-130H *Hercules*; KC-130H *Hercules*; L-100-30
TRANSPORT
  1 sqn with B-707
  1 sqn with DHC-6 *Twin Otter*; Saab 340
  1 sqn with F-27 *Friendship*
  1 sqn with F-28 *Fellowship*; Learjet 60
  1 (Pres) flt with B-757-23ER; S-70A *Black Hawk*, S-76B
TRAINING
  1 sqn with AT-63 *Pampa*
  1 sqn with EMB-312 *Tucano*
  1 sqn with Grob 120TP
  1 hel sqn with Hughes 369; SA-315B *Lama*
TRANSPORT HELICOPTER
  1 sqn with Hughes 369; MD-500; MD500D
EQUIPMENT BY TYPE
AIRCRAFT 72 combat capable
  ATK 52: 20 A-4 (A-4AR) *Skyhawk*†; 2 OA-4 (OA-4AR) *Skyhawk*†; 21 IA-58 *Pucara*; 9 IA-58M *Pucara*
  ELINT 1 Cessna 210
  TKR 2 KC-130H *Hercules*
  TPT 27: **Medium** 4: 3 C-130H *Hercules*; 1 L-100-30; **Light** 16: 1 Cessna 310; 6 DHC-6 *Twin Otter*; 4 Learjet 35A (test and calibration); 1 Learjet 60 (VIP); 4 Saab 340; **PAX** 7: 1 B-737; 1 B-757-23ER; 5 F-28 *Fellowship*
  TRG 59: 20 AT-63 *Pampa** (LIFT); 19 EMB-312 *Tucano*; 8 Grob 120TP; 6 P2002JF *Sierra*; 6 T-6C *Texan* II
HELICOPTERS
  MRH 27: 4 Bell 412EP; 11 Hughes 369; 3 MD-500; 4 MD-500D; 5 SA315B *Lama*
  TPT 12: **Medium** 3: 2 Mi-171E; 1 S-70A *Black Hawk*; **Light** 9: 7 Bell 212; 2 S-76B (VIP)
AIR DEFENCE
  GUNS 88: **20mm**: 86 Oerlikon/Rh-202 with 9 Elta EL/M-2106 radar; **35mm**: 2 Oerlikon GDF-001 with *Skyguard* radar
AIR-LAUNCHED MISSILES
  AAM • **IR** AIM-9L *Sidewinder*; R-550 *Magic*; *Shafrir* 2‡

Paramilitary 31,250

Gendarmerie 18,000
Ministry of Security
FORCES BY ROLE
COMMAND
  7 regional comd
SPECIAL FORCES
  1 SF unit
MANOEUVRE
  Other
  17 paramilitary bn

Aviation
1 (mixed) avn bn
EQUIPMENT BY TYPE
ARMOURED FIGHTING VEHICLES
  RECCE S52 *Shorland*
  APC (W) 87: 47 *Grenadier*; 40 UR-416
ARTILLERY • MOR 81mm
AIRCRAFT
  TPT 13: **Light** 12: 3 Cessna 152; 3 Cessna 206; 1 Cessna 336; 1 PA-28 *Cherokee*; 2 PC-6B *Turbo Porter*; 2 PC-12; PAX 1 Learjet 35
HELICOPTERS
  MRH 2 MD-500C
  TPT • **Light** 17: 5 Bell 205 (UH-1H *Iroquois*); 7 AS350 *Ecureuil*; 1 H135; 1 H155; 3 R-44 *Raven* II
  TRG 1 S-300C

Prefectura Naval (Coast Guard) 13,250

Ministry of Security
EQUIPMENT BY TYPE
PATROL AND COASTAL COMBATANTS 69
  PCO 7: 1 *Correa Falcon*; 1 *Delfin*; 5 *Mantilla* (F30 *Halcón* – undergoing modernisation)
  PCC 1 *Mariano Moreno*
  PB 58: 1 *Dorado*; 25 *Estrellemar*; 2 *Lynch* (US *Cape*); 18 *Mar del Plata* (Z-28); 1 *Surel*; 8 Damen Stan 2200; 3 Stan Tender 1750
  PBF 2 *Shaldag* II
  PBR 1 *Tonina*
LOGISTICS & SUPPORT 11
  AAR 1 *Tango*
  AFS 1 *Prefecto Garcia*
  AG 2
  ARS 1 *Prefecto Mansilla*
  AX 5: 1 *Mandubi*; 4 other
  AXS 1 *Dr Bernardo Houssay*
AIRCRAFT
  MP 1 Beech 350ER *King Air*
  TPT • **Light** 6: 5 C-212 *Aviocar*; 1 Beech 350ER *King Air*
  TRG 2 Piper PA-28 *Archer* III
HELICOPTERS
  SAR 3 AS565MA *Panther*
  MRH 1 AS365 *Dauphin* 2
  TPT 5: **Medium** 3: 1 H225 *Puma*; 2 SA330L (AS330L) *Puma*; **Light** 2 AS355 *Ecureuil* II
  TRG 4 S-300C

DEPLOYMENT

CENTRAL AFRICAN REPUBLIC: UN • MINUSCA 2 obs
CYPRUS: UN • UNFICYP 244; 2 inf coy; 1 hel flt; 2 Bell 212
MIDDLE EAST: UN • UNTSO 3 obs
WESTERN SAHARA: UN • MINURSO 2 obs

Bahamas BHS

Bahamian Dollar B$		2017	2018	2019
GDP	B$	12.2bn	12.9bn	
	US$	12.2bn	12.9bn	
per capita	US$	32,661	34,333	
Growth	%	1.4	2.3	
Inflation	%	1.4	2.5	
Def bdgt	B$	98.7m	90.6m	92.3m
	US$	98.7m	90.6m	
US$1=B$		1.00	1.00	
Population	332,634			

Age	0–14	15–19	20–24	25–29	30–64	65 plus
Male	11.4%	3.9%	4.2%	4.2%	22.2%	3.1%
Female	11.0%	3.8%	4.1%	4.1%	23.0%	4.9%

Capabilities

The Royal Bahamas Defence Force (RBDF) is an entirely naval force primarily tasked with disaster relief, maritime security and countering narcotics trafficking. Its single commando squadron is tasked with base and internal security. The Bahamas is a member of the Caribbean Community, and the RBDF maintains training relationships with the UK and US. The RBDF participates in US SOUTHCOM's multinational annual *Tradewinds* disaster-response exercise. There is very little independent capacity to deploy abroad, aside from recent regional disaster-relief efforts. The second phase of the Sandy Bottom Project was completed in April 2017; the final phase will see further infrastructure improvements and an increase in RBDF personnel numbers. A new permanent naval base on Grand Bahama is under discussion to bolster the RBDF's counter-narcotics work. The maritime wing is focused around patrol vessels and smaller patrol boats, while the air wing has a small inventory of light aircraft. Apart from limited maintenance facilities, the Bahamas has no indigenous defence industry.

ACTIVE 1,300

ORGANISATIONS BY SERVICE

Royal Bahamian Defence Force 1,300

FORCES BY ROLE
MANOEUVRE
  Amphibious
  1 mne coy (incl marines with internal- and base-security duties)
EQUIPMENT BY TYPE
PATROL AND COASTAL COMBATANTS 21
  PCC 2 *Bahamas*
  PBF 6 Nor-Tech
  PB 13: 4 *Arthur Dion Hanna*; 2 *Dauntless*; 3 *Lignum Vitae* (Damen 3007); 2 Sea Ark 12m; 2 Sea Ark 15m
LOGISTICS & SUPPORT 1
  AKR 1 *Lawrence Major* (Damen 5612)
AIRCRAFT • TPT • Light 3: 1 Beech A350 *King Air*; 1 Cessna 208 *Caravan*; 1 P-68 *Observer*

FOREIGN FORCES

Guyana Navy: Base located at New Providence Island

Barbados BRB

Barbados Dollar B$		2017	2018	2019
GDP	B$	9.98bn	10.3bn	
	US$	4.99bn	5.17bn	
per capita	US$	17,758	18,366	
Growth	%	-0.2	-0.5	
Inflation	%	4.4	4.2	
Def bdgt [a]	B$	77.m	78.5m	
	US$	38.5m	39.3m	
US$1=B$		2.00	2.00	

[a] Defence & security expenditure

Population 293,131

Age	0–14	15–19	20–24	25–29	30–64	65 plus
Male	8.9%	3.1%	3.1%	3.6%	24.6%	5.0%
Female	8.9%	3.1%	3.2%	3.6%	25.5%	7.3%

Capabilities

Maritime security and resource protection are the main tasks of the Barbados Defence Force (BDF), but it has a secondary public-safety role in support of the police force. The BDF has been active in counter-narcotics work in recent years, and troops have also been tasked with supporting law-enforcement patrols. The BDF has been taking steps to improve its disaster-relief capacity and is developing a company-size mobile field hospital. The Caribbean Regional Security System is headquartered in Barbados, and it is also a member of the Caribbean Community. The BDF participates in US SOUTHCOM's multinational annual *Tradewinds* disaster-response exercise. There is limited capacity to independently deploy within the region, most recently on hurricane-relief duties. The inventory consists principally of a small number of patrol vessels. Apart from limited maintenance facilities, Barbados has no indigenous defence industry.

ACTIVE 610 (Army 500 Coast Guard 110)
RESERVE 430 (Joint 430)

ORGANISATIONS BY SERVICE

Army 500
FORCES BY ROLE
MANOEUVRE
  Light
    1 inf bn (cadre)

Coast Guard 110
HQ located at HMBS Pelican, Spring Garden
EQUIPMENT BY TYPE
PATROL AND COASTAL COMBATANTS • PB 6:
1 *Dauntless*; 2 *Enterprise* (Damen Stan 1204); 3 *Trident* (Damen Stan Patrol 4207)

Belize BLZ

Belize Dollar BZ$		2017	2018	2019
GDP	BZ$	3.71bn	3.82bn	
	US$	1.85bn	1.91bn	
per capita	US$	4,806	4,830	
Growth	%	0.8	1.8	
Inflation	%	1.1	1.3	
Def bdgt [a]	BZ$	47.6m	45.7m	
	US$	23.8m	22.8m	
FMA (US)	US$	1m	0m	0m
US$1=BZ$		2.00	2.00	

[a] Excludes funds allocated to Coast Guard and Police Service

Population 385,854

Age	0–14	15–19	20–24	25–29	30–64	65 plus
Male	17.2%	5.4%	4.3%	4.4%	16.7%	2.1%
Female	16.4%	5.0%	4.1%	4.5%	17.7%	2.2%

Capabilities

Belize maintains a small Defence Force (BDF) and coastguard to provide national security, particularly control of the borders with Guatemala and Mexico. A new National Security and Defence Strategy (2017–20) identifies territorial defence and combating transnational crime as key objectives. An unresolved territorial dispute with Guatemala over Belize's southern border remains a source of concern. The UK has a long-standing security relationship with Belize and maintains a small training unit there, and the BDF also trains with US SOUTHCOM. Overall training levels are limited but generally sufficient for the BDF's tasks. Belize is a member of the Caribbean Community. The BDF does not deploy internationally and logistics support is adequate for border-security missions. The conventional equipment inventory is limited and there is no domestic defence industry other than limited maintenance facilities.

ACTIVE 1,500 (Army 1,500) Paramilitary 150
RESERVE 700 (Joint 700)

ORGANISATIONS BY SERVICE

Army ε1,500
FORCES BY ROLE
MANOEUVRE
  Light
    2 inf bn (3 inf coy)
COMBAT SERVICE SUPPORT
  1 spt gp
EQUIPMENT BY TYPE
ANTI-TANK/ANTI-INFRASTRUCTURE • RCL 84mm *Carl Gustav*
ARTILLERY • MOR 81mm 6

Air Wing
EQUIPMENT BY TYPE
AIRCRAFT
  TPT • Light 3: 1 BN-2A *Defender*; 1 BN-2B *Defender*; 1 Cessna 182 *Skylane*

TRG 1 T-67M-200 *Firefly*
HELICOPTERS
TPT • **Light** 3: 2 Bell 205 (UH-1H *Iroquois*); 1 Bell 407

Reserve
FORCES BY ROLE
MANOEUVRE
  Light
  1 inf bn (3 inf coy)

Paramilitary 150

Coast Guard 150
EQUIPMENT BY TYPE
All operational patrol vessels under 10t FLD

FOREIGN FORCES
United Kingdom BATSUB 12

Bolivia BOL

Bolivian Boliviano B		2017	2018	2019
GDP	B	259bn	287bn	
	US$	37.8bn	41.8bn	
per capita	US$	3,413	3,719	
Growth	%	4.2	4.3	
Inflation	%	2.8	3.2	
Def bdgt	B	3.73bn	3.45bn	
	US$	543m	503m	
US$1=B		6.86	6.86	
Population	11,306,341			

Age	0–14	15–19	20–24	25–29	30–64	65 plus
Male	16.0%	5.1%	4.7%	4.4%	16.9%	2.4%
Female	15.4%	5.0%	4.6%	4.4%	18.2%	3.0%

Capabilities

The armed forces are constitutionally tasked with maintaining sovereignty and territorial defence, but counter-narcotics and internal and border security are in practical terms the main tasks of the armed forces. Joint task forces have been formed and dispatched to border regions to combat smuggling activities, and a series of border posts are being established. Modest procurement programmes are intended to improve the services' ability to undertake these roles. Airspace control is an emerging strategic priority, and construction continues on 13 civilian and military radars to help address this requirement. There is defence-technology cooperation with Russia, but China remains a significant supplier of military materiel, and delivered logistics vehicles in late 2018. An agreement was signed in September 2018 on joint operations with Peru on countering illicit trafficking and disaster relief. Amid greater internal deployments to border areas on counter-trafficking tasks, the armed forces have stressed the need to improve conditions for personnel. An Aerospace Research and Development Centre was created in 2018 in the military engineering school with the objective of developing munitions and ISR UAVs. There is some local maintenance, repair and overhaul capacity for the services.

ACTIVE 34,100 (Army 22,800 Navy 4,800 Air 6,500)
Paramilitary 37,100

Conscript liability 12 months voluntary conscription for both males and females

ORGANISATIONS BY SERVICE

Army 9,800; 13,000 conscript (total 22,800)
FORCES BY ROLE
COMMAND
  6 mil region HQ
  10 div HQ
SPECIAL FORCES
  3 SF regt
MANOEUVRE
  Reconnaissance
  1 mot cav gp
  Armoured
  1 armd bn
  Mechanised
  1 mech cav regt
  2 mech inf regt
  Light
  1 (aslt) cav gp
  5 (horsed) cav gp
  3 mot inf regt
  21 inf regt
  Air Manoeuvre
  2 AB regt (bn)
  Other
  1 (Presidential Guard) inf regt
COMBAT SUPPORT
  6 arty regt (bn)
  6 engr bn
  1 int coy
  1 MP bn
  1 sigs bn
COMBAT SERVICE SUPPORT
  2 log bn
AVIATION
  2 avn coy
AIR DEFENCE
  1 ADA regt
EQUIPMENT BY TYPE
ARMOURED FIGHTING VEHICLES
  LT TK 54: 36 SK-105A1 *Kuerassier*; 18 SK-105A2 *Kuerassier*
  RECCE 24 EE-9 *Cascavel*
  APC 148+
    APC (T) 87+: 50+ M113, 37 M9 half-track
    APC (W) 61: 24 EE-11 *Urutu*; 22 MOWAG *Roland*; 15 V-100 *Commando*
  AUV 19 *Tiger* 4×4
ENGINEERING & MAINTENANCE VEHICLES
  ARV 4 *Greif*; M578 LARV
ANTI-TANK/ANTI-INFRASTRUCTURE
  MSL
    SP 2 *Koyak* with HJ-8
    MANPATS HJ-8
  RCL 90mm M67; 106mm M40A1

ARTILLERY 311+
  TOWED 61: **105mm** 25 M101A1; **122mm** 36 M-30 (M-1938)
  MOR 250+: **81mm** 250 M29; Type-W87; **107mm** M30;
  120mm M120
AIRCRAFT
  TPT • **Light** 4: 1 Fokker F-27-200; 1 Beech 90 *King Air*; 1
  C-212 *Aviocar*; 1 Cessna 210 *Centurion*
HELICOPTERS
  MRH 6 H425
  TRG 1 Robinson R55
AIR DEFENCE • GUNS • TOWED **37mm** 18 Type-65

Navy 4,800

Organised into six naval districts with HQ located at Puerto Guayaramerín

EQUIPMENT BY TYPE
PATROL AND COASTAL COMBATANTS • PBR 3: 1 *Santa Cruz*; 2 others
LOGISTICS AND SUPPORT 3
  AG 1
  AH 2

Marines 1,700 (incl 1,000 Naval Military Police)

FORCES BY ROLE
MANOEUVRE
  Mechanised
  1 mech inf bn
  Amphibious
  6 mne bn (1 in each Naval District)
COMBAT SUPPORT
  4 (naval) MP bn

Air Force 6,500 (incl conscripts)

FORCES BY ROLE
GROUND ATTACK
  1 sqn with K-8WB *Karakorum*
ISR
  1 sqn with Cessna 206; Cessna 402; Learjet 25B/25D (secondary VIP role)
SEARCH & RESCUE
  1 sqn with AS332B *Super Puma*; H125 *Ecureuil*; H145
TRANSPORT
  1 (TAM) sqn with B-727; B-737; BAe-146-100; MA60
  1 (TAB) sqn with C-130A *Hercules*; MD-10-30F
  1 sqn with C-130B/H *Hercules*
  1 sqn with F-27-400M *Troopship*
  1 (VIP) sqn with Beech 90 *King Air*; Beech 200 *King Air*; Beech 1900; *Falcon* 900EX; *Sabreliner* 60
  6 sqn with Cessna 152/206; IAI-201 *Arava*; PA-32 *Saratoga*; PA-34 *Seneca*
TRAINING
  1 sqn with DA40; T-25
  1 sqn with Cessna 152/172
  1 sqn with PC-7 *Turbo Trainer*
  1 hel sqn with R-44 *Raven* II
TRANSPORT HELICOPTER
  1 (anti-drug) sqn with Bell 205 (UH-1H *Iroquois*)
AIR DEFENCE
  1 regt with Oerlikon; Type-65

EQUIPMENT BY TYPE
AIRCRAFT 22 combat capable
  TPT 88: **Heavy** 1 MD-10-30F; **Medium** 4: 1 C-130A *Hercules*; 2 C-130B *Hercules*; 1 C-130H *Hercules*; **Light** 72: 1 *Aero Commander* 690; 3 Beech 90 *King Air*; 1 Beech 55 *Baron*; 2 Beech 200 *King Air*; 1 Beech 1900; 3 C-212-100; 10 Cessna 152; 2 Cessna 172; 19 Cessna 206; 3 Cessna 210 *Centurion*; 1 Cessna 402; 9 DA40; 3 F-27-400M *Troopship*; 4 IAI-201 *Arava*; 2 Learjet 25B/D; 2 MA60†; 1 PA-32 *Saratoga*; 4 PA-34 *Seneca*; 1 *Sabreliner* 60; **PAX** 11: 1 B-727; 5 B-737-200; 1 B-737-300; 1 BAe-146-100; 2 BAe-146-200; 1 *Falcon* 900EX (VIP)
  TRG 30: 6 K-8WB *Karakorum**; 6 T-25; 16 PC-7 *Turbo Trainer**; 2 Z-242L
HELICOPTERS
  MRH 1 SA316 *Alouette* III
  TPT 35: **Medium** 6 H215 *Super Puma*; **Light** 29: 2 H125 *Ecureuil*; 19 Bell 205 (UH-1H *Iroquois*); 2 H145; 6 R-44 *Raven* II
AIR DEFENCE • GUNS 18+: **20mm** Oerlikon; **37mm** 18 Type-65

Paramilitary 37,100+

National Police 31,100+
FORCES BY ROLE
MANOEUVRE
  Other
  27 frontier sy unit
  9 paramilitary bde
  2 (rapid action) paramilitary regt

Narcotics Police 6,000+
FOE (700) – Special Operations Forces

DEPLOYMENT

CENTRAL AFRICAN REPUBLIC: UN • MINUSCA 1; 2 obs
DEMOCRATIC REPUBLIC OF THE CONGO: UN • MONUSCO 3 obs
SOUTH SUDAN: UN • UNMISS 3 obs
SUDAN: UN • UNISFA 1; 3 obs

Brazil BRZ

Brazilian Real R		2017	2018	2019
GDP	R	6.56tr	6.88tr	
	US$	2.06tr	1.91tr	
per capita	US$	9,896	9,127	
Growth	%	1.0	1.4	
Inflation	%	3.4	3.7	
Def bdgt [a]	R	93.3bn	101bn	107bn
	US$	29.2bn	28.0bn	
US$1=R		3.19	3.60	

[a] Includes military pensions

Population	208,846,892					
Age	0–14	15–19	20–24	25–29	30–64	65 plus
Male	11.2%	4.2%	4.1%	4.0%	22.2%	3.7%
Female	10.7%	4.1%	4.0%	3.9%	23.1%	4.9%

Capabilities

The armed forces are among the most capable in the region. Brazil seeks to enhance its power-projection capabilities, boost surveillance of the Amazon region and coastal waters, and further develop its defence industry, though economic difficulties continue to affect its ability to develop these ambitions. However, security challenges from organised crime have seen the armed forces deploy on internal-security operations. Brazil maintains military ties with most of its neighbours including personnel-exchange programmes and joint military training with Chile and Colombia. There is also defence cooperation with France, Sweden and the US, centred on procurement, technical advice and personnel training. Brazil's air-transport fleet enables it to independently deploy forces. It contributes small contingents to several UN missions across Europe, the Middle East and sub-Saharan Africa. Despite substantial budgetary constraints, Brazil is attempting to modernise its equipment across all domains. Major platform programmes include PROSUB (one nuclear-powered and four diesel-electric submarines) and the recent acquisition of a former UK helicopter carrier. Brazil has a well-developed defence-industrial base, across all domains, with a capability to design and manufacture equipment for its armed forces. The aerospace sector is particularly strong, with some private companies such as Avibras and Embraer exporting to international customers. Local companies are also involved in the border-security programme SISFRON. There are industrial partnerships, including technology transfers and R&D support, with France's Naval Group (PROSUB) and Sweden's Saab (FX-2 fighter).

ACTIVE 334,500 (Army 198,000 Navy 69,000 Air 67,500) **Paramilitary 395,000**

Conscript liability 12 months (can go to 18; often waived)

RESERVE 1,340,000

ORGANISATIONS BY SERVICE

Space
EQUIPMENT BY TYPE
SATELLITES • COMMUNICATIONS 1 SGDC-1 (civil–military use)

Army 128,000; 70,000 conscript (total 198,000)
FORCES BY ROLE
COMMAND
 8 mil comd HQ
 12 mil region HQ
 7 div HQ (2 with regional HQ)
SPECIAL FORCES
 1 SF bde (1 SF bn, 1 cdo bn)
 1 SF coy
MANOEUVRE
 Reconnaissance
 3 mech cav regt
 Armoured
 1 (5th) armd bde (1 mech cav sqn, 2 tk regt, 2 armd inf bn, 1 SP arty bn, 1 engr bn, 1 sigs coy, 1 log bn)
 1 (6th) armd bde (1 mech cav sqn, 2 tk regt, 2 armd inf bn, 1 SP arty bn, 1 AD bty, 1 engr bn, 1 sigs coy, 1 log bn)
 Mechanised
 3 (1st, 2nd & 4th) mech cav bde (1 armd cav bn, 3 mech cav bn, 1 arty bn, 1 engr coy, 1 sigs coy, 1 log bn)
 1 (3rd) mech cav bde (1 armd cav bn, 2 mech cav bn, 1 arty bn, 1 engr coy, 1 sigs coy, 1 log bn)
 1 (15th) mech inf bde (3 mech inf bn, 1 arty bn, 1 engr coy, 1 log bn)
 Light
 1 (3rd) mot inf bde (1 mech cav sqn, 1 mech inf bn, 1 mot inf bn, 1 inf bn, 1 arty bn, 1 engr coy, 1 sigs coy, 1 log bn)
 1 (4th) mot inf bde (1 mech cav sqn, 1 mot inf bn, 1 inf bn, 1 mtn inf bn, 1 arty bn, 1 sigs coy, 1 log bn)
 1 (7th) mot inf bde (3 mot inf bn, 1 arty bn)
 1 (8th) mot inf bde (1 mech cav sqn, 3 mot inf bn, 1 arty bn, 1 log bn)
 1 (10th) mot inf bde (1 mech cav sqn, 4 mot inf bn, 1 inf coy, 1 arty bn, 1 engr coy, 1 sigs coy)
 1 (13th) mot inf bde (1 mot inf bn, 2 inf bn, 1 inf coy, 1 arty bn)
 1 (14th) mot inf bde (1 mech cav sqn, 3 inf bn, 1 arty bn)
 1 (11th) lt inf bde (1 mech cav regt, 3 inf bn, 1 arty bn, 1 engr coy, 1 sigs coy, 1 MP coy, 1 log bn)
 10 inf bn
 1 (1st) jungle inf bde (1 mech cav sqn, 2 jungle inf bn, 1 arty bn)
 4 (2nd, 16th, 17th & 22nd) jungle inf bde (3 jungle inf bn)
 1 (23rd) jungle inf bde (1 cav sqn, 4 jungle inf bn, 1 arty bn, 1 sigs coy, 1 log bn)
 Air Manoeuvre
 1 AB bde (1 cav sqn, 3 AB bn, 1 arty bn, 1 engr coy, 1 sigs coy, 1 log bn)
 1 (12th) air mob bde (1 cav sqn, 3 air mob bn, 1 arty bn, 1 engr coy, 1 sigs coy, 1 log bn)
 Other
 1 (9th) mot trg bde (3 mot inf bn, 1 arty bn, 1 log bn)
 1 (18th) sy bde (2 sy bn, 2 sy coy)
 1 sy bn
 7 sy coy
 3 gd cav regt
 1 gd inf bn

COMBAT SUPPORT
3 SP arty bn
6 fd arty bn
1 MRL bn
1 STA bty
6 engr bn
1 engr gp (1 engr bn, 4 construction bn)
1 engr gp (4 construction bn, 1 construction coy)
2 construction bn
1 EW coy
1 int coy
6 MP bn
3 MP coy
4 sigs bn
2 sigs coy
COMBAT SERVICE SUPPORT
5 log bn
1 tpt bn
4 spt bn
HELICOPTER
1 avn bde (3 hel bn, 1 maint bn)
1 hel bn
AIR DEFENCE
1 ADA bde (5 ADA bn)
EQUIPMENT BY TYPE
ARMOURED FIGHTING VEHICLES
MBT 393: 128 *Leopard* 1A1BE; 220 *Leopard* 1A5BR; 45 M60A3/TTS
LT TK 50 M41C
RECCE 408 EE-9 *Cascavel*
IFV 6 VBTP-MR *Guarani* 30mm
APC 1,153
 APC (T) 630: 584 M113; 12 M113A2; 34 M577A2
 APC (W) 523: 223 EE-11 *Urutu*; 300 VBTP-MR *Guarani* 6×6
ENGINEERING & MAINTENANCE VEHICLES
AEV 6+: *Greif*; 2 Sabiex HART; 4+ Pioneerpanzer 2 *Dachs*
ARV 4+: BPz-2; 4 M88A1; M578 LARV
VLB 4+: XLP-10; 4 *Leopard* 1 with *Biber*
ANTI-TANK/ANTI-INFRASTRUCTURE
MSL • MANPATS *Eryx*; *Milan*; MSS-1.2 AC
RCL 194+: **84mm** *Carl Gustav*; **106mm** 194 M40A1
ARTILLERY 1,865
SP 153: **105mm** 72 M7/108; **155mm** 81: 37 M109A3; 44 M109A5/A5+
TOWED 431
 105mm 336: 233 M101/M102; 40 L118 Light Gun; 63 Model 56 pack howitzer
 155mm 95 M114
MRL 127mm 36: 18 ASTROS II Mk3M; 18 ASTROS II Mk6
MOR 1,245: **81mm** 1,168: 453 L16, 715 M936 AGR; **120mm** 77 M2
HELICOPTERS
MRH 51: 29 AS565 *Panther* (HM-1); 5 AS565 K2 *Panther* (HM-1); 17 AS550U2 *Fennec* (HA-1 – armed)
TPT 38: **Heavy** 11 H225M *Caracal* (HM-4); **Medium** 12: 8 AS532 *Cougar* (HM-3); 4 S-70A-36 *Black Hawk* (HM-2); **Light** 15 AS350L1 *Ecureuil* (HA-1)

AIR DEFENCE
SAM • Point-defence RBS-70; 9K38 *Igla* (SA-18 *Grouse*); 9K338 *Igla*-S (SA-24 *Grinch*)
GUNS 100:
 SP 35mm 34 *Gepard* 1A2
 TOWED 66: **35mm** 39 GDF-001 towed (some with *Super Fledermaus* radar); **40mm** 27 L/70 (some with BOFI)

Navy 69,000

Organised into 9 districts with HQ I Rio de Janeiro, HQ II Salvador, HQ III Natal, HQ IV Belém, HQ V Rio Grande, HQ VI Ladario, HQ VII Brasilia, HQ VIII Sao Paulo, HQ IX Manaus

FORCES BY ROLE
SPECIAL FORCES
1 (diver) SF gp
EQUIPMENT BY TYPE
SUBMARINES • TACTICAL • SSK 5:
 2 *Tupi* (GER T-209/1400) with 8 single 533mm TT with Mk24 HWT (of which 1 in refit until 2019)
 2 *Tupi* (GER T-209/1400) with 8 single 533mm TT with Mk48 HWT
 1 *Tikuna* (GER T-209/1450) with 8 single 533mm TT with Mk24 HWT (in refit until 2019)
PRINCIPAL SURFACE COMBATANTS 11
DESTROYERS • DDGHM 2:
 1 *Greenhalgh* (ex-UK *Broadsword*) with 4 single lnchr with MM38 *Exocet* AShM, 2 sextuple lnchr with *Sea Wolf* SAM, 6 single STWS Mk2 324mm ASTT with Mk 46 LWT (capacity 2 *Super Lynx* Mk21A hel)
 1 *Greenhalgh* (ex-UK *Broadsword*) with 4 single lnchr with MM40 *Exocet* Block 2 AShM, 2 sextuple lnchr with *Sea Wolf* SAM, 6 single STWS Mk2 324mm ASTT with Mk 46 LWT (capacity 2 *Super Lynx* Mk21A hel)
FRIGATES 9
 FFGHM 6 *Niterói* with 2 twin lnchr with MM40 *Exocet* Block 2 AShM, 1 octuple *Albatros* lnchr with *Aspide* SAM, 2 triple Mk32 324mm ASTT with Mk 46 LWT, 1 twin 375mm A/S mor, 2 *Sea Trinity* Mk3 CIWS, 1 115mm gun (capacity 1 *Super Lynx* Mk21A hel)
 FFGH 3:
 2 *Inhaúma* with 2 twin lnchr with MM40 *Exocet* Block 2 AShM, 2 triple Mk32 324mm ASTT with Mk 46 LWT, 1 115mm gun (1 *Super Lynx* Mk21A hel)
 1 *Barroso* with 2 twin lnchr with MM40 *Exocet* Block 2 AShM, 2 triple Mk32 324mm ASTT with Mk 46 LWT, 1 *Sea Trinity* Mk3 CIWS, 1 115mm gun (capacity 1 *Super Lynx* Mk21A hel)
PATROL AND COASTAL COMBATANTS 44
 PSO 3 *Amazonas* with 1 hel landing platform
 PCO 6: 4 *Bracui* (ex-UK *River*); 1 *Imperial Marinheiro* with 1 76mm gun; 1 *Parnaiba* with 1 hel landing platform
 PCC 2 *Macaé*
 PCR 5: 2 *Pedro Teixeira* with 1 hel landing platform; 3 *Roraima*
 PB 24: 12 *Grajau*; 6 *Marlim*; 6 *Piratini* (US PGM)
 PBR 4 LPR-40
MINE WARFARE • MINE COUNTERMEASURES •
MSC 4 *Aratu* (GER *Schutze*)

AMPHIBIOUS
PRINCIPAL AMPHIBIOUS SHIPS 2
- **LPD** 1 *Bahia* (ex-FRA *Foudre*) (capacity 4 hels; 8 LCM, 450 troops)
- **LPH** 1 *Atlantico* (ex-UK *Ocean*) (capacity 18 hels; 4 LCVP; 40 vehs; 800 troops)

LANDING SHIPS 3
- **LST** 1 *Mattoso Maia* (ex-US *Newport*) with 1 *Phalanx* CIWS (capacity 3 LCVP; 1 LCPL; 400 troops)
- **LSLH** 2: 1 *Garcia D'Avila* (ex-UK *Sir Galahad*) (capacity 1 hel; 16 MBT; 340 troops); 1 *Almirante Saboia* (ex-UK *Sir Bedivere*) (capacity 1 med hel; 18 MBT; 340 troops)

LANDING CRAFT 16:
- **LCM** 12: 10 EDVM-25; 2 *Icarai* (ex-FRA CTM)
- **LCT** 1 *Marambaia* (ex-FRA CDIC)
- **LCU** 3 *Guarapari* (LCU 1610)

LOGISTICS AND SUPPORT 44
- **ABU** 5: 4 *Comandante Varella*; 1 *Faroleiro Mario Seixas*
- **ABUH** 1 *Almirante Graca Aranah* (lighthouse tender)
- **AFS** 1 *Potengi*
- **AGHS** 5: 1 *Caravelas* (riverine); 4 *Rio Tocantin*
- **AGOS** 2: 1 *Ary Rongel* with 1 hel landing platform; 1 *Almirante Maximiano* (capacity 2 AS350/AS355 *Ecureuil* hel)
- **AGS** 8: 1 *Aspirante Moura*; 1 *Cruzeiro do Sul*; 1 *Antares*; 3 *Amorim do Valle* (ex-UK *Rover*); 1 *Rio Branco*; 1 *Vital de Oliveira*
- **AGSH** 1 *Sirius*
- **AH** 5: 2 *Oswaldo Cruz* with 1 hel landing platform; 1 *Dr Montenegro*; 1 *Tenente Maximianol* with 1 hel landing platform; 1 *Soares de Meirelles*
- **AOR** 2: 1 *Almirante Gastão Motta*; 1 *Marajó*
- **AP** 3: 1 *Almirante Leverger*; 1 *Paraguassu*; 1 *Pará* (all river transports)
- **ASR** 1 *Felinto Perry* (NOR *Wildrake*) with 1 hel landing platform
- **ATF** 5: 3 *Triunfo*; 2 *Almirante Guihem*
- **AX** 1 *Brasil* (*Niterói* mod) with 1 hel landing platform
- **AXL** 3 *Nascimento*
- **AXS** 1 *Cisne Barco*

Naval Aviation 2,100

FORCES BY ROLE
GROUND ATTACK
- 1 sqn with A-4/4M (AF-1) *Skyhawk*; TA-4/4M (AF-1A/1C) *Skyhawk*

ANTI SURFACE WARFARE
- 1 sqn with *Super Lynx* Mk21A

ANTI SUBMARINE WARFARE
- 1 sqn with S-70B *Seahawk* (MH-16)

TRAINING
- 1 sqn with Bell 206B3 *Jet Ranger* III

TRANSPORT HELICOPTER
- 1 sqn with AS332 *Super Puma*; AS532 *Cougar*
- 1 sqn with AS350 *Ecureuil* (armed); AS355 *Ecureuil* II (armed); H225M *Caracal* (UH-15A)
- 3 sqn with AS350 *Ecureuil* (armed); AS355 *Ecureuil* II (armed)

EQUIPMENT BY TYPE
AIRCRAFT 11 combat capable
- **ATK** 11: 6 A-4 (AF-1) *Skyhawk*; 2 A-4M (AF-1B) *Skyhawk*; 2 TA-4 (AF-1A) *Skyhawk*; 1 TA-4M (AF-1C) *Skyhawk*

HELICOPTERS
- **ASW** 18: 11 *Super Lynx* Mk21A; 1 *Super Lynx* Mk21B; 6 S-70B *Seahawk* (MH-16)
- **CSAR** 2 H225M *Caracal* (UH-15A)
- **TPT** 53: **Heavy** 8 H225M *Caracal* (UH-15); **Medium** 7: 5 AS332 *Super Puma*; 2 AS532 *Cougar* (UH-14); **Light** 38: 15 AS350 *Ecureuil* (armed); 8 AS355 *Ecureuil* II (armed); 15 Bell 206B3 *Jet Ranger* III (IH-6B)

AIR-LAUNCHED MISSILES • AShM: AM39 *Exocet*; *Sea Skua*; AGM-119 *Penguin*

Marines 16,000

FORCES BY ROLE
SPECIAL FORCES
- 1 SF bn

MANOEUVRE
Amphibious
- 1 amph div (1 lt armd bn, 3 mne bn, 1 arty bn)
- 1 amph aslt bn
- 7 (regional) mne gp
- 1 rvn bn

COMBAT SUPPORT
- 1 engr bn

COMBAT SERVICE SUPPORT
- 1 log bn

EQUIPMENT BY TYPE
ARMOURED FIGHTING VEHICLES
- **LT TK** 18 SK-105 *Kuerassier*
- **APC** 60
  - **APC (T)** 30 M113A1 (incl variants)
  - **APC (W)** 30 *Piranha* IIIC
- **AAV** 47: 13 AAV-7A1; 20 AAVP-7A1 RAM/RS; 2 AAVC-7A1 RAM/RS (CP); 12 LVTP-7

ENGINEERING VEHICLES • ARV 2: 1 AAVR-7; 1 AAVR-7A1 RAM/RS

ANTI-TANK/ANTI-INFRASTRUCTURE
- **MSL • MANPATS** RB-56 *Bill*; MSS-1.2 AC

ARTILLERY 65
- **TOWED** 41: **105mm** 33: 18 L118 *Light Gun*; 15 M101; **155mm** 8 M114
- **MRL 127mm** 6 ASTROS II Mk6
- **MOR 81mm** 18 M29

AIR DEFENCE • GUNS 40mm 6 L/70 (with BOFI)

Air Force 67,500

Brazilian airspace is divided into 7 air regions, each of which is responsible for its designated air bases. Air assets are divided among 4 designated air forces (I, II, III & V) for operations (IV Air Force temporarily deactivated)

FORCES BY ROLE
FIGHTER
- 4 sqn with F-5EM/FM *Tiger* II

FIGHTER/GROUND ATTACK
- 2 sqn with AMX (A-1A/B)

GROUND ATTACK/ISR
  4 sqn with EMB-314 *Super Tucano* (A-29A/B)*
MARITIME PATROL
  1 sqn with P-3AM *Orion*
  2 sqn with EMB-111 (P-95A/B/M)
ISR
  1 sqn with AMX-R (RA-1)*
  1 sqn with Learjet 35 (R-35A); EMB-110B (R-95)
AIRBORNE EARLY WARNING & CONTROL
  1 sqn with EMB-145RS (R-99); EMB-145SA (E-99)
TANKER/TRANSPORT
  1 sqn with C-130H/KC-130H *Hercules*
TRANSPORT
  1 VIP sqn with A319 (VC-1A); EMB-190 (VC-2); AS355 *Ecureuil* II (VH-55); H135M (VH-35); H225M *Caracal* (VH-36)
  1 VIP sqn with EMB-135BJ (VC-99B); ERJ-135LR (VC-99C); ERJ-145LR (VC-99A); Learjet 35A (VU-35); Learjet 55C (VU-55C)
  2 sqn with C-130E/H *Hercules*
  2 sqn with C295M (C-105A)
  7 (regional) sqn with Cessna 208/208B (C-98); Cessna 208-G1000 (C-98A); EMB-110 (C-95); EMB-120 (C-97)
  1 sqn with ERJ-145 (C-99A)
  1 sqn with EMB-120RT (VC-97), EMB-121 (VU-9)
TRAINING
  1 sqn with EMB-110 (C-95)
  2 sqn with EMB-312 *Tucano* (T-27) (incl 1 air show sqn)
  1 sqn with T-25A/C
ATTACK HELICOPTER
  1 sqn with Mi-35M *Hind* (AH-2)
TRANSPORT HELICOPTER
  1 sqn with H225M *Caracal* (H-36)
  1 sqn with AS350B *Ecureuil* (H-50); AS355 *Ecureuil* II (H-55)
  1 sqn with Bell 205 (H-1H); H225M *Caracal* (H-36)
  2 sqn with UH-60L *Black Hawk* (H-60L)
ISR UAV
  1 sqn with *Hermes* 450/900
EQUIPMENT BY TYPE
AIRCRAFT 210 combat capable
  FTR 46: 43 F-5EM *Tiger* II; 3 F-5FM *Tiger* II
  FGA 49: 38 AMX (A-1); 11 AMX-T (A-1B)
  ASW 9 P-3AM *Orion*
  MP 19: 10 EMB-111 (P-95A *Bandeirulha*)*; 9 EMB-111 (P-95BM *Bandeirulha*)*
  ISR: 8: 4 AMX-R (RA-1)*; 4 EMB-110B (R-95)
  ELINT 6: 3 EMB-145RS (R-99); 3 Learjet 35A (R-35A)
  AEW&C 5 EMB-145SA (E-99)
  SAR 7: 1 C295M *Amazonas* (SC-105); 4 EMB-110 (SC-95B), 1 SC-130E *Hercules*
  TKR/TPT 2 KC-130H
  TPT 198: **Medium** 20: 4 C-130E *Hercules*; 16 C-130H *Hercules*; **Light** 170: 11 C295M (C-105A); 7 Cessna 208 (C-98); 9 Cessna 208B (C-98); 13 Cessna 208-G1000 (C-98A); 52 EMB-110 (C-95A/B/C/M); 16 EMB-120 (C-97); 4 EMB-120RT (VC-97); 5 EMB-121 (VU-9); 7 EMB-135BJ (VC-99B); 3 EMB-201R *Ipanema* (G-19); 2 EMB-202A *Ipanema* (G-19A); 2 ERJ-135LR (VC-99C); 7 ERJ-145 (C-99A); 1 ERJ-145LR (VC-99A); 9 Learjet 35A (VU-35); 1 Learjet 55C (VU-55); 9 PA-34 *Seneca* (U-7); 12 U-42 *Regente*; **PAX** 8: 1 A319 (VC-1A); 3 EMB-190 (VC-2); 4 Hawker 800XP (EU-93A – calibration)
  TRG 264: 100 EMB-312 *Tucano* (T-27); 39 EMB-314 *Super Tucano* (A-29A)*; 44 EMB-314 *Super Tucano* (A-29B)*; 81 T-25A/C
HELICOPTERS
  ATK 12 Mi-35M *Hind* (AH-2)
  MRH 2 H135M (VH-35)
  TPT 60: **Heavy** 14 H225M *Caracal* (12 H-36 & 2 VH-36); **Medium** 16 UH-60L *Black Hawk* (H-60L); **Light** 30: 24 AS350B *Ecureuil* (H-50); 4 AS355 *Ecureuil* II (H-55/VH-55); 2+ Bell 205 (H-1H)
UNMANNED AERIAL VEHICLES
  ISR • **Medium** 5: 4 *Hermes* 450; 1 *Hermes* 900
AIR-LAUNCHED MISSILES
  AAM • **IR** MAA-1 *Piranha*; R-550 *Magic* 2; *Python* 3; **IIR** *Python* 4; **SARH** Super 530F; **ARH** *Derby*
  AShM AM39 *Exocet*
  ARM MAR-1 (in development)

Paramilitary 395,000 opcon Army

Public Security Forces 395,000

State police organisation technically under army control. However, military control is reducing, with authority reverting to individual states

EQUIPMENT BY TYPE
UNMANNED AERIAL VEHICLES
  ISR • **Heavy** 3 *Heron* (deployed by Federal Police for Amazon and border patrols)

Cyber

Cyber was a key component of the 2008 National Defence Strategy and the July 2012 Defence White Paper. In 2011, the army inaugurated Brazil's cyber-defence centre (CDCiber) to coordinate existing army, navy and air-force activities. There is an active training programme, run by the Institute of Cyber Defence among others, and a Cyber Operations Simulator (SIMOC) was set up in 2013, within the Integrated Electronic Warfare Centre. In July 2015, the army activated two provisional cyber-defence units under CDCiber, a cyber-defence command and a national school of cyber defence. Brazil's cyber-defence command (ComDCiber), set up in 2016, plans, coordinates and controls operational, doctrinal, development and training activities relating to cyberspace. The 2018 *Cyber Guardian* exercise utilised the SIMOC and involved military and civil organisations.

DEPLOYMENT

CENTRAL AFRICAN REPUBLIC: UN • MINUSCA 4; 3 obs
CYPRUS: UN • UNFICYP 2
DEMOCRATIC REPUBLIC OF THE CONGO: UN • MONUSCO 7; 1 obs
LEBANON: UN • UNIFIL 222; 1 FFGHM
SOUTH SUDAN: UN • UNMISS 6; 5 obs
SUDAN: UN • UNAMID 1 obs; **UN** • UNISFA 3 obs
WESTERN SAHARA: UN • MINURSO 10 obs

Chile CHL

Chilean Peso pCh		2017	2018	2019
GDP	pCh	180tr	189tr	
	US$	277bn	300bn	
per capita	US$	15,068	16,143	
Growth	%	1.5	4.0	
Inflation	%	2.2	2.4	
Def bdgt [a]	pCh	2.60tr	2.68tr	
	US$	4.01bn	4.25bn	
US$1=pCh		648.85	631.07	

[a] Includes military pensions

Population	17,925,262				
Age	0–14	15–19	20–24	25–29	30–64	65 plus
Male	10.2%	3.5%	3.9%	4.2%	22.7%	4.7%
Female	9.8%	3.4%	3.8%	4.0%	23.4%	6.5%

Capabilities

Chile's 2017 defence white paper noted core roles of assuring sovereignty and territorial integrity, but also indicated an increasing shift towards non-traditional military roles such as disaster relief, humanitarian assistance and peacekeeping. Chile maintains military ties with most of it neighbours. Personnel-exchange programmes and R&D cooperation are under way with Brazil and Colombia. Defence cooperation with the US is centred on procurement, technical advisory and personnel training. Training takes place regularly on a national basis, and the armed forces routinely participate in international exercises. Chile has a limited capacity to deploy independently beyond its borders. Serviceability challenges may arise for some equipment in the absence of upgrades. One such case is Chile's F-16s, several of which are reaching the end of their operational life, though an upgrade plan was announced in late 2018. However, because of the reduced risk of conventional conflict and border crises, priorities have changed to reflect a new focus on littoral and blue-water surveillance capabilities and helicopters. Chile has a developed defence-industrial base, with ENAER conducting aircraft maintenance. ASMAR and FAMAE are key maritime and land firms respectively, with the former set to construct a new icebreaker that will enhance Chile's ability to support operations in Antarctica.

ACTIVE 77,200 (Army 46,350 Navy 19,800 Air 11,050) **Paramilitary 44,700**

Conscript liability Army 12 months; Navy 18 months; Air Force 12 months. Legally, conscription can last for 2 years

RESERVE 40,000 (Army 40,000)

ORGANISATIONS BY SERVICE

Space
EQUIPMENT BY TYPE
SATELLITES
ISR 1 SSOT (Sistema Satelital de Observación de la Tierra)

Army 46,350
6 military administrative regions

FORCES BY ROLE
Currently being reorganised into 1 SF bde, 4 armd bde, 1 armd det, 3 mot bde, 2 mot det, 4 mtn det and 1 avn bde
COMMAND
  6 div HQ
SPECIAL FORCES
  1 SF bde (1 SF bn, 1 (mtn) SF gp, 1 para bn, 3 cdo coy, 1 log coy)
MANOEUVRE
  Reconnaissance
  4 cav sqn
  2 recce sqn
  2 recce pl
  Armoured
  3 (1st, 2nd & 3rd) armd bde (1 armd recce pl, 1 armd cav gp, 1 mech inf bn, 1 arty gp, 1 AT coy, 1 engr coy, 1 sigs coy)
  1 (4th) armd bde (1 armd recce pl, 1 armd cav gp, 1 mech inf bn, 1 arty gp, 1 engr coy)
  1 (5th) armd det (1 armd cav gp, 1 mech inf coy, 1 arty gp)
  Mechanised
  1 (1st) mech inf regt
  Light
  1 (1st) mot inf bde (1 recce coy, 1 mot inf bn, 1 arty gp, 3 AT coy, 1 engr bn)
  1 (4th) mot inf bde (1 mot inf bn, 1 MRL gp, 2 AT coy, 1 engr bn)
  1 (24th) mot inf bde (1 mot inf bn, 1 arty gp, 1 AT coy)
  1 (6th) reinforced regt (1 mot inf bn, 1 arty gp, 1 sigs coy)
  1 (10th) reinforced regt (1 mot inf bn, 2 AT coy, 1 engr bn)
  1 (11th) mot inf det (1 inf bn, 1 arty gp)
  1 (14th) mot inf det (1 mot inf bn, 1 arty gp, 1 sigs coy, 1 AT coy)
  7 mot inf regt
  1 (3rd) mtn det (1 mtn inf bn, 1 arty gp, 1 engr coy)
  1 (9th) mtn det (1 mtn inf bn, 1 engr coy, 1 construction bn)
  2 (8th & 17th) mtn det (1 mtn inf bn, 1 arty coy)
COMBAT SUPPORT
  1 arty regt
  1 engr regt
  4 sigs bn
  1 sigs coy
  2 int regt
  1 MP regt
COMBAT SERVICE SUPPORT
  1 log div (2 log regt)
  4 log regt
  6 log coy
  1 maint div (1 maint regt)
AVIATION
  1 avn bde (1 tpt avn bn, 1 hel bn, 1 spt bn)
EQUIPMENT BY TYPE
ARMOURED FIGHTING VEHICLES
  MBT 246: 115 Leopard 1; 131 Leopard 2A4
  IFV 191: 173 Marder 1A3; 18 YPR-765 PRI
  APC 548
    APC (T) 369 M113A1/A2
    APC (W) 179 Piranha

ENGINEERING & MAINTENANCE VEHICLES
AEV 9 Pioneerpanzer 2 *Dachs*
ARV 35 BPz-2
VLB 16 *Biber*
MW 3+: Bozena 5; 3 *Leopard* 1

ANTI-TANK/ANTI-INFRASTRUCTURE
MSL • MANPATS *Spike*-LR; *Spike*-ER
RCL 84mm *Carl Gustav*; **106mm** 213 M40A1

ARTILLERY 1,407
SP **155mm** 48: 24 M109A3; 24 M109A5+
TOWED 240: **105mm** 192: 88 M101; 104 Model 56 pack howitzer; **155mm** 48 M-68
MRL **160mm** 12 LAR-160
MOR 1,107: **81mm** 743: 303 ECIA L65/81; 175 FAMAE; 265 Soltam; **120mm** 293: 173 ECIA L65/120; 17 FAMAE; 93 M-65; SP **120mm** 71: 35 FAMAE (on *Piranha* 6x6); 36 Soltam (on M113A2)

AIRCRAFT
TPT • **Light** 8: 2 C-212-300 *Aviocar*; 3 Cessna 208 *Caravan*; 3 CN235

HELICOPTERS
ISR 9 MD-530F *Lifter* (armed)
TPT 17: **Medium** 12: 8 AS532AL *Cougar*; 2 AS532ALe *Cougar*; 2 SA330 *Puma*; **Light** 5: 4 H125 *Ecureuil*; 1 AS355F *Ecureuil* II

AIR DEFENCE
SAM • Point-defence *Mistral*
GUNS 41:
SP **20mm** 17 *Piranha*/TCM-20
TOWED **20mm** 24 TCM-20

Navy 19,800

5 Naval Zones; 1st Naval Zone and main HQ at Valparaiso; 2nd Naval Zone at Talcahuano; 3rd Naval Zone at Punta Arenas; 4th Naval Zone at Iquique; 5th Naval Zone at Puerto Montt

FORCES BY ROLE
SPECIAL FORCES
1 (diver) SF comd

EQUIPMENT BY TYPE
SUBMARINES • TACTICAL • SSK 4:
2 *O'Higgins* (*Scorpène*) with 6 single 533mm TT with A-184 *Black Shark* HWT/SUT HWT/SM39 *Exocet* Block 2 AShM
2 *Thomson* (GER T-209/1400) with 8 single 533mm TT A-184 *Black Shark* HWT/SUT HWT/SM39 *Exocet* Block 2 AShM (of which 1 in refit)

PRINCIPAL SURFACE COMBATANTS 8
DESTROYERS • DDGHM 1 *Almirante Williams* (ex-UK *Broadsword* Type-22) with 2 quad Mk141 lnchr with RGM-84 *Harpoon* AShM, 2 octuple VLS with *Barak* SAM; 2 triple 324mm ASTT with Mk46 LWT, 1 76mm gun (capacity 1 AS532SC *Cougar*)

FRIGATES 7:
FFGHM 5:
3 *Almirante Cochrane* (ex-UK *Norfolk* Type-23) with 2 quad Mk141 lnchr with RGM-84C *Harpoon* AShM, 1 32-cell VLS with *Sea Wolf* SAM, 2 twin 324mm ASTT with Mk46 Mod 2 LWT, 1 114mm gun (capacity 1 AS-532SC *Cougar*) (MLU begun 2018)

2 *Almirante Riveros* (ex-NLD *Karel Doorman*) with 2 quad lnchr with MM40 *Exocet* Block 3 AShM, 1 octuple Mk48 lnchr with RIM-7P *Sea Sparrow* SAM, 4 single Mk32 Mod 9 324mm ASTT with Mk46 Mod 5 HWT, 1 76mm gun (capacity 1 AS532SC *Cougar*)

FFGM 2:
2 *Almirante Lattore* (ex-NLD *Jacob Van Heemskerck*) with 2 twin Mk141 lnchr with RGM-84 *Harpoon* AShM, 1 Mk13 GMLS with SM-1MR SAM, 1 octuple Mk48 lnchr with RIM-7P *Sea Sparrow* SAM, 2 twin Mk32 324mm ASTT with Mk46 LWT, 1 *Goalkeeper* CIWS

PATROL AND COASTAL COMBATANTS 12
PSOH 4: 2 *Piloto Pardo*; 2 *Piloto Pardo* with 1 76mm gun (ice-strengthened hull)
PCG 3:
2 *Casma* (ISR *Sa'ar* 4) with 4 single lnchr with *Gabriel* I AShM, 2 76mm guns
1 *Casma* (ISR *Sa'ar* 4) with 4 single lnchr with *Gabriel* I AShM, 2 twin lnchr with MM40 *Exocet* AShM, 2 76mm guns
PCO 5 *Micalvi*

AMPHIBIOUS
PRINCIPAL AMPHIBIOUS SHIPS
LPD 1 *Sargento Aldea* (ex-FRA *Foudre*) with 3 twin Simbad lnchr with *Mistral* SAM (capacity 4 med hel; 1 LCT; 2 LCM; 22 tanks; 470 troops)
LANDING SHIPS 3
LSM 1 *Elicura*
LST 2 *Maipo* (FRA *Batral*) with 1 hel landing platform (capacity 7 tanks; 140 troops)
LANDING CRAFT 3
LCT 1 CDIC (for use in *Sargento Aldea*)
LCM 2 (for use in *Sargento Aldea*)

LOGISTICS AND SUPPORT 13
ABU 1 *George Slight Marshall* with 1 hel landing platform
AFD 3
AGOR 1 *Cabo de Hornos*
AGHS 1 *Micalvi*
AGS 1 Type-1200 (ice-strengthened hull, ex-CAN) with 1 hel landing platform
AOR 2: 1 *Almirante Montt* with 1 hel landing platform; 1 *Araucano*
AP 1 *Aguiles* (1 hel landing platform)
ATF 2 *Veritas*
AXS 1 *Esmeralda*

Naval Aviation 600

EQUIPMENT BY TYPE
AIRCRAFT 14 combat capable
ASW 4: 2 C295ASW *Persuader*; 2 P-3ACH *Orion*
MP 4: 1 C295MPA *Persuader*; 3 EMB-111 *Bandeirante**
ISR 7 P-68
TRG 7 PC-7 *Turbo Trainer**
HELICOPTERS
ASW 5 AS532SC *Cougar*
MRH 8 AS365 *Dauphin*
TPT • **Light** 7: 3 Bell 206 *Jet Ranger*; 4 Bo-105S
AIR-LAUNCHED MISSILES • AShM AM39 *Exocet*

Marines 3,600
FORCES BY ROLE
MANOEUVRE
Amphibious
1 amph bde (2 mne bn, 1 cbt spt bn, 1 log bn)
2 coastal def unit
EQUIPMENT BY TYPE
ARMOURED FIGHTING VEHICLES
LT TK 15 FV101 *Scorpion*
APC • APC (W) 25 MOWAG *Roland*
AAV 12 AAV-7
ARTILLERY 39
TOWED 23: **105mm** 7 KH-178; **155mm** 16 M-71
MOR **81mm** 16
COASTAL DEFENCE • AShM MM38 *Exocet*
AIR DEFENCE • SAM • Point-defence 14: 4 M998 *Avenger*; 10 M1097 *Avenger*

Coast Guard
Integral part of the Navy
EQUIPMENT BY TYPE
PATROL AND COASTAL COMBATANTS 55
PBF 26 *Archangel*
PB 29: 18 *Alacalufe* (*Protector*-class); 4 *Grumete Diaz* (*Dabor*-class); 6 *Pelluhue*; 1 *Ona*

Air Force 11,050
FORCES BY ROLE
FIGHTER
1 sqn with F-5E/F *Tiger* III+
2 sqn with F-16AM/BM *Fighting Falcon*
FIGHTER/GROUND ATTACK
1 sqn with F-16C/D Block 50 *Fighting Falcon* (*Puma*)
ISR
1 (photo) flt with; DHC-6-300 *Twin Otter*; Learjet 35A
AIRBORNE EARLY WARNING
1 flt with B-707 *Phalcon*
TANKER/TRANSPORT
1 sqn with B-737-300; C-130B/H *Hercules*; KC-130R *Hercules*; KC-135 *Stratotanker*
TRANSPORT
3 sqn with Bell 205 (UH-1H *Iroquois*); C-212-200/300 *Aviocar*; Cessna O-2A; Cessna 525 *Citation* CJ1; DHC-6-100/300 *Twin Otter*; PA-28-236 *Dakota*; Bell 205 (UH-1H *Iroquois*)
1 VIP flt with B-737-500 (VIP); Gulfstream IV
TRAINING
1 sqn with EMB-314 *Super Tucano**
1 sqn with PA-28-236 *Dakota*; T-35A/B *Pillan*
TRANSPORT HELICOPTER
1 sqn with Bell 205 (UH-1H *Iroquois*); Bell 206B (trg); Bell 412 *Twin Huey*; Bo-105CBS-4; S-70A *Black Hawk*
AIR DEFENCE
1 AD regt (5 AD sqn) with *Crotale*; NASAMS; *Mistral*; M163/M167 *Vulcan*; Oerlikon GDF-005
EQUIPMENT BY TYPE
AIRCRAFT 88 combat capable
FTR 48: 10 F-5E *Tigre* III+; 2 F-5F *Tigre* III+; 29 F-16AM *Fighting Falcon*; 7 F-16BM *Fighting Falcon*
FGA 10: 6 F-16C Block 50 *Fighting Falcon*; 4 F-16D Block 50 *Fighting Falcon*
ATK 16 C-101CC *Aviojet* (A-36 *Halcón*)
ISR 3 Cessna O-2A
AEW&C 1 B-707 *Phalcon*
TKR 5: 2 KC-130R *Hercules*; 3 KC-135 *Stratotanker*
TPT 37: **Medium** 3: 1 C-130B *Hercules*; 2 C-130H *Hercules*; **Light** 29: 2 C-212-200 *Aviocar*; 1 C-212-300 *Aviocar*; 4 Cessna 525 *Citation* CJ1; 3 DHC-6-100 *Twin Otter*; 7 DHC-6-300 *Twin Otter*; 2 Learjet 35A; 10 PA-28-236 *Dakota*; **PAX** 5: 1 B-737-300; 1 B-737-500; 1 B-767-300ER; 2 Gulfstream IV
TRG 46: 4 Cirrus SR-22T; 14 EMB-314 *Super Tucano**; 28 T-35A/B *Pillan*
HELICOPTERS
MRH 12 Bell 412EP *Twin Huey*
TPT 28: **Medium** 7: 1 S-70A *Black Hawk*; 6 S-70i (MH-60M) *Black Hawk*; **Light** 21: 13 Bell 205 (UH-1H *Iroquois*); 5 Bell 206B (trg); 2 BK-117; 1 Bo-105CBS-4
UNMANNED AERIAL VEHICLES
ISR • **Medium** 3 *Hermes* 900
AIR DEFENCE
SAM
Short-range 17: 5 *Crotale*; 12 NASAMS
Point-defence *Mistral* (including some *Mygale/Aspic*)
GUNS • TOWED **20mm** M163/M167 *Vulcan*; **35mm** Oerlikon GDF-005
AIR-LAUNCHED MISSILES
AAM • IR AIM-9J/M *Sidewinder*; *Python* 3; *Shafrir*‡; IIR *Python* 4; ARH AIM-120C AMRAAM; *Derby*
ASM AGM-65G *Maverick*
BOMBS
Laser-guided *Paveway* II
INS/GPS guided JDAM

Paramilitary 44,700

Carabineros 44,700
Ministry of Interior; 15 zones, 36 districts, 179 *comisaria*
EQUIPMENT BY TYPE
ARMOURED FIGHTING VEHICLES
APC • APC (W) 20 MOWAG *Roland*
ARTILLERY • MOR 81mm
AIRCRAFT
TPT • **Light** 4: 1 Beech 200 *King Air*; 1 Cessna 208; 1 Cessna 550 *Citation* V; 1 PA-31T *Cheyenne* II
HELICOPTERS • TPT • Light 16: 5 AW109E *Power*; 1 AW139; 1 Bell 206 *Jet Ranger*; 2 BK-117; 5 Bo-105; 2 H135

Cyber
The Joint Staff coordinates cyber-security policies for the Ministry of National Defence and the armed forces. Each service has a cyber-security organisation. The Ministry of Interior and Public Security (Internal Affairs) released a National Cyber Security Strategy in 2017. There is active discussion with neighbouring states on cyber-security challenges. Chile and the US signed in 2018 a joint declaration on cooperation in cyber defence. In late 2017, Chile's Official Gazette detailed cyber plans including the creation of a Joint Cyberdefence Command and defence CERT teams, among other measures.

DEPLOYMENT

BOSNIA-HERZEGOVINA: EU • EUFOR • *Operation Althea* 15
CYPRUS: UN • UNFICYP 12
INDIA/PAKISTAN: UN • UNMOGIP 2 obs
MIDDLE EAST: UN • UNTSO 3 obs

Colombia COL

Colombian Peso pC		2017	2018	2019
GDP	pC	928tr	989tr	
	US$	314bn	337bn	
per capita	US$	6,380	6,761	
Growth	%	1.8	2.8	
Inflation	%	4.3	3.2	
Def bdgt [a]	pC	30.0tr	31.3tr	33.5tr
	US$	10.2bn	10.6bn	
FMA (US)	US$	38.5m	0m	20m
US$1=pC		2951.27	2936.46	

[a] Includes Defence and Security

Population 48,168,996

Age	0–14	15–19	20–24	25–29	30–64	65 plus
Male	12.2%	4.2%	4.4%	4.3%	21.0%	3.2%
Female	11.6%	4.1%	4.2%	4.2%	21.9%	4.5%

Capabilities

Colombia's armed forces have over recent decades significantly improved their level of training and their overall capabilities. Internal security remains a priority, and the armed forces are focused on fulfilling counter-insurgency and counter-narcotics operations, though the armed forces are looking towards new security roles and organisations for the post-FARC era. In response to the humanitarian and security challenge from Venezuela, Colombia is strengthening cooperation with Brazil on border controls, while also housing a large number of Venezuelan refugees. Colombia maintains good military ties with Argentina, Chile and Peru, although it withdrew from UNASUR in 2018. The US is Colombia's closest international military partner, with cooperation involving equipment procurement, technical advice and personnel training. In May 2018, Colombia joined NATO as a global partner and will participate in Alliance initiatives including in cyber and maritime security. Conscription was adjusted in 2017 and the government intends to grow the reserve component. The forces train regularly, including large multilateral exercises such as the US *Red Flag* air-combat exercise in 2018. Although the equipment inventory mainly comprises legacy systems, Colombia has the capability to independently deploy its forces beyond national borders. The army is planning to modernise its oldest APCs, while the navy may look to replace both its submarine and frigate fleets in the medium term. The air force's ground-attack capabilities remain limited, although a substantial number of multi-role and transport helicopters have been procured. In 2018, Colombia activated its first UAV squadron, which is set to carry out ISR missions. Colombia's defence industry is active in all domains. CIAC is developing its first indigenous UAVs, while CODALTEC is developing an air-defence system for regional export. COTECMAR has supplied patrol boats and amphibious ships for national and export markets.

ACTIVE 293,200 (Army 223,150, Navy 56,400 Air 13,650) **Paramilitary 187,900**

Conscript liability 18-months duration with upper age limit of 24, males only

RESERVE 34,950 (Army 25,050 Navy 6,500 Air 3,400)

ORGANISATIONS BY SERVICE

Army 223,150

FORCES BY ROLE
SPECIAL FORCES
  1 SF div (3 SF regt)
  1 (anti-terrorist) SF bn
MANOEUVRE
  Mechanised
  1 (1st) div (1 (2nd) mech bde (2 mech inf bn, 1 mtn inf bn, 1 engr bn, 1 MP bn, 1 cbt spt bn, 1 log bn, 1 Gaula anti-kidnap gp); 1 (10th) mech bde (1 armd recce bn, 1 mech cav bn, 1 mech inf bn, 1 mtn inf bn, 2 sy bn, 2 arty bn, 1 engr bn, 1 cbt spt bn, 2 Gaula anti-kidnap gp); 2 sy bn; 1 log bn)
  Light
  1 (2nd) div (1 (5th) lt inf bde (2 lt inf bn, 1 jungle inf bn, 1 sy bn, 1 arty bn, 1 AD bn, 1 engr bn, 1 cbt spt bn, 1 Gaula anti-kidnap gp); 1 (30th) lt inf bde (1 cav recce bn, 2 lt inf bn, 1 sy bn, 1 arty bn, 1 engr bn, 1 cbt spt bn, 1 log bn); 1 rapid reaction force (3 mobile sy bde))
  1 (3rd) div (1 (3rd) lt inf bde (2 lt inf bn, 1 mtn inf bn, 1 COIN bn, 1 arty bn, 1 engr bn, 1 cbt spt bn, 1 MP bn, 1 log bn, 1 Gaula anti-kidnap gp); 1 (23rd) lt inf bde (1 cav gp, 1 lt inf bn, 1 jungle inf bn, 1 cbt spt bn, 1 log bn); 1 (29th) mtn bde (1 mtn inf bn, 1 lt inf bn, 2 COIN bn, 1 cbt spt bn, 1 log bn); 2 rapid reaction force (total: 7 mobile sy bde))
  1 (4th) div (1 (7th) air mob bde (2 air mob inf bn, 1 lt inf bn, 1 COIN bn, 1 engr bn, 1 cbt spt bn, 1 log bn, 1 Gaula anti-kidnap gp); 1 (22nd) jungle bde (1 air mob inf bn, 1 lt inf bn, 1 jungle inf bn, 1 COIN bn, 1 cbt spt bn, 1 log bn); 1 (31st) jungle bde (1 lt inf bn, 1 jungle inf bn))
  1 (5th) div (1 (6th) lt inf bde (2 lt inf bn,1 mtn inf bn, 2 COIN bn, 1 cbt spt bn, 1 log bn, 1 Gaula anti-kidnap gp); 1 (8th) lt inf bde (1 lt inf bn, 1 mtn inf bn, 1 arty bn, 1 engr bn, 1 cbt spt bn, 1 Gaula anti-kidnap gp); 1 (9th) lt inf bde (1 SF bn, 2 lt inf bn, 1 arty bn, 1 COIN bn, 1 cbt spt bn, 1 sy bn, 1 log bn, 1 Gaula anti-kidnap gp); 1 (13th) lt inf bde (2 cav recce bn, 1 airmob inf bn, 3 lt inf bn, 1 COIN bn, 1 arty bn, 1 engr bn, 1 cbt spt bn, 2 MP bn, 1 log bn, 2 Gaula anti-kidnap gp); 1 rapid reaction force (3 mobile sy bde))
  1 (6th) div (1 (12th) lt inf bde (2 lt inf bn, 2 jungle inf bn, 1 COIN bn, 1 engr bn, 1 cbt spt bn, 1 Gaula anti-kidnap gp); 1 (13th) mobile sy bde (4 COIN bn); 1 (26th) jungle bde (1 lt jungle inf bn, 1 COIN bn, 1 cbt spt bn); 1 (27th) lt inf bde (2 lt inf bn, 1 jungle inf bn, 1 sy bn, 1 arty bn, 1 cbt spt bn, 1 log bn))
  1 (7th) div (1 (4th) lt inf bde (1 (urban) spec ops bn; 1 cav recce bn, 3 lt inf bn, 1 sy bn, 1 arty bn, 1 engr bn,

1 MP bn, 1 cbt spt bn, 1 log bn); 1 (11th) lt inf bde (2 lt inf bn, 1 sy bn, 1 engr bn, 1 cbt spt bn); 1 (14th) lt inf bde (3 lt inf bn, 1 sy bn, 1 engr bn, 1 cbt spt bn, 1 log bn); 1 (15th) jungle bde (1 lt inf bn, 1 COIN bn, 1 engr bn, 1 log bn); 1 (17th) lt inf bde (2 lt inf bn, 1 COIN bn, 1 engr bn, 1 cbt spt bn, 1 log bn); 1 rapid reaction force (1 (11th) mobile sy bde (3 COIN bn)))

1 (8th) div (1 (16th) lt inf bde (1 mech cav recce bn, 1 lt inf bn, 1 log bn, 1 Gaula anti-kidnap gp); 1 (18th) lt inf bde (1 air mob gp, 1 sy bn, 1 arty bn, 1 engr bn, 1 cbt spt bn, 1 log bn); 1 (28th) jungle bde (2 inf, 2 COIN, 1 cbt spt bn); 1 rapid reaction force (1 (5th) mobile sy bde (3 COIN bn); 1 (31st) mobile sy bde (5 COIN bn)))

3 COIN mobile bde (each: 4 COIN bn, 1 cbt spt bn)

Other
1 indep rapid reaction force (1 SF bde, 3 mobile sy bde)

COMBAT SUPPORT
1 cbt engr bde (1 SF engr bn, 1 (emergency response) engr bn, 1 EOD bn, 1 construction bn, 1 demining bn, 1 maint bn)
1 int bde (2 SIGINT bn, 1 log bn, 1 maint bn)

COMBAT SERVICE SUPPORT
2 spt/log bde (each: 1 spt bn, 1 maint bn, 1 supply bn, 1 tpt bn, 1 medical bn, 1 log bn)

AVIATION
1 air aslt div (1 counter-narcotics bde (3 counter-narcotics bn, 1 spt bn); 1 (25th) avn bde (4 hel bn; 5 avn bn; 1 avn log bn); 1 (32nd) avn bde (1 avn bn, 2 maint bn, 1 trg bn, 1 spt bn); 1 SF avn bn)

EQUIPMENT BY TYPE
ARMOURED FIGHTING VEHICLES
RECCE 121 EE-9 *Cascavel*
IFV 60: 28 *Commando Advanced*; 32 LAV III
APC 114
  APC (T) 54: 28 M113A1 (TPM-113A1); 26 M113A2 (TPM-113A2)
  APC (W) 56 EE-11 *Urutu*
  PPV 4 RG-31 *Nyala*
  AUV 38 M1117 *Guardian*
ANTI-TANK/ANTI-INFRASTRUCTURE
MSL
  SP 77 *Nimrod*
  MANPATS TOW; *Spike*-ER
RCL 106mm 73 M40A1
ARTILLERY 1,796
  TOWED 120: 105mm 107: 22 LG1 MkIII; 85 M101; 155mm 13 155/52 APU SBT-1
  MOR 1,676: 81mm 1,507; 120mm 169
AIRCRAFT
  ELINT 3: 2 Beech B200 *King Air*; 1 Beech 350 *King Air*
  TPT • Light 22: 2 An-32B; 2 Beech B200 *King Air*; 3 Beech 350 *King Air*; 1 Beech C90 *King Air*; 2 C-212 *Aviocar* (Medevac); 7 Cessna 208B *Grand Caravan*; 1 Cessna 208B-EX *Grand Caravan*; 4 *Turbo Commander* 695A
HELICOPTERS
  MRH 17: 6 Mi-17-1V *Hip*; 6 Mi-17MD; 5 Mi-17V-5 *Hip*
  TPT 93: Medium 54: 47 UH-60L *Black Hawk*; 7 S-70i *Black Hawk*; Light 39: 24 Bell 205 (UH-1H *Iroquois*); 15 Bell 212 (UH-1N *Twin Huey*)
AIR DEFENCE • GUNS • TOWED 40mm 4 M1A1

Navy 56,400 (incl 12,100 conscript)
HQ located at Puerto Carreño
EQUIPMENT BY TYPE
SUBMARINES • TACTICAL • SSK 4:
  2 *Pijao* (GER T-209/1200) each with 8 single 533mm TT each with HWT
  2 *Intrepido* (GER T-206A) each with 8 single 533mm TT each with HWT
PRINCIPAL SURFACE COMBATANTS 4
  FRIGATES • FFGHM 4 *Almirante Padilla* with 2 quad lnchr with *Hae Sung* I AShM, 2 twin *Simbad* lnchr with *Mistral* SAM, 2 triple B515 *ILAS-3* 324mm ASTT each with A244 LWT, 1 76mm gun (capacity 1 Bo-105/AS555SN *Fennec* hel)
PATROL AND COASTAL COMBATANTS 62
  CORVETTES • FS 1 *Narino* (ex-ROK *Dong Hae*) with 2 triple 324mm ASTT with Mk46 LWT, 1 76mm gun
  PSOH 3 *20 de Julio*
  PCO 2: 1 *Valle del Cauca Durable* (ex-US *Reliance*) with 1 hel landing platform; 1 *San Andres* (ex-US *Balsam*)
  PCC 3 *Punta Espada* (CPV-46)
  PCR 10: 2 *Arauca* with 2 76mm guns; 8 *Nodriza* (PAF-II) with hel landing platform
  PB 12: 1 *11 de Noviembre* (CPV-40) with 1 *Typhoon* CIWS; 2 *Castillo y Rada* (Swiftships 105); 2 *Jaime Gomez*; 1 *José Maria Palas* (Swiftships 110); 4 *Point*; 2 *Toledo*
  PBR 31: 6 *Diligente*; 7 LPR-40; 3 Swiftships; 9 *Tenerife*; 2 PAF-L; 4 others
AMPHIBIOUS 23
  LCM 3 LCM-8
  LCU 12: 5 *Golfo de Tribuga*; 7 *Morrosquillo* (LCU 1466)
  UCAC 8 *Griffon* 2000TD
LOGISTICS AND SUPPORT 8
  ABU 1 *Quindio*
  AG 2: 1 *Inirida*; 1 *Luneburg* (ex-GER, depot ship for patrol vessels)
  AGHS 1 *Roncador*
  AGOR 2 *Providencia*
  AGS 1 *Gorgona*
  AXS 1 *Gloria*

Naval Aviation 150
EQUIPMENT BY TYPE
AIRCRAFT
  MP 3 CN235 MPA *Persuader*
  ISR 1 PA-31 *Navajo* (upgraded for ISR)
  TPT • Light 11: 1 C-212 (Medevac); 4 Cessna 206; 3 Cessna 208 *Caravan*; 1 PA-31 *Navajo*; 1 PA-34 *Seneca*; 1 Beech 350 *King Air*
HELICOPTERS
  MRH 8: 1 AS555SN *Fennec*; 3 Bell 412 *Twin Huey*; 4 Bell 412EP *Twin Huey*
  TPT • Light 9: 1 Bell 212; 5 Bell 212 (UH-1N); 1 BK-117; 2 Bo-105

Marines 22,250
FORCES BY ROLE
SPECIAL FORCES
1 SF bde (4 SF bn)
MANOEUVRE
  Amphibious
  1 mne bde (1 SF (Gaula) bn, 5 mne bn, 2 rvn bn, 1 spt bn)

1 mne bde (1 SF bn, 2 mne bn, 2 rvn bn, 1 spt bn)
1 rvn bde (1 SF bn, 1 mne bn, 2 rvn bn, 1 spt bn)
1 rvn bde (4 rvn bn)
1 rvn bde (3 rvn bn)
COMBAT SERVICE SUPPORT
1 log bde (6 spt bn)
1 trg bde (7 trg bn, 1 spt bn)
EQUIPMENT BY TYPE
ARTILLERY • MOR 82: **81mm** 74; **120mm** 8
AIR DEFENCE • SAM Point-defence *Mistral*

Air Force 13,650
FORCES BY ROLE
FIGHTER/GROUND ATTACK
  2 sqn with *Kfir* C-10/C-12/TC-12
GROUND ATTACK/ISR
  1 sqn with A-37B/OA-37B *Dragonfly*
  1 sqn with AC-47T
  1 sqn with EMB-312 *Tucano**
  2 sqn with EMB-314 *Super Tucano** (A-29)
EW/ELINT
  2 sqn with Beech 350 *King Air*; Cessna 208; Cessna 560; C-26B *Metroliner*; SA 2-37; 1 *Turbo Commander* 695
TRANSPORT
  1 (Presidential) sqn with B-737BBJ; EMB-600 *Legacy*; Bell 412EP; F-28 *Fellowship*; UH-60L *Black Hawk*
  1 sqn with B-727; B-737-400; C-130B/H *Hercules*; C-212; C295M; CN235M; ; IAI *Arava*; KC-767
  1 sqn with Beech C90 *King Air*; Beech 350C *King Air*; Cessna 208B; Cessna 550; EMB-110P1 (C-95)
TRAINING
  1 sqn with Lancair *Synergy* (T-90 *Calima*)
  1 sqn with T-37B
  1 hel sqn with Bell 206B3
  1 hel sqn with TH-67
HELICOPTER
  1 sqn with AH-60L *Arpia* III
  1 sqn with UH-60L *Black Hawk* (CSAR)
  1 sqn with Hughes 500M
  1 sqn with Bell 205 (UH-1H)
  1 sqn with Bell 206B3 *Jet Ranger* III
  1 sqn with Bell 212
EQUIPMENT BY TYPE
AIRCRAFT 72 combat capable
  FGA 22: 10 *Kfir* C-10; 9 *Kfir* C-12; 3 *Kfir* TC-12
  ATK 12: 6 A-37B/OA-37B *Dragonfly*; 6 AC-47T *Spooky* (*Fantasma*)
  ISR 13: 1 Beech C90 *King Air*; 1 C-26B *Metroliner*; 5 Cessna 560 *Citation* II; 6 SA 2-37
  ELINT 13: 4 Beech 350 *King Air*; 6 Cessna 208 *Grand Caravan*; 2 Cessna 337G; 1 *Turbo Commander* 695
  TKR/TPT 1 KC-767
  TPT 64: **Medium** 7: 3 C-130B *Hercules* (3 more in store); 3 C-130H *Hercules*; 1 B-737F; **Light** 49: 10 ATR-42; 2 Beech 300 *King Air*; 2 Beech 350C *King Air*; 1 Beech 350i *King Air* (VIP); 4 Beech C90 *King Air*; 4 C-212; 6 C295M; 1 Cessna 182R; 12 Cessna 208B (medevac); 1 Cessna 550; 2 CN235M; 2 EMB-110P1 (C-95); 1 EMB-170-100LR; 1 IAI-201 *Arava*; **PAX** 8: 2 B-727; 1 B-737-400; 1 B-737BBJ;

1 EMB-600 *Legacy*; 1 F-28-1000 *Fellowship*; 1 F-28-3000 *Fellowship*; 1 Learjet 60
  TRG 78: 14 EMB-312 *Tucano**; 24 EMB-314 *Super Tucano* (A-29)*; 23 Lancair *Synergy* (T-90 *Calima*); 17 T-37B
HELICOPTERS
  MRH 18: 6 AH-60L *Arpia* III; 8 AH-60L *Arpia* IV; 2 Bell 412EP *Twin Huey* (VIP); 2 Hughes 500M
  TPT 48: **Medium** 13 UH-60L *Black Hawk* (incl 1 VIP hel); **Light** 35: 12 Bell 205 (UH-1H *Iroquois*); 12 Bell 206B3 *Jet Ranger* III; 11 Bell 212
  TRG 30 TH-67
UNAMMED AERIAL VEHICLES • ISR • **Medium** 8: 6 *Hermes* 450; 2 *Hermes* 900
AIR-LAUNCHED MISSILES
  AAM • IR *Python* 3; IIR *Python* 4; *Python* 5; ARH *Derby*; I-*Derby* ER (reported)
  ASM *Spike*-ER; *Spike*-NLOS
BOMBS
  Laser-guided *Paveway* II
  INS/GPS guided *Spice*

Paramilitary 187,900

National Police Force 187,900
EQUIPMENT BY TYPE
AIRCRAFT
  ELINT 5 C-26B *Metroliner*
  TPT • **Light** 42: 5 ATR-42; 3 Beech 200 *King Air*; 2 Beech 300 *King Air*; 2 Beech 1900; 1 Beech C99; 4 BT-67; 2 C-26 *Metroliner*; 3 Cessna 152; 3 Cessna 172; 9 Cessna 206; 2 Cessna 208 *Caravan*; 2 DHC-6 *Twin Otter*; 1 DHC-8; 3 PA-31 *Navajo*
HELICOPTERS
  MRH 4: 1 Bell 407GXP; 1 Bell 412EP; 2 MD-500D
  TPT 75: **Medium** 17: 5 UH-60A *Black Hawk*; 9 UH-60L *Black Hawk*; 3 S-70i *Black Hawk*; **Light** 58: 34 Bell 205 (UH-1H-II *Huey II*); 6 Bell 206B; 5 Bell 206L/L3/L4 *Long Ranger*; 8 Bell 212; 5 Bell 407

Cyber
Colombia's 2011 policy guidelines for cyber security and cyber defence set out three main organisations with cyber responsibilities: the CERT team (colCERT); the Police Cyber Centre; and the armed forces' Joint Cybersecurity and Cyberdefence Command. The defence ministry is the coordinating body for cyber defence, and Colombia has an active training and simulation programme in cyber defence, with the Higher War College also organising courses in cyber warfare for military (a staff course) and civil personnel.

DEPLOYMENT
CENTRAL AFRICAN REPUBLIC: UN • MINUSCA 2 obs
EGYPT: MFO 275; 1 inf bn
LEBANON: UN • UNIFIL 1

FOREIGN FORCES
United States US Southern Command: 50

Costa Rica CRI

Costa Rican Colon C		2017	2018	2019
GDP	C	32.8tr	34.6tr	
	US$	58.3bn	60.8bn	
per capita	US$	11,729	12,095	
Growth	%	3.3	3.3	
Inflation	%	1.6	2.4	
Sy Bdgt [a]	C	220bn	259bn	259bn
	US$	390m	454m	
FMA (US)	US$	5m	0m	0m
US$1=C		562.87	569.25	

[a] Paramilitary budget

Population 4,987,142

Age	0–14	15–19	20–24	25–29	30–64	65 plus
Male	12.2%	4.2%	4.4%	4.3%	21.0%	3.2%
Female	11.6%	4.1%	4.2%	4.2%	21.9%	4.5%

Capabilities

Costa Rica's armed forces were constitutionally abolished in 1949, and the country relies on paramilitary-type police organisations for internal-security and counter-narcotics tasks, as well as participation in regional peacekeeping operations. A new National Security Strategy was adopted in 2018 in order to help tackle rising crime. Colombia and the US have provided assistance and training, focused on policing and internal-security tasks rather than conventional military operations. The Special Intervention Unit (UEI) has received specialist training from non-regional states, including the US. The Public Force, Coast Guard and Air Surveillance Units have little heavy military equipment, and recent modernisation has depended on donations from countries such as China and the US. Apart from limited maintenance facilities, Costa Rica has no domestic defence industry.

PARAMILITARY 9,800

ORGANISATIONS BY SERVICE

Paramilitary 9,800

Special Intervention Unit
FORCES BY ROLE
SPECIAL FORCES
  1 spec ops unit

Public Force 9,000
11 regional directorates

Coast Guard Unit 400
EQUIPMENT BY TYPE
PATROL AND COASTAL COMBATANTS 10:
  PCC 2 *Libertador Juan Rafael Mora* (ex-US *Island*)
  PB 8: 2 *Cabo Blanco* (US *Swift* 65); 1 *Isla del Coco* (US *Swift* 105); 3 *Point*; 1 *Primera Dama* (US *Swift* 42); 1 *Puerto Quebos* (US *Swift* 36)

Air Surveillance Unit 400
EQUIPMENT BY TYPE
AIRCRAFT • TPT • Light 17: 4 Cessna T210 *Centurion*; 4 Cessna U206G *Stationair*; 1 DHC-7 *Caribou*; 2 PA-31 *Navajo*; 2 PA-34 *Seneca*; 1 Piper PA-23 *Aztec*; 1 Cessna 182RG; 2 Y-12E
HELICOPTERS • MRH 3: 2 MD-500E; 1 MD-600N

Cuba CUB

Cuban Peso P		2017	2018	2019
GDP	US$			
per capita	US$			
Growth				
Inflation				
Def exp	P			
	US$			
US$1=P				

Population 11,116,396
*definitive data not available

Age	0–14	15–19	20–24	25–29	30–64	65 plus
Male	8.5%	3.2%	3.1%	3.6%	24.5%	7.0%
Female	8.0%	2.9%	2.9%	3.3%	24.9%	8.3%

Capabilities

Cuba's armed forces are principally focused on protecting territorial integrity, and rely on a mass-mobilisation system. Military capability is limited by equipment obsolescence and a largely conscript-based force. Cuba maintains military ties with China and Russia, and the latter has stepped in to supply oil and fuel following Venezuela's economic collapse. Defence cooperation with Russia is largely centred around technical support for the maintenance of Cuba's ageing Soviet-era equipment. Cooperation with China appears to be on a smaller scale and involves training agreements and personnel exchanges. Training levels are uncertain and flying hours are likely to be low due to the limited availability of serviceable aircraft. The armed forces are no longer designed for expeditionary operations, and have little logistical capability to support deployments abroad. The inventory is almost entirely composed of legacy Soviet-era systems with varying degrees of obsolescence. Serviceability appears a problem, with much equipment at a low level of availability and maintenance demands growing as fleets age. Much of the aviation fleet is reported to be in storage. Russian assistance should improve availability, but is only a short-term solution given the advanced age of much of the inventory. It is unlikely that Havana will be in a position to finance significant equipment recapitalisation in the near term. Cuba has little in the way of domestic defence industry, bar some upgrade and maintenance capacity. Cuba has sent maintainers to South Africa, highlighting not just revenue-raising requirements for the forces but also the potential knock-on effect this might have on the level of maintenance capacity remaining in Cuba.

ACTIVE 49,000 (Army 38,000 Navy 3,000 Air 8,000)
Paramilitary 26,500
Conscript liability 2 years

RESERVE 39,000 (Army 39,000) Paramilitary 1,120,000
Ready Reserves (serve 45 days per year) to fill out Active and Reserve units; see also Paramilitary

ORGANISATIONS BY SERVICE

Army ε38,000
FORCES BY ROLE
COMMAND
  3 regional comd HQ
  3 army comd HQ
COMMAND
  3 SF regt
MANOEUVRE
  Armoured
  1 tk div (3 tk bde)
  Mechanised
  2 (mixed) mech bde
  Light
  2 (frontier) bde
  Air Manoeuvre
  1 AB bde
AIR DEFENCE
  1 ADA regt
  1 SAM bde

Reserves 39,000
FORCES BY ROLE
MANOEUVRE
  Light
  14 inf bde
EQUIPMENT BY TYPE†
ARMOURED FIGHTING VEHICLES
  MBT ε900 T-34/T-54/T-55/T-62
  LT TK PT-76
  ASLT BTR-60 100mm
  RECCE BRDM-2;
  AIFV ε50 BMP-1/1P
  APC ε500 BTR-152/BTR-50/BTR-60
ANTI-TANK/ANTI-INFRASTRUCTURE
  MSL
    SP 2K16 *Shmel* (AT-1 *Snapper*)
    MANPATS 9K11 *Malyutka* (AT-3 *Sagger*)
  GUNS 600+: **57mm** 600 ZIS-2 (M-1943); **85mm** D-44
ARTILLERY 1,715+
  SP 40+: **100mm** AAPMP-100; CATAP-100; **122mm** 2S1 *Gvozdika*; AAP-T-122; AAP-BMP-122; *Jupiter* III; *Jupiter* IV; **130mm** AAP-T-130; *Jupiter* V; **152mm** 2S3 *Akatsiya*
  TOWED 500: **122mm** D-30; M-30 (M-1938); **130mm** M-46; **152mm** D-1; M-1937 (ML-20)
  MRL • **SP** 175: **122mm** BM-21 *Grad*; **140mm** BM-14
  MOR 1,000: **82mm** M-41; **82mm** M-43; **120mm** M-43; M-38
AIR DEFENCE
  SAM
    Short-range 2K12 *Kub* (SA-6 *Gainful*)
    Pont-defence 200+: 200 9K35 *Strela*-10 (SA-13 *Gopher*); 9K33 *Osa* (SA-8 *Gecko*); 9K31 *Strela*-1 (SA-9 *Gaskin*); 9K36 *Strela*-3 (SA-14 *Gremlin*); 9K310 *Igla*-1 (SA-16 *Gimlet*); 9K32 *Strela*-2 (SA-7 *Grail*)‡
  GUNS 400
    SP 23mm ZSU-23-4; **30mm** BTR-60P SP; **57mm** ZSU-57-2
    TOWED 100mm KS-19/M-1939; **85mm** KS-12; **57mm** S-60; **37mm** M-1939; **30mm** M-53; **23mm** ZU-23

Navy ε3,000
Western Comd HQ at Cabanas; Eastern Comd HQ at Holquin
EQUIPMENT BY TYPE
PATROL AND COASTAL COMBATANTS 8
  PSO 1 *Rio Damuji* with two single P-15M *Termit* (SS-N-2C *Styx*) AShM, 2 57mm guns, 1 hel landing platform
  PCM 1 *Pauk* II† (FSU) with 1 quad lnchr (manual aiming) with 9K32 *Strela*-2 (SA-N-5 *Grail*) SAM, 4 single ASTT, 2 RBU 1200 A/S mor, 1 76mm gun
  PBF 6 *Osa* II† (FSU) each with 4 single lnchr (for P-15 *Termit* (SS-N-2B *Styx*) AShM – missiles removed to coastal-defence units)
MINE WARFARE AND MINE COUNTERMEASURES 5
  MHI 3 *Korund* (*Yevgenya*) (Project 1258)†
  MSC 2 *Sonya*† (FSU)
LOGISTICS AND SUPPORT 2
  ABU 1
  AX 1

Coastal Defence
ARTILLERY • TOWED 122mm M-1931/37; **130mm** M-46; **152mm** M-1937
COASTAL DEFENCE • AShM 4+: *Bandera* IV (reported); 4 4K51 *Rubezh* (SSC-3 *Styx*)

Naval Infantry 550+
FORCES BY ROLE
MANOEUVRE
  Amphibious
  2 amph aslt bn

Anti-aircraft Defence and Revolutionary Air Force ε8,000 (incl conscripts)
Air assets divided between Western Air Zone and Eastern Air Zone
FORCES BY ROLE
FIGHTER/GROUND ATTACK
  3 sqn with MiG-21ML *Fishbed*; MiG-23ML/MF/UM *Flogger*; MiG-29A/UB *Fulcrum*
TRANSPORT
  1 (VIP) tpt sqn with An-24 *Coke*; Mi-8P *Hip*; Yak-40
ATTACK HELICOPTER
  2 sqn with Mi-17 *Hip H*; Mi-35 *Hind*
TRAINING
  2 (tac trg) sqn with L-39C *Albatros* (basic); Z-142 (primary)
EQUIPMENT BY TYPE
AIRCRAFT 45 combat capable
  FTR 33: 16 MiG-23ML *Flogger*; 4 MiG-23MF *Flogger*; 4 MiG-23U *Flogger*; 4 MiG-23UM *Flogger*; 2 MiG-29A *Fulcrum*; 3 MiG-29UB *Fulcrum* (6 MiG-15UTI *Midget*; 4+ MiG-17 *Fresco*; 4 MiG-23MF *Flogger*; 6 MiG-23ML *Flogger*; 2 MiG-23UM *Flogger*; 2 MiG-29 *Fulcrum* in store)
  FGA 12: 4 MiG-21ML *Fishbed*; 8 MiG-21U *Mongol* A (up to 70 MiG-21bis *Fishbed*; 30 MiG-21F *Fishbed*; 28 MiG-21PFM *Fishbed*; 7 MiG-21UM *Fishbed*; 20 MiG-23BN *Flogger* in store)
  ISR 1 An-30 *Clank*

TPT 11: **Heavy** 2 Il-76 *Candid*; **Light** 9: 1 An-2 *Colt*; 3 An-24 *Coke*; 2 An-32 *Cline*; 3 Yak-40 (8 An-2 *Colt*; 17 An-26 *Curl* in store)
TRG 45: 25 L-39 *Albatros*; 20 Z-326 *Trener Master*
HELICOPTERS
  ATK 4 Mi-35 *Hind* (8 more in store)
  ASW (5 Mi-14 in store)
  MRH 8 Mi-17 *Hip* H (12 more in store)
  TPT • Medium 2 Mi-8P *Hip*
AIR DEFENCE • SAM
  Medium-range S-75 *Dvina* (SA-2 *Guideline*); S-75 *Dvina* mod (SA-2 *Guideline* – on T-55 chassis)
  Short-range S-125 *Pechora* (SA-3 *Goa*); S-125 *Pechora* mod (SA-3 *Goa* – on T-55 chassis)
AIR-LAUNCHED MISSILES
  AAM • IR R-3‡ (AA-2 *Atoll*); R-60 (AA-8 *Aphid*); R-73 (AA-11 *Archer*); **IR/SARH** R-23/24‡ (AA-7 *Apex*); R-27 (AA-10 *Alamo*)
  ASM Kh-23‡ (AS-7 *Kerry*)

Paramilitary 26,500 active

State Security 20,000
Ministry of Interior

Border Guards 6,500
Ministry of Interior
PATROL AND COASTAL COMBATANTS 20
  PCC 2 *Stenka*
  PB 18 *Zhuk*

Youth Labour Army 70,000 reservists

Civil Defence Force 50,000 reservists

Territorial Militia ε1,000,000 reservists

FOREIGN FORCES
United States US Southern Command: 1,000 (JTF-GTMO) at Guantanamo Bay

Dominican Republic DOM

Dominican Peso pRD		2017	2018	2019
GDP	pRD	3.61tr	4.01tr	
	US$	76.1bn	81.1bn	
per capita	US$	7,478	7,891	
Growth	%	4.6	6.4	
Inflation	%	3.3	4.3	
Def bdgt	pRD	23.5bn	29.8bn	
	US$	496m	603m	
US$1=pRD		47.48	49.45	
Population	10,298,756			

Age	0–14	15–19	20–24	25–29	30–64	65 plus
Male	14.0%	4.8%	4.6%	4.3%	20.1%	2.8%
Female	13.6%	4.6%	4.5%	4.2%	19.5%	3.1%

Capabilities
The principal tasks for the Dominican armed forces include internal- and border-security missions, as well as disaster relief. Training and operations increasingly focus on counter-narcotics and include collaboration with the police in an inter-agency task force. The US sends training teams to the country under the terms of a 2015 military-partnership agreement, and the navy has trained with French forces. The Dominican Republic is a regular participant in the US SOUTHCOM's annual *Tradewinds* disaster-response exercise. The army has strengthened its presence along the border with Haiti, establishing new surveillance posts. There is little capacity to deploy and sustain forces abroad. The army's equipment inventory is small and outdated, and the small number of armoured vehicles are obsolete and likely increasingly difficult to maintain. The Air Force operates a modest number of light fixed- and rotary-wing assets, and the Navy has a small fleet of mainly ex-US patrol craft of varying size. Aside from maintenance facilities, the country does not have a domestic defence industry.

ACTIVE 56,050 (Army 28,750 Navy 11,200 Air 16,100) **Paramilitary** 15,000

ORGANISATIONS BY SERVICE

Army 28,750
5 Defence Zones
FORCES BY ROLE
SPECIAL FORCES
  3 SF bn
MANOEUVRE
  Light
  4 (1st, 2nd, 3rd & 4th) inf bde (3 inf bn)
  2 (5th & 6th) inf bde (2 inf bn)
  Air Manoeuvre
  1 air cav bde (1 cdo bn, 1 (6th) mtn bn, 1 hel sqn with Bell 205 (op by Air Force); OH-58 *Kiowa*; R-22; R-44 *Raven* II)
  Other
  1 (Presidential Guard) gd regt
  1 (MoD) sy bn
COMBAT SUPPORT
  1 cbt spt bde (1 lt armd bn; 1 arty bn; 1 engr bn; 1 sigs bn)
EQUIPMENT BY TYPE
ARMOURED FIGHTING VEHICLES
  LT TK 12 M41B (76mm)
  APC • APC (W) 8 LAV-150 *Commando*
ANTI-TANK/ANTI-INFRASTRUCTURE
  RCL 106mm 20 M40A1
  GUNS 37mm 20 M3
ARTILLERY 104
  TOWED 105mm 16: 4 M101; 12 *Reinosa* 105/26
  MOR 88: **81mm** 60 M1; **107mm** 4 M30; **120mm** 24 Expal Model L
HELICOPTERS
  ISR 8: 4 OH-58A *Kiowa*; 4 OH-58C *Kiowa*
  TPT • Light 6: 4 R-22; 2 R-44 *Raven* II

Navy 11,200
HQ located at Santo Domingo
FORCES BY ROLE
SPECIAL FORCES
  1 (SEAL) SF unit

MANOEUVRE
Amphibious
1 mne sy unit
EQUIPMENT BY TYPE
PATROL AND COASTAL COMBATANTS 17
PCO 1 *Almirante Didiez Burgos* (ex-US *Balsam*)
PCC 2 *Tortuguero* (ex-US *White Sumac*)
PB 14: 2 *Altair* (Swiftships 35m); 4 *Bellatrix* (US Sewart Seacraft); 2 *Canopus* (Swiftships 101); 3 *Hamal* (Damen Stan 1505); 3 *Point*
AMPHIBIOUS • LCU 1 *Neyba* (ex-US LCU 1675)
LOGISTICS AND SUPPORT 8
AG 8

Air Force 16,100
FORCES BY ROLE
GROUND ATTACK
1 sqn with EMB-314 *Super Tucano**
SEARCH & RESCUE
1 sqn with Bell 205 (UH-1H *Huey II*); Bell 205 (UH-1H *Iroquois*); Bell 430 (VIP); OH-58 *Kiowa* (CH-136); S-333
TRANSPORT
1 sqn with C-212-400 *Aviocar*; PA-31 *Navajo*
TRAINING
1 sqn with T-35B *Pillan*
AIR DEFENCE
1 ADA bn with 20mm guns
EQUIPMENT BY TYPE
AIRCRAFT 8 combat capable
ISR 1 AMT-200 *Super Ximango*
TPT • Light 13: 3 C-212-400 *Aviocar*; 1 Cessna 172; 1 Cessna 182; 1 Cessna 206; 1 Cessna 207; 1 *Commander* 690; 3 EA-100; 1 PA-31 *Navajo*; 1 P2006T
TRG 12: 8 EMB-314 *Super Tucano**; 4 T-35B *Pillan*
HELICOPTERS
ISR 9 OH-58 *Kiowa* (CH-136)
TPT • Light 16: 8 Bell 205 (UH-1H *Huey* II); 5 Bell 205 (UH-1H *Iroquois*); 1 H155 (VIP); 2 S-333
AIR DEFENCE • GUNS 20mm 4

Paramilitary 15,000
National Police 15,000

Ecuador ECU

United States Dollar $		2017	2018	2019
GDP	US$	104bn	107bn	
per capita	US$	6,217	6,301	
Growth	%	2.4	1.1	
Inflation	%	0.4	-0.2	
Def bdgt	US$	1.57bn	1.70bn	
Population	16,498,502			

Age	0–14	15–19	20–24	25–29	30–64	65 plus
Male	13.6%	4.7%	4.6%	4.2%	19.0%	3.6%
Female	13.1%	4.5%	4.4%	4.2%	20.1%	4.0%

Capabilities

Ecuador's armed forces are able to fulfil internal-security tasks, although the crisis in Venezuela and resulting refugee flows transiting Colombia has added to existing security challenges in the northern border area. In 2018, Ecuador's defence ministry drafted an ambitious all-domain equipment-modernisation and -procurement plan, though this is reliant on budgetary approval. Due to the security conditions along the northern border area, the armed forces are standing up a new joint task force for counter-insurgency and counter-narcotics operations. Greater defence cooperation with Peru is focused on demining efforts on the border. Military ties with Washington have been revived, representing a turning point in bilateral relations after defence ties were curtailed in 2009 and US troops left Manta air base. The armed forces train regularly and have participated in large regional and international military exercises. There is limited capability to independently deploy beyond its borders. The equipment inventory is derived from a variety of sources and suffers from a general state of obsolescence and low availability. Modernisation plans will target the small fleet of fighter aircraft, transport and training aircraft, and the army's personnel carriers. Ecuador's defence industries are centred on the army's Office of Industries (DINE), which produces military equipment through army-run enterprises. The state-owned shipyard ASTINAVE has some construction, maintenance and repair capabilities; however, the navy's submarines are being modernised in Chile.

ACTIVE 40,250 (Army 24,750 Navy 9,100 Air 6,400)
Paramilitary 500
Conscript liability Voluntary conscription

RESERVE 118,000 (Joint 118,000)
Ages 18–55

ORGANISATIONS BY SERVICE

Army 24,750
FORCES BY ROLE
gp are bn sized
COMMAND
4 div HQ
SPECIAL FORCES
1 (9th) SF bde (3 SF gp, 1 SF sqn, 1 para bn, 1 sigs sqn, 1 log comd)
MANOEUVRE
Mechanised
1 (11th) armd cav bde (3 armd cav gp, 1 mech inf bn, 1 SP arty gp, 1 engr gp)
1 (5th) inf bde (1 SF sqn, 2 mech cav gp, 2 inf bn, 1 cbt engr coy, 1 sigs coy, 1 log coy)
Light
1 (1st) inf bde (1 SF sqn, 1 armd cav gp, 1 armd recce sqn, 3 inf bn, 1 med coy)
1 (3rd) inf bde (1 SF gp, 1 mech cav gp, 1 inf bn, 1 arty gp, 1 hvy mor coy, 1 cbt engr coy, 1 sigs coy, 1 log coy)
1 (7th) inf bde (1 SF sqn, 1 armd recce sqn, 1 mech cav gp, 3 inf bn, 1 jungle bn, 1 arty gp, 1 cbt engr coy, 1 sigs coy, 1 log coy, 1 med coy)
1 (13th) inf bde (1 SF sqn, 1 armd recce sqn, 1 mot cav gp, 3 inf bn, 1 arty gp, 1 hvy mor coy, 1 cbt engr coy, 1 sigs coy, 1 log coy)

2 (17th & 21st) jungle bde (3 jungle bn, 1 cbt engr coy, 1 sigs coy, 1 log coy)

1 (19th) jungle bde (3 jungle bn, 1 jungle trg bn, 1 cbt engr coy, 1 sigs coy, 1 log coy)

COMBAT SUPPORT

1 (27th) arty bde (1 SP arty gp, 1 MRL gp, 1 ADA gp, 1 cbt engr coy, 1 sigs coy, 1 log coy)

1 (23rd) engr bde (3 engr bn)

2 indep MP coy

1 indep sigs coy

COMBAT SERVICE SUPPORT

1 (25th) log bde

2 log bn

2 indep med coy

AVIATION

1 (15th) avn bde (2 tpt avn gp, 2 hel gp, 1 mixed avn gp)

AIR DEFENCE

1 ADA gp

EQUIPMENT BY TYPE

ARMOURED FIGHTING VEHICLES

LT TK 24 AMX-13

RECCE 67: 25 AML-90; 10 EE-3 *Jararaca*; 32 EE-9 *Cascavel*

APC 123

  APC (T) 95: 80 AMX-VCI; 15 M113

  APC (W) 28: 18 EE-11 *Urutu*; 10 UR-416

ANTI-TANK/ANTI-INFRASTRUCTURE

RCL 404: **90mm** 380 M67; **106mm** 24 M40A1

ARTILLERY 541+

SP **155mm** 5 Mk F3

TOWED 100: **105mm** 78: 30 M101; 24 M2A2; 24 Model 56 pack howitzer; **155mm** 22: 12 M114; 10 M198

MRL **122mm** 24: 18 BM-21 *Grad*; 6 RM-70

MOR 412+: **81mm** 400 M29; **107mm** M30; **160mm** 12 M-66

AIRCRAFT

TPT • Light 14: 1 Beech 200 *King Air*; 2 C-212; 1 CN235; 4 Cessna 172; 2 Cessna 206; 1 Cessna 500 *Citation* I; 3 IAI-201 *Arava*

TRG 6: 2 MX-7-235 *Star Rocket*; 2 T-41D *Mescalero*; 2 CJ-6A

HELICOPTERS

MRH 33: 7 H125M (AS550C3) *Fennec*; 6 Mi-17-1V *Hip*; 2 SA315B *Lama*; 18 SA342L *Gazelle* (13 with HOT for anti-armour role)

TPT 11: Medium 7: 5 AS332B *Super Puma*; 2 Mi-171E; (3 SA330 *Puma* in store); Light 4: 2 H125 (AS350B2) *Ecureuil*; 2 H125 (AS350B3) *Ecureuil*

AIR DEFENCE

SAM • Point-defence *Blowpipe*; 9K32 *Strela*-2 (SA-7 *Grail*)‡; 9K38 *Igla* (SA-18 *Grouse*)

GUNS 240

SP **20mm** 44 M163 *Vulcan*

TOWED 196: **14.5mm** 128 ZPU-1/-2; **20mm** 38: 28 M-1935, 10 M167 *Vulcan*; **40mm** 30 L/70/M1A1

AIR-LAUNCHED MISSILES • ASM HOT

Navy 9,100 (incl Naval Aviation, Marines and Coast Guard)

EQUIPMENT BY TYPE

SUBMARINES • TACTICAL • SSK 2:

2 *Shyri* (GER T-209/1300) with 8 single 533mm TT each with SUT HWT (1 undergoing refit in Chile)

PRINCIPAL SURFACE COMBATANTS • FRIGATES 1

FFGHM 1 *Moran Valverde*† (ex-UK *Leander* batch II) with 4 single lnchr with MM40 *Exocet* AShM, 3 twin lnchr with *Mistral* SAM, 1 *Phalanx* CIWS, 1 twin 114mm gun (capacity 1 Bell 206B *Jet Ranger* II hel)

PATROL AND COASTAL COMBATANTS 9

CORVETTES • FSGM 6 *Esmeraldas* (3†) with 2 triple lnchr with MM40 *Exocet* AShM, 1 quad *Albatros* lnchr with *Aspide* SAM, 2 triple B515 ILAS-3 324mm ASTT with A244 LWT (removed from two vessels), 1 76mm gun, 1 hel landing platform (upgrade programme ongoing)

PCFG 3 *Quito* (GER Lurssen TNC-45 45m) with 4 single lnchr with MM38 *Exocet* AShM, 1 76mm gun (upgrade programme ongoing)

LOGISTICS AND SUPPORT 8

AE 1 *Caluchima*

AGOS 1 *Orion* with 1 hel landing platform

AGS 1 *Sirius*

AK 1 *Galapagos*

ATF 1

AWT 2: 1 *Quisquis*; 1 *Atahualpa*

AXS 1 *Guayas*

Naval Aviation 380

EQUIPMENT BY TYPE

AIRCRAFT

MP 1 CN235-300M

ISR 3: 2 Beech 200T *King Air*; 1 Beech 300 *Catpass King Air*

TPT • Light 3: 1 Beech 200 *King Air*; 1 Beech 300 *King Air*; 1 CN235-100

TRG 6: 2 T-34C *Turbo Mentor*; 4 T-35B *Pillan*

HELICOPTERS

TPT • Light 9: 3 Bell 206A; 3 Bell 206B; 1 Bell 230; 2 Bell 430

UNMANNED AERIAL VEHICLES

ISR 5: Heavy 2 *Heron*; Medium 3 *Searcher* Mk.II

Marines 2,150

FORCES BY ROLE

SPECIAL FORCES

1 cdo unit

MANOEUVRE

Amphibious

5 mne bn (on garrison duties)

EQUIPMENT BY TYPE

ARTILLERY • MOR 32+ 60mm/81mm/120mm

AIR DEFENCE • SAM • Point-defence *Mistral*; 9K38 *Igla* (SA-18 *Grouse*)

Air Force 6,400

Operational Command

FORCES BY ROLE

FIGHTER

1 sqn with *Cheetah* C/D

FIGHTER/GROUND ATTACK
 2 sqn with EMB-314 *Super Tucano**
 1 sqn with *Kfir* C-10 (CE); *Kfir* C-2; *Kfir* TC-2

Military Air Transport Group

FORCES BY ROLE
SEARCH & RESCUE/TRANSPORT HELICOPTER
 1 sqn with Bell 206B *Jet Ranger* II
 1 sqn with PA-34 *Seneca*
TRANSPORT
 1 sqn with C-130/H *Hercules*; L-100-30
 1 sqn with HS-748
 1 sqn with DHC-6-300 *Twin Otter*
 1 sqn with B-727; EMB-135BJ *Legacy* 600; *Sabreliner* 40
TRAINING
 1 sqn with Cessna 206; DA20-C1; MXP-650; T-34C *Turbo Mentor*

EQUIPMENT BY TYPE
AIRCRAFT 42 combat capable
 FGA 25: 10 *Cheetah* C; 2 *Cheetah* D; 4 *Kfir* C-2; 7 *Kfir* C-10 (CE); 2 *Kfir* TC-2
 TPT 31: **Medium** 4: 2 C-130B *Hercules*; 1 C-130H *Hercules*; 1 L-100-30; **Light** 16: 1 Beech E90 *King Air*; 3 C295M; 1 Cessna 206; 3 DHC-6 *Twin Otter*; 1 EMB-135BJ *Legacy* 600; 2 EMB-170; 2 EMB-190; 1 M-28 *Skytruck*; 1 MXP-650; 1 PA-34 *Seneca*; **PAX** 11: 2 A320; 2 B-727; 1 *Falcon* 7X; 1 Gulfstream G-1159; 5 HS-748
 TRG 39: 11 DA20-C1; 17 EMB-314 *Super Tucano**; 11 T-34C *Turbo Mentor*
HELICOPTERS • TPT • **Light** 7 Bell 206B *Jet Ranger* II
AIR-LAUNCHED MISSILES • **AAM** • **IR** *Python* 3; R-550 *Magic*; *Shafrir*‡; **IIR** *Python* 4; **SARH** Super 530
AIR DEFENCE
 SAM • **Point-defence** 13+: 6 9K33 *Osa* (SA-8 *Gecko*); 7 M48 *Chaparral*; *Blowpipe*; 9K32 *Strela*-2 (SA-7 *Grail*)‡; 9K310 *Igla*-1 (SA-16 *Gimlet*); 9K38 *Igla* (SA-18 *Grouse*)
 GUNS
  SP 20mm 28 M35
  TOWED 64: **23mm** 34 ZU-23; **35mm** 30 GDF-002 (twin)

Paramilitary 500

Coast Guard 500
EQUIPMENT BY TYPE
PATROL AND COASTAL COMBATANTS 21
 PCC 4: 3 *Isla Fernandina* (*Vigilante*); 1 *Isla San Cristóbal* (Damen Stan Patrol 5009)
 PB 14: 1 *10 de Agosto*; 2 *Espada*; 2 *Manta* (GER Lurssen 36m); 1 *Point*; 4 *Rio Coca*; 4 *Isla Santa Cruz* (Damen Stan 2606)
 PBR 3: 2 *Río Esmeraldas*; 1 *Rio Puyango*

DEPLOYMENT

SUDAN: UN • UNAMID 1; 1 obs; UN • UNISFA 1 obs
WESTERN SAHARA: UN • MIURNSO 3 obs

El Salvador SLV

United States Dollar $		2017	2018	2019
GDP	US$	24.8bn	25.9bn	
per capita	US$	3,895	4,041	
Growth	%	2.3	2.5	
Inflation	%	1.0	1.2	
Def bdgt	US$	146m	141m	
FMA (US)	US$	1.9m	0m	0m
Population	6,187,271			

Age	0–14	15–19	20–24	25–29	30–64	65 plus
Male	13.0%	5.0%	5.0%	4.3%	17.3%	3.4%
Female	12.3%	4.9%	5.0%	4.5%	20.9%	4.3%

Capabilities

El Salvador's armed forces' primary challenge is tackling organised crime and narcotics trafficking in support of the National Civil Police. The country's 2015 security strategy focuses on tackling violent crime. El Salvador switched diplomatic recognition from Taiwan to China in 2018, a move which has halted planned equipment donations from Taiwan. El Salvador participates in a tri-national border task force with Guatemala and Honduras. The armed forces have long-standing training programmes, including with regional states and with the US, focused on internal security, disaster relief and support to civilian authorities. El Salvador has deployed on UN peacekeeping missions up to company strength but lacks the logistical support to sustain independent international deployments. The armed forces have received little new heavy military equipment in recent years and are dependent on an inventory of Cold War-era platforms; the majority of these are operational, indicating adequate support and maintenance. El Salvador lacks a substantive defence industry but has successfully produced light armoured vehicles domestically based upon commercial vehicle chassis.

ACTIVE 24,500 (Army 20,500 Navy 2,000 Air 2,000)
Paramilitary 17,000
Conscript liability 12 months (selective); 11 months for officers and NCOs

RESERVE 9,900 (Joint 9,900)

ORGANISATIONS BY SERVICE

Army 20,500
FORCES BY ROLE
SPECIAL FORCES
 1 spec ops gp (1 SF coy, 1 para bn, 1 (naval inf) coy)
MANOEUVRE
 Reconnaissance
 1 armd cav regt (2 armd cav bn)
 Light
 6 inf bde (3 inf bn)
 Other
 1 (special) sy bde (2 border gd bn, 2 MP bn)
COMBAT SUPPORT
 1 arty bde (2 fd arty bn, 1 AD bn)
 1 engr comd (2 engr bn)

EQUIPMENT BY TYPE
ARMOURED FIGHTING VEHICLES
RECCE 5 AML-90 (4 more in store)
APC • **APC (W)** 38: 30 VAL *Cashuat* (mod); 8 UR-416
ANTI-TANK/ANTI-INFRASTRUCTURE
RCL 399: **106mm** 20 M40A1 (incl 16 SP); **90mm** 379 M67
ARTILLERY 217+
TOWED **105mm** 54: 36 M102; 18 M-56 (FRY)
MOR 163+: **81mm** 151 M29; **120mm** 12+: 12 UBM 52; (some M-74 in store)
AIR DEFENCE • **GUNS** 35: **20mm** 31 M-55; 4 TCM-20

Navy 2,000
EQUIPMENT BY TYPE
PATROL AND COASTAL COMBATANTS 10
PB 10: 3 Camcraft (30m); 1 *Point*; 1 Swiftships 77; 1 Swiftships 65; 4 Type-44 (ex-USCG)
AMPHIBIOUS • **LANDING CRAFT** • **LCM** 4

Naval Inf (SF Commandos) 90
FORCES BY ROLE
SPECIAL FORCES
1 SF coy

Air Force 2,000
FORCES BY ROLE
FIGHTER/GROUND ATTACK/ISR
1 sqn with A-37B/OA-37B *Dragonfly*; O-2A/B *Skymaster**
TRANSPORT
1 sqn with BT-67; Cessna 210 *Centurion*; Cessna 337G; Commander 114; IAI-202 *Arava*; SA-226T *Merlin* IIIB
TRAINING
1 sqn with R-235GT *Guerrier*; T-35 *Pillan*; T-41D *Mescalero*; TH-300
TRANSPORT HELICOPTER
1 sqn with Bell 205 (UH-1H *Iroquois*); Bell 407; Bell 412EP *Twin Huey*; MD-500E; UH-1M *Iroquois*

EQUIPMENT BY TYPE
AIRCRAFT 25 combat capable
ATK 14 A-37B *Dragonfly*
ISR 11: 6 O-2A/B *Skymaster**; 5 OA-37B *Dragonfly**
TPT • **Light** 10: 2 BT-67; 2 Cessna 210 *Centurion*; 1 Cessna 337G *Skymaster*; 1 *Commander* 114; 3 IAI-201 *Arava*; 1 SA-226T *Merlin* IIIB
TRG 11: 5 R-235GT *Guerrier*; 5 T-35 *Pillan*; 1 T-41D *Mescalero*
HELICOPTERS
MRH 14: 4 Bell 412EP *Twin Huey*; 8 MD-500E; 2 UH-1M *Iroquois*
TPT• **Light** 9: 8 Bell 205 (UH-1H *Iroquois*); 1 Bell 407 (VIP tpt, govt owned)
TRG 5 TH-300
AIR-LAUNCHED MISSILES • **AAM** • **IR** *Shafrir*‡

Paramilitary 17,000
National Civilian Police 17,000
Ministry of Public Security
AIRCRAFT
ISR 1 O-2A *Skymaster*

TPT • **Light** 1 Cessna 310
HELICOPTERS
MRH 2 MD-520N
TPT • **Light** 3: 1 Bell 205 (UH-1H *Iroquois*); 2 R-44 *Raven* II

DEPLOYMENT
LEBANON: UN • UNIFIL 52; 1 inf pl
MALI: UN • MINUSMA 156; 1 hel sqn
SOUTH SUDAN: UN • UNMISS 1; 2 obs
SUDAN: UN • UNISFA 1 obs
WESTERN SAHARA: UN • MINURSO 1 obs

FOREIGN FORCES
United States US Southern Command: 1 Forward Operating Location (Military, DEA, USCG and Customs personnel)

Guatemala GUA

Guatemalan Quetzal q		2017	2018	2019
GDP	q	556bn	592bn	
	US$	75.6bn	79.1bn	
per capita	US$	4,469	4,583	
Growth	%	2.8	2.8	
Inflation	%	4.4	3.7	
Def bdgt	q	1.91bn	1.92bn	2.37bn
	US$	260m	256m	
FMA (US)	US$	1.74m	0m	0m
US$1=q		7.35	7.49	

Population	16,581,273					
Age	0–14	15–19	20–24	25–29	30–64	65 plus
Male	17.6%	5.2%	5.0%	4.4%	15.4%	2.0%
Female	16.9%	5.1%	4.9%	4.4%	16.5%	2.4%

Capabilities
The armed forces are refocusing on border security, having drawn down their decade-long direct support for the National Civil Police in 2018 as part of the inter-agency Plan Fortaleza. Guatemala maintains an inter-agency task force with neighbouring El Salvador and Honduras. The army has trained with US SOUTHCOM, as well as with regional partners such as Brazil and Colombia. Training for conventional military operations is limited by budget constraints and the long focus on providing internal security. Guatemala maintains a company-sized contingent as part of the UN mission to the DRC, but otherwise lacks the capability for significant international deployments. The equipment inventory is small and ageing. The US has provided several soft-skinned vehicles to the army, while the air force has undertaken some modest recapitalisation of its fixed-wing transport and surveillance capacity. Funding is being sought for additional maritime- and air-patrol capabilities. Aside from limited maintenance facilities, the country has no domestic defence industry.

ACTIVE 18,050 (Army 15,550 Navy 1,500 Air 1,000)
Paramilitary 25,000

RESERVE 63,850 (Navy 650 Air 900 Armed Forces 62,300)

(National Armed Forces are combined; the army provides log spt for navy and air force)

ORGANISATIONS BY SERVICE

Army 15,550
15 Military Zones
FORCES BY ROLE
SPECIAL FORCES
　1 SF bde (1 SF bn, 1 trg bn)
　1 SF bde (1 SF coy, 1 ranger bn)
　1 SF mtn bde
MANOEUVRE
　Light
　1 (strategic reserve) mech bde (1 inf bn, 1 cav regt, 1 log coy)
　6 inf bde (1 inf bn)
　Air Manoeuvre
　1 AB bde with (2 AB bn)
　Amphibious
　1 mne bde
　Other
　1 (Presidential) gd bde (1 gd bn, 1 MP bn, 1 CSS coy)
COMBAT SUPPORT
　1 engr comd (1 engr bn, 1 construction bn)
　2 MP bde with (1 MP bn)

Reserves
FORCES BY ROLE
MANOEUVRE
　Light
　ε19 inf bn
EQUIPMENT BY TYPE
ARMOURED FIGHTING VEHICLES
　RECCE (7 M8 in store)
　APC 47
　　APC (T) 10 M113 (5 more in store)
　　APC (W) 37: 30 *Armadillo*; 7 V-100 *Commando*
ANTI-TANK/ANTI-INFRASTRUCTURE
　RCL 120+: **75mm** M20; **105mm** 64 M-1974 FMK-1 (ARG); **106mm** 56 M40A1
ARTILLERY 149
　TOWED **105mm** 76: 12 M101; 8 M102; 56 M-56
　MOR 73: **81mm** 55 M1; **107mm** (12 M30 in store); **120mm** 18 ECIA
AIR DEFENCE • GUNS • TOWED 32: **20mm** 16 GAI-D01; 16 M-55

Navy 1,500
EQUIPMENT BY TYPE
PATROL AND COASTAL COMBATANTS 10
　PB 10: 6 *Cutlass*; 1 *Dauntless*; 1 *Kukulkan* (US *Broadsword* 32m); 2 *Utatlan* (US *Sewart*)

AMPHIBIOUS • LANDING CRAFT • LCP 2 *Machete*
LOGISTICS AND SUPPORT • AXS 3

Marines 650 reservists
FORCES BY ROLE
MANOEUVRE
　Amphibious
　2 mne bn(-)

Air Force 1,000
2 air comd
FORCES BY ROLE
FIGHTER/GROUND ATTACK/ISR
　1 sqn with A-37B *Dragonfly*
TRANSPORT
　1 sqn with BT-67; Beech 90/200 *King Air*
　1 (tactical support) sqn with Cessna 206
TRAINING
　1 sqn with T-35B *Pillan*
TRANSPORT HELICOPTER
　1 sqn with Bell 212 (armed); Bell 407GX; Bell 412 *Twin Huey* (armed); UH-1H *Iroquois*
EQUIPMENT BY TYPE
Serviceability of ac is less than 50%
AIRCRAFT 1 combat capable
　ATK 1 A-37B *Dragonfly*
　TPT • **Light** 16: 1 Beech 90 *King Air*; 2 Beech 200 *King Air*; 4 BT-67; 2 Cessna 206; 4 Cessna 208B; 3 Cessna 210 *Centurion*; (4 IAI-201 *Arava*; 5 Cessna R172K *Hawk* XP in store)
　TRG 4 T-35B *Pillan*† (7 PC-7 *Turbo Trainer** in store)
HELICOPTERS
　MRH 4: 2 Bell 412 *Twin Huey* (armed); 2 Bell 407GX
　TPT • **Light** 13: 2 Bell 205 (UH-1H *Iroquois*); 5 Bell 206B *Jet Ranger*; 6 Bell 212 (armed) (2 Bell 206B *Jet Ranger*; 4 Bell 212 (armed) in store)

Tactical Security Group
Air Military Police

Paramilitary 25,000

National Civil Police 25,000
FORCES BY ROLE
SPECIAL FORCES
　1 SF bn
MANOEUVRE
　Other
　1 (integrated task force) paramilitary unit (incl mil and treasury police)

DEPLOYMENT

CENTRAL AFRICAN REPUBLIC: UN • MINUSCA 2; 1 obs
DEMOCRATIC REPUBLIC OF THE CONGO: UN • MONUSCO 150; 5 obs; 1 SF coy
LEBANON: UN • UNIFIL 2
MALI: UN • MINUSMA 2
SOUTH SUDAN: UN • UNMISS 4; 3 obs
SUDAN: UN • UNISFA 1; 2 obs

Guyana GUY

Guyanese Dollar G$		2017	2018	2019
GDP	G$	749bn	780bn	
	US$	3.56bn	3.64bn	
per capita	US$	4,578	4,649	
Growth	%	2.1	3.4	
Inflation	%	2.0	1.3	
Def bdgt	G$	12.0bn	12.1bn	
	US$	57.1m	56.2m	
US$1=G$		210.26	214.52	

Population 740,685

Age	0–14	15–19	20–24	25–29	30–64	65 plus
Male	12.9%	5.7%	5.4%	4.4%	19.5%	2.6%
Female	12.5%	5.4%	5.1%	4.0%	18.7%	3.8%

Capabilities

The Guyana Defence Force (GDF) has minimal conventional military capability, and its activities are focused on border control and support for law-enforcement operations and assistance to the civil power. The government is planning to restructure the GDF to improve its flexibility. Guyana is part of the Caribbean Basin Security Initiative. It has close military ties with Brazil, with whom it cooperates on border security via annual military regional exchange meetings. The country also has bilateral agreements with France, China and the US, who provide military training and equipment. The GDF trains regularly and takes part in bilateral and multinational exercises. A training initiative with China helped two Guyanese pilots to acquire air-combat certification although Guyana has no combat aircraft in its inventory. There is no expeditionary or associated logistics capability. Equipment is mostly composed of second-hand platforms, mainly of Brazilian and North American manufacture. The air force has expanded its modest air-transport capabilities with some second-hand utility aircraft. Apart from maintenance facilities, there is no defence-industrial sector.

ACTIVE 3,400 (Army 3,000 Navy 200 Air 200)
Active numbers combined Guyana Defence Force

RESERVE 670 (Army 500 Navy 170)

ORGANISATIONS BY SERVICE

Army 3,000
FORCES BY ROLE
SPECIAL FORCES
 1 SF coy
MANOEUVRE
 Light
 1 inf bn
 Other
 1 (Presidential) gd bn
COMBAT SUPPORT
 1 arty coy
 1 (spt wpn) cbt spt coy
 1 engr coy
EQUIPMENT BY TYPE
ARMOURED FIGHTING VEHICLES
 RECCE 9: 6 EE-9 *Cascavel* (reported); 3 S52 *Shorland*

ARTILLERY 54
 TOWED 130mm 6 M-46†
 MOR 48: **81mm** 12 L16A1; **82mm** 18 M-43; **120mm** 18 M-43

Navy 200
EQUIPMENT BY TYPE
PATROL AND COASTAL COMBATANTS 5
 PCO 1 *Essequibo* (ex-UK *River*)
 PB 4 *Barracuda* (ex-US Type-44)

Air Force 200
FORCES BY ROLE
TRANSPORT
 1 unit with Bell 206; Cessna 206; Y-12 (II)
EQUIPMENT BY TYPE
AIRCRAFT • TPT • Light 4: 2 BN-2 *Islander*; 1 Cessna 206; 1 Y-12 (II)
HELICOPTERS
 MRH 1 Bell 412 *Twin Huey*†
 TPT • Light 2 Bell 206

Haiti HTI

Haitian Gourde G		2017	2018	2019
GDP	G	552bn	640bn	
	US$	8.61bn	9.72bn	
per capita	US$	784	874	
Growth	%	1.2	2.0	
Inflation	%	14.7	13.3	
Def bdgt	G	435m	514m	
	US$	6.8m	7.8m	
FMA (US)	US$	1.2m	0m	0m
US$1=G		64.12	65.82	

Population 10,788,440

Age	0–14	15–19	20–24	25–29	30–64	65 plus
Male	16.1%	5.4%	5.2%	4.6%	16.4%	1.9%
Female	16.2%	5.4%	5.2%	4.6%	16.9%	2.4%

Capabilities

Haiti possesses almost no military capability. A small coastguard is tasked with maritime security and law enforcement and, while the country's embryonic army is hoped to eventually number around 5,000 personnel, it is still in the very early stages of development. Plans for military expansion were outlined in the 2015 White Paper on Security and Defence. A road map for the re-establishment of the Haitian armed forces was distributed to ministers in early 2017 and in March 2018 an army high command was established. The army's primary missions will reportedly be disaster relief and border security. Haiti is a member of the Caribbean Community and participates in US Southern Command's annual *Tradewinds* disaster-response exercise. Ecuador and Brazil have both pledged to assist with training the new army. The plan is to recruit 500 troops initially, focusing on engineering and medical capability for disaster-relief tasks. However, it is unclear whether the current budgetary provision is sufficient to fund the level of capability required. There is no heavy military equipment, and no defence industry.

ACTIVE 150 (Army 150) Paramilitary 50

ORGANISATIONS BY SERVICE

Army 150

Paramilitary 50

Coast Guard ε50
EQUIPMENT BY TYPE
PATROL AND COASTAL COMBATANTS • PB 8: 5
Dauntless; 3 3812-VCF

Honduras HND

Honduran Lempira L		2017	2018	2019
GDP	L	540bn	576bn	
	US$	23.0bn	23.8bn	
per capita	US$	2,766	2,829	
Growth	%	4.8	3.5	
Inflation	%	3.9	4.4	
Def bdgt [a]	L	6.28bn	7.96bn	
	US$	267m	329m	
FMA (US)	US$	4.5m	0m	0m
US$1=L		23.49	24.18	

[a] Defence & national security budget

Population 9,182,766

Age	0–14	15–19	20–24	25–29	30–64	65 plus
Male	16.5%	5.5%	5.2%	4.6%	16.7%	1.9%
Female	15.8%	5.3%	5.0%	4.4%	16.6%	2.5%

Capabilities

The armed forces have been deployed in support of the police to combat organised crime and narcotics trafficking since 2011; this mission remains their prime focus. Honduras's 2014–18 strategy document outlines internal security as its primary concern. Honduras maintains diplomatic relations with Taiwan, which has supplied surplus military equipment, and also receives US security assistance, though this has been reduced in recent years. Honduras hosts a US base at the Soto Cano airfield. Honduras is also part of a tri-national border-security task force with neighbouring El Salvador and Guatemala, and a separate border-security force with Nicaragua. Training remains focused on internal- and border-security requirements, and training for conventional military action is limited. Honduras does not have the capability to maintain substantial overseas deployments. Most equipment is ageing, with serviceability in doubt. The air force and Public Order Military Police are working with Israel to modernise their inventories. Apart from limited maintenance facilities, the country has no domestic defence industry.

ACTIVE 14,950 (Army 7,300 Navy 1,350 Air 2,300 Military Police 4,000) Paramilitary 8,000

RESERVE 60,000 (Joint 60,000; Ex-servicemen registered)

ORGANISATIONS BY SERVICE

Army 7,300
FORCES BY ROLE
SPECIAL FORCES
  1 (special tac) spec ops gp (2 spec ops bn, 1 inf bn; 1 AB bn; 1 arty bn)
MANOEUVRE
  Mechanised
  1 inf bde (1 mech cav regt, 1 inf bn, 1 arty bn)
  Light
  1 inf bde (3 inf bn, 1 arty bn)
  3 inf bde (2 inf bn)
  1 indep inf bn
  Other
  1 (Presidential) gd coy
COMBAT SUPPORT
  1 engr bn
  1 sigs bn
AIR DEFENCE
  1 ADA bn
EQUIPMENT BY TYPE
ARMOURED FIGHTING VEHICLES
  LT TK 12 FV101 *Scorpion*
  RECCE 57: 1 FV105 *Sultan* (CP); 3 FV107 *Scimitar*; 40 FV601 *Saladin*; 13 RBY-1
ANTI-TANK/ANTI-INFRASTRUCTURE
  RCL 50+: **84mm** *Carl Gustav*; **106mm** 50 M40A1
ARTILLERY 118+
  TOWED 28: **105mm**: 24 M102; **155mm**: 4 M198
  MOR 90+: **81mm**; **120mm** 60 FMK-2; **160mm** 30 M-66
AIR DEFENCE • GUNS **20mm** 48: 24 M-55A2; 24 TCM-20

Navy 1,350
EQUIPMENT BY TYPE
PATROL AND COASTAL COMBATANTS 17
  PB 17: 2 *Lempira* (Damen Stan Patrol 4207 – leased); 1 *Chamelecon* (Swiftships 85); 1 *Tegucilgalpa* (US *Guardian* 32m); 4 *Guanaja* (ex-US Type-44); 3 *Guaymuras* (Swiftships 105); 5 *Nacaome* (Swiftships 65); 1 *Rio Coco* (US PB Mk III)
AMPHIBIOUS • LANDING CRAFT 4
  LCU 2: 1 *Gracias a Dios* (COL *Golfo de Tribuga*); 1 *Punta Caxinas*
  LCM 2 LCM 8

Marines 1,000
FORCES BY ROLE
MANOEUVRE
  Amphibious
  2 mne bn

Air Force 2,300
FORCES BY ROLE
FIGHTER/GROUND ATTACK
  1 sqn with A-37B *Dragonfly*
  1 sqn with F-5E/F *Tiger* II

GROUND ATTACK/ISR/TRAINING
  1 unit with Cessna 182 *Skylane*; EMB-312 *Tucano*; MXT-7-180 *Star Rocket*
TRANSPORT
  1 sqn with Beech 200 *King Air*; C-130A *Hercules*; Cessna 185/210; IAI-201 *Arava*; PA-42 *Cheyenne*; *Turbo Commander* 690
  1 VIP flt with PA-31 *Navajo*; Bell 412EP/SP *Twin Huey*
TRANSPORT HELICOPTER
  1 sqn with Bell 205 (UH-1H *Iroquois*); Bell 412SP *Twin Huey*
EQUIPMENT BY TYPE
AIRCRAFT 17 combat capable
  FTR 11: 9 F-5E *Tiger II†*; 2 F-5F *Tiger II†*
  ATK 6 A-37B *Dragonfly*
  TPT 17: **Medium** 1 C-130A *Hercules*; **Light** 16: 1 Beech 200 *King Air*; 2 Cessna 172 *Skyhawk*; 2 Cessna 182 *Skylane*; 1 Cessna 185; 2 Cessna 208B *Grand Caravan*; 2 Cessna 210; 1 EMB-135 *Legacy* 600; 1 IAI-201 *Arava*; 1 L-410 (leased); 1 PA-31 *Navajo*; 1 PA-42 *Cheyenne*; 1 *Turbo Commander* 690
  TRG 16: 9 EMB-312 *Tucano*; 7 MXT-7-180 *Star Rocket*
HELICOPTERS
  MRH 8: 1 Bell 412EP *Twin Huey* (VIP); 5 Bell 412SP *Twin Huey*; 2 Hughes 500
  TPT • **Light** 7: 6 Bell 205 (UH-1H *Iroquois*); 1 H125 *Ecureuil*
AIR-LAUNCHED MISSILES • AAM • IR *Shafrir‡*

Military Police 4,000
FORCES BY ROLE
MANOEUVRE
  Other
    8 sy bn

Paramilitary 8,000

Public Security Forces 8,000
Ministry of Public Security and Defence; 11 regional comd

DEPLOYMENT
WESTERN SAHARA: UN • MINURSO 12 obs

FOREIGN FORCES
United States US Southern Command: 380; 1 avn bn with CH-47F *Chinook*; UH-60 *Black Hawk*

Jamaica JAM

Jamaican Dollar J$		2017	2018	2019
GDP	J$	1.90tr	1.99tr	
	US$	14.8bn	15.4bn	
per capita	US$	5,193	5,393	
Growth	%	0.7	1.2	
Inflation	%	4.4	3.4	
Def bdgt	J$	18.2bn	29.4bn	
	US$	142m	228m	
US$1=J$		128.44	128.99	

Population 2,812,090

Age	0–14	15–19	20–24	25–29	30–64	65 plus
Male	13.2%	4.8%	4.5%	3.8%	19.0%	4.1%
Female	12.8%	4.6%	4.5%	3.9%	20.1%	4.6%

Capabilities
The Jamaica Defence Force (JDF) is focused principally on maritime and internal security, including support to police operations. Jamaica maintains military ties, including for training purposes, with Canada, the UK and the US and is a member of the Caribbean Community. The defence force participates in US SOUTHCOM's annual *Tradewinds* disaster-response exercise. In March 2018, financed by Canada, the JDF established the Caribbean Special Tactics Centre, which will train special-forces units from Jamaica and other Caribbean nations. The JDF does not have any capacity to support independent deployment abroad. Funds have been allocated to procure new vehicles and helicopters, and a new *King Air* maritime-patrol aircraft has arrived. Other than limited maintenance facilities, Jamaica has no domestic defence industry.

ACTIVE 3,950 (Army 3,400 Coast Guard 300 Air 250)
(combined Jamaican Defence Force)

RESERVE 980 (Army 900 Coast Guard 60 Air 20)

ORGANISATIONS BY SERVICE

Army 3,400
FORCES BY ROLE
MANOEUVRE
  Mechanised
    1 (PMV) lt mech inf coy
  Light
    2 inf bn
COMBAT SUPPORT
  1 engr regt (4 engr sqn)
COMBAT SERVICE SUPPORT
  1 spt bn (1 MP coy, 1 med coy, 1 log coy, 1 tpt coy)
EQUIPMENT BY TYPE
ARMOURED FIGHTING VEHICLES
  AUV 12 *Bushmaster*
ARTILLERY • MOR 81mm 12 L16A1

Reserves
FORCES BY ROLE
MANOEUVRE
  Light
    1 inf bn

Coast Guard 300
EQUIPMENT BY TYPE
PATROL AND COASTAL COMBATANTS 10
PBF 3
PB 7: 2 *County* (Damen Stan Patrol 4207); 4 *Dauntless*; 1 *Paul Bogle* (US 31m)

Air Wing 250
Plus National Reserve
FORCES BY ROLE
MARITIME PATROL/TRANSPORT
1 flt with Beech 350ER *King Air*; BN-2A *Defender*; Cessna 210M *Centurion*
SEARCH & RESCUE/TRANSPORT HELICOPTER
1 flt with Bell 407
1 flt with Bell 412EP
TRAINING
1 unit with Bell 206B3; DA40-180FP *Diamond Star*
EQUIPMENT BY TYPE
AIRCRAFT
MP 1 Beech 350ER *King Air*
TPT • Light 4: 1 BN-2A *Defender*; 1 Cessna 210M *Centurion*; 2 DA40-180FP *Diamond Star*
HELICOPTERS
MRH 2 Bell 412EP
TPT • Light 7: 2 Bell 206B3 *Jet Ranger*; 3 Bell 407; 2 Bell 429

Mexico MEX

Mexican Peso NP		2017	2018	2019
GDP	NP	21.8tr	23.5tr	
	US$	1.15tr	1.20tr	
per capita	US$	9,319	9,614	
Growth	%	2.0	2.2	
Inflation	%	6.0	4.8	
Def bdgt [a]	NP	86.4bn	102bn	
	US$	4.57bn	5.23bn	
FMA (US)	US$	5m	0m	0m
US$1=NP		18.93	19.56	

[a] National security expenditure

Population	125,959,205					
Age	0–14	15–19	20–24	25–29	30–64	65 plus
Male	13.6%	4.5%	4.3%	4.1%	19.3%	3.2%
Female	13.0%	4.3%	4.3%	4.1%	21.3%	4.0%

Capabilities
Mexico has the most capable armed forces in Central America. They have been committed to providing internal-security support within Mexico for nearly a decade. As articulated by the Program for National Security 2014–18, the armed forces are tasked with defending state sovereignty and territorial integrity, internal security and extending aid to civilian authorities. They are focused on tackling drugs cartels and other organised crime; the Military Police Corps has been expanded in recent years to allow it to take on a wider role as part of this tasking. Mexico has a close defence relationship with the US, which has provided equipment and training to Mexican forces under the Mérida Initiative, as well as via bilateral programmes via the Pentagon. There has been a training focus on internal-security tasks and low-intensity warfare. The armed forces have a moderate capability to deploy independently, but do not do so in significant numbers. There are plans to recapitalise diverse and ageing conventional combat platforms across all three services. State-owned shipyards have produced patrol craft for the navy and will produce modules for the frigates currently under construction. Army factories have produced light armoured utility vehicles for domestic use. Airbus Helicopters operates a manufacturing plant in Querétaro.

ACTIVE 277,150 (Army 208,350 Navy 60,300 Air 8,500) **Paramilitary 58,900**
Conscript liability 12 months (partial, selection by ballot) from age 18, serving on Saturdays; voluntary for women; conscripts allocated to reserves.

RESERVE 81,500 (National Military Service)

ORGANISATIONS BY SERVICE

Space
EQUIPMENT BY TYPE
SATELLITES • COMMUNICATIONS 2 *Mexsat*

Army 208,350
12 regions (total: 46 army zones)
FORCES BY ROLE
SPECIAL FORCES
1 (1st) SF bde (5 SF bn)
1 (2nd) SF bde (7 SF bn)
1 (3rd) SF bde (4 SF bn)
MANOEUVRE
Reconnaissance
3 (2nd, 3rd & 4th Armd) mech bde (2 armd recce bn, 2 lt mech bn, 1 arty bn, 1 (Canon) AT gp)
25 mot recce regt
Light
1 (1st) inf corps (1 (1st Armd) mech bde (2 armd recce bn, 2 lt mech bn, 1 arty bn, 1 (Canon) AT gp), 3 (2nd, 3rd & 6th) inf bde (each: 3 inf bn, 1 arty regt, 1 (Canon) AT gp), 1 cbt engr bde (3 engr bn))
3 (1st, 4th & 5th) indep lt inf bde (2 lt inf bn, 1 (Canon) AT gp)
92 indep inf bn
25 indep inf coy
Air Manoeuvre
1 para bde with (1 (GAFE) SF gp, 3 bn, 1 (Canon) AT gp)
Other
1 (Presidential) gd corps (1 SF gp, 1 mech inf bde (2 inf bn, 1 aslt bn), 1 mne bn (Navy), 1 cbt engr bn, 1 MP bde (3 bn, 1 special ops anti-riot coy))
COMBAT SUPPORT
1 indep arty regt
10 MP bde (3 MP bn)
EQUIPMENT BY TYPE
ARMOURED FIGHTING VEHICLES
RECCE 255: 19 DN-5 *Toro*; 127 ERC-90F1 *Lynx* (7 trg); 40 M8; 37 MAC-1; 32 VBL

IFV 390 DNC-1 (mod AMX-VCI)
APC 309
  APC (T) 73: 40 HWK-11; 33 M5A1 half-track
  APC (W) 236: 95 BDX; 16 DN-4; 2 DN-6; 28 LAV-100 (*Pantera*); 26 LAV-150 ST; 25 MOWAG *Roland*; 44 VCR (3 amb; 5 cmd post)
AUV 397: 150 DN-XI; 247 *Sandcat*
ENGINEERING & MAINTENANCE VEHICLES
  ARV 7: 3 M32 *Recovery Sherman*; 4 VCR ARV
ANTI-TANK/ANTI-INFRASTRUCTURE
  MSL • SP 8 VBL with *Milan*
  RCL • 106mm 1,187+ M40A1 (incl some SP)
  GUNS 37mm 30 M3
ARTILLERY 1,390
  TOWED 123: **105mm** 123: 40 M101; 40 M-56; 16 M2A1, 14 M3; 13 NORINCO M90
  MOR 1,267: **81mm** 1,100: 400 M1; 400 Brandt; 300 SB
  120mm 167: 75 Brandt; 60 M-65; 32 RT-61
AIR DEFENCE • GUNS • TOWED 80: **12.7mm** 40 M55; **20mm** 40 GAI-B01

Navy 60,300

Two Fleet Commands: Gulf (6 zones), Pacific (11 zones)

EQUIPMENT BY TYPE
PATROL AND COASTAL COMBATANTS 127
  PSOH 6:
    4 *Oaxaca* with 1 76mm gun (capacity 1 AS565MB *Panther* hel)
    2 *Oaxaca* (mod) with 1 57mm gun (capacity 1 AS565MB *Panther* hel)
  PCOH 16:
    4 *Durango* with 1 57mm gun (capacity 1 Bo-105 hel)
    4 *Holzinger* (capacity 1 MD-902 *Explorer*)
    3 *Sierra* with 1 57mm gun (capacity 1 MD-902 *Explorer*)
    5 *Uribe* (ESP *Halcon*) (capacity 1 Bo-105 hel)
  PCO 9: 6 *Valle* (US *Auk* MSF) with 1 76mm gun; 3 *Valle* (US *Auk* MSF) with 1 76mm gun
  PCGH 1 *Huracan* (ISR *Aliya*) with 4 single lnchr with *Gabriel* II AShM, 1 *Phalanx* CIWS
  PCC 2 *Democrata*
  PBF 73: 6 *Acuario*; 2 *Acuario* B; 48 *Polaris* (SWE CB90); 17 *Polaris* II (SWE IC 16M)
  PB 20: 3 *Azteca*; 3 *Cabo* (US *Cape Higgon*); 2 *Lago*; 2 *Punta* (US *Point*); 10 *Tenochtitlan* (Damen Stan Patrol 4207)
AMPHIBIOUS • LS • LST 4: 2 *Monte Azules* with 1 hel landing platform; 2 *Papaloapan* (ex-US *Newport*) with 4 76mm guns, 1 hel landing platform
LOGISTICS AND SUPPORT 25
  AGOR 3 *Altair* (ex-US *Robert D. Conrad*)
  AGS 7: 3 *Arrecife*; 1 *Onjuku*; 1 *Rio Hondo*; 1 *Rio Tuxpan*
  AK 1 *Rio Suchiate*
  AOTL 2 *Aguascalientes*
  AP 2: 1 *Isla Maria Madre* (Damen Fast Crew Supplier 5009); 1 *Nautla*
  ATF 4 *Otomi* with 1 76mm gun
  ATS 4 *Kukulkan*
  AX 2 *Huasteco* (also serve as troop transport, supply and hospital ships)
  AXS 1 *Cuauhtemoc* with 2 65mm saluting guns

Naval Aviation 1,250

FORCES BY ROLE
MARITIME PATROL
  5 sqn with Cessna 404 *Titan*; MX-7 *Star Rocket*; Lancair IV-P; T-6C+ *Texan* II
  1 sqn with Beech 350ER *King Air*; C-212PM *Aviocar*; CN235-300 MPA *Persuader*
  1 sqn with L-90 *Redigo*
TRANSPORT
  1 sqn with An-32B *Cline*
  1 (VIP) sqn with DHC-8 *Dash 8*; Learjet 24; *Turbo Commander* 1000
TRANSPORT HELICOPTER
  2 sqn with AS555 *Fennec*; AS565MB/AS565MBe *Panther*; MD-902
  2 sqn with Bo-105 CBS-5
  5 sqn with Mi-17-1V/V-5 *Hip*
TRAINING
  1 sqn with Z-242L; Z-143Lsi
EQUIPMENT BY TYPE
AIRCRAFT 3 combat capable
  MP 6 CN235-300 MPA *Persuader*
  ISR 4: 2 C-212PM *Aviocar*; 2 Z-143Lsi
  TPT 32: **Light** 30: 5 Beech 350ER *King Air* (4 used for ISR); 3 Beech 350i *King Air*; 4 C295M; 2 C295W; 1 Cessna 404 *Titan*; 1 DHC-8 *Dash 8*; 6 Lancair IV-P; 2 Learjet 31A; 1 Learjet 60; 5 *Turbo Commander* 1000; **PAX** 2: 1 CL-605 *Challenger*; 1 Gulfstream 550
  TRG 47: 3 L-90TP *Redigo**; 4 MX-7 *Star Rocket*; 13 T-6C+ *Texan* II; 27 Z-242L
HELICOPTERS
  MRH 29: 2 AS555 *Fennec*; 4 MD-500E; 19 Mi-17-1V *Hip*; 4 Mi-17V-5 *Hip*
  SAR 14: 4 AS565MB *Panther*; 10 AS565MBe *Panther*
  TPT 27: **Heavy** 3 H225M *Caracal*; **Medium** 10 UH-60M *Black Hawk*; **Light** 14: 1 AW109SP; 5 MD-902 (SAR role); 8 S-333
  TRG 4 Schweizer 300C

Marines 21,500 (Expanding to 26,560)

FORCES BY ROLE
SPECIAL FORCES
  3 SF unit
MANOEUVRE
  Light
    32 inf bn(-)
  Air Manoeuvre
    1 AB bn
  Amphibious
    1 amph bde (4 inf bn, 1 amph bn, 1 arty gp)
  Other
    1 (Presidential) gd bn (included in army above)
COMBAT SERVICE SUPPORT
  2 spt bn
EQUIPMENT BY TYPE
ARMOURED FIGHTING VEHICLES
  APC • APC (W) 29: 3 BTR-60 (APC-60); 26 BTR-70 (APC-70)

ANTI-TANK/ANTI-INFRASTRUCTURE
  RCL **106mm** M40A1
ARTILLERY 22+
  TOWED 105mm 16 M-56
  MRL 122mm 6 Firos-25
  MOR 81mm some
AIR DEFENCE • SAM • Point-defence 9K38 *Igla* (SA-18 *Grouse*)

Air Force 8,500

FORCES BY ROLE
GROUND ATTACK/ISR
  4 sqn with T-6C+ *Texan* II
  1 sqn with PC-7/PC-9M
ISR/AEW
  1 sqn with Beech 350ER *King Air*; EMB-145AEW *Erieye*; EMB-145RS; SA-2-37B; SA-227-BC *Metro* III (C-26B)
TRANSPORT
  1 sqn with C295M; PC-6B
  1 sqn with B-737; Beech 90
  1 sqn with C-27J *Spartan*; C-130E/K-30 *Hercules*; L-100-30
  5 (liaison) sqn with Cessna 182/206
  1 (anti-narcotic spraying) sqn with Bell 206; Cessna T206H;
  1 (Presidential) gp with AS332L *Super Puma*; AW109SP; B-737; B-757; B-787; Gulfstream 150/450/550; H225; Learjet 35A; Learjet 36; *Turbo Commander* 680
  1 (VIP) gp with B-737; Beech 200 *King Air*; Beech 350i *King Air*; Cessna 501/680 *Citation*; CL-605 *Challenger*; Gulfstream 550; Learjet 35A; Learjet 45; S-70A-24
TRAINING
  1 sqn with Cessna 182
  1 sqn with PC-7; T-6C+ *Texan* II
  1 sqn with Beech F33C *Bonanza*; Grob G120TP; SF-260EU
TRANSPORT HELICOPTER
  4 sqn with Bell 206B; Bell 212; Bell 407GX
  1 sqn with MD-530MF/MG
  1 sqn with Mi-17 *Hip*
  1 sqn with H225M *Caracal*; Bell 412EP *Twin Huey*; S-70A-24 *Black Hawk*
  1 sqn with UH-60M *Black Hawk*
ISR UAV
  1 unit with *Hermes* 450; S4 *Ehécatl*

EQUIPMENT BY TYPE
AIRCRAFT 56 combat capable
  ISR 8: 2 Cessna 501 *Citation*; 2 SA-2-37A; 4 SA-227-BC *Metro* III (C-26B)
  ELINT 8: 6 Beech 350ER *King Air*; 2 EMB-145RS
  AEW&C 1 EMB-145AEW *Erieye*
  TPT 112: **Medium** 9: 4 C-27J *Spartan*; 2 C-130E *Hercules*; 2 C-130K-30 *Hercules*; 1 L-100-30; **Light** 90: 2 Beech 90 *King Air*; 1 Beech 200 *King Air*; 1 Beech 350i *King Air*; 6 C295M; 59 Cessna 182; 3 Cessna 206; 8 Cessna T206H; 1 Cessna 501 *Citation*; 1 Cessna 680 *Citation*; 2 Learjet 35A; 1 Learjet 36; 1 Learjet 45XP; 3 PC-6B; 1 *Turbo Commander* 680; **PAX** 13: 6 B-737; 1 B-757; 1 B-787; 1 CL-605 *Challenger*; 2 Gulfstream 150; 1 Gulfstream 450; 1 Gulfstream 550
  TRG 144: 4 Beech F33C *Bonanza*; 25 Grob G120TP; 20 PC-7* (30 more possibly in store); 1 PC-9M*; 4 PT-17; 25 SF-260EU; 35 T-6C+ *Texan* II*
HELICOPTERS
  MRH 44: 15 Bell 407GXP; 11 Bell 412EP *Twin Huey*; 18 Mi-17 *Hip* H
  ISR 13: 4 MD-530MF; 9 MD-530MG
  TPT 125: **Heavy** 11 H225M *Caracal*; **Medium** 31: 3 AS332L *Super Puma* (VIP); 2 H225 (VIP); 2 Mi-8T *Hip*; 6 S-70A-24 *Black Hawk*; 18 UH-60M *Black Hawk* **Light** 83: 5 AW109SP; 45 Bell 206; 13 Bell 206B *Jet Ranger* II; 7 Bell 206L; 13 Bell 212
UNMANNED AERIAL VEHICLES • ISR 8: **Medium** 3 *Hermes* 450; **Light** 5 S4 *Ehécatl*
AIR-LAUNCHED MISSILES • AAM • IR AIM-9J *Sidewinder*

Paramilitary 62,900

Federal Police 41,000 (Incl 5,000 Gendarmerie)
Public Security Secretariat
EQUIPMENT BY TYPE
AIRCRAFT
  TPT 13: **Light** 7: 2 CN235M; 2 Cessna 182 *Skylane*; 1 Cessna 500 *Citation*; 2 *Turbo Commander* 695; **PAX** 6: 4 B-727; 1 *Falcon* 20; 1 Gulfstream II
HELICOPTERS
  MRH 3 Mi-17 *Hip* H
  TPT 27: **Medium** 13: 1 SA330J *Puma*; 6 UH-60L *Black Hawk*; 6 UH-60M *Black Hawk*; **Light** 14: 2 AS350B *Ecureuil*; 1 AS355 *Ecureuil* II; 6 Bell 206B; 5 H120 *Colibri*
UNMANNED AERIAL VEHICLES
  ISR 12: **Medium** 2 *Hermes* 900; **Light** 10 S4 *Ehécatl*

Federal Ministerial Police 4,500
EQUIPMENT BY TYPE
HELICOPTERS
  TPT • **Light** 25: 18 Bell 205 (UH-1H); 7 Bell 212
UNMANNED AERIAL VEHICLES
  ISR • **Heavy** 2 *Dominator* XP

Rural Defense Militia 17,400
FORCES BY ROLE
MANOEUVRE
Light
  13 inf unit
  13 (horsed) cav unit

Cyber

Press reports indicated that the cyberspace operations centre was completed within Sedena in 2017, the same year that Mexico published a National Cybersecurity Strategy. It is understood that another cyberspace operations centre will be created for the navy. Key documentation includes the 2013–18 National Defence Sector Programme, the 2013–18 National Development Programme and the 2014–18 National Security Programme.

DEPLOYMENT

CENTRAL AFRICAN REPUBLIC: UN • MINUSCA 1
MALI: UN • MINUSMA 3
WESTERN SAHARA: UN • MINURSO 4 obs

Nicaragua NIC

Nicaraguan Gold Cordoba Co		2017	2018	2019
GDP	Co	415bn	422bn	
	US$	13.8bn	13.4bn	
per capita	US$	2,221	2,127	
Growth	%	4.9	-4.0	
Inflation	%	3.9	5.9	
Def bdgt	Co	2.51bn	2.58bn	
	US$	83.5m	81.7m	
US$1=Co		30.05	31.55	

Population	6,085,213					
Age	0–14	15–19	20–24	25–29	30–64	65 plus
Male	13.6%	5.1%	5.3%	4.9%	17.4%	2.4%
Female	13.0%	5.0%	5.3%	5.1%	19.8%	3.0%

Capabilities

Nicaragua's armed forces are primarily a territorial light-infantry force, with a vestigial coastal-patrol capability. They are tasked with border and internal security, as well as with support for disaster-relief efforts and ecological protection. Nicaragua has training relationships with Russia and the US, as well as with neighbouring and regional states, including Cuba and Venezuela. Training is largely focused on key internal- and border-security tasks, although the mechanised brigade has received Russian training in conventional military operations. The armed forces do not undertake significant international deployments and lack the logistical support for large-scale military operations, although the strategic-reserve mechanised brigade can deploy internally. Equipment primarily consists of ageing Cold War-era platforms. Russia has supplied some second-hand tanks and armoured vehicles to help re-equip the mechanised brigade and has supported the establishment of a repair workshop to maintain the vehicles in-country. Barring maintenance facilities there is no domestic defence industry.

ACTIVE 12,000 (Army 10,000 Navy 800 Air 1,200)

ORGANISATIONS BY SERVICE

Army ε10,000
FORCES BY ROLE
SPECIAL FORCES
  1 SF bde (2 SF bn)
MANOEUVRE
  Mechanised
  1 mech inf bde (1 armd recce bn, 1 tk bn, 1 mech inf bn, 1 arty bn, 1 MRL bn, 1 AT coy)
  Light
  1 regional comd (3 lt inf bn)
  1 regional comd (2 lt inf bn; 1 arty bn)
  3 regional comd (2 lt inf bn)
  2 indep lt inf bn

Other
  1 comd regt (1 inf bn, 1 sy bn, 1 int unit, 1 sigs bn)
  1 (ecological) sy bn
COMBAT SUPPORT
  1 engr bn
COMBAT SERVICE SUPPORT
  1 med bn
  1 tpt regt
EQUIPMENT BY TYPE
ARMOURED FIGHTING VEHICLES
  MBT 82: 62 T-55 (65 more in store); 20 T-72B1
  LT TK (10 PT-76 in store)
  RECCE 20 BRDM-2
  IFV 17+ BMP-1
  APC • APC (W) 90+: 41 BTR-152 (61 more in store); 45 BTR-60 (15 more in store); 4+ BTR-70M
ENGINEERING & MAINTENANCE VEHICLES
  AEV T-54/T-55 AEV
  VLB TMM-3
ANTI-TANK/ANTI-INFRASTRUCTURE
  MSL
    SP 12 9P133 *Malyutka* (AT-3 *Sagger*)
    MANPATS 9K11 *Malyutka* (AT-3 *Sagger*)
  RCL 82mm B-10
  GUNS 281: **57mm** 174 ZIS-2; (90 more in store); **76mm** 83 ZIS-3; **100mm** 24 M-1944
ARTILLERY 766
  TOWED 12: **122mm** 12 D-30; (**152mm** 30 D-20 in store)
  MRL 151: **107mm** 33 Type-63: **122mm** 118: 18 BM-21 *Grad*; 100 *Grad* 1P (BM-21P) (single-tube rocket launcher, man portable)
  MOR 603: **82mm** 579; **120mm** 24 M-43; (**160mm** 4 M-160 in store)
AIR DEFENCE • SAM • Point-defence 9K36 *Strela*-3 (SA-14 *Gremlin*); 9K310 *Igla*-1 (SA-16 *Gimlet*); 9K32 *Strela*-2 (SA-7 *Grail*)‡

Navy ε800
EQUIPMENT BY TYPE
PATROL AND COASTAL COMBATANTS • PB 8: 3 *Dabur*; 4 *Rodman* 101, 1 *Zhuk*

Marines
FORCES BY ROLE
MANOEUVRE
  Amphibious
  1 mne bn

Air Force 1,200
FORCES BY ROLE
TRANSPORT
  1 sqn with An-26 *Curl*; Beech 90 *King Air*; Cessna U206; Cessna 404 *Titan* (VIP)
TRAINING
  1 unit with Cessna 172; PA-18 *Super Cub*; PA-28 *Cherokee*
TRANSPORT HELICOPTER
  1 sqn with Mi-17 *Hip* H (armed)
AIR DEFENCE
  1 gp with ZU-23

EQUIPMENT BY TYPE
AIRCRAFT
  TPT • **Light** 9: 3 An-26 *Curl*; 1 Beech 90 *King Air*; 1 Cessna 172; 1 Cessna U206; 1 Cessna 404 *Titan* (VIP); 2 PA-28 *Cherokee*
  TRG 2 PA-18 *Super Cub*
HELICOPTERS
  MRH 7 Mi-17 *Hip* H (armed)†
  TPT • **Medium** 2 Mi-171E
AIR DEFENCE • GUNS 23mm 18 ZU-23
AIR-LAUNCHED MISSILES • ASM 9M17 *Skorpion* (AT-2 *Swatter*)

Panama PAN

Panamanian Balboa B		2017	2018	2019
GDP	B	61.8bn	66.0bn	
	US$	61.8bn	66.0bn	
per capita	US$	15,089	15,877	
Growth	%	5.4	4.6	
Inflation	%	0.9	2.0	
Def bdgt [a]	B	746m	738m	
	US$	746m	738m	
FMA (US)	US$	2m	0m	0m
US$1=B		1.00	1.00	
[a] Public security expenditure				

Population		3,800,644				
Age	0–14	15–19	20–24	25–29	30–64	65 plus
Male	13.3%	4.3%	4.3%	4.0%	20.5%	3.9%
Female	12.8%	4.1%	4.1%	3.8%	20.2%	4.6%

Capabilities

Panama abolished its armed forces in 1990, but has a border service, a police force and an air/maritime service for low-level security tasks. The primary security focus is on the southern border with Colombia, and the majority of the border service is deployed there. Both Colombia and the US have provided training and support. Training is focused on internal and border security rather than conventional military operations and there is no capability to mount significant external deployments. None of Panama's security services maintain heavy military equipment, focusing instead on light transport, patrol and surveillance capabilities. Aside from limited maintenance facilities, the country has no domestic defence industry.

Paramilitary 26,000

ORGANISATIONS BY SERVICE

Paramilitary 26,000

National Border Service 4,000
FORCES BY ROLE
SPECIAL FORCES
  1 SF gp
MANOEUVRE
  Other
  1 sy bde (5 sy bn(-))
  1 indep sy bn

National Police Force 20,000
No hvy mil eqpt, small arms only
FORCES BY ROLE
SPECIAL FORCES
  1 SF unit
MANOEUVRE
  Other
  1 (presidential) gd bn(-)

National Aeronaval Service 2,000
FORCES BY ROLE
TRANSPORT
  1 sqn with C-212M *Aviocar*; Cessna 210; PA-31 *Navajo*; PA-34 *Seneca*
  1 (Presidential) flt with ERJ-135BJ; S-76C
TRAINING
  1 unit with Cessna 152; Cessna 172; T-35D *Pillan*
TRANSPORT HELICOPTER
  1 sqn with AW139; Bell 205; Bell 205 (UH-1H *Iroquois*); Bell 212; Bell 407; Bell 412EP; H145; MD-500E
EQUIPMENT BY TYPE
PATROL AND COASTAL COMBATANTS 17
  PCO 1 *Independencia* (ex-US *Balsam*)
  PCC 2 *Saettia*
  PB 14: 1 *Cocle*; 1 *Chiriqui* (ex-US PB MkIV); 2 *Panquiaco* (UK Vosper 31.5m); 5 3 *De Noviembre* (ex-US *Point*), 1 *Taboga*; 4 Type-200
AMPHIBIOUS • LANDING CRAFT • LCU 1 *General Estaban Huertas*
LOGISTICS AND SUPPORT • AG 2
AIRCRAFT
  TPT • **Light** 11: 1 DHC-6-400 *Twin Otter*; 3 C-212M *Aviocar*; 1 Cessna 152, 1 Cessna 172; 1 Cessna 210; 1 ERJ-135BJ; 1 PA-31 *Navajo*; 2 PA-34 *Seneca*
  TRG 6 T-35D *Pillan*
HELICOPTERS
  MRH 10: 8 AW139; 1 Bell 412EP; 1 MD-500E
  TPT • **Light** 21: 2 Bell 205; 13 Bell 205 (UH-1H *Iroquois*); 2 Bell 212; 2 Bell 407; 1 H145; 1 S-76C

Paraguay PRY

Paraguayan Guarani Pg		2017	2018	2019
GDP	Pg	219tr	238tr	
	US$	38.9bn	41.9bn	
per capita	US$	5,600	5,934	
Growth	%	4.8	4.4	
Inflation	%	3.6	4.0	
Def bdgt	Pg	1.53tr	1.78tr	1.77tr
	US$	273m	313m	
US$1=Pg		5618.94	5690.47	

Population 7,025,763

Age	0–14	15–19	20–24	25–29	30–64	65 plus
Male	13.3%	4.3%	4.3%	4.0%	20.5%	3.9%
Female	12.8%	4.1%	4.1%	3.8%	20.2%	4.6%

Capabilities

The armed forces are small by regional standards and the equipment inventory for all services is ageing and largely obsolete. The country faces internal challenges from insurgency and transnational organised crime, chiefly drug trafficking. Conscript numbers have reduced in recent years, and there are a significant number of higher ranks in the force structure. Key formations have long been under-strength. There has been some training support by the US, and the MOD reported in 2018 a training cooperation agreement with Germany. Paraguay has had a consistent if limited tradition of contributing to UN peacekeeping operations since 2001. There is only limited ability to self-sustain forces abroad, and no effective power-projection capacity. There is a small force of river-patrol craft, though some of the older of these have finally been retired. Armoured capability is very limited. While there are plans to acquire more modern equipment, including tanks, naval equipment and aircraft of all types for the air force, recent acquisitions of heavier materiel have been confined to small quantities of engineering and transport equipment. There is some local maintenance capacity but the effectiveness of systems is limited by age and while there is some R&D and manufacturing cooperation with local research institutes, there is no traditional defence-industrial base.

ACTIVE 11,900 (Army 7,400 Navy 2,700 Air 1,800)
Paramilitary 14,800
Conscript liability 12 months

RESERVE 164,500 (Joint 164,500)

ORGANISATIONS BY SERVICE

Army 7,400

Much of the Paraguayan army is maintained in a cadre state during peacetime; the nominal inf and cav divs are effectively only at coy strength. Active gp/regt are usually coy sized

FORCES BY ROLE
MANOEUVRE
  Light
    3 inf corps (total: 6 inf div(-), 3 cav div(-), 6 arty bty)
  Other
    1 (Presidential) gd regt (1 SF bn, 1 inf bn, 1 sy bn, 1 log gp)
COMBAT SUPPORT
  1 arty bde with (2 arty gp, 1 ADA gp)
  1 engr bde with (1 engr regt, 3 construction regt)
  1 sigs bn

Reserves
FORCES BY ROLE
MANOEUVRE
  Light
    14 inf regt (cadre)
    4 cav regt (cadre)
EQUIPMENT BY TYPE
ARMOURED FIGHTING VEHICLES
  RECCE 28 EE-9 *Cascavel*
  APC • APC (W) 12 EE-11 *Urutu*
ARTILLERY 99
  TOWED 105mm 19 M101
  MOR 81mm 80
AIR DEFENCE • GUNS 22:
  SP 20mm 3 M9 half track
  TOWED 19: 40mm 13 M1A1, 6 L/60

Navy 2,700

EQUIPMENT BY TYPE
PATROL AND COASTAL COMBATANTS 20
  PCR 1 *Itaipú*
  PBR 19: 1 *Capitan Cabral*; 2 *Capitan Ortiz* (ROC *Hai Ou*); 2 *Novatec*; 6 Type-701; 3 Croq 15; 5 others
AMPHIBIOUS • LANDING CRAFT • LCVP 3

Naval Aviation 100

FORCES BY ROLE
TRANSPORT
  1 (liaison) sqn with Cessna 150; Cessna 210 *Centurion*; Cessna 310; Cessna 401
TRANSPORT HELICOPTER
  1 sqn with AS350 *Ecureuil* (HB350 *Esquilo*)
EQUIPMENT BY TYPE
AIRCRAFT • TPT • Light 6: 2 Cessna 150; 1 Cessna 210 *Centurion*; 2 Cessna 310; 1 Cessna 401
HELICOPTERS • TPT • Light 2 AS350 *Ecureuil* (HB350 *Esquilo*)

Marines 700; 200 conscript (total 900)

FORCES BY ROLE
MANOEUVRE
  Amphibious
    3 mne bn(-)
ARTILLERY • TOWED 105mm 2 M101

Air Force 1,800

FORCES BY ROLE
GROUND ATTACK/ISR
  1 sqn with EMB-312 *Tucano**
TRANSPORT
  1 gp with C-212-200/400 *Aviocar*; DHC-6 *Twin Otter*
  1 VIP gp with Beech 58 *Baron*; Bell 427; Cessna U206 *Stationair*; Cessna 208B *Grand Caravan*; Cessna 210

Centurion; Cessna 402B; PA-32R *Saratoga* (EMB-721C *Sertanejo*); PZL-104 *Wilga* 80

TRAINING
  1 sqn with T-25 *Universal*; T-35A/B *Pillan*

TRANSPORT HELICOPTER
  1 gp with AS350 *Ecureuil* (HB350 *Esquilo*); Bell 205 (UH-1H *Iroquois*)

MANOEUVRE
  Air Manoeuvre
  1 AB bde

EQUIPMENT BY TYPE
AIRCRAFT 6 combat capable
  TPT • Light 18: 1 Beech 58 *Baron*; 4 C-212-200 *Aviocar*; 1 C-212-400 *Aviocar*; 2 Cessna 208B *Grand Caravan*; 1 Cessna 210 *Centurion*; 1 Cessna 310; 2 Cessna 402B; 2 Cessna U206 *Stationair*; 1 DHC-6 *Twin Otter*; 1 PA-32R *Saratoga* (EMB-721C *Sertanejo*); 2 PZL-104 *Wilga* 80
  TRG 21: 6 EMB-312 *Tucano**; 6 T-25 *Universal*; 6 T-35A *Pillan*; 3 T-35B *Pillan*
HELICOPTERS • TPT • Light 9: 3 AS350 *Ecureuil* (HB350 *Esquilo*); 5 Bell 205 (UH-1H *Iroquois*); 1 Bell 427 (VIP)

Paramilitary 14,800

  Special Police Service 10,800; 4,000 conscript (total 14,800)

DEPLOYMENT

CENTRAL AFRICAN REPUBLIC: UN • MINUSCA 1; 2 obs
CYPRUS: UN • UNFICYP 12
DEMOCRATIC REPUBLIC OF THE CONGO: UN • MONUSCO 1; 6 obs
SOUTH SUDAN: UN • UNMISS 1 obs

Peru PER

Peruvian Nuevo Sol NS		2017	2018	2019
GDP	NS	699bn	748bn	
	US$	214bn	229bn	
per capita	US$	6,732	7,118	
Growth	%	2.5	4.1	
Inflation	%	2.8	1.4	
Def bdgt	NS	7.06bn	7.51bn	7.47bn
	US$	2.17bn	2.30bn	
FMA (US)	US$	1m	0m	0m
US$1=NS		3.26	3.27	

Population	31,331,228					
Age	0–14	15–19	20–24	25–29	30–64	65 plus
Male	13.2%	4.4%	4.6%	4.3%	18.9%	3.6%
Female	12.8%	4.3%	4.6%	4.5%	20.7%	4.0%

Capabilities

Peru's armed forces have sufficient training and capabilities to fulfil domestic-security tasks, although they are limited by an increasingly ageing equipment inventory and economic constraints. The armed forces are primarily orientated towards preserving territorial integrity and security, focusing on counter-insurgency and counter-narcotics operations, while strengthening their disaster-relief capabilities. Peru maintains close military ties with Colombia. The two countries signed a cooperation agreement on air control, humanitarian assistance and counter-narcotics. The armed forces train regularly and take part in national and multilateral exercises. The armed forces are capable of independently deploying externally and contribute to UN missions abroad. There has been some modernisation of some air-combat assets, though not across the whole fleet. The navy is looking to acquire new corvettes and modernise its ageing submarines. The state-owned shipyard SIMA and aviation firm SEMAN are key players in Peru's defence industry, both in terms of manufacturing and maintenance. SEMAN completed in 2017 final assembly for the last Korean-designed KT-1 trainer, and the navy in 2018 commissioned the first locally built and South Korean-designed multipurpose vessel.

ACTIVE 81,000 (Army 47,500 Navy 24,000 Air 9,500)
Paramilitary 77,000
Conscript liability 12 months voluntary conscription for both males and females

RESERVE 188,000 (Army 188,000)

ORGANISATIONS BY SERVICE

Space
EQUIPMENT BY TYPE
SATELLITES • ISR PERÚSAT-1

Army 47,500
4 mil region

FORCES BY ROLE
SPECIAL FORCES
  1 (1st) SF bde (4 cdo bn, 1 airmob arty gp, 1 MP Coy, 1 cbt spt bn)
  1 (3rd) SF bde (3 cdo bn, 1 airmob arty gp, 1 MP coy)
  1 SF gp (regional troops)
MANOEUVRE
  Armoured
  1 (3rd) armd bde (2 tk bn, 1 armd inf bn, 1 arty gp, 1 AT coy, 1 AD gp, 1 engr bn, 1 cbt spt bn)
  1 (9th) armd bde (2 tk bn, 1 armd inf bn, 1 SP arty gp, 1 ADA gp)
  Mechanised
  1 (3rd) armd cav bde (3 mech cav bn, 1 mot inf bn, 1 arty gp, 1 AD gp, 1 engr bn, 1 cbt spt bn)
  1 (1st) cav bde (4 mech cav bn, 1 MP coy, 1 cbt spt bn)
  Light
  2 (2nd & 31st) mot inf bde (3 mot inf bn, 1 arty gp, 1 MP coy, 1 log bn)
  3 (1st, 7th & 32nd) inf bde (3 inf bn, 1 MP coy, 1 cbt spt bn)
  1 (4th) mtn bde (1 armd regt, 3 mot inf bn, 1 arty gp, 1 MP coy, 1 cbt spt bn)
  1 (5th) mtn bde (1 armd regt, 2 mot inf bn, 3 jungle coy, 1 arty gp, 1 MP coy, 1 cbt spt bn)
  1 (5th) jungle inf bde (1 SF gp, 3 jungle bn, 3 jungle coy, 1 jungle arty gp, 1 AT coy, 1 AD gp, 1 jungle engr bn)
  1 (6th) jungle inf bde (4 jungle bn, 1 engr bn, 1 MP coy, 1 cbt spt bn)
COMBAT SUPPORT
  1 (1st) arty bde (4 arty gp, 2 AD gp, 1 sigs gp)

1 (3rd) arty bde (4 arty gp, 1 AD gp, 1 sigs gp)
1 (22nd) engr bde (3 engr bn, 1 demining coy)
COMBAT SERVICE SUPPORT
1 (1st Multipurpose) spt bde
AVIATION
1 (1st) avn bde (1 atk hel/recce hel bn, 1 avn bn, 2 aslt hel/tpt hel bn)
AIR DEFENCE
1 AD gp (regional troops)
EQUIPMENT BY TYPE
ARMOURED FIGHTING VEHICLES
  MBT 165 T-55; (75† in store)
  LT TK 96 AMX-13
  RECCE 95: 30 BRDM-2; 15 Fiat 6616; 50 M9A1
  APC 295
    APC (T) 120 M113A1
    APC (W) 175: 150 UR-416; 25 Fiat 6614
ENGINEERING & MAINTENANCE VEHICLES
  ARV M578
ANTI-TANK-ANTI-INFRASTRUCTURE
  MSL
    SP 22 M1165A2 HMMWV with 9K135 *Kornet* E (AT-14 *Spriggan*)
    MANPATS 9K11 *Malyutka* (AT-3 *Sagger*); HJ-73C; 9K135 *Kornet* E (AT-14 *Spriggan*); Spike-ER
  RCL 106mm M40A1
ARTILLERY 1,011
  SP 155mm 12 M109A2
  TOWED 290: **105mm** 152: 44 M101; 24 M2A1; 60 M-56; 24 Model 56 pack howitzer; **122mm**; 36 D-30; **130mm** 36 M-46; **155mm** 66: 36 M114, 30 Model 50
  MRL 122mm 35: 22 BM-21 *Grad*; 13 Type-90B
  MOR 674+: **81mm/107mm** 350; **SP 107mm** 24 M106A1; **120mm** 300+ Brandt/Expal Model L
AIRCRAFT
  TPT • Light 16: 2 An-28 *Cash*; 3 An-32B *Cline*; 1 Beech 350 *King Air*; 1 Beech 1900D; 4 Cessna 152; 1 Cessna 208 *Caravan* I; 2 Cessna U206 *Stationair*; 1 PA-31T *Cheyenne* II; 1 PA-34 *Seneca*
  TRG 4 IL-103
HELICOPTERS
  MRH 7 Mi-17 *Hip* H
  TPT 36: **Heavy** (3 Mi-26T *Halo* in store); **Medium** 23 Mi-171Sh; **Light** 13: 2 AW109K2; 9 PZL Mi-2 *Hoplite*; 2 R-44
  TRG 5 F-28F
AIR DEFENCE
  SAM • Point-defence 9K36 *Strela*-3 (SA-14 *Gremlin*); 9K310 *Igla*-1 (SA-16 *Gimlet*); 9K32 *Strela*-2 (SA-7 *Grail*)‡
  GUNS 165
    SP 23mm 35 ZSU-23-4
    TOWED 23mm 130: 80 ZU-23-2; 50 ZU-23

Navy 24,000 (incl 1,000 Coast Guard)

Commands: Pacific, Lake Titicaca, Amazon River
EQUIPMENT BY TYPE
SUBMARINES • TACTICAL • SSK 6:
  4 *Angamos* (GER T-209/1200) with 8 single 533mm TT with AEG SST-4 HWT (of which 1 in refit)
  2 *Islay* (GER T-209/1100) with 8 single 533mm TT with AEG SUT-264 HWT

PRINCIPAL SURFACE COMBATANTS 7
  FRIGATES 7
    FFGHM 6:
      3 *Aguirre* (ex-ITA *Lupo*) with 8 single lnchr with Otomat Mk2 AShM, 1 octuple Mk29 lnchr with RIM-7P *Sea Sparrow* SAM, 2 triple 324mm ASTT with A244 LWT, 1 127mm gun (capacity 1 Bell 212 (AB-212)/SH-3D *Sea King*)
      3 *Carvajal* (mod ITA *Lupo*) with 8 single lnchr with Otomat Mk2 AShM, 1 octuple *Albatros* lnchr with *Aspide* SAM, 2 triple 324mm ASTT with A244 LWT, 1 127mm gun (capacity 1 Bell 212 (AB-212)/SH-3D *Sea King*)
    FFHM 1:
      1 *Aguirre* (ex-ITA *Lupo*) with 1 octuple Mk29 lnchr with RIM-7P *Sea Sparrow* SAM, 2 triple 324mm ASTT with A244 LWT, 1 127mm gun (capacity 1 Bell 212 (AB-212)/SH-3D *Sea King*) (is being fit with MM40 *Exocet* Block 3)
PATROL AND COASTAL COMBATANTS 12
  CORVETTES • FSG 6 *Velarde* (FRA PR-72 64m) with 4 single lnchr with MM38 *Exocet* AShM, 1 76mm gun
  PCR 6:
    2 *Amazonas* with 1 76mm gun
    2 *Manuel Clavero*
    2 *Marañon* with 2 76mm guns
AMPHIBIOUS
  PRINCIPAL AMPHIBIOUS SHIPS • LPD 1 *Pisco* (IDN *Makassar*) (capacity 2 LCM; 3 hels; 24 IFV; 450 troops)
  LANDING SHIPS • LST 2 *Paita* (capacity 395 troops) (ex-US *Terrebonne Parish*)
  LANDING CRAFT • UCAC 7 *Griffon* 2000TD (capacity 22 troops)
LOGISTICS AND SUPPORT 25
  AG 4 *Rio Napo*
  AGOR 1 *Humboldt*
  AGORH 1 *Carrasco*
  AGS 5: 1 *Carrasco* (ex-NLD *Dokkum*); 2 *Van Straelen*; 1 *La Macha*, 1 *Stiglich* (river survey vessel for the upper Amazon)
  AH 4 (river hospital craft)
  AO 2 *Noguera*
  AOR 1 *Mollendo*
  AORH 1 *Tacna* (ex-NLD *Amsterdam*)
  AOT 2 *Bayovar*
  ATF 1
  AWT 1 *Caloyeras*
  AXS 2: 1 *Marte*; 1 *Union*

Naval Aviation ε800

FORCES BY ROLE
MARITIME PATROL
  1 sqn with Beech 200T; Bell 212 ASW (AB-212 ASW); F-27 *Friendship*; Fokker 60; SH-2G *Super Seasprite*; SH-3D *Sea King*
TRANSPORT
  1 flt with An-32B *Cline*; Cessna 206; Fokker 50
TRAINING
  1 sqn with F-28F; T-34C *Turbo Mentor*
TRANSPORT HELICOPTER
  1 (liaison) sqn with Bell 206B *Jet Ranger* II; Mi-8 *Hip*

EQUIPMENT BY TYPE
AIRCRAFT
MP 8: 4 Beech 200T; 4 Fokker 60
ELINT 1 F-27 *Friendship*
TPT • **Light** 6: 3 An-32B *Cline*; 1 Cessna 206; 2 Fokker 50
TRG 5 T-34C *Turbo Mentor*
HELICOPTERS
ASW 6: 2 Bell 212 ASW (AB-212 ASW); 1 SH-2G *Super Seasprite*; 3 SH-3D *Sea King*
MRH 3 Bell 412SP
TPT 11: **Medium** 8: 2 Mi-8 *Hip*; 6 UH-3H *Sea King*; **Light** 3 Bell 206B *Jet Ranger* II
TRG 5 F-28F
MSL • **AShM** AM39 *Exocet*

Marines 4,000
FORCES BY ROLE
SPECIAL FORCES
3 cdo gp
MANOEUVRE
Light
2 inf bn
1 inf gp
Amphibious
1 mne bde (1 SF gp, 1 recce bn, 2 inf bn, 1 amph bn, 1 arty gp)
Jungle
1 jungle inf bn
EQUIPMENT BY TYPE
ARMOURED FIGHTING VEHICLES
APC • **APC (W)** 47+: 32 LAV II; V-100 *Commando*; 15 V-200 *Chaimite*
ANTI-TANK/ANTI-INFRASTRUCTURE
RCL **84mm** *Carl Gustav*; **106mm** M40A1
ARTILLERY 18+
TOWED **122mm** D-30
MOR 18+: **81mm** some; **120mm** ε18
AIR DEFENCE • **GUNS 20mm** SP (twin)

Air Force 9,500
Divided into five regions – North, Lima, South, Central and Amazon
FORCES BY ROLE
FIGHTER
1 sqn with MiG-29S/SE *Fulcrum* C; MiG-29UB *Fulcrum* B
FIGHTER/GROUND ATTACK
1 sqn with *Mirage* 2000E/ED (2000P/DP)
2 sqn with A-37B *Dragonfly*
1 sqn with Su-25A *Frogfoot* A†; Su-25UB *Frogfoot* B†
ISR
1 (photo-survey) sqn with Learjet 36A; SA-227-BC *Metro* III (C-26B)
TRANSPORT
1 sqn with B-737; An-32 *Cline*
1 sqn with DHC-6 *Twin Otter*; DHC-6-400 *Twin Otter*; PC-6 *Turbo Porter*
1 sqn with L-100-20
TRAINING
2 (drug interdiction) sqn with EMB-312 *Tucano*
1 sqn with MB-339A*

1 sqn with Z-242
1 hel sqn with Schweizer 300C
ATTACK HELICOPTER
1 sqn with Mi-25/Mi-35P *Hind*
TRANSPORT HELICOPTER
1 sqn with Mi-17 *Hip* H
1 sqn with Bell 206 *Jet Ranger*; Bell 212 (AB-212); Bell 412 *Twin Huey*
1 sqn with Bo-105C/LS
AIR DEFENCE
6 bn with S-125 *Pechora* (SA-3 *Goa*)
EQUIPMENT BY TYPE
AIRCRAFT 78 combat capable
FTR 20: 9 MiG-29S *Fulcrum* C; 3 MiG-29SE *Fulcrum* C; 6 MiG-29SMP *Fulcrum*; 2 MiG-29UBM *Fulcrum* B
FGA 12: 2 *Mirage* 2000ED (2000DP); 10 *Mirage* 2000E (2000P) (some†)
ATK 36: 18 A-37B *Dragonfly*;1 Su-25A *Frogfoot* A; 9 Su-25A *Frogfoot* A†; 8 Su-25UB *Frogfoot* B†
ISR 6: 2 Learjet 36A; 4 SA-227-BC *Metro* III (C-26B)
TPT 37: **Medium** 6: 4 C-27J *Spartan*; 2 L-100-20; **Light** 27: 4 An-32 *Cline*; 7 Cessna 172 *Skyhawk*; 3 DHC-6 *Twin Otter*; 12 DHC-6-400 *Twin Otter*; 1 PC-6 *Turbo-Porter*; **PAX** 4 B-737
TRG 68: 19 EMB-312 *Tucano*; 20 KT-1P; 10 MB-339A*; 6 T-41A/D *Mescalero*; 13 Z-242
HELICOPTERS
ATK 18: 16 Mi-25 *Hind* D; 2 Mi-35P *Hind* E
MRH 20: 2 Bell 412 *Twin Huey*; 18 Mi-17 *Hip* H
TPT 28: **Medium** 7 Mi-171Sh; **Light** 21: 8 Bell 206 *Jet Ranger*; 6 Bell 212 (AB-212); 1 Bo-105C; 6 Bo-105LS
TRG 4 Schweizer 300C
AIR DEFENCE • **SAM**
Short-range S-125 *Pechora* (SA-3 *Goa*)
Point-defence *Javelin*
AIR-LAUNCHED MISSILES
AAM • **IR** R-3 (AA-2 *Atoll*)‡; R-60 (AA-8 *Aphid*)‡; R-73 (AA-11 *Archer*); R-550 *Magic*; **IR/SARH** R-27 (AA-10 *Alamo*); **ARH** R-77 (AA-12 *Adder*)
ASM AS-30; Kh-29L (AS-14A *Kedge*)
ARM Kh-58 (AS-11 *Kilter*)

Paramilitary 77,000

National Police 77,000 (100,000 reported)
EQUIPMENT BY TYPE
ARMOURED FIGHTING VEHICLES
APC (W) 120: 20 BMR-600; 100 MOWAG *Roland*
HELICOPTERS
MRH 1 Mi-17 *Hip* H

General Police 43,000

Security Police 21,000

Technical Police 13,000

Coast Guard 1,000
Personnel included as part of Navy
EQUIPMENT BY TYPE
PATROL AND COASTAL COMBATANTS 38

PSOH 1 *Carvajal* (mod ITA *Lupo*) with 1 127mm gun (capacity 1 Bell 212 (AB-212)/SH-3D *Sea King*)
PCC 8: 1 *Ferré* (ex-ROK *Po Hang*) with 1 76mm gun; 2 *Río Cañete* (ROK *Tae Geuk*); 5 *Río Nepena*
PB 10: 6 *Chicama* (US *Dauntless*); 1 *Río Chira*; 3 *Río Santa*
PBR 19: 1 *Río Viru*; 8 *Parachique*; 10 *Zorritos*
LOGISTICS AND SUPPORT • AH 1 *Puno*
AIRCRAFT
  TPT • Light 3: 1 DHC-6 *Twin Otter*; 2 F-27 *Friendship*

Rondas Campesinas

Peasant self-defence force. Perhaps 7,000 rondas 'gp', up to pl strength, some with small arms. Deployed mainly in emergency zone

DEPLOYMENT

CENTRAL AFRICAN REPUBLIC: UN • MINUSCA 209; 4 obs; 1 engr coy
DEMOCRATIC REPUBLIC OF THE CONGO: UN • MONUSCO 3; 8 obs
SOUTH SUDAN: UN • UNMISS 1; 3 obs
SUDAN: UN • UNAMID 1; 1 obs; UN • UNISFA 2 obs

Suriname SUR

Suriname Dollar srd		2017	2018	2019
GDP	srd	25.6bn	28.7bn	
	US$	3.42bn	3.84bn	
per capita	US$	5,870	6,506	
Growth	%	1.9	2.0	
Inflation	%	22.0	7.8	
Def exp	srd	n.k.	n.k.	
	US$	n.k.	n.k.	
US$1=srd		7.49	7.47	
Population	597,927			

Age	0–14	15–19	20–24	25–29	30–64	65 plus
Male	12.3%	4.6%	4.3%	4.2%	22.3%	2.7%
Female	11.8%	4.4%	4.1%	4.0%	21.8%	3.5%

Capabilities

The armed forces are principally tasked with preserving territorial integrity. They also assist the national police in internal- and border-security missions, as well as tackling transnational criminal activity and drug trafficking. They have also been involved in disaster-relief and humanitarian-assistance operations. The country is a member of the Caribbean Disaster Emergency Management Agency and the Caribbean Basin Security Initiative. Ties with Brazil, China, India and the US have been crucial for the supply of equipment, including a limited number of armoured vehicles and helicopters, as well as training activity. The armed forces take part in the multilateral *Tradewinds* disaster-response exercise. The armed forces are not sized or equipped for power projection and are no longer engaged in any international peacekeeping operations. Resource challenges and limited equipment serviceability means the armed forces are constrained in providing sufficient border and coastal control and surveillance. There is no capability to design and manufacture modern military equipment and Suriname has looked to its foreign military cooperation to improve not just trade training but also military maintenance capacity.

ACTIVE 1,840 (Army 1,400 Navy 240 Air 200)
(All services form part of the army)

ORGANISATIONS BY SERVICE

Army 1,400
FORCES BY ROLE
MANOEUVRE
  Mechanised
  1 mech cav sqn
  Light
  1 inf bn (4 coy)
COMBAT SUPPORT
  1 MP bn (coy)
EQUIPMENT BY TYPE
ARMOURED FIGHTING VEHICLES
  RECCE 6 EE-9 *Cascavel*
  APC • APC (W) 15 EE-11 *Urutu*
ANTI-TANK/ANTI-INFRASTRUCTURE
  RCL 106mm M40A1
ARTILLERY • MOR 81mm 6

Navy ε240
EQUIPMENT BY TYPE
PATROL AND COASTAL COMBATANTS 10 **PB** 5: 3 Rodman 101†; 2 others
PBR 5 Rodman 55

Air Force ε200
EQUIPMENT BY TYPE
AIRCRAFT 2 combat capable
  TPT • Light 2: 1 BN-2 *Defender**; 1 Cessna 182
  TRG 1 PC-7 *Turbo Trainer**
HELICOPTERS • MRH 3 SA316B *Alouette* III (*Chetak*)

Trinidad and Tobago TTO

Trinidad and Tobago Dollar TT$		2017	2018	2019
GDP	TT$	154bn	158bn	
	US$	22.8bn	23.3bn	
per capita	US$	16,638	16,931	
Growth	%	-2.6	1.0	
Inflation	%	1.9	2.3	
Def bdgt	TT$	7.63bn	6.24bn	6.12bn
	US$	1.13bn	920m	
US$1=TT$		6.78	6.78	
Population	1,215,527			

Age	0–14	15–19	20–24	25–29	30–64	65 plus
Male	9.8%	3.0%	3.0%	3.6%	26.5%	4.8%
Female	9.4%	2.8%	2.7%	3.3%	24.8%	6.3%

Capabilities

The Trinidad and Tobago Defence Force (TTDF) focuses on border protection and maritime security, as well as counter-narcotics tasks. A larger role in law-enforcement support is planned for the army. Trinidad and Tobago is a member of the Caribbean Community, and cooperates with other countries in the region in disaster-relief efforts. It also takes part in US SOUTHCOM's annual *Tradewinds* disaster-response exercise and sends personnel to the US and UK for training. Trinidad and Tobago has no capacity to deploy and maintain troops abroad, and bar limited maintenance facilities has no domestic defence industry.

ACTIVE 4,050 (Army 3,000 Coast Guard 1,050)
(All services form the Trinidad and Tobago Defence Force)

ORGANISATIONS BY SERVICE

Army ε3,000
FORCES BY ROLE
SPECIAL FORCES
  1 SF unit
MANOEUVRE
  Light
  2 inf bn
COMBAT SUPPORT
  1 engr bn
COMBAT SERVICE SUPPORT
  1 log bn
EQUIPMENT BY TYPE
ANTI-TANK/ANTI-INFRASTRUCTURE
  RCL 84mm *Carl Gustav*
ARTILLERY • MOR 81mm 6 L16A1

Coast Guard 1,050
FORCES BY ROLE
COMMAND
  1 mne HQ
EQUIPMENT BY TYPE
PATROL AND COASTAL COMBATANTS 26
  PCO 1 *Nelson II* (ex-PRC)
  PCC 6: 2 *Point Lisas* (Damen Fast Crew Supplier 5009); 4 *Speyside* (Damen Stan Patrol 5009)
  PB 19: 2 *Gasper Grande*; 1 *Matelot*; 4 *Plymouth*; 4 *Point*; 6 *Scarlet Ibis* (Austal 30m); 2 *Wasp*; (1 *Cascadura* (SWE *Karlskrona* 40m) non-operational)

Air Wing 50
EQUIPMENT BY TYPE
AIRCRAFT
  TPT • Light 2 SA-227 *Metro* III (C-26)
HELICOPTERS
  MRH 2 AW139
  TPT • Light 1 S-76

Uruguay URY

Uruguayan Peso pU		2017	2018	2019
GDP	pU	1.70tr	1.85tr	
	US$	59.2bn	60.9bn	
per capita	US$	16,942	17,380	
Growth	%	2.7	2.0	
Inflation	%	6.2	7.6	
Def bdgt	pU	14.8bn	14.8bn	14.8bn
	US$	515m	486m	
US$1=pU		28.68	30.36	

Population 3,369,299

Age	0–14	15–19	20–24	25–29	30–64	65 plus
Male	10.1%	3.8%	4.0%	3.8%	20.8%	5.8%
Female	9.8%	3.7%	4.0%	3.7%	21.8%	8.6%

Capabilities

Principal tasks for the armed forces are assuring sovereignty and territorial integrity, restated in the 2018 draft military law. This also reinforced civilian control over the military. The 2018 draft law contained provisions to reduce the number of senior officers and address promotion issues across all services. Uruguay and Argentina have a joint peacekeeping unit and take part in joint exercises. In 2018 a defence cooperation agreement was signed with Russia, including training exchanges. The armed forces participate regularly in multinational exercises and deployments, notably on UN missions. The air force is focused on the counter-insurgency role, but ambitions to purchase a light fighter aircraft remain hampered by funding problems. The acquisition of air-defence radars may have improved the military's ability to monitor domestic airspace, but the lack of interdiction capability will continue to limit the capacity to respond to contingencies. Much of the equipment inventory is second-hand, and there is little capacity for independent power projection. Maintenance work is sometimes outsourced to foreign companies, such as Chile's ENAER.

ACTIVE 21,000 (Army 13,500 Navy 4,800 Air 2,700)
Paramilitary 1,400

ORGANISATIONS BY SERVICE

Army 13,500

Uruguayan units are substandard size, mostly around 30%. Div are at most bde size, while bn are of reinforced coy strength. Regts are also coy size, some bn size, with the largest formation being the 2nd armd cav regt

FORCES BY ROLE
COMMAND
  4 mil region/div HQ
MANOEUVRE
  Mechanised
  2 armd regt
  1 armd cav regt
  5 mech cav regt
  8 mech inf regt
  Light
  1 mot inf bn
  5 inf bn

Air Manoeuvre
1 para bn
COMBAT SUPPORT
1 (strategic reserve) arty regt
5 fd arty gp
1 (1st) engr bde (2 engr bn)
4 cbt engr bn
AIR DEFENCE
1 AD gp
EQUIPMENT BY TYPE
ARMOURED FIGHTING VEHICLES
  MBT 15 Tiran-5
  LT TK 38: 16 M24 Chaffee; 22 M41A1UR
  RECCE 15 EE-9 Cascavel
  IFV 18 BMP-1
  APC 376
    APC (T) 27: 24 M113A1UR; 3 MT-LB
    APC (W) 349: 54 Condor; 48 GAZ-39371 Vodnik; 53 OT-64; 47 OT-93; 147 Piranha
ENGINEERING & MAINTENANCE VEHICLES
  AEV MT-LB
ANTI-TANK/ANTI-INFRASTRUCTURE
  MSL • MANPATS Milan
  RCL 69: **106mm** 69 M40A1
ARTILLERY 185
  SP 122mm 6 2S1 Gvozdika
  TOWED 44: **105mm** 36: 28 M101A1; 8 M102; **155mm** 8 M114A1
  MOR 135: **81mm** 91: 35 M1, 56 Expal Model LN; **120mm** 44 Model SL
UNMANNED AERIAL VEHICLES • ISR • Light 1 Charrua
AIR DEFENCE • GUNS • TOWED 14: **20mm** 14: 6 M167 Vulcan; 8 TCM-20 (w/Elta M-2106 radar)

Navy 4,800 (incl 1,400 Prefectura Naval Coast Guard)

HQ at Montevideo
EQUIPMENT BY TYPE
PRINCIPAL SURFACE COMBATANTS • FRIGATES 2
  FF 2 Uruguay (PRT Joao Belo) with 2 triple Mk32 324mm ASTT with Mk46 LWT, 2 100mm gun
PATROL AND COASTAL COMBATANTS 15
  PB 15: 2 Colonia (ex-US Cape); 1 Paysandu; 9 Type-44 (coast guard); 3 PS (coast guard)
MINE WARFARE • MINE COUNTERMEASURES 3
  MSO 3 Temerario (Kondor II)
AMPHIBIOUS 3: 2 LCVP; 1 LCM
LOGISTICS AND SUPPORT 9
  ABU 2
  AG 2: 1 Artigas (GER Freiburg, general spt ship with replenishment capabilities); 1 Maldonado (also used as patrol craft)
  AGS 2: 1 Helgoland; 1 Trieste
  ARS 1 Vanguardia
  AXS 2: 1 Capitan Miranda; 1 Bonanza

Naval Aviation 210
FORCES BY ROLE
MARITIME PATROL
1 flt with Beech 200T*; Cessna O-2A Skymaster

SEARCH & RESCUE/TRANSPORT HELICOPTER
1 sqn with AS350B2 Ecureuil (Esquilo); Bell 412SP Twin Huey
TRANSPORT/TRAINING
1 flt with T-34C Turbo Mentor
EQUIPMENT BY TYPE
AIRCRAFT 2 combat capable
  ISR 5: 2 Beech 200T*; 3 Cessna O-2A Skymaster
  TRG 2 T-34C Turbo Mentor
HELICOPTERS
  MRH 2 Bell 412SP Twin Huey
  TPT • Light 1 AS350B2 Ecureuil (Esquilo)

Naval Infantry 700
FORCES BY ROLE
MANOEUVRE
  Amphibious
  1 mne bn(-)

Air Force 2,700
FORCES BY ROLE
FIGHTER/GROUND ATTACK
1 sqn with A-37B Dragonfly
ISR
1 flt with EMB-110 Bandeirante
TRANSPORT
1 sqn with C-130B Hercules; C-212 Aviocar; EMB–110C Bandeirante; EMB-120 Brasilia
1 (liaison) sqn with Cessna 206H; T-41D
1 (liaison) flt with Cessna 206H
TRAINING
1 sqn with PC-7U Turbo Trainer
1 sqn with Beech 58 Baron (UB-58); SF-260EU
TRANSPORT HELICOPTER
1 sqn with AS365 Dauphin; Bell 205 (UH–1H Iroquois); Bell 212
EQUIPMENT BY TYPE
AIRCRAFT 13 combat capable
  ATK 12 A-37B Dragonfly
  ISR 1 EMB-110 Bandeirante*
  TPT 23: **Medium** 2 C-130B Hercules; **Light** 21: 1 BAe-125-700A; 2 Beech 58 Baron (UB-58); 6 C-212 Aviocar; 9 Cessna 206H; 1 Cessna 210; 2 EMB-110C Bandeirante; 1 EMB-120 Brasilia; **PAX** 1 C-29 Hawker
  TRG 17: 5 PC-7U Turbo Trainer; 12 SF-260EU
HELICOPTERS
  MRH 2 AS365N2 Dauphin II
  TPT • Light 9: 5 Bell 205 (UH–1H Iroquois); 4 Bell 212

Paramilitary 1,400

Guardia Nacional Republicana 1,400

DEPLOYMENT

CENTRAL AFRICAN REPUBLIC: UN • MINUSCA 2
DEMOCRATIC REPUBLIC OF THE CONGO: UN • MONUSCO 930; 7 obs; 1 inf bn; 1 mne coy; 1 hel sqn
EGYPT: MFO 41; 1 engr/tpt unit

INDIA/PAKISTAN: UN • UNMOGIP 3 obs
LEBANON: UN • UNIFIL 2

Venezuela VEN

Venezuelan Bolivar Fuerte Bs		2017	2018	2019
GDP	Bs	2.93bn	3.41tr	
	US$	210bn	96bn	
per capita	US$	6,890	3,300	
Growth	%	-14	-18	
Inflation	%	1,088	1,370,000	
Def bdgt	Bs	10.3m	n.k	
	US$ [a]	741m	n.k	
US$1=Bs		0.01	354.40	

[a] US dollar figures should be treated with caution due to high levels of currency volatility as well as wide differentials between official and parallel exchange rates

Population	31,689,176					
Age	0–14	15–19	20–24	25–29	30–64	65 plus
Male	13.9%	4.3%	4.2%	4.2%	19.9%	3.3%
Female	13.2%	4.1%	4.1%	4.1%	20.5%	4.0%

Capabilities

The armed forces and national guard are tasked with protecting sovereignty, assuring territorial integrity and assisting with internal-security and counter-narcotics operations. They have sufficient capabilities and funding to fulfil internal-security tasks and fulfil their regime-protection role, but the economic crisis will impact future equipment availability and training levels. Incidents such as the apparent attempted assassination of President Maduro in 2018 and the attack on the supreme court by a police helicopter pilot in 2017 point to some internal stresses in the armed forces. Venezuela is almost completely isolated regionally, with frictions relating to the humanitarian crisis leading to troop deployments near the Colombia–Venezuela border. There are close ties with China and Russia. Caracas relies on both countries for procurements and technical support. The armed forces train regularly, with a recent increase in large-scale, civil–military cooperation. Venezuela has also taken part in joint combined exercises with China, Cuba and Russia. There is little logistics capability that would support deployment abroad. Equipment is relatively modern and mainly of Chinese and Russian manufacture, with advanced Su-30MKV combat aircraft and S-300VM air-defence systems in the inventory. However, the economic crisis has seriously affected the government's ability to sustain its military expenditure; maintenance and further procurement may suffer as a consequence. Venezuela's defence industry is based on a series of small, state-owned companies, mainly focused on the production of small arms, ammunition and explosives. Venezuela has no capability to design modern defence equipment, and local platform production is limited to small coastal-patrol boats.

ACTIVE 123,000 (Army 63,000 Navy 25,500 Air 11,500 National Guard 23,000) **Paramilitary 220,000**

Conscript liability 30 months selective, varies by region for all services

RESERVE 8,000 (Army 8,000)

ORGANISATIONS BY SERVICE

Space
EQUIPMENT BY TYPE
SATELLITES • COMMUNICATIONS 1 Venesat-1

Army ε63,000
FORCES BY ROLE
MANOEUVRE
  Armoured
    1 (4th) armd div (1 armd bde, 1 lt armd bde, 1 AB bde, 1 arty bde)
  Mechanised
    1 (9th) mot cav div (1 mot cav bde, 1 ranger bde, 1 sy bde)
  Light
    1 (1st) inf div (1 SF bn, 1 armd bde, 1 mech inf bde, 1 ranger bde, 1 inf bde, 1 arty unit, 1 spt unit)
    1 (2nd) inf div (1 mech inf bde, 1 inf bde, 1 mtn inf bde)
    1 (3rd) inf div (1 inf bde, 1 ranger bde, 1 sigs bde, 1 MP bde)
    1 (5th) inf div (1 SF bn, 1 cav sqn, 2 jungle inf bde, 1 engr bn)
COMBAT SUPPORT
  1 cbt engr corps (3 engr regt)
COMBAT SERVICE SUPPORT
  1 log comd (2 log regt)
AVIATION
  1 avn comd (1 tpt avn bn, 1 atk hel bn, 1 ISR avn bn)

Reserve Organisations 8,000
FORCES BY ROLE
MANOEUVRE
  Armoured
    1 armd bn
  Light
    4 inf bn
    1 ranger bn
COMBAT SUPPORT
  1 arty bn
  2 engr regt
EQUIPMENT BY TYPE
ARMOURED FIGHTING VEHICLES
  MBT 173: 81 AMX-30V; 92 T-72B1
  LT TK 109: 31 AMX-13; 78 Scorpion-90
  RECCE 121: 42 Dragoon 300 LFV2; 79 V-100/V-150
  IFV 237: 123 BMP-3 (incl variants); 114 BTR-80A (incl variants)
  APC 81
    APC (T) 45: 25 AMX-VCI; 12 AMX-PC (CP); 8 AMX-VCTB (Amb)
    APC (W) 36 Dragoon 300
ENGINEERING & MAINTENANCE VEHICLES
  ARV 5: 3 AMX-30D; BREM-1; 2 Dragoon 300RV; Samson
  VLB Leguan
NBC VEHICLES 10 TPz-1 Fuchs NBC
ANTI-TANK/ANTI-INFRASTRUCTURE
  MSL • MANPATS IMI MAPATS
  RCL 106mm 175 M40A1
  GUNS • SP 76mm 75 M18 Hellcat

ARTILLERY 515+
  SP 60: **152mm** 48 2S19 *Msta-S* (replacing Mk F3s); **155mm** 12 Mk F3
  TOWED 92: **105mm** 80: 40 M101A1; 40 Model 56 pack howitzer; **155mm** 12 M114A1
  MRL 56: **122mm** 24 BM-21 *Grad*; **160mm** 20 LAR SP (LAR-160); **300mm** 12 9A52 *Smerch*
  GUN/MOR 120mm 13 2S23 NONA-SVK
  MOR 294+: **81mm** 165; **SP 81mm** 21 *Dragoon* 300PM; AMX-VTT; **120mm** 108: 60 Brandt; 48 2S12
AIRCRAFT
  TPT • Light 28: 1 Beech 90 *King Air*; 1 Beech 200 *King Air*; 1 Beech 300 *King Air*; 1 Cessna 172; 6 Cessna 182 *Skylane*; 2 Cessna 206; 2 Cessna 207 *Stationair*; 1 IAI-201 *Arava*; 2 IAI-202 *Arava*; 11 M-28 *Skytruck*
HELICOPTERS
  ATK 10 Mi-35M2 *Hind*
  MRH 32: 10 Bell 412EP; 2 Bell 412SP; 20 Mi-17V-5 *Hip* H
  TPT 9: **Heavy** 3 Mi-26T2 *Halo*; **Medium** 2 AS-61D; **Light** 4: 3 Bell 206B *Jet Ranger*, 1 Bell 206L3 *Long Ranger* II

Navy ε22,300; ε3,200 conscript (total ε25,500)
EQUIPMENT BY TYPE
SUBMARINES • TACTICAL • SSK 2:
  2 *Sabalo* (GER T-209/1300) with 8 single 533mm TT with SST-4 HWT
PRINCIPAL SURFACE COMBATANTS • FRIGATES 6
  FFGHM 6 *Mariscal Sucre* (ITA mod *Lupo*) with 8 single lnchr with *Otomat* Mk2 AShM, 1 octuple *Albatros* lnchr with *Aspide* SAM, 2 triple 324mm ASTT with A244 LWT, 1 127mm gun (capacity 1 Bell 212 (AB-212) hel)
PATROL AND COASTAL COMBATANTS 10
  PSOH 3 *Guaiqueri* with 1 *Millennium* CIWS, 1 76mm gun (1 damaged in explosion in 2016)
  PBG 3 *Federación* (UK Vosper 37m) with 2 single lnchr with *Otomat* Mk2 AShM
  PB 4: 3 *Constitucion* (UK Vosper 37m) with 1 76mm gun; 1 *Fernando Gomez de Saa* (Damen 4207)
AMPHIBIOUS
  LANDING SHIPS • LST 4 *Capana* (capacity 12 tanks; 200 troops) (FSU *Alligator*)
  LANDING CRAFT 3:
    LCU 2 *Margarita* (river comd)
    UCAC 1 *Griffon* 2000TD
LOGISTICS AND SUPPORT 10
  AGOR 1 *Punta Brava*
  AGS 2
  AKL 4 *Los Frailes*
  AORH 1 *Ciudad Bolivar*
  ATF 1
  AXS 1 *Simon Bolivar*

Naval Aviation 500
FORCES BY ROLE
ANTI-SUBMARINE WARFARE
  1 sqn with Bell 212 (AB-212)
MARITIME PATROL
  1 flt with C-212-200 MPA

TRANSPORT
  1 sqn with Beech 200 *King Air*; C-212 *Aviocar*; Turbo Commander 980C
TRAINING
  1 hel sqn with Bell 206B *Jet Ranger* II; TH-57A *Sea Ranger*
TRANSPORT HELICOPTER
  1 sqn with Bell 412EP *Twin Huey*; Mi-17V-5 *Hip* H
EQUIPMENT BY TYPE
AIRCRAFT 2 combat capable
  MP 2 C-212-200 MPA*
  TPT • Light 7: 1 Beech C90 *King Air*; 1 Beech 200 *King Air*; 4 C-212 *Aviocar*; 1 Turbo Commander 980C
HELICOPTERS
  ASW 4 Bell 212 ASW (AB-212 ASW)
  MRH 12: 6 Bell 412EP *Twin Huey*; 6 Mi-17V-5 *Hip*
  TPT • Light 1 Bell 206B *Jet Ranger* II (trg)
  TRG 1 TH-57A *Sea Ranger*

Marines ε15,000
FORCES BY ROLE
COMMAND
  1 div HQ
SPECIAL FORCES
  1 spec ops bde
MANOEUVRE
  Amphibious
  1 amph aslt bde
  3 mne bde
  3 (rvn) mne bde
COMBAT SUPPORT
  1 cbt engr bn
  1 MP bde
  1 sigs bn
COMBAT SERVICE SUPPORT
  1 log bn
EQUIPMENT BY TYPE
ARMOURED FIGHTING VEHICLES
  LT TK 10 VN-16
  IFV 21: 11 VN-1; 10 VN-18
  APC • APC (W) 37 EE-11 *Urutu*
  AAV 11 LVTP-7
ENGINEERING & MAINTENANCE VEHICLES
  ARV 1 VN-16 ARV
  AEV 1 AAVR7
ANTI-TANK/ANTI-INFRASTRUCTURE
  RCL 84mm Carl Gustav; **106mm** M40A1
ARTILLERY 30
  TOWED 105mm 18 M-56
  MOR 120mm 12 Brandt
PATROL AND COASTAL COMBATANTS • PBR 23: 18 *Constancia*; 2 *Manaure*; 3 *Terepaima* (*Cougar*)
AMPHIBIOUS • LANDING CRAFT • 1 LCM; 1 LCU; 12 **LCVP**

Coast Guard 1,000
EQUIPMENT BY TYPE
PATROL AND COASTAL COMBATANTS 22
  PSO 3 *Guaicamacuto* with 1 *Millennium* CIWS, 1 76 mm gun (capacity 1 Bell 212 (AB-212) hel) (1 additional vessel in build)

PB 19: 12 *Gavion*; 1 *Pagalo* (Damen Stan 2606); 4 *Petrel* (US *Point*); 2 *Protector*

LOGISTICS AND SUPPORT 5
AG 2 *Los Tanques* (salvage ship)
AKSL 1
AP 2

Air Force 11,500
FORCES BY ROLE
FIGHTER/GROUND ATTACK
1 sqn with F-5 *Freedom Fighter* (VF-5)
2 sqn with F-16A/B *Fighting Falcon*
4 sqn with Su-30MKV
2 sqn with K-8W *Karakorum**

GROUND ATTACK/ISR
1 sqn with EMB-312 *Tucano**; OV-10A *Bronco*

ELECTRONIC WARFARE
1 sqn with *Falcon* 20DC; SA-227 *Metro* III (C-26B)

TRANSPORT
1 sqn with Y-8; C-130H *Hercules*; KC-137
1 sqn with A319CJ; B-737
4 sqn with Cessna T206H; Cessna 750
1 sqn with Cessna 500/550/551; *Falcon* 20F; *Falcon* 900
1 sqn with G-222; Short 360 *Sherpa*

TRAINING
1 sqn with Cessna 182N; SF-260E
2 sqn with DA40NG; DA42VI
1 sqn with EMB-312 *Tucano**

TRANSPORT HELICOPTER
1 VIP sqn with AS532UL *Cougar*; Mi-172
3 sqn with AS332B *Super Puma*; AS532 *Cougar*
2 sqn with Mi-17 *Hip* H

EQUIPMENT BY TYPE
AIRCRAFT 93 combat capable
FTR 21: 17 F-16A *Fighting Falcon*; 4 F-16B *Fighting Falcon*
FGA 23 Su-30MKV
ATK 7 OV-10A *Bronco*
EW 4: 2 *Falcon* 20DC; 2 SA-227 *Metro* III (C-26B)
TKR 1 KC-137
TPT 75: **Medium** 14: 5 C-130H *Hercules* (some in store); 1 G-222; 8 Y-8; **Light** 56: 6 Beech 200 *King Air*; 2 Beech 350 *King Air*; 10 Cessna 182N *Skylane*; 12 Cessna 206 *Stationair*; 4 Cessna 208B *Caravan*; 1 Cessna 500 *Citation* I; 3 Cessna 550 *Citation* II; 1 Cessna 551; 1 Cessna 750 *Citation* X; 2 Do-228-212; 1 Do-228-212NG; 11 Quad City Challenger II; 2 Short 360 *Sherpa*; **PAX** 5: 1 A319CJ; 1 B-737; 1 *Falcon* 20F; 2 *Falcon* 900
TRG 84: 24 DA40NG; 6 DA42VI; 18 EMB-312 *Tucano**; 24 K-8W *Karakorum**; 12 SF-260E
HELICOPTERS
MRH 8 Mi-17 (Mi-17VS) *Hip* H
TPT 23: **Medium** 15: 3 AS332B *Super Puma*; 8 AS532 *Cougar*; 2 AS532UL *Cougar*; 2 Mi-172 (VIP); **Light** at least 8 Enstrom 480B

AIR-LAUNCHED MISSILES
AAM • **IR** AIM-9L/P *Sidewinder*; R-73 (AA-11 *Archer*); PL-5E; R-27T/ET (AA-10B/D *Alamo*); **IIR** *Python* 4; **SARH** R-27R/ER (AA-10A/C *Alamo*); **ARH** R-77 (AA-12 *Adder*)
ASM Kh-29L/T (AS-14A/B *Kedge*); Kh-59M (AS-18 *Kazoo*)
AShM Kh-31A (AS-17B *Krypton*); AM39 *Exocet*
ARM Kh-31P (AS-17A *Krypton*)

Air Defence Command (CODAI)
Joint service command with personnel drawn from other services
FORCES BY ROLE
AIR DEFENCE
5 AD bde
COMBAT SERVICE SUPPORT
1 log bde (5 log gp)

EQUIPMENT BY TYPE
AIR DEFENCE
SAM
Long-range S-300VM
Medium-range 9K317M2 *Buk*-M2E (SA-17 *Grizzly*); S-125 *Pechora*-2M (SA-26)
Point-defence 9K338 *Igla*-S (SA-24 *Grinch*); ADAMS; *Mistral*; RBS-70
GUNS 440+
SP 40mm 12+: 6+ AMX-13 *Rafaga*; 6 M42
TOWED 428+: **20mm**: 114 TCM-20; **23mm** ε200 ZU-23-2; **35mm**; **40mm** 114+: 114+ L/70; Some M1

National Guard (Fuerzas Armadas de Cooperacion) 23,000
(Internal sy, customs) 9 regional comd
EQUIPMENT BY TYPE
ARMOURED FIGHTING VEHICLES
APC • **APC (W)** 44: 24 Fiat 6614; 20 UR-416
ARTILLERY • **MOR** 50 81mm
PATROL AND COASTAL COMBATANTS • **PB** 34: 12 *Protector*; 12 *Punta*; 10 *Rio Orinoco* II
AIRCRAFT
TPT • **Light** 34: 1 Beech 55 *Baron*; 1 Beech 80 *Queen Air*; 1 Beech 90 *King Air*; 1 Beech 200C *King Air*; 3 Cessna 152 *Aerobat*; 2 Cessna 172; 2 Cessna 402C; 4 Cessna U206 *Stationair*; 6 DA42 MPP; 1 IAI-201 *Arava*; 12 M-28 *Skytruck*
TRG 3: 1 PZL 106 *Kruk*; 2 PLZ M2-6 *Isquierka*
HELICOPTERS
MRH 13: 8 Bell 412EP; 5 Mi-17V-5 *Hip* H
TPT • **Light** 19: 9 AS355F *Ecureuil* II; 4 AW109; 5 Bell 206B/L *Jet Ranger*/*Long Ranger*; 1 Bell 212 (AB 212); **TRG** 5 F-280C

Paramilitary ε220,000

Bolivarian National Militia ε220,000

Arms procurements and deliveries – Latin America and the Caribbean

Significant events in 2018

- Spanish company Indra and Colombian company Codaltec signed in June an agreement to develop an air-defence system. The two companies will begin work on a command-and-control system that will integrate data from different sensors. It is unclear if the system will eventually include ground-based air defence or will comprise an air-surveillance network.

- In July, Boeing and Brazil's Embraer agreed a deal that will see Boeing acquire through a new US$4.75bn joint venture (JV) a controlling stake in Embraer's commercial-aircraft business. Embraer will retain control of its defence business but the two companies are also discussing creating a JV for sales, support and manufacturing of Embraer's KC-390 transport aircraft.

- Brazil announced the shortlist for its *Tamandaré* corvette programme in October, which will see four vessels acquired for US$1.5bn:
  - Saab and Damen Schelde with Consub – SIGMA 10514 with the Saab 9LV combat-management system;
  - TKMS with Embraer and Oceana shipyard – MEKO A100;
  - Leonardo and Fincantieri with Vard Promar shipyard – a modification of the *Barroso*-class design;
  - Naval Group – *Gowind* 2500.

- The first series-production Embraer KC-390 was flown on its maiden flight on 9 October. This allowed the aircraft to be awarded its civil certificate of airworthiness. The first KC-390 for the Brazilian Air Force is expected to be delivered in the first half of 2019 with full operating capability to be achieved by the end of the year.

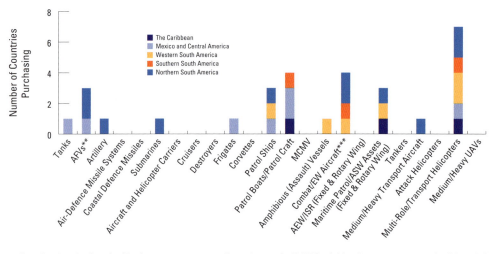

Figure 26 **Latin America and the Caribbean: selected ongoing or completed procurement priorities in 2018**

*Data reflects the number of countries with equipment-procurement contracts either ongoing or completed in 2018. Data includes only procurement programmes for which a production contract has been signed. The data does not include upgrade programmes.
**Armoured fighting vehicles not including main battle tanks   ***Includes combat-capable training aircraft

Figure 27 Naval Group: Programa de Desenvolvimento de Submarinos (PROSUB)

The Brazilian Navy has operated conventionally powered submarines (SSKs) since the 1920s. Patrol requirements in the southern Atlantic and in Brazil's exclusive economic zone, including hydrocarbon fields, has led Brasilia to recently sharpen focus on developing a nuclear-propulsion capacity. These ambitions are long-standing and pre-date the 1978 beginning of the Submarino com Propulsão Nuclear Brasileiro (SN-BR) programme.

This project languished until the 2000s. In 2008, France and Brazil signed a series of defence-cooperation agreements. This was followed later that year by the establishment of the Programa de Desenvolvimento de Submarinos (PROSUB) office in Brazil, with the intention of developing an indigenous nuclear-propulsion capability, as well as acquiring new SSKs.

Brazil's National Defence Strategy was published in 2009, which restated the intent to 'maintain and develop [Brazil's] ability to design and manufacture both conventional and nuclear-propelled submarines'. Contracts signed with France in 2009 formalised many of the 2008 agreements: Naval Group would transfer technology and support Brazil's efforts to build four *Scorpène*-class SSKs and a larger nuclear-powered submarine (SSN) based on that design. The first of each type was planned to enter service in 2015 and 2021 respectively.

Despite construction starting on the first SSK in 2010, the programme is now several years behind schedule, largely due to budgetary challenges that have affected many government programmes. PROSUB has also been caught up in Brazilian anti-corruption investigations. The first SSK is now expected to be delivered in 2020 and the SSN in 2029.

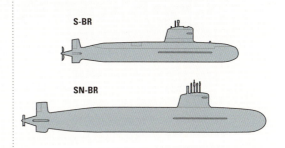

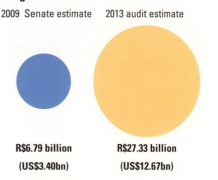

Programme costs

2009 Senate estimate: R$6.79 billion (US$3.40bn)

2013 audit estimate: R$27.33 billion (US$12.67bn)

Contractor(s) and responsibilities

- Naval Group (formerly DCNS): technology transfer, construction of some submarine parts, supply of torpedoes and countermeasures
- Itaguaí Construções Navais (ICN): construction of the five submarines
- Odebrecht: design and construction of the new ICN shipyard and naval base
- Nuclebrás Equipamentos Pesados (NUCLEP): production of the nuclear-propulsion system
- Amazônia Azul Tecnologias de Defesa (AMAZUL): development of nuclear-propulsion and nuclear-fuelling site in new naval base

Programme	Vessel name	Pennant number	First-steel cut	Launched	Commissioned
SN-BR	*Álvaro Alberto*	SN-10	-	-	-
S-BR	*Riachuelo*	S-40	27 May 2010	-	-
S-BR	*Humaitá*	S-41	04 Sep 2013	-	-
S-BR	*Tonelero*	S-42	13 Jan 2015	-	-
S-BR	*Angostura*	S-43	23 Feb 2016	-	-

© IISS

Chapter Nine
Sub-Saharan Africa

- With few exceptions, a combination of ageing inventories and a lack of procurement investment is limiting the region's ability to generate combat air power.
- Amid continuing conflict and crises in the region, positive developments included the rapprochement between Ethiopia and Eritrea.
- The African Union continues to work towards harmonising its African Standby Force concept with the range of ad hoc groupings that have developed, such as the G-5 Sahel and the MNJTF combating Boko Haram.
- China has deepened its defence presence in the region with the establishment of its first overseas military base at Djibouti.
- With regional budgets still constrained, defence spending declined by 5% between 2017 and 2018.

Sub-Saharan Africa defence spending, 2018 – top 5

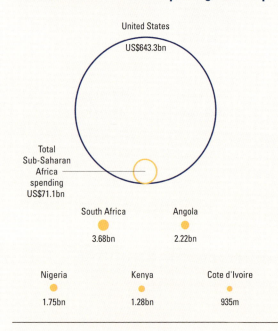

Active military personnel – top 10
(10,000 per unit)

Patrol and coastal combatants
(10 per unit)

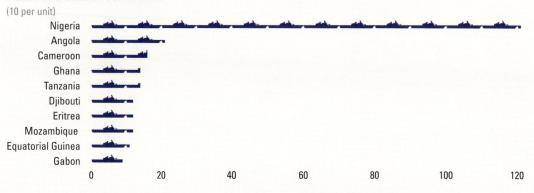

Regional defence policy and economics	440 ▶
Armed forces data section	451 ▶
Arms procurements and deliveries	501 ▶

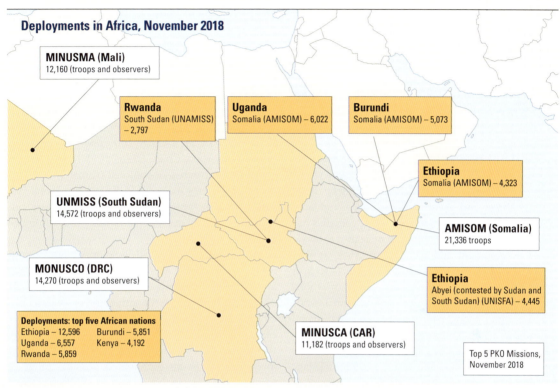

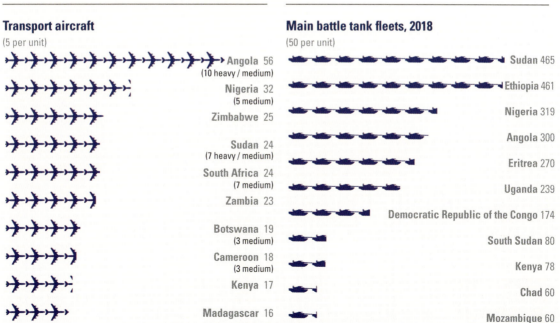

Sub-Saharan Africa

Regional defence establishments remain preoccupied with the causes and consequences of conflict and instability. The eruption of new crises, such as that in Cameroon, and flare-ups in areas long afflicted by conflict and instability, such as the Democratic Republic of the Congo (DRC), act as a reminder of the fragility of peace and security in parts of the continent.

Threats remain multifaceted, ranging from institutional weakness to direct challenges from state and non-state actors, including terrorists. The duration and fluid nature of some conflicts – which cross borders and challenge states including by direct military threat and asymmetric activity – not only highlight the adaptability of regional adversaries but also the requirement for long-term measures to tackle wider development and security priorities, as well as more immediate military imperatives. As well as combat capabilities, good logistics, communications and intelligence, surveillance and reconnaissance are important. Along with regional and continental institutions, some defence organisations continue to make progress in capacity-building, supported by a range of external actors. However, a continuing task for local governments and international partners is ensuring that these efforts are sustainable.

Nonetheless, there were positive developments in 2018, including the rapprochement between Ethiopia and Eritrea and the declaration on cooperation between Eritrea, Ethiopia and Somalia. Measures also continue on the continent to support the development of peace and security, such as those of the African Union (AU). An issue now identified by the AU is to bring into step measures developed due to necessity – such as the ad hoc Multinational Joint Task Force (MNJTF), tackling Boko Haram, and the African Capacity for Immediate Response to Crises (ACIRC), which emerged after conflict erupted in Mali in 2013 – with structures like the African Standby Force (ASF), which are intended to be a long-term and sustainable means of contending with the continent's security crises.

Conflict, terrorism and instability

The roster of regional security challenges grew longer in 2018. The activity of secessionist groups in Cameroon's anglophone regions, together with the military response by the government, have led to particular concern over the impact that the fighting is having on people in affected regions, including those who are internally displaced. The actions of Boko Haram have also had an impact on Cameroon's population in the north of the country, and the group also remains active in northern Nigeria. Armed forces from the MNJTF (which comprises troops from Benin, Cameroon, Chad, Niger and Nigeria) remain engaged on combat operations against this group in the area of the Lake Chad Basin. The group has suffered a series of setbacks and has lost territory, but retains significant operational capacity and continues its terrorist activity.

Amid continuing ground deployments and ground combat, including internal deployments to counter instability in Zamfara State, and the consequent operational stresses on the armed forces, Nigeria has looked to increase its air-to-ground combat-support capacities. Two Mi-35 helicopters arrived in 2018, while Nigerian President Muhammadu Buhari's visit to the United States highlighted possible progress towards the sale to Nigeria of 12 EMB-314 *Super Tucano* aircraft, which was earlier blocked by the Obama administration.

The challenge from insurgents has been enabled by weak institutions and governance in the region, as well as the effect of conflicts both in the region and further north; Libya is a prime example. The 2013 near-collapse in Mali, which followed rapid advances by Islamist groups, led to rapid French military action to forestall a takeover by these groups and to bolster local security forces. French forces remain engaged on combat operations and capacity-building tasks in Mali and regional states as part of *Operation Barkhane*, which began in 2014. The challenges to this mission are many, not least because of the terrain. It is also challenging in terms of intelligence, surveillance and combat- and logistics-support requirements.

France's operations are conducted alongside missions by regional states of the G5 Sahel grouping (Burkina Faso, Chad, Mali, Mauritania and Niger). In July 2017, the group created the G5 Sahel Cross-

Border Joint Force. The European Union financially supports the joint force to the tune of €50 million (US$56m), among other types of support for the G5 Sahel. At full operational capability, the force is planned to have some 5,000 military and police personnel, with seven battalions spread across three zones (centre, east and west). It is understood that the force headquarters, based in Mali, relocated in late 2018 from Sévaré to Bamako. (The base at Sévaré was targeted by terrorists earlier in the year.)

Further east, Somalia has long suffered from the actions of al-Shabaab, as well as years of clan violence and weak governance. International support for the reconstruction of the Somali security sector continues, with military training taking place in Mogadishu. The African Union Mission in Somalia (AMISOM) continues to engage in combat operations against al-Shabaab, as do external actors, including the US. The Somali authorities are to assume security responsibility eventually and, according to the United Nations, the government is planning for transfer of responsibility in four areas: operational handover of locations from AMISOM to the Somali security forces; institutional capacity-building; the implementation of the national-security architecture; and the alignment of supporting activities, such as local governance and stabilisation. However, with al-Shabaab still demonstrating its operational capability through continued attacks, any drawdown in AMISOM's strength or areas of responsibility will need to be carefully managed.

Continental initiatives

Such security crises and conflicts involve the deployment of military personnel and materiel from multiple African states. However, external actors are vital, not just in terms of the materiel and logistical support they can offer, but also in financial terms.

Improving regional states' capacity to act in support of continental security requirements is key to realising the ambition of regional standby forces, which are part of the African Peace and Security Architecture pursued by the AU. Each Regional Economic Community (REC) is developing a standby force and regional logistics depot, while in early 2018 the AU inaugurated the planned Continental Logistics Base at Douala in Cameroon. RECs continue to develop their standby forces, although the ASF was declared operational by the AU in early 2016, following the end of exercise *Amani Africa* II. The RECs are increasingly active in addressing regional security requirements. For instance, in September 2018 the Intergovernmental Authority on Development mandated Djibouti and Somalia to deploy troops to South Sudan. This builds on the UN-authorised Regional Protection Force, which began to deploy in late 2017 – principally to the Juba area – in order to allow United Nations Mission in South Sudan (UNMISS) forces to redeploy to other locations. Another example is the Economic Community of West African States (ECOWAS) mission to Gambia in 2017.

Nonetheless, the challenge lies in synchronising the ASF with the range of ad hoc groupings that have developed, including the ACIRC, the G5 Sahel, the MNJTF and the Regional Cooperation Initiative for the Elimination of the Lord's Resistance Army. The AU is pursuing initiatives in this regard, and has been in discussion with the RECs, including on a legal framework concerning the deployment and use of the ASF. At its October 2018 Chiefs of Defence meeting, the AU said that it would provide 'mission and logistical support, technical assistance and financial support and resource mobilisation', as part of its plan to boost cooperation with ad hoc coalitions. The AU's Maputo Strategic Five-Year Work Plan on the African Standby Force (2016–20) 'underscored that the RECs … are part of the overall security architecture of the Union'. The plan charges key AU leaders with ensuring that the activities of the RECs are consistent with the aims and objectives of the AU.

However, the Maputo work plan is being revised. The AU sees it as a 'living document', intended to tackle political, technical and operational gaps identified in lessons-learned processes coming out of AU Peace Support Operations (PSOs). The AU said in 2018 that the work plan incorporated new elements 'that include the revision and development of an AU PSO Doctrine and ASF concept; harmonisation between the ASF Framework and ACIRC activities; and enhanced cooperation between the ASF and ad-hoc coalitions'.

Work is also under way, through the Maputo work plan, to identify routine gaps in regional military capacity, such as in strategic airlift. The possibility of pursuing pre-approved contracts for strategic-lift capabilities has been raised. Uganda, meanwhile, has pledged a C-130 to the AU for ASF strategic lift, and the AU's Peace and Security Commission is looking for more contributions. The AU was due to conduct the last two of its REC strategic-lift assessments in late 2018, for the North African Regional

Capability and the Southern African Development Community. An important development has been the establishment of the AU's Peace Fund, which should provide more predictable funding for AU PSOs. If fully operationalised, a source of African funding for African peace-support operations could fundamentally change the relationship between the AU, UN and EU as well as other influential donors such as the US, United Kingdom and France.

Foreign military presence: new influences

Foreign military support for multinational operations and national armed forces continued in 2018. French forces in West Africa and the Sahel region remain engaged on operations, while France maintains a significant presence in Djibouti, which is also home to the US Combined Joint Task Force–Horn of Africa. From this location, US forces carry out regional training activities, as well as military operations, particularly in Somalia. US training activities on the continent are broad, ranging from pre-deployment training to mission-specific tasks, and a set of exercise and support programmes continue, such as the *Flintlock* counter-terrorism exercises and the Africa Contingency Operations Training and Assistance initiative. The US has been active in supporting counter-terrorist operations in the Sahel. As part of a deployment that has built up in recent years, by May 2018 the US had about 800 personnel deployed to Niger. The deployment includes training teams dedicated to building local counter-terrorist capacities, and armed *Reaper* uninhabited aerial vehicles (UAVs) based at Niamey. Nonetheless, the United States' largest regional contingent remains based at Djibouti's Camp Lemonnier.

As well as France and the US, China is now resident in Djibouti. For some years, Beijing has deployed ships off the Horn of Africa on counter-piracy patrols, though not as part of multinational missions, and has increasingly taken part in UN peacekeeping missions and developed defence and security ties – as well as a range of economic links – across the continent. Beijing has pledged to establish a China–Africa peace fund and to continue military assistance to the AU. Chinese press sources quoted an intended 50 security-assistance programmes. However, China's construction of port facilities in Djibouti, and a military deployment there to the country's first overseas military base, has generated a new level of scrutiny. A marine company is assessed to be present at the base, though at the time of writing no principal surface combatants were believed to have yet moored alongside, though the PLA Navy has docked vessels there including an amphibious vessel.

Other nations continue to deploy to sub-Saharan Africa as part of multinational missions, including EU operations from the Sahel to the Central African Republic (CAR), as well as on national engagements like bilateral training assistance. For example, a report in May 2018 by the UN secretary-general referenced a 14 March 2018 agreement between Somaliland and the United Arab Emirates (UAE) that the UAE 'would support training of "Somaliland" security forces and that the construction of the military airbase and naval base at Berbera would proceed as planned'. The potential training of Somaliland forces was not greeted positively in Mogadishu. The UK, meanwhile, has long maintained advisory and training teams on the continent. The establishment of the new regional British Defence Staff in 2016 signalled a renewal of the UK's relationship with West African states.

Russia too has a relatively long history of involvement on the continent, though in recent years this has been restricted to the supply of military equipment. Moscow's involvement deepened in late 2017 when the UN Security Council granted it an exemption to the arms embargo on the CAR. In early 2018, it was reported that Russian shipments of small arms had taken place, along with the provision of civilian instructors to train two battalions of CAR troops. Non-governmental organisations have expressed concern that the influx of new weapons to government forces would in turn drive rebel groups to increase their armament. Meanwhile, CAR President Faustin-Archange Touadéra was reported to have a Russian security adviser, as well as Russian nationals in the presidential guard. Media sources allege that the civilian instructors are in fact from the same Russian private military company, labelled 'Wagner', that has been reported as active in Syria and Ukraine, though this remains unconfirmed.

DEFENCE ECONOMICS

Macroeconomics

Economic growth firmed up across the continent, rising from 2.7% in 2017 to 3.1% in 2018, according to the International Monetary Fund (IMF). This was driven largely by increasing commodity prices, notably in oil and metals, and a rebounding economy in Nigeria. Other factors include improved agricultural output and rising domestic consumption.

Figure 28 China: military engagement in Africa

China takes part in UN peacekeeping operations in Africa as well as counter-piracy missions in the Gulf of Aden. It also provides maritime-security training off the east coast. Beijing has also built more permanent military infrastructure and now has a military base in Djibouti. It has also financed and built military infrastructure in Ghana, Tanzania and Zimbabwe, including training centres, barracks, defence colleges and defence-ministry buildings. Between 2016 and 2017, China also exported military equipment to 20 states in North and sub-Saharan Africa, including offshore-patrol vessels, armoured personnel carriers, surface-to-air missile systems, uninhabited aerial vehicles and training aircraft. Meanwhile, China has invested heavily in the construction of ports, some with major railway connections as part of regional connectivity projects. While some of these may be associated with China's Belt and Road Initiative, China's presence in Africa has moved beyond solely economic or humanitarian impulses, and there is now a distinct security and defence focus to its engagement.

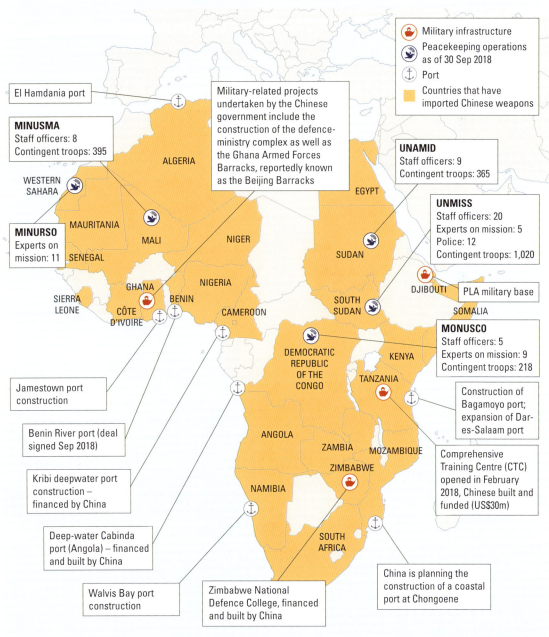

444 THE MILITARY BALANCE 2019

The rise in commodity prices was noteworthy. According to the World Bank, oil prices rose from a yearly average of around US$51 per barrel in 2015 to around US$80 per barrel in October 2018, while prices for South African coal rose from US$57 per metric tonne (mt) in 2015 to US$100 per mt in October 2018. Metal prices have also increased in recent years – for instance in aluminium, copper, iron ore, nickel and zinc – which enabled metal-exporting countries to increase their mining output.

Despite this increase in commodity prices – including in agricultural prices – which helped resource-intensive economies, most regional economies remained fragile. Although fiscal deficits narrowed in central African states such as Cameroon, Chad and Gabon, widening deficits and deteriorating fiscal positions have led to rising debt levels in other countries. Rising debt levels were also caused by exchange-rate depreciation, while the interest payments needed to service these debts further constrained countries' fiscal space. The IMF said that, for oil exporters, interest payments accounted for almost 15% of their total revenue in 2017; the figure was almost 10% for the whole region.

Inflation rates fell in 2018 and stabilised at 8.6%, a positive development explained by tighter monetary policies in key countries such as Angola and Nigeria. Other contributory factors were improved currency stability and a more moderate increase in agricultural prices than between 2011 and 2014.

However, regional growth was again weighed down by the slower recovery in some of the larger countries, such as South Africa, and persistent conflict or instability in others, such as Burundi, the Democratic Republic of the Congo and South Sudan. The economic disruption caused by conflict-

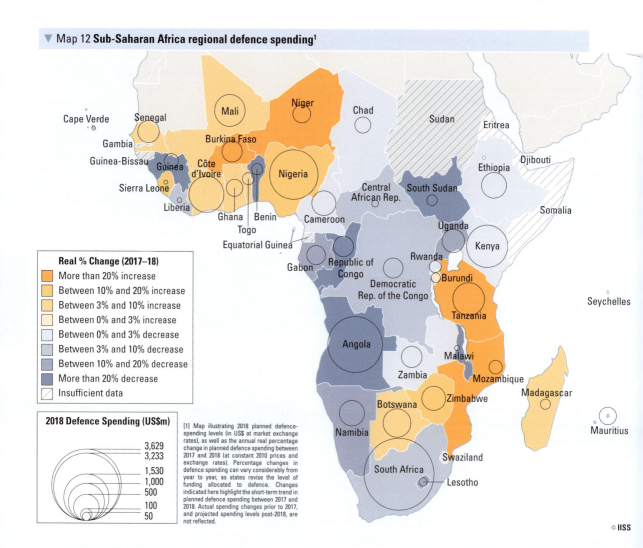

Map 12 Sub-Saharan Africa regional defence spending[1]

[1] Map illustrating 2018 planned defence-spending levels (in US$ at market exchange rates), as well as the annual real percentage change in planned defence spending between 2017 and 2018 (at constant 2010 prices and exchange rates). Percentage changes in defence spending can vary considerably from year to year, as states revise the level of funding allocated to defence. Changes indicated here highlight the short-term trend in planned defence spending between 2017 and 2018. Actual spending changes prior to 2017, and projected spending levels post-2018, are not reflected.

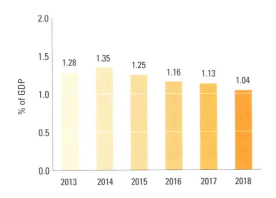

▲ Figure 29 **Sub-Saharan Africa regional defence expenditure** as % of GDP

related population displacement continues to affect neighbouring states, as well as the area where conflict takes place.

Economic success stories include Côte d'Ivoire, where GDP was expected to grow by 7.4% in 2018 and 7.0% in 2019, slightly lower than the 7.8% figure seen in 2017. Like Senegal, which grew by 7.0% in 2018, Côte d'Ivoire has reaped the benefits of infrastructure investments. Senegal's 'Emerging Senegal Plan', which launched in 2013, began a series of large infrastructure projects, including power plants. However, the fastest-growing region remained East Africa. Ethiopia's GDP grew by 7.5% in 2018, also driven by infrastructure investments. In Kenya, where growth was 6.0% in 2018, the main factor was private consumption.

Growth in South Africa slowed down, from 1.3% in 2017 to 0.8% in 2018. Overall, South Africa's economic prospects remain mixed, with rising wages and inflation under control, but also rising unemployment. However, a change in government in South Africa – as well as in Angola and Zimbabwe – helped regenerate confidence over these countries' economic trajectory.

Defence budgets and procurement

With economies still constrained, defence spending in sub-Saharan Africa declined by 5.0% in real terms between 2017 and 2018, after a decline of 5.1% between 2016 and 2017.

In particular, the fall in Angola's defence spending drove totals down. While the budget rose in local-currency terms, this still resulted in a decline in US-dollar terms, given currency problems the country experienced in 2018. Angola introduced a floating exchange rate early in 2018 to protect its foreign reserves, which led to a depreciation in its currency. As a result, defence spending declined in US-dollar terms from AOA536 billion (US$3.2bn) in 2017 to AOA546bn (US$2.2bn) in 2018.

In South Africa, years of economic underperformance led defence spending to fall further when measured in rand, although exchange rates resulted in a slight increase in US-dollar terms, from R48.6bn (US$3.65bn) in 2017 to R47.9bn (US$3.68bn) in 2018. The most significant budget cuts have been to those of the air force and navy. As a result, the Department of Defence stated in its 2018 Annual Performance Plan that the proposals elaborated in the 2015 defence review could not be realised. This review restated South Africa's ambition to be the major regional power, though these economic challenges will likely limit South Africa's aspirations until more funds can be generated.

By contrast, the budget in Nigeria rose from N465bn (US$1.5bn) in 2017 to N567bn (US$1.7bn) in 2018. While significant costs are disbursed on ongoing operations in the north of the country, the 2018 budget bill provides funds for developing naval capacities, including hydrographic survey ships, landing ships, patrol craft and patrol boats. The budget also indicated that the navy will acquire an uninhabited aerial vehicle. Nigeria's principal maritime threats relate to piracy, illegal fishing and the theft of oil in the country's inland waterways, deltas and coastal areas. Maritime-equipment deliveries in 2018 included FPB 72 and FPB 110 MkII patrol boats from French shipyard OCEA. Germany also donated five patrol boats in 2018 to help Nigerian forces patrol Lake Chad and to help in the fight against Boko Haram.

Significantly in 2018, the United States changed its stance regarding arms transfers to Nigeria. While the Obama administration limited arms sales due to security and humanitarian reasons, US President Donald Trump lifted the ban as part of a general push to increase US arms sales. This means that progress might now be made on the plan to acquire 12 EMB-314 *Super Tucano* aircraft, in addition to related training and spare parts, for a total estimated by the US Defense Security Cooperation Agency at US$593 million. These aircraft are used elsewhere in a light-attack role, and on arrival in Nigeria should further reinforce the country's capabilities for counter-terrorism operations.

Meanwhile, there were significant increases in the defence budgets of some smaller sub-Saharan African countries. Burkina Faso's budget rose from Fr112bn (US$192m) to Fr174bn (US$315m), while budgets in Côte d'Ivoire and Tanzania also increased – from Fr482bn (US$829m) to Fr517bn (US$935m) in the former and from Sh1.19 trillion (US$532m) to Sh1.73trn (US$757m) in the latter. The increase in Tanzania may be explained by funds allocated to enable the delivery of *Super Puma* helicopters in 2018, a deal valued at €190m (US$225m), according to a French parliamentary report on arms exports.

Defence industry

South Africa is home to the region's most advanced defence industries. However, limited defence spending by the state in recent years has not helped the country's defence manufacturers, and exports have not entirely compensated for this.

In 2017, the latest year for which data is available, total export values declined to R3.62bn (US$272m), from the 2016 total of R4.17bn (US$283m). Armoured vehicles remained the principal export products, with Paramount and Denel the key manufacturers.

Denel encountered difficulties that reflected some of the broader challenges facing South African defence firms. The company faced a liquidity crisis in the wake of questions over governance. Attempts to open Denel Asia in 2016, a joint venture in India with VR Laser Asia, have been highlighted in the media. It was intended to be a stepping stone to enable Denel to penetrate Asian markets, but became involved in broader allegations of corruption levelled against the Gupta family – with whom the firm VR Laser Asia was linked. Press reports alleged that had the joint venture been set up as planned, it would likely have benefited the Gupta family through preferential terms. The company's financial position was also not helped by its acquisition of BAE Systems Land Systems South Africa for R855m (US$67m) in 2015.

Reports indicated that as a result of its liquidity problems, Denel had experienced difficulties in paying its employees and suppliers on at least one occasion. In turn, reportedly delayed payments to suppliers generated knock-on delays in programme production. In a bid to improve matters, Denel's entire board was replaced in April 2018, and the new leadership is engaged in efforts to improve governance.

At the same time, South Africa is implementing a national strategy to revive its defence industry. Two important initiatives were launched in 2018: a Defence Industry Fund (DIF) and a defence science and engineering programme. The DIF is structured around a public–private partnership (the private firm Crede Capital Partners will operate the fund). DIF will be able to lend money to defence companies to develop their supply chain or guarantee exports. The defence science and engineering programme, meanwhile, targets universities in order to train skilled personnel for the defence sector.

In other regional countries, defence manufacturing remains limited in scale and at the lower end of the technological spectrum. Most firms are involved in the land sector, such as Uganda's Impala Services and Logistics, which produces armoured personnel carriers. Nigeria's defence-industrial base is the most advanced after South Africa's, and in 2018 an agreement was signed with Poland's PGZ to manufacture rifles under licence in the Ordnance Factory Complex in Kaduna, which is operated by the state-run Defence Industries Corporation of Nigeria. Nigeria also has a small-scale naval shipbuilding capacity, with firms including Epenal Group shipyard, Nautic Africa and Nigeria Naval Dockyard.

SOUTH AFRICA

South Africa's defence review was conducted in 2011–13 and released in 2015. It set out a robust regional role for the South African National Defence Force (SANDF) and was accepted across government. However, the review warned that the defence budget was not only inadequate to support that ambition, but also insufficient to prevent further decline in South Africa's defence capability. Nonetheless, funding dropped to less than 1% of GDP in 2018, and the SANDF has been warned to expect yet further cuts, making any notion of an expanded regional security role unrealistic.

The primary driver for the review's recommendations about South Africa's regional role was economic. The country needs a stable environment within which it can continue to develop and to expand exports into Africa; for most of the continent it remains the most important manufacturing economy. As then-president Thabo Mbeki set out at the 2001 World Economic Forum in Davos, this requires 'peace, security and stability' – a prerequisite if South Africa is to attract the scale of fixed capital investment it needs.

This desire motivated the decisions to deploy SANDF personnel to Lesotho (1998), Burundi (2001–

09), the Democratic Republic of the Congo (DRC) (2001 to date), Comoros (2006) and the Central African Republic (CAR) (2007–13). A vision of wider African solidarity led to the deployments to Darfur (2004–16), the provision of staff officers to African Union and United Nations missions in Eritrea, Ethiopia and Liberia for various periods, as well as engagement in Côte d'Ivoire (2006) and Libya (2011) in support of the South African president's peace efforts.

However, the security challenge remains. South Africa's immediate region – the Southern African Development Community (SADC) – is unstable: the DRC remains beset by conflict; Lesotho, Swaziland and Zimbabwe are fragile; and Mozambique is at risk of renewed insurgency by Renamo rebels and now faces what appears to be Islamist terrorism in the north along the border with Tanzania. Angola, meanwhile, faces the risk of renewed insurgency in its oil-rich Cabinda exclave should it lose influence in either of the Congos, which could provide safe haven for guerrillas. Some analysts think that either the Republic of Congo or the DRC will in future dispute Angola's possession of Cabinda, which is geographically, ethnically and historically a part of the former Congo kingdoms. Countries adjacent to the SADC are even less stable: the Republic of Congo is fragile, the CAR is a failed state, South Sudan is embroiled in civil war and Burundi faces renewed political and security problems.

The need for South Africa to remain engaged with regional security issues therefore continues, but for Pretoria to play a credible and effective role, it needs the military capability to respond quickly to crises, to participate in extended peace-support missions, deal with disruptive state or non-state actors and conduct constabulary operations, such as counter-piracy patrols. It will not be possible, analysts argue, to regenerate and develop the necessary military capabilities at current funding levels.

A force challenged

Current funding levels place in question the ability of the SANDF to meet even the objective of the review's first planning milestone – to 'arrest the decline in critical capabilities' (the target date was 2018). The entire concept of 'milestones' in the review has been undermined by budget cuts in 2018, which will result in further capability reductions and the generation of a 'bow wave' of requirements, as more equipment becomes obsolete or non-operational as a result of inadequate maintenance. Meanwhile, training, which has also reduced over the past two decades due to lack of funding, will be further affected.

Government funding works on a three-year medium-term expenditure framework (MTEF) that is intended to ensure a smooth funding flow. The 2018 budget was reduced from the amount that had been originally set for this and the next two years in the MTEF. A second wave of cuts is expected in the budget issued halfway through the financial year, with a real likelihood of more cuts during the current five-year medium-term strategic framework (MTSF).

The impact of this is summed up in a key paragraph of the Department of Defence's (DoD's) 2018 Annual Performance Plan (APP). The APP says that 'the persistent disconnect between government's defence expectations and the resources allocated to defence has eroded capabilities to the point where the SANDF will be unable to fulfil its defence commitments. The SANDF therefore cannot even support the current modest level of ambition. South Africa's defence ambition and defence capacity are clearly at odds with one another.'

The plan also says that a full review of the department might be needed in order to align it with available resources. It posits that the DoD may instead have to plan against the defence review's 'Strategic Policy Option 1', which was based on an assumption that reduced defence funding translates into 'vastly reduced defence capability', which 'does not support a continental leadership role' and is 'unable to fully comply with the constitutional requirements'.

The pressure on the army was lifted to an extent by the decision in 2016 to withdraw the SANDF battalion deployed in Darfur, meaning that the only major deployed South African force was an army combat formation and air-force contingent attached to the MONUSCO Force Intervention Brigade in the DRC. The government has at various times talked of additional deployments, including a return to the CAR, but at the same time, the army lacks the troops for effective border patrols. Meanwhile, the navy is conducting patrols along the west coast of Africa when it lacks sufficient ships (possessing in its surface fleet only four frigates and four patrol and coastal craft, barring minesweepers and auxiliaries) to patrol home waters and the Mozambique Channel – the route for half of South Africa's oil imports. The disconnect between what government expects of the SANDF and what it is willing to fund remains a critical problem.

Meanwhile, the country's foreign and national-security policies are seen by analysts as incoherent. Some cabinet ministers, at least in the former Zuma administration, reportedly alleged Western plans for 'regime change' in South Africa. And there have been closer ties with countries regarded as hostile to the West, such as China and Russia as well as Cuba, Iran and Venezuela. This attitude may also explain other actions by the DoD or the SANDF, such as the last-minute cancellation of live-fire missile exercises at the Denel Overberg Test Range scheduled by the Italian and Turkish navies in 2014 (the latter was reinstated after protests by Ankara). There was also a last-minute refusal of overflight rights (reinstated after protest at ministerial level) for German *Tornado*s for their long-planned 2017 live-fire exercise at the same range. The undertaking by the South African ambassador to Venezuela on 18 July 2018 that Pretoria would provide troops to defend that country against the United States was quickly repudiated by the Department of International Relations and Cooperation.

Equipment and training

Tight funding and a decade of overstretch have left their mark: training exercises are fewer and dramatically smaller in scale; equipment and facilities cannot be properly maintained; and critical equipment gaps remain unaddressed.

The air force still operates, for example, 1940s-era C-47TPs for maritime surveillance and 1963-vintage C-130s that lack the payload and range performance for regional missions. The navy may soon have only eight viable ships (four frigates and three submarines, delivered between 2006 and 2008, and a 30-year-old support ship), as its fleet of ageing patrol craft and minehunters will need to be retired. The army has not been able to replace its 1980s-vintage soft-skinned vehicles or armoured personnel carriers, and has funding for only 15 infantry companies to conduct border patrols, instead of the planned 22. However, the army may finally receive two battalion sets of the new *Badger* infantry combat vehicle (ICV).

Political factors also pose challenges. For instance, some assert that political pressure to award the contract for three offshore patrol vessels (OPVs) to China's Poly Technologies may have been a factor in the project being delayed after the tender process saw Dutch company Damen being the preferred bidder. Similarly, instead of training its own mechanics, the army is employing Cuban mechanics to repair its vehicles to an ad hoc standard rather than to baseline.

Operational lessons

At the same time, lessons have been learned from South Africa's deployments abroad. For instance, a study of the combat in Bangui in March 2013 led to some changes to the SANDF contingent deployed to the DRC. For example, battalion commanders are allowed to decide which weapons they take for each mission, and each battalion is given some experienced officers and NCOs for the duration of its deployment. Meanwhile, officers who served in the CAR during the clash in March 2013 support pre-deployment training. And there are also three *Rooivalk* attack helicopters for close support, in addition to five *Oryx* helicopters to help air mobility and other tasks. When the United Nations mooted replacing the *Rooivalk* detachment with 'cheaper' Mi-24s, the South African government objected, apparently to the extent of warning that if the *Rooivalk* was withdrawn, the *Oryx* helicopters and the South African battalion would also be withdrawn.

South African contingents performed well in the DRC, as previously in Burundi and in Darfur. Similarly, anecdotal evidence from the Mozambique Navy and from the South African tourism sector suggests that the navy's patrols in the northern parts of the Mozambique Channel have reduced general maritime crime – illegal fishing, smuggling and people trafficking; there has been no pirate activity since the patrols began in 2011.

SANDF engagement in peace-support and constabulary missions has also proved useful in building professionalism and boosting morale and retention: there is a sense that personnel are carrying out tasks for which they were trained. One indicator of this is that the army now has middle-ranking officers and senior NCOs that have completed ten to 12 deployments. Professionalism has become more evident among officers moving up through the system, even if the mission and funding mismatch continues to frustrate and concern service chiefs and senior officers. That said, there remain some senior officers whose appointments seem perplexing to outside observers, and there have been reports that senior personnel have been arrested on suspicion of illicit activities, although this could become less of a concern as operationally experienced officers and NCOs are promoted.

There is, however, a near-term challenge in the form of succession planning regarding the top posts. The secretary for defence, the chief of the defence force, the chief of defence staff, the chief of the army, the chief of the air force and the general officer commanding special forces are all due to retire over the next two years, and suitable successors are not immediately apparent. There is no lack of suitable officers, but poor succession planning has caused a gap between officers due to retire too soon to be available for these posts and others that will still be too junior in rank in two years. This may require some officers to be fast-tracked, but there is precedent for that in the former South African Defence Force.

Defence economics

The primary challenge facing South Africa's armed forces remains the mismatch between funding and commitments. While the budget has remained more or less constant in US-dollar terms over the past few years, it was inadequate to begin with and has not matched inflation. In addition, with unemployment a significant problem there is no specific SANDF exit mechanism to plan for and manage departures, such as improved severance packages. As a consequence, the average age of SANDF personnel is steadily increasing, while an increasing proportion of junior ranks have families. The result has been that direct (57.1% of the budget) and indirect personnel costs absorb, according to treasury budget papers, almost 80% of the available funding.

This has put the SANDF in a difficult situation, resulting in, according to official documents, reductions in training exercises, air-force flying hours and sea days (500 sea days for the entire fleet in the first two years of the current three-year MTEF, shrinking to 417 in FY2020/21). It also makes it difficult to maintain equipment and facilities properly, let alone close strategic capability gaps or replace old equipment. The present budget plan is to cut personnel from just over 75,500 to about 74,660 by 2020 and reduce the use of reserve personnel. However, this will depend on finding an exit mechanism and the funds needed to buy out those personnel who are no longer required, and on the government not entering into new tasks requiring significant personnel commitments.

With the economy shrinking, there are only slim prospects for any real increase in defence funding, even looking beyond the present three-year MTEF and five-year MTSF. The DoD has, however, taken a new approach in arguing its case for funding. It has set out the importance of exports to the region – which depend on stability that, in turn, can depend on peace-support or constabulary operations – and foreign-currency earnings from defence exports. The *Rooivalk* attack helicopter, for instance, cost some R6.2 billion (US$642 million) to develop and manufacture, and had by the end of 2013 generated foreign-exchange revenues of more than R15bn (US$1.55bn) from the export of subsystems (both 2013 rand).

There were some positive developments in the medium-term (three-year) budget, but there remains the chance of further cuts during the year. The army may receive the first *Badger* ICVs, artillery command systems and new water-purification equipment, and the air force the first A-*Darter* infrared air-to-air missiles and a new mobile communications system. Some funds had been allocated to maritime and light-transport aircraft, although those seem unlikely to materialise since the money has been diverted to personnel costs. The navy has been disappointed by the fate of its planned three OPVs, which have been

Table 20 **SANDF budget by programme (in rand/US$ at yearly exchange rates)**

Programme/Year	2017/18	2018/19		2019/20		2020/21
	Final	Planned	Actual	Planned	Revised	Planned
Administration	5.5bn (409m)	5.6bn (432m)	5.5bn (426m)	5.9bn (437m)	5.8bn (430m)	6.3bn (448m)
Force Employment	3.4bn (358m)	3.7bn (281m)	3.4bn (259m)	3.8bn (276m)	3.6bn (264m)	3.8bn (270m)
Landward Defence	16.7bn (1.25bn)	17.1bn (1.3bn)	16.2bn (1.2bn)	18.2bn (1.3bn)	16.6bn (1.2bn)	17.0bn (1.2bn)
Air Defence	6.8bn (510m)	7.1bn (548m)	6.4bn (492m)	8.6bn (630m)	7.3bn (535m)	8.2bn (586m)
Maritime Defence	4.6bn (346m)	4.89bn (375m)	4.4bn (339m)	4.5bn (330m)	4.4bn (324m)	5.1bn (363m)
Military Health Support	4.6bn (349m)	4.91bn (376m)	4.7bn (362m)	5.4bn (395m)	5.3bn (387m)	5.8bn (416m)
Defence Intelligence	908m (68m)	948m (73m)	1bn (73m)	1bn (74m)	1bn (73m)	1.1bn (76m)
General Support	6.5bn (490m)	6.3bn (483m)	6.3bn (482m)	6.7bn (491m)	6.7bn (492m)	6.9bn (494m)
Total	**R49bn (US$3.7bn)**	**R50.6bn (US$3.9bn)**	**R48bn (US$3.7m)**	**R50.4bn (US$4.0bn)**	**R50.7bn (US$3.7bn)**	**R54.0bn (US$3.9bn)**

Source: South African defence budget 2018

deferred, although contracts for three inshore patrol vessels and a new survey ship have been signed. However, it remains to be seen how far these plans will be realised in the face of the weakening economy.

The Special Defence Account, which covers the acquisition of equipment and systems, is due to receive only R5.36bn (US$411m) in 2018/19, R5.29bn (US$406m) in 2019/20 and R5.51bn (US$423m) in 2020/21, assuming that there are no further cuts.

Defence industry

The South African defence industry is much smaller than it was in 1989, down from 130,000 employees to 15,000 and from some 3,000 companies to fewer than 200; it has also lost some key capabilities. The main factor in this reduction was the 50% cut in defence funding between 1989 and 1994, years that saw operational costs increase. This was followed by the costs of integrating the non-statutory forces and the former SADF, moving to a regular force and then nearly a decade of operational overstretch from 2001.

An outcome is that SANDF-funded research and development (R&D), accounting for about 11.2% of acquisition funding in the 2018/19 financial year, is set to decline to 10.2% by 2020/21, forcing many projects to be put on hold or even cancelled.

For a considerable time, the defence industry was able to offset the shrinking SANDF acquisition budget by exporting, and it continues to be successful in the international market. The reduction in defence-funded R&D has meant that companies have fewer new products, which has affected export potential, with exports in 2015 dropping below the level reached in 2006.

Pretoria now appreciates the economic potential of the defence industry, and a new defence-industry strategy was approved in April 2018. The strategy calls for streamlining the SANDF acquisition and procurement processes, as well as focused government support, but it will not succeed if defence-acquisition funding cannot be increased and if there is no support for joint ventures or partnerships with foreign and international defence groups. However, there is potential for such cooperation, given South Africa's success in secure communications, electronic warfare, guided weapons and protected vehicles. However, there will need to be a shift in government thinking on foreign partnerships, given that the only viable partners will often be Western states, rather than favoured friends such as China and Russia (who are also the defence industry's primary competitors). Another challenge lies in attempting to draft an implementation plan when there is no certainty regarding acquisition funding. That will make it difficult for the defence industry to plan ahead and may see more companies exit the sector.

Angola ANG

New Angolan Kwanza AOA		2017	2018	2019
GDP	AOA	21.0tr	28.2tr	
	US$	127bn	115bn	
per capita	US$	4,466	3,924	
Growth	%	-2.5	-0.1	
Inflation	%	29.8	20.5	
Def bdgt	AOA	536bn	546bn	
	US$	3.23bn	2.22bn	
USD1=AOA		165.92	246.31	

Population 30,355,880

Ethnic groups: Ovimbundu 37%; Kimbundu 25%; Bakongo 13%

Age	0–14	15–19	20–24	25–29	30–64	65 plus
Male	23.0%	4.9%	4.0%	3.3%	11.5%	1.0%
Female	24.2%	5.1%	4.3%	3.7%	12.7%	1.4%

Capabilities

Though numerically one of the region's largest and best-equipped armed forces, the available inventory is limited in scale with maintenance and readiness a challenge. The armed forces are constitutionally tasked with ensuring sovereignty and territorial integrity, though maritime security and the protection of offshore resources is an increasing focus. There are growing military ties with China. Luanda is looking to Beijing to help modernise its armed forces, and to develop its defence-industrial base. Defence ties persist with Russia, which also provides support to the armed forces. Angola retains conscription and, in recent years, force health and education have been investment priorities. The armed forces train regularly and have participated in multinational exercises with the US and others. Angola is the only regional state with a strategic-airlift capacity and has a comparatively large transport fleet, though availability remains an issue. Improving the military-logistics system has been identified as a key requirement, but progress is unclear. Modernisation plans have been curtailed by the fall in oil prices. However, there have been some acquisitions. The country ordered the C295 maritime-patrol aircraft in 2018 in light of security concerns in the Gulf of Guinea. Defence industry is limited to in-service maintenance facilities, but Angola has ambitions to develop greater capacity by partnering with countries such as China, Brazil, Russia and Portugal.

ACTIVE 107,000 (Army 100,000 Navy 1,000 Air 6,000) Paramilitary 10,000

ORGANISATIONS BY SERVICE

Army 100,000
FORCES BY ROLE
MANOEUVRE
  Armoured
   1 tk bde
  Light
   1 SF bde
   1 (1st) div (1 mot inf bde, 2 inf bde)
   1 (2nd) div (3 mot inf bde, 3 inf bde, 1 arty regt)
   1 (3rd) div (2 mot inf bde, 3 inf bde)
   1 (4th) div (1 tk regt, 5 mot inf bde, 2 inf bde, 1 engr bde)
   1 (5th) div (2 inf bde)
   1 (6th) div (1 mot inf bde, 2 inf bde, 1 engr bde)
COMBAT SUPPORT
  Some engr units
COMBAT SERVICE SUPPORT
  Some log units
EQUIPMENT BY TYPE†
ARMOURED FIGHTING VEHICLES
  MBT 300: ε200 T-55AM2; 50 T-62; 50 T-72
  LT TK 10 PT-76
  ASLT 3+ PTL-02 *Assaulter*
  RECCE 600 BRDM-2
  IFV 250 BMP-1/BMP-2
  APC 246
    APC (T) 31 MT-LB
    APC (W) 170+: ε170 BTR-152/BTR-60/BTR-80; WZ-551 (CP)
    PPV 45 *Casspir* NG2000
  ABCV BMD-3
ENGINEERING & MAINTENANCE VEHICLES
  ARV T-54/T-55
  MW *Bozena*
ARTILLERY 1,439+
  SP 16+: **122mm** 2S1 *Gvozdika*; **152mm** 4 2S3 *Akatsiya*; **203mm** 12 2S7 *Pion*
  TOWED 575: **122mm** 523 D-30; **130mm** 48 M-46; **152mm** 4 D-20
  MRL 98+: **122mm** 98: 58 BM-21 *Grad*; 40 RM-70; **240mm** BM-24
  MOR 750: **82mm** 250; **120mm** 500
ANTI-TANK/ANTI-INFRASTRUCTURE
  MSL • MANPATS 9K11 (AT-3 *Sagger*)
  RCL 500: 400 **82mm** B-10/**107mm** B-11†; **106mm** 100†
  GUNS • SP 100mm SU-100†
AIR DEFENCE
  SAM • Point-defence 9K32 *Strela*-2 (SA-7 *Grail*)‡; 9K36 *Strela*-3 (SA-14 *Gremlin*); 9K310 *Igla*-1 (SA-16 *Gimlet*)
  GUNS
    SP 23mm ZSU-23-4
    TOWED 450+: **14.5mm** ZPU-4; **23mm** ZU-23-2; **37mm** M-1939; **57mm** S-60

Navy ε1,000
EQUIPMENT BY TYPE
PATROL AND COASTAL COMBATANTS 21
  PCO 2 *Ngola Kiluange* with 1 hel landing platform (Ministry of Fisheries)
  PCC 5 *Rei Bula Matadi* (Ministry of Fisheries)
  PBF 5 PVC-170
  PB 9: 4 *Mandume*; 5 *Comandante Imperial Santana* (Ministry of Fisheries)

Coastal Defence
EQUIPMENT BY TYPE
COASTAL DEFENCE • AShM 4K44 *Utyos* (SS-C-1B *Sepal* – at Luanda)

Air Force/Air Defence 6,000
FORCES BY ROLE
FIGHTER
 1 sqn with MiG-21bis/MF *Fishbed*
 1 sqn with Su-27/Su-27UB/Su-30K *Flanker*
FIGHTER/GROUND ATTACK
 1 sqn with MiG-23BN/ML/UB *Flogger*
 1 sqn with Su-22 *Fitter* D
 1 sqn with Su-25 *Frogfoot*
MARITIME PATROL
 1 sqn with F-27-200 MPA; C-212 *Aviocar*
TRANSPORT
 3 sqn with An-12 *Cub*; An-26 *Curl*; An-32 *Cline*; An-72 *Coaler*; BN-2A *Islander*; C-212 *Aviocar*; Do-28D *Skyservant*; EMB-135BJ *Legacy* 600 (VIP); Il-76TD *Candid*
TRAINING
 1 sqn with Cessna 172K/R
 1 sqn with EMB-312 *Tucano*
 1 sqn with L-29 *Delfin*; L-39 *Albatros*
 1 sqn with PC-7 *Turbo Trainer*; PC-9*
 1 sqn with Z-142
ATTACK HELICOPTER
 2 sqn with Mi-24/Mi-35 *Hind*; SA342M *Gazelle* (with HOT)
TRANSPORT HELICOPTER
 2 sqn with AS565; SA316 *Alouette* III (IAR-316) (trg)
 1 sqn with Bell 212
 1 sqn with Mi-8 *Hip*; Mi-17 *Hip* H
 1 sqn with Mi-171Sh
AIR DEFENCE
 5 bn/10 bty with S-125 *Pechora* (SA-3 *Goa*); 9K35 *Strela*-10 (SA-13 *Gopher*)†; 2K12 *Kub* (SA-6 *Gainful*); 9K33 *Osa* (SA-8 *Gecko*); 9K31 *Strela*-1 (SA-9 *Gaskin*); S-75M *Volkhov* (SA-2 *Guideline*)

EQUIPMENT BY TYPE†
AIRCRAFT 88 combat capable
 FTR 26: 6 Su-27/Su-27UB *Flanker*; 2 Su-30K *Flanker*; 18 MiG-23ML *Flogger*
 FGA 42+: 20 MiG-21bis/MF *Fishbed*; 8 MiG-23BN/UB *Flogger*; 13 Su-22 *Fitter* D; 1+ Su-24 *Fencer*
 ATK 10: 8 Su-25 *Frogfoot*; 2 Su-25UB *Frogfoot*
 ELINT 1 B-707
 TPT 56: **Heavy** 4 Il-76TD *Candid*; **Medium** 6 An-12 *Cub*; **Light** 46: 12 An-26 *Curl*; 2 An-32 *Cline*; 8 An-72 *Coaler*; 8 BN-2A *Islander*; 2 C-212; 5 Cessna 172K; 6 Cessna 172R; 1 Do-28D *Skyservant*; 1 EMB-135BJ *Legacy* 600 (VIP); 1 Yak-40
 TRG 42: 13 EMB-312 *Tucano*; 6 EMB-314 *Super Tucano**; 6 L-29 *Delfin*; 2 L-39C *Albatros*; 5 PC-7 *Turbo Trainer*; 4 PC-9*; 6 Z-142
HELICOPTERS
 ATK 56: 34 Mi-24 *Hind*; 22 Mi-35 *Hind*
 MRH 60: 8 AS565 *Panther*; 9 SA316 *Alouette* III (IAR-316) (incl trg); 8 SA342M *Gazelle*; 27 Mi-8 *Hip*/Mi-17 *Hip* H; 8 Mi-171Sh *Terminator*
 TPT • Light 8 Bell 212

AIR DEFENCE • SAM 122
 Medium-range 40 S-75M *Volkhov* (SA-2 *Guideline*)‡
 Short-range 37: 25 2K12 *Kub* (SA-6 *Gainful*); 12 S-125 *Pechora* (SA-3 *Goa*)
 Point-defence 45: 10 9K35 *Strela*-10 (SA-13 *Gopher*)†; 15 9K33 *Osa* (SA-8 *Gecko*); 20 9K31 *Strela*-1 (SA-9 *Gaskin*)
AIR-LAUNCHED MISSILES
 AAM
  IR R-3 (AA-2 *Atoll*)‡; R-60 (AA-8 *Aphid*); R-73 (AA-11 *Archer*)
  IR/SARH R-23/24 (AA-7 *Apex*)‡; R-27 (AA-10 *Alamo*)
 ASM AT-2 *Swatter*; HOT
 ARM Kh-28 (AS-9 *Kyle*)

Paramilitary 10,000

Rapid-Reaction Police 10,000

Benin BEN

CFA Franc BCEAO fr		2017	2018	2019
GDP	fr	5.37tr	5.81tr	
	US$	9.25bn	10.5bn	
per capita	US$	831	923	
Growth	%	5.606	6.039	
Inflation	%	0.144	2.3	
Def bdgt	fr	67.9bn	50.1bn	
	US$	117m	91m	
US$1=fr		580.91	550.84	

Population	11,340,504					
Age	0–14	15–19	20–24	25–29	30–64	65 plus
Male	21.6%	5.7%	4.8%	3.9%	13.2%	1.1%
Female	20.7%	5.5%	4.6%	3.8%	13.4%	1.8%

Capabilities

The country's small armed forces focus on border- and internal-security issues, as well as combating illicit trafficking. Border patrols increased and security was tightened after increased concern over the regional threat from Islamist groups. Maritime security is a priority in light of continuing piracy in the Gulf of Guinea. In 2018, the government merged the police and gendarmerie into a new body called the Republican Police. There is a military-cooperation agreement with France, whose Senegal-based forces have delivered training to boost Benin's border-surveillance capacity. The US has provided similar training to the army and national police. US forces have also delivered pre-deployment training to the armed forces and training in professional ethics, anti-corruption and accountability to the Republican Police. Benin's forces took part in the academic section of the US AFRICOM *Unified Focus 2018* exercise in Cameroon. Benin contributes personnel to the Multi-National Joint Task Force fighting Boko Haram. There is a limited capacity to deploy beyond neighbouring states without external support. The country has no domestic defence-industrial capability.

ACTIVE 7,250 (Army 6,500 Navy 500 Air 250)
Paramilitary 4,800

Conscript liability 18 months (selective)

ORGANISATIONS BY SERVICE

Army 6,500
FORCES BY ROLE
MANOEUVRE
  Armoured
    2 armd sqn
  Light
    1 (rapid reaction) mot inf bn
    8 inf bn
  Air Manoeuvre
    1 AB bn
COMBAT SUPPORT
  2 arty bn
  1 engr bn
  1 sigs bn
COMBAT SERVICE SUPPORT
  1 log bn
  1 spt bn
EQUIPMENT BY TYPE
ARMOURED FIGHTING VEHICLES
  LT TK 18 PT-76†
  RECCE 34: 3 AML-90; 14 BRDM-2; 7 M8; 10 VBL
  APC 34 • **APC (T)** 22 M113; **APC (W)** 2 *Bastion* APC; **PPV** 10 *Casspir* NG
ARTILLERY 16+
  TOWED 105mm 16: 12 L118 Light Gun; 4 M101
  MOR 81mm some; 120mm some

Navy ε500
EQUIPMENT BY TYPE
PATROL AND COASTAL COMBATANTS
  PB 6: 2 *Matelot Brice Kpomasse* (ex-PRC); 3 FPB 98; 1 27m (PRC)

Air Force 250
EQUIPMENT BY TYPE
AIRCRAFT
  TPT 3: **Light** 1 DHC-6 *Twin Otter*†; **PAX** 2: 1 B-727; 1 HS-748†
  TRG 2 LH-10 *Ellipse*
HELICOPTERS
  TPT • **Light** 5: 4 AW109BA; 1 AS350B *Ecureuil*†

Paramilitary 4,800
  Police Republicaine 4,800

DEPLOYMENT

CENTRAL AFRICAN REPUBLIC: UN • MINUSCA 4; 2 obs
CHAD: Lake Chad Basin Commission • MNJTF 150
DEMOCRATIC REPUBLIC OF THE CONGO: UN • MONUSCO 49; 4 obs
MALI: UN • MINUSMA 258; 1 mech inf coy(+)
SOUTH SUDAN: UN • UNMISS 3; 1 obs
SUDAN: UN • UNISFA 2 obs

Botswana BWA

Botswana Pula P		2017	2018	2019
GDP	P	180bn	195bn	
	US$	17.4bn	19.1bn	
per capita	US$	7,584	8,168	
Growth	%	2.36	4.618	
Inflation	%	3.296	3.792	
Def bdgt [a]	P	5.30bn	5.85bn	
	US$	512m	572m	
US$1=P		10.36	10.23	

[a] Defence, Justice and Security Budget

Population	2,249,104					
Age	0–14	15–19	20–24	25–29	30–64	65 plus
Male	15.9%	4.7%	4.5%	4.2%	16.5%	2.3%
Female	15.6%	4.8%	4.7%	4.5%	19.3%	3.1%

Capabilities

The Botswana Defence Force (BDF) mainly comprises ground forces and a small, but comparatively well-equipped, air wing. The major task for the BDF is to ensure territorial integrity, coupled with domestic missions such as tackling poachers. There is also a history of involvement in peacekeeping operations. The BDF has reportedly been working on a defence doctrine that is believed to be influenced by US concepts and practices. Botswana has a good relationship with the US and regularly sends its officers to train there. The armed forces also train with other African nations, including Namibia, with whom it holds biannual exercises. The operations centre for the Southern African Development Community Standby Force is located in Gaborone. The BDF is an all-volunteer force. Recent personnel priorities include improving conditions of service, overhauling retirement ages and boosting capability. Growing relations with Beijing have seen some military personnel travel to China for training. The air force has a reasonable airlift capacity, given the size of its armed forces, and the BDF is able to deploy a small force by air if required. There is an ongoing effort to identify a successor for the air arm's primary combat aircraft, the F-5, while, in recent years, ground-based air defence has been improved. Local reports suggest a limited capacity in armoured-vehicle maintenance; beyond this, the country has no defence-industrial base.

ACTIVE 9,000 (Army 8,500 Air 500)

ORGANISATIONS BY SERVICE

Army 8,500
FORCES BY ROLE
MANOEUVRE
  Armoured
    1 armd bde(-)
  Light
    2 inf bde (1 armd recce regt, 4 inf bn, 1 cdo unit, 1 engr regt, 1 log bn, 2 ADA regt)
COMBAT SUPPORT
  1 arty bde
  1 engr coy
  1 sigs coy

COMBAT SERVICE SUPPORT
  1 log gp
AIR DEFENCE
  1 AD bde(-)
EQUIPMENT BY TYPE
ARMOURED FIGHTING VEHICLES
  LT TK 45: ε20 SK-105 *Kurassier*; 25 FV101 *Scorpion*
  RECCE 72+: RAM-V-1; ε8 RAM-V-2; 64 VBL
  APC 157: **APC (W)** 145: 50 BTR-60; 50 LAV-150 *Commando* (some with 90mm gun); 45 MOWAG *Piranha* III; **PPV** 12 *Casspir*
  AUV 6 FV103 *Spartan*
ENGINEERING & MAINTENANCE VEHICLES
  ARV *Greif*; M578
  MW *Aardvark* Mk2
ANTI-TANK/ANTI-INFRASTRUCTURE
  MSL
    SP V-150 TOW
    MANPATS TOW
  RCL 84mm *Carl Gustav*
ARTILLERY 78
  TOWED 30: **105mm** 18: 12 L118 Light Gun; 6 Model 56 pack howitzer; **155mm** 12 Soltam
  MRL 122mm 20 APRA-40
  MOR 28: **81mm** 22; **120mm** 6 M-43
AIR DEFENCE
  SAM • Point-defence *Javelin*; 9K310 *Igla*-1 (SA-16 *Gimlet*); 9K32 *Strela*-2 (SA-7 *Grail*)‡
  GUNS • TOWED 20mm 7 M167 *Vulcan*

Air Wing 500
FORCES BY ROLE
FIGHTER/GROUND ATTACK
  1 sqn with F-5A *Freedom Fighter*; F-5D *Tiger* II
ISR
  1 sqn with O-2 *Skymaster*
TRANSPORT
  2 sqn with BD-700 *Global Express*; BN-2A/B *Defender**; Beech 200 *Super King Air* (VIP); C-130B *Hercules*; C-212-300 *Aviocar*; CN-235M-100; Do-328-110 (VIP)
TRAINING
  1 sqn with PC-7 MkII *Turbo Trainer**
TRANSPORT HELICOPTER
  1 sqn with AS350B *Ecureuil*; Bell 412EP/SP *Twin Huey*; EC225LP *Super Puma*
EQUIPMENT BY TYPE
AIRCRAFT 28 combat capable
  FTR 13: 8 F-5A *Freedom Fighter*; 5 F-5D *Tiger* II
  ISR 5 O-2 *Skymaster*
  TPT 19: **Medium** 3 C-130B *Hercules*; **Light** 15: 4 BN-2 *Defender**; 6 BN-2B *Defender**; 1 Beech 200 *King Air* (VIP); 1 C-212-300 *Aviocar*; 2 CN-235M-100; 1 Do-328-110 (VIP); **PAX** 1 BD700 *Global Express*
  TRG 5 PC-7 MkII *Turbo Trainer**
HELICOPTERS
  MRH 7: 2 Bell 412EP *Twin Huey*; 5 Bell 412SP *Twin Huey*
  TPT 9: **Medium** 1 EC225LP *Super Puma*; **Light** 8 AS350B *Ecureuil*

Burkina Faso BFA

CFA Franc BCEAO fr		2017	2018	2019
GDP	fr	7.30tr	7.87tr	
	US$	12.6bn	14.3bn	
per capita	US$	655	734	
Growth	%	6.4	5.9	
Inflation	%	0.4	2.0	
Def bdgt	fr	112bn	174bn	
	US$	192m	321m	
US$1=fr		580.94	550.83	

Population   19,742,715

Age	0–14	15–19	20–24	25–29	30–64	65 plus
Male	22.5%	5.8%	4.3%	3.7%	11.3%	1.4%
Female	21.8%	5.6%	4.5%	4.1%	13.3%	1.8%

Capabilities

An increased terrorist threat has challenged Burkina Faso's security forces in recent years. The country is part of the G5 Sahel grouping and, as part of its support for this, France has supplied armed pick-up trucks. The terrorist threat has led Ouagadougou to refocus its military efforts to the north. There is cooperation with France and Mali, particularly on border security. Aviation capacities are slowly improving, with the arrival of more helicopters. However, financial challenges hinder broader military-capability developments. Military deployment capabilities are limited to neighbouring countries without external support. Maintenance capacities are limited and the country has no traditional defence industry.

ACTIVE 11,200 (Army 6,400 Air 600 Gendarmerie 4,200) **Paramilitary 250**

ORGANISATIONS BY SERVICE

Army 6,400

Three military regions. In 2011, several regiments were disbanded and merged into other formations, including the new 24th and 34th *régiments interarmes*

FORCES BY ROLE
MANOEUVRE
  Mechanised
    1 cbd arms regt
  Light
    1 cbd arms regt
    6 inf regt
  Air Manoeuvre
    1 AB regt (1 CT coy)
COMBAT SUPPORT
  1 arty bn (2 arty tp)
  1 engr bn
EQUIPMENT BY TYPE
ARMOURED FIGHTING VEHICLES
  RECCE 91+: 19 AML-60/AML-90; 8+ *Bastion Patsas*; 24 EE-9 *Cascavel*; 30 *Ferret*; 2 M20; 8 M8
  APC 44+
    APC (W) 13+: 13 Panhard M3; Some *Bastion* APC
    PPV 31 *Puma* M26-15

ANTI-TANK/ANTI-INFRASTRUCTURE
RCL 75mm Type-52 (M20); **84mm** *Carl Gustav*
ARTILLERY 50+
TOWED 14: **105mm** 8 M101; **122mm** 6
MRL 9: **107mm** ε4 Type-63; **122mm** 5 APR-40
MOR 27+: **81mm** Brandt; **82mm** 15; **120mm** 12
AIR DEFENCE
SAM • **Point-defence** 9K32 *Strela*-2 (SA-7 *Grail*)‡
GUNS • **TOWED** 42: **14.5mm** 30 ZPU; **20mm** 12 TCM-20

Air Force 600
FORCES BY ROLE
GROUND ATTACK/TRAINING
1 sqn with SF-260WL *Warrior**; Embraer EMB-314 *Super Tucano**
TRANSPORT
1 sqn with AT-802 *Air Tractor*; B-727 (VIP); Beech 200 *King Air*; CN235-220; PA-34 *Seneca*
ATTACK/TRANSPORT HELICOPTER
1 sqn with AS350 *Ecureuil*; Mi-8 *Hip*; Mi-17 *Hip* H; Mi-35 *Hind*
EQUIPMENT BY TYPE
AIRCRAFT 5 combat capable
ISR 1 DA42M (reported)
TPT 9: **Light** 8: 1 AT-802 *Air Tractor*; 2 Beech 200 *King Air*; 1 CN235-220; 1 PA-34 *Seneca*; 3 *Tetras*; **PAX** 1 B-727 (VIP)
TRG 5: 3 EMB-314 *Super Tucano**; 2 SF-260WL *Warrior**
HELICOPTERS
ATK 2 Mi-35 *Hind*
MRH 3: 2 Mi-17 *Hip* H; 1 AW139
TPT 4: **Medium** 1 Mi-8 *Hip*; **Light** 3: 1 AS350 *Ecureuil*; 2 UH-1H *Huey*

Gendarmerie 4,200
FORCES BY ROLE
SPECIAL FORCES
1 spec ops gp (USIGN)
EQUIPMENT BY TYPE
ARMOURED FIGHTING VEHICLES
APC • **APC (W)** some Bastion APC

Paramilitary 250

People's Militia (R) 45,000 reservists (trained)

Security Company 250

DEPLOYMENT
CENTRAL AFRICAN REPUBLIC: UN • MINUSCA 1; 1 obs
DEMOCRATIC REPUBLIC OF THE CONGO: UN • MONUSCO 1; 3 obs
MALI: UN • MINUSMA 1,720; 2 inf bn
SUDAN: UN • UNAMID 1; 1 obs; **UN** • UNISFA 1 obs

FOREIGN FORCES
France *Operation Barkhane* 250; 1 SF gp; 1 H225M; 1 *Gazelle*

Burundi BDI

Burundi Franc fr		2017	2018	2019
GDP	fr	5.87tr	6.18tr	
	US$	3.40bn	3.44bn	
per capita	US$	312	307	
Growth	%	0.0	0.1	
Inflation	%	16.6	1.2	
Def bdgt	fr	110bn	117bn	
	US$	63.5m	64.8m	
US$1=fr		1729.18	1799.57	

Population   11,844,520

Ethnic groups: Hutu 85%; Tutsi 14%

Age	0–14	15–19	20–24	25–29	30–64	65 plus
Male	22.9%	5.2%	4.3%	3.7%	12.4%	1.1%
Female	22.6%	5.2%	4.4%	3.7%	12.7%	1.5%

Capabilities
The country's political crisis has tested the cohesion of the armed forces. Military-training activity with international partners largely stalled in 2015 as a result. However, Burundi reportedly signed a cooperation agreement with Russia in 2018 on counter-terrorism and joint training. The experience accumulated during UN operations, where troops have gained valuable combat experience and military skills, partly compensates for the otherwise low level of training. The armed forces have a limited capability to deploy externally, though they maintain a deployment to the AMISOM mission in Somalia. Peacekeeping missions help to fund the armed forces, though financial challenges otherwise limit their effectiveness. Apart from limited maintenance facilities, the country has no domestic defence-industrial capability.

ACTIVE 30,050 (Army 30,000 Navy 50) **Paramilitary 21,000**

DDR efforts continue, while activities directed at professionalising the security forces have taken place, some sponsored by United Nations agencies.

ORGANISATIONS BY SERVICE

Army 30,000
FORCES BY ROLE
MANOEUVRE
  Mechanised
  2 lt armd bn (sqn)
  Light
  7 inf bn
  Some indep inf coy
COMBAT SUPPORT
  1 arty bn
  1 engr bn
AIR DEFENCE
  1 AD bn
EQUIPMENT BY TYPE
ARMOURED FIGHTING VEHICLES
  RECCE 55: 6 AML-60; 12 AML-90; 30 BRDM-2; 7 S52 *Shorland*

APC 94
  APC (W) 60: 20 BTR-40; 10 BTR-80; 9 Panhard M3; 15 Type-92; 6 *Walid*
  PPV 34: 12 *Casspir*; 12 RG-31 *Nyala*; 10 RG-33L
  AUV 15 *Cougar* 4×4
ARTILLERY 120
  TOWED 122mm 18 D-30
  MRL 122mm 12 BM-21 *Grad*
  MOR 90: 82mm 15 M-43; 120mm ε75
ANTI-TANK/ANTI-INFRASTRUCTURE
  MSL • MANPATS *Milan* (reported)
  RCL 75mm Type-52 (M20)
AIR DEFENCE
  SAM • Point-defence 9K32 *Strela*-2 (SA-7 *Grail*)‡
  GUNS • TOWED 150+: 14.5mm 15 ZPU-4; 135+ 23mm ZU-23/37mm Type-55 (M-1939)

Air Wing 200
EQUIPMENT BY TYPE
AIRCRAFT 1 combat capable
  TPT 2: Light 2 Cessna 150L†
  TRG 1 SF-260W *Warrior**
HELICOPTERS
  ATK 2 Mi-24 *Hind*
  MRH 2 SA342L *Gazelle*
  TPT • Medium (2 Mi-8 *Hip* non-op)

Reserves
FORCES BY ROLE
MANOEUVRE
  Light
  10 inf bn (reported)

Navy 50
EQUIPMENT BY TYPE
PATROL AND COASTAL COMBATANTS • PB 4
AMPHIBIOUS • LCT 2

Paramilitary ε1,000

General Administration of State Security
ε1,000

DEPLOYMENT
CENTRAL AFRICAN REPUBLIC: UN • MINUSCA 760; 9 obs; 1 inf bn
MALI: UN • MINUSMA 2
SOMALIA: AU • AMISOM 5,073; 6 inf bn
UN • UNSOM 1 obs
SUDAN: UN • UNAMID 3; 1 obs; UN • UNISFA 2 obs

Cameroon CMR

CFA Franc BEAC fr		2017	2018	2019
GDP	fr	20.3tr	21.3tr	
	US$	35.0bn	38.4bn	
per capita	US$	1,441	1,545	
Growth	%	3.5	3.8	
Inflation	%	0.6	1.0	
Def bdgt	fr	239bn	239bn	
	US$	411m	432m	
US$1=fr		580.93	553.07	

Population   25,640,965

Age	0–14	15–19	20–24	25–29	30–64	65 plus
Male	21.3%	5.3%	4.5%	4.0%	13.4%	1.5%
Female	21.0%	5.2%	4.5%	3.9%	13.4%	1.7%

Capabilities

Although internal stability has long been a focus for Cameroon's armed forces, the threat from Boko Haram and separatist movements have generated a significant response, particularly in the northern area of the country bordering Nigeria. The government continues to boost the size of the armed forces. In 2018, a fifth military region was created in response to security challenges in the west stemming from separatist activity. Cameroon is part of the Multinational Joint Task Force engaged on operations against Boko Haram. There are long-standing military ties with France and the US, including for support and training. The US has trained naval personnel as part of the Africa Maritime Law Enforcement Partnership. A military-assistance agreement was signed with China in 2018. The two countries have cooperated over the new floating dock at Kribi, which it is hoped will improve operational readiness. The AU's continental logistic base was inaugurated at Douala in early 2018. The armed forces are considered disciplined and well organised, though in 2018 there were some allegations of abuse. In late 2018, the US said it would continue assisting the armed forces, but urged accountability in the wake of the abuse allegations. The army has contributed personnel to UN peacekeeping operations and has strengthened its participation to deployments in the CAR. There is only limited capability for power projection and deployment capabilities are limited to neighbouring countries without external support. Many elements of the equipment inventory are ageing, but infantry fighting vehicles and protected patrol vehicles were acquired from China and South Africa and gifted by the US. The armed forces are improving their ISR capability with fixed-wing aircraft and small UAVs. Maritime capabilities improved in recent years with the acquisition of more patrol vessels, both new and second-hand. Cameroon has no defence-industrial capacity, bar maintenance facilities.

ACTIVE 15,400 (Army 13,500 Navy 1,500 Air 400)
Paramilitary 9,000

ORGANISATIONS BY SERVICE

Army 13,500
3 Mil Regions
FORCES BY ROLE
MANOEUVRE
  Light
  1 rapid reaction bde (1 armd recce bn, 1 AB bn, 1 amph bn)

1 mot inf bde (4 mot inf bn, 1 spt bn)
2 mot inf bde (3 mot inf bn, 1 spt bn)
2 mot inf bde (2 mot inf bn, 1 spt bn)
3 (rapid reaction) inf bn
Air Manoeuvre
1 cdo/AB bn
Other
1 (Presidential Guard) gd bn
COMBAT SUPPORT
1 arty regt (5 arty bty)
5 engr regt
AIR DEFENCE
1 AD regt (6 AD bty)
EQUIPMENT BY TYPE
ARMOURED FIGHTING VEHICLES
ASLT 18: 6 AMX-10RC; ε12 PTL-02 mod (*Cara* 105)
RECCE 64: 31 AML-90; 15 *Ferret*; 8 M8; 5 RAM Mk3; 5 VBL
IFV 42: 8 LAV-150 *Commando* with 20mm gun; 14 LAV-150 *Commando* with 90mm gun; 12 *Ratel*-20 (Engr); ε8 Type-07P
APC 64
  APC (T) 12 M3 half-track
  APC (W) 36: 15 *Bastion* APC (reported); 21 LAV-150 *Commando*
  PPV 16 Gaia *Thunder*
  AUV 6+: 6 *Cougar* 4×4; Panthera T6
ENGINEERING & MAINTENANCE VEHICLES
ARV WZ-551 ARV
ANTI-TANK/ANTI-INFRASTRUCTURE
MSL
  SP 24 TOW (on Jeeps)
  MANPATS *Milan*
RCL 53: **75mm** 13 Type-52 (M20); **106mm** 40 M40A2
ARTILLERY 106+
  SP 155mm 18 ATMOS 2000
  TOWED 52: **105mm** 20 M101; **130mm** 24: 12 M-1982 (reported); 12 Type-59 (M-46); **155mm** 8 M-71
  MRL 122mm 20 BM-21 *Grad*
  MOR 16+: **81mm** (some SP); **120mm** 16 Brandt
AIR DEFENCE • GUNS
  SP 20mm RBY-1 with TCM-20
  TOWED 54: **14.5mm** 18 Type-58 (ZPU-2); **35mm** 18 GDF-002; **37mm** 18 Type-63

Navy ε1,500
HQ located at Douala
EQUIPMENT BY TYPE
PATROL AND COASTAL COMBATANTS 16
  PCC 3: 1 *Dipikar* (ex-FRA *Flamant*); 2 *Le Ntem* (PRC *Limam El Hidrami*) with 1 76mm gun
  PB 11: 2 Aresa 2400; 2 Aresa 3200; 2 Rodman 101; 4 Rodman 46; 1 *Quartier Maître Alfred Motto*
  PBR 2 *Swift*-38
AMPHIBIOUS • LANDING CRAFT 4
  LCM 2: 1 Aresa 2300; 1 *Le Moungo*
  LCU 2 *Yunnan*

Fusiliers Marin
FORCES BY ROLE
MANOEUVRE
  Amphibious
  3 mne bn

Air Force 300–400
FORCES BY ROLE
FIGHTER/GROUND ATTACK
  1 sqn with MB-326K; *Alpha Jet**†
TRANSPORT
  1 sqn with C-130H/H-30 *Hercules*; IAI-201 *Arava*; PA-23 *Aztec*
  1 VIP unit with AS332 *Super Puma*; AS365 *Dauphin* 2; Bell 206B *Jet Ranger*; Gulfstream III
TRAINING
  1 unit with *Tetras*
ATTACK HELICOPTER
  1 sqn with SA342 *Gazelle* (with HOT); Mi-24 *Hind*
TRANSPORT HELICOPTER
  1 sqn with Bell 206L-3; Bell 412; SA319 *Alouette* III
EQUIPMENT BY TYPE
AIRCRAFT 9 combat capable
  ATK 5: 1 MB-326K *Impala* I; 4 MB-326K *Impala* II
  ISR 2 Cessna 208B *Grand Caravan*
  TPT 18: **Medium** 3: 2 C-130H *Hercules*; 1 C-130H-30 *Hercules*; **Light** 14: 1 CN235; 1 IAI-201 *Arava* (in store); 2 J.300 *Joker*; 1 MA60; 2 PA-23 *Aztec*; 7 *Tetras*; **PAX** 1 Gulfstream III
  TRG 4 *Alpha Jet**†
HELICOPTERS
  ATK 2 Mi-24 *Hind*
  MRH 13: 1 AS365 *Dauphin* 2; 1 Bell 412 *Twin Huey*; 2 Mi-17 *Hip* H; 2 SA319 *Alouette* III; 4 SA342 *Gazelle* (with HOT); 3 Z-9
  TPT 7: **Medium** 4: 2 AS332 *Super Puma*; 2 SA330J *Puma*; **Light** 3: 2 Bell 206B *Jet Ranger*; 1 Bell 206L3 *Long Ranger*
AIR-LAUNCHED MISSILES
  ASM HOT

Fusiliers de l'Air
FORCES BY ROLE
MANOEUVRE
  Other
  1 sy bn

Paramilitary 9,000

Gendarmerie 9,000
FORCES BY ROLE
MANOEUVRE
  Reconnaissance
  3 (regional spt) paramilitary gp

DEPLOYMENT
CENTRAL AFRICAN REPUBLIC: UN • MINUSCA 755; 3 obs; 1 inf bn

MALI: UN • MINUSMA 1; 1 obs

DEMOCRATIC REPUBLIC OF THE CONGO: UN • MONUSCO 2; 4 obs

FOREIGN FORCES
United States 300; MQ-1C *Gray Eagle*

Cape Verde CPV

Cape Verde Escudo E		2017	2018	2019
GDP	E	173bn	183bn	
	US$	1.78bn	1.97bn	
per capita	US$	3,301	3,622	
Growth	%	4.013	4.259	
Inflation	%	0.784	1.002	
Def bdgt	E	954m	1.04bn	
	US$	9.8m	11.2m	
US$1=E		97.63	92.99	

Population	568,373					
Age	0–14	15–19	20–24	25–29	30–64	65 plus
Male	14.4%	4.9%	5.0%	4.8%	17.6%	2.0%
Female	14.3%	4.9%	5.0%	4.8%	19.3%	3.3%

Capabilities

In its legislative programme for 2016–21, the government outlined the priorities for Cape Verde's defence forces, including territorial defence, maritime security, and EEZ and airspace protection. Although the armed forces are small and presently have limited capability, the government has suggested reorganising around marines, engineering and paramilitary national-guard units. The government is interested in greater regional and international defence engagement; international partners provide some maritime-security training support. The armed forces take part in multinational regional exercises and cooperative activities; the 2018 *Africa Endeavour* senior leaders' symposium was held in Cape Verde. Equipment capabilities remain limited, given the country's geographical position, though the US donated patrol boats in 2018 to bolster its maritime-security capacities. There is no defence industry, beyond limited maintenance facilities.

ACTIVE 1,200 (Army 1,000 Coast Guard 100 Air 100)
Conscript liability Selective conscription (14 months)

ORGANISATIONS BY SERVICE

Army 1,000
FORCES BY ROLE
MANOEUVRE
Light
2 inf bn (gp)
COMBAT SUPPORT
1 engr bn
EQUIPMENT BY TYPE
ARMOURED FIGHTING VEHICLES
RECCE 10 BRDM-2
ARTILLERY • MOR 18: **82mm** 12; **120mm** 6 M-1943
AIR DEFENCE
SAM • Point-defence 9K32 *Strela* (SA-7 Grai*l*)‡
GUNS • TOWED 30: **14.5mm** 18 ZPU-1; **23mm** 12 ZU-23

Coast Guard ε100
EQUIPMENT BY TYPE
PATROL AND COASTAL COMBATANTS 5
PCC 2: 1 *Guardião*; 1 *Kondor I*
PB 2: 1 *Espadarte*; 1 *Tainha* (PRC-27m)
PBF 1 *Archangel*
AIRCRAFT • TPT • Light 1 Do-228

Air Force up to 100
FORCES BY ROLE
MARITIME PATROL
1 sqn with An-26 *Curl*
EQUIPMENT BY TYPE
AIRCRAFT • TPT • Light 3 An-26 *Curl*†

Central African Republic CAR

CFA Franc BEAC fr		2017	2018	2019
GDP	fr	1.13tr	1.22tr	
	US$	1.94bn	2.31bn	
per capita	US$	389	454	
Growth	%	4.3	4.3	
Inflation	%	4.1	4.0	
Def exp	fr	17.7bn	17.2bn	
	US$	30.5m	32.5m	
US$1=fr		580.88	529.15	

Population	5,745,062					
Age	0–14	15–19	20–24	25–29	30–64	65 plus
Male	20.0%	5.3%	4.7%	4.2%	14.1%	1.3%
Female	19.8%	5.3%	4.6%	4.2%	14.3%	2.1%

Capabilities

Effective military and security organisations remain largely absent in the wake of the violence in 2013 and the armed forces are insufficient for the country's internal-security challenges. Instability continues to affect the country and – due to refugee flows – neighbouring states. The May 2015 Bangui Forum on National Reconciliation agreed principles governing DDR. Under the National Recovery and Peacebuilding Plan 2017–21, attempts to improve security focus on DDR and SSR, among others. A National Superior Council on Security will be set up to oversee the overall reform process. However, the UN's MINUSCA mission remains the principal security provider in the country. The CAR benefits from defence partnerships with France and Russia. Moscow has been deepening its military ties in the country and has donated small arms. There are also reports of Russian nationals in the presidential guard, as well as personnel – according to some reports, from a private military company – operating in the country more broadly in a military training and assistance role. Reports in 2018 indicated that China delivered military vehicles. Apart from some equipment deliveries, the country remains under a UN arms embargo. The armed forces receive training from UN forces and the European Training Mission. Poor infrastructure and logistics capacity are other factors limiting the ability of the CAR armed forces to provide security across the country. There is no independent capability to deploy troops externally, while the lack of financial resources and defence-industrial capacity makes equipment maintenance problematic.

ACTIVE 7,150 (Army 7,000 Air 150) **Paramilitary 1,000**
Conscript liability Selective conscription 2 years; reserve obligation thereafter, term n.k.

ORGANISATIONS BY SERVICE

Army ε7,000
FORCES BY ROLE
MANOEUVRE
  Light
    1 inf bn
EQUIPMENT BY TYPE
ARMOURED FIGHTING VEHICLES
  MBT 3 T-55†
  RECCE 9: 8 *Ferret*†; 1 BRDM-2
  IFV 18 *Ratel*
  APC • APC (W) 14+: 4 BTR-152†; 10+ VAB†
ARTILLERY • **MOR** 12+: **81mm**†; **120mm** 12 M-1943†
ANTI-TANK/ANTI-INFRASTRUCTURE
  RCL **106mm** 14 M40†
PATROL AND COASTAL COMBATANTS • **PBR** 9†

Air Force 150
EQUIPMENT BY TYPE
AIRCRAFT • **TPT** 7: **Medium** 1 C-130A *Hercules*; **Light** 6: 3 BN-2 *Islander*; 1 Cessna 172RJ *Skyhawk*; 2 J.300 *Joker*
HELICOPTERS • **TPT** • **Light** 1 AS350 *Ecureuil*

FOREIGN FORCES

MINUSCA unless stated
Argentina 2 obs
Bangladesh 1,010; 9 obs; 1 cdo coy; 1 inf bn; 1 med coy
Benin 4; 3 obs
Bhutan 2; 2 obs
Bolivia 1; 2 obs
Bosnia-Herzegovina EUTM RCA 2
Brazil 4; 3 obs
Burkina Faso 1; 1 obs
Burundi 760; 9 obs; 1 inf bn
Cambodia 221; 6 obs; 1 engr coy
Cameroon 755; 3 obs; 1 inf bn
Colombia 2 obs
Congo 10; 2 obs
Egypt 1,015; 9 obs; 1 inf bn; 1 tpt coy
France 10; 1 UAV unit • EUTM RCA 40
Gabon 436; 1 inf bn(-)
Gambia 2; 3 obs
Georgia EUTM RCA 35
Ghana 11; 4 obs
Guatemala 2; 1 obs
Hungary 2; 2 obs
Indonesia 208; 4 obs; 1 engr coy
Italy EUTM RCA 3
Jordan 7; 3 obs
Kenya 7; 6 obs
Lithuania EUTM RCA 1
Mauritania 744; 9 obs; 1 inf bn
Mexico 1
Moldova 2; 3 obs
Morocco 765; 2 obs; 1 inf bn
Nepal 340; 4 obs; 1 MP coy
Niger 3; 1 obs
Nigeria 1
Pakistan 1,259; 10 obs; 1 inf bn; 1 engr coy; 1 hel sqn
Paraguay 1; 2 obs
Peru 209; 4 obs; 1 engr coy
Poland EUTM RCA 1
Portugal 165; 1 AB coy • EUTM RCA 45
Romania EUTM RCA 14
Rwanda 1,378; 8 obs; 2 inf bn; 1 fd hospital
Senegal 111; 1 atk hel sqn
Serbia 73; 2 obs; 1 med coy • EUTM RCA 7
Spain EUTM RCA 8
Sri Lanka 115; 6 obs; 1 avn unit
Sweden EUTM RCA 9
Tanzania 445; 1 inf bn(-)
Togo 6; 4 obs
United States 8
Uruguay 2
Vietnam 4; 1 obs
Zambia 942; 8 obs; 1 inf bn

Chad CHA

CFA Franc BEAC fr		2017	2018	2019
GDP	fr	5.75tr	6.08tr	
	US$	9.87bn	11.1bn	
per capita	US$	810	890	
Growth	%	-3.1	3.5	
Inflation	%	-0.9	2.1	
Def bdgt	fr	102bn	101bn	
	US$	176m	185m	
US$1=fr		582.10	547.04	

Population 15,833,116

Age	0–14	15–19	20–24	25–29	30–64	65 plus
Male	24.4%	5.5%	4.2%	3.6%	10.7%	1.0%
Female	23.8%	5.4%	4.2%	3.7%	12.1%	1.4%

Capabilities

Chad's most pressing security concerns are instability in West Africa and the Sahel and the need to prosecute counter-insurgency operations against Boko Haram in the Lake Chad Basin area. The forces are combat experienced, though some observers assess additional work is required in improving military strategy, doctrine and command and control. The country is a key contributor to the G5 Sahel and is an important component of the Multi-National Joint Task Force fighting Boko Haram. There is strong defence cooperation with France and *Operation Barkhane* is headquartered in N'Djamena. Chadian military skills are widely recognised by partners, though there are some differences in training levels across the force. French forces delivered training to Chadian combat engineers in 2018. A lack of logistical capacity has hindered routine rotations for deployed forces. The country's ISR capability has been improved with the arrival of aircraft from the US, following improvements in ground-attack and medium-airlift capability. Barring maintenance facilities, there is no domestic defence-industrial capacity.

ACTIVE 30,350 (Army 25,000 Air 350 State Security Service 5,000) **Paramilitary 4,500**

Conscript liability Conscription authorised

ORGANISATIONS BY SERVICE

Army ε25,000
7 Mil Regions
FORCES BY ROLE
MANOEUVRE
  Armoured
   1 armd bn
  Light
   7 inf bn
COMBAT SUPPORT
  1 arty bn
  1 engr bn
  1 sigs bn
COMBAT SERVICE SUPPORT
  1 log gp
EQUIPMENT BY TYPE
ARMOURED FIGHTING VEHICLES
  MBT 60 T-55
  ASLT 30 PTL-02 *Assaulter*
  RECCE 309+: 132 AML-60/AML-90; 22 *Bastion Patsas*; ε100 BRDM-2; 20 EE-9 *Cascavel*; 4 ERC-90F *Sagaie*; 31+ RAM Mk3
  IFV 131: 80 BMP-1; 42 BMP-1U; 9 LAV-150 *Commando* with 90mm gun
  APC • APC (W) 99: 24 BTR-80; 12 BTR-3E; ε20 BTR-60; ε10 *Black Scorpion*; 25 VAB-VTT; 8 WZ-523
ARTILLERY 26+
  SP 122mm 10 2S1 *Gvozdika*
  TOWED 105mm 5 M2
  MRL 11+: **107mm** some Type-63; **122mm** 11: 6 BM-21 *Grad*; 5 Type-81
  MOR 81mm some; **120mm** AM-50
ANTI-TANK/ANTI-INFRASTRUCTURE
  MSL • MANPATS *Eryx*; *Milan*
  RCL 106mm M40A1
AIR DEFENCE
  SAM
    Short-range 2K12 *Kub* (SA-6 *Gainful*)
    Point-defence 9K310 *Igla-1* (SA-16 *Gimlet*)
  GUNS • TOWED 14.5mm ZPU-1/ZPU-2/ZPU-4; **23mm** ZU-23

Air Force 350
FORCES BY ROLE
GROUND ATTACK
  1 unit with PC-7; PC-9*; SF-260WL *Warrior**; Su-25 *Frogfoot*
TRANSPORT
  1 sqn with An-26 *Curl*; C-130H-30 *Hercules*; Mi-17 *Hip* H; Mi-171
  1 (Presidential) Flt with B-737BBJ; Beech 1900; DC-9-87; Gulfstream II
ATTACK HELICOPTER
  1 sqn with AS550C *Fennec*; Mi-24V *Hind*; SA316 *Alouette* III
EQUIPMENT BY TYPE
AIRCRAFT 14 combat capable
  FTR 1 MiG-29S *Fulcrum* C†
  ATK 10: 8 Su-25 *Frogfoot*; 2 Su-25UB *Frogfoot* B
  ISR 2 Cessna 208B *Grand Caravan*
  TPT 10: Medium 3: 2 C-27J *Spartan*; 1 C-130H-30 *Hercules*; **Light** 4: 3 An-26 *Curl*; 1 Beech 1900; **PAX** 3: 1 B-737BBJ; 1 DC-9-87; 1 Gulfstream II
  TRG 4: 2 PC-7 (only 1*); 1 PC-9 *Turbo Trainer**; 1 SF-260WL *Warrior**
HELICOPTERS
  ATK 5 Mi-24V *Hind*
  MRH 8: 3 AS550C *Fennec*; 3 Mi-17 *Hip* H; 2 SA316
  TPT • Medium 2 Mi-171

State Security Service General Direction (DGSSIE) 5,000 active

Paramilitary 4,500 active
  Gendarmerie 4,500

DEPLOYMENT

MALI: UN • MINUSMA 1,447; 3 obs; 1 SF coy; 2 inf bn

FOREIGN FORCES

Benin MNJTF 150
France Operation Barkhane 1,500; 1 mech inf BG; 1 FGA det with 4 *Mirage* 2000C/D; 1 tpt det with 1 C-130H; 4 CN235M

Congo, Republic of COG

CFA Franc BEAC fr		2017	2018	2019
GDP	fr	5.06tr	6.31tr	
	US$	8.72bn	11.5bn	
per capita	US$	2,005	2,572	
Growth	%	-3.1	2.0	
Inflation	%	0.5	1.2	
Def bdgt	fr	284bn	162bn	
	US$	490m	295m	
US$1=fr		580.94	550.81	

Population 5,062,021

Age	0–14	15–19	20–24	25–29	30–64	65 plus
Male	21.1%	4.5%	4.0%	3.6%	15.6%	1.4%
Female	20.7%	4.4%	4.0%	3.8%	15.2%	1.7%

Capabilities

Congo's small armed forces have low levels of training and limited overall capability, and utilise ageing equipment. They have struggled to recover from the brief but devastating civil war in the late 1990s. France provides advisory assistance and capacity-building support in military administration and military and police capability. Reports in late 2017 indicated some Chinese security assistance. The troop contingent deployed to the CAR was withdrawn by the government in mid-2017, amid allegations of indiscipline. Deployment capability is limited to neighbouring countries without external support. The air force is effectively grounded for lack of spares and serviceable equipment. The navy is largely a riverine force, despite the need for maritime security on the country's small coastline. A modernisation effort is under way and several MRAPs have been bought. Maintenance facilities are limited and the country has no domestic defence-industrial capability.

ACTIVE 10,000 (Army 8,000 Navy 800 Air 1,200)
Paramilitary 2,000

ORGANISATIONS BY SERVICE

Army 8,000
FORCES BY ROLE
MANOEUVRE
  Armoured
   2 armd bn
  Light
   2 inf bn (gp) each with (1 lt tk tp, 1 arty bty)
   1 inf bn
  Air Manoeuvre
   1 cdo/AB bn
COMBAT SUPPORT
  1 arty gp (with MRL)
  1 engr bn
EQUIPMENT BY TYPE†
ARMOURED FIGHTING VEHICLES
  MBT 40: 25 T-54/T-55; 15 Type-59; (some T-34 in store)
  LT TK 13: 3 PT-76; 10 Type-62
  RECCE 25 BRDM-1/BRDM-2
  APC 133+
    APC (W) 78+: 28 AT-105 *Saxon*; 20 BTR-152; 30 BTR-60; Panhard M3
    PPV 55: 18 *Mamba*; 37 *Marauder*
  ARTILLERY 56+
    SP **122mm** 3 2S1 *Gvozdika*
    TOWED 15+: **122mm** 10 D-30; **130mm** 5 M-46; **152mm** D-20
    MRL 10+: **122mm** 10 BM-21 *Grad*; **140mm** BM-14; **140mm** BM-16
    MOR 28+: **82mm**; **120mm** 28 M-43
  ANTI-TANK/ANTI-INFRASTRUCTURE
    RCL **57mm** M18
    GUNS 15: **57mm** 5 ZIS-2 (M-1943); **100mm** 10 M-1944
  AIR DEFENCE • GUNS
    SP **23mm** ZSU-23-4 *Shilka*
    TOWED **14.5mm** ZPU-2/ZPU-4; **37mm** 28 M-1939; **57mm** S-60; **100mm** KS-19

Navy ε800
EQUIPMENT BY TYPE
PATROL AND COASTAL COMBATANTS 8
  PCC 4 *5 Février 1979*
  PBR 4

Air Force 1,200
FORCES BY ROLE
FIGHTER/GROUND ATTACK
  1 sqn with *Mirage* F-1AZ
TRANSPORT
  1 sqn with An-24 *Coke*; An-32 *Cline*; CN235M-100
ATTACK/TRANSPORT HELICOPTER
  1 sqn with Mi-8 *Hip*; Mi-35P *Hind*
EQUIPMENT BY TYPE†
AIRCRAFT
  FGA 2 *Mirage* F-1AZ
  TPT • **Light** 4: 1 An-24 *Coke*; 2 An-32 *Cline*; 1 CN235M-100
HELICOPTERS†
  ATK (2 Mi-35P *Hind* in store)
  TPT • **Medium** (3 Mi-8 *Hip* in store)
AIR-LAUNCHED MISSILES • AAM • IR R-3 (AA-2 *Atoll*)‡

Paramilitary 2,000 active

Gendarmerie 2,000
FORCES BY ROLE
MANOEUVRE
  Other
   20 paramilitary coy

Presidential Guard some
FORCES BY ROLE
MANOEUVRE
  Other
   1 paramilitary bn

DEPLOYMENT
CENTRAL AFRICAN REPUBLIC: UN • MINUSCA 10; 2 obs

Côte d'Ivoire CIV

CFA Franc BCEAO fr		2017	2018	2019
GDP	fr	23.5tr	25.4tr	
	US$	40.5bn	45.9bn	
per capita	US$	1,621	1,791	
Growth	%	7.8	7.4	
Inflation	%	0.8	1.7	
Def bdgt [a]	fr	482bn	517bn	
	US$	829m	935m	
US$1=fr		580.93	553.07	

[a] Defence, order and security expenses

Population 26,260,582

Age	0–14	15–19	20–24	25–29	30–64	65 plus
Male	19.9%	5.3%	4.6%	4.3%	14.9%	1.2%
Female	19.7%	5.3%	4.6%	4.2%	14.4%	1.5%

Capabilities

The armed forces are still undergoing reconstruction, and SSR initiatives remain in place. A law on the defence forces' organisation was enacted in 2015. This detailed defence zones and military regions, the creation of a general staff and general inspectorate for the armed forces, and stressed the armed forces' role in assisting Ivorian society. In 2016 a Military Programme Law for 2016–20 was adopted, planning for an incremental reduction in military strength up to 2020, to enable an increase in the gendarmerie. In April 2016, the United Nations lifted the arms embargo that had previously been imposed on the country. This allowed Côte d'Ivoire to start recapitalising its air force, notably with the delivery of Mi-24 helicopters from Russia. As part of the SSR process, an aviation academy was established in Abidjan, with limited rotary-wing-pilot and maintenance training. The latter is also an issue for the small naval unit. The administration has moved to regulate promotion and salary structures to aid professionalisation, and also improve military infrastructure. There is strong defence cooperation with France, which has a significant training mission in the country. Except limited maintenance facilities, Côte d'Ivoire does not have domestic defence-industrial capabilities.

ACTIVE 27,400 (Army 23,000 Navy 1,000 Air 1,400 Special Forces 2,000) Paramilitary n.k.

Moves to restructure and reform the armed forces continue

ORGANISATIONS BY SERVICE

Army ε23,000
FORCES BY ROLE
MANOEUVRE
　Armoured
　　1 armd bn
　Light
　　7 inf bn
　Air Manoeuvre
　　1 cdo/AB bn
COMBAT SUPPORT
　1 arty bn
　1 engr bn
COMBAT SERVICE SUPPORT
　1 log bn
AIR DEFENCE
　1 AD bn
EQUIPMENT BY TYPE
ARMOURED FIGHTING VEHICLES
　MBT 10 T-55†
　RECCE 18: 13 BRDM-2; 5 *Cayman* BRDM
　IFV 10 BMP-1/BMP-2†
　APC 41
　　APC (W) 40: 9 Bastion APC; 6 BTR-80; 12 Panhard M3; 13 VAB
　　PPV 1 *Snake*
ENGINEERING & MAINTENANCE VEHICLES
　VLB MTU
ANTI-TANK/ANTI-INFRASTRUCTURE
　MSL • MANPATS 9K111-1 *Konkurs* (AT-5 *Spandrel*) (reported); 9K135 *Kornet* (AT-14 *Spriggan*) (reported)
　RCL 106mm ε12 M40A1
ARTILLERY 36+
　TOWED 4+: 105mm 4 M-1950; 122mm (reported)
　MRL 122mm 6 BM-21
　MOR 26+: 81mm; 82mm 10 M-37; 120mm 16 AM-50
AIRCRAFT • TPT • Medium 1 An-12 *Cub*†
AIR DEFENCE
　SAM • Point-defence 9K32 *Strela*-2 (SA-7 *Grail*)‡ (reported)
　GUNS 21+
　　SP 20mm 6 M3 VDAA
　　TOWED 15+: 20mm 10; 23mm ZU-23-2; 40mm 5 L/60

Navy ε1,000
EQUIPMENT BY TYPE
PATROL AND COASTAL COMBATANTS 4
　PB 4: 3 *L'Emergence*; 1 *Atchan*
AMPHIBIOUS • LANDING CRAFT • LCM 1 *Aby*

Air Force ε1,400
EQUIPMENT BY TYPE†
AIRCRAFT
　TPT • PAX 1 B-727
HELICOPTERS
　ATK 4 Mi-24 *Hind*
　TPT • Medium 2 SA330L *Puma* (IAR-330L)

Special Forces ε2,000
FORCES BY ROLE
SPECIAL FORCES
　1 spec ops bde

Paramilitary n.k.
　Republican Guard n.k.
　Gendarmerie n.k.
EQUIPMENT BY TYPE†
ARMOURED FIGHTING VEHICLES
　RECCE 3 *Cayman* BRDM
　APC • APC (W) some VAB
PATROL AND COASTAL COMBATANTS • PB 1 *Bian*

DEPLOYMENT
MALI: UN • MINUSMA 162; 1 obs; 1 sy coy

FOREIGN FORCES
France 950; 1 (Marine) inf bn; 2 SA330 *Puma*; 1 *Gazelle*

Democratic Republic of the Congo DRC

Congolese Franc fr		2017	2018	2019
GDP	fr	58.2tr	71.4tr	
	US$	41.4bn	42.7bn	
per capita	US$	478	478	
Growth	%	3.414	3.824	
Inflation	%	41.5	23	
Def bdgt	fr	422bn	483bn	
	US$	301m	289m	
US$1=fr		1403.57	1671.60	

Population　85,281,024

Age	0–14	15–19	20–24	25–29	30–64	65 plus
Male	20.8%	5.7%	5.0%	4.2%	13.0%	1.1%
Female	20.5%	5.6%	5.0%	4.2%	13.2%	1.5%

Capabilities

On paper, the DRC has the largest armed forces in Central Africa. However, given the country's size and the poor levels of training, morale and equipment, they are unable to provide security throughout the country. Kinshasa has pursued several military-modernisation programmes, though plans to re-examine doctrine and organisation have seen little positive impact. When conflict finally abates in the east, significant attention to wide-ranging

DDR and SSR will be required, to continue the work intermittently undertaken over the past decade. The mandate of the MONUSCO mission was renewed for another 12 months in March 2018. The UN's Force Intervention Brigade (FIB) remains active in the east of the country. Training will have improved for units operating with the FIB, while external-partner training and capacity-building assistance is also commonplace. The armed forces, which have incorporated a number of non-state armed groups, struggle with conflicting loyalties. There remains significant scope to improve training, recruitment and retention. Deployment capability is limited and the lack of logistics vehicles significantly reduces transport capacity even within the country. The lack of sufficient tactical airlift and helicopters is a brake on military effectiveness and there is some reliance on MONUSCO capabilities, which are also insufficient given the geographical scale of the country. Much equipment is in poor repair and while new equipment has been acquired, the absence of any domestic defence-industrial capacity will mean that maintenance levels also hinder military capability.

ACTIVE ε134,250 (Central Staffs ε14,000, Army 103,000 Republican Guard 8,000 Navy 6,700 Air 2,550)

ORGANISATIONS BY SERVICE

Army (Forces du Terre) ε103,000

The DRC has 11 Military Regions. In 2011, all brigades in North and South Kivu provinces were consolidated into 27 new regiments, the latest in a sequence of reorganisations designed to integrate non-state armed groups. The actual combat effectiveness of many formations is doubtful

FORCES BY ROLE
MANOEUVRE
  Light
  6 (integrated) inf bde
  ε3 inf bde (non-integrated)
  27+ inf regt
COMBAT SUPPORT
  1 arty regt
  1 MP bn
EQUIPMENT BY TYPE†
(includes Republican Guard eqpt)
ARMOURED FIGHTING VEHICLES
  MBT 174: 12–17 Type-59†; 32 T-55; 25 T-64BV-1; 100 T-72AV
  LT TK 40: 10 PT-76; 30 Type-62†
  RECCE up to 52: up to 17 AML-60; 14 AML-90; 19 EE-9 *Cascavel*; 2 RAM-V-2
  IFV 20 BMP-1
  APC 104+:
    APC (T) 9: 3 BTR-50; 6 MT-LB
    APC (W) 95+: 30–70 BTR-60PB; 58 Panhard M3†; 7 TH 390 *Fahd*
ANTI-TANK/ANTI-INFRASTRUCTURE
  RCL 57mm M18; **73mm**; **75mm** M20; **106mm** M40A1
  GUNS 85mm 10 Type-56 (D-44)
ARTILLERY 726+
  SP 16: **122mm** 6 2S1 *Gvozdika*; **152mm** 10 2S3 *Akatsiya*
  TOWED 125: **122mm** 77 M-30 (M-1938)/D-30/Type-60; **130mm** 42 Type-59 (M-46)/Type-59-I; **152mm** 6 D-20 (reported)
  MRL 57+: **107mm** 12 Type-63; **122mm** 24+: 24 BM-21 *Grad*; some RM-70; **128mm** 6 M-51; **130mm** 3 Type-82; **132mm** 12

  MOR 528+: **81mm** 100; **82mm** 400; **107mm** M30; **120mm** 28: 10 Brandt; 18 other
AIR DEFENCE
  SAM • **Point-defence** 9K32 *Strela*-2 (SA-7 *Grail*)‡
  GUNS • **TOWED** 64: **14.5mm** 12 ZPU-4; **37mm** 52 M-1939

Republican Guard 8,000
FORCES BY ROLE
MANOEUVRE
  Armoured
  1 armd regt
  Light
  3 gd bde
COMBAT SUPPORT
  1 arty regt

Navy 6,700 (incl infantry and marines)
All operational patrol vessels under 10t FLD

Air Force 2,550
EQUIPMENT BY TYPE
AIRCRAFT 4 combat capable
  ATK 4 Su-25 *Frogfoot*
  TPT 5: **Medium** 1 C-130H *Hercules*; **Light** 2 An-26 *Curl*; **PAX** 2 B-727
HELICOPTERS
  ATK 7: 4 Mi-24 *Hind*; 3 Mi-24V *Hind*
  TPT • **Medium** 3: 1 AS332L *Super Puma*; 2 Mi-8 *Hip*

Paramilitary

National Police Force
Incl Rapid Intervention Police (National and Provincial forces)

People's Defence Force

FOREIGN FORCES
All part of MONUSCO unless otherwise specified
Algeria 3 obs
Bangladesh 1,710; 5 obs; 1 inf bn; 1 engr coy; 1 avn coy; 2 hel coy
Belgium 1; 1 obs
Benin 49; 4 obs
Bhutan 2 obs
Bolivia 3 obs
Bosnia-Herzegovina 3 obs
Burkina Faso 1; 3 obs
Cameroon 2; 4 obs
Canada (*Operation Crocodile*) 8
China, People's Republic of 223; 9 obs; 1 engr coy; 1 fd hospital
Czech Republic 1; 1 obs
Egypt 155; 16 obs; 1 SF coy
France 2
Ghana 469; 15 obs; 1 inf bn(-)
Guatemala 150; 5 obs; 1 SF coy
India 2,625; 22 obs; 3 inf bn; 1 med coy

Indonesia 180; 9 obs; 1 engr coy
Ireland 4
Jordan 4; 6 obs
Kenya 7; 5 obs
Malawi 857; 4 obs; 1 inf bn
Malaysia 2; 4 obs
Mali 1 obs
Mongolia 2 obs
Morocco 527; 2 obs; 1 inf bn; 1 fd hospital
Nepal 884; 10 obs; 1 inf bn; 1 engr coy
Niger 5; 4 obs
Nigeria 2; 6 obs
Pakistan 2,758; 18 obs; 4 inf bn; 1 hel sqn
Paraguay 1; 6 obs
Peru 3; 8 obs
Poland 1 obs
Romania 4; 7 obs
Russia 2; 14 obs
Senegal 7; 1 obs
Serbia 1
South Africa (*Operation Mistral*) 1,175; 7 obs; 1 inf bn; 1 atk hel sqn; 1 hel sqn
Sweden 1; 1 obs
Switzerland 3
Tanzania 1,003; 2 obs; 1 SF coy; 1 inf bn
Tunisia 11; 4 obs
Ukraine 255: 8 obs; 2 atk hel sqn
United Kingdom 2
United States 3
Uruguay 930; 7 obs; 1 inf bn; 1 mne coy; 1 hel sqn
Zambia 3; 7 obs

Djibouti DJB

Djiboutian Franc fr		2017	2018	2019
GDP	fr	361bn	389bn	
	US$	2.03bn	2.19bn	
per capita	US$	1,989	2,085	
Growth	%	6.7	6.7	
Inflation	%	0.7	1	
Def exp	fr	n.k	n.k	
	US$	n.k	n.k	
FMA (US)	US$	0.5m	0m	
US$1=fr		177.76	177.72	

Population 884,017
Ethnic groups: Somali 60%; Afar 35%

Age	0–14	15–19	20–24	25–29	30–64	65 plus
Male	15.4%	5.0%	4.9%	4.5%	14.1%	1.7%
Female	15.3%	5.3%	5.8%	5.9%	19.9%	2.1%

Capabilities

Djibouti's strategic location and relative stability have led a number of foreign states to base forces there. The armed forces' main responsibility is internal and border security, and counter-insurgency operations. The northern border dispute with Eritrea might abate in the wake of the late 2018 diplomatic rapprochement. The 2017 defence white paper highlighted a requirement to modernise key capabilities, including intelligence and command, as well as equipment, but funds for these remain limited. Djibouti maintains strong defence cooperation with France; Djibouti hosts its largest foreign military base. The US also operates its Combined Joint Task Force–Horn of Africa from Djibouti. Japan has based forces there for regional counter-piracy missions and the EU and NATO have at various times maintained a presence to support their operations. China's first overseas military base, including dock facilities, was officially opened in Djibouti in 2017. Djibouti's armed forces benefit from training received from France and the US. EU NAVFOR Somalia has delivered training to the navy and coastguard to strengthen their maritime-security capabilities. Djibouti participates in a number of regional multinational exercises and contributed to the AMISOM mission in Somalia, but has limited capacity to independently deploy beyond its territory. Army equipment consists predominantly of older French and Soviet-era equipment and while recent acquisitions have focused on mobility and artillery, armoured-warfare capability remains limited. Bar limited maintenance facilities, the country has no defence-industrial capacity.

ACTIVE 10,450 (Army 8,000 Navy 200 Air 250 Gendarmerie 2,000) **Paramilitary 2,650**

ORGANISATIONS BY SERVICE

Army ε8,000
FORCES BY ROLE
4 military districts (Tadjourah, Dikhil, Ali-Sabieh and Obock)
MANOEUVRE
  Mechanised
    1 armd regt (1 recce sqn, 3 armd sqn, 1 (anti-smuggling) sy coy)
  Light
    4 inf regt (3-4 inf coy, 1 spt coy)
    1 rapid reaction regt (4 inf coy, 1 spt coy)
  Other
    1 (Republican Guard) gd regt (1 sy sqn, 1 (close protection) sy sqn, 1 cbt spt sqn (1 recce pl, 1 armd pl, 1 arty pl), 1 spt sqn)
COMBAT SUPPORT
  1 arty regt
  1 demining coy
  1 sigs regt
  1 CIS sect
COMBAT SERVICE SUPPORT
  1 log regt
  1 maint coy
EQUIPMENT BY TYPE
ARMOURED FIGHTING VEHICLES
  ASLT 1 PTL-02 *Assaulter*
  RECCE 38: 4 AML-60†; 17 AML-90; 2 BRDM-2; 15 VBL
  IFV 28: 8 BTR-80A; 16-20 *Ratel*
  APC 43
    APC (W) 30+: 12 BTR-60†; 4+ AT-105 *Saxon*; 14 *Puma*
    PPV 13: 3 *Casspir*; 10 RG-33L
  AUV 22: 10 *Cougar* 4×4 (one with 90mm gun); 2 CS/VN3B; 10 PKSV AUV
ANTI-TANK/ANTI-INFRASTRUCTURE
  RCL 106mm 16 M40A1

ARTILLERY 76
  SP 155mm 10 M109L
  TOWED 122mm 9 D-30
  MRL 12: 107mm 2 PKSV AUV with PH-63; 122mm 10: 6 (6-tube Toyota Land Cruiser 70 series); 2 (30-tube Iveco 110-16); 2 (30-tube)
  MOR 45: 81mm 25; 120mm 20 Brandt
AIR DEFENCE • GUNS 15+
  SP 20mm 5 M693
  TOWED 10: 23mm 5 ZU-23-2; 40mm 5 L/70

Navy ε200
EQUIPMENT BY TYPE
PATROL AND COASTAL COMBATANTS 12
  PBF 2 Battalion-17
  PB 10: 1 *Plascoa*†; 2 *Sea Ark 1739*; 1 *Swari*†; 6 others
AMPHIBIOUS • LCT 1 EDIC 700

Air Force 250
EQUIPMENT BY TYPE
AIRCRAFT
  TPT • Light 6: 1 Cessna U206G *Stationair*; 1 Cessna 208 *Caravan*; 2 Y-12E; 1 L-410UVP *Turbolet*; 1 MA60
HELICOPTERS
  ATK (2 Mi-35 *Hind* in store)
  MRH 5: 1 Mi-17 *Hip* H; 4 AS365 *Dauphin*
  TPT 3: Medium 1 Mi-8T *Hip*; Light 2 AS355F *Ecureuil* II

Gendarmerie 2,000+
Ministry of Defence
FORCES BY ROLE
MANOEUVRE
  Other
  1 paramilitary bn
EQUIPMENT BY TYPE
  AFV • AUV 2 CS/VN3B
  PATROL AND COASTAL COMBATANTS • 1 PB

Paramilitary ε2,650

National Police Force ε2,500
Ministry of Interior

Coast Guard 150
EQUIPMENT BY TYPE
PATROL AND COASTAL COMBATANTS 11
  PB 11: 2 *Khor Angar*; 9 other

DEPLOYMENT
SOMALIA: AU • AMISOM 1,872; 2 inf bn
WESTERN SAHARA: UN • MINURSO 2 obs

FOREIGN FORCES
China 240: 1 mne coy(-); 1 med unit; 2 ZTL-11; 8 ZBL-08; 1 LPD; 1 ESD
France 1,450: 1 SF unit; 1 (Marine) combined arms regt (2 recce sqn, 2 inf coy, 1 arty bty, 1 engr coy); 1 hel det with 2 SA330 *Puma*; 1 SA342 *Gazelle*; 1 LCM; 1 air sqn with 4 *Mirage* 2000-5; 1 C-160 *Transall*; 2 SA330 *Puma*
Germany Operation Atalanta 1 AP-3C *Orion*
Italy 90
Japan 170; 2 P-3C *Orion*
New Zealand 1 P-3K2 *Orion*
Spain Operation Atalanta 1 P-3M *Orion*
United States US Africa Command: 4,700; 1 tpt sqn with C-130H/J-30 *Hercules*; 1 spec ops sqn with MC-130H; PC-12 (U-28A); 1 CSAR sqn with HH-60G *Pave Hawk*; 1 CISR sqn with MQ-9A *Reaper*; 1 naval air base

Equatorial Guinea EQG

CFA Franc BEAC fr		2017	2018	2019
GDP	fr	7.27tr	7.28tr	
	US$	12.5bn	13.2bn	
per capita	US$	14,818	15,294	
Growth	%	-3.2	-7.7	
Inflation	%	0.7	0.9	
Def exp	fr	n.k	n.k	
	US$	n.k	n.k	
US$1=fr		582.08	550.83	

Population   797,457

Age	0–14	15–19	20–24	25–29	30–64	65 plus
Male	20.0%	5.4%	4.7%	4.0%	14.2%	1.6%
Female	19.4%	5.2%	4.5%	3.8%	14.8%	2.3%

Capabilities
The army dominates the armed forces, with internal security the principal task. Equatorial Guinea has been trying for several years to modernise its armed forces. France maintains a military-cooperation detachment in Malabo, advising on defence-institutional development issues and providing capacity-building support through the naval-focused regional school at Tica, as well as some training activities with French forces based in Gabon and in the region as part of the *Corymbe* mission. There is only limited capability for power projection and deployments are limited to neighbouring countries without external support. There has been significant naval investment in recent years, including in both equipment and onshore infrastructure at Bata and Malabo, although naval capabilities remain limited. Maritime-security concerns in the Gulf of Guinea have resulted in an increased emphasis on bolstering the country's maritime-patrol capacity. The air force has received several new transport aircraft. Equatorial Guinea has only limited maintenance capacity and no traditional defence industry.

ACTIVE 1,450 (Army 1,100 Navy 250 Air 100)

ORGANISATIONS BY SERVICE

Army 1,100
FORCES BY ROLE
MANOEUVRE
  Light
  3 inf bn(-)
EQUIPMENT BY TYPE
ARMOURED FIGHTING VEHICLES
  MBT 3 T-55
  RECCE 6 BRDM-2
  IFV 20 BMP-1

APC 35
APC (W) 10 BTR-152
PPV 25 *Reva* (reported)

Navy ε250
EQUIPMENT BY TYPE
PATROL AND COASTAL COMBATANTS 11
  PSO 2:
    1 *Bata* with 1 76mm gun, 1 hel landing platform
    1 *Wele Nzas* with 2 AK630M CIWS, 2 76mm gun, 1 hel landing platform
  PCC 2 OPV 62
  PBF 2 *Shaldag* II
  PB 5: 1 *Daphne*; 2 *Estuario de Muni*; 2 *Zhuk*
LOGISTICS AND SUPPORT
  AKRH 1 *Capitan David Eyama Angue Osa* with 1 76mm gun

Air Force 100
EQUIPMENT BY TYPE
AIRCRAFT 4 combat capable
  ATK 4: 2 Su-25 *Frogfoot*; 2 Su-25UB *Frogfoot* B
  TPT 4: **Light** 3: 1 An-32B *Cline*; 2 An-72 *Coaler*; **PAX** 1 *Falcon* 900 (VIP)
  TRG 2 L-39C *Albatros*
HELICOPTERS
  ATK 5 Mi-24P/V *Hind*
  MRH 1 Mi-17 *Hip* H
  TPT 4: **Heavy** 1 Mi-26 *Halo*; **Medium** 1 Ka-29 *Helix*; **Light** 2 Enstrom 480

Paramilitary

Guardia Civil
FORCES BY ROLE
MANOEUVRE
  Other
    2 paramilitary coy

Coast Guard n.k.

Eritrea ERI

Eritrean Nakfa ERN		2017	2018	2019
GDP	ERN	89.4bn	103bn	
	US$	5.81bn	6.72bn	
per capita	US$	980	1,112	
Growth	%	5.0	4.2	
Inflation	%	9.0	9.0	
Def exp	ERN	n.k	n.k	
	US$	n.k	n.k	
USD1=ERN		15.37	15.37	

Population 5,970,646

Ethnic groups: Tigrinya 50%; Tigre and Kunama 40%; Afar; Saho 3%

Age	0–14	15–19	20–24	25–29	30–64	65 plus
Male	19.9%	5.3%	4.6%	3.7%	14.1%	1.6%
Female	19.7%	5.3%	4.7%	3.8%	15.0%	2.3%

Capabilities

Eritrea has maintained large armed forces in response to historic military tensions and conflict with neighbouring Ethiopia. Efforts to sustain and modernise capabilities were restricted by a UN arms embargo, which was lifted in November 2018 following a diplomatic rapprochement with Ethiopia. The armed forces have focused on border defence but now may have an opportunity to restructure accordingly. Maritime security remains an issue, including piracy. The UAE has established a military presence in Eritrea and has continued to refurbish and expand port and airfield facilities at Assab to support Gulf states participating in the Yemen campaign. Eritrea maintains a large army due to mandatory conscription. For some the term of service is indefinite, and significant numbers of conscripts have chosen to leave the country or otherwise evade service. These factors likely affect overall military cohesion and effectiveness. A UN report alleged that the UAE had trained some air-force and navy personnel. A private European company has allegedly provided pilot training. Eritrea has not demonstrated any capacity to deploy beyond its borders. The armed forces' inventory primarily comprises outdated Soviet-era systems and modernisation was restricted by the UN arms embargo. The embargo will have resulted in serviceability issues, notwithstanding allegations of external support, with some aircraft likely cannibalised for parts and others illicitly overhauled abroad. The navy remains capable of only limited coastal-patrol and interception operations. Apart from limited maintenance facilities, the country has no domestic defence-industrial capacity.

ACTIVE 201,750 (Army 200,000 Navy 1,400 Air 350)
Conscript liability 18 months (4 months mil trg) between ages 18 and 40

RESERVE 120,000 (Army ε120,000)

ORGANISATIONS BY SERVICE

Army ε200,000
Heavily cadreised
FORCES BY ROLE
COMMAND
  4 corps HQ
MANOEUVRE
  Mechanised
    1 mech bde
  Light
    19 inf div
    1 cdo div

Reserve ε120,000
FORCES BY ROLE
MANOEUVRE
  Light
    1 inf div
EQUIPMENT BY TYPE
ARMOURED FIGHTING VEHICLES
  MBT 270 T-54/T-55
  RECCE 40 BRDM-1/BRDM-2
  IFV 15 BMP-1
  APC 35
    APC (T) 10 MT-LB†
    APC (W) 25 BTR-152/BTR-60

ENGINEERING & MAINTENANCE VEHICLES
ARV T-54/T-55 reported
VLB MTU reported
ANTI-TANK/ANTI-INFRASTRUCTURE
MSL • MANPATS 9K11 *Malyutka* (AT-3 *Sagger*); 9K111-1 *Konkurs* (AT-5 *Spandrel*) GUNS 85mm D-44
ARTILLERY 258
SP 45: **122mm** 32 2S1 *Gvozdika*; **152mm** 13 2S5 *Giatsint*-S
TOWED 19+: **122mm** D-30; **130mm** 19 M-46
MRL 44: **122mm** 35 BM-21 *Grad*; **220mm** 9 9P140 *Uragan*
MOR 150+: **82mm** 50+; **120mm/160mm** 100+
AIR DEFENCE
SAM • Point-defence 9K32 *Strela*-2 (SA-7 *Grail*)‡
GUNS 70+
  SP **23mm** ZSU-23-4 *Shilka*
  TOWED **23mm** ZU-23

Navy 1,400
EQUIPMENT BY TYPE
PATROL AND COASTAL COMBATANTS 12
  PBF 9: 5 *Battalion-17*; 4 *Super Dvora*
  PB 3 *Swiftships*
AMPHIBIOUS 3
  LS • LST 2: 1 *Chamo*† (Ministry of Transport); 1 *Ashdod*†
  LC • LCU 1 T-4† (in harbour service)

Air Force ε350
FORCES BY ROLE
FIGHTER/GROUND ATTACK
  1 sqn with MiG-29/MiG-29SE/MiG-29UB *Fulcrum*
  1 sqn with Su-27/Su-27UBK *Flanker*
TRANSPORT
  1 sqn with Y-12(II)
TRAINING
  1 sqn with L-90 *Redigo*
  1 sqn with MB-339CE*
TRANSPORT HELICOPTER
  1 sqn with Bell 412EP *Twin Huey*
  1 sqn with Mi-17 *Hip H*
EQUIPMENT BY TYPE
AIRCRAFT 14 combat capable
  FTR 8: 4 MiG-29 *Fulcrum*; 2 MiG-29UB *Fulcrum*; 1 Su-27 *Flanker*; 1 Su-27UBK *Flanker*
  FGA 2 MiG-29SE *Fulcrum*
  TPT • Light 5: 1 Beech 200 *King Air*; 4 Y-12(II)
  TRG 16+: 8 L-90 *Redigo*; 4 MB-339CE*; 4+ Z-143/Z-242
HELICOPTERS
  MRH 8: 4 Bell 412EP *Twin Huey* (AB-412EP); 4 Mi-17 *Hip H*
AIR-LAUNCHED MISSILES
  AAM • IR R-60 (AA-8 *Aphid*); R-73 (AA-11 *Archer*); IR/SARH R-27 (AA-10 *Alamo*)

FOREIGN FORCES
United Arab Emirates Operation Restoring Hope 1,000; 1 armd BG; *Leclerc*; BMP-3; G-6; *Agrab* Mk2; 2 FSGHM; 2 LST; 6 LCT; 4 *Archangel*; 3 AH-64D *Apache*; 2 CH-47F *Chinook*; 4 UH-60M *Black Hawk*; *Wing Loong* I (GJ-1) UAV; 4 MIM-104F *Patriot* PAC-3

Ethiopia ETH

Ethiopian Birr EB		2017	2018	2019
GDP	EB	1.81tr	2.14tr	
	US$	80.9bn	83.8bn	
per capita	US$	873	891	
Growth	%	10.9	7.5	
Inflation	%	9.9	12.7	
Def bdgt	EB	11bn	12bn	
	US$	492m	469m	
FMA (US)	US$	0.5m	0m	
US$1=EB		22.34	25.58	

Population 108,386,391

Ethnic groups: Oromo 34.4%; Amhara 27%; Somali 6.2%; Tigray 6.1%; Sidama 4%; Guragie 2.5%; other or unspecified 19.2%

Age	0–14	15–19	20–24	25–29	30–64	65 plus
Male	21.7%	5.5%	4.6%	3.8%	12.8%	1.3%
Female	21.5%	5.5%	4.6%	3.9%	13.1%	1.6%

Capabilities

Ethiopia maintains one of the region's largest and most capable armed forces. It is a significant contributor to regional peacekeeping. The 2018 rapprochement with Eritrea might affect military dispositions. Countering al-Shabaab remains an ongoing military commitment. Ethiopia maintains long-standing defence and security ties with the US. Addis Ababa continues to support the Federal Government of Somalia militarily. The armed forces are experienced by regional standards, following a history of combat operations. Training and experience is also gained through international peacekeeping deployments. Ethiopia has demonstrated the capability to make significant contributions to the UN missions in Darfur and South Sudan. It is the largest overall troop contributor to UN peacekeeping missions and provides significant numbers to the AMISOM mission in Somalia. The country's inventory comprises mostly Soviet-era equipment. Despite engaging in a ten-year (2005–15) modernisation plan, most platform recapitalisation is based on surplus stock from Hungary, Ukraine and the US. Ethiopia has developed a modest local defence-industrial base, primarily centred on small arms, with some license production of light armoured vehicles. There is adequate maintenance capability but only a limited capacity to support advanced platforms.

ACTIVE 138,000 (Army 135,000 Air 3,000)

ORGANISATIONS BY SERVICE

Army 135,000
4 Mil Regional Commands (Northern, Western, Central and Eastern) each acting as corps HQ
FORCES BY ROLE
MANOEUVRE
  Light
  1 (Agazi Cdo) SF comd
  1 (Northern) corps (1 mech div, 4 inf div)
  1 (Western) corps (1 mech div, 3 inf div)
  1 (Central) corps (1 mech div, 5 inf div)
  1 (Eastern) corps (1 mech div, 5 inf div)

EQUIPMENT BY TYPE
ARMOURED FIGHTING VEHICLES
  MBT 461+: 246+ T-54/T-55/T-62; 215 T-72B
  RECCE ε100 BRDM-1/BRDM-2
  IFV ε20 BMP-1
  APC 300+
    APC (T) some Type-89
    APC (W) 300+: ε300 BTR-60/BTR-152; some Type-92
  AUV some Ze'ev
ENGINEERING & MAINTENANCE VEHICLES
  ARV T-54/T-55 reported; 4 BTS-5B
  VLB MTU reported
  MW Bozena
ANTI-TANK/ANTI-INFRASTRUCTURE
  MSL • MANPATS 9K11 *Malyutka* (AT-3 *Sagger*); 9K111 *Fagot* (AT-4 *Spigot*); 9K135 *Kornet-E* (AT-14 *Spriggan*)
  RCL 82mm B-10; **107mm** B-11
  GUNS 85mm D-44
ARTILLERY 524+
  SP 10+: **122mm** 2S1 *Gvozdika*; **152mm** 10 2S19 *Msta-S*
  TOWED 464+: **122mm** 464 D-30/M-30 (M-1938); **130mm** M-46; **155mm** AH2
  MRL 122mm ε50 BM-21 *Grad*
  MOR 81mm M1/M29; **82mm** M-1937; **120mm** M-1944
AIR DEFENCE
  SAM
    Medium-range S-75 *Dvina* (SA-2 *Guideline*)
    Short-range S-125 *Pechora* (SA-3 *Goa*)
    Point-defence 9K32 *Strela-2* (SA-7 *Grail*)‡
  GUNS
    SP 23mm ZSU-23-4 *Shilka*
    TOWED 23mm ZU-23; **37mm** M-1939; **57mm** S-60

Air Force 3,000
FORCES BY ROLE
FIGHTER/GROUND ATTACK
  1 sqn with MiG-23ML *Flogger* G/MiG-23UB *Flogger* C
  1 sqn with Su-27/Su-27UB *Flanker*
TRANSPORT
  1 sqn with An-12 *Cub*; An-26 *Curl*; An-32 *Cline*; C-130B *Hercules*; DHC-6 *Twin Otter*; L-100-30; Yak-40 *Codling* (VIP)
TRAINING
  1 sqn with L-39 *Albatros*
  1 sqn with SF-260
ATTACK/TRANSPORT HELICOPTER
  2 sqn with Mi-24/Mi-35 *Hind*; Mi-8 *Hip*; Mi-17 *Hip* H; SA316 *Alouette* III
EQUIPMENT BY TYPE
AIRCRAFT 19 combat capable
  FTR 11: 8 Su-27 *Flanker*; 3 Su-27UB *Flanker*
  FGA 8 MiG-23ML/UB *Flogger* G/C
  TPT 15: **Medium** 9: 3 An-12 *Cub*; 2 C-130B *Hercules*; 2 C-130E *Hercules*; 2 L-100-30; **Light** 6: 1 An-26 *Curl*; 1 An-32 *Cline*; 3 DHC-6 *Twin Otter*; 1 Yak-40 *Codling* (VIP)
  TRG 16: 12 L-39 *Albatros*; 4 SF-260
HELICOPTERS
  ATK 18: 15 Mi-24 *Hind*; 3 Mi-35 *Hind*
  MRH 19: 1 AW139; 6 SA316 *Alouette* III; 12 Mi-8 *Hip*/Mi-17 *Hip* H

AIR-LAUNCHED MISSILES
  AAM • IR R-3 (AA-2 *Atoll*)‡; R-60 (AA-8 *Aphid*); R-73 (AA-11 *Archer*); **IR/SARH** R-23/R-24 (AA-7 *Apex*); R-27 (AA-10 *Alamo*)

DEPLOYMENT
SOMALIA: AU • AMISOM 4,323; 6 inf bn
SOUTH SUDAN: UN • UNMISS 2,122; 17 obs; 3 inf bn
SUDAN: UN • UNAMID 1,684; 5 obs; 2 inf bn; **UN •** UNISFA 4,368; 77 obs; 1 recce coy; 3 inf bn; 2 arty coy; 1 engr coy; 1 sigs coy; 5 fd hospital; 1 hel sqn

Gabon GAB

CFA Franc BEAC fr		2017	2018	2019
GDP	fr	8.67tr	9.48tr	
	US$	14.9bn	17.2bn	
per capita	US$	7,373	8,385	
Growth	%	0.451	2.042	
Inflation	%	2.7	2.8	
Def bdgt [a]	fr	155bn	145bn	
	US$	267m	263m	
US$1=fr		580.93	550.82	

[a] Includes funds allocated to Republican Guard

Population	2,119,036					
Age	0–14	15–19	20–24	25–29	30–64	65 plus
Male	19.1%	5.9%	5.7%	4.9%	14.4%	1.9%
Female	18.3%	5.5%	5.0%	4.0%	13.2%	2.0%

Capabilities

Oil revenues have allowed the government to support small but regionally capable armed forces, while the country has benefited from the long-term presence of French troops acting as a security guarantor. There is regular training with French forces and with the regionally deployed French navy, as well as with the US and other international partners. Military medicine is well regarded. Gabonese forces took part in the 2018 *Obangame Express* exercise. The armed forces retain sufficient airlift to ensure mobility within the country and even a limited capability to project power by sea and air. Apart from limited maintenance facilities, there is no domestic defence-industrial capacity.

ACTIVE 4,700 (Army 3,200 Navy 500 Air 1,000)
Paramilitary 2,000

ORGANISATIONS BY SERVICE

Army 3,200
Republican Guard under direct presidential control
FORCES BY ROLE
MANOEUVRE
  Light
  1 (Republican Guard) gd gp (bn)
    (1 armd/recce coy, 3 inf coy, 1 arty bty, 1 ADA bty)
  8 inf coy

Air Manoeuvre
  1 cdo/AB coy
COMBAT SUPPORT
  1 engr coy
EQUIPMENT BY TYPE
ARMOURED FIGHTING VEHICLES
  RECCE 77: 24 AML-60/AML-90; 12 EE-3 *Jararaca*; 14 EE-9 *Cascavel*; 6 ERC-90F4 *Sagaie*; 7 RAM V-2; 14 VBL
  IFV 12 EE-11 *Urutu* (with 20mm gun)
  APC 64
    APC (W) 30: 9 LAV-150 *Commando*; 5 *Bastion* APC; 3 WZ-523; 12 VXB-170; 1 *Pandur*
    PPV 34 Ashok Leyland MPV
    AUV 12 *Aravis*
ANTI-TANK/ANTI-INFRASTRUCTURE
  MSL • MANPATS *Milan*
  RCL 106mm M40A1
ARTILLERY 67
  TOWED 105mm 4 M101
  MRL 24: 107mm 16 PH-63; 140mm 8 *Teruel*
  MOR 39: 81mm 35; 120mm 4 Brandt
AIR DEFENCE • GUNS 41
  SP 20mm 4 ERC-20
  TOWED 37+: 14.5mm ZPU-4; 23mm 24 ZU-23-2; 37mm 10 M-1939; 40mm 3 L/70

Navy ε500

HQ located at Port Gentil
EQUIPMENT BY TYPE
PATROL AND COASTAL COMBATANTS 9
  PB 9: 4 *Port Gentil* (FRA VCSM); 4 Rodman 66; 1 *Patra*†
AMPHIBIOUS LANDING CRAFT • LCM 1 Mk 9 (ex-UK)

Air Force 1,000

FORCES BY ROLE
FIGHTER/GROUND ATTACK
  1 sqn with *Mirage* F-1AZ
TRANSPORT
  1 (Republican Guard) sqn with AS332 *Super Puma*; ATR-42F; *Falcon* 900; Gulfstream IV-SP/G650ER
  1 sqn with C-130H *Hercules*; CN-235M-100
ATTACK/TRANSPORT HELICOPTER
  1 sqn with Bell 412 *Twin Huey* (AB-412); SA330C/H *Puma*; SA342M *Gazelle*
EQUIPMENT BY TYPE
AIRCRAFT 8 combat capable
  FGA 6 *Mirage* F-1AZ
  ATK 2 MB-326 *Impala* I
  MP (1 EMB-111* in store)
  TPT 6: Medium 1 C-130H *Hercules*; (1 L-100-30 in store); Light 2: 1 ATR-42F; 1 CN-235M-100; PAX 3: 1 *Falcon* 900; 1 Gulfstream IV-SP; 1 Gulfstream G650ER
  TRG (4 CM-170 *Magister* in store)
HELICOPTERS
  MRH 2: 1 Bell 412 *Twin Huey* (AB-412); 1 SA342M *Gazelle*; (2 SA342L *Gazelle* in store)
  TPT 7: Medium 4: 1 AS332 *Super Puma*; 3 SA330C/H *Puma*; Light 3: 2 H120 *Colibri*; 1 H135
AIR-LAUNCHED MISSILES • AAM • IR U-*Darter* (reported)

Paramilitary 2,000

Gendarmerie 2,000

FORCES BY ROLE
MANOEUVRE
  Armoured
    2 armd sqn
  Other
    3 paramilitary bde
    11 paramilitary coy
  Aviation
    1 unit with AS350 *Ecureuil*; AS355 *Ecureuil* II
EQUIPMENT BY TYPE
HELICOPTERS • TPT • Light 4: 2 AS350 *Ecureuil*; 2 AS355 *Ecureuil* II

DEPLOYMENT

CENTRAL AFRICAN REPUBLIC: UN • MINUSCA 436; 1 inf bn(-)

FOREIGN FORCES

France 450; 1 AB bn
Spain *Operation Barkhane* 45: 1 C295M

Gambia GAM

Gambian Dalasi D		2017	2018	2019
GDP	D	69.4bn	77.1bn	
	US$	1.48bn	1.61bn	
per capita	US$	705	740	
Growth	%	4.6	5.4	
Inflation	%	8.0	6.2	
Def bdgt	D	n.k	n.k	
	US$	n.k	n.k	
US$1=D		46.84	48.05	

Population	2,092,731					
Age	0–14	15–19	20–24	25–29	30–64	65 plus
Male	18.6%	5.2%	4.8%	4.4%	14.7%	1.6%
Female	18.4%	5.3%	5.0%	4.6%	15.5%	1.9%

Capabilities

The armed forces are undergoing SSR in the wake of political instability in 2016–17. Gambia's small forces have traditionally focused on maritime security and countering human trafficking. The US provides limited military training assistance. France resumed military assistance in 2017 and supports training and SSR. There is also cooperation with neighbouring states. A security and defence cooperation agreement was signed with Senegal in 2017, aimed at generating joint patrols and exercises. ECOWAS maintains its ECOMIG mission of 500 troops in Gambia, with financial support from the EU. Following the departure of long-serving president Jammeh, there has been a focus on clarifying political–military relations. Personnel are being trained to form a new presidential guard. The armed forces participate in multinational exercises, including the US-led *Obangame Express*, and have deployed in support of UN missions across the continent. Its largest deployment is of more than 200 troops to the UNAMID mission in Sudan. The equipment inventory is limited, with serviceability in doubt for some types. Gambia has no significant defence-industrial capabilities.

ACTIVE 800 (Army 800)

ORGANISATIONS BY SERVICE

Gambian National Army 800
FORCES BY ROLE
MANOEUVRE
  Light
  2 inf bn
COMBAT SUPPORT
  1 engr sqn

Marine Unit ε300
EQUIPMENT BY TYPE
PATROL AND COASTAL COMBATANTS 8
  PBF 4: 2 Rodman 55; 2 *Fatimah* I
  PB 4: 1 *Bolong Kanta*†; 3 *Taipei* (ROC *Hai Ou*) (one additional damaged and in reserve)

Air Wing
EQUIPMENT BY TYPE
AIRCRAFT
  TPT 5: **Light** 2 AT-802A *Air Tractor*; **PAX** 3: 1 B-727; 1 CL-601; 1 Il-62M *Classic* (VIP)

DEPLOYMENT
CENTRAL AFRICAN REPUBLIC: UN • MINUSCA 2; 3 obs
MALI: UN • MINUSMA 3; 2 obs
SUDAN: UN • UNAMID 211; 1 inf coy

FOREIGN FORCES
Ghana ECOMIG 50
Nigeria ECOMIG 200
Senegal ECOMIG 250

Ghana GHA

Ghanaian New Cedi C		2017	2018	2019
GDP	C	205bn	243bn	
	US$	47.0bn	51.8bn	
per capita	US$	1,663	1,787	
Growth	%	8.4	6.3	
Inflation	%	12.4	9.5	
Def bdgt	C	822m	991m	
	US$	189m	211m	
US$1=C		4.35	4.69	

Population 28,102,471

Age	0–14	15–19	20–24	25–29	30–64	65 plus
Male	19.0%	5.0%	4.3%	3.8%	15.2%	2.0%
Female	18.8%	5.0%	4.4%	4.0%	16.2%	2.3%

Capabilities
Ghana's armed forces are among the most capable in the region, with a long-term development plan covering both the current and the next decade. The ability to control its maritime EEZ is of increasing importance due to piracy and resource exploitation, and this underpins the navy's expansion plans. Internal and maritime security are central military tasks, along with participation in peacekeeping missions. The US delivers training and support and there is also significant and long-standing defence engagement with the UK, which in 2017 ran a strategic-leadership programme for Ghanaian and other regional participants at the Kofi Annan peacekeeping centre. Air-force training, close-air support and airlift capabilities have developed in recent years. There are plans to organise additional realistic training programmes and exercises, as well as to improve military infrastructure. The army is a regular contributor to UN peacekeeping operations and has pledged to maintain 1,000 personnel in readiness for such missions. Ghana has started to develop forward operating bases, principally with the objective of protecting the country's oil resources. Plans persist to develop air capabilities; a contract for *Super Tucano* aircraft was awarded in 2015. There have been some defence acquisitions from China. Apart from maintenance facilities and some ammunition production, the country has no traditional defence-industrial base. The formation of the Defence Industries Holding Company was intended to enable the armed forces to engage in civil–military collaborative projects.

ACTIVE 15,500 (Army 11,500 Navy 2,000 Air 2,000)

ORGANISATIONS BY SERVICE

Army 11,500
FORCES BY ROLE
COMMAND
  2 comd HQ
MANOEUVRE
  Reconnaissance
  1 armd recce regt (3 recce sqn)
  Light
  1 (rapid reaction) mot inf bn
  6 inf bn
  Air Manoeuvre
  2 AB coy
COMBAT SUPPORT
  1 arty regt (1 arty bty, 2 mor bty)
  1 fd engr regt (bn)
  1 sigs regt
  1 sigs sqn
COMBAT SERVICE SUPPORT
  1 log gp
  1 tpt coy
  2 maint coy
  1 med coy
  1 trg bn
EQUIPMENT BY TYPE
ARMOURED FIGHTING VEHICLES
  RECCE 3 EE-9 *Cascavel*
  IFV 48: 24 *Ratel*-90; 15 *Ratel*-20; 4 *Piranha* 25mm; 5+ Type-05P 25mm
  APC 105
    APC (W) 55+: 46 *Piranha*; 9+ Type-05P
    PPV 50 Streit *Typhoon*

ARTILLERY 87+
 TOWED **122mm** 6 D-30
 MRL 3+: **107mm** Type-63; **122mm** 3 Type-81
 MOR 78: **81mm** 50; **120mm** 28 Tampella
ENGINEERING & MAINTENANCE VEHICLES
 AEV 1 Type-05P AEV
 ARV *Piranha* reported
ANTI-TANK/ANTI-INFRASTRUCTURE
 RCL **84mm** *Carl Gustav*
AIR DEFENCE
 SAM • **Point-defence** 9K32 *Strela*-2 (SA-7 *Grail*)‡
 GUNS • **TOWED** 8+: **14.5mm** 4+: 4 ZPU-2; ZPU-4;
 23mm 4 ZU-23-2

Navy 2,000
Naval HQ located at Accra; Western HQ located at Sekondi; Eastern HQ located at Tema
EQUIPMENT BY TYPE
PATROL AND COASTAL COMBATANTS 14
 PCO 2 *Anzone* (US)
 PCC 10: 2 *Achimota* (GER Lurssen 57m) with 1 76mm gun; 2 *Dzata* (GER Lurssen 45m); 2 *Warrior* (GER Gepard); 4 *Snake* (PRC 47m)
 PBF 1 *Stephen Otu* (ROK *Sea Dolphin*)
 PB 1 *David Hansen* (US)

Air Force 2,000
FORCES BY ROLE
GROUND ATTACK
 1 sqn with K-8 *Karakorum**; L-39ZO*; MB-339A*
ISR
 1 unit with DA-42
TRANSPORT
 1 sqn with BN-2 *Defender*; C295; Cessna 172
TRANSPORT HELICOPTER
 1 sqn with AW109A; Bell 412SP *Twin Huey*; Mi-17V-5 *Hip* H; SA319 *Alouette* III; Z-9EH
EQUIPMENT BY TYPE†
AIRCRAFT 8 combat capable
 ATK (3 MB-326K in store)
 TPT 10: **Light** 10: 1 BN-2 *Defender*; 3 C295; 3 Cessna 172; 3 DA42; (**PAX** 1 F-28 *Fellowship* (VIP) in store)
 TRG 8: 4 K-8 *Karakorum**; 2 L-39ZO*; 2 MB-339A*
HELICOPTERS
 MRH 10: 1 Bell 412SP *Twin Huey*; 3 Mi-17V-5 *Hip* H; 2 SA319 *Alouette* III; 4 Z-9EH
 TPT 6: **Medium** 4 Mi-171Sh; **Light** 2 AW109A

DEPLOYMENT
CENTRAL AFRICAN REPUBLIC: UN • MINUSCA 11; 4 obs
DEMOCRATIC REPUBLIC OF THE CONGO: UN • MONUSCO 469; 15 obs; 1 inf bn(-)
GAMBIA: ECOWAS • ECOMIG 50
LEBANON: UN • UNIFIL 870; 1 mech inf bn
MALI: UN • MINUSMA 163; 1 obs; 1 engr coy
SOMALIA: UN • UNSOS 2 obs
SOUTH SUDAN: UN • UNMISS 861; 10 obs; 1 inf bn
SUDAN: UN • UNAMID 9; 4 obs; UN • UNISFA 6; 2 obs
SYRIA/ISRAEL: UN • UNDOF 12
WESTERN SAHARA: UN • MINURSO 7; 6 obs

Guinea GUI

Guinean Franc fr		2017	2018	2019
GDP	fr	93.2tr	107tr	
	US$	10.3bn	11.5bn	
per capita	US$	790	865	
Growth	%	8.2	5.8	
Inflation	%	8.9	8.2	
Def bdgt	fr	n.k	n.k	
	US$	n.k	n.k	
US$1=fr		9,087.89	9,263.73	

Population 11,855,411

Age	0–14	15–19	20–24	25–29	30–64	65 plus
Male	20.9%	5.3%	4.4%	3.7%	14.0%	1.7%
Female	20.5%	5.2%	4.4%	3.7%	14.1%	2.1%

Capabilities
Guinea's armed forces remain limited in size and capacity, although reforms since 2010 have brought them back under political control and begun a process of professionalisation. SSR, supported by the EU, is ongoing, with improvements seen in units dispatched to Mali. Internal-security challenges reportedly led to the composition of mixed army–gendarmerie units. Piracy in the Gulf of Guinea is a key concern, as is illegal trafficking and fishing. A military-programme law for the period 2015–20 may not be fully implemented due to funding issues. Defence cooperation with France and the US has led to financial and training assistance, including AFRICOM support for Guinea's MINUSMA deployment to Mali. France has also supported the Mali deployment. Guinea participates in multilateral exercises, such as the US-led *Obangame Express*, and a small airborne detachment trained with Moroccan troops in early 2018. In late 2017, the government announced that it would reinstate military service for students in 2018. This is expected to include 45 of days military training and six months of local service. Much of the country's military equipment is ageing and of Soviet-era vintage; serviceability will be questionable for some types. There is very limited organic airlift and France is supporting the development of a light aviation observation capability. In 2018, Guinea refurbished patrol boats originally donated by the US in the late 1980s, as part of general plans to reinforce its maritime units. Guinea is also attempting to improve its logistics and military-health capacities. There are no significant defence-industrial capabilities, though the president reportedly said that the armed forces should take on more of a role in national industry.

ACTIVE 9,700 (Army 8,500 Navy 400 Air 800)
Paramilitary 2,600
Conscript liability 2 years

ORGANISATIONS BY SERVICE

Army 8,500
FORCES BY ROLE
MANOEUVRE
 Armoured
  1 armd bn
 Light
  1 SF bn
  5 inf bn

1 ranger bn
1 cdo bn
Air Manoeuvre
1 air mob bn
Other
1 (Presidential Guard) gd bn
COMBAT SUPPORT
1 arty bn
1 AD bn
1 engr bn
EQUIPMENT BY TYPE
ARMOURED FIGHTING VEHICLES
  MBT 38: 30 T-34; 8 T-54
  LT TK 15 PT-76
  RECCE 27: 2 AML-90; 25 BRDM-1/BRDM-2
  IFV 2 BMP-1
  APC 59
    APC (T) 10 BTR-50
    APC (W) 30: 16 BTR-40; 8 BTR-60; 6 BTR-152
    PPV 19: 10 *Mamba*†; 9 *Puma* M36
ENGINEERING & MAINTENANCE VEHICLES
  ARV T-54/T-55 reported
ANTI-TANK/ANTI-INFRASTRUCTURE
  MSL • MANPATS 9K11 *Malyutka* (AT-3 *Sagger*); 9K111-1 *Konkurs* (AT-5 *Spandrel*)
  RCL 82mm B-10
  GUNS 6+: 57mm ZIS-2 (M-1943); 85mm 6 D-44
ARTILLERY 47+
  TOWED 24: 122mm 12 M-1931/37; 130mm 12 M-46
  MRL 220mm 3 9P140 *Uragan*
  MOR 20+: 82mm M-43; 120mm 20 M-1938/M-1943
AIR DEFENCE
  SAM • Point-defence 9K32 *Strela*-2 (SA-7 *Grail*)‡
  GUNS • TOWED 24+: 30mm M-53 (twin); 37mm 8 M-1939; 57mm 12 Type-59 (S-60); 100mm 4 KS-19

Navy ε400
EQUIPMENT BY TYPE
PATROL AND COASTAL COMBATANTS • PB 4: 1 Swiftships†; 3 RPB 20

Air Force 800
EQUIPMENT BY TYPE†
AIRCRAFT
  FGA (3 MiG-21 *Fishbed* non-op)
  TPT • Light 4: 2 An-2 *Colt*; 2 *Tetras*
HELICOPTERS
  ATK 4 Mi-24 *Hind*
  MRH 5: 2 MD-500MD; 2 Mi-17-1V *Hip* H; 1 SA342K *Gazelle*
  TPT 2: Medium 1 SA330 *Puma*; Light 1 AS350B *Ecureuil*
AIR-LAUNCHED MISSILES
  AAM • IR R-3 (AA-2 *Atoll*)‡

Paramilitary 2,600 active

Gendarmerie 1,000

Republican Guard 1,600

People's Militia 7,000 reservists

DEPLOYMENT
MALI: UN • MINUSMA 865; 3 obs; 1 inf bn
SOUTH SUDAN: UN • UNMISS 2; 1 obs
SUDAN: UN • UNISFA 1; 1 obs
WESTERN SAHARA: UN • MINURSO 5 obs

Guinea-Bissau GNB

CFA Franc BCEAO fr		2017	2018	2019
GDP	fr	784bn	818bn	
	US$	1.35bn	1.48bn	
per capita	US$	794	852	
Growth	%	5.9	4.5	
Inflation	%	1.1	2.0	
Def bdgt	fr	n.k	n.k	
	US$	n.k	n.k	
US$1=fr		580.73	553.02	

Population 1,833,247

Age	0–14	15–19	20–24	25–29	30–64	65 plus
Male	21.9%	5.4%	4.5%	3.7%	12.0%	1.3%
Female	21.7%	5.6%	4.8%	4.1%	13.4%	1.7%

Capabilities

Guinea-Bissau's armed forces have limited capabilities and are in the midst of both DDR and SSR programmes. There are embryonic schemes to recruit professionals. Defence policy is focused mainly on tackling internal-security challenges, in particular drug trafficking. International defence cooperation has reduced since the 2012 *coup d'état*. The US lifted its restrictions on foreign assistance only in 2014. The ECOWAS mission in Guinea-Bissau has been extended until September 2019. The authorities have looked elsewhere for defence cooperation; in 2017 a letter of intent was signed with Indonesia. Training remains limited and there are problems with recruitment and retention, as well as in developing adequate non-commissioned-officer structures. The number of generals and admirals more than doubled between 2009 and 2017. A pension system was established and funded only in 2015, with international financing. The armed forces participate in multinational exercises, such as the US-led *Obangame Express* in 2018. China has donated some non-lethal military and civilian equipment, but much of the country's military equipment is ageing. With no significant defence industry, equipment maintenance will remain a limiting factor on military capability.

ACTIVE 4,450 (Army 4,000 Navy 350 Air 100)
Conscript liability Selective conscription
Manpower and eqpt totals should be treated with caution. A number of draft laws to restructure the armed services and police have been produced

ORGANISATIONS BY SERVICE

Army ε4,000 (numbers reducing)
FORCES BY ROLE
MANOEUVRE
  Reconnaissance
  1 recce coy

Armoured
1 armd bn (sqn)
Light
5 inf bn
COMBAT SUPPORT
1 arty bn
1 engr coy
EQUIPMENT BY TYPE
ARMOURED FIGHTING VEHICLES
MBT 10 T-34
LT TK 15 PT-76
RECCE 10 BRDM-2
APC • APC (W) 55: 35 BTR-40/BTR-60; 20 Type-56 (BTR-152)
ANTI-TANK/ANTI-INFRASTRUCTURE
RCL 75mm Type-52 (M20); 82mm B-10
GUNS 85mm 8 D-44
ARTILLERY 26+
TOWED 122mm 18 D-30/M-30 (M-1938)
MOR 8+: 82mm M-43; 120mm 8 M-1943
AIR DEFENCE
SAM • Point-defence 9K32 *Strela*-2 (SA-7 *Grail*)‡
GUNS • TOWED 34: 23mm 18 ZU-23; 37mm 6 M-1939; 57mm 10 S-60

Navy ε350
EQUIPMENT BY TYPE
PATROL AND COASTAL COMBATANTS 4
PB 4: 2 *Alfeite*†; 2 Rodman 55m

Air Force 100
EQUIPMENT BY TYPE
AIRCRAFT • TPT • Light 1 Cessna 208B

FOREIGN FORCES
Nigeria ECOMIB 100

Kenya KEN

Kenyan Shilling sh		2017	2018	2019
GDP	sh	8.20tr	9.15tr	
	US$	79.2bn	89.6bn	
per capita	US$	1,695	1,865	
Growth	%	4.9	6.0	
Inflation	%	8.0	5.0	
Def bdgt [a]	sh	124bn	130bn	
	US$	1.20bn	1.27bn	
FMA (US)	US$	1m	0m	
US$1=sh		103.45	102.15	

[a] Includes national intelligence funding

Population 48,397,527
Ethnic groups: Kikuyu ε22–32%

Age	0–14	15–19	20–24	25–29	30–64	65 plus
Male	19.6%	5.5%	4.3%	4.1%	15.1%	1.3%
Female	19.5%	5.5%	4.4%	4.1%	15.0%	1.8%

Capabilities

The armed forces are concerned with maintaining regional stability and combating security threats, particularly from neighbouring Somalia. There are plans to establish a separate Coast Guard Service, to assume some maritime-security responsibilities from the navy. A long-standing defence and security agreement with the UK includes a permanent UK training unit, which is to increase support for maritime security and open a counter-IED training centre. There are also significant defence ties with the US and evidence of developing relationships with the Chinese and Jordanian armed forces. Involvement in a number of regional security missions and multinational exercises may also foster improved levels of cooperation and interoperability. Training has received attention, given the need to prepare for AU deployments. Regular operational deployments have increased military experience and confidence. Kenya's armed forces regularly participate in multinational exercises. Kenya remains a key contributor to AMISOM in Somalia, demonstrating limited capacity to project power immediately beyond its own territory. The armed forces also provide smaller contributions to other UN missions and are a leading element of the East African Standby Force. Recent equipment investments have focused on improving counter-insurgency capabilities, including the procurement of helicopters, armoured vehicles and ISR systems. There are plans to renew the fixed-wing transport fleet to support regional deployments. There is a limited defence industry focused on equipment maintenance and the manufacture of small-arms ammunition.

ACTIVE 24,100 (Army 20,000 Navy 1,600 Air 2,500)
Paramilitary 5,000

ORGANISATIONS BY SERVICE

Army 20,000
FORCES BY ROLE
MANOEUVRE
Armoured
1 armd bde (1 armd recce bn, 2 armd bn)
Light
1 spec ops bn
1 ranger bn 1 inf bde (3 inf bn)
1 inf bde (2 inf bn)
1 indep inf bn
Air Manoeuvre
1 air cav bn
1 AB bn
COMBAT SUPPORT
1 arty bde (2 arty bn, 1 mor bty)
1 ADA bn
1 engr bde (2 engr bn)
EQUIPMENT BY TYPE
ARMOURED FIGHTING VEHICLES
MBT 78 Vickers Mk 3
RECCE 92: 72 AML-60/AML-90; 12 *Ferret*; 8 S52 *Shorland*
APC 200
  APC (W) 95: 52 UR-416; 31 Type-92; 12 *Bastion* APC; (10 M3 Panhard in store)
  PPV 105 *Puma* M26-15
ENGINEERING & MAINTENANCE VEHICLES
ARV 7 Vickers ARV
MW *Bozena*

ARTILLERY 111
 SP 155mm 2+ *Nora B-52*
 TOWED 105mm 47: 40 L118 Light Gun; 7 Model 56 pack howitzer
 MOR 62: **81mm** 50; **120mm** 12 Brandt
ANTI-TANK/ANTI-INFRASTRUCTURE
 MSL • MANPATS *Milan*
 RCL 84mm *Carl Gustav*
HELICOPTERS
 MRH 37: 2 Hughes 500D†; 12 Hughes 500M†; 10 Hughes 500MD *Scout Defender*† (with TOW); 10 Hughes 500ME†; 3 Z-9W
AIR DEFENCE • GUNS • TOWED 94: **20mm** 81: 11 Oerlikon; ε70 TCM-20; **40mm** 13 L/70
AIR-LAUNCHED MISSILES • ASM TOW

Navy 1,600 (incl 120 marines)
EQUIPMENT BY TYPE
PATROL AND COASTAL COMBATANTS 7
 PCO 1 *Jasiri* with 1 76mm gun
 PCF 2 *Nyayo*
 PCC 3: 1 *Harambee II* (ex-FRA P400); 2 *Shujaa* with 1 76mm gun
 PBF 1 *Archangel*
AMPHIBIOUS • LCM 2 *Galana*
LOGISTICS AND SUPPORT • AP 2

Air Force 2,500
FORCES BY ROLE
FIGHTER/GROUND ATTACK
 2 sqn with F-5E/F *Tiger* II
TRANSPORT
 Some sqn with DHC-5D *Buffalo*†; DHC-8†; F-70† (VIP); Y-12(II)†
TRAINING
 Some sqn with *Bulldog* 103/*Bulldog* 127†; EMB-312 *Tucano*†*; *Hawk* Mk52†*; Hughes 500D†
TRANSPORT HELICOPTER
 1 sqn with SA330 *Puma*†
EQUIPMENT BY TYPE†
AIRCRAFT 37 combat capable
 FTR 21: 17 F-5E *Tiger* II; 4 F-5F *Tiger* II
 TPT 17 **Light** 16: 4 DHC-5D *Buffalo*†; 3 DHC-8†; 9 Y-12(II)†; (6 Do-28D-2 in store); **PAX** 1 F-70 (VIP)
 TRG 29: 8 *Bulldog* 103/127†; 11 EMB-312 *Tucano*†*; 5 Grob 120A; 5 *Hawk* Mk52†*
HELICOPTERS
 ATK 3 AH-1F *Cobra*
 MRH 9 H125M (AS550) *Fennec*
 TPT 20: **Medium** 12: 2 Mi-171; 10 SA330 *Puma*†; **Light** 8 Bell 205 (UH-1H *Huey* II)
AIR-LAUNCHED MISSILES
 AAM • IR AIM-9 *Sidewinder*
 ASM AGM-65 *Maverick*

Paramilitary 5,000
Police General Service Unit 5,000
EQUIPMENT BY TYPE
ARMOURED FIGHTING VEHICLES
 APC • PPV 25 CS/VP3

PATROL AND COASTAL COMBATANTS • PB 5 (2 on Lake Victoria)

Air Wing
EQUIPMENT BY TYPE
AIRCRAFT • TPT • Light 6: 2 Cessna 208B *Grand Caravan*; 3 Cessna 310; 1 Cessna 402
HELICOPTERS
 MRH 3 Mi-17 *Hip* H
 TPT 5: **Medium** 1 Mi-17V-5; **Light** 4: 2 AW139; 1 Bell 206L *Long Ranger*; 1 Bo-105
 TRG 1 Bell 47G

DEPLOYMENT
CENTRAL AFRICAN REPUBLIC: UN • MINUSCA 7; 6 obs
DEMOCRATIC REPUBLIC OF THE CONGO: UN • MONUSCO 7; 5 obs
LEBANON: UN • UNIFIL 1
MALI: UN • MINUSMA 8; 3 obs
SOMALIA: AU • AMISOM 4,046: 3 inf bn
SOUTH SUDAN: UN • UNMISS 11; 7 obs
SUDAN: UN • UNAMID 89; 2 obs; 1 MP coy

FOREIGN FORCES
United Kingdom BATUK 350; 1 trg unit

Lesotho LSO

Lesotho Loti M		2017	2018	2019
GDP	M	35.7bn	38.5bn	
	US$	2.75bn	2.98bn	
per capita	US$	1,361	1,466	
Growth	%	-1.6	0.8	
Inflation	%	5.3	6.3	
Def bdgt	m	723m	661m	
	US$	55.6m	51.2m	
US$1=M		13.00	12.92	

Population 1,962,461

Age	0–14	15–19	20–24	25–29	30–64	65 plus
Male	16.0%	4.9%	4.4%	4.3%	17.0%	2.8%
Female	15.8%	5.1%	5.0%	5.1%	16.8%	2.7%

Capabilities

Lesotho has a small ground force and an air wing for light transport and liaison. A SADC force deployed in country at the end of 2017 to support the government following the assassination of the army chief. The force was due to leave in late 2018. Lesotho's armed forces are charged with protecting territorial integrity and sovereignty and ensuring internal security. Lesotho is a SADC member state. The armed forces are a voluntary service. Morale may have been undermined by instability in the country and by the requirement for a SADC force to provide stability. There is no independent capacity to deploy and support an operation beyond national borders. Lesotho's limited inventory is obsolescent by modern standards, and there is little possibility of any significant procurement to replace ageing equipment. The acquisition of light helicopters has been identified as a goal. Barring very limited maintenance, there is no defence-industrial capacity.

ACTIVE 2,000 (Army 2,000)

ORGANISATIONS BY SERVICE

Army ε2,000
FORCES BY ROLE
MANOEUVRE
  Reconnaissance
  1 recce coy
  Light
  7 inf coy
  Aviation
  1 sqn
COMBAT SUPPORT
  1 arty bty(-)
  1 spt coy (with mor)
EQUIPMENT BY TYPE
ARMOURED FIGHTING VEHICLES
  MBT 1 T-55
  RECCE 30: 4 AML-90; 2 BRDM-2†; 6 RAM Mk3; 10 RBY-1; 8 S52 *Shorland*
ANTI-TANK/ANTI-INFRASTRUCTURE
  RCL 106mm 6 M40
ARTILLERY 12
  TOWED 105mm 2
  MOR 81mm 10

Air Wing 110
AIRCRAFT
  TPT • Light 3: 2 C-212-300 *Aviocar*; 1 GA-8 *Airvan*
HELICOPTERS
  MRH 3: 1 Bell 412 *Twin Huey*; 2 Bell 412EP *Twin Huey*
  TPT • Light 1 Bell 206 *Jet Ranger*

Liberia LBR

Liberian Dollar L$		2017	2018	2019
GDP	L$	3.29bn	3.22bn	
	US$	3.29bn	3.22bn	
per capita	US$	694	663	
Growth	%	2.5	3.0	
Inflation	%	12.4	21.3	
Def bdgt	L$	14.4m	16.0m	15.5m
	US$	14.4m	16.0m	
FMA (US)	US$	2.5m	0m	
US$1=L$		1.00	1.00	

Population 4,809,768

Ethnic groups: Americo-Liberians 5%

Age	0–14	15–19	20–24	25–29	30–64	65 plus
Male	22.1%	5.5%	4.5%	3.4%	13.1%	1.4%
Female	21.6%	5.4%	4.5%	3.6%	13.4%	1.5%

Capabilities

Liberia's developing armed forces and security institutions are now operating without in-country support formerly provided by UNMIL, which completed its mandate in March 2018. A revised National Security Strategy was produced in 2017, reportedly clarifying the roles of Liberia's security institutions. The government is emphasising national security as part of its development agenda, in order to fill the gap left by the end of UNMIL. However, some UN-level support continues for the security and justice sectors. The army chief of staff has said that priorities include improving training, operational readiness and personnel welfare. There are plans to establish an air wing to boost the country's search-and-rescue, movement and logistics, medevac and maritime-patrol capacities. Historical ties with the US have led to a deep defence relationship, which in recent years has focused on areas such as force health, including schemes to improve recruitment and retention. A US mentoring mission that ended in 2017 worked on defence administration, engineering and explosive-ordnance disposal. Subsequent US assistance has focused on maritime security and medical skills. There is cooperation also in military medicine, coming only years after significant US assistance as part of the Ebola response. A military-cooperation agreement with Nigeria was signed in 2007 and has led to training for soldiers and personnel for the embryonic air wing. In 2018, the first two pilots graduated after a new round of fixed-wing-aircraft training in Nigeria. The armed forces are able to deploy and sustain small units, such as to the MINUSMA mission in Mali. Equipment recapitalisation will be dependent on finances as well as the development of a supporting force structure. Liberia has no domestic defence industry, bar limited maintenance support capacities.

ACTIVE 2,010 (Army 1,950, Coast Guard 60)

ORGANISATIONS BY SERVICE

Army 1,950
FORCES BY ROLE
MANOEUVRE
  Light
  1 (23rd) inf bde with (2 inf bn, 1 engr coy, 1 MP coy)
COMBAT SERVICE SUPPORT
  1 trg unit (forming)

Coast Guard 60
All operational patrol vessels under 10t FLD

DEPLOYMENT

MALI: UN • MINUSMA 115; 1 obs; 1 inf coy(-)

Madagascar MDG

Malagsy Ariary fr		2017	2018	2019
GDP	fr	35.8tr	40.5tr	
	US$	11.5bn	12.5bn	
per capita	US$	449	475	
Growth	%	4.2	5.0	
Inflation	%	8.3	7.8	
Def bdgt	fr	208bn	243bn	
	US$	66.8m	74.9m	
US$1=fr		3,116.06	3,244.13	

Population 25,683,610

Age	0–14	15–19	20–24	25–29	30–64	65 plus
Male	19.9%	5.3%	4.8%	4.1%	14.3%	1.5%
Female	19.6%	5.3%	4.8%	4.1%	14.3%	1.8%

Capabilities

The army dominates the country's modest armed forces, and there remains the risk of military intervention in domestic politics. Ensuring sovereignty and territorial integrity are principal defence aspirations; maritime security is also an area of focus. Madagascar is a member of SADC and its regional Standby Force. In 2018, the country signed an 'umbrella defence agreement' with India to explore closer defence ties and an intergovernmental agreement with Russia on military cooperation. There is no independent capacity to deploy and support an operation beyond national borders. The equipment inventory is obsolescent and with economic development a key government target, equipment recapitalisation is unlikely to be a priority.

ACTIVE 13,500 (Army 12,500 Navy 500 Air 500)
Paramilitary 8,100
Conscript liability 18 months (incl for civil purposes)

ORGANISATIONS BY SERVICE

Army 12,500+
FORCES BY ROLE
MANOEUVRE
  Light
   2 (intervention) inf regt
   10 (regional) inf regt
COMBAT SUPPORT
  1 arty regt
  3 engr regt
  1 sigs regt
COMBAT SERVICE SUPPORT
  1 log regt
AIR DEFENCE
  1 ADA regt
EQUIPMENT BY TYPE
ARMOURED FIGHTING VEHICLES
  LT TK 12 PT-76
  RECCE 73: ε35 BRDM-2; 10 FV701 *Ferret*; ε20 M3A1; 8 M8
APC • APC (T) ε30 M3A1 half-track
ANTI-TANK/ANTI-INFRASTRUCTURE
  RCL 106mm M40A1
ARTILLERY 25+
  TOWED 17: 105mm 5 M101; 122mm 12 D-30
  MOR 8+: 82mm M-37; 120mm 8 M-43
AIR DEFENCE • GUNS • TOWED 70: 14.5mm 50 ZPU-4; 37mm 20 PG-55 (M-1939)

Navy 500 (incl some 100 Marines)
EQUIPMENT BY TYPE
PATROL AND COASTAL COMBATANTS 8
  PCC 1 *Trozona*
  PB 7 (ex-US CG MLB)
AMPHIBIOUS • LCT 1 (ex-FRA EDIC)

Air Force 500
FORCES BY ROLE
TRANSPORT
  1 sqn with An-26 *Curl*; Yak-40 *Codling* (VIP)
  1 (liaison) sqn with Cessna 310; Cessna 337 *Skymaster*; PA-23 *Aztec*
TRAINING
  1 sqn with Cessna 172; J.300 *Joker*; *Tetras*
TRANSPORT HELICOPTER
  1 sqn with SA318C *Alouette* II
EQUIPMENT BY TYPE
AIRCRAFT • TPT 16: **Light** 14: 1 An-26 *Curl*; 4 Cessna 172; 1 Cessna 310; 2 Cessna 337 *Skymaster*; 2 J.300 *Joker*; 1 PA-23 *Aztec*; 1 *Tetras*; 2 Yak-40 *Codling* (VIP); **PAX** 2 B-737
HELICOPTERS • MRH 4 SA318C *Alouette* II

Paramilitary 8,100

Gendarmerie 8,100

Malawi MWI

Malawian Kwacha K		2017	2018	2019
GDP	K	4.53tr	5.03tr	
	US$	6.24bn	6.89bn	
per capita	US$	326	349	
Growth	%	4.0	3.3	
Inflation	%	12.2	9.2	
Def bdgt	K	27.6bn	15.3bn	22.0bn
	US$	38.0m	21.0m	
US$1=K		725.62	730.39	

Population 19,842,560

Age	0–14	15–19	20–24	25–29	30–64	65 plus
Male	23.0%	5.6%	4.6%	3.7%	11.4%	1.2%
Female	23.2%	5.7%	4.7%	3.7%	11.7%	1.5%

Capabilities

The army is the largest element of the Malawi Defence Force (MDF). In recent years, the army has been used to help with transport-infrastructure development and to attempt to control illegal deforestation. The Malawi Defence Force Act came into operation in 2004. The armed forces are constitutionally tasked with ensuring sovereignty and territorial integrity. Providing military assistance to civil authorities in times of emergencies and support to the police are additional tasks. Counter-trafficking is a role for the MDF's small air wing and the naval unit. Development plans include enhancing combat readiness and improving military medicine and engineering. Malawi is a member of the SADC and its Standby Force. In 2018, the country signed an 'umbrella defence agreement' with India to explore closer defence ties. The armed forces have contributed to AU and UN peacekeeping operations, including in Côte d'Ivoire and the DRC. The armed services are all-volunteer. There is no independent capacity to deploy and support an operation beyond national borders. The UK provided training and support for the armed forces' deployment to the DRC, where troops contribute to the Force Intervention Brigade. Although the military inventory is obsolescent, there are no public requirements for modernisation. Apart from limited maintenance facilities, the country has no defence industry.

ACTIVE 10,700 (Army 10,700) Paramilitary 4,200

ORGANISATIONS BY SERVICE

Army 10,700
FORCES BY ROLE
MANOEUVRE
  Mechanised
  1 mech bn
  Light
  1 inf bde (4 inf bn)
  1 inf bde (1 inf bn)
  Air Manoeuvre
  1 para bn
COMBAT SUPPORT
  3 lt arty bty
  1 engr bn
COMBAT SERVICE SUPPORT
  12 log coy
EQUIPMENT BY TYPE
ARMOURED FIGHTING VEHICLES
  RECCE 66: 30 *Eland-90*; 8 FV701 *Ferret*; 20 FV721 *Fox*; 8 RAM Mk3
  APC • PPV 31: 14 *Casspir*; 9 *Marauder*; 8 *Puma* M26-15
ARTILLERY 107
  TOWED 105mm 9 L118 Light Gun
  MOR 81mm 98: 82 L16A1; 16 M3
AIR DEFENCE • GUNS • TOWED 72: **12.7mm** 32; **14.5mm** 40 ZPU-4

Navy 220
EQUIPMENT BY TYPE
PATROL AND COASTAL COMBATANTS 1
  PB 1 *Kasungu* (ex-FRA *Antares*)

Air Wing 200
EQUIPMENT BY TYPE
AIRCRAFT • TPT • Light 1 Do-228
HELICOPTERS • TPT 8: **Medium** 3: 1 AS532UL *Cougar*; 1 SA330H *Puma*; 1 H215 *Super Puma* **Light** 5: 1 AS350L *Ecureuil*; 4 SA341B *Gazelle*

Paramilitary 4,200

Police Mobile Service 4,200
EQUIPMENT BY TYPE
ARMOURED FIGHTING VEHICLES
  RECCE 8 S52 *Shorland*
AIRCRAFT
  TPT • Light 4: 3 BN-2T *Defender* (border patrol); 1 SC.7 3M *Skyvan*
HELICOPTERS • MRH 2 AS365 *Dauphin 2*

DEPLOYMENT
DEMOCRATIC REPUBLIC OF THE CONGO: UN • MONUSCO 857; 4 obs; 1 inf bn
SUDAN: UN • UNAMID 2; UN • UNISFA 1
WESTERN SAHARA: UN • MINURSO 3 obs

Mali MLI

CFA Franc BCEAO fr		2017	2018	2019
GDP	fr	8.93tr	9.59tr	
	US$	15.4bn	17.4bn	
per capita	US$	813	892	
Growth	%	5.4	5.1	
Inflation	%	1.8	2.5	
Def bdgt [a]	fr	381bn	403bn	423bn
	US$	655m	731m	
US$1=fr		580.93	550.82	

[a] Defence and interior security budget

Population 18,429,893

Ethnic groups: Tuareg 6–10%

Age	0–14	15–19	20–24	25–29	30–64	65 plus
Male	24.1%	5.1%	3.9%	3.0%	11.0%	1.5%
Female	23.9%	5.4%	4.4%	3.7%	12.3%	1.5%

Capabilities

The armed forces are focused on countering rebel and Islamist groups. A defence-reform process is ongoing, with assistance from external partners. A 2015–19 military-programming law aims to improve recruitment and training. Mali is supported by neighbouring states in the G5 Sahel partnership, and benefits from training assistance from France, the EU and the US. France maintains bases, personnel and equipment in Mali as part of *Operation Barkhane*. The EU Training Mission, whose mandate has been extended to March 2020, has trained more than 10,000 soldiers, many at the Koulikoro training centre. The EUTM has also delivered training to the air force. The armed forces also participate in multinational exercises, particularly those focused on counter-terrorism capabilities. There are no deployments of formed units abroad. Equipment and maintenance capabilities are limited, and the serviceability of some vehicles is in doubt. The air force has no combat aircraft and only a small number of attack helicopters. Strengthening air capability is a priority and contracts have recently been signed with Brazil for training aircraft, France for transport helicopters and Russia for attack helicopters. The country has no significant defence industry.

ACTIVE 10,000 (Army 10,000) Paramilitary 7,800

ORGANISATIONS BY SERVICE

Army ε10,000
FORCES BY ROLE
The remnants of the pre-conflict Malian army are being reformed into new combined-arms battlegroups, each of which comprise one lt mech coy, three mot inf coy, one arty bty and additional recce, cdo and cbt spt elms
MANOEUVRE
  Light
    8 mot inf BG
  Air Manoeuvre
    1 para bn
COMBAT SUPPORT
  1 engr bn
COMBAT SERVICE SUPPORT
  1 med unit
EQUIPMENT BY TYPE
ARMOURED FIGHTING VEHICLES
  RECCE BRDM-2†
  APC • APC (W) 23+: 4+ *Bastion* APC; 10+ BTR-60PB; 9 BTR-70
ARTILLERY 30+
  TOWED 122mm D-30
  MRL 122mm 30+ BM-21 *Grad*

Air Force
FORCES BY ROLE
TRANSPORT
  1 sqn with BT-67; C295W; Y-12E
TRAINING
  1 sqn with *Tetras*
TRANSPORT/ATTACK HELICOPTER
  1 sqn with H215; Mi-24D *Hind*; Mi-35M *Hind*
EQUIPMENT BY TYPE
AIRCRAFT 4 combat capable
  TPT • Light 11: 1 BT-67; 1 C295W; 7 *Tetras*; 2 Y-12E (1 An-24 *Coke*; 2 An-26 *Curl*; 2 BN-2 *Islander* all in store)
  TRG 4 A-29 *Super Tucano** (6 L-29 *Delfin*; 2 SF-260WL *Warrior** all in store)
HELICOPTERS
  ATK 4: 2 Mi-24D *Hind*; 2 Mi-35M *Hind*
  MRH (1 Z-9 in store)
  TPT • Medium 2 H215; (1 Mi-8 *Hip* in store); **Light** (1 AS350 *Ecureuil* in store)

Paramilitary 7,800 active

Gendarmerie 1,800
FORCES BY ROLE
MANOEUVRE
  Other
    8 paramilitary coy

National Guard 2,000
FORCES BY ROLE
MANOEUVRE
  Reconnaissance
    6 (camel) cav coy

National Police 1,000
Militia 3,000

DEPLOYMENT
DEMOCRATIC REPUBLIC OF THE CONGO: UN • MONUSCO 1 obs

FOREIGN FORCES
All under MINUSMA comd unless otherwise specified
Albania EUTM Mali 4
Armenia 1
Austria 3 • EUTM Mali 12
Bangladesh 1,415; 3 obs; 1 inf bn; 1 engr coy; 2 sigs coy; 1 tpt coy
Belgium 130; 1 recce unit; 1 tpt flt with 1 C-130H *Hercules* • EUTM Mali 20
Benin 258; 1 mech inf coy
Bhutan 4
Bosnia-Herzegovina 2
Bulgaria EUTM Mali 5
Burkina Faso 1,720; 2 inf bn
Burundi 2
Cambodia 303; 2 eng coy; 1 EOD coy
Cameroon 1; 1 obs
Canada 138; 1 hel sqn with 2 CH-47F; 5 Bell 412
Chad 1,447; 3 obs; 1 SF coy; 2 inf bn
China 403; 1 sy coy; 1 engr coy; 1 fd hospital
Côte d'Ivoire 162; 1 obs; 1 sy coy
Czech Republic 3; 2 obs • EUTM Mali 41
Denmark 1
Egypt 327; 3 obs; 2 sy coy; 1 MP coy
El Salvador 156; 1 hel sqn
Estonia 3 • *Operation Barkhane* 50 • EUTM Mali 4
Finland 4 • EUTM Mali 1
France 24 • *Operation Barkhane* 1,750; 1 mech inf BG; 1 log bn; 1 hel unit with 4 *Tiger*; 3 NH90 TTH; 6 SA330 *Puma*; 4 SA342 *Gazelle* • EUTM Mali 13
Gambia 3; 2 obs
Georgia EUTM Mali 1
Germany 430; 1 obs; 1 sy coy; 1 int coy; 1 UAV sqn • EUTM Mali 147
Ghana 163; 1 obs; 1 engr coy; 1 avn flt
Greece EUTM Mali 2
Guatemala 2
Guinea 865; 3 obs; 1 inf bn
Hungary EUTM Mali 7
Indonesia 9; 1 obs
Ireland EUTM Mali 20
Italy 2 • EUTM Mali 12
Jordan 61; 1 obs
Kenya 8; 3 obs
Latvia 17 • EUTM Mali 3
Liberia 115; 1 obs; 1 inf coy(-)
Lithuania 38; 1 obs • EUTM Mali 2
Luxembourg EUTM Mali 2
Mauritania 8

Mexico 3
Montenegro EUTM Mali 1
Nepal 153; 3 obs; 1 EOD coy
Netherlands 241; 1 recce coy • EUTM Mali 1
Niger 861; 2 obs; 1 inf bn
Nigeria 83; 4 obs; 1 fd hospital
Norway 15
Pakistan 3
Portugal 2 • EUTM Mali 12
Romania 3 • EUTM Mali 3
Senegal 1,095; 2 inf bn
Serbia EUTM Mali 3
Sierra Leone 10; 2 obs
Slovenia EUTM Mali 4
Spain 1 • EUTM Mali 292
Sri Lanka 200; 7; 1 sy coy
Sweden 241; 1 int coy • EUTM Mali 6
Switzerland 6
Togo 937; 2 obs; 1 inf bn; 1 fd hospital
Tunisia 4; 1 obs
United Kingdom 2 • *Operation Barkhane* 90; 1 hel flt with 3 CH-47SD *Chinook* HC3; • EUTM Mali 8
United States 24

Mauritius MUS

Mauritian Rupee R		2017	2018	2019
GDP	R	460bn	479bn	
	US$	13.3bn	14.0bn	
per capita	US$	10,504	11,015	
Growth	%	3.8	3.9	
Inflation	%	3.7	5.1	
Def bdgt [a]	R	8.06bn	7.54bn	8.49bn
	US$	234m	221m	
US$1=R		34.48	34.14	

[a] Police service budget

Population	1,364,283					
Age	0–14	15–19	20–24	25–29	30–64	65 plus
Male	10.2%	3.7%	3.7%	4.0%	23.5%	4.2%
Female	9.7%	3.5%	3.7%	3.9%	24.1%	6.0%

Capabilities

The country has no standing armed forces; instead, security tasks are met by the police force's Special Mobile Force (SMF), formed as a motorised infantry battalion. The SMF is tasked with ensuring internal and external territorial and maritime security. India provides support to the Mauritian National Coast Guard, which is a branch of the police force. The SMF trains along traditional military lines but has no ability to deploy beyond national territory. There is no defence industry, beyond very limited maintenance facilities.

ACTIVE NIL Paramilitary 2,550

ORGANISATIONS BY SERVICE

Paramilitary 2,550

Special Mobile Force ε1,750
FORCES BY ROLE
MANOEUVRE
  Reconnaissance
    2 recce coy
  Light
    5 (rifle) mot inf coy
COMBAT SUPPORT
  1 engr sqn
COMBAT SERVICE SUPPORT
  1 spt pl
EQUIPMENT BY TYPE
ARMOURED FIGHTING VEHICLES
  IFV 2 VAB with 20mm gun
  APC • APC (W) 12: 3 *Tactica*; 9 VAB
ARTILLERY • MOR 81mm 2

Coast Guard ε800
EQUIPMENT BY TYPE
PATROL AND COASTAL COMBATANTS 17
  PCC 2 *Victory* (IND *Sarojini Naidu*)
  PCO 1 *Barracuda* with 1 hel landing platform
  PB 14: 10 (IND *Fast Interceptor Boat*); 1 P-2000; 1 SDB-Mk3; 2 *Rescuer* (FSU *Zhuk*)
AIRCRAFT • **TPT** • **Light** 4: 1 BN-2T *Defender*; 3 Do-228-101

Police Air Wing
EQUIPMENT BY TYPE
HELICOPTERS
  MRH 9: 1 H125 (AS555) *Fennec*; 2 *Dhruv*; 1 SA315B *Lama* (*Cheetah*); 5 SA316 *Alouette* III (*Chetak*)

Mozambique MOZ

Mozambique New Metical M		2017	2018	2019
GDP	M	804bn	878bn	
	US$	12.6bn	14.6bn	
per capita	US$	426	481	
Growth	%	3.7	3.5	
Inflation	%	15.3	6.0	
Def bdgt	M	5.97bn	7.86bn	
	US$	93m	131m	
US$1=M		63.92	60.16	

Population	27,233,789					
Age	0–14	15–19	20–24	25–29	30–64	65 plus
Male	22.4%	5.8%	4.9%	3.8%	10.8%	1.3%
Female	22.1%	5.8%	5.1%	4.2%	12.2%	1.6%

Capabilities

The country faces a growing internal threat from Islamist groups, with attacks being carried out in the north of the country. The May 2018 death of RENAMO opposition leader Afonso Dhlakama also raised concerns over renewed armed clashes between the former resistance movement and the government. The armed forces are tasked with ensuring territorial integrity and internal security, as well as tackling piracy and human trafficking. The integration of RENAMO personnel into the military is a long-standing objective.

Mozambique has defence relationships with China, Portugal and Russia. In 2017, the UN raised concerns that Mozambique was receiving defence support from North Korea, a claim the government rejected. The armed forces use conscription to meet their personnel requirements. The ministry is reportedly to implement a military HIV policy, including more screening, to try to reduce HIV incidence. The armed forces have no capacity to deploy beyond Mozambique's borders without assistance. Maintaining ageing Soviet-era equipment, which makes up the bulk of its inventory, will be problematic, not least in the absence of any local defence industry. Moreover, Mozambique's recent economic performance will likely limit the government's ability to recapitalise.

ACTIVE 11,200 (Army 10,000 Navy 200 Air 1,000)
Conscript liability 2 years

ORGANISATIONS BY SERVICE

Army ε9,000–10,000
FORCES BY ROLE
SPECIAL FORCES
　3 SF bn
MANOEUVRE
　Light
　　7 inf bn
COMBAT SUPPORT
　2-3 arty bn
　2 engr bn
COMBAT SERVICE SUPPORT
　1 log bn
EQUIPMENT BY TYPE†
Equipment estimated at 10% or less serviceability
ARMOURED FIGHTING VEHICLES
　MBT 60+ T-54
　RECCE 30 BRDM-1/BRDM-2
　IFV 40 BMP-1
　APC 326
　　APC (T) 30 FV430
　　APC (W) 285: 160 BTR-60; 100 BTR-152; 25 AT-105 *Saxon*
　　PPV 11 *Casspir*
ANTI-TANK/ANTI-INFRASTRUCTURE
　MSL • MANPATS 9K11 *Malyutka* (AT-3 *Sagger*); 9K111 *Fagot* (AT-4 *Spigot*)
　RCL 75mm; **82mm** B-10; **107mm** 24 B-12
　GUNS 85mm 18: 6 D-48; 12 PT-56 (D-44)
ARTILLERY 126
　TOWED 62: **100mm** 20 M-1944; **105mm** 12 M101; **122mm** 12 D-30; **130mm** 6 M-46; **152mm** 12 D-1
　MRL 122mm 12 BM-21 *Grad*
　MOR 52: **82mm** 40 M-43; **120mm** 12 M-43
AIR DEFENCE • GUNS 290+
　SP 57mm 20 ZSU-57-2
　TOWED 270+: **20mm** M-55; **23mm** 120 ZU-23-2; **37mm** 90 M-1939; (10 M-1939 in store); **57mm** 60 S-60; (30 S-60 in store)

Navy ε200
EQUIPMENT BY TYPE
PATROL AND COASTAL COMBATANTS 12
　PBF 8: 2 DV 15; 6 HSI 32
　PB 4: 3 *Ocean Eagle* 43 (capacity 1 *Camcopter* S-100 UAV); 1 *Pebane* (ex-ESP *Conejera*)
UNMANNED AERIAL VEHICLES
　ISR • Light 1 S-100 *Camcopter*

Air Force 1,000
FORCES BY ROLE
FIGHTER/GROUND ATTACK
　1 sqn with MiG-21bis *Fishbed*; MiG-21UM *Mongol* B
TRANSPORT
　1 sqn with An-26 *Curl*; FTB-337G *Milirole*; Cessna 150B; Cessna 172; PA-34 *Seneca*
ATTACK/TRANSPORT HELICOPTER
　1 sqn with Mi-24 *Hind*†
EQUIPMENT BY TYPE
AIRCRAFT 8 combat capable
　FGA 8: 6 MiG-21bis *Fishbed*; 2 MiG-21UM *Mongol* B
　ISR 2 FTB-337G *Milirole*
　TPT 6: **Light** 5: 1 An-26 *Curl*; 2 Cessna 150B; 1 Cessna 172; 1 PA-34 *Seneca*; (4 PA-32 *Cherokee* non-op); **PAX** 1 Hawker 850XP
HELICOPTERS
　ATK 2 Mi-24 *Hind*†
　TPT • Medium (2 Mi-8 *Hip* non-op)
AD • SAM • TOWED: (S-75 *Dvina* (SA-2 *Guideline*) non-op‡; S-125 *Pechora* SA-3 *Goa* non-op‡)

Namibia NAM

Namibian Dollar N$		2017	2018	2019
GDP	N$	176bn	184bn	
	US$	13.2bn	14.1bn	
per capita	US$	5,589	5,923	
Growth	%	-0.8	1.1	
Inflation	%	6.1	3.5	
Def bdgt	N$	6.40bn	5.96bn	
	US$	481m	457m	
US$1=N$		13.32	13.04	

Population	2,533,224				
Age	0–14	15–19	20–24	25–29	30–64	65 plus
Male	18.5%	5.4%	4.8%	4.2%	14.4%	1.7%
Female	18.1%	5.3%	4.9%	4.4%	16.1%	2.3%

Capabilities

The defence authorities aim to develop a small, mobile professional force. According to the constitution, the Namibian Defence Force's (NDF's) primary mission is territorial defence. Secondary roles include assisting the civil power in domestic support operations, assisting the AU and the SADC and supporting UN missions. The NDF Development Strategy 2012–22 states that the NDF design should be based on a conventional force with a force-projection capability. Namibia is a member of the AU and the SADC, with which the navy exercises as part of its Standing Maritime Committee. There is a permanent commission on defence and security with Zambia that meets annually. An MoU on training and cooperation was signed with Botswana in late 2018. While the NDF receives a comparatively large proportion of the state budget, the government has acknowledged that funding problems led training to almost cease, especially for recruits, though the services continued training at low levels. Namibia has deployed on AU and UN missions, but there is only limited capacity for independent power projection. The NDF is equipped for the most part with ageing or obsolescent systems, which it has ambitions to replace.

However, economic difficulties make this unlikely in the near term. The country has a limited defence-manufacturing sector covering armoured vehicles, tactical communications and ammunition, as well as some broader industrial business interests.

ACTIVE 9,900 (Army 9,000 Navy 900) Paramilitary 6,000

ORGANISATIONS BY SERVICE

Army 9,000
FORCES BY ROLE
MANOEUVRE
  Reconnaissance
  1 recce regt
  Light
  3 inf bde (total: 6 inf bn)
  Other
  1 (Presidential Guard) gd bn
COMBAT SUPPORT
  1 arty bde with (1 arty regt)
  1 AT regt
  1 engr regt
  1 sigs regt
COMBAT SERVICE SUPPORT
  1 log bn
AIR DEFENCE
  1 AD regt
EQUIPMENT BY TYPE
ARMOURED FIGHTING VEHICLES
  MBT T-54/T-55†; T-34†
  RECCE 12 BRDM-2
  IFV 7: 5 Type-05P mod (with BMP-1 turret); 2 *Wolf Turbo* 2 mod (with BMP-1 turret)
  APC 61
    APC (W) 41: 10 BTR-60; 3 Type-05P; 28 *Wolf Turbo* 2
    PPV 20 *Casspir*
ENGINEERING & MAINTENANCE VEHICLES
  ARV T-54/T-55 reported
ANTI-TANK/ANTI-INFRASTRUCTURE
  RCL 82mm B-10
  GUNS 12+: **57mm**; **76mm** 12 ZIS-3
ARTILLERY 72
  TOWED **140mm** 24 G-2
  MRL **122mm** 8: 5 BM-21 *Grad*; 3 PHL-81
  MOR 40: **81mm**; **82mm**
AIR DEFENCE
  SAM • Point-defence FN-6; 9K32 *Strela*-2 (SA-7 *Grail*)‡
  GUNS 65
    SP **23mm** 15 *Zumlac*
    TOWED 50+: **14.5mm** 50 ZPU-4; **57mm** S-60

Navy ε900
EQUIPMENT BY TYPE
PATROL AND COASTAL COMBATANTS 7
  PSO 1 *Elephant* with 1 hel landing platform
  PCC 3: 2 *Daures* (ex-PRC *Haiqing* (Type-037-IS)) with 2 FQF-2300 A/S mor; 1 *Oryx*
  PB 3: 1 *Brendan Simbwaye* (BRZ *Grajaú*); 2 *Terrace Bay* (BRZ *Marlim*)

AIRCRAFT • TPT • Light 1 F406 *Caravan II*
HELICOPTERS • TPT • Medium 1 S-61L

Marines ε700

Air Force
FORCES BY ROLE
FIGHTER/GROUND ATTACK
  1 sqn with F-7 (F-7NM); FT-7 (FT-7NG)
ISR
  1 sqn with O-2A *Skymaster*
TRANSPORT
  Some sqn with An-26 *Curl*; *Falcon* 900; Learjet 36; Y-12
TRAINING
  1 sqn with K-8 *Karakorum**
ATTACK/TRANSPORT HELICOPTER
  1 sqn with H425; Mi-8 *Hip*; Mi-25 *Hind* D; SA315 *Lama* (*Cheetah*); SA316B *Alouette* III (*Chetak*)
EQUIPMENT BY TYPE
AIRCRAFT 12 combat capable
  FTR 8: 6 F-7NM; 2 FT-7 (FT-7NG)
  ISR 5 Cessna O-2A *Skymaster*
  TPT 6: Light 5: 2 An-26 *Curl*; 1 Learjet 36; 2 Y-12; PAX 1 *Falcon* 900
  TRG 4+ K-8 *Karakorum**
HELICOPTERS
  ATK 2 Mi-25 *Hind* D
  MRH 5: 1 H425; 1 SA315 *Lama* (*Cheetah*); 3 SA316B *Alouette* III (*Chetak*)
  TPT • Medium 1 Mi-8 *Hip*

Paramilitary 6,000

Police Force • Special Field Force 6,000 (incl Border Guard and Special Reserve Force)

DEPLOYMENT
SOUTH SUDAN: UN • UNMISS 2
SUDAN: UN • UNAMID 1; 3 obs; UN • UNISFA 3; 1 obs

Niger NER

CFA Franc BCEAO fr		2017	2018	2019
GDP	fr	4.77tr	5.23tr	
	US$	8.22bn	9.46bn	
per capita	US$	438	489	
Growth	%	4.9	5.3	
Inflation	%	2.4	3.9	
Def bdgt	fr	100bn	128bn	
	US$	172m	231m	
US$1=fr		580.92	553.06	

Population 19,866,231

Ethnic groups: Gourma 55.3%; Djerma Sonrai 21%; Touareg 9.3%; Peuhl 8.5%; Kanouri Manga 4.6%; other or unspecified 1.3%

Age	0–14	15–19	20–24	25–29	30–64	65 plus
Male	24.6%	5.4%	4.1%	3.2%	11.5%	1.3%
Female	24.1%	5.5%	4.3%	3.4%	11.2%	1.3%

Capabilities

Maintaining internal and border security are key roles for the armed forces, in light of the regional threat from Islamist groups. Defence-policy developments in recent years have enabled Niger's armed forces to professionalise. The country is a member of the G5 Sahel group and part of the Multinational Joint Task Force fighting Boko Haram in the Lake Chad Basin. France has conducted joint counter-terrorism operations with Niger's armed forces, while Germany has developed an air-transport base at Niamey to supply its troops in neighbouring Mali. France maintains an air contingent at Niamey, where there is also a detachment of US UAVs. Niger's armed forces are combat experienced and relatively well trained, receiving training support from France, Italy and the US. Deployment capabilities are limited to neighbouring countries without external support. Operations in austere environments have demonstrated adequate sustainment and manoeuvre capacity. However, the armed forces are generally under-equipped and -resourced for the tasks they face. Apart from limited maintenance facilities, the country has no domestic defence-industrial capability.

ACTIVE 5,300 (Army 5,200 Air 100) **Paramilitary 5,400**

Conscript liability Selective conscription, 2 years

ORGANISATIONS BY SERVICE

Army 5,200
3 Mil Districts

FORCES BY ROLE
MANOEUVRE
  Reconnaissance
  4 armd recce sqn
  Light
  7 inf coy
  Air Manoeuvre
  2 AB coy
COMBAT SUPPORT
  1 engr coy
COMBAT SERVICE SUPPORT
  1 log gp
AIR DEFENCE
  1 AD coy
EQUIPMENT BY TYPE
ARMOURED FIGHTING VEHICLES
  RECCE 132: 35 AML-20/AML-60; 90 AML-90; 7 VBL
  APC 45
    APC (W) 24: 22 Panhard M3; 2 WZ-523
    PPV 21 *Puma* M26-15
ANTI-TANK/ANTI-INFRASTRUCTURE
  RCL 14: **75mm** 6 M20; **106mm** 8 M40
ARTILLERY • MOR 40: **81mm** 19 Brandt; **82mm** 17; **120mm** 4 Brandt
AIR DEFENCE • GUNS 39
  SP 20mm 10 Panhard M3 VDAA
  TOWED 20mm 29

Air Force 100
EQUIPMENT BY TYPE
AIRCRAFT 2 combat capable
  ATK 2 Su-25 *Frogfoot*
  ISR 6: 4 Cessna 208 *Caravan*; 2 DA42 MPP *Twin Star*
  TPT 7: Medium 1 C-130H *Hercules*; **Light** 5: 1 An-26 *Curl*; 2 Cessna 208 *Caravan*; 1 Do-28 *Skyservant*; 1 Do-228-201; **PAX** 1 B-737-700 (VIP)
HELICOPTERS
  ATK 2 Mi-35P *Hind*
  MRH 5: 2 Mi-17 *Hip*; 3 SA342 *Gazelle*

Paramilitary 5,400

Gendarmerie 1,400

Republican Guard 2,500

National Police 1,500

DEPLOYMENT

CENTRAL AFRICAN REPUBLIC: UN • MINUSCA 3; 1 obs
DEMOCRATIC REPUBLIC OF THE CONGO: UN • MONUSCO 5; 4 obs
MALI: UN • MINUSMA 861; 2 obs; 1 inf bn

FOREIGN FORCES

France Opération Barkhane 500; 1 FGA det with 2 *Mirage* 2000C; 2 *Mirage* 2000D; 1 tkr/tpt det with 1 C-135FR; 1 C-160; 1 UAV det with 4 MQ-9A *Reaper*
Germany Opération Barkhane 2 C-160
Italy MISIN 70
United States 800

Nigeria NGA

Nigerian Naira N		2017	2018	2019
GDP	N	115tr	129tr	
	US$	376bn	397bn	
per capita	US$	1,995	2,050	
Growth	%	0.8	1.9	
Inflation	%	16.5	12.4	
Def bdgt	N	465bn	567bn	
	US$	1.53bn	1.75bn	
FMA (US)	US$	0.5m	0m	
US$1=N		305.29	325.00	

Population 203,452,505
Ethnic groups: North (Hausa and Fulani), Southwest (Yoruba), Southeast (Ibo); these tribes make up ε65% of population

Age	0–14	15–19	20–24	25–29	30–64	65 plus
Male	21.7%	5.6%	4.5%	3.6%	13.6%	1.5%
Female	20.8%	5.4%	4.4%	3.6%	13.7%	1.7%

Capabilities

Nigeria is the region's principal military power and faces numerous security challenges, including from Boko Haram and militants in the Delta. The challenge from Boko Haram, and the relative weaknesses exposed in the armed forces, have led to reform initiatives. There have been operational changes, including attempts to implement counter-insurgency tactics and generate forward-operating bases and quick-reaction groups. Nigeria is central to several regional security initiatives and is part of the Multinational Joint Task Force. It is a key member of the ECOWAS Standby Force. Military and security assistance is either discussed or under way with Germany, the UK and the US. The UK bases its British Defence Staff West Africa in Nigeria. Efforts have been made to improve training, notably in the air force, with the establishment of Air Training Command and Ground Training Command. The UK has deployed short-term training teams to Nigeria. Contractors have also been used to improve training levels. Nigeria is able to mount regional operations, though its deployable capacities remain limited. There is a plan (with finance allocated in the 2018 budget) to acquire JF-17 combat aircraft. Deliveries of attack helicopters continue, and an effort has been made to refurbish previously stored aircraft. A number of small coastal-patrol boats have been acquired in recent years in light of security requirements in the Delta region. Nigeria is developing its defence-industrial capacity, including the development of local production facilities for small arms and protected patrol vehicles.

ACTIVE 135,000 (Army 100,000 Navy 25,000 Air 10,000) **Paramilitary 80,000**
Reserves planned, none org

ORGANISATIONS BY SERVICE

Army 100,000
FORCES BY ROLE
SPECIAL FORCES
  1 spec ops bn
  3 (mobile strike team) spec ops units
  1 ranger bn
MANOEUVRE
  Armoured
  1 (3rd) armd div (1 armd bde, 1 arty bde)
  Mechanised
  1 (1st) mech div (1 recce bn, 1 mech bde, 1 mot inf bde, 1 arty bde, 1 engr regt)
  1 (2nd) mech div (1 recce bn, 1 armd bde, 1 arty bde, 1 engr regt)
  1 (81st) composite div (1 recce bn, 1 mech bde, 1 arty bde, 1 engr regt)
  Light
  1 (6th) inf div (1 amph bde, 2 inf bde)
  1 (7th) inf div (1 spec ops bn, 1 recce bn(-), 1 armd bde, 7 (task force) inf bde, 1 arty bde, 1 engr regt)
  1 (8th Task Force) inf div (2 inf bde)
  1 (82nd) composite div (1 recce bn, 3 mot inf bde, 1 arty bde, 1 engr regt)
  1 (Multi-national Joint Task Force) bde (2 inf bn(-))
  Other
  1 (Presidential Guard) gd bde (4 gd bn)
AIR DEFENCE
  1 AD regt
EQUIPMENT BY TYPE
ARMOURED FIGHTING VEHICLES
  MBT 319: 176 Vickers Mk 3; 100 T-55†; 12 T-72AV; 31 T-72M1
  LT TK 157 FV101 *Scorpion*
  RECCE 342: 90 AML-60; 40 AML-90; 70 EE-9 *Cascavel*; 50 FV721 *Fox*; 20 FV601 *Saladin* Mk2; 72 VBL
  IFV 32: 10 BTR-4EN; 22 BVP-1

  APC 655+
    APC (T) 317: 250 4K-7FA *Steyr*; 67 MT-LB
    APC (W) 282+: 110 *Cobra*; 10 FV603 *Saracen*; 110 AVGP *Grizzly* mod/*Piranha* I 6x6; 47 BTR-3UN; 5 BTR-80; some EE-11 *Urutu* (reported)
    PPV 56+: 16 *Caiman*; 8 *Maxxpro*; 9 Proforce *Ara*; 23 REVA III 4×4; Streit *Spartan*; Streit *Cougar* (*Igirigi*); Streit *Typhoon*; *Bigfoot*
ENGINEERING & MAINTENANCE VEHICLES
  ARV 17+: AVGP *Husky*; 2 *Greif*; 15 Vickers ARV
  VLB MTU-20; VAB
ANTI-TANK/ANTI-INFRASTRUCTURE
  RCL **84mm** *Carl Gustav*; **106mm** M40A1
ARTILLERY 517+
  SP 155mm 39 *Palmaria*
  TOWED 106: **105mm** 50 M-56; **122mm** 49 D-30/D-74; **130mm** 7 M-46; (**155mm** 24 FH-77B in store)
  MRL 122mm 42: 10 BM-21 *Grad*; 25 APR-21; 7 RM-70
  MOR 330+: **81mm** 200; **82mm** 100; **120mm** 30+
AIR DEFENCE
  SAM • Point-defence 16+: 16 *Roland*; *Blowpipe*; 9K32 *Strela*-2 (SA-7 *Grail*)‡
  GUNS 90+
    SP 23mm 30 ZSU-23-4 *Shilka*
    TOWED 60+: **20mm** 60+; **23mm** ZU-23; **40mm** L/70

Navy 25,000 (incl Coast Guard)
Western Comd HQ located at Apapa; Eastern Comd HQ located at Calabar; Central Comd HQ located at Brass
EQUIPMENT BY TYPE
PRINCIPAL SURFACE COMBATANTS 1
  FRIGATES • FFGHM 1 *Aradu*† (GER MEKO 360) with 8 single lnchr with *Otomat* AShM, 1 octuple *Albatros* lnchr with *Aspide* SAM, 2 triple STWS 1B 324mm ASTT with A244 LWT, 1 127mm gun (capacity 1 med hel)
PATROL AND COASTAL COMBATANTS 121
  CORVETTES • FSM 1 *Erinomi*† (UK Vosper Mk 9) with 1 triple lnchr with *Seacat*† SAM, 1 twin 375mm A/S mor, 1 76mm gun
  PSOH 4: 2 *Centenary* with 1 76mm gun; 2 *Thunder* (ex-US *Hamilton*) with 1 76mm gun
  PCFG 1 *Sipri*† (FRA *Combattante*) with 2 twin lnchr with MM38 *Exocet* AShM, 1 76mm gun
  PCF 2 *Siri* (FRA *Combattante* IIIB) with 1 76mm gun
  PCO 4 *Kyanwa* (ex-US CG *Balsam*)
  PCC 2 *Ekpe*† (GER Lurssen 57m) with 1 76mm gun
  PBF 33: 21 *Manta* (Suncraft 17m); 4 *Manta* MkII; 3 *Shaldag* II; 2 *Torie* (Nautic Sentinel 17m); 3 *Wave Rider*
  PB 74: 1 *Andoni*; 1 *Dorina* (FPB 98); 5 *Okpoku* (FPB 72); 1 *Karaduwa*; 1 *Sagbama*; 2 *Sea Eagle* (Suncraft 38m); 15 *Stingray* (Suncraft 16m); 40 Suncraft 12m; 4 Swiftships; 2 *Town* (of which one laid up); 2 *Yola*†
MINE WARFARE • MINE COUNTERMEASURES 2:
  MCC 2 *Ohue* (ITA *Lerici* mod)
AMPHIBIOUS 4
  LC • LCVP 4 *Stingray* 20
LOGISTICS AND SUPPORT 1
  AX 1 *Prosperity*

Naval Aviation
EQUIPMENT BY TYPE
HELICOPTERS
  MRH 2 AW139 (AB-139)
  TPT • Light 3 AW109E *Power*†

Special Boat Service 200
EQUIPMENT BY TYPE
FORCES BY ROLE
SPECIAL FORCES
  1 SF unit

Air Force 10,000
FORCES BY ROLE
Very limited op capability
FIGHTER/GROUND ATTACK
  1 sqn with F-7 (F-7NI); FT-7 (FT-7NI)
MARITIME PATROL
  1 sqn with ATR-42-500 MP; Do-128D-6 *Turbo SkyServant*; Do-228-100/200
TRANSPORT
  2 sqn with C-130H *Hercules*; C-130H-30 *Hercules*; G-222
  1 (Presidential) gp with B-727; B-737BBJ; BAe-125-800; Beech 350 *King Air*; Do-228-200; *Falcon* 7X; *Falcon* 900; Gulfstream IV/V
TRAINING
  1 unit with *Air Beetle*†
  1 unit with *Alpha Jet**
  1 unit with L-39 *Albatros*†*; MB-339A*
  1 unit with *Super Mushshak*; DA40NG
  1 hel unit with Mi-34 *Hermit* (trg)
ATTACK HELICOPTER
  1 sqn with Mi-24/Mi-35 *Hind*†
TRANSPORT HELICOPTER
  1 sqn with H215 (AS332) *Super Puma*; (AS365N) *Dauphin*; AW109LUH; H135
EQUIPMENT BY TYPE†
AIRCRAFT 60 combat capable
  FTR 12: 10 F-7 (F-7NI); 2 FT-7 (FT-7NI)
  ELINT 2 ATR-42-500 MP
  TPT 32: **Medium** 5: 1 C-130H *Hercules* (4 more in store†); 1 C-130H-30 *Hercules* (2 more in store); 3 G.222† (2 more in store†); **Light** 18: 3 Beech 350 *King Air*; 1 Cessna 550 *Citation*; 8 Do-128D-6 *Turbo SkyServant*; 1 Do-228-100; 5 Do-228-200 (incl 2 VIP); **PAX** 9: 1 B-727; 1 B-737BBJ; 1 BAe 125-800; 2 *Falcon* 7X; 2 *Falcon* 900; 1 Gulfstream IV; 1 Gulfstream V
  TRG 118: 58 *Air Beetle*† (up to 20 awaiting repair); 3 *Alpha Jet* A*; 10 *Alpha Jet* E*; 2 DA40NG; 23 L-39ZA *Albatros*†*; 12 MB-339AN* (all being upgraded); 10 *Super Mushshak*
HELICOPTERS
  ATK 15: 2 Mi-24P *Hind*; 4 Mi-24V *Hind*; 3 Mi-35 *Hind*; 2 Mi-35P *Hind*; 4 Mi-35M *Hind*
  MRH 11+: 6 AW109LUH; 2 Bell 412EP; 3+ SA341 *Gazelle*
  TPT 19: **Medium** 11: 2 AW101; 5 H215 (AS332) *Super Puma* (4 more in store); 3 AS365N *Dauphin*; 1 Mi-171Sh; **Light** 9: 4 H125 (AS350B) *Ecureuil*; 1 AW109; 1 Bell 205; 3 H135
UNMANNED AERIAL VEHICLES 2+
  CISR • **Heavy** 1+ CH-3

ISR 1: **Medium** (9 *Aerostar* non-operational); **Light** 1+ *Tsaigami*
AIR-LAUNCHED MISSILES
  AAM • **IR** R-3 (AA-2 *Atoll*)‡; PL-9C
  ASM AR-1
BOMBS • **INS/GPS guided** FT-9

Paramilitary ε80,000

Security and Civil Defence Corps 80,000
EQUIPMENT BY TYPE
ARMOURED FIGHTING VEHICLES
  APC 80+
    APC (W) 74+: 70+ AT105 *Saxon*†; 4 BTR-3U; UR-416
    PPV 6 *Springbuck* 4x4
  AIRCRAFT • **TPT** • **Light** 4: 1 Cessna 500 *Citation* I; 2 PA-31 *Navajo*; 1 PA-31-350 *Navajo Chieftain*
  HELICOPTERS • **TPT** • **Light** 5: 2 Bell 212 (AB-212); 2 Bell 222 (AB-222); 1 Bell 429

DEPLOYMENT
CENTRAL AFRICAN REPUBLIC: UN • MINUSCA 1
DEMOCRATIC REPUBLIC OF THE CONGO: UN • MONUSCO 2; 6 obs
GAMBIA: ECOWAS • ECOMIG 200
GUINEA-BISSAU: ECOWAS • ECOMIB 100
LEBANON: UN • UNIFIL 1
MALI: UN • MINUSMA 83; 4 obs; 1 fd hospital
SOMALIA: UN • UNSOS 1 obs
SOUTH SUDAN: UN • UNMISS 5; 7 obs
SUDAN: UN • UNAMID 126; 7 obs; 1 sigs unit; 1 fd hospital; UN • UNISFA 2; 2 obs
WESTERN SAHARA: UN • MINURSO 4 obs

FOREIGN FORCES
United Kingdom 50 (trg teams)

Rwanda RWA

Rwandan Franc fr		2017	2018	2019
GDP	fr	7.60tr	8.39tr	
	US$	9.14bn	9.71bn	
per capita	US$	772	800	
Growth	%	6.1	7.2	
Inflation	%	4.8	3.3	
Def bdgt	fr	90.4bn	92.3bn	101bn
	US$	109m	107m	
US$1=fr		831.55	863.97	

Population 12,187,400
Ethnic groups: Hutu 80%; Tutsi 19%

Age	0–14	15–19	20–24	25–29	30–64	65 plus
Male	20.7%	5.3%	4.4%	4.2%	13.3%	1.0%
Female	20.3%	5.3%	4.4%	4.3%	15.3%	1.5%

Capabilities

Rwanda is one of the principal security actors in the East African region, with disciplined and well-trained armed forces. Their principal missions are to defend territorial integrity and national sovereignty. The country fields a relatively large army, but units are lightly equipped, with little mechanisation. Rwanda signed a Mutual Defence Treaty with Kenya and Uganda in 2014 and participates in the East African Standby Force. A law on downsizing and demobilising elements of the armed forces was published in October 2015 and there have in recent years been official retirement ceremonies for those reaching rank-related retirement ages. The lack of fixed-wing aircraft limits the armed forces' ability to independently deploy much beyond personnel overseas. There have been some acquisitions of modern artillery and armoured vehicles. There is limited maintenance capacity but Rwanda does not possess a defence-industrial base

ACTIVE 33,000 (Army 32,000 Air 1,000) **Paramilitary 2,000**

ORGANISATIONS BY SERVICE

Army 32,000

FORCES BY ROLE
MANOEUVRE
  Light
  2 cdo bn
  4 inf div (3 inf bde)
COMBAT SUPPORT
  1 arty bde
EQUIPMENT BY TYPE
ARMOURED FIGHTING VEHICLES
  MBT 34: 24 T-54/T-55; 10 *Tiran*-5
  RECCE 106: ε90 AML-60/AML-90; 16 VBL
  IFV 35+: BMP; 15 *Ratel*-90; 20 *Ratel*-60
  APC 90+
    APC (W) 50+: BTR; *Buffalo* (Panhard M3); 30 *Cobra*; 20 WZ-551 (reported)
    PPV 40 RG-31 *Nyala*
ENGINEERING & MAINTENANCE VEHICLES
  ARV T-54/T-55 reported
ARTILLERY 171+
  SP 11: **122mm** 6 SH-3; **155mm** 5 ATMOS 2000
  TOWED 35+: **105mm** some; **122mm** 6 D-30; **152mm** 29 Type-54 (D-1)†
  MRL 10: **122mm** 5 RM-70; **160mm** 5 LAR-160
  MOR 115: **81mm**; **82mm**; **120mm**
  AIR DEFENCE SAM • Point-defence 9K32 *Strela*-2 (SA-7 *Grail*)‡
  GUNS ε150: **14.5mm**; **23mm**; **37mm**

Air Force ε1,000

FORCES BY ROLE
ATTACK/TRANSPORT HELICOPTER
  1 sqn with Mi-17/Mi-17MD/Mi-17V-5/Mi-17-1V *Hip* H; Mi-24P/V *Hind*
EQUIPMENT BY TYPE
HELICOPTERS
  ATK 5: 2 Mi-24V *Hind* E; 3 Mi-24P *Hind*
  MRH 12: 1 AW139; 4 Mi-17 *Hip* H; 1 Mi-17MD *Hip* H; 1 Mi-17V-5 *Hip* H; 5 Mi-17-1V *Hip* H
  TPT • Light 1 AW109S

Paramilitary

District Administration Security Support Organ ε2,000

DEPLOYMENT

CENTRAL AFRICAN REPUBLIC: UN • MINUSCA 1,378; 8 obs; 2 inf bn; 1 fd hospital

SOUTH SUDAN: UN • UNMISS 2,774; 23 obs; 3 inf bn; 2 hel sqn

SUDAN: UN • UNAMID 1,671; 5 obs; 2 inf bn; **UN** • UNISFA 2; 3 obs

Senegal SEN

CFA Franc BCEAO fr		2017	2018	2019
GDP	fr	12.3tr	13.4tr	
	US$	21.1bn	24.2bn	
per capita	US$	1,331	1,485	
Growth	%	7.2	7.0	
Inflation	%	1.3	0.4	
Def bdgt	fr	179bn	193bn	201bn
	US$	309m	348m	
FMA (US)	US$	0.3m	0m	
US$1=fr		580.94	553.08	

Population 15,020,945

Ethnic groups: Wolof 36%; Fulani 17%; Serer 17%; Toucouleur 9%; Man-dingo 9%; Diola 9% (of which 30–60% in Casamance)

Age	0–14	15–19	20–24	25–29	30–64	65 plus
Male	20.7%	5.4%	4.7%	4.0%	12.3%	1.3%
Female	20.5%	5.4%	4.8%	4.2%	15.1%	1.7%

Capabilities

Senegal's armed forces have robust international relationships and experience in deployments abroad. Their focus is internal and border security, including countering insurgency in the country's south and Islamist activity in neighbouring states, as well as combating narcotics trafficking. Under the 'Horizon 2025' programme, the defence authorities intend to reorganise and re-equip key defence organisations and renew infrastructure. Areas for improvement include mobility and firepower. Despite limited resources, there are plans to improve operational capabilities and introduce cohesive training regimes for garrisoned troops and in tactical training centres. There are also plans to increase personnel numbers by around 4,000. Senegal's principal defence relationship is with France, which has a military presence in country of some 350 troops and with which it signed a defence-cooperation agreement in 2013. French military forces deliver training assistance, including in search and rescue. The US also provides security assistance, including to the national police and gendarmerie. In September 2018, Senegal opened a counter-terrorism training centre at the CET-7 military base at Thies, funded through the US State Department's Anti-Terrorism Assistance programme. Senegal takes part in the US *Flintlock* counter-terrorism exercise and with US partner nations from the Trans-Sahara Counterterrorism Partnership. The armed forces are able to deploy personnel using organic airlift, as demonstrated during the deployment to Gambia, but short-notice movements of heavy equipment would be problematic without external assistance. Modernisation of the air force is a priority, and Senegal is looking to revive a modest jet capability with the intended purchase of two L-39s, having ordered a small number of turboprop trainers. Refurbished Mi-24 helicopters have been returned to the inventory, while land-force recapitalisation is taking place in light of the Horizon 2025 programme. Bar limited maintenance facilities, the country has no domestic defence-industrial capability.

ACTIVE 13,600 (Army 11,900 Navy 950 Air 750)
Paramilitary 5,000
Conscript liability Selective conscription, 24 months

ORGANISATIONS BY SERVICE

Army 11,900 (incl conscripts)
7 Mil Zone HQ
FORCES BY ROLE
MANOEUVRE
  Reconnaissance
  4 armd recce bn
  Light
  1 cdo bn
  6 inf bn
  Air Manoeuvre
  1 AB bn
  Other
  1 (Presidential Guard) horse cav bn
COMBAT SUPPORT
  1 arty bn
  1 engr bn
  3 construction coy
  1 sigs bn
COMBAT SERVICE SUPPORT
  1 log bn
  1 med bn
  1 trg bn
EQUIPMENT BY TYPE
ARMOURED FIGHTING VEHICLES
  ASLT 27 PTL-02 *Assaulter*
  RECCE 145: 30 AML-60; 74 AML-90; 10 M8; 4 M20; 27 RAM Mk3
  IFV 26 *Ratel*-20
  APC 81
    APC (T) 12 M3 half-track
    APC (W) 22: 2 *Oncilla*; 16 Panhard M3; 4 WZ-551 (CP)
    PPV 47: 8 *Casspir*; 39 *Puma* M26-15
ENGINEERING & MAINTENANCE VEHICLES
  ARV 1 *Puma* M36
ANTI-TANK/ANTI-INFRASTRUCTURE
  MSL • MANPATS *Milan*
ARTILLERY 82
  TOWED 20: **105mm** 6 HM-2/M101; **155mm** 14: ε6 Model-50; 8 TR-F1
  MRL 122mm 6 BM-21 *Grad* (UKR *Bastion*-1 mod)
  MOR 56: **81mm** 24; **120mm** 32

AIR DEFENCE • GUNS • TOWED 39: **14.5mm** 6 ZPU-4 (tch); **20mm** 21 M693; **40mm** 12 L/60

Navy (incl Coast Guard) 950
FORCES BY ROLE
SPECIAL FORCES
  1 cdo coy
EQUIPMENT BY TYPE
PATROL AND COASTAL COMBATANTS 5
  PCO 1 *Fouladou* (OPV 190 Mk II)
  PCC 1 *Njambour* (FRA SFCN 59m) with 2 76mm gun
  PBF 1 *Ferlo* (RPB 33)
  PB 2: 1 *Conejera*; 1 *Kedougou*
AMPHIBIOUS • LANDING CRAFT 2
  LCT 2 *Edic* 700
LOGISTICS AND SUPPORT 1
  AG 1

Air Force 750
FORCES BY ROLE
MARITIME PATROL/SEARCH & RESCUE
  1 sqn with C-212 *Aviocar*; CN235; Bell 205 (UH-1H *Iroquois*)
ISR
  1 unit with BN-2T *Islander* (anti-smuggling patrols)
TRANSPORT
  1 sqn with B-727-200 (VIP); F-27-400M *Troopship*
TRAINING
  1 sqn with R-235 *Guerrier**; TB-30 *Epsilon*
ATTACK/TRANSPORT HELICOPTER
  1 sqn with AS355F *Ecureuil* II; Bell 206; Mi-35P *Hind*; Mi-171Sh
EQUIPMENT BY TYPE
AIRCRAFT 1 combat capable
  TPT 10: **Light** 8: 1 BN-2T *Islander* (govt owned, mil op); 1 C-212-100 *Aviocar*; 2 CN235; 2 Beech B200 *King Air*; 2 F-27-400M *Troopship* (3 more in store); **PAX** 2: 1 A319; 1 B-727-200 (VIP)
  TRG 7: 1 R-235 *Guerrier**; 6 TB-30 *Epsilon*
HELICOPTERS
  ATK 5: 3 Mi-24V *Hind* D; 2 Mi-35P *Hind*
  MRH 1 AW139
  TPT 8: **Medium** 2 Mi-171Sh; **Light** 6: 1 AS355F *Ecureuil* II; 1 Bell 205 (UH-1H *Iroquois*); 2 Bell 206; 2 PZL Mi-2 *Hoplite*

Paramilitary 5,000

Gendarmerie 5,000
EQUIPMENT BY TYPE
ARMOURED FIGHTING VEHICLES
  RECCE 11 RAM Mk3
  APC 35:
    APC (W) 23: 6 *Bastion* APC; 5 EE-11 *Urutu*; 12 VXB-170
    PPV 12 *Gila*
  AUV 25 *Ejder Yalcin*

DEPLOYMENT

CENTRAL AFRICAN REPUBLIC: UN • MINUSCA 111; 1 atk hel sqn

DEMOCRATIC REPUBLIC OF THE CONGO: UN • MONUSCO 7; 1 obs

GAMBIA: ECOWAS • ECOMIG 250

LIBERIA: UN • UNMIL 1

MALI: UN • MINUSMA 1,095; 2 inf bn

SOUTH SUDAN: UN • UNMISS 1; 2 obs

SUDAN: UN • UNAMID 39

FOREIGN FORCES

France 350; 1 *Falcon* 50MI

Spain *Operation Barkhane* 57; 1 C-130H *Hercules*

Seychelles SYC

Seychelles Rupee SR		2017	2018	2019
GDP	SR	20.4bn	21.9bn	
	US$	1.50bn	1.56bn	
per capita	US$	15,859	16,377	
Growth	%	5.3	3.6	
Inflation	%	2.9	4.4	
Def exp	SR	n.k	n.k	
	US$	n.k	n.k	
US$1=SR		13.65	14.01	
Population	94,633			

Age	0–14	15–19	20–24	25–29	30–64	65 plus
Male	10.0%	3.3%	3.6%	4.0%	27.5%	3.1%
Female	9.5%	3.0%	3.2%	3.5%	24.7%	4.7%

Capabilities

The Seychelles maintains one of the smallest standing armed forces in the world. Its proximity to key international shipping lanes is of strategic significance. The Seychelles People's Defence Force (PDF) primarily focus on maritime security and counter-piracy operations. The country hosts US military forces conducting maritime-patrol activities on a rotational basis, including the operation of unarmed UAVs. India maintains strong defence ties with the Seychelles, donating equipment, providing maintenance and supporting efforts to enhance its maritime-patrol and -surveillance capability. There are ongoing plans to further the Seychelles' defence cooperation with China. The Seychelles has participated in and hosted a number of multinational maritime-security exercises. The PDF does not deploy overseas and has a limited capacity to deploy and support troops operating in the archipelago. Modern platforms in the air force and coastguard comprise donations from China, India and the UAE. There is no traditional domestic defence industry.

ACTIVE 420 (Land Forces 200; Coast Guard 200; Air Force 20)

ORGANISATIONS BY SERVICE

People's Defence Force

Land Forces 200
FORCES BY ROLE
SPECIAL FORCES
  1 SF unit
MANOEUVRE
  Light
  1 inf coy
  Other
  1 sy unit
COMBAT SUPPORT
  1 MP unit
EQUIPMENT BY TYPE
ARMOURED FIGHTING VEHICLES
  RECCE 6 BRDM-2†
ARTILLERY• MOR 82mm 6 M-43†
AIR DEFENCE • GUNS • TOWED 14.5mm ZPU-2†; ZPU-4†; **37mm** M-1939†

Coast Guard 200 (incl 80 Marines)
EQUIPMENT BY TYPE
PATROL AND COASTAL COMBATANTS 8
  PCO 3: 1 *Andromache* (ITA *Pichiotti* 42m); 2 *Topaz* (ex-IND *Trinkat*)
  PBF 1 *Hermes* (ex-IND *Coastal Interceptor Craft*)
  PB 4: 2 *Le Vigilant* (ex-UAE Rodman 101); 1 *Etoile* (*Shanghai* II mod); 1 *Fortune* (UK *Tyne*)

Air Force 20
EQUIPMENT BY TYPE
AIRCRAFT
  TPT • Light 5: 1 DHC-6-320 *Twin Otter*; 2 Do-228; 2 Y-12

Sierra Leone SLE

Sierra Leonean Leone L		2017	2018	2019
GDP	L	26.6tr	30.1tr	
	US$	3.61bn	3.75bn	
per capita	US$	488	496	
Growth	%	3.7	3.7	
Inflation	%	18.2	15.6	
Def bdgt	L	86.5bn	107bn	127bn
	US$	11.7m	13.3m	
US$1=L		7,366.21	8,028.44	
Population	6,312,212			

Age	0–14	15–19	20–24	25–29	30–64	65 plus
Male	20.8%	4.9%	4.2%	3.7%	13.4%	1.6%
Female	20.9%	5.1%	4.4%	4.0%	14.7%	2.2%

Capabilities

The armed forces' primary task is to ensure internal and border security and provide forces for continental peacekeeping missions. With international support, there remains a focus on building defence institutions, generating formal defence documentation and improving planning functions. The UK is heavily involved in supporting the development of Sierra Leone's security institutions and improving training. UK training has developed command-and-control systems around disaster response, and readiness training for peace-support operations. UK training is also intended to boost the capacity of the police force, so that military support is only needed in major emergencies. The intent is for Freetown's Horton Academy to develop into a regional centre of excellence for SSR. Defence ties with China include personnel exchanges and capacity-building for peacekeeping operations. The armed forces' ability to deploy anything other than small units is constrained by force size and logistics-support capacity. Logistics support received a boost in 2017 with the donation by ECOWAS states of soft-skinned vehicles, water bowsers and fuel trucks. Capability remains limited in other areas, including in assets that would enable air and maritime surveillance. There is no domestic defence-industrial capability.

ACTIVE 8,500 (Joint 8,500)

ORGANISATIONS BY SERVICE

Armed Forces 8,500
FORCES BY ROLE
MANOEUVRE
  Reconnaissance
  1 recce unit
  Light
  3 inf bde (total: 12 inf bn)
COMBAT SUPPORT
  1 engr regt
  1 int unit
  1 MP unit
  1 sigs unit
COMBAT SUPPORT
  1 log unit
  1 fd hospital
EQUIPMENT BY TYPE
ARMOURED FIGHTING VEHICLES
  APC • PPV 4: 3 *Casspir*; 1 *Mamba* Mk5
ANTI-TANK/ANTI-INFRASTRUCTURE
  RCL 84mm *Carl Gustav*
ARTILLERY 37
  TOWED 122mm 6 Type-96 (D30)
  MOR 31: 81mm ε27; 82mm 2; 120mm 2
HELICOPTERS • MRH 2 Mi-17 *Hip* H/Mi-8 *Hip*†
AIR DEFENCE • GUNS 7: 12.7mm 4; 14.5mm 3

Maritime Wing ε200
EQUIPMENT BY TYPE
PATROL AND COASTAL COMBATANTS • PB 2: 1 *Shanghai* III†; 1 *Isle of Man*

DEPLOYMENT
LEBANON: UN • UNIFIL 3
MALI: UN • MINUSMA 10; 2 obs
SOMALIA: UN • UNSOM 2 obs; UN • UNSOS 1 obs
SUDAN: UN • UNAMID 4; UN • UNISFA 2; 1 obs

Somalia SOM

Somali Shilling sh		2017	2018	2019
GDP	US$	7.05bn	7.41bn	
per capita	US$	7.05bn	7.41bn	
Growth	%	2.3	3.1	
Inflation	%	n.k.	n.k.	
Def bdgt	US$	n.k.	n.k.	
US$1=sh		1.00	1.00	

*Definitive economic data unavailable

Population	11,259,029					
Age	0–14	15–19	20–24	25–29	30–64	65 plus
Male	21.4%	5.4%	4.3%	4.0%	14.4%	0.9%
Female	21.5%	5.4%	4.2%	3.8%	13.5%	1.3%

Capabilities
Internal stability remains fragile following decades of conflict and insurgency. Deployed international forces provide security, stabilisation and capacity building, with a transition plan in place for the country to assume full security responsibility. The Somali National Army (SNA) remains weak in terms of both organisation and military capability. US forces are deployed independently to Somalia and target militant groups. Plans to professionalise, legitimise and unite the loose collections of clan-based militia groups that form the SNA have yet to be fully realised. Although training programmes have been delivered by a number of countries, organisations and private-security companies there are no common training standards throughout the army. There is no capacity to deploy beyond national borders, while there is minimal national infrastructure available to support domestic operations. The equipment inventory is limited, and government plans to re-establish and equip Somalia's air and maritime forces remain unfulfilled. There is no domestic defence-industrial capability.

ACTIVE 19,800 (Army 19,800)

ORGANISATIONS BY SERVICE

Army 19,800 (plus further militias (to be integrated))
FORCES BY ROLE
COMMAND
  4 div HQ
MANOEUVRE
  Light
  Some cdo bn(+)
  12 inf bde (3 inf bn)
  2 indep inf bn
  Other
  1 gd bn
EQUIPMENT BY TYPE
ARMOURED FIGHTING VEHICLES
  APC 47+
    APC (W) 38+: 25+ AT-105 *Saxon*; 13 *Bastion* APC; Fiat 6614
    PPV 9+: *Casspir*; MAV-5; 9+ *Mamba* Mk5; RG-31 *Nyala*
  AUV 12 *Tiger* 4×4

Paramilitary

Coast Guard
All operational patrol vessels under 10t FLD

FOREIGN FORCES

Under UNSOM command unless stated
Burundi 1 obs • AMISOM 5,073; 6 inf bn
Djibouti AMISOM 1,872; 2 inf bn
Ethiopia AMISOM 4,323; 6 inf bn
Finland EUTM Somalia 7
Ghana UNSOS 2 obs
Hungary EUTM Somalia 4
India 1 obs
Italy EUTM Somalia 123
Kenya AMISOM 4,046; 3 inf bn
Mauritania UNSOS 1 obs
Netherlands EUTM Somalia 11
Nigeria UNSOS 1 obs
Pakistan UNSOS 1 obs
Portugal EUTM Somalia 4
Romania EUTM Somalia 3
Serbia EUTM Somalia 6
Sierra Leone 2 obs • UNSOS 1 obs
Spain EUTM Somalia 13
Sweden EUTM Somalia 4
Turkey 1 obs • 200 (trg base)
Uganda 530; 2 obs; 1 sy bn • AMISOM 6,022; 7 inf bn • UNSOS 1 obs
United Kingdom 43; 3 obs • UNSOS 40; 2 obs • EUTM Somalia 4
United States Africa Command 500

TERRITORY WHERE THE GOVERNMENT DOES NOT EXERCISE EFFECTIVE CONTROL

Data presented here represents the de facto situation. This does not imply international recognition as a sovereign state. Much of this equipment is in poor repair or inoperable.

Somaliland

Army ε12,500
FORCES BY ROLE
MANOEUVRE
 Armoured
  2 armd bde
 Mechanised
  1 mech inf bde
 Light
  14 inf bde
COMBAT SUPPORT
 2 arty bde
COMBAT SERVICE SUPPORT
 1 spt bn
EQUIPMENT BY TYPE†
ARMOURED FIGHTING VEHICLES
 MBT T-54/55
 RECCE Fiat 6616
 APC • APC(W) Fiat 6614
ARTILLERY • MRL various incl BM-21 *Grad*
AIR DEFENCE • GUNS • 23mm ZU-23

Ministry of the Interior

Coast Guard 600
All operational patrol vessels under 10t FLD

Puntland

Army ε3,000 (to be integrated into Somali National Army)

Maritime Police Force ε1,000
EQUIPMENT BY TYPE
AIRCRAFT • TPT 4: **Light** 3 Ayres S2R; **PAX** 1 DC-3
HELICOPTERS • MRH SA316 *Alouette* III
PATROL AND COASTAL COMBATANTS
All operational patrol vessels under 10t FLD

South Africa RSA

South African Rand R		2017	2018	2019
GDP	R	4.65tr	4.91tr	
	US$	349bn	377bn	
per capita	US$	6,180	6,560	
Growth	%	1.3	0.8	
Inflation	%	5.3	4.8	
Def bdgt	R	48.6bn	48.0bn	50.7bn
	US$	3.65bn	3.68bn	
FMA (US)	US$	0.3m	0m	
US$1=R		13.32	13.04	

Population	55,380,210					
Age	0–14	15–19	20–24	25–29	30–64	65 plus
Male	21.4%	5.4%	4.3%	4.0%	14.4%	0.9%
Female	21.5%	5.4%	4.2%	3.8%	13.5%	1.3%

Capabilities

While on paper the region's most capable armed forces, economic problems have undermined the armed forces' effectiveness. Roles include protecting the state and maintaining territorial integrity, as well as supporting the police service in specific circumstances. The Department of Defence Strategic Plan 2015–2020 is the force's primary policy instrument. This maps out five strategic-planning milestones, the first of which is to arrest the decline of critical military capabilities. South Africa contributes to UN operations and has been a key component of the Force Intervention Brigade in the Democratic Republic of the Congo (DRC) since its inception. It is a member of the SADC Standby Force. Historically, South African forces have also played a significant role in training and supporting other regional forces. Continuing budget cuts are likely to have an adverse effect on training. The SANDF can independently deploy its forces across the continent, deploys regularly on peacekeeping missions, and participates in national and multinational exercises. Equipment availability on some deployments, such as helicopter units in the DRC, has been a cause for concern. While the SANDF has a well-established modernisation plan, the ability to deliver on this is hindered by funding problems and a number of programmes are behind schedule. There is concern in the army over the obsolescence of principal equipment. South Africa has the continent's most capable defence industry, including the state-owned Armaments Corporation of South Africa (ARMSCOR) and weapons manufacturer Denel. However, defence-budget cuts and reduced domestic procurement have increasingly required South Africa to look to export markets. A National Defence Industry Council was launched in 2016 to support arms exports.

ACTIVE 65,350 (Army 40,200 Navy 7,100 Air 9,900 South African Military Health Service 8,150)

RESERVE 15,050 (Army 12,250 Navy 850 Air 850 South African Military Health Service Reserve 1,100)

ORGANISATIONS BY SERVICE

Space
EQUIPMENT BY TYPE
SATELLITES • ISR 1 *Kondor-E*

Army 40,200
FORCES BY ROLE
Regt are bn sized. A new army structure is planned with 3 mixed regular/reserve divisions (1 mechanised, 1 motorised and 1 contingency) comprising 12 brigades (1 armoured, 1 mechanised, 7 motorised, 1 airborne, 1 air-landed and 1 sea landed)
COMMAND
  2 bde HQ
SPECIAL FORCES
  2 SF regt(-)
MANOEUVRE
  Reconnaissance
  1 armd recce regt
  Armoured
  1 tk regt(-)
  Mechanised
  2 mech inf bn
  Light
  8 mot inf bn
  1 lt inf bn
  Air Manoeuvre
  1 AB bn
  1 air mob bn
  Amphibious
  1 amph bn
COMBAT SUPPORT
  1 arty regt
  1 engr regt
  1 construction regt
  3 sigs regt
COMBAT SERVICE SUPPORT
  1 engr spt regt
AIR DEFENCE
  1 ADA regt

Reserve 12,250 reservists (under-strength)
FORCES BY ROLE
MANOEUVRE
  Reconnaissance
  3 armd recce regt
  Armoured
  4 tk regt
  Mechanised
  6 mech inf bn
  Light
  14 mot inf bn
  3 lt inf bn (converting to mot inf)
  Air Manoeuvre
  1 AB bn
  2 air mob bn
  Amphibious
  1 amph bn
COMBAT SUPPORT
  7 arty regt
  2 engr regt
AIR DEFENCE
  5 AD regt

EQUIPMENT BY TYPE
ARMOURED FIGHTING VEHICLES
  MBT 24 *Olifant* 2 (133 *Olifant* 1B in store)
  ASLT 50 *Rooikat-76* (126 in store)
  IFV 534 *Ratel-20/Ratel-60/Ratel-90*
  APC • PPV 810: 370 *Casspir*; 440 *Mamba*
ENGINEERING & MAINTENANCE VEHICLES
  ARV *Gemsbok*
  VLB *Leguan*
  MW *Husky*
ANTI-TANK/ANTI-INFRASTRUCTURE
  MSL
    SP ZT-3 *Swift*
    MANPATS *Milan* ADT/ER
  RCL 106mm M40A1 (some SP)
ARTILLERY 1,240
  SP 155mm 2 G-6 (41 in store)
  TOWED 155mm 6 G-5 (66 in store)
  MRL 127mm 6 *Valkiri* Mk II MARS *Bataleur*; (26 *Valkiri* Mk I and 19 *Valkiri* Mk II in store)
  MOR 1,226: 81mm 1,190 (incl some SP on *Casspir* & *Ratel*); 120mm 36
UNMANNED AERIAL VEHICLES
  ISR • Light up to 4 *Vulture*
AIR DEFENCE
  SAM • Point-defence *Starstreak*
  GUNS 76
    SP 23mm (36 *Zumlac* in store)
    TOWED 35mm 40: 22 GDF-002; 18 GDF-005A/007

Navy 7,100
Fleet HQ and Naval base located at Simon's Town; Naval stations located at Durban and Port Elizabeth
EQUIPMENT BY TYPE
SUBMARINES • TACTICAL • SSK 2 *Heroine* (Type-209/1400 mod) with 8 533mm TT with AEG SUT 264 HWT (1 additional boat in refit since 2014, awaiting funds to complete)
PRINCIPAL SURFACE COMBATANTS • FRIGATES 4:
  FFGHM 4 *Valour* (MEKO A200) with 2 quad lnchr with MM40 *Exocet* Block 2 AShM (upgrade to Block 3 planned); 2 16-cell VLS with *Umkhonto*-IR SAM, 1 76mm gun (capacity 1 *Super Lynx* 300 hel)

PATROL AND COASTAL COMBATANTS 4
 PCC 3: 2 *Warrior* (ISR *Reshef*) with 1 76mm gun; 1 *Warrior* (ISR *Reshef*)
 PB 1 *Tobie* (2 additional in reserve)
MINE WARFARE • MINE COUNTERMEASURES 2
 MHC 3 *River* (GER *Navors*) (Limited operational roles; training and dive support)
LOGISTICS AND SUPPORT 2
 AORH 1 *Drakensberg* (capacity 2 *Oryx* hels; 100 troops)
 AGHS 1 *Protea* (UK *Hecla*) with 1 hel landing platform

Maritime Reaction Squadron
FORCES BY ROLE
MANOEUVRE
 Amphibious
 1 mne patrol gp
 1 diving gp
 1 mne boarding gp
 COMBAT SERVICE SUPPORT
 1 spt gp

Air Force 9,900
Air Force HQ, Pretoria, and 4 op gps
Command & Control: 2 Airspace Control Sectors, 1 Mobile Deployment Wg, 1 Air Force Command Post
FORCES BY ROLE
FIGHTER/GROUND ATTACK
 1 sqn with *Gripen* C/D (JAS-39C/D)
GROUND ATTACK/TRAINING
 1 sqn with *Hawk* Mk120*
TRANSPORT
 1 (VIP) sqn with B-737 BBJ; Cessna 550 *Citation* II; *Falcon* 50; *Falcon* 900
 1 sqn with C-47TP
 2 sqn with Beech 200/300 *King Air*; C-130B/BZ; C-212
ATTACK HELICOPTER
 1 (cbt spt) sqn with AH-2 *Rooivalk*
TRANSPORT HELICOPTER
 4 (mixed) sqn with AW109; BK-117; *Oryx*
EQUIPMENT BY TYPE
AIRCRAFT 50 combat capable
 FGA 26: 17 *Gripen* C (JAS-39C); 9 *Gripen* D (JAS-39D)
 TPT 24: **Medium** 7: 2 C-130B *Hercules*; 5 C-130BZ *Hercules*; **Light** 13: 3 Beech 200C *King Air*; 1 Beech 300 *King Air*; 3 C-47TP (maritime); 2 C-212-200 *Aviocar*†; 1 C-212-300 *Aviocar*†; 2 Cessna 550 *Citation* II; 1 PC-12; (9 Cessna 208 *Caravan* in store) PAX 4: 1 B-737BBJ; 2 *Falcon* 50; 1 *Falcon* 900
 TRG 59: 24 *Hawk* Mk120*; 35 PC-7 Mk II *Astra*
HELICOPTERS
 ATK 11 AH-2 *Rooivalk*
 MRH 4 *Super Lynx* 300
 TPT 70: **Medium** 36 *Oryx*; **Light** 34: 26 AW109; 8 BK-117
AIR-LAUNCHED MISSILES • AAM • IIR IRIS-T
BOMBS • **Laser-guided** GBU-12 *Paveway* II

Ground Defence
FORCES BY ROLE
MANOEUVRE
 Other
 12 sy sqn (SAAF regt)

South African Military Health Service 8,150; ε1,100 reservists (total 9,250)

Cyber
South Africa published a National Cybersecurity Policy Framework in 2011. Since then, the defence-intelligence branch of the Department of Defence has been tasked with developing a comprehensive cyber-warfare strategy and a cyber-warfare implementation plan. A Cyber Security Incident Response Team (CSIRT) operates under the State Security Agency.

DEPLOYMENT
DEMOCRATIC REPUBLIC OF THE CONGO: UN • MONUSCO • *Operation Mistral* 1,175; 7 obs; 1 inf bn; 1 atk hel sqn; 1 hel sqn
MOZAMBIQUE CHANNEL: Navy • 1 FFGHM
SUDAN: UN • UNAMID • *Operation Cordite* 3; 10 obs

South Sudan SSD

South Sudanese Pound ssp		2017	2018	2019
GDP	ssp	348bn	631bn	
	US$	3.06bn	3.98bn	
per capita	US$	243	307	
Growth	%	-5.2	-3.2	
Inflation	%	188	106	
Def bdgt [a]	ssp	11.0bn	13.0bn	15.9bn
	US$	97.2m	81.7m	
US$1=ssp		113.62	158.66	

[a] Security and law enforcement spending

Population 10,204,581

Age	0–14	15–19	20–24	25–29	30–64	65 plus
Male	21.5%	6.0%	4.9%	4.0%	13.6%	1.4%
Female	20.8%	5.9%	4.2%	3.6%	13.1%	1.1%

Capabilities
South Sudan has been in a state of civil war with armed opposition groups since 2013, which has delayed plans to rationalise and transform the former militia force. In November 2018, the Sudan People's Liberation Army (SPLA) was officially renamed the South Sudan People's Defence Force (SSPDF) and previous plans to professionalise and restructure the force were renewed, including the establishment of two separate new commands for air-defence and riverine units. Allegations continue of child-soldier recruitment. It is unclear if the 2018 peace agreement will be successfully implemented. In 2018, South Sudan reportedly signed a defence agreement with South Africa, including scope to cooperate on procurement and training. There is no capacity to deploy and sustain military units beyond national borders. Equipment is primarily of Soviet origin with some light arms of Chinese origin. There have been efforts to expand the small air force in recent years and the two newly acquired L-39 combat-capable trainers are reportedly operational. US sanctions and an EU arms embargo remain in place, although a December 2016 vote for a wider UN arms embargo was unsuccessful. South Sudan has no established

domestic defence industry but has reportedly sought to develop an ammunition-manufacturing capacity in recent years.

ACTIVE 185,000 (Army 185,000)

ORGANISATIONS BY SERVICE

Army ε185,000
FORCES BY ROLE
3 military comd
MANOEUVRE
  Light
    8 inf div
COMBAT SUPPORT
  1 engr corps
EQUIPMENT BY TYPE
ARMOURED FIGHTING VEHICLES
  MBT 80+: some T-55†; 80 T-72AV†
  APC • PPV Streit *Typhoon*; Streit *Cougar*; *Mamba*
ANTI-TANK/ANTI-INFRASTRUCTURE
  MSL • MANPATS HJ-73; 9K115 *Metis* (AT-7 *Saxhorn*)
  RCL 73mm SPG-9 (with SSLA)
ARTILLERY
  SP 122mm 2S1 *Gvozdika*; 152mm 2S3 *Akatsiya*
  TOWED 130mm Some M-46
  MRL 122mm BM-21 *Grad*; 107mm PH-63
  MOR 82mm; 120mm Type-55 look-alike
AIR DEFENCE
  SAM
    Short-range 16 S-125 *Pechora* (SA-3 *Goa*) (reported)
    Point-defence 9K32 *Strela*-2 (SA-7 *Grail*)‡; QW-2
  GUNS 14.5mm ZPU-4; 23mm ZU-23-2; 37mm Type-65/74

Air Force
EQUIPMENT BY TYPE
AIRCRAFT 2 combat capable
  TPT • Light 1 Beech 1900
  TRG ε2 L-39 *Albatros**
HELICOPTERS
  ATK 5: 2 Mi-24V *Hind*; 3 Mi-24V-SMB *Hind*
  MRH 9 Mi-17 *Hip H*
  TPT 3: **Medium** 1 Mi-172 (VIP); **Light** 2 AW109 (civ livery)

FOREIGN FORCES
All UNMISS, unless otherwise indicated
Australia 23; 1 obs
Bangladesh 1,601; 7 obs; 1 inf coy; 2 rvn coy; 2 engr coy
Benin 3; 1 obs
Bhutan 2; 2 obs
Bolivia 3 obs
Brazil 6; 5 obs
Cambodia 79; 6 obs; 1 MP unit
Canada 5; 5 obs
China, People's Republic of 1,040; 5 obs; 1 inf bn; 1 engr coy; 1 fd hospital
Denmark 11
Egypt 1; 2 obs
El Salvador 1; 2 obs
Ethiopia 2,122; 17 obs; 3 inf bn
Fiji 2
Germany 3; 11 obs
Ghana 861; 10 obs; 1 inf bn
Guatemala 4; 3 obs
Guinea 2; 1 obs
India 2,351; 18 obs; 2 inf bn; 1 engr coy; 1 fd hospital
Indonesia 2; 3 obs
Japan 4
Jordan 4
Kenya 11; 7 obs
Korea, Republic of 273; 2 obs; 1 engr coy
Kyrgyzstan 1 obs
Moldova 1; 2 obs
Mongolia 867; 7 obs; 1 inf bn
Myanmar 1; 1 obs
Namibia 2
Nepal 1,745; 13 obs; 2 inf bn
Netherlands 6
New Zealand 2; 3 obs
Nigeria 5; 7 obs
Norway 14
Pakistan 4; 2 obs
Papua New Guinea 2 obs
Paraguay 1 obs
Peru 1; 3 obs
Philippines 2 obs
Poland 1 obs
Romania 2; 5 obs
Russia 3; 2 obs
Rwanda 2,774; 23 obs; 3 inf bn; 2 hel sqn
Senegal 1; 2 obs
Sri Lanka 172; 2 obs; 1 fd hospital; 1 hel sqn
Sweden 2 obs
Tanzania 5; 4 obs
Togo 2
Uganda 2
Ukraine 1; 3 obs
United Kingdom 333; 1 engr coy
United States 7
Vietnam 1; 2 obs
Zambia 2; 4 obs
Zimbabwe 1; 2 obs

Sudan SDN

Sudanese Pound sdg		2017	2018	2019
GDP	sdg	830bn	119bn	
	US$	45.8bn	33.2bn	
per capita	US$	1,123	792	
Growth	%	1.4	-2.3	
Inflation	%	32.4	61.8	
Def exp	sdg	n.k	n.k	
	US$	n.k	n.k	
US$1=sdg		18.12	35.66	

Population 43,120,843

Ethnic and religious groups: Muslim 70% mainly in North; Christian 10% mainly in South; Arab 39% mainly in North

Age	0–14	15–19	20–24	25–29	30–64	65 plus
Male	21.9%	5.8%	4.5%	3.7%	12.8%	1.6%
Female	21.2%	5.7%	4.2%	3.6%	13.6%	1.4%

Capabilities

Sudan's armed forces focus on continued tensions with neighbouring South Sudan. There are also ongoing concerns regarding opposition groups operating in the south, including in Darfur, with the government relying on paramilitary forces to provide internal security. The UN maintains two significant peacekeeping missions in Sudan. Sudan is part of the Saudi-led coalition intervention in Yemen. A defence agreement was signed with Iran in 2008; it is believed to have included assistance in the development of Sudan's domestic arms industry. The armed forces are conscript-based and will have gained operational experience from internal-security deployments and the Saudi-led coalition. By regional standards, Sudan's armed forces are relatively well equipped, with significant holdings of both ageing and modern systems. While there is a UN arms embargo in place, it is limited to equipment used within the Darfur region. Recent acquisitions have been Russian and Ukrainian government surplus, apart from new Chinese jet trainers. The state-run Military Industry Corporation manufactures a range of ammunition, small arms and armoured vehicles for the domestic and export market. The majority of the corporation's products are based on older Chinese and Russian systems.

ACTIVE 104,300 (Army 100,000 Navy 1,300 Air 3,000) **Paramilitary 20,000**

Conscript liability 2 years for males aged 18–30

RESERVE NIL Paramilitary 85,000

ORGANISATIONS BY SERVICE

Army 100,000+
FORCES BY ROLE
SPECIAL FORCES
  5 SF coy
MANOEUVRE
  Reconnaissance
  1 indep recce bde
  Armoured
  1 armd div
  Mechanised
  1 mech inf div
  1 indep mech inf bde
  Light
  15+ inf div
  6 indep inf bde
  Air Manoeuvre
  1 air aslt bde
  Amphbious
  1 mne div
  Other
  1 (Border Guard) sy bde
COMBAT SUPPORT
  3 indep arty bde
  1 engr div (9 engr bn)
EQUIPMENT BY TYPE
ARMOURED FIGHTING VEHICLES
  MBT 465: 20 M60A3; 60 Type-59/Type-59D; 305 T-54/T-55; 70 T-72AV; 10 *Al-Bashier* (Type-85-IIM)
  LT TK 115: 70 Type-62; 45 Type-63
  RECCE 206: 6 AML-90; 70 BRDM-1/2; 50–80 FV701 *Ferret*; 30–50 FV601 *Saladin*
  IFV 152+: 135 BMP-1/2; 10 BTR-3; 7 BTR-80A; WZ-523 IFV
  APC 415+
    APC (T) 66: 20-30 BTR-50; 36 M113
    APC (W) 349+: 10 BTR-70M *Kobra* 2; 50–80 BTR-152; 20 OT-62; 50 OT-64; 3+ *Rakhsh*; 10 WZ-551; WZ-523; 55-80 V-150 *Commando*; 96 *Walid*
ANTI-TANK/ANTI-INFRASTRUCTURE
  MSL • MANPATS 9K11 *Malyutka* (AT-3 *Sagger*); HJ-8; 9K135 *Kornet* (AT-14 *Spriggan*)
  RCL 106mm 40 M40A1
  GUNS 40+: 40 76mm ZIS-3/100mm M-1944; 85mm D-44
ARTILLERY 860+
  SP 66: 122mm 56 2S1 *Gvozdika*; 155mm 10 Mk F3
  TOWED 128+: 105mm 20 M101; 122mm 21+: 21 D-30; D-74; M-30; 130mm 75 M-46/Type-59-I; 155mm 12 M114A1
  MRL 666+: 107mm 477 Type-63; 122mm 188: 120 BM-21 *Grad*; 50 *Saqr*; 18 Type-81; 302mm 1+ WS-1 MOR 81mm; 82mm; 120mm AM-49; M-43
AIR DEFENCE
  SAM • Point-defence 4+: 9K32 *Strela*-2 (SA-7 *Grail*)‡; FN-6; 4+ 9K33 *Osa* (SA-8 *Gecko*)
  GUNS 966+
    SP 20: 20mm 8 M163 *Vulcan*; 12 M3 VDAA
    TOWED 946+: 740+ 14.5mm ZPU-2/14.5mm ZPU-4/37mm Type-63/57mm S-60/85mm M-1944; 20mm 16 M167 *Vulcan*; 23mm 50 ZU-23-2; 37mm 80 M-1939; (30 M-1939 unserviceable); 40mm 60

Navy 1,300
EQUIPMENT BY TYPE
PATROL AND COASTAL COMBATANTS 11
  PBR 4 *Kurmuk*
  PB 7: 1 13.5m; 1 14m; 2 19m; 3 41m (PRC)
AMPHIBIOUS • LANDING CRAFT 5
  LCVP 5

LOGISTICS AND SUPPORT 3
AG 3

Air Force 3,000
FORCES BY ROLE
FIGHTER
  2 sqn with MiG-29SE/UB *Fulcrum*
FIGHTER/GROUND ATTACK
  1 sqn with FTC-2000*
GROUND ATTACK
  1 sqn with A-5 *Fantan*
  1 sqn with Su-24M *Fencer*
  1 sqn with Su-25/Su-25UB *Frogfoot*
TRANSPORT
  Some sqn with An-30 *Clank*; An-32 *Cline*; An-72 *Coaler*; An-74TK-200/300; C-130H *Hercules*; Il-76 *Candid*; Y-8
  1 VIP unit with *Falcon* 20F; *Falcon* 50; *Falcon* 900; F-27; Il-62M *Classic*
TRAINING
  1 sqn with K-8 *Karakorum**
ATTACK HELICOPTER
  2 sqn with Mi-24/Mi-24P/Mi-24V/Mi-35P *Hind*
TRANSPORT HELICOPTER
  2 sqn with Mi-8 *Hip*; Mi-17 *Hip* H; Mi-171
AIR DEFENCE
  5 bty with S-75 *Dvina* (SA-2 *Guideline*)‡

EQUIPMENT BY TYPE
AIRCRAFT 71 combat capable
  FTR 22: 20 MiG-29SE *Fulcrum* C; 2 MiG-29UB *Fulcrum* B
  ATK 32: 15 A-5 *Fantan*; 6 Su-24/M *Fencer*; 9 Su-25 *Frogfoot*; 2 Su-25UB *Frogfoot* B
  ISR 2 An-30 *Clank*
  TPT 24: **Heavy** 1 Il-76 *Candid*; **Medium** 6: 4 C-130H *Hercules*; 2 Y-8; **Light** 13: ε3 An-26 *Curl*; 2 An-32 *Cline*; 2 An-72 *Coaler*; 4 An-74TK-200; 2 An-74TK-300; **PAX** 4: 1 *Falcon* 20F (VIP); 1 *Falcon* 50 (VIP); 1 *Falcon* 900; 1 Il-62M *Classic*
  TRG 21: 6 FTC-2000*; 11 K-8 *Karakorum**; 3 UTVA-75
HELICOPTERS
  ATK 40: 25 Mi-24 *Hind*; 2 Mi-24P *Hind*; 7 Mi-24V *Hind* E; 6 Mi-35P *Hind*
  MRH ε3 Mi-17 *Hip* H
  TPT 27: **Medium** 23: 21 Mi-8 *Hip*; 2 Mi-171; **Light** 4: 1 Bell 205; 3 Bo-105
AIR DEFENCE • SAM • Medium-range: 90 S-75 *Dvina* (SA-2 *Guideline*)‡
AIR-LAUNCHED MISSILES • AAM • IR R-3 (AA-2 *Atoll*)‡; R-60 (AA-8 *Aphid*); R-73 (AA-11 *Archer*); **ARH** R-77 (AA-12A *Adder*)

Paramilitary 20,000

Popular Defence Force 20,000 (org in bn 1,000); 85,000 reservists (total 105,000)
mil wing of National Islamic Front

DEPLOYMENT
SAUDI ARABIA: *Operation Restoring Hope* 3 Su-24 *Fencer*
YEMEN: *Operation Restoring Hope* 950; 1 mech BG; T-72AV, BTR-70M *Kobra* 2

FOREIGN FORCES
All UNAMID, unless otherwise indicated
Bangladesh 356; 3 obs; 2 inf coy
Benin UNISFA 2 obs
Bhutan 1; 1 obs • UNISFA 1; 1 obs
Bolivia UNISFA 1; 3 obs
Brazil 1 obs • UNISFA 3 obs
Burkina Faso 1; 1 obs • UNISFA 1 obs
Burundi 3; 1 obs • UNISFA 2 obs
Cambodia 1 obs
China, People's Republic of 374; 1 engr coy
Ecuador 1; 1 obs; • UNISFA 1 obs
Egypt 854; 20 obs; 1 inf bn
El Salvador UNISFA 1 obs
Ethiopia 1,684; 5 obs; 2 inf bn • UNISFA 4,368; 77 obs; 1 recce coy; 3 inf bn; 2 arty coy; 1 engr coy; 1 sigs coy; 5 fd hospital; 1 hel sqn
Gambia 211; 1 inf coy
Germany 7
Ghana 9; 4 obs • UNISFA 6; 2 obs
Guatemala UNISFA 1; 2 obs
Guinea UNISFA 1; 1 obs
India UNISFA 2; 2 obs
Indonesia 800; 4 obs; 1 inf bn • UNISFA 2 obs
Iran 1; 3 obs
Jordan 11; 5 obs
Kenya 87; 2 obs; 1 MP coy
Korea, Republic of 2
Kyrgyzstan 1 obs
Malawi 2 • UNISFA 1
Malaysia 3; 1 obs • UNISFA 1 obs
Mongolia 2 • UNISFA 1; 2 obs
Namibia 1; 3 obs • UNISFA 3; 1 obs
Nepal 359; 7 obs; 2 inf coy • UNISFA 5; 1 obs
Nigeria 126; 7 obs; 1 sigs unit; 1 fd hospital • UNISFA 2; 2 obs
Pakistan 1,170; 2 obs; 1 inf bn; 1 engr pl; 1 med pl
Peru 1; 1 obs • UNISFA 2 obs
Russia UNISFA 1 obs
Rwanda 1,671; 5 obs; 2 inf bn • UNISFA 2; 3 obs
Senegal 39
Sierra Leone 4 • UNISFA 2; 1 obs
South Africa 3; 10 obs
Sri Lanka UNISFA 2; 5 obs
Tanzania 818; 5 obs; 1 inf bn • UNISFA 1; 2 obs
Thailand 9; 1 obs
Togo 2; 5 obs
Ukraine UNISFA 2; 3 obs
Zambia 5; 4 obs • UNISFA 1; 2 obs
Zimbabwe 2; 5 obs • UNISFA 1; 2 obs

Tanzania TZA

Tanzanian Shilling sh		2017	2018	2019
GDP	sh	116tr	127tr	
	US$	51.8bn	55.6bn	
per capita	US$	1,034	1,090	
Growth	%	6.0	5.8	
Inflation	%	5.3	3.8	
Def bdgt	sh	1.19tr	1.73tr	
	US$	532m	757m	
US$1=sh		2,230.92	2,279.11	

Population 55,451,343

Age	0–14	15–19	20–24	25–29	30–64	65 plus
Male	21.9%	5.5%	4.5%	3.8%	12.9%	1.3%
Female	21.5%	5.5%	4.5%	3.8%	13.1%	1.8%

Capabilities

Non-state actors pose the principal threat to Tanzania's security, with terrorism, poaching and piracy of concern. A developing relationship with China has led to a series of procurements and training contacts. There are also defence-related ties with Israel, Pakistan and Russia. The armed forces take part in multinational exercises in Africa and have provided some training assistance to other African forces. Training relationships also exist with extra-regional armed forces, including the US. Tanzania's contribution to the UN's Force Intervention Brigade in the eastern DRC, notably its special forces, will have provided many lessons for force development as well as direct combat experience. However, there is only a limited capacity to project power independently beyond the country's borders. Budget constraints have limited recapitalisation ambitions and, although heavy equipment is ageing, airlift capacity has improved with the delivery of new helicopters. There are local ammunition facilities, but otherwise Tanzania relies on imports for its military equipment.

ACTIVE 27,000 (Army 23,000 Navy 1,000 Air 3,000)
Paramilitary 1,400
Conscript liability Three months basic military training combined with social service, ages 18–23

RESERVE 80,000 (Joint 80,000)

ORGANISATIONS BY SERVICE

Army ε23,000
FORCES BY ROLE
SPECIAL FORCES
  1 SF unit
MANOEUVRE
  Armoured
  1 tk bde
  Light
  5 inf bde
COMBAT SUPPORT
  4 arty bn
  1 mor bn
  2 AT bn
  1 engr regt (bn)

COMBAT SERVICE SUPPORT
  1 log gp
AIR DEFENCE
  2 ADA bn
EQUIPMENT BY TYPE†
ARMOURED FIGHTING VEHICLES
  MBT 45: 30 T-54/T-55; 15 Type-59G
  LT TK 57+: 30 FV101 *Scorpion*; 25 Type-62; 2+ Type-63A
  RECCE 10 BRDM-2
  APC • APC (W) 14: ε10 BTR-40/BTR-152; 4 Type-92
ANTI-TANK/ANTI-INFRASTRUCTURE
  RCL 75mm Type-52 (M20)
  GUNS 85mm 75 Type-56 (D-44)
ARTILLERY 344+
  TOWED 130: **122mm** 100: 20 D-30; 80 Type-54-1 (M-30); **130mm** 30 Type-59-I
  GUN/MOR 120mm 3+ Type-07PA
  MRL 61+: **122mm** 58 BM-21 *Grad*; **300mm** 3+ A100
  MOR 150: **82mm** 100 M-43; **120mm** 50 M-43

Navy ε1,000
EQUIPMENT BY TYPE
PATROL AND COASTAL COMBATANTS 14
  PCC 2 *Mwitongo* (ex-PRC *Haiqing*)
  PHT 2 *Huchuan* each with 2 533mm ASTT
  PB 10: 2 *Ngunguri*; 2 *Shanghai* II (PRC); 2 VT 23m; 4 *Mambwe* (Damen Fast Crew Supplier 3307)
AMPHIBIOUS 3
  LCM 2 *Mbono* (ex-PRC *Yunnan*)
  LCT 1 *Kasa*

Air Defence Command ε3,000
FORCES BY ROLE
FIGHTER
  3 sqn with F-7/FT-7; FT-5; K-8 *Karakorum**
TRANSPORT
  1 sqn with Cessna 404 *Titan*; DHC-5D *Buffalo*; F-28 *Fellowship*; F-50; Gulfstream G550; Y-12 (II)
TRANSPORT HELICOPTER
  1 sqn with Bell 205 (AB-205); Bell 412EP *Twin Huey*
EQUIPMENT BY TYPE†
AIRCRAFT 17 combat capable
  FTR 11: 9 F-7TN; 2 FT-7TN
  ISR 1 SB7L-360 *Seeker*
  TPT 12: **Medium** 2 Y-8; **Light** 7: 2 Cessna 404 *Titan*; 3 DHC-5D *Buffalo*; 2 Y-12(II); **PAX** 3: 1 F-28 *Fellowship*; 1 F-50; 1 Gulfstream G550
  TRG 9: 3 FT-5 (JJ-5); 6 K-8 *Karakorum**
HELICOPTERS
  MRH 1 Bell 412EP *Twin Huey*
  TPT 2: **Medium** 1+ H225M; **Light** 1 Bell 205 (AB-205)
AIR DEFENCE
  SAM
    Short-range 2K12 *Kub* (SA-6 *Gainful*)†; S-125 *Pechora* (SA-3 *Goa*)†
    Point-defence 9K32 *Strela*-2 (SA-7 *Grail*)‡
  GUNS 200
    TOWED **14.5mm** 40 ZPU-2/ZPU-4†; **23mm** 40 ZU-23; **37mm** 120 M-1939

Paramilitary 1,400 active

Police Field Force 1,400
18 sub-units incl Police Marine Unit

Air Wing
EQUIPMENT BY TYPE
AIRCRAFT • TPT • Light 1 Cessna U206 *Stationair*
HELICOPTERS
  TPT • Light 4: 2 Bell 206A *Jet Ranger* (AB-206A);
  2 Bell 206L *Long Ranger*
  TRG 2 Bell 47G (AB-47G)/Bell 47G2

Marine Unit 100
EQUIPMENT BY TYPE
PATROL AND COASTAL COMBATANTS
All operational patrol vessels under 10t FLD

DEPLOYMENT

CENTRAL AFRICAN REPUBLIC: UN • MINUSCA 445; 1 inf bn(-)

DEMOCRATIC REPUBLIC OF THE CONGO: UN • MONUSCO 1,003; 2 obs; 1 SF coy; 1 inf bn

LEBANON: UN • UNIFIL 159; 1 MP coy

SOUTH SUDAN: UN • UNMISS 5; 4 obs

SUDAN: UN • UNAMID 818; 5 obs; 1 inf bn; **UN •** UNISFA 1; 2 obs

Togo TGO

CFA Franc BCEAO fr		2017	2018	2019
GDP	fr	2.77tr	2.96tr	
	US$	4.77bn	5.35bn	
per capita	US$	611	668	
Growth	%	4.4	4.7	
Inflation	%	-0.7	0.4	
Def bdgt	fr	51.9bn	58.0bn	
	US$	89.4m	105m	
US$1=fr		580.97	553.12	
Population	8,176,449			

Age	0–14	15–19	20–24	25–29	30–64	65 plus
Male	20.1%	5.1%	4.5%	4.1%	14.3%	1.5%
Female	20.0%	5.1%	4.5%	4.2%	14.7%	2.0%

Capabilities

The armed forces are adequate for the internal-security role, but they have limited deployment capacity. Togo is increasingly concerned by piracy in the Gulf of Guinea and other illegal maritime activities and is strengthening its cooperation with neighbours to address these threats. Military-training cooperation continues with France, which provides peacekeeping training for Togolese personnel participating in MINUSMA. There is also a peacekeeping training centre in Lomé. The US Africa Contingency Operations Training and Assistance programme has also provided training assistance. Togo's deployment capabilities are limited to its region without external support. Financial challenges limit the armed forces' capabilities, including air-transport and maritime capacities. Apart from limited maintenance facilities, the country has no domestic defence-industrial capability.

ACTIVE 8,550 (Army 8,100 Navy 200 Air 250)
Paramilitary 750
Conscript liability Selective conscription, 2 years

ORGANISATIONS BY SERVICE

Army 8,100+
FORCES BY ROLE
MANOEUVRE
  Reconnaissance
  1 armd recce regt
  Light
  2 cbd arms regt
  2 inf regt
  1 rapid reaction force
  Air Manoeuvre
  1 cdo/para regt (3 cdo/para coy)
  Other
  1 (Presidential Guard) gd regt (1 gd bn, 1 cdo bn, 2 indep gd coy)
COMBAT SUPPORT
  1 cbt spt regt (1 fd arty bty, 2 ADA bty, 1 engr/log/tpt bn)
EQUIPMENT BY TYPE
ARMOURED FIGHTING VEHICLES
  MBT 2 T-54/T-55
  LT TK 9 FV101 *Scorpion*
  RECCE 86: 3 AML-60; 7 AML-90; 29 *Bastion Patsas*; 36 EE-9 *Cascavel*; 6 M8; 3 M20; 2 VBL
  IFV 20 BMP-2
  APC 34
    APC (T) 4 M3A1 half-track
    APC (W) 30 UR-416
ANTI-TANK/ANTI-INFRASTRUCTURE
  RCL 75mm Type-52 (M20)/Type-56; **82mm** Type-65 (B-10)
  GUNS 57mm 5 ZIS-2
ARTILLERY 30+
  SP 122mm 6
  TOWED 105mm 4 HM-2
  MRL 122mm Type-81 mod (SC6 chassis)
  MOR 82mm 20 M-43
AIR DEFENCE • GUNS • TOWED 43 **14.5mm** 38 ZPU-4; **37mm** 5 M-1939

Navy ε200 (incl Marine Infantry unit)
EQUIPMENT BY TYPE
PATROL AND COASTAL COMBATANTS 3
  PBF 1 *Agou* (RPB 33)
  PB 2 *Kara* (FRA Esterel)

Air Force 250
FORCES BY ROLE
FIGHTER/GROUND ATTACK
  1 sqn with *Alpha Jet**; EMB-326G*
TRANSPORT
  1 sqn with Beech 200 *King Air*
  1 VIP unit with DC-8; F-28-1000

TRAINING
  1 sqn with TB-30 *Epsilon**
TRANSPORT HELICOPTER
  1 sqn with SA315 *Lama*; SA316 *Alouette* III; SA319 *Alouette* III

EQUIPMENT BY TYPE†
AIRCRAFT 10 combat capable
  TPT 5: **Light** 2 Beech 200 *King Air*; **PAX** 3: 1 DC-8; 2 F-28-1000 (VIP)
  TRG 10: 3 *Alpha Jet**; 4 EMB-326G *; 3 TB-30 *Epsilon**
HELICOPTERS
  MRH 4: 2 SA315 *Lama*; 1 SA316 *Alouette* III; 1 SA319 *Alouette* III
  TPT • **Medium** (1 SA330 *Puma* in store)

Paramilitary 750

Gendarmerie 750
Ministry of Interior
FORCES BY ROLE
2 reg sections
MANOEUVRE
  Other
    1 (mobile) paramilitary sqn

DEPLOYMENT
CENTRAL AFRICAN REPUBLIC: UN • MINUSCA 6; 4 obs
LIBERIA: UN • UNMIL 1
MALI: UN • MINUSMA 937; 2 obs; 1 inf bn; 1 fd hospital
SOUTH SUDAN: UN • UNMISS 2
SUDAN: UN • UNAMID 2; 5 obs
WESTERN SAHARA: UN • MINURSO 2 obs

Uganda UGA

Ugandan Shilling Ush		2017	2018	2019
GDP	Ush	96.8tr	107tr	
	US$	26.6bn	27.9bn	
per capita	US$	707	717	
Growth	%	4.5	5.9	
Inflation	%	5.6	3.8	
Def bdgt	Ush	1.58tr	1.47tr	1.47tr
	US$	434m	384m	
US$1=Ush		3,635.79	3,835.06	
Population	40,853,749			

Age	0–14	15–19	20–24	25–29	30–64	65 plus
Male	23.9%	5.6%	4.8%	3.9%	10.6%	0.9%
Female	24.0%	5.7%	4.9%	4.0%	10.5%	1.1%

Capabilities
Uganda's armed forces are well equipped and are important contributors to East African security. Operational experience and training have led to improvements in administration and planning, as well as in military skills including counter-IED and urban patrolling. A number of years spent targeting the Lord's Resistance Army has also ensured experience in counter-insurgency tactics. There are plans to establish a National Defence College. Uganda is one of the largest contributors to the East Africa Standby Force and in 2014 signed a Mutual Defence Treaty with Kenya and Rwanda. Training levels are adequate, particularly for the special forces, and are improving after recent experiences. There is regular training with international partners, including at Uganda's own facilities, and Ugandan forces have gained experience at the US Joint Readiness Training Centre. Airlift is limited, though the country was able to deploy an armoured element to southern Sudan in 2013. Rotary-wing aviation has improved in recent years, partly due to US assistance. While logistical support remains superior to that of many other regional states, the motorised infantry still lacks sufficient transport and logistics capacity. Uganda's mechanised forces are relatively well equipped in these areas, though heavy equipment is disparate and ageing. Improvements include the arrival of MRAP and other protected vehicles. There is limited defence-industrial capacity, though there is some manufacturing of light armoured vehicles. Uganda's 2015–19 Security Sector Development plan included the establishment of an engineering centre at Magamaga, as well as a defence-research centre at Lugazi.

ACTIVE 45,000 (Ugandan People's Defence Force 45,000) Paramilitary 1,400

RESERVE 10,000

ORGANISATIONS BY SERVICE

Ugandan People's Defence Force ε40,000–45,000
FORCES BY ROLE
MANOEUVRE
  Armoured
    1 armd bde
  Light
    1 cdo bn
    5 inf div (total: 16 inf bde)
  Other
    1 (Special Forces Command) mot bde
COMBAT SUPPORT
  1 arty bde
AIR DEFENCE
  2 AD bn

EQUIPMENT BY TYPE†
ARMOURED FIGHTING VEHICLES
  MBT 239+: 185 T-54/T-55; 10 T-72; 44 T-90S; ZTZ-85-IIM
  LT TK ε20 PT-76
  RECCE 46: 40 Eland-20; 6 FV701 *Ferret*
  IFV 31 BMP-2
  APC 150
    APC (W) 58: 15 BTR-60; 20 *Buffel*; 4 OT-64; 19 *Bastion* APC
    PPV 92: 42 *Casspir*; 40 *Mamba*; 10 RG-33L
  AUV 15 *Cougar*
ENGINEERING & MAINTENANCE VEHICLES
  ARV T-54/T-55 reported
  VLB MTU reported
  MW *Husky*
ARTILLERY 333+
  SP 155mm 6 ATMOS 2000

TOWED 243+: **122mm** M-30; **130mm** 221; **155mm** 22: 4 G-5; 18 M-839
MRL 6+: **107mm** (12-tube); **122mm** 6+: BM-21 *Grad*; 6 RM-70
MOR 78+: **81mm** L16; **82mm** M-43; **120mm** 78 *Soltam*
AIR DEFENCE
  SAM
    Short-range 4 S-125 *Pechora* (SA-3 *Goa*)
    Point-defence 9K32 *Strela*-2 (SA-7 *Grail*)‡; 9K310 *Igla*-1 (SA-16 *Gimlet*)
  GUNS • TOWED 20+: **14.5mm** ZPU-1/ZPU-2/ZPU-4; **37mm** 20 M-1939

Marines ε400
All operational patrol vessels under 10t FLD

Air Wing
FORCES BY ROLE
FIGHTER/GROUND ATTACK
  1 sqn with MiG-21bis *Fishbed*; MiG-21U/UM *Mongol A/B*; Su-30MK2 *Flanker*
TRANSPORT
  1 unit with Y-12
  1 VIP unit with Gulfstream 550; L-100-30
TRAINING
  1 unit with L-39 *Albatros*†*
ATTACK/TRANSPORT HELICOPTER
  1 sqn with Bell 206 *Jet Ranger*; Bell 412 *Twin Huey*; Mi-17 *Hip* H; Mi-24 *Hind*; Mi-172 (VIP)
EQUIPMENT BY TYPE
AIRCRAFT 16 combat capable
  FGA 13: 5 MiG-21bis *Fishbed*; 1 MiG-21U *Mongol* A; 1 MiG-21UM *Mongol* B; 6 Su-30MK2 *Flanker*
  TPT 6: **Medium** 1 L-100-30; **Light** 4: 2 Cessna 208B; 2 Y-12; **PAX** 1 Gulfstream 550
  TRG 3 L-39 *Albatros*†*
HELICOPTERS
  ATK 1 Mi-24 *Hind* (2 more non-op)
  MRH 5: 2 Bell 412 *Twin Huey*; 3 Mi-17 *Hip* H (1 more non-op)
  TPT 4: **Medium** 2: 1 Mi-172 (VIP), 1 Mi-171 (VIP); **Light** 2 Bell 206A *Jet Ranger*
AIR-LAUNCHED MISSILES
  AAM • IR R-73 (AA-11 *Archer*); **SARH** R-27 (AA-10 *Alamo*); **ARH** R-77 (AA-12 *Adder*) (reported)
  ARM Kh-31P (AS-17A *Krypton*) (reported)

Paramilitary ε600 active

Border Defence Unit ε600
Equipped with small arms only

DEPLOYMENT
SOMALIA: AU • AMISOM 6,022; 7 inf bn; **UN •** UNSOM 530; 2 obs; 1 sy bn; **UN •** UNSOS 1 obs
SOUTH SUDAN: UN • UNMISS 2

Zambia ZMB

Zambian Kwacha K		2017	2018	2019
GDP	K	245bn	281bn	
	US$	25.7bn	25.8bn	
per capita	US$	1,491	1,450	
Growth	%	3.4	3.8	
Inflation	%	6.6	8.5	
Def bdgt	K	3.20bn	3.50bn	
	US$	337m	320m	
US$1=K		9.52	10.92	
Population	16,445,079			

Age	0–14	15–19	20–24	25–29	30–64	65 plus
Male	23.1%	5.4%	4.6%	3.8%	12.1%	1.0%
Female	22.9%	5.4%	4.6%	3.8%	12.1%	1.3%

Capabilities
Zambia faces no immediate external threat, though its border with the Democratic Republic of the Congo presents a security challenge. China has become an important investor in the country over the past decade, including military training and weapons sales. Ensuring territorial integrity and border security, and a commitment to international peacekeeping operations, are the armed forces' key tasks. Given equipment obsolescence and a comparatively small establishment strength, there could be challenges in adequately fulfilling this role. Zambia is a member of the AU and SADC and the services have participated in exercises with international and regional partners including for the SADC Standby Force. Zambia's largest peacekeeping contribution is to the MINUSCA operation in the Central African Republic. As well as growing defence ties with China, in April 2017 Zambia signed a defence deal with Russia for equipment spare-parts support. The armed forces are all-volunteer. The US has provided funding and material support for army and air-force pre-deployment training for the CAR peacekeeping mission. In the air force, procedural trainers and full-mission simulators have been bought to support the L-15 advanced jet trainer/light-attack aircraft from China. The armed forces have limited capacity to self-deploy and sustain forces beyond national borders. While there is a need to modernise the equipment inventory, funds remain limited. The country has no defence-industrial base, apart from limited ammunition production.

ACTIVE 15,100 (Army 13,500 Air 1,600) **Paramilitary 1,400**

RESERVE 3,000 (Army 3,000)

ORGANISATIONS BY SERVICE

Army 13,500
FORCES BY ROLE
COMMAND
  3 bde HQ
SPECIAL FORCES
  1 cdo bn
MANOEUVRE
  Armoured
    1 armd regt (1 tk bn, 1 armd recce regt)

Light
6 inf bn
COMBAT SUPPORT
1 arty regt (2 fd arty bn, 1 MRL bn)
1 engr regt
EQUIPMENT BY TYPE
Some equipment†
ARMOURED FIGHTING VEHICLES
MBT 30: 20 Type-59; 10 T-55
LT TK 30 PT-76
RECCE 70 BRDM-1/BRDM-2 (ε30 serviceable)
IFV 23 Ratel-20
APC • **APC (W)** 33: 13 BTR-60; 20 BTR-70
ENGINEERING & MAINTENANCE VEHICLES
ARV T-54/T-55 reported
ANTI-TANK/ANTI-INFRASTRUCTURE
MSL • **MANPATS** 9K11 *Malyutka* (AT-3 *Sagger*)
RCL 12+: **57mm** 12 M18; **75mm** M20; **84mm** *Carl Gustav*
ARTILLERY 182
TOWED 61: **105mm** 18 Model 56 pack howitzer; **122mm** 25 D-30; **130mm** 18 M-46
MRL **122mm** 30 BM-21 *Grad* (ε12 serviceable)
MOR 91: **81mm** 55; **82mm** 24; **120mm** 12
AIR DEFENCE
SAM • **MANPAD** 9K32 *Strela*-2 (SA-7 *Grail*)‡
GUNS • **TOWED** 136: **20mm** 50 M-55 (triple); **37mm** 40 M-1939; **57mm** ε30 S-60; **85mm** 16 M-1939 *KS-12*

Reserve 3,000
FORCES BY ROLE
MANOEUVRE
Light
3 inf bn

Air Force 1,600
FORCES BY ROLE
FIGHTER/GROUND ATTACK
1 sqn with K-8 *Karakorum**
1 sqn with L-15*
TRANSPORT
1 sqn with MA60; Y-12(II); Y-12(IV); Y-12E
1 (VIP) unit with AW139; CL-604; HS-748
1 (liaison) sqn with Do-28
TRAINING
2 sqn with MB-326GB; MFI-15 *Safari*
TRANSPORT HELICOPTER
1 sqn with Mi-17 *Hip* H
1 (liaison) sqn with Bell 47G; Bell 205 (UH-1H *Iroquois*/AB-205)
AIR DEFENCE
3 bty with S-125 *Pechora* (SA-3 *Goa*)
EQUIPMENT BY TYPE†
Very low serviceability
AIRCRAFT 21 combat capable
TPT 23: **Light** 21: 5 Do-28; 2 MA60; 4 Y-12(II); 5 Y-12(IV); 5 Y-12E; **PAX** 2: 1 CL-604; 1 HS-748
TRG 51: 15 K-8 *Karakourm**; 6 L-15*; 10 MB-326GB; 8 MFI-15 *Safari*; 12 SF-260TW
HELICOPTERS
MRH 5: 1 AW139; 4 Mi-17 *Hip* H
TPT • **Light** 12: 9 Bell 205 (UH-1H *Iroquois*/AB-205); 3 Bell 212
TRG 5 Bell 47G
UNMANNED AERIAL VEHICLES 3+
ISR • **Medium** 3+ *Hermes* 450
AIR DEFENCE
SAM • **Short-range** S-125 *Pechora* (SA-3 *Goa*)
AIR-LAUNCHED MISSILES
AAM • **IR** PL-5E-II
ASM 9K11 *Malyutka* (AT-3 *Sagger*)

Paramilitary 1,400

Police Mobile Unit 700
FORCES BY ROLE
MANOEUVRE
Other
1 police bn (4 police coy)

Police Paramilitary Unit 700
FORCES BY ROLE
MANOEUVRE
Other
1 paramilitary bn (3 paramilitary coy)

DEPLOYMENT
CENTRAL AFRICAN REPUBLIC: UN • MINUSCA 942; 8 obs; 1 inf bn
DEMOCRATIC REPUBLIC OF THE CONGO: UN • MONUSCO 3; 7 obs
SOUTH SUDAN: UN • UNMISS 2; 4 obs
SUDAN: UN • UNAMID 5; 4 obs; **UN** • UNISFA 1; 2 obs

Zimbabwe ZWE

Zimbabwe Dollar Z$ [a]		2017	2018	2019
GDP	US$	17.6bn	19.4bn	
per capita	US$	1,185	1,269	
Growth	%	3.7	3.6	
Inflation	%	0.9	3.9	
Def bdgt	US$	341m	420m	
US$1=Z$		1.00	1.00	

[a] Zimbabwe dollar no longer in active use
Population 14,030,368

Age	0–14	15–19	20–24	25–29	30–64	65 plus
Male	19.1%	5.5%	4.5%	4.4%	13.6%	1.8%
Female	19.5%	5.6%	4.8%	4.5%	14.0%	2.7%

Capabilities

Political instability and a weak economy are the key challenges for the state. The August 2018 presidential election resulted in victory for Emmerson Mnangagwa, though it saw troops deployed on the streets amid unrest. Ensuring sovereignty, territorial integrity and border security, and providing internal-security support to the police, are tasks for the armed forces. They also take an active political role, evidenced by their role in toppling former president

Robert Mugabe. Zimbabwe is a member of the AU and the SADC, and takes part in SADC Standby Force exercises. In March 2018, Russian Foreign Minister Sergei Lavrov met with President Mnangagwa with future defence cooperation an agenda item. Zimbabwe and China have defence ties, while Belarus is also looking to improve ties with the country. The armed forces are all-volunteer. In 2018, a 'special allowance' was paid to military personnel to boost overall pay. Military leaders have identified training as a development priority. Small numbers of personnel have deployed on peacekeeping operations, but there is no capacity to sustain a force far beyond national borders. Recapitalising an obsolescent equipment inventory is also a priority. This, however, will depend on economic recovery, and perhaps the extent to which China and Russia will provide support. State-owned small-arms and munitions manufacturer Zimbabwe Defence Industries has struggled after nearly two decades of Western sanctions, but there are plans to revive the plant.

ACTIVE 29,000 (Army 25,000 Air 4,000) **Paramilitary 21,800**

ORGANISATIONS BY SERVICE

Army ε25,000
FORCES BY ROLE
COMMAND
  1 SF bde HQ
  1 mech bde HQ
  5 inf bde HQ
SPECIAL FORCES
  1 SF regt
MANOEUVRE
  Armoured
  1 armd sqn
  Mechanised
  1 mech inf bn
  Light
  15 inf bn
  1 cdo bn
  Air Manoeuvre
  1 para bn
  Other
  3 gd bn
  1 (Presidential Guard) gd gp
COMBAT SUPPORT
  1 arty bde
  1 fd arty regt
  2 engr regt
AIR DEFENCE
  1 AD regt
EQUIPMENT BY TYPE
ARMOURED FIGHTING VEHICLES
  MBT 40: 30 Type-59†; 10 Type-69†
  RECCE 115: 20 *Eland*-60/90; 15 FV701 *Ferret*†; 80 EE-9 *Cascavel* (90mm)
  IFV 2+ YW307
  APC • APC (T) 30: 8 ZSD-85 (incl CP); 22 VTT-323
ENGINEERING & MAINTENANCE VEHICLES
  ARV T-54/T-55 reported; ZJX-93 ARV
  VLB MTU reported
ARTILLERY 254
  SP 122mm 12 2S1 *Gvozdika*
  TOWED 122mm 20: 4 D-30; 16 Type-60 (D-74)
  MRL 76: **107mm** 16 Type-63; **122mm** 60 RM-70
  MOR 146: **81mm/82mm** ε140; **120mm** 6 M-43
AIR DEFENCE
  SAM • Point-defence 9K32 *Strela*-2 (SA-7 *Grail*)‡
  GUNS • TOWED 116: **14.5mm** 36 ZPU-1/ZPU-2/ZPU-4; **23mm** 45 ZU-23; **37mm** 35 M-1939

Air Force 4,000
FORCES BY ROLE
FIGHTER
  1 sqn with F-7 II†; FT-7†
FIGHTER/GROUND ATTACK
  1 sqn with K-8 *Karakorum**
  (1 sqn Hawker *Hunter* in store)
GROUND ATTACK/ISR
  1 sqn with Cessna 337/O-2A *Skymaster**
ISR/TRAINING
  1 sqn with SF-260F/M; SF-260TP*; SF-260W *Warrior**
TRANSPORT
  1 sqn with BN-2 *Islander*; CASA 212-200 *Aviocar* (VIP)
ATTACK/TRANSPORT HELICOPTER
  1 sqn with Mi-35 *Hind*; Mi-35P *Hind* (liaison); SA316 *Alouette* III; AS532UL *Cougar* (VIP)
  1 trg sqn with Bell 412 *Twin Huey*, SA316 *Alouette* III
AIR DEFENCE
  1 sqn
EQUIPMENT BY TYPE
AIRCRAFT 45 combat capable
  FTR 9: 7 F-7 II†; 2 FT-7†
  ISR 2 O-2A *Skymaster*
  TPT • Light 25: 5 BN-2 *Islander*; 7 C-212-200 *Aviocar*; 13 Cessna 337 *Skymaster**; (10 C-47 *Skytrain* in store)
  TRG 33: 10 K-8 *Karakorum**; 5 SF-260M; 8 SF-260TP*; 5 SF-260W *Warrior**; 5 SF-260F
HELICOPTERS
  ATK 6: 4 Mi-35 *Hind*; 2 Mi-35P *Hind*
  MRH 10: 8 Bell 412 *Twin Huey*; 2 SA316 *Alouette* III
  TPT • Medium 2 AS532UL *Cougar* (VIP)
AIR-LAUNCHED MISSILES • AAM • IR PL-2; PL-5 (reported)
AD • GUNS 100mm (not deployed); **37mm** (not deployed); **57mm** (not deployed)

Paramilitary 21,800

Zimbabwe Republic Police Force 19,500
incl air wg

Police Support Unit 2,300
PATROL AND COASTAL COMBATANTS
All operational patrol vessels under 10t FLD

DEPLOYMENT

SOUTH SUDAN: UN • UNMISS 1; 2 obs

SUDAN: UN • UNAMID 2; 5 obs; **UN • UNISFA** 1; 2 obs

Arms procurements and deliveries – Sub-Saharan Africa

Significant events in 2018

- In June, Airbus signed a memorandum of understanding with Côte d'Ivoire to develop the country's aerospace industry.

- South Africa launched its Defence Industry Fund (DIF) in July, the creation of which was recommended in 2015. The DIF will raise money from private investors and for the South African defence industry. South Africa's defence SMEs have struggled to source investment in recent years.

- South Africa's long-running A-*Darter* air-to-air missile programme completed qualification tests in September and deliveries will likely begin in 2019. The A-*Darter* was co-developed with Brazil and has an imaging infrared (IIR) seeker, making it more resistant to countermeasures. The South African Air Force already operates the IIR IRIS-T missile. It is not clear if A-*Darter* is intended to replace the IRIS-T in South African service.

- The Pakistani government reportedly provided a US$184.3m guarantee for the production of three JF-17 fighter aircraft for Nigeria in October. Nigeria set aside a small amount of funding for three JF-17s in 2016 and has since continued adding to the fund. Nigeria's 2018 budget included funding for a second batch of three fighters. It is not clear how many JF-17s Nigeria plans to acquire in total.

- In November, the South African authorities announced further delays to the *Project Hoefyster* programme. Local company Denel was supposed to begin supplying in 2015 over 200 *Badger* 8x8 armoured vehicles based on Patria's AMV, but software problems, delays in developing different variants and problems with Denel's finances mean that deliveries are now expected to begin in 2022.

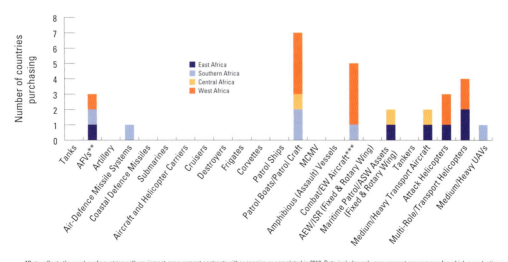

▼ Figure 30 **Sub-Saharan Africa: selected ongoing or completed procurement priorities in 2018**

*Data reflects the number of countries with equipment-procurement contracts either ongoing or completed in 2018. Data includes only procurement programmes for which a production contract has been signed. The data does not include upgrade programmes.
**Armoured fighting vehicles not including main battle tanks   ***Includes combat-capable training aircraft

© IISS

Table 21 South Africa: major equipment-procurement programmes

Equipment	Project name	Type	Quantity	Value (ZAR)	Value (US$)	Prime contractor	Contract date	Notes
Land								
Starstreak and ESR 220 Thutwa	Guardian	Point-defence SAM and radar	n.k.	801m	72.6m	Denel Dynamics	Dec 2002	Ground-Based Air Defence System (GBADS) Phase I; in-service date 2014
Badger 8x8	Hoefyster	IFV	242	15.4bn	1.6bn	Denel Land Systems	Sep 2013	To replace Ratel; deliveries significantly delayed, now expected to begin in 2022
Skyshield Fire Control System	Protector	35 mm anti-aircraft-gun upgrade	n.k.	n.k.	n.k.	Denel Integrated Solutions and Maritime	2014	GBADS Phase II: upgrade of 35mm guns and acquisition of Skyshield fire-control system; deliveries ongoing
Umkhonto Ground-Based Launcher (GBL)	Outcome	Short-range SAM	n.k.	-	-	Denel Dynamics	-	GBADS Phase III: C4I upgrade for GBADS and acquisition of Umkhonto GBL SAM
Maritime								
Vard 9 105 (UK Echo)	Hotel	AGHS	1	ε1.8bn	ε135.2m	Southern African Shipyards	Dec 2017	To be completed by end of 2021
Damen Stan Patrol 6211	Biro	PCC	3	n.k.	n.k.	DCST	Feb 2018	Inshore Patrol Vessel; original requirement for additional three offshore-patrol vessels dropped in 2017 due to budget cuts
Heroine class	n.k.	SSK mid-life upgrade	3	-	-	TBD	-	Feasibility studies ongoing; contract expected by 2020
Valour class	Syne	FFGHM mid-life upgrade	4	-	-	TBD	-	Concept phase begun Feb 2016
Aerospace								
A-Darter	Assegai	AAM IR	n.k.	939m	73.63m	Denel	Mar 2015	Project begun late 1990s; Brazil joined 2007. Deliveries one year behind production-contract schedule
TBD	Metsi	MPA ac	TBD	-	-	TBD	-	To replace C-47TP and C-212; procurement processes expected to begin 2019/20
	Kiepie	Lt Tpt ac						
Seeker 400	Itambo	Heavy ISR UAV	TBD	-	-	Denel Dynamics	-	Plan to reactivate UAV squadron announced in 2016

PART TWO
Explanatory notes

The Military Balance provides an assessment of the armed forces and defence expenditures of 171 countries and territories. Each edition contributes to the provision of a unique compilation of data and information, enabling the reader to discern trends by studying editions as far back as 1959. The data in the current edition is accurate according to IISS assessments as of November 2018, unless specified. Inclusion of a territory, country or state in *The Military Balance* does not imply legal recognition or indicate support for any government.

General arrangement and contents

The introduction is an assessment of global defence developments and key themes in the 2019 edition. There are three analytical essays, followed by a graphical section analysing comparative defence statistics by domain, as well as key trends in defence economics.

Regional chapters begin with analysis of the military and security issues that drive national defence policy developments, and key trends in regional defence economics. These are followed by focused analysis, for certain countries, of defence policy and capability issues, and defence economics. Next, detailed data on regional states' military forces and equipment, and defence economics, is presented in alphabetical order. Graphics assessing important regional arms procurements and deliveries complete each region.

The book closes with comparative and reference sections containing comparisons of expenditure and personnel statistics.

The Military Balance wall chart

The Military Balance 2019 wall chart is an assessment of the dispositions of China's armed forces, also highlighting key features of its military-modernisation process. It provides detail on each armed service, as well as the Strategic Support Force, People's Armed Police and the China Coast Guard. The graphical display is complemented by a timeline showing major modernisation events and relevant equipment events.

Using *The Military Balance*

The country entries assess personnel strengths, organisation and equipment holdings of the world's armed forces. Force-strength and equipment-inventory data is based on the most accurate data available, or on the best estimate

Abbreviations and definitions

Qualifier	
'At least'	Total is no less than the number given
'Up to'	Total is at most the number given, but could be lower
'About'	Total could be higher than given
'Some'	Precise inventory is unavailable at time of press
'In store'	Equipment held away from front-line units; readiness and maintenance varies
Billion (bn)	1,000 million (m)
Trillion (tr)	1,000 billion
$	US dollars unless otherwise stated
ε	Estimated
*	Aircraft counted by the IISS as combat capable
-	Part of a unit is detached/less than
+	Unit reinforced/more than
†	IISS assesses that the serviceability of equipment is in doubt[a]
‡	Equipment judged obsolete (weapons whose basic design is more than four decades old and which have not been significantly upgraded within the past decade)[a]

[a] Not to be taken to imply that such equipment cannot be used

that can be made. In estimating a country's total capabilities, old equipment may be counted where it is considered that it may still be deployable.

The data presented reflects judgements based on information available to the IISS at the time the book is compiled. Where information differs from previous editions, this is mainly because of changes in national forces, but it is sometimes because the IISS has reassessed the evidence supporting past entries. Given this, care must be taken in constructing time-series comparisons from information given in successive editions.

Country entries

Information on each country is shown in a standard format, although the differing availability of information and differences in nomenclature result in some variations. Country entries include economic, demographic and military data. Population figures are based on demographic statistics taken from the US Census Bureau. Data on ethnic and religious minorities is also provided in some country entries. Military data includes personnel numbers, conscript liability where relevant, outline organisation, number of formations and units, and an inventory of the major equipment of each service. Details of national forces stationed abroad and of foreign forces stationed within the given country are also provided.

Arms procurements and deliveries

A series of thematic tables, graphics and text follow the regional data. These are designed to illustrate key trends, principal programmes and significant events in regional defence procurements. More detailed information on defence procurements, organised by country, equipment type and manufacturing company, can be found on the IISS Military Balance+ database (*https://www.iiss.org/publications/the-military-balance-plus*). The information in this section meets the threshold for a *Military Balance* country entry and as such does not feature information on sales of small arms and light weapons.

Defence economics

Country entries include defence expenditures, selected economic-performance indicators and demographic aggregates. All country entries are subject to revision each year as new information, particularly regarding actual defence expenditure, becomes available. On pp. 503–08, there are also international comparisons of defence expenditure and military personnel, giving expenditure figures for the past three years in per capita terms and as a % of gross domestic product (GDP). The aim is to provide a measure of military expenditure and the allocation of economic resources to defence.

Individual country entries show economic performance over the past two years and current demographic data. Where this data is unavailable, information from the last available year is provided. All financial data in the country entries is shown in both national currency and US dollars at current – not constant – prices. US-dollar conversions are calculated from the exchange rates listed in the entry.

Definitions of terms

Despite efforts by NATO and the UN to develop a standardised definition of military expenditure, many countries prefer to use their own definitions (which are often not made public). In order to present a comprehensive picture, *The Military Balance* lists three different measures of military-related spending data.

- For most countries, an official defence-budget figure is provided.
- For those countries where other military-related outlays, over and above the defence budget, are known or can be reasonably estimated, an additional measurement referred to as defence expenditure is also provided. Defence-expenditure figures will naturally be higher than official budget figures, depending on the range of additional factors included.
- For NATO countries, a defence-budget figure, as well as defence expenditure reported by NATO in local currency terms and converted using IMF exchange rates, is quoted.

NATO's military-expenditure definition (the most comprehensive) is cash outlays of central or federal governments to meet the costs of national armed forces. The term 'armed forces' includes strategic, land, naval, air, command, administration and support forces. It also includes other forces if they are trained, structured and equipped to support defence forces and are realistically deployable. Defence expenditures are reported in four categories: Operating Costs, Procurement and Construction, Research and Development (R&D) and Other Expenditure. Operating Costs include salaries and pensions for military and civilian personnel; the cost of maintaining and training units, service organisations, headquarters and support elements; and the cost of servicing and repairing military equipment and infrastructure. Procurement and Construction expenditure covers national equipment and infrastructure spending, as well as common infrastructure programmes. R&D is defence expenditure up to the point at which new equipment can be put in service, regardless of whether new equipment is actually procured. Foreign Military Aid (FMA) contributions are also noted.

For many non-NATO countries the issue of transparency in reporting military budgets is fundamental. Not every UN member state reports defence-budget data (even fewer report real defence expenditures) to their electorates, the UN, the IMF or other multinational organisations. In the case of governments with a proven record of transparency, official figures generally conform to the standardised definition of defence budgeting, as adopted by the UN, and consistency problems are not usually a major issue. The IISS cites official defence budgets as reported by either national governments, the UN, the OSCE or the IMF.

For those countries where the official defence-budget figure is considered to be an incomplete measure of total military-related spending, and appropriate additional data is available, the IISS will use data from a variety of sources to arrive at a more accurate estimate of true defence expenditure. The most frequent instances of budgetary manipulation or falsification typically involve equipment procurement, R&D, defence-industrial investment, covert weapons programmes, pensions for retired military and civilian personnel, paramilitary forces and non-budgetary sources of revenue for the military arising from ownership of industrial, property and land assets. There will be several countries listed in *The Military Balance* for which only an official defence-budget figure is provided but where, in reality, true defence-related expenditure is almost certainly higher.

Percentage changes in defence spending are referred to in either nominal or real terms. Nominal terms relate to the percentage change in numerical spending figures, and do not account for the impact of price changes (i.e. inflation) on defence spending. By contrast, real terms account for inflationary effects, and may therefore be considered a more accurate representation of change over time.

The principal sources for national economic statistics cited in the country entries are the IMF, the OECD, the World Bank and three regional banks (the Inter-American, Asian and African Development banks). For some countries, basic economic data is difficult to obtain. GDP figures are nominal (current) values at market prices. GDP growth is real, not nominal growth, and inflation is the year-on-year change in consumer prices.

General defence data
Personnel
The 'Active' total comprises all servicemen and women on full-time duty (including conscripts and long-term assignments from the Reserves). When a gendarmerie or equivalent is under control of the defence ministry, they may be included in the active total. Only the length of conscript liability is shown; where service is voluntary there is no entry. 'Reserve' describes formations and units not fully manned or operational in peacetime, but which can be mobilised by recalling reservists in an emergency. Some countries have more than one category of reserves, often kept at varying degrees of readiness. Where possible, these differences are denoted using the national descriptive title, but always under the heading of 'Reserves' to distinguish them from full-time active forces. All personnel figures are rounded to the nearest 50, except for organisations with under 500 personnel, where figures are rounded to the nearest ten.

Other forces
Many countries maintain forces whose training, organisation, equipment and control suggest that they may be used to support or replace regular military forces, or be used more broadly by states to deliver militarily relevant effect; these are called 'paramilitary'. They include some forces that may have a constabulary role. These are detailed after the military forces of each country, but their personnel numbers are not normally included in the totals at the start of each entry.

Units and formation strength

Company	100–200
Battalion	500–1,000
Brigade	3,000–5,000
Division	15,000–20,000
Corps or Army	50,000–100,000

Cyber
The Military Balance includes detail on selected national cyber capacities, particularly those under the control of, or designed to fulfil the requirements of, defence organisations.

Forces by role and equipment by type
Quantities are shown by function (according to each nation's employment) and type, and represent what are believed to be total holdings, including active and reserve operational and training units. Inventory totals for missile systems relate to launchers and not to missiles. Equipment held 'in store' is not counted in the main inventory totals.

Deployments
The Military Balance mainly lists permanent bases and operational deployments, including peacekeeping operations, which are often discussed in the regional text. Information in the country-data sections details, first, deployments of troops and, second, military observers and, where available, the role and equipment of deployed units. Personnel figures are not generally included for embassy staff, standing multinational headquarters, or deployments of purely maritime and aerospace assets, such as Iceland Air Policing or anti-piracy operations. Personnel deployed on OSCE missions are listed as 'personnel' rather than 'observers'.

Land forces
To make international comparison easier and more consistent, *The Military Balance* categorises forces by role and translates national military terminology for unit and formation sizes. Typical personnel strength, equipment holdings and organisation of formations such as brigades and divisions vary from country to country. In addition, some unit terms, such as 'regiment', 'squadron', 'battery' and 'troop', can refer to significantly different unit sizes in different countries. Unless otherwise stated, these terms should be assumed to reflect standard British usage where they occur.

Naval forces

Classifying naval vessels according to role is complex. A post-war consensus on primary surface combatants revolved around a distinction between independently operating cruisers, air-defence escorts (destroyers) and anti-submarine-warfare escorts (frigates). However, ships are increasingly performing a range of roles. For this reason, *The Military Balance* classifies vessels according to full-load displacement (FLD) rather than a role-classification system. These definitions will not necessarily conform to national designations.

Air forces

Aircraft listed as combat capable are assessed as being equipped to deliver air-to-air or air-to-surface ordnance. The definition includes aircraft designated by type as bomber, fighter, fighter/ground attack, ground attack and anti-submarine warfare. Other aircraft considered to be combat capable are marked with an asterisk (*). Operational groupings of air forces are shown where known. Typical squadron aircraft strengths can vary both between aircraft types and from country to country. When assessing missile ranges, *The Military Balance* uses the following range indicators:
- Short-range ballistic missile (SRBM): less than 1,000 km;
- Medium-range ballistic missile (MRBM): 1,000–3,000 km;
- Intermediate-range ballistic missile (IRBM): 3,000–5,000 km;
- Intercontinental ballistic missile (ICBM): over 5,000 km.

Attribution and acknowledgements

The International Institute for Strategic Studies owes no allegiance to any government, group of governments, or any political or other organisation. Its assessments are its own, based on the material available to it from a wide variety of sources. The cooperation of governments of all listed countries has been sought and, in many cases, received. However, some data in *The Military Balance* is estimated. Care is taken to ensure that this data is as accurate and free from bias as possible. The Institute owes a considerable debt to a number of its own members, consultants and all those who help compile and check material. The Director-General and Chief Executive and staff of the Institute assume full responsibility for the data and judgements in this book. Comments and suggestions on the data and textual material contained within the book, as well as on the style and presentation of data, are welcomed and should be communicated to the Editor of *The Military Balance* at: IISS, Arundel House, 6 Temple Place, London, WC2R 2PG, UK, email: *milbal@iiss.org*. Copyright on all information in *The Military Balance* belongs strictly to the IISS. Application to reproduce limited amounts of data may be made to the publisher: Taylor & Francis, 4 Park Square, Milton Park, Abingdon, Oxon, OX14 4RN. Email: *society.permissions@tandf.co.uk*. Unauthorised use of data from *The Military Balance* will be subject to legal action.

Principal land definitions

FORCES BY ROLE

Command:	free-standing, deployable formation headquarters (HQs).
Special Forces (SF):	elite units specially trained and equipped for unconventional warfare and operations in enemy-controlled territory. Many are employed in counter-terrorist roles.
Manoeuvre:	combat units and formations capable of manoeuvring. These are subdivided as follows:
Reconnaissance:	combat units and formations whose primary purpose is to gain information.
Armoured:	units and formations principally equipped with main battle tanks (MBTs) and infantry fighting vehicles (IFVs) to provide heavy mounted close-combat capability. Units and formations intended to provide mounted close-combat capability with lighter armoured vehicles, such as light tanks or wheeled assault guns, are classified as light armoured.
Mechanised:	units and formations primarily equipped with lighter armoured vehicles such as armoured personnel carriers (APCs). They have less mounted firepower and protection than their armoured equivalents, but can usually deploy more infantry.
Light:	units and formations whose principal combat capability is dismounted infantry, with few, if any, organic armoured vehicles. Some may be motorised and equipped with soft-skinned vehicles.
Air Manoeuvre:	units and formations trained and equipped for delivery by transport aircraft and/or helicopters.
Amphibious:	amphibious forces are trained and equipped to project force from the sea.
Other Forces:	includes security units such as Presidential Guards, paramilitary units such as border guards and combat formations permanently employed in training or demonstration tasks.
Combat Support:	combat support units and formations not integral to manoeuvre formations. Includes artillery, engineers, military intelligence, nuclear, biological and chemical defence, signals and information operations.
Combat Service Support (CSS):	includes logistics, maintenance, medical, supply and transport units and formations.

EQUIPMENT BY TYPE

Light Weapons:	small arms, machine guns, grenades and grenade launchers and unguided man-portable anti-armour and support weapons have proliferated so much and are sufficiently easy to manufacture or copy that listing them would be impractical.
Crew-Served Weapons:	crew-served recoilless rifles, man-portable ATGW, MANPADs and mortars of greater than 80mm calibre are listed, but the high degree of proliferation and local manufacture of many of these weapons means that estimates of numbers held may not be reliable.
Armoured Fighting Vehicles (AFVs):	armoured combat vehicles with a combat weight of at least six metric tonnes, further subdivided as below:
Main Battle Tank (MBT):	armoured, tracked combat vehicles, armed with a turret-mounted gun of at least 75mm calibre and with a combat weight of at least 25 metric tonnes.
Light Tank (LT TK):	armoured, tracked combat vehicles, armed with a turret-mounted gun of at least 75mm calibre and with a combat weight of less than 25 metric tonnes.
Wheeled Assault Gun (ASLT):	armoured, wheeled combat vehicles, armed with a turret-mounted gun of at least 75mm calibre and with a combat weight of at least 15 metric tonnes.
Armoured Reconnaissance (RECCE):	armoured vehicles primarily designed for reconnaissance tasks with no significant transport capability and either a main gun of less than 75mm calibre or a combat weight of less than 15 metric tonnes, or both.
Infantry Fighting Vehicle (IFV):	armoured combat vehicles designed and equipped to transport an infantry squad and armed with a cannon of at least 20mm calibre.

Armoured Personnel Carrier (APC):	lightly armoured combat vehicles designed and equipped to transport an infantry squad but either unarmed or armed with a cannon of less than 20mm calibre.
Airborne Combat Vehicle (ABCV):	armoured vehicles designed to be deployable by parachute alongside airborne forces.
Amphibious Assault Vehicle (AAV):	armoured vehicles designed to have an amphibious ship-to-shore capability.
Armoured Utility Vehicle (AUV):	armoured vehicles not designed to transport an infantry squad, but capable of undertaking a variety of other utility battlefield tasks, including light reconnaissance and light transport.
Specialist Variants:	variants of armoured vehicles listed above that are designed to fill a specialised role, such as command posts (CP), artillery observation posts (OP), signals (sigs) and ambulances (amb), are categorised with their parent vehicles.
Engineering and Maintenance Vehicles:	includes armoured engineer vehicles (AEV), armoured repair and recovery vehicles (ARV), assault bridging (VLB) and mine warfare vehicles (MW).
Nuclear, Biological and Chemical Defence Vehicles (NBC):	armoured vehicles principally designed to operate in potentially contaminated terrain.
Anti-Tank/Anti-Infrastructure (AT):	guns, guided weapons and recoilless rifles designed to engage armoured vehicles and battlefield hardened targets.
Surface-to-Surface Missile Launchers (SSM):	launch vehicles for transporting and firing surface-to-surface ballistic and cruise missiles.
Artillery:	weapons (including guns, howitzers, gun/howitzers, multiple-rocket launchers, mortars and gun/mortars) with a calibre greater than 100mm for artillery pieces and 80mm and above for mortars, capable of engaging ground targets with indirect fire.
Coastal Defence:	land-based coastal artillery pieces and anti-ship-missile launchers.
Air Defence (AD):	guns and surface-to-air-missile (SAM) launchers designed to engage fixed-wing, rotary-wing and uninhabited aircraft. Missiles are further classified by maximum notional engagement range: point-defence (up to 10 km); short-range (10–30 km); medium-range (30–75 km); and long-range (75 km+). Systems primarily intended to intercept missiles rather than aircraft are categorised separately as Missile Defence.

Principal naval definitions

To aid comparison between fleets, the following definitions, which do not always conform to national definitions, are used:

Submarines:	all vessels designed to operate primarily under water. Submarines with a dived displacement below 250 tonnes are classified as midget submarines (SSW); those below 500 tonnes are coastal submarines (SSC).
Principal surface combatants:	all surface ships designed for combat operations on the high seas, with an FLD above 1,500 tonnes. Aircraft carriers (CV), including helicopter carriers (CVH), are vessels with a flat deck primarily designed to carry fixed- and/or rotary-wing aircraft, without amphibious capability. Other principal surface combatants include cruisers (C) (with an FLD above 9,750 tonnes), destroyers (DD) (with an FLD above 4,500 tonnes) and frigates (FF) (with an FLD above 1,500 tonnes).
Patrol and coastal combatants:	surface vessels designed for coastal or inshore operations. These include corvettes (FS), which usually have an FLD between 500 and 1,500 tonnes and are distinguished from other patrol vessels by their heavier armaments. Also included in this category are offshore-patrol ships (PSO), with an FLD greater than 1,500 tonnes; patrol craft (PC), which have an FLD between 250 and 1,500 tonnes; and patrol boats (PB) with an FLD between ten and 250 tonnes. Vessels with a top speed greater than 35 knots are designated as 'fast'.

Mine warfare vessels:	all surface vessels configured primarily for mine laying (ML) or countermeasures. Countermeasures vessels are either: sweepers (MS), which are designed to locate and destroy mines in an area; hunters (MH), which are designed to locate and destroy individual mines; or countermeasures vessels (MC), which combine both roles.
Amphibious vessels:	vessels designed to transport personnel and/or equipment onto shore. These include landing helicopter assault vessels (LHA), which can embark fixed- and/or rotary-wing air assets as well as landing craft; landing helicopter docks (LHD), which can embark rotary-wing or VTOL assets and have a well dock; landing platform helicopters (LPH), which have a primary role of launch and recovery platform for rotary-wing or VTOL assets with a dock to store equipment/personnel for amphibious operations; and landing platform docks (LPD), which do not have a through deck but do have a well dock. Landing ships (LS) are amphibious vessels capable of ocean passage and landing craft (LC) are smaller vessels designed to transport personnel and equipment from a larger vessel to land or across small stretches of water. Landing ships have a hold; landing craft are open vessels. Landing craft air cushioned (LCAC) are differentiated from Utility craft air cushioned (UCAC) in that the former have a bow ramp for the disembarkation of vehicles and personnel.
Auxiliary vessels:	ocean-going surface vessels performing an auxiliary military role, supporting combat ships or operations. These generally fulfil five roles: replenishment (such as oilers (AO) and solid stores (AKS)); logistics (such as cargo ships (AK) and logistics ships (AFS)); maintenance (such as cable-repair ships (ARC) or buoy tenders (ABU)); research (such as survey ships (AFS)); and special purpose (such as intelligence-collection ships (AGI) and ocean-going tugs (ATF)).
Weapons systems:	weapons are listed in the following order: land-attack cruise missiles (LACM), anti-ship missiles (AShM), surface-to-air missiles (SAM), heavy (HWT) and lightweight (LWT) torpedoes, anti-submarine weapons (A/S), CIWS, guns and aircraft. Missiles with a range less than 5 km and guns with a calibre less than 57 mm are generally not included.
Organisations:	naval groupings such as fleets and squadrons frequently change and are shown only where doing so would aid qualitative judgements.

Principal aviation definitions

Bomber (Bbr):	comparatively large platforms intended for the delivery of air-to-surface ordnance. Bbr units are units equipped with bomber aircraft for the air-to-surface role.
Fighter (Ftr):	aircraft designed primarily for air-to-air combat, which may also have a limited air-to-surface capability. Ftr units are equipped with aircraft intended to provide air superiority, which may have a secondary and limited air-to-surface capability.
Fighter/Ground Attack (FGA):	multi-role fighter-size platforms with significant air-to-surface capability, potentially including maritime attack, and at least some air-to-air capacity. FGA units are multi-role units equipped with aircraft capable of air-to-air and air-to-surface attack.
Ground Attack (Atk):	aircraft designed solely for the air-to-surface task, with limited or no air-to-air capability. Atk units are equipped with fixed-wing aircraft.
Attack Helicopter (Atk hel):	rotary-wing platforms designed for delivery of air-to-surface weapons, and fitted with an integrated fire-control system.
Anti-Submarine Warfare (ASW):	fixed- and rotary-wing platforms designed to locate and engage submarines, many with a secondary anti-surface-warfare capability. ASW units are equipped with fixed- or rotary-wing aircraft.
Anti-Surface Warfare (ASuW):	ASuW units are equipped with fixed- or rotary-wing aircraft intended for anti-surface-warfare missions.
Maritime Patrol (MP):	fixed-wing aircraft and unmanned aerial vehicles (UAVs) intended for maritime surface surveillance, which may possess an anti-surface-warfare capability. MP units are equipped with fixed-wing aircraft or UAVs.

Electronic Warfare (EW):	fixed- and rotary-wing aircraft and UAVs intended for electronic warfare. EW units are equipped with fixed- or rotary-wing aircraft or UAVs.
Intelligence/ Surveillance/ Reconnaissance (ISR):	fixed- and rotary-wing aircraft and UAVs intended to provide radar, visible-light or infrared imagery, or a mix thereof. ISR units are equipped with fixed- or rotary-wing aircraft or UAVs.
Combat/Intelligence/ Surveillance/ Reconnaissance (CISR):	aircraft and UAVs that have the capability to deliver air-to-surface weapons, as well as undertake ISR tasks. CISR units are equipped with armed aircraft and/or UAVs for ISR and air-to-surface missions.
COMINT/ELINT/ SIGINT:	fixed- and rotary-wing platforms and UAVs capable of gathering electronic (ELINT), communications (COMINT) or signals intelligence (SIGINT). COMINT units are equipped with fixed- or rotary-wing aircraft or UAVs intended for the communications-intelligence task. ELINT units are equipped with fixed- or rotary-wing aircraft or UAVs used for gathering electronic intelligence. SIGINT units are equipped with fixed- or rotary-wing aircraft or UAVs used to collect signals intelligence.
Airborne Early Warning (& Control) (AEW (&C)):	fixed- and rotary-wing platforms capable of providing airborne early warning, with a varying degree of onboard command and control depending on the platform. AEW(&C) units are equipped with fixed- or rotary-wing aircraft.
Search and Rescue (SAR):	units are equipped with fixed- or rotary-wing aircraft used to recover military personnel or civilians.
Combat Search and Rescue (CSAR):	units are equipped with armed fixed- or rotary-wing aircraft for recovery of personnel from hostile territory.
Tanker (Tkr):	fixed- and rotary-wing aircraft designed for air-to-air refuelling. Tkr units are equipped with fixed- or rotary-wing aircraft used for air-to-air refuelling.
Tanker Transport (Tkr/Tpt):	platforms capable of both air-to-air refuelling and military airlift.
Transport (Tpt):	fixed- and rotary-wing aircraft intended for military airlift. Light transport aircraft are categorised as having a maximum payload of up to 11,340 kg; medium up to 27,215 kg; and heavy above 27,215 kg. Light transport helicopters have an internal payload of up to 2,000 kg; medium transport helicopters up to 4,535 kg; heavy transport helicopters greater than 4,535 kg. PAX aircraft are platforms generally unsuited for transporting cargo on the main deck. Tpt units are equipped with fixed- or rotary-wing platforms to transport personnel or cargo.
Trainer (Trg):	fixed- and rotary-wing aircraft designed primarily for the training role; some also have the capacity to carry light to medium ordnance. Trg units are equipped with fixed- or rotary-wing training aircraft intended for pilot or other aircrew training.
Multi-role helicopter (MRH):	rotary-wing platforms designed to carry out a variety of military tasks including light transport, armed reconnaissance and battlefield support.
Uninhabited Aerial Vehicles (UAVs):	remotely piloted or controlled unmanned fixed- or rotary-wing systems. Light UAVs are those weighing 20–150 kg; medium: 150–600 kg; and large: more than 600 kg.

Reference

Table 22 **List of abbreviations for data sections**

AAA	anti-aircraft artillery	armd	armoured	CV/H/L/N/S	
AAM	air-to-air missile	ARS/H	rescue and salvage ship/with hangar		aircraft carrier/helicopter/light/nuclear powered/VSTOL
AAR	search-and-rescue vessel			CW	chemical warfare/weapons
AAV	amphibious assault vehicle	arty	artillery	DD/G/H/M	
AB	airborne	ARV	armoured recovery vehicle		destroyer/with AShM/with hangar/with SAM
ABM	anti-ballistic missile	AS	anti-submarine/submarine tender		
ABU/H	sea-going buoy tender/with hangar	ASBM	anti-ship ballistic missile	DDR	disarmament, demobilisation and reintegration
		ASCM	anti-ship cruise missile		
ABCV	airborne combat vehicle	AShM	anti-ship missile	DDS	dry deck shelter
ac	aircraft	aslt	assault	def	defence
ACV	air-cushion vehicle/armoured combat vehicle	ASM	air-to-surface missile	det	detachment
		ASR	submarine rescue craft	div	division
ACS	crane ship	ASTT	anti-submarine torpedo tube	ECM	electronic countermeasures
AD	air defence	ASW	anti-submarine warfare	ELINT	electronic intelligence
ADA	air-defence artillery	ASuW	anti-surface warfare	elm	element/s
ADEX	air-defence exercise	AT	tug/anti-tank	engr	engineer
adj	adjusted	ATBM	anti-tactical ballistic missile	EOD	explosive ordnance disposal
AE	auxiliary, ammunition carrier	ATF	tug, ocean going	EPF	expeditionary fast transport vessel
AEM	missile support ship	ATGW	anti-tank guided weapon	eqpt	equipment
AEV	armoured engineer vehicle	Atk	attack/ground attack	ESB	expeditionary mobile base
AEW	airborne early warning	ATS	tug, salvage and rescue ship	ESD	expeditionary transport dock
AFD/L	auxiliary floating dry dock/small	AUV	armoured utility vehicle	EW	electronic warfare
AFS/H	logistics ship/with hangar	AVB	aviation logistic support ship	excl	excludes/excluding
AFSB	afloat forward staging base	avn	aviation	exp	expenditure
AFV	armoured fighting vehicle	AWT	water tanker	FAC	forward air control
AG	misc auxiliary	AX/L/S	training craft/light/sail	fd	field
AGB/H	icebreaker/with hangar	BA	Budget Authority (US)	FF/G/H/M	frigate/with AShM/with hangar/with SAM
AGE/H	experimental auxiliary ship/with hangar	Bbr	bomber		
		BCT	brigade combat team	FGA	fighter ground attack
AGF/H	command ship/with hangar	bde	brigade	FLD	full-load displacement
AGHS	hydrographic survey vessel	bdgt	budget	flt	flight
AGI	intelligence collection vessel	BG	battlegroup	FMA	Foreign Military Assistance
AGM	space tracking vessel	BMD	ballistic-missile defence	FS/G/H/M	corvette/with AShM/with hangar/with SAM
AGOR	oceanographic research vessel	BMEWS	ballistic missile early warning system		
AGOS	oceanographic surveillance vessel			Ftr	fighter
AGS/H	survey ship/with hangar	bn	battalion/billion	FTX	field training exercise
AH	hospital ship	bty	battery	FY	fiscal year
AIP	air-independent propulsion	C2	command and control	GBU	guided bomb unit
AK/L	cargo ship/light	casevac	casualty evacuation	gd	guard
aka	also known as	cav	cavalry	GDP	gross domestic product
AKEH	dry cargo/ammunition ship	cbt	combat	GLCM	ground-launched cruise missile
AKR/H	roll-on/roll-off cargo ship/with hangar	CBRN	chemical, biological, radiological, nuclear, explosive	GMLS	Guided Missile Launching System
AKS/L	stores ship/light	cdo	commando	gp	group
ALCM	air-launched cruise missile	C/G/H/M/N	cruiser/with AShM/with hangar/with SAM/nuclear-powered	HA/DR	humanitarian assistance/disaster relief
amb	ambulance				
amph	amphibious/amphibian			hel	helicopter
AO/S	oiler/small	CISR	combat ISR	how	howitzer
AOE	fast combat support ship	CIMIC	civil–military cooperation	HQ	headquarters
AOR/L/H	fleet replenishment oiler with RAS capability/light/with hangar	CIWS	close-in weapons system	HUMINT	human intelligence
		COIN	counter-insurgency	HWT	heavyweight torpedo
AOT/L	oiler transport/light	comd	command	hy	heavy
AP	armour-piercing/anti-personnel/transport ship	COMINT	communications intelligence	IBU	inshore boat unit
		comms	communications	ICBM	intercontinental ballistic missile
APB	barracks ship	coy	company	IFV	infantry fighting vehicle
APC	armoured personnel carrier	CP	command post	IIR	imaging infrared
AR/C/D/L	repair ship/cable/dry dock/light	CPX	command post exercise	IMINT	imagery intelligence
ARG	amphibious ready group	CS	combat support	imp	improved
ARH	active radar homing	CSAR	combat search and rescue	indep	independent
ARL	airborne reconnaissance low	CSS	combat service support	inf	infantry
ARM	anti-radiation missile	CT	counter-terrorism	info ops	information operations

INS	inertial navigation system
int	intelligence
IOC	Initial Operating Capability
IR	infrared
IRBM	intermediate-range ballistic missile
ISD	in-service date
ISR	intelligence, surveillance and reconnaissance
ISTAR	intelligence, surveillance, target acquisition and reconnaissance
JOINTEX	joint exercise
LACM	land-attack cruise missile
LC/A/AC/H/M/PA/P/L/T/U/VP	landing craft/assault/air cushion/heavy/medium/personnel air cushion/personnel/large/tank/utility/vehicles and personnel
LCC	amphibious command ship
LGB	laser-guided bomb
LHA	landing ship assault
LHD	amphibious assault ship
LIFT	lead-in ftr trainer
LKA	amphibious cargo ship
LLI	long-lead items
lnchr	launcher
LoA	letter of acceptance
log	logistic
LoI	letter of intent
LP/D/H	landing platform/dock/helicopter
LRIP	low-rate initial production
LS/D/L/LH/M/T	landing ship/dock/logistic/logistic helicopter/medium/tank
lt	light
LWT	lightweight torpedo
maint	maintenance
MANPAD	man-portable air-defence system
MANPATS	man-portable anti-tank system
MAREX	maritime exercise
MBT	main battle tank
MC/C/CS/D/I/O	mine countermeasure coastal/command and support/diving support/inshore/ocean
MCM	mine countermeasures
MCMV	mine countermeasures vessel
MD	military district
MDT	mine diving tender
mech	mechanised
med	medium/medical
medevac	medical evacuation
MH/C/D/I/O	mine hunter/coastal/drone/inshore/ocean
mil	military
MIRV	multiple independently targetable re-entry vehicle
mk	mark (model number)
ML	minelayer
MLU	mid-life update
mne	marine
mod	modified/modification
mor	mortar
mot	motorised/motor
MoU	memorandum of understanding
MP	maritime patrol/military police
MR	maritime reconnaissance/motor rifle
MRBM	medium-range ballistic missile
MRH	multi-role helicopter
MRL	multiple rocket launcher
MS/A/C/D/I/O/R	mine sweeper/auxiliary/coastal/drone/inshore/ocean/river
msl	missile
mtn	mountain
MW	mine warfare
n.a.	not applicable
n.k.	not known
NBC	nuclear, biological, chemical
NCO	non-commissioned officer
nm	nautical mile
nuc	nuclear
O & M	operations and maintenance
obs	observation/observer
OCU	operational conversion unit
OP	observation post
op/ops	operational/operations
OPFOR	opposition training force
org	organised/organisation
OPV	offshore patrol vessel
para	paratroop/parachute
PAX	passenger/passenger transport aircraft
PB/C/F/G/I/M/R/T	patrol boat/coastal/fast/with AShM/inshore/with SAM/riverine/with torpedo
PC/C/F/G/H/I/M/O/R/T	patrol craft/coastal/fast/guided missile/with hangar/inshore/with CIWS missile or SAM/offshore/riverine/with torpedo
pdr	pounder
pers	personnel
PG/G/GF/H	patrol gunboat/guided missile/fast attack craft/hydrofoil
PGM	precision-guided munitions
PH/G/M/T	patrol hydrofoil/with AShM/with SAM/with torpedo
pl	platoon
PKO	peacekeeping operations
PoR	programme of record
PPP	purchasing-power parity
PPV	protected patrol vehicle
PRH	passive radar-homing
prepo	pre-positioned
PSO/H	peace support operations or offshore patrol ship/with hangar
PTF	semi-submersible vessel
ptn	pontoon bridging
quad	quadruple
R&D	research and development
RCL	recoilless launcher
recce	reconnaissance
regt	regiment
RFI	request for information
RFP	request for proposals
RIB	rigid inflatable boat
RL	rocket launcher
ro-ro	roll-on, roll-off
RRC/F/U	rapid-reaction corps/force/unit
RV	re-entry vehicle
rvn	riverine
SAM	surface-to-air missile
SAR	search and rescue
SARH	semi-active radar homing
sat	satellite
SDV	swimmer delivery vehicles
SEAD	suppression of enemy air defence
SF	special forces
SHORAD	short-range air defence
SIGINT	signals intelligence
sigs	signals
SLBM	submarine-launched ballistic missile
SLCM	submarine-launched cruise missile
SLEP	service-life-extension programme
SP	self-propelled
Spec Ops	special operations
SPAAGM	self-propelled anti-aircraft gun and missile system
spt	support
sqn	squadron
SRBM	short-range ballistic missile
SS	submarine
SSA	submersible auxiliary support vessel
SSAN	submersible auxiliary support vessel (nuclear)
SSBN	nuclear-powered ballistic-missile submarine
SSC	coastal submarine
SSG	guided-missile submarine
SSI	inshore submarine
SSGN	nuclear-powered guided-missile submarine
SSK	attack submarine (hunter-killer)
SSM	surface-to-surface missile
SSN	nuclear-powered attack submarine
SSR	security-sector reform
SSW	midget submarine
str	strength
surv	surveillance
sy	security
t	tonnes
tac	tactical
tch	technical
temp	temporary
tk	tank
tkr	tanker
TMD	theatre missile defence
torp	torpedo
tpt	transport
tr	trillion
trg	training
TRV	torpedo recovery vehicle
TT	torpedo tube
UAV	unmanned/uninhabited aerial vehicle
UCAC	utility craft air cushioned
UCAV	unmanned combat air vehicle
utl	utility
UUV	unmanned/uninhabited underwater vehicle
veh	vehicle
VLB	vehicle launched bridge
VLS	vertical launch system
VSHORAD	very short-range air defence
WFU	withdrawn from use
wg	wing

Table 23 **International comparisons of defence expenditure and military personnel**

	Defence Spending current US$ m 2016	2017	2018	Defence Spending per capita (current US$) 2016	2017	2018	Defence Spending % of GDP 2016	2017	2018	Active Armed Forces (000) 2019	Estimated Reservists (000) 2019	Active Paramilitary (000) 2019
North America												
Canada	15,738	18,563	18,235	445	521	508	1.02	1.12	1.05	67	27	5
United States	593,371	598,722	643,266	1,831	1,833	1,954	3.17	3.07	3.14	1,359	846	0
Total	**609,109**	**617,285**	**661,501**	**1,695**	**1,704**	**1,812**	**3.01**	**2.92**	**2.97**	**1,426**	**873**	**5**
Europe												
Albania	114	110	131	39	37	43	0.99	0.86	0.87	8	0	1
Austria	2,888	3,158	3,384	331	361	385	0.74	0.76	0.74	21	158	0
Belgium	3,861	4,513	4,984	338	393	431	0.83	0.91	0.93	27	0	5
Bosnia-Herzegovina	165	165	172	43	43	45	0.97	0.00	0.86	11	0	0
Bulgaria	671	677	724	94	95	103	1.26	1.19	1.14	31	3	0
Croatia	591	658	758	137	153	178	1.14	1.20	1.26	15	18	3
Cyprus	335	397	417	278	325	337	1.66	1.83	1.74	15	50	1
Czech Republic	1,955	2,247	2,748	183	211	257	1.00	1.04	1.12	23	0	0
Denmark	3,514	3,780	4,246	628	674	731	1.15	1.16	1.20	15	46	0
Estonia	499	544	641	396	434	515	2.14	2.09	2.17	6	28	0
Finland	3,100	3,195	3,406	564	579	615	1.30	1.26	1.23	22	216	3
France	46,784	48,699	53,365	700	726	792	1.90	1.88	1.91	204	36	103
Germany	37,943	41,784	45,686	470	518	568	1.09	1.13	1.13	180	28	0
Greece	4,598	4,731	4,896	427	439	455	2.39	2.36	2.25	142	221	4
Hungary	1,061	1,290	1,637	107	131	167	0.84	0.93	1.05	28	20	12
Iceland	46	55	41	136	162	119	0.22	0.22	0.15	0	0	0
Ireland	994	1,040	1,122	201	208	221	0.33	0.31	0.31	9	4	0
Italy	22,112	22,887	24,870	357	368	400	1.19	1.18	1.19	171	18	176
Latvia	407	531	684	207	273	355	1.48	1.75	1.99	6	16	0
Lithuania	637	817	1,057	223	289	378	1.49	1.73	2.02	20	7	14
Luxembourg	205	280	404	352	471	668	0.35	0.45	0.59	1	0	1
Macedonia (FYROM)	106	114	125	50	54	59	0.99	1.01	1.01	8	5	8
Malta	58	64	70	139	155	156	0.51	0.51	0.49	2	0	0
Montenegro	68	75	79	106	117	129	1.56	1.57	1.47	2	0	10
Netherlands	9,121	10,113	11,297	536	592	659	1.16	1.22	1.24	35	5	6
Norway	6,000	6,196	6,798	1,140	1,165	1,265	1.62	1.55	1.54	23	40	0
Poland	9,101	9,981	10,812	236	259	281	1.93	1.90	1.97	118	0	73

Table 23 International comparisons of defence expenditure and military personnel

	Defence Spending current US$ m 2016	2017	2018	Defence Spending per capita (current US$) 2016	2017	2018	Defence Spending % of GDP 2016	2017	2018	Active Armed Forces (000) 2019	Estimated Reservists (000) 2019	Active Paramilitary (000) 2019
Portugal	2,443	2,527	2,582	225	233	249	1.19	1.16	1.09	27	212	25
Romania	2,763	3,643	4,631	128	169	216	1.46	1.72	1.93	69	50	57
Serbia	501	546	707	70	77	100	1.31	1.32	1.48	28	50	4
Slovakia	974	1,118	1,283	179	205	236	1.09	1.16	1.20	16	0	0
Slovenia	446	474	532	225	240	253	1.00	0.97	0.97	7	2	0
Spain	9,975	13,353	15,117	205	273	306	0.81	1.02	1.05	120	15	76
Sweden	5,738	5,935	6,224	581	596	620	1.12	1.11	1.12	30	0	0
Switzerland	4,653	4,786	4,972	569	581	600	0.69	0.70	0.70	21	135	0
Turkey	8,664	7,885	7,897	108	98	97	1.00	0.93	1.11	355	379	157
United Kingdom	52,965	52,350	56,105	822	808	862	1.98	1.99	2.00	148	80	0
Total	**246,056**	**260,718**	**284,605**	**393**	**415**	**452**	**1.33**	**1.35**	**1.37**	**1,966**	**1,841**	**738**
Russia and Eurasia												
Armenia	431	435	506	141	143	166	4.09	3.77	4.04	45	210	4
Azerbaijan	1,395	1,554	1,611	141	156	160	3.69	3.82	3.53	67	300	15
Belarus	506	531	604	53	56	63	1.06	0.98	1.06	45	290	110
Georgia	319	307	322	65	62	65	2.22	2.02	1.93	21	0	5
Kazakhstan	1,134	1,265	1,590	62	68	85	0.83	0.79	0.86	39	0	32
Kyrgyzstan	n.k.	n.k.	n.k.	n.k.	n.k.	n.k.	n.k.	n.k.	n.k.	11	0	10
Moldova	27	31	37	8	9	11	0.34	0.32	0.32	5	58	2
Russia [a]	44,470	45,695	45,349	312	321	319	3.46	2.90	2.88	900	2,000	554
Tajikistan	194	194	217	23	23	25	2.79	2.72	2.95	9	0	8
Turkmenistan	n.k.	n.k.	n.k.	n.k.	n.k.	n.k.	n.k.	n.k.	n.k.	37	0	5
Ukraine	2,555	2,798	3,272	58	64	74	2.74	2.50	2.59	209	900	88
Uzbekistan	n.k.	n.k.	n.k.	n.k.	n.k.	n.k.	n.k.	n.k.	n.k.	48	0	20
Total**	**51,033**	**52,811**	**53,509**	**179**	**185**	**187**	**2.91**	**2.54**	**2.51**	**1,435**	**3,758**	**853**
Asia												
Afghanistan	2,593	2,169	2,064	78	64	59	13.35	10.72	10.13	174	0	149
Australia	23,617	24,446	26,555	1,027	1,052	1,131	1.87	1.77	1.86	58	21	0
Bangladesh	2,629	2,930	3,159	17	19	20	1.12	1.12	1.10	157	0	64
Brunei	409	327	367	936	738	815	3.59	2.70	2.50	7	1	1
Cambodia	656	788	951	41	49	58	3.27	3.57	3.94	124	0	67
China	143,668	151,455	168,202	104	109	121	1.28	1.26	1.25	2,035	510	660
Fiji	52	51	50	56	55	54	1.13	1.04	0.95	4	6	0

Table 23 International comparisons of defence expenditure and military personnel

	Defence Spending current US$ m 2016	2017	2018	Defence Spending per capita (current US$) 2016	2017	2018	Defence Spending % of GDP 2016	2017	2018	Active Armed Forces (000) 2019	Estimated Reservists (000) 2019	Active Paramilitary (000) 2019
India	51,438	58,026	57,874	41	45	45	2.26	2.23	2.15	1,445	1,155	1,586
Indonesia	7,380	8,596	7,318	29	33	28	0.79	0.85	0.73	396	400	280
Japan	46,456	45,692	47,256	367	361	375	0.94	0.94	0.93	247	56	14
Korea, DPR of	n.k.	n.k.	n.k.	n.k.	n.k.	n.k.	n.k.	n.k.	n.k.	1,280	600	189
Korea, Republic of	33,648	35,876	39,211	661	701	763	2.38	2.33	2.37	625	3,100	9
Laos	n.k.	n.k.	n.k.	n.k.	n.k.	n.k.	n.k.	n.k.	n.k.	29	0	100
Malaysia	4,187	3,476	3,869	135	111	122	1.41	1.11	1.11	113	52	23
Mongolia	101	85	105	33	28	34	0.90	0.76	0.82	10	137	8
Myanmar	2,282	2,149	1,951	40	39	35	3.61	3.19	2.73	406	0	107
Nepal	314	336	431	11	11	14	1.48	1.35	1.49	97	0	15
New Zealand	2,163	2,353	2,365	483	522	520	1.17	1.17	1.15	9	2	0
Pakistan	9,188	9,746	11,204	45	48	54	3.30	3.20	3.65	654	0	282
Papua New Guinea	82	71	63	12	10	9	0.43	0.36	0.30	4	0	0
Philippines	2,475	2,727	2,792	24	26	26	0.81	0.87	0.84	142	131	11
Singapore	10,017	10,288	11,000	1,733	1,747	1,835	3.23	3.18	3.17	73	313	8
Sri Lanka	2,005	1,863	1,739	90	83	77	2.46	2.13	1.88	255	6	62
Taiwan	9,902	10,488	11,041	422	446	469	1.87	1.83	1.83	163	1,657	11
Thailand	5,820	6,294	6,508	85	92	95	1.41	1.38	1.33	361	200	94
Timor-Leste	26	25	26	21	20	20	1.04	0.92	0.84	2	0	0
Vietnam	4,073	4,372	4,829	43	45	50	2.02	1.98	2.00	482	5,000	40
Total**	**365,180**	**384,630**	**410,929**	**91**	**95**	**101**	**1.46**	**1.44**	**1.43**	**9,350**	**13,346**	**3,779**
Middle East and North Africa												
Algeria	10,218	10,077	9,928	254	246	238	6.38	6.01	5.27	130	150	187
Bahrain	1,523	1,480	1,480	1,105	1,049	1,026	4.73	4.19	3.77	8	0	11
Egypt	5,300	3,212	2,900	56	33	29	1.59	1.36	1.16	439	479	397
Iran	17,456	20,957	19,591	211	256	236	4.32	4.87	4.56	523	350	40
Iraq	16,976	19,271	17,259	445	492	429	9.95	10.02	7.47	64	0	145
Israel	19,868	18,892	18,536	2,430	2,276	2,200	6.25	5.39	5.07	170	465	8
Jordan	1,474	1,635	1,635	180	160	156	3.81	4.07	3.90	101	65	15
Kuwait	5,743	5,791	6,179	2,027	2,014	2,119	5.18	4.80	4.28	18	24	7
Lebanon	1,740	1,866	2,122	279	300	348	3.38	3.44	3.74	60	0	20
Libya	n.k.	n.k.	n.k.	n.k.	n.k.	n.k.	n.k.	n.k.	n.k.	n.k.	n.k.	n.k.

Table 23 International comparisons of defence expenditure and military personnel

	Defence Spending current US$ m 2016	2017	2018	Defence Spending per capita (current US$) 2016	2017	2018	Defence Spending % of GDP 2016	2017	2018	Active Armed Forces (000) 2019	Estimated Reservists (000) 2019	Active Paramilitary (000) 2019
Mauritania	138	145	158	37	39	41	2.94	2.93	3.04	16	0	5
Morocco	3,327	3,491	3,633	99	103	106	3.22	3.19	3.07	196	150	50
Oman	9,102	8,687	8,947	2,713	2,537	2,561	13.80	12.27	10.95	43	0	4
Palestinian Territories	n.k.	n.k.	n.k.	n.k.	n.k.	n.k.	n.k.	n.k.	n.k.	0	0	n.k.
Qatar	n.k.	n.k.	n.k.	n.k.	n.k.	n.k.	n.k.	n.k.	n.k.	17	0	5
Saudi Arabia	81,526	89,067	82,933	2,895	3,117	2,506	12.64	12.97	10.77	227	0	25
Syria	n.k.	n.k.	n.k.	n.k.	n.k.	n.k.	n.k.	n.k.	n.k.	139	0	100
Tunisia	975	833	915	88	73	79	2.33	2.09	2.20	36	0	12
United Arab Emirates	n.k.	n.k.	n.k.	n.k.	n.k.	n.k.	n.k.	n.k.	n.k.	63	0	0
Yemen	n.k.	n.k.	n.k.	n.k.	n.k.	n.k.	n.k.	n.k.	n.k.	40	0	0
Total**	**175,367**	**185,404**	**176,217**	**411**	**431**	**394**	**5.76**	**5.88**	**5.10**	**2,287**	**1,683**	**1,031**
Latin America and the Caribbean												
Antigua and Barbuda	7	6	7	73	66	74	0.47	0.41	0.44	0	0	0
Argentina	5,205	6,172	4,234	119	139	95	0.94	0.97	0.89	74	0	31
Bahamas	121	99	91	369	299	272	1.02	0.81	0.70	1	0	0
Barbados	38	39	39	132	132	134	0.79	0.77	0.76	1	0	0
Belize	22	24	23	63	66	59	1.23	1.28	1.19	2	1	0
Bolivia	443	543	503	40	49	44	1.29	1.44	1.20	34	0	37
Brazil	23,516	29,245	27,952	114	141	134	1.31	1.42	1.46	335	1,340	395
Chile	3,444	4,006	4,249	195	225	237	1.38	1.45	1.42	77	40	45
Colombia	9,201	10,150	10,642	195	213	221	3.25	3.23	3.16	293	35	188
Costa Rica	409	390	454	84	79	91	0.71	0.67	0.75	0	0	10
Cuba	n.k.	n.k.	n.k.	n.k.	n.k.	n.k.	n.k.	n.k.	n.k.	49	39	27
Dominican Republic	458	496	603	43	46	59	0.63	0.65	0.74	56	0	15
Ecuador	1,565	1,565	1,698	97	96	103	1.57	1.50	1.58	40	118	1
El Salvador	146	146	141	24	24	23	0.61	0.59	0.55	25	10	17
Guatemala	289	260	256	19	17	15	0.42	0.34	0.32	18	64	25
Guyana	51	57	56	69	77	76	1.46	1.60	1.55	3	1	0
Haiti	7	7	8	1	1	1	0.09	0.08	0.08	0	0	0
Honduras	297	267	329	33	30	36	1.37	1.16	1.38	15	60	8
Jamaica	139	142	228	47	47	81	0.99	0.96	1.48	4	1	0
Mexico	4,917	4,568	5,227	40	37	41	0.46	0.40	0.44	277	82	59
Nicaragua	73	84	82	12	14	13	0.55	0.60	0.61	12	0	0

Table 23 International comparisons of defence expenditure and military personnel

	Defence Spending current US$ m 2016	2017	2018	Defence Spending per capita (current US$) 2016	2017	2018	Defence Spending % of GDP 2016	2017	2018	Active Armed Forces (000) 2019	Estimated Reservists (000) 2019	Active Paramilitary (000) 2019
Panama	751	746	738	203	199	194	1.30	1.21	1.12	0	0	26
Paraguay	267	273	313	39	39	45	0.74	0.70	0.75	12	165	15
Peru	2,225	2,166	2,301	72	70	73	1.14	1.01	1.00	81	188	77
Suriname	n.k.	n.k.	n.k.	n.k.	n.k.	n.k.	n.k.	n.k.	n.k.	2	0	0
Trinidad and Tobago	1,622	1,125	920	1,329	923	757	7.16	4.94	3.95	4	0	0
Uruguay	489	515	486	146	153	144	0.93	0.87	0.80	21	0	1
Venezuela	1,273	741	n.k.	41	24	n.k.	0.54	0.35	n.k.	123	8	220
Total**	**56,975**	**63,831**	**61,582**	**92**	**102**	**97**	**1.14**	**1.16**	**1.18**	**1,559**	**2,151**	**1,195**
Sub-Saharan Africa												
Angola	2,968	3,233	2,215	147	110	73	3.11	2.60	1.85	107	0	10
Benin	98	117	91	9	11	8	1.14	1.27	0.82	7	0	5
Botswana	561	512	572	254	231	254	3.58	2.98	3.07	9	0	0
Burkina Faso	150	192	315	8	10	16	1.32	1.53	2.16	11	0	0
Burundi	66	64	65	6	6	5	2.12	1.87	1.70	30	0	1
Cameroon	388	411	432	16	16	17	1.20	1.21	1.11	15	0	9
Cape Verde	11	10	11	19	17	20	0.64	0.56	0.56	1	0	0
Central African Rep	27	31	33	5	5	6	1.53	1.58	1.50	7	0	1
Chad	159	176	185	13	15	12	1.58	1.78	1.61	30	0	5
Congo	562	490	295	116	99	58	7.22	5.75	2.82	10	0	2
Côte d'Ivoire	755	829	935	32	34	36	2.08	2.05	1.94	27	0	n.k.
Dem Republic of the Congo	442	301	289	5	4	3	1.12	0.73	0.68	134	0	0
Djibouti	n.k.	n.k.	n.k.	n.k.	n.k.	n.k.	n.k.	n.k.	n.k.	10	0	3
Equatorial Guinea	n.k.	n.k.	n.k.	n.k.	n.k.	n.k.	n.k.	n.k.	n.k.	1	0	0
Eritrea	n.k.	n.k.	n.k.	n.k.	n.k.	n.k.	n.k.	n.k.	n.k.	202	120	0
Ethiopia	451	492	469	4	5	4	0.62	0.61	0.55	138	0	0
Gabon	203	267	263	117	150	124	1.45	1.75	1.51	5	0	2
Gambia	n.k.	n.k.	n.k.	n.k.	n.k.	n.k.	n.k.	n.k.	n.k.	1	0	0
Ghana	195	189	211	7	7	8	0.45	0.40	0.41	16	0	0
Guinea	162	200	165	13	16	14	1.91	2.06	1.52	10	0	3
Guinea-Bissau	n.k.	n.k.	n.k.	n.k.	n.k.	n.k.	n.k.	n.k.	n.k.	4	0	0
Kenya	1,222	1,199	1,275	26	25	26	1.73	1.51	1.44	24	0	5
Lesotho	44	56	51	23	28	26	1.82	2.01	1.75	2	0	0

Table 23 International comparisons of defence expenditure and military personnel

	Defence Spending current US$ m 2016	2017	2018	Defence Spending per capita (current US$) 2016	2017	2018	Defence Spending % of GDP 2016	2017	2018	Active Armed Forces (000) 2019	Estimated Reservists (000) 2019	Active Paramilitary (000) 2019
Liberia	13	14	16	3	3	3	0.39	0.44	0.48	2	0	0
Madagascar	59	67	75	2	3	3	0.59	0.58	0.59	14	0	8
Malawi	29	38	21	2	2	1	0.53	0.61	0.31	11	0	4
Mali	546	655	731	31	37	40	3.89	4.28	4.08	10	0	8
Mauritius	215	234	221	160	172	162	1.77	1.88	1.66	0	0	3
Mozambique	102	93	131	4	4	5	0.91	0.74	0.91	11	0	0
Namibia	404	481	457	166	194	180	3.69	3.79	3.44	10	0	6
Niger	166	172	231	9	9	12	2.21	2.09	2.34	5	0	5
Nigeria	1,751	1,525	1,746	9	8	9	0.43	0.41	0.43	135	0	80
Rwanda	95	109	107	7	9	9	1.12	1.19	1.07	33	0	2
Senegal	254	309	348	18	21	23	1.73	1.88	1.77	14	0	5
Seychelles	n.k.	n.k.	n.k.	n.k.	n.k.	n.k.	n.k.	n.k.	n.k.	0	0	0
Sierra Leone	13	12	13	2	2	2	0.35	0.32	0.35	9	0	0
Somalia	n.k.	n.k.	n.k.	n.k.	n.k.	n.k.	n.k.	n.k.	n.k.	20	0	0
South Africa	3,211	3,651	3,678	59	67	66	1.09	1.05	0.99	65	0	15
South Sudan	98	97	82	8	7	8	3.19	3.39	2.56	185	0	0
Sudan	n.k.	n.k.	n.k.	n.k.	n.k.	n.k.	n.k.	n.k.	n.k.	104	0	20
Tanzania	525	532	757	10	10	14	1.10	1.03	1.34	27	80	1
Togo	82	89	105	11	11	13	1.84	1.87	1.88	9	0	1
Uganda	463	434	384	12	11	9	1.83	1.65	1.39	45	10	1
Zambia	305	337	320	20	21	19	1.46	1.32	1.22	15	3	1
Zimbabwe	394	341	420	27	25	30	2.44	1.95	2.17	29	0	22
Total**	**17,190**	**17,955**	**17,714**	**17**	**18**	**17**	**1.16**	**1.13**	**1.04**	**1,555**	**213**	**228**
Summary												
North America	609,109	617,285	661,501	1,695	1,704	1,812	3.01	2.92	2.97	1,426	873	5
Europe	246,056	260,718	284,605	393	415	452	1.33	1.35	1.37	1,966	1,841	738
Russia and Eurasia	51,033	52,811	53,509	179	185	187	2.91	2.54	2.51	1,435	3,758	853
Asia	365,180	384,630	410,929	91	95	101	1.46	1.44	1.43	9,350	13,346	3,779
Middle East and North Africa	175,367	185,404	176,217	411	431	394	5.76	5.88	5.10	2,287	1,683	1,031
Latin America and the Caribbean	56,975	63,831	61,582	92	102	97	1.14	1.16	1.18	1,559	2,151	1,195
Sub-Saharan Africa	17,190	17,955	17,714	17	18	17	1.16	1.13	1.04	1,555	213	228
Global totals	**1,520,909**	**1,582,632**	**1,666,057**	**208**	**214**	**223**	**2.02**	**1.99**	**1.98**	**19,578**	**23,863**	**7,829**

* Estimates. **Totals exclude defence-spending estimates for states where insufficient official information is available in order to enable approximate comparisons of regional defence-spending between years [a] 'National Defence' budget chapter. Excludes other defence-related expenditures included under other budget lines (e.g. pensions) – see Table 11, p.175

Table 24 Index of country/territory abbreviations

Code	Country	Code	Country	Code	Country
AFG	Afghanistan	GAB	Gabon	NOR	Norway
ALB	Albania	GAM	Gambia	NPL	Nepal
ALG	Algeria	GEO	Georgia	NZL	New Zealand
ANG	Angola	GER	Germany	OMN	Oman
ARG	Argentina	GF	French Guiana	PT	Palestinian Territories
ARM	Armenia	GHA	Ghana	PAN	Panama
ATG	Antigua and Barbuda	GIB	Gibraltar	PAK	Pakistan
AUS	Australia	GNB	Guinea-Bissau	PER	Peru
AUT	Austria	GRC	Greece	PHL	Philippines
AZE	Azerbaijan	GRL	Greenland	POL	Poland
BDI	Burundi	GUA	Guatemala	PNG	Papua New Guinea
BEL	Belgium	GUI	Guinea	PRC	China, People's Republic of
BEN	Benin	GUY	Guyana	PRT	Portugal
BFA	Burkina Faso	HND	Honduras	PRY	Paraguay
BGD	Bangladesh	HTI	Haiti	PYF	French Polynesia
BHR	Bahrain	HUN	Hungary	QTR	Qatar
BHS	Bahamas	IDN	Indonesia	ROC	Taiwan (Republic of China)
BIH	Bosnia-Herzegovina	IND	India	ROK	Korea, Republic of
BIOT	British Indian Ocean Territory	IRL	Ireland	ROM	Romania
BLG	Bulgaria	IRN	Iran	RSA	South Africa
BLR	Belarus	IRQ	Iraq	RUS	Russia
BLZ	Belize	ISL	Iceland	RWA	Rwanda
BOL	Bolivia	ISR	Israel	SAU	Saudi Arabia
BRB	Barbados	ITA	Italy	SDN	Sudan
BRN	Brunei	JAM	Jamaica	SEN	Senegal
BRZ	Brazil	JOR	Jordan	SER	Serbia
BWA	Botswana	JPN	Japan	SGP	Singapore
CAM	Cambodia	KAZ	Kazakhstan	SLB	Solomon Islands
CAN	Canada	KEN	Kenya	SLE	Sierra Leone
CAR	Central African Republic	KGZ	Kyrgyzstan	SLV	El Salvador
CHA	Chad	KWT	Kuwait	SOM	Somalia
CHE	Switzerland	LAO	Laos	SSD	South Sudan
CHL	Chile	LBN	Lebanon	STP	São Tomé and Príncipe
CIV	Côte d'Ivoire	LBR	Liberia	SUR	Suriname
CMR	Cameroon	LBY	Libya	SVK	Slovakia
COG	Republic of Congo	LKA	Sri Lanka	SVN	Slovenia
COL	Colombia	LSO	Lesotho	SWE	Sweden
CPV	Cape Verde	LTU	Lithuania	SYC	Seychelles
CRI	Costa Rica	LUX	Luxembourg	SYR	Syria
CRO	Croatia	LVA	Latvia	TGO	Togo
CUB	Cuba	MDA	Moldova	THA	Thailand
CYP	Cyprus	MDG	Madagascar	TJK	Tajikistan
CZE	Czech Republic	MEX	Mexico	TKM	Turkmenistan
DJB	Djibouti	MHL	Marshall Islands	TLS	Timor-Leste
DNK	Denmark	MLI	Mali	TTO	Trinidad and Tobago
DOM	Dominican Republic	MLT	Malta	TUN	Tunisia
DPRK	Korea, Democratic People's Republic of	MMR	Myanmar	TUR	Turkey
DRC	Democratic Republic of the Congo	MNE	Montenegro	TZA	Tanzania
ECU	Ecuador	MNG	Mongolia	UAE	United Arab Emirates
EGY	Egypt	MOR	Morocco	UGA	Uganda
EQG	Equitorial Guinea	MOZ	Mozambique	UK	United Kingdom
ERI	Eritrea	MRT	Mauritania	UKR	Ukraine
ESP	Spain	MUS	Mauritius	URY	Uruguay
EST	Estonia	MWI	Malawi	US	United States
ETH	Ethiopia	MYS	Malaysia	UZB	Uzbekistan
FIN	Finland	NAM	Namibia	VEN	Venezuela
FJI	Fiji	NCL	New Caledonia	VNM	Vietnam
FLK	Falkland Islands	NER	Niger	YEM	Yemen, Republic of
FRA	France	NGA	Nigeria	ZMB	Zambia
FYROM	Macedonia, Former Yugoslav Republic	NIC	Nicaragua	ZWE	Zimbabwe
		NLD	Netherlands		

Table 25 Index of countries and territories

Country	Code	Page
Afghanistan	AFG	247
Albania	ALB	87
Algeria	ALG	332
Angola	ANG	451
Antigua and Barbuda	ATG	393
Argentina	ARG	393
Armenia	ARM	184
Australia	AUS	248
Austria	AUT	88
Azerbaijan	AZE	185
Bahamas	BHS	396
Bahrain	BHR	334
Bangladesh	BGD	251
Barbados	BRB	397
Belarus	BLR	188
Belgium	BEL	89
Belize	BLZ	397
Benin	BEN	452
Bolivia	BOL	398
Bosnia-Herzegovina	BIH	91
Botswana	BWA	453
Brazil	BRZ	400
Brunei	BRN	253
Bulgaria	BLG	92
Burkina Faso	BFA	454
Burundi	BDI	455
Cambodia	CAM	254
Cameroon	CMR	456
Canada	CAN	44
Cape Verde	CPV	458
Central African Republic	CAR	458
Chad	CHA	459
Chile	CHL	404
China, People's Republic of	PRC	256
Colombia	COL	407
Congo, Republic of	COG	460
Costa Rica	CRI	410
Côte d'Ivoire	CIV	461
Croatia	CRO	94
Cuba	CUB	410
Cyprus	CYP	96
Czech Republic	CZE	98
Democratic Republic of the Congo	DRC	462
Denmark	DNK	99
Djibouti	DJB	464
Dominican Republic	DOM	412
Ecuador	ECU	413
Egypt	EGY	336
El Salvador	SLV	415
Equatorial Guinea	EQG	465
Eritrea	ERI	466
Estonia	EST	101
Ethiopia	ETH	467
Fiji	FJI	265
Finland	FIN	103
France	FRA	105
Gabon	GAB	468
Gambia	GAM	469
Georgia	GEO	189
Germany	GER	110
Ghana	GHA	470
Greece	GRC	113
Guatemala	GUA	416
Guinea	GUI	471
Guinea-Bissau	GNB	472
Guyana	GUY	418
Haiti	HTI	418
Honduras	HND	419
Hungary	HUN	116
Iceland	ISL	118
India	IND	266
Indonesia	IDN	272
Iran	IRN	340
Iraq	IRQ	344
Ireland	IRL	118
Israel	ISR	346
Italy	ITA	119
Jamaica	JAM	420
Japan	JPN	276
Jordan	JOR	349
Kazakhstan	KAZ	191
Kenya	KEN	473
Korea, Democratic People's Republic of	DPRK	280
Korea, Republic of	ROK	283
Kuwait	KWT	351
Kyrgyzstan	KGZ	193
Laos	LAO	287
Latvia	LVA	123
Lebanon	LBN	353
Lesotho	LSO	474
Liberia	LBR	475
Libya	LBY	355
Lithuania	LTU	125
Luxembourg	LUX	126
Macedonia, Former Yugoslav Republic	FYROM	127
Madagascar	MDG	476
Malawi	MWI	476
Malaysia	MYS	288
Mali	MLI	477
Malta	MLT	128
Mauritania	MRT	357
Mauritius	MUS	479
Mexico	MEX	421
Moldova	MDA	194
Mongolia	MNG	291
Montenegro	MNE	129
Morocco	MOR	358
Mozambique	MOZ	479
Multinational Organisations		130
Myanmar	MMR	292
Namibia	NAM	480
Nepal	NPL	294
Netherlands	NLD	130
New Zealand	NZL	295
Nicaragua	NIC	424
Niger	NER	481
Nigeria	NGA	482
Norway	NOR	133
Oman	OMN	360
Pakistan	PAK	296
Palestinian Territories	PT	362
Panama	PAN	425
Papua New Guinea	PNG	300
Paraguay	PRY	426
Peru	PER	427
Philippines	PHL	300
Poland	POL	135
Portugal	PRT	138
Qatar	QTR	363
Romania	ROM	140
Russia	RUS	195
Rwanda	RWA	484
Saudi Arabia	SAU	365
Senegal	SEN	485
Serbia	SER	142
Seychelles	SYC	487
Sierra Leone	SLE	487
Singapore	SGP	303
Slovakia	SVK	144
Slovenia	SVN	145
Somalia	SOM	488
South Africa	RSA	489
South Sudan	SSD	491
Spain	ESP	147
Sri Lanka	LKA	305
Sudan	SDN	493
Suriname	SUR	430
Sweden	SWE	150
Switzerland	CHE	152
Syria	SYR	368
Taiwan (Republic of China)	ROC	307
Tajikistan	TJK	210
Tanzania	TZA	495
Thailand	THA	310
Timor-Leste	TLS	313
Togo	TGO	496
Trinidad and Tobago	TTO	430
Tunisia	TUN	371
Turkey	TUR	154
Turkmenistan	TKM	211
Uganda	UGA	497
Ukraine	UKR	212
United Arab Emirates	UAE	372
United Kingdom	UK	158
United States	US	47
Uruguay	URY	431
Uzbekistan	UZB	217
Venezuela	VEN	433
Vietnam	VNM	314
Yemen, Republic of	YEM	375
Zambia	ZMB	498
Zimbabwe	ZWE	499